DISCOVER SOCIOLOGY

William J. Chambliss
Daina S. Eglitis

P9-CRT-060

SOCIOLOGY STARTS WITH CURIOSITY...

What key social forces construct and transform our lives as individuals and as members of society? How does our social world shape us? How do we shape our world?

Join William J. Chambliss and Daina S. Eglitis as they journey beyond the classroom to help students answer these questions. Putting students at the center, **Discover Sociology** inspires curiosity about the social world and then provides the academic tools to help them understand it, analyze it, and maybe even change it.

Discover sociology through the theme of
SOCIOLOGICAL IMAGINATION

Private Lives, Public Issues boxes bring to the forefront the foundational theme of the sociological imagination by getting students to adopt a broader perspective in order to understand how individual lives are shaped by larger social forces.

"I like how the **Private Lives, Public Issues** *feature makes an attempt to speak directly to students and get them to consider sociology in a more practical way."*

—Matthew Green, *College of DuPage*

Discover sociology through the theme of
POWER

Inequality Matters boxes examine power as a crucial theme in sociology. This engaging feature gives students a critical perspective on how power is distributed, reproduced, and exercised in society.

"I really liked the **Inequality Matters** *feature. I think it brings to the surface a lot of issues that get swept under the rug."*

—Brian Brutlag, *Rio Hondo College*

Discover sociology through the theme of
TECHNOLOGICAL TRANSFORMATION

Digital Society boxes provide a valuable sociological perspective on the ever-evolving and transformational nature of technology, considering both the positive and negative effects on our increasingly connected global society.

*"The section on **Digital Society** stands out as exemplary and engaging."*

—Jeffrey Debies-Carl, *University of New Haven*

Discover sociology through the theme of
GLOBALIZATION

Global Issues boxes show that societal changes and challenges are happening all over the world. Shining a thematic light on how individual lives, communities, and countries are inextricably linked to a multicultural and interconnected international environment, this feature helps students develop a more informed global perspective.

*"**Global Issues** makes this text stand out in comparison to many others on the market."*

—Keri Diggins, *Scottsdale Community College*

"I am very glad to see that this book covers many more global issues than most introductory books. This may be the book's strongest advantage, or at least the piece that makes this text stand out compared to the majority of introductory books that only give token mentions to the world outside the U.S."

—Paul D. Breitkreutz, *University of Nebraska-Lincoln*

Discover sociology by becoming
CRITICAL CONSUMERS of RESEARCH

Behind the Numbers boxes ask students to consider the myriad of information and data bombarding us at all times. This feature helps students become stronger critical thinkers and savvy consumers of information by encouraging them to consider the source of information, how questions are framed, and what might be obscured by data.

Discover what you can do with a SOCIOLOGY DEGREE

By linking sociology and career success, **Discover Sociology** helps students chart a career path by highlighting the knowledge and skills they can acquire by majoring in sociology, as well as learn how to parlay these skills into a wide array of occupations and sectors.

"I like the very direct and clear focus on relating sociological concepts to students' career paths."

—Barb LaPilusa, *Montgomery College*

"Thinking about one's future career is what most students are doing."

—Brian Thomas, *Saginaw Valley State University*

"Students are eager for this kind of guidance."

—Wesley Jennings, *University of South Florida*

Discover the ANCILLARIES

Discover Sociology includes a comprehensive ancillary package that utilizes new media and a wide range of instructional technologies designed to support instructor course preparation and student learning.

CQ PRESS STATE STATS

Giving students the opportunity to work with real data helps them develop as sociologists and researchers. Through the Interactive eBook, students have access to **CQ Press State Stats**, a unique database where you and your students will find reliable, easy-to-use data from more than 80 different sources covering more than 15 years on topics ranging from health and mortality, to poverty and crime, to education and the economy. At the end of each chapter there is a **Discover CQ Press State Stats** activity perfectly geared to get students thinking sociologically about the world around them. To learn more and take a tour, visit **www.library.cqpress.com/statestats**

"I think students will enjoy the interactive aspect. Rather than the instructor showing students how to analyze data or indicate patterns, students can discover those for themselves."

—Jung-Whan de Jong, *SUNY Fashion Institute of Technology*

"Many of the issues listed on the site, such as the comparison of earnings by gender and the changing composition of the racial makeup of different states and the U.S., are always topics that garner a lot of discussion in class."

—Rebecca Nees, *Middle Georgia State College*

"Students like being able to customize and tailor the information to their specific research. Also, the freedom that it gives students to explore other areas is phenomenal."

—Caazena Hunter, *Tarleton State University*

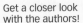

INTERACTIVE EBOOK

Discover Sociology is also available as an Interactive eBook, which can be packaged free with the book or purchased separately. Ideal for students in online and traditional courses who prefer a more contemporary, multimedia-integrated presentation for learning, this incredibly Interactive eBook provides students with the identical content and page layout of the traditional printed book in a flexible electronic format. Users of the eBook can link directly from the "page" to video, audio, additional enrichment readings, glossary terms, and other relevant resources that bring sociology to life in a way that a traditional print text can't. Students will also have immediate access to study tools such as highlighting, bookmarking, note-taking, helpful links to video, podcasts, SAGE journal articles, reference links, and much more!

 SOCview
Get a closer look with the authors!

 AUDIO

 CQ RESEARCHER

 VIDEO

 RESEARCH/ SOCIAL ACTION

 WEB LINK

 REFERENCE

JOURNAL

▶ **STUDENT STUDY SITE: www.sagepub.com/chamblissintro**

The **Open-Access Student Study Site** provides a variety of additional resources to build students' understanding of the book content and extend their learning beyond the classroom. Students will have access to the following features for each chapter:

- **SOCView Videos:** These original author videos provide students with a review of chapter content.
- **SAGE Journal Articles:** EXCLUSIVE! Access to specific full-text journal articles that have been carefully selected for each chapter.
- **Reference, CQ Researcher, and Pacific Standard Magazine Links:** Each chapter includes links to relevant articles from SAGE handbooks and encyclopedias, as well as links to articles from CQ Researcher and Pacific Standard Magazine.
- **Video, Audio, and Web Links**
- **Learning Objectives**
- **Mobile-Friendly eFlashcards and Web Quizzes**

▶ **INSTRUCTOR TEACHING SITE: www.sagepub.com/chamblissintro**

A **password-protected instructor teaching site** provides one integrated source for all instructor materials, including the following key components for each chapter:

- Microsoft® Word® Test Bank
- Diploma Electronic Test Bank
- PowerPoint® Slides
- Lecture Notes
- Sample Course Syllabi

- Chapter-Specific Discussion Questions
- Ideas for Class Activities
- Social Media Guidelines and Resources
- Learning Objectives
- And much more!

DISCOVER
SOCIOLOGY

To Pernille with thanks for everything and Neil, Cece, Timmy, and John who make me smile with pride. —WJC

This work is dedicated to Joe, for his tremendous patience and support, and to Anna and Niklavs, who are just all-around awesome. —DSE

DISCOVER SOCIOLOGY

William J. Chambliss
Daina S. Eglitis

The George Washington University

Los Angeles | London | New Delhi
Singapore | Washington DC

Los Angeles | London | New Delhi
Singapore | Washington DC

FOR INFORMATION:

SAGE Publications, Inc.
2455 Teller Road
Thousand Oaks, California 91320
E-mail: order@sagepub.com

SAGE Publications Ltd.
1 Oliver's Yard
55 City Road
London, EC1Y 1SP
United Kingdom

SAGE Publications India Pvt. Ltd.
B 1/I 1 Mohan Cooperative Industrial Area
Mathura Road, New Delhi 110 044
India

SAGE Publications Asia-Pacific Pte. Ltd.
3 Church Street
#10-04 Samsung Hub
Singapore 049483

Acquisitions Editor: Diane McDaniel
Associate Editor: Nathan Davidson
Editorial Assistant: Lauren Johnson
Production Editor: Brittany Bauhaus
Copy Editor: Melinda Masson
Typesetter: C&M Digitals (P) Ltd.
Proofreader: Theresa Kay
Indexer: Naomi Linzer
Cover Designer: Scott Van Atta
Marketing Manager: Erica DeLuca
Permissions Editor: Karen Ehrmann

Copyright © 2014 by SAGE Publications, Inc.

All rights reserved. No part of this book may be reproduced or utilized in any form or by any means, electronic or mechanical, including photocopying, recording, or by any information storage and retrieval system, without permission in writing from the publisher.

Printed in Canada

Library of Congress Cataloging-in-Publication Data

Chambliss, William J.

Discover sociology / William J. Chambliss, George Washington University, Daina Stukuls Eglitis, George Washington University.

pages cm
Includes bibliographical references and index.

ISBN 978-1-4129-9620-4 (pbk.: alk. paper) — ISBN 978-1-4833-0083-2 (web pdf) 1. Sociology. I. Eglitis, Daina Stukuls. II. Title.

HM585.C4473 2014
301—dc23   2013008877

This book is printed on acid-free paper.

13 14 15 16 17 10 9 8 7 6 5 4 3 2 1

ABOUT THE AUTHORS

William J. Chambliss (PhD, Indiana University) is a professor of sociology at The George Washington University. He has written and edited more than 25 books and numerous articles for professional journals in sociology, criminology, and law. His work integrating the study of crime with the creation and implementation of criminal law has been a central theme in his writings and research. His articles on the historical development of vagrancy laws, the legal process as it affects different social classes and racial groups, and his attempt to introduce the study of state-organized crimes into the mainstream of social science research have punctuated his career. He is the recipient of numerous awards and honors including a doctorate of laws honoris causa, University of Guelph, Guelph, Ontario, Canada, 1999; the 2009 Lifetime Achievement Award, Sociology of Law, American Sociological Association; the 2009 Lifetime Achievement Award, Law and Society, Society for the Study of Social Problems; the 2001 Edwin H. Sutherland Award, American Society of Criminology; the 1995 Major Achievement Award, American Society of Criminology; the 1986 Distinguished Leadership in Criminal Justice, Bruce Smith Sr. Award, Academy of Criminal Justice Sciences; and the 1985 Lifetime Achievement Award, Criminology, American Sociological Association. Professor Chambliss is a past president of the American Society of Criminology and past president of the Society for the Study of Social Problems. His current research covers a range of lifetime interests in international drug control policy, class, race, gender, and criminal justice, and the history of piracy on the high seas.

Daina S. Eglitis (PhD, University of Michigan–Ann Arbor) is an associate professor of sociology and international affairs and the director of undergraduate studies in the Department of Sociology at The George Washington University. Her scholarly interests include class and social stratification, historical sociology, contemporary theory, gender, and culture. She is the author of *Imagining the Nation: History, Modernity, and Revolution in Latvia* (Penn State Press, 2002), as well as numerous articles on social life and social change in postcommunism. She has held two Fulbright awards in Latvia. Dr. Eglitis is also the author of "The Uses of Global Poverty: How Economic Inequality Benefits the West," a widely used article for undergraduate sociology students. At GWU, she particularly enjoys teaching contemporary sociological theory, class and inequality, and introduction to sociology. She has written on her pedagogical approach in the *Teaching Sociology* article, "Performing Theory: Dramatic Learning in the Theory Classroom" (October 2010). Outside of the classroom, Dr. Eglitis loves to travel to new places and enjoys the company of her fantastic husband Joe and wonderful kids, Nik and Anna.

BRIEF CONTENTS

DETAILED CONTENTS

Chapter 3: Culture   50

Chapter 4: Socialization and Social Interaction   76

Chapter 5: Groups, Organizations, and Bureaucracies 100

Chapter 6: Deviance and Social Control 126

Chapter 7: Class and Inequality 152

Chapter 8: Race and Ethnicity 180

Chapter 9: Gender and Society 206

Chapter 10: Families and Society 237

Chapter 11: Education and Society 264

Chapter 12: Religion and Society 290

Chapter 13: The State, Politics, and Power   318

Chapter 14: Work, Consumption, and the Economy   344

Chapter 15: Health and Medicine 370

Chapter 16: War, Terror, and Genocide 394

Chapter 17: Population, Urbanization, and the Environment   414

Chapter 18: Social Change and Social Movements   444

PREFACE

Years ago a sociologist wrote that if you are the kind of person who walks down a dark street and wonders what is going on inside the houses whose lights shine through the windows, then you are a sociologist by nature. *Curiosity* is the bedrock of all scientific inquiry because curiosity underlies the motivation and passion to seek answers to hard questions. But curiosity is not enough. To be a component of good sociology, curiosity must be disciplined: Answers must be sought within the scientific tradition of gathering data through systematic observations and explaining the findings with carefully constructed explanations or theories. In this text, our goal is to pique students' curiosity about the social world—and then to give them the academic tools to understand it, analyze it, and maybe even change it.

There are many sociology textbooks, some of which are very good. We believe that our contribution to the marketplace of sociological texts and ideas is a book that engages the sociology student's curious mind—and then offers him or her the theoretical, conceptual, and empirical tools to analyze and understand the issues that affect our world, both local and global. The book has been written in a way that we hope will encourage students to keep reading, not only because of assigned pages, but because, with the encouragement of the instructor and the text, they have a desire to know more! We also endeavor to show the value of the discipline of sociology as a source of critical skills that students take with them as they prepare to pursue a career and begin the search for a job or undertake graduate education. Below we detail the special features of this book.

CHAPTER OPENERS THAT SPEAK TO STUDENTS

In this book, you will find chapters that begin with openers drawn from the real world and that endeavor to speak to students and to the kinds of experiences or concerns that they have as students, as well as in other roles in the family or at work. From the question of whether the use of "study drugs" should be considered cheating to an examination of research showing a correlation between rising student debt and declining rates of marriage, the book's openers offer instructors a terrific way to begin a discussion to which students will be eager to contribute. The beginning of each chapter also features three "What do you think?" questions that engage students' curiosity and give a small preview of interesting issues that will be covered in the chapter.

SOCIOLOGY IS A SCIENTIFIC DISCIPLINE

Every chapter in the book integrates empirical research from sociology, highlighting the point that sociology is about the *scientific understanding* of the social world—rigorous research can illuminate the social roots of diverse phenomena and institutions, ranging from poverty and deviance to capitalism and the nuclear family. Research may also draw conflicting or ambiguous conclusions. Students learn that social life is complex and sociological research is an ongoing effort to explain why things are as they are—and how they might change.

KEY THEMES AND BOXED FEATURES

Each chapter has a mix of boxed features that highlight key themes in this book.

- The **sociological imagination**, of course, is a foundational concept in the discipline. It is important throughout the book, and we also feature **Private Lives, Public Issues** boxes that illustrate the relationship between our individual lives and the social forces that shape them.

- Second, **power** is a key theme in sociology—and in this text. Sociologists want to know how power is distributed, how it is reproduced, and how it is exercised in social relationships and institutions. The unequal distribution of power is one important topic of sociological inquiry, and this text offers **Inequality Matters** boxes that probe manifestations of and explanations for power and resource disparities.

- Third, we emphasize **the importance of being a critical consumer of information.** We are surrounded by sources of data that stream into our lives from the Internet, newspapers, peers and colleagues, friends and family, and academic studies. Sociology asks us to look carefully at information and to understand its sources and assumptions in order to ascertain what it illuminates and what it obscures. To this end, we have included **Behind the Numbers** boxes to give students the opportunity to look critically and carefully at statistical information on social problems such as unemployment and poverty, among others.

- Fourth, we live in a world of unprecedented **technological transformation,** and new technologies are rapidly changing our world in ways that are both thrilling and worrisome. The book's **Digital Society** boxes provide a sociological perspective on some of these important developments.

- Finally, the book highlights **globalization** and **global perspectives** in an effort to help students develop a fuller understanding of the place of their lives, community, and country in an interconnected, interdependent, and multicultural international environment—and to see how other countries around the world are experiencing societal changes and challenges. **The Global Society** boxes are part of this effort.

Boxed features include questions for students to help them reflect on the material and link it back to the chapter's larger themes.

DISCOVER STATE STATS

This book introduces students to the process of gathering sociological data and using it to create hypotheses about sociological issues. Instructors and students who use *Discover Sociology* have access to CQ Press's extensive State Stats database. This database has a rich store of compelling data on topics that range from health and mortality to poverty and crime. Each chapter offers an exercise that invites students to use the database to find statistics and use these social indicators to explore a particular sociological issue.

RECOGNIZING CONTEMPORARY CONCERNS: A CHAPTER ON WAR, TERROR, AND GENOCIDE

Our book is pioneering a chapter not found in other introductory sociology texts—"War, Terror, and Genocide." It is our sense that sociologists should engage these very important issues and should engage with students about them. While historians and political scientists commonly weigh in on these issues, we believe that sociologists have unique perspectives to contribute to understanding and addressing these problems and imagining a world in which war, terror, and genocide play a far less prominent and devastating role.

CONNECTING SOCIOLOGY AND CAREER SUCCESS

As an instructor of introductory sociology, you are probably frequently asked by students, "What can I do with a sociology degree?" This is an important question for students (and, often, their parents) and instructors. This book offers instructors and students a unique feature that speaks directly, clearly, and specifically to this question. In each chapter, this book provides an essay that accomplishes two major tasks. First, early essays guide students through key steps in the *career development process* that can begin as early as freshman year. Second, later essays *highlight specific skills students learn as sociology majors, describe those skills, and then connect those skills to particular occupational fields and jobs where employers seek those skills.* This feature gives students critical information for charting a path to a career and offers instructors information from the perspective of a career development professional that can help them show students the linkage between sociological skills and future careers in a wide array of jobs and occupational fields.

PHOTOS AND GRAPHICS

Photos have been carefully selected to help students put images together with ideas, events, and phenomena. A good photo can engage a student's curiosity and give him or her a visual vehicle for remembering the material under discussion. This is our goal in the photo program. We have also carefully prepared visually appealing graphics, including tables, figures, and maps, that attract students' attention and enhance learning.

GLOSSARIES FOR LEARNING

This book features marginal glossaries, offering students easy access to definitions of key concepts, phenomena, and institutions. Additionally, key terms are bolded in the text, and a comprehensive glossary is available at the end of the book.

CHAPTER REVIEW

Every chapter ends with a summary of key learning points and a set of discussion questions to review what students have learned and to foster critical thinking about the materials.

ANCILLARIES

Discover Sociology includes a comprehensive ancillary package that utilizes new media and a wide range of instructional technologies designed to support instructor course preparation and student learning.

STUDENT STUDY SITE

An open-access student study site, available at www.sagepub.com/chamblissintro, provides a variety of additional resources to build students' understanding of the book content and extend their learning beyond the classroom. Students will have access to the following features for each chapter:

- **SOC View Videos:** These original author videos provide students and professors with a visual learning tool to experience a review of chapter content, explore riveting examples, and contemplate questions for further discussion in and out of the classroom.

- **SAGE Journal Articles:** Exclusive! Certain full-text journal articles have been carefully selected for each chapter. Each article supports and expands on the concepts presented in the chapter. This feature also provides questions to focus and guide student interpretation. Combine cutting-edge academic journal scholarship with the topics in your course for a robust classroom experience.

- **Reference, *CQ Researcher,* and *Pacific Standard* magazine links:** Each chapter includes links to relevant articles from SAGE handbooks and encyclopedias, as well as links to articles from *CQ Researcher* and *Pacific Standard* magazine.

- **Video, Audio, and Web Links:** These carefully selected, web-based resources feature relevant interviews, lectures, personal stories, inquiries, and other content for use in independent or classroom-based explorations of key topics.

- **Learning Objectives:** Several learning objectives are outlined for each chapter to help students focus their study goals and understand the comprehensive focus of the chapter.

- **eFlashcards and Web Quizzes:** These mobile-friendly resources reinforce understanding of key terms and concepts that have been outlined in the chapters.

- **CQ Press State Stats Activities:** These exclusive exercises allow students to explore the statistics of their sociological world with access to CQ Press State Stats.

- And much more!

INSTRUCTOR TEACHING SITE

A password-protected instructor teaching site, available at www.sagepub.com/chamblissintro, provides integrated sources for all instructor materials, including the following key components for each chapter:

- The **Microsoft Word test bank** contains multiple-choice, true/false, short-answer, and essay questions for each chapter. The test bank provides you with a diverse range of prewritten options as well as the opportunity for editing any question and/or inserting your own personalized questions to effectively assess students' progress and understanding.

- The **Diploma electronic test bank** can be used on PCs and Macs. Containing multiple-choice, true/false, short-answer, and essay questions per chapter, the test bank provides you with a diverse range of prewritten options as well as the opportunity for editing any questions and/or inserting your own personalized questions to effectively assess students' progress and understanding.

Diploma is also compatible with many popular learning management systems so you can easily get your test questions into your online course.

- Editable, chapter-specific Microsoft **PowerPoint slides** offer you complete flexibility in easily creating a multimedia presentation for your course. Highlight essential content, features, and artwork from the book.

- **Lecture notes** summarize key concepts on a chapter-by-chapter basis to help with preparation for lectures and class discussions.

- **Sample course syllabi** for semester and quarter courses provide suggested models for use when creating the syllabi for your courses.

- **Chapter-specific discussion questions** can help you launch classroom interaction by prompting students to engage with the material and by reinforcing important content.

- Lively and stimulating **ideas for class activities** can be used in class to reinforce active learning. The activities apply to individual or group projects.

- **Social media guidelines and resources** provide information on how to best use social media to enhance learning.

- **Learning objectives** are outlined for each chapter to help students focus their study goals and understand the comprehensive focus of the chapter.

- And much more!

INTERACTIVE E-BOOK

Discover Sociology is also available as an interactive e-book, which can be packaged free with the book or purchased separately. This interactive e-book offers links to web, audio, and video resources, as well as original author video.

ACKNOWLEDGMENTS

The authors are grateful to the terrific editors and staff at Sage including Nathan Davidson, David Repetto, Elisa Adams, Melinda Masson, Jonathan Mason, Megan Koraly, Brittany Bauhaus, and Erica DeLuca. It has been a privilege to work with such a creative, encouraging, and supportive group. We are also indebted to colleagues and graduate students who helped with the materials that went into the book. Among those who contributed ideas and assistance are the Department of Sociology at GWU's Michelle Kelso, Steven Tuch, Greg Squires, Ivy Ken, Carolyn Vasques Scalera, and Fran Buntman. We would like to extend special thanks to our excellent research assistants: Chris Moloney, Jee Jee Kim, Claire Cook, Scott Grether, Ken Leon, Ceylan Engin, and Adam Bethke. For their unending good humor and patience we also thank the Sociology department staff, Maureen Kentoff and Octavia Kelsey. This project could not have been brought to completion without the valuable help and skills of all of the people named.

We are also grateful to our families for their support. Daina would like to acknowledge in particular the extraordinary patience and support of her children, Niklavs and Anna, and husband, Joseph Burke. Daina is also grateful to her mother, Silvia Stukuls, whose help is irreplaceable. There is really no way to thank them all enough. Thanks as well to Nik's buddies—Daiyan, Erica, Dane, and Eric—who shared ideas for interesting chapter openers and inspired a few valuable thoughts on what young people might be curious about. Best wishes to you all as you pursue your own college studies. Bill would like to thank Pernille, whose intelligence, help, and support goes far beyond anything words can express.

Finally, we wish to thank all of the reviewers who contributed greatly to the textbook through excellent suggestions, creative insights, and helpful critiques: Kristian P. Alexander, *Zayed University*; Lori J. Anderson, *Tarleton State University*; Shannon Kay Andrews, *University of Tennessee at Chattanooga*; Joyce Apsel, *New York University*; Gabriel Aquino, *Westfield State College*; Janet Armitage, *St. Mary's University*; Dionne Mathis Banks, *University of Florida*; Michael S. Barton, *University at Albany*; Jeffrey W. Basham, *College of the Sequoias*; Paul J. Becker, *University of Dayton*; Alison J. Bianchi, *The University of Iowa*; Kimberly Boyd, *Piedmont Virginia Community College*; Mariana Branda, *College of the Canyons*; Jennifer Brennom, *Kirkwood Community College*; Denise Bump, *Keystone College*; Nicolette Caperello, *Sierra College*; Michael J. Carter, *California State University, Northridge*; Vivian L. Carter, *Tuskegee University*; Shaheen A. Chowdhury, *College of DuPage*; Jacqueline Clark, *Ripon College*; Susan Eidson Claxton, *Georgia Highlands College*; Debbie Coats, *Maryville University*; Angela M. Collins, *Ozarks Technical Community College*; Scott N. Contor, *Idaho State University*; Denise A. Copelton, *The College at Brockport, State University of New York*; Carol J. Corkern, *Franklin University*; Jennifer Crew Solomon, *Winthrop University*; William F. Daddio, *Georgetown University*; Jeffrey S. Debies-Carl, *University of New Haven;* Melanie Deffendall, *Delgado Community College*; Marc Jung-Whan de Jong, *State University of New York, Fashion Institute of Technology*; David R. Dickens, *University of Nevada, Las Vegas*; Keri Diggins, *Scottsdale Community College*; Amy M. Donley, *University of Central Florida*; Amanda Donovan, *Bristol Community College*; Heather A. Downs, *Jacksonville University*; Daniel D. Doyle, *Bay College*; Dorothy E. Everts, *University of Arkansas-Monticello*; Gary Feinberg, *St. Thomas University*; Bernie Fitzpatrick, *Western Connecticut State University*; Tonya K. Frevert, *University of North Carolina at Charlotte*; Cherly Furdge, *North Central Texas College*; S. Michael Gaddis, *University of North Carolina at Chapel Hill*; Robert Garot, *John Jay College of Criminal Justice*; Todd A. Garrard, *The University of Texas at San Antonio*; Cherly Gary-Furdge, *North Central Texas College*; Marci Gerulis-Darcy, *Metropolitan State University*; Louis Gesualdi, *St. John's University*; Jennifer E. Givens, *University of Utah*; John Glass, *Collin College*; Malcolm Gold, *Malone University*; Thomas B. Gold, *University of California, Berkeley*; Matthew Green, *College of DuPage*; Johnnie M. Griffin, *Jackson State University*; Randolph M. Grinc, *Caldwell College*; Greg Haase, *Western State College of Colorado*; Dean H. Harper, *University of Rochester*; Anne S. Hastings, *University of North Carolina at Chapel Hill*; Anthony L. Haynor, *Seton Hall University*; Roneiko Henderson-Beasley, *Tidewater Community College*; Marta T. Henriksen, *Central New Mexico Community College*; Klaus Heyer, *Nunez Community College*; Jeremy D. Hickman, *University of Kentucky*; Bonniejean Alford Hinde, *College of DuPage*; Joy Crissey Honea, *Montana State University Billings*; Caazena P. Hunter, *University of North Texas*; John Iceland, *Pennsylvania State University*; Robert B. Jenkot, *Coastal Carolina University*; Wesley G. Jennings, *University of South Florida*; Audra Kallimanis, *Wake Technical Community College*; Ali Kamali, *Missouri Western State University;* Leona Kanter, *Mercer University*; Earl A. Kennedy, *North Carolina State University*; Julie A. Kmec, *Washington State University*; Lloyd Klein, *York College, The City University of New York*; Todd M. Krohn, *The University of Georgia*; Veena S. Kulkarni, *Arkansas State University*; Karen F. Lahm, *Wright State University*; Amy G. Langenkamp, *Georgia State University*; Barbara LaPilusa, *Montgomery College*; Jason

LaTouche, *Tarleton State University*; Ke Liang, *Baruch College, The City University of New York*; Carol S. Lindquist, *Bemidji State University*; Travis Linnemann, *Kansas State University*; Stephen Lippmann, *Miami University*; David G. LoConto, *Jacksonville State University*; Rebecca M. Loew, *Middlesex Community College*; Jeanne M. Lorentzen, *Northern Michigan University*; Betsy Lucal, *Indiana University South Bend*; George N. Lundskow, *Grand Valley State University*; Crystal V. Lupo, *Auburn University*; Brian M. Lynch, *Quinebaug Valley Community College*; Kim A. Mac Innis, *Bridgewater State University*; Mahgoub El-Tigani Mahmoud, *Tennessee State University*; Lori Maida, *The State University of New York*; Hosik Min, *Norwich University*; Amanda Moras, *Sacred Heard University*; Madeline H. Moran, *Lehman College, The City University of New York*; Rebecca Nees, *Middle Georgia College*; Christopher Oliver, *University of Kentucky*; Sophia M. Ortiz, *San Antonio College;* Kathleen N. Overmiller, *Marshall University*; Josh Packard, *Midwestern State University*; Marla A. Perry, *Nashville State Community College*; Daniel Poole, *Salt Lake Community College*; Shana L. Porteen, *Finlandia University*; Eric Primm, *University of Pikeville*; Jeffrey Ratcliffe, *Drexel University*; Jo Reger, *Oakland University*; Daniel Roddick, *Rio Hondo College*; David Rohall, *Western Illinois University*; Olga I. Rowe, *Oregon State University*; Josephine A. Ruggiero, *Providence College*; Frank A. Salamone, *Iona College*; Stephen J. Scanlan, *Ohio University*; Michael D. Schulman, *North Carolina State University*; Maren T. Scull, *University of Colorado Denver*; Shane Sharp, *Northern Illinois University*; Mark Sherry, *The University of Toledo*; Amber M. Shimel, *Liberty University*; Vicki Smith, *University of California, Davis*; Dan Steward, *University of Illinois at Urbana-Champaign*; Myron T. Strong, *Community College of Baltimore County*; Richard Sullivan, *Illinois State University*; Sara C. Sutler-Cohen, *Bellevue College*; Joyce Tang, *Queens College of the City University of New York*; Debra K. Taylor, *Metropolitan Community College–Maple Woods*; Richard Tewksbury, *University of Louisville*; Kevin A. Tholin, *Indiana University—South Bend*; Brian Thomas, *Saginaw Valley State University*; Lorna Timmerman, *Indiana University East*; Cynthia Tooley-Heddlesten, *Metropolitan Community Colleges–Blue River*; Okori Uneke, *Winston-Salem State University*; Paula Barfield Unger, *McLennan Community College*; PJ Verrecchia, *York College of Pennsylvania*; Joseph M. Verschaeve, *Grand Valley State University*; Edward Walker, *University of California, Los Angeles*; Tom Ward, *New Mexico Highlands University*; Lisa Munson Weinberg, *Florida State University*; Casey Welch, *Flagler College*; Shonda Whetstone, *Blinn College*; S. Rowan Wolf, *Portland Community College*; Loreen Wolfer, *University of Scranton*; Jason Wollschleger, *Whitworth University*; and Kassia R. Wosick, *New Mexico State University*.

1

DISCOVER SOCIOLOGY

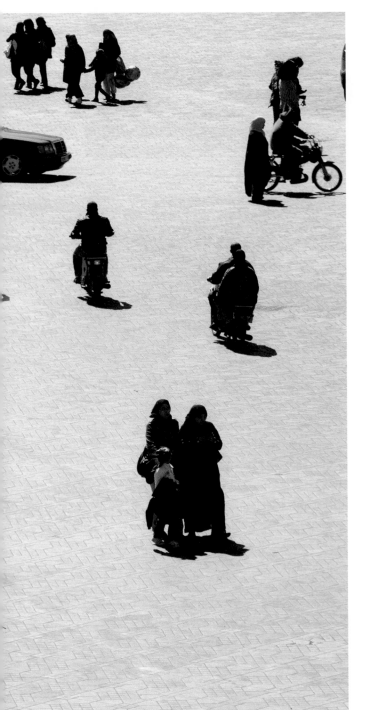

WHAT DO YOU THINK?

1. Can societies be studied scientifically? What does the scientific study of societies entail?
2. What is a theory? What is the role of theories in sociology?
3. In your opinion, what social issues or problems are most pressing today? What questions about them would you like to study?

SOC *VIEW*

Get a closer look with the authors!

1

A goal of this book is to take you on a sociological journey. But let's begin with a basic question: **What is sociology?** First of all, sociology is a discipline of and for curious minds! Sociologists are deeply committed to answering the question "Why?" Why are some people desperately poor and others fabulously wealthy? Why does racial segregation exist, and why does it persist half a century after civil rights laws were enacted? What accounts for the declining marriage rate among the working class and the poor in the United States? How can we explain the fact that low-income people are more likely to be overweight or obese than their middle-class counterparts? Why is the proportion of women entering and completing college rising, while the proportion of men has fallen? Why, in spite of this, do men as a group still earn higher incomes than women as a group? And how is it that social media are being simultaneously praised as an instrument of transformational activism and criticized as a cause of social alienation and civic disengagement? Take a moment now to think about some *why* questions you have about society and social life: As you look around you, hear the news, and interact with other people, what strikes you as fascinating—but perhaps difficult to understand? What are you curious about?

Sociology is an academic discipline that takes a scientific approach to answering the kinds of questions our curious minds propose. When we say that sociology is **scientific**, we mean that it is *a way of learning about the world that combines logically constructed theory and systematic observation*. The goal of sociological study and research is to base answers to questions like those above on a careful examination of the roots of social problems and phenomena such as poverty, segregation, and the wage gap. Sociologists do this with *research methods*—surveys, interviews, observations, and archival research, among others—which yield data that can be tested, challenged, and revised. In this text, you will see how sociology is done—and you will learn how to do sociology yourself.

. . . .

Scientific: A way of learning about the world that combines logically constructed theory and systematic observation.

Concisely stated, **sociology** is *the scientific study of human social relationships, groups, and societies.* Unlike *natural sciences* such as physics, chemistry, and biology, sociology is one of several *social sciences* engaged in the scientific study of human beings and the social worlds they consciously create and inhabit. The purpose of sociology is to understand and generate new knowledge about human behavior, social relations, and social institutions on a larger scale. The sociologist adheres to the principle of **social embeddedness**: the idea that *economic, political, and other forms of human behavior are fundamentally shaped by social relationships.* Thus, sociologists pursue studies on a wide range of issues occurring within and between families, communities, states, the nation, and the world. Other social sciences, some of which you may be studying, include anthropology, economics, political science, and psychology.

Sociology is a field in which students have the opportunity to build a broad spectrum of important skills, ranging from gathering and analyzing information to identifying and solving problems to effective written and oral communication. Throughout the book, we draw your attention to important skills you can gain through the study of sociology and what kinds of skills employers in different occupational fields seek. Sociology opens the door to both greater understanding of the social world and a range of career and graduate study possibilities.

Doing sociology requires building a foundation upon which the knowledge you gain will rest. Some of the key foundations of sociology are the *sociological imagination* and *critical thinking*. We turn to these below. ■

. . . .

Sociology: The scientific study of human social relations, groups, and societies.

Social embeddedness: The idea that economic, political, and other forms of human behavior are fundamentally shaped by social relations.

Sociological imagination: The ability to grasp the relationship between our individual lives and the larger social forces that help to shape them.

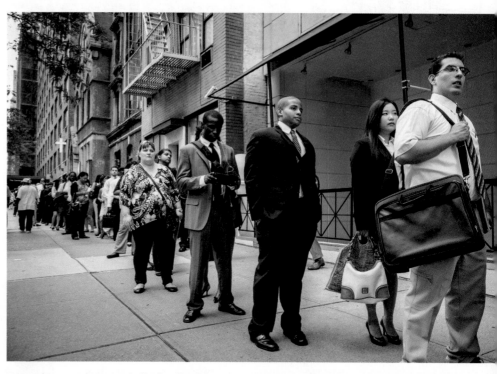

Unemployment is not equally distributed among U.S. demographic groups; those without a high school diploma or college degree have been hit hard by the loss of well-paying jobs in manufacturing since the 1970s. The cost of not getting an education increasingly includes not just higher rates of unemployment but also diminished earning power. ■

THE SOCIOLOGICAL IMAGINATION

As we go about our daily routines, we may forget that large-scale economic, political, and cultural forces shape even the most personal aspects of our lives. When parents divorce, for example, we tend to focus on individual explanations: A father was devoted more to his work than to his family; a mother may have felt trapped in an unhappy marriage but stuck with it for the sake of young children. Yet while personal issues are inevitable parts of a breakup, they can't tell the whole story. When so many U.S. marriages end in divorce, forces larger than incompatible personalities or marital discord are at play. But what are those greater social forces, exactly?

As sociologist C. Wright Mills (1959/2000b) suggested half a century ago, uncovering the relationship between what he called *personal troubles* and *public issues* calls for a **sociological imagination**. The sociological imagination is *the ability to grasp the relationship between individual lives and the larger social forces that shape them*—that is, to see where biography and history intersect.

In a country like the United States, where individualism is part of the national heritage, people tend to believe that each person creates his or her life's path and to largely disregard the social context in which this happens. When we cannot get a job, fail to earn enough to support a family, or experience marital separation,

What is Sociology?

Mills's Sociologicals Imagination

WHY ARE DIVORCE RATES SO HIGH?

The probability of a first marriage ending in separation or divorce within 5 years is 22%; after 10 years, it rises to 36%. Over the longer term, the rate of marital dissolution is closer to 50% (Goodwin, 2010). Just half a century ago, most marriages were "'til death do us part." What accounts for the change?

The sociological imagination shows us that marriage and divorce, seemingly the most private of matters, are as much public issues as personal ones. Consider the fact that when wages for working people lagged from the mid-'70s to the late-'90s, growing numbers of women went to work to help make ends meet. Many middle-class women also went to college and pursued careers as a means of personal fulfillment. In fact, today more women finish undergraduate degrees than men. As a result of trends like these, women today enjoy a higher measure of economic independence than ever before. The combination of educational attainment and satisfying careers reinforces women's independence, making it easier for those who are in unhappy marriages to leave them. Greater social acceptance of divorce has also removed much of the stigma once associated with a failed marriage.

Social trends like those described have made it more likely that an unhappy couple will divorce rather than stay in a failing marriage. Thus, this *private trouble* is in many respects strongly influenced by *public issues* such as women's rising economic independence and the dynamism of cultural norms related to marriage and divorce.

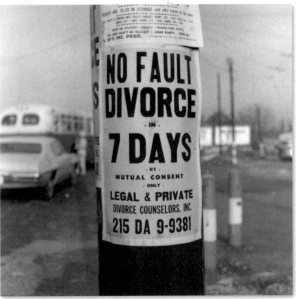

Marriage is one of the most private and personal forms of a relationship between two people. How can marriage—and divorce—be viewed through a sociological lens? ■

THINK IT THROUGH

■ *What other private troubles might sociologists identify as public issues?*

for example, we tend to see it as a personal trouble. We do not necessarily see it as a public issue. The sociological imagination, however, invites us to make the connection and to step away from the vantage point of a single life experience to see how powerful social forces—for instance, changes in social norms, ethnic or sex discrimination, large shifts in the economy, or the beginning or end of a military conflict—shape the obstacles and opportunities that contribute to the unfolding of our own life's story. Among Mills's (1959/2000b) most often cited examples is the following:

> When, in a city of 100,000, only one man is unemployed, that is his personal trouble, and for its relief we properly

Sociological Imagination

look to the character of the man, his skills, and his immediate opportunities. But when in a nation of 50 million employees, 15 million men are unemployed, that is an issue, and we may not hope to find its solution within the range of opportunities open to any one individual. The very structure of opportunities has collapsed. Both the correct statement of the problem and the range of possible solutions require us to consider the economic and political institutions of the society, and not merely the personal situation and character of a scatter of individuals. (p. 9)

To apply the idea to contemporary economic conditions, we might look at recent college graduates. If many of the young people who graduated from college in the middle years of the 2000s found the jobs they wanted, they may have accounted for their success by citing personal effort or solid academic qualifications; these are, of course, very important. The sociological imagination, however, suggests that there are also larger social forces at work—a booming economy in this period contributed to the low rate of unemployment among the college-educated. Consider, for instance, that while unemployment among young male college graduates was just under 7% in 2007 (just before the economic crisis hit in the United States), by 2010 it had peaked at over 12%. For young female college graduates, it grew from under 5% in 2007 to a peak of over 9% in 2010. In 2012, it took a downward turn for both groups (Figure 1.1 on page 6). If your friends who graduated into the labor market during the economic crisis or even the first years following encountered difficulties securing a solid first job, that suggests that personal effort and qualifications are only part of the explanation for the success of one graduating class and the frustration of another.

C. Wright Mills highlighted the use of the sociological imagination in studying social issues. When 20% of urban residents are poor by the government's official measure, we cannot assume the sole cause is personal failings but must ask what large-scale social and economic forces have fostered such widespread destitution. ■

Understanding this relationship is particularly critical for people in the United States, who often regard individuals as fully responsible for their own successes and failures. For instance, it is easy to fault the poor for their poverty, assuming they only need to "pull themselves up by their bootstraps." We may neglect the powerful role of social forces like racial discrimination, the outsourcing or automation of manufacturing jobs that used to employ those with less education, or the poor state of education in many economically distressed rural and urban areas. The sociological imagination implores us to seek the intersection between private troubles, such as a family's poverty, and public issues, such as lack of access to good schooling or jobs, to develop a more informed and comprehensive understanding of the social world and social issues.

It is useful, when we talk about the sociological imagination, to bring in the concepts of agency and structure. Sociologists often talk about social actions—individual and group behavior—in these terms. **Agency** can be understood as *the ability of individuals and groups to exercise free will and to make social change* on a small or large scale. **Structure** is a complex term but may be defined as *patterned social arrangements that have an effect on agency*—structure may enable or constrain social action. For example, sociologists talk about the *class structure,* which is composed of social groups who hold varying amounts of resources such as money, political voice, and social status. They also identify *normative structures*—for instance, they might analyze patterns of social norms regarding "appropriate" gender behaviors in different cultural contexts.

Sociologists take a strong interest in the relationship between structure and agency. Consider that, on the one hand, we all have the ability to make choices—so we have free will and we can opt for one path over another. On the other hand, the structures that surround us impose obstacles or opportunities for us: We can make choices, but they may be enabled or constrained by structure. For instance, in the early 1900s, we would surely have found bright young women in the U.S. middle class who wanted to study to be doctors or lawyers. The social norms of the time, however, suggested young women were better off marrying and starting a family. There were also legal constraints to women's entry into higher education and the paid labor force. So while the women in our example might have individually argued and pushed to go to college and have professional careers, the dreams of this group were constrained by powerful normative and legal structures that identified women's place as being in the home.

. . . .

Agency: The ability of individuals and groups to exercise free will and to make changes on a small or large scale.

Structure: Patterned social arrangements that have an effect on agency.

Sociological Imagination Critique

Agency-Structure Debate

■ **FIGURE 1.1** Unemployment Rate Among Young College Graduates in the U.S., 1989–2012

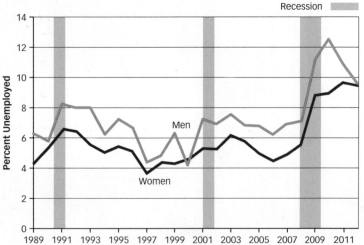

SOURCE: Shierholz, H., Sabadish, N., & Wething, H. (2012). *The class of 2012: Labor market for young graduates remains grim*. Washington, DC: Economic Policy Institute.

Consider the relationship between the class structure and individual agency as another way of thinking about social mobility in U.S. society. If, for instance, a young man today whose parents are well educated and whose family is economically prosperous wishes to go to college and become a doctor, his position in the class structure (or the position of his family) is *enabling*—that is, it makes it likely that he will be able to make this choice and to realize it. If, however, a young man from a poor family with no college background dreams of being an engineer and wants to study in college, his position in the class structure is likely to be *constraining*: Not only does his family have insufficient economic means to pay for college, but he may also be studying in an underfunded or underperforming school that cannot provide the advanced courses he needs to prepare for college. His lack of college role models may also be a factor. This does not mean that the first young man will inevitably go to college and the second will not; it does, however, suggest that probabilities favor the first college aspirant over the second.

Put succinctly, in order to understand why some students go to college and others do not, sociologists would say that we cannot rely on individual choice or will (agency) alone—structures, whether subtly or quite obviously, exercise an influence on social behavior and outcomes. At the same time, we should not see structures as telling the whole story of social behavior because history shows the power of human agency in making change even in the face of obstacles. Agency itself can transform structures (for example, think about the ways women's historical activism has helped to transform limiting gender norms for women today). Sociologists weight both agency and structure and continue to seek to understand how the two interact and connect to influence social behavior. For the most part, sociologists understand the relationship

as reciprocal—that is, it goes in both directions, as structure affects agency and agency, in turn, can change the dimensions of a structure (Figure 1.2).

CRITICAL THINKING

The sociological perspective requires more than an ability to use the sociological imagination. It also demands **critical thinking**, *the ability to evaluate claims about truth by using reason and evidence*. In everyday life, we frequently accept things as "true" because they are familiar, feel right, or are consistent with our beliefs. Critical thinking takes a different approach—recognizing poor arguments, rejecting statements not supported by evidence, and questioning our assumptions. One of the founders of modern sociology, Max Weber, captured the spirit of critical thinking in two words when he said that a key task of sociological inquiry was to openly acknowledge "inconvenient facts."

Critical thinking requires us to be open-minded, but it does not mean all arguments are equally valid. Those supported by logic and backed by evidence are clearly preferable to those that are not. For instance, we may passionately agree with Thomas Jefferson's famous statement, "That government is best that governs least." However, as sociologists we must also ask, "What evidence backs up the claim that less government is better under all circumstances?"

To think critically, it is useful to follow six simple rules (adapted from Wade & Tavris, 1997):

1. **Be willing to ask any question, no matter how difficult.** The belief in small government is a cherished U.S. ideal. But sociologists who study the role of government in modern society must be willing to ask whether there are circumstances under which more—not less—government is better. Government's role in areas such as homeland security, education, and health care has grown in the past several years—what are the positive and negative aspects of this growth?

2. **Think logically and be clear.** Logic and clarity require us to define concepts in a way that allows us to study them. "Big government" is a vague concept that must be made more precise and measurable before it provides for useful research. Are we speaking of federal, state, or local government, or all these? Is "big"

■ **FIGURE 1.2** Structure and Agency

· ·

Critical thinking: The ability to evaluate claims about truth by using reason and evidence.

Smile, you're on camera! Major metropolitan areas like Washington, DC, New York City, and London are heavily monitored by security cameras, especially since the September 11, 2001, terrorist attacks. Defining the appropriate balance between privacy and increased security is a contemporary challenge for governments and societies. ■

measured by the cost of government services, the number of agencies or offices within the government, the number of people working for it, or something else? What did Jefferson mean by "best," and what would that "best" government look like? Who would have the power to define this notion in any case?

3. **Back up your arguments with evidence.** Founding Father Thomas Jefferson is a formidable person to quote, but quoting him does not *prove* that smaller government is better in the 21st century. To find evidence, we need to seek out studies of contemporary societies to see whether there is a relationship between a population's well-being and the size of government or the breadth of services it provides. Because studies may offer contradictory evidence, we also need to be able to assess the strengths and weaknesses of arguments on different sides of the issue.

4. **Think about the assumptions and biases—including your own—that underlie all studies.** You may insist that government has a key role to play in modern society. On the other hand, you may believe with equal passion that big government is one root of the problems in the United States. Critical thinking, however, requires that we recognize our beliefs and biases. Otherwise we might unconsciously seek out only evidence that supports our argument, ignoring evidence to the contrary. Passion has a role to play in research: It can motivate us to devote long hours to studying an issue. But passion should not play a role when we are weighing evidence and drawing conclusions.

5. **Avoid anecdotal evidence.** It is tempting to draw a general conclusion from a single experience or anecdote, but that experience may illustrate the exception rather than the rule. For example, you may know someone who just yesterday received a letter mailed two years ago, but that is not evidence that the U.S. Postal Service is inefficient or does not fulfill its mandates. To determine whether this government agency is working well, you would have to study its entire mail delivery system and its record of work over time.

6. **Be willing to admit when you are wrong or uncertain about your results.** Sometimes we expect to find support for an argument only to find that things are not so clear. For example, consider the position of a sociologist who advocates small government and learns that Japan and Singapore initially became economic powerhouses because their governments played a leading role in promoting growth, or the sociologist who champions an expanded role for government but learns from the downturn of the 1990s in the Asian economies that some things can be better achieved by private enterprise. The answers we get are sometimes contradictory, and we learn from recognizing the error of our assumptions and beliefs as well.

Critical thinking means becoming a "critical consumer" of the information—news, blogs, surveys, texts, magazines, and scientific studies—that surrounds us. To be a good sociologist, it is important to look beyond the commonsense understanding of social life and develop a critical perspective. Being a critical

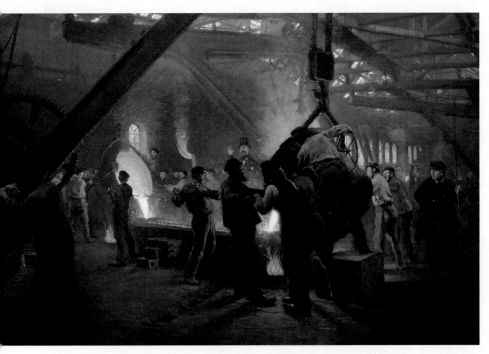

The harnessing of waterpower and the steam engine in textile production helped give rise to the industrial era and to factories, immortalized by writers such as Charles Dickens, in which men, women, and even children toiled for hours in wretched working conditions. Poet William Blake called these workplaces the "dark satanic mills." ∎

consumer of information also means paying attention to the sources of information we encounter and asking questions about how data were gathered.

THE DEVELOPMENT OF SOCIOLOGICAL THINKING

Humans have been asking questions about the nature of social life as long as people have lived in societies. Aristotle and Plato wrote extensively about social relationships more than 2,000 years ago. Ibn Khaldun, an Arab scholar writing in the 14th century, advanced a number of sociological concepts we recognize today. Yet modern sociological concepts and research methods did not emerge until the 19th century, after the Industrial Revolution, and then largely in those European nations undergoing dramatic changes in the form of industrialization and urbanization.

THE BIRTH OF SOCIOLOGY: SCIENCE, PROGRESS, INDUSTRIALIZATION, AND URBANIZATION

We can trace sociology's roots to four interrelated historical developments that gave birth to the modern world: the *scientific revolution,* the *Enlightenment, industrialization,* and *urbanization.* Since all these developments initially occurred in Europe, it is not surprising that sociological perspectives and ideas evolved there during the 19th century. By the end of the 19th century, sociology had taken root in North America as well; somewhat later, it gained a foothold in Central and South America, Africa,

and Asia. Sociology throughout the world initially bore the stamp of its European and North American origins, though recent decades have brought a greater diversity of perspectives to the discipline.

THE SCIENTIFIC REVOLUTION The rise of modern natural and physical sciences, beginning in Europe in the 16th century, offered scholars a more advanced understanding of the physical world. The success of natural science contributed to the belief that science could also be fruitfully applied to human affairs, thereby enabling people to improve society or even perfect it. Auguste Comte (1798–1857) coined the term *sociology* to characterize what he believed would be a new "social physics"—that is, the scientific study of society.

THE ENLIGHTENMENT Inspired in part by the success of the physical sciences, French philosophers in the 18th century such as Voltaire (1694–1778), Montesquieu (1689–1755), Diderot (1719–1784), and Rousseau (1712–1778) promised that humankind could attain lofty heights by applying scientific understanding to human affairs. Enlightenment ideals such as equality, liberty, and fundamental human rights found a home in the emerging social sciences, particularly sociology. Émile Durkheim (1858–1917), considered by many to be the first modern sociologist, argued that sociological understanding would create a more egalitarian, peaceful society, in which individuals would be free to realize their full potential. Many of sociology's founders shared the hope that a fairer and more just society would be achieved through the scientific understanding of society.

THE INDUSTRIAL REVOLUTION The Industrial Revolution, which began in England in the mid-18th century and soon spread to other countries, dramatically changed European societies. Traditional agricultural economies and the small-scale production of handicrafts in the home gave way to more efficient, profit-driven manufacturing based in factories. For instance, in 1801 in the English city of Leeds, there were about 20 factories manufacturing a variety of goods. By 1838, there were 106 woolen mills alone, employing 10,000 people.

Small towns including Leeds were transformed into bustling cities, showcasing extremes of wealth and poverty as well as opportunity and struggle. In the face of rapid social change and growing inequality, sociologists sought to gain a social scientific perspective on what was happening and how it had come about. For example, German theorist and revolutionary Karl Marx, who had an important impact on later sociological theorizing about modern societies and economies, predicted that industrialization would make life increasingly intolerable for the masses. He believed that private property ownership by the wealthy allowed for the exploitation of working people, and that its elimination, and revolution, would bring about a utopia of equality and genuine freedom for all.

URBANIZATION: THE POPULATION SHIFT TOWARD CITIES Industrialization fostered the growth of cities, as people streamed from rural fields to urban factories in search of work. By the end of the 19th century, more than 20 million people lived in English cities: The population of London alone exceeded 7 million by 1910.

Early industrial cities were often fetid places, characterized by pollution and dirt, crime, and crowded housing tenements. In Europe, early sociologists lamented the passing of communal village life and its replacement by a savage and alienating urban existence. Émile Durkheim, for example, worried about the potential breakdown of stabilizing beliefs and values in modern urban society. He argued that whereas traditional communities were held together by shared culture and **norms**, or *accepted social behaviors and beliefs,* modern industrial communities were threatened by **anomie**, or *a state of normlessness that occurs when people lose sight of the shared rules and values that give order and meaning to their lives.* In a state of anomie, individuals often feel confused and anxious, because they do not know how to interact with each other and their environment. Durkheim raised the question of what would hold societies and communities together as they shifted from homogeneity and shared cultures and values to heterogeneous masses of diverse and different occupations, cultures, and norms.

19TH-CENTURY FOUNDERS

Despite its largely European origins, early sociology sought to develop universal understandings that would apply to other peoples, times, and places. The discipline's principal acknowledged founders—Auguste Comte, Harriet Martineau, Émile Durkheim, Karl Marx, and Max Weber—left their mark on sociology in different ways.

AUGUSTE COMTE Auguste Comte (1798–1857), a French social theorist, is credited with founding modern sociology, naming it, and associating it with the scientific study of social relationships. The twin pillars of Comte's sociology were the study of **social statics**, *the way society is held together,* and the analysis of **social dynamics**, *the laws that govern social change.* Comte believed social science could be used effectively to manage the social change resulting from modern industrial society, but always with a strong respect for traditions and history.

Comte proclaimed that his new science of society was **positivist**. This meant that it was to be *based on facts alone,* which should

. . . .

Norms: Accepted social behaviors and beliefs.

Anomie: A social condition of normlessness; a state of normative uncertainty that occurs when people lose touch with the shared rules and values that give order and meaning to their lives.

Social statics: The way society is held together.

Social dynamics: The laws that govern social change.

Positivist: Science that is based on facts alone.

As a founding figure in the social sciences, Auguste Comte is associated with positivism, or the belief that social sciences must be anchored in facts and the scientific method. ■

be determined scientifically and allowed to speak for themselves. Comte argued that this purely factual approach was the proper method for sociology. He argued that all sciences—and all societies—go through three stages. The first stage is a *theological* one, in which explanations of the world are framed in terms of superstition, imagination, and religion. The second stage is a *metaphysical* one, characterized by abstract speculation, but framed by the basic belief that society is the product of natural rather than supernatural forces. The third and last stage is one in which knowledge is based on *scientific reasoning* "from the facts." Comte saw himself as leading sociology toward its final positivist stage.

Comte left a lasting mark on modern sociology. The scientific study of social life continues to be the goal of sociological research. His belief that social institutions have a strong impact on individual behavior—that is, that our actions are the product of personal choices *and* the surrounding social context—remains at the heart of sociology.

HARRIET MARTINEAU Harriet Martineau (1802–1876) was an English sociologist who, despite deafness and other physical challenges, became a prominent social and historical writer. Her greatest handicap was being a woman in male-dominated intellectual circles that failed to value female voices. Today she is generally acclaimed as the first woman sociologist.

Deeply influenced by Comte's work, Martineau translated his six-volume treatise on politics into English. Her editing helped make Comte's esoteric prose accessible to the English-speaking world, ensuring his standing as a leading figure in sociology.

Interestingly, Harriet Martineau translated into English the work of Auguste Comte, who dismissed women's intellect, saying, "Biological philosophy teaches us that . . . radical differences, physical and moral, distinguish the sexes . . . biological analysis presents the female sex . . . as constitutionally in a state of perpetual infancy, in comparison with the other" (Kandal, 1988, p. 75). ■

Martineau was also a distinguished scholar in her own right. She wrote dozens of books, more than a thousand newspaper columns, and 25 novels, including a three-volume study, *Society in America* (1837), based on observations of the United States she made during a tour there.

Martineau, like Comte, sought to identify basic laws that govern society. She derived three of her four "laws" from other theorists. The fourth law, however, was her own and reflected her feminist principles: For a society to evolve, it must ensure social justice for women and other oppressed groups. In her study of U.S. society, Martineau treated slavery and women's experience in marriage as indicators of the limits of moral development of the United States. In her view, the United States was unable to achieve its full social potential while it was morally stunted by persistent injustices like slavery and women's inequality. The question of whether the provision of social justice is critical to societal development remains a relevant and compelling one today.

ÉMILE DURKHEIM Auguste Comte founded and named the discipline of sociology, but French scholar Émile Durkheim (1858–1917) set the field on its present course. Durkheim established the early subject matter of sociology, laid out rules for conducting research, and developed an important theory of social change.

For Durkheim, sociology's subject matter was **social facts**, *qualities of groups that are external to individual members yet constrain their thinking and behavior.* Durkheim argued that such social facts as religious beliefs and social duties are external—that is, they are part of the social context and are larger than our individual lives. They also have the power to shape our behavior. You may feel compelled to act in certain ways in different contexts—in the classroom, on a date, at a religious ceremony—even if you are not always aware of such social pressures.

Durkheim also argued that *only social facts can explain other social facts.* For example, there is no scientific evidence that men have a superior, innate knack for business compared with women—but in 2012, women headed just 18 of the Fortune 500 companies. A Durkheimian approach would highlight the fact that women's experience in society—where historically they have been socialized into more domestic values or restricted to certain noncommercial professions—and the fact that the social networks that foster mobility in the corporate world today are still primarily male, can help explain why men dominate the upper ranks of the business world.

Émile Durkheim pioneered some of sociology's early research on such topics as social solidarity and suicide. His work continues to inform sociological study and understanding of social bonds and the consequences of their unraveling. ■

Social facts: Qualities of groups that are external to individual members yet constrain their thinking and behavior.

Durkheim's principal concern was explaining the impact of modern society on **social solidarity**, *the bonds that unite the members of a social group.* In his view, in traditional society these bonds are based on similarity—people speak the same language, share the same customs and beliefs, and do similar work tasks. He called this *mechanical solidarity.* In modern industrial society, however, bonds based on similarity break down. Everyone has a different job to perform in the industrial division of labor, and modern societies are more likely to be socially diverse. However, workers in different occupational positions are dependent upon one another for things like safety, education, and the provision of food and other goods essential to survival. The people filling these positions may not be alike in culture, beliefs, or language, but their dependence on one another contributes to social cohesion. Borrowing from biology, Durkheim called this *organic solidarity,* suggesting that modern society functioned as an interdependent organic whole, like a human body.

Yet organic solidarity, Durkheim argued, is not as strong as mechanical solidarity. People no longer necessarily share the same norms and values. The consequence, according to Durkheim, is anomie. In this weakened condition, the social order disintegrates and pathological behavior increases (Durkheim, 1922/1973).

Consider whether the United States, a modern and diverse society, is held together primarily by organic solidarity, or whether the hallmark of mechanical solidarity, a **collective conscience**—*common beliefs and values that bind a society together*—is in evidence. Does general patriotism on nationally significant anniversaries such as September 11 and July 4 indicate mechanical solidarity built on a collective sense of shared values, norms, and practices? Or do the deeply divisive politics of recent years suggest bonds based more fully on practical interdependence?

KARL MARX The views of Karl Marx (1818–1883) influenced the development of economics and political science as well as sociology. They also shaped world politics and helped inspire communist revolutions in Russia (later the Soviet Union), China, and Cuba, among others.

Marx's central idea was deceptively simple: Virtually all societies throughout history have been divided into economic classes, with one class prospering at the expense of others. All human history, Marx believed, should be understood as the product of **class conflict**, *competition between social classes over the distribution of wealth, power, and other valued resources in society* (Marx & Engels, 1848/1998).

. . . .

Social solidarity: The bonds that unite the members of a social group.

Collective conscience: Encompasses the common beliefs and values that bind a society together.

Class conflict: The product of competition between social classes over the distribution of wealth and power in society.

Proletariat: The working class; wage workers.

Bourgeoisie: The capitalist (or property-owning) class.

Means of production: The sites and technology that produce the goods we need and use.

Karl Marx was a major scholar and critic of early capitalism. His work has been thoroughly studied and critiqued around the world. ∎

In the period of early industrialization in which he lived, Marx condemned capitalism's exploitation of *working people,* the **proletariat**, by the *ownership class,* the **bourgeoisie.** As we will see in the book, Marx's views on conflict and inequality are still influential in contemporary sociological thinking, even among sociologists who do not share his views on society.

Marx focused his attention on the emerging capitalist industrial society (Marx, 1867/1992a, 1885/1992b, 1894/1992c). Unlike his contemporaries in sociology, however, Marx saw capitalism as a transitional stage to a final period in human history, in which economic classes and the unequal distribution of rewards and opportunities linked to class inequality would disappear and be replaced by a utopia of equality.

Although many of Marx's predictions have not proven to be correct, his critical analysis of the dynamics of capitalism proved insightful. Among other things, Marx posited that capitalism would lead to accelerating technological change, the replacement of workers by machines, and the growth of monopoly capitalism.

Marx also presciently predicted that ownership of the **means of production**, *the sites and technology that produce the goods*

Weber and Marx

(and sometimes services) we need and use, would come to be concentrated in fewer and fewer hands. As a result, he believed, a growing wave of people would be thrust down into the proletariat, which owned only its own labor power. In modern society, large corporations have progressively swallowed up or pushed out smaller businesses; where small lumber yards and pharmacies used to serve many communities, corporate giants such as Home Depot, CVS, and Best Buy have moved in, putting locally owned establishments out of business.

In many U.S. towns, small business owners have joined forces to protest the construction of enormous "box" stores like Walmart (now the largest private employer in the United States), arguing that these establishments, while they offer cheap goods, also wreak havoc on local retailers and bring only the meager economic benefit of masses of entry-level, low-wage jobs. From a Marxist perspective, we might say that the local retailers, in resisting the incursion of the capitalist behemoth Walmart, are fighting their own "proletarianization." Even physicians, many of whom used to own their own means of production in the form of private medical offices, have increasingly been driven by economic necessity into work in large health maintenance organizations (HMOs), where they become salaried employees.

Unlike Comte and Durkheim, Marx thought social change would be revolutionary, not evolutionary, and would be the product of oppressed workers rising up against a capitalist system that exploited the many to benefit the few.

MAX WEBER Max Weber (1864–1920), a German sociologist who wrote at the turn of the 20th century, left a substantial academic legacy. Among his contributions were an analysis of how Protestantism fostered the rise of capitalism in Europe (Weber, 1904–1905/2002) and insights into the emergence of modern bureaucracy (Gerth & Mills, 1958). Weber, like other founders of sociology, took up various political causes, condemning injustice wherever he found it. Although pessimistic about capitalism, he did not believe, as did Marx, that some alternative utopian form of society would arise. Nor did he see sociologists enjoying privileged insights into the social world that would qualify them to wisely counsel rulers and industrialists, as Comte (and, to some extent, Durkheim) had envisioned.

Weber believed that an adequate explanation of the social world begins with the individual and takes into account the *meaning* of what people say and do. While he argued that research should be scientific and value free, Weber also believed that to explain what people do, we must use a method he termed *Verstehen,* the German word for *interpretive understanding.* This methodology, rarely used by sociologists today, sought to explain social relationships by having the sociologist/observer imagine how the subjects being studied might have perceived and interpreted the situation. Studying social life, Weber felt, was not like studying plants or chemical reactions, because human beings act on the basis of meanings and motives.

Weber's theories of social and economic organization have also been highly influential (Weber, 1921/2012). Weber argued that the modern Western world showed an ever-increasing reliance on logic, efficiency, and reason. According to him, modern societies were

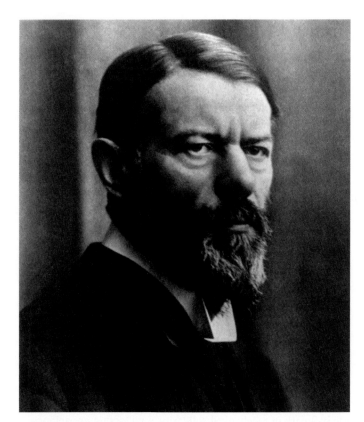

Max Weber made significant contributions to the understanding of how capitalism developed in Western countries, and its relationship to religious beliefs. Here is an easy trick to distinguish freshman from senior sociology students: See if they pronounce his last name as "Weber" or "Veiber!" ■

characterized by the development and growing influence of **formal rationality,** *a context in which people's pursuit of goals is increasingly shaped by rules, regulations, and larger social structures.* One of Weber's best known illustrations of formal rationality is his study of **bureaucracies,** *formal organizations characterized by written rules, hierarchical authority, and a paid staff, intended to promote organizational efficiency.* Bureaucracies, for Weber, epitomized formally rational systems: on the one hand, they offered clear, knowable rules and regulations for the efficient pursuit of an end, like obtaining a passport or getting financial aid for higher education. On the other hand, he feared, the bureaucratization of modern society would also progressively strip people of their humanity and creativity.

Weber's ideas about bureaucracy were remarkably prescient in their characterization of our bureaucratic (and formally rationalized) modern world. Today we are also confronted regularly with both the incredible efficiency and the baffling irrationality of

. . . .

Verstehen: The German word for interpretive understanding.

Formal rationality: A characteristic of modern societies, which means that people's pursuit of goals is shaped by rules, regulations, and larger social structures.

Bureaucracies: Formal organizations characterized by written rules, hierarchical authority, and a paid staff, intended to promote organizational efficiency.

modern bureaucratic structures. Within moments of entering an efficiently concluded contract with a wireless phone service provider, we can become consumers of a cornucopia of technological opportunities with the ability to chat on the phone or receive text messages from virtually anywhere, post photographs or videos online, and pass the time playing downloaded games. Should we later be confused by a bill and need to speak to a company representative, however, we may be shuttled through endless repetitions of an automated response system that never seems to offer the option to speak to another human being. Today, Weber's irrationality of rationality is alive and well.

EARLY 20TH-CENTURY U.S. SOCIOLOGY

Sociology was born in Europe, but it took firm root in U.S. soil, where it was heavily influenced by turn-of-the-century industrialization and urbanization, as well as racial strife and discrimination. Strikes by organized labor, corruption in government, an explosion of European immigration, racial segregation, and the growth of city slums all helped mold early sociological thought in the United States. By the late 1800s, a number of universities in the United States were offering sociology courses. The first faculties of sociology were established at the University of Kansas (1889), the University of Chicago (1892), and Atlanta University (1897).

ROBERT EZRA PARK The sociology department at the University of Chicago, which gave us what is often known as the "Chicago School" of sociology, dominated the new discipline in the United States at the start of the 20th century. Chicago sociologist Robert Ezra Park (1864–1944) pioneered the study of urban sociology and race relations. Once a muckraking journalist, Park was an equally colorful academic, reportedly coming to class in disheveled clothes and with shaving soap still in his ears. But his students were devoted to him and his work was widely recognized. His 1921 textbook *An Introduction to the Science of Sociology,* co-authored with his Chicago colleague Ernest Burgess, helped shape the discipline. The Chicago school studied a broad spectrum of social phenomena, from hoboes and flophouses (inexpensive dormitory-style housing) to movie houses, dance halls, and slums, and from youth gangs and mobs to residents of Chicago's ritzy Gold Coast.

Park was a champion of racial integration, having once served as personal secretary to the African American educator Booker T. Washington. Yet racial discrimination was evident in the treatment of Black sociologists, including W. E. B. Du Bois, a contemporary of many of the sociologists working in the Chicago School.

W. E. B. DU BOIS A prominent Black sociologist and civil rights leader at the African American Atlanta University, W. E. B. Du Bois (1868–1963) developed ideas that were considered too radical to find broad acceptance in the sociological community. At a time when the U.S. Supreme Court had ruled that segregated "separate but equal" facilities for Blacks and Whites were constitutional

W. E. B. Du Bois, the first African American to receive a PhD from Harvard, wrote 20 books and more than 100 scholarly articles on race and race relations. Today many of his works are classics in the study of African American lives and race relations in the United States. ■

and when lynching of Black Americans had reached an all-time high, Du Bois condemned the deep-seated racism of White society. Today, his writings on race relations and the lives of U.S. Blacks are classics in the field.

Du Bois sought to show that racism was widespread in U.S. society. He was also critical of Blacks who had "made it" and then turned their backs on those who had not. One of his most enduring ideas is that in U.S. society, African Americans are never able to escape a fundamental awareness of race. They experience a **double consciousness**, as he called it—*an awareness of themselves both as Americans and as Blacks, never free of racial stigma.* He wrote, "The Negro is sort of a seventh son . . . gifted with second sight . . . the sense of always looking at oneself through the eyes of others" (Du Bois, 1903/2011). Today as in Du Bois's time, physical traits such as skin color may shape people's perceptions and interactions in significant and complex ways.

THE MID-20TH CENTURY IN U.S. SOCIOLOGY After World War II, sociology began to apply sophisticated quantitative

. . . .

Double consciousness: An awareness of oneself both as American and as Black, never free of racial stigma.

Double-Consciousness

Tuskeegee Airmen and Double Consciousness

The "sociological imagination" involves viewing seemingly personal issues through a sociological lens. C. Wright Mills is best known for coining this catchy and popular term. ■

models to the study of social processes. There was also a growing interest in the grand theories of the European founders. At Columbia University, Robert K. Merton's (1910–2003) wide-ranging studies helped further establish sociology as a scientific discipline. Merton is best known for his theory of deviance (Merton, 1938), his work on the sociology of science (Merton, 1996), and his iteration of the distinction between *manifest* and *latent* functions (Merton, 1967). He emphasized the development of theories in what he called the "middle range"—midway between the grand theories of Weber, Marx, and Durkheim and quantitative studies of specific social problems.

Another Columbia University sociologist, C. Wright Mills (1916–1962), renewed interest in Max Weber by translating many of his works into English and applying his ideas to the contemporary United States. But Mills, who also drew on Marx, identified himself as a "plain Marxist." His concept of the sociological imagination can be traced in part to Marx's famous statement that "man makes history, but not under circumstances of his own choosing," meaning that while we are agents of free will, the social context may determine the obstacles or opportunities in our lives.

Sociological History

Mills synthesized Weberian and Marxian traditions, applying sociological thinking to the most pressing problems of the day, particularly inequality. He advocated an activist sociology with a sense of social responsibility. Like many sociologists, he was willing to turn a critical eye on "common knowledge," including the belief that the United States is a democracy that represents the interests of all the people. In a provocative study, he examined the workings of the "power elite," a small group of wealthy businessmen, military leaders, and politicians who Mills believed ran the country largely in their own interests (Mills, 1956/2000a).

WHY SO FEW FOUNDING MOTHERS?

Why did so few women social scientists find a place among sociology's founders? After all, the American (1776) and French (1789) revolutions elevated such lofty ideals as freedom, liberty, and equality. Yet long after these historical events, women and minorities were still excluded from public life in Europe and North America. Democracy—which gives people the right to participate in their governance—was firmly established as a principle for nearly a century and a half in the United States before women achieved the right to vote in 1920. In France, it took even longer—until 1945.

Sociology as a discipline emerged during the first modern flourishing of feminism in the 19th century. Yet women and people of non-European heritage were systematically excluded from influential positions in the European universities where sociology and the other modern social sciences originated. When women did pursue lives as scholars, the men who dominated the social sciences largely ignored their writings. Feminist scholar Julie Daubié won a prize from the Lyon Academy for her essay "Poor Women in the Nineteenth Century," yet France's public education minister denied her a diploma on the grounds that he would be "forever holding up his ministry to ridicule" (Kandal, 1988, pp. 57–58). Between 1840 and 1960, almost no women held senior academic positions in any sociology department at any European or U.S. university, with the exception of exclusively women's colleges.

A number of woman scholars managed to overcome the obstacles to make significant contributions to sociological inquiry. For example, in 1792 the British scholar Mary Wollstonecraft published *A Vindication of the Rights of Women,* arguing that scientific progress could not occur unless women were allowed to become men's equals by means of universal education. In France in 1843, Flora Tristan called for equal rights for women workers, "the last remaining slaves in France." Also in France, Aline Valette published *Socialism and Sexualism* in 1893, nearly three quarters of a century before the term *sexism* found its way into spoken English (Kandal, 1988).

One of sociology's most prominent early figures, Jane Addams (1860–1935), never won a full-time position at the University of Chicago in spite of the school's "progressive" leanings. The University of Chicago even denied her an honorary degree—though she wrote 11 books and hundreds of articles and was awarded the Nobel Peace Prize in 1931 for her dedication to social reform.

Addams is best known as the founder of Hull House, a settlement house for the poor, sick, and aged that became a center for

Underappreciated during her time, Jane Addams was a prominent scholar and early contributor to sociology. She is also known for her political activism and commitment to social reform. ■

political activists and social reformers. Less well known is the fact that under Addams's guidance, the residents of Hull House engaged in important research on social problems in Chicago. *Hull House Maps and Papers,* published in 1895, pioneered the study of Chicago neighborhoods, helping to shape the research direction of the Chicago School of sociology. Following Addams's lead, Chicago sociologists mapped the city's neighborhoods, studied their residents, and helped create the field of community studies.

As sociologists like Harriet Martineau, Jane Addams, Julie Daubié, and others experienced, early female sociologists were not accorded the same status as their male counterparts. Only recently were many of their writings "rediscovered" and their contributions acknowledged in sociology.

. . . .

Sociological theories: Logical, rigorous frameworks for the interpretation of social life that make particular assumptions and ask particular questions about the social world.

Macro-level paradigm: Theories of the social world that are concerned with large-scale patterns and institutions.

Micro-level paradigm: Models or images of the world that are concerned with social relations and interactions in specific, individual situations.

Structural functionalism (functionalist perspective): A theory that seeks to explain social organization and change in terms of the roles performed by different social structures and institutions.

SOCIOLOGY: ONE WAY OF LOOKING AT THE WORLD— OR MANY?

Sociologists often look at the same events, phenomena, or institutions and draw different conclusions. How can this be? One reason is that they may approach their analysis from different theoretical perspectives. In this section, we explore the key theoretical paradigms in sociology and look at how they are used as tools for the analysis of society.

Sociological theories are *logical, rigorous frameworks for the interpretation of social life that make particular assumptions and ask particular questions about the social world.* The word *theory* is rooted in the Greek word *theoria*, which means "a viewing." An apt metaphor for a theory is a set of glasses. You can view a social phenomenon such as socioeconomic inequality or poverty, deviance, or consumer culture, or an institution like capitalism or the family using different theories as lenses.

As you will see in the next section, in the discipline of sociology, there are several major categories of theories that seek to examine and explain social phenomena and institutions. Imagine the various sociological theories as different sets of glasses, each with colored lenses that change the way you see an image: As you put on each one, you may look at the same institution or phenomenon, but it will appear different, depending on the glasses you are wearing. Keep in mind that sociological theories are not "truths" about the social world. They are logical, rigorous analytical tools that we can use to inquire about, interpret, and make educated predictions about the world around us. From the vantage point of any sociological theory, some aspects of a phenomenon or an institution are illuminated, while others are obscured. In the end, theories are more or less useful depending on how well *empirical data*—that is, knowledge gathered by researchers through scientific methods—support their analytical conclusions. Below, we outline the basic theoretical perspectives that we will be using in this text.

The three dominant theoretical perspectives in sociology are *structural functionalism, social conflict theory,* and *symbolic interactionism.* We'll outline their basic characteristics below and revisit them again throughout the book. Symbolic interactionism shares with the functionalist and social conflict paradigms an interest in interpreting and understanding social life. However, the first two are **macro-level paradigms,** *concerned with large-scale patterns and institutions.* Symbolic interactionism is a **micro-level paradigm.** That is, it is *concerned with social relations and interactions in specific, individual situations.*

Structural functionalism, social conflict theory, and symbolic interactionism form the basic foundation of contemporary sociological theorizing (Table 1.1 on page 16). In the book, we will be introducing variations on these theories, as well as new and evolving theoretical ideas in sociology.

THE FUNCTIONALIST PARADIGM

Structural functionalism (or functionalism—the term we use in this book) *seeks to explain social organization and change in*

Theoretical Perspective and Founding Theorist(s)	Structural Functionalism *Émile Durkheim*	Social Conflict *Karl Marx*	Symbolic Interactionism *Max Weber, George Herbert Mead*
Assumptions About Self and Society	Society is a system of interdependent, interrelated parts, like an organism, with groups and institutions contributing to the stability and equilibrium of the whole social system.	Society consists of conflicting interests, but only some groups have the power and resources to realize their interests. Some groups benefit from the social order at the expense of other groups.	The self is a social creation; social interaction occurs by means of symbols such as words, gestures, and adornments; shared meanings are important to successful social interactions.
Key Focus and Questions	Macrosociology: What keeps society operating smoothly? What functions do different societal institutions and phenomena serve for society as a whole?	Macrosociology: What are the sources of conflict in society? Who benefits, and who loses from the existing social order? How can inequalities be overcome?	Microsociology: How do individuals experience themselves, one another, and society as a whole? How do they interpret the meanings of particular social interactions?

terms of the roles performed by different social structures and institutions. Functionalism characterizes society as made up of many interdependent parts—an analogy often cited is the human body. Each part serves a different function, but all parts work together to ensure the equilibrium and health of the entity as a whole. Society too is composed of a spectrum of different parts with a variety of different functions, such as the government, the family, religious and educational institutions, and the media. Together they contribute to the smooth functioning and equilibrium of a society.

The key question posed by the functionalist perspective is "What function does a particular institution, phenomenon, or social group serve for the maintenance of society?" That is, what contribution does a given institution, phenomenon, or social group make to the equilibrium, stability, and functioning of the whole? Note the underlying assumption of functionalism: Any existing institution or phenomenon *does* serve a function; if it served no function, it would evolve out of existence. Consequently, the central task of the functionalist sociologist is to discover what function an institution or a phenomenon—for instance, the traditional family, capitalism, social stratification, or deviance—serves in the maintenance of the social order.

Émile Durkheim is credited with developing the early foundations of functionalism. Among other ideas, Durkheim observed that all known societies have some degree of deviant behavior, such as crime. The notion that deviance is functional for societies may seem counterintuitive: Ordinarily, we do not think of deviance as beneficial or necessary to society. Durkheim, however, reasoned that since deviance is universal, it must serve a social function—if it did not serve a function, it would cease to exist. Durkheim

Symbolic Interactionism

concluded that one function of deviance—specifically, of society's labeling of some acts as deviant—is to remind members of society what is "normal" or "moral"; when a society punishes deviant behavior, it reaffirms people's beliefs in what is right and good.

Talcott Parsons (1902–1979) expanded functionalist analysis by looking at whole social systems such as government, the economy, and the family, and how they contribute to the functioning of the whole social system (Parsons, 1964/2007, 1967). For example, he wrote that traditional sex roles for men and women contribute to stability on both the micro familial level and the macro societal level. Parsons argued that traditional socialization produces *instrumental* or rational and work-oriented males, and *expressive* or sensitive, nurturing, and emotional females. Instrumental males, he reasoned, were well suited for the competitive world of work, while their expressive female counterparts were appropriately prepared to care for the family. According to Parsons, these roles are complementary and positively functional, leading men and women to inhabit different spheres of the social world. Complementary rather than competing roles contribute to solidarity in a marriage by reducing competition between husband and wife. Critics have rejected this idea as a justification of inequality.

As this example suggests, functionalism is conservative in that it tends to accept rather than question the status quo; it holds that any given institution or phenomenon exists because it is functional for society, rather than asking whether it might benefit one group to the detriment of others, as critics say Parsons's position on gender roles does. One of functionalism's longstanding weaknesses is a failure to recognize inequalities in the distribution of power and resources and how those affect social relationships.

Robert Merton attempted to refine the functionalist paradigm by demonstrating that not all social structures work to maintain or strengthen the social organism, as Durkheim and other early functionalists seemed to suggest. According to Merton, a social institution or phenomenon can have both positive functions and problematic dysfunctions. Merton broadened the functionalist

The manifest function of a vehicle is to transport a person efficiently from point A to point B. One latent function is to say something about the status of the driver. ■

idea by suggesting that **manifest functions** are *the obvious and intended functions of a given phenomenon or institution.* **Latent functions**, by contrast, are *functions that are not recognized or expected.* A manifest function of war, for instance, is usually to vanquish an enemy, perhaps to defend a territory or to claim it. Latent functions of war—those that are not the overt purpose but may still have a powerful effect—may include increased patriotism in countries engaged in the war, a rise in the profits of companies manufacturing military equipment or contracting workers to the military, and a change in national budgetary priorities.

THE SOCIAL CONFLICT PARADIGM

In contrast to functionalism, the **social conflict paradigm** (which we refer to in the book as conflict theory) *seeks to explain social organization and change in terms of the conflict built into social relationships.* Conflict theory is rooted in the ideas about class and power put forth by Karl Marx. While Durkheim's structural functionalist lens asked how different parts of society contribute to stability, Marx asked about the roots of conflict. Conflict theorists pose the questions "Who benefits from the way social institutions and relationships are structured?" and "Who loses?" The social

conflict paradigm focuses on what divides people, rather than what unites them. It presumes that group interests (such as social class interests) drive relationships, and that each group in society (for instance, social classes or genders or ethnic or racial groups) will act in its own interests. Conflict theory thus assumes not that interests are shared but rather that they may be irreconcilable and, importantly, that only some groups have the power and resources to realize their interests. Because of this, conflict is—sooner or later—inevitable.

From Marx's perspective, the bourgeoisie benefits directly from the capitalist social order. If, as Marx suggests, the capitalist class has an interest in maximizing productivity and profit and minimizing costs (like the cost of labor in the form of workers' wages), and the working class has an interest in earning more and working less, then their interests are difficult to reconcile. The more powerful group in society generally has the upper hand in furthering its interests.

After Marx, the body of conflict theory has expanded tremendously. In the 20th century and today, theorists have expanded the reach of the perspective to consider, for instance, how control of culture and the rise of technology (rather than just control of the means of production) underpinned class domination (Adorno, 1975; Horkheimer, 1947), as well as how the expanded middle class could be accommodated in a Marxist perspective (Wright, 1998). Some of feminist theory's key ideas also reflect a conflict-oriented perspective, though the focus shifts from social class to gender power and conflict (Connell, 2005), as well as ways that race is implicated in relations of power (Collins, 1990).

Recall Durkheim's functionalist analysis of crime and deviance. According to this perspective, society defines crime to reaffirm people's

Manifest functions: Functions of an object, an institution, or a phenomenon that are obvious and intended.

Latent functions: Functions of an object, an institution, or a phenomenon that are not recognized or expected.

Social conflict paradigm (conflict perspective): A theory that seeks to explain social organization and change in terms of the conflict that is built into social relations.

WHY ARE SOME PEOPLE POOR AND OTHERS RICH?

The concentration of wealth in the hands of a small elite and the widespread struggle of billions to make do with scant resources is a critical issue on both the domestic and global levels.

One common explanation of the disparity in the United States is that it results from individual differences in talent and ambition. While such factors play a role, the fact that over 15% of the population lives below the poverty line, including disproportionate numbers of Blacks, Latinos, and women (DeNavas-Walt, Proctor, & Smith, 2012), should lead our sociological imaginations to recognize that social and economic forces also underlie inequality.

Discrimination can place entire groups of people at an economic disadvantage. Women as a group continue to earn less than men as a group—as do Blacks and Latinos relative to White Americans. Importantly as well, educational opportunity is not equally distributed because in most U.S. states schools are still primarily funded by local property taxes; consequently, high-value areas have more funds to spend on teachers, textbooks, and technology than low-value areas. Without a strong educational foundation that prepares

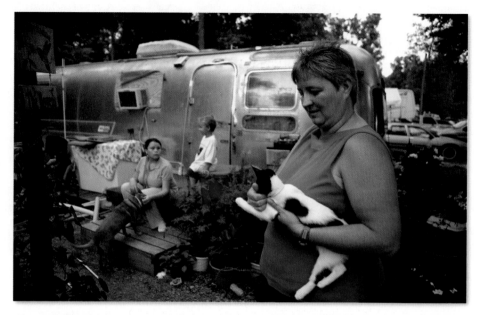

Why are children of poor parents are more likely to be poor as adults? This is a question of fundamental interest to sociologists. ■

them for a competitive economy, already poor children are likely to remain poor as adults.

Economic changes have also spurred the growth of inequality. Automation and the movement abroad of factory work have significantly reduced employment opportunities for less educated workers. Service jobs, including restaurant and retail work, have expanded as the manufacturing sector contracts, but they are far less likely to pay a living wage or give a worker a lift into the middle class.

Education is thus more critical than ever, but poor children are the least likely to get the solid skills they need to succeed.

THINK IT THROUGH

■ *In his inaugural address of 2013, President Obama stated that one of his goals in his second term as president was to see that a young girl born into poverty would know that she had every opportunity to realize her hopes. How are such opportunities created? What do you think?*

---

beliefs about what is right and dissuade them from deviating. A conflict theorist might argue that the behaviors labeled criminal or deviant are defined by dominant groups in society, *because they have the power to do so.* For example, street crimes such as mugging someone to get his wallet or carjacking are clearly defined and punished as criminal behavior. They are also amply represented in reality television programs, movies, and other cultural products as the image of criminal deviance. On the other hand, corporate or white-collar crime, which may cause a loss of money or even life, is less likely to be clearly defined,

represented, and punished as criminal. From a conflict perspective, white-collar crime is more likely to be committed by the upper class (for instance, business or political leaders or financiers) but is less likely to be punished harshly than street crime, which is associated with the lower-income classes, though white-collar crime may have even greater economic and health consequences. A social conflict theorist would draw our attention to the fact that the decision makers who pass our laws are mostly members of the upper class and govern in the interests of capitalism and their own socioeconomic peers.

A key weakness of the social conflict paradigm is that it overlooks the forces of stability, equilibrium, and consensus in society. The assumption that groups have conflicting, even irreconcilable interests, and that those interests are realized by those with power at the expense of those with less power, fails to account for forces of cohesion and stability in societies.

SYMBOLIC INTERACTIONISM

Symbolic interactionism argues that both the individual self and society as a whole are the product of social interactions based on language and other symbols. The term *symbolic interactionism* was coined by U.S. sociologist Herbert Blumer (1900–1987) in 1937, but the approach itself originated in the lectures of George Herbert Mead (1863–1931), a University of Chicago philosopher allied with the Chicago School of sociology. The symbolic interactionist paradigm argues that people acquire their sense of who they are only through interaction with others. They do this by means of **symbols**, *representations of things that are not immediately present to our senses*. Symbols include such things as words, gestures, emoticons, and tattoos, among others.

Recall our earlier discussions of the theoretical interpretations of deviance and crime. A symbolic interactionist might focus on the ways in which people label one another as deviant (a symbolic act that uses language), the factors that make such a label stick, and the meanings underlying such a label. If you are falsely accused of committing a crime you did not commit, how will the label of "criminal" affect the way others see you? How will it affect the way you see yourself, and will you begin to act differently as a result? Can being labeled "deviant" be a self-fulfilling prophecy? For the symbolic interactionist, sociological inquiry is the study of how people interact, and how they create and interpret symbols in the social world.

While symbolic interactionist perspectives draw our attention to important micro-level processes in society, they may miss the larger structural context of those processes, such as discovering who has the power to make laws defining what or who is deviant. For this reason, many sociologists seek to utilize both macro- and micro-level perspectives when analyzing social phenomena such as deviance.

These three paradigms lead to diverse images of society, research questions, and conclusions about the patterns and nature of social life. Each set of "glasses" can provide a different perspective on the social world. Throughout this text, the three major

· ·

Symbolic interactionism: A microsociological perspective that posits that both the individual self and society as a whole are the result of social interactions based on language and other symbols.

Symbols: Representations of things that are not immediately present to our senses.

Power: The ability to mobilize resources and achieve goals despite the resistance of others.

Inequality: Differences in wealth, power, and other valued resources.

Globalization: The process by which people all around the planet become increasingly interconnected economically, politically, culturally, and environmentally.

theoretical paradigms—and some new ones we will encounter in later chapters—will help us understand key issues and themes of sociology.

PRINCIPAL THEMES IN THIS TEXT

We began this chapter with a list of *why* questions with which sociologists are concerned—and about which any one of us might be curious. Behind these questions, we find several major themes—these also are some of the main themes in this book. Three important themes for sociology—and for us—are (1) *power and inequality* and the ways in which the unequal distribution of social, economic, and political power and resources shape opportunities, obstacles, and relationships; (2) the societal changes occurring as a result of *globalization* and the rising *social diversity* of modern societies; and (3) the powerful impact of *technological change* and the global expansion of digital societies.

POWER AND INEQUALITY

As we consider broad social topics such as gender, race, social class, and sexual orientation and their effects on social relationships and resources, we will be asking who has **power**—*the ability to mobilize resources and achieve goals despite the resistance of others*—and who does not. We will also ask about variables that influence the uneven distribution of power, and how some groups use power to create advantages for themselves (and disadvantages for others)—and how disadvantaged groups mobilize to challenge the powerful.

Power is often distributed unequally and can be used by those who possess it to marginalize other social groups. **Inequality** refers to *differences in wealth, power, opportunity, and other valued resources.* The existence of inequality not only raises moral and ethical questions about fairness; it can tear at the very fabric of societies, fostering social alienation and instability. It may also have negative effects on local and national economies. Notably, economic inequality is increasing both within and between many countries around the globe, a fact that makes understanding the roots and consequences of this phenomenon—that is, asking the *why* questions—ever more important.

GLOBALIZATION AND DIVERSITY

Globalization is the *process by which people all over the planet become increasingly interconnected economically, politically, culturally, and environmentally.* Globalization is not new. It began nearly 200,000 years ago when humans first spread from their African cradle into Europe and Asia. For thousands of years, humans have traveled, traded goods, and exchanged ideas over much of the globe, using seaways or land routes such as the famed Silk Road, a stretch of land that links China and Europe. But the rate of globalization took a giant leap forward with the Industrial Revolution, which accelerated the growth of global trade. It made another dramatic jump with the advent of the information age,

YOU, THE GLOBAL CONSUMER

Try a simple experiment. Walk through your dorm room, apartment, or house and make a list of the places of manufacture of some of the products you find. Be sure to examine electronic equipment such as your television, laptop, or smartphone. Go through your closet and drawers, checking the labels on your clothing. What about your bicycle or your car? If you are a good detective, you will find that people who live outside the United States made many of the necessities of your everyday life. Even your U.S.-manufactured car is likely to have parts that have passed through the hands of workers abroad.

According to a recent story in the *New York Times,* fully 90% of footwear sold in the United States is manufactured elsewhere (Manning, 2009). So much of our apparel is made abroad that some student groups have campaigned to ensure that the college apparel marketed by their schools is not made in sweatshops. United Students Against Sweatshops now has chapters across the United States.

While global production based on the use of cheap labor around the world has lowered the cost of many things we consume, it has also contributed to lower wages and lost jobs for manufacturing workers

The expensive sneakers that many Americans enjoy wearing in and outside the gym are often made by poorly compensated female labor abroad. Do labor conditions matter to U.S. consumers? ■

in the United States, as well as the employment of millions of people around the world in low-wage factories. On the one hand, these new industrial workers benefit from expanded job opportunities. On the other hand, the world's workers, many of whom are women, are also vulnerable to exploitation and their wages are often very low, their hours long, and their work sites unpleasant or even hazardous. The conditions under which some workers toil today recall the 19th-century English factories that inspired

Karl Marx to a powerful critique of capitalism's darker side.

THINK IT THROUGH

■ *Many questions remain for sociological investigation: Who benefits and who loses as a result of the explosive growth in global production? Will globalization bring a better world to all or to only a select few? What is our role as consumers in the global chain of production, and how do our choices affect industries and economies at home and abroad?*

DIGITAL SOCIETY

THE EXPLOSIVE GROWTH OF THE INTERNET

The Internet, which has revolutionized the way the world shares information, is barely four decades old. The first Internet message was sent from the University of California at Los Angeles to Stanford in 1969 on a small, experimental Department of Defense network. The initial effort experienced a glitch—the system reportedly crashed as the letter *G* of the word *LOGIN* was typed! Not until the mid-1980s was Internet technology sufficiently developed to make it possible for anyone with a computer to plug into the network. Since it was initially difficult to send anything more than simple text-based messages, the Internet was used mainly by a handful of researchers and scholars.

Part-time University of Illinois programmer Marc Andreessen developed the easy-to-use World Wide Web, with its graphical interface and ability to send sound and images, in 1992. Andreessen called his new program *Mosaic* and gave it away free on the Internet. Within a year and a half, the number of Internet users had tripled to 20 million, and Mosaic had morphed into the Netscape browser. In 1998, Netscape spun off Mozilla, a company that today maintains the Firefox browser. In the summer of 2000, there were 93 million Internet hosts worldwide. By the summer of 2012 there were 908 million and counting, along with about 200 million active

"OMG IT'S 2013 AND THIS HOTEL DOESN'T HAVE WI-FI!" Today's digital age has given us Internet access virtually everywhere, whether we are 35,000 miles in the sky, traveling on a bus, or waiting for class to begin. ■

websites and more than 240 billion Internet users worldwide. The rate of growth shows no signs of slowing (International Telecommunication Union, 2011; Internet Systems Consortium, 2012; Netcraft, 2012).

A recent study by the Pew Internet and American Life Project estimated that 90% of U.S. adults own some type of portable electronic device (Gahran, 2011). As you pass through a public space such as an airport or a mall or ride on public transportation in a metropolitan area, you see people engaging in a multitude of behaviors and activities, all facilitated

by the growth of high-tech gadgetry. Social media platforms like YouTube, Facebook, and Tumblr allow individuals across the globe to post videos and other media to share within the Internet community of millions.

THINK IT THROUGH

■ *Will such widely accessible and vastly powerful technology enable people to play a greater role in shaping their own destinies? Will technology be emancipating, or will it come to threaten our privacy and security in ways we cannot yet grasp? What do you think?*

drawing together individuals, cultures, and countries into a common global web of information exchange. In this book, we consider the variable manifestations, functions, and consequences of globalization on areas like the economy, culture, and the environment.

Growing contacts between people and cultures have made us increasingly aware of social diversity as a feature of modern societies. **Social diversity** is *the social and cultural mixture of different groups in society and the societal recognition of difference as significant.* The spread of culture through the globalization of media and the rise of migration has created a world in which virtually no place is isolated. As a result, many nations today, including the United States, are characterized by a high degree of social diversity.

Social diversity brings a unique set of sociological challenges. People everywhere tend to be **ethnocentric**—that is, *they judge other cultures by the standards of their own culture,* and regard their own way of life as "normal"—and better. From a sociological perspective, no group can be said to be more human than any other. Yet history abounds with examples of people lashing out at others whose religion, language, customs, race, or sexual orientation differed from their own.

TECHNOLOGY AND DIGITAL SOCIETY

Technology refers to *the practical application of knowledge to transform natural resources for human use.* The first human technology was probably the use of rocks and other blunt instruments as weapons, enabling humans to hunt large animals for food. Planting rice or corn in hopes of reaping a yearly harvest, otherwise known as agriculture, represents another technological advance, one superior to simple foraging in the wild for nuts and berries. The use of modern machinery, which ushered in the Industrial Revolution, represents still another technological leap, multiplying the productivity of human efforts.

Today we are in the midst of another revolutionary period of technological change: the information revolution. Thanks to the microchip, the Internet, and mobile technology, an increasing number of people around the world now have instant access to a mass of information that was unimaginable just 10 or 20 years ago. The information revolution is creating postindustrial economies based far more heavily on the production of knowledge than on the production of goods—as well as new ways of communicating that have the potential to draw people around the world together, as well as tear them apart.

WHY STUDY SOCIOLOGY?

A sociological perspective highlights the many ways that we both influence and are powerfully influenced by the social world around us: Society shapes us, and we, in turn, shape society. It also helps us to see the social world through a variety of different lenses (recall the glasses metaphor we used when talking about theory): There are many ways that sociologists might explain class differences, for instance, and why they persist. Each one may illuminate different aspects of the phenomenon, enabling us to assemble a fuller, more rigorous perspective on social life. In this sense, "the" sociological perspective is really a *collection* of sociological perspectives we can use as analytical tools.

Why are the issues and questions posed by sociology incredibly compelling for all of us to understand? One reason is that, as we will see throughout the book, many social issues sociologists study—marriage, fertility, poverty, unemployment, consumption, discrimination, and many others—are related to one another in ways we may not immediately see. *The sociological perspective helps us to make connections between diverse social phenomena.* When we understand these connections, we are better able to address social problems and to make (or vote for) policy choices that benefit society.

For example, a phenomenon like the *decline of marriage among the working class*, which we mentioned at the start of the chapter, is related to growing globalization, declining employment in the manufacturing sector, and the persistently high rate of poverty among single mothers. Consider these social phenomena as pieces of a puzzle. One of the defining characteristics of economic globalization is the movement of manufacturing industries away from the United States to lower-wage countries. As a result, jobs in U.S. manufacturing, an economic sector dominated by men, have been falling since the 1970s. The decreasing number of less educated men able to earn a good enough wage to support a family in turn is related to a decline in marriage among the working class. While marriage rates fall, however, many women still desire to have a family, so the proportion of nonmarital births rises. Single mothers with children are among the demographic groups in the United States most likely to be poor, and their poverty rate has remained relatively high even in periods of economic prosperity.

While the relationships between sociological factors are complex and sometimes indirect, when sociology helps us fit them together, we gain a better picture of the issues confronting all of us—as well as U.S. society and the larger world. Let's begin our journey.

Sociologists' Focus
on Technology

Social diversity: The social and cultural mixture of different groups in society and the recognition of difference as significant.

Ethnocentric: Judging other cultures by the standards of one's own culture, and regarding one's own way of life as "normal"—and better.

Technology: The practical application of knowledge to transform natural resources for human use.

WHAT CAN I DO WITH A SOCIOLOGY DEGREE?

CAREER DEVELOPMENT & SKILLS AND CAREERS: AN INTRODUCTION

A short feature will appear near the end of each chapter of *Discover Sociology* that links your study of sociology to potential careers. It is intended to help you answer the question "What can I do with a sociology degree?" An important goal of these features is to highlight the core knowledge and professional skills that you will develop through a sociology major. This set of competencies and skills, which range from critical thinking and writing skills to aptitude in qualitative and quantitative research to the understanding of diversity and conflict dynamics, prepares you for the workforce, as well as graduate and professional school. Many of the chapters ahead will highlight information about the *occupational fields, job titles, and work activities* that can be linked to the knowledge and skills you will learn as a sociology major. The *Skills & Careers* essays (Chapters 5–10 and 13–17) will describe professional skills, discuss their development through the study of sociology, and link them with specific occupational fields and jobs in which employers seek the skills discussed.

A second goal of the feature is to help you more fully identify and articulate your current and developing job-related skills, interests, and values, as well as to show you how to begin to explore careers, how to perform an effective internship or job search, and how to create a personal career action plan (see the career development wheel). These *Career Development* features are intended to benefit both sociology and nonsociology majors—career planning is important no matter your chosen field. The first chapter essays (Chapters 2–4) discuss the basics of career development. Two later chapters (Chapters 10 and 11) offer

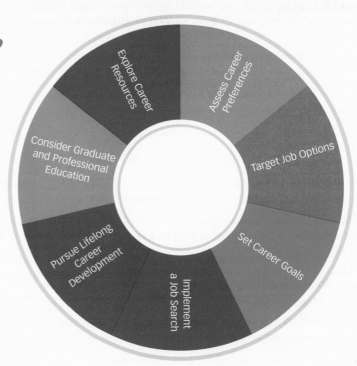

a discussion of how graduate or professional school may fit into your career development plans. We hope that you find these features useful!

THINK ABOUT CAREERS

■ *What are your potential career interests? Did you come to college with a specific interest, or have you developed new interests during your studies?*

■ *Have you spoken with anyone—family members, career counselors, professors, practitioners, or others—about your career interests? With whom might you speak to learn more about your field of interest?*

▶ *Access additional web links on the student study site to learn more.*

SUMMARY

To test your knowledge further, find additional study material on the Student Study Site at www.sagepub.com/chamblissintro

- **Sociology** is the scientific study of human social relationships, groups, and societies. Its central task is to ask what the dimensions of the social world are, how they influence our behavior, and how we in turn shape and change them.

- Sociology adheres to the principle of **social embeddedness**, the idea that economic, political, and other forms of human behavior are fundamentally shaped by social relationships. Sociologists seek to study through scientific means the social worlds that human beings consciously create.

- The **sociological imagination** is the ability to grasp the relationship between our individual lives and the larger social forces that help to shape them. It helps us see the connection between our private lives and public issues.

- **Critical thinking** is the ability to evaluate claims about truth by using reason and evidence. Often we accept things as true because they are familiar, seem to mesh with our own experiences, and sound right. Critical thinking instead asks us to recognize poor arguments, reject statements not supported by evidence, and even question our own assumptions.

- Sociology's roots can be traced to the scientific revolution, the Enlightenment, industrialization and the birth of modern capitalism, and the urbanization of populations. Sociology emerged in part as a tool to enable people to understand dramatic changes taking place in modern societies.

- Sociology generally traces its classical roots to Auguste Comte, Émile Durkheim, Max Weber, and Karl Marx. Early work in sociology reflected the concerns of the men who founded the discipline.

- In the United States, scholars at the University of Chicago focused on reforming social problems stemming from industrialization and urbanization. Women and people of color worked on the margins of the discipline because of persistent discrimination.

- Sociologists base their study of the social world on different theoretical perspectives that shape theory and guide research, often resulting in different conclusions. The major sociological paradigms are **structural functionalism**, the **social conflict paradigm**, and **symbolic interactionism**.

- Major themes in sociology include the distribution of **power** and growing inequality, **globalization** and its accompanying social changes, the growth of **social diversity**, and the way advances in **technology** have changed communication, commerce, and communities.

- The early founders believed that scientific knowledge could lead to shared social progress. Some modern sociologists question whether such shared scientific understanding is indeed possible.

KEY TERMS

Study terms on the go with the smartphone-friendly key term flashcards, available at www.sagepub.com/chamblissintro

scientific, 2

sociology, 3

social embeddedness, 3

sociological imagination, 3

agency, 5

structure, 5

critical thinking, 6

norms, 9

anomie, 9

social statics, 9

social dynamics, 9

positivist, 9

social facts, 10

social solidarity, 11

collective conscience, 11

class conflict, 11

proletariat, 11

bourgeoisie, 11

means of production, 11

Verstehen, 12

formal rationality, 12

bureaucracies, 12

double consciousness, 13

sociological theories, 15

macro-level paradigm, 15

micro-level paradigm, 15

structural functionalism, 15

manifest functions, 17

latent functions, 17

social conflict paradigm, 17

symbolic interactionism, 19

symbols, 19

power, 19

inequality, 19

globalization, 19

social diversity, 20

ethnocentric, 22

technology, 22

DISCUSSION QUESTIONS

1. Think about Mills's concept of the "sociological imagination" and its ambition to draw together what Mills called *private troubles* and *public issues*. Think of a private trouble that sociologists might classify as also being a public issue. Share your example with your classmates.

2. In the chapter, we asked why there are so few "founding mothers" in sociology. What factors explain the dearth of women's voices? What effect do you think this may have had on the development of the discipline?

3. Recall the three key theoretical paradigms discussed in the chapter—structural functionalism, conflict theory, and symbolic interactionism. Discuss the way these diverse "glasses" analyze deviance, its labeling, and its punishment in society. Try applying the analysis to another social phenomenon such as class inequality or traditional gender roles.

DISCOVER ⊕ STATE STATS

Log-in to the eBook and click on the title to the left for access to State Stats in order to complete the exercise.

In this activity, you will use your "sociological imagination." Begin by entering the State Stats database and locating "Employment and Labor." Find the unemployment rate statistics and examine the changing national unemployment rate across the available years. What do you find? Study the unemployment rate for your home state. What do you see here, and how does it compare to the national picture?

Imagine a young college graduate, a middle-aged restaurant worker, and an older industrial worker who are unemployed in the years you looked at. What sociological factors might you use to explain their unemployment?

STUDENT STUDY SITE

Visit the Student Study Site at **www.sagepub.com/chamblissintro** to access additional study tools, including eFlashcards, web quizzes, video resources, web resources, audio resources, links to SAGE journal, handbook, and research articles, and much more!

2 DISCOVER SOCIOLOGICAL RESEARCH

WHAT DO YOU THINK?

1. What kinds of research questions could one pose in order to better understand sociological issues like deviance, poverty, or the high dropout rate in some high schools?
2. What factors do you think affect the honesty of people's responses to survey questions?
3. What makes a sociological research project ethical or unethical?

SOC*VIEW*

Get a closer look
with the authors!

RESEARCHING THE UNDERGROUND ECONOMY

n *Off the Books: The Underground Economy of the Urban Poor* (2006), sociologist Sudhir Alladi Venkatesh writes that his work

> explores how people work beneath the radar, earning a living and providing for themselves and their families. It examines how people cope with the attendant risks and consequences, and ultimately, it tries to understand how a community lives and breathes—how it continues to function—within a very different set of rules. (p. 17)

Venkatesh explores the norms and practices that govern the shadow economy and how they offer impoverished neighborhoods an opportunity to make money, both legally and illegally, to meet basic needs.

While the underground economy provides some economic activity and earnings in distressed communities, Venkatesh (2006) suggests, "the participants are not actively creating the foundations for human capital and skills enhancement. They cannot use accumulated money to spur investment or to build a line of credit. They are exposed to unsafe work conditions, and . . . there is little of the foundation for upward social mobility that is at the core of the American way of life" (p. 384). No less importantly, the underground economy is disconnected from the mainstream economy, which increases the segregation of depressed neighborhoods from the outside world. Thus, Venkatesh concludes, where the underground economy is central to economic and social life, it simultaneously supports and damages urban communities.

Venkatesh conducted research in the city of Chicago over a span of several years (Figure 2.1 on page 29). His work combines in-depth interviews with participant and nonparticipant observation of the social environment. He also reviews the work of other sociologists who have contributed to the literature on urban life and discusses ways in which his work expands this body of knowledge. Venkatesh's work is a solid example of sociological research. It utilizes a scientific approach and rigorous research methodologies to cast light on how residents of some of the United States' most economically ravaged neighborhoods survive and how the underground economy carries benefits and costs for communities and individuals. ■

In this chapter, we examine the ways sociologists such as Venkatesh study and understand the social world. First, we distinguish between *sociological understanding* and common sense. Then we discuss the key steps in the research process itself. We examine how sociologists test their theories using a variety of research methods, and finally, we consider the ethical implications of doing research on human subjects.

SOCIOLOGY AND COMMON SENSE

Science is a unique way of seeing and investigating the world around us. The essence of the **scientific method** is straightforward: It is *a process of gathering empirical (scientific and specific) data, creating theories, and rigorously testing theories*. In sociological research, theories and empirical data exist in a dynamic relationship (Figure 2.2 on page 30). Some research begins from general theories,

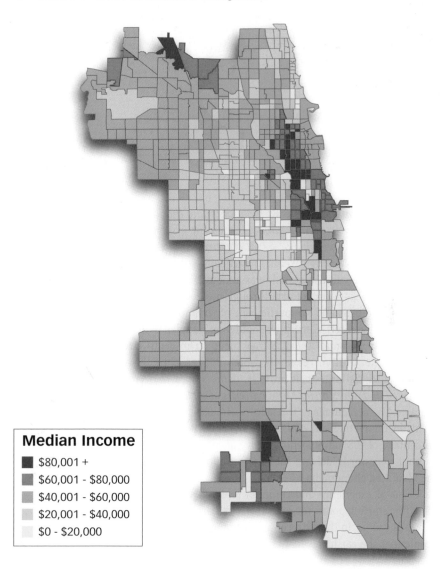

■ **FIGURE 2.1** Income Distribution in Chicago, 2000

Median Income
■ $80,001 +
■ $60,001 - $80,000
■ $40,001 - $60,000
■ $20,001 - $40,000
□ $0 - $20,000

SOURCE: https://www.cityofchicago.org/content/dam/city/depts/doit/general/GIS/Chicago_Maps/Census_Maps/Income_MedianHousehold.pdf

Scientific method: A way of learning about the world that combines logically constructed theory and systematic observation to provide explanations of how things work.

Deductive reasoning: The process of taking an existing theory and logically deducing that if the theory is accurate, we should discover other patterns of behavior consistent with it.

Hypothesis: An idea about the world, derived from a theory that can be disproved when tested against observations.

Inductive reasoning: The process of generalizing to an entire category of phenomena from a particular set of observations.

Qualitative research: Typically highlights data that cannot be quantified (or converted into numbers), focusing instead on generating in-depth knowledge of social life, institutions, and processes.

which offer "big picture" ideas about social life: **Deductive reasoning** *starts from broad theories but proceeds to break them down into more specific and testable hypotheses*. Sociological **hypotheses** are *ideas about the world that describe a possible relationship between social phenomena*. Some research begins from the ground up: **Inductive reasoning** *starts from specific data, such as interviews or field notes, which may focus on a single community or event, and endeavors to identify larger patterns from which to derive more general theories*.

Sociologists employ the scientific method in both qualitative and quantitative research. **Qualitative research**, such as that

Research Ethics

Theory

Research

conducted by Venkatesh, typically *highlights data that cannot be quantified (or converted into numbers), focusing instead on generating in-depth knowledge of social life, institutions, and processes* (for example, why parents in particular social groups are more or less likely to use spanking as a method of punishment). It relies on the gathering of data through methods such as focus groups, participant and nonparticipant observation, interviews, and archival research. Generally, population samples in qualitative research are small because they focus on in-depth understanding. **Quantitative research**, which is often done through methods such as large-scale surveys, *gathers data that can be quantified and offers insight into patterns of social behavior* (for example, the percentage of U.S. adults who use corporal punishment on their children) *and social attitudes* (for example, the percentage of U.S. adults who approve of corporal punishment), without necessarily delving into the meaning of or reasons for the identified phenomena.

Personal experience and common sense about the world are often fine starting points for sociological research. They can, however, mislead us. In the 14th century, common sense suggested to people that the earth was flat; after all, it *looks* flat. Today, influenced by stereotypes and media portrayals of criminal behaviors, many people believe Black high school and college students are more likely to use illegal drugs such as marijuana, cocaine, crack, and heroin than White high school and college students. But common sense misleads on both counts. The earth is not flat (as you know!), and Black high school and college students are *less* likely to use illegal drugs than their White counterparts (Table 2.1).

Consider the following ideas, which many believe to be true—though all are false:

Common Wisdom:

I know women who earn more than their husbands or boyfriends. The gender wage gap is no longer an issue in the United States.

Qualitative vs.
Quantitative Research

Sociological Research:

Data show that men as a group earn more than women as a group. For example, in 2011, men had a weekly median income of $832 compared to $684 for women for all full-time occupations (Hegewisch, Williams, & Harbin, 2012). According to statistical data, women earn about 82% of what men earn. This statistic compares all men and all women who work full-time and year-round. Reasons for this gap include worker characteristics (such as experience and education), job characteristics (such as hours required), devaluation of "women's work" by society, and discrimination against female workers and occupations (Cabeza, Johnson, & Tyner, 2011; Reskin & Padavic, 2002). So while some women, of course, earn more than some men, the overall pattern of men outearning women remains in place today. This topic is discussed in greater detail in Chapter 9.

Common Wisdom:

Homeless people are poor and lack adequate shelter because they do not work.

Sociological Research:

Some of the homeless cannot find work or are too disabled by mental or physical problems to work. Many, however, do work. Research suggests that about 44% of homeless adults work for pay (National Coalition for the Homeless, 2009), and the U.S. Conference of Mayors (2011) reports that 15% of the homeless were regularly employed full- or part-time. However, low wages and poor benefits in the service industry, where many less educated people work, as well as a shortage of adequate housing options for low-income families, can make finding permanent shelter a challenge even for those who work for pay. To illustrate how declining wages magnify the strain on low-income families, consider this: In many

■ **TABLE 2.1** Percent of High School Seniors Who Use Illegal Drugs by Race and Ethnicity, 2010

	Marijuana	Cocaine	Crack	LSD	Ecstasy
White	34.8%	3.4%	1.2%	2.7%	4.5%
Black	30.8%	0.9%	0.7%	0.8%	2.6%
Hispanic	31.6%	3.5%	1.8%	0.9%	4.6%

SOURCE: Johnston, L. D., O'Malley, P. M., Bachman, J. G., & Schulenberg, J. E. (2011). Demographic subgroup trends for various licit and illicit drugs, 1975–2010. *Monitoring the Future Occasional Paper No. 74.* Ann Arbor, MI: Institute for Social Research. Available from http://www.monitoringthefuture.org/

Quantitative research: Gathers data that can be quantified and offers insight into patterns of social behavior and social attitudes.

cities, to make ends meet, a household would need more than one full-time minimum-wage employee to afford the fair market rent price for a two-bedroom apartment (National Low Income Housing Coalition, 2009). The contemporary reality is that wages are not keeping up with the rate of inflation, which further adds to the economic hardships that low-income families endure. These topics are discussed in fuller detail in Chapter 7.

Common Wisdom:

"A rising tide lifts all boats." The economic boom years of the 1980s and 1990s reduced poverty and inequality in the United States.

Sociological Research:

Statistics from the U.S. Census Bureau show that the gap between the richest and the poorest has grown steadily since the 1970s. Even in periods of economic prosperity, gains by those in the middle and lower rungs of earners have been dwarfed by those at the top (Reich, 2010). In 1979, the richest 20% of households took in just over 44% of aggregate (or total) U.S. income. By 2012, this group earned over half the total income. In addition, the top 5% of households accounted for over 21% of aggregate income—up from about 17% in 1979. Households in the bottom fifth fell from about 4% to just over 3% over the same period. The middle quintiles (fifths) of earners have also experienced declines (U.S. Census Bureau, 2012). Periods of economic prosperity do expand the prospects of individuals and families across the income spectrum, but the gains in recent decades have been skewed toward the top of the income ladder, and the consequences of economic downturns have weighed heavily on the middle and bottom earners. We discuss these economic changes further in Chapter 14.

Even deeply held and widely shared beliefs about society and social groups may be inaccurate—or more nuanced and complex than they appear on the surface. Until it is tested, common sense is merely conjecture. Careful research allows us to test our beliefs to gauge whether they are valid or merely anecdotal. From a sociological standpoint, empirical evidence is granted greater weight than common sense. By basing their decisions on scientific evidence rather than personal beliefs or common wisdom, researchers and

The Metropolitan Washington Council of Governments distinguishes between the "permanently supported homeless," who have housing but are at risk due to extreme poverty and/or disability, and the "chronically homeless," who are continually homeless for a year or more, or at least four times in three years. Do you think that these categories fully encompass the homeless population? ■

students can draw informed conclusions, and policy makers can ensure that policies and programs are data driven and maximally effective.

RESEARCH AND THE SCIENTIFIC METHOD

Scientific theories *answer questions about how and why scientific observations are as they are.*

A good scientific theory has the following characteristics:

- *It is logically consistent.* One part of the theory does not contradict another part.
- *It can be disproved.* If the findings contradict the theory, then we can deduce that the theory is wrong. While we can say that testing has failed to disprove the theory, however, we cannot assume the theory is "true" if testing confirms it. Theories are always subject to further testing, which may point to needed revisions, highlight limitations, or strengthen conclusions.

Theories are made up of **concepts**, *terms used to summarize a set of phenomena.* Concepts are the building blocks of research and prepare a solid foundation for sociological work. Some of the key concepts in sociology are *social stratification, social class,*

· ·

Scientific theories: An explanation of how and why scientific observations are as they are.

Concept: An idea that describes a number of things that have something in common.

Quantitative Research Methods

Some research on bullying relies on self-reports, while other data come from peer reports. Recent research (Branson & Cornell, 2009) suggests that more than twice as many students (11%) were labeled bullies in peer reports than in self-reports (5%), highlighting the fact that any method of data collection has limitations. ■

power, inequality, and *diversity,* which we introduced in the opening chapter.

In order to gather data and create viable theories, we need to define concepts in ways that are precise and measurable. A study of social class, for example, would need to begin with a working definition of that term. An **operational definition** *defines the concept in such a way that we can observe and measure it.* Many sociologists define social class in terms of dimensions such as income, wealth, education, occupation, and consumption patterns. Each of these aspects of class has the potential to be measurable. We may construct operational definitions in terms of *qualities* or *quantities* (Babbie, 1998; Neuman, 2000). In terms of qualities, we might say, for instance, that the "upper middle class" is composed of those who have completed a graduate or professional degree, even though there may be a broad income spread between those with a master's degree in English and those with a master's of business administration. This definition is based on an assumption of class as a social position that derives from educational attainment. Alternatively, using quantity as a key measure, we might operationally define "upper class" as households with annual income greater than $150,000 and "lower class" as households with annual income of less than $20,000. This definition takes income as the preeminent determinant of class position, irrespective of education.

Consider a social issue of contemporary interest—bullying. Imagine that you wanted to conduct a research study of bullying to determine how many female middle schoolers have experienced bullying in the past academic year. You would need to begin with a clear definition of bullying that operationalizes the term: In order to measure how many girls had experienced bullying, you would need to articulate *what constitutes bullying.* Would you include physical bullying? If so, how many instances of being pushed or punched would constitute bullying? Would you include cyberbullying? What kinds of behaviors would be included in that category? To study a phenomenon like bullying, it is not enough to assume that we "know it when we see it." Empirical research relies on the careful and specific definition of terms and the recognition of how definitions and methods affect research outcomes.

RELATIONSHIPS BETWEEN VARIABLES

In studying social relationships, sociologists also need *variables.* A **variable** is *a concept that can take on two or more possible values.* For instance, sex can be male or female, work status can be employed or unemployed, and geographic location can be inner-city, suburbs, or rural area. We can measure variables both *quantitatively and qualitatively.* **Quantitative variables** include *factors we can count,* such as crime rates, unemployment rates, and drug use frequency. **Qualitative variables** are *variables that express a quality and do not have a numerical value.* Qualitative variables might include a physical characteristic (such as gender or eye color) or an attitudinal characteristic such as a parent's preference for a private or public school or a commuter's preference for riding public transportation or driving to work.

Sociological research often tries to establish a relationship between two or more variables. Suppose you want to find out whether more education is associated with higher earnings. After asking people about their years of schooling and their annual income, both of which are quantitative variables, you could estimate the degree of *correlation* between the two. **Correlation**—literally, "co-relationship"—is *the degree to which two or more variables are associated with one another.* Correlating the two variables "years of education" and "annual income" demonstrates

Operational definition: Definition of a concept that allows it to be observed and measured.

Variable: A concept or its empirical measure that can take on multiple values.

Quantitative variables: Factors we can count.

Qualitative variables: Variables that express a quality and do not have a numerical value.

Correlation: The degree to which two or more variables are associated with one another.

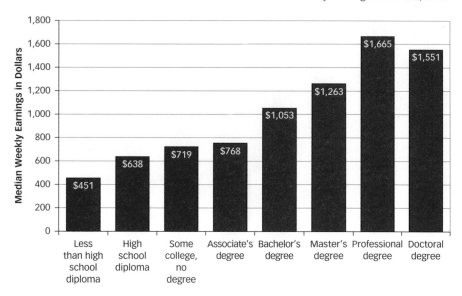

SOURCE: Bureau of Labor Statistics. (2012). Education pays. *Employment projections.* Washington, DC: U.S. Government Printing Office.

that the greater the education, the higher the income (Figure 2.3). (Do you see the exception to that relationship? How might you explain it?)

When two variables are correlated, we are often tempted to infer a **causal relationship,** *a relationship between two variables in which one is the cause of the other.* However, just because two variables are correlated, we cannot assume that one causes the other. For example, ice cream sales significantly rise during the summer, as does the homicide rate. These two events are correlated in the sense that both increase during the hottest months. However, because the sharp rise in ice cream sales does not *cause* rates of homicide to increase (nor, clearly, does the rise in homicide rates cause a spike in ice cream consumption), these two phenomena do not have a causal relationship. *Correlation does not equal causation.*

Sometimes an observed correlation between two variables is the result of a **spurious relationship.** A spurious relationship is *a correlation between two or more variables*

· ·

Causal relationship: A relationship in which one variable is the cause of another.

Spurious relationship: A correlation between two or more variables that is actually the result of something else that is not being measured, rather than a causal link between the variables themselves.

caused by another factor that is not being measured. In the example above, the common factor missed in the relationship is, in fact, the temperature. When it's hot, more people want to eat ice cream. Studies also show that rising temperatures are linked to an increase in violent crime—though after a certain temperature threshold (about 90 degrees), crimes wane again (Gamble & Hess, 2012). Among the reasons for more violent crime in hot weather is the fact that people spend more time outdoors in social interactions that can lead to confrontations.

Let's take another example that is close to home: Imagine that your school paper publishes a study concluding that coffee drinking causes poor test grades. The story is based on a survey of students that found those who reported drinking a lot of coffee the night before an exam scored lower than their peers who had consumed little or no coffee. Having studied sociology, you wonder whether this relationship might be spurious. What is the "something else" that is not being measured here? Could it be that students who did not study in the days and weeks prior to the test and stayed up late the night before cramming—probably consuming a lot of coffee as they fought sleep—received lower test grades than peers who studied earlier and got adequate sleep the night before the test? The overlooked variable, then, is the amount of studying students did in the weeks preceding the exam, and we are likely to find a positive correlation and

Getting enough sleep is one factor that can help students maintain good grades in college. How would you design a research study to examine the question of which factors correlate most strongly with solid grades? ■

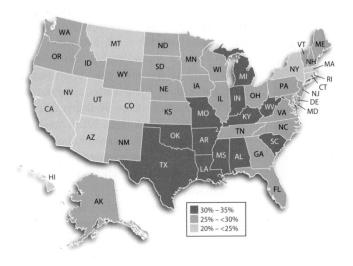

■	30% – 35%
■	25% – <30%
■	20% – <25%

SOURCE: Centers for Disease Control and Prevention. (2011). Prevalence of self-reported obesity among U.S. adults. *Behavioral Risk Factor Surveillance System*. Washington, DC.

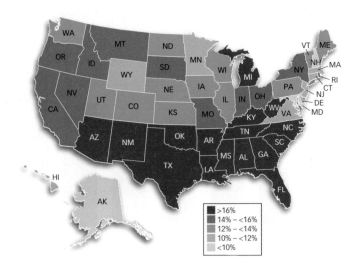

■	>16%
■	14% – <16%
■	12% – <14%
■	10% – <12%
■	<10%

SOURCE: U.S. Census Bureau, "American FactFinder," 2010 American Community Survey.

evidence of causation in looking at time spent studying and grade outcomes.

Sociologists attempt to develop theories systematically by offering clear operational definitions, collecting unbiased data, and accurately identifying relationships between variables. Sociological research methods usually yield credible and useful data, but we must always critically analyze the results to ensure their validity and reliability and to check that hypothesized relationships are not spurious.

TESTING THEORIES AND HYPOTHESES

Once we have defined concepts and variables with which to work, we can endeavor to test a theory by positing a hypothesis. Hypotheses enable scientists to check the accuracy of their theories. For example, consider state-level data on obesity and poverty (Figures 2.4 and 2.5). Data from the U.S. Census Bureau for 2010 shows that some positive correlation exists between obesity and poverty rates at the state level. A positive correlation is *a relationship showing that as one variable rises or falls, the other does as well*. Their common trajectory suggests a possible relationship between poverty and obesity (Table 2.2 on page 35), though, as we noted above, sociologists are quick to point out that correlation does not equal causation. Researchers are interested in creating and testing hypotheses to explain cases of positive correlation—they are also interested in explaining exceptions to the pattern of correlation between two (or more) variables.

In fact, researchers have explored and hypothesized the relationship between poverty and obesity. Among the conclusions they have drawn is that living in poverty—and particularly living in a poor neighborhood—puts people at higher risk of obesity, though the risk is greater among women than men (Centers for Disease Control and Prevention, 2012; Hedwig, 2011; Smith, 2009). Among the factors that researchers identify as contributing to a causal path between poverty and obesity are the lack of access to healthy food choices, the lack of access to safe and close spaces for physical exercise, and a deficit of time to cook healthy foods and exercise. They also cite the stress induced by poverty. While the data cannot lead us to conclude decisively that poverty is a cause of obesity, research can help us to gather evidence that supports or refutes a hypothesis about their relationship. We look at this issue in greater depth in Chapter 15.

In the case of a **negative correlation**, *one variable increases as the other decreases*. As we discuss later in Chapter 10, which focuses on the family and society, researchers have found a negative correlation between male unemployment and rates of marriage. That is, as rates of male unemployment in a community rise, rates of marriage in the community fall (Edin & Kefalas, 2005). Observing this relationship, a sociologist might design a research study to test possible explanations for it.

Keep in mind that we can never prove theories to be decisively right—we can only prove them wrong. Proving a theory right would require the scientific testing of absolutely every possible hypothesis based on that theory—a fundamental impossibility. In fact, good theories are constructed in a way that makes it logically possible to prove them wrong. This is Karl Popper's (1959)

. . . .

Negative correlation: One variable increases as the other decreases.

■ TABLE 2.2 Top 10 States: Obesity and Poverty, 2010

State	Percent Obese	State	Percent in Poverty
Mississippi	34.9	Mississippi	24.3%
Louisiana	33.4	Louisiana	22.4%
West Virginia	32.4	Georgia	19.6%
Alabama	32	Texas	19.3%
Michigan	31.3	Arizona	19.2%
Oklahoma	31.1	New Mexico	18.3%
Arkansas	30.9	Alabama	18%
Indiana	30.8	Indiana	17.9%
South Carolina	30.8	North Carolina	17.8%
Kentucky	30.4	Nevada	17.8%

SOURCE: Trust for America's Health. (2010). "F as in Fat: How Obesity Threatens America's Future." Available from http://healthyamericans.org/reports/obesity2010/; U.S. Census Bureau. (2010). POV46: Poverty status by state: 2010. *Annual social and economic (ASEC) supplement*. Washington, DC: U.S. Government Printing Office.

famous **principle of falsification,** or **falsifiability,** which holds that *to be scientific, a theory must lead to testable hypotheses that can be disproved if they are wrong.*

VALIDITY AND RELIABILITY

For theories and hypotheses to be testable, both the concepts used to construct them and the measurements used to test them must be accurate. When our observations adequately reflect the real world, then our findings have **validity**—that is, *the concepts and measurements accurately represent what they claim to represent.* For example, suppose you want to know whether the crime rate in the United States has gone up or down. For years sociologists

. . . .

Principle of falsification: The principle, advanced by philosopher Karl Popper, that a scientific theory must lead to testable hypotheses that can be disproved if they are wrong.

Falsifiability: The ability for a theory to be disproven; the logical possibility for a theory to be tested and proven false.

Validity: The degree to which concepts and their measurements accurately represent what they claim to represent.

Reliability: The extent to which researchers' findings are consistent with different studies of the same thing, or with the same study over time.

Bias: A characteristic of results that systematically misrepresent the true nature of what is being studied.

depended on police reports to measure crime. However, researchers could assess the validity of these tallies only if a subsequent survey was administered nationally to victims of crime. If the victim tallies matched those of the police reports, then we could say the police reports are a valid measure of crime in the United States. The National Crime Victimization Survey (NCVS) enables researchers to assess validity because it offers data on victimization, even for crimes that have not been reported to authorities.

Sociologists are also concerned with the reliability of their findings. **Reliability** is *the extent to which the findings are consistent with different studies of the same phenomenon or with the same study over time.* Sociological research may suffer from problems of validity and reliability because of **bias,** *a characteristic of results that systematically misrepresent the full dimensions of what is being studied.* Bias can creep into research due to the use of inappropriate measurement instruments. For example, suppose the administrator of a city wants to know whether homelessness has risen in recent years. She operationally defines the homeless as those who sleep in the street or in shelters and dispatches her team of researchers to city shelters to count the number of people occupying shelter beds or sleeping on street corners or park benches. A sociologist reviewing her results might question her operational definition of what it means to be "homeless" and, by extension, her findings. Are the homeless solely those spending the night in a shelter or on the street? What about those who stay with a friend after eviction or camp out in a car? In this instance, a sociologist might suggest that city's measure is biased because it misrepresents (and undercounts) the homeless population by failing to define the concept in a way that captures the broad manifestations of homelessness.

Bias can also occur in research when respondents do not tell the truth. A good example of this is a study in which respondents were asked whether they used illegal drugs or had driven while impaired (Table 2.3 on page 37). All were asked the same questions, but some were wired to a machine they were told was a lie detector. The subjects who thought their truthfulness was being monitored by a lie detector reported higher rates of illegal drug use than subjects who did not. Based on the assumption that actual drug use would be about the same for both groups, the researchers concluded that the subjects who were not connected to the device were underreporting their actual illegal drug use, and that simply asking people about drug use would lead to *biased* findings because respondents would not tell the truth. Do you think truthfulness of respondents is a general problem, or one we would encounter only where sensitive issues such as drug use or racism are at issue?

OBJECTIVITY IN SCIENTIFIC RESEARCH

Even if sociologists develop theories based on good operational definitions and collect valid and reliable data, like all human

Stephen Colbert on
Validity Research

INEQUALITY MATTERS

HOW MANY PEOPLE SUFFER FROM HOMELESSNESS?

Homelessness is a social problem in the United States. But how extensive is it? The National Law Center on Homelessness and Poverty (2012) estimates that more than 3 million U.S. people experience homelessness over the course of a year. Of these, 1.3 million are children; more than one third of the entire homeless population is made up of families. While the majority of the homeless have access to transitional housing or emergency shelters, approximately 4 out of 10 are unsheltered, living in improvised conditions that are not suited for human habitation. Despite the homeless population decreasing nationally, the rates for 24 individual states and the District of Columbia increased between 2009 and 2011 (National Alliance to End Homelessness, 2012).

Statistics vary, however, depending upon the definitions and counting methodologies employed. In the early 1980s, the U.S. government was under pressure to provide services and assistance to a population of homeless that some claimed was large and growing. In response, the U.S. Department of Housing and Urban Development (HUD) conducted a study to determine the number of homeless people in cities and towns across the country. After analyzing all existing studies, government researchers called homeless service providers and other experts in 60 cities and asked them to estimate the number of homeless people in their communities. Based on this research, the government concluded there were 250,000 to 350,000 homeless people in the United States. This figure was considerably

Understanding of research methods will help you recognize the challenges in gathering reliable statistics on populations that are outside the mainstream. In this photo, volunteers conduct an interview with a homeless man, which helps local authorities assess how many homeless people are in the city. ■

lower than the estimate of 2 million that came from other sources outside the government (Burt, 1992).

Politicians used the HUD figures extensively, although some sociologists were skeptical (Appelbaum, 1986; Appelbaum, Dolny, Dreier, & Gilderbloom, 1991). First, HUD's *operational definition* of homelessness included only people on streets and in shelters; it effectively excluded homeless people living in cars or abandoned buildings or taking temporary shelter with friends. Second, HUD based its figures on the estimates of shelter providers, police officers, and other local experts who admitted they were often only guessing. Finally, the HUD figures were based almost entirely on homeless estimates for the downtown areas of big cities, a methodological bias that excluded the numerous homeless people who lived in surrounding towns and suburbs. As a result of these problems, HUD's estimate

of a national homeless figure lacked validity.

THINK IT THROUGH

■ *Subsequent research has confirmed that by the early 1990s there were as many as 1 million homeless in the United States—three to four times the estimate produced by the government study. An axiom of sociological research is that it is not what you think you know that matters, but how you came to know it. The homeless represent a transient population that is challenging to count. The homeless have no fixed address, no consistent billing statements, and no easy way for a researcher to locate them. What methods might you employ to attempt to systematically count the number of homeless people in your community? What kinds of resources do you think you would need?*

■ TABLE 2.3 How Truthful Are Survey Respondents?

Survey Question	Threat of Validation		No Threat of Validation	
	Anonymous	Named	Anonymous	Named
Ever smoked?	63.5%	72.9%	60.5%	67.8%
Smoked in the last month?	34.5%	39.5%	25.9%	21.8%
Smoked in the last week?	26.0%	25.5%	14.4%	17.6%

SOURCE: Adams, J., Parkinson, L., Sanson-Fisher, R. W., & Walsh, R. A. (2008). Enhancing self-report of adolescent smoking: The effects of bogus pipeline and anonymity. *Addictive Behaviors, 33*(10), 1291–1296.

beings they have passions and biases that may color their research. For example, criminologists long ignored the criminality of women because they assumed that women were not disposed toward criminal behavior. Researchers therefore did not have an accurate picture of women and crime until the bias was recognized and rectified.

Personal values and beliefs may affect the researcher's **objectivity**, or *ability to represent the object of study accurately.* Nineteenth-century sociologist Max Weber argued that in order for scientific research to be objective it has to be **value neutral**— that is, *personal beliefs and opinions do not influence the course of research.* The sociologist should acknowledge personal biases and assumptions, make them explicit, and prevent them from getting in the way of observation and reporting.

How can we best achieve objectivity? First, recall Karl Popper's principle of falsification, which proposes that the goal of research is not to prove our ideas correct, but to find out whether they are wrong. To accomplish this, researchers must be willing to accept that data might contradict their most passionate convictions. Research should deepen human understanding, not prove a particular point of view.

A second way to ensure objectivity is to invite others to draw their own conclusions about the validity of our data through

· ·

Objectivity: The ability to represent the object of study accurately.

Value neutrality: Freedom from personal beliefs and opinions that would influence the course of research.

Replication: The repetition of a previous study using a different sample or population to verify or refute the original findings.

Research method: A specific technique for systematically gathering data.

Survey: A questionnaire or interviews administered to a group of people in person or by telephone or e-mail to determine their characteristics, opinions, and behaviors.

replication, *the repetition of a previous study using a different sample or population to verify or refute the original findings.* For research to be replicated, the original study must spell out in detail the research methods employed. If potential replicators cannot conduct the study exactly as it was originally performed, they might accidentally introduce unwanted variables. To ensure the most accurate replication of their work, researchers should archive original materials such as questionnaires or field notes and allow replicators access to them.

Karl Popper (1959) described scientific discovery as an ongoing process of "confrontation and refutation." Sociologists usually subject their work to this process by publishing their results in scholarly journals. Submitted research undergoes a rigorous peer review process from other experts in the field of study before being finalized and published. Once research has been published in a reputable journal such as the *American Sociological Review* or the *Journal of Health and Social Behavior,* other scholars read it with a critical eye. The study may then be replicated in a different setting.

DOING SOCIOLOGICAL RESEARCH

Sociological research requires careful preparation and a clear plan that guides the work. The purpose of a sociological research project may be to obtain preliminary knowledge that will help formulate a theory, or to evaluate an already-existing theory about society and social life. As part of the strategy, the researcher selects from a variety of **research methods**— *specific techniques for systematically gathering data.* In the following sections, we look at a range of research methods, including their advantages and disadvantages. We also discuss how you might prepare a sociological research project of your own.

SOCIOLOGICAL RESEARCH METHODS

Sociologists employ a variety of methods to learn about the social world (Table 2.4 on page 38). Since each has strengths and weaknesses, a good research strategy may be to use several different methods. If each yields similar findings, researchers are more likely to have confidence in the results. The principal methods are the survey, fieldwork—either participant observation or detached observation—experiments, working with existing information, and participatory research.

SURVEY RESEARCH

A **survey** relies on a *questionnaire or interviews with a group of people in person or by telephone or e-mail to determine their characteristics, opinions, and behaviors.* Surveys are versatile,

Validity and Reliability

Method	Appropriate Circumstances
Survey Research	When basic information about a large population is desired. Sociologists usually conduct survey research by selecting a sample representative of the entire population.
Fieldwork	When detailed information is sought, and when surveys are impractical for getting the information desired (for example, in studying youth gangs). Fieldwork usually relies on relatively small samples, especially compared to surveys.
Detached Observation	When researchers desire to stay removed from the people being studied and must gather data in a way that minimizes impact on the subjects. Detached observations are often supplemented with face-to-face interviews.
Participant Observation	When firsthand knowledge of the subjects' direct experience is desired, including a deeper understanding of their lives.
Experiments	When it is possible to create experimental and control groups that are matched on relevant variables but provided with different experiences in the experiment.
Use of Existing Information	When direct acquisition of data is either not feasible or not desirable because the event studied occurred in the past, or because gathering the data would be too costly or too difficult.
Participatory Research	When a primary goal is training people to gain political or economic power and acquire the necessary skills to do the research themselves.

and sociologists often use them to test a theory or simply to gather data. Some, such as National Opinion Research Center questionnaires, consist of *closed-ended questions* for which the respondent checks his or her preferred response. Others, such as the University of Chicago's Social Opportunity Survey, consist of *open-ended questions* that permit the respondent to answer in his or her own words.

An example of survey research conducted for data collection is the largest survey in the nation, the U.S. Census, which is conducted every 10 years. The census is not designed to test any particular theory. Rather, it gathers voluminous data about U.S. residents that researchers, including sociologists, use to test and develop a variety of theories.

Usually, surveys are conducted on *a relatively small number of people*, a **sample**, selected to represent a **population**, *the whole group of people to be studied.*

The first step in designing a survey is to identify your population of interest. Imagine doing a study of behavioral factors that affect grades in college: Who would you survey? Members of a certain age group only? People in the airline industry? Pet owners? To conduct a study well, we need to clearly identify the survey population that will most effectively help us answer the research question. In your study you would most likely choose to survey students now in college, because they offer the best opportunity to correlate grades with particular behaviors.

Once they have identified a population of interest, researchers will usually select a sample, as they seldom have the time or money to talk to all the members of a given population, especially if it is a large one. Other things being equal, larger samples better represent the population than smaller ones. However, with proper

sampling techniques, sociologists can use relatively small (and therefore inexpensive) samples to represent large populations. For instance, a well-chosen sample of 1,000 voters can be used to represent 100,000 U.S. voters with a fair degree of accuracy, enabling surveys to make election predictions with reasonable confidence. Sampling is also used for looking at social phenomena such as drug or alcohol use in a population: CNN reported recently that 17% of high schoolers drink, smoke, or use drugs during the school day, based on a 1,000-student sample polled by the National Center on Addiction and Substance Abuse at Columbia University (Azuz, 2012).

Ideally, a sample should reflect the composition of the population we are studying. For instance, if you wanted to be able to use research data about college students to generalize about the entire college student population of the United States, you would want to collect proportional samples from two-year colleges, four-year colleges, large universities, community colleges, online schools, and such. It would not be adequate to survey only students at online colleges or only female students at private four-year schools.

To avoid bias in surveys, sociologists may use **random sampling,** whereby *everyone in the population of interest has an*

· ·

Sample: A portion of the larger population selected to represent the whole.

Population: The whole group of people studied in sociological research.

Random sample: A sample in which everyone in the population of interest has an equal chance of being chosen for the study.

equal chance of being chosen for the study. Typically, they make or obtain a list of everyone in the population of interest. Then they draw names or phone numbers, for instance, by chance until the desired sample size is reached (today, most such work is done by computers). Large-scale random sample surveys permit the researcher to draw conclusions about large numbers of people on the basis of a relatively small number of respondents. This is an advantage in terms of time and money.

In constructing surveys, sociologists must take care to ensure that the questions and their possible responses will capture the respondents' points of view. The wording of questions is an important factor; poor wording can produce misleading results, as the following example illustrates. In 1993, an American Jewish Committee/Roper poll was taken to examine public attitudes and beliefs about the Holocaust. To the astonishment of many, results indicated that fully 22% of survey respondents expressed a belief the Holocaust had never happened. Not immediately noticed was the fact that the survey contained some very awkward wording, including the question: "Does it seem possible or does it seem impossible to you that the Nazi extermination of the Jews never happened?" Can you see why such a question might produce a questionable result? The question's compound structure and double negative wording almost certainly confused many respondents.

The American Jewish Committee released a second survey with different wording: "Does it seem possible to you that the Nazi extermination of the Jews never happened, or do you feel certain that it happened?" The results of the second poll were quite different. Only about 1% of respondents thought it was possible the Holocaust never happened, while 8% were unsure (Kagay, 1994). Despite the follow-up poll that corrected the mistaken perception of the previous poll's results, the new poll was not as methodologically rigorous as it could have been; a single survey question should ask for only one type of response. The American Jewish Committee's second survey contained a question that attempted to simultaneously gauge two different responses.

A weakness of surveys is that they may reveal what people say rather than what they do. Responses are sometimes self-serving, intended to make the interviewee look good in the eyes of the researcher. As we saw in an earlier example, a respondent may not wish to reveal his or her drinking or drug habits.

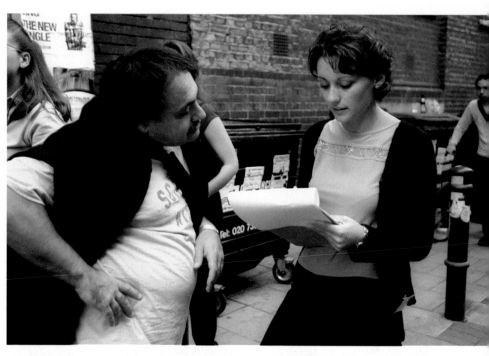

Since it is often impossible to sample every person in a target population, being well versed in research methodology enables a researcher to produce empirically rigorous data with a representative population sample. ■

A well-constructed survey, however, can overcome these problems. Assuring the respondent of anonymity, assigning interviewers with whom respondents feel comfortable, and building in questions that ask for the same information in different ways can reduce self-serving bias in survey research.

FIELDWORK

Fieldwork is *a method of research that uses in-depth and often extended study to describe and analyze a group or community.* Sometimes called *ethnography,* it takes the researcher into the "field," directly observing—and sometimes interacting with—subjects in their social environment. Social scientists, including sociologists and anthropologists, have employed fieldwork to study everything from hoboes and working-class gangs in the 1930s (Anderson, 1940; Whyte, 1943) to prostitution and drug use among inner-city women (Maher, 1997) and Vietnam veterans motorcycling across the country to the Vietnam Veterans Memorial in Washington, DC (Michalowski & Dubisch, 2001). Sudhir Venkatesh's (2006) work on the underground economy is another example of the use of fieldwork in sociological research.

Most fieldwork combines several different methods of gathering information. These include interviews, detached observation, and participant observation.

An **interview** is *a detailed conversation designed to obtain in-depth information about a person and his or her activities.*

. . . .

Fieldwork: A research method relying on an in-depth and often extended study of a group or community.

Interview: A detailed conversation designed to obtain in-depth information about a person and his or her activities.

Survey v. Public Opinion

When used in surveys, interview questions may be either open-ended or closed-ended. They may also be formal or informal. In fieldwork, the questions are usually open-ended to allow the respondent to answer in his or her own words. Sometimes the interviewer prepares a detailed set of questions; at other times, the best approach is simply to have a list of relevant topics to cover.

Good researchers guard against influencing the respondent's answers. In particular, they should avoid **leading questions,** *which elicit a particular response.* Imagine a question on attitudes toward the marine environment that read, "Do you believe tuna fishing with broad nets, which leads to the violent death of dolphins, should be regulated?" The bias in this question is obvious—the stated association of broad nets with violent dolphin deaths creates a bias in favor of a yes answer. Accurate data depends upon good questions that do not lead the respondent.

Sometimes a study requires that researchers in the field keep a distance from the people they are studying and simply observe without getting involved. The people being observed may or may not know they are being observed. This approach is called *detached observation.* In his study of two delinquent gangs (the "Saints" and the "Roughnecks"), this text's coauthor, William J. Chambliss, spent many hours observing gang members without actually being involved in what they were doing. With the gang members' permission, he sat in his car with the window rolled down so he could hear them talk and watch their behavior while they hung out on a street corner. At other times, he would observe them playing pool while he played at a nearby table. Chambliss sometimes followed gang members in his car as they drove around in theirs and sat near enough to them in bars and cafés to hear their conversations. Through his observations at a distance, he was able to observe in detail the kinds of delinquencies the gangs engaged in. He was also able to unravel some of the social processes that led to their behavior and observe other people's reactions to it.

Detached observation is particularly useful when the researcher has reason to believe other forms of fieldwork might influence the behavior of the people to be observed. It also helps in checking the validity of what the researcher has been told in interviews. A great deal of sociological information about illegal behavior has been gathered through detached observation.

One problem with detached observation is that the information gathered is likely to be incomplete. Without actually talking to people, it is impossible to check our impressions against their experiences. For this reason, detached observation is usually supplemented by in-depth interviews. In his study of the delinquent gang members, Chambliss (1973, 1999) periodically interviewed them to complement his findings and check the accuracy of his detached observations.

Another type of fieldwork is *participant observation,* a mixture of active participation and detached observation. Participant-observation research can at times be dangerous. Chambliss's (1988) research on organized crime and police corruption in Seattle, Washington, exposed him to threats from the police and organized crime network members who feared he would reveal their criminal activities. Venkatesh's (2006) work also included participant observation; for instance, he sometimes mediated disputes in the Chicago neighborhoods he studied. He also cultivated a relationship with the leader of a neighborhood gang that was involved in, among other activities, crack dealing (Venkatesh, 2008).

EXPERIMENTATION

Experiments are *research techniques for investigating cause and effect under controlled conditions.* We construct experiments to measure the effects of **independent** or **experimental variables,** *variables we change intentionally,* on **dependent variables,** which *change as a result of our alterations to the independent variables.* To put it another way, researchers modify one controllable variable (such as diet or exposure to violent movie scenes) to see what happens to another variable (such as willingness to socialize or to display aggression). Some variables, such as sex, ethnicity, and height, do not change in response to stimuli and thus do not make useful dependent variables.

In a typical experiment, researchers select participants who share characteristics such as age, education, social class, or experiences that are relevant to the experiment. The participants are then randomly assigned to two groups. The first, called the *experimental group,* is exposed to the independent variable—the variable the researchers hypothesize will affect the subjects' behavior. The second group is assigned to the *control group.* These subjects are not exposed to the independent variable—they receive no special attention. The researchers then measure both groups for the dependent variable. For example, if a neuroscientist wanted to conduct an experiment on whether listening to classical music affects performance on a math exam, he or she might have an experimental group listen to Mozart, Bach, or Chopin for an hour before taking a test. The control group would take the same test but would not listen to any music beforehand. In this example, exposure to classical music is the independent variable, and the quantifiable results of the math test are the dependent variable.

. . . .

Leading question: A question that solicits a particular response.

Experiments: Research techniques for investigating cause and effect under controlled conditions.

Independent or experimental variable: A variable that causes changes in another variable.

Dependent variable: A variable that changes as a result of changes in another variable.

Survey Research

Teenage Spending Habits

To study the relationship between violent video game play and aggression, researchers took a longitudinal approach by examining the sustained violent video game play and aggressive behavior of 1,492 adolescents in Grades 9 through 12 (Willoughby, Adachi, & Good, 2012). Their results showed a strong correlation between playing violent video games and being more likely to engage in, or approve of, violence. This body of literature represents another example of how important research methodology is; the same researchers, in a separate study, found that the level of competitiveness in a video game, and not the violence itself, had the greatest influence on aggressive behavior (Adachi & Willoughby, 2011). More research on this topic may help differentiate between the effects of variables and avoid conclusions based on spurious relationships.

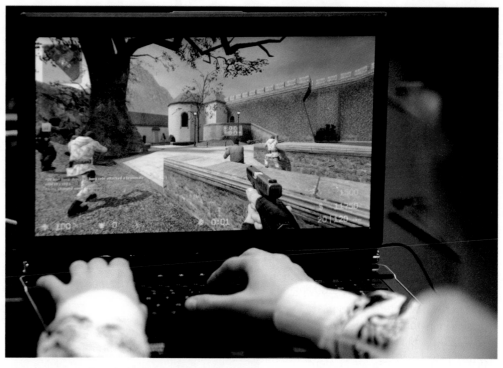

When looking at the relationship between violent video games and violent behaviors, researchers must account for many variables. What variables would you choose to test? ■

WORKING WITH EXISTING INFORMATION

Sociologists frequently work with existing information and data gathered by other researchers. Why would researchers choose to reinterpret existing data? Perhaps they want to do a secondary analysis of statistical data collected by an agency such as the U.S. Census Bureau, which makes its materials available to researchers studying issues ranging broadly from education to poverty to racial residential segregation. Or they may want to work with archival data to examine the cultural products—posters, films, pamphlets, and such—used by an authoritarian regime in a given time period to legitimate its power or disseminated by a social movement like the civil rights movement to spread its message to the masses.

Statistical data include *quantitative information obtained from government agencies, businesses, research studies, and other entities that collect data for their own or others' use.* The Bureau of Justice Statistics, for example, provides a rich

· ·

Statistical data: Quantitative information obtained from government agencies, businesses, research studies, and other entities that collect data for their own or others' use.

Document analysis: Examines written materials or cultural products: previous studies, newspaper reports, court records, campaign posters, digital reports, films, pamphlets, and other forms of text or images produced by individuals, government agencies, or private organizations.

storehouse of information on a number of criminal justice social indicators, such as prison populations, incidents of crime, and criminal justice expenditures. Many other government agencies routinely conduct surveys of commerce, manufacturing, agriculture, labor, and housing. International organizations such as the United Nations and the World Bank collect annual data on the health, education, population, and economies of nearly all countries in the world. Many businesses publish annual reports that yield basic statistical information about their financial performance.

Document analysis *examines written materials or cultural products: previous studies, newspaper reports, court records, campaign posters, digital reports, films, pamphlets, and other forms of text or images produced by individuals, government agencies, private organizations, and others.* However, because such documents are not always compiled with accuracy in mind, good researchers exercise caution in using them. People who keep records are often aware that others will see the records and take pains to avoid recording anything unflattering. The diaries and memoirs of politicians are a good example of documents that are an invaluable source of data, but that must be interpreted with great caution. The expert researcher looks at such materials with a critical eye, double-checking with other sources for accuracy where possible.

This type of research may include *historical research,* which entails the analysis of historical documents. Often such research is comparative, examining historical events in several different countries for similarities and differences. Unlike historians, sociologists usually identify patterns common to different times and places,

DOES TECHNOLOGY AFFECT STUDYING?

In 2011, as it has every year since 2000, the National Survey of Student Engagement (NSSE) surveyed about 416,000 U.S. students at 673 institutions of higher education, asking about student relationships with faculty, note taking and study habits, and hours spent studying. One of the 2011 findings, consistent with the results of other recent surveys, was that students are spending far fewer hours studying than did their counterparts in past decades. If in 1961 the average student reported studying about 24 hours per week, by 2011 the average student reported about 14 hours of study time (Babcock & Marks, 2010; National Survey of Student Engagement, 2012). Within this figure are variations by major, ranging from about 24 hours per week for architecture majors to 10 for speech majors. Sociology majors reported studying an average of 13.8 hours per week (de Vise, 2012).

Has technology helped or hindered your studying in college? Does it mostly provide research help—or additional distractions? ■

This study presents a number of interesting research questions, few of which are answered by the NSSE survey, which collected quantitative data but did not analyze the results. What factors might be behind the precipitous decline in self-reported hours spent studying?

Some existing hypotheses implicate modern technology for at least two reasons. First, it has been suggested that students study less because they are spending substantial time using social media such as Facebook. One pilot study at Ohio State University (Karpinski & Duberstein, 2009) concluded that students who used Facebook had poorer grades than those who did not. These data suggest that another study could profitably look for correlations between social media use and study time.

Second, students may be reporting less study time because technology has cut the hours of work needed for some tasks. While preparing a research paper in the past may have demanded hours in the library stacks or in pursuit of an expert to interview, today a search engine can bring up a wealth of data earlier generations could not have imagined. Far fewer students consult research librarians or use library databases today. Notably, however, a new study suggests the quality of data students have the skills to find in their searches is mixed and often low (Kolowich, 2011).

Technology is only one possible factor in the decline in student studying. Two economists, for instance, suggest that studying has declined as achievement standards have fallen (Babcock & Marks, 2010). But there is no denying that one of the most dramatic differences between the 1960s and today is the proliferation of technology, which suggests that an explanatory relationship may exist.

THINK IT THROUGH

■ *Imagine that your final paper for this semester involves answering the research question "What is the impact of technology on studying and learning?" How would you go about answering this question?*

whereas historians focus on a particular time and place and are less likely to draw broad generalizations from their research. An early master of the sociological approach to historical research was Max Weber (1919/1946, 1979), who contributed to our understanding of—among many other things—the differences between religious traditions in the West and those in East Asia.

Content analysis systematically analyzes forms of documented communication. A study can take a content analysis approach by coding and analyzing patterns in cultural products like music, laws, tweets, blogs, and works of art. An exciting aspect of social science research is that your object of curiosity can become a research question. In 2009, sociologists conducted a content analysis of 403 gangsta rap songs to assess whether rap's reputation of being misogynistic (hostile to women) was justified (Weitzer & Kubrin, 2009). The analysis found that the songs did contain significant misogynistic undertones, which reflect larger stereotypical views of male and female characteristics.

PARTICIPATORY RESEARCH

While sociologists usually try to avoid having an impact on the people they study, one research method is employed specifically to foster change. *Participatory research* supports an organization or community trying to improve its situation when it lacks the necessary economic or political power to do so by itself. The researcher fully participates by training the members to conduct research on their own while working with them to enhance their power (Freire, 1972; Park, 1993; Whyte, 1991). Such research might be part of, for instance, empowering a community to act against the threat of HIV/AIDS, as has been done in places like San Francisco and Nairobi, Kenya. Participatory research is an effective way of conducting an empirical study while also furthering a community or organizational goal that will benefit from the results of the study.

DOING SOCIOLOGY: A STUDENT'S GUIDE TO RESEARCH

Sociological research seldom follows a formula that indicates exactly how to proceed. Sociologists often have to feel their way as they go, responding to the challenges that arise during research and adapting new methods to fit the circumstances. Thus, the stages of research can vary even when sociologists agree about the basic sequence. At the same time, for student sociologists, it is useful to understand the key building blocks of good sociological research. As you read through the stages described below, think about a topic of interest to you and how you might use that as the basis for an original research project.

FRAME YOUR RESEARCH QUESTION

"Good research," Thomas Dewey observed, "scratches where it itches." Sociological research begins with the formulation of a question or questions to be answered. Society offers an endless spectrum of compelling issues to study: Does exposure to violent video games affect the probability of aggressive behavior in

■ **FIGURE 2.6** Sociological Research Formula

adolescents? Does religious faith affect voting behavior? Is family income a good predictor of performance on standardized college-entrance tests such as the SAT? Beyond the descriptive aspects of social phenomena, sociologists are also interested in *how* we can explain relationships between variables we examine.

Formulating a research question precisely and carefully is one of the most important steps to ensuring a successful research project. Research questions come from many sources. Some arise from problems that form the foundation of sociology, including an interest in socioeconomic inequalities and their causes and effects, or the desire to understand how power is exercised in social relationships. Sociologists are also mindful that solid empirical data are important to public policies on issues of concern such as poverty, occupational mobility, and domestic violence.

Keep in mind that you also need to define your terms. Recall our discussion of operationalizing concepts. For example, if you are studying middle school bullying, you need to make explicit your definition of the term and how that will be measured. The same would hold true if you were studying topics such as illiteracy or aggressive behavior.

Field Work Methods

Ethnography in Context

REVIEW EXISTING KNOWLEDGE

Once you identify the question you want to ask, you need to conduct a review of the existing literature on your topic. Literature may include published studies, unpublished papers, books, dissertations, government documents, newspapers and other periodicals, and, increasingly, data disseminated on the Internet. The key focus of the literature review, however, is usually published and peer-reviewed research studies. The purpose of the literature review is to learn about studies that have already been done on your topic of interest and to set your research in the context of existing studies. The researcher also uses the literature review to highlight how he or she will contribute to this body of knowledge.

SELECT THE APPROPRIATE METHOD

Now you are ready to think about how your research question can best be answered. Which of the research methods described earlier (1) will give the best results for the project and (2) is most feasible for your research circumstances, experience, and budget?

If you wish to obtain basic information from a relatively large population in a short period of time, then a survey is the best method to use. If you want to obtain detailed information about a smaller group of people, then interviews might be most beneficial. Participant observation and detached observation are ideal research methods to verify research obtained through interviews, or, for the latter, when the presence of a researcher might alter the research results. Document analysis and historical research are good choices for projects focused on inaccessible subjects and historical sociology. Remember, sociological research often uses multiple methods.

WEIGH THE ETHICAL IMPLICATIONS

Research conducted on other human beings—as much of sociological research is—poses certain ethical problems. An outpouring of outrage after the discovery of gruesome experiments conducted by the Nazis during World War II prompted the adoption of the *Nuremberg Code,* a collection of ethical research guidelines developed to help prevent such atrocities from ever happening again (Table 2.5). In addition to these basic guidelines, scientific societies throughout the world have adopted their own codes of ethics to safeguard against the misuse and abuse of human subjects.

Before beginning your research, it is important to familiarize yourself with the American Sociological Association's Code of Ethics (www.asanet.org/about/ethics.cfm), as well as the standards of your school, and carefully follow both. Ask yourself whether your research will cause the subjects any emotional or physical harm. How will you guarantee their anonymity? Does the research violate any of your own ethical principles?

Most universities and research institutes require researchers to complete particular forms for experiments using human

■ TABLE 2.5 The Nuremberg Code

	Directives for Human Experimentation
1.	The voluntary consent of the human subject is absolutely essential.
2.	The experiment should be such as to yield fruitful results for the good of society.
3.	The experiment should be so designed and based on the results of animal experimentation and a knowledge of the natural history of the disease.
4.	The experiment should be so conducted as to avoid all unnecessary physical and mental suffering and injury.
5.	No experiment should be conducted where there is an a priori reason to believe that death or disabling injury will occur.
6.	The degree of risk to be taken should never exceed that determined by the humanitarian importance of the problem to be solved by the experiment.
7.	Proper preparations should be made and adequate facilities provided to protect the experimental subject against even remote possibilities of injury, disability, or death.
8.	The experiment should be conducted only by scientifically qualified persons.
9.	During the course of the experiment the human subject should be at liberty to bring the experiment to an end.
10.	During the course of the experiment the scientist in charge must be prepared to terminate the experiment at any stage, if he has probable cause to believe, in the exercise of the good faith, superior skill, and careful judgment required of him that a continuation of the experiment is likely to result in injury, disability, or death to the experimental subject.

SOURCE: U.S. Department of Health and Human Services.

subjects, describing the research methods to be used and the groups of subjects who will take part. Depending on the type of research, a researcher may need to obtain written agreement from the subjects for their participation. Today, a study like that conducted by Philip Zimbardo at Stanford University (described in the *Private Lives, Public Issues* box) would be unlikely to be approved because of the stress put on the experiment's subjects in the course of the research. Human subjects approval is granted with an eye to both fostering good research and protecting the interests of those partaking in a given study.

COLLECT AND ANALYZE THE DATA

Collecting data is the heart of research. It is time-consuming, but exciting. During this phase, you will gather the information that will allow you to make a contribution to the sociological understanding of your topic. If your data set is qualitative—for example, open-ended responses to interview questions or observations of

Milgram's Experiment

Participatory Research

ZIMBARDO'S EXPERIMENT: THE INDIVIDUAL AND THE SOCIAL ROLE

Social psychologist Philip Zimbardo (1974; Haney, Banks, & Zimbardo, 1973) wanted to investigate how role expectations shape behavior. He was intrigued by the possibility that the frequently observed cruelty of prison guards was a consequence of the institutional setting and role, not the guards' personalities.

In a well-known experiment, Zimbardo converted the basement of a Stanford University building into a makeshift prison. Seventy young men responded to a newspaper ad to take part in the experiment for pay. They were first given a battery of physical and psychological tests to assess their emotional stability and maturity. The most mature 24 subjects were selected for the experiment and randomly assigned to the role of "guards" or "prisoners." Those assigned to be prisoners were "arrested," handcuffed, and taken to the makeshift prison by the Palo Alto police. The behavior of the guards and the prisoners was filmed. Within a week, the prison setting took on many of the characteristics of actual prisons. The guards were often aggressive and seemed to take pleasure in being cruel. The prisoners began planning escapes and expressed hostility and bitterness toward the guards.

The subjects in the experiment so identified with their respective roles that many of them displayed

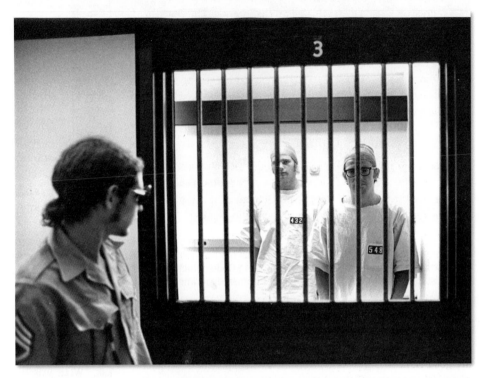

Despite questions about the ethics of Philip Zimbardo's experiment, sociologists still study his work. Is it wrong to use research data gathered by means we now consider unethical? Do the results of research ever justify subjecting human beings to physical or psychological discomfort, invasion of privacy, or deception? ■

signs of depression and anxiety. As a result, some were released early, and the experiment was canceled before the first week was over. Since the participants had all been screened for psychological and physical problems, Zimbardo concluded that the results could not be attributed to their personalities. Instead, the prison setting itself—the *independent variable*—appeared to be at the root of the guards' brutal behavior and the prisoners' hostility and rebelliousness— the *dependent variable*. Zimbardo's

research shows how profoundly private lives are shaped by the behavioral expectations of the roles we occupy in social institutions.

THINK IT THROUGH

■ *Zimbardo's experiment could not be repeated today, as it would violate guidelines for ethical human subjects research. How might a researcher de- sign an ethical experiment to test the question of the circumstances under which apparently "normal" individuals will engage in violent or cruel acts?*

people—you will proceed by carefully reviewing and organizing your field notes, documents, and other sources of information. If your data set is quantitative—for example, completed closed-ended

surveys—you will proceed by entering data into spreadsheets, comparing results, and analyzing your findings using statistical software.

During the Nuremberg Trials, which brought key figures of the Nazi Party of Germany to justice, the practices of some Nazi medical personnel were found to be unethical and even criminal. The Nuremberg Code, which emerged from these trials, established principles for any type of human experimentation. ■

Your analysis should offer answers to the research questions with which you began the study. Be mindful in interpreting your data and avoid conclusions that are speculative or not warranted by the actual research results. Do your data support or contradict your initial hypothesis? Or are they simply inconclusive? Report *all* your results. Do your findings have implications for larger theories in the discipline? Do they suggest the need for further study of another dimension of the issue at hand? Good research need not have results that unequivocally support your hypothesis. A finding that refutes the hypothesis can be instructive as well.

SHARE THE RESULTS

However fascinating your research may be to you, its benefits are amplified when you take advantage of opportunities to share it with others. You can share your findings with the sociological community by publishing the results in academic journals. Before submitting research for publication, sociologists must learn which journals cover their topic areas and review those journals' standards for publication. Some colleges and universities sponsor undergraduate journals that offer an opportunity for students to publish original research.

Other outlets for publication include books, popular articles, newspapers, video documentaries, and websites. Another way to communicate your findings is to give a presentation at a professional meeting. Many professional meetings are held each year; at least one will offer a panel suited to your topic. In some cases, high-quality undergraduate papers are selected for presentation. If your paper is one, relevant experts at the meeting will likely help you interpret your findings further.

SOCIOLOGY AND YOU: WHY LEARN TO DO SOCIOLOGICAL RESEARCH?

The news media provide us with an immense amount of round-the-clock information. Some of it is very good; some of it is misleading. Reported "facts" may come from sources that have agendas or are motivated by self-interest, such as political interest groups, lobbying groups, media outlets, and even government agencies. Perhaps the most problematic are "scientific" findings that are agenda driven, not scientifically unbiased. In particular because we live in a time of information saturation, it is important that we learn to be critical consumers of information and to ask questions about the quality of the data presented to us. Carefully gathered and precise data are important not only as sources of information, but also as the basis of informed decision making on the part of elected officials and others in positions of power.

Because you now understand how valid and reliable data are gathered, you can better question the veracity and reliability of others' claims. For example, when a pollster announces that 80% of the "American people" favor Joe Conman for Congress, you can ask, "What was the size of the sample? How representative is it of the population? How was the survey questionnaire prepared? Exactly what questions were asked?" If it turns out that the data are based on the responses of 25 residents of a gated Colorado community or that the random sample used was given leading questions, you know the results do not give an accurate picture.

Similarly, a broader grasp of the research process allows you to have greater confidence in research that was conducted properly. You should put more stock in the results of a nationwide Centers for Disease Control and Prevention survey of college students' drug use or safe-sex choices that used carefully prepared questionnaires tested for their validity and reliability, and less stock in data gathered by a reporter untrained in scientific methods who interviewed a small, nonrandom sample of students on a single college campus.

You have also taken the first step in learning how to gather and evaluate data yourself. Realizing the value of theories that can be tested and proven false if they are wrong is the first step in developing your own theories and hypotheses. By using the concepts, processes, and definitions introduced in this chapter, you can conduct research that is valid, appropriate, and even publishable.

In short, these research tools will help you be a more critical consumer of information and better understand the social world around you. Other benefits of learning sociology will become apparent throughout the following chapters as you discover how the research process is applied to an understanding of cultures, societies, and the institutions that shape your life.

WHAT CAN I DO WITH A SOCIOLOGY DEGREE?

CAREER DEVELOPMENT: GETTING STARTED AND ASSESSING YOUR INTERESTS, VALUES, AND SKILLS

The skills and knowledge of career development and your job search are learned, practiced, and mastered over time. You will learn about yourself, make career decisions, manage workplace expectations, and pursue new opportunities throughout your professional life. Your career success starts with *self-reflection, exploration, the effective implementation of career and job search action plans, and a personal and professional commitment to your career.* The basic activities linked to these processes are shown in the career development wheel.

In this chapter, we focus on your assessment of career interests and preferences and your exploration of career and job options.

Assessment of Individual Career Interests and Preferences

Self-knowledge is an important element of career assessment and development. Learning about your career identity—*the values, aspirations, interests, talents, skills, and preferences related to careers*—is fundamental to your career success.

Careful self-assessment will help you determine what you do well and enjoy, what skills and talents you possess, how you prefer to work, what interests you actively pursue, what values drive your choices, and where your strengths and weaknesses lie. By matching your characteristics to careers and occupations, you will establish a basis for identifying your career options and a guide to further research and exploration.

Assessments may be completed individually, online, in a group setting, and/or with a career professional. Assessments often include information linking your career interests to

potential academic majors. You may want to access the following *online assessment resources* to research your career identity:

- www.jobhuntersbible.com (*What Color Is Your Parachute?*)
- www.focuscareer.com (*Focus 2* Online Career Planning System)
- www.humanesources.com/products/program/do-what-you-are (*Do What You Are*)
- www.careerinfonet.org/occupations (CareerOneStop)

THINK ABOUT CAREERS

■ *Consider the components of a* career identity *noted above. What characteristics of your career identity can you identify at this point? How will you begin to establish the key aspects of your career identity?*

▶ *Access additional web links on the student study site to learn more.*

SUMMARY

To test your knowledge further, find additional study material on the Student Study Site at **www.sagepub.com/chamblissintro**

- Unlike commonsense beliefs, sociological understanding puts our biases, assumptions, and conclusions to the test.

- As a science, sociology combines logically constructed theory and systematic observation in order to explain human social relations.

- **Inductive reasoning** generalizes from specific observations; **deductive reasoning** consists of logically deducing the empirical implications of a particular theory or set of ideas.

- A good theory is logically consistent, testable, and valid. The principle of **falsification** holds that if theories are to be scientific, they must be formulated in such a way that they can be disproved if wrong.

- Sociological **concepts** must be operationally defined to yield measurable or observable variables. Often, sociologists operationally define variables so they can measure these in quantifiable values and assess **validity** and **reliability**, to eliminate **bias** in their research.

- Quantitative analysis permits us to measure correlations between the variables and identify **causal relationships**. Researchers must be careful not to infer causation from correlation.

- Qualitative analysis is often better suited than **quantitative research** to producing a deep understanding of how the people being studied view the social world. On the other hand, it is sometimes difficult to measure the reliability and validity of **qualitative research**.

- Sociologists seek **objectivity** when conducting their research. One way to help ensure objectivity is through the **replication** of research.

- Research strategies are carefully thought-out plans that guide the gathering of information about the social world. They also suggest the choice of appropriate **research methods**.

- Research methods in sociology include **survey** research (which often relies on random sampling), **fieldwork** (including participant observation and detached observation), **experiments**, working with existing information, and participatory research.

- Sociological research typically follows seven steps: framing the research question, reviewing the existing knowledge, selecting appropriate methods, weighing the ethical implications of the research, collecting data, analyzing data, and sharing the results.

- To be ethical, researchers must be sure their research protects the privacy of subjects and does not cause them unwarranted stress. Scientific societies throughout the world have adopted codes of ethics to safeguard against the misuse and abuse of human subjects.

KEY TERMS

Study terms on the go with the smartphone-friendly key term flashcards, available at **www.sagepub.com/chamblissintro**

scientific method, 29

deductive reasoning, 29

hypothesis, 29

inductive reasoning, 29

qualitative research, 29

quantitative research, 30

scientific theories, 31

concept, 31

operational definition, 32

variable, 32

quantitative variables, 32

qualitative variables, 32

correlation, 32

causal relationship, 33

spurious relationship, 33

negative correlation, 34

principle of falsification, 35

falsifiability, 35

validity, 35

reliability, 35

bias, 35

objectivity, 37

value neutrality, 37

replication, 37

research method, 37

survey, 37

sample, 38

population, 38

random sample, 38

fieldwork, 39

interview, 39

leading question, 40

experiments, 40

independent or experimental variable, 40

dependent variable, 40

statistical data, 41

document analysis, 41

DISCUSSION QUESTIONS

1. Think about a topic of contemporary relevance in which you may be interested (for example, poverty, juvenile delinquency, teen births, or racial neighborhood segregation). Using what you learned in this chapter, create a simple research question about the topic. Match your research question to an appropriate research method. Share your ideas with classmates.

2. Imagine that your school has recently documented a dramatic rise in plagiarism reported by teachers. Your sociology class has been invited to study this issue. Consider what you learned in this chapter about survey research and design a project to assess the problem.

3. In this chapter, you learned about the issue of ethics in research and read about the Zimbardo prison experiment. How should knowledge collected under unethical conditions (whether that is sociological, medical, psychological, or other scientific knowledge) be treated? Should it be used just like data collected under ethically rigorous conditions?

DISCOVER ⊕ STATE STATS

Log-in to the eBook and click on the title to the left for access to State Stats in order to complete the exercise.

Go to the State Stats "Education" database and search out the "Averaged Freshman Graduation Rate for Public High Schools." You will find several items, including a national rate and a breakdown of rates by race/ethnicity. First, check the "Source" note to see how the rate was calculated so you understand what the rate represents (note an adjustment in the rate calculation between 2005 and 2006). Second, examine the rates for different races/ethnicities and the rate change across the years indicated. Third, come up with two or three research questions a sociologist might ask about the data. What kinds of research methods could you use to answer them?

STUDENT STUDY SITE

Visit the Student Study Site at **www.sagepub.com/chamblissintro** to access additional study tools, including eFlashcards, web quizzes, video resources, web resources, audio resources, links to SAGE journal, handbook, and research articles, and much more!

3 CULTURE

WHAT DO YOU THINK?

1. Is the decision to cheat—whether in school, in a relationship, or otherwise—solely an individual choice, or should it be understood in the context of the culture in which a person lives?

2. Why do the covers of many fashion, sports, and lifestyle magazines depict body types that are unrepresentative of the general U.S. population? What might this tell us about the functions or dysfunctions of U.S. popular culture?

3. How many times have you been in an argument or a debate where someone says, "It's all relative"? Do you agree, or is there an objective standard by which to evaluate diverse customs, norms, and values of different cultures?

SOC **VIEW**

Get a closer look with the authors!

CULTURE, LANGUAGE, AND LOSS

Well over a billion people on our planet speak a dialect of Chinese as their first language. English and Spanish are the first languages of another 300 million people each. More than 182 million people speak Hindi, the primary official language of India, as a first language. In contrast, the world's 3,500 least widely spoken languages share just 8.25 million speakers. Aka, another language of India, has between 1,000 and 2,000 native speakers. The Mexican language of Seri has between 650 and 1,000. Euchee, a Native American language, has four fluent speakers left. According to a recent article in *National Geographic,* "one language dies every 14 days," and we can expect to lose about half the 7,000 languages spoken around the world by the end of the century (Rymer, 2012). What is the significance of language loss for human culture?

Symbols, like the names we assign to the objects around us, are *cultural representations of social realities.* They may take the form of letters or words, images, rituals, or actions. When we use language, we imbue these symbols with meaning. **Language** is *a particular kind of symbolic system, composed of verbal, nonverbal, and sometimes written representations that are vehicles for conveying meaning.* Language is thus a key vehicle of culture.

In the 1930s, Edward Sapir and Benjamin Whorf articulated the *Sapir-Whorf hypothesis,* which posits that our understandings and actions emerge from language—that is, the words and concepts we learn and use structure our perceptions of the social world. Language is also closely tied to cultural objects and practices. Consider that the Aka language has more than 26 words to describe beads, a rich vocabulary suited for a culture in which beads not only are decorative objects but also convey status and facilitate market transactions. In the Seri language, to inquire where someone

. . . .

Symbols: Cultural representations of social realities.

Language: A system of symbolic verbal, nonverbal, and written representations rooted within a particular culture.

■ FIGURE 3.1 Endangered Languages Worldwide

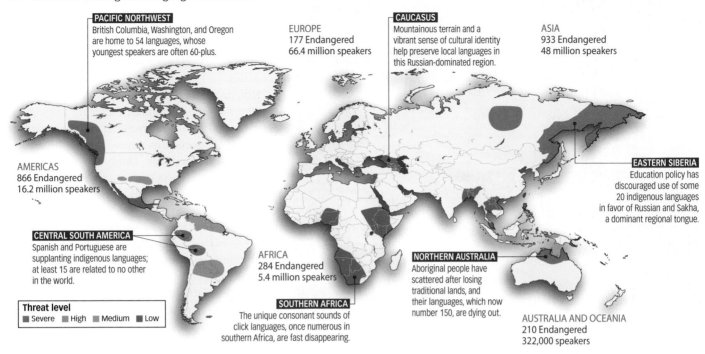

PACIFIC NORTHWEST
British Columbia, Washington, and Oregon are home to 54 languages, whose youngest speakers are often 60-plus.

EUROPE
177 Endangered
66.4 million speakers

CAUCASUS
Mountainous terrain and a vibrant sense of cultural identity help preserve local languages in this Russian-dominated region.

ASIA
933 Endangered
48 million speakers

AMERICAS
866 Endangered
16.2 million speakers

EASTERN SIBERIA
Education policy has discouraged use of some 20 indigenous languages in favor of Russian and Sakha, a dominant regional tongue.

CENTRAL SOUTH AMERICA
Spanish and Portuguese are supplanting indigenous languages; at least 15 are related to no other in the world.

AFRICA
284 Endangered
5.4 million speakers

NORTHERN AUSTRALIA
Aboriginal people have scattered after losing traditional lands, and their languages, which now number 150, are dying out.

Threat level
■ Severe ■ High ■ Medium ■ Low

SOUTHERN AFRICA
The unique consonant sounds of click languages, once numerous in southern Africa, are fast disappearing.

AUSTRALIA AND OCEANIA
210 Endangered
322,000 speakers

SOURCE: Mason, Virginia W. National Geographic Stock. Reprinted with permission.

is from you ask, "Where is your placenta buried?" This question references a historical cultural practice of burying a newborn's afterbirth by covering it with sand, rocks, and ashes (Rymer, 2012).

As languages like Aka and Seri die out, usually replaced by dominant tongues like Spanish, English, Chinese, Arabic, and Russian, we lose the opportunity to more fully understand the historical and contemporary human experience and the natural world. For instance, the fact that some small languages have no words linked to specific numbers but make use of relative designations like "few" or "many" opens the possibility that our number system may be a product of culture, rather than of innate cognition as many believe. Or consider that the Seri culture, based in the Sonoran Desert, has names for animal species describing behaviors that natural scientists are only beginning to document (Rymer, 2012). Language is a cultural vehicle that enables communication, illuminates beliefs and practices, roots a community in its environment, and contributes to the cultural richness of our world. Each language lost represents the erasure of history, knowledge, and human diversity (Living Tongues Institute for Endangered Languages, n.d.). ■

Culture: The beliefs, norms, behaviors, and products common to the members of a particular group.

We begin this chapter with an examination of the concept of culture, taking a look at material and nonmaterial culture globally, as well as ideal and real culture in the United States. We also explore issues of ethnocentrism and multiculturalism, phenomena that have grown in significance in a mobile and diverse world. We then turn to the topic of culture and class, how the two are related and whether culture and taste are linked to both class identity and social reproduction. The chapter also addresses the issue of culture and violence, raising questions about whether and how culturally conveyed messages about violence contribute to risk, particularly the risk of sexual violence against women. Finally, we examine the evolving relationship between global and local cultures.

CULTURE: CONCEPTS AND APPLICATIONS

What is culture? The word *culture* might evoke images of song, dance, and literature—the beat of Latin salsa, Polish folk dances performed by girls with red ribbons knitted into their braids, or the latest in a popular series of fantasy novels. It might remind you of a dish from the Old Country made by a beloved grandmother, or a spicy Indian meal you ate with friends from New Delhi.

Culture, from a sociological perspective, is composed of *the beliefs, norms, behaviors, and products common to the members of a particular group.* Culture is integral to our social experience of the world. It offers diversion and entertainment, but it also helps form our identities and gives meaning to the artifacts and experiences of our lives. Culture shapes and permeates material

Many people find flag burning offensive because the flag, an object of material culture, is a symbol of the country and its ideals. The Supreme Court, however, has held in a series of cases that symbolic expression is also protected by the First Amendment, which explicitly protects free speech. ■

objects like folk costumes; rituals like nuptial and burial ceremonies; and language, as expressed in conversation, poetry, stories, or music. We as social beings make culture, but culture also makes us, in ways that are both apparent and subtle.

MATERIAL AND NONMATERIAL CULTURE

Every culture has both material and nonmaterial aspects. We can broadly define **material culture** as the *physical objects created, embraced, or consumed by society that help shape people's lives.* Material culture includes television programs, computer games, software, and other artifacts of human creation. It also emerges from the physical environment inhabited by the community. For example, in the countries surrounding the Baltic Sea, such as Poland, Latvia, and Lithuania, amber—a substance created when the resin of fallen seaside pines is hardened and smoothed by decades or centuries in the salty waters—is an important part of local cultures. It is valued both for its decorative properties in jewelry and for its therapeutic properties; it is said to relieve pain. Amber has become a part of the material culture in these countries rather than elsewhere because it is a product of the physical environment in which these communities dwell.

Material culture also includes the types of shelters that characterize a community. For instance, in seaside communities, homes are often built on stilts to protect against flooding. The materials used to construct homes have historically been those available in the immediate environment—wood, thatch, or mud, for instance—though the global trade in timber, marble and granite, and other components of modern housing has transformed the relationship between place and shelter in many countries.

Nonmaterial culture is composed of the *abstract creations of human cultures, including ideas about behavior and living.* Nonmaterial culture embraces aspects of the social experience, such as behavioral norms, values, language, family forms, and institutions. It also reflects the natural environment in which the culture has evolved: Recall our opening vignette's discussion of unique Seri language terms for the wildlife of the Sonoran Desert.

While material culture is concrete and nonmaterial culture is abstract, the two are intertwined: Nonmaterial culture may attach particular meanings to the objects of material culture. For example, people will go to great lengths to protect an object of material culture, say a national flag, not because of what it is—imprinted cloth—but because of the nonmaterial culture it represents, such as ideals about freedom or patriotic pride. In order to grasp the full extent of nonmaterial culture, you must first understand three of the sociological concepts that shape it: *beliefs, norms,* and *values* (Table 3.1).

■ **TABLE 3.1** Values, Norms, Folkways, Mores, Taboos, Laws, and Beliefs

Concept	Characteristics
Values	General ideas about what is good, right, or just in a culture
Norms	Culturally shared rules governing social behavior ("oughts" and "shoulds")
Folkways	Conventions (or weak norms), the violation of which is not very serious
Mores	Strongly held norms, the violation of which is considered very offensive to the community or culture
Taboos	Very strongly held norms, the violation of which is highly offensive and even unthinkable
Laws	Norms that have been codified into law
Beliefs	Particular ideas that people accept as true

Material culture: The physical objects that are created, embraced, or consumed by society that help shape people's lives.

Nonmaterial culture: The abstract creations of human cultures, including language and social practices.

Consumer Culture

BELIEFS We broadly define **beliefs** as *particular ideas that people accept as true.* We can believe based on faith, superstition, science, tradition, or experience: To paraphrase the words of sociologists W. I. and D. S. Thomas (1928), beliefs may be understood as real when they are real in their consequences. They need not be objectively true. For example, during the witch hunts in early colonial America, rituals of accusation, persecution, and execution could be sustained in communities such as Salem, Massachusetts, because there was a shared belief in the existence of witches and diabolical power. Between 1692 and 1693, more than 200 people were accused of practicing witchcraft and 20 were executed, 19 by hanging and one by being pressed to death between heavy stones. Beliefs, like other aspects of culture, are dynamic rather than static: When belief in the existence of witchcraft waned, so did the witch hunts. In 1711, a bill was passed that restored "the rights and good names" of the accused, and in 1957, the state of Massachusetts issued a formal apology for the events of the past (Blumberg, 2007).

NORMS In any culture, there exists a set of ideas about what is right, just, and good, as well as what is wrong and unjust. **Norms** are *the common rules of a culture that govern the behavior of people belonging to it.*

Sociologist Robert Nisbet (1970) writes, "The moral order of society is a kind of tissue of 'oughts': negative ones which forbid certain actions and positive ones which [require certain] actions" (p. 226). We can think of norms as representing a set of "oughts" and "ought nots" that guide behavioral choices like where to stand relative to others in an elevator, how long to hold someone's gaze in conversation, how to conduct the rites of passage that mark different stages of life, and how to resolve a disagreement or conflict. Some norms are enshrined in legal statutes; others are inscribed in our psyches and consciences. Weddings bring together elements of both.

The wedding ceremony is a central ritual of adult life with powerful social, legal, and cultural implications. It is also significant economically: The term *wedding industrial complex* (Ingraham, 1999) has been used to describe a massive industry that in 2011, for instance, generated more than $53 billion in revenues. This comes as little surprise when we consider that in 2011, the estimated average amount spent on a wedding was just over $25,000 (*The Wedding Report*, 2012). The wedding as a key cultural image

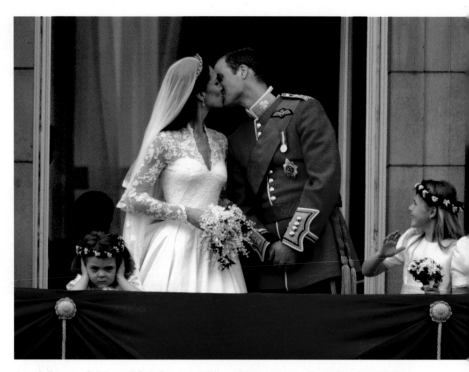

One folkway of the traditional U.S. wedding dates to the reign of Queen Victoria (1819–1901). In her 1840 wedding to the handsome Prince Albert, the "plain" Victoria wore a beautiful white gown. By the end of her life, the tradition was firmly in place, and the white gown had acquired new symbolism, representing purity and virginity (Ingraham, 1999). The royal wedding between Prince William and Catherine Middleton, pictured here, attracted broad public interest. ■

and icon is cultivated in families, religions, and the media. Wedding images are used to sell products ranging from cosmetics to furniture and are an important theme in popular movies, including *My Big Fat Greek Wedding* (2002), *Wedding Crashers* (2005), *Rachel Getting Married* (2008), and *Bridesmaids* (2011). Popular television series such as *The Office* and *Sex and the City* have used weddings as narratives for highly anticipated season finales. Today, the reality program *Say Yes to the Dress* enthralls viewers with the drama of choosing a wedding gown, while *Bridezillas* follows the adventures of brides behaving badly. Clearly, the wedding ritual is a powerful artifact of our culture. In light of this, a sociologist might ask, "What are the cultural components of the ritual of entering matrimony, the wedding ceremony?"

Sociologist William Graham Sumner (1906/1959) distinguished between several different kinds of norms, each of which can be applied to weddings. **Folkways** are *fairly weak norms that are passed down from the past, whose violation is generally not considered serious within a particular culture.* A folkway that has become part of many U.S. wedding rituals is the "giving away" of the bride: The father of the bride symbolically gives his daughter to the groom, signaling a change in the woman's identity from daughter to wife. Some couples today reject this ritual

....

Beliefs: Particular ideas that people accept as true.

Norms: The common rules of a culture that govern the behavior of people belonging to that culture.

Folkways: Fairly weak norms that are passed down from the past, whose violation is generally not considered serious within a particular culture.

Appearance Cultures

Do you think that loneliness is stigmatized in our connected and busy world? Could it be considered a violation of U.S. cultural norms? ■

as patriarchal because it recalls earlier historical periods when a woman was treated as chattel given—literally—to her new husband by her previous keeper, her father.

Some modern couples are choosing to walk down the aisle together to signal an equality of roles and positions. While the sight of a couple going to the altar together might raise a few eyebrows among more traditional guests, this violation of the "normal" way of doing things does not constitute a serious cultural transgression and, because culture is dynamic, may in time become a folkway itself.

Mores (pronounced MOR-ays) are strongly held norms; violating them seriously offends the standards of acceptable conduct of most people within a particular culture. In U.S. weddings, the person conducting the ceremony plays an important role in directing the events, and the parties enacting the ritual are expected to respond in conventional ways. For instance, when guests are asked whether anyone objects to the union, the convention is for no one to object. When an objector surfaces (more often in films than in real life), the response of the guests is shock and dismay: The ritual has been disrupted and the scene violated.

Taboos are *powerful mores, the violation of which is considered serious and even unthinkable.* The label of taboo is commonly reserved for behavior that is extremely offensive: Incest is a nearly universal taboo. There may not be taboos regarding the wedding ritual itself, but there are some relating to marital relationships. For instance, while in some states it is not illegal to marry a first cousin, in most modern communities doing so violates a basic taboo against intermarriage in families.

Culture Jamming

Laws are *codified norms or rules of behavior.* Laws formalize and institutionalize society's norms. There are laws that govern marriage in general: For instance, in most U.S. states, marriage is legally open only to heterosexual adults who are not already married to other people. As of December 2012, only nine states and the District of Columbia permit same-sex marriage: Connecticut, Iowa, Maine, Maryland, Massachusetts, New Hampshire, New York, Vermont, and Washington. While 10 offer some form of civil union or domestic partnership, fully 39 explicitly ban same-sex marriage (Freedom to Marry, 2012).

Marriage equality groups and their supporters continue to fight prohibitions against same-sex marriage. A poll conducted by the Pew Research Center (2012) found that in 2011 47% of U.S. adults agreed same-sex marriage should be recognized as legally valid—43% disagreed. Just three years earlier, 39% of adults agreed while 51% disagreed, suggesting that norms codified in laws are dynamic, too, and are not necessarily shared by all.

VALUES Like norms, values are a component of nonmaterial culture in every society. **Values** are *the abstract and general standards in society that define ideal principles, like those governing notions of right and wrong.* Sets of values attach to the institutions of society at multiple levels. You may have heard about national or patriotic values, community values, and family values. These can all coexist harmoniously within a single society. Because we use values to legitimate and justify our behavior as members of a country or community, or as individuals, we tend to staunchly defend the values we embrace (Kluckhohn & Strodtbeck, 1961).

Is there a specific set of values we can define as "American"? According to a classic study by Robin Williams (1970), "American values" include personal achievement, hard work, material comfort, and individuality. U.S. adults value science and technology, efficiency and practicality, morality and humanitarianism, equality, and "the American way of life." A joint 1998 study on American values by Harvard University, the *Washington Post,* and the Kaiser Family Foundation

. . . .

Mores: Strongly held norms, violation of which would seriously offend the standards of acceptable conduct of most people within a particular culture.

Taboos: Powerful mores, the violation of which is considered serious and even unthinkable.

Laws: Codified norms or rules of behavior.

Values: The general standards in society that define ideal principles, like those governing notions of what is right or wrong.

identified similar points—hard work, self-reliance, tolerance, and the embrace of equal rights—though respondents also voiced important disagreements about such issues as the ideal size of the U.S. government and the degree to which the government should promote economic equality (Kaiser Family Foundation, 1998).

A 2010 study found an interesting split between those who agreed they would like to see "the federal government provide more services, even if it costs more in taxes" (49%) and those who agreed they would like to see "the federal government cost less in taxes," even if it meant the provision of fewer services (47%). In 2010, the percentage in favor of more services (even with higher taxes) rose 10 percentage points (Kaiser Family Foundation, 2010). What we value, then, varies across time and communities and may even be contradictory. Do these differences matter? Can we still speak of a unified body of "American values"? What do you think?

Structural functionalists including Talcott Parsons (1951) have proposed that values play a critical role in the social integration of a society. However, values do not play this role by themselves. They are abstract—vessels into which any generation or era pours its meanings in a process that can be both dynamic and contentious. For instance, equality is a value that has been strongly supported in the United States since the country's founding. The pursuit of equality was a powerful force in the American Revolution, and the Declaration of Independence declares that "all men are created equal" (Wood, 1993). However, equality has been defined quite differently across various eras of U.S. history. In the first half of the country's existence, "equality" did not include women or African Americans, who were by law excluded from its benefits. Through the 20th century, equality became *more* equal, as the rights of all citizens of the United States, regardless of race, gender, or class status, were formally recognized as equal before the law.

IDEAL AND REAL CULTURE IN U.S. SOCIETY

Beauty is only skin deep. Don't judge a book by its cover. All that glitters is not gold. These bits of common wisdom are part of U.S. culture. We rarely recall where we first heard them; we simply know them, because they are part of the cultural framework of our lives. These three statements represent a commitment of sorts that society will value our inner qualities more than our outward appearances. They are also examples

. . . .

Ideal culture: The values, norms, and behaviors that people in a given society profess to embrace.

Real culture: The values, norms, and behaviors that people in a given society actually embrace and exhibit.

Ursula, a character from the Disney film *The Little Mermaid,* is one of many children's story characters who combine an unattractive appearance with a flawed personality. How do we reconcile the idea that "beauty is only skin deep" with messages of popular culture? ∎

of **ideal culture,** *the values, norms, and behaviors that people in a given society profess to embrace,* even though the actions of our society often contradict them.

Real culture represents *the values, norms, and behaviors that people in a given society actually embrace and exhibit.* In the United States, for instance, empirical research shows that conventional attractiveness offers consistent advantages (Hamermesh, 2011). From our childhood, the stories told to us by parents, teachers, and the media seem to sell the importance of beauty. Stories such as *Snow White, Cinderella,* and *Sleeping Beauty* connect beauty with morality and goodness, and unattractiveness with malice, jealousy, and other negative traits. The link between unattractive (or unconventional) appearance and unattractive behavior is unmistakable, especially in female figures. Think of other characters introduced to many U.S. children early in life, such as nasty Cruella de Vil in *101 Dalmatians,* the dastardly Queen of Hearts of *Alice in Wonderland,* and angry octopod Ursula in *The Little Mermaid.*

On television, another medium that disseminates important cultural stories, physical beauty and social status are powerfully linked. Overweight or average-looking characters populate shows featuring working- or lower-middle-class people, for example *Family Guy, The Office,* and *New Girl.* Programs such as *Modern Family* and *Mike & Molly* offer leading characters who are pleasant and attractive—and often overweight. In the latter, for instance, Mike is a police officer and Molly an elementary school teacher. They have not broken the glass ceiling of high-status jobs that remain largely reserved for their thinner prime-time peers. Characters such as those we encounter on *Gossip Girl, Privileged, Sex and the City,* and *Mad Men* are almost invariably svelte and stylish—and occupy higher rungs on the status hierarchy.

Mike and Molly, Roseanne, and *The Honeymooners* are examples of sitcoms that feature main characters who are working-class people who also happen to be overweight. The next time you're flipping through the channels or watching a movie, take note of the correlation between socioeconomic status and appearance. ■

A reality television program that achieved popularity until its end in 2007 was *Extreme Makeover.* As the name suggests, this program featured radical transformations of guests and the realization of, in the program's words, their "fairy tale fantasies." One of *Extreme Makeover*'s many thematic successors, *Bridalplasty,* ran from November 2010 to January 2011. On the program, 12 brides-to-be were in competition to win their desired plastic surgery procedure. While each week's winner would win a single surgery from her wish list, the final champion had her entire dream surgery list fulfilled. Her "new look" was to be revealed to her groom on their wedding day.

There is a clear **cultural inconsistency**, *a contradiction between the goals of ideal culture and the practices of real culture,* in our society's treatment of conventional attractiveness. Do we "judge a book by its cover"? Studies suggest this is precisely what many of us do in a variety of social settings:

- In the workplace, conventionally attractive job applicants appear to have an advantage in securing jobs (Hamermesh, 2011; Marlowe, Schneider, & Nelson, 1996; Shahani-Denning, 2003; Tews, Stafford, & Zhu, 2009). Another study found a significant earnings penalty for those who were perceived as short or unattractive (Harper, 2000).
- Women in one study who were an average of 65 pounds heavier than the norm of the study group earned about 7% less than their slimmer counterparts, an effect equivalent to losing about one year of education or two years of experience. The link between obesity and a "pay penalty" has been confirmed by other studies (Harper, 2000; Lempert, 2007). Interestingly, some research does not find strong evidence that weight affects wages of African

American or Hispanic female workers (Cawley, 2001; DeBeaumont, 2009).

- In the courtroom, some defendants who do not meet conventional standards of attractiveness are disadvantaged (DeSantis & Kayson, 1997; Gunnell & Ceci, 2010; Taylor & Butcher, 2007). Mazzella and Feingold (1994) note that defendants charged with certain crimes like rape and robbery benefit from being attractive. This is consistent with the "beautiful is good" hypothesis (Dion, Berscheid, & Walster, 1972), which attributes a tendency toward leniency to the belief that attractive people have more socially desirable characteristics. Ahola, Christianson, and Hellstrom (2009) suggest that female defendants in particular are advantaged by attractive appearance.
- In studies of college students, attractive people are more likely to be perceived as intelligent (Chia, Allred, Grossnickle, & Lee, 1998; Poteet, 2007). This bias has also been detected in students' evaluations of their instructors:

· ·

Cultural inconsistency: The contradiction between the goals of ideal culture and the practices of real culture.

PRIVATE LIVES, PUBLIC ISSUES

THE CULTURE OF THINNESS IN AMERICA

Whether you are male or female, you may sometimes experience feelings of inadequacy as you leaf through magazines like *Cosmopolitan, GQ, Vogue,* and *Maxim.* You may get a sense that, in this media-constructed universe, your face, hair, body, and clothing do not fit the feminine (or masculine) ideal. You may wish that you had the "right look" or that you were thinner. You would not be alone.

One survey of college-age women found that 83% desired to lose weight. Among these, 44% of women of normal weight intentionally ate less than they wanted, and most women did not have healthy dieting habits (Malinauskas, Raedeke, Aeby, Smith, & Dallas, 2006). According to a Canadian study, chronic dieters' sense of identity is often frail and reflects others' perceptions of them (Polivy & Herman, 2007). Indeed, a recent study examining body weight perceptions among college students found that women with an exaggerated body weight perception were more likely to engage in unhealthy weight management strategies and were more depressed than those women with an accurate perception of their weight (Harring, Montgomery, & Hardin, 2011).

Using our sociological imaginations, we can deduce that the weight concerns many people experience as personal troubles are in fact linked to public issues: Worrying about (and even obsessing over) weight is a widely shared phenomenon. Millions of women diet regularly, and some manifest extreme attention to weight in the form of eating disorders. By one estimate, fully 9 million people in the

United States are afflicted with eating disorders over the courses of their lives (Hudson, Hiripi, Pope, & Kessler, 2007), most of them women. The National Institute of Mental Health (2010) recently reported that "women are three times as likely to experience anorexia (0.9 percent of women vs. 0.3 percent of men) and bulimia (1.5 percent of women vs. 0.5 percent of men) during their life. They are also 75 percent more likely to have a binge eating disorder (3.5 percent of women vs. 2.0 percent of men)."

The diet industry in the United States is extremely profitable—by some estimates worth $60.9 billion a year (LaRosa, 2011). The fashion industry (among others) primarily employs models who are abnormally thin and whose images are airbrushed or digitally altered to perfection. Psychologist Sarah Grogan (2008) writes that the dieting, fashion, cosmetic surgery, and advertising industries are fueled by the successful manipulation and oppression of women. That is, manufacturers and marketers create a beauty culture based on total but artificial perfection and then sell products to "help" women achieve a look that is unachievable.

As individuals, we experience the consequences of this artificially

The billboard here appeared in Milan during Fashion Week to raise awareness of the dangers of excessive thinness. Can such a message get through in a cultural context that equates a very slim female figure with glamour? ■

created ideal as a personal trouble—unhappiness about our appearance—but the deliberate construction and dissemination of an unattainable ideal for the purpose of generating profits is surely a public issue. Reflecting a conflict perspective, psychologist Sharlene Hesse-Biber (1997) has suggested that to understand the eating disorders and disordered eating so common among U.S. women, we ought to ask not "'What can women do to meet the ideal?' but 'Who benefits from women's excessive concern with thinness?'" (p. 32). This is the sociological imagination at work.

THINK IT THROUGH

■ *How would you summarize the key factors that explain the broad gap between ideal culture, which entreats us not to judge a book by its cover, and real culture, which pushes women and men to pursue unattainable physical perfection?*

A pair of economists recently found that the independent influence of attractiveness gives some instructors an advantage on undergraduate teaching evaluations (Hamermesh & Parker, 2005).

Another example of cultural inconsistency is in our commitment to the ideal that honesty is "the best policy." We find an unambiguous embrace of honesty in the stories of our childhood. Think of *Pinocchio*: Were you warned as a child not to lie because it might cause your nose to grow? Did you ever promise a friend not to reveal his or her secret with a pinky swear and the words "Cross my heart and hope to die; stick a needle in my eye"? Yet most people do lie.

Why is this so? We may lie to protect or project a certain image of ourselves. Sociologist Erving Goffman (1959), a symbolic interactionist, called this *misrepresentation*. Goffman argued that all of us, as social actors, engage in this practice because we are concerned with "defining a situation"—whether it be a date or a job interview or a meeting with a professor or boss—in a manner favorable to ourselves. It is not uncommon for job seekers to pad their résumés, for instance, in order to leave the impression on potential employers that they are qualified or worthy. According to an overview of the issue posted on the Society for Human Resource Management (SHRM) website, almost half of 3,100 hiring managers surveyed by CareerBuilder indicated that they had detected lying on a job candidate's résumé. Common lies included misrepresentations of educational credentials, salary level, and even criminal record. About 43% of hiring managers also said they spent less than a minute looking at a single résumé during the initial screening process, suggesting that some dishonesty probably goes unnoticed (SHRM, 2008).

Studies also suggest that cheating and plagiarism are common among high school students (Table 3.2). According to one study of 23,000 high school students, about half reported that they had cheated on a test in the past year. Just under a third also responded that they had used the Internet to plagiarize assigned work (Josephson Institute Center for Youth Ethics, 2012).

Why do you think there is such a big gap between what we say and what we do? Do you think most people are culturally inconsistent? What about you?

ETHNOCENTRISM

Much of the time, a community or society's cultural norms, values, and practices are internalized to the point where they become part of the natural order. Sociologist Pierre Bourdieu (1977) describes these internalized beliefs as **doxic**: *To a member of a given community or cultural group, common norms*

Ethnocentrism

■ **TABLE 3.2** Ethical and Unethical Behavior Among High School Students in 2012

	NEVER	ONCE	TWO or more times
Copied an Internet document for a class assignment	45%	26%	29%
Cheated on a test	49%	24%	28%
Lied to a teacher about something significant	45%	26%	29%

SOURCE: Josephson Institute Center for Youth Ethics. (2012). *2012 report card on the ethics of American youth*. Retrieved from http://charactercounts.org/programs/reportcard/2012/index.html.

and practices appear as a part of the social order—just the way things are. But the social organization of our lives is not natural, though it comes to appear that way. Instead, norms, values, and practices are *socially constructed*. That is, they are the product of decisions and directions chosen by groups and individuals (often, a conflict theorist would argue, those with the most power). And though all human societies share certain similarities, different societies construct different norms, values, and practices and then embrace them as "just the way things are."

Because we tend to perceive our own culture as "natural" and "normal," it emerges as the standard by which we tend to judge everything else. This is indicative of **ethnocentrism**, *a worldview whereby we judge other cultures by the standards of our own.* That which deviates from our own "normal" social order can appear exotic, even shocking. Other societies' rituals of death, for example, can look astonishingly different from those to which we are accustomed, as in this description of an ancient burial practice from the North Caucasus:

> Scythian-Samartian burials were horrible but spectacular. A royal would be buried in a kurgan [burial mound] alongside piles of gold, weapons, horses, and . . . various members of the household: one of his concubines, his butler, his cook, his groom, his steward, and his chamberlain—all of them strangled. A year later, 50 fine horses and 50 young men would be strangled, gutted, stuffed with chaff, sewn up, and then impaled and stuck around the kurgan to mount a ghoulish guard for their departed king. (Smith, 2001, pp. 33–34)

. . . .

Doxic: That which is taken for granted as "natural" or "normal" in society, though it may be socially constructed.

Ethnocentrism: A worldview whereby one judges other cultures by the standards of one's own culture.

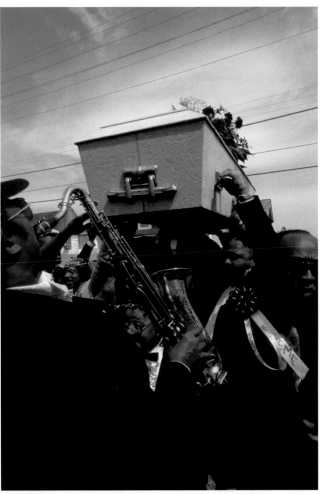

In the Tibetan sky burial, the body is left on a mountaintop exposed to the elements. This once-common practice of "giving alms to the birds" represented belief in rebirth and the idea that the body is just an unneeded empty shell. In Indonesia, mass cremations take place where bodies are placed in sarcophagi of various sizes with animal representations. In New Orleans, a casket is paraded through the street. Death and burial rituals are components of culture. ■

Let us interpret this historical fragment using two different cultural perspectives. From an **etic perspective**—that is, *the perspective of the outside observer*—the burial ritual looks bizarre and shockingly cruel. However, in order to understand it fully and avoid a potentially ethnocentric perspective, we need to call upon an **emic perspective**, *the perspective of the insider,* and ask, "What did people in this time period believe about the royals? What did they believe about the departed and the experience of death itself? What did they believe about the utility of material riches in the afterlife and the rewards the afterlife would confer on the royals and those loyal to them?"

. . . .

Etic perspective: The perspective of the outside observer.

Emic perspective: The perspective of the insider, the one belonging to the cultural group in question.

Cultural relativism: A worldview whereby the practices of another society should be understood sociologically in terms of that society's own norms and values, and not one's own.

Are there death rituals in the U.S. cultural repertoire that might appear exotic or strange to an outsider even though we see them as "normal"?

Putting aside the ethnocentric perspective allows us to embrace **cultural relativism**, *a worldview whereby we understand the practices of another society sociologically, in terms of that society's own norms and values and not our own.* In this way we can come closer to an understanding of cultural beliefs and practices such as those that surround the end of life. Whether the body of the departed is viewed or hidden, buried or burned, feasted with or feasted for, danced around or sung about, a culturally relativist perspective allows the sociologist to conduct his or her examination of the roots of these practices most rigorously.

Ideas and Customs

We may also call on cultural relativism to help us understand the rituals of another people, the *Nacirema*, described here by anthropologist Herbert Miner (1956):

Nacirema culture is characterized by a highly developed market economy which has evolved in a rich natural habitat. While much of the people's time is devoted to economic pursuits, a large part of the fruits of these labors and a considerable portion of the day are spent in ritual activity. The focus of this activity is the human body, the appearance and health of which loom as a dominant concern in the ethos of the people . . .

The fundamental belief underlying the whole system appears to be that the human body is ugly and that its tendency is to debility and disease. Incarcerated in such a body, man's only hope is to avert these characteristics through the use of powerful influences of ritual and ceremony. Every household has one or more shrines devoted to this purpose. The more powerful individuals in this society have several shrines in their houses . . .

The focal point of the shrine is a box or chest which is built into the wall. In this chest are kept many charms and magical potions without which no native believes he could live. These preparations are secured from a variety of specialized practitioners . . . However, the medicine men do not provide the curative potions for their clients, but decide what the ingredients should be and then write them down in an ancient and secret language. This writing is understood only by the medicine men and by the herbalists who, for another gift, provide the required charm. (pp. 503–504)

What looks strange here, and why? Did you already figure out that *Nacirema* is *American* spelled backwards? Miner invites his readers to see U.S. rituals linked to the body and health not as natural, but as *part of a culture.* Can you think of other U.S. norms or practices we could view from this perspective? What about the all-American game of baseball, the high school graduation ceremony, the youth language of texting, or the cultural obsession with celebrities or automobiles?

SUBCULTURES

When sociologists study culture, they do not presume that in any given country—or even

community—there is a single culture. They may identify a dominant culture within any group, but significant cultural identities exist in addition to, or sometimes in opposition to, the dominant one. These are **subcultures**, *cultures that exist together with a dominant culture but differ from it in some important respects.*

Some subcultures, including ethnic subcultures, may embrace most of the values and norms of the dominant culture while simultaneously choosing to preserve the values, rituals, and languages of their native (or their parents' or grandparents' native) countries. Members of ethnic subcultures such as Armenian Americans and Cuban Americans may follow political events in their home countries or prefer their children to marry within the group. It is comfort in the subculture rather than rejection of the dominant culture that supports the vitality of many ethnic subcultures.

In a few cases, though, ethnic or other subcultures do reject the dominant culture surrounding them. The Amish choose to elevate tradition over modernity in areas such as transportation (many still use buggies), occupations (they rely on simple farming), and family life (women are seen as subordinate to men), and they lead a *retreatist* lifestyle in which their community is intentionally separated from the dominant culture.

Sociologists sometimes also use the term *counterculture* to designate a subcultural group whose norms, values, and practices deviate from those of the dominant culture. The hippies of the 1960s, for example, are commonly cited as a

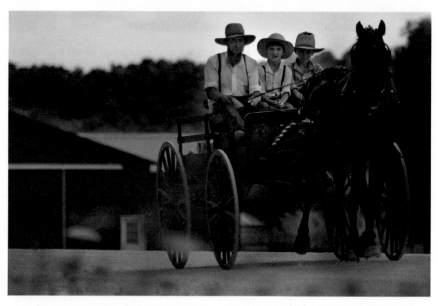

"Father drives a mustang, and I'm not talking about the car . . ." While most Americans elect to use automobiles as a primary method of transportation, most Amish communities still rely on horse-drawn carriages. When you're committed to preserving traditional elements of your culture and religion, a horse-drawn buggy beats a Volkswagen Bug. ■

Hate Rock

Subcultures: Cultures that exist together with a dominant culture, but differ in some important respects from that dominant culture.

THE FRENCH MELTING POT—OR SALAD BOWL?

The "melting pot" image of the United States implies a melding of different cultures that lose their individual shapes by dissolving into a single, larger culture. While mainstream U.S. culture is itself changed by the addition of new customs and communities, immigrant culture is dissolved into the larger entity. In contrast, the "salad bowl" image suggests a cultural mix in which different parts make up a whole but maintain their distinctive and individual characteristics, just as tomatoes, lettuce, and carrots are all parts of the salad but each retains its distinctive character. The salad bowl image more closely reflects the idea of U.S. society as a multicultural mixture of cultures, traditions, languages, and communities. Just as the United States, long a destination for immigrants from across the globe, has struggled over time to resolve debates over whether assimilation or multicultural integration is more culturally desirable, so too have European states like France, which are more recent mass immigration destinations, begun to contend with questions about their culture and identity as the population undergoes changes unprecedented in its modern history.

France is home to about 6 million Muslims, many of them immigrants from countries such as Algeria. In recent years, the growth of this population has provoked a firestorm of controversy over the national and cultural integration of migrant populations and their France-born children. One subject of controversy is the French government's effort to ban the burqa or niqab, the full, face-covering veil worn by a small number of Muslim women. In July 2010, the French National Assembly, France's parliamentary body, voted to enact a ban on the wearing of the burqa in public spaces including schools, hospitals, public transport facilities, and government offices.

France had already banned from public schools the head scarves worn by some Muslim schoolgirls in accordance with Muslim norms about female modesty. The 2004 prohibition joined a broader ban on religious symbols in French public schools, a prohibition that has been in force since the French state took control of schools from the Catholic Church over a hundred years ago.

France is a largely secular country. Photographs of women forced to wear burqas in Taliban-era Afghanistan have arguably reinforced deeply negative feelings regarding the garment, which became a key symbol of this oppressive era. On the other hand, of the few hundred women who wear a full veil, many are French converts

In France, legislation was introduced to ban the burqa that is worn by some Muslim women. Proponents of this legislation argued that the prohibition of the burqa would eliminate a symbol of repression, yet opponents point out that the government would be trampling the right of women to freely elect to wear the burqa. ■

to Islam. They say they have freely chosen the full veil after marriage, and "that to stigmatize or ban the veil would only cause more women to wear it out of protest" (Erlanger, 2009). Muslims and non-Muslims alike who oppose the ban argue, among other things, that it threatens diversity and women's rights and that France should embrace multiculturalism over assimilation.

THINK IT THROUGH

■ Is the melting pot an anachronism, or is assimilation of immigrant communities still a desirable and achievable goal? Is the salad bowl a fitting road to a harmonious and diverse community, or is it an unachievable ideal? What are the risks and rewards of these different approaches to the integration of immigrants?

counterculture to mainstream "middle America," though many of those who participated in hippie culture aged into fairly conventional middle-class lives. Subcultures may generate anxiety in or hostility among those in the mainstream culture: For example, the Amish have been targets of hate crimes (Byers & Crider, 2002). In 2011, seven people were arrested for forcibly cutting the hair off several Amish men and women (*CBS News*, 2011). The Amish consider such an act to be highly offensive because of their belief that the Bible instructs women to grow their hair long and advises men to stop cutting their beards after marriage. Interestingly, in this unusual instance, the alleged perpetrators were also Amish.

Though there are exceptions, the vast majority of U.S. subcultures are permeated by the dominant culture, and the influence runs both ways. What, for example, is an "all-American" meal? Your answer may be a hamburger and fries. But what about other U.S. staples, such as Chinese takeout and Mexican burritos? Mainstream culture has also absorbed the influence of the United States' multicultural heritage: Salsa music, created by Cuban and Puerto Rican American musicians in 1960s New York, is widely popular, and world music, a genre that reflects a range of influences from the African continent to Brazil, has a broad U.S. following. Contemporary pop, as performed by artists such as Lady Gaga, incorporates elements of British glam, U.S. hip-hop, and central European dance. The influence is apparent in sports as well: Soccer, now often the youth game of choice in U.S. suburbs, was popularized by players and fans from South America and Europe. Mixed martial arts, a combat sport popularized by the U.S. organization Ultimate Fighting Championship, incorporates elements of Greco-Roman wrestling, Japanese karate, Brazilian jujitsu, and Muay Thai (from Thailand).

CULTURE, CLASS, AND LANGUAGE

From the sociological perspective, we are all *cultured* because we all participate in and identify with a culture or cultures. According to the conventional use of the term, however, some classes of people are considered *more cultured* than others. We refer to people who attend the symphony, are knowledgeable about classic literature and fine wines, and possess a set of distinctive manners as cultured, and we often assume a value judgment in believing that being cultured is better than being uncultured.

We commonly distinguish between high culture and popular culture. **High culture** refers to *music, theater, literature, and*

Gun Culture

Skateboarding Culture

other cultural products that are held in particularly high esteem in society. It can also encompass a particular body of literature or a set of distinctive tastes. High culture is usually associated with the wealthier, more educated classes in society, but this association can shift over time. William Shakespeare's plays were popular with the English masses when they were staged in open public theaters during his lifetime. Lobster was a meal of the poor in colonial America. This suggests that high culture's association with educated and upper-income elites may be more a function of accessibility—the prohibitive cost of theater tickets and lobster meat today, for instance—than with "good taste" as such.

Popular culture encompasses *the entertainment, culinary, and athletic tastes shared by the masses.* It is more accessible than high culture because it is widely available and less costly to consume. Popular culture can include music that gets broad airplay on the radio, television shows and characters that draw masses of viewers (e.g., *The Voice, How I Met Your Mother*, the *Real Housewives* franchise, and *Mad Men*), blockbuster films such as the *Hunger Games* and the *Twilight* series, Oprah's Book Club, and spectator sports such as wrestling and professional baseball. Because it is an object of mass consumption, popular culture obviously plays a key role in shaping values, attitudes, and consumption in society. It is an optimal topic of sociological study because it not only *shapes* but *is shaped by* a society and its members.

CULTURE, CLASS, AND INEQUALITY

In their studies of culture and class, sociologists consider whether the musical and artistic tastes of different socioeconomic classes vary and, if so, why. While the answer may be interesting in itself, researchers are also likely to go a step further and examine the links between culture, power, and class inequality. Particularly when using a social conflict lens, sociologists have long sought to show how elites use culture to gain or maintain power over other groups.

Sociologist Pierre Bourdieu has used culture to help explain the phenomenon of **social class reproduction**, *the way class status is reproduced from generation to generation.* Bourdieu (1984) discusses the concept of **cultural capital**, *wealth in the form of knowledge, ideas, verbal skills, and ways of thinking and behaving.* Karl Marx argued that the key to power in a capitalist system is *economic capital*, particularly possession of the

....

High culture: The music, theater, literature, and other cultural products that are held in particularly high esteem in society.

Popular culture: The entertainment, culinary, and athletic tastes shared by the masses.

Social class reproduction: The way that class status is reproduced from generation to generation, with parents "passing on" a class position to their offspring.

Cultural capital: Wealth in the form of knowledge, ideas, verbal skills, and ways of thinking and acting.

means of production. Bourdieu extends this idea by suggesting that cultural capital can also be a source of power. Children from privileged backgrounds have access to markedly different stores of cultural capital than do children from working-class backgrounds.

Children of the upper and middle classes come into the education system—the key path to success in modern industrial societies—with a set of language and academic skills, beliefs, and models of success and failure that fit into and are validated by mainstream schools. Children from less privileged backgrounds enter with a smaller amount of validated cultural capital; their skills, knowledge base, and styles of speaking are not those that schools conventionally recognize and reward. For example, while a child from a working-class immigrant family may know how to care for her younger siblings, prepare a good meal, or translate for non-English-fluent parents, her parents (like many first-generation immigrants) may have worked multiple jobs and may not have had the skills to read to her or the time or money to take her to enriching activities. By contrast, her middle-class peers are more likely to have grown up with parents who regularly read to them, took them to shows and museums, and quizzed them on multiplication problems. While both children come to school with *knowledge and skills,* the cultural capital of the middle-class child can be more readily "traded" for academic success—and eventual economic gains.

In short, schools serve as locations at which the cultural capital of the better-off classes is exchanged for educational success and credentials. This difference in scholastic achievement then translates into economic capital, as high achievers assume prestigious, well-paid positions in the workplace. Those who do not have the cultural capital to trade for academic success are often tracked into jobs in society's lower tiers. Class is reproduced as cultural capital begets academic achievement, which begets economic capital, which again begets cultural capital for the next generation.

Clearly, however, the structure of institutional opportunities, while unequal, cannot alone account for broad reproduction of social class across generations. Individuals, after all, make choices about education, occupations, and the like. They have free will—or, as sociologists put it, *agency,* which is understood as the capacity of individuals to make choices and to act independently. Bourdieu (1977) argues that agency must be understood in the context of structure. To this end, he introduces the concept of **habitus,** *the internalization of objective probabilities and the expression of those probabilities as choice.* Put another way, people come to want what they can realistically have—and they act accordingly.

Consider the following hypothetical example of habitus in action. In a poor rural community where few people go to college, fewer can afford it, and the payoff is not obvious because there are no immediate role models with higher education, Bourdieu would argue that an individual's "choice" not to prioritize getting into college reflects both agency *and* structure. That is, she makes the choice not to prepare herself for college or to apply to college—but going to college would likely not have been possible for her anyway due to her economic circumstances and perhaps due to an inadequate education in an underfunded school. By contrast, the habitus of a young upper-middle-class person makes the choice of going to college almost unquestionable. Nearly everyone around her has gone or is going to college, the benefits of a college education are broadly discussed, and she is socialized from her early years to understand that college will follow high school—alternatives are rarely considered. No less importantly, a college education is accessible—she is prepared for college work in a well-funded public school or a private school, and family income, loans, or scholarships will contribute to making higher education a reality. Bourdieu thus suggests that social class reproduction appears on its face to be grounded in individual choices and merit, but fundamental structural inequalities that underlie class reproduction often go unrecognized, a fact that benefits the well-off.

LANGUAGE AND SOCIAL INTEGRATION

Conflict theorists focus on disintegrative forces in society, while functionalists study integrative forces. Where social conflict theorists see culture as serving the interests of the elite, functionalists argue that shared values and norms maintain social bonds both between people and between people and society (Parsons & Smelser, 1956). By serving as a vehicle for the dissemination of these values and norms, culture functions to keep society stable and harmonious and gives people a sense of belonging in a complex, even alienating, social world (Smelser, 1962). To illustrate, we consider the issue of language use in the United States.

In part a response to the increased use of Spanish and other languages spoken by the United States' large immigrant population, an English-only movement has arisen that supports the passage of legislation to make English the only official language of the United States and its government. Modern proponents argue that they want to "restore the great American melting pot," though the movement has roots in the early 20th century, when President Theodore Roosevelt wrote, "We have room for but one language in this country, and that is the English language, for we intend to see that the crucible turns our people out as Americans . . . and not as dwellers in a polyglot boarding house." Like today, Roosevelt's era was characterized by high rates of emigration to the United States.

How would a functionalist analyze the English-only movement? He or she might highlight language as a vehicle of social

....

Habitus: The internalization of objective probabilities and subsequent expression of those probabilities as choice.

Health and Illness

INEQUALITY MATTERS

POWER AND CONTROL OF CULTURAL IDEAS

While Karl Marx argued that an elite class, or *bourgeoisie*, dominates society through its control of the economic means of production such as factories, Antonio Gramsci (1971) believed that elites' power also drew from their control of the means of production of *ideas*. That is, Gramsci argued that through *cultural hegemony,* or the domination of culture and the vehicles that disseminate it, elites facilitate mass acceptance of the ideas that promote their power and survival. These ideas become dominant in society—in other words, they evolve into *hegemonic ideas* about social institutions such as capitalism, education, and family life.

Gramsci's ideas provide tools for a conflict-oriented analysis of powerful cultural ideas in U.S. society. For example, there is a pervasive sense—a hegemonic idea—in the United States that individuals are fully responsible for their own destinies. According to a 2010 Kaiser Family Foundation survey, two thirds of U.S. adults agree that "most people who want to get ahead can make it if they're willing to work hard" (p. 7). Well-known personal stories form an effective vehicle for this belief. Abraham Lincoln, Bill Clinton, and Barack Obama rose from modest beginnings to become U.S. presidents, while Henry Ford made his way up from poverty to become a wealthy industrialist, and more than one groundbreaking high-tech firm got started in somebody's dorm or garage. Such stories have inspired many to strive and achieve, but they may also have the power to mislead.

Hard work is absolutely important to educational success, but so too is opportunity. However, unlike the capacity to work hard, opportunities are not equally distributed. In two decades of publications, ranging from *Savage Inequalities* (1991) to *The Shame of the Nation* (2010), writer Jonathan Kozol has documented startling inequalities in U.S. public schools: Upper- and middle-class children have access to skilled teachers, modern textbooks, and advanced technology, while children schooled in poor urban and rural (and often minority) areas experience packed classrooms, rounds of substitute teachers, inadequate supplies of textbooks, outdated technology, and unsanitary, unhealthful conditions for learning.

Schools matter. So too do activities outside of school, particularly those that build literacy or other educationally vital competencies. A recent article in the *New York Times* points out that "one reason for the growing gap in achievement, researchers say, could be that wealthy parents invest more time and money than ever before in their children (in weekend sports, ballet, music lessons, math tutors, and in overall involvement in their children's schools), while lower-income families, which are now more likely than ever to be headed by a single parent, are increasingly stretched for time and resources" (Tavernise, 2012).

Is the classroom a site for the reduction or the reproduction of social inequalities in society? This is a question debated by sociologists. ■

A Gramscian perspective would argue that most people in the United States fail to recognize (or to see as a problem) the lack of social mobility in the bottom rungs of U.S. society, because this fundamental inequality is obscured by the hegemonic cultural belief—perpetuated through cultural stories that shape our perceptions of the social world—that individual effort is the key determinant of educational and, by extension, economic success and that "most people who want to get ahead can make it if they're willing to work hard." No less importantly, this belief also legitimates the position of the elite class, which is presumed to be the outcome of merit and hard work rather than a product, at least in part, of privilege.

THINK IT THROUGH

■ *How do schools today contribute to the reduction of social inequality? How do they contribute to its reproduction? Which function, on balance, is more powerful? What do you think?*

integration and a form of social glue. Indeed, the English-only movement focuses on the function of language as an integrative mechanism; its website (www .englishfirst.org) states that "this nation of immigrants must be able to talk to each other. [We] believe that the English language unites America. [We] are tired of seeing the government use [our] tax money to divide Americans on the basis of language or ancestry." From this perspective, the use of different primary languages in a single country is dysfunctional to the extent that it undermines the common socialization that comes from a shared language and culture.

Is the nation threatened by residents who speak several languages or, for that matter, by the presence of people who speak English poorly or not at all? Some in the English-only movement think so. Former Republican congressman, House of Representatives speaker, and presidential candidate Newt Gingrich has argued that bilingualism poses "long-term dangers to the fabric of our nation" and that "allowing bilingualism to continue to grow is very dangerous" (cited in Hunt, 2007). Census data suggest that about 80% of U.S. residents 5 years of age and older use only English at home. Just under 20% use a language other than English. Of this 20%, the majority of respondents (about 56%) indicate that they speak English "very well," though there is variation by age and primary language (Shin & Kominski, 2010).

Many people embrace cultural diversity and emphasize the value of **multiculturalism**, *a commitment to respecting cultural differences rather than submerging them into a larger, dominant culture.* Multiculturalism recognizes that the country is as likely to be enriched as divided by its differences. In a globalizing world, knowledge of other cultures and proficiency in languages other than English is important. In fact, a functionalist might also regard the U.S. Census data cited above as indicative of *both* the common language English-only proponents see as crucial to national unity, and the cultural diversity that enriches the country and allows it to incorporate a variety of languages in its national and global political, cultural, and

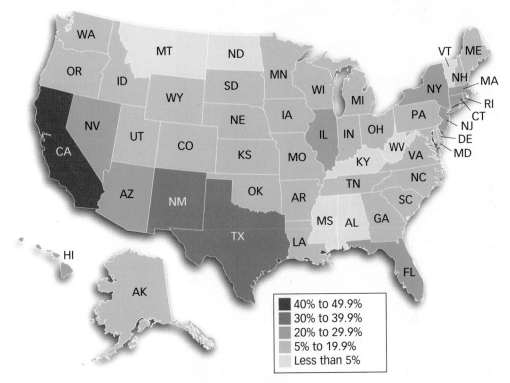

■ **FIGURE 3.2** Percent of Population Speaking a Language Other Than English at Home, 2010

- 40% to 49.9%
- 30% to 39.9%
- 20% to 29.9%
- 5% to 19.9%
- Less than 5%

SOURCE: U.S. Census Bureau. (2010). "Population 5 years and older who spoke a language other than English at home by Hispanic origin and race: 2009." *American Community Survey* Briefs.

economic dealings—which is also positively functional for the country (Figure 3.2).

CULTURE AND VIOLENCE

In this section, we turn our attention to another dimension of culture and discuss the relationship between culture and a negative but pervasive sociological phenomenon—sexual violence against women.

Recent statistics suggest that rape and sexual assault devastate the lives of thousands of U.S. women every year. According to the National Crime Victimization Survey (NCVS), in 2010 there were 188,380 rapes, attempted rapes, or sexual assaults in the United States (U.S. Bureau of Justice Statistics, 2011). Men and boys also fall prey to these crimes, but women are the most commonly victimized.

One explanation for this number might be that sexual assaults are perpetrated by thousands of deviant individuals and are the outcomes of particular and individual circumstances. Applying the sociological imagination, however, means recognizing the magnitude of the problem and considering the idea that examination

· ·

Multiculturalism: A commitment to respect cultural differences rather than to try to submerge them into a larger, dominant culture.

Cultural Control

The hero of many popular culture stories—particularly in films and video games—is often the most violent character. John Rambo (Sylvester Stallone) and Batman (Christian Bale most recently) often practice violence against other men. Many films and games also depict violence against women, rendering aggressive interactions a form of entertainment. ■

[the law] punishes takings by force (robbery), by coercive threats (extortion), by stealth (larceny), by breach of trust (embezzlement), and by deception (fraud and false pretenses) . . . Yet sexual autonomy, almost alone among our important personal rights, is not fully protected. The law of rape, as if it were only a law against the "robbery" of sex, remains focused almost exclusively on preventing interference by force. (pp. 100–101)

Schulhofer (2000) notes that this problem is linked to a culture that treats male sexual aggression as "natural." Taslitz (1999) adds that the cultural stories brought into courtrooms also render proceedings around rape problematic by situating them in myths, such as the idea that a female victim was "asking for it."

Some research in the fields of sociology and communications suggests that popular culture promotes rape culture by *normalizing violence*. That is not to argue that culture is a direct cause of sexual violence, but rather to suggest that popular culture renders violence part of the social scenery by making its appearance so common in films, video games, and music videos that it evolves from being shocking to being utterly ordinary (Katz & Jhally, 2000a, 2000b). How does this process occur?

Some scholars argue that popular media embraces *violent masculinity*, a form of masculinity that associates "being a man" with being aggressive and merciless. As well, the messages of popular culture may serve to normalize violence against women in particular. Tyler, The Creator, winner of the 2011 MTV Video Music Award for Best New Artist, has come under fire from parents, media outlets, and fellow musicians for his violently misogynistic and homophobic lyrics. Hip-hop has long been associated with the use of misogynistic lyrics (Morgan, 1999; Pough, 2004; Weitzer & Kubrin, 2009). Many commercial films and music videos also feature rough—even very violent—treatment of women, offered as entertainment. The most gratuitous violence in films such as *The Girl With the Dragon Tattoo* (2011), *The Killer Inside Me* (2010), *The Last Exorcism* (2010), and *Final Destination 5* (2011) is reserved for female victims. In early 2010, citizens in Japan and around the world expressed dismay and disgust when reports emerged about the popular dissemination of the videogame *RapeLay*, in which a player stalks a young woman, her mother, and her sister on a train. In the game, the player uses the mouse to grope—and eventually rape—his victims.

Popular culture's most predictable normalization of violence against women occurs in pornography, a multibillion-dollar-a-year industry in the United States. Fictionalized portrayals of sexual activity range from coercion of a compliant and always willing female to violent rape simulations in which consent is clearly refused.

While researchers do not propose that lyrics or images cause sexual violence *directly*, some suggest that popular culture's persistent use of sex-starved, compliant, and easily victimized female

of individual cases alone is inadequate for fully understanding the phenomenon of rape and sexual assault in the United States. To paraphrase C. Wright Mills, it is clearly a personal trouble *and* a public issue.

Some researchers (Boswell & Spade, 1996; Buchwald, Fletcher, & Roth, 1993/2005; Sanday, 1990) have posited the existence of a **rape culture**, *a social culture that provides an environment conducive to rape.* According to some scholars, rape culture has been pervasive in the U.S. legal system. Feminist theorist and legal scholar Catherine MacKinnon (1989) argues that legislative and judicial processes regarding rape utilize a male viewpoint. Consider, for instance, that until the late 1970s most states did not treat spousal rape as a crime. This conclusion was based, at least in part, on the notion that a woman could not be raped by her husband because sexual consent was taken as implied in the marital contract.

Some researchers argue that the legal culture takes rape less seriously than other crimes of violence (Taslitz, 1999). Legal scholar Stephen J. Schulhofer (2000) has written that

. . . .

Rape culture: A social culture that provides an environment conducive to rape.

characters sends messages that forced sex is no big deal, that women really want to be raped, and that some invite rape by their appearance. In a study of 400 male and female high school students, Cassidy and Hurrell (1995, cited in Workman & Freeburg, 1999) determined that respondents who heard a vignette about a rape scenario and then viewed a picture of the "victim" (in reality, a model for the research) dressed in provocative clothing were more likely than those who saw her dressed in conservative clothing, or who saw no picture at all, to judge her responsible for her assailant's behavior, and to say his behavior was justified and not really rape. More recent studies have reproduced findings that rape myths are widely used to explain and even justify sexual violence (Hammond, Berry, & Rodriguez, 2011).

A 2003 study found that victims' attire is not a significant factor in sexual assault. Instead, rapists look for signs of passivity and submissiveness (Beiner, 2007). Why, with evidence to the contrary, do such rape myths, common but rarely true beliefs about rapists and rape victims, exist? Recent studies link regular exposure to popular print, television, film, and Internet media with acceptance of rape myths among college-aged men and women (Kahlor & Morrison, 2007; Lonsway et al., 2009, citing Katz, 2006; Reinders, 2006). Is this indicative of the existence of a rape culture? Is culture, particularly vehicles like music or movies that give a platform to expressions of violence against women, a sociological antecedent of real sexual violence? What do you think?

CULTURE AND GLOBALIZATION

There is a pervasive sense around the world that globalization is creating a homogenized culture—a landscape dotted in every corner of the globe with the Golden Arches and the face of Colonel Sanders beckoning the masses to consume hamburgers and fried chicken. The familiar songs of Lady Gaga, Justin Bieber, and Beyoncé are broadcast on radio stations from Bangladesh to Bulgaria to Belize, while rebroadcasts of such popular U.S. soap operas as *The Bold and the Beautiful* provide a picture of ostensibly "average" U.S. lives on the world's television screens.

We see the effects of globalization—and of Americanization in particular—in cultural representations like McDonald's restaurants, U.S. pop music and videos, and bottles of Coca-Cola spreading around the world. According to press reports, even in the Taliban era in Afghanistan, a time when a deeply conservative Islamist ideology was enforced throughout society, the culture of global Hollywood seeped in through the cracks of fundamentalism's wall. In January 2001, the Taliban rounded up dozens of barbers in the capital city of Kabul because they had been cutting men's hair in a style known locally as the "Titanic": "At the time, Kabul's cooler young men wanted that Leonardo DiCaprio look, the one he sported in the movie. It was an interesting moment

The worldwide success of North American pop artists such as Lady Gaga (shown here) fosters imitation abroad. The threat of a homogenized global culture does not just mean the music of these artists is played everywhere—it means locally produced music often sounds nearly identical as well. ■

because under the Taliban's moral regime, movies were illegal . . . Yet thanks to enterprising video smugglers who dragged cassettes over mountain trails by mule, urban Afghans knew perfectly well who DiCaprio was and what he looked like" (Freund, 2002, p. 24).

How should a sociologist evaluate the spread of a globalized culture? Is globalization, on balance, positive or negative for countries, communities, and corporate entities? Is it just business, or does it also have political implications? The conflict and functionalist perspectives offer us different ways of seeing a contemporary **global culture** that *draws heavily, though by no means exclusively, on U.S. trends and tastes*.

A functionalist examining the development and spread of a broad global culture might begin by asking, "What is its function?" He or she could deduce that globalization spreads not only material culture in the form of food and music, but also nonmaterial culture in the form of values and norms. Globalized norms and values can strengthen social solidarity and consequently serve

Global culture: A type of culture—some would say U.S. culture—that has spread across the world in the form of Hollywood films, fast-food restaurants, and popular music heard in virtually every country.

Melting Pot

GLOBAL ISSUES

THE TALIBAN AND CULTURE IN AFGHANISTAN

From about 1996 through the end of 2001, the Taliban ruled the war-torn Middle Eastern country of Afghanistan with a fundamentalist, antimodern Islamic ideology. The regime provides a stark picture of a government attempting to radically transform the culture of a country, not least by brutally suppressing traditional cultural practices. Ahmed Rashid (2000), writing on the Taliban's rule, has suggested that "the Taliban did not recognize the very idea of culture" (p. 115). If culture is a vehicle for transmitting a group's history, beliefs, and practices, then suppression of culture is a means of denying a group its fundamental identity. While the Taliban itself was a carrier of a particular culture, it rejected traditional cultural vehicles such as music, dancing, and art, which formed a key foundation for Afghan life. The Taliban's recent efforts to reestablish its dominance make it particularly important to understand its early rule (McGirk, 2009).

During the Taliban's five-year regime, official policy forbade the playing of music, and the Afghan culture's tradition of keeping pigeons and other birds. The government did not permit the depiction of human figures in art, citing the blasphemy of idol worship: In an official decree, it noted that "in vehicles, shops, hotels, room [sic] and any other place pictures/portraits should be abolished" (Rashid, 2000, p. 249). In Afghanistan's museums, works of art depicting human figures were destroyed or the figures were painted over. Rashid (2000) writes that an Afghan artist, Mohammed Mashal, "who was painting a huge mural showing 500 years of Herat's [an Afghan city] history was forced to watch as the Taliban whitewashed over it" (p. 115).

In the wake of the Taliban's defeat and removal from power in 2001, music, birds, and art were reclaimed and reincorporated into cultural practices. But cultural freedom in Afghanistan remains tenuous, and journalists have documented recent attempts by the Taliban to reestablish their control of culture in some areas of the country through, for instance, shuttering music stores (Shukoor, 2010). A Taliban resurgence in Afghanistan may signal a new era of political control—and cultural suppression.

Among the prohibitions in Taliban-ruled Afghanistan was women's participation in education and work outside the home. ■

THINK IT THROUGH

■ *Can you write an argument to support the idea that repressive states suppress culture because they fear it? What might an authoritarian state have to fear from culture? Consider the questions from a sociological perspective that highlights culture's role in societies and communities.*

---

to reduce conflict between states and societies. Therefore, globalization plays an integrative function by creating some semblance of a common culture that can foster mutual understanding and a foundation for dialogue.

Recall from Chapter 1 that functionalism assumes the social world's many parts are interdependent. Indeed, globalization highlights both the cultural and the economic interdependence of countries and communities. The book *Global Hollywood* (Miller, Govil, McMurria, & Maxwell, 2002) describes what its authors call a *new international division of cultural labor,* a system of cultural production that crosses the globe, making the creation of culture an international rather than a national phenomenon (though profits still flow primarily into the core of the filmmaking industry in Hollywood).

The blockbuster film *Slumdog Millionaire* (2008) offers an example of the international division of cultural labor. The film was directed by Englishman Danny Boyle and co-directed by

Honor Killings

New Delhi native Loveleen Tandan from a screenplay by Boyle's fellow countryman, Simon Beaufoy, that was based on the 2005 novel *Q & A* by Indian writer Vikas Swarup. In 2009, the film, distributed in the United States by Warner Independent Pictures but shown internationally, received nine Academy Awards, including Best Picture. *Slumdog Millionaire* cast both established local actors and young slum dwellers, some of whom were later found to have earned very little from their efforts. Boyle has argued, however, that the film-makers worked to ensure future educational opportunities and shelter for the young actors. The film's global appeal was huge, generating almost $378 million in box office returns and leading the *Wall Street Journal* to label it "the film world's first globalized masterpiece" (Morgenstern, 2008).

From the social conflict perspective, we can view the globalization of culture as a force with the potential to perpetuate economic inequality—particularly because globalization is a product of the developed world. While a functionalist would highlight the creative global collaboration and productive interdependence of a film like *Slumdog Millionaire,* a conflict theorist would ask, "Who benefits from these productions?" While Western film companies, producers, and directors walk away with huge profits, the slum dwellers used as actors or extras garner far less sustained global interest or financial gain.

A conflict theorist might also describe how the globalization of cheap fast food can cripple small independent eateries that serve indigenous (and arguably healthier) cuisine. An influx of global corporations inhibits some local people from owning their own means of production and providing employment to others. The demise of local restaurants, cafés, and food stalls represents a loss of the cuisines and thus the unique cultures of indigenous peoples. It also forces working people to depend on large corporations for their livelihoods, depriving them of economic independence.

While functionalism and conflict theory offer different interpretations of globalization, both offer us valuable insights. Globalization may bring people together through common entertainment, eating experiences, and communication technologies, and at the same time, it may represent a threat—real or perceived—to local cultures and economies as indigenous producers are marginalized and the sounds and styles of different cultures are replaced by a single mold set by Western entertainment marketers.

Journalist Thomas Friedman has suggested that while most countries cannot resist the forces of globalization, it is not inevitably homogenizing. In *The Lexus and the Olive Tree: Understanding Globalization,* Friedman (2000) writes that "the most important filter is the ability to 'glocalize.' I define healthy glocalization as the ability of a culture, when it encounters other

Did all of the actors who were part of *Slumdog Millionaire,* a blockbuster film, benefit from its success? The local extras—as well as some of the central characters—took away little financial gain from the film. ■

strong cultures, to absorb influences that naturally fit into and can enrich that culture, to resist those things that are truly alien and to compartmentalize those things that, while different, can nevertheless be enjoyed and celebrated as different" (p. 295). The concept of *glocalization* highlights the idea of cultural hybrids born of a pastiche of both local and global influences.

In *The Globalization of Nothing* (2007), sociologist George Ritzer proposes a view of globalization that also integrates what he calls *grobalization,* the product of "the imperialistic ambitions of nations, corporations, organizations, and the like and their desire . . . to impose themselves on various geographic areas" (p. 15). Ritzer adds that the "main interest of the entities involved in grobalization is in seeing their power, influence, and in many cases profits grow (hence the term *grobalization*) throughout the world" (p. 16). The concept of grobalization draws from classical sociological theorists like Karl Marx and Max Weber. For instance, where Marx theorized capitalism's imperative of economic imperialism, Ritzer offers contemporary examples of grobalization's economic and cultural imperialism, exporting not only brand-name products but also the values of consumerism and the practical vehicles of mass consumption, such as credit cards.

How will the world's cultures shift in the decades to come? Will they globalize or remain localized? Will they glocalize or grobalize? Clearly, the material culture of the West, particularly of the United States, is powerful: It is pushed into other parts of the world

Power and Cultural Ideas

In its more than half-century of operation, McDonald's has become one of the most recognized icons of U.S. life and culture; Ronald McDonald is said to be the most recognized figure in the world after Santa Claus. McDonald's serves 47 million customers every day in an estimated 31,000 restaurants in 119 countries around the globe. ■

by markets and merchants, but it is also pulled in by people eager to hitch their stars to the modern Western world. Local identities and cultures continue to shape people's views and actions, but there is little reason to believe that McDonald's, Kentucky Fried Chicken, and Coca-Cola will drop out of the global marketplace. The dominance of U.S. films, music, and other cultural products is also likely to remain a feature of the world cultural stage.

WHY STUDY CULTURE THROUGH A SOCIOLOGICAL LENS?

Culture is a vital component of a community's identity—through language, objects, and practices, cultures embody a community and its environment. Each culture is a unique mirror. The loss of culture—whether through the disappearance of ancient languages or the political suppression of culture—is a loss for the community

Indigenous Cultures

Social Interaction

and for the world. Culture is also dynamic, however, and humans are constantly creating new forms and manifestations of it.

Culture can be a source of integration and harmony, as functionalists assert, or it can be a vehicle of manipulation and oppression, as conflict theorists sometimes see it. There is compelling evidence for both perspectives, and context is critical for recognizing which better captures the character of a given cultural scenario.

The study of culture is much more than just an intellectual exercise. Will the evolution of a more global culture play an integrative role in world affairs, or will smaller cultures resist homogenization and assert their own local power? Or perhaps both? These are questions of profound importance in a globalized and changing world. Understanding the norms, perspectives, and structures that drive your own culture—as well as those that drive the cultures of others—is of real consequence when negotiating your way in a society and world that are increasingly complex, diverse, and inextricably interconnected. We make culture, but culture also makes us: We must be able to look both critically and carefully at our own cultural communities, and to step beyond their boundaries, to embrace the broad mix of cultures that make up the global community in which we all dwell.

WHAT CAN I DO WITH A SOCIOLOGY DEGREE?

CAREER DEVELOPMENT: EXPLORING CAREERS AND SETTING GOALS

EXPLORE AND TARGET CAREERS AND JOB OPTIONS

When you have completed an initial career identity assessment, reflect on your career options. Enlist the support of friends, family, and career professionals as you review career options. You can start by using online tools and library resources. Review general information about occupational fields and industries to identify a wide spectrum of career options. Examine specific aspects of careers and occupations, including *types of employers, job skills and titles, responsibilities, entry-level educational requirements, advancement potentials, work environments, salaries and benefits, and employment trends.*

Use your research results to identify potential employers and link to their websites. Compare results for a variety of employers. Your career and occupational exploration and your employer research are the best ways to support and validate your career aspirations. *Online career exploration and employer resources* include the following:

- www.careerinfonet.org/Occupations/select_occupation .aspx (CareerOneStop)
- www.vault.com (Vault Career Intelligence)
- www.bls.gov/ooh/home.htm (Bureau of Labor Statistics, *Occupational Outlook Handbook*)
- www.onetonline.org (O*Net Online)

In addition to researching career trends and data, learn about career options firsthand through *informational interviews.* An informational interview is similar to any interview, except that you interview the individual working in your career field of interest to learn about his or her profession, career skills, education, current position, and/or employer. To request an informational interview, target your family, friends, or school faculty and alumni and their networks.

Another option to explore careers is through an internship, field study, or a part-time job. Internships offer the opportunity to learn about career options in a real-world setting, to test your career skills and interests, and to meet professionals in your field.

MAKE CAREER DECISIONS AND SET CAREER GOALS

Making *career decisions* is a key aspect of the career development process. Evaluate your alternatives and identify the advantages and disadvantages of each career. From here, you can begin to make a career choice, which will influence your career goals.

Career goals are important milestones that provide a structure for you to evaluate progress on your career path. Goals are not absolute, and may be updated and changed as you continue to move ahead. Long-term goals are generally accomplished in one, five, or ten years and incorporate your dreams and aspirations. Short-term goals (or objectives) are completed on a daily, weekly, monthly, or annual basis and identify specific tasks associated with the career plan.

THINK ABOUT CAREERS

■ *Explore some sample employer websites to gather information. What are the career and employment options in this organization? What information is highlighted and what do you learn about the employer? What can you conclude about the industry?*

■ *Create three goals that you hope to accomplish in the next five years. Then, add short-term goals that support the completion of the long-term goal.*

▶ *Access additional web links on the student study site to learn more.*

SUMMARY

To test your knowledge further, find additional study material on the Student Study Site at www.sagepub.com/chamblissintro

- **Culture** consists of the beliefs, norms, behaviors, and products common to members of a particular social group. **Language** is an important component of cultures. The Sapir-Whorf hypothesis points to language's role in structuring perceptions and actions. Culture is a key topic of sociological study because as human beings we have the capacity to develop it through the creation of artifacts such as songs, foods, values, and more. Culture also influences our social development: We are products of our cultural beliefs, behaviors, and biases.

- Sociologists and others who study culture generally distinguish between material and nonmaterial culture. **Material culture** encompasses physical artifacts—the objects created, embraced, and consumed by a given society. **Nonmaterial culture** is generally abstract and includes culturally accepted ideas about living and behaving. The two are intertwined, because nonmaterial culture often gives particular meanings to the objects of material culture.

- **Norms** are the common rules of a culture that govern people's actions. **Folkways** are fairly weak norms, the violation of which is tolerable. **Mores** are strongly held norms; violating them is subject to social or legal sanction. **Taboos** are the most closely held mores; violating them is socially unthinkable. **Laws** codify some, though not all, of society's norms.

- **Beliefs** are particular ideas that people accept as true, though they need not be objectively true. Beliefs can be based on faith, superstition, science, tradition, or experience.

- **Values** are the general, abstract standards of a society and define basic, often idealized principles. We identify national values, community values, institutional values, and individual values. Values may be a source of cohesion or conflict.

- **Ideal culture** represents the norms and values that people of a society profess to embrace. **Real culture** represents the real practices of people in that society.

- **Ethnocentrism** is the habit of judging other cultures by the standards of our own.

- Sociologists entreat us to embrace **cultural relativism**, a perspective that allows us to understand the practices of another society in terms of that society's own norms and values rather than our own.

- Multiple cultures may exist and thrive within any country or community. Some of these are **subcultures**, which exist together with the dominant culture but differ in some important respects from it.

- **High culture** is an exclusive culture often limited in its accessibility and audience. High culture is widely associated with the upper class, which both defines and embraces its content. **Popular culture** represents entertainment, culinary, and athletic tastes that are broadly shared. As "mass culture," popular culture is more fully associated with the middle and working classes.

- **Rape culture** is a social culture that provides an environment conducive to rape. Some sociologists argue that we can best understand the high number of rapes and attempted rapes in the United States by considering both individual circumstances and the larger social context, which contains messages that marginalize and normalize the problem of sexual assault.

- **Global culture**—some would say U.S. culture—has spread across the world in the form of Hollywood films, fast-food restaurants, and popular music heard in virtually every country.

KEY TERMS

Study terms on the go with the smartphone-friendly key term flashcards, available at www.sagepub.com/chamblissintro

symbols, 52

language, 52

culture, 53

material culture, 54

nonmaterial culture, 54

beliefs, 55

norms, 55

folkways, 55

mores, 56

taboos, 56

laws, 56

values, 56

DISCUSSION QUESTIONS

1. As we will see in later chapters, the United States has some of the highest rates of overweight and obesity in the world. Is there a relationship between the "culture of thinness" discussed in this chapter and U.S. rates of obesity and overweight? How might a sociologist explain this seemingly paradoxical phenomenon?

2. The chapter presents an argument on the relationship between culture and sexual violence with a discussion of the concept of a rape culture. Do you agree or disagree with the argument? Explain your position.

3. Sociologist George Ritzer sees within globalization two processes—that of glocalization and that of grobalization. What is the difference between the two? Which is, in your opinion, the more powerful process, and why do you believe this? Support your point with evidence.

DISCOVER ⌐q|p⌐ STATE STATS

Log-in to the eBook and click on the title to the left for access to State Stats in order to complete the exercise.

Begin by finding the population database and locating "Population by Race." Here you will find population percentages for Hispanics, Blacks, Asians, American Indians, and Whites for 1995, 2000, and 2005, and projections for 2015 and 2025. Look up the national percentages, and then look up percentages for your home state and three other states in different regions of the country. How is the demographic face of the United States changing? Which populations are growing, and which are declining? Write a sociological research question that asks about the relationship of changing demographics to changes in U.S. material and nonmaterial culture.

STUDENT STUDY SITE

Visit the Student Study Site at **www.sagepub.com/chamblissintro** to access additional study tools, including eFlashcards, web quizzes, video resources, web resources, audio resources, links to SAGE journal, handbook, and research articles, and much more!

4 SOCIALIZATION AND SOCIAL INTERACTION

WHAT DO YOU THINK?

1. Is the personality of an individual determined at birth?
2. Are the media today as important in a child's socialization as his or her family? Might the media be more important?
3. Do people adjust the presentation of their personality in interactions in order to leave a particular impression? Might we say that we have different "social selves" that we present in different settings?

SOC*VIEW*

Get a closer look
with the authors!

POP CULTURE AND TEEN SOCIALIZATION

Today, young people devote considerable time to media—television; texting; music videos; movies; social networking sites such as Facebook, Twitter, Tumblr, and Instagram; and the like. By one recent estimate, young people 8 to 18 spend an average of seven and a half hours per day immersed in the media world (Rideout, Foehr, & Roberts, 2010). The media are an important agent of socialization in the lives of the young, both reflecting and reproducing social norms, roles, and values.

While other media forms have grown in influence, television remains a powerful agent of socialization. Interestingly, it is not only the writers and producers of programs who shape these social norms, roles, and values. In 2012, the popular television comedy *Raising Hope* featured a scene in which the main character, a middle-aged woman who had been a teenage mother, catches a teen girl in bed with her boyfriend. She scolds the couple, declaring that, "I'm your ghost of teen pregnancy future!" What follows is a sharp scene outlining teenage pregnancy's problems and worries. This anti–teen pregnancy message was inserted by writers who had met with representatives of the National Campaign to Prevent Teen and Unwanted Pregnancy (Ulaby, 2012).

Unlike consumer products companies, which pay for "product placement," the nonprofit organization does not pay for placement of its message. But it has been relentless in its efforts to set that message into a variety of programs that appeal to teens, and it has made broad connections in Hollywood (Ulaby, 2012). Television is a powerful vehicle for conveying norms, roles, values, and aspirations that young people internalize. In this case, some popular shows are offering a pointed message about teen pregnancy to the young. Do you think such efforts can have a tangible effect on teen pregnancy? What would you predict based on what you know about TV as an agent of socialization in young people's lives? ■

In this chapter, we examine the process of socialization and the array of agents—including but hardly limited to television—that help shape our social selves and our behavioral choices. We begin by looking into the debate on nature versus nurture and learning what sociology says about that debate. We follow with a look at the key agents of socialization, as well as ways socialization may differ in total institutions and across the life course. We then examine theoretical perspectives on socialization. Finally, we look at social interaction and ways in which sociologists conceptualize our presentation of self and our group interactions.

THE BIRTH OF THE SOCIAL SELF

Socialization is *the process by which people learn the culture of their society.* It is a lifelong and active process in which individuals construct their sense of who they are, how to think, and how to act as members of their culture. Socialization is our primary way of reproducing culture, including norms and values and the belief that our culture represents "normal" social practices and perceptions.

The principal agents of socialization—including parents, teachers, religious institutions, friends, television, and the Internet—exert an enormous influence on us. Much socialization takes place every day, usually without our thinking about it: when we speak, when others react to us, when we observe others' behavior—even if only in the movies or on television—and in virtually every other human interaction.

Debate has raged in the social sciences over the relative influence of genetic inheritance—"nature"—and cultural and social experiences—"nurture"—in shaping people's lives (Coleman & Hang, 2008; Ridgeway & Correll, 2004). If inborn biological predispositions explain differences between, say, sixth-grade boys' and girls' behavior or between a professional thief and the police officer who apprehends him, then understanding socialization will do little to help us understand them. On the other hand, if biology cannot explain much about differences in attitudes, characters, and behaviors, then socialization must account for them.

Almost no one today argues that behavior is entirely determined by either socialization or biology. There is doubtless an interaction between the two. What social scientists disagree about, however, is which is more important in shaping a person's personality, life chances, philosophy of life, and behavior. In this text we lean toward socialization because we think the evidence points in that direction.

Social scientists have found little evidence to support the idea that personalities and behaviors are rooted exclusively in "human

. . . .

Socialization: The process by which people learn the culture of their society.

A young girl prays for the New Year on the shoulders of her father at the Meiji shrine in Tokyo. Many components of one's culture are seamlessly passed down through habit, observational learning, and family practices. ■

nature." Indeed, very little human behavior is actually "natural." For example, humans have a biological capacity for language, but language is learned and develops only through interaction. The weight of socialization in the development of language, reasoning, and social skills is dramatically illustrated in children raised in isolation. If a biologically inherited mechanism alone triggered language, it would do so even in people who grow up deprived of contact with other human beings. If socialization plays a key role, however, then such people would not only have difficulty learning to speak like human beings; they would lack the capacity to play the social roles to which most of us are so fully accustomed.

One of the best documented cases of social isolation occurred about 210 years ago, when a "wild boy," later named Victor, was seen by hunters in the forests of Aveyron, a rural area of France (Shattuck, 1980). Victor had been living alone in the woods for most of his 12 or so years and could not speak, and although he stood erect, he ran using both arms and legs like an animal. Victor was taken into the home of Jean-Marc-Gaspard Itard, a young medical doctor who, for the next 10 years, tried to teach him the social and intellectual skills expected of a child his age. According to Itard's careful records, Victor managed to learn a

Given the choice in an experiment between a wire mother surrogate and a surrogate covered with cloth, the infant monkey almost invariably chose the cloth figure. How are human needs similar to and different from those we find in the animal kingdom? ■

few words, but he never spoke in complete sentences. Although he eventually learned to use the toilet, he continued to evidence "wild" behavior, including public masturbation. Despite the efforts of Itard and others, Victor was incapable of learning more than the most rudimentary social and intellectual skills; he died in Paris in 1828.

Other studies of the effects of isolation have centered on children raised by their parents, but in nearly total isolation. For 12 years, from the time she was 1 ½ years old, "Genie" (a pseudonym) saw only her father, mother, and brother, and only when one of them came to feed her. Genie's father did not allow his wife or Genie to leave the house or have any visitors. Genie was either strapped to a child's potty-chair or placed in a sleeping bag that limited her movements. Genie rarely heard any conversation. If she made noises, her father beat her (Curtiss, 1977; Rymer, 1993).

When Genie was 13, her mother took her and fled the house. Genie was unable to cry, control her bowels, eat solid food, or talk. Because of her tight confinement, she had not even learned to focus her eyes beyond 12 feet. She was constantly salivating and spitting, and she had little controlled use of her arms or legs (Rymer, 1993).

Gradually Genie learned some of the social behavior expected of a child. For example, she became toilet-trained and learned to wear clothes. However, although intelligence tests did not indicate reasoning disability, even after five years of concentrated effort on the part of a foster mother, social workers, and medical doctors, Genie never learned to speak beyond the level of a 4-year-old, and she never spoke with other people. Although she responded positively to those who treated her with sympathy, Genie's social behavior remained severely underdeveloped for the rest of her life (Rymer, 1993).

Genie's and Victor's experiences underscore the significance of socialization, especially during childhood. Their cases show that however rooted in biology certain capacities may be, they do not develop into recognizable human ways of acting and thinking unless the individual interacts with other humans in a social environment. Children raised in isolation fail to develop complex language, abstract thinking, notions of cooperation and sharing, or even a sense of themselves as people. In other words, they do not develop the hallmarks of what we know as humanity (Ridley, 1998).

Sociologists and other social scientists have developed a number of theories to explain the role of socialization in the development of social selves. What these theories recognize is that whatever the contribution of biology, ultimately people are made, not born. We'll explore four approaches to understanding socialization: behaviorism, symbolic interactionism, developmental stage theories, and psychoanalytic theories.

BEHAVIORISM AND SOCIAL LEARNING THEORY

Behaviorism is *a psychological perspective that emphasizes the effect of rewards and punishments on human behavior.* It arose during the late 19th century to challenge the then-popular belief that human behavior results primarily from biological instincts and drives (Baldwin & Baldwin, 1986, 1988; Dishion, McCord, & Poulin, 1999). Early behaviorist researchers such as Ivan Pavlov (1849–1936) and John Watson (1878–1958), and later B. F. Skinner (1904–1990), demonstrated that even behavior thought to be purely instinctual (like a dog salivating when it sees food) can be produced or extinguished through the application of rewards and punishments. Thus a pigeon will learn to press a bar if that triggers the release of food (Skinner, 1938, 1953; Watson, 1924). Behaviorists concluded that both

. . . .

Behaviorism: A psychological perspective that emphasizes the effect of rewards and punishments on human behavior.

animal and human behavior can be learned, and neither is just instinctive.

When they turned to human beings, behaviorists focused on **social learning**, *the way people adapt their behavior in response to social rewards and punishments* (Baldwin & Baldwin, 1986; Bandura, 1977; Bandura & Walters, 1963). Of particular interest was the satisfaction people get from imitating others. Social learning theory thus combines the reward-and-punishment effects identified by behaviorists with the idea that we model the behavior of others; that is, we observe the way people respond to others' behavior.

Social learning theory would predict, for example, that if a boy gets high-fives from his friends for talking trash to his teacher—a form of encouragement rather than punishment—he is likely to repeat this behavior. What's more, other boys may imitate it. Social learning researchers have developed formulas for predicting how rewards and punishments affect behavior. For example, rewards given repeatedly may become less effective when the individual becomes satiated. If you have just eaten a huge piece of cake, you are less likely to feel rewarded by the prospect of another.

Social behaviorism is not widely embraced today as a rigorous perspective on human behavior. One reason is that only in carefully controlled laboratory environments is it easy to demonstrate the power of rewards and punishments. In real social situations the theory is of limited value as a predictor. For example, whether a girl teased ("punished") for playing football will lose interest in the sport depends on many other experiences, such as the support of family and friends and her own enjoyment of the activity. The simple application of rewards and punishments is hardly sufficient to explain why people repeat some behaviors and not others.

In addition, behaviorist theories violate Popper's principle of falsification (see Chapter 2). Since what was previously rewarding may lose effectiveness if the person is satiated, if a reward does not work, we can always attribute its failure to satiation. Therefore, no matter the outcome of the experiment, the theory has to be true; it cannot be proven false. For these reasons sociologists find

. . . .

Social learning: The way people adapt their behavior in response to social rewards and punishments.

Looking-glass self: The concept developed by Charles Horton Cooley that our self-image results from how we interpret other people's views of us.

Primary group: A small group characterized by intense emotional ties, face-to-face interaction, intimacy, and a strong, enduring sense of commitment.

Secondary group: A group that is large and impersonal and characterized by fleeting relationships.

Reference group: A group that provides standards for judging one's attitudes or behaviors.

I: According to George Herbert Mead, the part of the self that refers to the impulse to act; it is creative, innovative, unthinking, and largely unpredictable.

behaviorism an inadequate theory of socialization. To explain how people become socialized, they highlight theories that emphasize *symbolic interaction*.

SOCIALIZATION AS SYMBOLIC INTERACTION

Recall from the introductory chapter that *symbolic interactionism* views the self and society as resulting from social interaction based on language and other symbols. Symbolic interactionism has proven especially fruitful in explaining how individuals develop a social identity and a capacity for social interaction (Blumer, 1969, 1970; Hutcheon, 1999; Mead, 1934, 1938).

An early contribution to symbolic interactionism was Charles Horton Cooley's (1864–1929) concept of the **looking-glass self**, the *self-image that results from our interpretation of other people's views of us*. For example, children who are frequently told they are smart or talented will tend to come to see themselves as such and act accordingly. On the other hand, children who are repeatedly told they lack intelligence or are "slow" will lose pride in themselves and act the part. According to Cooley (1902/1964), we are constantly forming ideas about how others perceive and judge us, and the resulting self-image—the way we view ourselves—is in turn the basis of our social interaction with others.

Cooley recognized that not everyone we encounter is equally important in shaping our self-image. **Primary groups** are *small groups characterized by intense emotional ties, face-to-face interaction, intimacy, and a strong, enduring sense of commitment*. Families, close friends, and lovers are all examples of primary groups likely to shape the self-image. **Secondary groups**, on the other hand, are *large and impersonal, characterized by fleeting relationships*. Much of our adult life is spent in secondary groups, such as college classrooms and workplaces, but secondary groups typically have less influence in forming our self-image than do primary groups. Both groups act on us throughout our lives; the self-image is not set in concrete at some early stage but continues to develop throughout adulthood (Barber, 1992; Berns, 1989).

Both primary and secondary groups also serve as **reference groups**, or *groups that provide standards for judging our attitudes or behaviors*. When you consider your friends' reactions to your dress or hairstyle or the brand of mobile phone you plan to buy, you are using your peers as a reference in shaping your decisions.

George Herbert Mead (1863–1931), widely regarded as the founder of symbolic interactionism, explored the ways in which self and society shape one another. Mead proposed that the self comprises two parts: the "I" and the "me." The I is *the impulse to act; it*

Mental Institutions

Socialization and Men

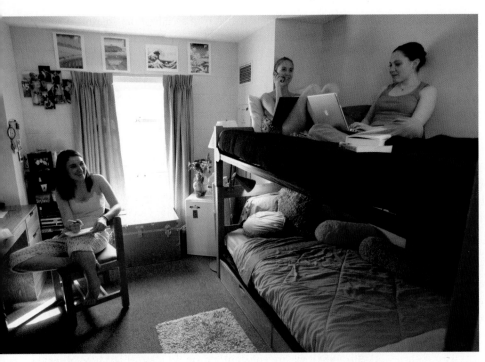

As a powerful reference group, high school peers may provide the normative standards for a young person to judge his or her fashion sense, musical tastes, behavioral choices, and academic commitment. How does the power of peers as a reference group change in the college years? ■

is creative, innovative, unthinking, and largely unpredictable. The **me** is *the part of the self through which we see ourselves as others see us.* (Note the similarity between Mead's "me" and Cooley's "looking-glass self.") The "I" represents innovation; the "me" social convention and conformity. In the tension between them, the "me" is often capable of controlling the "I." When the "I" initiates a spontaneous act, the "me" raises society's response: *How will others regard me if I act this way?*

Mead further argued that people develop a sense of self through **role-taking,** *the ability to take the role of others in interaction.* For example, a young girl playing soccer may pretend to be a coach; in the process, she learns to see herself from a coach's perspective. Mead proposed that childhood socialization relies on an ever-increasing ability to take on such roles, moving from the extreme self-centeredness of the infant to an adult ability to take the standpoint of society as a whole. He outlined four principal stages in socialization that reflect this progression: the preparatory, play, game, and adult stages. The completion of each stage results in an increasingly complete sense of self.

1. During the *preparatory stage,* children under 3 relate to the world as though they are the center of the universe. They do not engage in true role-taking but respond primarily to things in their immediate environment, such as their mother's breast, the color of a toy, or the sound of a voice.

2. Children 3 or 4 years old enter the *play stage,* during which they learn to take the attitude and role of the people with

whom they interact. **Significant others** are *the specific people important in children's lives, and whose views have the greatest impact on their self-evaluations.* By role-playing at being mother or father, for example, children come to see themselves as their parents see them. However, according to Mead, they have not yet acquired the complex sense of self that lets them see themselves through the eyes of *many* different people—or society.

3. The *game* stage begins when children are about 5 and learn to take the role of multiple others. The game is an effective analogy for this stage. When children participate in a game of basketball, for example, they must see themselves from the perspective of teammates, the other team, and the coach, and must play accordingly. They must know the rules of the game. This stage signals the development of a self that is aware of societal positions and perspectives.

4. Game playing takes the child to the final, *adult stage,* which can appear as early as the first and second grades. Here children have internalized the **generalized other,** *the sense of society's norms and values by which people evaluate themselves.* They take into account a set of general principles that may or may not serve their self-interest— for example, voluntarily joining the army to fight in a war that might injure or kill them because patriotic young people are expected to defend their country. By now, a person is capable of understanding abstract and complex cultural symbols, such as love and hate, success and failure, friendship and morality.

Mead also had a vision that in the future people would be able to assimilate a multitude of *generalized others,* adapting their behavior in terms of their own but also other people's cultures. Mead's "dream of a highly multicultural world" may

· ·

Me: According to George Herbert Mead, the part of the self through which we see ourselves as others see us.

Role-taking: The ability to take the role of others in interaction.

Significant others: According to George Herbert Mead, the specific people who are important in children's lives and whose views have the greatest impact on their self-evaluations.

Generalized other: The abstract sense of society's norms and values by which people evaluate themselves.

someday be a reality as globalization makes ever more people aware of the value of other cultures.

STAGES OF DEVELOPMENT: PIAGET AND KOHLBERG

Like Mead and Cooley, the Swiss social psychologist Jean Piaget (1896–1980) believed humans are socialized in stages. Piaget devoted a lifetime to researching how young children develop the ability to think abstractly and make moral judgments (Piaget, 1926, 1928, 1930, 1932). His theory of **cognitive development**, based largely on studies of Swiss children at play (including his own), argues that *the ability to make logical decisions increases as a person grows older.* Piaget noted that infants are highly **ego-centric**, *experiencing the world as if it were centered entirely on them.* In stages, socialization lets them learn to use language and symbols, to think abstractly and logically, and to see things from different perspectives.

Piaget also developed a theory of moral development, which holds that as they grow, people learn to act according to abstract ideas about justice or fairness. This theory parallels his idea of cognitive development, since both describe overcoming egocentrism and acquiring the ability to take other points of view. Eventually children come to develop abstract notions of fairness, learning that rules should be judged relative to the circumstances. For example, even if the rules say "three strikes and you're out," an exception might be made for a child who has never played the game or is physically challenged.

Lawrence Kohlberg (1927–1987) extended Piaget's ideas about moral development. In his best known study, subjects were told the story of the fictitious "Heinz," unable to afford a drug that might prevent his wife from dying of cancer. As the story unfolds, Heinz breaks into the druggist's shop and steals the medication. Kohlberg asked his subjects what they would have done, emphasizing that there is no "right" or "wrong" answer. Using experiments such as this, Kohlberg (1969, 1983, 1984) proposed three principal stages (and several substages) of moral development:

1. The *preconventional stage,* during which people seek simply to achieve personal gain or avoid punishment. A person might support Heinz's decision to steal on the grounds that it would be too difficult to get the medicine by other means, or oppose it on the grounds that Heinz might get caught and go to jail. Children are typically socialized into this rudimentary form of morality between ages 7 and 10.

2. The *conventional stage,* during which the individual is socialized into society's norms and values and would feel

. . . .

Cognitive development: As theorized by Jean Piaget, the increasing ability to make logical decisions as a person grows older.

Egocentric: Experiencing the world as if it were centered entirely on oneself.

Game playing is an activity that is seen in virtually every culture; what varies is the type of game and the materials used. Some games, including basketball and soccer, require teamwork, while others, including checkers and mancala, are played with one person against another. Games such as these provide many socialization benefits, as young children learn how to interact with one another and develop their motor skills. ∎

shame or guilt about violating them. The person might support Heinz's decision to steal on the grounds that society would judge him callous if he let his wife die, or oppose it because people would call Heinz a thief if he were caught. Children are socialized into this more developed form of morality at about age 10, and most people remain in this stage throughout their adult lives.

3. Finally, the *postconventional stage,* during which the individual invokes general, abstract notions of right and wrong. Even though Heinz has broken the law, his transgression has to be weighed against the moral cost of sacrificing his wife's life. People at the highest levels of postconventional morality will go beyond social convention entirely, appealing to a higher set of abstract principles.

Some scholars have argued that Kohlberg's theory reflects a strong male bias because it derives from male rather than female experience. Foremost among Kohlberg's critics is Carol Gilligan (1982; Gilligan, Ward, & Taylor, 1989), who argues that men may be socialized to base moral judgment on abstract principles of fairness and justice, but women are socialized to base theirs on compassion and caring. She showed that women scored lower on Kohlberg's measure of moral development because they valued how other family members were affected by Heinz's decision more than abstract considerations of justice. Because it assumed that abstract thinking represents a "higher stage" of development, Gilligan suggested, Kohlberg's measure was necessarily biased in favor of male socialization.

Research testing Gilligan's ideas has found that men and women alike adhere to *both* care-based *and* justice-based forms of moral reasoning (Gump, Baker, & Roll, 2000; Jaffee & Hyde, 2000). Differences between the sexes in these kinds of reasoning are in fact small or nonexistent. Studies of federal employees (Peek, 1999), a sample of men and women using the Internet (K. Anderson, 2000), and a comparison of Mexican American and Anglo American students (Gump et al., 2000) all found no significant difference between men and women in the degree to which they employed care-based and justice-based styles of moral reasoning. In her effort to correct Kohlberg's research, which looked only at men, might Gilligan have also contributed to gender stereotypes?

BIOLOGICAL NEEDS VERSUS SOCIAL CONSTRAINTS: FREUD

Sigmund Freud (1856–1939), an Austrian psychiatrist, had a major impact on the study of socialization as well as the disciplines of psychology and psychiatry. Freud (1905, 1929, 1933) founded the field of **psychoanalysis**, *a psychological perspective that emphasizes the complex reasoning processes of the conscious and unconscious mind.* He stressed the role of the unconscious mind in shaping human behavior and theorized that early childhood socialization was essential in molding the adult personality by age 5 or 6. In addition, Freud sought to demonstrate that, for a society to thrive, it must socialize its members to curb their instinctive needs and desires.

According to Freud, the human mind has three components: the id, the ego, and the superego (Figure 4.1). The **id** is *the repository of basic biological drives and needs,* which Freud believed to be primarily bound up in sexual energy. (*Id* is Latin for "it," reflecting Freud's belief that this aspect of the human personality is not even truly human.) The **ego** (Latin for "I") is *the "self," the core of what we regard as a person's unique personality.* The **superego** consists of *the values and norms of society, insofar as they are internalized, or taken in, by the individual.* It is similar to the notion of a conscience.

Freud believed that babies are all id. Left to their own devices, they will seek instant gratification of their biological needs for food, physical contact, and nurturing. Therefore, according to Freud, to be socialized they must eventually learn to suppress such gratification. The child's superego, consisting of cultural "shoulds" and "should nots," struggles constantly with the biological impulses of the id. Serving as mediator between id and superego is the child's emerging ego. In Freud's view,

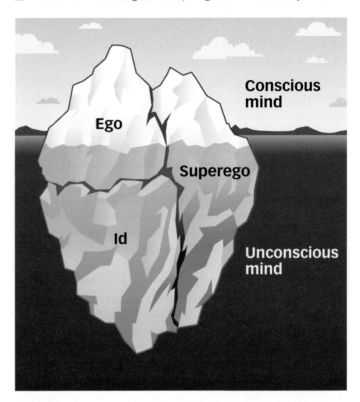

■ **FIGURE 4.1** The Id, Ego, and Superego, as Conceived by Freud

the child will grow up to be a well-socialized adult to the extent that the ego succeeds in bending the biological desires of the id to meet the social demands of the superego.

Since Freud claimed that personality is set early in life, he viewed change as difficult for adults, especially if psychological troubles originate in experiences too painful to face or remember. Individuals must become fully aware of their repressed or unconscious memories and unacceptable impulses if they ever hope to change (Freud, 1933). Freud's psychoanalytic therapy focused on accessing deeply buried feelings in order to help patients alter current behaviors and feelings. While Mead saw socialization as a lifelong process relying on many socialization agents, for Freud it stopped at a young age. Table 4.1 on page 85 compares Mead's and Freud's view point by point.

....

Psychoanalysis: A psychological perspective that emphasizes the complex reasoning processes of the conscious and unconscious mind.

Id: According to Sigmund Freud, the part of the mind that is the repository of basic biological drives and needs.

Ego: According to Sigmund Freud, the part of the mind that is the "self," the core of what is regarded as a person's unique personality.

Superego: According to Sigmund Freud, the part of the mind that consists of the values and norms of society, insofar as they are internalized, or taken in, by the individual.

AGENTS OF SOCIALIZATION

Among primary groups, the family is for most people the single most critical agent of socialization. Other significant agents are school, peer groups, work, religion, and technology and mass media, including the Internet and social media (Figure 4.2).

THE FAMILY

The family is a primary group in which children, especially during the earliest years of their lives, are physically and emotionally dependent on adult members. It plays a key role in transmitting norms, values, and culture across generations, and as a result it is the first and usually the foremost source of socialization in all societies.

Children usually first encounter their society in the family, learning socially defined roles like father, mother, sister, brother, uncle, aunt, and grandparent, and the expected behaviors attached to them. Parents often hold stereotypical notions of how boys and girls should be, and they reinforce gender behaviors in countless subtle and not-so-subtle ways. A father may be responsible for grilling and yard work, while a mother cooks dinner

■ FIGURE 4.2 Agents of Socialization

and cleans the house. On the other hand, some families embrace egalitarian or nonconventional gender roles. Although gay- and same-sex couple families are more likely to challenge gender-normative roles and behaviors, they sometimes still enforce or support typical gender roles for their children (Ackbar, 2011; Bos & Sandfort, 2010).

The way parents relate to their children affects virtually all aspects of the child's behavior, including the ability to resolve conflicts through the use of reason instead of violence, and the propensity for emotional stability or distress. The likelihood that young people will be victims of homicide, commit suicide or acts of aggression against other people, use drugs, complete their secondary education, or have an unwanted pregnancy also is greatly influenced by childhood experiences in the family (Campbell & Muncer, 1998; McLoyd & Smith, 2002; Muncer & Campbell, 2000). For example, children who are regularly spanked or otherwise physically punished often learn that violence is an acceptable means of achieving goals and are more likely to engage in aggressive delinquent behavior. They are also more likely to have low self-esteem, suffer depression, and do poorly in school; see the *Private Lives, Public Issues* box on page 87 (Borgeson, 2001; Straus, Sugarman, & Giles-Sims, 1997).

Child-rearing practices within families can vary by ethnicity or religious affiliation. Because U.S. culture is ethnically diverse, it is difficult to describe a "typical" family (Glazer, 1997; Stokes

■ TABLE 4.1 Comparison of Mead's and Freud's Theories of Socialization

Mead's Stages	Freud's Psychoanalytic Theory
Preparatory: Highly limited role-taking in which the individual views the world through his or her own eyes.	**Id:** The repository of basic biological drives and needs, which seeks instant gratification.
Play: The individual takes on the role of significant others, one at a time.	**Ego:** The "self" that, once developed, balances the forces of the id and superego. The ego is necessary in the socialization process to become a well-adjusted adult
Game: The individual is able to view the world through the eyes of multiple others, simultaneously.	**Superego:** The values and norms of society. May conflict with the id.
Maturity: The individual is able to take the attitude of the generalized other and can view the world through the eyes of society as a whole.	

SOURCE: Adapted from Mead, G. H. (1934). *Mind, self, and society.* Chicago: University of Chicago Press.

Family and Community

Today, household and child-related tasks are shared more evenly by heterosexual couples than in the past, a change one may note both in families and in media representations. But some aspects of the gender division of household labor have changed only marginally. Why do you think that is the case? ■

& Chevan, 1996). Among Latinos, for example, the family often includes grandparents, aunts, uncles, cousins, and in-laws, who share child-rearing responsibilities. Among Black Americans as well, child rearing may be shared among a broader range of family members than in White families (Lubeck, 1985). Extended-family patterns also occur among Afro-Caribbean immigrants and the Amish religious community of Pennsylvania (Forsythe-Brown, 2007; Ho, 1993; Stokes & Chevan, 1996).

Child-rearing practices may vary by social class as well. Parents whose jobs require them to be subservient to authority and to follow orders without raising questions typically stress obedience and respect for authority at home, while parents whose work gives them freedom to make their own decisions and be creative are likely to socialize their children into norms of creativity and spontaneity. Since many working-class jobs demand conformity while middle- and upper-middle-class jobs are more likely to offer independence, social class is a key factor in explaining differences in child-rearing (Kohn, 1989; Lareau, 2002).

Family patterns are changing rapidly, partly because of declining marriage rates and high rates of divorce. Such changes affect socialization. For example, children raised by a single parent may lack role models for the parent who is missing or experience economic hardship that in turn determines where they go to school or with whom they socialize. Children raised in blended families (the result of remarriage) may have a stepparent and stepsiblings whose norms, values, and behavior are unfamiliar.

Socialization and Education

TEACHERS AND SCHOOL

Children in the United States often begin "schooling" when they enter day care or preschool as infants or toddlers, and they spend more hours each day and more days each year in school than was the case a hundred years ago (although less than their peers in Europe and Asia). Indeed, education has taken on a large role in helping young people prepare for adult society. In addition to reading, writing, and arithmetic, schools are expected to teach values and norms like patriotism, competitiveness, morality, and respect for authority, as well as basic social skills. Some sociologists call this the **hidden curriculum**, that is, *an unspoken classroom socialization to the norms, values, and roles of a culture that school provides along with the "official" curriculum.* The hidden curriculum may include "lessons" in gender roles taught through teachers' differing expectations of boys and girls with, for instance, boys pushed to pursue higher math while girls are encouraged to embrace language and literature (Sadker, Zittleman, & Sadker, 2003). It may also entail "lessons" that reinforce class status, with middle- and upper-class children having access to classes and schools with advanced subjects and poor children limited to a smaller selection of less academically challenging or vocational classes (Bowles & Gintis, 1976; Kozol, 2010).

PEERS

Peers are people of the same age and, often, the same social standing. Peer socialization begins when the child starts to play with other children outside the family, usually during the first year of life, and grows more intense in school. Conformity to the norms and values of friends is especially compelling during adolescence and continues into adulthood (Harris, 2009; Ponton, 2000; Sebald, 2000). In U.S. society, adolescents spend far more time with their peers than with their families thanks to school, athletic activities, and other social and academic commitments. Sociological theories thus often focus on young people's peer groups to account for a wide variety of adult behavioral patterns, including the development of self-esteem and self-image, career choices, ambition, and deviant behavior (Cohen, 1958; Hine, 2000; Sebald, 2000).

Judith Rich Harris (2009) argues that after the first few years of life, friends' opinions outweigh the opinions of parents. To manage these predominant peer group influences, parents must make certain their children have the "right" friends. But this is an increasingly complex problem when "friends" may be Internet

Hidden curriculum: An unspoken classroom socialization to the norms, values, and roles of a culture that a school provides along with the "official" curriculum.

SPANKING AND AGGRESSIVE BEHAVIOR

While many people still believe in the old adage "spare the rod and spoil the child," the use of physical punishment in socializing children varies largely by social class. At a rate that has largely held steady in the past decades, about 65% of U.S. adults approve of spanking under certain circumstances. Interestingly, these adults are most likely to be members of the working class, rather than the middle or upper class (Berlin et al., 2009; Borgeson, 2001; Rosellini & Mulrine, 1998). Remember Kohn's (1989) research, which concluded that the experience of people in working-class employment is reflected in their child-rearing practices: Working-class parents are more likely to emphasize obedience than are middle-class parents, who tend to stress independent thinking. The use of corporal punishment, however, is not only a matter of social class or a private decision made by parents in the home. It is a public issue with considerable social consequences.

Murray Straus, a prominent sociologist at the University of New Hampshire, found that when boys and girls 6 to 9 years old were spanked, they became more antisocial—more likely to cheat, tell lies, act cruelly to others, break things deliberately, and get into trouble at school (Straus, Sugarman, & Giles-Sims, 1997; also see McKee et al., 2007). Straus and his colleagues concluded that reducing corporal punishment would not only benefit children, but could even reduce antisocial behavior.

Other research supports Straus's conclusions (Borgeson, 2001; de Paul & Domenech, 2000). For example, one study concluded that corporal

Should parents spank their children? Ask some friends or classmates what they think. You may find a wide range of opinions on this practice. ■

punishment, and even some lesser forms of parental punishment, could have a strong effect on a child's ability to cope later in life (Welsh, 1998). Similarly, the authors of a study of Israeli high school students found that adolescents whose parents routinely resorted to physical punishment were more likely than others to have psychiatric symptoms and lower levels of well-being in general (Bachar, Canetti, Bonne, DeNour, & Shalev, 1997). On the other hand, research by psychologist Marjorie Lindner Gunnoe (1997), which tracked more than 1,100 children over a 5-year period, found that while some 8- to 11-year-old boys, but not girls, who had been spanked regularly got into more fights at school, children of both sexes aged 4–7 who had been spanked regularly got into fewer fights than children who were not spanked. Most

research, however, confirms the negative effects of spanking.

Although not all the research on the effects of physical punishment is in agreement, it does suggest that spanking—an aggressive form of punishment—often results in aggressive behavior on the part of children. The parents' "private" decision to use corporal punishment becomes a "public issue," since children who are physically punished at home are more likely to become physically abusive outside the home.

THINK IT THROUGH

■ *Using the knowledge you have gained through the study of socialization, and knowing the results of research on the effects of physical punishment on children's behavior, could you design a social policy to reduce the use of physical punishment in the home?*

acquaintances who are difficult to monitor and about whom parents may be unaware.

The adolescent subculture plays an extremely important part in the socialization of adolescents in the modern world. It reveals the following characteristics (Hine, 2000; Sebald, 2000):

1. A set of norms not shared with the adult or childhood cultures and governing interaction, statuses, and roles.

2. An *argot* (the special vocabulary of a particular group) that is not shared with nonadolescents and is often frowned upon by adults and school officials. Think about the jargon used by young people who text—many adults can read it only with difficulty!

3. Various underground media and preferred media programs, music, and Internet sites.

4. Unique fads and fashions in dress and hairstyles that often lead to conflict with parents and other adult authorities over their "appropriateness."

5. A set of "heroes, villains, and fools." Sometimes adults are the "villains and fools," while the adults' "villains and fools" are heroes in the adolescent subculture.

6. A more open attitude toward experimentation with drugs and at times violence (fighting, for example) than the attitude of the general culture.

Teenagers differ in the degree to which they are caught up in, and therefore socialized by, the adolescent subculture. Harris's (2009) claim that parents are largely irrelevant is no doubt an overstatement. Yet peer socialization in Western cultures does play a crucial part in shaping many of the ideas, self-images, and attitudes that will persist throughout a person's life.

Sociologists use the term **anticipatory socialization** to describe the process of *adopting the behavior or standards of a group you emulate or hope to join.* For example, teens who seek membership into a tough, streetwise gang will abandon their upper-middle-class norms for the dress and talk of the tougher youth they seek to emulate. Anticipatory socialization looks to future expectations, rather than present experience. Because a great deal of anticipatory socialization in children looks toward the kind of adults they will be, it includes their expectations about where they will fit in the workforce on leaving school.

RELIGION

Religion is a central part of the lives of many people around the world. While the United States has a notable proportion of inhabitants who identify as atheists, 83% of U.S. adults indicate they are members of a religion. About 70% believe in God, 56% say religion is an important part of their lives, and nearly 40% attend religious services at least once a week (Pew Forum on Religion and Public Life, 2008). Beginning with Émile Durkheim sociologists have noted the role of religion in fostering social solidarity. Talcott Parsons (1970) pointed out that religion also acts as an agent

of socialization, teaching fundamental values and beliefs that contribute to a shared normative culture.

Different religions function in similar ways, giving their followers a sense of what is right and wrong, how to conduct themselves in society, and how to organize their lives. Some socialize their followers with abstract teachings about morality, service, or self-discipline, directing believers to, for example, serve their fellow human beings or to avoid the sin of vanity. Others contain abstract teachings but specific rules about dress and hairstyles. The Amish faith entreats young men to remain clean-shaven prior to marriage, but married men must grow beards. Sikh men of India do not cut their hair but rather wrap it in a turban they wear on the head.

Like other agents of socialization and social control, religion directs its followers to choose certain paths and behaviors and not others. This is to say not that we are forced to behave a certain way, but rather that socialization often leads us to control our own behavior because we fear social ostracism or other negative consequences.

WORK

For most U.S. adults postadolescent socialization begins with entry into the workforce. While workplace norms calling for conformity or individuality are frequently taught by parents in the home, expectations at work often differ substantially from those we experience in primary groups, such as the family and peer groups.

Workplace socialization has had a particular influence on women, dramatically changing gender roles. Beginning in the 1960s, paid work afforded women greater financial independence, allowing them to marry later—or not at all—and bringing new opportunities for social interaction.

Employment also often socializes us into the wider aspects of the job role itself. Becoming a teacher, cook, factory worker, professor, or lawyer requires learning specific skills and the norms and values associated with each role. Even "occupations" outside the bounds of legality are governed by rules and roles. Harry King, a professional thief studied by one of the authors, not only learned how to break into buildings and open safes; he learned the culture of the professional thief. You never "rat" on a partner, for example, and a professional never steals from "Mom and Pop" stores. In addition, he acquired a unique language that enabled him to talk to other thieves while in the company of nonthieves ("Square Johns"), police officers, and prison guards (King & Chambliss, 1984).

MASS MEDIA, THE INTERNET, AND SOCIAL MEDIA

Much of what we experience today is filtered through the lens of technology and the **mass media**, *forms of communication*

. . . .

Anticipatory socialization: Adopting the behavior or standards of a group one emulates or hopes to join.

Mass media: Forms of communication that permit a flow of information from a single source to a wide audience.

Sibling Socialization

Journalists and Social Media

Teen Shaming

that permit a flow of information from a single source to a wide audience. Newspapers, magazines, movies, radio, and television are all forms of mass media. As an agent of socialization, television is especially alluring for the average U.S. child aged 2–11, who spends over 26 hours a week in front of the TV (Nielsen, 2011; see also Figure 4.3). By the time the typical young viewer reaches 18, he or she will have viewed nearly 18,000 hours of television, including depictions of as many as 8,000 murders. The Internet is another powerful agent of socialization, not just for the young. Unlike the mass media, however, the Internet offers a flow of information that is dynamic rather than one-way.

Child psychologists, sociologists, and parents' groups pay special attention to the impact of TV and other media violence on children and young adults. Media studies during the past 20 years have largely come to a common conclusion: Media violence has the clear potential to socialize children, teenagers, and even adults into a greater acceptance of real-life violence. This is true for males and females, Whites and non-Whites. Much media violence is directed against women, and a large body of research supports the conclusion that media violence promotes tolerance among men for sexual violence, including rape (C. Anderson et al., 2003; Greene & Kramar, 2005). The argument is not that viewing violent shows is a direct cause of violence; rather, viewers may become immunized to the sight of violence. Still, because most people who are exposed to violence in the media do not themselves become violent, the part played by the media as an agent of socialization is probably less important than the contribution made by other agents, such as family and peers.

The media do play a definite role in socialization by creating fads and fashions for how people should look, what they should wear, and what kind of friendships they should have. These influences, and accompanying gender stereotypes, are particularly strong during adolescence. Children's cartoons, prime-time television, TV advertisements, and popular networks like MTV depict males, females, races, and ethnicities in stereotyped ways. Teenage girls, for example, are likely to be depicted as boy-crazy and obsessed with their looks; teenage boys are active, independent, and sexually and physically aggressive (Kahlenberg & Hein, 2010; Maher, Herbst, Childs, & Finn, 2008). Females' roles also portray mostly familial or romantic ideals, whereas males fulfill work-related roles (Lauzen, Dozier, & Horan, 2008). These stereotypes have been found to influence children's gender perception (Aubrey & Harrison, 2004).

Nielsen (2010) estimates that people in the United States now spend 906 million hours a month using social networking sites, 407 million hours participating in online gaming, and 329 million hours e-mailing. While the long-term impact of this massive level of use has yet to be determined, one clear way the Internet affects socialization is by changing social interaction. To name just one effect that was impossible 20 years ago, large groups of semianonymous individuals, often separated by great distances, can interact with one another in virtual communities, even forming close ties and friendships.

On the positive side, especially when online interactions are mixed with off-line face-to-face interactions, Internet use can foster new personal relationships and build stronger communities (Rule, 1999; Valentine, 2006; Wellman & Hampton, 1999). The types of friendships adolescents create and maintain through social media reflect the friendships they have off-line (Mazur & Richards, 2011). Since interaction is often anonymous and occurs from the safety of familiar places, people with characteristics society tends to stigmatize, such as obesity or a stutter, can enter virtual communities where differences are not perceived or punished (McKenna & Bargh, 1998) and interests such as chess or movies can be shared. Finally, the moderate use of e-mail and the Internet can help children and teens maintain and strengthen interpersonal relationships (Subrahmanyam & Lin, 2007).

The Internet can have negative social consequences, too. Researchers have linked high levels of use with declines in communication within the same household, shrinking social circles, and increased depression and loneliness (Dokoupil, 2012; Kraut et al., 1998; Yen, Yen, & Ko, 2010). Extreme cases can develop into Internet addiction, a relatively recent phenomenon characterized by a search for social stimulation and escape from real-life problems (Armstrong, Phillips, & Saling, 2000; Block, 2008). Although the Internet can be a valuable learning tool for children, it can also damage their development by decreasing the time they spend in face-to-face interactions and exposing them to inappropriate information and images (Bremer & Rauch, 1998; Livingstone & Brake, 2010).

Another form of negative socialization is *cyberbullying*— taunting, teasing, or verbal attacks through e-mail, text, or social

■ **FIGURE 4.3** Average Weekly Television Viewing by Age Group in the U.S., 2011

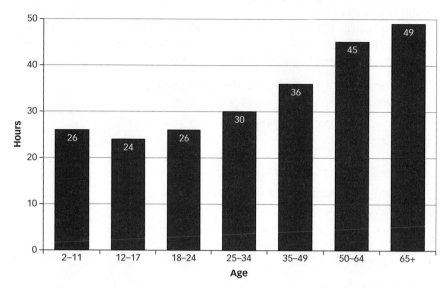

SOURCE: Data from Nielsen (2011) *State of the Media: The Cross Platform Report.* New York City: Nielsen Media Research.

Television offers a variety of female images ranging from independent working women to "fashionistas." From the *Mary Tyler Moore Show* (1970–1977) to *Sex and the City* (1998-2004) to *Pretty Little Liars* (2010–Present), images can both reflect and construct ideas about femininity. ■

networking sites with the intent to hurt the victim (Van DeBosch & Van Cleemput, 2008). Cyberbullying is a growing problem of acute concern to social workers, child psychologists, and school administrators (Slovak & Singer, 2011). Children and adolescents who are bullied in real life are sometimes both cyberbullies and victims of cyberbullying (Dilmac, 2009; Smith et al., 2008; Tyman, Saylor, Taylor, & Comeaux, 2010). Victims take to the Internet to get revenge, often through an anonymous attack, but this perpetuates the bullying cycle online and in real life. One study found that hurtful cyberteasing between adolescents in a romantic relationship can escalate into real-life shouting, throwing objects, or hitting (Madlock & Westerman, 2011).

Modern technology may foster positive socialization, but it also has the potential to be detrimental on both the micro level of individual and small group interactions and the level of communities and countries. Consider the role played today by social media in turning interest groups, or even ethnic groups, against one another. The Internet can be a powerful source of information, but it can also be a source of profound disinformation and hatred, as we discuss in the *Global Issues* box on page 91.

TOTAL INSTITUTIONS AND RESOCIALIZATION

Although individuals typically play an active role in their own socialization, in one setting—the total institution—they experience little choice. **Total institutions** are *institutions that isolate individuals from the rest of society in order to achieve administrative control over most aspects of their lives.* Examples include prisons, the military, hospitals—especially mental hospitals—and live-in drug and alcohol treatment centers. Administrative control is achieved through rules that govern all aspects of daily life, from dress to schedules to interaction with other people. The residents of total institutions are subject to inflexible routines rigidly enforced by staff supervision (Goffman, 1961; Malacrida, 2005).

A major purpose of total institutions is **resocialization**, *the process of altering an individual's behavior through total control of his or her environment.* The first step is to break down the resident's sense of self. The staff monitor every aspect of the resident's life. Residents are stripped of all identification with the outside world on which their personalities are based and surrender their privacy. Institutional haircuts, uniforms, round-the-clock inspections, and abuse, such as the harassment of new recruits to a military school, contribute to breaking down the individual's sense of self. In extreme situations, psychological and even physical torture, as in concentration camps, may also be used.

Once the institutionalized person is "broken," the institution begins rebuilding the personality. Desirable behaviors are rewarded with small privileges, such as choice of work duty in prisons. Undesirable behaviors are severely punished, as by the

Total institution: An institution that isolates individuals from the rest of society in order to achieve administrative control over most aspects of their lives.

Resocialization: The process of altering an individual's behavior through control of his or her environment, for example, within a total institution.

Nicki Minaj in Media

Media Socialization of Children

Political Socialization

GLOBAL ISSUES

SOCIALIZING HATRED IN A REGION OF CONFLICT

Throughout history, human beings everywhere have engaged in conflicts that pit members of one ethnic group against those of another. In the South Caucasus, conflict between ethnic groups has a long and bloody history. Nagorno-Karabakh, for example, is a sliver of land to which both Armenia and Azerbaijan lay historical claim. From 1988 to 1994, the two countries fought a deeply destructive war over the territory that killed 30,000 people and displaced over a million others. While armed conflict is now limited to border skirmishes, formal and informal media in both countries exacerbate tensions—and perhaps increase the risk of future conflict—by socializing Armenians and Azeris to hate one another.

In 2011, London-based nongovernmental organization International Alert (www .international-alert.org) used document analysis to study the way Armenians and Azeris perceive one another. Examining sources from school texts to online news sites and blogs to political speeches, the researchers hoped "to identify key words, narratives, and other innuendos that reference the concept of 'us vs. them' or 'friend vs. enemy'" (Geybullayeva, 2012). They found some alarming trends, particularly in the blogosphere.

Armenians and Armenia were common topics in the Azeri blogosphere, and many posts offered deeply negative

A woman walks past a wall decorated with the national colors in a street of Stepanakert, the capital of the self-proclaimed Republic of Nagorno-Karabakh, a mostly Armenian-populated enclave claimed by Azerbaijan. The final status of the republic has yet to be resolved, and it is recognized only by Armenia. ■

and dehumanizing characterizations. Geybullayeva (2012) writes that in one post, "the author compared Armenia to a disease that should be eradicated." Other posts celebrated the killing of a civilian Armenian shepherd living near the border, lauding it as "happy news" because there was one fewer Armenian. Geybullayeva suggests that youth, who are the most active users of the Internet, are the most likely to be affected by such messages, which both reflect and reproduce hatred for their ethnic neighbors.

Azeris are hardly alone in the blogosphere of hate. The Internet can bring people together through social networking and other means, but it can also tear them apart, functioning as a platform for socializing groups, and even generations, into hostility and hatred.

THINK IT THROUGH

■ *Should national laws or international agreements seek to restrict the use of the Internet as a platform for expressing or disseminating hatred of other social groups? Would such laws violate the democratic value of "free speech"?*

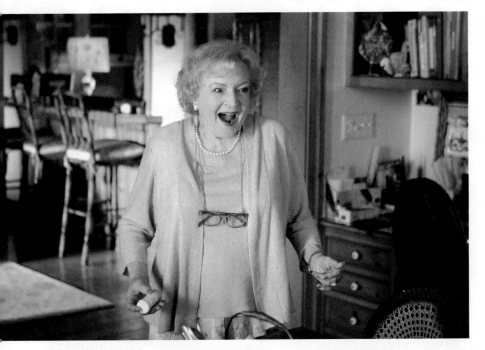

Meyrowitz (1985) writes that "Old people are respected [in media portrayals] to the extent that they can behave like young people." Betty White is a highly recognized actress, whose roles are often humorous and appealing to younger crowds. Think about portrayals of the elderly you have seen recently in movies or on television. Do you agree with this assessment? ■

assignment of humiliating or painful work chores. Since the goal of the total institution is to change attitudes as well as behaviors, even a hint that the resident continues to harbor undesirable ideas may provoke disciplinary action.

How effective are total institutions in resocializing individuals? The answer depends partly on the methods used, partly on the individual, and partly on peer pressure. In the most extreme total institution imaginable, the Nazi concentration camp, some inmates came to identify with their guards and torturers, even helping them keep other prisoners under control. Most, however, resisted resocialization until their death (Bettelheim, 1979).

Prisons often fail at resocialization because the inmates identify more with their fellow prisoners than with the administration's agenda. Inmates in U.S. prisons may well be resocialized, but it is not likely to be to the norms of prison officials or the wider society. Rather, prisoners learn the norms of other prisoners, and as a result, many come out of prison more hardened in their criminal behavior than before.

Even when an institution is initially successful at resocialization, individuals who return to their original social environments often revert to earlier behavior. This reversal confirms that socialization is an ongoing process, continuing throughout a person's lifetime as a result of changing patterns of social interaction.

Total
Institutions

Lifespan
Socialization

Virtual
Identities

LIFE SPAN SOCIALIZATION

Most theories of socialization focus on infancy, childhood, and adolescence. But as the example of total institutions shows us, people do not stop changing once they become adults. Work, marriage, and parenting, for example, shape socialization over the life course. Through social interaction we are not only constantly shaped by others, we are also shaping ourselves and the way others respond to us.

As people near the end of their working life, anticipatory socialization again kicks in to help them envision their future lives. They may pay more attention to how friends react to retirement, whether they are treated differently as they begin to age, and how they are portrayed in the media. In U.S. media programming and advertisements, in fact, seniors are seriously underrepresented relative to their numbers. Older characters that are present are often gender-stereotyped and wealthier than in the real world, but portrayals are usually positive, perhaps reflecting an attempt to appeal to this growing group (Kessler, Racoczy, & Staudinger, 2004; Lee, Carpenter, & Meyers, 2007).

Health and dying may also become increasingly important. Married couples face the prospect of losing a spouse; what will it mean to live alone? For women this question is more urgent than for men, since men on average die several years younger than women. Very old people in particular are likely to spend time in the hospital, which requires being socialized into a total institution. Growing older is thus influenced by socialization as significant and challenging as in earlier life stages.

SOCIAL INTERACTION

Socialization at every stage of life occurs primarily through *social interaction*—the ordinary, taken-for-granted rules that enable people to live, work, and socialize together (Ridgeway & Smith-Lovin, 1999). Spoken words, gestures, body language, and other symbols and cues come together in complex ways to create human communication. The sociologist must look behind the everyday aspects of social interaction to identify how it actually occurs and how social norms and language make it possible.

Social interaction usually requires conformity to social conventions. According to Scheff (1966), violation of the norms of interaction is generally interpreted as a sign that the person is "abnormal," perhaps even dangerous. A person in a crowded elevator who persists in loud, face-to-face conversations with strangers, for example, and disheveled, homeless people shuffling down the street muttering to themselves evoke anxiety if not repugnance.

Norms govern a wide range of interactive behaviors. For example, making eye contact when speaking to someone is valued in U.S. culture; people who don't make eye contact are considered dishonest and shifty. Conversely, among the Navajo and the Australian Aborigines, as well as in many East Asian cultures, direct eye contact is considered disrespectful, especially with a person of greater authority. Norms also govern how close we stand to friends and strangers in making conversation. In North American and Northern European cultures, people avoid standing closer than a couple of feet from one another unless they are on intimate terms (Hall, 1973). U.S. men are socialized to avoid displays of intimacy, such as walking arm in arm. In Nigeria, however, men who are close friends or relatives hold hands when walking together, while in Italy, Spain, Greece, and some Middle Eastern countries, men commonly throw their arms around each others' shoulders, hug, and even kiss.

Two different approaches to studying interaction are Erving Goffman's metaphor of interaction-as-theater, and conversation analysts' efforts to study the way people manage routine talk. First, however, we will look briefly at some sociologists' studies of social interaction.

STUDIES OF SOCIAL INTERACTION

Studies of social interaction have frequently drawn on the symbolic interactionist perspective. They illuminate nearly every form and aspect of social interaction. For example, research on battered women shows how victims of domestic violence redefine their situation to come to grips with abusive relationships (Hattery, 2001). One strategy is to deny the partner's violent behavior altogether. Another is to minimize the partner's responsibility, attributing it to external factors like unemployment, alcoholism, or mental illness. Or the victim will define her own role as caretaker and assume responsibility for "saving" the abusive partner. But women who eventually decide to leave the relationship must redefine the situation so as to change their self-image. They must come to see themselves as victims of abuse who are capable of ending the abusive relationship, rather than someone responsible for "solving" their mate's "problem" (Johnson & Ferraro, 1984).

Recent studies of social interaction have covered:

- The way online gamers coordinate their individual actions with one another and through the user interface in order to succeed at computer games such as *World of Warcraft* (Williams & Kirschner, 2012).

Actors use *dramatic realization*, sometimes with exaggerated behaviors, to leave a particular impression upon the audience. Goffman argues that we also use it in our own more ordinary performances. Have you ever made a concerted effort to "look busy" as your supervisor or teacher walked by although you were engaged in something unrelated to the assigned work? ■

- The strategies homeless youth used in order to manage and alleviate stigma, including creating friendships or attempting to pass as nonhomeless, as well as acting aggressive and fighting back (Roschelle & Kaufman, 2004).
- The ways in which a sense of "corporate social responsibility" is promoted and learned by corporate executives in the work environment (Shamir, 2011).

THE DRAMATURGICAL APPROACH: ERVING GOFFMAN

Erving Goffman (1961, 1963, 1967, 1972, 1973), a major figure in the study of social interaction, developed a set of theoretical ideas that make it possible to observe and describe social interaction. Goffman used what he termed the **dramaturgical approach**, *the study of social interaction as if it were governed by the norms of theatrical performance.*

According to Goffman, people, much like actors on a stage, are concerned with the **presentation of self**, that is, *the creation of impressions in the minds of others in order to define and control a social situation.* For instance, to serve many customers simultaneously, waiters must take charge with a "presentation of self" that is polite but firm and does not allow customers to usurp control by taking too much time ordering. After only a short time, the waiter asserts control by saying, "I'll give you a few minutes to decide what you want" and walks away.

Dramaturgical approach: Erving Goffman's theory of social interaction that studies it as if it were governed by the norms of theatrical performance.

Presentation of self: The creation of impressions in the minds of others in order to define and control a social situation.

Social Interaction

Peer Socialization

The film *The Wizard of Oz* offers a good example of *mystification*. Though the wizard is really, in his own words, "just a man," he maintains his status in Oz by hiding behind a curtain and using a booming voice and fiery mask to convey the impression of awesome power. ∎

- *Idealization* is an actor's effort to embody in his or her behaviors the officially accredited norms and values of a community or society. Those with fewer economic resources might purchase faux designer bags or watches in order to conform to perceived societal expectations of material wealth.
- *Misrepresentation* is part of every actor's repertoire, ranging from kind deception (telling a friend she looks great) to self-interested untruth (telling a professor a paper was lost in a computer crash when it was never written) to bald-faced prevarication (lying to conceal an affair). The actor wants to maintain a desired impression in the eyes of the audience: The friend would like to be perceived as kind and supportive, the student as conscientious and hardworking, and the spouse as loyal and loving.
- *Mystification* is largely reserved for those with status and power and serves to maintain distance from the audience in order to keep people in awe. Corporate leaders keep their offices on a separate floor and don't mix with employees, while celebrities may avoid interviews and allow their on-screen roles to define them as savvy and smart.

As people interact, they monitor themselves and each other, looking for clues that reveal the impressions they are making on others. This ongoing effort at *impression management* results in a continual realignment of the individual's "performance," as the "actors" refit their roles using dress, objects, voice, and gestures in a joint enterprise.

Continuing the metaphor of a theatrical performance, Goffman divides spheres of interaction into two stages. In the *front stage,* we are social actors engaged in a process of impression management through the use of props, costumes, gestures, and language. A professor lecturing to her class, a young couple on their first date, and a job applicant in an interview all are governed by existing social norms, so the professor will not arrive in her nightgown, nor will the prospective employee greet his interviewer with a high-five rather than a handshake. Just as actors in a play must stick with their scripts, so too, suggests Goffman, do we as social actors risk consequences (like a failed interaction) if we diverge from the normative script.

Goffman offers insights into the techniques we as social actors have in our repertoire. Among them are the following:

- *Dramatic realization* is the actor's effort to mobilize his or her behavior to draw attention to a particular characteristic of the role he or she is assuming. What impression does a baseball umpire strive to leave on his audience (the teams and fans)? Arguably, he would like to embody authority, so he makes his calls loudly and with bold gestures.

We may also engage in impression management as a team. *Teams* consist of two or more actors cooperating to create a definition of the situation favorable to them. For example, members of a sports team work together, though some may be more skilled than others, to convey a definition of themselves as a highly competent and competitive group. Or the members of a family may work together to convey to their dinner guests that they are content and happy by acting cooperatively and smiling at one another during the group interaction.

The example of the family gives us an opportunity to explore Goffman's concept of the *back stage,* where actors let down their masks and relax or even practice their impression management. Before the party, the home is a back stage. One parent is angry at the other for getting cheap rather than expensive wine, one sibling refuses to speak to the parent who grounded her, and the other won't stop texting long enough to set the table. Then the doorbell rings. Like magic, the home becomes the front stage as the adults smilingly welcome their guests and the kids begin to carry out trays of snacks and drinks. The guests may or may not sense some tension in the home, but they play along with the scenario so as not to create discomfort. When the party ends, the home reverts to the back stage, and each actor can relax his or her performance.

Goffman's work, like Mead's and the work of other sociologists focusing on socialization, sees the social self as an outcome of society and social interactions. Goffman, however, characterizes the social self not as a *possession*—a dynamic but still essentially real self—but rather as a *product* of a given social interaction, which can change as we seek to manage impressions for different audiences. Would you say that Mead or Goffman offers a better characterization of us as social actors?

Deprivation of Social Interaction

INEQUALITY MATTERS

GENDER AND CONVERSATION

Men often claim they "cannot get a word in edgewise" when talking to women. However, conversation analysis research challenges this claim: In hundreds of recorded conversations between men and women, researchers found that men more frequently interrupted women than women interrupted men, and that men used the interruptions to dominate the conversation. Men tended to speak more loudly and to be less polite than women, using loudness and rudeness (such as sarcastic remarks about what a woman had said) to control the conversation (Campbell, Klein, & Olson, 1992; Fishman, 1978; West, 1979; West & Zimmerman, 1977, 1983; Zimmerman & West, 1975, 1980). While men set the agenda and otherwise dominated the conversation, women often did the "work" of maintaining conversations by nodding their heads, saying "a-hah," and asking questions (DeFrancisco, 1991; Fishman, 1978; Leaper & Robnett, 2011; Tannen, 2001; West & Zimmerman, 1977, 1983).

This research shows that the rules and conventions governing ordinary talk are grounded in the larger society—society's gender roles, in which men generally assume a dominant position in interaction with women without even realizing it. In fact, not only do men not realize they are dominating the conversation; they think women dominate and "talk too much."

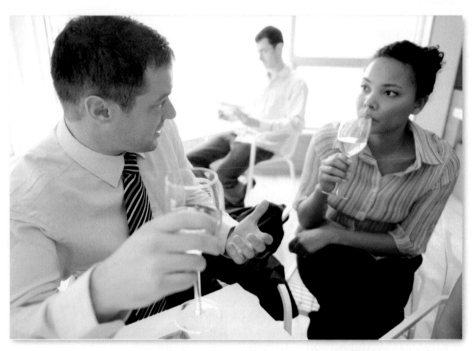

Do you think that men and women communicate differently? How would you articulate differences you observe? Would you attribute them to nature or nurture? ■

The apparently private conversations between men and women thus reflect a fundamental issue in contemporary society: inequality between the sexes, including how inequality gets reproduced in subtle ways. The cultural stereotype of women as talkative and emotional and men as quiet and rational affects women even though it's basis in reality is weak. No matter that men talk more and dominate conversations— women are made to feel unequal by the reproduction of the stereotype, and inequality between the sexes is reinforced. The private lives of people in conversations thus cannot be divorced from the way the larger society shapes relationships between men and women.

THINK IT THROUGH

■ *This box demonstrates how sociological research can shed light on commonsense assumptions by empirically testing the assumption that women dominate conversations more than do men. What other generally stereotypical notions are challenged by research described in the text?*

ETHNOMETHODOLOGY AND CONVERSATION ANALYSIS

Routine, day-to-day social interactions are the building blocks of social institutions and ultimately of society itself. **Ethnomethodology** studies *the body of commonsense knowledge and procedures by which ordinary members of a society make sense of their social circumstances and interactions. Ethno* refers to "folk," or ordinary people; *methodology* to the methods they use to govern interaction—as distinct as the methods used by sociologists to study them. Ethnomethodology was created through Harold Garfinkel's work in the early 1960s. Garfinkel (1963, 1985) sought to understand exactly what goes on in social interactions, after observing that our interpretation of social interaction depends on the context. For example, if a child on a playground grabs another child's ball and runs with it, the teacher may see this as a sign of the child's aggressiveness, while fellow students see it as a display of courage. Social interaction and communication would be impossible unless most people have learned to assign similar meanings to the same interactions. By studying the specific contexts of concrete social interactions, Garfinkel sought to understand how people come to share the same interpretation of social interactions.

Garfinkel also believed that in all cultures people expect others to talk in a way that is coherent and understandable and become anxious and upset when this does not happen. Making sense of one another's conversations is even more fundamental to social life than cultural norms, Garfinkel argued, since without ways of arriving at meaningful understandings, communication, and hence culture, is not possible. Because the procedures that determine how we make sense of conversations are so important to social interaction, another field developed from ethnomethodology that focused on talk itself: conversation analysis.

Conversation analysis investigates *the way participants in social interaction recognize and produce coherent conversation* (Sacks, Schegloff, & Jefferson, 1974; Schegloff, 1990, 1991). The term *conversation* includes virtually any form of verbal communication, from routine small talk to emergency phone calls to congressional hearings and court proceedings (Heritage & Greatbatch, 1991; Hopper, 1991, Whalen & Zimmerman, 1987, 1990; Zimmerman, 1984, 1992).

Conversation analysis research suggests that social interaction is not simply a random succession of events. Rather, people construct conversations through a reciprocal process that makes the interaction coherent. One way in which we sequentially organize conversations is *turn taking,* a strategy that allows us to understand an utterance as a response to an earlier one and a cue to take our turn in the conversation. A person's turn ends once the other conversants indicate they have understood the message. For example, by answering "Fine" to the question "How are you?" you show that you have understood the question and are ready to move ahead.

On the other hand, answering "What do you mean?" or "Green" to the question "How are you?" is likely to lead to conversational breakdown. Conversational analysts have identified a number of techniques commonly used to repair such breakdowns. For example, if you begin speaking but realize midsentence that the other person is already speaking, you can "repair" this awkward situation by pausing until the original speaker finishes his or her turn and then restarting your turn.

Later research emphasized the impact of the larger social structure on conversations (T. Wilson, 1991). Sociologists looked at the use of power in conversations, whether the power of the dispatcher over the caller in emergency phone calls (Whalen, Zimmerman, & Whalen, 1990; Zimmerman, 1984, 1992), of the questioner over the testifier in governmental hearings (Molotch & Boden, 1985), or of men in male-female interactions (Campbell, Klein, & Olson, 1992; Fishman, 1978; West, 1979; West & Zimmerman, 1977, 1983; Zimmerman & West, 1975, 1980). The last instance, in particular, illustrates how the larger social structure—in this case, gender structure—affects conversation. Even at the most basic and personal level—a private conversation between two people—social structures exercise a potentially powerful influence.

WHY STUDY SOCIALIZATION AND SOCIAL INTERACTION?

Have you ever wondered why you and some of your classmates or neighbors differ in worldviews, coping strategies for stress, or values concerning right and wrong? Understanding socialization and social interaction sheds light on such differences and what they mean to us in everyday life. For example, if you travel abroad, you will have a sense of how cultural differences come to be and appreciate that no culture is more "normal" than another—each may have its own norms, values, and roles taught from earliest childhood.

By studying socialization, you also know how critical are the peers, schools, and work environments to which children and young people are exposed. The growing role of the mass media, the Internet, and other technological innovations means we must pay close attention to these sources of socialization and social interaction as well. As people spend more time on the Internet talking to friends and strangers, experimenting with new identities, and seeking new forms of and forums for social interaction, sociologists may need to rethink some of their ideas about the influence of agents like parents and schools; perhaps these may recede in importance—or grow. Sociologists also ask how our presentation of self is transformed when we create social selves in the anonymous space of social media. What kinds of research could you imagine conducting to learn more about the digital world as an agent of socialization and a site of modern social interaction?

. . . .

Ethnomethodology: A sociological method that studies the body of commonsense knowledge and procedures by which ordinary members of a society make sense of their social circumstances and interaction.

Conversation analysis: The study of how participants in social interaction recognize and produce coherent conversation.

Social Interaction Theories

WHAT CAN I DO WITH A SOCIOLOGY DEGREE?

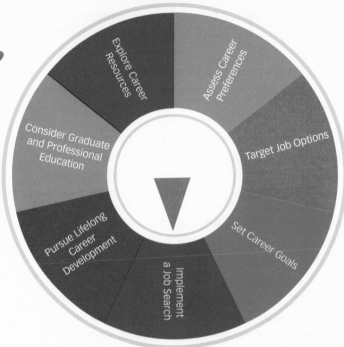

Explore Career Resources · Assess Career Preferences · Target Job Options · Set Career Goals · Implement a Job Search · Pursue Lifelong Career Development · Consider Graduate and Professional Education

CAREER DEVELOPMENT: CREATING A JOB SEARCH PLAN AND PUTTING IT INTO ACTION

CREATE AND IMPLEMENT A JOB SEARCH ACTION PLAN

Your job search action plan builds on your career goals and focuses on short- and medium-term activities. Break your goals into specific and manageable tasks to create action items. Strive to be as specific as possible with your action items by providing details about who and what is involved in completing the task, identifying measureable outcomes, and noting time-based deadlines about when an activity will be completed. Include in your *job search action plan* job search strategies likely to produce results.

In the remainder of this essay, we briefly discuss each of these strategies. Additional resources for each can be found on the book's student study site, www.sagepub.com/chamblissintro.

Target Employers

Develop a list of 10–15 potential employers based on your research that align with your career and job search goals. Track the employer regularly to update your organizational knowledge and learn about new opportunities. Utilize LinkedIn and other social media sites to identify individuals and groups with whom you might connect in the organization for information, introductions, and leads.

Network

Networking is about building relationships for the purpose of making connections to enhance your career and/or job search. People build their networks online, at their place of employment, at internships, and in their community, as well as with professors, friends, friends of friends, family, former employers, and fellow alumni. Consider informational interviews, previously used for career exploration, to network and to learn about particular employers, industries, and individuals.

Market Yourself: Résumés

A résumé reviews your education, academic awards, employment and volunteer experiences, college and leadership activities, and language and technical skills. Start your experience descriptions with action verbs and omit all personal pronouns. Use qualifiers and quantifiers to describe the breadth and depth of your involvement in an activity. Your résumé should be one page, written in a standard 10–12 font, printed on bond paper, and error free.

Market Yourself: Cover Letters

Cover letters are a form of business writing and should follow a business letter format. The first paragraph of your cover letter should start with information about the reason for writing, identify how you learned of the position, and succinctly state how your skills, degree, and experience match the requirements of the position. The second paragraph should expand on information about your fit for the position, discuss your accomplishments, and use specific examples that parallel the experience and skills that the employer seeks. The third paragraph identifies career-related characteristics that will support your success in the position, such as resourcefulness, time management, and persistence, among others. The final paragraph should restate your interest in the position, your availability to discuss the opportunity, and a reference to your contact information.

Market Yourself: Utilizing the Online Advantage

Utilize resources online to brand and market yourself, connect with individuals and groups, access job listings, link to employer and job listing sites, research employer information and occupational trends, and/or create a website or write a blog to highlight career and professional activities and accomplishments. Expand your network by connecting with individuals and groups via social media and job listing sites.

Interview Strategies

An interview is your opportunity to articulate to the employer your skills, abilities, and accomplishments that best match the attributes that he or she is seeking in an ideal candidate. Be sure that you have researched the employer so that you can ask informed questions. Plan ahead so that you are able to arrive early for the interview. When you greet the interviewer, make eye contact, smile, and shake his or her hand firmly. As the interview begins, be professional, but be yourself. Listen to the interviewer's question without interruption and allow yourself time to form a response before answering the question. Speak clearly and enthusiastically about experiences and skills and offer detailed responses about your experience, skills, and knowledge.

E-mail or mail a thank-you letter to each person with whom you met within 24 hours of your interview. Learn more about interviewing strategies, as well as questions frequently asked by employers and interviewees, at our online data source.

Evaluate and Negotiate Offers

When you receive a job offer, consider your offer carefully by reviewing the entire compensation package, which includes your salary and benefits. In addition to the compensation package, review the related "pros" or "cons" of accepting the position. To negotiate a change in the package, start with the salary and state the preferred range of your salary. Restate your selling points including why you believe that your skills, knowledge, and experience are the best fit for the position and how you will add value to the organization. Always frame your argument in relation to the employer's hiring needs and the goals of the organization rather than your preferences.

Reflect and Pursue Lifelong Career Development

Even when a specific job search is complete, your career development is continuous. Practice lifelong learning and actively engage in professional development. Build your network, develop connections to colleagues, and demonstrate ethical behaviors in your professional activities. Continue to explore new opportunities and review and update your career goals. Seek to know and remain true to your career identity—the values, aspirations, interests, talents, skills, and preferences related to careers that are fundamental to your career satisfaction and success.

▶ *Access additional web links on the student study site to learn more.*

SUMMARY

To test your knowledge further, find additional study material on the Student Study Site at **www.sagepub.com/chamblissintro**

- **Socialization** is a lifelong, active process by which people learn the cultures of their society and construct a sense of who they are.

- What we often think of as "human nature" is in fact learned through socialization. Sociologists argue that human behavior is not determined biologically, though biology plays some role, but develops primarily through social interaction.

- Although some theories emphasize the early years, sociologists generally argue that socialization takes place throughout the life course. The theories of Sigmund Freud and Jean Piaget emphasize the early years, while those of George Herbert Mead (although his **role-taking** theory focused on the earlier stages of the life course), Lawrence Kohlberg, and Judith Harris give more consideration to the whole life course. According to Mead, children acquire a sense of self through symbolic interaction, including the role-taking that eventually enables the adult to take the standpoint of society as a whole.

- Kohlberg built on Piaget's ideas to argue that a person's sense of morality develops through different stages, from that in which people strictly seek personal gain or avoid punishment to the stage in which they base moral decisions on abstract principles.

- The immediate family provides the earliest and typically foremost source of socialization, but school, work, peers, mass media, and the Internet all play a significant role.

- Socialization may differ by social class. Middle-class families place a somewhat greater emphasis on creativity and independence, while working-class families often stress obedience to authority. These differences, in turn, reflect the corresponding workplace differences associated with social class.

- In **total institutions,** such as prisons, the military, and hospitals, individuals are isolated so that society can achieve administrative control of their lives. By enforcing rules that govern all aspects of daily life, from dress to schedules to interaction with other people, total institutions can open the way to **resocialization,** which is the breaking down of the person's sense of self and rebuilding of the personality.

- According to Erving Goffman's **dramaturgical approach,** we are all actors concerned with the presentation of ourselves in social interaction. People perform their social roles on the "front stage," while they are able to avoid performing on the "back stage."

- **Ethnomethodology** is a method of analysis that examines the body of commonsense knowledge and procedures by which ordinary members of a society make sense of their social circumstances and interaction.

- **Conversation analysis,** which builds on ethnomethodology, studies the way participants in social interaction recognize and produce coherent action.

KEY TERMS

Study terms on the go with the smartphone-friendly key term flashcards, available at **www.sagepub.com/chamblissintro**

DISCUSSION QUESTIONS

1. Think about your own experiences with family and peers. What conclusions might you draw about their relative importance as agents of socialization in your life? Is it possible to generalize these conclusions beyond your own experience to say something about their effects in the larger society?

2. What importance does the way people react to you play in the development of your personality and your self-image? How can the reaction of others influence whether or not you develop skills as an athlete or a student or a musician, for example?

3. Recall Goffman's ideas in the chapter about social interaction and the presentation of self. How have social media sites such as Facebook and Instagram affected the presentation of self? Have there been changes to what Goffman saw as our front and back stages?

DISCOVER STATE STATS

Log-in to the eBook and click on the title to the left for access to State Stats in order to complete the exercise.

In the Education database, find the percentage of public school females proficient or better in reading for either fourth or eighth grade, and the same item for males. There is a pretty big difference between males and females. Look at data for the nation and for a few states, note them in a chart, and think about how sociologists might use the concept of gender socialization to explain this gap. What hypotheses might you want to test?

STUDENT STUDY SITE

Visit the Student Study Site at **www.sagepub.com/chamblissintro** to access additional study tools, including eFlashcards, web quizzes, video resources, web resources, audio resources, links to SAGE journal, handbook, and research articles, and much more!

5

GROUPS, ORGANIZATIONS, AND BUREAUCRACIES

WHAT DO YOU THINK?

1. Do most people conform to the expectations of the groups to which they belong?
2. Why do many people think of bureaucracies as inefficient and annoying? What would be the alternative?
3. Could a group of college students working together on a societal issue such as rising student debt, child hunger, or veteran homelessness bring about significant social change?

SOC VIEW

Get a closer look with the authors!

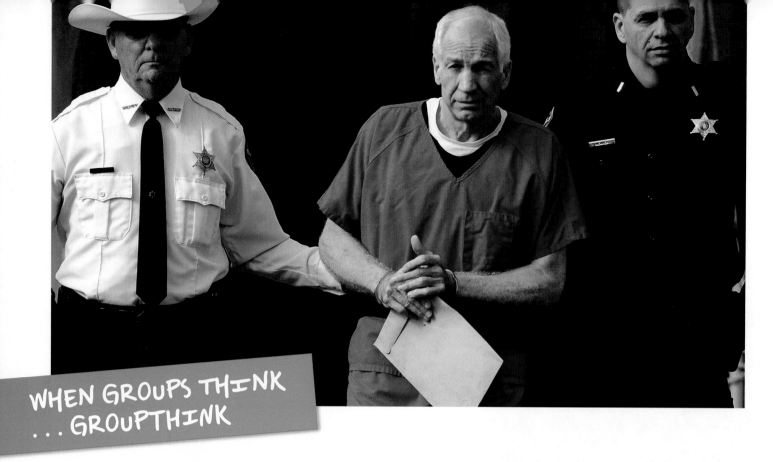

WHEN GROUPS THINK . . . GROUPTHINK

In June 2012, former Pennsylvania State University football assistant coach Jerry Sandusky was convicted by a Pennsylvania court of sexually abusing children who were under his care and supervision. Sandusky had contact with many boys through his respected position at Penn State and his Second Mile charity, a service organization with a mission to help disadvantaged young people through sports. The charges, witness testimonies, and some of Sandusky's own admissions about, for instance, showering with boys in the PSU locker room were shocking to most who heard them.

But they may not have been a shock to a number of Sandusky's colleagues at Penn State. According to an investigative report prepared by former FBI director Louis Freeh at the behest of the Penn State Board of Regents, many people were already aware of Sandusky's abusive activities. Some, like head football coach Joe Paterno and Penn State president Graham Spanier, had been aware of allegations against Sandusky for years. So why did no one act to halt the abuse? Why were allegations and evidence of Sandusky's actions covered up by colleagues in the football program and the university administration?

The case is complex, and a spectrum of answers to this question exists. One possibility, however, is *groupthink,* a phenomenon characterized by a group choosing to elevate consensus and conformity—and preservation of the group—above other values. In an opinion piece published by *Time* magazine on groupthink at Penn State, two authors, a psychologist and a physician, argue that Penn State's athletic and administrative leadership chose to protect Sandusky, who was one of their elite group, rather than the victimized children, nearly all of whom were poor. They wanted to shield Sandusky—and the Penn State image and program—from damaging scrutiny. Their logic, deduced from e-mail traffic uncovered by Freeh, is characterized by the authors as follows: "[T]his particular insider group managed to twist logic to the point where they thought it was more 'humane' to cover up the repeated allegations of Sandusky's abuse than to report them to police" (Cohen & Debenedet, 2012, p. 26).

When decisions are primarily based on how group members will react, rather than on ethical, professional, or legal considerations, groupthink can, as this case shows, lead to devastating outcomes. The influence of the group can foster deviance—but at the same time, group bonds are fundamental to our lives and a key part of socialization and social integration. The role that groups play in society is clearly complex, and a key focus of sociological study. ∎

We begin this chapter with an overview of the nature of social groups, looking at primary and secondary groups and their effects on our lives. We also examine the power of groups in fostering integration and enforcing conformity, among other key functions. The chapter then turns to the importance of capital in social group formation and action. We follow with an exploration of the place of organizations in society. The chapter then turns to a topic about which Max Weber wrote extensively and with which we all have some experience—bureaucracies. We end with a consideration of the modern role of governmental and nongovernmental organizations in the pursuit of social change.

Secondary groups may evolve into primary groups for some of their members. For example, when students taking the same course begin to socialize after class, they may create bonds of friendship that come to constitute a primary group. ∎

THE NATURE OF GROUPS

The male elephant is a solitary creature, spending much of its life wandering alone, interacting with other elephants only when it is time to mate or if another male intrudes on its territory. Female elephants, by contrast, live their lives in groups. Both male and female human beings are like the female elephant: We are social animals who live our entire lives in the company of others. Our lives are, in essence, social, and we can organize and understand them based on the types of groups with which we are associated. We are born into an emotionally and biologically connected group we know as "the family." As we mature, we become increasingly interconnected with other people, some our own age and others not, at school, on sports teams, and through various other social interactions and increasingly via the Internet and other social media. We consolidate and accumulate friends, teammates, and classmates—different groups with whom we interact on a regular basis. Eventually we obtain jobs and engage with coworkers and other people we encounter in the course of our work. Along the way we may form and maintain friendship groups, either in person or virtually, that share an interest in a particular activity or lifestyle, like poker, model airplanes, or

music. Sometimes we are part of groups that gather for special circumstances, like watching a football game or going to a presidential inauguration.

A moment's reflection on these types of groups reveals that they differ in many important ways, particularly in the degree of intimacy and social support their members experience in them. Sociologists find this difference so fundamental that they use it to distinguish between *primary* and *secondary* groups. Primary groups are characterized by *intense emotional ties, intimacy, and identification with membership in the group*. Secondary groups are *large, impersonal groups with minimal emotional and intimate ties* (Cooley, 1909). Today, social networking sites and virtual, online groups that people are part of can include primary or secondary groups. Moreover, the Internet is increasingly blurring the boundary distinctions between primary and secondary groups—very large, ostensibly impersonal groups can take on a very intimate feeling thanks to the power of virtual communication and information sharing. As we will discuss later in this chapter, technology and the Internet have changed quite a lot about how we think of social relations and social groups.

Primary groups are of great significance because they exert a long-lasting influence on the development of our social selves (Cooley, 1902/1964). Charles Horton Cooley (1864–1929), who

Extremist Groups

Characteristic	Primary Group	Secondary Group
Social distance of relationships	Low: face-to-face	High: indirect, remote
Intimacy	High: "fusion of personalities"	Low: relatively impersonal
Importance in forming the "social self"	Fundamental: earliest complete experience of social unity	Secondary: occurs later in life, no all-embracing experience of social unity
Degree of mutual identification with others	High: "we"	Low: "they"
Degree of permanence	High: change but slowly over time	Low: likely to change over time
Examples	Family; children's playgroups; neighborhood and community groups; clubs, fraternities, and sororities	Secondary schools, colleges, and universities; businesses and other workplaces; government agencies; bureaucracies of all sorts

first introduced the distinction, argued that people belong to primary groups mainly because they satisfy personal needs of belonging and fulfillment. People join secondary groups such as business organizations, schools, work groups, athletic clubs, and governmental bodies to achieve some specific goal: to earn a living, get a college degree, or compete in sports. For a summary of the characteristics of primary and secondary groups, see Table 5.1.

THE POWER OF GROUPS

As you learned in Chapter 4, we often judge ourselves by how we think we appear to others, which Cooley termed the "looking-glass self." Groups as well as individuals provide the standards by which we make these self-evaluations. Robert K. Merton (1938/1968), following Herbert Hyman (1942), elaborated on the concept of the reference group as a measure by which we evaluate ourselves. Importantly, a reference group provides a standard for judging our own attitudes or behaviors.

For most people, the family is the reference group with the greatest impact in shaping our early view of ourselves. As we mature, and particularly during adolescence, peer groups replace or at least compete with the family as the reference group through which we define ourselves. Today, thanks to the growth of social media, many people establish "virtual" reference groups and intimate primary groups with people they have never seen face-to-face.

Reference groups may be primary, such as the family, or secondary, such as a group of soldiers in the same branch of service in the military. They may even be fictional. One of the chief functions of advertising, for example, is to create a set of

imaginary reference groups that will influence consumers' buying habits. When lean female models with flawless complexions are shown in ads for cosmetics, the message to women is simple: "If you want to look as though you are part of a group of highly attractive, eternally youthful women, buy this product." In reality, of course, models seldom have unblemished features and have been given the benefit of artful lighting, photographic techniques, computer enhancement, and sometimes even cosmetic surgery. Similarly, the happy-go-lucky, physically perfect young men and women seen sailing or playing volleyball or hang gliding in beer commercials have little to do with the reality of most of our lives—or even the actors' own.

THE EFFECTS OF SIZE

Another significant way in which groups differ has to do with their size. The German sociologist Georg Simmel (1858–1918) was one of the first to call attention to the influence of group size on people's behavior. Since Simmel's time, small group researchers have conducted a number of laboratory experiments to discover how group size affects both the quality of interaction in the group and the group's effectiveness in accomplishing certain tasks (Levine & Crowther, 2008; Lucas & Lovaglia, 1998).

The simplest group, which Simmel (1955) called a **dyad**, *consists of two persons*. Simmel reasoned that dyads, which offer both intimacy and conflict, are likely to be simultaneously intense and unstable. To survive, they require the full attention and cooperation of both parties. Dyads are typically the source of our most elementary social bonds, often constituting the group in which we are most likely to share our deepest secrets. The commitment two people make through marriage is one way to form a dyadic group. But dyads can also be very fragile. If one person withdraws

Types of Groups

Group Size and Conformity

Dyad: A group consisting of two persons.

DIGITAL SOCIETY

SOCIAL INTERACTIONS IN A NEW AGE OF COMMUNICATION

The technologies of social media can strengthen ties among members of primary and secondary groups, aid social change, and disseminate unfiltered news immediately as events unfold. At the same time, they allow anyone to disseminate information about anyone else with relative anonymity and no fact-checking, provide an avenue for those with dangerous or sinister causes or desires to unite, and present an opportunity for new forms of exploitation, bullying, and harassment. Whether human social interaction today is better or worse than in the past is irrelevant; it is simply significantly different.

Estimates place the number of individuals with access to the Internet around the world at roughly 2.3 billion people and climbing—so the Internet is already accessible to some degree to about 33% of the world's population (Internet World Stats, 2012). Facebook, the world's most dominant social networking website, has 552 million daily users and more than 1 billion monthly users, the majority of them outside the United States (Facebook, 2012). Nearly 1 in 5 people in the United States have gone out with someone they met online. Since its creation in 2003, LinkedIn has drawn more than 150 million members in more than 200 countries (LinkedIn, 2012). Pinterest allows users to create virtual pinboards to save and share links, recipes, photos, fashions, and countless other preferences (Pinterest, 2012). Increasingly, digital

"This child is old enough to have an iPhone!" The dissemination of technology has resulted in nearly one third of the global population having access to the Internet. Many children today are growing up in a truly digital society, where technology is deeply entwined with their upbringing and socialization. ■

communications are becoming integrated and "intelligent," letting users link their Pinterest board to their Facebook account and access it from their smartphone.

Not only does technology provide a means of increasing social interactions among individuals and groups; it also presents opportunities for interactions that might otherwise never have taken place. The wife of a Washington state corrections officer received a "People You May Know" update on her Facebook page suggesting she might want to be friends with another woman. When she clicked on the other woman's profile, she found wedding photos of her husband and the other woman. Not only had her husband never told her he had been married before; he was still married to the woman in the pictures. He was subsequently arrested and charged with bigamy (Rabiner, 2012).

There is a very good chance that the theorizing sociologists have done about social groups and interactions in the 20th century will look quite different in the 21st century as our means of forming groups, feeling integrated, and interacting with others change.

THINK IT THROUGH

■ *What kinds of research questions might sociologists use in theorizing about the qualities of groups in the digital age?*

Dyad Relationship

Triad Relationship

from the dyad, it vanishes. That is why, as Simmel believed, a variety of cultural and legal norms arise to support dyadic groups, including marriage, in societies where such groups are regarded as an important source of social stability.

Adding one other person to a dyad changes the group relationship considerably, making what Simmel termed a **triad**. Triads are apt to be more stable than dyads, since the presence of a third person relieves some of the pressure on the other two members to always get along and energize the relationship. One person can temporarily withdraw his or her attention from the relationship without necessarily threatening it. In addition, if two members have a disagreement, the third can play the role of mediator, as when you try to patch up a falling-out between two friends or coworkers (see Figure 5.1).

On the other hand, however, **alliances**, sometimes termed **coalitions**, may form between two members, enabling them to "gang up" on the third member, thereby destabilizing the group. Alliances are most likely to form when no member is clearly dominant and all three are competing for the same thing—for example, when three friends are given a pair of tickets to a concert and have to decide which two will go. Larger groups share some characteristics of triads. For instance, on the TV series *Survivor*, many alliances form within the group of castaways, as the program's characters forge special relationships with one another to avoid being eliminated by a group vote.

In forming an alliance, a member is most likely to choose the weaker of the two other members, if there is one. But why would this be the case if picking a stronger member would strengthen the alliance? Choosing a weaker member enables the existing alliance member to exercise more power and control within the alliance. However, in some "revolutionary" coalitions, the two weaker members form an alliance to overthrow the stronger one (Goldstone, 2001; Grusky, Bonacich, & Webster, 1995).

Going from a dyad to a triad illustrates an important sociological principle first identified by Georg Simmel: *As group size increases, the intensity of relationships within the group decreases, while overall group stability increases.* There are exceptions to every principle, however. Intensity of interaction among individuals within a group decreases as the size of the group increases because, for instance, a larger number of outlets or alternative arenas for interaction exists for individuals who are not getting along (Figure 5.2 on page 107). In a dyad, only a single relationship is possible; however, in a triad, three different two-person relationships can occur. Adding a fourth person leads to six possible two-person relationships, not counting subgroups that may form. In a 10-person group, the number of possible two-person relationships increases to 45! When one relationship doesn't work out to your liking, you can easily move on to another, as you sometimes may do at large parties.

Larger groups tend to be more stable than smaller ones because the withdrawal of some members does not threaten the survival of the entire group. For example, sports teams do not cease to exist simply because of the loss of one player, even though that player might have been important to the team's overall success. Beyond a certain size, perhaps a dozen people, groups may also develop a formal structure. Formal leadership roles may arise, such as president or secretary, and official rules may develop to govern what the group does. We discuss formal organizations later in this chapter.

Larger groups can sometimes be exclusive, since it is easier for their members to limit their social relationships to the group itself, avoiding relationships with nonmembers. This sense of being part of an in-group or clique is often what unites fraternities, sororities, and other campus organizations. Cliquishness is especially likely to occur when the group consists of members who are similar to one another in such social characteristics as age, gender, class, race, or ethnicity. Members of rich families, for example, may sometimes be reluctant to fraternize with people from the working class, men may prefer to play basketball only with other men, and students who belong to a particular ethnic group may seek out each other's company in the dormitory or cafeteria. The concept of **social closure**, originally developed by Max Weber, is especially relevant here, insofar as it speaks to the *ability of groups to strategically and consciously exclude outsiders or those deemed "undesirable" from participating in the group or enjoying the group's resources* (Murphy, 1988; Parkin, 1979).

. . . .

Triad: A group consisting of three persons.

Alliances (or coalitions): Groups that may form between members, enabling them to "gang up" on another member, thereby destabilizing the group.

Social closure: The ability of groups to strategically and consciously exclude outsiders or those deemed "undesirable" from participating in the group or enjoying the group's resources.

Groups don't always exclude outsiders, however (Blau, 1977; Stolle, 1998). For example, if your social group or club is made up of members from different social classes or ethnic groups, you are more likely to appreciate diversity thanks to your firsthand experience. This experience with difference may perhaps lead you to be more inclusive of others not like yourself in other aspects of your life, for example, in bringing together a group to work on a project. This, of course, is an optimistic outlook and one that we embrace and hope holds true in practice.

At the same time, researchers have shown that exposure to differences of race, ethnicity, religion, social class, and other characteristics may in fact lead to negative consequences and exclusion—thus highlighting that there are two sides to every coin. The idea here is that exposure to "different" things may heighten the "threat" level that people feel and associate with differences, causing them to want to exclude those people or things from their lives (Blalock, 1967; Markert, 2010).

TYPES OF GROUP LEADERSHIP

A leader is a person able to influence the behavior of other members of a group. All groups tend to have leaders, even if the leader does not have a formal title. Leaders come in a variety of forms: autocratic, charismatic, democratic, laissez-faire, bureaucratic, and so on. Some leaders are especially effective in motivating members of their groups or organizations, inspiring them to achievements they might not ordinarily accomplish. Such **transformational leaders** go beyond the merely routine, *instilling in group members a sense of mission or higher purpose and thereby changing (transforming) the nature of the group itself* (Burns, 1978; Kanter, 1983; Mehra, Dixon, Brass, & Robertson, 2006).

Transformational leaders leave their mark on their organizations and can also be a vital inspiration for social change in the world. Nelson Mandela, the first African president of post-apartheid South Africa, spent 27 years in prison, having been convicted of treason against the White-dominated government. Nonetheless, his moral and political position was so strong that upon his release he immediately assumed leadership of the African National Congress (ANC), leading that political group to the pinnacle of power in South Africa and then assuming the office of president of the entire nation.

Most leaders are not as visionary as Mandela, however. Leaders who simply "get the job done" are **transactional leaders**,

- -

Transformational leader: A leader who is able to instill in the members of a group a sense of mission or higher purpose, thereby changing the nature of the group itself.

Transactional leader: A leader who is concerned with accomplishing the group's tasks, getting group members to do their jobs, and making certain that the group achieves its goals.

Legitimate authority: A type of power that is recognized as rightful by those over whom it is exercised.

■ **FIGURE 5.2** A Complex Network of Relationships

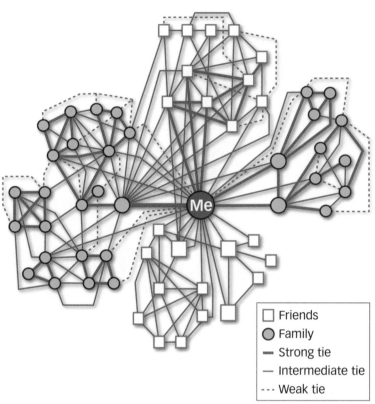

☐ Friends
⬤ Family
— Strong tie
— Intermediate tie
--- Weak tie

concerned with accomplishing the group's tasks, getting group members to do their jobs, and making certain the group achieves its goals. Transactional leadership is routine leadership. For example, the teacher who effectively gets through the lesson plan each day—but does not necessarily transform the classroom into a place where students explore new ways of thinking and behaving that change their educational lives—is exercising transactional leadership.

For leaders to be effective, they must somehow get others to follow them. How do they do that? At one end of the spectrum, the leader can coerce people into compliance and subordination; at the other end, people may willingly comply and subordinate themselves. The basic sociological notion of *power,* the ability to mobilize resources and achieve a goal despite the resistance of others, captures the first point (Emerson, 1962; Hall, 2003; Weber, 1947). The related notion of **legitimate authority,** *power exercised over those who recognize it as deserved or earned,* captures the second (Blau, 1964). For example, prison guards often rely on the use of force to ensure compliance with their orders, whereas professors must depend on their legitimate authority if they hope to keep their students attentive.

Sociologists have typically found authority to be more interesting than the exercise of raw force. After all, it is not surprising

Leadership

Nelson Mandela played an influential role in leading South Africa out of apartheid in the late 1980s and early 1990s. Prior to assuming the presidency of the postapartheid South African government, Mandela, writing from a prison cell, inspired many South Africans to form antiapartheid coalitions and groups. ■

that people will follow orders when someone holds a gun to their head. But why do they go along with authority when they are *not* overtly compelled to do so?

Part of the answer is that people often regard authority as legitimate when it seems to naturally accompany the leadership position. A teacher, for example, seems to possess the right to expect students to listen attentively and behave respectfully. Power stemming from an official leadership position is termed **positional power**; *it depends on the leader's role in the group* (Chiang, 2009; Hersey, Blanchard, & Natemeyer, 1987; Raven & Kruglianski, 1975). At the same time, some leaders derive their power from their unique ability to inspire others. Power that derives from the leader's personality is termed **personal power**; *it depends on the ability to persuade rather than command* (van Dijke & Poppe, 2006).

In most situations, the effective exercise of personal power, rather than positional power, is more likely to result in highly motivated and satisfied group members. Yet, when group members are confused or ill prepared to undertake a particular task, they seem to prefer the more command-oriented style associated with positional leadership (Hersey et al., 1987; Mizruchi & Potts, 1998; Patterson, 1989; Podsakoff & Schriesheim, 1985; Schaefer, 2011).

CONFORMITY TO GROUPS

Following group and societal norms like getting a tattoo or a piercing, or wearing the trendiest brand of jeans, seems relatively

Groupthink

harmless. At the same time, conformity to group pressure can lead to destructive behavior such as drug abuse or serious crimes against others. For this reason, sociologists and social psychologists have long sought to understand why most people tend to go along with others—and under what circumstances they do not.

Some of the earliest studies of conformity to group pressures were conducted by psychologist Solomon Asch over 50 years ago. In one of his classic experiments, Asch (1952) asked subjects to decide which of three lines of different length most closely matched a fourth (Figure 5.3). The difference between the line lengths was clearly obvious; subjects had no difficulty making the correct match. Asch then arranged a version of the experiment in which the lines to match were presented in a group setting, with each person calling out the answer one at a time.

In this second version of the experiment, all but one of the subjects were secret accomplices of Asch's, who intentionally attempted to deceive the outsider in the group by saying that two lines— *clearly* unequal in length—were identical. The unwitting subject, always one of the last to call out an answer, was placed under group pressure to conform, even though the other answers given were wrong. Amazingly, in the experimental groups, one third of the subjects gave the same wrong answer as that put forth by Asch's accomplices. In the experiments where no intentionally misleading answers were given, the subjects offered an incorrect response less than 1% of the time. Although

■ **FIGURE 5.3** The Asch Experiments: A Study in Conformity

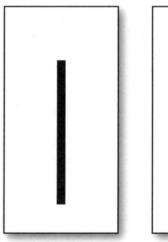

Positional power: Power that stems officially from the leadership position itself.

Personal power: Power that derives from a leader's personality.

the duped subjects sometimes stammered and fidgeted, they still yielded to the unspoken pressure to conform to the group's decision. Asch's experiments demonstrated that many people are willing to discount their own perceptions rather than contradict group consensus. How do you think you would respond if you were the subject in such an experiment (and had not read this account first)? Would you conform or dissent?

OBEDIENCE TO AUTHORITY Another classic study of conformity was Stanley Milgram's (1963) research. One of his specific research questions was what allowed ordinary German citizens to go along with and even participate in the mass killing of Jews, Romani (also known as Gypsies), homosexuals, the disabled, and others who were judged socially undesirable by the Nazis in World War II. Obedience is a kind of conformity. Milgram thus desired to find the boundaries of obedience, to identify how far a person would be willing to go if an authority figure encouraged him or her to complete a given task. His study produced some chilling answers.

Most people would say that they are not capable of committing horrendous acts, yet Stanley Milgram's famous experiment illustrated how obedience to authority can lead people to commit actions that they know are injurious. ■

In Milgram's experiment male volunteers were told by an actor dressed in a white lab coat (an authoritative prop) to read aloud pairs of words from a list someone in another room was to memorize and repeat. Whenever the "learner" made a mistake, the subject was instructed to give him an electric shock by flipping a switch on a fake but official-looking machine. With each mistake, the voltage (intensity) of the shock was to be increased, until it eventually reached the highest levels, visibly labeled "450 volts—danger, severe shock."

In reality the learner never received any electric shocks but reacted audibly and physically as if he had, with cries that grew louder and more pained, pounding on the table, and moving about in his chair (the cries were prerecorded and played back). Meanwhile the "scientist" ordered the subject to proceed with the experiment and continue administering shocks, saying things like "The experiment requires that you continue," even when the learner expressed concern about his "bad heart."

More than half the participants in the study obeyed the commands to keep going, administering electric shocks up to the maximum voltage until nothing but an eerie silence came from the other room. What happened here? How could ordinary, basically good people so easily conform to orders that turned them into potential accomplices to injury or death?

The answer, Milgram found, was deceptively simple: Ordinary people will conform to orders given by someone in a position of power or authority, even if those orders have consequences. Many ordinary Germans who participated in the mass execution of Jews in Nazi concentration camps did so on

the ground that they were "just following orders." Milgram's research, though ethically questionable, produced sobering findings for those who believed that only "other people" would bow to authority.

A recent film called *Compliance* follows real-life events that unfold as a result of a prank phone caller. The prankster, an unidentified male, called fast-food establishments, often pretending to be a police officer. He would enlist the aid of the store manager to help him crack an ostensibly important case. Once the manager agreed to help the "officer," the prankster would tell the store manager to perform increasingly invasive acts against a female employee. Obeying a figure he believed to be a legitimate (though unseen) authority, in several instances managers strip-searched female employees (Kavner, 2012; Wolfson, 2005).

In another example of obedience to authority even in the face of dangerous consequences, the Edgewood Arsenal in Maryland was the site of top-secret military experiments involving over 7,000 U.S. soldiers from the 1950s through the 1970s. Many soldiers volunteered for duty at Edgewood unaware of, or even deceived about, exactly what would be asked of them. Once at Edgewood, they were informed that if they refused to participate in any "required" duties they could face jail time for insubordination or receive an unsatisfactory review in their

Stanley Milgram's Work

Conformity

While humorous, this parody of groupthink points to group members' reduced inclination to differ from the consensus of the group. ■

personnel files, and during the Vietnam era some were reportedly threatened with being sent to war. The soldiers were experimented on repeatedly, often exposed to a variety of dangerous chemical and biological toxins, including sarin gas, VX gas, LSD, tranquilizers, and barbiturates, some of which produced extended and untreated hallucinations (Martin, 2012; Young & Martin, 2012).

The Edgewood Arsenal experiments highlight the point that individuals, when encountering those in a position of authority, are likely to comply with any demands out of fear of the repercussions, even if what they are asked to do seems dangerous or even potentially lethal to others—or to themselves.

GROUPTHINK Common sense tells us that "two minds are better than one." But, as our opening story on the abuse scandal at Penn State University suggests, pressures to go along with the crowd sometimes result in worse decisions rather than creative new solutions to problems. You have probably had the experience of feeling uneasy about voicing your opinion while in a group struggling with a difficult decision. Irving L. Janis (1972, 1989; Janis & Mann, 1977) coined the term **groupthink** to describe *what happens when members of a group ignore anything that goes against the group consensus.* Not only does groupthink frequently embarrass potential dissenters into conforming, but it can also produce a shift in perceptions so that alternative

possibilities are ruled out without being seriously considered. Groupthink may facilitate reaching a quick consensus, but the consensus may also be ill chosen.

Janis undertook historical research to see whether groupthink had characterized U.S. foreign policy decisions, including the infamous Bay of Pigs invasion of Cuba in 1961. Newly elected president John F. Kennedy inherited from the preceding administration a plan to provide U.S. supplies and air cover while an invasion force of exiled Cubans parachuted into Cuba's Bay of Pigs, to liberate the country from Fidel Castro's communist government. A number of Kennedy's top advisers were certain the plan was fatally flawed but refrained from countering the emerging consensus. As it happened, the invasion was a disaster. The ill-prepared exiles were immediately defeated, Kennedy suffered public embarrassment, and the cold war standoff between the Soviet Union and the United States deepened.

How could Kennedy's advisers, people of strong will and independent judgment educated at elite universities, have failed to adequately voice their concerns? Janis identified a number of possible reasons. For one, they were hesitant to disagree with the president lest they lose his favor. Nor did they want to diminish group harmony in a crisis situation where teamwork was all-important. In addition, there was little time to consult outside experts who might offer radically different perspectives. All these circumstances contributed to a single-minded pursuit of the president's initial ideas, rather than an effort to generate effective alternatives.

Think about your own experiences working with groups either at work, on a class project, or in a campus organization. Have you ever "gone along to get along" or felt pressured to choose a particular path of action in spite of your own reservations? Or, conversely, did you choose to refuse in spite of the pressure? What factors affected your decision in either case?

ECONOMIC, CULTURAL, AND SOCIAL CAPITAL

One of the most important additions to the sociological study of groups is the contribution of the French school of thought known as **structuralism,** or *the idea that there exists an overarching structure within which culture and other aspects of society must be understood.* A leading proponent, the French sociologist Pierre Bourdieu, provides an analytical framework that extends our understanding of the way group relationships shape our lives. Bourdieu argues that several forms of *capital*—that is,

. . . .

Groupthink: A process by which the members of a group ignore ways of thinking and plans of action that go against the group consensus.

Structuralism: The idea of an overarching structure within which culture and other aspects of society must be understood.

Groupthink and Cognitive Perceptions

Groupthink Defined

social currency—stem from our membership in different groups. These forms of capital are of importance in the reproduction of social status and position.

Economic capital is the most basic and consists of *money and material that can be used to produce goods and services.* Depending upon the social class you are born into and the development of your own career, you will have more or less access to economic capital and ability to take advantage of this form of capital. Another form is *cultural capital,* or your interpersonal skills, habits, manners, linguistic styles, tastes, and lifestyles. In some social circles, having refined table manners and speaking with a distinctive accent place a person in a social class that enhances his or her access to jobs, social activities, and friendship groups.

Friendship groups and other social contacts also provide **social capital**, *the personal connections and networks that enable people to accomplish their goals and extend their influence* (Bourdieu, 1984; Coleman, 1990; Putnam, 2000). College students who join fraternities and sororities expect and trust that their "brothers" or "sisters" will help them get through the often challenging social and academic experiences of college. Many new—as well as more seasoned—employees (and prospective employees) join LinkedIn, a social media site that offers possibilities for people to expand their professional social networks, a key part of nurturing social capital.

Social capital, while strongly influenced by socioeconomic class status, may also be related to gender, to race, and intersectionally to both gender and race (McDonald & Day, 2010; McDonald, Lin, & Ao, 2009). In a study of social networks and their relationship to people's information about job leads, sociologists Matt Huffman and Lisa Torres (2002) found that women benefited from being part of networks that included more men than women; those who had more women in their social network had a diminished probability of hearing about a good job lead. Interestingly, the predominance of men or women in a man's social network made no discernible difference. The researchers suggested that perhaps women were less likely to learn about job leads and, notably, that when they knew of leads, they were more likely to pass them along to men than to other women. Similarly, research by McDonald and Mair (2010) and Trimble and Kmec (2011) explores issues of networking in relation to women's career opportunities over their lifetime and also the extent to which networks aid women in attaining jobs, each finding that social capital in the form of networks of relations has very distinct and important repercussions for women. The advent of professional networking sites such as LinkedIn, which we discussed above, offers sociologists the potential opportunity to expand this research

We often hear the phrase "It's not what you know; it's who you know." Indeed, history shows that social networks are important. Former president George W. Bush comes from an influential political family, and he made key connections while a student at Yale University, an institution that has educated many U.S. leaders. ■

to see if and how gender affects social networks and their professional benefits, with research from the field of psychology indicating that job networking sites including LinkedIn play an important role in the job acquisition process (Bohnert & Ross, 2010).

Economic, cultural, and social capital confer benefits to individuals at least in part through their membership in a particular social group. Characteristics such as class, race, ethnicity, and gender, among others, can have an effect on the capital one has. Membership in organizations, like a fraternity or an exclusive golf club, can offer powerful network access. These are just small examples, however, of the kinds of organizations that shape our lives and society, sometimes to our benefit,

. . . .

Economic capital: Money and material that can be used to produce goods and services.

Social capital: The social knowledge and connections that enable people to accomplish their goals and extend their influence.

Social Networking

sometimes to our disadvantage. Below we look at organizations and their societal functions through the sociological lens.

ORGANIZATIONS

People frequently band together to pursue activities they could not readily accomplish by themselves. A principal means for accomplishing such cooperative actions is the **organization**, *a group with an identifiable membership that engages in concerted collective actions to achieve a common purpose* (Aldrich & Marsden, 1988). An organization can be a small primary group, but it is more likely to be a larger, secondary one: Universities, churches, armies, and business corporations are all examples of organizations. Organizations are a central feature of all societies, and their study is a core concern of sociology today.

Organizations tend to be highly formal in modern industrial and postindustrial society. A **formal organization** is *rationally designed to achieve particular objectives by means of explicit rules, regulations, and procedures.* Examples could include a state or county's Department of Motor Vehicles or the federal Internal Revenue Service. As Max Weber (1919/1946) first recognized almost a hundred years ago, modern societies are increasingly dependent on formal organizations. One reason is that formality is often a requirement for legal standing. For a college or university to be legally accredited, for example, it must satisfy explicit written standards governing everything from faculty hiring to fire safety. Today, formal organizations are the dominant form of organization across the globe.

TYPES OF FORMAL ORGANIZATIONS

Thousands of different kinds of formal organizations serve every imaginable purpose. Sociology seeks to simplify this diversity by identifying the principal types. Amitai Etzioni (1975) grouped organizations into three main types based on the reasons people join them: utilitarian, coercive, and normative. In practice, of course, many organizations, especially utilitarian and normative, include elements of more than one type.

Utilitarian organizations are *those that people join primarily because of some material benefit they expect to receive in return for membership.* For example, you probably enrolled in college not only because you want to expand your knowledge and skills but also because you know that a college degree will help you get a better job and earn more money later in life. In exchange, you have paid tuition and fees, devoted countless hours to studying, and agreed to submit to the rules that govern your school, your major, and your courses. Many of the organizations people join are utilitarian, particularly those in which they earn a living, such as corporations, factories, and banks.

Coercive organizations are *those in which members are forced to give unquestioned obedience to authority.* People are often forced to join coercive organizations because they have been either sentenced to punishment (prisons) or remanded for mandatory treatment (mental hospitals or drug treatment centers). Coercive organizations may use force or the threat of force, and sometimes confinement, to ensure compliance with rules and regulations. Guards, locked doors, barred windows, and monitoring are all features of jails, prisons, and mental hospitals. Sometimes we may join coercive organizations voluntarily, although once a member, you may not have the option of leaving as you desire. An example of this is the military; while enlisting is voluntary in the United States, once you join, you are subject to close discipline and the demand for submission to authority in a rigidly hierarchical structure. These coercive institutions are examples of *total institutions,* which you read about in Chapter 4. By encompassing all aspects of people's lives, total institutions can radically alter people's thinking and behavior.

Normative organizations, or *voluntary associations, are those that people join of their own will, to pursue a morally worthwhile goal without expectation of material reward.* Belonging to such organizations may offer social prestige or moral or personal satisfaction. (Of course, such organizations may also serve utilitarian purposes, such as a charitable group you join partly to hand out your business card and boost your chances for monetary gain.)

The United States is a nation of normative organization joiners. Individuals affiliate with volunteer church groups, such as the YMCA, Hillel, and Women's Missionary Society of the African Methodist Episcopal Church; charitable organizations such as the Red Cross; social clubs and professional organizations; politically oriented groups such as the National Association for the Advancement of Colored People (NAACP); and self-help groups such as Alcoholics Anonymous and Overeaters Anonymous. According to the National Center for Charitable Statistics (2009) there are over 110,000 civic leagues and social welfare organizations, 77,000 fraternal societies, and 57,000 social and recreational clubs nationwide. They provide their members with

. . . .

Organization: A group with an identifiable membership that engages in concerted collective actions to achieve a common purpose.

Formal organization: An organization that is rationally designed to achieve its objectives, often by means of explicit rules, regulations, and procedures.

Utilitarian organization: An organization that people join primarily because of some material benefit they expect to receive in return for membership.

Coercive organization: An organization in which people are forced to give unquestioned obedience to authority.

Normative organization: An organization that people join of their own will to pursue a morally worthwhile goal, without expectation of material reward; sometimes called a voluntary association.

Bureaucracy

Voluntary Associations

INEQUALITY MATTERS

AFRICAN AMERICAN WOMEN IN VOLUNTARY ASSOCIATIONS

Antislavery organizations are one kind of normative, or voluntary, association that played a little known but pivotal role in the fight for civil rights among African Americans before and during the Civil War. Abolitionist organizations, such as the Anti-Slavery Societies in the northern states, fought slavery before the war and provided charity for the poor throughout much of the 19th century. African Americans were active members and leaders of many of these organizations. Philadelphia alone had almost 60 African American charitable associations in the 1830s, many run by Black women. After the Civil War, these organizations widened their focus to include teaching as well as charity, fighting for the rights of Blacks, and ending lynching in the South.

One crusader, Margaret Murray Washington (1865–1925), exemplifies the efforts of these organizations. Born to a poverty-stricken family in Macon, Georgia, she began teaching school at the age of 14, earned a degree from Fisk University in 1889, and became affiliated with the Tuskegee Institute, where she married the prominent Black educator Booker T. Washington. She was later president of the National Association of Colored Women. In the following passage, Ruskin and Washington (1929/1973) describe a particular goal, antilynching, of the National Association of Colored Women's Clubs, which in 1929 had 300,000 members in the United States and other countries:

> Our club women work incessantly to help mold sentiment against lynching, and

African American women played an important role in protesting injustices and advocating for civil rights before the start of the Civil War. The women pictured here are picketing the White House in protest of a quadruple lynching in Georgia. ■

although it is a slow process, there is a strong and growing feeling against this form of punishment for any cause whatsoever. . . . The Georgia State Federation of White Women's Clubs in their last convention came out strongly in favor of law and order as against mob violence and lynching. When the Women's State Federation of other Southern States takes a stand against this evil, the men in authority in these States will see to it that lynching is put down and not until then will it be done. It is women's work now as always. (pp. 445–447)

These associations represented unions of citizens who individually were voiceless in a society that oppressed them based on race. Together, however, they were part of a network of associations that asserted strong positions against racial inequality and, over time, saw the fruits of their labor realized in civil rights legislation.

THINK IT THROUGH

■ *How do the actions of voluntary associations fighting for a cause look in the digital age? How do the tools of social media enhance social action? How might they detract from it?*

The individuals here are part of a total institution, in which they are subject to complete regimentation and control of their daily activities by an authoritative body. Whether eating, exercising, or partaking in therapy or education, they are closely monitored and managed. ■

a sense of connectedness while enabling them to accomplish personal and moral goals. They have even played a central but little recognized role in U.S. history, fighting slavery and asserting the rights of African Americans after the Civil War (see the *Inequality Matters* box on page 113).

Normative organizations may also erect barriers based on social class, race, ethnicity, and gender. Those traditionally excluded from such organizations, including women, Latinos, Native Americans, African Americans, and other people of color, have, in response, formed their own voluntary associations. Although it may seem that they, too, are exclusionary, these groups have a different basis for their creation—remedying social inequality. Social justice, as a result, is often their primary concern.

Below we shift our gaze from voluntary and coercive organizations to a phenomenon that is familiar to most of us—the bureaucracy. While we have some control over our membership in many organizations, we are all—as U.S. residents, taxpayers, students, or recipients of mortgage or college loans, among others—subject to the reach of modern bureaucracy.

BUREAUCRACIES

The authority structure of most large organizations today is bureaucratic. In this section we will look at the modern bureaucracy—the way it operates and some of its shortcomings.

We will also see how these structures have been modified or reformed to offer an alternative type of organization.

Max Weber (1919/1946) was the first sociologist to examine the characteristics of bureaucracy in detail. Weber defined **bureaucracy** as *a type of formal organization based on written procedural rules, arranged into a clear hierarchy of authority, and staffed by full-time paid officials*. Although Weber showed that bureaucracies could be found in many different societies throughout history, he argued that they became a dominant form of social organization only in modern society, where they had or would come to touch key aspects of our daily lives. In particular, Weber suggested that bureaucracies were a highly rational form of organization because they were devised to achieve organizational goals with the greatest degree of efficiency—that is, to optimize the achievement of a task.

Note that when Weber characterized bureaucracies as *rational*, he did not assume that they would always be *reasonable*. By rational, he meant that they were organized *based on knowable rules and regulations that laid out a particular path to a goal rather than on general or abstract principles or ideologies*. As we know from our own contacts with bureaucratic structures—whether they involve long waits on the phone to speak to a human being

· ·

Bureaucracy: A type of formal organization based on written procedural rules, arranged into a clear hierarchy of authority, and staffed by full-time paid officials.

rather than a computer or the confusing pursuit of the correct person to turn to in a critical student loan application—they are not, in fact, always reasonable.

To better understand the modern bureaucracy, Weber (1919/1946) identified what he referred to as the *ideal type* of this form of organization: the characteristics that would be found if the quintessential bureaucracy existed (Figure 5.4). While Weber recognized that no actual bureaucracy necessarily possesses all of the characteristics he identifies, he argued that, by clearly articulating them, he was describing a standard against which actual bureaucracies could be judged and understood.

WRITTEN RULES AND REGULATIONS

The routine operation of the bureaucracy is governed by written rules and regulations, whose purpose is to ensure that universal standards govern all aspects of bureaucratic behavior. Typically rules govern everything from hiring employees to reporting an absence due to illness. They are usually spelled out in an organizational manual or handbook, and now often on an employee human resources website, which describes in detail the requirements of each organizational position. While these rules and regulations can be lengthy and complex, they are, in theory, knowable, and the expectation is that those who work in and seek the services of a given organization will adhere to them—sometimes even if they don't seem to make sense!

- **Specialized offices.** Positions in bureaucracies are organized into "offices" that create a division of labor within the organization. The duties of each office, such as bookkeeping or paying invoices, are described in the organizational manual. Each office specializes in one particular bureaucratic function to the exclusion of all others. Such specialization is one of the reasons that bureaucratic organization is said to be efficient; bureaucratic officials are supposed to become experts at their particular tasks, efficient cogs in a vast machine. The efficiency is, ideally, beneficial for the organization and its clients. If you are seeking to clear up a problem with your tuition bill, you will not visit the admissions office because you know the expert advice you seek is to be found in student accounts.
- **Hierarchy.** Bureaucracies are organized according to the vertical principle of hierarchy, so that each office has authority over one or more lower-level offices, and each in turn is responsible to a higher-level office. At the top, the leader of the organization stands alone; in the well-known words of former U.S. President Harry S. Truman, "the buck stops here." The organizational chart of a bureaucracy therefore generally looks like a pyramid. Again, efficiency is achieved by having a knowable hierarchy of power that governs an organization.
- **Impersonality in record keeping.** Within the bureaucracy, communications are likely to be formal and impersonal.

■ **FIGURE 5.4** The Ideal Typical Bureaucracy

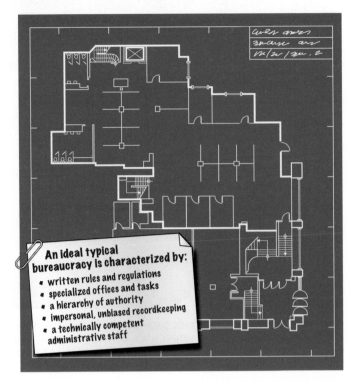

An ideal typical bureaucracy is characterized by:
- written rules and regulations
- specialized offices and tasks
- a hierarchy of authority
- impersonal, unbiased recordkeeping
- a technically competent administrative staff

Written forms—"paperwork" or the electronic equivalent—substitute for more personalized human contact, because bureaucracies must maintain written records or databases of all important actions. Modern computer technology has vastly increased the ability of organizations to maintain and access records. In some ways, this is an advantage—for example, when you register for classes via smartphone instead of standing in line for hours waiting to fill out forms. On the other hand, you may regret the loss of human contact and the inflexibility of the process, however efficient it may be. This "impersonality" also, ideally, has the effect of supposedly ensuring that all clients are treated equally and efficiently rather than capriciously, although bureaucracies are often easiest to navigate for those people with greater economic, social, or cultural capital.

- **A technically competent administrative staff.** Bureaucracies generally seek to employ a qualified professional staff. Anyone who by training and expertise is able to perform the duties of the offices of the organization is deemed eligible to fill the office. Work in the bureaucracy is a full-time job, ideally providing a career path for the bureaucrat, who must demonstrate the training and expertise necessary to fill each successive position. In its "ideal" form, the system is a meritocracy—that is, a bureaucracy in which positions are filled on the basis of a person's merit or qualifications typically demonstrated by performance on competitive exams, rather than by knowing the "right" people. In

Today, a great deal of bureaucratic paperwork is done online. If we wish to apply for a passport, open a bank account, or renew a license, many of these tasks can be accomplished in front of a computer screen. What are some of the positive functions of this development? What are some dysfunctions? ■

As you think about this metaphor of the iron cage, consider encounters with bureaucratic structures that you have had: If you've ever had the feeling that solving a personal or family problem with something like tuition, taxes, or immigration would require speaking to a human being with the power to make a decision or to see that your case is an exception in some way—but no such human was available!—then you can see what Weber meant. We make rules and regulations to keep order and to have a set of knowable guidelines for action and decisions, but what happens when the rules and regulations and their enforcement become the *ends* of an organization rather than *a means to an end*? Then we are in the iron cage.

Sociologists have identified a number of specific problems that plague bureaucracies, many of which may be familiar and could be thought of as representing *irrationalities of rationality*:

practice, however—as is true of the other characteristics listed above—an actual bureaucracy is unlikely to fully meet this standard. In fact, getting hired into the organization and advancing in it are likely to be influenced not strictly by objective criteria such as education and experience, but also by such social variables as age, gender, race, and social connections.

BUREAUCRACIES: A CRITICAL EVALUATION

Bureaucracies popularly evoke images of "paper pushers" and annoying red tape. In their studies of bureaucracy, sociologists, too, have had much to say about this form of organization, with mixed conclusions. Max Weber recognized that bureaucracies can, indeed, provide organizational efficiency in getting the job done. In contrast to earlier organizational forms, many of which filled offices through nepotism, bribes, or other non–merit-based forms of promotion, and were founded to serve the needs of a leader or small elite, modern bureaucracies have many redeeming qualities in spite of the frustrations they cause.

At the same time, Weber argued that a bureaucracy may create what he termed an *iron cage*—a prison of rules and regulations from which there is little escape (DiMaggio & Powell, 1983; Weber, 1904–1905/1977). The iron cage, which Weber memorably described as having the potential to be a "polar night of icy darkness," is a metaphor. We become "caged" in bureaucratic structures when we build them to serve us (as rules and regulations would ideally do), but they ultimately come to trap us by denying our humanity, creativity, and autonomy.

- **Waste and incompetence.** As long as administrators appear to be doing their jobs—filing forms, keeping records, responding to memos, and keeping busy—nobody really wants to question whether the organization as a whole is performing effectively or efficiently. Secure in their positions, bureaucrats may become inefficient, incompetent, and often indifferent to the clients they are supposed to serve.

- **Trained incapacity.** We have all known bureaucrats who "went by the book," even when the situation clearly called for fresh thinking. Thorstein Veblen (1899), a U.S. sociologist and contemporary of Weber's, termed this tendency *trained incapacity*, a learned inability to exercise independent thought. However intelligent they may otherwise be, such bureaucrats make poor judgments when it comes to decisions not covered by the rule book. They become so obsessed with following the rules and regulations that they lose the ability and flexibility to respond to new situations.

- **Goal displacement.** Bureaucracies may lose sight of the original goals they were created to accomplish. Large corporations such as General Motors or Hewlett-Packard or government organizations such as the Department of Homeland Security employ thousands of "middle managers" whose job it is to handle the paperwork required in manufacturing automobiles or computers, or in protecting the country. Perhaps understandably, such people may over time become preoccupied with getting their own jobs done and, driven by the need to ensure the continuation of a particular practice or program linked to their position, eventually lose touch with the larger goals of the organization. The organization then becomes a sanctuary for bureaucrats who know and care little about making high-quality cars or computers. This process adds to costs, lowers efficiency, and may prove detrimental to corporations that compete in a global economy and governments seeking to accomplish goals and stay within tight budgets.

Although Weber presented a sometimes chilling picture of bureaucracies operating as vast, inhuman machines, we all recognize that, in practice, there is often a human face behind the counter. In fact, much important work done in bureaucratic organizations is achieved through informal channels and personal ties and connections rather than official channels, as Peter Blau showed (Blau & Meyer, 1987). For example, students who wish to register late for a class may avoid having to get half a dozen signatures if they know the professor or a staff person in the registrar's office. However, because of the shortcomings of bureaucratic forms of organization, some theorists have argued for the development of alternative organizational forms. We will discuss some of these after looking at the relationship between bureaucracy and democracy.

BUREAUCRACY AND DEMOCRACY

Max Weber argued that bureaucracies were an inevitable outgrowth of modern society, with its large-scale organizations, complex institutional structure, and concern with rationality and efficiency. Yet many observers have viewed bureaucracy as a stifling, irrational force that dominates our lives and threatens representative government. In *Les Employés,* French novelist Honoré de Balzac, who popularized the term *bureaucracy*, called it "the giant power wielded by pigmies" and a "fussy and meddlesome" government. Do bureaucracies inevitably lead to a loss of freedom and erosion of democracy? Are there more humanistic alternatives to bureaucracies that allow freer, more fulfilling participation in the organization? Let's look briefly at the views of sociologist Robert Michels on the incompatibility between democracy and bureaucracy, then see what some people have done to try to reform this organizational structure.

Michels (1876–1936), another contemporary of Weber's, argued that bureaucracy and democracy are fundamentally at odds. He observed that the Socialist Party in Germany, originally created to democratically represent the interests of workers, had become an oligarchy, a form of organization in which a small number of people exert great power. For him this was an example of what he termed the **iron law of oligarchy,** an inevitable

. . . .

Iron law of oligarchy: Robert Michels's theory that there is an inevitable tendency for large-scale bureaucratic organizations to become ruled undemocratically by a handful of people.

tendency for large-scale bureaucratic organizations to become ruled undemocratically by a handful of people. (*Oligarchy* means the rule of a small group over many people.)

Following Weber, Michels argued that in large-scale bureaucratic organizations, the closer you are to the top, the greater the concentration of power. People typically get to the top because they are ambitious, hard-driving, and effective in managing the people below, or because they have economic and social capital to trade for proximity to power. Once there, leaders increase their social capital through specialized access to information, resources, and influential people, access that reinforces their power. They also often appoint subordinates who are loyal supporters and thus further enhance their position. Such leaders may come to regard the bureaucracy as a means to meet their own needs or those of their social group. The democratic purposes of an organization may become subordinate to the needs of the dominating group.

Since all modern societies require large-scale organizations to survive, Michels believed that democracies—or, in some cases, organizations—may sow the seeds of their own destruction by breeding bureaucracies that eventually grow into undemocratic oligarchies. While there are few signs that, for instance, the United States, which has many large-scale bureaucracies, is drifting from democracy, one could make a case that institutions like the U.S. Congress show some tendencies to act in the interests of political parties or powerful members rather than the interests of constituents. For example, bills on disaster relief or unemployment insurance may be held up when a party leader feels that stalling the bill might confer political advantage on his or her party.

In response to what they feel is the stifling effect of bureaucratic organizations, some people have sought alternatives designed to allow greater freedom and more fulfilling participation in these organizations. For example, as part of the sweeping countercultural spirit of the late 1960s and early 1970s, many youthful activists joined collectives, small organizations that operate by cooperation and consensus. Food cooperatives, employee-run newspapers and health clinics, and "free schools" sprang up as organizations that sought to operate by consensus rather than by bureaucracy. Members of these organizations shunned hierarchy, avoided a division of labor based on expertise, and happily sacrificed efficiency in favor of more humanistic relationships.

The founders of these organizations believed they were reviving more personal organizational arrangements that could better enable us to reach our goals as a society. Although these organizations initially met with some success and left a legacy, they also confronted a larger society in which more conventional forms of organization effectively shut them out.

Members of such organizations as the food cooperatives and employee-run newspapers and health clinics of the 1960s and 1970s favored such values as cooperation and service over the more competitive and materialistic values of the larger society. In the exuberance of that period, members of collectives believed they were forging a radically new kind of antibureaucratic organization.

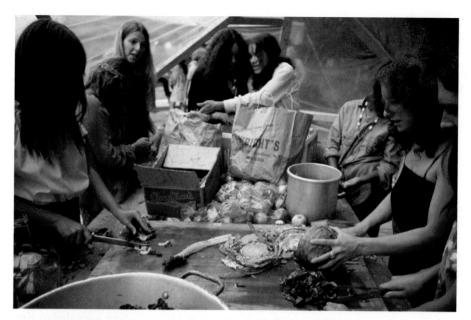

Food collective, anyone? An alternative to a bureaucratic style of managing an organization, the "collective" emphasizes cooperation, consensus, and humanistic relations. The women here are preparing a meal as part of the activities of their organization, called the "Hog Farm," in Woodstock, New York. ■

In her examination of early collectives, sociologist Joyce Rothschild-Whitt (1979) studied several that self-consciously rejected bureaucracy in favor of more cooperative forms. In one health clinic, for example, all jobs were shared (to the extent legally possible) by all members: Doctors would periodically answer telephones and clean the facility, while nurses and paramedical staff would conduct examinations and interview patients. While the doctors were paid somewhat more than the other staff members, the differences were not large and were the subject of negotiation by everyone who worked at the clinic.

As long as the collectives remained small, they were able to maintain their founders' values. On the other hand, vastly reduced pay differentials between professional and nonprofessional staff, job sharing, and collective decision making often made it difficult to compete for employees with organizations that shared none of these values (Rothschild-Whitt, 1979). Doctors, for example, could make much more money in conventional medical practice, without being expected to answer telephones or sweep the floor. Over time the original cooperative values tended to erode, and many of the new organizations came to resemble conventional organizations in the larger society. Still, more than two decades after Rothschild-Whitt studied them, a number of these original groups still exist. Although they may have lost some of their collective zeal, they still operate more cooperatively than most traditional organizations.

Sociological research suggests that when these new groups grow in size, they too will run the risk of spawning bureaucratic structures and losing their more personal, humanistic orientation—just as did the original collectives of the 1960s.

THE GLOBAL ORGANIZATION

Organizations from multinational corporations to charitable foundations span the globe and increasingly contribute to what some sociologists believe is a "homogenization" of the world's countries (McNeely, 1995; Neyazi, 2010; Scott & Meyer, 1994; Thomas, Meyer, Ramirez, & Boli, 1987). You can listen to the same music, employ the same Internet search engine, see the same films, and eat the same meals (if you wish) in Bangalore and Baku as you do in Berlin and Boston.

Global organizations are not new. The Hanseatic League, a business alliance between German merchants and cities, dominated trade in the North and Baltic Seas from the mid-12th to the mid-18th centuries. The British East India Company virtually owned India and controlled the vast bulk of trade throughout the Far East for several centuries. In 1919, following World War I, the League of Nations was formed, uniting the most economically and militarily powerful nations of the world in an effort to ensure peace and an end to war. When Germany withdrew and began expanding its borders throughout Europe, however, the league dissolved.

After World War II, a new effort at international governance was made in the form of the United Nations (UN), begun in 1945. The UN is still important and active today: Its power is limited, but its influence has grown. It not only mediates disputes between nations; it is ever present in international activities ranging from fighting hunger and HIV/AIDS to mobilizing peacekeepers and intervening to address conflicts and their consequences.

International organizations exist in two major forms: those consisting of national governments and those consisting of private organizations. We will consider each separately.

INTERNATIONAL GOVERNMENTAL ORGANIZATIONS

The first type of global organization is the **international governmental organization (IGO)** established by treaties between governments. Most IGOs *exist to facilitate and regulate trade*

- -

International governmental organization (IGO): An international organization established by treaties between governments for purposes of commerce, security, promotion of social welfare and human rights, and environmental protection.

IGOs

■ FIGURE 5.5 Increase in Number of IGOs, 1909–2011

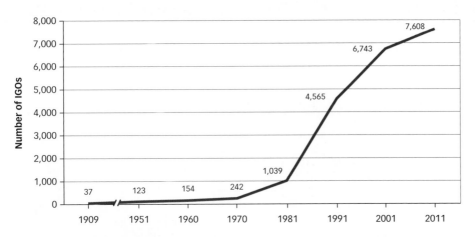

SOURCE: Union of International Associations. (2011). Historical overview of number of international organizations by type, 1909–2011. *Yearbook of International Organizations, 2011/2012 Edition.* Herndon, VA: Brill.

between the member countries, promote national security (both the League of Nations and the United Nations were created after highly destructive world wars), *protect social welfare or human rights, or, increasingly, ensure environmental protection.*

Some of the most powerful IGOs today were created to unify national economies into large and powerful trading blocs. One of the most complex IGOs is the European Union (EU), whose rules now govern 27 countries in Europe. Six additional countries have applied for entry. The EU was formed to create a single European economy, in which businesses could operate freely across borders in search of markets and labor, and workers could move freely in search of jobs without having to go through customs or show passports at border crossings. EU members have common economic policies, and 12 of them share a single currency (the euro). Not all Europeans welcome economic unity, however, since it means their countries must surrender some of their economic power to the EU as a whole. Being economically united by a single currency also means the economic problems felt by one country are distributed among all the other countries to some degree. Thus, in recent years when economic crisis hit Europe, the severe economic woes of Greece, Portugal, and Spain, among others, caused serious problems for stronger EU economies, like that of Germany.

IGOs can also wield considerable military power, provided their member countries are willing to do so. The North Atlantic Treaty Organization (NATO) and the UN, for example,

International nongovernmental organization (INGO): An international organization established by agreements between the individuals or private organizations making up its membership and existing to fulfill an explicit mission.

have sent troops from some of their participating nations into war zones in Iraq, Afghanistan, Liberia, and Kosovo in recent years. Yet because nations ultimately control the use of their own military force, there are limits to the authority of even the most powerful military IGOs, whose strength derives from the voluntary participation of their member nations.

IGOs often reflect inequalities in power between their members. For example, the UN Security Council is responsible for maintaining international peace and security and is therefore the most powerful organization within the UN. Its five permanent members include Britain, the United States, China, France, and Russia, which gives these countries significant clout over the security council's actions. The remaining 10 countries are elected by the UN General Assembly for two-year terms and therefore have less lasting power than the permanent members.

At the beginning of the 20th century, there were only about three dozen IGOs in the world, although data for that time are incomplete. By 1981, when consistent reporting criteria were adopted, there were 1,039; by 2011, the most recent year for which data are available, there were 7,608 (Union of International Associations [UIA], 2011; see also Figures 5.5 and 5.6).

INTERNATIONAL NONGOVERNMENTAL ORGANIZATIONS

The second type of global organization is the **international nongovernmental organization (INGO)**, *established by agreements between the individuals or private organizations making up the membership and existing to fulfill an explicit mission.* Examples include the International Planned Parenthood Federation, the International Sociological Association, the International

■ FIGURE 5.6 Increase in Number of INGOs, 1909–2011

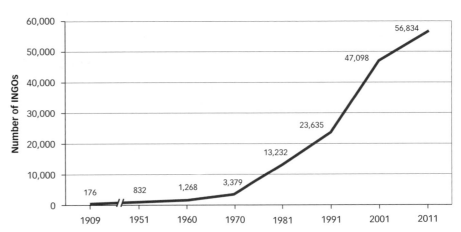

SOURCE: Union of International Associations. (2011). Historical overview of number of international organizations by type, 1909–2011. *Yearbook of International Organizations, 2011/2012 Edition.* Herndon, VA: Brill.

AMNESTY INTERNATIONAL AND THE GLOBAL CAMPAIGN FOR HUMAN RIGHTS

In 2011, Jalila al-Salman, vice president of the Bahrain Teachers' Association (BTA), was arrested, held in solitary confinement for a week, and beaten. Both she and Mahdi Abu Dheeb, president of BTA, were charged with using their positions "to call for a strike by teachers, halting the educational process, 'inciting hatred of the regime' and 'attempting to overthrow the ruling system by force'" (Amnesty International, 2012). Although al-Salman was released on bail, Abu Dheeb has been sentenced to 10 years in prison. In April 2012, he testified that he was being tortured, but his request to be released on bail was denied. Amnesty International (2012), a *normative organization* pursuing global human rights, believes al-Salman and Abu Dheeb are *prisoners of conscience*, arrested for no crime greater than being leaders of the BTA and "peacefully exercising their rights to freedom of expression and assembly." The organization also believes their status as civilians makes their prosecution in military court inappropriate and illegal.

According to Amnesty International (2012), governments in more than 20 countries executed 676 prisoners in 2011—the total is likely much higher. A record number of protests occurred worldwide that year, leading to widespread brutalities, arrests, and torture since 91 countries uphold laws that restrict freedom of expression. Amnesty International also reports that

Arrested in Bahrain for organizing peaceful protests against conditions for teachers and public school children, the woman pictured here, Jalila al-Salman, was arrested for "inciting hatred of the regime." Amnesty International engaged in a human rights campaign to help al-Salman escape injustice. ■

tens of thousands of people throughout the world are imprisoned without having been charged with any crime.

Amnesty International has more than 5,000 affiliated local groups and 2.8 million members in over 150 countries and territories, including 250,000 in the United States. One of its key purposes is to help secure the freedom of people imprisoned because of their political beliefs or actions, especially those in immediate danger of torture or execution. Amnesty International has helped thousands of individual prisoners since it was founded in Britain in 1961. It functions as a global pressure group made up of ordinary citizens. Anyone can join,

pay nominal annual dues, and become part of a global "urgent action network" that is regularly mobilized to send government officials faxes, express mail, and e-mail requests on behalf of prisoners. Amnesty International also sends delegations to countries where abuse is rampant. The reports these delegations write draw worldwide media attention to the world's prisons.

THINK IT THROUGH

■ *In cases of groups like Amnesty International, does size matter? Is a larger group more effective than a smaller collective of activists? What do you think?*

Council of Women, and the environmental group Greenpeace. Global business organizations (GBOs) represent a subtype within the broader INGO literature. The concept of the GBO captures the fluid and highly interconnected nature of our modern, globalized labor market in which employees often interact and communicate with people from other nations and cultures, facilitated by technology and online networks. Like the number of IGOs, the number of INGOs, including GBOs, has increased exponentially in recent years—from fewer than 200 near the beginning of the 20th century to over 20,000 by 1985 and up to 56,834 in 2011 (UIA, 2011).

INGOs are primarily concerned with promoting the global interests of their members, largely through influencing the United Nations, other IGOs, or individual governments. They also engage in research, education, and the spread of information by means of international conferences, meetings, and journals. INGOs have succeeded in shaping the policies of powerful nations.

One prominent (and highly successful) INGO is the International Campaign to Ban Landmines (ICBL). The Committee, along with its founder Jody Williams, was awarded the Nobel Peace Prize in 1997 for its success in getting a majority of the world's countries to agree to a treaty banning the devastating use of land mines. The Nobel Prize commended the Committee for changing "a vision to a feasible reality," adding that "this work has grown into a convincing example of an effective policy for peace that could prove decisive in the international effort for disarmament" (ICBL, 2012).

The ICBL is affiliated with over a thousand other INGOs in some 60 countries. Together they have focused public attention on the dangers posed to civilians of the more than 100 million antipersonnel mines that are a deadly legacy of past wars fought in Europe, Asia, and Africa. These mines are unlike other weapons. They can remain active for decades after a war, terrorizing and trapping whole populations. In Cambodia, for example, fertile croplands have been mined, threatening starvation to farmers who are not willing to risk a misstep that would reduce them or their family to a shower of scraps. The campaign's efforts resulted in a treaty banning the use, production, stockpiling, and transfer of antipersonnel landmines. The treaty, which became international law in March 2012, has been signed and ratified by 160 countries (ICBL, 2012).

Although they are far more numerous than IGOs and have achieved some successes, INGOs have far less power over state actions and policies, since legal power (including enforcement) ultimately lies with governmental organizations and treaties. In the effort to ban landmines, for instance, although most of the major powers in the world signed the treaty, the United States, citing security concerns in Korea, refused, as did Russia. Some INGOs, like Amnesty International and Greenpeace, nonetheless wield considerable influence (see the *Global Issues* box on page 120).

WHY STUDY GROUPS AND ORGANIZATIONS?

You now have a good idea of how the groups and organizations to which you belong exert an influence over your life. They help to determine who you know and, in many ways, who you are. The primary groups of your earliest years were crucial in shaping your sense of self—a sense that changes only very slowly thereafter. Throughout your life, groups are the wellspring of the norms and values that enable and enrich your social life. At the same time, they are the source of nonconforming behavior; the rebel is shaped by group membership as much as the more mainstream and conventional citizen.

Although groups remain central in our lives, group affiliation in the United States is rapidly changing. To some degree, longstanding conventional groups appear to be losing ground. For example, today's typical college students are less likely to join civic groups and organizations—or even vote—than were their parents. At the same time, many are active "netizens," joining and creating groups for both amusement and civic or political causes through such vehicles as Facebook and Twitter.

The global economy and information technology are also redefining group life in ways we can already perceive. For instance, workers in earlier generations spent much of their careers in a relatively small number of long-lasting, bureaucratic organizations; younger workers today are much more likely to be part of a succession of networked, "flexible," and even virtual organizations.

How will these trends affect the quality of our social relationships? Will the blurring between primary and secondary groups continue and expand? Will our growing reliance on social media as a key forum for interaction foster integration or alienation? In our changing social environment, these questions pose important frontiers for sociological analysis.

INGOs in Africa Spoof

INGOs

WHAT CAN I DO WITH A SOCIOLOGY DEGREE?

SKILLS AND CAREERS: UNDERSTANDING AND FOSTERING SOCIAL CHANGE

Social change comes about as a result of shifts in the social order of society. While the changes may be evolutionary or revolutionary in pace, change is inevitable. *Understanding social change* and the factors that underlie its dynamics is key to bringing about positive change, whether at the micro or the macro level. Sociologists study factors that bring about large-scale social change—for instance, shifts in population growth or health, technological progress, economic changes, the mobilization of civil society, or the rise of a charismatic leader—and seek to understand barriers to normative or structural change. They are also interested in factors that affect change or resistance to change in smaller groups and communities. Skills in the areas of leadership, communications, strategic thinking, motivation and mobilization, and advocacy can evolve from knowledge gained in the study of social change. Students interested in social change may also take advantage of internships or practicums in community or political organizations involved in fostering positive change. Supervised practice and the opportunity for reflection on your work nurture skills in the area of social change.

In Chapter 5, we examined the phenomenon of *groupthink*—a form of decision making that elevates consensus and conformity over a critical, multidimensional approach to a problem. Groupthink may be a powerful obstacle to social action and social change. Consider the chapter's opening story, which focused on Penn State University and the decision of a small group of administrators and coaches to keep silent about the pedophilia of a colleague in order to maintain his and the athletic program's respectability. Could a trained leader have overcome the obstacles to action and challenged the consensus of resistance to altering the status quo? Could a skilled advocate have spoken out in favor of interests—like those of the victimized children—that diverged from the perceived interests of the Penn State leaders? Sociologists are deeply interested in social change, which comes in many forms—it can range from normative changes in a small group to massive national political revolutions. Sociology is a discipline dedicated to understanding how change comes about, knowledge that is at the foundation of transformation.

Careers in social change may focus on specific areas, including the environment, labor, human rights, free speech, legal reform, social justice, conflict resolution, poverty, health care, gender equity, economic justice, and corporate ethics. They may be careers in public service (like the federal, state, or local government) or in the private sector (with advocacy organizations or in research-focused organizations, for instance). The understanding of social change and the development of skills associated with fostering positive social change are important in *occupational fields* that include government, social services, nonprofit management and advocacy, education, health care, entrepreneurship, politics and lobbying, community service and volunteerism, and the law, among others. Some specific *job titles* associated with these fields are community outreach and education specialist, policy analyst, advocacy and public policy coordinator, community organizer, labor union organizer, human rights advocate, social worker, lobbyist, social policy analyst, program evaluator, and researcher.

THINK ABOUT CAREERS

■ *What kinds of social, political, economic, ecological, or other issues are of interest to you?*

■ *What kinds of career paths might you envision emerging from your interests?*

▶ *Access additional web links on the student study site to learn more.*

SUMMARY

To test your knowledge further, find additional study material on the Student Study Site at www.sagepub.com/chamblissintro

- The importance of social groups in our lives is one of the salient features of the modern world. Social groups are collections of people who share a sense of common identity and regularly interact with one another based on shared expectations. There are many conceptual ways to distinguish social groups sociologically in order to better understand them.

- Among the most important characteristics of a group is whether or not it serves as a reference group—that is, a group that provides standards by which we judge ourselves in terms of how we think we appear to others, what sociologist Charles Horton Cooley termed the "looking-glass self."

- Group size is another variable that is an important factor in group dynamics. Although their intensity may diminish, larger groups tend to be more stable than smaller groups of two (**dyads**) or three (**triads**) people. While even small groups can develop a formal group structure, larger groups develop a formal structure.

- Formal structures include some people in leadership roles—that is, those group members who are able to influence the behavior of the other members of a group. The most common form of leadership is **transactional**—that is, routine leadership concerned with getting the job done. Less common is **transformational leadership,** which is concerned with changing the very nature of the group itself.

- Leadership roles imply that the role occupant is accorded some power, the ability to mobilize resources and get things done despite resistance. Power derives from two principal sources: the personality of the leader (**personal power**) and the position that the leader occupies (**positional power**). Max Weber highlighted the importance of charisma as a source of leadership as well as leadership deriving from traditional authority (a queen inherits a throne, for example).

- In general people are highly susceptible to group pressure. Many people will do what others tell them to do, even when the consequences involve injury or death to others or oneself.

- Important aspects of groups are the networks that are formed between groups and people in them. Networks constitute a broad source of relationships, direct and indirect, including connections that may be extremely important in business and politics. Women, people of color, and lower-income people typically have less access to the most influential economic and political networks than do upper-class White males in U.S. society.

- As a consequence of access to powerful social networks, there is an unequal division of social capital in society. **Social capital** refers to the knowledge and connections that enable people to cooperate with one another for mutual benefit and extend their influence. Some social scientists have argued that social capital has declined in the United States during the last quarter-century—a process they worry indicates a decline in Americans' commitment to civic engagement.

- **Formal organizations** are organizations that are rationally designed to achieve their objectives by means of rules, regulations, and procedures. They may be **utilitarian, coercive,** or **normative,** depending on the reasons for joining. One of the most common types of formal organizations in modern society is the bureaucracy. **Bureaucracies** are characterized by written rules and regulations, specialized offices, a hierarchical structure, impersonality in record keeping, and a professional administrative staff.

- The **iron law of oligarchy** holds that large-scale organizations tend to concentrate power in the hands of a few people. As a result, even supposedly democratic organizations, when they become large, tend to become undemocratic.

- A number of organizational alternatives to bureaucracies exist. These include collectives, which emphasize cooperation, consensus, and humanistic relations. Networked organizations, which increase flexibility by reducing hierarchy, are like collectives in organization.

- Two important forms of global organization are **international governmental organizations (IGOs)** and **international nongovernmental organizations (INGOs).** Both play an increasingly important role in the world today, and IGOs—particularly the United Nations—may become key organizational actors as the pace of globalization increases.

KEY TERMS

Study terms on the go with the smartphone-friendly key term flashcards, available at **www.sagepub.com/chamblissintro**

dyad, 104

triad, 106

alliances, 106

social closure, 106

transformational leader, 107

transactional leader, 107

legitimate authority, 107

positional power, 108

personal power, 108

groupthink, 110

structuralism, 110

economic capital, 111

social capital, 111

organization, 112

formal organization, 112

utilitarian organization, 112

coercive organization, 114

normative organization, 114

bureaucracy, 114

iron law of oligarchy, 117

international governmental organization (IGO) , 118

international nongovernmental organization (INGO) , 119

DISCUSSION QUESTIONS

1. This chapter began with a look at the Penn State University child abuse scandal through the conceptual lens of *groupthink*. Can you think of a time when a group to which you belonged was making a decision you thought was wrong—ethically, legally, or otherwise—but you went along anyway? How do your experiences confirm or refute Janis's characterization of groupthink and its effects?

2. List the primary and secondary groups of which you are a member. Then make another list of the primary and secondary groups to which you belonged five years ago. Which groups in these two periods were most important for shaping (1) your view of yourself, (2) your political beliefs, (3) your goals in life, and (4) your friendships?

3. Max Weber suggested that bureaucracy, while intended to maximize efficiency in tasks and organizations, could also be highly irrational. He coined the term *the iron cage* to talk about the web of rules and regulations he feared would ensnare modern societies and individuals. On the one hand, societies create rules and regulations to maintain social order and foster the smooth working of institutions such as the state and the economy. On the other hand, members of society may often feel trapped and dehumanized by them. Explain this paradox using an example of your own encounters with an "iron cage" of bureaucracy.

DISCOVER ⓐⓅ STATE STATS

Log-in to the eBook and click on the title to the left for access to State Stats in order to complete the exercise.

Begin this activity by going to the Households and Housing database in State Stats. From there, go to the database listing the average number of persons per household in the United States and by state. Make a note of national statistics for the available time periods. Also note the average for your home state and another state you choose.

Now estimate what you think is the percentage of U.S. households occupied by just a single person. Next find the actual data about the size of this group. What did you find? How closely did the data match your estimate? Using your sociological imagination, hypothesize both the roots of this trend and its implications for U.S. civic life and family life.

STUDENT STUDY SITE

Visit the Student Study Site at **www.sagepub.com/chamblissintro** to access additional study tools, including eFlashcards, web quizzes, video resources, web resources, audio resources, links to SAGE journal, handbook, and research articles, and much more!

6

DEVIANCE AND SOCIAL CONTROL

WHAT DO YOU THINK?

1. Is everyone deviant at least some of the time? Does this make deviance *normal*?
2. How do we know what deviance is? Who has the power to define it?
3. Which modern countries do you think have the highest rates of incarceration in the world?

SOC *VIEW*

Get a closer look with the authors!

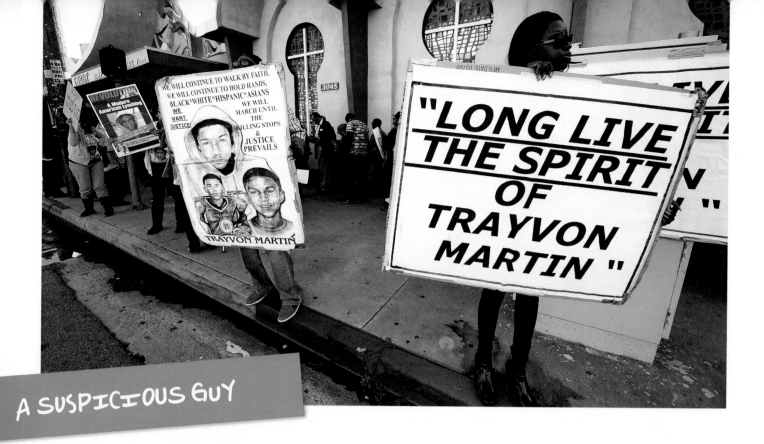

A SUSPICIOUS GUY

"There's a real suspicious guy . . ."

On February 26, 2012, 17-year-old Trayvon Martin was killed inside a gated community in Sanford, Florida, by George Zimmerman, a local community crime watch volunteer (Epps, 2012; Timoney, 2012). After calling police to report Martin as a "suspicious" person—and ignoring police orders not to follow him—Zimmerman confronted the unarmed teenager. Zimmerman alleged that Martin attacked him, and that he retrieved his 9-mm pistol and fired a fatal shot into Martin's chest because he feared for his life (Alcindor, Bello, & Welch, 2012).

The death of Martin, and the reticence of Sanford Police to charge Zimmerman due to Florida's "Stand Your Ground" self-defense law, sparked widespread public outrage, especially among African Americans. The conflict centered on the question of why Zimmerman confronted Martin in the first place. By Zimmerman's account, Martin looked "out of place" in the gated community—despite the fact that he was staying with family friends in the neighborhood—and seemed to be acting suspiciously; in fact, Martin was taking the shortest path home through the rain, cutting through the backyards of some homes. In short, Zimmerman's decision to call 911 and confront Martin came from his perception that Martin looked "suspicious" and was possibly about to engage in some form of unlawful, criminally deviant behavior (excerpt from George Zimmerman's 911 phone call on February 26, 2012; see City of Sanford, Florida, n.d.).

The Trayvon Martin case, which as of this writing was ongoing, highlights one of the most important aspects of the topic of deviance: The perception of deviance almost always relies on a judgment by one individual or group about the behavior or condition of another. As you might imagine, this fundamental fact makes the study of deviance complicated, but also fascinating. As you will see in this chapter, *deviance* is an extremely broad term, encompassing a diverse array of behaviors and conditions, of which only a small part fall into the category of "crime." Likewise, explanations of deviance are as expansive and diverse as the manifestations deviance itself. ■

We begin this chapter by addressing the basic question of how deviant behavior is defined. We follow by examining the array of perspectives that sociologists take in their efforts to understanding deviance in society. Deviance comes in many forms, and the chapter continues with an elaboration of the distinction between deviance and criminal deviance. Finally, we consider how societies exercise social control over those it defines as deviant.

WHAT IS DEVIANT BEHAVIOR?

Deviance refers to *any behavior, practice, or condition, including those that violate cultural norms or societal laws, that results in disapproval, hostility, or sanction if it becomes known.* By contrast a **crime** is *an act defined in the law as punishable by fines, imprisonment, or both.* The definition of deviance highlights several important points. First, deviance is a broad term that can encompass crimes, but also encompasses many noncriminal actions, behaviors, and conditions. Second, deviance is not restricted to a specific group, gender, or age range; both adults and youth can engage in deviance at any time. Third, what is considered deviant can include things that are not consciously chosen, such as medical conditions, illnesses, and physical defects and abnormalities. Finally, this definition suggests that deviance is primarily a label applied by people or groups to other people or groups who engage in certain acts or behaviors or who look a certain way. As such, moral and social, as well as legal, judgments play a role in deciding what is or is not deviant.

Although individuals may disagree about what should be included in the category of "deviance," there is widespread agreement that acts of violence against another person, stealing someone else's property, and sexually molesting children are deviant acts that should be punished by law. In other cases, such as having multiple body piercings, smoking marijuana, and engaging in certain sexual acts, we often lack consensus about what is deviant. This lack of consensus stems directly from the fact that most societies in the modern world are pluralistic.

. . . .

Deviance: Any behavior, action, practice, or condition, including those that violate cultural norms or societal laws, that results in disapproval, hostility, or sanction if it becomes known.

Crime: An act defined in the law as punishable by fines, imprisonment, or both.

Pluralistic societies: Societies made up of many diverse groups with different norms and values.

Polygamy: The act of having multiple wives.

Capital offenses: Crimes considered so heinous they are punishable by death.

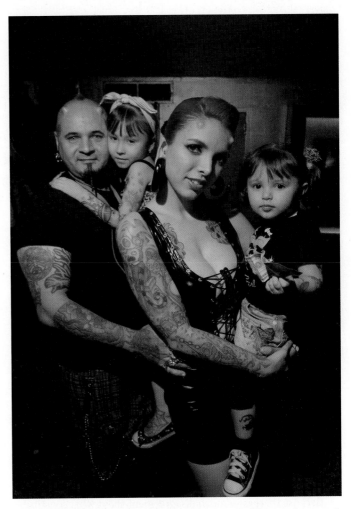

Sociologists suggest that what is labeled deviant depends on cultural norms and is subject to change. Tattoos, once limited to a few subcultures, are widely accepted and displayed with pride by people of different backgrounds, including celebrities, athletes, and military veterans. ■

Pluralistic societies are *made up of many different groups with different norms and values,* which may or may not change over time. In a pluralistic society, what is deviant for one group may be acceptable or normal in another, and even long-held beliefs and practices are sometimes subject to radical transformation over time. For example, in the 1800s the Church of Jesus Christ of Latter-Day Saints (Mormons) practiced **polygamy**—*the act of having multiple wives*—but by the end of that century, polygamy was officially condemned by the church. Similarly, in 2005, after centuries of supporting the execution of juveniles for **capital offenses**, *crimes considered so heinous they are punishable by death,* the U.S. Supreme Court ruled that it was unconstitutional to execute anyone who committed a capital crime before the age of 18. Prior to this ruling, 22 individuals were executed for crimes committed

Self-Identity and Deviance

When was the last time a law enforcement officer arrested you because of what you were wearing to the pool or beach? In this old photo, a woman in Chicago is arrested for wearing a one-piece bathing suit without the "required" leg coverings. What are other examples of how definitions of deviance have evolved over time? ■

humans (Lombroso, 1896) and that they also had different body types than noncriminals (Sheldon, 1949). These early biological theories have been disproven, but the search for biological causes of deviance continues, with some success in individual cases (Wright, Tibbetts, & Daigle, 2008). Advances in medical technology, especially increased use of magnetic resonance imaging (MRI and fMRI), are proving fruitful in enabling researchers to uncover patterns of brain function, physiology, and response unique to some deviant or criminal individuals (Giedd, 2004). However, most modern biological theories do not attribute deviance to biology alone. Instead, they argue that deviance may be the product of an interaction between biological and environmental factors (Denno, 1990; Kanazawa & Still, 2000; Mednick, Moffitt, & Stack, 1987; Stewart, 2000).

One method for testing biological theories is to compare children with their parents to see whether children of parents with deviant lifestyles are more likely to re-create those lifestyles than are children whose parents are not deviant. Research has found that people who suffer from alcoholism and some forms of mental illness (particularly schizophrenia, chronic depression, and bipolar personality disorder) are indeed more likely to have parents with similar problems than are people who do not suffer from them (Dunner, Gershon, & Barrett, 1988; Scheff, 1988).

while under the age of 18 (Death Penalty Information Center, 2010). In each case, norms pertaining to practices or punishment shifted over time, creating a "new normal."

Because there is so much disagreement about what constitutes deviant behavior, we should not be surprised to find that most people deviate from some of the established norms a good deal of the time. As the data in Table 6.1 show, deviance is not limited solely to violating norms like not spitting on the sidewalk—even behaviors defined as criminal are committed much more often than most people might think.

HOW DO SOCIOLOGISTS EXPLAIN DEVIANCE?

What explains deviance? Below we look at a spectrum of theoretical perspectives that seek to explain why people engage in deviance. We can divide these theories into biological, functional, conflict, and symbolic interactionist perspectives.

BIOLOGICAL PERSPECTIVES

Early social scientists were convinced that deviance—from alcoholism to theft to murder—was caused by biological or anatomical abnormalities (Hooton, 1939). For example, some early researchers claimed that *skull configurations of deviant individuals differed from those of nondeviants,* a theory known as **phrenology**. Other theorists claimed that deviants were **atavisms**, *throwbacks to primitive early*

■ **TABLE 6.1** Deviant Behavior Among High School Seniors in the U.S., 2009

Deviant Act	Percent
Robbery	5%
Auto theft	7%
Been arrested	9%
Hurt someone who then needed medical help	13%
Shoplifting	27%
Traffic ticket/warning	30%

SOURCE: Johnston, L. D., Bachman, J. G., & O'Malley, P. M. (2010). *Monitoring the future: Questionnaire responses from the nation's high school seniors, 2009.* Ann Arbor, MI: Institute for Social Research.

Phrenology: A theory that the skull shapes of deviant individuals differ from those of nondeviants.

Atavisms: A word utilized by earlier proponents of biological explanations of deviance that means deviant people are more like primitive humans.

However, studies comparing the frequency of deviance between generations do not always control for the possibility that children of alcoholic, schizophrenic, depressed, or bipolar parents may have learned coping strategies that show up as symptoms of these problems, rather than having inherited a biological predisposition. Children of farmers are more likely to be farmers than are children of urban office workers, but we would not therefore argue that farming is a biologically determined trait. Furthermore, many children of parents who are deviant are not deviant themselves, and many people with deviant lifestyles come from mainstream families (Chambliss & Hass, 2011; Katz & Chambliss, 1995; Scheff, 1988).

Studies that compare similarities in patterns of deviant behavior between twins are often cited as evidence in support of biological theories of deviance and crime. The Danish sociologist Karl Christiansen (1977) examined the life histories of 7,172 twins. Among these, 926 had been convicted of a crime. Christiansen found that 35% of the identical male twins who had been convicted of a crime had twin brothers who had

Cesare Lombroso, an early criminologist, theorized that criminals were throwbacks to primitive humans. Although his theory has been disproved by research, the search for biological causes of criminality continues. ■

also been convicted of a crime. Among male fraternal twins, 21% who had committed a crime had brothers who also had committed a crime (Christiansen, 1977; Mednick, Gabrielli, & Hutchings, 1987). Biological theorists interpret these findings as support for the theory that biological factors contribute to deviant and criminal behavior (Mednick, Gabrielli, & Hutchings, 1987).

Interestingly, critics of biological theories see this evidence as *disproving* the influence of biology. Among both men and women, in the vast majority of cases where one twin has committed a crime, the other twin has not. Moreover, if criminal behavior were genetically determined, we should expect that nearly all twin brothers or sisters of identical twins who are criminal should also be criminals (Katz & Chambliss, 1991). To the extent that identical twins do show similar patterns of deviance as adults, we can attribute these patterns to their common socialization: Identical twins are more likely than other siblings to be treated the same, dressed alike, and sometimes even confused with one another by acquaintances, teachers, and friends (Lyons, 2007; Stewart, 2000).

A more nuanced approach to biological explanations of deviance attempts to incorporate *both* sets of factors. The nature *versus* nurture paradigm is essentially converted to nature *and* nurture. Kevin Beaver (Beaver, Wright, DeLisi, & Vaughn, 2008) and a team of criminologists took a more critical approach to this question by examining a general theory of crime posited by Gottefredson and Hirschi. A major tenet of this theory is that low self-control is largely a result of parental management influences and not biogenetic factors. Beaver's study analyzed twin data drawn from the National Longitudinal Study of Adolescent Health and estimated that genetic factors accounted for 52% to 64% of the variance in low self-control, with twins' nonshared environment accounting for the remaining variance (Beaver et al., 2008). As accessibility to more rigorous and valid genetic and biological data become available, a school of thought within criminology is pursuing the question of how biological factors may play a part in crime and deviance.

FUNCTIONALIST PERSPECTIVES

Functionalist theories embrace the assumption that we must examine culture, especially shared norms and values, to understand why people behave the way they do. Recall that functionalist theory assumes society is characterized by a high degree of consensus on norms and values. It regards deviance as an abnormality that society seeks to eliminate, much as an organism seeks to rid itself of a parasite. At the same time, functionalist theory sees a certain amount of deviant behavior as useful—or functional—for society. It suggests that deviance—or the labeling of some behaviors as deviant—contributes to social solidarity by enhancing members' sense of the boundary between right and wrong (Durkheim, 1892/1997a).

DEVIANCE AND SOCIAL SOLIDARITY Émile Durkheim (1858–1917), the father of functionalist theories of deviance, hypothesized that deviant behavior served a useful purpose (a "function") in society by drawing "moral boundaries" of what behavior is acceptable and what is not within a community. Durkheim argued that we can describe a society lacking consensus on what is right and wrong as being in a condition of *anomie,* a state of confusion that occurs when people lose sight of the shared

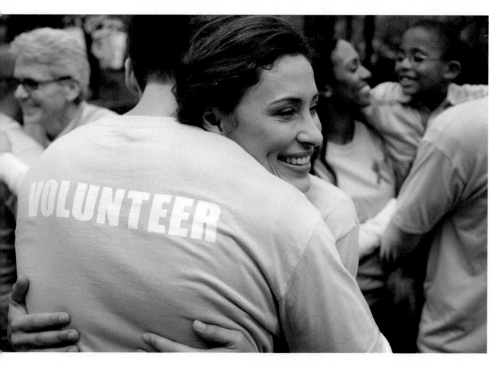

If you were to hypothesize that higher levels of social solidarity, or meaningful connections to others, are associated with lower levels of suicide, Émile Durkheim would agree. Volunteering for a cause that is meaningful to you is one of many channels that can strengthen social bonds. ■

rules and values that give order and meaning to their lives. In one of his most famous studies, Durkheim sought to show that anomie was a principal cause of suicide, itself a deviant act.

Durkheim gathered extensive data on suicide in France and Italy and found that it supported the theory that societies characterized by high levels of anomie also had high levels of suicide (Durkheim, 1897/1997b). Moreover, Durkheim argued that his research demonstrated that suicide rates varied depending on the level of *social solidarity,* or the social bonds that unite members of a group. Durkheim discovered, for example, that single men had higher rates of suicide than married men, Protestants a higher rate than Catholics, and men higher rates than women. Durkheim suggested that the higher rates were correlated with lower levels of social solidarity in the groups to which people were attached.

Durkheim's research methods—the statistics as well as the sampling procedures—were primitive compared to modern-day methods. Since he first published his research, however, hundreds of studies have looked at suicide differences between men and women, differences between industrialized and developing countries, and even among the homeless. Most of these empirical studies find considerable support for Durkheim's anomie theory (Cutright & Fernquist, 2000; Diaz, 1999; Kubrin, 2005; Lester, 2000; Simpson & Conklin, 1989; Wasserman, 1999). Durkheim's theory has spawned some of the most influential contemporary

Anti-Doping in Sports

Deviance in Technology

theories of deviance, including those of Robert Merton, Richard Cloward, and Lloyd Ohlin, which we discuss below.

STRUCTURAL STRAIN THEORY In the 1930s, U.S. sociologist Robert K. Merton (1968b) adapted Durkheim's concept of anomie into a general theory of deviance. According to Merton's theory, **structural strain** is *a form of anomie that occurs when a gap exists between the culturally defined goals of a society and the means available in society to achieve those goals.*

Merton argued that most people in a given society share a common understanding of the goals they should pursue, as well as the legitimate means for achieving those goals. For example, success, as measured in terms of wealth, consumption, or prestige, is widely regarded as an important goal in U.S. society. Moreover, there appears to be widespread consensus on the legitimate means for achieving success—education, an enterprising spirit, and hard work, among others.

Most people pursue the goal of "success" by following established social norms. Merton referred to such behavior as *conformity.* However, success is not always attainable through conventional means, or conformity. When this occurs, Merton argued, the resulting contradiction between societal goals and the means of achieving them creates *strain,* which may result in four different types of deviant behavior. His **strain theory** suggests that *when there is a discrepancy between the cultural goals for success and the means available to achieve those goals, rates of deviance will be high.* Reactions to the discrepancy will lead to the types of deviance depicted in the first column in Table 6.2 on page 133. It is important to note that since Merton's original formulation of strain theory, other researchers have expanded upon his work. For example, Kaufman (2009) explored the relation between general strains and gender, finding that serious strains may affect men and women differently and influence their inclination to engage in deviance. Women, Kaufman found, are especially likely to engage in deviance in response to depression.

OPPORTUNITY THEORY Although Merton's theory helps us understand the structural conditions leading to high rates of deviance, it neglects the fact that not everyone has the same access to deviant solutions. This is the point made by Richard Cloward

· ·

Structural strain: In Merton's reformulation of Durkheim's functionalist theory, a form of anomie that occurs when a gap exists between society's culturally defined goals and the means society makes available to achieve those goals.

Strain theory: Argues that societal pressures inhibit the ability of people to fulfill their needs, causing them to experience stress, or strain, and turn to crime to satisfy those needs.

■ TABLE 6.2 Merton's Typology of Deviance

Type of Response	Cultural Goals	Legitimacy of Means
Conformity	Accept	Accept
Innovation	Accept	Reject
Ritualism	Reject	Accept
Retreatism	Reject	Reject
Rebellion	Reject/substitute	Reject/substitute

SOURCE: Merton, R. K. (1968). *Social theory and social structure* (pp. 230–246). New York: Free Press. (Original work published 1938)

and Lloyd Ohlin (1960), who developed **opportunity theory** as an extension of Merton's strain theory.

According to Cloward and Ohlin, *people differ not only in their motivation to engage in deviant acts, but also in their opportunity to do so.* For instance, only the presence of a demand for drugs, plus access to drug supplies through producers, offers opportunities to be a dealer. Similarly, unless you have access to funds you can secretly convert to your own use, you are unlikely ever to consider embezzlement as an option, much less carry it out. Deviance is widespread in a community only when the opportunities for it exist.

CONTROL THEORY Agreeing with the functionalist claim that a society's norms and values are the starting point for understanding deviance, Gottfredson and Hirschi's (1990, 2004) **control theory** *explains that the cause of delinquency or deviance* among children and teenagers *lies in the arena of social control.* Gottfredson and Hirschi differ from Durkheim and Merton, however, regarding the importance of a general state of anomie in creating deviance, arguing instead that accepting or rejecting societal norms depends on the individual's life experiences.

Gottfredson and Hirschi (also Hirschi, 2004) believe deviance arises from **social bonds,** or *connections to others,* especially institutions, rather than from anomie. Forming strong social bonds with people and institutions that disapprove of deviance, they believe, keeps people from engaging in deviant behaviors. Conversely, people who do not form strong social bonds will engage in deviant acts because they have nothing to lose by acting on their impulses and do not fear the consequences of their actions.

· ·

Opportunity theory: Argues that people differ not only in their motivation to engage in deviant acts, but also in their *opportunity* to do so.

Control theory: Explains that the cause of deviance lies in the arena of social control and, specifically, the life experiences and relationships people form.

Social bonds: Our connections to others (see also *control theory*).

Subcultural theories: Explain deviance in terms of the conflicting interests of more and less powerful segments of a population.

Furthermore, control theorists argue that most deviant acts are spontaneous. For example, a group of teenagers sees a drunken homeless man walking down the street and decides to rob him, or a man learns of a house whose owners are on vacation and decides to burglarize it. Some people will succumb to such temptations. Those who do not, according to Gottfredson and Hirschi, have a greater willingness to conform. This willingness, in turn, comes from associating with people who are committed to conventional roles and morality.

Some evidence supports control theory. For example, delinquency is somewhat less common among youth who have strong family attachments, perform well in school, and feel they have something to lose by appearing deviant in the eyes of others (Gottfredson & Hirschi, 1990; Hirschi, 1969). On the other hand, we could scarcely argue that white-collar criminals such as Bernie Madoff, who pleaded guilty to massive financial fraud in 2009, did not have strong social bonds to society. The success of many white-collar criminals in business suggests a life of conforming to societal norms, yet they also commit criminal acts that cost U.S. taxpayers, investors, and pension holders billions of dollars (McLean & Elkind, 2003). Thus, while control theory explanations of deviance and crime may prove useful in certain instances, they have limitations.

CONFLICT PERSPECTIVES

Recall that the conflict perspective makes the assumption that groups in society have different interests and differential access to resources with which to realize those interests. In contrast to the functionalist perspective, it does not assume shared norms and values. The conflict perspective presumes that groups with power will use that power to maintain control in society and keep other groups at a disadvantage. As we will see below, conflict theory can be fruitfully used in the study of deviance.

SUBCULTURES AND DEVIANCE Three quarters of a century ago, Thorsten Sellin (1938) pointed out that the cultural diversity of modern societies results in conflicts between social groups over what kinds of behavior are right and wrong. Sellin argued that deviance was best explained through **subcultural theories** that *identify the conflicting interests of certain segments of the population,* whether it be over culture (as in Sellin's case) or more generally over certain rituals or behaviors. For example, immigrants to the United States bring norms and values with them from their original cultures and, to the extent that these conflict with the norms and values of the adopted country, they may be perceived as deviant by the dominant culture.

Such deviance might create only minor breaches of U.S. conventions. For instance, an Indian woman wears a traditional *sari,* or a Middle Eastern man wears a scarf. Other customary practices, however, might be serious violations of criminal laws. The

Deviance in the Mining Industry

THE WAR ON DRUGS: WHO GETS BUSTED FOR DRUG USE?

Behind drawn shades and by the dim light of candles, a small group of White teens gathers in a New York suburban mansion to get high on cocaine. There are no police cruisers in the leafy neighborhood—this is a safe area, and crime has never been a problem. A few miles away, on the streets of the South Bronx in New York City, a young Black addict smokes in a neighborhood crack house. That night, the police make a bust in the area, and together with a dozen other inhabitants of the house, the addict is arrested and taken to jail.

What is the difference between the drug activities in these two scenarios?

Survey data from the 2010 National Survey on Drug Use and Health (Substance Abuse and Mental Health Services Administration, 2011) indicate that of the 871,000 respondents aged 12 or older who self-reported usage of crack cocaine, 64 percent were White, 24 percent were Black, and 10 percent were Hispanic. Yet in 2009 African Americans still constituted more than 80 percent of federal crack cocaine convictions (The Sentencing Project, 2009).

While Whites are more likely to use cocaine, they are much less likely to be prosecuted for the offense (Chambliss & Hass, 2011; Johnston, O'Malley, Bachman, & Schulenberg, 2011b). Why is this the case? First, law enforcement efforts are not likely to be concentrated in the neighborhoods

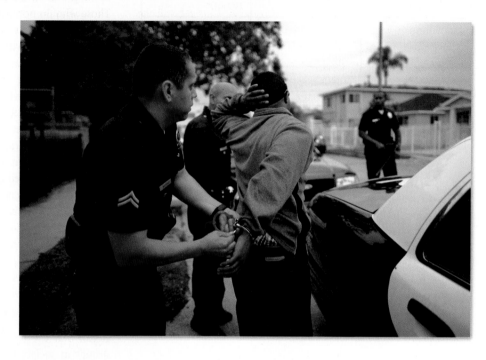

where White youths, particularly those of middle- and upper-class background, live (Chambliss, 2001). Police surveillance in higher-income neighborhoods is limited. Surveillance on the streets of impoverished urban areas is more intense, and minority youth—particularly young Black men—are a frequent target of police interest, whether or not a crime has been committed.

Second, if they are busted, White youths will most likely be represented by a private attorney in court. They may be referred to their parents, turned over to drug treatment programs, or put on probation rather than being sent to jail. Minority youth, on the other hand, are much more likely to be jailed without

the benefit of a private attorney, or the benefit of the doubt.

Data show us that the criminal justice system's treatment of someone's private drug habit depends a great deal on the person's race and social class. Commenting on the difference in treatment, Jeffrey Reimer (2003) has asked whether the system is one of criminal *justice* or criminal justice. What do you think?

THINK IT THROUGH

■ *Can you identify theories you have studied in this book that might shed light on the practices of legislators and law enforcement that target minority drug users more often than White drug users?*

practice of female circumcision by some immigrants to France from North Africa is a violation of French law. Domestic violence may be customary in some countries, but immigrants to the United States who practice domestic violence are in violation of U.S. law.

It is not only cultural differences between immigrants and the host country that create subcultures of deviance; sociologists also analyze juvenile gangs, professional thieves, White racist groups, and a host of other deviant groups as subcultures in which criminality is the norm, despite the fact that these values contradict the norms of the wider society (Chambliss & King, 1984; Cohen, 1955; Etter, 1998; Hamm, 2002).

CLASS-DOMINANT THEORY Class-dominant theories propose that what is labeled deviant or criminal—and therefore who gets punished—is determined by the interests of the dominant class (Quinney, 1970). For example, since labor is central to the functioning of capitalism, those who do not work are labeled deviant (Spitzer, 1975). In a similar vein, since private property is a key foundation of capitalism, those who engage in acts against property, such as stealing or vandalism, will be defined as deviant and likely as criminal. And, because profits are realized through buying and selling things in the capitalist marketplace, uncontrolled market activities (like selling drugs on the street or making alcohol without a license) will also be defined as deviant and criminal.

Critics of class-dominant theory point out that laws against the interests of the ruling class do get passed. Laws prohibiting insider trading on the stock market, governing the labor practices of corporations, and giving workers the right to strike and form trade unions were all signed over the strident opposition of capitalists (Chambliss, 2001). To incorporate these facts, William J. Chambliss (1988a) proposes a structural contradiction theory that takes into account the limitations, as well as the ultimate power, of capitalists in a capitalist society.

STRUCTURAL CONTRADICTION THEORY Rather than seeing the ruling class as all-powerful in determining what is deviant or criminal, structural contradiction theory argues that *conflicts generated by fundamental contradictions in the structure of society produce laws defining certain acts as deviant or criminal* (Chambliss, 1988a; Chambliss & Hass, 2011; Chambliss & Zatz, 1994).

For instance, there is a fundamental structural contradiction in capitalist economies between the need to maximize profits (which keeps wages down) and the need to maximize consumption (which requires high wages). Consider a U.S. business that, to maximize profits, keeps wages and salaries down, perhaps by moving its factories to a part of the world where labor is cheap. As jobs are transferred to low-wage countries, the availability of jobs to unskilled and semiskilled workers in the United States declines. The loss of jobs produces downward pressure on wages and a loss of purchasing power. Yet, capitalism depends on people buying the things that are produced—corporations cannot profit unless they sell their products.

Trapped in the contradiction between norms valuing consumerism and an economic system that can make consumption of desired material goods and services difficult for many and impossible for some, some, but not all, people will resolve the consumption-resources conflict by resorting to deviant and criminal acts such as cheating on income taxes, writing bad checks, or profiting from illegal markets, such as by selling drugs or committing theft.

Of course it is not just lower-income people who deviate in order to increase their consumption of material goods. Everyone who wants to enjoy a higher standard of living is a candidate for deviant or criminal behavior, according to structural contradiction theory. The head of a giant corporation may be as tempted to violate criminal laws in order to increase company profits (and personal income) as is the 13-year-old from a poor family who snatches a pair of sunglasses from the drugstore.

Structural contradiction theory holds that societies with the greatest gap between what people earn and what they are normatively enticed to buy will have the highest levels of deviance. Since industrial societies differ substantially in this regard, we can compare them to test this theory. Societies such as Finland, Denmark, Sweden, and Norway, for instance, provide a "safety net" that guarantees all citizens a decent standard of living. Therefore, the lower classes in Scandinavian countries are able to come much closer to what their societies have established as a "normal" level of consumption. The fact that rates of assault, robbery, and homicide are anywhere from 3 to 35 times higher in the United States than in these countries (depending on which country is compared) is exactly what structural contradiction theory would predict (Archer & Gartner, 1984).

Globalization is another example of the way structural contradictions lead to changes in deviant behavior. The ability to trade worldwide increases the wealth of the nations that are able to take advantage of global markets. However, it also increases opportunities for criminal activities such as money laundering, stealing patents and copyrights, and smuggling people, arms, and drugs.

FEMINIST THEORY The sociological study of deviance—like most areas of academic study—has for centuries been dominated by men. As a result, most theories and research have reflected a male point of view. Recent years bear witness to a sea change in the sociological perspective, as women have become better represented in sociology.

In the 1980s, a **feminist perspective on deviance** emerged within the sociological tradition (Campbell, 1984; Chesney-Lind,

· ·

Class-dominant theories: Propose that what is labeled deviant or criminal—and therefore who gets punished—is determined by the interests of the dominant class in a particular culture or society.

Structural contradiction theory: Argues that conflicts generated by fundamental contradictions in the structure of society produce deviance laws defining certain deviant acts as criminal.

Feminist perspective on deviance: Suggests that studies of deviance are biased and that both gender-specific cultural norms and the particular ways in which women are victimized by virtue of their gender help to account for deviance among women.

GLOBALIZATION AND CRIMINAL OPPORTUNITIES

Globalization vastly increases the potential for crime networks to gain wealth and political power (Block & Weaver, 2004; Naylor, 2002). At the top of the list of crimes facilitated by processes linked to globalization are (1) money laundering; (2) smuggling, including the smuggling of human beings, military equipment, drugs, and stolen merchandise; and (3) terrorism.

Nearly every major bank in Europe and the United States has been found guilty of laundering money at one time or another. In December 2012, the British bank HSBC was fined $1.9 billion for laundering billions of dollars in drug profits and for allowing terrorist groups to launder money through its Mexican affiliate (Douglas, 2013). In 2011, Swiss bank UBS and the Royal Bank of Scotland were found guilty of international rigging of interest rates by fraudulently setting the interest rates established through LIBOR, a benchmark for interest rates covering everything from home mortgages to student loans (Douglas, 2013). There are no reliable data on how many of these crimes occur annually, in part because sociological and political awareness is only now coming to the fore. It is clear, however, that hundreds of billions of dollars are illegally laundered annually (Block & Weaver, 2004; Naylor, 2002).

The economies of entire nations depend at least in part on supporting criminal enterprises through money laundering: Switzerland and Lichtenstein's bank secrecy laws as well as banking policies in numerous Caribbean nations enable money launderers from international criminal syndicates and terrorist organizations, as well as individuals evading taxes, to enjoy massive profits through criminal enterprises (Block & Weaver, 2004; Naylor, 2002).

The international drug trade in cocaine, opium, heroin, methamphetamines, and marijuana is estimated to be between $300 and $400 billion a year—a sum larger than the wealth of most nations (Glenny, 2009; Woodiwiss, 2005). The production of opium, coca, methamphetamines, and marijuana is a major contributor to the economies of Afghanistan, Malaysia, Laos, Thailand, Pakistan, Turkey, Colombia, Peru, Bolivia, and Mexico (Global Commission on Drug Policy, 2011; Woodiwiss, 2005). Some of these countries—Afghanistan and Bolivia, for example—have a disproportionately high value of illicit drug revenue as a percentage of their gross domestic product (Naylor, 2002).

Trafficking in exotic and endangered plants and animals has always been a lucrative business, but in recent years smuggling of these products has increased in part due to the rise of consumer markets for plant and animal products in rising economies such as China and Vietnam (Bremer, 2012). Goods ranging from traditional Asian medicines, to carved ivory, to high-priced furs, to exotic pets are smuggled from their place of origin and sold clandestinely in back-room operations or on Internet websites and messaging boards. The stunning value of the trade explains its growth and persistence: It is estimated to generate more than $10 billion per year (U.S. Fish and Wildlife

Service, Office of Law Enforcement Intelligence Unit, 2003).

The smuggling of people has also become a major international criminal enterprise. People pay large sums of money to be smuggled from poorer countries into wealthier ones where they imagine an opportunity for a better life. Women and girls are smuggled across borders for prostitution, sometimes under false pretenses such as promising them work in bars and restaurants as waitresses or as nannies. The extent of trafficking in women and girls for prostitution can only be estimated, but law enforcement and international task forces point to an alarming increase in the smuggling of human beings (Polaris Project, 2013).

Globalization has brought many benefits to countries and communities. It has also, as we have seen, contributed to the expansion of criminal enterprises.

THINK IT THROUGH

■ *Who is responsible for addressing the problem of globalized crime in the contemporary world? What sociological factors make the prevention and prosecution of globalized crime particularly challenging?*

1989, 2004; Messerschmidt, 1986). The starting point of feminist explanations of deviance is the observation that *studies of deviance are biased because almost all the research is done by, and about, males, largely ignoring female perspectives on deviant behavior, as well as analyses of differences in the types and causes of female deviance* (Messerschmidt, 1993). By ignoring the female population, deviance theory avoided one of the most challenging issues in the field: Why do rates of deviance—and especially criminal deviance—vary by gender?

Early feminist theory argued that gender-specific cultural norms partly account for the different rates of deviance of men and women (Adler, 1975; Steffensmeier & Allen, 1998). For example, women traditionally have been socialized into the roles of wife and mother, where behavior is more tightly prescribed than it is for men. Moreover, women's deviant behavior is more likely to be **stigmatized**—that is, *branded as highly disgraceful*—than is comparable male behavior. For example, a woman who has multiple sexual partners is shamed as a "slut," while a sexually promiscuous man is not disdained and might even be praised for being a "stud."

Feminists have argued that an adequate theory of deviance must take into account the particular ways in which women are victimized by virtue of their gender (Chesney-Lind, 2004; Mann & Zatz, 1998; Sokoloff & Raffel, 1995). For example, studies show that before becoming involved in the juvenile justice system, many girls labeled delinquent were runaways escaping sexual and physical abuse. Phelps's (1982) study of girls in the Wisconsin juvenile justice system found that 79% had been victims of physical abuse, while fully half had been subjected to sexual abuse, a third at the hands of parents or relatives. This research supports the hypothesis that many girls labeled delinquent were driven out of their homes by abusive parents or relatives. Their lives on the streets, marked by petty crime, resulted from their need to survive.

Women also continue to be disproportionately represented in cases of inmate sexual assault and victimization. While they only constitute 7% of the total inmate population, they make up one third of all sexual victimization cases (U.S. Bureau of Justice Statistics, 2011c).

. . . .

Stigmatized: Branded as highly disgraceful (see also *labeling theory*).

Labeling theory: A symbolic interactionist approach holding that deviance is a product of the labels people attach to certain types of behavior.

Primary deviance: A term developed by Edwin Lemert; the first step in the labeling of deviance, it occurs at the moment an activity is labeled deviant (see also *secondary deviance*).

Girls sometimes form gangs in neighborhoods where male street gangs are prevalent. These girl gangs are often "auxiliaries" of male gangs engaged in selling drugs and committing petty crimes. Joining a gang may require an initiation ritual that includes violence and even rape. ∎

SYMBOLIC INTERACTIONIST PERSPECTIVES

Symbolic interaction theories provide a language and framework for looking at how an individual is connected to the social structure and to explain why some people are labeled deviant and behave in deviant ways while others do not. According to symbolic interactionist theories, we see ourselves through the eyes of others, and our resulting sense of ourselves conditions how we behave. This idea has been applied to the study of deviant behavior in the development of both labeling theory and differential association theory.

LABELING THEORY Labeling theory holds that *deviant behavior is a product of the labels people attach to certain types of behavior* (Asencio & Burke, 2011; Lemert, 1951; Tannenbaum, 1938). From this perspective, deviance is seen as being socially constructed. That is, labeling theory holds that deviance is the product of interactions wherein the response of some people to certain types of behaviors produces a label of *deviant* or *not deviant*. In turn, these labels, which also end up being applied to people engaging in certain types of behavior, can influence how people conduct themselves. Thus, labeling theory is sometimes referred to as *societal reaction theory*.

One of the founders of labeling theory, Edwin Lemert (1951), argued that the labeling process has two steps: primary deviance and secondary deviance. **Primary deviance** occurs *at the moment an*

Labeling Theory

THE SAINTS AND THE ROUGHNECKS

Using detached observation and interviewing as his research methods, William Chambliss (2001) studied two gangs of teenage boys for two years. With the permission and cooperation of the boys, Chambliss was able to follow them, talk to them, and watch them during and after school hours. He named the two gangs "the Saints" and "the Roughnecks."

Eight young men—children of good, stable, white upper-middle-class families, active in school affairs and destined for college—were some of the most delinquent boys at Hannibal High School. The Saints were frequently truant from school and drunk on the weekends. They drove their cars wildly and committed numerous acts of petty theft . . . and vandalism. Yet in school, among parents, and in the rest of the community they had the reputation of being "good kids, headed in the right direction." Not one was arrested for any misdeed during the two years of observation. . . .

Six working-class white boys [Chambliss] called the Roughnecks hung out at the local drug store, where their harassment of passersby, public drinking, boisterous antics and fighting often got them into trouble with the community and with the police. To the school, the police, and the rest of the community the upper-middle-class boys were good, upstanding youths with bright futures. They were like Saints. But this same community treated the Roughnecks, whose delinquencies were comparable to those of the Saints, as though they were tough young criminals headed for even more serious trouble.

Years later, Chambliss followed the after-high-school careers of the members of the two gangs . . . All but one of the Saints had gone on to college and graduated, while several of the Roughnecks had become involved in criminal activities as adults: one was sentenced to prison for murder, another for manslaughter, and one became a member of an organized crime network.

Why did the Roughnecks and the Saints have such different careers after high school—careers that, by and large, lived up to the community's expectations?

First, the delinquencies of the Roughnecks were far more visible than those of the Saints. With their access to automobiles, the Saints were able to remove themselves from the sight of the community.

But the Roughnecks congregated in a crowded area that everyone in the community passed frequently, including teachers and law enforcement officers. Second, the demeanor of gang members differed. While the Saints showed remorse and respect, the Roughnecks offered a barely veiled contempt for authority. This resulted in different responses to their misdeeds. Third, adults in the community showed bias in favor of the Saints, who were presumed to be "good boys sowing wild oats" rather than "bad boys."

Labels matter. Those who were labeled as "bad" did, in fact, largely live up (or down) to this standard. Those whose youthful transgressions were not transformed into labels lived up to more positive expectations and became successful adults. These self-fulfilling prophecies suggest that the ways in which we opt to label individuals and groups can have an important effect on actions and outcomes.

THINK IT THROUGH

■ *W. I. Thomas observed that if people define a situation as real, it is real in its consequences even if objectively it may not be true. Using Thomas's theory, how would you explain the different response of the teachers, the police, and the community to the Saints and the Roughnecks?*

activity is labeled as deviant by others. **Secondary deviance** occurs *when a person labeled deviant accepts the label as part of his or her identity and, as a result, begins to act in conformity with the label.* To illustrate his theory, Lemert reported on a group of people in the Northwest with an unusually high incidence of stuttering. Observing the interaction between people in this group, he concluded that stuttering was common partly because people were stigmatized and labeled as "stutterers" (primary deviance). These "stutterers" then began to view themselves through this label, and increasingly acted in accordance with it—which included a greater amount of stuttering than otherwise would have been the case (secondary deviance).

Chambliss's (2001) observations of the Saints and the Roughnecks, discussed in the *Inequality Matters* box on page 138, also support labeling theory. The working-class boys he studied were labeled deviant, while the middle-class boys he observed were not. Eventually, the adult careers of the two groups of boys evolved to be largely consistent with the labels attached to them and their behaviors during adolescence.

DIFFERENTIAL ASSOCIATION THEORY Another symbolic interactionist approach to the study of deviance looks at how deviance is transmitted culturally and argues that we learn deviant behaviors through our social interactions. **Differential association theory** holds that *deviant and criminal behavior results from regular exposure to attitudes favorable to acting in ways that are deviant or criminal* (Burgess & Akers, 1966; Church, Jaggers, & Taylor, 2012; Sutherland, 1929). For example, the corporate executive who embezzles company funds may learn the norms and values appropriate to this type of criminal activity by associating with others already engaged in it. Similarly, kids and teenagers living in areas where selling and using drugs are common practices will be more likely to develop attitudes favorable to using and selling drugs than kids and teenagers who are not exposed to that subculture. Conversely, populations that possess a different subculture or attitude toward a particular form of deviance (such as illicit drug usage) may not experience the same rates of crime.

· ·

Secondary deviance: A term developed by Edwin Lemert; the second step in the labeling of deviance, it occurs when a person labeled deviant accepts the label as part of his or her identity and, as a result, begins to act in conformity with the label (see also *primary deviance*).

Differential association theory: Holds that deviant and criminal behavior results from exposure attitudes favorable to acting in ways that are deviant or criminal.

In the Netherlands (pictured), where marijuana can legally be sold in licensed cafés, the incidence of lifetime use is lower than in the United States, where criminal penalties for possession and use are still common. How would you explain this unexpected difference? ■

According to Sutherland's differential association theory, the more we associate with people whose behavior is deviant, the greater the likelihood that our behavior will also be deviant. Sutherland, therefore, linked deviance with such factors as the frequency and intensity of our associations with other people, how long they last, and how early in our lives they occur. Much has changed since Sutherland developed his theory, and today many of our interactions take place through technologies such as the Internet and smartphones. A modern adaptation of Sutherland's theory would certainly have to take into account the importance of the unique methods of interacting today in promoting both deviant and conforming behavior.

Symbolic interactionist theories, like functional and conflict theories, provide us with considerable insight into the social processes that lead to deviance and crime in society. We might come to the conclusion that each of the competing theories "makes sense" and has some empirical support, yet also fails to explain all the behaviors we classify as deviant or criminal. This debate and interaction between theories is essential to the development of scientific knowledge (Popper, 1939). Thus, while there are so many unique ways to examine the same topic without necessarily reaching one perfect answer with any of them, we should be reassured that each theoretical orientation presented in this chapter can be useful in explaining certain facets of deviance and crime. It is up to the researcher to decide which theory to use and why, and for others to determine whether the use of the theory was a success or failure.

Differential
Association Theory

Deviance is not restricted to any particular class or social group. The powerful and elite commit deviance as well. Infidelity may happen all the time, but it is more sensational when it is done by high-ranking officials and esteemed leaders of society. Retired General David Petraeus's affair with his biographer cost him his job as CIA director. ■

TYPES OF DEVIANCE

As noted in the opening to this chapter, deviance comes in many varieties, from the relatively benign to the extremely harmful. In this section, we explore some of the manifestations that deviance can take in society.

EVERYDAY DEVIANCE

A broad spectrum of acts could fall under the label of "everyday deviance": plagiarism among high school or college students, shoplifting, under-age alcohol consumption, spitting, using pornography, smoking, binge eating, eating meat, or calling in sick to work or school when you actually feel fine. All of these are considered deviant behaviors, actions, or conditions by some individuals and/or groups. Many of you reading this text engage in at least some types of deviance on a fairly regular basis.

In the commission of everyday deviance, we clearly recognize the pluralistic nature of U.S. society. Taking a subcultural perspective, we see that smoking is more acceptable among some specific societal subgroups—for instance, truck drivers—and not among others, like fitness instructors. So too with eating meat: The owner of a BBQ restaurant and a vegan are likely to hold starkly different views regarding the deviance of eating meat or subsisting on a vegan diet. In turn, these views are representative of the broader societal subcultures and groups to which these individuals belong.

Everyday deviance can be explained in a multitude of ways. For instance, we might utilize labeling theory. Pornography represents an interesting example in which both the behavior (using pornography) and the physical object (the pornographic movie or magazine) have been labeled as deviant. We could therefore easily make the argument that pornography is deviant simply because people have chosen to label it as such. Yet, this explanation, as you might have sensed, is pretty basic. We could strengthen our understanding of what makes pornography deviant by including a conflict perspective. Thus, we could look at who in society has had the power to define pornography as deviant, and what goals such a definition might have served for that particular group. The point is that deviance in its various forms has many potential explanations, which can be strengthened by combining various theoretical perspectives.

SEXUAL DEVIANCE

Sex, sexual orientations, and sexual practices are diverse, as are the responses to them. We are witnessing a process of redefinition of what deviance means within the context of our intimate relationships. Look no further than the wildly popular *Fifty Shades of Grey* novel, which made headlines for its depiction of kinky sex and for being on the nightstands of many "ordinary" men and women. As the success of the *Fifty Shades of Grey* series indicates, we might even argue that some *traditional* notions regarding sex, sexual orientations, and sexual activities are themselves increasingly becoming viewed as deviant, because they simply do not reflect the realities of modern social life.

Definitions of sexual deviance can include many things—from the choices we make in terms of whom we begin intimate relationships with, to how and where those relationships are carried out. While we could utilize many explanations to examine sexual deviance, looking at the current debate over same-sex marriage from a conflict perspective we see an ongoing struggle between those groups that have long determined what passes for acceptable sexual behavior (for instance, religious groups), and those that seek to redefine sexual behavior to include things other than heterosexual sex and marriage.

DEVIANCE OF THE POWERFUL

The crimes of the powerful are ubiquitous and wide ranging, from fraudulently reporting corporate profits to misleading investors to bribery, corruption, and the misuse of public trust. The most powerful people in public life engage in many of the same types of deviance as ordinary men and women (McLean & Elkind, 2003; McLean & Nocera, 2010; Reiman & Leighton, 2012).

The media has a heyday when deviance committed by political leaders, celebrities, or athletes becomes public. When it was revealed that golfer Tiger Woods had a multitude of women with whom he had sexual relations while married with children, the press spent weeks following the story in detail. Recently, the world-champion cyclist Lance Armstrong was stripped of his multiple Tour de France wins and banned from competitive cycling for life for his use of performance-enhancing drugs. Sociologically what must be taken into account is that deviance knows no class bounds.

The response of the public to the deviance of political leaders is often particularly pointed given the immense trust, responsibility, and power we vest in those individuals. For example, in 2012, the head of the Central Intelligence Agency,

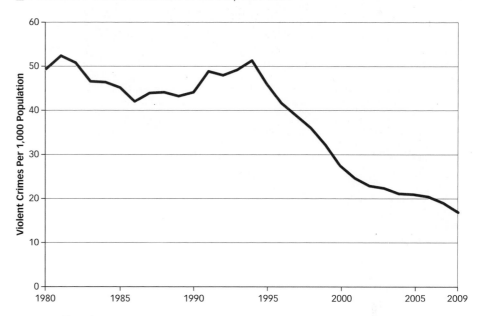

FIGURE 6.1 Violent Crime Rate in the U.S., 1980–2009

SOURCE: Office of Justice Programs, U.S. Bureau of Justice Statistics. (2013b). National Crime Victimization Survey violent crime trends, 1980–2009. *Key Facts at a Glance*. Retrieved from http://bjs.ojp.usdoj.gov/content/glance/tables/viortrdtab.cfm

retired General David Petraeus, previously the commanding general of coalition forces in Afghanistan, was engaged in an affair with his biographer while both were married. As a result of the affair becoming public, Petraeus had to resign as CIA director. The public response to deviance committed by powerful individuals reflects not only dismay at the fact of deviance but disdain for the hypocrisy; lawyer and former New York governor Eliot Spitzer prosecuted prostitution in New York with a vengeance, only to be caught hiring a high-priced call girl to accompany him on a trip from New York to Washington, DC.

On the one hand, empirical data show that the powerful are more likely to escape punishment for deviance. On the other hand, those who are caught are often subject in social media to acute public disdain. Should public figures be subject to particular scrutiny for their behavior, or should they be treated like everyone else?

CRIMINAL DEVIANCE

Our discussion thus far has primarily been concerned with deviance in a general sense—those behaviors and actions that are widespread but are generally not condemned by all or seen as especially serious. In this section, we discuss **criminal deviance,** or

....

Criminal deviance: Deviance that violates established laws.

Crimes: An act defined in the law as punishable by fines, imprisonment, or both.

Violent crime: Involves force or threat of force and includes robbery, murder, assault, and rape.

Property crime: Involves violating the ownership rights of someone else and includes crimes like burglary, larceny/theft, arson, and motor vehicle theft.

especially serious forms of deviance that violate established laws. Criminal deviance is often simply referred to as crime. **Crimes** are *acts defined in the law as punishable by fines, imprisonment, or both.* Law enforcement agencies take rigorous steps to record how much criminal deviance occurs.

VIOLENT AND PROPERTY CRIMES A great deal of effort is expended measuring crime in U.S. society. This is accomplished through official, limited records like the FBI's Uniform Crime Reports (UCR) and the collection of survey data from individuals and households across the country via the National Crime Victimization Survey (NCVS). These measures of crime, especially the UCR, focus predominantly on violent and property crimes, serious forms of deviance that nearly every person in society agrees should be made illegal.

Violent crimes *include robbery (taking something from someone by physical force), murder, assault, and rape.* **Property crimes** *include burglary (taking something from a person's home), arson, larceny/theft, and motor vehicle theft.* Property crimes are much more common in U.S. society than violent crimes, although their number, like the number of violent crimes (Figure 6.1), has been steadily declining (Figure 6.2 on page 142).

Most property crimes are committed against those who can least afford them—poor and low-income people. For example, two of every five victims of theft, including car theft, had household income under $25,000. Almost half of all burglary victims also fell into this category (FBI Uniform Crime Report, 2009).

Life of a Handgun

CSI and Deviance in Media

Moscow special police arrest a suspected mafia car thief in the Russian capital. Both organized and everyday crime have risen dramatically in the period following the collapse of the Soviet Union in 1991. ■

As variations of serious deviance, violent and property crimes could be explained from a multitude of theories. For instance, violent crimes could be seen from an opportunity theory perspective—property crimes in terms of societal strain. How would such analyses look?

ORGANIZED CRIME Sociologists define **organized crime** as *crimes committed by criminal groups that provide illegal goods and services*. Gambling, prostitution, selling and trafficking illegal drugs, black marketeering, loan sharking, and money laundering are some of the most prominent activities of organized crime (Block & Chambliss, 1981; Glenny, 2009; McCoy, 1991; Paoli, 2003).

To meet the demand for illegal goods and services, criminal organizations have flourished in U.S. urban areas since the 1800s (Woodiwiss, 2000). Over the years, they have recruited members and leadership from more impoverished groups in society, such as new immigrants in big cities, who may have great aspirations but limited means of achieving them (Block & Weaver, 2004). Consequently, organized crime has been dominated by the most recent arrivals to urban areas: Irish, Jewish, and Italian "mobs" in the past, and Asian, African, South American, and Russian "mobs" today (Albanese, 1989; Hess, 1973; National Institute of Justice [NIJ], 2012).

Sex Trafficking

Movie and television depictions of organized crime such as *The Sopranos, The Godfather, Scarface,* and *Goodfellas* popularize the erroneous impression that there is an international organization of criminals (the "Mafia") dominated by Italian Americans. The reality is that organized crime consists of thousands of different groups throughout the United States and the world. No single ethnic group or organization has control over most or even a major share of these activities, which include human trafficking and weapons smuggling (Block & Weaver, 2004; Chambliss, 1988a; NIJ, 2012).

CRIMES OF THE POWERFUL When most people think of criminal deviance, or crime, they think of the violent and property crimes discussed above—and they think of crimes committed by those in lower socioeconomic groups. But the forms of criminal deviance perpetrated by individuals and groups who possess great power, authority, and influence are also often deeply harmful to society and its members.

White-collar crime is *crime committed by people of high social status in connection with their work* (Sutherland, 1949/1993). There are two principal types: crimes for the benefit of the individual who commits them, and crimes for the benefit of the organization for which the individual works.

Among the many white-collar crimes that benefit the individual are the theft of money by accountants who alter an employer's or client's books, and the overcharging of clients by lawyers. A much more costly type of white-collar crime occurs when

■ **FIGURE 6.2** Property Crime Rate in the U.S., 1980–2008

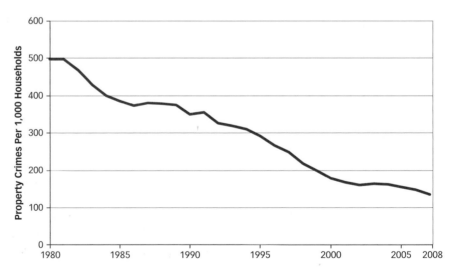

SOURCE: Office of Justice Programs, Bureau of Justice Statistics. (2013a). National Crime Victimization Survey property crime trends, 1980–2008. *Key Facts at a Glance*. Retrieved http://bjs.ojp.usdoj.gov/content/glance/tables/proptrdtab.cfm

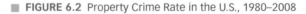

Organized crime: Crimes committed by groups that provide illegal goods and services.

White-collar crime: Crimes committed by people of high social status in connection with their work.

corporate executives commit criminal acts that benefit the companies for which they work at the expense of those to whom the company owes a financial or other obligation.

White-collar crimes have received considerable media attention in recent years. For example:

- The bankruptcy of Enron, the seventh-largest corporation in the United States, in 2001 caused the loss of thousands of jobs and millions of dollars in investment, savings, and retirement funds (McLean & Elkind, 2003). Leading executives lied about the company's profits and, through elaborate accounting fraud, concealed debts, making it appear that Enron was prospering when in fact it was bankrupt.
- In 2008, Bernard "Bernie" Madoff, a former Wall Street executive, was arrested and charged with managing an intricate criminal scheme that stole at least $50 billion from corporate and individual investors. Madoff pled guilty to 11 criminal counts in Manhattan's federal district courthouse and was sentenced to 150 years in prison (Rosoff, Pontell, & Tillman, 2010).
- In 2010, financial giant JPMorgan Chase was fined $48.6 million by British financial regulators for "failing to keep clients' funds separate from those of the firm." The error went undetected for more than seven years and placed billions of dollars of client funds at risk of being lost (Werdigier, 2010).

POLICE CORRUPTION AND POLICE BRUTALITY Policing is a job invested with trust, responsibility, and authority. Police officers are the frontline enforcers of laws expected to limit the amount of criminal deviance that occurs in society. When violent or property crimes are committed, we rely upon them for both protection and investigation. Thus, when instances of police corruption—whether it be accepting bribes or engaging in criminal activities—and other forms of deviance come to light, the public is often shocked and outraged.

Such was the case in 2010 when a video surfaced that showed a University of Maryland student being beaten by several Prince George's County, Maryland, police officers following a collegiate basketball game. The student can be seen on the video drunkenly walking down the street toward several police officers sitting on horseback. He stops short when one of the officers moves his horse to block his path, and in an instant several other policemen on foot rush from behind the mounted officers, slam him into a brick wall, and begin beating him with their batons (Blackburn, 2010). Prior to publication of the video, which showed that the young man was neither aggressive nor capable of defending himself, the officers claimed he had assaulted them and resisted arrest.

Financier Bernie Madoff pleaded guilty in 2009 to orchestrating a massive financial fraud. His fraud involved a complex Ponzi scheme that appeared to defy markets in its profitability for investors, but earnings were fictitious. ■

Police brutality has a long history in the United States. The response of southern police officers and sheriffs, such as Birmingham, Alabama's Bull Connor to the 1960s civil rights marches, provides a well-documented example. Police brutality continues to occur, however, although few instances garner public attention, because often they go unseen and unrecorded. The videotaped beating of Rodney King in the 1990s by four White members of the Los Angeles Police Department and L.A. County Sheriff's Office served as one vivid example of the treatment many minority city residents suffered at the hands, and batons, of the police. Even more recently, a drunken off-duty Chicago policeman named Anthony Abbate was caught on tape viciously beating and stomping a female bartender after she refused to serve him any more drinks (Walberg, 2009). Had the video not been found, it is possible the 250-pound Abbate's claim that he acted in self-defense in pummeling the 125-pound bartender would have been substantiated.

Police corruption is no less serious than police brutality, and in fact it may be more so if we consider that entrenched corruption may significantly undermine the ability of the police to effectively enforce laws and can also lead to acts of targeted violence in some cases. Both corruption and brutality represent important forms of criminal deviance committed by official representatives of state authority. But how can we make sense of these forms of deviance?

In the case of both police corruption and use of excessive force, Sutherland's differential association theory may provide valuable insights. Some studies and first-person accounts demonstrate that police officers are often exposed to various forms of deviance once

White-Collar Crime

Detainees at Abu Ghraib in Iraq were subject to humiliation and torture at the hands of some of their U.S. military overseers. The appearance of the photos, many of them taken by guards complicit in the abuse, caused a scandal in the United States in 2004. ■

they become members of the force (Kappeler, Sluder, & Alpert, 1998; Maas, 1997). Exposure to attitudes favorable to the commission of deviance and crime, especially in light of the intensity and duration of the relationships police officers form with one another, may lead some to engage in those same types of deviant or criminal behaviors. We can also view the police as having a distinct culture, explaining brutality and corruption in terms of the subcultural expectations that accompany police work. Certain behaviors, actions, and perspectives, especially regarding the use of force or engaging in corrupt practices, may be seen as both necessary and normal parts of accomplishing the demands of police work.

STATE CRIMES Finally, we turn to perhaps the most harmful and underanalyzed form of criminal deviance among the powerful: state crime. While police brutality and corruption are especially egregious examples of criminal deviance occurring among those with power, state crimes rank above even them in terms of the seriousness and potential harm that may result from their commission.

Can Computers
Predict Crime?

Organized Crime

State crime is defined as *criminal acts committed by state and government officials in the pursuit of their jobs as representatives of the government*. Needless to say, governments do not normally keep statistics on their own criminal behavior. Nonetheless we know that such crimes are not uncommon (Chambliss, Michalowski, & Kramer, 2011; Green & Ward, 2004; Rothe, 2009). Contemporary examples of state crime involving the United States include the torture of detainees at the U.S. military prison in Guantánamo Bay, Cuba; the secret transportation and torture of battlefield detainees in foreign prisons; and even the violation of international laws leading up to the 2004 invasion of Iraq (Grey, 2006; Kramer & Michalowksi, 2005; Paglen & Thompson, 2006; Ratner & Ray, 2004). Globally, many studies have drawn attention to state crime, including the Chinese government's role in the trafficking of human body parts. In the latter study, the author found that the organs of executed prisoners were harvested by government-approved doctors and sold to corporations and other entities for use in organ transplantation and cosmetic surgery, often at substantial profits, without the consent of the prisoners' families (Lenning, 2007).

SOCIAL CONTROL OF DEVIANCE

The persistence of deviant behavior in society leads inevitably to a variety of measures designed to control it. Social control is defined as the *attempts by certain people or groups in society to control the behaviors of other individuals and groups in order to increase the likelihood that they will conform to established norms or laws*. Thus, deviance, whose definition tends to require some sort of moral judgment, also attracts attempts at social control, usually exercised by those people or groups who possess social power, or *the ability to exercise social control*.

INFORMAL SOCIAL CONTROL

Informal social control is *the unofficial means through which deviance is sanctioned in everyday interactions*. It ranges from frowning at someone's sexist assertion to threatening to take away a child's cell phone in order to coerce conformity to the parent's wishes. Informal social control mechanisms explain why people

. . . .

State crime: Criminal acts committed by state and government officials in the pursuit of their jobs as representatives of the government.

Social control: Refers to the attempts by certain people or groups in society to control the behaviors of other individuals and groups in order to increase the likelihood that they will conform to established norms or laws.

Social power: The ability to exercise social control.

Informal social control: Most often occurs among ordinary people during the course of their interactions and is the unofficial mechanism through which deviance and deviant behaviors are sanctioned in society.

don't spit on the floor in a restaurant, do choose to pay back a friend who lent them $5, or say "thank you" in response to a favor. These behaviors and responses are governed not by formal laws, but by informal expectations that we are all aware of and that lead us to make certain choices. Much of the time these informal social controls lead us into conformity with societal or group norms—and away from deviance.

Socialization, which we have discussed in earlier chapters, thus plays a significant role in the success of informal social controls. When parents seek to get their children to conform to the values and norms of their society, they teach them to do one thing and not another. Peer groups of workers, students, and friends also implement informal social controls, such as embarrassment and criticism, that work to control behavior and thus deviance. Bonds to institutions and people enact various informal social controls on our behavior. They have been shown to be crucial in explaining why some people engage in deviance and others do not (Laub & Sampson, 2003; Sampson & Laub, 1990).

FORMAL SOCIAL CONTROL AND CRIMINAL DEVIANCE

The street corner drug dealer who gets chased by the police, cornered, and forced violently to the ground is handcuffed, packed into the back of a squad car, and hauled to jail. This is the experience of **formal social control**, *attempts to officially sanction certain behaviors and visibly punish others*. In the modern world, formal social control is most often exercised by societal institutions associated with the state, including the police, prosecutors, courts, and prisons. The goal of all these institutions is to suppress, reduce, and punish those individuals or groups who engage in criminal deviance. Stealing, assaulting someone, vandalizing property, cheating on income taxes, fraudulently reporting corporate earnings, and insider trading on the stock market—all have been deemed crimes and represent forms of criminal deviance. As such they are subject to formal social control.

For an act to be criminal, several elements must be present: There must be a specific law prohibiting the act, and a punishment of either prison or a fine, or both, must be specified.

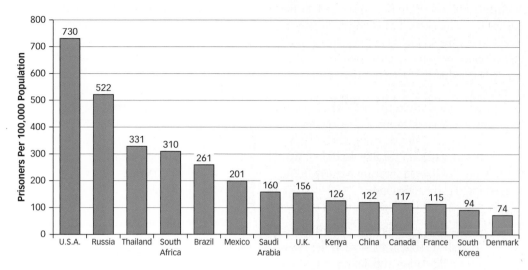

■ **FIGURE 6.3** Incarceration Rates in Selected Countries, 2011

SOURCE: Chambliss, W. J., & Hass, A. (2011). *Criminology: Theory, research and practice*. New York: McGraw-Hill.

Most importantly, the act must be *intended, and the person committing the act must be capable of having the intent*. Someone judged to be mentally ill, which U.S. criminal law defines as the person "not knowing right from wrong" at the time of the act, cannot have the required legal intent and therefore cannot be held criminally liable for committing an act. However, the insanity defense does not apply to all states: Idaho, Montana, Kansas, and Utah do not recognize insanity as a defense. In other state courts and federal courts, the burden of proof is on the defendant to prove he or she is insane. The U.S. Supreme Court refused to hear a case from Idaho where a defendant claimed he had a constitutional right to claim insanity as a defense (Barnes, 2012).

RISING PRISON POPULATIONS Controlling criminal deviance typically includes the arrest and prosecution of individuals who have committed violent crime or property crime, and to a lesser extent individuals engaged in police brutality or corruption, white-collar, organized, or state crimes. Common sense would seem to indicate that most of the people subject to various formal social controls would be those implicated in some type of violent criminal deviance, such as rape, robbery, or murder. Interestingly, though, of the roughly 13 million U.S. arrests in 2010, fewer than 1 in 20 were for a violent crime (FBI Uniform Crime Report, 2010).

Another indication of the importance of formal social control in the modern world is the unprecedented increase in the number of people imprisoned today (Figure 6.3). The 2010 imprisonment rate in the United States was 500 per 100,000 U.S. residents, or

· ·

Formal social control: Is most often exercised by the state, including the police and courts, and is society's *attempt to officially sanction certain behaviors and visibly punish others.*

Future of Crime

Wrongful Convictions

Organized Criminals and Crime

1 prisoner out of every 200 residents (U.S. Bureau of Justice Statistics, 2011b). Indeed, while the U.S. prison population has declined slightly in recent years, the United States still imprisons a vastly higher percentage of its population than any other industrial society (U.S. Bureau of Justice Statistics, 2011b).

The rapid increase in the number of people in prison is particularly intriguing to sociologists, since it has occurred during a period when the crime rate has been steadily declining. Why has this unprecedented increase occurred? The reasons include the following:

1. **Mandatory minimum sentences:** Federal and state legislators in the 1980s passed legislation stipulating that a person found guilty of a particular crime had to be sentenced to a minimum number of years in prison. This reduced judges' ability to use their discretion in sentencing and led to a substantial increase in the average prison term.

2. **"Three strikes" laws:** Many states and the federal government can sentence anyone to life in prison who is found guilty of committing three *felonies*, or serious crimes punishable by a minimum of one year in jail. In November 2012, California passed a ballot initiative reducing the impact (slightly) of applications of three-strikes laws.

3. **The "war on drugs":** Efforts to reduce the trafficking of illegal drugs are responsible for a significant increase in the number of people in prison. For example, in 2010 there were just under 13 million U.S. arrests, of which 1.6 million were for minor drug law violations—not for serious trafficking or distribution offenses (FBI Uniform Crime Report, 2010). As a result of increased arrest and sentencing for minor drug-related offenses, about 60% of federal prison inmates and over 30% of state prison inmates are serving time for the sale or possession of illegal drugs (Boncar & Beck, 1997).

Over the last several decades, changes in criminal laws and criminal sentencing have resulted in much stricter forms of social control in relationship to certain types of criminal deviance. In turn, this has led to a huge increase in the U.S. prison population. Currently, 1 in 33 U.S. adults is under some form of correctional supervision—prison, jail, parole, or probation (U.S. Bureau of Justice Statistics, 2011b). At the same time, the application of these formal mechanisms of social control have not been applied equally, or proportionally, to all groups in society.

RACE, ETHNICITY, GENDER, AND CRIMINAL DEVIANCE

Three-strikes laws, mandatory minimum sentences, and the "war

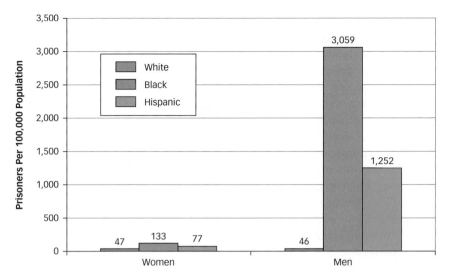

■ **FIGURE 6.4** Incarceration Rate by Gender and Race in the U.S., 2010

SOURCE: Guerino, P., Harrison, P. M., & Sabol, W. (2011). *Prisoners in 2010*. Washington, DC: U.S. Bureau of Justice Statistics.

on drugs" have all contributed to high U.S. prison populations. However, those most likely to be imprisoned and punished for engaging in criminal deviance are disproportionately people of color. Blacks and Hispanics are disproportionately arrested and imprisoned at much higher rates than Whites, despite the fact that Whites make up a much larger proportion of the total U.S. population (Chambliss, 2001; U.S. Bureau of Justice Statistics, 2011b).

For example, 1 in 3 Black males will enter state or federal prison during his lifetime, compared to 1 in 6 Hispanic males and 1 in 17 White males (The Sentencing Project, 2012). Black males are incarcerated at a rate of over 4,300 per 100,000; for Hispanic males the rate is over 1,700 per 100,000 (Boncar & Beck, 1997).

White males, by contrast, have an incarceration rate of only 678 per 100,000 (Boncar & Beck, 1997). If current trends continue, Black males between the ages of 19 and 34 will experience an even greater overrepresentation in the prison population (Figure 6.4). The incarceration rates for females, while lower overall than those for men, exhibit a similar disproportionate trend, with Black females twice as likely as Hispanic females and three times more

· ·

Mandatory minimum sentences: Federal and state legislators in the 1980s passed legislation stipulating that a person found guilty of a particular crime had to be sentenced to a minimum number of years in prison. This reduced judges' ability to use their discretion in sentencing and led to a substantial increase in the average prison term.

"Three strikes" laws: Many states and the federal government can sentence anyone to life in prison who is found guilty of committing three felonies, or serious crimes punishable by a minimum of one year in jail.

The "war on drugs": Actions taken by the U.S. government that are intended to curb the illegal drug trade and reduce drug use.

likely than White females to end up in jail or prison (Boncar & Beck, 1997).

People of color are more likely than Whites to be arrested and imprisoned for a number of reasons, all of which relate to the extension of formal social controls over criminal deviance (Mann & Zatz, 1998). First, impoverished inner-city residents are disproportionately non-White, and the inner city is where the "war on drugs" has been most avidly waged (Anderson, 1999; Chambliss, 2001). As a consequence, drug-related arrests fall disproportionately upon people of color (Figure 6.5).

Second, the work of policing generally focuses on poor neighborhoods, where crowded living conditions force many activities onto the streets. Illegal activities are therefore much more likely to attract police attention in poor neighborhoods than in dispersed suburban neighborhoods.

Finally, racism in practices of prosecution and sentencing may also account for greater arrest and imprisonment rates of people of color. Even though many more Whites than non-Whites are arrested for crimes, people of color are more likely to be imprisoned for their offenses (Austin, Dimas, & Steinhart, 1992).

WHY STUDY DEVIANCE?

The sociological perspective focuses the lens through which we view deviant behavior. It highlights the fact that the line between "deviant" and "normal" behavior is often arbitrary: What is deviant to one group is normal and even expected behavior to another.

Mainstream media and "official" depictions of deviance often overlook or ignore some of the more serious manifestations of deviance in the culture. So too do local communities: For example, in research on "the Saints and the Roughnecks," Chambliss (2001) found that middle-class boys were much more likely to have their deviant behavior written off as simply "sowing their wild oats," even though it was dangerous and costly. On the other hand, the community was quick to judge, and apply deviant labels, to a lower-income group of boys. This suggests a need for sociologists to delve more deeply into stereotypes of "gangs"

■ **FIGURE 6.5** Drug Offenders in Federal Prison by Race and Ethnicity, 1999–2005

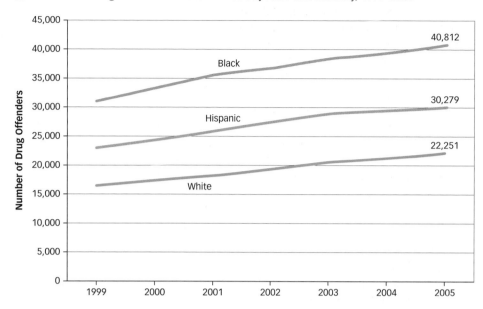

SOURCE: Mauer, M. (2009). *The changing racial dynamics of the war on drugs.* Washington, DC: The Sentencing Project.

and "delinquency" as phenomena associated almost exclusively with poor urban youth.

Similarly, sociological research and theory remind us that focusing on the deviance of the poor and minorities blinds us to an understanding of deviance among the rich and powerful. Criminal deviance, as discussed earlier in this chapter, is widespread throughout modern societies. Some of the most dangerous and costly patterns of deviant behavior are systematically practiced by corporate executives, politicians, and government officials. The sociological perspective demands that we ask questions, in such a case, about power and who has the power to define deviance and to enforce their definitions.

The findings of sociologists who study deviant behavior generally and criminal deviance in particular suggest the limited effect of social control policies such as imprisonment. Instead, these findings point to the need to change the social conditions that lead to criminality in the first place. The implications of most sociological studies of deviance is that street crimes and gangs in poor urban neighborhoods can best be controlled by creating jobs and opportunities for those who otherwise cannot hope to succeed. For white-collar, political, and governmental crimes, the organizational structures that make it rewarding to violate laws and social norms will have to change if there is any hope of reducing deviance among the elite.

WHAT CAN I DO WITH A SOCIOLOGY DEGREE?

SKILLS AND CAREERS: PROBLEM SOLVING

Problem solving is a fundamental skill in social scientific disciplines such as sociology—and in a wide variety of contemporary occupational fields. Managing and addressing complex problems by identifying the dimensions of a problem, researching the roots of the problem, and using the knowledge rigorously and thoughtfully to craft well-reasoned responses is a skill set that is developed through careful study, research training, and practice. Problem solving is, in many respects, composed of other key skills we will discuss in the *Skills and Careers* features in this book, including data and information literacy, critical thinking, quantitative and qualitative research competency, understanding conflict dynamics, understanding diversity and global perspectives, and written communication. At the same time, it is a skill that has its own characteristics as a product of sociological training. Sociological research data, which forms the centerpiece of much of what sociologists do and teach, does not itself solve problems; rather, it contributes to the informed understanding of the dimensions of a problem. It is also used to hypothesize the roots of a problem. Once the roots of a problem are identified, they can be addressed through, for instance, policy or community interventions. Research can be used to follow up on whether and how solutions worked and to rework a hypothesis based on new information.

In Chapter 6, we learned about a variety of theories that seek to explain deviant or criminal activities. Consider the problem, for instance, of illegal drugs as a community concern. Drugs can be a problem for a community when, for instance, illicit drug markets contribute to a rise in neighborhood violence. How might a sociologist approach this problem? First, it is important to ascertain the dimensions of a problem. How will the problem at issue be defined, operationalized, and measured? Second, having established the dimensions of a problem, sociologists would look for the roots of the problem. Sociologists may choose to study a particular neighborhood closely and to draw conclusions and perhaps make generalizations from data they gather through interviews, observations, examination of police records, or surveys, for instance. Or they might begin from an existing theory of deviance, such as opportunity theory or structural contradiction theory, and opt to test the theory through the collection of empirical evidence. Researching the roots of a problem can involve a spectrum of different approaches, and you often need to try more than one to generate a comprehensive picture of the problem. Third, sociologists can use the knowledge they have developed through research to craft possible approaches to a problem that get at the roots of the issue. Further research can be used to test the effects of these approaches and to refine the analysis of the community drug problem. Social life is complex, and most serious social problems are not amenable to simple solutions. At the same time, the probability of successfully addressing a problem is appreciably greater when careful research has been used to understand its causes.

Problems encountered in different occupational fields vary, but the need for skills to break down a problem, define it, analyze it, craft solutions based on good data, and effectively communicate identified paths of action is common across many areas. Among the *occupational fields* where problem-solving skills are very important are business and management, nonprofit and volunteer management, nongovernmental organization management, education and training, criminal justice, politics, law, mediation and negotiation, health administration, marketing, public relations, and research. Among the *job titles* that are associated with these fields are the following: social worker or youth counselor, caseworker, psychologist, educator or education administrator, policy director or analyst, researcher, business manager or executive, social media manager, advertising manager or executive, Peace Corps volunteer, labor relations manager, criminologist, detective, corporate trainer, and organizational development consultant.

THINK ABOUT CAREERS:

■ *Think about career fields that might be of interest to you. What kinds of problems do people who work in this career field confront and address?*

▶ *Access additional web links on the student study site to learn more.*

SUMMARY

To test your knowledge further, find additional study material on the Student Study Site at **www.sagepub.com/chamblissintro**

- Notions of what constitutes **deviance** vary considerably and are relative to the norms and values of particular cultures as well as the labels applied by certain groups or individuals to specific behaviors, actions, practices, or conditions. Even **crimes,** which are particular forms of especially serious deviance, differ from place to place and over time, and they depend on social and political processes.

- The fact that the United States is a **pluralistic society** makes it difficult to establish universally accepted notions of deviance.

- Most sociologists do not believe there is a direct causal link between biology and deviance. Whatever the role of biology, deviant behaviors are culturally defined and socially learned.

- Functionalist theorists explain deviance in terms of the functions it performs for society. Émile Durkheim argued that some degree of deviance serves to reaffirm society's normative boundaries. Robert K. Merton argued that deviance reflects structural strain between the culturally defined goals of a society and the means society provides for achieving those goals. **Opportunity theory** emphasizes access to deviance as a major source of deviance. **Control theories** focus on the presence of interpersonal bonds as a means of keeping deviance in check.

- Conflict theories explain deviance in terms of the conflict between different groups, classes, or subcultures in society. **Class-dominant theories** of deviance emphasize how wealthy and powerful groups are able to define as deviant any behavior that runs counter to their interests. **Structural contradiction theory** argues that conflicts are inherent in social structure; it sees the sorts of structural strains identified by Merton as being built into society itself. Feminist perspectives on deviance remind us that, until relatively recently, research on deviance was almost exclusively conducted on males. Recent feminist theories have argued that many women labeled as deviant are themselves victims of deviant behavior, such as "delinquent" girls who are, in fact, runaways escaping sexual and physical abuse.

- Symbolic interactionist theorists argue that deviance, like all forms of human behavior, results from the ways in which we come to see ourselves through the eyes of others. One version of symbolic interactionism is **labeling theory,** which argues that deviance results mainly from the labels others attach to our behavior.

- Although crime is often depicted as concentrated among poor racial minorities, crimes are committed by people from all walks of life. **White-collar crime** and **state crime** are two examples of crime committed by people in positions of wealth and power. They exact enormous financial and personal costs from society.

- Deviance and **criminal deviance** are both controlled socially through the use of **informal social controls,** such as socialization, and **formal social controls,** such as arrests and imprisonment.

- Criminal deviance is controlled formally, and in modern societies including the United States this most often means incapacitating criminals by imprisoning them. Among industrialized nations, the United States currently has the highest proportion of its population in prison, giving rise to a large and powerful crime control industry.

- Although there is a public perception that crime is increasing, crime has steadily decreased over the 35 years the government has been collecting systematic data on it. **Violent crimes** are the most heavily publicized, but the most common are **property crimes** and victimless crimes.

- A disproportionate number of people of color are arrested and incarcerated in the United States. In addition, the **"war on drugs"** is focused on urban areas where poor people of color are concentrated.

KEY TERMS

Study terms on the go with the smartphone-friendly key term flashcards, available at **www.sagepub.com/chamblissintro**

deviance, 129

crime, 129

pluralistic societies, 129

polygamy, 129

capital offenses, 129

phrenology, 130

atavisms, 130

structural strain, 132

strain theory, 132

opportunity theory, 133

control theory, 133

social bonds, 133

subcultural theories, 133

class-dominant theories, 135

structural contradiction theory, 135

feminist perspective on deviance, 135

stigmatized, 137

labeling theory, 137

primary deviance, 137

secondary deviance, 139

differential association theory, 139

criminal deviance, 141

crime, 141

violent crime, 141

property crime, 141

organized crime, 142

white-collar crime, 142

state crime, 144

social control, 144

social power, 144

informal social control, 144

formal social control, 145

mandatory minimum sentences, 146

"three strikes" laws, 146

the "war on drugs", 146

DISCUSSION QUESTIONS

1. Measuring crime, including property crimes and violent crimes, can be challenging. Often, a single source is not enough to provide a comprehensive picture. What kinds of factors could affect the accuracy of statistics on the incidence of crime? How can the problems be overcome to render an accurate picture?

2. Labeling theories in the area of criminology suggest that labeling particular groups as deviant can be a self-fulfilling prophecy. That is, people may become that which is expected of them—including becoming deviant or even criminally deviant. Can you think of other social settings where labeling theory might be applied?

3. Think about some theoretical explanations for why people commit crime—differential association, social control, labeling. You might conclude that they all make sense on an intuitive level. Yet there is contradictory evidence for each of these theories; that is, some data support each theory, and some data contradict it. What is the difference between seeing intuitive sense in a theory and testing it empirically?

DISCOVER STATE STATS

Log-in to the eBook and click on the title to the left for access to State Stats in order to complete the exercise.

Go to the Education database and locate the subsection titled "Safety and Discipline," which compiles state and national data on related issues in U.S. schools. Find the most recent statistics on three forms of deviance for which data have been collected. Note their prevalence in the country as a whole and in three specific states representing different regions of the country. Write a brief paragraph that describes one of these forms of deviance and its prevalence (based on the statistical data), and that offers specific research questions a sociologist might ask about the phenomenon of deviance in U.S. schools.

STUDENT STUDY SITE

Visit the Student Study Site at **www.sagepub.com/chamblissintro** to access additional study tools, including eFlashcards, web quizzes, video resources, web resources, audio resources, links to SAGE journal, handbook, and research articles, and much more!

7

CLASS AND INEQUALITY

WHAT DO YOU THINK?

1. Why has income inequality in the United States grown since the 1970s?
2. What explains the existence and persistence of widespread poverty in the United States, one of the richest countries on earth?
3. Why are some countries poor and others wealthy?

SOC *VIEW*

Get a closer look with the authors!

THE NOUVEAU POOR

The term *nouveau riche,* French for "new rich," refers to those who once occupied a lower socioeconomic status but experienced substantial gains in income and wealth during their lifetime. The idea has roots in the early Industrial Revolution, which created masses of impoverished and exploited industrial workers and a new class of rich merchants (Rhodes, 2010). The *nouveau riche* were those who rose rapidly up the socioeconomic ladder, the top of which was already occupied by old nobility or the landed classes, sometimes called "old money." In the early American South, for instance, new factory owners in early industrialism were often looked down upon by the Southern gentry, who saw the newcomers as lacking the ability and knowledge to use their wealth and who resented the intrusion of the newly rich on their economic territory.

The Great Recession, our most recent financial crisis, began at the end of 2007 and officially ended in 2009. Its effects, however, continued to be felt even after economists declared the crisis past, as unemployment rates and home foreclosures remained high. Like early industrialism, the Great Recession gave birth to a new vocabulary, including the term *nouveau poor.*

In March 2012, the radio program *Marketplace* profiled a Georgia couple in their 50s who have experienced downward mobility. The interviewer meets Suellen and Steve in their renovated kitchen, where, when they had money for good food, Suellen loved to cook.

In 2008, when Steve lost his job, it was a shock. They'd just gotten back from a trip to Europe, where they celebrated their 30th wedding anniversary. Steve was sure he'd bounce back, but within a matter of months, they'd emptied their retirement accounts, and they went from middle class to the working poor.

The interviewer, David Gura, describes their struggle, as well as their effort to help others in their community through the creation of a small organization that offers fresh cooked food to poor families. Clearly, they are not the only ones in this dire economic situation, as the director of the

Inequality and the
Economic Crisis

Atlanta Food Bank suggests with his observation that about 20% of those seeking help in recent years have never sought help in the past. At the end of the interview, Gura (2012) adds that

> Suellen has come up with a term to describe the situation she's in. You've got nouveau riche, you become wealthy overnight. She calls herself nouveau poor. Suddenly poor, she's got to figure out how to get benefits, how to sort of survive without the money, without what she used to have.

As Suellen and Steve's story points out, even the middle class is not immune to the sting of downward mobility and economic struggles.

On the lower rungs of the economic ladder, millions in the United States fight to keep their heads above water, meet their mortgage or rental payments and other bills, avoid costly pitfalls like doctors' bills, and economize on groceries and other necessities. Some are unemployed, while others work multiple part-time jobs, cleaning homes or babysitting on some days, working in a supermarket or restaurant on others. Many still fall into poverty: In 2011, about 15% of the U.S. population was officially poor—over 46 million people were classified by the U.S. Census Bureau (2012a) as falling beneath the government's poverty line.

At the other end of the economic spectrum, in upper-middle-class and wealthy communities, neighborhoods are virtually crime-free, and public schools provide a solid education. Many parents have the means to send their children to private schools, where a high-quality education is virtually ensured. Most children go on to college, and a substantial proportion continue through graduate or professional school. Many will live comfortable lives as adults and pass their advantages on to their children.

In the United States today, there is substantial **social inequality**—a *disparity in income, wealth, power, prestige, and other resources.* Sociologists capture these disparities conceptually with an image from geology: They suggest that

· ·

Social inequality: A high degree of disparity in income, wealth, power, prestige, and other resources.

Social stratification: The systematic ranking of different groups of people in a hierarchy of inequality.

society, like the earth's surface, is made up of different layers. **Social stratification** is thus *the systematic ranking of different groups of people in a hierarchy of inequality.* Sociologists seek to outline the quantitative dimensions and the qualitative manifestations of social stratification in the United States and around the globe, but—even more importantly—they try to identify the social roots of stratification. ■

This chapter opens with an examination of forms of stratification in traditional and modern societies. We follow with a discussion of key aspects of social class and stratification. We consider theoretical perspectives on stratification that address the analytical questions of why economic inequality exists and persists. Next, we look at the quantitative and qualitative dimensions of

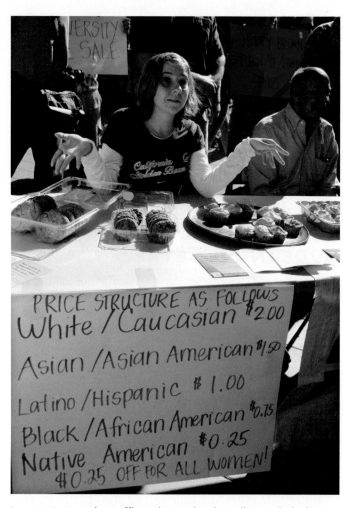

In a protest against affirmative action in college admissions, a "diversity bake sale" held at a California college by the College Republicans set pastry prices by racial and gender group. The action provoked anger among those who argue that affirmative action is a means of ensuring equal access to educational opportunities. Interest has grown recently in focusing affirmative action policies on class rather than race or gender. Is this likely to provoke controversy as well? ■

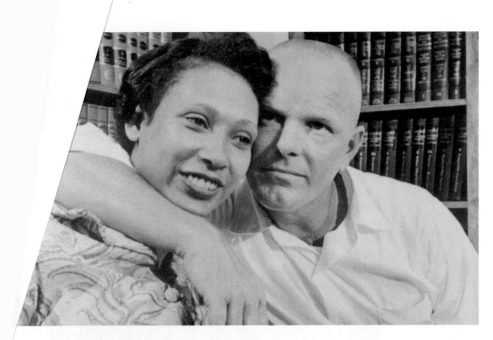

In *Loving v. Virginia* (1967), the U.S. Supreme Court ruled unanimously that a law forbidding interracial marriage was unconstitutional. Richard and Mildred Loving, shown here, were married in the District of Columbia in 1958. Their arrest in Virginia, where they resided, prompted the case. ■

inequality and poverty in the United States. Finally, we shift our gaze to the global picture, asking why some countries in the global system are poor and others wealthy.

STRATIFICATION IN TRADITIONAL AND MODERN SOCIETIES

Stratification systems are considered "closed" or "open," depending on how much mobility between layers is available to groups and individuals within a society. Caste societies (closed) and class societies (open) represent two important examples of systems of stratification.

CASTE SOCIETIES

In **caste societies** *the social levels are closed, so that all individuals remain at the social level of their birth throughout life.* Social status is based on personal characteristics—such as race or ethnicity, parental religion, or parental caste—that are present at birth, and mobility is virtually impossible. Social status, then, is the outcome of ascribed rather than achieved characteristics.

Historically, castes have largely appeared in agricultural societies that have not yet developed advanced industrial economies, such as rural India or South Africa prior to the end of White rule in 1992. In the United States before the end of the Civil

War in 1865, slavery imposed a racial caste system because, unless a slave escaped or was freed by his or her White master, it was usually a permanent condition. In the eyes of the law, the slave was a form of property without personal rights. Some argue that institutionalized racial inequality has remained a fixture of the U.S. landscape even after the end of slavery (Alexander, 2010; Dollard, 1957; Immerwahr, 2007). Indeed, enforced separation of Blacks and Whites was supported by federal, state, and local laws on education, family formation, public spaces, and housing as late as the 1960s.

Caste systems are far less common in countries and communities today than they were in centuries past. As we will see later in the chapter, India is home to a rising middle class. At the same time, India has long been characterized as a caste system because of its historical categorization of the population into four basic castes (or *varnas*): priests, warriors, traders, and workmen. These categories, which can be further divided, are based on the country's majority Hindu religion. At the bottom of the caste hierarchy, one finds the *Dalits* or "untouchables," the lowest caste.

Since the 1950s, India has passed laws to integrate the lowest caste members into positions of greater economic and political power. Some norms have also changed, permitting members of different castes to intermarry. While members of the lowest castes still lag in educational attainment compared to higher-caste groups, India today is moving closer to a class system.

CLASS SOCIETIES

Class societies are *societies in which social mobility allows someone to change his or her socioeconomic position.* Class societies exist in modern economic systems and are defined by several characteristics. First, they are *economically based,* at least in theory: That is, they determine class position by economic status (whether earned or inherited) rather than by religion or tradition. Second, class systems are *relatively fluid:* Boundaries between classes are violable and can be crossed. In fact, unlike the situation in caste systems, mobility is looked at favorably. Finally, class status is understood to be *achieved rather than ascribed:* Status is, ideally, given not by birth or religion or race or other inherited categories, but by merit or achievement in areas such as education and occupation.

As we will see in this chapter, these ideal-typical characteristics of class societies do not necessarily characterize reality, and class

....

Caste society: A social system in which social status is given for life. Caste societies are closed to social mobility.

Class society: A social system in which social level is open to movement so that changing class status is possible.

Hollywood's American Dream

status can be profoundly affected by factors like race, gender, or class of birth as much as by achievement.

SOCIOLOGICAL BUILDING BLOCKS OF STRATIFICATION AND SOCIAL CLASS

Nearly all socially stratified systems share three characteristics. First, rankings apply to **social categories** of people—that is, to *people who share a common characteristic without necessarily interacting or identifying with one another.* In many societies, women may be ranked differently than men, wealthy people differently than the poor, and highly educated people differently than those with little schooling. Individuals may be able to change their rank (through education, for instance), but the categories themselves will continue to exist as part of the social hierarchy.

Second, people's life experiences and opportunities are powerfully influenced by how their social category is ranked. Ranking may be linked to **achieved status**, which is *social position linked to one's acquisition of socially valued credentials or skills,* or **ascribed status**, which is *social position linked to characteristics that are socially significant but cannot generally be altered (such as race or gender).* While anyone can exercise individual agency, membership in a social category may influence whether the path forward (and upward) is characterized by obstacles or opportunities.

The third characteristic of a socially stratified system is that the hierarchical positions of social categories tend to change slowly

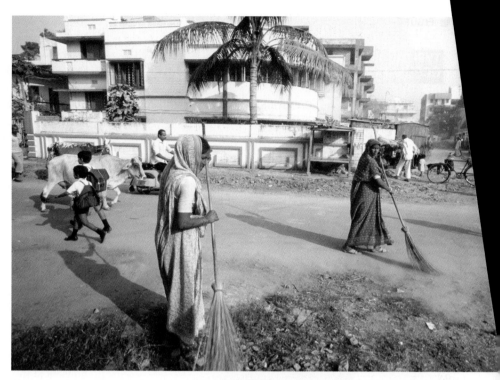

While discrimination on the basis of caste is not legal in modern India, members of low castes including the *Dalits* continue to be subject to unequal opportunities and justice—women's experience of discrimination is particularly acute. In some parts of India, incidents of sexual abuse of lower-caste girls and women by higher-caste men go unreported because of the improbability of punishment. ■

over time. Those groups who enjoy prestigious and preferential rankings in the social order tend to remain at the top, though the expansion of opportunities may change the composition of the group over time.

Societal stratification has evolved through different stages. The earliest societies, based on hunting and gathering, had little social stratification; there were few resources to divide, so differences within communities were less pronounced, at least materially. The development of agriculture produced considerably more wealth and a consequent rise in social stratification. The hierarchy in agricultural societies increasingly came to resemble a pyramid, with a large number of poor people at the bottom and successively smaller numbers in the upper tiers of more economically advantaged members.

Modern capitalist societies are, predictably, even more complex: Some sociologists suggest that class stratification resembles a teardrop (Figure 7.1 on page 158), with a large number of people in the middle ranks, a slightly smaller number of people at the bottom, and very few people at the top.

Before we continue, let's look at what sociologists mean when they use the term class. **Class** refers to *a person's economic position in society, which is associated with differences in income, wealth, and occupation.* Class position at birth strongly influences a person's **life chances**, *the opportunities and obstacles the person will encounter in education, social life, work, and other areas critical to social mobility.* **Social mobility** is *the upward or downward status movement of individuals or groups*

- -

Social categories: People sharing a common characteristic without necessarily interacting or identifying with one another.

Achieved status: An individual's social position is linked to his or her acquisition of socially valued credentials or skills.

Ascribed status: An individual's social position is linked to characteristics that are socially significant but cannot generally be altered (such as race or gender).

Class: A person's economic status in society, usually associated with income, wealth, and occupation, and sometimes associated with political voice.

Life chances: The opportunities and obstacles one will encounter in education, social life, work, and other areas critical to social mobility.

Social mobility: The upward or downward status movement of individuals or groups over time.

CAL CUPATIONS		TYPICAL INCOMES
stors, s, and ecutives	capitalist class	Top 1% make about $1.5 Million per year
Upper managers, Professionals, and Medium-sized business owners	upper middle class	14% make about $80,000 per year
Lower managers, Semi-professionals, Craftsmen, Foremen, and Non-retail sales	middle class	30% make about $45,000 per year
Low-skill manual, Clerical, and Retail sales	working class	30% make about $30,000 per year
Lowest-paid manual, retail, and service workers	working poor	13% make about $20,000 per year
Unemployed or part-time menial jobs, public assistance	under class	Bottom 13% make about $10,000 per year

SOURCE: Gilbert, D. L. (2011). *The American class structure in an age of growing inequality*. Thousand Oaks, CA: Pine Forge Press.

over time. Suellen and Steve, whom we met in our opening story, have experienced downward mobility due to the economic crisis. Upward social mobility may be experienced by those who earn educational credentials or have social networks they can tap. A college degree is one important step for many students toward upward mobility.

People who perform manual labor or work in low-wage sectors like food service are generally understood to be working class. Those who provide skilled professional services of some kind (whether legal advice, electrical wiring, nursing, or accounting services) and work for someone else are considered—and consider themselves—middle class. Dentists, teachers, managers, plumbers, auto sales representatives, and store managers are widely considered to be middle class, though there may be significant income, wealth, and educational differences between them, leading some writers to make the distinctions lower-middle, middle-middle, and upper-middle class. Notably, nailing down the quantitative dimensions of a U.S. middle class is so difficult that in 2012 the White House Task Force on the Middle Class, led by Vice President Joe Biden, opted for a descriptive rather than

Affirmative Action Bans

statistical definition of the middle class: its members are "defined by their aspirations more than their income. [It is assumed that] middle class families aspire to homeownership, a car, college education for their children, health and retirement security and occasional family vacations" (U.S. Department of Commerce Economics and Statistics Administration, 2010). Those who own or exercise substantial financial control over large businesses, financial institutions, or factories, or have achieved wealth through inheritance or talent, are generally seen to be part of the upper class.

Let's look more closely at some components of social class position: *income, wealth, occupation,* and *political voice*.

INCOME

Income refers to *the amount of money a person or household earns in a given period of time*. Income is earned most commonly at a job and less commonly through investments. Household income also includes government transfers such as Social Security payments or disability checks. Income typically goes to pay for food, clothing, shelter, health care, and other costs of daily living. It has a fluid quality in that it flows into a household in the form of a pay-period check and then flows out again as mortgages or rents are settled, groceries purchased, and other daily expenses paid.

U.S. household incomes have largely stagnated over the past decades, a topic we cover in detail later in the chapter. Between 2000 and 2011, median income for working-age households decreased in constant dollars from $63,535 to $55,640, a decline of $7,895—or more than 12% (U.S. Census Bureau, 2012). Effects of the recent economic crisis have not been evenly felt, but they have been experienced by all U.S. ethnic and racial groups (Figure 7.2). Income gains in the United States, however, have been disproportionately concentrated among the top earning groups.

WEALTH

Wealth, sometimes referred to as **net worth**, differs from income and is *the value of everything a person owns, minus the value of everything he or she owes*. Wealth becomes a more important source of status as people rise on the income ladder.

For most people in the United States who possess any measurable wealth, the key source of wealth is home equity, which is essentially the difference between the market value of their home and what they owe on their mortgage. This form of wealth is *illiquid* (as opposed to *liquid*); illiquid assets are those that are logistically difficult to transform into cash because the process is lengthy and complicated. So a family needing money to finance car repairs, meet educational expenses, or even ride out a period

Income: The amount of money a person or household earns in a given period of time, usually a year.

Wealth (or net worth): The value of everything a person owns, minus the value of everything owed.

of unemployment cannot readily transform its illiquid wealth into cash.

Economists and sociologists treat **net financial assets** as *a measure of wealth that excludes illiquid personal assets such as home and car.* Examples of net financial assets are stocks, bonds, cash, and other forms of investment assets. These are the principal sources of wealth used by the rich to secure their position in the economic hierarchy and, through reinvestment and other financial vehicles, to accumulate still more wealth.

Wealth, unlike income, is built up over a lifetime and passed down to the next generation. It is used to create new opportunities rather than merely to cover routine expenditures. Income buys shoes, coffee, and car repairs; wealth buys a high-quality education, business ventures, and access to travel and leisure that are out of reach of most, as well as financial security and the creation of new wealth. Those who possess wealth have a decided edge at getting ahead in the stratification system.

As we will see later in the chapter, wealth in the United States is largely concentrated at the top of the economic ladder.

OCCUPATION

An **occupation** is *a person's main vocation.* In the modern world, it generally refers to *paid employment.* Occupation is an important determinant of social class because it is the main source of income in modern societies. The U.S. Bureau of Labor Statistics (BLS) cites 840 detailed occupational categories in the United States. Sociologists have used various classifications to reduce this to a far smaller number of categories. For example, jobs are classified as *blue-collar* if they are based primarily on manual labor (factory workers, agricultural laborers, truck drivers, and miners) and *white-collar* if they require mainly analytic skills or formal education (doctors, lawyers, and business managers). The term *pink-collar* characterizes jobs that primarily employ women in semi-skilled, low-paid service positions (waitresses, sales clerks, and receptionists).

In the 1990s, some writers adopted the term *gold-collar* to classify young professionals who commanded huge salaries and high occupational positions very early in their professional careers, thanks to the technology bubble and economic boom of the 1990s (Wonacott, 2002). After the bubble burst, gold-collar workers were more often found in the financial sector, earning very substantial salaries and benefits. The economic recession that commenced in

· ·

Net financial assets: A measure of wealth that excludes such personal assets as home and car.

Occupation: A person's main vocation or paid employment.

Status: The prestige associated with a social position.

■ **FIGURE 7.2** U.S. Real Median Household Income by Racial and Ethnic Group, 1967–2011

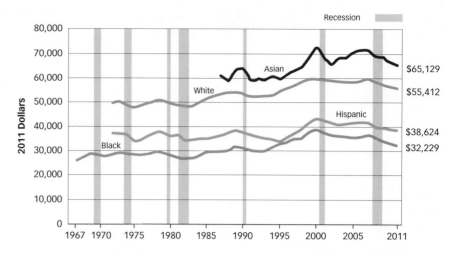

SOURCE: DeNavas-Walt, C., Proctor, B. D., & Smith, J. C. (2012). Income, poverty, and health insurance coverage in the United States: 2011. *Current Population Reports.* Washington, DC: U.S. Census Bureau.

2007 put a damper on growth in salaries and benefits of gold-collar workers, but they have risen again.

STATUS

Status refers to *the prestige associated with social position.* It varies based on factors such as family background and occupation. A considerable amount of social science research has gone into classifying occupations according to the degree of status or prestige they hold in public opinion.

We might expect white-collar jobs to rank more highly in prestige than blue-collar jobs, but do they? Doctors and scientists are indeed at the top of the prestige scale—but so are less highly paid professionals such as nurses and firefighters (who top the poll discussed in this section with 62% of respondents indicating they have "very great prestige"). Also in the top ranks are teachers and military officers (both with 51% conferring "very great prestige" on them). At the bottom are actors, stockbrokers, accountants, and real estate agents (just 5% of respondents indicated "very great prestige" for real estate agents). It seems occupations that require working with ideas (scientist, engineer) or providing professional services that contribute to the public welfare (teacher, doctor, firefighter) have the highest prestige, and, perhaps surprisingly, the U.S. public does not always relate prestige to income (Harris Interactive, 2009).

Prestige rankings of specific occupations are rather stable over time and across cultures, though changes do occur. For instance, since 1977 both scientists and lawyers have lost ground, falling 9 points to 57% and 10 points to 26%, respectively. What factors might explain these drops? Have societal changes taken

Low-Income and College

Income Mobility

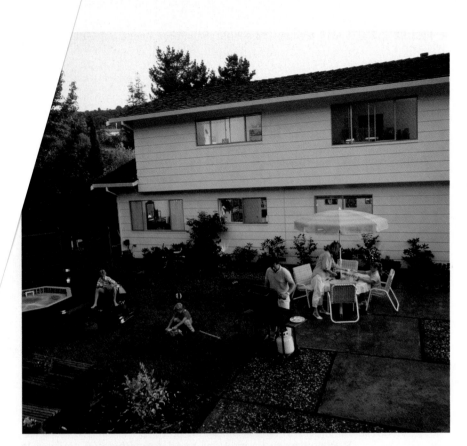

How would you define the U.S. middle class? Is the definition used by the White House Task Force on the Middle Class too broad, or not broad enough? Should aspirations or achievements be the foundation of a definition of a socioeconomic class? ■

place that might contribute to our understanding of why occupations like these rise and fall on the prestige scale?

POLITICAL VOICE

Political power refers to a particular type of power—*the ability to exercise influence on political institutions and/or actors in order to realize personal or group interests.* It encompasses the mobilization of resources (such as money or technology or political support of a desired constituency) and the successful achievement of political goals (such as the passage of legislation favorable to a particular group).

Sociological analyses of power have revealed a pyramid-like stratification system in the United States—as well as in most advanced industrial societies including those of Western Europe. At the top are a handful of political figures, businesspeople, and other leaders with substantial power over political decision making and the national economy. Moving down the pyramid, we encounter more people—and less power (Domhoff, 2009).

Sociologist C. Wright Mills began to write as early as the 1950s about the existence of a "power elite," which he defined as a group

comprising elites from the executive branch, the military, and the corporate community who shared social ties, a common "worldview" born of socialization in prestigious schools and clubs, and professional links that created revolving doors between positions in these three areas (Mills, 1956).

In contrast to the *pluralist perspective* on U.S. democracy, which suggests that political power is fluid and passes, over time, between a spectrum of groups and interests who compete in the political arena, Mills offered a critical perspective. He described a concentration of political power in the hands of a small elite. While some power over local issues remained in the hands of elected legislatures and interest groups, decision making power over issues of war and peace, global economic interests, and other matters of international and national consequence remained with the power elite. The power of the masses was little more than an illusion for Mills, and he saw the masses as composed of "entirely private" individuals wrapped up in personal concerns and largely disconnected from the political process. (We discuss the power elite and pluralism more fully in Chapter 13.)

Today, the middle class is at the center of electoral discourse. But are its fundamental economic concerns being addressed by decision makers? Or do the interests of the wealthy guide policy making? Are the voices of the poor present in politics? What do you think?

WHY DOES STRATIFICATION EXIST AND PERSIST IN CLASS SOCIETIES?

We find stratification in virtually all societies, a fact that the functionalist and social conflict perspectives seek to explain. The functionalist perspective highlights the ways in which stratification is functional for society as a whole. Social conflict theorists, in contrast, argue that inequality weakens society as a whole and exists because it benefits those in the upper economic, social, and political spheres. We take a closer look at these theoretical perspectives below.

THE FUNCTIONALIST EXPLANATION

Functionalism is rooted in part in the writings of sociologist Émile Durkheim (1893/1964), who suggested that we could best understand economic positions as performing interdependent functions

Genetics and Inequality

....

Political power: The ability to exercise influence on political institutions and/or actors in order to realize personal or group interests.

for society as a whole. Using this perspective, we can think of social classes as equivalent to the different organs in the human body: Just as the heart, lungs, and kidneys serve different yet indispensable functions for human survival, so do the different positions in the class hierarchy.

In the middle of the 20th century, Kingsley Davis and Wilbert Moore (1945) built on these foundations to offer a detailed functionalist analysis of social stratification. They argued that in all societies some positions—the most "functionally important" positions—require more skill, talent, and training than others. These positions are thus difficult to fill—that is, they may suffer a "scarcity of personnel." To ensure they get filled, societies can offer valued rewards like money, prestige, and leisure to induce the best and brightest to make "sacrifices," such as getting a higher education, and to do these important jobs conscientiously and competently. According to Davis and Moore social inequality is an "unconsciously evolved device by which societies ensure that the most important positions are conscientiously filled by the most qualified persons" (p. 243).

An implication of this perspective is that U.S. society is a **meritocracy**, *a society in which personal success is based on talent and individual effort.* That means your position in the system of stratification depends primarily upon your talents and efforts: Each person gets more or less what he or she deserves or has earned, and society benefits because the most functionally important positions are occupied by the most qualified individuals. Stratification is then ultimately functional for society, because the differential distribution of rewards ensures that highly valued positions are filled by well-prepared and motivated people: After all, Davis and Moore might say, we all benefit when we get economic information from good economists, drive across bridges designed by well-trained engineers, and cure our ills with pharmaceuticals discovered by capable medical scientists.

Clearly the idea that the promise of higher pay and prestige motivates people to work hard has some truth. Yet it is difficult to argue that the actual difference in rewards between positions is necessarily a measure of their relative worth to society (Tumin, 1953, 1963, 1985; Wrong, 1959). Are NBA point guards really worth more than a teacher or nurse, for instance? Are hedge fund managers that much more important than scientists (particularly given that both positions require extensive education)?

Moreover, when people acquire socially important, higher-status positions by virtue of their skills and efforts, they are then often able to pass along their economic privilege, and the educational opportunities and social connections that go with it, to their children, even if their children are not particularly bright, motivated,

. . . .

Meritocracy: A society in which personal success is based on talent and individual effort.

Herbert Gans suggests that poverty ensures a pool of workers "unable to be unwilling" to do difficult and dirty jobs for low pay. Such jobs could also be filled in the absence of poverty—through better pay and benefits. But, says Gans, this would be costly, and thus dysfunctional, to the nonpoor. ■

or qualified. As Melvin Tumin (1953) points out in his critique of Davis and Moore, stratification may *limit* the discovery of talent in society rather than *ensuring* it, by creating a situation in which those who are born to privilege are given fuller opportunities and avenues to realize occupational success, while others are limited by poor schooling, little money, and lack of networks upon which to call. Such a result would surely be dysfunctional for society, rather than positively functional.

How would functionalism account for the fact that people are often discriminated against because of their skin color, sex, and other characteristics determined at birth that have nothing to do with their talents or motivations, resulting in an enormous waste of society's human skills and talents? Can you see other strengths or weaknesses to Davis and Moore's perspective on stratification?

In a twist on the functionalist perspective, sociologist Herbert Gans (1972) poses this provocative question: How is poverty positively functional in U.S. society? Gans begins with a bit of functionalist logic, namely that if a social phenomenon exists and persists, it must serve a function or else it would evolve out of existence. But he does not assume that poverty is functional for everyone. So *for whom* is it functional? Gans suggests that eliminating poverty would be costly to the better-off. Thus poverty is functional for the nonpoor, but not functional for the poor—or even for society as a whole.

Among the "benefits" to the nonpoor of having a stratum of poor people, Gans includes the following:

- Poverty ensures there will be low-wage laborers prepared—or driven by circumstances—to do society's "dirty work." These are the jobs no one else wants because they are demeaning, dirty, and sometimes dangerous. A large pool of laborers desperate for jobs also pushes down wages, a benefit to employers.

- Poverty creates a spectrum of jobs for people who help the poor (social welfare workers), protect society from those poor people who transgress the boundaries of the law (prison guards), or profit from them (owners of welfare motels or cheap grocery shops). Even the author of the piece, esteemed sociologist Herbert Gans, has built an academic career on analyzing poverty.

- Poverty provides a market for goods and services that would otherwise go unused. Day-old bread, wilting fruits and vegetables, and old automobiles are not generally purchased by the better-off. The services of second-rate doctors and lawyers, among others, are also peddled to the poor when no one else wants them.

- Beyond economics, the poor also serve cultural functions. They provide scapegoats for society's problems and help guarantee some status for those who are not poor. They also give the upper crust of society a socially valued reason for lavish charity functions.

Gans's (1972) point is stark. He notes that the "functions" served by the poor have *functional alternatives*—that is, they could be fulfilled by other means than poverty. However, he suggests, those who are better off in society are not motivated to comprehensively fight poverty because its existence is demonstrably functional for them. While he is not arguing that anyone is in favor of poverty (which is difficult to imagine), he is suggesting that "phenomena like poverty can be eliminated only when they become dysfunctional for the affluent or powerful, or when the powerless can obtain enough power to change society" (p. 288). Do you agree with his argument? Why or why not?

THE SOCIAL CONFLICT EXPLANATION

Social conflict theory draws heavily from the work of Karl Marx. As we saw in the opening chapter, Marx divided society into two broad classes: workers and capitalists, or *proletarians* and *bourgeoisie*. The workers do not own the factories and machinery needed to produce wealth in capitalist societies—they possess nothing of real value except their labor power. The capitalists own the necessary equipment—the *means of production*—but require the labor power of the workers to run it.

These economic classes are unequal in their access to resources and power, and their interests are opposed. Capitalists seek to keep labor costs as low as possible in order to produce goods cheaply and make a profit. Workers seek to be paid adequate wages and to secure safe, decent working conditions and hours. At the same time, the two groups are interdependent: The capitalists need the labor of the workers, and the workers depend on the wages they earn (regardless of how meager) to survive.

Although over a century has passed since Marx formulated his theory, a struggle between workers and owners (or, in our times, between workers and owners, managers, and even stockholders, who all depend on the company's profits) still exists. Conflict is often based on the irreconcilability of their competing interests. A recent study found that collective action lawsuits alleging wage and hour violations have skyrocketed, increasing 400% in the past 11 years. Among companies such as Bank of America, Walmart, and Starbucks, Taco Bell has been one of the latest to be sued for allegedly forcing employees to work overtime without pay (Eichler, 2012).

The source of inequality, from this perspective, lies in the fact that the bourgeoisie own the means of production and can use their assets to make more money and secure their position in society. Most workers do not own substantial economic assets aside from their own labor power, which they use to earn a living. While successful lawsuits for lost wages show that workers have avenues for asserting their rights against employers, the conflict perspective contrasts these small victories with the far more significant power and control exercised by large economic actors in modern society.

In short, the conflict perspective suggests that significant and persistent stratification exists because those who have power use it to create economic, political, or social conditions that favor them and their children, even if they are detrimental to the lower classes. Inequality thus is not functional, as Davis and Moore argued. Rather, it is dysfunctional, because it keeps power concentrated in the hands of the

The poor often face limited choices in terms of housing, employment, and transportation due to financial constraints. Their options are restricted by affordability with little room for personal preference. They may find themselves forced to purchase low-quality products, such as the decrepit vehicles pictured above. ■

DIGITAL SOCIETY

POWER AND MODERN TECHNOLOGY

Most conflict theorists, following the lead of Karl Marx, maintain that capitalism is a system characterized by oppression and rife with inequality. If this is so, why do working people, victimized by an economic order that enriches the upper socioeconomic classes at their expense, not rise up in protest? Sociologists Herbert Marcuse and Douglas Kellner have a few ideas.

Marcuse, writing in the 1960s and 1970s, saw technology in modern capitalist society as paving the road to a "comfortable, smooth, reasonable, democratic unfreedom" (Marcuse, 1964, p. 1). He believed that modern technology, employed in the service of capitalist interests, would lead to ever more effective—and even pleasant—methods of exerting external control over individuals. After all, spending the evening immersed in a reality program or an action film is much easier than rising up in protest or revolution. And we may not like the conditions of our work, but we are willing to work hard so we can get our hands on the newest iPhone. From this perspective, mass media (for instance, television) are used to socialize and pacify populations and are thus instruments of domination. Marcuse (1964) argued that the freedom of individuals had been "invaded and whittled down" by modern technology, and that the result was a "one-dimensional" society in which the ability to think negatively and critically about the

social order was progressively crushed (p. 10).

Kellner (1990) expanded the argument that modern technology—and television in particular—constitutes a threat to human freedom of thought and action in the realm of social change. Kellner suggests that the television industry "has the crucial ideological functions of legitimating the capitalist mode of production and delegitimating its opponents" (p. 9). That is, he suggests that mainstream television appears to offer a broad spectrum of opinions but opinions that seem to question the fundamental values of capitalism (for example, the right to accumulate unlimited wealth and power) or to critique not individual politicians, parties, and policies but the system within which they operate,

are systematically excluded. Because television is such a pervasive force in our lives, the boundaries it draws around debates on capitalism, social change, and genuine democracy are significant.

THINK IT THROUGH

■ *Karl Marx wrote that the ruling ideas of any society are those of the ruling class. Arguably, many of those ideas are conveyed through the vehicle of TV. Does television, which delivers images and messages to our homes for an average of seven hours a day, foster passivity and make us vulnerable to manipulation? What about the Internet? How does it expand human action, creativity, and freedom? How does it limit them?*

few, rather than creating conditions of meritocracy that would give equal opportunity to all. In the *Digital Society* box on page 163, we look at a modern perspective on this conflict and, in particular, why those who are economically disadvantaged by it do not rise up in protest.

Like the functionalist perspective, the conflict perspective has analytical weaknesses. It overlooks cooperative aspects of modern capitalist businesses, some of which have taken a more democratic approach to management, offering workers the opportunity to participate in decision making processes in the workplace. Modern workplaces in, for instance, the technology sector thrive when decision making and the production of ideas come from various levels rather than just from the top down.

CLASS AND INEQUALITY IN THE UNITED STATES: DIMENSIONS AND TRENDS

The United States prides itself on being a nation of equals. Indeed, except for the Great Depression of the 1930s, inequality declined throughout much of the 20th century, reaching its lowest levels during the 1960s and early 1970s. But during the past three decades, inequality has been on the rise again. The rich have gotten much richer, middle-class incomes have stagnated, and a growing number of poor are struggling to make ends meet.

INCOME INEQUALITY

Sociologist Richard Sennett (1998) writes that "Europeans from [Alexis de] Tocqueville on have tended to take the face value for reality; some have deduced we Americans are indeed a classless society, at least in our manners and beliefs—a democracy of consumers; others, like Simone de Beauvoir, have maintained we are hopelessly confused about our real differences" (p. 64). Was Tocqueville right, or Beauvoir? Are we classless or confused? Are we all just members of a vast middle class? What are the dimensions of our differences? Let us look at what statistics tell us and then discuss what they might mean for addressing these questions.

Every year the U.S. Census Bureau calculates how income is distributed across the population of earners. All households are ranked by annual income and then categorized into *quintiles,* or fifths. The Census Bureau calculates how much of the aggregate income, or total income, generated in the United States each quintile gets. In other words, imagine all legally earned and reported income thrown into a big pot—that is the aggregate income. The Census Bureau wants to know (and we do too!) how much of this income goes to each quintile of earners. In a society with equal distribution across quintiles, each fifth of earners would get one fifth of the income in the pot. Conversely, in a society with complete inequality across quintiles, the top would get everything, and the bottom quintiles would be left empty-handed. The United States, like all other countries, falls between these two hypothetical extremes. In Figure 7.3, we see how aggregate income in the United States is divided among quintiles of earners.

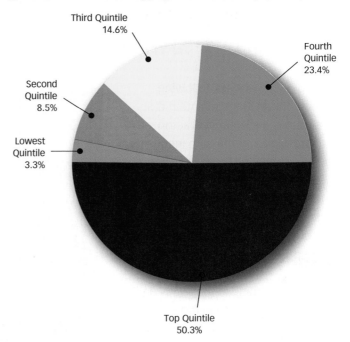

■ **FIGURE 7.3** Shares of Aggregate U.S. Income by Quintile, 2011

SOURCE: DeNavas-Walt, C., Proctor, B. D., & Smith, J. C. (2012). Income, poverty, and health insurance coverage in the United States: 2011. *Current Population Reports.* Washington, DC: U.S. Census Bureau.

When we look at the pie, we see that income earners at different levels take in disparate proportions of the income total. Those in the bottom quintile take in just over 3% of the aggregate income, while those in the top quintile get more than half; that means the top 20% of earners bring in as much as all in the bottom 80% combined. No less significantly, the top 5% take in over 22% of the total income—more than the bottom 40% combined (U.S. Census Bureau, 2012).

Data compiled by economists Emmanuel Saez and Thomas Piketty, with a slightly different formula that uses pretax income (as do the census figures) and includes capital gains, suggests an even more stratified picture: About 50% of pretax income goes to the top 10% of earners. Within this well-off decile (or tenth) of earners, there is a still more dramatic division of income, because the top *1%* of earners takes about a fifth of the aggregate income (Saez, 2010). Clearly, gains have been concentrated at the top of the income ladder: As economist Joseph Stiglitz (2012) points out, the fraction of the aggregate income taken by the upper 1% has doubled since 1980, while the fraction that goes to the upper 0.1% has nearly tripled over that period.

When we study issues like income inequality, we benefit from understanding the data we gather in its historical context. The pie we looked at is a snapshot of one moment in time, but what about decades past? The economic prosperity of the middle to late 1990s brought some benefit to most workers: The median U.S. income rose faster at the end of the 1990s than it had since the period from the late 1940s to the middle. Saez (2010) calculates that the real annual growth of income among the bottom 99% of earners grew 2.7% in the period he terms the "Clinton Expansion" (1993–2000), but it dropped during the 2000–2002 recession (by 3.3%) and again during the 2007–2008 period (by 6.9%). On the whole, the period from 1993 to 2008 saw a real annual growth of just 0.75% for the incomes of the bottom 99%. Over the same period, the top 1% of earners experienced a real annual growth of under 4% (though this group too experienced significant losses in the recessionary periods).

From about World War II until the middle 1970s, the top 10% earned less than a third of the national income pool (Pearlstein, 2010). In the years since, however, the incomes of people at or near the top have risen far faster than those of earners at the bottom or middle of the income scale (Figure 7.4). The stagnation of wages can be illustrated by looking at the poor growth (and even decline) of average wages of new college graduates. As we see in Figure 7.5, in the period between 2000 and 2011, the wages of new college graduates fell by more than 5% (Shierholz, Sabadish, & Wething, 2012).

WEALTH INEQUALITY

We see the growth of inequality in the distribution of income, but what about the wealth gap? What are its dimensions? Is it growing or shrinking?

Recall that while income has a fluid quality—flowing into the household with a weekly or monthly check and flowing out again as bills are paid and other goods of daily life purchased—wealth has a more solid quality. Wealth represents possessions that do not flow into and out of the household regularly but instead provide a set of assets that can buy security, educational opportunity, or comfortable retirement years. The distribution of wealth gives us another important gauge of how U.S. families are doing relative to one another in terms of security, opportunity, and prospects.

More people than ever have invested money in the stock market. Does that mean wealth is more evenly spread across the population than before? In fact, the distribution of wealth is even more unequal than the income gap and, like that gap, is growing. If we exclude the ownership of cars and homes—which, as we noted, are not really sources of wealth that people can use to pay the bills or get richer—the difference in wealth between high-income families and everyone else is particularly pronounced. Figure 7.6 on page 167 shows the expanding ratio of the average wealth of the top 1% and the national median wealth.

Minority groups hold far fewer net financial assets than Whites. The wealth held by minority households has lagged dramatically in the past; for instance, in 1990, Black households held about 1% of total U.S. wealth (Conley, 1999). This percentage rose markedly in the economic boom years of the 1990s and continued to expand into the 2000s. Black household wealth reached an average of just over $12,000 in 2005. This climb, however, has been reversed by the housing crisis and the Great Recession, which saw a 53% fall in household wealth among Blacks to just $5,677. Among Hispanics, the fall was even

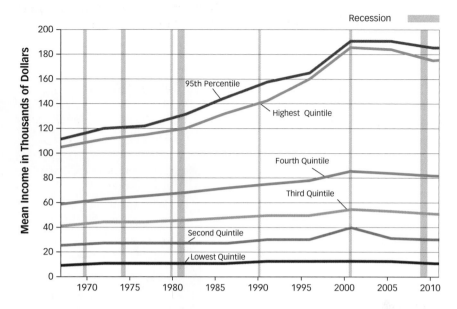

■ **FIGURE 7.4** Changes in Income Inequality in the U.S., 1967–2011

SOURCE: DeNavas-Walt, C., Proctor, B. D., & Smith, J. C. (2012). Income, poverty, and health insurance coverage in the United States: 2011. *Current Population Reports*. Washington, DC: U.S. Census Bureau.

FIGURE 7.5 Average Hourly Wages of U.S. College Graduates Aged 21–24, 1989–2011

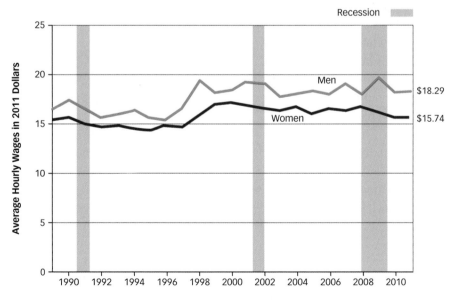

SOURCE: Shierholz, H., Sabadish, N., & Wething, H. (2012). *Wages of young college graduates have failed to grow in the last decade.* Washington, DC: Economic Policy Institute.

Income Inequality

INEQUALITY MATTERS

THE MINIMUM WAGE DEBATE

In July 2009, the federal minimum wage rose to $7.25 an hour, the third and final increase mandated by the amended Fair Labor Standards Act (FLSA). A full-time employee earning the minimum wage makes a yearly pretax income of $15,504. Clearly, no one gets rich on the minimum wage—it is a *minimum* wage level legally mandated for U.S. workers (though exceptions in the law exist, for instance, for full-time students under the age of 20). But is it enough to ensure a minimum standard of living? Should it be raised further? Or should it be lowered or even abolished altogether?

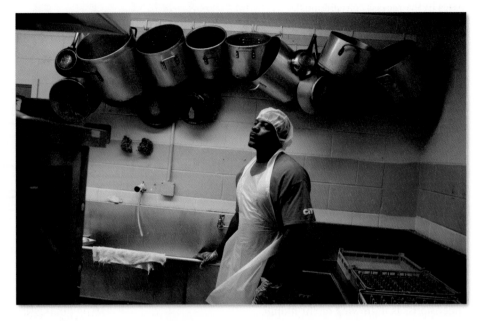

Proponents of minimum wage laws and increases argue that the current wage does not support the idea that "work pays." Many minimum wage workers earn below or just barely above the U.S. official poverty line. A single parent with one child working full-time at a minimum wage job is scarcely above the poverty threshold of $15,504 for one adult under 65 supporting one child (U.S. Census Bureau, 2011). An increased minimum wage, they argue, has the potential to increase the standard of living of the neediest U.S. workers and their children.

From a macroeconomic perspective, higher wages also push up consumption because the poor spend all or most of their wages. This is beneficial for the economy, which is highly dependent upon consumption.

Other benefits that proponents cite include greater employee motivation and retention, which lowers the cost of training new employees, and less need for government support of low-wage workers in the form of food stamps and housing subsidies.

Opponents of minimum wage laws suggest that a federally mandated minimum wage hurts both low-wage workers and private businesses. They argue that mandated increases may reduce hiring as businesses seek to cut labor costs—the result is fewer jobs for those in the low-wage sector. Further, a rising minimum wage, say opponents, can discourage high school students from completing their education by enticing them to join the job market prematurely. Consumers may also be harmed as higher labor costs are passed on in

the form of higher prices for goods and services. Finally, profit margins for small businesses, already slim, may be further reduced by mandated wage increases. If minimum wage laws were abolished, markets would set the minimum wage by balancing what employers will pay and what employees will accept.

THINK IT THROUGH

■ *So what is the answer to the minimum wage conundrum? Should it be raised at the federal level? (Sixteen states and the District of Columbia already have higher minimum wages than the law requires.) How strong are the competing arguments on the two sides of the debate? What do you think?*

more stark, with household wealth dropping 66% from a high of $18,359 in 2005. In the aftermath of the economic crisis, the median household wealth of Whites is fully 20 times that of Black households and 18 times that of Hispanic households (Kochhar, Fry, & Taylor, 2011).

Many U.S. families have zero or negative net worth, a condition worsened by the recent recession. Consider a Pew Research Center (2011) finding that while the median wealth of Latino households in 2009 was just over $6,000, nearly a third had zero or negative net worth, a figure that put them between White households (15% had zero or negative net worth) and Black households (35% had zero or negative net worth).

OTHER GAPS: INEQUALITIES IN HEALTH CARE, HEALTH, AND ACCESS TO CONSUMER GOODS

Along with the gap in income and wealth, there is a critical gap in employer benefits, including health coverage. From the 1980s to the 1990s, health care coverage for workers in the bottom quintile of earners fell more dramatically than for any other segment of workers: From a rate of 41% coverage it dropped to just 32% in the late 1990s (Reich, 2001). In 2011, about 25% of those living in households earning less than $25,000 a year were uninsured, along with over 21% of those in households earning $25,000–$49,999 (U.S. Census Bureau, 2012). Altogether, more than 15% (48.6 million) of the U.S. population was without health insurance, including 7 million children under age 18 (U.S. Census Bureau, 2012). One goal of President Obama's Patient Protection and Affordable Care Act, signed into law in 2010, is to expand insurance coverage for the working poor. The results of this effort are, as yet, not clear because all parts of the law have not been implemented as of this writing.

Many of the jobs created in the 1990s were positions in the service sector, which includes retail sales and food service. While the strong job growth of this period helped push down the unemployment rate, the quality of jobs created for those with less education was not on par with many of the jobs lost as U.S. manufacturing became automated or moved overseas. Many service sector jobs pay wages at or just above minimum wage and have been increasingly unlikely to offer benefits.

Perhaps predictably, there is a powerful relationship between health and class status. Empirical data show that those with greater income and education are less likely than their less well-off peers to have and die of heart disease, diabetes, and many types of cancer. Just as income is distributed unevenly in the population,

. . . .

Food deserts: Sites bereft of places selling competitively priced, healthy, and fresh food.

■ **FIGURE 7.6** Wealth of Top 1%, 1962–2010

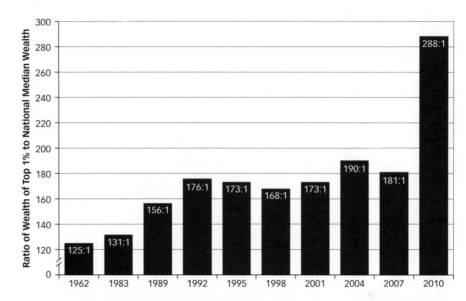

SOURCE: Economic Policy Institute. (2012). Ratio of average top 1% household wealth to median wealth, 1962–2010. *The State of Working America.* Washington, DC: Wolff.

so is good health. Notably, modern medical advances have disproportionately provided benefits for those at the top of the income spectrum (Scott, 2005).

The physical and mental health of children in disadvantaged families is more likely to be poor than that of their better-off peers. The Kaiser Family Foundation (2008) found that the rate of hospitalization for asthma for Black children is 4 to 5 times higher than that for White children. The problem is not only a lack of health insurance in families—though this factor is important—but also the lack of physical activity that may result from a lack of safe places to play and exercise, and a lack of healthy foods when both money and access are limited.

The problem of health and good food is linked to another disadvantage experienced by those on the lower economic rungs, which is lack of access to high-quality goods at competitive prices. Most middle-class shoppers purchase food at large chain grocery stores that stock items like fresh fruit and vegetables and meat at competitive prices, while inhabitants of poor neighborhoods are more likely to shop at small groceries that have less stock and higher prices because large chains choose not to locate in poor areas. If they want to shop at big grocery stores, poor residents may need to travel a greater distance, a substantial challenge for those less likely to own cars.

Some writers refer to areas with few or no easily accessible sources of fresh food as **food deserts**, *sites bereft of places selling competitively priced, healthy, and fresh food.* A *USA Today* article quoted Louisville retiree Jessie Caldwell, who regularly

Economic Inequality

Many city neighborhoods lack access to large, well-stocked supermarkets with competitive prices. Residents must often choose between overpriced and often poor-quality goods, and a long trip to a suburban market. The low rates of private vehicle ownership among the urban poor can make shopping for healthy food a burden. ■

makes an hourlong bus trip to get fresh vegetables or meat: "[F]or her and many others, it's often tempting to go to a more convenient mini-market or grab some fast food. 'The corner stores just sell a lot of potato chips, pop and ice cream,' she said. 'But people are going to eat what's available'" (Kenning & Halladay, 2008).

While we do not always think of access to competitive prices, fresh goods, and accessible stores as issues in class inequality, they affect the quality of life, conferring advantage on the already advantaged and disadvantage on those who struggle to make ends meet. Writer Barbara Ehrenreich (2001) highlights this point with her argument that

> There are no secret economies that nourish the poor; on the contrary, there are a host of special costs. If you can't put up the two months' rent you need to secure an apartment, you end up paying through the nose for a room by the week. If you have only a room, with a hot plate at best, you can't save by cooking up huge lentil stews that can be frozen for the week ahead. You eat fast food and hot dogs and Styrofoam cups of soup that can be microwaved in a convenience store. (p. 27)

Health Inequalities

Poor Neighborhoods and Food Deserts

WHY HAS INEQUALITY GROWN?

There is a significant split between the fortunes of those who are well educated and those who do not or cannot attend college. The demand for labor over the past several decades has been differentiated on the basis of education and skills—workers with more education are more highly valued, while those with little education are becoming less valuable. These effects result from the United States' transition to a postindustrial economy.

Our earlier industrial economy was founded heavily on manufacturing. The United States produced a substantial proportion of the goods we used—cars, washing machines, textiles, and the like—and a big part of the economy depended on this production for its prosperity. This is no longer the case. In the postindustrial economy of today, the United States manufactures a smaller proportion of the goods it consumes and fewer goods overall. Many manufacturing jobs have either been mechanized or gone abroad, drawn to the low-cost labor in developing countries. The new focus is on the production of knowledge and information and the provision of services.

One group that has grown is professionals who engage in what former Secretary of Labor Robert Reich (1991) has called "symbolic analysis" or "problem-solving, problem-identifying, and strategic-brokering activities" (p. 111). These occupational categories—law, engineering, business, technology, and the like—typically pay well and offer some job security, but they also require a high level of skill and at least a college education. Even well-educated, middle-class workers, however, have been touched by automation and outsourcing. As well, a rising proportion of middle-level jobs have converted from relatively stable and secure long-term positions to contractual work. We examine these issues in greater detail in Chapter 14.

The fastest-growing sector of the postindustrial economy beginning in the 1980s was the service sector: That includes jobs in food service, retail sales, health care (for instance, home health aides or nurse's aides), janitorial and housecleaning services, and security. These jobs do not require advanced education or technical skills, but they typically pay poorly and offer weak job security and few benefits.

In the period following the official end of the Great Recession, the bulk of new jobs were low-wage positions in the service sector. While middle-wage, middle-skill jobs have failed to recover in the years after the economic crisis, jobs on the low end of the pay scale have multiplied (Figure 7.7 on page 169).

By providing jobs to those with less education, the service sector has, in a sense, moved into the void left by the manufacturing sector of the industrial economy over the past few decades. The service sector, which offers lower pay scales and fewer benefits, does not typically provide the kinds of jobs that offer a solid road to the middle class. Another difference is that manufacturing, especially automaking and steel, was overwhelmingly a male bastion, while service jobs favor women. The "advantage" enjoyed by less educated women over their male counterparts does not, however, translate into substantial economic gains for females or their families. Female wage gains have been more fully driven by gains made by college-educated women.

The stratification of the U.S. labor force into a low-wage service sector and a better-paid knowledge and technology sector appears to be continuing unabated. The narrative of a "disappearing middle class" has become a common theme in both social science and mainstream political discourse. Do you see such a trend in your own community? How does this narrative coexist with our long-existing tendency to self-identify as middle class, almost regardless of income?

AT THE BOTTOM OF THE LADDER: POVERTY IN THE UNITED STATES

There is a familiar America. It is celebrated in speeches and advertised on television and in the magazines. It has the highest mass standard of living the world has ever known.

In the 1950s this America worried about itself, yet even its anxieties were products of abundance . . . There was introspection about Madison Avenue and tail fins; there was discussion of the emotional suffering taking place in the suburbs. In all this, there was an implicit assumption that the basic grinding economic problems had been solved in the United States . . .

While this discussion was being carried on, there existed another America. In it dwelt between 40,000,000 and 50,000,000 citizens of this land. They were poor. They still are.

To be sure, the other America is not impoverished in the same sense as those poor nations where millions cling to hunger as a defense against starvation. This country has escaped such extremes. That does not change the fact that tens of millions of Americans are, at this very moment, maimed in body and spirit, existing at levels beneath those necessary for human decency. If these people are not starving, they are hungry, and sometimes fat with hunger, for that is what cheap foods do. They are without adequate housing and education and medical care. (Harrington, 1963, pp. 1–2)

These words, first published in 1963, helped to open the eyes of many to the plight of the U.S. poor, who were virtually invisible to a postwar middle class comfortably ensconced in suburbia.

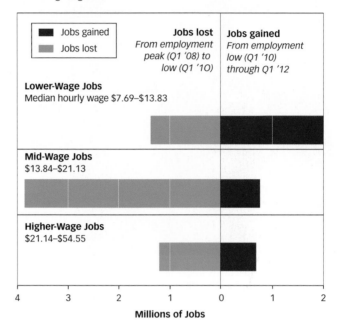

■ **FIGURE 7.7** Job Losses and Gains in the U.S. Economy, 2008–2012

Missing Middle

Most of the jobs added during the recovery have come in the lower-wage segment.

SOURCE: Bernhardt, A. (2012). *The low-wage recovery and growing inequality.* New York: National Employment Law Project, p. 2.

Michael Harrington's classic book, *The Other America: Poverty in the United States,* also caught the interest of President John F. Kennedy's administration and later the Johnson administration, which inaugurated the War on Poverty in 1964.

When President Lyndon B. Johnson began his War on Poverty, around 36 million U.S. citizens lived in poverty. Within a decade, the number had dropped sharply, to around 23 million. But then, beginning in the early 1970s, poverty again began to climb, reaching a high of 39 million people in 1993 before receding. It has climbed once more, and since 2008 poverty has surpassed the peak set in 1993 (Figure 7.8 on page 170). In 2011, the number of officially poor stood at over 46 million people—or about 15% of the population (U.S. Census Bureau, 2012).

We pause on the topic of "official poverty" for a moment, because it is important for us to be critical consumers of information. We are surrounded by statistics, subject to a barrage of information about the proportion of the population who support the president or reject the health care initiatives of a political party, about the number of teen pregnancies and births, about the percentage who are unemployed or in poverty. These statistics illuminate the social world around us and offer us a sense of what we as a nation are thinking or earning or debating. On the other hand, statistics—including social indicators like the poverty numbers (Table 7.1 on page 171)—may also obscure some important issues. To use indicators such as the poverty numbers wisely, we should know where they come from and what their limitations are.

Periods of economic crisis foster heavy demand on spaces in homeless shelters. At the same time, city budgets also suffer shortfalls, and demand may exceed supply. In some cities, the law requires that shelter be provided when temperatures fall beneath a set minimum, but even freezing temperatures cannot expand limited beds. ■

What is poverty from the perspective of the U.S. government? How were these numbers generated? The **official poverty line** is the dollar amount set by the government as the minimum amount of money needed to meet the basic needs for a family. In 2011, the government used the following thresholds:

- One person, under 65: $11,702
- One person, 65 or older: $10,788
- Three persons (one adult, two children): $18,106
- Four persons (two adults, two children): $22,811
- Five persons (two adults, three children): $26,844.

From the federal government's perspective, those whose pretax income falls beneath the threshold are officially poor; those whose pretax income is above the line (whether by $10 or $10 million) are "nonpoor." How are these thresholds generated? The *Behind the Numbers* box on page 173 explains.

Inequality and poverty in the United States are serious issues that demand both analysis and attention. While inequality is part of any modern capitalist state, the steep rise of inequality in recent decades presents a challenge to societal mobility and perhaps, ultimately, stability. Below we continue with an examination of another important challenge—global inequality, and its roots and consequences.

GLOBAL INEQUALITY

In this section, we look at the some of the dimensions of global inequality, examining such factors as per capita income, literacy, and health in order to understand more about the class hierarchy that exists not only between social groups but also between countries in our global system. We then ask why these deep global disparities exist and persist and consider some answers offered by social scientists.

DIMENSIONS OF GLOBAL INEQUALITY

Much of the world is poor. According to the Population Reference Bureau (2011), about 48% of the earth's inhabitants live on less than $2 a day, a generally accepted definition of absolute poverty worldwide. Almost all of these deeply impoverished populations live in the developing world. Just

■ **FIGURE 7.8** Poverty Levels in the U.S., 1959–2010

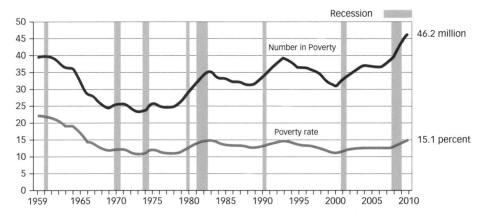

SOURCE: U.S. Census Bureau. (2012). Historical poverty tables: People. Retrieved from http://www.census.gov/hhes/www/poverty/data/historical/people.html

Aid That Works

Impoverished Neighborhoods

Official poverty line: The dollar amount set by the government as the minimum amount of money needed to meet the basic needs for a family.

a small fraction of the world's population consumes much of its valued resources: The United States is home to less than 5% of the world's population but uses about a fifth of the oil, coal, and natural gas produced globally (U.S. Energy Information Administration, 2011).

We can identify a global class system with some very wealthy states (though, of course, not all their inhabitants share the good fortune), some very poor states, and a wide swath of countries in between (see Table 7.2). Next, we look at some of the dimensions of this inequality, comparing the gross national income–purchasing power parity per capita, or **GNI-PPP**, *a comparative economic measure that uses international dollars to indicate the amount of goods and services someone could buy in the United States with a given amount of money*. We also examine the percentage of the population living in absolute poverty (that is, on less than $2 a day), life expectancy at birth, and infant mortality rate.

At one end of the class spectrum, we find countries with a very high GNI-PPP, such as the United States ($47,310), Canada ($38,370), Norway ($58,570), Switzerland ($49,960), and Japan

■ **TABLE 7.1** Poverty Rates of Selected U.S. Subgroups, 2011

Category	Percent
All people	**15%**
Whites	9.8%
Blacks	27.6%
Hispanics	25.3%
Asian	12.3%
Married couples	6.2%
Female heads of household, no husband present	31.2%

SOURCE: DeNavas-Walt, C., Proctor, B. D., & Smith, J. C. (2012). Income, poverty, and health insurance coverage in the United States: 2011. *Current Population Reports.* Washington, DC: U.S. Census Bureau.

($34,610). In the middle are countries ranging from South Korea ($29,110) and Estonia ($19,810) to Turkey ($15,530) and Brazil ($11,000). At the bottom are countries whose GNI-PPP can be as low as that of Nicaragua ($2,790) or Kenya ($1,640). While GNI-PPP cannot tell us a great deal about the resources of individual families in the given countries, it gives us some insight into the economic resources available to the state and society from a macro perspective, and it offers a comparative measure for looking at stratification in the global system.

As we saw in our discussion of U.S. stratification, one important indicator of inequality is health. In looking at the global order, we might consider a comparison of the **infant mortality rate**, which *measures the number of deaths of infants under age 1 per 1,000 live births per year*. This figure gives some insight into the health status of populations, but of women and children in particular, because rates are lowest in states that offer access to safe pre- and antenatal care and sanitary childbirth facilities, as well as good nutrition during pregnancy. In 2012, in the United States and Canada, infant mortality rates were 6.0 and 5.1, respectively, while in Norway they are as low as 2.4. In middle-level states including Brazil and Thailand they were slightly higher, at 20 and 12, respectively, while in the least developed countries they can be staggeringly high, as in Kenya (59), Pakistan (68), and Nigeria (77).

■ **TABLE 7.2** Global Inequality Indicators

Country	GNI-PPP	Percent of Population Living on Less Than $2/Day	Infant Mortality Rate per 1,000 Live Births
World	**$10,760**	**53%**	**41**
United States	$47,310	n/a	6.0
Germany	$38,100	n/a	3.4
Hungary	$19,550	2%	4.9
China	$7,640	47%	17
Mexico	$14,400	26%	15
India	$3,400	81%	47
Bangladesh	$1,810	83%	43
Nigeria	$2,240	91%	77

SOURCE: Population Reference Bureau. (2011). 2011 World Population Data Sheet; http://www.prb.org/pdf11/2011population-data-sheet_eng.pdf

· ·

GNI-PPP: A comparative economic measure that uses international dollars to indicate the amount of goods and services someone could buy in the United States with a given amount of money.

Infant mortality rate: Measures the number of deaths of infants under age 1 per 1,000 live births per year.

Modernization theory: A market-oriented development theory that envisions development as evolutionary and guided by modern institutions and cultures.

THEORETICAL PERSPECTIVES ON GLOBAL INEQUALITY

What explains global inequality? We can call on some sociological perspectives to help us understand global stratification. Later in the chapter we will evaluate these theories.

Modernization theory is *a market-oriented development theory* associated with the work of writers including Walt Rostow

Global Inequality

(1961). In contrast to many perspectives on stratification, the modernization perspective asks not why some countries are poor, but why some are wealthy. The answer it proposes is that affluent states have "modern" institutions, markets, and worldviews; by "modern" Rostow meant those that emulate the democratic and capitalist states of the West. He argued that economically underdeveloped states can progress if they adopt Western institutions, markets, and worldviews. Rostow used the analogy of an airplane taking flight to illustrate his key ideas about the stages of development:

- *The traditional stage:* In this "pre-Newtonian" (that is, pre-scientific) stage, societies are present and past time oriented, looking back into history for models of economic and political behavior rather than looking forward and seeking new models. They embrace tradition over innovation. Economic development is limited by low rates of savings and investment, and a work orientation that elevates subsistence over ambition and prosperity. The airplane is grounded and has not yet begun its journey to affluence. Today, few such countries exist. One might look at individual communities within developing countries to find these traditional orientations.

   In some developing countries, however, traditional beliefs about women's roles hinder their educational attainment and access to the labor market. Arguably, this is a cultural norm that also stifles national development, as it keeps a segment of the population that could potentially constitute half the workforce (women) from contributing its talents and skills.
- *The takeoff stage:* In this stage, societies are moving away from traditional cultural norms, practices, and institutions and are embracing economic development with a sense of purpose and growing practices of savings and investment. The plane rises as the weight of tradition is cast overboard in favor of modernity.

   Walt Rostow, an originator of modernization theory, was an adviser to President Kennedy, whose administration was responsible for the development of the Peace Corps. The Peace Corps, which has for decades sent young U.S. workers abroad to spread innovations in agriculture and technology, to teach English, and to train leaders in developing countries in methods of modern governance, could be seen as a vehicle for moving countries from the traditional to the takeoff stage. Today, some African countries with modernity-oriented leadership like Liberia might be categorized as members of the "takeoff" group.
- *In flight with technological progress and cultural modernity:* In the next stage, as the plane moves forward, technology is spreading to areas like agriculture and industry, innovation is increasing, and resistance to change is declining. Many people are adopting "modern" cultural values. Advanced countries facilitate these processes by offering advice and money.

   Progress may take the form of industrialization, which drives greater urbanization, as rural dwellers leave poor agricultural areas to seek their fortunes in cities.

It may also be accompanied by lower fertility, driven by the increased use of contraception, as opportunities for women grow in education and the labor market. India might be considered a modern example of this stage, as it has a growing educated middle class, rising urbanization and industrialization, and (for better or worse) soaring consumer ambitions.
- *The stage of high mass consumption and high living standards:* In this stage, there is a greater emphasis on the satisfaction of consumer desires, as new affluence expands the ranks of those with disposable income. This is the stage that advanced countries like those of Western and Northern Europe, the United States, and Japan have reached. The plane cruises forth . . . maybe to Disney World?

As these stages show, modernization theory assumes we can understand a given state's level of development by looking at its political, economic, and social institutions and its cultural orientation. That is, it uses a country's *internal variables* as key measuring sticks. In contrast, two later theories take a conflict perspective, focusing on countries' conflicting interests, unequal resources, and exploitive relationships, though they emphasize different aspects of inequality.

Just as Marx posited a fundamentally exploitive relationship between the bourgeoisie and the proletariat, so too does **dependency theory** (Emmanuel, 1972; Frank, 1966, 1979; Ghosh, 2001). Dependency theorists argue that the poverty of some countries is a consequence of their exploitation by wealthy states, who control the global capitalist system. While exploitation originated in colonial relationships, when powerful Western states such as Britain, the Netherlands, and Belgium dominated countries such as the Congo, South Africa, and India, it continues through the modern vehicle of multinational corporations that reap great profits from the cheap labor and raw materials of poor countries, while local populations draw only bare subsistence from their human and natural resources.

Dependency theory draws its name from the idea that prices on the global market for human and natural resources held by poor states are intentionally kept low to benefit high-income states, so low-income states cannot fully develop industrially, technologically, or economically. Thus these states remain in a *dependency relationship* with the well-off states that buy and exploit their labor and raw materials. While modernization theory implies that high-income states want to encourage the full development of low-income countries, dependency theory suggests there is a direct relationship between the affluence of one and the poverty of the other.

World systems theory shares some of these basic ideas. Immanuel Wallerstein (1974/2011a, 1980/2011b, 1989/2011c,

· ·

Dependency theory: Argues that the poverty of some countries is a consequence of their exploitation by wealthy states, which control the global capitalist system.

World systems theory: Argues that the global capitalist economic system has long been shaped by a few powerful economic actors, who have ordered it in a way that favors their economic and political interests.

BEHIND THE NUMBERS

CALCULATING U.S. POVERTY

How does the U.S. government measure poverty? In the early 1960s, an economist at the Social Security Administration, Mollie Orshansky, used a 1955 U.S. Department of Agriculture study to establish a poverty line. She learned from the study that about one third of household income went to food, so she calculated the cost of a "thrifty food basket" and tripled it to take into account other family needs such as transportation and housing. Then she adjusted the figure again to take into account the size and composition of the family and the age of the head of household. The result was the poverty threshold, which is illustrated in Figure 7.10.

Orshansky's formula represented the first systematic federal attempt to count the poor, and it has been in use for about half a century. But its age makes it a problematic indicator for the 21st century. Some critics argue that it may underestimate the number of those struggling with material deprivation. Consider the following points:

- The multiplier of 3 was used because food was estimated to constitute one third of a family budget in the 1960s. Food is a smaller part of budgets today (about one fifth), and housing

and transport are much bigger ones. Using a higher multiplier would raise the official poverty line and, consequently, increase the number of households classified as poor.

- There is no adjustment for where people live, though costs of living vary tremendously by region. While a family of four may be able to make basic ends meet on a pretax income of $15,000 in South Dakota or Nebraska, it is doubtful that the housing costs of such areas as Boston, San Francisco, Washington, DC, and New York City would permit our hypothetical family to survive in basic decency.

On the other hand, some critics have suggested that the poverty rate overestimates the problem, because it does not account for noncash benefits that some poor families receive, including food stamps and public housing vouchers. Adding the value of those (though they cannot be converted into cash) would increase the income of some families, possibly raising them above the poverty line.

■ **FIGURE 7.10** The Poverty Threshold Calculation

3 x Crisis Food Basket
Adjusted for family size and age of head of household

U.S. Census Bureau. (2010). *Poverty: 2008 and 2009. American community survey briefs.* Washington, DC: A. Bishaw & S. Macartney.■

We might thus conclude that while the official poverty statistics give us some sense of the problem of poverty and poverty trends over time, they must be read with a critical eye.

THINK IT THROUGH

■ *Taking into consideration forms of inequality and issues of poverty discussed in this chapter, how would you create an instrument to measure poverty in the United States? The current measurement focuses on a "crisis food basket." What variables would you include?*

2011d), one of the pioneers of the theory, argues that the global capitalist economic system has long been shaped by a few powerful economic actors, who have ordered it in a way that favors their economic and political interests. He suggests that the world economy is populated by three key categories of countries:

- *Core countries:* The core countries are economically advanced, technologically sophisticated, and well educated. They control the vast majority of the world's wealth and reap the greatest benefits from the world economic order. They include the United States, Canada, the states of Western and Northern Europe, and Japan, among others.

Port Harcourt, located in Nigeria's River State, is a key exporter of crude oil. Despite its economic strength, many citizens in the region still face extreme hardship, including poverty and environmental threats. ■

- *Peripheral countries:* The peripheral states have low national incomes and low levels of technological and industrial development; many still depend on agriculture. They have been exploited by the core states for their cheap labor (and, historically, slave labor) and for cheap raw materials that are exported to advanced countries and made into finished goods that bring far greater profit to core companies and consumers. Peripheral countries include parts of Central and Latin America, Asia, and many of sub-Saharan Africa's states. Some of the latter provide the critical mineral components of modern electronics for which consumers pay top dollar, such as smartphones and iPads, but they still suffer dire poverty.
- *Semiperipheral states:* The semiperiphery shares some characteristics with both the core and peripheral states, occupying an intermediate and sometimes stabilizing position between them. Semiperipheral states such as China, India, and Brazil may be exploited by core states, but they may in turn have the capacity to exploit the resources of peripheral states. For example, China, which has advanced industrial capacity and a growing middle class of consumers, has begun to foster economic relationships with African countries that can offer oil resources for the populous and economically growing state.

World systems theory sees the world as dynamic rather than static, with peripheral and semiperipheral states seeking to rise in the ranks and core countries attempting to hold fast to global power.

Judgment of Fairness

Inequality in Early Cultures

Below we use these perspectives to examine the case of Nigeria, a developing African country. Application of the perspective will help us to assess the utility of the perspectives as analytical tools for understanding development and global inequality.

APPLYING THE THEORIES: THE CASE OF NIGERIAN OIL WEALTH

A *National Geographic* story on the Niger Delta begins like this:

> Oil fouls everything in southern Nigeria. It spills from the pipelines, poisoning soil and water. It stains the hands of politicians and generals, who siphon off its profits. It taints the ambitions of the young, who will try anything to scoop up a share of the liquid riches—fire a gun, sabotage a pipeline, kidnap a foreigner.
>
> Nigeria had all the makings of an uplifting tale: poor African nation blessed with enormous sudden wealth . . . By the mid-1970s, Nigeria had joined OPEC (Organization of Petroleum Exporting Countries), and the government's budget bulged with petrodollars. (O'Neill, 2007)

Using the case of Nigeria and its vast oil reserves in the southern Niger Delta, we can evaluate the theories we've just described and compare how well they illuminate the case of this devastatingly poor state, where about 84% of the population lives on less than $2 a day and, in spite of the wealth of natural resources, gross national income in purchasing power parity (GNI-PPP) is just $2,240 (Population Reference Bureau, 2012).

Recall that the modernization perspective highlights internal variables; the lack of modern state, economic, and legal institutions; and inadequately modern cultures to explain why some

THE RISING MIDDLE CLASS IN INDIA

India, one of only two countries in the world with over a billion inhabitants (China is the other), has long been home to populations ravaged by poverty. Even today, about half of Indians live on less than $2 a day (Population Reference Bureau, 2011). But a new middle class in India, born in the age of technology and market liberalization and globalization, is rising rapidly to national and demographic prominence. According to a recent analysis, "Over the next two decades, the country's middle class will grow from about 5 percent of the population to more than 40 percent and create the world's fifth-largest consumer market" (Beinhocker, Farrell, & Zainulbhai, 2007). Much of this transformation will take place in the country's massive cities such as Delhi and Bombay.

The Indian middle class is a rising power with the potential to change both markets and politics in significant ways. As is the case around the globe, a hallmark of the middle class in India is consumption; having achieved some disposable income, the middle class aspires to new automobiles, bigger dwellings, and more educational and cultural opportunities. The U.S. Department of State (2012) estimates that today at least 50 million Indians have disposable incomes in a middle-class range (between about $4,100 and $20,800 annually), and the next 15 years will see a tenfold rise in those who have the means to join the new class of consumers.

While middle-class Indians promise to drive growth in the consumer market, they are also putting their stamp on government institutions and practices. A recent *Washington Post* article (Denyer & Lakshmi, 2011) on the efforts of the new urban middle class to battle pervasive corruption in state structures points out that,

As India's middle class grows in number and economic resources, it is attracting more political attention. While the group is still of modest size in comparison to the number of Indian poor, middle-class politics is of growing significance in this rapidly developing country. ■

in the past, cynical lawmakers figured that they could get away with almost anything as long as they threw a few sops to the rural poor at election time every five years. But two decades of economic liberalization have brought into being a new Indian middle class . . . whose votes and opinions can no longer be taken for granted.

"The consumer revolution that we have experienced in the past two decades has told the citizen that he can expect a higher quality of governance," social anthropologist Shiv Viswanathan said. "The information revolution has created a revolution of rising expectation."

So how do states become "modern"—that is, economically and technologically developed and responsively governed? In its pursuit of entrepreneurial opportunities and cleaner governance, the Indian middle class has embraced what Rostow would have described as components of modernity. India has also changed from a British colony growing cotton for the profit of British mills to an independent, increasingly well-educated and entrepreneurial regional powerhouse with the potential to exercise global power in markets and politics. Although neither modernization theory nor dependency theory looked at the middle class as an agent of change, in India, the new middle class is challenging both internal and external obstacles and transforming the country domestically and globally.

THINK IT THROUGH

■ *Why do growing middle-class populations in many developing states have an interest in addressing governmental corruption? How does corruption undermine the interests of the middle class?*

countries have lagged in development. A modernization theorist would thus point to the rampant culture of corruption and lack of rule of law that have characterized Somalia and North Korea: In 2011 Transparency International, a corruption watchdog agency, ranked these countries as the most corrupt countries in the world. Nigeria is also near the top of the list (Transparency International, 2011). Clearly, there is a link between the failing state, the lack of an effective legal and civic structure, and the dire poverty in and around Port Harcourt. Though it is the capital of the oil-rich Rivers State, it has "no electricity, no clean water, no medicine, no schools" (O'Neill, 2007). But does the modernization perspective miss some key aspects of the problem of global poverty?

Critics argue that in attending almost exclusively to internal variables, the modernization perspective fails to recognize the external obstacles to development and the ways in which well-off states benefit from the inferior economic position of poor states. According to *National Geographic,* in the wake of independence from colonial Britain, few observers expected that Nigeria would become a global oil source. In the decades that followed, however, five multinational oil companies, Royal Dutch Shell, Total, Italy's Agip, ExxonMobil, and Chevron, transformed the Rivers state. "The imprint: 4,500 miles . . . of pipelines, 159 oil fields, and 275 flow stations" (O'Neill, 2007). The United Nations Development Programme and the International Crisis Group point to decades of problematic economic strategies employed by oil companies, which have taken advantage of weak environmental controls, offered little compensation for land and few employment opportunities to local communities, engaged in corrupt deals for oil, and used private security forces to commit violence against those who resisted their efforts to control the oil fields of the Niger Delta (Brock & Cocks, 2012; O'Neill, 2007).

From the dependency and world systems perspectives, a relationship of fundamental exploitation exists between Nigeria and high-income countries including the United States and Britain, for which Nigeria provides a critically important resource. If the United States is a core state, Nigeria appears from this perspective a peripheral state supplying oil, the basic raw building block of modern economies, without seeing the benefit of its own natural wealth. Semiperipheral states aggressively seeking to develop their own economies and wealth are also part of the picture: "China, India, and South Korea, all energy-hungry, have begun buying stakes in Nigeria's offshore [oil] blocks" (O'Neill, 2007). The dependency theory perspective suggests that developed and rapidly developing states benefit from lax government oversight of environmental pollution, low-wage pools of local labor, and corruptible officials willing to bend rules to accommodate corporate wishes.

Like modernization theory, the dependency and world systems theoretical perspectives illuminate some aspects of the case while obscuring others. Variables like the exploitive power of Western oil companies are a key part of understanding the failure of Nigeria to develop in a way that benefits the broader population, but conflict-oriented perspectives pay little attention to the agency of poor states and, in particular, their governing bodies, in setting a solid foundation for development.

WHY STUDY INEQUALITY?

We began this chapter by recognizing that many people today struggle to make ends meet on wages that have stagnated in the decades of postindustrialism. We've looked at the dimensions of both class and inequality in the United States and asked why inequality exists and persists.

The questions raised by the theoretical perspectives we studied are not just academic: They are critical to understanding the world in which we live and in which (if we so choose) we will raise our children. Is it the case, as functionalists Davis and Moore asserted, that inequality is positively functional for all society, and that we all benefit from it because it ensures that the best and brightest take the most important jobs? Or, as Tumin argues, does inequality ensure just the opposite—does stratification limit the discovery of the full range of talent in society? How much should we worry about inequality and its growth? The answer depends quite a lot on whether we subscribe to the functionalist or the conflict view of socioeconomic stratification.

What about poverty? Poverty in individual cases may be the result of bad luck or poor choices, but the sheer magnitude of the problem of poverty suggests that it has structural roots as well and a fuller explanation cannot be found at the individual level. Why does crushing poverty exist in a country that is arguably the wealthiest in the world? This is a question that asks us to fire up our sociological imaginations.

At the global level, we find countries arranged in a stratified hierarchy of positions, with some exercising economic and political dominance and others on the brink of social crisis and financial failure. What accounts for these differences? Again, sociology offers us some insights. It's up to us to study different cases and to test a variety of explanations. Global inequality matters because in an ever more populated, interconnected, and interdependent world, the misfortunes and good fortunes of different countries will not remain isolated in their effects.

WHAT CAN I DO WITH A SOCIOLOGY DEGREE?

SKILLS AND CAREERS:
QUANTITATIVE RESEARCH SKILLS

Sociologists use quantitative research skills to conduct systematic empirical investigations of social phenomena using statistical methods. *Quantitative research comprises those studies in which data are expressed in terms of numbers.* The objective of quantitative research in sociology is to gather rigorous data and to use those numerical data to characterize the dimensions of an issue or the extent of a problem (this could include, for instance, the collection of statistical data on rates of obesity and poverty in neighborhoods or states and the calculation of the correlation of the two phenomena) and, often, to use those data to develop or test hypotheses about the roots of the problem at hand.

In Chapter 7, we saw a broad spectrum of quantitative data, which is key to both academic studies and policy making on issues such as poverty, wealth and income inequality, and postindustrial changes in the labor market. We cited data collected by the U.S. government to measure household incomes and to establish the dimensions of the division of aggregate income across quintiles of earners. We also read about data collected by the Pew Research Center on the gap in net worth between Whites, Blacks, and Latinos. As you advance in your sociological studies, you will have the opportunity to become familiar with quantitative data on important sociological issues and to see how these data are used in analyses—and you will have the opportunity to learn how to do quantitative sociology. For example, you might learn to measure and compare trends in income differences by race, ethnicity, and gender or to assess the significance of variables such as neighborhood unemployment, educational attainment, and median income as predictors of neighborhood street crime.

Knowledge of quantitative methods is a valuable skill in today's job market. Learning quantitative methods of research, which is an important part of a sociological education, prepares you to do a wide variety of *job tasks*, including survey development, questionnaire design, market research, brand health tracking, and financial quantitative modeling and analysis. These kinds of tasks are commonly part of the *job description* of, among others, market research analysts, marketing specialists, social science research assistants, clinical research coordinators, criminal justice and law enforcement teachers, financial quantitative analysts, markets quantitative analysts, and statistical research analysts. These are jobs that can be found in a variety of *occupational fields*, including education, marketing, criminal justice, health and medicine, business and management, finance, and social science research, among others.

THINK ABOUT CAREERS

■ *Social statistics are used in a broad variety of analyses of the social world, and researchers often use quantitative methods to study relationships between different sociological variables. How do you think the job tasks of people who use quantitative data in occupational fields such as marketing, health, criminal justice, or business might be similar to and different from what quantitative sociologists do?*

▶ *Access additional web links on the student study site to learn more.*

SUMMARY

To test your knowledge further, find additional study material on the Student Study Site at www.sagepub.com/chamblissintro

- Class societies are more open than caste societies. In **caste societies**, a person's position in the hierarchy is determined by ascribed characteristics such as race or birth status. In **class societies**, position is determined by what someone achieves, and mobility is looked upon favorably. However, caste-like barriers to mobility still exist in class societies.

- **Class** refers to a person's economic role in society, associated with differences in income, wealth, and the type of work that he or she does. Class position strongly influences an individual's **life chances**—the opportunities and obstacles one encounters in areas such as education, social life, and work. Important components of class position are occupation, income, and wealth.

- Functionalist theorists argue that inequality exists and persists because it is positively functional for society. Inequality is necessary to motivate the best people to assume the most important occupational positions.

- Conflict theorists argue that the privileged classes benefit from inequality and that inequality inhibits the discovery of talented people rather than fostering it. Conflict theory suggests that classes, with differential access to power and resources, are in conflict. The interests of the well-off are most likely to be realized.

- We can measure inequality in the United States by looking at disparities in **income, wealth,** health, and access to credit and goods. All these indicators show that inequality in the United States is substantial and growing.

- Since the early 1970s, the gap has grown between the rich and the poor, and between the rich and everyone else. Some of the gap is attributable to the transformation of the U.S. economy from industrial to postindustrial, which has helped the best educated and hurt the least educated.

- Poverty is a significant problem in the United States: Over 15% of the population was officially poor in 2011. The formula used to measure poverty gives us a sense of the problem, but it has limitations of which we should be aware.

- **Modernization theorists** posit that global underdevelopment exists in states that cling to traditional cultures and fail to build modern state and market institutions. **Dependency theorists** and **world systems theorists** highlight external variables that point out how high-income states benefit from the economic marginality of low-income states.

KEY TERMS

Study terms on the go with the smartphone-friendly key term flashcards, available at www.sagepub.com/chamblissintro

social inequality, 155

social stratification, 155

caste society, 156

class society, 156

social categories, 157

achieved status, 157

ascribed status, 157

class, 157

life chances, 157

social mobility, 157

income, 158

wealth (or net worth), 159

net financial assets, 159

occupation, 159

status, 160

political power, 160

meritocracy, 161

food deserts, 167

official poverty line, 170

GNI-PPP, 171

infant mortality rate, 171

modernization theory, 171

dependency theory, 172

world systems theory, 172

DISCUSSION QUESTIONS

1. What are the key dimensions and trends related to income inequality in the United States today? How would you expect these trends to evolve or change in the coming decade? Explain your reasoning.

2. Herbert Gans talks about the "uses of poverty" for the nonpoor. Recall some of his points and then add some of your own. Would you agree with the argument he makes about the existence and persistence of poverty? Why or why not?

3. How do theorists such as Rostow and Wallerstein explain inequalities of income and development between countries? What are the relative strengths and weaknesses of each theory? Which do you see as more persuasive and why?

DISCOVER 〇🆂 STATE STATS

Log-in to the eBook and click on the title to the left for access to State Stats in order to complete the exercise.

In the Social Welfare database, gather data on the percentage of children living in poverty for your home state, for another state of your choosing from a different part of the country, and for the country as a whole. Choose the earliest and latest data available to compare, and consider the possible sociological roots of differences between the states. How do the states compare to the country as a whole? Can you begin to explain the existence and persistence of poverty over time, using the chapter information as a basis?

STUDENT STUDY SITE

Visit the Student Study Site at **www.sagepub.com/chamblissintro** to access additional study tools, including eFlashcards, web quizzes, video resources, web resources, audio resources, links to SAGE journal, handbook, and research articles, and much more!

8

RACE AND ETHNICITY

WHAT DO YOU THINK?

1. What makes a group a "minority"? Does this term have qualitative and quantitative dimensions?
2. Why does racial residential segregation exist and persist in major U.S. cities?
3. How is the ethnic and racial composition of the United States changing today? What factors are driving this change?

SOC*VIEW*

Get a closer look with the authors!

African American poet Langston Hughes (1902–1967) is known for, among other writings, the poem "A Dream Deferred" (sometimes called "Harlem").

What happens to a dream deferred

> Does it dry up
> like a raisin in the sun?
> Or fester like a sore—
> And then run?
> Does it stink like rotten meat?
> Or crust and sugar over—
> like a syrupy sweet?
>
> Maybe it just sags
> like a heavy load.
>
> *Or does it explode?*

In the 1920s and 1930s, Hughes was one of the writers of the Harlem Renaissance, highlighting issues of race relations and inequality. Hughes's most famous poem contemplated the consequences of a "dream deferred." Indeed, the dreams of many African Americans were deferred—or denied. Mary Jean Price Walls was among them.

Mary Jean Price Walls, the child of a Black mother and White father, dreamed of being a teacher. In 1950, Mary Jean was the salutatorian of her graduating class at Lincoln High School, an all-Black school. She applied for admission to Missouri State University, the only institution of higher education near her home and, thus, the only one she could afford to attend. She never received an answer and never went to college, instead becoming mother to eight children and, later, cleaning homes and working as a janitor (Moore, 2012).

At age 52, one of Walls's sons, Terry Walls, went back to college, enrolling at Missouri State University. As a student, he sought to find out why his mother had been denied admission to the school. Using the university archives, he tracked down the thin, onion-skinned letter with which his mother applied for admission. He also learned that MSU's regents had held a special meeting: "Formal minutes reveal that her application was denied because those same classes were available at the all-black college four hours away" (Moore, 2012). Without funds to attend a college away from home, Mary Jean's dream of being a teacher could not be realized. Desegregation of U.S. education would begin slowly, with the Supreme Court ruling in *Brown vs. Board of Education* in 1954, too late for Mary Jean to realize her ambition.

In 2010, MSU granted Mary Jean an honorary degree, recognizing the opportunity that had been closed to her by racism. In 2012, MSU awarded a diploma to Terry Walls, her son, for completion of his college work.

What are we to conclude from Mary Jean's story? Clearly, her dream was denied. Today, African Americans like Mary Jean's children have legally protected opportunities for education and professional success. But race is still a powerful social force, influencing interpersonal interactions and institutional arrangements in the United States. And racism, though often more subtle than that experienced by Mary Jean, remains a potent obstacle for many who seek to fulfill dreams of education, housing, and professional achievement. ■

Race and ethnicity are key issues in sociology. We begin this chapter with a discussion of the social construction of race and ethnicity. A consideration of forms that minority-majority group relations may take is next. We also look at theoretical perspectives on ethnicity, racism, and minority group status. This leads to a discussion of prejudice and discrimination and the consequences of these social phenomena. We then examine the experience of different racial and ethnic groups in the United States and how group membership may shape people's political, economic, and social status. Finally, we consider race and ethnicity in a global perspective.

THE SOCIAL CONSTRUCTION OF RACE AND ETHNICITY

Sociologists W. I. and Dorothy Thomas (1928) observed that "if [people] define situations as real, they are real in their consequences" (pp. 571–572). The wisdom of the Thomases' observation is powerfully demonstrated by the way societies construct definitions of racial and ethnic groups and then respond as though the definitions represent objective realities.

RACE

One of the most dynamic areas of scientific research in recent years is the Human Genome Project. Among its compelling findings is the discovery that genetically all human beings are nearly identical. Less than .01% of the total gene pool contributes to racial differences (as manifested in physical characteristics), whereas thousands of genes contribute to traits that include intelligence, artistic or athletic talent, and social skills (Angier, 2000; Cavalli-Sforza, Menozzi, & Piazza, 1994). Based on this research, many scientists agree, "Race is a *social concept,* not a *scientific* one . . . we all evolved in the last 100,000 years from the same small number of tribes that migrated out of Africa and colonized the world" (Angier, 2000).

Sociologists define a **race** as *a group sharing apparent physical traits deemed by society to be socially significant.* Notice that this definition says physical characteristics are not the only—or even necessarily the most important—way of defining "races." For many years, Catholics and Protestants in Ireland defined one another as separate races, and the United States long considered Jews a separate racial category from Europeans, even though distinctive physical characteristics among these groups are in the eye of the beholder rather than objectively verifiable (Schaefer, 2009).

While sociologists do not treat race as scientifically significant, it is, as we will see in the chapter, *socially significant.* Following the observation of the Thomases, we can conclude that because race is defined as real, it is real in its consequences. Racial differentiation has historically been linked to power: Racial categories have facilitated the treatment (or maltreatment) of others based on membership in a given racial group.

Notably, race is also *social scientifically* significant. Statistical data on phenomena ranging from obesity and poverty to crime

Race: A group sharing apparent physical traits deemed by society to be socially significant.

Racism on the Internet

Whiteness in America

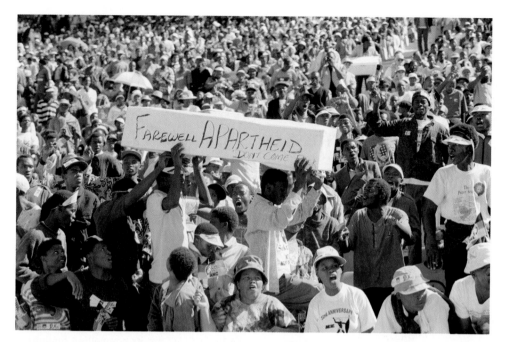
South Africa's apartheid was a system of privilege based on race. With racial identity determining social status and access to resources in society, Whites sat atop a hierarchy of power, while Black South Africans were at the bottom. ■

and educational attainment are gathered and sorted by race. This book features such data throughout its pages. While sociologists generally agree that races cannot be objectively, biologically differentiated, it is a fact that they also use race to sort statistics and establish social facts about groups in society. This implicitly acknowledges the fact that this "social concept" is profoundly real as a differentiating mechanism with historical and contemporary consequences.

ETHNICITY

Although *race* may be a particularly significant social category in terms of the consequences for people's lives, other socially constructed categorizations are very important. Among these, ethnicity ranks next to race in significance. **Ethnicity** refers to *a group's national origin, language, and cultural or religious practices.* While ethnicity can be based on cultural self-identification, an acknowledgment or degree of acceptance by a larger group is often necessary. For example, a third-generation Italian American may choose to self-identify as Italian. If he cannot speak Italian, however, others in the group may not see him as "authentically" Italian. The sociological significance of belonging to a particular racial or ethnic group is that society may treat group members differently, judging them or giving favorable or unfavorable treatment based on membership and perceived affiliation.

Rise of the Minority

MINORITIES

Any racial, ethnic, religious, or other group can constitute a "minority" in a society. **Minorities** are less powerful groups who are dominated politically and economically by a more powerful group and, often, who experience discrimination on the basis of socially constructed characteristics. Minorities are usually distinguished by gender or physical and cultural attributes, which make them recognizable to the dominant group. Minorities often are fewer in number than the dominant population: In the United States, African Americans, Latinos, and Asians are less numerous than the White majority, though the higher number of births among non-Whites, combined with immigration, will begin to change this fact in coming decades (Figure 8.1).

Although one usually thinks of minorities as being fewer in number (the term implies a numerical difference), the important aspect of being a minority group is that the group has relatively less access to power and resources valued by society. Thus, sociologically, women in the United States, and in most cultures worldwide, may be considered a minority despite the fact that they outnumber men. In Rwanda, the "minority" ethnic Hutu population makes up over 80% of the population, but they are sociologically a minority that

■ **FIGURE 8.1** Projected Racial and Ethnic Composition of the United States, 2010–2040

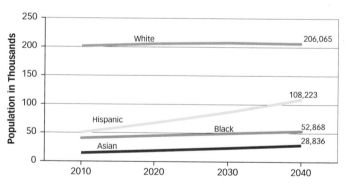

SOURCE: U.S. Census Bureau. (2009). *2009 national population projections.* Retrieved from http://www.census.gov/population/projections/data/national/2009.html

. . . .

Ethnicity: The attribution of characteristics to groups of people who share a common cultural (including religious) heritage.

Minorities: Groups of people who are discriminated against on the basis of socially constructed characteristics.

is dominated by the 15% of the population that is Tutsi. In South Africa before the end of apartheid rule in the early 1990s, a small number of Whites dominated the much larger minority of what were termed Black, colored, and mixed races.

MINORITY AND DOMINANT GROUP RELATIONS

Modern societies are characterized by racial and ethnic heterogeneity, as well as by divisions between dominant and minority groups. The coexistence of racial and ethnic groups can be a source of social conflict. Among minorities' most frequently used methods of resolving conflicts are social movements designed to challenge and change existing social relations. In extreme cases, resolution may be sought in revolution or rebellion. Dominant populations respond with a variety of social and political policies, ranging from expulsion and segregation to assimilation of minorities and the acceptance of cultural pluralism. We discuss this spectrum of relationships below.

EXPULSION

Conflicts between White settlers and American Indians over land and resources in the United States in the 1800s often ended with the removal of Native Americans to isolated reservations. Sociologically, *the process of forcibly removing people from one part of the country to another* is referred to as **expulsion**. Native Americans populated broad swaths of the United States when European settlers arrived. The Native Americans were driven under military arms to march, sometimes thousands of miles, to areas designated by the government as Native American reservations. These reservations continue to be socially and economically marginal (Figure 8.2).

Today, across the globe, people are being forced from their homes due to civil wars, ethnic or sectarian conflict, and rebellions. It is estimated that in 2010 the number of displaced people and refugees reached the highest level since 1990 with over 43 million people displaced: 27 million internally displaced and more than 15 million refugees. While not all are victims of an official policy

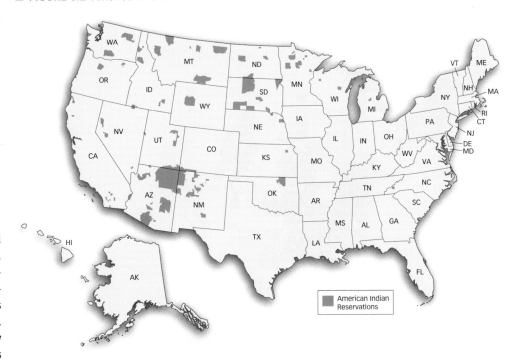

■ **FIGURE 8.2** American Indian Reservations in the U.S.

SOURCE: U.S. Parks Service.

of expulsion, many suffer the dire consequences of ethnic clashes between dominant and minority groups (United Nations High Commissioner for Refugees, 2010).

SEGREGATION

Racial and ethnic conflict and tensions can also be linked to institutionalized and enforced segregation: **Segregation** is *the practice of spatially or socially segregating people on the basis of race or ethnicity.*

In South Africa, apartheid was a state policy until the beginning of the 1990s. The release of antiapartheid activist Nelson Mandela in 1990 and the end of a ban on previously forbidden groups began the process of desegregation, which has slowly evolved in the wake of the establishment of democracy in 1994. Apartheid was an extreme form of segregation that included not only prohibitions on where different racial and ethnic groups could live, but where they could travel and at what hours of the day they could be in different parts of the city. While apartheid is no longer a policy in South Africa, the legacy of segregation lives on in many communities, where the White, Black, and colored populations still live separately and unequally.

Before the 1960s, segregation on the basis of race was common practice and legally upheld in many parts of the United States. In some places it was a crime for Whites to rent apartments or sell homes to non-Whites (Molotch, 1972). In the South, Blacks could not sit in the same restaurants as Whites. When they rode the same buses, Blacks were required by law to sit at the back. In other parts of the country, restaurants and hotels could refuse to serve dark-skinned customers.

. . . .

Expulsion: The forcible removal of a population.

Segregation: The physical and social separation of different categories of people.

More than 75% White

More than 75% Black

More than 75% Hispanic

SOURCE: Center for Governmental Studies, Northern Illinois University.

The civil rights movement of the 1960s succeeded in securing the passage of federal laws that outlawed segregation. Despite this success, high levels of segregation remain a reality in U.S. cities. Why is this the case in the post–civil rights era? First, it is legal and commonplace to segregate housing markets by income. Since minorities tend to be poorer then Whites, many cannot afford to live in predominantly White neighborhoods, where people are wealthier and housing costs higher. Second, laws outlawing residential segregation are not always followed by realtors and lenders, who may steer minorities away from predominantly White neighborhoods (Squires, 2003; Squires et al., 2002). Third, some ethnic minorities choose to live in neighborhoods where their own ethnic groups predominate, as exemplified by, for instance, San Francisco's Chinatown or

Boston's Italian North End. Finally, White residents sometimes move out of neighborhoods when increasing numbers of minority residents move in (Woldoff, 2011).

Low-income African Americans and Latinos are especially likely to live in highly segregated communities in the largest U.S. cities such as Los Angeles and Chicago (Figure 8.3). According to the U.S. Census Bureau (2010b), some urban neighborhoods are over 90% White, and others are over 90% Black or Hispanic. The average White household lives in a neighborhood where over 75% of its neighbors are White. On the other hand, more than 50% of the Black population lives in neighborhoods that vary from 34% to 54% Black. It is important to note that metropolitan areas around the United States vary greatly in racial composition, and that some cities have less racially segregated neighborhoods than others. Racial residential segregation remains a significant phenomenon, though positive changes have taken place in many metropolitan areas in recent decades (Turner & McDade, 2012).

Segregation has negative consequences for minority groups. Apart from denying them residential choice, it compels them to live in poorer neighborhoods that offer less access to high-quality schools and medical facilities (Kozol, 1995; Massey & Denton, 1993). Poor and segregated neighborhoods and regions are also more likely to be home to hazardous waste facilities and other sources of pollution, a problem that plagues minority communities from urban Los Angeles to rural Louisiana.

In sum, racial segregation of minorities contributes to the concentration of poverty and disadvantage. Pursuing greater opportunities, members of minority groups may seek to move to racially integrated areas. Unfortunately, historically and today, powerful social forces of poverty and discrimination have kept many from achieving this goal.

ASSIMILATION AND CULTURAL PLURALISM

Throughout much of the 20th century, sociologists who studied minorities, race, and ethnicity assumed that the ultimate destiny of most minority groups was **assimilation**, or *absorption into the dominant culture.* U.S. citizens have long prided themselves on being part of a vast "melting pot," in which fundamental ethnic differences gradually disappear and the population is boiled into a single cultural soup. This view was strengthened by the experience of many immigrant groups, particularly from Northern European countries, who adopted the norms, values, and folkways

· ·

Assimilation: The absorption of a minority group into the dominant culture.

Residential Segregation

Sharia Law vs. Western Law

of the dominant culture to increase their social acceptance as well as their economic success.

While migrant groups have historically sought to assimilate into the dominant majority group, many also want to retain their unique identity. Some American Indian nations, for example, have long sought to keep alive their own traditions and beliefs. In **cultural pluralism**, *the coexistence of different racial and ethnic groups is characterized by acceptance of one another's differences.* Such a society resembles a *salad bowl* rather than a *melting pot.* Cultural differences are respected for their contribution to the richness of society as a whole. While cultural pluralists criticize the forced segregation that results from prejudice and discrimination, they argue that the *voluntary* segregation of people into their own ethnic communities helps preserve their cultural heritages and, at the same time, provides networks of mutual social and economic support.

"Chemical Alley," an area of Louisiana where chemical plants spew toxic pollutants into the air, water, and soil, is populated almost exclusively by poor African Americans. Those with the least political voice in society are also most likely to find themselves in highly polluted residential areas. ■

The relative merits of assimilation and cultural pluralism remain controversial, but sociologists generally agree that the debates over these issues are at the heart of racial and ethnic relations in the modern world.

THEORETICAL APPROACHES TO ETHNICITY, RACISM, AND MINORITY STATUS

Throughout this text, we seek to highlight ways that key theoretical perspectives in sociology illuminate social phenomena including socioeconomic stratification, poverty, deviance, and the like. In this section, we look at ethnicity, racism, and minority group status using the functionalist, conflict, and symbolic interactionist theoretical lenses.

THE FUNCTIONALIST PERSPECTIVE

One of functionalism's key assumptions is that a social phenomenon exists and persists because it serves a positive function in a community or society, contributing to order and harmony. Beginning with classical sociologists Auguste Comte and Émile Durkheim and extending to contemporary functionalist theorizing,

· ·

Cultural pluralism: The coexistence of different racial and ethnic groups characterized by acceptance and respect for one another's differences.

Racism: Institutionalized relationships between dominant and minority groups that create a structure of economic, social, and political inequality based on socially constructed racial or ethnic categories.

the basic functionalist assumption is that solidarity characterizes social groupings. Durkheim believed social groups held together by mechanical solidarity and based on homogeneity in, among other things, language and culture are more culturally durable than those based on organic solidarity, which is based on interdependence (for instance, economic interdependence). This may help us understand the cohesion of many ethnic groups in the United States. Whether they are Armenian Americans, Egyptian Americans, Cuban Americans, or some other group, people gravitate toward those who are like them, a process rooted in shared pasts and practices.

It is far more challenging to apply the functionalist perspective to *racism* as a phenomenon. Racism cannot be positively functional for a community or society because, by definition, it marginalizes some members of the group. It can, however, be positively functional for some groups while being detrimental for others. Asking "How is this functional for some groups?" takes us close to the key conflict question: "Who benefits from this phenomenon or institution—and who loses?" In the section below, we examine *who benefits* from racism.

THE CONFLICT PERSPECTIVE

Consider that **racism**, *the idea that one group is inherently superior to another group,* offers a justification for racial inequality and interlinked forms of stratification such as socioeconomic inequality. If a powerful group defines itself as "better" than another group, then the unequal treatment and distribution of resources can be rationalized as acceptable.

Parading Race

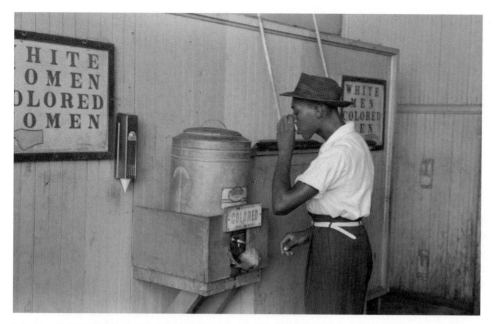

Prior to the passage of civil rights legislation in the 1960s, many U.S. societal institutions and places—from public transportation and education to public restrooms and access to housing—were legally separated along racial lines. Signs like the one in the photo were commonplace. ■

After the end of slavery, racism continued to manifest in new forms, including Jim Crow laws, which followed in the decade after slavery and lasted until the middle of the 20th century. These laws legally mandated segregation of public facilities in the South and fundamentally limited Blacks' ability to exercise their rights. The schools, accommodations, and opportunities afforded to Blacks were invariably inferior to those offered to Whites. Local and state governments could therefore expend fewer funds on their Black populations, and White populations benefited from reduced competition in higher education and the labor market. Racism made Jim Crow laws both possible and widely acceptable, because it offered a basic justification for their existence and persistence.

While racism is clearly of no benefit to its victims and has negative effects on society as a whole, the conflict perspective entreats us to recognize ways in which it has provided benefits for some more powerful groups in society, helping to explain its existence and persistence over time.

Slavery was a fundamentally racist phenomenon. It was possible for Southern (and many Northern) Whites to justify the maltreatment of Blacks because they were not seen as fully human. Senator John Calhoun, who represented South Carolina and died just over a decade before the Civil War, wrote in a letter that "the African is incapable of self-care and sinks into lunacy under the burden of freedom. It is a mercy to him to give him the guardianship and protection from mental death" (quoted in Silva, 2001, p. 71).

In legal terms, racism was clear in the Three-Fifths Compromise, which emerged from the Philadelphia Convention of 1787. Southern and Northern delegates agreed that for purposes of taxation and political representation, the slave would be counted as three fifths of a person. The compromise was needed because abolitionists wanted to count only free people. Slaveholders and their supporters wanted to count slaves, whose presence would add to their population count and representation in Congress. Those who held slaves but did not permit them to be free or to vote still gained politically from their presence. In economic terms, slavery was of benefit to plantation owners and their families, who could reap the financial benefits of a population of workers who could be bought and sold, be exploited and abused, and perform difficult and demanding work without pay.

It can be argued that early U.S. capitalism and economic development would not have been so robust without reliance on an enslaved labor force, which contributed most fully to the development of a growing agricultural economy in the South. The North too had numerous beneficiaries and proponents of slavery.

THE SYMBOLIC INTERACTIONIST PERSPECTIVE

Sociologist Louis Wirth (1945) wrote that minority groups share particular traits. First, membership in the minority group is essentially involuntary—that is, someone is socially classified as a member of the discriminated group and is not, in most instances, free to opt out. Second, as we discussed above, minority status is a question not of numbers ("minorities" may outnumber the dominant group), but rather of control of valued resources. Third, minorities do not share the full privileges of mobility or opportunity enjoyed by the dominant group. Finally, membership in the minority group conditions the treatment of group members by others in society. Specifically, Wirth writes that societal minorities are "treated as members of a category, irrespective of their individual merits" (p. 349).

Wirth's definition recalls symbolic interactionist Erving Goffman's explanation of a **stigma,** an *attribute that is deeply discrediting to an individual or a group because it overshadows other attributes and merits the individual or group may possess.* Goffman (1963b) writes of the unlikely scenario of a young woman born without a nose. While the young woman has a spectrum of interesting and engaging characteristics—she is a bright student and a good dancer—she is defined by her stigma, and her treatment by others is ever defined and determined by her "difference."

Side-Effects of Racism

. . . .

Stigma: An attribute that is deeply discrediting to an individual or a group because it overshadows other attributes and merits the individual or group may possess.

Goffman examined what he called **mixed contacts**—that is, *interactions between those who are stigmatized and those who are "normal"* (by *normal*, he meant only those who are members of the dominant, nonstigmatized group—the term was not intended to denote normality as contrasting with deviance). Goffman concluded that mixed contacts are shaped by the presence of the stigma, which influences the way a social interaction unfolds. While the stigmatized identity may not be the point of the interaction, it is inevitably a part of it. Think about your own social interactions: Have you experienced what Goffman describes? How would you expand or modify his sociological description based on those experiences?

In the section below, we turn to issues of prejudice and discrimination, considering how our judgments about someone's race or ethnicity—or about the racial or ethnic identity of an entire group—are manifested in practice.

PREJUDICE AND DISCRIMINATION

Prejudice is *a belief about an individual or a group that is not subject to change on the basis of evidence.* Prejudices are thus inflexible attitudes toward others. Sociologist Zygmunt Bauman (2001), writing about the Holocaust, eloquently captures this idea: "Man *is* before he *acts;* nothing he does may change what he is. That is, roughly, the philosophical essence of racism" (p. 60). Recall Wirth's point about the characteristics of a social minority: Membership in the disadvantaged group matters more than individual merit.

When prejudices are strongly held, no amount of evidence is likely to change the belief. Among neo-Nazis, for example, prejudice against Jews runs deep. Some neo-Nazis even deny the occurrence of the Holocaust, despite clearly authentic firsthand accounts, films, and photographs of Nazi Germany's concentration camps, where millions of Jews were killed during World War II. Why do prejudicial beliefs trump evidence in cases such as Holocaust denial? Why is prejudice difficult to overcome, even with facts? We may gain some insight into these questions by looking at another social phenomena linked to prejudice—stereotyping.

Stereotyping means *generalizing a set of characteristics to all members of a group.* Ethnic and racial stereotypes are often produced and reproduced in films: Think about popular film images in U.S. action films of scheming Italian mafiosi, tough African American street gangs, or violent Asian gangsters or martial artists. Or consider the ways that we may attribute

· ·

Mixed contacts: Interactions between those who are stigmatized and those who are "normal."

Prejudice: A belief about an individual or a group that is not subject to change on the basis of evidence.

Stereotyping: Generalizing a set of characteristics to all members of a group.

The cognitive dissonance of espousing values of freedom, equality, and justice for all, while simultaneously maintaining an inhumane system of slave labor, required some kind of rationalization. The vicious wounds on the back of this man could be the result of the fact that many White Americans at the time did not view Blacks as fully human. ■

characteristics—intelligence, entrepreneurship, sloth, or slyness—to entire groups based upon experiences with or information about no or just a few members of that group. Stereotyping offers a way for human beings to organize and categorize the social world—but the attributions we make may be deeply flawed.

From a sociological perspective, we might argue that while stereotypes are often flawed, they are also functional for some groups—though dysfunctional for others. Consider that one of the social forces contributing to racism is the desire of one group to exploit another. Research on early contacts between Europeans and Africans suggests that negative stereotypes of Africans developed *after* Europeans discovered the economic value of exploiting their labor and the natural resources of the African continent. That is, Black Africans were stereotyped by

White Privilege

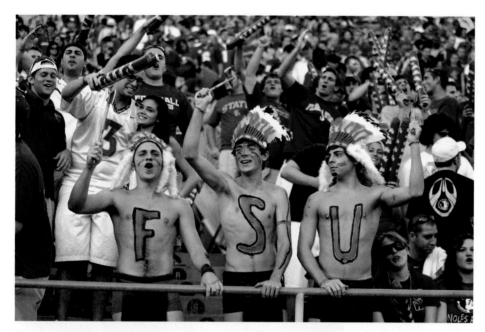

"Scalp 'em!" Many popular sports teams proudly utilize Native Americans as their mascots, without realizing the negative effect of stereotypes. Fans at some universities, for example, encourage their players with chants implicitly portraying Native Americans as savages. ■

In 1866, Congress passed the first civil rights act giving Black men the right to vote, hold public office, use public accommodations, and serve on juries. In 1883, however, the U.S. Supreme Court declared the 1866 law unconstitutional, and states then passed laws restricting where minorities could live, go to school, receive accommodations, and such. These laws were upheld by the U.S. Supreme Court in the case of *Plessy v. Ferguson* in 1896. It took more than 75 years for the Court to reverse itself.

In the 1960s, the Supreme Court held that laws institutionalizing discrimination were unconstitutional. Open forms of discrimination, such as signs and advertisements that said "Whites only" or "Jews need not apply," were deemed illegal. Research and experience suggest, however, that discrimination often continues in more subtle and complex forms. Consider, once again, the case of housing and discrimination. Institutionalized discrimination affects opportunities for housing and, by extension, opportunities for building individual and community wealth through broad homeownership. We noted earlier in the chapter that African Americans often still live in segregated neighborhoods. Discrimination is part of the reason; for example, Blacks have been historically less likely to secure mortgages. Paired testing studies, which send Black and White applicants with nearly identical financial profiles to apply for mortgages, have determined that Whites as a group continue to be advantaged in their treatment by lending institutions (Silverman, 2005). Among other benefits, they enjoy higher rates of approval and better loan conditions (Turner, Popkin, & Rawlings, 2009).

These practices have had a powerful effect on the Black-White wealth gap. Because most wealth held by the U.S. middle class exists in the form of home equity, the opportunity to own an affordable home in a neighborhood with good property values is a key way to accrue wealth.

The turn of the millennium, however, ushered in a shift in mortgage lending. Lending money for home purchases was plentiful, and among those targeted by banks eager to make mortgage loans were minorities, even those with low incomes and poor credit. The lending bonanza was no boon for these groups,

White Europeans as, for instance, unintelligent or less than human, when such images suited the need to justify enslavement and economic exploitation of this population.

Discrimination is *the unequal treatment of individuals on the basis of their membership in a group.* Discrimination is often targeted and intentional, but it may also be unintentional—in either case, it denies groups and individuals equal opportunities and blocks access to valued resources.

Sociologists distinguish between individual and institutional discrimination. **Individual discrimination** is *overt and intentional unequal treatment, often based on prejudicial beliefs.* If the manager of an apartment complex refuses to rent a place to someone on the basis of his or her skin color or an employer chooses not to hire someone, even if qualified, because he or she is foreign-born, that is individual discrimination.

Institutionalized discrimination is discrimination enshrined in law, public policy, or common practice—it is *unequal treatment that has become a part of the routine operation of major social institutions such as businesses, schools, hospitals, and the government.* Institutionalized discrimination is particularly pernicious because, while it may be clearly targeted and intentional (as in the 1831 act prohibiting the teaching of slaves to read), it may also be the outcome of customary practices and bureaucratic decisions that result in discriminatory outcomes.

Discrimination against African Americans and women was initially institutionalized in the Constitution of the United States, which excluded them from voting and holding public office.

Racial Prejudice

· ·

Discrimination: The unequal treatment of individuals on the basis of their membership in a group.

Individual discrimination: Overt and intentional unequal treatment, often based on prejudicial beliefs.

Institutionalized discrimination: Unequal treatment that has become a part of the routine operation of such major social institutions as businesses, schools, hospitals, and the government.

however, because many loans were subprime (subprime loans carry a higher risk that the borrower will default, and the terms are more stringent to compensate for this risk). Subprime loans were five times more common in predominantly Black neighborhoods than in White ones (Pettit & Reuben, 2010), and many borrowers did not fully understand their terms, such as "balloon" interest rates that rose dramatically over the life of the loan. One consequence was a massive wave of foreclosures beginning in 2008.

While minority and poor communities have not been the only ones affected, they have been disproportionately harmed. The Center for Responsible Lending (2011) estimates that "property depreciation related to foreclosures between 2009 and 2012 [will] end up costing black communities $194 billion and Latino communities $177 billion." Foreclosures have hit these communities hard: In 2011, the Latino foreclosure rate was nearly 12%, and for Blacks it was just under 10%. By comparison, the foreclosure rate for Asians was over 6%; for Whites it was 5% (Weller, Ajinkya, & Farrell, 2012).

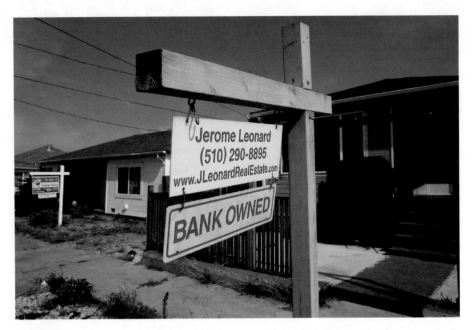

Foreclosures are more common in minority communities, with devastating impact on both individual and neighborhood wealth. In 2005, about two thirds of the wealth held by Latinos in the United States was linked to home equity; it has fallen faster than the wealth of any other ethnic or racial group. ▪

TECHNOLOGIES OF DISCRIMINATION

Have you recently rented or purchased an apartment or a home? Did you consult the classified ads in your local newspaper, or drive around desirable neighborhoods looking for rental or sale signs? In all likelihood, you went to the Internet and headed for a site such as Craigslist, which offers, among many other things, rental units of all sizes and price points. Between 50% and 70% of all renters utilize the Internet in their search for a home, up from just 2% in 1995 (National Association of Realtors, 2006). Among those seeking a home to buy, the figure is even higher. Enforcement of the standard Fair Trading Act, whose primary purpose is to keep discriminatory practices in check, has not kept pace with the explosive growth of the online housing market. While racial and ethnic discrimination are illegal, new forms of digital discrimination are challenging integration efforts and reinforcing old patterns of segregation in U.S. communities. From blatant "Whites only" statements to more veiled implications that people of color will not be accepted, the Internet is rife with the potential for housing discrimination.

In a subtler manner, housing providers and sellers are simply picking interested parties who have "White"-sounding names over those whose names sound "ethnic." For example, a recent study used Craigslist to analyze responses of potential housing providers to home seekers giving their names as Neil, Tyrone, and Jorge (Friedman, Squires, & Chadwick, 2010). The researchers found that respondents with "White-sounding" names (for example, Neil) were more likely to get multiple responses, be put in touch with the housing provider, be offered the opportunity to look at the house, and be told the property is available. While racial and ethnic discrimination are not legal in modern America, new forms of digital discrimination are challenging integration efforts and reinforcing long-existing patterns of segregation in U.S. communities. The Internet can also be the source of other forms of prejudice and discrimination, as we discuss in the *Digital Society* box on page 192.

PRISON, POLITICS, AND POWER

One of the key rights of U.S. citizenship is the right to vote—that is, the right to have a voice in the country's political process. Some citizens, however, are denied this right. Many of those have been legally disenfranchised because of state laws that prohibit ex-felons who have served their prison sentences from voting. Statistically speaking, this translates into about 5.3 million disenfranchised individuals and, among them, roughly 1.4 million Black men. A staggering 13% of the Black population cannot legally vote as a direct result of these laws (The Sentencing Project, 2011).

In the mid-20th century, more than 70% of those incarcerated were White; by the end of the 20th century those numbers had reversed, and most prisoners were non-White (Wacquant, 2002; Western & Pettit, 2010). This has had a profound effect on African Americans: 48 states prohibit inmates from voting while they are incarcerated, 35 prohibit parolees from voting, and 30 prohibit

What Is Prejudice?

Concepting Discrimination

DIGITAL SOCIETY

HATE GOES DIGITAL

Sociologists use the term **scapegoating** to describe one group blaming another for problems they face. As early as the 14th century, social theorist Ibn Khaldun observed that the perception of an outside threat serves to increase solidarity within a society. Scapegoating also aids the bonding of social groups that share a fear or hatred of other populations. In the United States, scapegoating is a characteristic shared by "hate groups," whose numbers have spiraled upwards in recent years.

In the United States, organized White separatist and supremacist groups target their appeals primarily to lower-income Whites, blaming their poor economic position on other groups, in particular immigrants and Blacks, though Jews have also historically been a target. According to the Southern Poverty Law Center (2011), which tracks hate groups in the United States, in 2011, there were 1,002 known active hate groups across the United States. These include neo-Nazis, Klansmen, racist skinheads, neo-Confederate groups, Black separatists, and border vigilantes, and a growing number of antigovernment militias. Hate group activities range from criminal acts to marches, rallies, speeches, pamphlet and book publication, video production, and public or secret meetings.

Since 2000, there has been a staggering 54% increase in the number of hate groups. Why have these numbers risen? Key reasons include Latino immigration and an associated perception of threat as

the demographic composition shifts away from White dominance in some states, including Texas and California, and among the youngest generations; the election of the first Black president; and the economic crisis, which, even before its official beginning in 2008, hit many communities hard (Southern Poverty Law Center, 2011).

Another potential factor in the growth of hate groups is the Internet. The ease of interaction with like-minded individuals on popular social networking sites has provided fertile soil for hate groups to form, recruit, and spread their message. The ease of forming or joining a group on the Internet (and the anonymity it offers), combined with changing U.S. demographics and economic uncertainty, are a powerful mix: A recent study of online hate group activity identified more than 14,000 "problematic" sites, which included blogs, Twitter accounts, Facebook groups, and other forums associated with the spread of hate. The study also suggested that "digital hate" is on the rise: The number of sites identified as problematic rose by 12% from 2010 to 2011 (Simon Wiesenthal Center, 2011).

"Digital hate" can be manifested as "trolling," taking over a targeted web user's identity and damaging his or her reputation. Antihate activists and groups including the Southern Poverty Law Center are among those

The Internet is a powerful method of exercising one's freedom of speech. Some racist groups, like this White pride organization, have taken advantage of the Internet to spread messages of hate. ■

targeted by hackers representing hate groups or working alone to discredit them. Another digital aspect of the subculture of hate is the popularity of "hate games" that transform violence against gays, immigrants, people of color, or Jews into "entertainment" (Simon Wiesenthal Center, 2011).

Hate groups have a long history in the United States, but the Internet has transformed the social landscape by offering new forums for communication and recruitment, as well as new and anonymous means of expressing hate and prejudice. While the Internet is also home to groups and organizations actively engaged in combating these trends, the broad proliferation of digital hate remains a problem to be addressed and solved.

THINK IT THROUGH

■ *Can hate speech—or hateful speech—be controlled on the Internet? Should communities or states try to control it through legislation? What are other means of addressing it?*

....

Scapegoating: Scapegoating involves one group blaming another for problems they face.

BEHIND THE NUMBERS

BLACK WOMEN, "COLORISM," AND PRISON SENTENCING

In 2009, more than 3,000 African American women were serving time in U.S. prisons for federal crimes, a statistic that has held relatively steady since the beginning of the new millennium (U.S. Bureau of Justice Statistics, 2011d). What characterizes these female prisoners? Most were convicted of nonviolent crimes, including drug crimes. Many are parents from poor communities. According to researchers at Villanova University, another characteristic of imprisoned women is darker skin tone. Related to racism, but useful to distinguish from it, is the phenomenon of *colorism*—that is, discrimination based on skin tone. What does colorism look like in practice?

Researchers examined more than 12,000 cases of Black women sentenced to prison in North Carolina. In order to ensure comparability of cases, they took into account the types of crimes for which the women were sentenced, as well as their criminal history. They concluded that women with lighter skin tone were given more lenient sentences and served shorter prison terms than their darker-skinned peers. Specifically, lighter-skinned

women were sentenced to about 12% less time and served about 11% less time (Viglione, Hannon, & DeFina, 2011).

Does colorism explain the difference in sentencing? Researchers believe the perception of how "White" someone is does matter—to both Whites and Blacks. William Darity, a professor of African American studies and economics at Duke University and director of the Research Network on Racial and Ethnic Inequality, has conducted research on the impact of skin tone on marriage rates for women and employment for men. Darity points out that "all blacks don't face the same type or degree of discrimination." Furthermore, the preference for lighter-skinned women is expressed by both Black and White men (quoted in Sanders, 2011).

While understanding and combating racism remains a key issue on the agenda of researchers and policy makers, *colorism*, reacting to others on the basis of skin color, has also appeared on the radar screen. A 2008 initiative by the U.S. Equal Employment Opportunity Commission (EEOC) explicitly includes colorism as a form of discrimination (Sanders, 2011).

THINK IT THROUGH

■ *How might a sociologist explain the more acute discrimination faced by those with darker skin?*

---

people on probation from voting. In addition, Virginia, Kentucky, Iowa, and Florida all have a lifetime voting ban on anyone who has been convicted of a felony (The Sentencing Project, 2011).

Among those disenfranchised African Americans is Jarvious Cotton. Author and law professor Michelle Alexander writes about Cotton in her book, *The New Jim Crow: Mass Incarceration in the Age of Colorblindness* (2010):

> Like his father, grandfather, great-grandfather, and great-great-grandfather, [Jarvious Cotton] has been denied the right to participate in our electoral democracy . . . Cotton's great-great-grandfather could not vote as a slave. His great-grandfather was beaten to death by the Ku Klux Klan for

attempting to. His grandfather was prevented from voting by Klan intimidation. His father was barred from voting by poll taxes and literacy tests. Today, Jarvious Cotton cannot vote because he, like many black men in the United States, has been labeled a felon and is currently on parole. . . .

Once you're labeled a felon, the old forms of discrimination—employment discrimination, housing discrimination, denial of the right to vote, denial of educational opportunity, denial of food stamps and other public benefits, and exclusion from jury service—are suddenly legal. . . . We have not ended racial caste in America; we have merely redesigned it. (pp. 1–2)

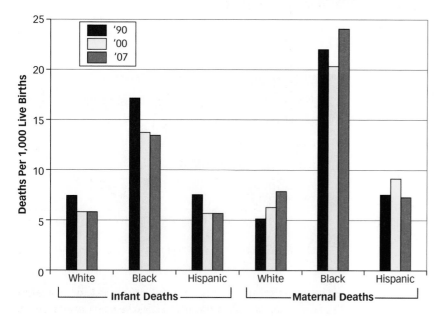

SOURCE: Centers for Disease Control and Prevention. (2012e). Estimated pregnancy rates and rates of pregnancy outcomes for the United States, 1990–2008. *National Vital Statistics Reports, 60*(7).

Alexander (2010) posits that the U.S. criminal justice system effectively functions as a modern incarnation of the Jim Crow laws. Today, she suggests, the expansion of the prison population to include nonviolent offenders, particularly people of color, has contributed to the development of a population segment denied opportunities to have a political voice, as well as education, work, and housing. Prison populations also include women of color (though they are fewer in number). The *Behind the Numbers* box on page 193 points to another aspect of discrimination in the criminal justice system—*colorism*.

CONSEQUENCES OF PREJUDICE AND DISCRIMINATION: RACE AND HEALTH

Sociologists studying discrimination are also interested in the health of populations. Some argue that racism and other disadvantages suffered by Black women in the United States contribute to the much higher level of negative birth outcomes in this population, including low birth weight and infant mortality (Colen et al., 2006). Consider the following statistics: Black women are 60% more likely than White women to experience premature births, and Black babies are about 230% more likely to die before the age of 1 (Norris, 2011). Black women are also more than twice as likely to give birth to very low-weight infants

Color Wheel of Incarceration

than their White or Latina sisters (Centers for Disease Control and Prevention, 2012e).

These data suggest that race trumps other identified predictors of health, including age, income, and educational attainment (Norris, 2011). While health outcomes are predictably favorable among White women as they gain economic status and give birth in their 20s and early 30s (rather than their teens), Black women's birth outcomes do not appear to follow this pattern (Colen et al., 2006). Why is race such a powerful predictor of birth outcomes?

Answers are varied and complex. Public health researcher Arline Geronimus (1992) argues that the racial disparity in birth outcomes—and its stubborn resistance to improvement even as Black women make educational and economic gains—can be attributed to a phenomenon she terms *weathering*. Geronimus describes weathering as an amalgamation of racism and stressors ranging from environmental pollutants to crime to poor health care. These lead, she argues, to a demonstrable deterioration of health, including poor birth outcomes, advanced aging, and even early death.

Geronimus's argument was met with skepticism when she proposed it two decades ago, but it has increasingly gained acceptance. Even in their 20s and 30s, she says, African American women "[suffer] from hypertension at two or three times the rate of whites their own age . . . African-Americans at age 35 have the rates of disability of white Americans who are 55, and we haven't seen much traction over 20 to 30 years of trying to reduce and eliminate these disparities" (Norris, 2011). To see such medical statistics through the prism of social science is a goal of **social epidemiology**, which *studies communities and their social status, practices, and problems to understand patterns of health and disease.*

It is challenging to draw a direct connection between race-related social stressors and negative health outcomes; critics have questioned the link, and more work remains to be done. However, the work of Geronimus demonstrates how sociology can highlight connections between private troubles—such as the birth of a low-weight or preterm infant—and public issues (Figure 8.4). As Geronimus points out, we are just beginning to see the impact of public policy choices in areas such as housing and economics on women's health (Norris, 2011).

Prejudice and discrimination have a long history and take a multitude of forms, some overt, many quite subtle. Will the United States see a decline in prejudice and discrimination as ethnic and

. . . .

Social epidemiology: Studies communities and their social status, practices, and problems to understand patterns of health and disease.

racial diversity grow—or will a different demographic picture make conflicts more acute? Below we look at some of the major groups that make up the U.S. population and see how their numbers are changing.

RACIAL AND ETHNIC GROUPS IN THE UNITED STATES

The area now called the United States was once occupied by hundreds of Indian nations. Later came Europeans, most of whom were English, though early settlers also included the French, Dutch, and Spanish, among others. Beginning in 1619, Africans were brought as slaves and added a substantial minority to the European population. Hundreds of thousands of Europeans continued to arrive from Norway, Sweden, Germany, and Russia to start farms and work in the factories of early industrial America. In the mid-1800s, Chinese immigrants were brought in to provide the heavy labor for building railroads and mining gold and silver. Between 1890 and 1930, nearly 28 million people emigrated to the United States. After the 1950s, immigrants came mostly from Latin America and Asia (Figure 8.5).

Today, non-Whites make up just under 30% of the U.S. population. If current trends hold, non-Whites will constitute a numeric majority nationwide about 2040. Non-Whites already constitute a majority in Texas, which has a growing Latino population. Between 2000 and 2010, the U.S. Latino population nearly doubled to more than 16% percent of the U.S. population, surpassing African Americans (about 12.6%). Asians also experienced double-digit growth from 2000 to 2010 and now constitute about 5% of the U.S. population (U.S. Census Bureau, 2011a).

The rapid growth of minority populations reflects growth from both new births and migration. Migration is the primary engine of population growth in the United States. In fact, demographers estimate that by the middle of the century, fully a fifth of the U.S. population will be immigrants. In a population estimated to reach over 438 million by 2050, 67 million will be immigrants, and about 50 million will be the children and grandchildren of immigrants (Pew Hispanic Center, 2008). Overall, the trend toward a more racially and ethnically diverse country is clear: According to the 2010 census, the majority of babies under 2 years old were non-White.

In the following sections we look in more depth at the racial and ethnic groups that have come together to constitute U.S. culture and society today.

AMERICAN INDIANS

There is no agreement on how many people lived in North America when the Europeans arrived, but anthropologists' best guess is about 20 million. When the Europeans arrived there were

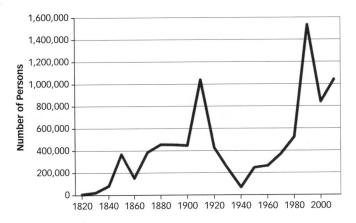

■ **FIGURE 8.5** Number of Persons Obtaining Legal Permanent U.S. Resident Status, 1820–2010

SOURCE: Department of Homeland Security, Office of Immigration Statistics, *Yearbook of Immigration Statistics*, 2010.

thousands of thriving societies throughout North and South America. Encounter soon became conquest, and despite major resistance, the indigenous populations were eventually defeated and their lands confiscated by European settlers. It is believed that between 1500 and 1800 the North American Indian population was reduced from over 20 million to fewer than 600,000 people (Haggerty, 1991; Schaefer, 1993). American Indians, like conquered and oppressed people everywhere, did not passively accept the European invasion. The "Indian Wars" are among the bloodiest in U.S. history, but resistance was not enough. First, White settlers had access to superior weaponry that Native Americans' weaponry could not effectively counter. Second, their control of political, economic, and environmental policies gave Whites a powerful advantage. Consider, for instance, the U.S. government's decision to permit the unregulated slaughter of bison (buffalo) in the post–Civil War era. From about 1866, when millions of bison roamed the American West and the Great Plains, to the 1890s, this key Native American resource was decimated until just a few thousand remained (Moloney, 2012; Smits, 1994).

Since the 1960s, some Native Americans have focused on efforts to force the U.S. government to honor treaties and improve their living conditions, particularly on reservations. In 1969, the group Indians of All Tribes (IAT), citing the Treaty of Fort Laramie (1868), which stated that all unused or abandoned federal land be returned to the Indians, seized the abandoned island of Alcatraz, a former prison island in the San Francisco Bay, and issued a proclamation, which contained the following (deliberately ironic) declarations: "We, the native Americans, re-claim the land known as Alcatraz Island in the name of all American Indians by right of discovery . . . We feel that this so-called Alcatraz Island is more than suitable for an Indian

2008 Presidential Election and Race

American Indians lived in the territorial United States long before the political state was established. They suffered the loss of territory and population as a result of U.S. government policies. Even today, American Indian communities face unique challenges. ■

Reservation, as determined by the white man's own standards." They went on to note its "suitability" by pointing out that, among other things, it had no fresh running water, no industries to provide employment, no health care facilities, and no oil or mineral rights for inhabitants. This comparison was intended to point to the devastating conditions in most reservations.

Alcatraz was occupied by the IAT for more than 18 months. The occupation ended when IAT members either left due to poor living conditions, as the federal government shut off all power and water to the island, or were removed when the government took control of the island in June 1971.

Despite centuries of struggle, more than 60% of the 4.9 million American Indians in the United States today live in urban areas and are among the poorest people in the nation: Over half of all Native American children are born into poverty, three times the rate of White children. About 1.9 million Native Americans live on reservations, where unemployment rates run as high as 50%. With limited economic opportunities, Native Americans also have relatively low educational attainment: Just 13% have earned a bachelor's degree (Ogunwole, Drewery, & Rios-Vargas, 2012).

The *Inequality Matters* box on page 198 raises another issue pertinent to the status of Native Americans in the United States, which is who has the power to name this population.

AFRICAN AMERICANS

In 1903, W. E. B. Du Bois penned the following words: "The problem of the twentieth century is the problem of the color line"

Native American Struggles

(1968, p. 19). By that he meant that grappling with that legacy of 250 years of slavery would be one of the great problems of the 20th century. Indeed, as this chapter shows, Du Bois was right although he did not foresee that the "color line" would incorporate not just African Americans but Hispanics, Asians, American Indians, and other minorities as well.

Slavery forcibly brought more than 9 million people, mostly from the west of Africa, to North and South America. While the stereotype of slaves gratefully serving their White masters dominated U.S. culture for many years, slave revolts were frequent throughout the South. Over 250 Black uprisings against slavery were recorded from 1700 to 1865, and many others were not recorded (Greenberg, 1996; Williams-Meyers, 1996).

Immediately following the end of slavery, during the Reconstruction period, African Americans sought to establish political and economic equality. Former slaves gained the right to vote, and in some jurisdictions, they comprised the majority of registered voters. Black legislators were elected in every Southern state. Between 1870 and 1901, 22 blacks served in the U.S. Congress, while hundreds of others served in state legislatures, on city councils, and as elected and appointed officials throughout the South (Holt, 1977). Their success was short-lived. White Southern legislators, still a majority, passed Jim Crow laws excluding Blacks from voting and using public transportation. In time, every aspect of life was constrained, including access to hospitals, schools, restaurants, churches, jobs, recreation sites, and cemeteries. By 1901, because literacy was required to vote and most Blacks had been effectively denied even a basic education, the registration of Black voters had dwindled to a mere handful (Morrison, 1987).

The North's higher degree of industrialization offered a promise of economic opportunity, even though social and political discrimination existed there as well. Between 1940 and 1970, over 5 million African Americans left the rural South for what they hoped would be a better life in the North (Lemann, 1991). Whether they stayed in the South or moved north, however, many Blacks were still denied fundamental rights nearly a hundred years after slavery was abolished.

By the 1950s, the social landscape was changing— consider the fact that having fought against a racist regime in Nazi Germany in the 1940s, the United States found it far more difficult to justify continued discrimination against its own minority populations. Legal mandates, however, do not necessarily translate to actual practices, and the 1960s saw a wave of protest from African Americans eager to claim greater rights and opportunities for themselves. The civil rights movement was committed to nonviolent forms of protest. It used strikes, boycotts, voter registration drives, sit-ins, and freedom rides in its efforts to achieve racial equality. In 1964, following what was at the time the largest march on Washington in the nation's history, the federal government passed the first in a series of civil rights laws that made it illegal to discriminate on the basis of race, sex, religion, physical disability, or ethnic origin.

All African Americans have not benefited from legislation aimed at abolishing discrimination (Wilson, 2010). In particular, the poorest Blacks—those living in disadvantaged urban and rural areas—lack the opportunities that could make a difference in their lives. Many poor Black Americans suffer from having very little social capital, including uneducated parents, inadequate schools, lack of skills and training, and poor local job opportunities. As a result, nearly half of all African American workers are today employed in unskilled or semiskilled service jobs such as health aides, janitorial service, or food service, compared with only a quarter of all Whites. Few of these occupations offer the opportunity to earn a living wage.

Over time, African Americans have been broadly successful in improving their economic circumstances. The economic gains of African Americans, however, have been more tenuous than those of most other groups, and the Great Recession that began in 2007 substantially eroded Black wealth and income in America. Consider that in late 2010, Black median weekly earnings were $623, but by 2011, the figure had fallen by over 7%. By comparison, income drops for Whites were about 4%, for Asian Americans they were about 4% percent, and for Latinos they were just under 5% (Center for American Progress, 2011).

Gains in economic power, as we see, have been mixed. In spite of this, African Americans have seen important gains in political power. In the early 1960s, there were only 103 African Americans holding public office in the United States. By 1970, about 715 Blacks held elected office at the city and county levels. By the 1990s, however, the figure had surpassed 5,000 and in intervening years, major cities including New York City, Los Angeles, Chicago, and Washington have elected Black mayors in recent decades, and representation on city and town councils and state bodies has grown dramatically. At the federal level, there have been fewer gains, though, clearly, President Obama's election in November 2008 and reelection in 2012 represented a profound political breakthrough for Blacks. Following the November 2012 elections, there were 42 Black members in the House of Representatives, but only 1 in the Senate.

LATINOS/LATINAS

The category of *Latino/a* (or *Hispanic*, the term used by the U.S. Census Bureau) includes people from the many different cultures in Latin America. Latinos largely share the Spanish language as part of their ethnic heritage. According to official estimates, there are 32 million Latinos living in the United States, making them the largest minority group. It's probable that official

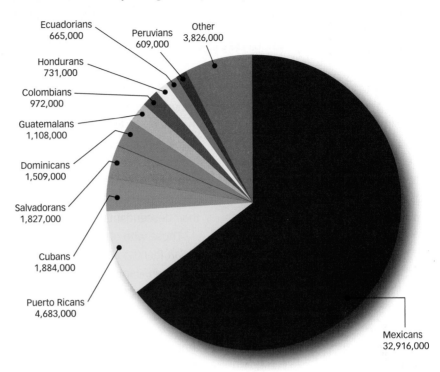

■ **FIGURE 8.6** Country of Origin of Hispanic Population in the U.S., 2010

SOURCE: Pew Research Center. (2012a). *Hispanic origins profiles, 2010* by Seth Motel and Eileen Patten. Pew Hispanic Center.

data actually underestimate the total Latino population, given that they likely miss a sizable number of undocumented immigrants. Latinos are increasing in numbers more rapidly than any other minority group, because of both high immigration rates and higher birthrates. By 2025, they are expected to number nearly 59 million and make up about a fifth of the U.S. population.

Many Latinos trace their ancestry to a time when the southwestern states were part of Mexico. During the mid-19th century, the United States sought to purchase from Mexico what are now Texas and California. Mexico refused to sell, leading to the 1846–1848 U.S.-Mexican War. Following its victory, the U.S. government forced Mexico to sell two fifths of its territory, enabling the United States to acquire all the southwestern states, including California, Texas, New Mexico, and Arizona. Along with this vast territory came the people who inhabited it, including tens of thousands of Mexicans who were forced by White settlers to forfeit their property and who suffered discrimination at the hands of the Whites (Valenzuela Arce, 1992).

Latinos have experienced some of the same obstacles of prejudice and discrimination in the United States as have African Americans. They continue to be discriminated against and live below the standards of the dominant population. At the same time, the very category of *Latino* is problematic for sociologists because it encompasses several different ethic groups with very different experiences of immigration. Latinos are often referred to in such a way that implies uniformity, when in reality, Latinos are a diverse

INEQUALITY MATTERS

WHO HAS THE POWER TO NAME?

"A language is a dialect that has an army and a navy," said sociolinguist Max Weinreich. Before White Europeans came to North America, one of the largest Indian nations was the *Dineh,* a name that means "the People of the Earth." No one knows exactly why, but the Spaniards renamed them "Navajo," the designation by which the Europeans have referred to them ever since. While Native Americans were being outgunned and oppressed by the wave of White European settlers, their language was also subject to marginalization, as was their power to name themselves.

Sociologist Pierre Bourdieu (1999) has pointed out that language is a medium of power, a vehicle that may confer either status or function as a means of devaluation and exclusion. Historically, minority groups have been denied opportunities to name themselves. What is the appropriate name for the people who lived for thousands of years in what today is known as North and South America? They are commonly referred to as Indians, Native Americans, indigenous people, or simply "Natives." Two

prominent organizations—the National Congress of American Indians and the American Indian Movement— use *American Indian* to describe themselves. Yet others object to the term since, like the word *Navajo,* it was given to them by European settlers and their descendants.

Those who object to *American Indian* feel the alternative, *Native American,* captures the fact that they alone among ethnic groups are truly native to this continent, but this name also was given by European settlers. Others argue that nothing short of the correct name for each nation (such as Sioux, Pawnee, Cheyenne, Dineh, or Cherokee) is acceptable. However, referring to each separate nation is problematic when we speak of the collective of Native Americans. After years of controversy among the members of the various nations, their leaders agreed to accept *American Indian* to refer to themselves collectively (Scott, Tehranian, & Mathias, 2002).

The name for a particular racial or ethnic group may be highly contested, since it carries with it information about

the group's social history. The effort by many groups to "name themselves" reflects their belief that to passively accept the name given by society's dominant group is to potentially accept being silenced. American Indian activists Laura Waterman Wittstock and Elaine J. Salinas (1998) suggest in their history of the American Indian Movement that "in the 30 years of its formal history, the American Indian Movement (AIM) has given witness to a great many changes. We say formal history, because the movement existed for 500 years without a name. The leaders and members of today's AIM never fail to remember all of those who have traveled on before, having given their talent and their lives for the survival of the people."

THINK IT THROUGH

■ *Bourdieu highlights the "power to name" as one which is more likely to be held and exercised by dominant groups in society. Can you name another situation in which the power to name gives an advantage to one group and disadvantage to another?*

ethnic population, coming from a range of countries in Central America, South America, and the Caribbean (Figure 8.6). To add to the complexity, Latinos who are born in the United States, or who have the majority of their family anchored in the United States, are increasingly different from the people who permanently reside in their family's country of origin. We discuss two of the most prominent Latino groups below.

MEXICAN AMERICANS Mexicans are the largest group of Latinos in the United States. A large proportion of the Mexican American population lives in California, New Mexico, Texas, and Arizona, though migration to the American South has grown

substantially. The immigration of Mexican Americans has long reflected the immediate labor needs of the U.S. economy (Barrera, 1979; Muller & Espenshade, 1986). During the 1930s, state and local governments forcibly sent hundreds of thousands of Mexican immigrants back to Mexico, but when the United States experienced a labor shortage during World War II, immigration was again encouraged. After the war the *bracero* ("laborer") program enabled 4 million Mexicans to work as temporary farm laborers in the United States, often under exploitive conditions. The program was repealed in 1964, but by the 1980s, immigration was on the upsurge, with millions of people fleeing poverty and political turmoil in Latin America by illegally entering the United States.

Political rhetoric about the threat of illegal immigrants seeking U.S. jobs has become increasingly heated in the recession that began in 2008, although their number has likely been falling. In fact, recent data suggest that a host of factors—including the dangers of crossing the U.S.-Mexican border due to drug violence on the Mexican side, harsher immigration laws in states from Georgia to Arizona, and the dearth of employment in the wake of the recession—have pushed illegal immigration down, perhaps to the point that more undocumented migrants are leaving the United States than entering it (Massey, 2011).

Most ethnic Mexicans in the United States are legal residents, and the number of those rising into the middle class has grown considerably, though the number living in poverty has also risen, particularly in the wake of the economic crisis.

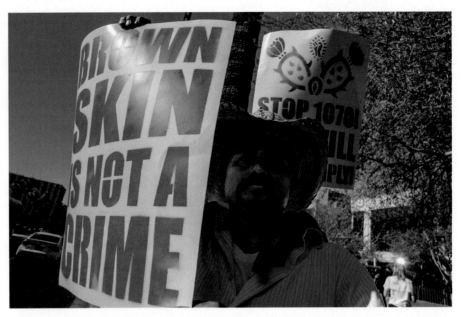

Arizona's SB 1070 legislation gives law enforcement officers the right to ask for proof of legal residency within the United States. This controversial law allows officers to exercise discretion in determining who "looks" like a legal or illegal resident. ■

CUBAN AMERICANS When Fidel Castro came to power in Cuba in 1959, Cubans who opposed his communist regime sought to emigrate to the United States. These included some of Castro's political opponents, but mostly middle-class Cubans whose standard of living was declining under Castro's economic policies and the U.S. economic embargo of Cuba. About half a million entered the United States, mostly through Florida, which is just 90 miles away.

The Cuban community has enjoyed both economic and, perhaps as a result, political success in Florida (Ferment, 1989; Stepick & Grenier, 1993). In contrast to many immigrants, who tend to come from the poorer strata of their native countries, Cuban immigrants were often highly educated professionals and businesspeople before they fled to the United States. They brought with them a considerable reserve of training, skill, and sometimes wealth.

The anticommunist stance of the new migrants was also a good fit with U.S. foreign policy and the effort to crush communist politics in the Western Hemisphere. The U.S. government provided financial assistance such as small-business loans to Cuban immigrants. It also offered a spectrum of language classes, job-training programs, and recertification classes for physicians, architects, nurses, teachers, and lawyers who sought to reestablish their professional credentials in the United States. About three quarters of all Cubans arriving before 1974 received some form of government benefit, the highest rate of any minority community.

While Cuban migrants have tended to have higher levels of education than Mexican immigrants, their status in the United States has also been strongly influenced by the political and economic (that is, the structural) needs of the U.S. government. U.S. economic needs have determined whether the government encouraged or discouraged the migration of manual labor power from Mexico, while political considerations have fostered a support network for migrants endorsing the U.S. government's effort to end the communist Castro regime in Cuba.

ASIAN AMERICANS

Asian immigrants were instrumental in the development of industrialization in the United States. In the mid-1900s, construction began on the transcontinental railroad that would link California with the industrializing East. At the same time, gold and silver were discovered in the American West. Labor was desperately needed to develop the natural resources and work on the railroad. At the time, China was suffering a severe drought. U.S. entrepreneurs seeking labor quickly saw the potential fit of supply and demand, and hundreds of thousands of Chinese were brought to the United States as inexpensive manual labor. Most came voluntarily, but some were kidnapped by U.S. ship captains and brought to the West Coast.

About 4% of the U.S. population trace their origins to Asian countries such as India, China, Japan, Korea, and Vietnam. The number of Asian Americans is growing, primarily because of immigration (Asian American birthrates, following the pattern in their home countries, are low). As with Latinos, the ethnic diversity of this population cannot be fully captured by the term *Asian American* (Figure 8.7 on page 200).

Asian Americans, like other minorities, have experienced prejudice and discrimination. For example, during World War II, many Japanese Americans were forcibly placed in internment camps, and their property was confiscated (Daniels, 2004; Harth, 2001). The U.S. government feared their allegiances were with Japan—an enemy in World War II—rather than the United States. While the teaching of German was banned in some schools, drastic measures were not taken against German or Italian Americans, although Germany and Italy were allied with Japan during the war.

In spite of obstacles, the Asian American population has been successful in making economic gains. Asian Americans as a whole have the highest median household income of any minority group, as well as the lowest rates of divorce, teenage

Beginning in 1942, the U.S. government relocated an estimated 110,000 Japanese Americans living on the West Coast to internment camps. The government feared disloyalty after the Japanese attack on Pearl Harbor, in spite of the fact that more than 60% of those interned were U.S. citizens. ■

pregnancy, and unemployment. Their economic success reflects the fact that, like Cuban Americans, recent Asian immigrants have come from higher socioeconomic backgrounds, bringing greater financial resources and more human capital (Zhou & Bankston, 1998). Family networks and kinship obligations also play an important role. In many Asian-American communities, informal community-based lending organizations provide capital for businesses, families and friends support one another as customers and employees, and profits are reinvested in the community (Ferment, 1989; Gilbertson & Gurak, 1993; Kasarda, 1993).

At the same time, there are substantial differences within the Asian American population. Nearly half of all Asian Indian Americans, for example, are professionals, compared with fewer than a quarter of Korean Americans, who are much more likely to run small businesses and factories. Poverty and hardship are more prevalent among those from Southeast Asia, particularly immigrants from Cambodia and Laos, which are deeply impoverished countries with less educated populations.

ARAB AMERICANS

Arab Americans are an ethnic group that began coming to the United States in the 1880s. The last major wave of migration occurred in the decade following World War II. (PBS, 2011). Contrary to popular perceptions, most Arab Americans are born in the United States, and the majority trace their roots back to

Discrimination and Terrorism

Lebanon, Syria, Palestine, Egypt, and Iraq (Arab American Institute, 2012).

Arab Americans face a unique set of challenges and obstacles. Immediately following the September 11, 2001, terrorist attacks, Arab Americans as a group suffered stigma; acts of discrimination against them increased sharply. The terror attacks provided an avenue for legitimizing the views of racists and xenophobes (Salaita, 2005), but institutionalized prejudice was also obvious in the increase in "random" screenings and searches that targeted Arab Americans.

At the same time, Arab Americans represent a "model minority"—a racial or ethnic group with higher levels of achievement than the general population in areas such as education and income. Like Asian Americans, Arab Americans as a demographic group have been notably successful in these two fields; 45% have at least a bachelor's degree or higher (compared to 28% for the general population), and in 2008 their mean individual income was 27% higher than the national average (Arab American Institute Foundation, 2010).

WHITE ETHNIC AMERICANS

The United States has always had a high percentage of the foreign-born population that is White. The stereotype of minorities

■ **FIGURE 8.7** Country of Origin of Asian Population in the United States, 2010

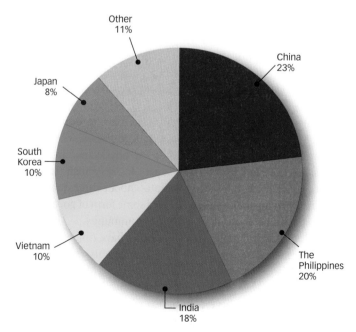

SOURCE: Pew Research Center. (2012c). *The rise of Asian Americans*. Pew Social & Demographic Trends.

as people of color leaves out significant pockets of White ethnic minorities. In the early days of mass migration to the United States, the dominant group was White Protestants from Europe. Whites from Europe who were not Protestant—particularly Catholics and Jews—were defined as ethnic minorities—and their status was clearly marginal in U.S. society.

In mid-19th-century Boston, for example, Irish Catholics made up a large portion of the city's poor and were stereotyped as drunken, criminal, and generally immoral (Handlin, 1991). The term *paddy wagon,* used to describe the police van that picks up the drunk and disorderly, came from the story that the Irish were the van's most common occupants. (*Paddy* was a derogatory term for an Irishman.) Over time, however, White ethnic groups could more easily assimilate because, for the most part, they looked much like the dominant population (Prell, 1999). To further ease assimilation, some families changed their names and encouraged their children to speak English only. Today, most of these White ethnic groups—the Irish, Italians, Russians, and others—have integrated fully into U.S. society (Figure 8.8). They are, on the whole, born wealthier, have more social capital, and encounter fewer barriers to mobility than other racial and ethnic groups.

If dark skin has historically been an obstacle in U.S. society, white skin has been an advantage. That advantage, however, may go unrecognized, according to Peggy McIntosh. In her thought-provoking article, "White Privilege: Unpacking the Invisible Knapsack" (1990), McIntosh writes, "As a white person, I realized I had been taught about racism as something that puts others at a disadvantage, but had been taught not to see one of its corollary aspects, white privilege, which puts me at an advantage . . . I have come to see white privilege as an invisible package of unearned assets that I can count on cashing in each day, but about which I was 'meant' to remain oblivious" (p. 31).

She goes on to outline these "assets," including the following. When Whites are told about their national heritage, or the origins of "civilization," they are shown that White people shaped it. Posters, picture books, greeting cards, toys, and dolls all overwhelmingly feature White images. As a White person, she need not worry that her coworkers at an affirmative action employer will suspect she got the job only because of her race. If she needed any medical or legal help, her race alone would not be considered a risk factor or hindrance in obtaining such services. These are just a few among the 50 unearned privileges of White skin that McIntosh identifies. Her argument is essentially that obliviousness to the advantages of White skin "maintain[s] the myth of meritocracy, the myth that democratic choice is equally available to all." Recognition of skin privilege, in contrast, would be a challenge to the structure of power, which prefers to ignore whatever does not support the story of achievement as an outcome of merit.

Is the recognition of racial or ethnic *advantages* as important as recognition of racial or ethnic *disadvantages*? Can this help to even the field of opportunity for all Americans? What do you think?

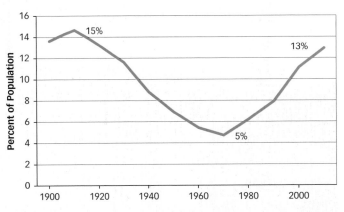

■ **FIGURE 8.8** Foreign-Born Population in the U.S., 1900–2010

SOURCE: U.S. Census Bureau *Statistical Abstracts of the United States: 2000* and *The Foreign Born Population in the United States: 2003;* U.S. Census Bureau. (2010). Nation's foreign-born population nears 37 million. *Newsroom;* Center for Immigration Studies (2012).

RACE AND ETHNICITY IN A GLOBAL PERSPECTIVE

While our focus to this point has been on the United States, issues of racial and ethnic identities and inequalities are global in scope. Around the world, unstable minority and majority relationships, fears of rising migration from developing countries, and even ethnic and racial hatreds that explode into brutal violence highlight again how important it is for us to understand the causes and dynamics of categories that, while socially constructed, are powerfully real in their consequences.

European countries such as France, Germany, and Denmark have struggled in recent years to deal with challenges of immigration, discrimination, and prejudice. Migration to northern and western Europe from developing states, particularly those in North Africa and the Middle East, has risen, driven by a combination of *push factors* (social forces such as dire economic conditions or inadequate educational opportunities that encourage migrants to leave their home countries) and *pull factors* (forces that draw migrants to a given country, such as labor shortages that can be filled by low- or high-skilled migrants or an existing ethnic network that can offer new migrants support). In a short period of time, the large number of job seekers from developing countries in search of a better life has transformed many European countries from largely ethnically homogeneous homelands to multicultural mixtures—and caused some political and social tensions.

Tensions in Europe revolve at least in part around the fact that a substantial proportion of migrants from developing states are Muslim, and some have brought with them religious practices such as veiling that are not perceived to be a good fit with largely secular European societies. By some estimates, Muslims will account for about a fifth of the population of the European Union by 2050 (Migration Policy Institute, 2011). In 2011, France,

The award-winning film *Hotel Rwanda* captured just a fragment of the 1994 genocide in Rwanda. Nearly a million ethnic Tutsis were systematically killed by ethnic Hutus in less than 100 days. ▪

From that time, the Tutsis remained in control of the government and the military (BBC News, 2008). In 1994, the majority Hutus rebelled, and because they outnumbered the Tutsis, they attacked and slaughtered indiscriminately, murdering at least 800,000 people.

Ethnicity and race are powerful forms of identity. They can have positive functions in generating a sense of belonging and integration through a collective conscience and common roots. On the other hand, they also contribute to acute—sometimes deeply prejudicial and dangerous—feelings of social distance from other groups. Racial and ethnic group identity are complex—and their societal effects, challenges, and consequences present a challenge as we move forward in an increasingly multicultural world.

in which about 10% of the population is Muslim, became the first country in Europe to ban the full face veil, also known as the burqa, which is the customary dress for many Muslim women. Similar legislation has been introduced, but not passed, in Belgium and the Netherlands. Earlier, when France banned all overt religious symbols from schools in 2004, civil defiance and violence followed. The Parisian suburbs burned as young French Muslims rioted, demanding opportunity and acceptance in a society that has traditionally narrowly defined who is "French."

In some cases, ethnic and racial tensions have had even more explosive effects. Consider the case of Rwanda, where in 1994, no fewer than 800,000 ethnic Tutsis were killed by ethnic Hutus in the space of just 100 days. Many killings were perpetuated by machete, and women and girls were also targeted for sexual violence. What was at the root of this brutality? By most accounts, Tutsis and Hutus are not so different from one another; they are members of the same ethnic group, live in the same areas, and share a common language. However, for over 500 years the minority Tutsis representing approximately 14% of the population have subjugated the majority Hutus (Kapuscinski, 2001). One cultural difference of considerable importance, however, is that for the Tutsis the cow is sacred and cannot be killed or used for food. The Hutus, who survive almost exclusively by farming, are forced to leave large areas open for cattle grazing, thus limiting the fertile ground available for farming. As the cattle herds have multiplied, so have the Tutsi and Hutu populations, which in turn has led to increasing poverty, especially among the Hutus.

Rwanda was a colony of Belgium, but in the 1950s the Tutsis began to demand independence, as did many other colonized people in Africa. The Belgians incited the Hutus to rebel against the Tutsi ruling class. The rebellion was unsuccessful, but the seeds for genocide were planted in fertile soil. Belgium finally relinquished power and granted Rwanda independence in 1962.

WHY STUDY RACE AND ETHNICITY FROM A SOCIOLOGICAL PERSPECTIVE?

Living in the United States, we are surrounded by serious and casual discussions and comments about race, ethnic jokes and anecdotes, and stories and studies about race and ethnicity. Rarely do we stop to ask ourselves what these categories really mean and why they are significant. Who decided they should be significant, and why? What institutions in society reinforce this belief? What institutions challenge it? As a society we have simply accepted such categories as "Black" and "White" as real. Sociologists, however, argue that they are "socially constructed"—what is real is not race but rather the consequences of racism, with its accompanying prejudice and discrimination.

Sociologically defined concepts such as "race"—as well as prejudice, discrimination, assimilation, and the like—help us see domestic and international conflicts in a different light. We may begin to understand that socially constructed categories marginalize and even dehumanize certain groups, and that we must recognize these symbolic acts, as well as the violent acts that often accompany them.

We benefit in our personal lives too from recognizing the socially constructed nature of categories such as race. We ought to pause and ask ourselves: Why is treatment of individuals often conditioned on skin color? Why has our society opted to define this marker as significant? What must we do culturally, socially, politically, educationally, and economically to pull down the artificial barriers imposed by socially constructed categories?

WHAT CAN I DO WITH A SOCIOLOGY DEGREE?

SKILLS AND CAREERS: CRITICAL THINKING SKILLS

Critical thinking is the ability to evaluate claims about society, politics, the economy, culture, the environment, or any other area of knowledge by using reason and evidence. Critical thinking skills are very broad, but they encompass the ability to logically and rigorously evaluate and interpret data to form ideas and understandings, determine actions, and identify solutions to problems. They also include the inclination and knowledge to be a critical consumer of information, thoughtfully questioning rather than simply accepting arguments or solutions at face value. Critical thinking is not about *criticizing*, but about deeply understanding.

Every chapter in this book seeks to help you sharpen your critical thinking by helping you to see more deeply into the social processes and structures that affect our lives and society and to raise questions about social phenomena we may take for granted. In this chapter we saw, for instance, that racial residential segregation is still widespread in the United States—that is, people of different racial groups often live in different neighborhoods. As well, neighborhoods dominated by Whites tend to have the greatest access to desired resources such as good public schools, safe places to play, and a variety of shopping options. Applying critical thinking to this issue means *asking questions about the existence and persistence of racial residential segregation in the contemporary United States, assessing and addressing our own assumptions about the issue, and working to reason out answers by seeking reliable information and evidence that can be applied to the analysis of the issue.* As sociologists-in-training you will develop a more comprehensive understanding of your social world and will learn both to ask critical questions about why things are as they are and to seek out and find evidence-based answers to those questions.

The ability to exercise critical thinking skills is of great value in both graduate education and the world of work.

Critical thinking skills are a key part of *job tasks* that include analysis, argumentation, research, and investigation. These kinds of tasks are commonly part of the *job description* of, among others, lawyers and judges, government investigators, reporters and correspondents, intelligence analysts, professors and researchers, and management consultants, among others. These jobs are to be found in a diverse array of *occupational fields* that include business/management, government, criminal justice, media, education, health care, and the law.

THINK ABOUT CAREERS

■ *How is critical thinking different from criticizing? How does it differ from other kinds of "thinking" we might apply to issues or problems?*

■ *Notice that critical thinking is a skill often associated with occupations and jobs that demand investigation and analysis. What is the connection between these kinds of tasks and critical thinking?*

▶ *Access additional web links on the student study site to learn more.*

SUMMARY

To test your knowledge further, find additional study material on the Student Study Site at **www.sagepub.com/chamblissintro**

- **Race** is not a biological category but a social construct. Its societal significance derives from the fact that people in a particular culture believe, falsely, that there are biologically distinguishable races and then act on the basis of this belief. The perceived differences are often distorted and lead to **prejudice** and **discrimination**.

- Many societies include different ethnic groups whose history, culture, and practices differ from one another.

- **Minority** groups, typically because of their race or **ethnicity**, may experience prejudice and discrimination. Different types of minority/dominant group relations include **expulsion, assimilation, segregation,** and **cultural pluralism**.

- Prejudice usually relies on **stereotyping** and **scapegoating**. During difficult economic times prejudice may increase, as people seek someone to blame for their predicament.

- The civil rights struggles beginning over 60 years ago led to passage of civil rights and affirmative action legislation that has reduced, but not eliminated, the effects of prejudice and discrimination against minorities.

- Although discrimination is against the law in the United States, it is still widely practiced. **Institutionalized discrimination** in particular results in the unequal treatment of minorities in employment, housing, education, and other areas.

- The United States is a multiethnic, multiracial society. Minority groups—including American Indians, African Americans, Latinos, and Asian Americans—make up over 30% of the population. The U.S. Census Bureau has projected that this figure will rise to nearly 50% in the next 40 years.

- Historically, the vast majority of immigrants to the United States have come from Europe, but in recent years the pattern has changed, with most coming from Latin America and Asia.

- With a few exceptions, minority groups are disadvantaged in the United States relative to the majority White population in terms of income, the number living in poverty, and the quality of education and health, as well as political voice. Though the disadvantages of dark skin are recognized, the privileges of white skin have not been widely acknowledged.

KEY TERMS

Study terms on the go with the smartphone-friendly key term flashcards, available at **www.sagepub.com/chamblissintro**

race, 183

ethnicity, 184

minorities, 184

expulsion, 185

segregation, 185

assimilation, 186

cultural pluralism, 187

racism, 187

stigma, 188

mixed contacts, 189

prejudice, 189

stereotyping, 189

discrimination, 190

individual discrimination, 190

institutionalized discrimination, 190

scapegoating, 192

social epidemiology, 194

DISCUSSION QUESTIONS

1. If genetic differences between people who have different physical characteristics (like skin color) are minor, why do we as a society continue to use race as a socially significant category?

2. Racial residential segregation, as you learned in this chapter, remains a key problem in the United States. What sociological factors explain its persistence in an era when housing discrimination is illegal?

3. Do you think immigration will continue to grow in coming decades in the United States? What kinds of factors might influence immigration trends?

DISCOVER ⊡ STATE STATS

Log-in to the eBook and click on the title to the left for access to State Stats in order to complete the exercise.

In the Health database, compare infant mortality rates for Blacks and Whites across two decades. Note differential health outcomes by race that you discover. How do researchers explain these differences?

STUDENT STUDY SITE

Visit the Student Study Site at **www.sagepub.com/chamblissintro** to access additional study tools, including eFlashcards, web quizzes, video resources, web resources, audio resources, links to SAGE journal, handbook, and research articles, and much more!

9

GENDER AND SOCIETY

WHAT DO YOU THINK?

1. Why do boys as a group outscore girls as a group on the SAT, even though girls on average do better in school?
2. Why are women today more likely to enroll in and complete college than their male peers?
3. Why do men as a group continue to outearn women as a group?

SOC *VIEW*

Get a closer look
with the authors!

207

WHERE THE BOYS ARE (NOT)

I f you attend a coed campus and suspect there are fewer men than women in many of your courses, it is not your imagination. A recent article about campus life at a U.S. college begins as follows:

Another ladies' night, not by choice.

After midnight on a rainy night last week in Chapel Hill, N.C., a large group of sorority women at the University of North Carolina squeezed into the corner booth of a gritty basement bar. Bathed in a neon glow, they splashed beer from pitchers, traded jokes and belted out lyrics to a Taylor Swift heartache anthem thundering overhead. As a night out, it had everything— except guys.

"This is so typical, like all nights, 10 out of 10," said Kate Andrew, a senior from Albemarle, N.C. The experience has grown tiresome: they slip on tight-fitting tops, hair sculpted, makeup just so, all for the benefit of one another, Ms. Andrew said, "because there are no guys."

North Carolina, with a student body that is nearly 60 percent female, is just one of many large universities that at times feels eerily like a women's college. Women have represented about 57 percent of enrollments at American colleges since at least 2000, according to a recent report by the American Council on Education. Researchers there cite several reasons: women tend to have higher grades; men tend to drop out in disproportionate numbers; and female enrollment skews higher among older students, low-income students, and Black and Hispanic students. (A. Williams, 2010)

The story suggests that women are moving ahead in academic achievement—and men are falling behind. This is a significant social phenomenon that we'll explore in this chapter.

Women's advancements in higher education represent a powerful social transformation. This change, however, is only part of a story that still finds women earning less than their male counterparts in the workforce and reaching fewer positions at the top of the corporate ladder and politics. Women across the globe remain deeply vulnerable to violence and exploitation. Deep-seated prejudices hamper both men and women who do not behave as their society expects: Gays, lesbians, transgendered individuals, and others who "do gender" differently are frequently subject to ostracism, discrimination, and abuse. In this chapter, we will look at the social category of gender and its continuing significance in modern society, examining its effects on individuals, groups, and societies.

We begin with a discussion of key concepts of sex and gender and how those are used in sociological study. We next discuss the construction of gendered selves, looking at agents of socialization including the family, media, and schools and examining the idea that gender is as much an action and a process as an identity. This leads us to a wide-ranging discussion of gender and society. We focus on gender and family life, higher education, the wage gap, and sexual harassment to understand how gender norms, roles, and expectations shape the experiences of men and women in key societal institutions. Then we turn to both the classical canon and contemporary feminist thinking about gender, ending with a section on women's global concerns, including maternal mortality and sex trafficking, asking about the marginality of women and the steps being taken to empower them to change their own lives and communities. ■

- -

Gender roles: The attitudes and behaviors that are considered appropriately "masculine" or "feminine" in a particular culture.

Sex: Anatomical or other biological differences between males and females that originate in genetic differences.

Gender: Behavioral differences between males and females that are culturally based and socially learned.

Are gender differences between little girls and little boys more natural or learned? Before reading the rest of the chapter, think about evidence you would use to support both arguments. Which seems more persuasive? Why? ■

SOCIOLOGICAL CONCEPTS OF SEX AND GENDER

Sociologists acknowledge that a complex interaction between biology and culture shapes behavioral differences associated with gender. They seek to take both forces into account, though most believe culture and society play more important roles in structuring gender and **gender roles**, *the attitudes and behaviors considered appropriately "masculine" or "feminine" in a particular culture.* Sociologists thus argue that gender-specific behaviors are not reducible to biological differences; rather, biology, culture, and social learning all interact to shape human behaviors.

To highlight the distinction between biological and social factors, sociologists use the term *sex* to refer to biological identity and *gender* to refer to the "masculine" or "feminine" roles associated with sex. **Sex** encompasses the *anatomical or other biological differences between males and females that originate in human genes.* Many of these biologically based sex differences, such as differences in genitalia, are usually present at birth. Others, triggered by male or female hormones, develop later—for example, female menstruation and differences in muscle mass, facial hair, height, and vocal characteristics.

Sociologists use the term **gender** to refer to *norms, roles, and behaviors associated in a given society with being male or female.* Gender is less about being biologically male or female

Gender Stereotyping

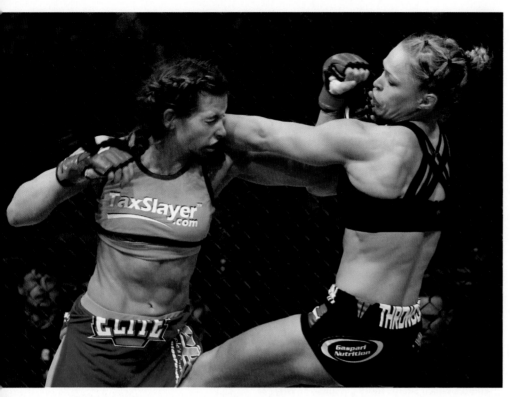

Ronda Rousey (on right) is the first female fighter to join the Ultimate Fighting Championship (UFC), a mixed martial arts organization. Women have also begun to enter other sports traditionally defined as masculine, including boxing and football. ■

assigned sex at birth or is outside the two gender categories. Transgender can refer to people who were female assigned at birth (FAAB) but identify as a man (FTM), or were male assigned at birth (MAAB) but identify as a woman (MTF). It also includes, but is not limited to, other categories and identities such as transsexual, cross-dresser, androgynous, genderqueer, bigender, third gender, and gender nonconforming. **Transsexual** usually refers to *people who use surgery and hormones to change their sex to match their preferred gender*. It is important to note that being trans is a *gender orientation*, not a **sexuality**. Transgendered people may have heterosexual, lesbian, gay, or bisexual sexual orientation.

Clearly, both sex and gender can be complicated. In early 2012, officials of the Miss Universe Canada competition disqualified Jenna Talackova, born a male, by claiming she was required to have been born a female to compete. Within days, the judges decided Talackova could compete (Schabner, 2012). In a YouTube video for Miss International Queen, an earlier transgender/transsexual pageant in which she competed, Talackova said she began hormone therapy at 14 and had sexual reassignment surgery at age 19. She defines herself as a woman, and her gender display is clearly feminine. Is sex at birth an immutable category? Or should individuals have the freedom to define themselves, pushing boundaries of both gender and sex?

In spite of the controversy that surrounded her entry in the May 2012 Miss Universe Canada pageant, transgender contestant Jenna Talackova placed among the top 12 finalists and earned one of four "Miss Congeniality" ribbons.

than about conforming to mainstream notions of *masculinity* and *femininity*, though the characteristics we associate with gender vary across time and space. Biologically based sex differences are not unimportant in shaping social norms of gender. Only biological women can bear and nurse children, with enormous implications for women's roles in all societies (Huber, 2006), but this does not mean that, as Sigmund Freud asserted, biology is destiny.

Before moving on, it is worth noting that both sex and gender are considered by many sociologists to be dynamic concepts. While it's clear that *gender,* which is associated with norms, roles, and behaviors that shift over time, is socially constructed, a growing number of researchers also suggest that *sex* is also socially constructed rather than solely biological (Preves, 2003). They cite cases of infants born with ambiguous sex characteristics and/or an abnormal chromosomal makeup. Such uncertainties in sex categorization are rarely tolerated by doctors, parents, or society. As a result, children are subject to surgeries and medications that will render them "categorizable" in societally normative terms.

Transgender is *an umbrella term to describe those whose gender identity, expression, or behavior differs from their*

CONSTRUCTING GENDERED SELVES

In the diverse cultures of our planet, males are generally expected to behave in "masculine" ways and females in "feminine" ways. Few people fully conform to these stereotypes: Most exhibit a blend of characteristics. Still, in many cultures people believe male and

Transgender: An umbrella term used to describe all those who identify outside of their assigned sex or outside the gender binary.

Transsexuals: People who use surgery and hormones to change their sex to match their preferred gender.

Sexuality: The ways in which people construct their sexual desires and relationships, including the norms governing sexual behavior.

Gender Norms

female stereotypes represent fundamental gender differences, and while some "blending" is acceptable, there are social consequences for diverging too far from the social scripts of gender.

What we consider "masculine" and "feminine" differs across cultures, and gender displays can vary dramatically. Among the Canela of Brazil, for example, large, colorful disks called *kui* are inserted into holes pierced into a boy's ears. Repeated piercings and insertions stretch the holes to a large size, in order to enable the ears to eventually accommodate disks that are several inches across. This painful process is performed to enable the boy to better hear the wisdom of his elders, as well as make him attractive to women (Crocker, 1986, 1990, 1994). This practice would not be considered masculine in U.S. culture, although earrings, once considered a mark of femininity, are now commonplace symbols of masculinity in some U.S. subcultures.

In all cultures, there are pressures to conform to conventional gender roles. At the same time, norms and characteristics are dynamic, meaning men and women both shape and

Thomas Beatie (left) attracted attention in 2007 as the first "pregnant man." Beatie is a transgender male who preserved his female reproductive organs after transitioning. Jenna Talackova (right) attracted the public's attention in 2012 as the first male-to-female transgender contestant in the Miss Universe Canada pageant. Both individuals transgress traditional sex and gender boundaries, inviting both positive and negative reactions in society. ■

are shaped by these expectations. We can think of gender roles as being continuously learned and relearned through social interaction (Fenstermaker & West, 2002). That is, they are neither biologically determined nor passively acquired from others. Rather, each of us plays a dynamic role in learning what it means to be a boy or a girl and a man or a woman in a particular culture. In becoming accomplished actors of these roles, we often forget we are playing a part and become fully identified with the role itself. Yet, because we are constantly renegotiating our gender roles in social interaction, we can change and challenge "rules" we find to be limiting.

Important early influences on gender roles include family, religion, peer groups, the mass media, and schools. These are the *agents of gender socialization* that contribute to the creation of our gendered selves.

AGENT NUMBER ONE: THE FAMILY

Children learn a great deal about socially normative gender roles from their families, particularly their parents. The power of the family in the production and reproduction of gender has led some sociologists to call the home a "factory of gendered personalities" (Fenstermaker Berk, 1985; Goldscheider & Waite, 1991).

Often parents have particular beliefs about how their infant daughters and sons are supposed to behave, and they communicate

these attitudes in countless subtle and not-so-subtle ways. A girl may play with a toy truck with few social consequences, while a boy can face acute teasing from enjoying a baby doll. This distinction may seem to favor girls, but we can also argue that it illustrates the stigmatization and marginalization of practices or objects associated with femininity.

A number of studies have shown that many parents have a sense of gender differences that affect their behaviors toward children, often from birth (Eliot, 2009; Marini, 1990). One study found that mothers spoke differently to their baby in utero if they knew it was a boy than if they knew it was a girl (D. Smith, 2005).

Hillary Lips (2008) has written that parents give their daughters "roots" and their sons "wings," nurturing closer and more dependent ties with girls than their brothers. Some studies also show that boys are more likely to be taught to complete a task on their own, while girls are instructed to ask for help or have the task completed for them (Lindsey & Mize, 2001), a difference that has been documented in the early-education classroom (Sadker & Zittleman, 2009).

Gender Identity Disorder

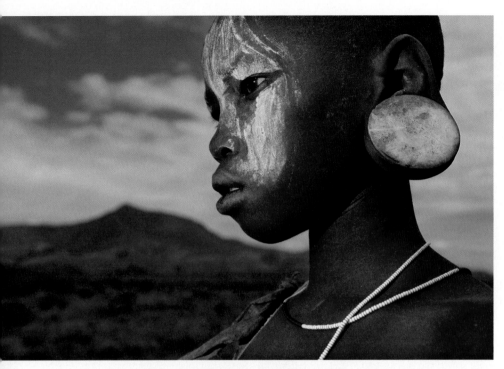

The Surma people of the Omo Valley in Ethiopia use body adornments as part of members' gender display. Ear labrets are worn by women as well as men, though lip plates, which stretch the lower lip away from the mouth, are only worn by women. ■

When parents interact with their children on the basis of gender stereotypes, they may reinforce them. Yet parents can play an equally important part in countering such patterns, by being role models and socializing their children into norms and values reflecting greater gender equality. For example, daughters encouraged to excel in traditionally "male" areas like science and mathematics are more likely to grow up to pursue science- or math-related careers (Bhanot & Jovanovic, 2005; Tenenbaum & Leaper, 2003). Just a few decades ago, women were a clear minority in most institutions of higher education. Legal measures such as Title IX, which in 1972 prohibited discrimination in educational institutions receiving federal funding, opened more educational opportunities to women. By the 1960s and 1970s, young women had greater social and economic support at home as well. Both society and families have been part of the revolution in women's higher education, though women still lag in well-paid but historically male-dominated science, math, and engineering fields.

GENDER AMONG FRIENDS: PEER INFLUENCES

The actions and judgments of our peers affect the way we enact our gender roles. Beginning at an early age, girls and boys learn stereotypical gender roles in peer groups (Martin & Fabes, 2001). Aina & Cameron (2011) suggest that friendship patterns and peer pressure reflect and affirm stereotypes. This is particularly acute among boys who "police" peers, stigmatizing perceived feminine traits. Playing in same-sex peer groups, interestingly enough, may have a different effect from playing more often in mixed groups. Martin and

Fabes (2001) point to a "social dosage effect," such that play among young girls who stayed with all-girl groups tended to reflect norms of encouragement and support, while young boys in same-gender groups developed a tendency toward more aggressive and competitive play.

Research on elementary school playgroups reports that girls often gather in smaller groups, playing games that include imitation and the taking of turns. Boys, on the other hand, play in larger groups at rule-governed games that occur over larger physical distances than girls occupy (Richards, 2012; Thorne, 1993). Long before they become teenagers, young people learn that gender matters and that roles, norms, and expectations of boys and girls are often different.

During late childhood and adolescence, children are especially concerned about what their friends think of them—far more than about what their parents think. In her ethnography of a racially diverse working-class high school, C. J. Pascoe (2011) uncovered how teenage boys reinforced norms of masculinity and heterosexuality by disciplining behavior deemed inappropriate, feminine, or otherwise "unmanly," using slurs like "fag" or "faggot."

Pressures for peer conformity remain strong into college, where sororities, fraternities, athletic teams, and other social groups may reproduce stereotypical gender behavior (Edwards, 2007). Homophobia can be acute during this period and, as we will see later in the chapter, may result in sexual harassment (D'Augelli, Pilkington, & Hershberger, 2002; Wyss, 2007). As young adults move into adulthood, the pressures for gender conformity decline somewhat—or perhaps more models for gender roles become available to those who opt not to conform to dominant expectations.

MEDIA POWER: REFLECTING AND REINFORCING GENDER

Scholars have written extensively on the role television plays in reinforcing gender identities in society (Barner, 1999; Condry, 1989; Gauntlett, 2008). According to the American Academy of Child and Adolescent Psychiatry (2011), the average U.S. child spends three to four hours per day in front of the TV, more when a child has a television in his or her room. We might therefore predict that the often highly gendered messages conveyed by everything from characters to themes to advertisements will have a powerful impact on images, norms, and identities. While much has changed, media images often appear frozen in time, persistently peddling domestic or highly sexualized images of women—or cattiness, a popular trait for women on "reality" shows—and aggressive if also analytic and often financially successful men.

Cartoons also convey gendered images. One study found that male cartoon characters outnumbered female characters four to one—the same ratio as 25 years before. Moreover, male cartoon characters tended to be powerful, dominant, smart, and aggressive; females generally lacked personalities altogether (Spicher & Hudak, 1997; Thompson & Scantlin, 2007). Another study found that male cartoon characters used more physical aggression, while females were more likely to display behaviors that were fearful, polite and supportive, or romantic (Gokcearslan, 2010; Leaper, Breed, Hoffman, & Perlman, 2002). An analysis of prime-time TV sitcoms in Canada concluded that the body type of female characters was often a factor in the humor; the heavier the character, the more likely she was to be the target of negative comments by male characters, as a means of getting a laugh (Fouts & Burggraf, 2000; Himes & Thompson, 2007).

A recent report in the *New York Times* documents the harassment of females in online gaming communities, a phenomenon that is now pervasive, particularly in competitive games with strangers. Some women seek safer playing environments in smaller online "clans" of identified gamers (O'Leary, 2012). ■

Video games offer an area for expanding this research. By some estimates, fully 92% of children ages 2 to 17 play video games, with "heavy gamers" concentrated in the 6 to 17 age group. The majority are still male, though the proportion of girls has been growing (NPD Group, 2006). This is significant because content studies suggest popular video games consistently convey stereotypical gender images. Downs and Smith (2010), in an analysis of 60 video games with a total of 489 characters, determined that women were likely to be presented in hypersexualized ways that included being partially nude or wearing revealing attire. Reflecting common findings that men are "action" figures while women are largely passive, Haninger and Thompson (2004) discovered that in the 81 teen-rated games they sampled, fully 72 had playable male characters, while just 42 had playable female characters.

In an age of growing media influence, where stories and images and ideas reach us not only through television, films, and games but through computers, phones, and other devices, it is important to consider what kinds of gender images are being "sold" to us. Do new media sources offer more diverse images? Are old stereotypes still pervasive?

GENDER IN THE CLASSROOM: SCHOOLS AND SOCIALIZATION

According to some researchers, in addition to providing instruction in basic subjects, schools are an important site of a "hidden curriculum," or the unspoken socialization to norms, values, and roles—including gender roles (Basow, 2004; Margolis, 2001). The roles of teachers, administrators, and other adults in the school provide some early lessons to students about their future career prospects. Pre-K and elementary teaching is still largely female-dominated, while in many schools, the only men are administrators, physical education teachers or coaches, or janitors (Figure 9.1 on page 214).

Classroom materials reflect gender power and position too. Books on history, for instance, are still heavily populated by male characters, the great heroes and villains of the global and local past. Until very recently, when books began to present a more diverse cast of historical characters,

women were not viewed as an integral part of the historical record. The vast majority remained silent and invisible, their history subsumed under general descriptions of men's lives . . . Extraordinary figures like the queens of sixteenth-century Europe or the nineteenth-century reformers in the United States, active agents in their own right, fared no better. Though [they were] sometimes praised for having successfully assumed male roles, traditional, patronizing phrases and denigrating stereotypes abstracted and diminished even their exceptional personalities and experiences. (Zinsser, 1993, p. 3)

Gender Segregation at School

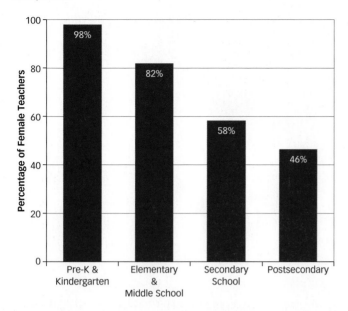

SOURCE: U.S. Bureau of Labor Statistics. (2012c). Table 11: Employed persons by detailed occupation, sex, race, and Hispanic or Latino ethnicity. *Household Data Annual Averages*. Washington, DC: U.S. Government Printing Office. Retrieved from http://www.bls.gov/cps/cpsaat11.pdf

Even today, where women (and, often, minorities) appear, they may still be shown in special features (such as essay boxes) outside the main text that are more likely to be overlooked. In their book, *Failing at Fairness* (1997), David Sadker and Myra Sadker argue that in most history texts students see few women. Their study of one 819-page text yielded less than a full page of references devoted to women. Another book revealed four pictures of men for every one of women, and just about 3% of the text was allotted to telling about women.

The authors write about challenging high school seniors to name 20 famous U.S. women, past or present (not including sports or entertainment figures). In the allotted five minutes, most students were able to come up with just a handful, but had little trouble naming famous men (Sadker & Sadker, 1997). Clearly, changes have been made in the teaching of history since Sadker and Sadker's work. Have those altered the gender balance in history teaching? How would you perform on such a quiz, and what sociological factors would you cite to explain your performance?

THE SAT EXAM: WHY DO BOYS OUTSCORE GIRLS?

Girls outperform boys on many academic measures: earning high grades, enrolling in Advanced Placement (AP) courses, achieving academic honors, finishing in the top 10% of their class,

and graduating, to name a few. One measure where boys have consistently outpaced their female peers, however, is the Scholastic Aptitude Test or SAT. In 2010, the average mathematics score for males was 534 out of 800; females scored an average of 500. While both boys' and girls' scores have risen over time, the gap has remained largely steady (Figure 9.2). While boys' advantage on the verbal section of the SAT is smaller, it too has persisted, though girls tend to earn markedly better average grades in courses like English.

What explains the difference? Some suggest the gap points to a gender bias in the test (Sadker & Sadker, 1997; Sadker & Zittleman, 2009). Why, they ask, do boys continue to outscore girls if girls do better in school and continue doing better in college? After all, the SAT is intended to measure college readiness. A study published in 1989 (Rosser) argued that girls did better than boys on questions focused on relationships, aesthetics, and the humanities, while boys performed better when questions involved sports, the natural sciences, or business. Rosser's study followed an earlier report by Carol Dwyer of the Educational Testing Service (ETS). Dwyer (1976) concluded that gender differences could be altered through selective use of test items. In an effort to "balance" the test, she writes, ETS added more test items highlighting politics, sports, and business, areas on which boys did better. Questions about whether the test favors boys continue to be raised 40 years later (Sadker & Zittleman, 2009).

On the other hand, some observers argue that boys' higher scores on math are a result of a different phenomenon. Christina Hoff Summers (2000) argues that more girls—and girls representing more varying levels of achievement and ability—take the test, explaining their lower average score. Boys' higher average score, to some researchers, is the product of a limited pool of test takers representing the best-prepared young men.

■ **FIGURE 9.2** Average SAT Mathematics Scores for Males and Females, 1972–2010

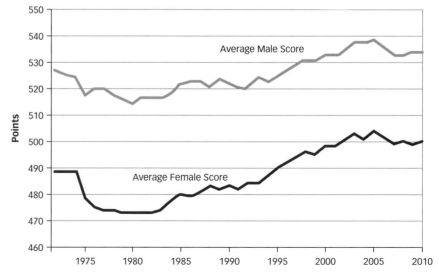

SOURCE: College Board. (2010). *2010 College-bound seniors:* Total group profile report. Retrieved from http://professionals.collegeboard.com/profdownload/2010-sat-trends.pdf

Is the SAT gender-biased because it shows boys outperforming girls, even though girls end up earning better grades and dropping out less frequently? Or is it evidence of girls' advantages, because girls are more likely to take college entrance exams and go to college? Might other factors be at play here?

DOING GENDER

Sociologists commonly define gender as a product of agents of socialization, the combined influence of which creates gendered selves. The implication is that gender is an internalized identity, not natural, but still a fundamental aspect of the social self. Another sociological perspective, described below, suggests that gender is less an identity than an activity.

As we saw in Chapter 4, sociologist Erving Goffman (1959) argued that the social self is the *product* of a social interaction. Thus could the individual engage in "impression management" to tailor his or her presentation of self in a way most favorable to the given situation. Goffman argued that the individual (or a group) was concerned with defining the situation and ensuring a believable performance.

Goffman's work does not have gender at its center, though some of his examples of impression management are telling. For instance, he illustrates *idealization,* in which we present ourselves in ways that exemplify the values and norms of society, with a young woman choosing not to appear smarter than her male date. While her decision to "play dumb" may have gone the way of the 1950s (when Goffman's book was written), it demonstrates how individuals seek to perform gender in accordance with societal expectations.

Building on some of Goffman's ideas, Candace West and Don Zimmerman's (1987) article "Doing Gender" suggests that gender is an activity we *do,* rather than a fixed identity. West and Zimmerman posit that *sex* is a biological category for classifying people as male or female; **sex category** is the *socially required identification display that confirms someone's membership in a given category,* including displaying and enacting gender as social norms and expectations determine. Thus, *gender* is an activity that creates differences between men and women that, while not biological, appear natural because they are so consistently enacted. Membership in a sex category also brings differential access to power and resources, affecting our interpersonal relationships and social status.

Think back to our discussion of other agents of gender socialization. Are there any clues in these materials about why boys outscore girls on standardized math tests such as the SAT? ■

Recall Jenna Talackova, the transsexual Miss Universe Canada contestant. Since she was raised as a male, she had to learn to "do gender" in a way consistent with the sex she aspired to be—female. While most women "do gender" largely without effort, thanks to socialization, for a trans individual, the process may be more conscious, deliberate, and apparent—and no less important for acceptance as a member of his or her new sex category.

GENDER AND SOCIETY

Anthropological studies have found that inequalities in almost all known societies, past and present, favor men over women (Huber, 2006). Women are occasionally equal to men economically, politically, or socially, but in no known society do they have greater control over economic and political resources, exercise greater power and authority, or enjoy more prestige than men (Chafetz, 1984). Many sociologists explain this inequality by noting that women alone can give birth to and (before modern bottle-feeding) nurse infants, two activities essential to a society's continuation but usually lacking in social status. Given that a major source of power, wealth, and status is the ability to earn money or acquire other goods of value, any limitations on women's ability to pursue these rewards affects their social position.

· ·

Sex category: The socially required identification display that confirms someone's membership in a given category.

Adidas Gender Roles   Doing Gender

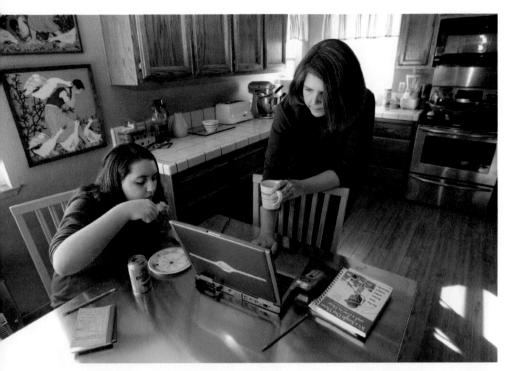

How do you see the future division of labor in your family? If you are already a spouse or parent, think about your level of satisfaction with how household work is divided in your family. What might you want to change and why? ■

In hunting and gathering and early horticultural societies, women produced nearly as much food as men and were more equal in power and prestige, though wealth differences in such subsistence economies were minimal (Huber, 1990, 1993; Mukhopadhyay & Higgins, 1988). With the emergence of agricultural societies and the development of metallurgy, trade and warfare became much more central features of social organization. Because women spent their active years pregnant or nursing infants, they were less likely to become merchants or warriors. Strong states emerged to manage warfare and trade, and these were controlled by men. Women's status suffered accordingly (Friedl, 1975; Grant, 1991).

In modern industrial societies, the requirements of physical survival, reproduction, and economic organization no longer exert the same sorts of constraints. The ability to have fewer children, along with the invention of bottle-feeding around 1910, has freed women from long periods of pregnancy and nursing. Mass education, established in most industrial nations by the end of the 19th century, encouraged women to seek knowledge and eventually careers outside the home.

Today, gender stratification persists, but in a rapidly changing and dynamic social environment. Families, the educational system, and the labor force are all in flux. Below we examine these areas and the ways women's and men's status and roles are changing.

Gender Gap in Politics

GENDER AND FAMILY LIFE

Domestic tasks—child care, cooking, cleaning, and shopping for necessities of living—may entail long hours of work. In the United States, women still do the disproportionate share of housework and child care. Men are more likely to engage in nonroutine tasks, such as making home repairs or taking the children on outings.

Attitudes and practices change, though slowly. Just over a generation ago, a study found that fewer than 5% of husbands did as much housework as their wives (Coltrane & Ishii-Kuntz, 1992). In a 15-year study that tracked thousands of men and women born after World War II, Goldscheider and Waite (1991) found that, in two-parent families with teenage boys and girls, girls were assigned five times as many household chores as their brothers.

More recently, a 2007 *Time* magazine survey found that 84% of respondents (men and women) agreed that husbands and wives "negotiate the rules, relationships and responsibilities more than those earlier generations did" (Gibbs, 2009). A study by the University of Michigan (Achen & Stafford, 2005; Reaney & Goldsmith, 2008) found that the total amount of housework done by women had fallen since 1976 from an average of 26 hours per week to about 17, while the amount done by men had grown from 6 hours to 13 hours. Clearly, there has been some convergence. Labor-saving devices (like the microwave) have contributed to changes, as has the ability of more dual-earner households to pass the burden of domestic work to housekeepers, gardeners, and the like. At the same time, women are still primarily responsible for domestic work in most two-parent households (Davis, Greenstein, & Marks, 2007). Arlie Hochschild and Anne Machung (2003) call this responsibility the **second shift**—*the unpaid housework women typically do after they come home from their paid employment.*

Some data show that unmarried women who live with men spend less time on housework than do married women—even when the number of children and hours of paid work are taken into account (Davis et al., 2007). The division of household labor is more likely to be equal among lesbian and gay couples (Kurdek, 2007). What might explain these differences? Interestingly, one recent study (Davis et al., 2007), with about 17,000 respondents in 28 countries, suggests that marriage has a "traditionalizing" effect on couples, even those who describe themselves and their practices in egalitarian terms.

Second shift: A phrase used by sociologists to characterize the unpaid housework that women typically do after they come home from their paid employment.

GENDER AND HIGHER EDUCATION

We began the chapter by noting that more women than men are studying in U.S. institutions of higher education. Consider that by age 24, nearly 28% of women today have earned a bachelor's degree, while just 19% of men have done so (U.S. Bureau of Labor Statistics, 2012a). The gap is smaller for Whites and larger in Black and Hispanic populations.

Today women make up the larger share of college students; in the past they were actively discouraged from pursuing higher education. In the late 19th century, powerful social barriers stood in the way, like beliefs about women's capacity to succeed at *both* education and reproduction. Some believed that the "ovaries—not the brain—were the most important organ in a woman's body" (Brumberg, 1997, p. 8). Author Joan Brumberg (1997) writes,

> The most persuasive spokesperson for this point of view was Dr. Edward Clarke, a highly regarded professor at Harvard Medical School, whose popular book *Sex in Education; Or, A Fair Chance for the Girls* (1873) was a powerful statement of the ideology of "ovarian determinism." In a series of case studies drawn from his clinical practice, Clarke described adolescent women whose menstrual cycles, reproductive capacity, and general health were all ruined, in his opinion, by inattention to their special monthly demands [menstruation] . . . Clarke argued against higher education because he believed women's bodies were more complicated than men's; this difference meant that young girls needed time and ease to develop, free from the drain of intellectual activity. (p. 8)

While the idea of a "brain-womb conflict" faded as the United States entered the 20th century, other beliefs persisted. Ordinary families with resources to support college study were more likely to invest them in their sons, who were expected to be the primary breadwinners. Families that did seek education for their daughters ran into structural barriers. For example, until the passage of Title IX in 1972, some U.S. colleges and universities, particularly at the graduate and professional school level, limited or prohibited female enrollment.

Although Title IX is often associated with increasing equity in women's access to collegiate athletic opportunities, in fact it requires gender equity for men and women in every educational program receiving federal funding. In 1972, women were earning just 7% of law degrees and 9% of medical degrees in the United States (National Organization for Women, n.d.). By contrast, the U.S. Census Bureau reported in 2010 that 11% of men and 10% of women 25 and older had attained an education higher than a bachelor's degree. As well, women make up 60% of advanced

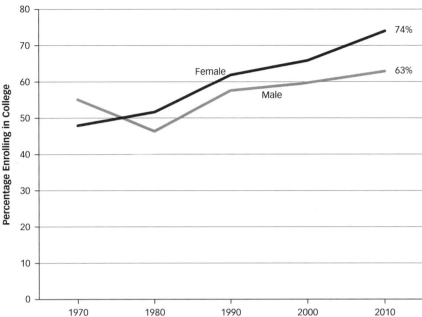

■ **FIGURE 9.3** Percentage of Male and Female High School Graduates Enrolling in College, 1970–2010

SOURCE: National Center for Education Statistics. (2011). Recent high school completers and their enrollment in college, by sex: 1960 through 2010. *Digest of Education Statistics*. Retrieved from http://nces.ed.gov/programs/digest/d11/tables/dt11_209.asp

degree holders aged 25–29. In addition, according to the latest data from the U.S. Census Bureau (2011), more women than men now hold degrees overall, with 37% having earned at least a bachelor's degree compared to 35% of men.

The *proportion* of women enrolled in college has been greater than the proportion of men since 1991, though the actual *number* of women has been greater since the early 1980s, since women make up a larger share of the population (Figure 9.3). Women's climb to equality in educational opportunity was long and slow, but their gains in higher education since Title IX have been dramatic and rapid (National Center for Education Statistics, 2011).

Researchers suggest several reasons for women's growing presence in higher education. First, a high school degree is a prerequisite to college. More men than women leave high school without a degree. In 2007, about 86% of all young people 25–29 had completed high school (Figure 9.4 on page 218). Within this figure, however, lie some notable differences. For instance, White males and White females have almost equal completion rates, while Black and especially Hispanic males drop out in greater numbers than females.

Second, young women as a group have higher grades than young men: In 2009, the mean high school grade point average for female students was 3.10 of a possible 4.0, while for male students

Breaking Gender Barriers

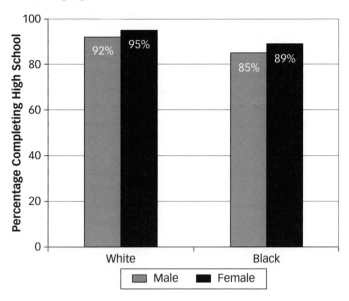

SOURCE: U.S. Department of Education. (2012). *Trends in high school dropout and completion rates in the United States: 1972–2009*. Retrieved from http://nces.ed.gov/pubs2012/2012006.pdf

it was 2.90 (National Center for Education Statistics, 2009). This makes women more likely candidates for college matriculation.

Third, the numbers are affected by substantially higher female enrollment among some demographic groups, including Black and Hispanic, low-income, and older students. Black women substantially outpace their male peers in completing college: Fully 63% of college-educated young Black adults are female, while just 37% are male (Wang & Parker, 2011). Among older ("nontraditional") students, women outnumber men by about two to one (U.S. Department of State, 2008). Finally, more men than women drop out of college, a topic we cover in greater depth in Chapter 11.

Interestingly, a 2011 Pew Research Center survey found that women are more likely than men to say college was "very useful" in increasing their knowledge and helping them grow intellectually (81% compared to 67%), as well as helping them grow and mature as a person (73% compared to 64%). Public perceptions about the necessity of a college education for "getting ahead in life" were also split by gender: 77% of respondents indicated this was true for women, while 68% felt it was true for men (Wang & Parker, 2011).

In 2009, the U.S. Commission on Civil Rights began an investigation into whether some college admissions offices discriminate against qualified female applicants in order to support a desired "gender balance" in admitted classes (Jaschik, 2009). Ironically, the 1972 amendments to Title IX do give admissions departments in private liberal arts colleges the legal right to consider gender. As of March 2011, the investigation was shelved due to disagreements

Gender Wage Gap

over the data collected from 19 schools (Lederman, 2011). What does the general public believe about women's gains (and men's proportional losses) in the attainment of higher education? The *Behind the Numbers* box on page 219 suggests some answers.

GENDER AND ECONOMICS: MEN, WOMEN, AND THE GENDER WAGE GAP

Given their rising achievements in education, are women enjoying earnings that equal or surpass those of men? Women have made tremendous gains in the workplace, but in the United States and across the globe, as a group they continue to lag behind men in earnings in most occupational categories. The **gender wage gap** is *the difference between the earnings of women who work full-time year-round as a group and those of men who work full-time year-round as a group*. Why does it persist?

At the turn of the 19th century, only one in five women 16 or older was paid for her work; most paid workers were young, unmarried, or poor (often all three) and held very low-wage jobs. By 1950, five years after the end of World War II, the proportion of women working outside the home for pay rose to a third. But the enormous economic expansion that continued through the 1970s drew even more women into the paid workforce, attracted by higher pay and supported by the passage of laws such as the Equal Pay Act of 1963, which made unequal pay for equal work illegal. Women's educational gains also opened up more professional and well-paid positions to them. By 1980, more than half of U.S. women were in the paid workforce.

At the beginning of the 20th century, median earnings for women working in full-time, year-round jobs were only half as much as those for men. In 1963 they were still only about three-fifths as much, but by 1999 the gap had narrowed and women earned just over 72% of the median male wage. These gains were partly the result of postwar "baby boom" women, many of them educated and skilled, entering the workforce and moving into higher-paying jobs as they gained experience.

Figures from 2011 show that women working full-time and year-round earned 77% of what their male counterparts earned, with variations by race and ethnicity (see Figure 9.7 on page 220). This translates to average weekly earnings of $684 for women and $832 for men. This continuing difference has two key components, which we look at next.

One important aspect of the gender wage gap is the fact that *men and women are still*, and more than we might think, *concentrated in different occupations*—researchers label this **occupational segregation by gender**. When we identify the 20 most

· ·

Gender wage gap: The difference between the earnings of women who work full-time year-round as a group and those of men who work full-time year-round as a group.

Occupational segregation by gender: The concentration of men and women in different occupations.

BEHIND THE NUMBERS

GENDER AND HIGHER EDUCATION—QUESTIONS AND PERCEPTIONS

Experienced social researchers will tell you that myriad variables can affect the findings of a survey, including the wording and order of the questions. Consider the questions asked by the Pew Research Center on the shifting proportion of men and women in higher education.

When asked whether the fact that "*more women than men* are graduating from college is a good thing, rather than a bad thing," 52% of respondents evaluated the trend positively, 7% said it was a "bad thing," and 39% said it "made no difference" (Figure 9.5; Pew Research Center, 2011). In contrast, when asked whether the fact that

"*fewer men than women* are graduating from college" is a good or bad thing for society, only 46% said it was a "bad thing"; 12% said it was good and 38% that it "made no difference" (Figure 9.6; Pew Research Center, 2011).

While the percentage of people who thought the phenomenon was not important did not change significantly, the difference in the number who thought it was good was quite dramatic. When a positive trend (more women graduating) was emphasized, survey respondents reacted positively. When a negative trend (fewer men graduating) was emphasized, survey respondents reacted negatively. In evaluating social

research, we need to be critical and informed consumers of information and pay attention not only to survey responses, but to the questions the researchers posed as well.

THINK IT THROUGH

■ *What does the Pew study tell us about public attitudes toward the phenomenon of changing demographics in higher education? What does it tell us about the significance of question wording in public surveys? Would your responses have differed depending on the question wording?*

■ **FIGURE 9.5** Attitudes Toward Female Graduation Rates

More Women Than Men Are Graduating From College—Is This a Good Thing or a Bad Thing?

% saying this is a . . . for our society

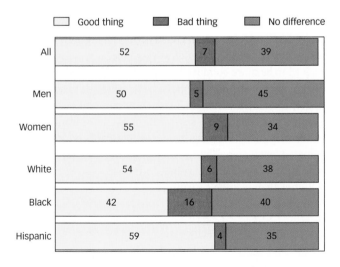

■ **FIGURE 9.6** Attitudes Toward Male Graduation Rates

Fewer Men Than Women Are Graduating From College—Is This a Good Thing or a Bad Thing?

% saying this is a . . . for our society

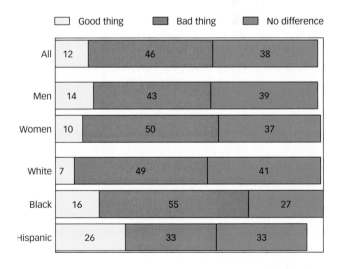

SOURCE: Wang, W., & Parker, K. (2011). *Women see value and benefits of college: Men lag on both fronts, survey finds.* Washington, DC: Pew Research Center.

common occupations for women and for men, only four names appear on both lists. Nearly 40% of women are employed in "traditionally female" occupations, and about 44% of men in "traditionally male" occupations (Hegewisch & Liepmann, 2012).

Why does gender occupational segregation exist and persist? To answer, we borrow some terms from economics. For the purposes of our analysis, **labor supply factors** *highlight reasons that women or men may "prefer" particular occupations,* preparing for, pursuing, and accepting these positions in the labor force. **Labor demand factors** highlight *needs and preferences of the employer.*

Labor supply factors draw our attention to the agency we exercise in choosing a career path and the decisions we make about how and when to be a part of the paid labor force. A generation ago many high school– or college-educated working women were likely to work in three occupational categories: secretarial work, nursing, and teaching (below the college level). Why did they opt for these occupations? One key factor was socialization; women were encouraged to choose "feminine" occupations, and many did. Another factor may be choices women base on their families' needs; a teacher's daytime hours and summers off better fit her children's schedules than a full year of full-time work.

Today, women are far less limited by either imagination or structural obstacles, as we've seen in educational and occupational statistics. At the same time, the top 10 jobs women occupy today still include the heavily and traditionally "feminine" jobs done by women since they entered the workforce en masse in the 1970s (see Table 9.1 on page 221).

We can also use labor supply factors to talk about men's "preferences" in the workforce. Men are more broadly spread throughout the U.S. Census Bureau's occupational categories than women, though in many categories, such as engineer and pilot, they make up a substantial share of all workers. Imagine a young man interested in health and medicine. Would he be encouraged to pursue a career as a nurse? There is still a powerful sense in our society that nursing is a "female" occupation. The film *Meet the Parents* (2000) centers on a daughter's young male suitor, a nurse, whose occupation is the object of both jokes and concern that he is not smart enough to be doctor. We even use the term *male nurse* when referring to men in the nursing profession because our default understanding of "nurse" is a woman. Perhaps it is not surprising then that men still make up just a small fraction of nurses.

Labor demand factors highlight what employers need and prefer—employees with **human capital** or *skills valuable in the particular workplace.* A landscaper seeking a partner will want to hire someone with skills in landscaping; an office manager will seek a receptionist who is tech savvy and organized; an accounting firm will want a competent accountant. These preferences are not gendered but instead focus on skills and credentials.

But other labor supply factors may introduce gender into employer preferences. For example, some employers believe they will incur higher *indirect labor costs* by hiring females. **Indirect**

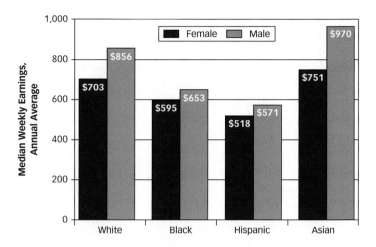

■ **FIGURE 9.7** The Gender Wage Gap by Race and Ethnicity for Full-Time U.S. Workers 16 and Older, 2011

SOURCE: U.S. Bureau of Labor Statistics. (2012b). Median usual weekly earnings of full-time wage and salary workers by selected characteristics, annual averages. *Economic News Release.* Washington, DC: U.S. Government Printing Office. Retrieved from http://www.bls.gov/news.release/wkyeng.t07.htm

labor costs include the time, training, or money spent when an employee takes time off to care for sick family members, opts for parental leave, arrives at work late, or leaves after receiving employer-provided training. Because women are still associated with the roles of wife and mother, employers often assume they are more likely than men to be costly employees.

Stereotypes may also condition an employer's views, especially when jobs are strongly perceived as "feminine" or "masculine." Just as a preschool or child care center might be wary of hiring a man to work with small children or infants (because women are perceived to be nurturing), a construction firm might hesitate to hire a woman to head a team of workers (because men are widely perceived to be more comfortable under male leadership).

Labor supply and labor demand factors help us to sort out factors that concentrate men and women in different occupations.

Gender occupational segregation is significant because jobs dominated by men have historically paid more than jobs dominated by women. That is, those jobs have higher pay scales, which means that men's earnings will tend to start higher and end higher than women's earnings.

· ·

Labor supply factors: Factors that highlight reasons that women or men may "prefer" particular occupations.

Labor demand factors: Factors that highlight the needs and preferences of the employer.

Human capital: The skills and knowledge a person possesses that makes them valuable in a particular workplace.

Indirect labor costs: The time, training, or money spent when an employee takes time off to care for sick family members, opts for parental leave, arrives at work late, or leaves a position after receiving employer-provided training.

Even *within* occupational categories, men tend to earn more than their female counterparts. Data from the U.S. Bureau of Labor Statistics (2012b) show that, for example, among retail salespersons (an occupation that is 41% female), women earn about 75% of men's median weekly earnings. For waiters and waitresses, the gap is larger: Women earn just 64% of the median weekly earnings of their male counterparts. In other occupations, such as bookkeeping/accounting, there is no gap, but this is an exception. Table 9.2 (on page 222) offers some additional comparisons.

What explains these differences within occupations? First, while the Equal Pay Act of 1963 made it illegal to pay men and women a different wage for the same work, numerous violations have been documented in fields from journalism to construction to academia. Second, in some occupations, men and women concentrate in different specialties; men tend to occupy the most lucrative sectors. For instance, male physicians are more likely to be in cardiology, which pays better than areas where women

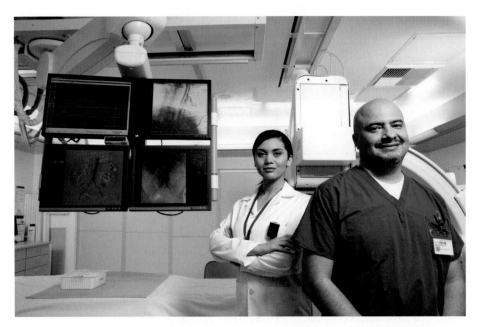

The proportion of female physicians and surgeons is slowly rising: Between 2003 and 2011, their share rose from about 30% to nearly 34%. The proportion of male registered nurses has also grown, to about 9% in 2011 from 8% in 2003. What factors might account for these shifts? ■

concentrate, such as pediatrics. Similarly, women realtors are more likely to sell residential properties, while men are more likely to sell commercial properties for higher profit and commissions. Even male waiters tend to concentrate in high-end restaurants, while women dominate in diners and chain restaurants.

MEN, WOMEN, AND WORKPLACE PROMOTION: GLASS CEILINGS AND GLASS ESCALATORS

When it comes to the positions with the highest status and pay, qualified women still encounter a **glass ceiling,** *an artificial boundary that allows them to see the next occupational level even as structural obstacles keep them from reaching it.* A 2006 study of 1,200 executives in eight countries including the United States, Austria, and Australia found that a substantial percentage of women (70%) and a majority of men (57%) agreed a glass ceiling prevents women from moving ahead in the business hierarchy (Clark, 2006). They may be correct; CNN reports that women occupied just 18 chief executive officer (CEO) positions in the Fortune 500 companies in 2012 (Hoare, 2012).

An earlier study of women of color in corporate management found that female managers in general earned significantly less than White male managers, and that Black, Latina, and Asian American female managers earned less than their male

■ **TABLE 9.1** Top 10 Jobs for U.S. Women, 2010

Rank	Occupations
1	Secretaries and administrative assistants
2	Elementary and middle school teachers
3	Registered nurses
4	Nursing, psychiatric, and home health aides
5	First-line supervisors/managers of retail sales workers
6	First-line supervisors/managers of office and administrative support workers
7	Customer service representatives
8	Cashiers
9	Accountants and auditors
10	Managers, all other

SOURCE: Institute for Women's Policy Research. (2011). Gender wage gap by occupation. *IWPR #C350a,* Table 1. Retrieved from http://www.iwpr.org/initiatives/employment-job-quality/#publications

Glass ceiling: An artificial boundary that allows women to see the next occupational or salary level even as structural obstacles keep them from reaching it.

Gender Gap in Employment

TABLE 9.2 The Pay Gap in Selected Occupations, 2011

Occupation	Median Weekly Pay	
	Men	Women
Chief Executive Officers	$2,122	$1,464
Physicians and surgeons	$1,935	$1,527
Bookkeeping, accounting, and auditing clerks	$654	$656
Real estate brokers and sales agents	$992	$676
Waiters and waitresses	$466	$389
Elementary and middle school teachers	$1,022	$993
First-line supervisors of retail sales workers	$1,016	$781
Office and administrative support occupations	$668	$615

SOURCE: U.S. Bureau of Labor Statistics. (2012d). Table 39: Median weekly earnings of full-time wage and salary workers by detailed occupation and sex. *Household Data Annual Averages*. Washington, DC: U.S. Government Printing Office. Retrieved from http://www.bls.gov/cps/cpsaat39.pdf

counterparts. Non-White female managers also tended to be concentrated in the lowest-paying management positions. Those who did reach the senior management level often complained about lacking influential mentors and not having "a style men are comfortable with" as barriers to their advancement (Catalyst, 1997, 1999).

Recent data show that just under 6% of women are working in traditionally male occupations and just 4.6% of men work in traditionally female occupations (Hegewisch & Liepmann, 2012). While these figures are small, sociologist Christine Williams's (1995) work suggests that when men work in traditional "women's" jobs such as librarianship, social work, nursing, and elementary school teaching, they benefit from a **glass escalator,** *the nearly invisible promotional boost men gain in female-dominated occupations.* Williams found that bosses often presumed the men in her study wanted to move up, so a teacher was assumed to want an administrative position or a nurse to be a head nurse. Many were put on a promotional track—even when they were ambivalent about leaving positions in which they felt satisfied. However, it should be noted that men experience the escalator effect differently based on their race. Wingfield (2008),

Women in the Military

for example, found that African American male nurses did not benefit from their gender in the same way that White men did, despite their dedication to the field.

SEXUAL HARASSMENT

According to federal Equal Employment Opportunity Commission (EEOC) guidelines, **sexual harassment** consists of *unwelcome sexual advances, requests for sexual favors, or physical conduct of a sexual nature when such conduct is used as a condition of employment, instruction, evaluation, benefits, or other opportunities; or when such conduct interferes with an individual's performance or contributes to an intimidating, hostile, or offensive environment.* This definition describes two key types of sexual harassment. **Quid pro quo sexual harassment** is "something for something," or the demand or implication that a sexual favor will buy a promotion or just an opportunity to keep your job. **Hostile environment harassment** is defined by conditions someone perceives as intimidating, uncomfortable, or otherwise distressing.

Quid pro quo sexual harassment typically occurs in a situation of unequal power—for example, between supervisor and employee, or professor and student. It ranges from crude and explicit efforts to coerce someone into a clearly unwanted sexual relationship, to subtle innuendoes that carry the same meaning.

Sexual harassment is found between peers in school as well. In a 1990s study of 1,600 students from 79 high schools across the country, 4 of 5 young people reported being sexually harassed at least once, mainly by other students. Harassment ranged from unwanted sexual comments to forced sexual activity. Only a moderately higher percentage of girls than boys reported being harassed. Girls were harassed more frequently, however, and about a quarter reported the experience was so distressing it forced them to stay home or cut class, interfering with their studies (American Association of University Women, 1993).

Has growing awareness of the problem changed the situation? A survey conducted in 2011 found that, in fact, "sexual harassment is part of everyday life in middle and high schools. About

Glass escalator: The nearly invisible promotional boost men gain in female-dominated occupations.

Sexual harassment: Unwelcome sexual advances, requests for sexual favors, or physical conduct of a sexual nature when such conduct is used as a condition of employment, instruction, evaluation, benefits, or other opportunities; or when such conduct interferes with an individual's performance or contributes to an intimidating, hostile, or offensive environment.

Quid pro quo sexual harassment: The demand or implication that a sexual favor will buy a promotion or an opportunity to keep one's job.

Hostile environment harassment: Conditions in the workplace that someone perceives as intimidating, uncomfortable, or otherwise distressing.

LEGAL GENDER DISCRIMINATION IN THE UNITED STATES

Until 1963, it was legal for employers to pay male and female workers different wages for doing the same job. The Equal Pay Act (EPA) of 1963 prohibits employers from discriminating on the basis of sex for jobs that entail "equal skill, effort, and responsibility, and which are performed under similar working conditions." While some objected that the EPA would increase unemployment among women, it was broadly supported and has been credited with narrowing the gender wage gap.

The Equal Pay Act was followed by Title VII of the Civil Rights Act of 1964, which forbade discrimination on the basis of sex in hiring, promotion, and other basic conditions of employment. While conditions of work for women have yet to achieve full equality, legal protections have significantly improved women's opportunities to achieve economic independence, to support their families, and to contribute to the economic growth of the country.

Advocacy organizations, including the Human Rights Campaign (www.hrc.org), argue that these opportunities are not fully afforded to U.S. workers who are gay, lesbian, bisexual, or transgender. According to the HRC (2013), it is legal in 29 states to discriminate based on sexual orientation, and in 35 states

Is employment discrimination on the basis of gender, race, ethnicity, religion, or sexual orientation ever acceptable? ■

to do so based on gender identity or expression. As a result, LGBT people may face legal discrimination in employment, including in hiring, firing, or promotion. As of early 2012, however, 16 states and the District of Columbia prohibited discrimination based on either sexual orientation or gender identity, while 5 others forbade discrimination based on sexual orientation. Similar federal legislation has not been enacted; the Employment Non-Discrimination Act (ENDA) has been proposed to prohibit public and private employers, employment agencies, and labor

unions from "using an individual's sexual orientation or gender identity as the basis for employment decisions, such as hiring, firing, promotion or compensation," but it has not passed Congress.

THINK IT THROUGH

■ *Why would it be in the interest of an employer to discriminate on the basis of race, gender, sexual orientation, sexual identity, or other group membership? What sociological factors might be used to explain discrimination in the workplace?*

48 percent of the students surveyed experienced some form of sexual harassment in the 2010–2011 school year, and the majority of those students (87 percent) said it had a negative effect on them" (Hill & Kearl, 2011, p. 2). New means of harassment have grown, too, including texts, e-mails, and Facebook, and nearly one third of students reported experiencing harassment through electronic

media. The American Association of University Women report (Hill & Kearl, 2011) points out that even witnessing sexual harassment, as a third to a quarter of students do, can negatively affect perceptions of safety and appear to "normalize" the offense.

The most likely victims of sexual harassment continue to be girls and students of both sexes who are or are perceived to be gay or lesbian. Girls are more likely to report physical or sexual harassment. They also report more acutely negative effects, from emotional to academic consequences (Hill & Kearl, 2011). Many harassers have themselves been victims, and paradoxically, many also characterized their behavior toward others as "no big deal" or funny. Yet a recent study found sexual harassment at school had a more negative effect on teens' health than bullying, even though bullying was more common (Gruber & Fineran, 2008).

What, then, is the relationship between sexual harassment and gender? It may be indirect. If, for instance, media frequently portray women as hypersexualized, sexually available, and passive, this image may influence the ways boys see girls and girls see themselves (Jhally, 2007). Or consider that heterosexuality is elevated as the norm; just 12 U.S. states and the District of Columbia recognize same-sex marriage, nearly all media portrayals of relationships highlight heterosexual couples, and adolescents still commonly use the word *gay* as an insult. What other connections between sexual harassment and societal messages about gender can we as sociologists make to more fully understand the persistence of this problem?

CLASSICAL THEORIES AND FEMINIST THINKING

Until the middle of the 20th century, most sociological theories assumed existing sex roles and norms were positively functional for society—and natural. Contemporary scholarship, particularly by feminist sociologists, challenges this perspective.

CLASSICAL SOCIOLOGICAL APPROACHES TO GENDER

For the "founding fathers" of sociology, whom we met in Chapter 1, gender stratification was all but invisible. While Friedrich Engels did address women's experience of inequalities, a common theme was that men and women were organically and naturally suited to the unequal gender roles in European society. Auguste Comte and Émile Durkheim drew on earlier philosophers including Jean-Jacques Rousseau to argue that women were best suited to "private" family roles such as nurturance, childbearing, and child rearing and were in many ways "naturally" subordinate to men. Men were seen as possessing inherent advantages in such "public" spheres as science, industry, and government (Comte, 1975; Durkheim, 1895/1964).

The roots of this perspective were sought in human physiology. In one popular theory, women were reported to have smaller brain capacity than men based on their relative skull sizes. (By this standard, elephants should be more intelligent than humans, because their skulls are larger.) Because of ostensible differences in brain size, men were assumed to be biologically more rational,

Sexual Harassment

with an advantage in pursuits that required skills of reasoning and logic such as business or governance. Women were seen as inherently more emotional and better at pursuits requiring emotional skills, such as nurturing.

Few women's voices were present or prominent in early sociology. Charlotte Perkins Gilman (1898) was one of the first female and feminist sociologists. Gilman viewed heterosexual marriage between males and females as a *sexuoeconomic relation*. Women were expected to be financially dependent upon men, and in turn serve as caregivers for their husband and children. Their gender socialization included significant pressure to find a husband, who in turn felt obligated to support them. Thus, the sexual relationship between men and women also became an economic one, with negative effects for the relationship, as well as women's autonomy.

Until relatively recently, some sociologists (largely male) argued that sex-role differences—whether biological or social in origin— were positively functional for social harmony, order, and stability. For example, functionalist sociologist Talcott Parsons, one of the most influential midcentury U.S. sociologists, offered a theory of sex roles in the U.S. kinship system that sought to explain them in terms of their functionality (Parsons,1954; Parsons & Bales, 1955).

Parsons argued that, in industrial society, women make their societal contribution by raising children and maintaining the family unit; men do so by earning the family income through outside labor. Parsons did not attribute this role specialization to biology; rather, he argued, women were socialized in the family to acquire such "expressive" qualities as sympathy and emotionality needed in the private sphere of the home. Men were socialized into such "instrumental" qualities as rationality and competitiveness, needed for the capitalist workplace. Competition for standing in the family was thus avoided, and the family's status in society was clear because it derived from the man's position. Hence, sex roles functioned on both the micro (family) and macro (society) levels.

Feminist theorists rejected Parsons's theory. While he did recognize sex roles as the product of socialization rather than nature, his perspective appeared to justify what many feminists saw as a sex-role division rooted in, and reproducing, fundamental inequalities. In a capitalist society, power derives from the ability to earn independently, and the role Parsons foresaw for women was one of economic and social dependence.

CONTEMPORARY U.S. FEMINIST THINKING ON GENDER

If you were a woman . . . 40 years ago, the odds were good that your husband provided the money to buy [this magazine]. That you voted the same way he did. That if you got breast cancer, he might be asked to sign the form authorizing a mastectomy. That your son was heading to college but not your daughter. That your boss, if you had a job, could explain that he was paying you less because, after all, you were probably working just for pocket money. (Gibbs, 2009)

Activists have long sought to bring attention to conditions of female oppression and male dominance. While mid-20th-century activists including Bella Abzug highlighted problems such as limited roles for women outside of motherhood, 21st-century activists have come out against societal practices such as the shaming of women who violate conventional norms of dress or sexuality. ■

The fact that the world looks fundamentally different today is to a large degree thanks to the feminist movements of both the distant and the recent past.

Feminism is *the belief that social equality should exist between the sexes.* It also refers to *social movements aimed at achieving that goal.* Feminism is directly tied to both analysis and action. It seeks to explain, expose, and eliminate **sexism,** *the belief that one sex is innately superior to the other and is therefore justified in having a dominant social position.* In U.S. and most societies, sexism refers to men's dominance over women. Feminists seek to analyze why it exists and how it can be eliminated.

Feminism emerged in the United States in connection with abolitionism and attempts to end slavery during the 1830s, giving birth to the struggle by women for basic rights such as the right to vote and own land. The first wave began in 1848, when Elizabeth Cady Stanton and Lucretia Mott organized a convention in Seneca Falls, New York, to pursue women's expanded rights. While these efforts were a landmark in women's history, the results they sought were achieved only much later (women gained the vote in 1920). Activism was also limited to a small group of women and their male supporters in an environment that saw sex differences as natural.

The 1963 publication of Betty Friedan's *The Feminine Mystique,* which argued that U.S. stereotypes of femininity distorted women's actual experiences and contributed to their unhappiness, helped initiate the second wave of the women's movement, with social theorizing and activism that was much broader in scope (Bernard, 1981, 1982; Epstein, 1988; Friedan, 1963, 1981). Women's experiences in the civil rights and anti–Vietnam War social movements also helped shape a growing feminist consciousness.

The second wave, like the first, called for the equal treatment of women. Women and men were to be viewed not as fundamentally different but as similar; given equal opportunity, women would show themselves the equals of men in all respects. This revival of feminist thinking strongly appealed to the growing number of well-educated, professional women drawn to work and public life during the 1960s (Buechler, 1990), and an explosion of feminist thinking and activism followed.

Women in their 20s, 30s, and 40s today came of age when the feminist social movement had already made great strides and are less likely to have experienced the same degree of discrimination as their predecessors. At the same time, although only about a quarter of all U.S. women describe themselves as "feminist," more than two thirds believe the women's movement has made their lives better—including 75% of all women under 35. Eighty-two percent of

Feminism: The belief that social equality should exist between the sexes, as well as the social movements aimed at achieving that goal.

Sexism: The belief that one sex is innately superior to the other, and is therefore justified in having a dominant social position.

Gender Theory

U.S. women believe the status of women has improved over the past 25 years, and about half of all younger women believe there is still a need for a strong women's movement (Alfano, 2009).

Several broad streams of feminist thinking agree on the importance of basic economic, social, and political equality for women—equal pay for equal work and the sharing of housework. They differ in their analyses of the causes of inequality—and the solutions. Below we provide an brief overview of feminism's varied manifestations.

Liberal feminism, reflected in the work of Betty Friedan and those who followed her lead, holds that *women's inequality is primarily the result of imperfect institutions, which can be corrected by reforms that do not fundamentally alter society itself*. To solve this inequality, liberal feminists have fought to elect women to the U.S. House and Senate, enact an Equal Rights Amendment (ERA) to the U.S. Constitution, and protect women's right to make choices about fertility and family.

As its name implies, **socialist feminism** is rooted in the socialist tradition. It is deeply critical of capitalist institutions and practices and regards *women's inequality as the result of the combination of capitalistic economic relations and male domination (patriarchy), arguing that both must be fundamentally transformed before women can achieve equality* (Chafetz, 1997). This viewpoint originated in the writings of Marx and Engels, who argued that inequality, including that of women, was an inevitable feature of capitalism. Engels (1884/1942), for example, sought to demonstrate that the family unit was historically based on the exploitation and male "ownership" of women (the practice of a father "giving away" his daughter in marriage is rooted in the symbolic "giving" of a young woman from one "keeper" to the a new one). Socialist feminism in the United States emerged in the 1960s, when liberal feminists became frustrated by the pace of social reform and began to address more fundamental sources of women's oppression (Hartmann, 1984; Jaggar, 1983; MacKinnon, 1982; Rowbotham, 1973).

Some feminists grew frustrated with the civil rights and anti-war organizations of the 1960s and 1970s, headed by male leaders who often treated women as second-class citizens. Mindful that true equality for women has yet to be achieved under any existing economic-political system, **radical feminism** argues that *women's inequality underlies all other forms of inequality*. Radical feminists point to gender inequality in the economy, religion, and other institutions to argue that relations between the sexes must be radically transformed before women can hope to achieve true equality. Radical feminists thus focus their attention on the nature of **patriarchy**, *any set of social relationships in which men dominate women*, pointing to male dominance in economics and politics as chief examples.

Radical feminists argue that if patriarchal norms and values go unchallenged, many women will accept them as normal, even natural. Thus while men should also work to end male domination, it is only with other women that women can hope to truly empower themselves and confront male domination in whatever form. Radical feminists advocate all-women efforts to provide shelters for battered women, rape crisis intervention, and other issues that affect women directly (Barry, 1979; Dworkin, 1981, 1987, 1989; Faludi, 1991; Firestone, 1971; Griffin, 1978, 1979, 1981; Millett, 1970).

Multicultural feminism aims to *understand and end inequality for all women, regardless of race, class, nationality, age, sexual orientation, physical ability, or other characteristics* (B. Smith, 1990). Multicultural feminists seek to build coalitions among women, creating international and global organizations, networks, and programs to achieve women's equality. They acknowledge that much of the contemporary women's movement originated among heterosexual, White, and middle- or upper-class women in Europe and North America, and that as a result its central ideas reflect their perspectives. These perspectives are being challenged and changed by feminists of color from Africa, Asia, and Latin America, as well as homosexual, bisexual, and trans women, contributing to an enriched multicultural feminist understanding (Andersen & Collins, 1992; Anzaldúa, 1990; Chafetz, 1997; Narayan & Harding, 2000; Zinn, Weber, Higginbotham, & Dill, 1990).

Third-wave feminism emerged in the early 1990s as a response to some of the perceived shortcomings of second-wave feminism. While issues such as gender violence and rape, reproductive rights, and "reclamation of femininity" have received significant attention by third-wave feminists, they also argue that any issue a feminist finds important can and should be talked about. Choice is a central tenet; whether a woman wants to wear makeup, dress in feminine clothing, and be a stay-at-home mother, or whether she wants to cut her hair short, wear ambiguous clothing, and work in a male-dominated field, any choice is valid.

There is also an emphasis on *intersectional feminism*, which recognizes the intersecting oppressions of race, class, gender, sexuality, and so on. Intersectional feminism is a response to the critique of second-wave feminism that has suggested it caters mainly to the needs of middle-class, White, heterosexual women. Third-wave feminists also use the Internet and social media as vehicles of activism. Although not often recognized as a "wave"

. . . .

Liberal feminism: The belief that women's inequality is primarily the result of imperfect institutions, which can be corrected by reforms that do not fundamentally alter society itself.

Socialist feminism: The belief that women's inequality results from the combination of capitalistic economic relations and male domination, arguing that both must be transformed fundamentally before women can achieve equality.

Radical feminism: The belief that women's inequality underlies all other forms of inequality, including economic inequality.

Patriarchy: Any set of social relationships in which men dominate women.

Multicultural feminism: The belief that inequality must be understood—and ended—for all women, regardless of race, class, nationality, age, sexual orientation, physical ability, or other characteristics.

Feminism

We could argue that popular movie heroines Bella of *Twilight* and Katniss of *The Hunger Games* embody different versions of modern femininity. How would you characterize Bella and Katniss? How might female audiences in particular relate to them in different ways? ■

by academics, perhaps because of its broad focus and lack of definition, many young people identify as third-wave feminists (Baumgardner & Richards, 2010).

Do you identify with any of the types of feminism mentioned above? What would you identify as important feminist issues today?

FEMINIST PERSPECTIVES ON DOING SOCIOLOGY

Sociologists Dorothy Smith and Patricia Hill Collins offer valuable perspectives on what it means to do sociology from a feminist perspective, explicitly recognizing women as both subjects and creators of new knowledge. Smith (1987, 1990, 2005) is a key originator of **standpoint theory**, which says *the knowledge we create is conditioned by where we stand—that is, by our subjective social position.* Our sociological picture of the world has emerged from a variety of standpoints, but until recently they were largely the perspectives of educated and often economically privileged White males. Smith thus suggests that our world of knowledge is incomplete.

Standpoint theory offers a challenge to the sociological (and general scientific) idea that researchers can be, in Max Weber's words, "value-free." Smith argues that standpoint does matter,

. . . .

Standpoint theory: A perspective that says the knowledge we create is conditioned by where we stand, or our subjective social position.

Standpoint epistemology: A philosophical perspective that argues that what we can know is affected by the position we occupy in society.

Matrix of domination: A system of social positions in which any individual may concurrently occupy a status (for example, gender, race, class, or sexual orientation) as a member of a dominated group and a status as a member of a dominating group.

since we do not so much *discover* knowledge as we *create* it from data we gather and interpret from our own standpoint. Recall Victorian doctor Edward Clarke's influential book about the "brain-womb" conflict, positing that higher education could damage young women's reproductive capacity. Could such "knowledge" emerge from the research of a female physician of that time? Would the theorizing of Karl Marx or Talcott Parsons look the same from a woman's perspective? What do you think?

Patricia Hill Collins (1990) has integrated elements of these ideas into her articulation of "Black feminist thought." She offers **standpoint epistemology**, *a philosophical perspective that what we can know is affected by the position we occupy in society.* Epistemology is the study of how we know what we know and how we discern what we believe to be valid knowledge. Collins argues that Black women have long been denied status as "agents of knowledge"—that is, creators of knowledge about their lives and experiences. Other groups have used their power to define Black women, creating a picture that is incomplete and disempowering. Collins calls for recognition of Black women as agents of knowledge and the use of Black feminist thought as a tool for resisting oppression.

Collins points to race, class, sexual orientation, and other factors as those that fundamentally affect status and standpoint. The concept of a **matrix of domination**, *a system of social positions in which any individual may concurrently occupy a status (for example, gender, race, class, or sexual orientation) as a member of a dominated group and a status as a member of a dominating group,* highlights this point. Collins (1990) writes that "all groups possess varying amounts of penalty and privilege in one historically created system . . . Depending on the context, an individual may be an oppressor, a member of an oppressed group, or simultaneously oppressor and oppressed" (p. 225).

Black women's experience of multiple oppressions makes them wary of dominant frames of knowledge, few of which have emerged from their own experience. Thus to Collins, comprehensive knowledge is born of a multitude of standpoints, and creation of knowledge is a form of power that should extend across social groups.

TOWARD A SOCIOLOGY OF MASCULINITY

Integrating women's voices into contemporary sociology is an important goal. At the same time, argues sociologist Michael Kimmel (1986), because men still dominate sociology, it is also necessary to develop a *sociology of masculinity*. Sociologist Raewyn Connell (2010) notes that "masculinities" are not the same as men, adding that masculinities concern in particular the position of men in the gender order.

Kimmel (1996) follows David and Brannon's (1976) idea that in U.S. culture, there are four "basic rules of manhood":

- No "sissy stuff"—avoid any hint of femininity.
- Be a "big deal"—acquire wealth, power, and status.
- Be a "sturdy oak"—never show your emotions.
- "Give 'em hell"—exude a sense of daring and aggressiveness.

These "rules" reflect the concept of *hegemonic masculinity*, or the culturally normative idea of male behavior, which often emphasizes strength, domination, and aggression (Connell & Messerschmidt, 2005). Kimmel argues that such notions of masculinity are so deeply ingrained in culture that when we discuss social problems, ranging from "teen violence" in U.S. schools to "ethnic cleansing" in Bosnia-Herzegovina, we forget that we are really talking almost entirely about the behavior of men. Masculinity as a factor in violence remains obscured.

Before sociologists can understand these social problems, says Kimmel, they must understand how masculine socialization contributes to them. This means "men's studies"—the study of masculinity—should become as much a part of the college curriculum as "women's studies." Of course, Kimmel acknowledges that men are already well integrated into college curricula. In fact,

> if you look at the college curriculum, every course that doesn't have the word "women" in the title is about men. Every course that isn't in "women's studies" is de facto a course in men's studies. Except we call it history, political science, literature, chemistry. But it's always about men as political leaders, military heroes, scientists, writers, artists. Men, themselves, are invisible *as men*. Rarely, if ever do we see a course that examines the lives of men as men. What is the impact of gender on the lives of these famous men? How does masculinity play a part in the lives of great artists, writers, presidents, etc.? (Kimmel, 2000, pp. 5–6)

Gender and Globalization

Notably then, the role played by gender in shaping power relations is largely overlooked. Kimmel's research reminds us how unstated notions of masculinity run through the ideas and pronouncements of men who "shaped history." For example, Louis Stack Sullivan, the inventor of the skyscraper, once said his ambition was to create "masculine forms," and former U.S. President Lyndon Johnson, during the Vietnam War, said of North Vietnam's communist leader, "I didn't just screw Ho Chi Minh, I cut his pecker off" (Kimmel, 1996, p. 268).

Only by studying the social construction of masculinity can we hope to understand that "men" are made and not born. And that, Kimmel believes, is an important step toward achieving gender equality in both attitudes and practices.

GENDER IN A GLOBAL PERSPECTIVE

Being born a woman is a risk. If you are reading these words in the United States, you might feel that is an exaggeration. Certainly, U.S. women are at greater risk than their male counterparts of falling victim to crimes such as sexual assault or rape, of experiencing discrimination the workplace, or being subjected to sexual harassment on the street, at work, or in school. U.S. women are also much more likely to be poor or uninsured than their female counterparts in many European states, including Sweden, Denmark, and Germany.

At the same time, as we have seen in the chapter, women have made dramatic gains in areas such as education, which have brought them independence, earning power, and greater workplace opportunities. Women are in positions of power in politics, the economy, culture, and education. Being born a woman carries risks—and opportunities.

In many places across the globe where you might be reading these words you are likely a male, because millions of women are denied education and cannot read. They are also more likely to be denied medical care, trafficked into the sex trade, and denied the right to own or inherit property. They are less likely to go to school, earn wages equivalent to their work, and eat when a family's food is scarce. In this section, we highlight issues of gender and equality from a global perspective.

MOTHERS AND CHILDREN: THE THREAT OF MATERNAL MORTALITY

In a small hospital in Yokadouma, Cameroon, 24-year-old Prudence died in childbirth. Here is a small piece of her story:

> Prudence had been living with her family in a village seventy-five miles away [from the hospital], and she had received no prenatal care. She went into labor at full term, assisted by a traditional birth attendant who had no training. But Prudence's cervix was blocked, and the baby couldn't come out. After three days of labor, the birth attendant sat on Prudence's stomach and jumped up and down.

That ruptured Prudence's uterus. The family paid a man with a motorcycle to take Prudence to the hospital. The hospital's doctor . . . realized that she needed an emergency cesarean. But he wanted $100 for the surgery, and Prudence's husband and parents said that they could raise only $20 . . . If she had been a man, the family probably would have sold enough possessions to raise $100. (Kristof & WuDunn, 2009, pp. 109–110)

The dangers of childbirth have been nearly alleviated in industrialized countries, and maternal mortality is a rarity. In many developing countries, however, the dangers are just as much social, cultural, and economic as physical (Table 9.3). Kristof and WuDunn (2009) write that Prudence died due to a massive infection, but apart from physical and biological factors, her history also included lack of schooling, lack of rural health care capacity, and cultural disregard for women.

Hospitals in many industrialized countries have tried to cope with nursing shortages by enticing trained nurses from developing countries to migrate. Because modern hospitals offer good pay and clean, safe, well-supplied working conditions, many nurses, by choice or necessity, leave their home countries behind to work abroad. ■

WOMEN AND EDUCATION Educated, literate women are healthier women; there is a powerful correlation between education and health. A 2010 global study also showed a conclusive link between greater education of mothers and lower child mortality, as more educated mothers are more likely to understand and practice good hygiene and health practices (Brown, 2010). Lower child mortality also correlates with fewer pregnancies and smaller families, because if women feel confident their children will survive, they are less inclined to feel the need for "extra" children who can reach adulthood and support the family.

A better-educated birth attendant can treat her patient more effectively; she is clearly less likely to sit on a patient's stomach and risk rupturing her uterus. By raising income potential, education can also offer families like Prudence's the opportunity to pay for needed medical services without delay.

LACK OF RURAL HEALTH SYSTEMS Kristof and WuDunn (2009) write that "if Cameroon had a better health care structure, the hospital would have operated on Prudence as soon as she arrived. It would have had powerful antibiotics to treat her infection. It would have trained rural birth attendants in the area, equipped with cell phones to summon an ambulance. Any one of these factors might have saved Prudence" (p. 114). The global ratio of physicians to population is dramatically skewed, with wealthy countries far more likely to have more doctors per 1,000 population than poor states (see Table 9.4 on page 230). Global "brain drain" is also an obstacle to the development of rural health care systems.

DISREGARD FOR WOMEN Countries where women are marginalized have high rates of maternal mortality. Indeed, where women have little social, cultural, economic, or political voice,

■ **TABLE 9.3** Maternal Mortality Rate for Selected Countries, 2010

Country	Maternal Deaths Per 100,000 Live Births
Cameroon	690
Afghanistan	460
Bangladesh	240
India	200
Brazil	56
China	37
United States	21
Turkey	20
Canada	12
Denmark	12

SOURCE: World Health Organization. (2013). Maternal mortality country profiles. *Global Health Observatory (GHO)*. Retrieved from http://www.who.int/gho/maternal_health/countries/en/index.html#U

In 1997, Madeleine Albright became the first female U.S. Secretary of State in history. She served until 2001. Condoleezza Rice served from 2005 to 2009, when she was replaced by Hillary Clinton (pictured), who occupied the position until early 2013. ■

their lives seem to carry little significance and scarce resources may be directed elsewhere (Hausmann, Tyson, & Zahidi, 2011). In 21st-century China, "39,000 girls die annually . . . because parents don't give them the same medical care and attention that boys receive—and that is just in the first year of life" (Kristof & WuDunn, 2009, p. xiv).

In spite of the power of some women on the global stage (recent U.S. Secretaries of State Condoleezza Rice, Madeleine Albright, and Hillary Clinton come to mind), women's global voice is still limited. Inadequate funding of "women's concerns" including maternal health initiatives—and perhaps even their definition as "women's concerns" rather than family or national concerns—speak to the priority they hold.

THE PRICE OF (BEING) A GIRL

On the illicit global market, available goods include weapons, drugs, pirated software and films, and women and girls. Impoverished girls from the developing world are particularly vulnerable to sexual exploitation and trafficking. According to the annual *Trafficking in Persons* (TIP) report published by the U.S. Department of State (2012), it is difficult to pin down the extent of this "modern-day slavery." The International Labour Organization estimates that over 12 million adults and children experience forced or bonded labor or sexual servitude, with 55% of forced labor and 98% of sex trafficking victims being women and girls. Of these, just under a million and a half may be victims of commercial sexual exploitation (U.S. Department of State, 2012).

In India, the sex trade and sex trafficking are pervasive (Kara, 2009). "India almost certainly has more modern [sex] slaves . . . than any other country. There are 2 to 3 million prostitutes in India. . . . One

2008 study of Indian brothels found that of Indian and Nepali prostitutes who started as teenagers, a significant number have said that they had been coerced into the brothels; women who began working in their twenties were more likely to have made the choice themselves, often to feed their children" (Kristof & WuDunn, 2009, p. 5). Among the reasons are, first, in conservative societies such as India, Pakistan, and other neighboring states, societal norms dictate that young couples wait until marriage to consummate a relationship. "Respectable" middle-class girls are expected to save their virginity for a husband. For young men, then, access to prostitutes offers a penalty-free way to gain sexual pleasure and experience before marriage. Second, the girls and young women in the brothels are usually poor, illiterate villagers with no power or voice and few advocates or protectors (Kara, 2009). Police are not only unlikely to help them but may participate in their exploitation as well.

The diminished status conferred by deep poverty and being female imposes a profound double burden on girls and women. It is no coincidence that in a global environment that so often marginalizes women and girls, the trade in their bodies and lives is vast, widespread, and often ignored by authorities.

CHANGE HAPPENS

It is possible to empower women across the globe. The nonprofit organization Oxfam America, for example, features a program called "Saving for Change" (www.oxfamamerica.org/issues/community-finance). This initiative emphasizes "savings-led

■ TABLE 9.4 Physicians Density Rate in Selected Countries

Country	Physicians Per 1,000 Population
Germany	3.5 (2008)
Denmark	3.4 (2007)
Austria	2.99 (2009)
Egypt	2.8 (2009)
United States	2.6 (2004)
Brazil	1.7 (2007)
India	.59 (2005)
Cameroon	.19 (2004)
Mali	.04 (2008)
Afghanistan	.02 (2009)

SOURCE: World Health Organization. (2012). Health workforce: Aggregated data, density per 1,000. *Data Repository: World Health Statistics.* Retrieved from http://apps.who.int/ghodata/?vid=92100

GLOBAL ISSUES

SON PREFERENCE IN MODERNIZING SOCIETIES

In the natural order of things, 104 to 106 boys are born for every 100 girls. We don't know the precise reasons for this difference, though as far as we do know, it has always existed.

In the societal order of things, from the ancient Greeks to the modern world, many families have pursued the goal of bringing forth a male heir. Aristotle counseled that "men should tie off their left testicle during intercourse if they wanted a son" (Hvistendahl, 2011, p. xv) because the Greeks believed it was the right testicle that produced boys. Far more sophisticated techniques for sex selection are available today, including prenatal identification of sex through ultrasound.

Intuitively, we might associate son preference and the determined pursuit of a male child with traditional societies. After all, greater opportunity and equality for women are among the hallmarks of modern societies. Some researchers suggest, however, that rising sex ratio gaps in regions including East Asia (China, Vietnam), South Asia (India, Pakistan), and Asia Minor (Armenia, Azerbaijan, Georgia) are associated with societal *modernization* (Guilmoto, 2007; Hvistendahl, 2011). That is, while son preference is rooted in traditional cultural norms, the means to ensure the birth of a son are decidedly modern.

How skewed are sex ratios in these regions? In some parts of China, Hvistendahl (2011) discovered dramatic divergence from the natural ratio: "In Yichun, Jiangxi, there are 137 boys for every 100 girls under age four. In Fangchenggang, Guangxi, the number jumps to 153. And in Tianmen, Hubei, 176" (p. 23). While these figures are statistical outliers, the country figures are also striking; in 2010,

Son preference has led to substantially skewed gender ratios in some regions of China. How might the overrepresentation of boys in a school classroom affect the dynamics of teaching, learning, and socializing? ■

China's male-to-female birth ratio was estimated at 121:100, and India's was 112:100 (Hvistendahl, 2011).

Demographer Christophe Guilmoto points to three commonalties among the regions where sex ratios have become acutely skewed. First, health care brought by rapid development has made prenatal screening widely available. Second, fertility rates have often shown steep declines. Third, abortion is pervasive. The first two factors are clearly correlated with modernization, though their relationship to skewing sex ratios is unexpected. Guilmoto notes, however, that low fertility translates into a lowered natural probability of having a son. (Vietnam has a total fertility rate—that is, average births per woman—of just 1.9, and in China it is 1.5.) This fact, together with the technological means to select for sex, is one of the drivers of the higher number of boys. "Guilmoto found sex

selection typically starts with the urban, well educated stratum of society. Elites are the first to gain access to a new technology . . . But like any new technology, sex selection does not remain the domain of the elite" (Hvistendahl, 2011, pp. 10–11).

Modernization has brought women new opportunities, gains in education and pay, and a more prominent voice in society. It has also brought new and perhaps unexpected threats to the female sex, particularly where it meets the currents of traditional cultural norms such as son preference.

THINK IT THROUGH

■ *How should states and societies respond to the manifestation of son preference in sex-selective abortions? Is a solution to the problem more likely to be a product of changes in attitudes or policies?*

According to the British nonprofit organization Oxfam, by 2012 more than 7,000 Saving for Change groups existed in 2,625 villages in Mali. The women make small weekly deposits into a common fund and lend to one another from the fund at a 10% monthly interest rate. ■

women who step out of traditionally subjugated roles is a risk.

On the other hand, greater independence—social or economic—may allow women to leave violent relationships or challenge norms that marginalize them. The effects of women's economic empowerment can also go beyond their own lives, improving prospects for their children and communities. Studies suggest that when women earn and control economic resources, family money is more likely to go toward needs such as food, medicine, and housing (Kristof & WuDunn, 2009). Maternal and child mortality are reduced with women's empowerment, as are the poverty, marginality, and illiteracy that may lead desperate girls and women to the global sex trade. Mobilization of human and intellectual capital is a critical part of domestic development for a country. It is not a coincidence that countries offering opportunity and mobility to women prosper economically; where fully half the population is deprived of rights, education, and access to the labor market, the consequences are ultimately borne by the whole society and state.

microfinance," in which groups of women save and pool their money, agree on guidelines for investing or lending in their communities, and organize their resources to serve local needs. The groups enhance not only their economic but also their social capital, building ties that support them in times of economic or other crisis. While Oxfam funds coaches who help the women get started, "Saving for Change" groups are not financed or managed from the outside; they are fully autonomous and run by the women themselves.

According to Hausmann, Tyson, and Zahidi (2011), Mali has a female literacy rate of just 18% (men's literacy rate is also low at 35%), high rates of early marriage, and few legal protections for women. But Mali, a site of "Saving for Change," also has a growing practice of savings-led microfinance empowering women to save, earn, lend, and invest. With coaching, women can gain financial literacy and empowerment despite their lack of schooling. More mature savings groups are serving the global market for local commodities such as shea butter, a popular cosmetic ingredient. Other hosts to savings-led microfinance programs are Senegal, with a female literacy rate of 39% (compared to men's rate of 62%), and Cambodia, where female literacy is somewhat higher at 71% (to men's 85%). Expansion continues around the world.

Some fear that women's empowerment can foster backlash, manifested as violence or social repercussions. Some patriarchal, conservative societies may not be ready to see women take the initiative to address sexual exploitation, bring attention to crimes against women, or grow economically independent of men, and the victimization of

WHY STUDY GENDER FROM A SOCIOLOGICAL PERSPECTIVE?

Gender matters. Whether we are talking about the toys a child may receive on a birthday, encouragement to study different academic subjects, or pay and promotions on the job, gender can make a difference in someone's experience. It can determine whether someone has the opportunity to visit a health clinic, attend school, or work in a paid job. Historically and often today it still gives men the power to choose whom women will marry, what they can own, and whether they can assert control over their own lives, fertility, economic independence, and physical safety.

When we study gender roles, we have the opportunity to recognize the power of sex and gender as categories that offer opportunities and construct obstacles. Girls and women have made tremendous strides in schools, families, and workplaces, and for many, equality seems achievable. For many others, marginality is still the hallmark of societal experiences. But women have agency, and even women in deprived circumstances can develop economic and political and social voice. Public interest and political will can open doors to better lives for millions of girls and women.

Boys and men are part of this picture too. Women's growing roles challenge men to reconsider long-held ideas about sex and gender and to imagine, along with women, a world in which gender equality improves not only individual lives but families, communities, and countries.

WHAT CAN I DO WITH A SOCIOLOGY DEGREE?

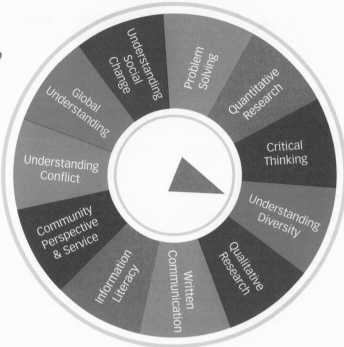

SKILLS AND CAREERS: ACTIVE UNDERSTANDING OF DIVERSITY

The development of an *understanding of diversity* is central to sociological study. As a sociology student, you will gain knowledge related to the histories, practices, and perspectives of diverse groups and will develop intercultural competence. You will also study and apply theories that lend themselves to the analysis of diversity and ways in which it can underpin societal harmony as well as conflict. The close understanding of diversity can inform important research about societal challenges and potential solutions. Active reflection on this knowledge supports the development of skills to effectively work through and with differences that may divide communities and individuals by race, gender, sexuality, culture, religion, and class, among others.

A key part of developing an active understanding of diversity is learning to see the world from the perspectives of others. In this chapter, we learned about the feminist sociological perspectives of Dorothy Smith and Patricia Hill Collins. Recall Smith's *standpoint theory,* which suggests that the knowledge we construct is conditioned by where we stand—that is, by our subjective social position. Collins points to the idea that some groups have historically had the power to create knowledge about and mainstream images of themselves—while other groups, including African American women, have been denied this power. These theorists advocate for the integration of more "standpoints" and a more diverse discipline, which recognizes that creation of knowledge and even "facts" is not just an objective process, but can also reflect one's social position and power. As a major in the social scientific discipline of sociology, you will be exposed to a breadth of theoretical and empirical work that illuminates the social world from a variety of perspectives and helps you to see how the position of different groups in the social structure may affect perceptions, practices, and opportunities. You will be well prepared for the diverse and dynamic workplace of the future . . . and the present.

An understanding of diversity and possession of the skills to work effectively with diverse groups of colleagues, clients, students, and leaders are important assets in today's job market. Among the many *job titles* for which diversity knowledge and skills are essential are diversity workshop trainer, equal employment officer, cultural diversity liaison, manager of diversity initiatives, organizational development and leadership consultant, director of college/university diversity services, and case manager. These are jobs are to be found in a broad range of *occupational fields,* including higher education, human resources, business and management, media, medicine, law, government, the nonprofit sector, and human services.

THINK ABOUT CAREERS:

■ *How would you describe to an employer the skill of understanding diversity (or intercultural competence)?*
■ *How would you explain to a colleague or friend the importance of this skill?*

▶ *Access additional web links on the student study site to learn more.*

SUMMARY

To test your knowledge further, find additional study material on the Student Study Site at **www.sagepub.com/chamblissintro**

- **Gender roles** refer to the attitudes and behaviors considered appropriately "masculine" or "feminine" in a particular culture. In understanding such roles, sociologists use the term **sex** to refer to biological differences between males and females, and **gender** to refer to differences that are socially learned.

- Children begin to learn culturally appropriate masculine and feminine gender identities as soon as they are born, and these roles are reinforced and renegotiated throughout life.

- Gender roles are learned through social interaction with others. Early family influences, peer pressure, the mass media, and the hidden curriculum in schools are especially important sources of gender socialization.

- Gender stratification is found in virtually all known societies, largely because, until the advent of modern industrial production, the requirements of childbearing and nursing constrained women to roles less likely to provide major sources of food. In modern societies, technological changes have removed such barriers to full equality, although stratification continues to persist.

- Women do more housework than men in all industrial societies, even when they hold paid employment outside the home.

- Women typically hold lower-paying occupations than men and are paid less than men for similar jobs. They have made gains but are still less likely to be promoted in most positions than their male peers.

- **Sexual harassment** continues to be a problem. Schools are sites of harassment that can target young people based on gender or sexual orientation.

- **Liberal feminism** argues that women's inequality is primarily the result of imperfect institutions. **Socialist feminism** argues that women's inequality results from the combination of capitalistic economic relations and male domination. **Radical feminism** focuses on patriarchy as the source of domination. Finally, **multicultural feminism** emphasizes ending inequality for all women, regardless of race, class, nationality, age, sexual orientation, or other characteristics. Third wave feminism is a nascent movement highlighting women's agency.

- Globally, being born female is still a risk. Women are disadvantaged in access to power, health care, and safety. At the same time, women are taking the initiative in many developing areas to improve their own lives and those of their communities and families.

KEY TERMS

Study terms on the go with the smartphone-friendly key term flashcards, available at **www.sagepub.com/chamblissintro**

gender roles, 209

sex, 209

gender, 209

sexuality, 210

transgender, 210

transsexual, 210

sex category, 215

second shift, 216

gender wage gap, 218

occupational segregation by gender, 218

labor supply factors, 220

labor demand factors, 220

human capital, 220

indirect labor costs, 220

glass ceiling, 221

glass escalator, 222

sexual harassment, 222

quid pro quo sexual harassment, 222

hostile environment harassment, 222

feminism, 225

sexism, 225

liberal feminism, 226

socialist feminism, 226

radical feminism, 226

patriarchy, 226

multicultural feminism, 226

standpoint theory, 227

standpoint epistemology, 227

matrix of domination, 227

DISCUSSION QUESTIONS

1. How does one "become" a man or a woman? Explain how the individual is socialized into a gender at the following life stages: early childhood, adolescence, teenage years, young adulthood, parenthood. Now consider the other gender. How is this socialization different?

2. Throughout the chapter, we learned about gender inequalities in institutions including the family, education, and the workplace. Think about another institution such as religion, politics, or criminal justice. What kinds of research questions could we create to study gender inequality there?

3. There have been several waves of feminism, and women have gained a spectrum of legal rights and new opportunities. Is feminism as an ideology still needed in our society? Explain your answer.

DISCOVER qᴵᵖ STATE STATS

Log-in to the eBook and click on the title to the left for access to State Stats in order to complete the exercise.

In the Employment and Labor database, find median earnings of both male and female full-time workers. Gather data for your home state, for another state of your choosing, and for the country as a whole. What sociological factors that you learned about in Chapter 9 can help explain differences you find? What other hypotheses might you want to test to explain your findings?

STUDENT STUDY SITE

Visit the Student Study Site at www.sagepub.com/chamblissintro to access additional study tools, including eFlashcards, web quizzes, video resources, web resources, audio resources, links to SAGE journal, handbook, and research articles, and much more!

10 FAMILIES AND SOCIETY

WHAT DO YOU THINK?

1. What is the relationship between rising student loan debt among young adults and the delay and decline of marriage in the United States today?

2. Why are poor and working-class women in the United States less likely than their middle-class counterparts to marry—and more likely to divorce?

3. What is a family? Who should have the power to decide what constitutes a family?

SOC *VIEW*

Get a closer look
with the authors!

THE DRAG OF DEBT: STUDENT LOANS AND FAMILY FORMATION TODAY

According to *CNN Money*, students today are graduating from college with unprecedented levels of debt:

College seniors who took out loans to fund their college education owed an average of $25,250, [or] 5% more than the class of 2009 owed, according to a report from the Institute for College Access & Success' Project on Student Debt. . . .

"Most students in the Class of 2010 started college before the recent economic downturn, but the economy soured while they were still in school, widening the gap between rising college costs and what students and their parents could afford," the report stated. (Ellis, 2011)

Student loan debt now exceeds consumer credit card debt. The New York Federal Reserve Bank estimates that it tops about $905 billion, and over 14% is past due (Brown, Haughwout, Lee, Mabutas, & van der Klaauw, 2012).

Why is this topic of interest to us in a chapter on families in the United States? Here is why: Research has begun to show a correlation between the student debt burden and the ability or willingness of young adults to start families—that is, to marry and have children (Smock, Manning, & Porter, 2000). If, in the past, young people in their early to middle 20s were marrying and perhaps purchasing first homes, today's substantial and widespread student debt may be delaying entry into both family life and the associated consumption of "big-ticket items" such as houses and cars. Indeed, students graduating from higher education in the past decade are the first U.S. generation to finance so much of their education with interest-bearing loans. If this has an effect on family

Student
Loan Debt

formation, it is a topic of interest to sociologists, students, and society.

So what does research show? A 2002 survey from Nellie Mae, a nonprofit corporation and until recently the largest private source of student loans, offers some early insights into the relationship between debt and delayed family formation. In the survey, 14% of borrowers indicated that "loans delayed marriage," a rise from 9% in 1987, when the debt burden was smaller. Over one fifth responded that they had "delayed having children because of student loan debt," an increase from 12% in 1987. Among low-income recipients of Pell grants, the figures were still higher: 19% indicated they delayed marriage, and 24% delayed childbearing due to debt (Baum & O'Malley, 2003).

A report discussing debt and life choices further reinforces this point, noting that about half the young single adults in the study "indicate that their current debts will probably delay their plans to start a family" (Manning, 2005, p. 56). More recently, an IHS Global Insight report highlights that while other types of debt have declined, student loan debt continues to rise—and it correlates with a discernible trend among young adults of delaying marriage and childbearing (Dwoskin, 2012).

As we will see later in this chapter, marriage rates among today's young adults have declined compared to those of earlier generations. Some suggest that marriage is an outdated institution, or that more economically independent women are choosing singlehood over marriage, while others cite a shortage in some communities of "marriageable" men. There are a host of possible explanations. Might debt be one that sociologists should further explore? Is it an obstacle to family formation, and is this a generational and "public issue" rather than just a "personal trouble"? ∎

. . . .

Family: A group of people who identify themselves as being related to one another, usually by blood, marriage, or adoption, and who share intimate relationships and dependency.

Marriage: A culturally approved relationship, usually between two individuals, which provides a degree of economic cooperation, emotional intimacy, and sexual activity.

Monogamy: A form of marriage in which a person may have only one spouse at a time.

Polygamy: A form of marriage in which a person may have more than one spouse at a time.

Polygyny: A form of marriage in which a man may have multiple wives.

Polyandry: A form of marriage in which a woman may have multiple husbands.

In this chapter, we focus our attention on the U.S. family, its demographics, trends, variations, and challenges. We begin by introducing the key concepts used in the sociological study of families and discuss the idea of the family as an institution. Then we review the functionalist and feminist perspectives on families and, in particular, on the character of sex roles in marital relationships. We devote a broad section of the chapter to an overview of U.S. families today, looking at trends in marriage and divorce, as well as family life in a sampling of subcultures—migrant, Native American, and deaf families. Sociologists take a strong interest in issues of social class and its roots and effects, so next we explore practices of child rearing and differences across class, the decline of marriage in the poor and working classes, and work and family life in the middle class. Finally, we explore the relationship between globalization and family in the United States and beyond.

SOME CONCEPTS SOCIOLOGISTS USE TO STUDY FAMILIES

Families come in a broad spectrum of forms, but they share basic qualities. A **family**, at the most basic level, is *two or more individuals who live together and have a legally or normatively recognized relationship* based on, among other things, marriage, birth, or adoption. The family is a key social institution. Though families and their structures vary, the family as an institution is an organized system of social relationships that both reflects societal norms and expectations, and meets important societal needs. It plays a role in society as a site for the reproduction of a community and citizenry, socialization and transmission of culture, and the care of the young and old. Families, as micro units in the social order, also serve as sites for the allocation of social roles, like "breadwinner" and "caregiver," and contribute to the economy as consumers.

Many families are formed through marriage. Sociologists define **marriage** as a *culturally normative relationship, usually between two individuals, that provides a framework for economic cooperation, emotional intimacy, and sexual relations.* Marriages may be legitimized by legal or religious authorities or, in some instances, by the norms of the prevailing culture. Although marriage has historically united partners of different sexes, same-sex marriages have become more common in the United States and other modern countries, though their legal recognition is still incomplete.

Most societies have clear and widely accepted norms regarding the institution and practice of marriage that have varied across time and space. Two common patterns are **monogamy**, in which *a person may have only one spouse at a time,* and **polygamy**, in which *a person may have more than one marital partner at a time.* Within the latter category are **polygyny**, in which *a man may have multiple wives,* and **polyandry**, in which *a woman*

Imagine being a man and having 21 children, conceived by three different wives. The polygynist practice of a man taking multiple wives is unusual (and not legally recognized) in the United States, but according to researchers at Brigham Young University, an estimated 30,000–50,000 U.S. residents practice polygamy. Many are members of breakaway sects of the Mormon church. ■

is permitted to have multiple husbands. In feudal Europe and Asia monogamy prevailed, though in some parts of Asia, wealthy men supported concubines (similar to mistresses; Goody, 1983). George Peter Murdock's (1949) classic anthropological study of 862 preindustrial societies found that 16% had norms supportive of monogamy, 80% had norms that underpinned the practice of polygyny, and just 4% permitted polyandry.

Some sociologists and other social observers have suggested that, because divorce and remarriage are so common in postindustrial countries such as the United States, our marriage pattern might be labeled **serial monogamy**, the *practice of having more than one wife or husband, but only one at a time.* Most modern societies are strongly committed to monogamy, and to the selection of a lifelong mate—in principle, if not always in actual practice. Later in this chapter, we will explore another key trend in families: More women and men in modern countries are forgoing marriage altogether, turning the tables on an institution that has long been considered normative and necessary in the life course—and the social order.

In many societies, marriages tend to be **endogamous**— that is, *limited to partners who are members of the same social group or caste.* Sexual or marital partnerships outside the group may be cause for a range of sanctions from family

Interracial Marriage

disapproval to social ostracism to legal consequences. Consider that in the United States, **antimiscegenation laws**—that is, *laws passed by states to prohibit interracial sexual relations and marriage*—were ruled unconstitutional only in 1967. Until then, some states defined miscegenation as a felony, prohibiting residents from marrying outside the racial group. Today such laws are history. In fact, the Pew Research Center, using data from 2008 and 2009, reported in 2010 that nearly 15% of new marriages were between spouses of different races or ethnicities. The data show that among newlyweds in 2008, about 9% of Whites, 16% of Blacks, 26% of Hispanics, and 31% of Asians married outside their own race or ethnicity.

At the same time, there may still be social consequences for those who venture outside the dating and marital confines of their class, ethnic, racial, or other social group. While intermarriage has increased, more than doubling between 1980 and 2008, most people who marry still do so within their own racial or ethnic group. Think about married couples you know: Would you say that most "match up" on the basis of characteristics such as race, ethnicity, religion, and class? How much of this matching might be attributable to chance or personal preferences? To exposure in the "marriage markets" such as college or places of worship? To normative pressures?

Clearly, marriage in modern societies is most often the outcome of choices made by two people in a relationship. At the same time, as sociologists, we need to attend to the social context in which "choice" is exercised. Later in this chapter we examine U.S. patterns of partnership and family dissolution in greater detail.

FAMILIES AND THE WORK OF RAISING CHILDREN

The role of *parent* or primary caregiver in the United States and much of Europe has traditionally been assumed by the biological parents (occasionally stepparents), but this is one of many possible solutions humans have reached in different times and places. Consider the Baganda tribe of Central Africa, in which the biological father's brother was traditionally responsible for raising the children

. . . .

Serial monogamy: The practice of having more than one wife or husband, but only one at a time.

Endogamous: A characteristic of marriages in which partners are limited to members of the same social group or caste.

Antimiscegenation laws: Laws passed by states to prohibit interracial sexual relations and marriage.

(Queen, Habenstein, & Adams, 1961). The Nayars of southern India offer another variation, assigning responsibility to the mother's eldest brother (Renjini, 2000; Schneider & Gough, 1974). In Trinidad and other Caribbean communities, extended family members have often assumed the care of children whose parent or parents migrate north (to the United States in most instances) to seek work (Ho, 1993).

A substantial minority of U.S. children also live in **extended families**, *social groups consisting of one or more parents, children, and other kin, often spanning several generations, living in the same household.* An extended family may include grandparents, aunts and uncles, cousins, and other close relatives. Most Northern and Western European, Canadian, U.S., and Australian families are **nuclear**—that is, *they are characterized by parents living with their biological children and apart from other kin*—while extended families are more common in Eastern and Southern Europe, Africa, Asia, and Central and Latin America. Extended U.S. families are more common in lower-income households, in rural areas, and among recent migrants and minorities.

For close and extended family to function as caregivers is neither new nor unusual. In fact, a growing number of U.S. children live with one or a pair of grandparents, though the percentage who live with neither parent is still just 4%. In 2011, 69% of children lived with two parents, and just under 24% lived with only their mothers, while only 3% resided with just their father (U.S Census Bureau, 2011b).

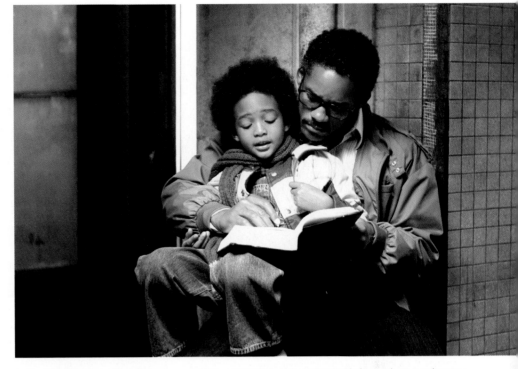

In the film *The Pursuit of Happyness* (2006), actor Will Smith portrays Chris Gardner, a salesman and single father who loses his home after a poor investment and struggles to regain a financial foothold. Gardner, whose real-life story is played out in the film, cares for his young son alone through a long bout of homelessness, which he never reveals to his colleagues and employers. The movie concludes with Gardner's successful professional rebirth as a stockbroker. ■

THEORETICAL PERSPECTIVES ON FAMILIES

When sociologists study families, their perspectives are shaped by their overall theoretical orientations toward society. Thus, as in the study of other institutions, it is helpful to distinguish between the functionalist and conflict perspectives, though, as we will see, there are some important variations and additions to these classic categories.

. . . .

Extended family: A social group consisting of one or more parents, children, and other kin, often spanning several generations, living in the same household.

Nuclear family: A social group consisting of one or two parents and their biological, dependent children with no other kin.

THE FUNCTIONALIST PERSPECTIVE ON THE FAMILY

Recall a key functionalist question: What positive functions does a given institution or phenomenon serve in society? Based on this question and the foundational assumption that if something exists and persists, it must serve a function, functionalist theory has tended to highlight in particular the economic, social, and cultural functions of the family. Arguably, the shift from agricultural to industrial to postindustrial economies has made the family's economic purpose less central than its reproductive and socializing functions, though the family's micro-level consumption decisions continue to drive a macro-economy deeply dependent on consumer activity and acquisition.

In his work on sex roles in the U.S. kinship system, functionalist sociologist Talcott Parsons (1954a) theorized that men and women play different but complementary roles in families. In the "factory of personalities"—in other words, the family—socialization produced males and females prepared for different roles in the family and society. He posited that women were socially prepared for the *expressive* role of mothers and wives, while men were prepared for *instrumental* roles in the public sphere, working and earning money to support the family. As well, socialization prepared men and women to *want* to enact the roles that society needed them to do. These complementary roles, he suggested, were positively functional, as they ensured harmony rather than the conflict that might emerge from competing for status or position. Distinct sex

According to the Census Bureau, about one fifth of U.S. households today consist of married couples with children. In 1950, about 43% of households fit this description. Some contemporary television shows including *Family Guy* both parody and reproduce traditional family images and gender roles. ■

roles also clarified the social status of the family, which was derived from the male's social position.

Aside from his belief that the family served the function of primary socialization—that is, the process of learning and internalizing social roles and norms (such as those relating to gender)—Parsons also suggested that the nuclear family of his time functioned to support adult family members emotionally, a phenomenon he called *personality stabilization* (Parsons & Bales, 1955). In industrial societies, in which the nuclear family unit was often disconnected from the extended kin networks that characterized earlier eras, this stabilization function was of particular value.

Writing in the 1950s, Parsons worried that disruption of the roles he observed in families could have dysfunctions for the family and society. Indeed, though he did not live to see it, there has been some correlation between women's assumption of autonomous roles outside the home and the rise of divorce. Correlation is, of course, not causation. Possible explanations for the link include the advent of no-fault divorce laws, decline in the normative stigma related to divorce, and women's greater economic independence, which has enabled them to leave unhappy marriages that might earlier have been sustained by their dependence on a spouse's wage.

Critics see Parsons's work as reinforcing and legitimating traditional roles that have both positive functions and problematic dysfunctions. The functionalist perspective—and Parsons's expression of it—has been criticized for neglecting the power differentials inherent in a relationship where one party (the wife) is economically dependent on the other (the husband). In a capitalist system, power tends to accrue to those who hold economic resources. Functionalists also neglect family dysfunctions, including ways in

which the nuclear family, central to modern society yet in many respects isolated from support systems such as kin, may also perpetuate gender inequality and even violence.

THE FEMINIST APPROACH: A CONFLICT PERSPECTIVE . . . AND BEYOND

You can probably anticipate that in looking at the family, the conflict perspective will ask how it might produce and reproduce inequality. Feminist theorizing about the family has reflected a conflict orientation in its efforts to unpack and understand the family as a potential site of both positive support and unequal power. From the 1970s, a period following the intense activity of the women's movement and an increase in the number of women taking jobs outside the home, feminist perspectives became central to sociological debates on the family.

While early theorizing about the family highlighted its structure and roles, as well as its evolution from the agricultural to the industrial era, feminist theorizing in the late 20th century turned its attention to women's experiences of domestic life and their status in the family and social world. Feminists endeavored to critique the **sexual division of labor in modern societies**, *the phenomenon of dividing production by gender (men produce, and women reproduce) and designating different spheres of activity, the "private" to women and the "public" to men*. While theorists including Parsons saw this division as fundamentally functional,

. . . .

Sexual division of labor in modern societies: The phenomenon of dividing production functions by gender and designating different spheres of activity, the "private" to women and the "public" to men.

feminists challenged a social order that gave males privileged access to the sphere offering capitalism's prized rewards, including status, independence, opportunities for advancement, and, of course, money.

HIS AND HER MARRIAGE An important sociological analysis that captures some of liberal feminism's key concerns is Jessie Bernard's *The Future of Marriage* (1982). (See Chapter 9 for a fuller discussion of varieties of modern feminism, including liberal feminism.) Bernard confronts the issue of equality in marriage, positing that a husband and wife each experience a different marriage. In her analysis of marriage as a cultural system comprising beliefs and ideals, an institutional arrangement of norms and roles, and a complicated individual-level interactional and intimate experience, Bernard identified *his and her marriage experiences:*

- *His* marriage is one in which he may define himself as burdened and constrained (following societal norms that indicate this is what he *should* be experiencing), while at the same time experiencing authority, independence, and a right to the sexual, domestic, and emotional "services" of his wife.
- *Her* marriage is one in which she may seek to define herself as fulfilled through her achievement of marriage (following societal norms that indicate this is what she *should* be experiencing), while at the same time experiencing associated female dependence and subjugation.

Bernard understood these gender-differentiated experiences as rooted in the cultural and institutional foundations of marriage in the era she studied. Marriage functioned, from this perspective, to allocate social roles and expectations—but not to women's advantage. In a good example of the sociological imagination, she saw a connection between the personal experiences of individual men and women and the norms, roles, and expectations that create the context in which their relationship is lived.

Bernard's analysis pointed to data showing that married women, ostensibly "fulfilled" by marriage and family life, and unmarried men, ostensibly privileged by "freedom," scored highest on stress indicators, while their unmarried female and married male counterparts scored lowest. While she was writing several decades ago, recent social indicators show a mix of patterns. Some are similar to those she identified. For instance, the *Harvard Men's Health Watch Newsletter* recently wrote,

> A major survey of 127,545 American adults found that married men are healthier than men who were never married or whose marriages ended in divorce or widowhood. Men who have marital partners also live longer than men without spouses; men who marry after age 25 get more protection than those who tie the knot at a younger age, and the longer a man stays married, the greater his survival advantage over his unmarried peers. (Harvard Medical School, 2010)

Other studies paint a different picture. For instance, a 2007 examination of a spectrum of marriage studies determined that married women were less likely to experience depression than their unmarried counterparts. Researchers controlled for such factors as the possibility that less-depressed people were more likely to get married (which would confound results) and found that self-selection was not an issue. That is, marriage did seem to have positive health effects for women (Wood, Goesling, & Avellar, 2007).

In fact, however, the issue is more complex than either Bernard or recent scientific studies can embrace in a single narrative. Consider some other variables at play here. For example, men do seem to have *more* health benefits than women from marriage, even if women have some. Yet marriage as an institution does not appear to confer health benefits; rather, it is the *quality* of marriage that matters. Solid and low-conflict marriages are healthy, and unstable high-conflict marriages are not. The never-married are better off than those in high-conflict marriages (Parker-Pope, 2010).

Bernard's work gives us an opportunity to look at the institution of marriage as a *gendered institution*—that is, one in which gender fundamentally affects the experience on a large scale. While her 30-year-old analysis cannot fully capture the reality of today's U.S. marriages, her recognition that men and women can experience marriage in quite different ways remains an important insight.

The feminist perspective and other conflict-oriented perspectives offer a valuable addition to functionalist theorizing. However, their focus on the divisive and unequal aspects of family forms and norms may overlook the valuable functions of caring, socializing, and organizing that families have long performed and continue to perform in society. Indeed, both these macro-level approaches may have difficulty capturing the complexities of any family's lived experiences, particularly as they evolve and change over years through interpersonal negotiations and decisions. Nonetheless, they offer us a useful way of thinking about families and family members, their place in the larger social world, and the way they influence and are influenced by societal institutions and cultures.

THE PSYCHODYNAMIC FEMINIST PERSPECTIVE Sociologist Nancy Chodorow (1999) asks, "Why do women mother?" She suggests that to explain women's choice to "mother," a verb that describes a commitment to the care and nurturing of children, and men's choice to not "mother" (that is, to assume a more distant role from child rearing), we must look at personality development and relational psychology. While mothering is rooted in biology, Chodorow argues that biology cannot fully explain "mothering," because fathers or other kin can perform key "mothering" functions as well.

Drawing from Sigmund Freud's object-relations perspective, Chodorow argues that infants of both sexes form their initial bond to the mother, who satisfies all the infant's basic needs. Later, mothers push sons away emotionally while maintaining the bond to the daughter. Through this early socialization,

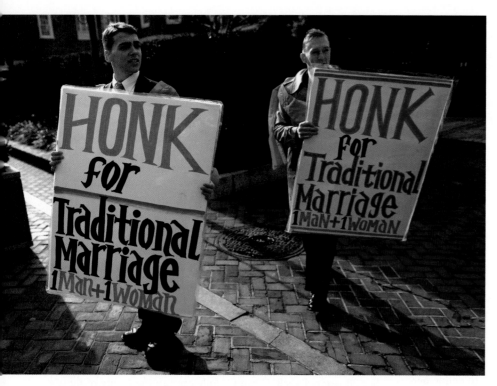

In U.S. political discourse, we encounter discussions of "family values," which are often linked to traditional heterosexual marriage. How would you define family values? Do you think most people could agree on a common definition? ■

associated traits may be reflected in the societal institutions that men still dominate. That is, the higher valuation of traits associated with masculinity in areas such as politics, business, and the labor market is, at least in part, linked to the *devaluation* of the feminine that men carry with them from their early childhood experiences.

Chodorow's work on sex roles and socialization in the family offers a merger of Freud and feminism that is both challenging and compelling, asking us to consider the effects that psychological processes in early childhood have on social institutions from the family to politics and the economy.

U.S. FAMILIES TODAY AND YESTERDAY

The traditional nuclear family often appears in popular media and political debates as a nostalgic pinnacle of values and practices to which U.S. families should return. Historian Stephanie Coontz (2000, 2005), who has written about the history of U.S. families, points out that this highly venerated traditional nuclear family model is, in fact, a fairly recent development.

Consider that in the preindustrial era, when the U.S. economy was primarily agricultural, families were both social and economic units. Households often included multiple generations, and sometimes boarders or farmworkers too. The family was large, and children were valued for their contributions to its economic viability, participating along with the other members of the family in its productive activities. Marriages tended to endure; divorce was neither normative nor especially easy to secure. At the same time, average life expectancy was about 45 years (Rubin, 1996). As life spans increased, divorce also rose, replacing death as the factor most likely to end a marriage.

The period of early industrialization shifted these patterns somewhat, not least because it was accompanied by urbanization, which brought workers and their families to cities for work. The family's economic function declined; some children worked in factories, but the passage of child labor laws and the rise of mass public schooling made this increasingly uncommon (though, according to one source, at the end of the 19th century a quarter of Southern textile workers were children, whose cheap labor was a boon to employers; Wertheimer, 1977). Over time, children became more of an economic cost than a wage-earning benefit; in a related development, families became smaller and began to evolve toward the nuclear family model.

The basic nuclear family model, with a mother working in the private sphere of the home while focused on child rearing

daughters come to more fully identify with mothers; boys, on the other hand, develop "masculine" personalities, but those draw from societal models of masculinity (or, sometimes, hypermasculinity) rather than predominantly from the father, who takes a far less prominent role in child rearing than the mother. Chodorow suggests that "masculinity" in boys may thus develop in part as a "nonfemininity," a negation and marginalization of qualities associated with femininity, which is rejected for both social and psychological reasons.

Women, reared by mothers who nurture a close and critical bond, are rendered "relational" through this process, seeking close bonds and defining themselves through relationships (Anna's mom, Joe's wife, and the like). Men, by contrast, define themselves more autonomously and have a harder time forming close bonds. Again, the roots of this difficulty are social (society defines men as autonomous and independent) and psychological (the pain of an early break in the mother-son bond results in fear or avoidance of these deep bonds). So why do women "mother" then? Because men in heterosexual relationships are not socially or psychologically well prepared for close relational bonding, women choose to mother in order to reproduce this connection with someone else.

While these processes play out primarily on the micro level of the family and relationships, Chodorow also recognizes macro-level effects. For instance, if, for lack of available male role models at home, the masculine personality develops in part as a negation of the feminine personality, when the boy makes his psychological break from the mother, this devaluation of the feminine and its

"White flight" to residential suburbs in the middle of the 20th century left many minority families behind in economically struggling neighborhoods. Suburban advantages in access to good education, housing, and recreation were in many cases a stark contrast to the disadvantages of poor urban areas. ■

and a father working in the public sphere for pay, evolved among middle-class families in the late 19th century. It was far less common among the working class at this time; working-class women, in fact, often toiled in the homes of the burgeoning middle class, as housekeepers and nursemaids.

Coontz (2000) points out that, just as the popular imagination suggests, the mother-as-homemaker and father-as-breadwinner model of the nuclear family is most characteristic of the widely idealized era of the 1950s. The post–World War II era witnessed a range of interconnected social phenomena, including suburbanization, supported by federal government initiatives to build a network of highways and encourage homeownership; a boom in both economic growth (and wages) that brought greater consumption power, and technologies that made the home more comfortable and convenient; and a "baby boom," as a wave of pregnancies delayed by the years of war came to term.

While prosperity and technology brought new opportunities to many, mass suburbanization largely left behind minorities, including Black Americans, who were not given access to the government's subsidized mortgages and were left in segregated, devalued neighborhoods. As the jobs followed White workers to the suburbs, the economic condition of many Black families was further diminished.

Further, it is not clear that all was well in the prosperous suburbs either. As we noted in the section on feminist theoretical perspectives, some sociological observers detected a streak of discontent that ran through the nuclear family so idealized today. Betty Friedan's book *The Feminine Mystique* (1963) highlighted "the problem that has no name," a broad discontent born of women's exclusion from or marginalization in the workplace, and the disconnect between their low status and opportunities and society's expectation that marriage and children were the

ultimate feminine fulfillment. Coontz (2000) points out that tranquilizers, one of many medical innovations of the era, were largely consumed by women, and in considerable quantities—at least 1.15 million pounds in 1959 alone.

MARRIAGE, DIVORCE, AND FAMILY IN THE MODERN UNITED STATES

The traditional nuclear family with men as breadwinners and women as caregivers is still in existence, though it has changed in many respects since the 1950s and today represents only about 7% of U.S. households (see the *Behind the Numbers* box on page 247). At the same time, while commentators often lament the "decline of the family," most children (69% in 2011) still live in two-parent households, and, as we saw above, all but 4% live with at least one parent (U.S. Census Bureau, 2011b). More children are living with single parents than in the past, but more adults are also living in nonfamily households, consisting of either a single householder or unrelated individuals. The trend toward living alone—which about 27% of people in the United States do (Figure 10.1 on page 248)—is one we'll discuss more below.

One reason for the growth of single-person households is the rising age at first marriage, now about 29 for men and 27 for women (Taylor et al., 2011), which means many people are not marrying until their 30s or even later. Most U.S. adults indicate a wish to marry, and most will at some point in their lives; more than 2.1 million married in 2011, and the U.S.

Divorce in Families

■ **FIGURE 10.1** Changes in U.S. Household Composition, 1940–2010

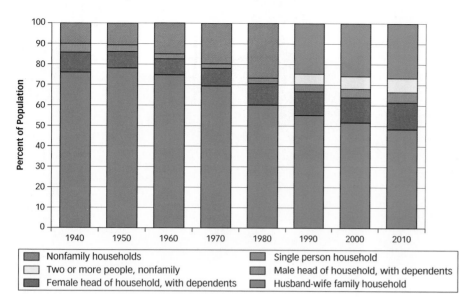

Legend:
- Nonfamily households
- Two or more people, nonfamily
- Female head of household, with dependents
- Single person household
- Male head of household, with dependents
- Husband-wife family household

SOURCE: U.S. Census Bureau. (2003). *Statistical Abstract of the United States, No. HS-12. Households by Type and Size: 1900 to 2002*. Washington, DC: U.S. Government Printing Office; U.S. Census Bureau. (2012). *Households and Families: 2010*. Washington, DC: U.S. Government Printing Office.

marriage rate exceeds that of most other modern societies (Centers for Disease Control and Prevention, 2013). By contrast, Western and Northern Europe are home to very high rates of **cohabitation**, or **common law marriage**, *in which partners live as if married but without marriage's formal legal framework.*

At the same time, rates of marriage have declined (Figure 10.2). Between 1960 and 2010, the rate per 1,000 women declined by about 20 percentage points, and today only about half of U.S. adults over age 18 are married, compared to about 72% in 1960 (Taylor et al., 2011). These declines have been far more pronounced among the less educated than among those who have a college education, though the latter also marry later. In the section below on class and marriage, we will look at some of the factors driving this decline, particularly among poor women.

With the decline of marriage, the United States has also experienced a decline in divorce. After rising through the 1960s and 1970s, the rate of divorce has leveled off. There is a logic to these two phenomena, since a smaller number of marriages reduces the pool of people who can divorce. The rate overall is still high, however, and the United States has one of the highest divorce rates in the world, with the rate for second and

later marriages exceeding that for first marriages (Figure 10.3 on page 248).

Why is the U.S. divorce rate, while declining, persistently high? Historian Stephanie Coontz (2005) argues that divorce is in part driven by our powerful attachment to the belief that marriage is the outcome of romantic love. While historically many societies accepted marriage primarily as part of an economic or social contract, and some still do, modern U.S. adults are smitten with love. Yet the powerful early feelings and passion that characterize many relationships are destined to wane over time. In a social context that elevates romantic love and passion in films, music, and books, we may have less tolerance for the more measured emotions inherent in most long-term marriages. Could our strong focus on romantic love be a driver of both marriage *and* divorce? What do you think?

Families are surely in the process of changing—and not only in the United States. See the box *Global Issues* on page 250 for a look at family issues in Japan.

■ **FIGURE 10.2** Marital Status in the U.S., 1960–2010

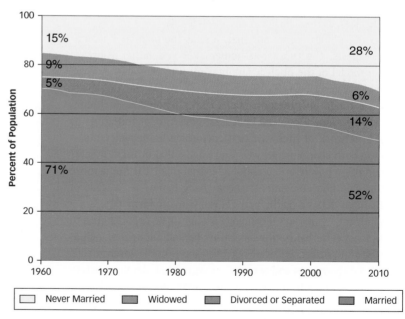

Legend:
- Never Married
- Widowed
- Divorced or Separated
- Married

SOURCE: U.S. Census Bureau. (2012). *Aggregate data 1960–2010*. Washington, DC: U.S. Government Printing Office.

· ·

Cohabitation: Living together as a couple without being legally married.

Common law marriage: A type of relationship in which partners live as if married but without marriage's formal legal framework.

Marriage and Divorce

BEHIND THE NUMBERS

WHAT IS A FAMILY?

The U.S. Census Bureau uses the household as a key unit in calculating a spectrum of national statistics, from income to poverty. A *household* is composed of all the people who occupy a given housing unit. The Census Bureau further distinguishes between *family households*—consisting of immediate relatives such as a husband, wife, and children or a mother and her children—and *nonfamily households,* which include just about everyone else, such as those who live alone and those who live with "nonrelative" household members. Implicit in these bureaucratic categories is a definition of what a family is from the government's perspective.

In 2009, of more than 117 million households, nearly a third was nonfamily households (U.S. Census Bureau, 2010). But aside from those living alone, are these households necessarily "nonfamilies" from a sociological perspective? Sociologist Brian Powell sought to answer this question in his study *Counted Out: Same-Sex Relations and Americans' Definitions of Family* (Powell, Bolzendahl, Geist, & Steelman, 2010), which surveyed more than 2,300 U.S. adults about their definition of family. Powell and his team identified three categories of respondents in the study: "exclusionists," who embrace a narrow and largely traditional definition of family; "moderates," who expand beyond the traditional to include, for instance, same-sex couples if there are children; and "inclusionists," who hold an expansive view of what can constitute a family, ranging from opposite- or same-sex cohabiters to people with pets. Children seemed to be a decisive factor in whether a

For same-sex couples, the struggles and joys of family life do not differ significantly from those of heterosexual couples. ■

household was seen as a family: For instance, while only 33% of respondents agreed that a gay male couple was a family, the addition of children to this unit raised the figure to 64%.

The public's definition of what constitutes a family is changing fast. Powell noted a significant change even in a short period of time; for instance, the percentage of respondents favoring a narrowly traditional view of a family as married parents and children dropped by 11% between 2003 and 2010. More people are accepting cohabiting and gay or lesbian couples as families as well.

The definitions used by the Census Bureau and other institutions, including those that govern estates and inheritance, adoption, and hospitalization and medical consent, lag behind those embraced by a growing number of U.S. adults. Perhaps within the third of the population living in "nonfamily" households, we would find quite a few families too.

THINK IT THROUGH

■ *How would you define the term* family? *What experiences or influences led you to that particular definition?*

GAY MARRIAGE . . . AND DIVORCE

In the *Behind the Numbers* box on page 247 we asked "What is a family?" As we saw, by the definition of the federal government, many household configurations are *not* counted as "families," including same-sex partners. At the same time, in 2010, there were over 130,000 married same-sex households and over 500,000 nonmarried same-sex partner households. Over 100,000 same-sex households were raising children (U.S. Census Bureau, 2011c).

Many states follow the federal government in their rejection of same-sex marriage; in 2012, fully 35 states prohibited it while just 9 states and the District of Columbia permitted it. States that reject same-sex marriage have often used the same language as the federal law, the Defense of Marriage Act (DOMA): "[T]he word 'marriage' means only a legal union between one man and one woman as husband and wife." DOMA was signed into law by President Bill Clinton in 1996. It also includes the provision that states are not obligated to recognize same-sex marriages conducted in states or cities that permit them.

Some states that reject same-sex marriage do recognize **civil unions**, which are *legal unions that fall short of marriage but provide some state-level legal rights and benefits*, or **domestic partnerships**, which are *legal unions that provide a circumscribed spectrum of rights and benefits to same-sex couples*. The more expansive set of social and economic opportunities available to

The 2010 U.S. Census showed that about 130,000 married same-sex couples and over half a million unmarried same-sex couples reside in the United States. About a quarter of these households are raising children. Sixteen states permit same-sex couples to adopt; most others permit it on a case-by-case basis. In some couples, one partner is the biological parent of the children, while the other becomes a legal parent through second-parent adoption. ■

couples recognized as legally married by the federal government, including Social Security and survivor benefits and joint filing of income taxes, is not available to those in civil unions or domestic partnerships.

While state legislatures and Congress have not been as quick to adopt broad definitions of marriage and family as many individuals have, the picture of legal prohibition and recognition around the country makes for a rapidly changing map. Figure 10.4 on page 249 shows the laws in effect at the time of publication.

Same-sex couples who seek to marry—and their advocates—often argue that they face mass denial of a basic civil right on the grounds of sexual orientation. Why should those in a committed relationship be denied the right to sanctify and legalize it regardless of sexual orientation? Those who object to same-sex marriage respond that this broad definition of marriage constitutes a threat to traditional marriage and families, not least because same-sex marriage cannot produce shared biological children. As well, say some opponents, legitimating same-sex marriage could lead to its spread, threatening heterosexual marriage. While more people are beginning to favor the legalization of same-sex marriage, a substantial minority remains vehemently opposed (Figure 10.5 on page 249).

■ **FIGURE 10.3** U.S. Divorce Rate, 1950–2010

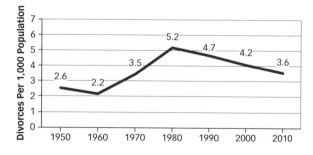

SOURCE: National Center for Health Statistics. (2012). *Aggregate data 1950–2010*. Atlanta, GA: Centers for Disease Control and Prevention.

Same-Sex Couple Rights

Civil unions: Legal unions that fall short of marriage but provide some state-level legal rights and benefits.

Domestic partnerships: Legal unions that provide a circumscribed spectrum of rights and benefits to same-sex couples.

With about half of all U.S. marriages ending in divorce, it's not surprising that the battle for same-sex partners to secure marriage rights has recently evolved into a fight for the right to divorce, particularly where there are children or property. U.S. divorce rates may be driven by many factors, including frustration with waning passion, economic stress, and poor compatibility of partners, among others. One factor sometimes noted by observers, however—the ease of divorce in the United States, partly a product of no-fault divorce laws—does not apply to same-sex partners.

A problem arises when same-sex couples married in a state permitting their legal union seek a divorce in a state that does not recognize gay and lesbian marriages. In a 2012 case in the state of Maryland, a lesbian couple married in 2008 in California sought a divorce. They were, according to the *Washington Post*, expecting a smooth and simple legal procedure; their property had been divided, the divorce was uncontested, and they had no children. The couple was stunned when the judge denied them. As the *Post*'s story points out, the "case represents just one of the many blind spots in the legal infrastructure of same-sex marriage in America. Couples often have different rights when they cross jurisdictional lines and may not have the same status in the eyes of the federal government as they do in their home states. The laws are constantly evolving" (McCarthy, 2012). A Maryland court ruled in May 2012, however, that the couple could proceed with their divorce—though, ironically, same-sex couples were denied the right to marry in Maryland until 2013.

Cases like these represent a conundrum in a country where states may make their own laws governing the prohibition or recognition of unions the federal government has not legally recognized. While

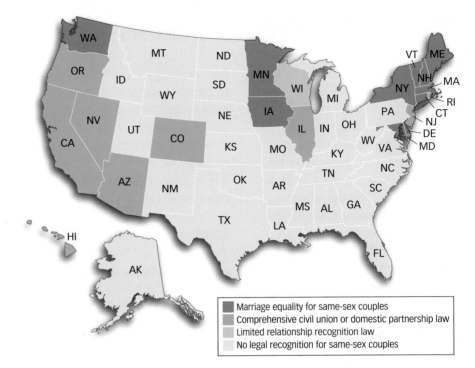

■ **FIGURE 10.4** Same-Sex Marriage Laws by State, August 2013

- ■ Marriage equality for same-sex couples
- ■ Comprehensive civil union or domestic partnership law
- ■ Limited relationship recognition law
- ■ No legal recognition for same-sex couples

SOURCE: National Public Radio. (2012). *State by state: The legal battle over gay marriage.*

Maryland had no law in place expressly banning the recognition of same-sex marriage from another state, it also had no law allowing it. Is the manifest function of divorce law to permit a couple to legally end a union that is no longer viable—or is it to act as a symbol of a state's position on marriage and family? How can a conflict between these two functions of divorce law be resolved?

IMMIGRATION AND FAMILY PATTERNS

The United States has more foreign-born residents than any other country in the world. Given its low fertility rate, a substantial proportion—about a third—of the country's population growth is the result of immigration (Table 10.1 and Figure 10.6 on page 251). With the percentage of foreign-born residents at about 13%, it is not surprising that immigrants and the cultures they carry with them have important effects on U.S. family patterns.

Predictably, more recent immigration correlates with a group's stronger ties to its homeland culture (Moore & Pinderhughes, 2001). Many scholars are now focusing on the *transnational* nature of immigrant families.

■ **FIGURE 10.5** Changing Attitudes of U.S. Adults Toward Same-Sex Marriage, 2001–2012

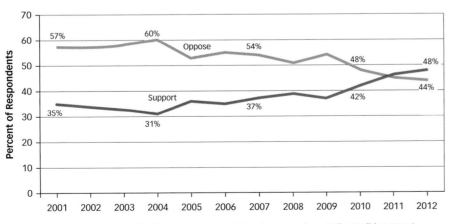

SOURCE: Newport, F. (2012). *Half of Americans support legal gay marriage.* Gallup Politics, May 8.

Same-Sex Marriage Controversies

GLOBAL ISSUES

LOVE AND COMMERCE: THE FAMILY RENTAL MARKET IN JAPAN

People need and want families for a wide variety of reasons. Some are emotional: Families can provide warmth, comfort, and pleasurable interactions. Others are social and cultural: Families are expected to be in attendance at key cultural rituals in our lives, such as holidays, weddings, and religious ceremonies. But what if families are estranged or far away? Or if someone has no living relatives?

In Japan, modernity has brought a functional alternative with the advent of "rental" families a mouse click away. In the early 1990s, Japan Efficiency Corporation was "doing a booming business renting families to the lonely," especially the elderly. Asked to comment on the nascent phenomenon, a Japanese sociologist commented, "It's extremely strange to me that people would want to rent families, and even more surprising that they seem to be satisfied . . . I suppose people nowadays really

find the need for kinship. Compared to 50 years ago, the family system in Japan has really changed, and family-like relationships are gradually disappearing" (Watanbe, 1992).

Today the market has expanded further. Office Agents, a Tokyo firm, offers friends and family for rent as event guests. "Many in Japan see weddings as a formal event that must be attended by as many family members, friends, and co-workers as possible . . . But what if you've got no one to do that for you?" Office Agents has about 1,000 "fakes" available for occasions that may vary from weddings to funerals to training seminars. The company's head notes that sometimes even a marriage partner is unaware there are fake guests at the party (Kubota, 2009).

The Hagemashi Tai agency (a name that translates to *I Want to Cheer Up Limited*) also rents relatives for parties—as well as temporary

husbands for single mothers who want one. According to a British Broadcasting Company report on the topic, the firm's website advertises that "dad" will "help the children with homework. He will sort out problems with the neighbours. He will take the kids to a barbeque or park. He could also appear at the daunting interview with a nursery school head teacher which parents are required to endure in order to persuade the principal to give their child a good start in life" (Kubota, 2009).

THINK IT THROUGH

■ *While this phenomenon is not extensive in Japan, it has grown and continues to expand. What does this say about family and its functions? Are rented relatives a viable functional alternative for people who lack a family? Could you see such a phenomenon taking root in the United States? Why or why not?*

Embodying transnationalism may mean living, working, worshipping, and being politically active in one nation, while still maintaining strong political, social, religious, and/or cultural ties to other nations (Levitt, 2004). Family members may send back remittance, keep in contact using technology such as Skype, and travel back and forth frequently in order to maintain close emotional ties.

Many immigrant parents also prefer their children to marry within the group. According to research by the Center for Immigration Studies (Pipes & Duran, 2002), in some devout Muslim communities parents' traditional values exist in a tense relationship with new norms embraced by their children:

Just when Muslim girls traditionally would be separated from boys, taken out of school, and perhaps start wearing

a head covering, their American counterparts begin to discover and experiment with their sexuality. To prevent such experimentation, Muslim parents seek to enforce the traditional rules and sometimes even cloistering their daughters. [However . . .] by law, girls must go to school until 16 or so; and at 18, they acquire additional rights. . . .

To encourage the young to marry within the faith, American Muslims are developing a number of novel solutions, including summer camps, socials for singles, and marriage advertisements. But even these Muslim institutions have a difficult time keeping boys and girls apart.

Interestingly, reflecting the influence of home cultures on migrants that we discussed in the opening of this section, first-generation migrants often have birthrates above those of the native-born U.S. population. One study even found that among some groups, immigrant women in the United States were having more children on average (2.9) than women in their home

Small Town Immigrants

countries (2.3; Camarota, 2005). In the second generation, however, the rate typically declines to the average U.S. rate—that is, approximately 2.1 children per woman (Hill & Johnson, 2002). However, some studies have found that the trend toward decreasing fertility in first- and second-generation immigrant women may actually be reversed in the third generation for some groups (Parrado & Morgan, 2008). Historically, fertility rates have decreased for immigrant families the longer they reside in the United States. However, it is important to note that factors such as country of origin, education, religion, and cultural attitudes make understanding these trends more complex.

Below we narrow our focus to look at a pair of specific examples of U.S. family subcultures—those of Native Americans and deaf families.

AMERICA'S FIRST NATIONS: NATIVE AMERICAN FAMILIES

Family patterns among Native Americans are highly diverse. There are nearly 500 different nations, although over half of all American Indians identify as coming from just six of these (U.S. Census Bureau, 2011f). American Indian households are often composed of extended families, including uncles, aunts, cousins, and grandparents. According to the *Journal of American Indian Education,*

> The central unit of Indian society is the family . . . Indian families do not have the rigid structure of relationships found in Western white culture. Instead, Indians relate to people outside the immediate family in supportive and caring ways. (Levine & Laurie, 1974)

TABLE 10.1 Top 10 Feeder Countries for Migration to the U.S., 2010

Country of Birth	Population	Percentage of U.S. Migrants by Country of Origin
Mexico	11,711,103	29%
China	1,608,095	5%
India	1,780,322	4%
Philippines	1,777,588	4%
Vietnam	1,240,542	3%
El Salvador	1,214,049	3%
Cuba	1,104,679	3%
Korea	1,100,422	3%
Dominican Republic	879,187	2%
Guatemala	830,824	2%

SOURCE: Migration Policy Institute. (2012). *Region of birth as a percentage of the total immigrant population, 1960–2011.* Retrieved from http://www.migrationinformation.org/datahub/charts/fb.2.shtml

■ FIGURE 10.6 Region of Birth as Percent of Total Migrant Population, 2010

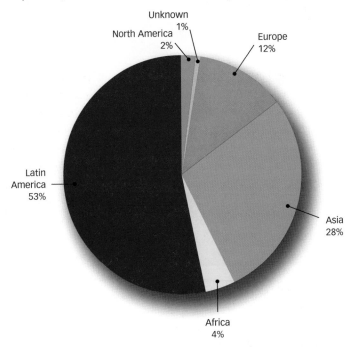

SOURCE: Migration Policy Institute. (2012). *Region of birth as a percentage of the total immigrant population, 1960–2011.* Retrieved from http://www.migrationinformation.org/datahub/charts/fb.2.shtml

An example of family involvement outside the immediate parents is found in Sioux families. This involvement begins early in life when a second set of parents are selected for newborn babies (Sandoz, 1961). Therefore, the "total" family involved in child rearing and support includes unrelated members of the Indian community (Ryan, 1981). This community support and protection can be viewed as responsibility for others' actions (Light & Martin, 1996).

More recent studies have shown how Native American family ties extend across generations. Native American grandparents have shown high levels of involvement in the care of their grandchildren (Mutchler, Baker, & Lee, 2007). Native Americans also report high levels of caregiving to their elderly relatives (McGuire, Okoro, Goins, & Anderson, 2008). Indeed, Native American culture and families traditionally emphasize sensitivity toward kin, tribe, and land and value the collective over the individual, in contrast to the mainstream U.S. emphasis on individual fulfillment and achievement (Light & Martin, 1996; Newcomb, 2008).

Research on Native Americans of the Southwest suggests that many members of these groups see their children as belonging to the entire nation: to the land, the sky, the tribe, and its history, customs, and traditions (Nicholas, 2009). Yet the migration of American Indian families from reservations to urban areas has led to increased assimilation and acculturation,

Defining "Family"

The 2010 U.S. Census counted just over half a million (557,185) American Indian and Alaska Native families in the United States. About 57% were reported to be married-couple families. ■

and urban American Indian families, like migrant families from abroad, are likely to evolve over a generation or two to resemble the families of the dominant culture. Nicholas (2009) found in her study of Hopi youth that although some members of the community felt the children who didn't speak the traditional Hopi language were alienating themselves from the community, the Hopi children still felt deeply connected to the culture.

DEAF CULTURE AND FAMILY LIFE

Census Bureau data show about a fifth of the U.S. population has a disability of some kind. How does this affect family life? In this subsection, we examine the case of deaf people and the choices and challenges that family life brings. According to the Gallaudet Research Institute (2005), approximately 2 to 4 of every 1,000 people in the United States are "functionally deaf," or unable to hear normal conversation even with the use of a hearing aid. Fewer than 1 in 1,000 were deaf before the age of 18; more than half became deaf at some point after childhood. Family life poses unique challenges for many deaf people, and as a consequence, some prefer to practice endogamy, marrying others who are deaf and therefore share a common experience.

There has been a movement within the deaf community to redefine the meaning of deafness not as a form of disability, but as a positive culture. Some deaf people see themselves as similar to an ethnic group, sharing a common language (American Sign Language, or ASL), possessing a strong sense of cultural identity, and taking pride in their heritage. Identifying as an ethnic group rather than as a disability group, some deaf people believe that cochlear implant surgery, a procedure by which one can become hearing, is problematic, especially when it is performed on children who cannot consent. Oftentimes, deaf people who undergo this surgery are still unable to obtain mastery of any oral language

(Lane, 2005). The National Association of the Deaf (2000) takes a cautionary stance on cochlear implants, advising hearing parents of deaf children to conduct thorough research, create a support system, and, most importantly, communicate with their child before undertaking the transition.

Julie Mitchiner takes pride in being deaf. She writes,

> Growing up with deaf parents and attending deaf schools, I have a strong sense of pride of being deaf and being part of the Deaf community. I do not look at myself as disabled. I often say if I were given a choice to hear or stay deaf, I'd choose to stay deaf. It is who I am. My family, my friends, and my community have taught me that being deaf is part of our culture and is a way of life. (Paludneviciene & Leigh, 2011, p. 3)

The desire for a deaf identity reflects the challenge for deaf people of learning to communicate with hearing people through lipreading and simulated speech. People who have never heard find it very difficult to utter sounds that most hearing people can recognize as words. Lipreading is equally difficult and fraught with error. Reading text, which depends on understanding the meaning of spoken words, may prove a frustrating experience (Dolnick, 1993). Yet for those fluent in ASL, a rich form of communication is possible, and with it comes a strong sense of shared identity (Lane, 2005).

Many people have succeeded in the hearing world, but they can confront daunting problems (Heppner, 1992). Often they will not be able to speak in a way that hearing people fully understand, and most hearing people will not know ASL. It is not surprising that an estimated 85% of deaf people choose to marry others who share their own language and culture (Cichowski & Nance, 2004), or that many deaf parents are wary when their deaf children form relationships with hearing people. What happens when a deaf couple has a hearing child? The family must often make difficult choices, as they negotiate not only the ordinary challenges of child rearing, but also the raising of children who may be "functionally hearing" but "culturally deaf" (Bishop & Hicks, 2009; Preston, 1994).

Families ordinarily confer their own cultural status on their children, but this may not be true for 9 of 10 deaf children born to hearing parents. On the one hand, hearing parents want the same sorts of things for their deaf children as do any parents: happiness, fulfillment, and successful lives as adults. Many would like their children to mainstream into the hearing world as well as possible, in spite of challenges. On the other hand, some in the deaf community argue that the deaf children of hearing parents can never fully belong to the hearing world. Many in the deaf community believe hearing parents should send their deaf children to residential schools for the deaf, where they will be fully accepted, learn deaf culture, and be with people who share their experience of deafness (Dolnick, 1993; Lane, 1992; Sparrow, 2005).

Deaf parents raising a hearing child and hearing parents raising a deaf child raise interesting and fundamental questions about what happens when family members are also members of different cultures and how the obstacles of difference within a micro unit such as the family are overcome.

SOCIOECONOMIC CLASS AND FAMILY IN THE UNITED STATES

An array of family differences are linked to social class differences. In this section we consider research showing that social class may have an effect on both child-rearing practices and family formation through marriage.

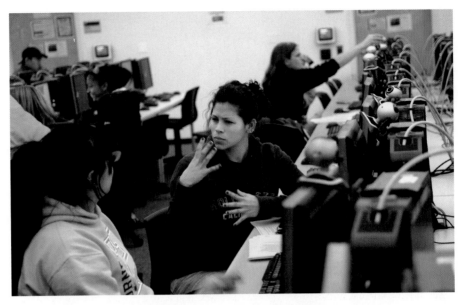

Gallaudet University in Washington, DC, is unique in serving specifically the deaf and hearing-impaired, offering bilingual instruction in English and ASL. The rising proportion of students who are hearing or come from mainstream schools and do not know ASL has led to debates over the centrality of deaf culture at the school. ■

SOCIAL CLASS AND CHILD REARING

Parents are often caught in a dilemma. They must instill some degree of conformity in their children as they attempt to socialize them into the norms and values that will be socially appropriate for adult behavior. At the same time, they must foster a degree of independence; after all, the child must eventually leave the nest and survive in the adult world. Given the tension between protecting and instilling independence, it should not be surprising that in most families neither is fully achieved. Parents may understand that they need to help build their children's independence yet still be unwilling to trust their children's judgment, especially during adolescence. They may hang on to their children, prolonging dependence long past the point where the children are ready to make decisions on their own. Growing up includes some degree of conflict no matter what approach is used.

Some studies suggest that parental attitudes toward children's independence differ markedly by social class. In U.S. culture, middle- and upper-class families tend to value self-direction and individual initiative in their children. Working-class parents, by contrast, have been observed by some researchers to value respect for authority, obedience, and a higher degree of conformity, and to rely on punishment when these norms are violated. Sociologist Melvin Kohn (1977), who spent many years studying class differences in child rearing, attributes them to differences in the parents' work experiences: Middle- and upper-class jobs often require individual initiative and innovation, while working-class jobs tend to emphasize conformity.

Annette Lareau (2003) goes beyond Kohn's focus on work experiences to argue that social class, which we experience in a multitude of ways, has an impact on family life, in particular on the styles of child rearing in which parents engage. In reporting her study, in which 88 White and Black American families were interviewed and 12 closely observed at home, Lareau writes,

> It is the interweaving of life experiences and resources, including parents' economic resources, occupational conditions, and educational backgrounds, that appears to be most important in leading middle-class parents to engage in concerted cultivation and working-class and poor parents to engage in the accomplishment of natural growth. (pp. 771–772)

These two concepts, concerted cultivation and accomplishment of natural growth, form a key foundation for Lareau's argument. She defines *concerted cultivation* as a style of parenting associated most fully with the middle class and characterized by the emphasis on negotiation, discussion, questioning of authority, and cultivation of talents and skills through, among other things, participation in organized activities. Lareau explains the *accomplishment of natural growth* as the parenting style associated with the working class or poor families. Directives rather than negotiation and explanation, a focus on obedience, and an inclination to care for children's basic needs characterize this style, in which parents leave children to play and grow in a largely unstructured environment. Notably, Lareau identified a tension between obedience and trust in this style, suggesting it is characterized by something close to distrustful consent born of frustration with authority and dominant institutions, but a sense of powerlessness in

Immigrant Family Issues

Social Class and Childrearing

Are middle-class parents "overparenting," raising risk-averse young people characterized by a sense of entitlement? Popular magazines have run articles with provocative titles such as "How to Land Your Kid in Therapy" (Gottlieb, 2011), expounding the virtues of less-involved parenting. How might this debate fit into Lareau's characterization of middle-class parenting styles? ■

their presence. From this, she suggests, children take away an emerging sense of constraint.

Consider the following observation by Edin and Kefalas (2005):

> While poor mothers see keeping a child housed, fed, clothed, and safe as noteworthy accomplishments, their middle-class counterparts often feel they must earn their parenting stripes by faithfully cheering at soccer league games, chaperoning boy scout camping trips and attending ballet recitals or martial arts competitions. (p. 141)

What are the outcomes of these differing styles of child rearing, which Lareau argues are associated with class status? Examining the outcomes for children of parents she studied in the years of young adulthood, Lareau (2011) concludes that the accomplishment of natural growth style tends to cultivate early independence, but also to lead young people toward jobs that require respect for authority and obedience to directives, like those associated with the working class. In contrast, the concerted cultivation approach to child raising leads young people both to hold a sense of entitlement and to pursue careers that require a broad vocabulary and ease in negotiating with people in authority. Following up with the families she had studied, Lareau found that all the middle-class children had completed high school and most were attending college. Many of the children of low-income families had left high school and few were in college. "In sum," she writes, "differences in family life lie not only in the advantages parents obtain for their children, but also in the skills they transmit to children for negotiating their own life paths."

These studies strongly suggest that family life, and practices of child rearing in particular, contribute to the reproduction of class status. While structural factors, including obstacles related to education and other important resources for mobility, are part of the picture, Lareau suggests that the development of orientations and skills in childhood, which become part of a young adult's human capital as he or she negotiates the path through school and toward a job, are key to understanding socioeconomic outcomes and the reproduction of class status.

ECONOMY, CULTURE, AND FAMILY FORMATION

Class status is linked with changing patterns of family life in another important way. Some sociologists (Edin & Kefalas, 2005; Wilson, 1997, 2010) believe macro-level economic changes, in particular the rise of a postindustrial economy and associated labor market, have had a powerful effect on micro-level practices of family formation. In the section below, we examine the sociological roots of the decline of marriage and the rise of nonmarital births in poor and working-class Black, White, and Latino communities.

In 1965, the late Daniel Patrick Moynihan, a former professor of sociology and U.S. senator from New York, published a controversial study of the African American family, "The Negro Family: The Case for National Action," which later came to be called the Moynihan Report. In it, Moynihan argued that lower-class Black family life was often dysfunctional, as reflected in high rates of family dissolution, single parenting, and the dominance of female-headed families.

Moynihan saw the breakdown of Black families, together with continued racial inequality, as leading to "a new crisis in race relations." He identified the legacy of slavery, which intentionally broke up Black families, as one of the roots of the problem. He also claimed that many rural Blacks had failed to adapt adequately to urban environments. Moynihan concluded that these patterns in lower-class Black family life were at least in part responsible for the failure of many Black Americans to make it into the economic mainstream in the United States. He saw Black poverty and urban violence, which exploded in the urban riots of the 1960s, as partly the result of Black family breakdown.

The Moynihan Report was widely criticized as racist and sexist, and Moynihan was accused of blaming the victims of racism and poverty (primarily Black female heads of household) for their disadvantages. Many critiques ignored Moynihan's attention to *structural* as well as *cultural* factors in his analysis, however. While he wrote that "at the center of the tangle of pathology is the weakness of the family structure," he also implicated social phenomena such as unemployment, poverty, and racial segregation in the decline of families and the rise of dysfunctions. Still, critics focused largely on his cultural analysis, and Moynihan's findings were disregarded while sociologists avoided examining the connection between race, family characteristics, and poverty for at least two decades.

In 1987, however, sociologist William Julius Wilson revisited the issues Moynihan had raised in the 1965 report. In the two intervening decades, much had changed—and much had stayed the same. The family patterns identified by Moynihan as problematic, including nonmarital births and high levels of family dissolution, had become more pronounced among poor and working-class Black Americans. At the same time, social problems including joblessness in the inner city had grown more acute, as deindustrialization and the movement of more work to the suburbs dramatically reduced the number of jobs available for less-educated and low-skill workers. These changes, Wilson noted, would have important consequences for family formation.

Ten years later, Wilson (1997) argued that falling rates of marriage and rising numbers of nonmarital births were, at least in part, rooted in the declining number of "marriageable men" in inner-city neighborhoods. He posited that the ratio of unmarried Black women to single and "marriageable" Black men of a similar age was skewed by male joblessness, high rates of incarceration, and high death rates for young Black men. The loss of jobs in the inner city had a powerfully negative effect on male employment opportunities. The consequences were felt not only in the economic fortunes of communities but, no less importantly, in families, where women were choosing motherhood, but options for marriage were deeply diminished by the uneven ratio of single women to marriageable men. While rates of nonmarital births had previously been high in Black communities, where extended families have traditionally been available to support mothers and children (Gerstel & Gallagher, 1994), Wilson now saw new urban circumstances as central to the rise of nonmarital births among Black Americans from one quarter in 1965 (when Moynihan wrote his report) to about 70% by the middle 1990s, where it remains today (Figure 10.7 on page 256). By then about half of Black American families were headed by a woman (Wilson, 2010).

When Wilson revisited this issue in 2010, he found that research on the relationship between male employment and rates of marriage and single parenthood offered mixed findings:

> Joblessness among black men is a significant factor in their delayed entry into marriage and in the decreasing rates of marriage after a child has been born, and this relationship has been exacerbated by sharp increases in incarceration that in turn lead to continued joblessness. Nevertheless, much of the decline in marriages in the inner city, including marriages that occur after a child has been born, remains unexplained when only structural factors are examined. (p. 108)

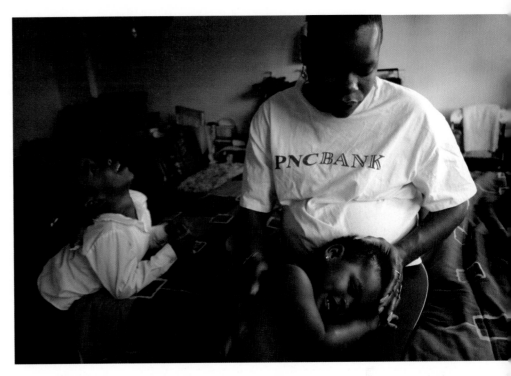

Some studies suggest that poor women value motherhood more than marriage. Sociologists link this in part to the lack of marriageable males in their peer group. Why do you think women who choose to have children without a marriage partner are still stigmatized in U.S. society? ■

Wilson (2010) also cited cultural factors in the fragmentation of the poor Black family. While sociologists have been reluctant to use culture as an explanation, not least due to fear of the backlash generated by the Moynihan report, Wilson writes that structure and culture interact to create normative contexts for behavior. He points out, for instance, that "both inner-city black males and females believe that since most marriages will eventually break up and no longer represent meaningful relationships, it is better to avoid the entanglements of wedlock altogether . . . Single mothers who perceive the fathers of their children as unreliable or as having limited financial means will often—rationally—choose single parenthood" (p. 125). In this social context, the stigma of unmarried parenthood is minimal, and behaviors rooted in structure become culturally normative.

Examining the phenomenon of low marriage rates and high nonmarital births in some communities, sociologists Kathryn Edin and Maria Kefalas (2005) looked at data on low-income White, Black, and Puerto Rican single mothers in Camden, New Jersey, and Philadelphia, Pennsylvania. While Black communities have historically had higher nonmarital birth rates and lower rates of marriage than Whites and Latinos, in low-income White and Latino communities these phenomena have grown.

Edin and Kefalas found that the women in their study placed a high value on both motherhood and marriage. They saw motherhood as a key role and central achievement in their lives, and few took efforts to delay motherhood. If anything, they saw early motherhood as something that had forced them to mature and kept them from getting into trouble.

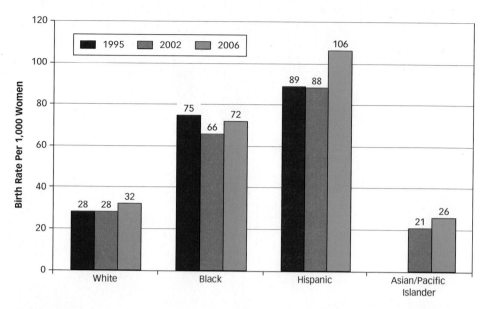

■ **FIGURE 10.7** Nonmarital Birthrate by Race/Ethnicity in the U.S., 1995–2006

SOURCE: Centers for Disease Control and Prevention. (2012). *National Vital Statistics System: Birth Data.* Washington, DC: U.S. Government Printing Office. Retrieved from http://www.cdc.gov/nchs/births.htm

FAMILY LIFE IN THE MIDDLE CLASS

Middle-class family life is often characterized by a strong commitment to constructive and active child rearing (as we saw in Lareau's study) and to the parents' pursuit of careers. These competing commitments often leave parents without the time to do everything, to do it well, and to feel satisfied instead of rushed and stressed.

Sociologist Arlie Russell Hochschild (2001b) came to some interesting and perhaps surprising conclusions about this modern dilemma. Hochschild conducted a series of interviews with employees at a well-known Fortune 500 firm that had gone to some lengths to be family-friendly, offering flextime, the option of part-time work, parental leave, job sharing, and even a course titled "Work-Life Balance for Two-Career Couples." But she noticed that family-friendly measures didn't make much of a difference. Most employees said they put "family first," but they also felt strained to the limit, and almost no one cut back on work time. Few took advantage of parental leave or the option of part-time employment.

Why do people say they want to strike a better balance between work and the rest of their lives yet do nothing about it when they have the opportunity? Some reasons are practical; a number of employees in Hochschild's study feared that taking advantage of liberal work policies would count against them in their careers, while others simply needed the money. Yet Hochschild identified a more surprising reason why people worked long hours: They liked it better than being at home. Previous research had shown that many men regard work as a haven, and Hochschild found that a notable number of working women now feel the same way. Despite the stress of long hours and guilt about being away from their families, they are reluctant to cut back on their commitment to paid work.

Hochschild found that both men and women often derive support, companionship, security, pride, and a sense of being valued when they are working. In the absence of family time and kin and community support at home, some parents sought and found—and sometimes preferred—a sense of competence and achievement in the workplace. In about a fifth of families, work rather than home was the site at which they derived the most satisfaction.

Many studies since have found that workplaces with more "family-friendly" policies have higher levels of degrees of workplace satisfaction and productivity, as well as lower levels of stress (Bilal, Zia-ur-Rehman, & Raza, 2010; Frye & Breaugh, 2004). Still, Hochschild's (2001b) research suggests that many people derive satisfaction from being workaholics. As she concludes, "working families are both prisoners and architects of the time bind in which they find themselves" (p. 249).

At the same time, they held a utopian view of marriage that may, ironically, have put it out of their reach. Many dreamed of achieving financial security and owning a home before marrying—but their poverty made this a challenge. More problematically, perhaps, they did not consider the men in their lives—often the fathers of their children—to be good partners, their marriageability undermined by low education, joblessness, poor economic prospects, criminal records, violence, drug and alcohol abuse, and infidelity.

Notably, then, while they highly valued marriage, the women had few realistic opportunities to achieve stability and independence first, and little hope of finding a stable partner. Motherhood, however, was an achievable dream, an opportunity to occupy an important social role and to achieve success as a parent, where other paths of opportunity were often blocked by poor structural circumstances. Ironically, children in single-mother homes are among those most likely to be born and to grow up impoverished. They are also more likely than their better-off peers to repeat the patterns of their parents and to remain in poverty. An interesting question emerges: Is single parenthood a cause (not the only one) of poverty, or is living in poverty a sociological root of single parenthood? Or perhaps both are true?

The relationship between class, poverty, and family patterns is complex, but Wilson and Edin and Kefalas offer sociological lenses for understanding some of the structural and cultural causes of low marriage rates and high nonmarital birth rates in many poor U.S. communities. As Wilson notes in his 2010 book, "how families are formed among America's poorest citizens is an area that cries out for further research" (p. 129). What other factors should sociologists examine? How would you conduct such a study? What kinds of questions would you ask?

Family stresses reach across the socio-economic spectrum and create a variety of challenges. Sometimes problems also manifest as violence, an issue we tackle below.

VIOLENCE AND THE FAMILY

Domestic or **family violence** is *physical or sexual abuse committed by one family member against another.* It may be perpetrated by adults toward their children, by one spouse against another, among siblings, and occasionally by adult children against their elderly parents. Thirty to forty years ago, domestic violence was rarely studied. Many people regarded violence in the home as a private matter, an attitude that was reflected in lawmaking as well, which provided few sanctions for violence that did not reach the level of severe injury or death. Today domestic violence is a serious public issue, as researchers have come to realize that it is sadly commonplace (Bureau of Justice Statistics, 2012).

Accurate data on family violence are difficult to obtain for a variety of reasons. Abused partners or children are reluctant to call attention to the fact that they are abused. Police do not want to mediate or make arrests in family conflicts, and, even today, the courts are hesitant to intervene in what is often perceived as a family matter (Tolan, Gorman-Smith, & Henry, 2005). Some good estimates of the prevalence of this crime are available, however. According to the U.S. Bureau of Justice Statistics (2005), family violence accounted for about 11% of both reported and unreported violence between 1998 and 2002. Of the 3.5 million violent crimes committed against family members, 49% were crimes against spouses, 11% victimized sons or daughters, and 41% were crimes against other family members.

The National Intimate Partner and Sexual Violence Survey, a national and ongoing survey developed and administered by the Centers for Disease Control and Prevention, found in its 2010 survey that 1 in 3 women and 1 in 4 men had been victims of *intimate partner violence* (IPV) in their lifetime, a term that includes physical violence, rape, and/or stalking by a former or current partner or spouse. About 1 in 4 women and 1 in 7 men surveyed had experienced severe physical violence by their partner. While these data are for experiences over the life course, even data from a single year (2010) reveal a serious epidemic of intimate partner violence. According to the survey, more than 12 million people experienced IPV in 2010 (Centers for Disease Control and Prevention, 2010).

According to the U.S. Bureau of Labor Statistics' (2012) survey on time use, in 2011, Americans spent more time at work than engaged in any other activity (8.8 hours). Sleep was a close second. Household activities and caring for others together constituted just 2.3 hours of the average day. ■

Child abuse—sexual and/or physical assaults on children by adult members of their family—is also common in our society. According to the U.S. Department of Health and Human Services (2010), approximately 3.3 million child abuse reports and allegations were made in 2009 involving about 6 million children. On any given day, no fewer than 5 children are killed by abuse (U.S. Government Accountability Office, 2011), though the main form of abuse is neglect (U.S. Department of Health and Human Services, 2010). Boys and girls are equally likely to be physically abused, but girls are more likely to be sexually abused as well. According to Childhelp, an organization dedicated to prevention of child abuse, the cycle of abuse is difficult to break. One study suggests that about 30% of abused and neglected children will later abuse their own children (Childhelp, 2010).

Elder abuse is the victimization of the elderly by family members or other caregivers. According to a 2009 National Institute of Justice study, 11% of elderly U.S. adults (those 65 or older) reported experiencing either emotional, physical, or sexual abuse or potential neglect (Aclemo, Hernandez-Tejada, Muzzy, & Steve, 2009). Like child abuse, elder abuse is likely underreported, because victims are often in a subordinate position in the family and unable

Domestic Abuse
in Families

. . . .
Domestic (family) violence: Physical or sexual abuse committed by one family member against another.

The effects of economic globalization on families have been uneven, with negative consequences borne disproportionately by those with less education. Can you identify any current trends that suggest the circumstances of these families will improve or get worse in coming decades? ■

People have become far more aware of child and spouse abuse and its spectrum of consequences in recent years, largely because of efforts by the women's movement to bring them into the open (see the *Inequality Matters* box on page 259). Shelters for battered women and children enable victims to be protected from violence. While still limited in number, such refuges have enabled women to get counseling while terminating abusive relationships in relative safety (Hajyahia & Cohen, 2009). Family violence is clearly a dysfunctional social phenomenon. It is both a personal trouble and a public issue. Understanding more fully its roots and consequences can contribute to both a fuller national conversation of the problem and more robust efforts to address it.

to access help outside the home. Elder abuse also shares with child abuse some of its forms, including neglect—the failure of caregivers to provide for basic needs like nutritious food and hygienic conditions—and physical abuse. Some aspects of elder abuse differ, however. For example, elder abuse may take the form of financial exploitation or outright theft of property. Those who care for elderly relatives may feel entitled to the resources possessed by the victim—or they may just take advantage of an older person's vulnerabilities.

As sociologists examining a problem that is both a private trouble and a public issue, we need to ask, why does domestic violence as a widespread phenomenon exist and persist? The right of a husband to physically discipline his wife has deep roots in Anglo-American culture. British common law permitted a man to discipline his wife and children with a stick, provided the stick was no thicker than his thumb; the phrase "rule of thumb" originates in this practice. Through the end of the 19th century in the United States, men could legally beat their wives (Renzetti & Curran, 1992). Research has found that domestic violence is most likely to be prevalent in societies in which family relationships are characterized by high emotional intensity and attachment, there is a pattern of male dominance and sexual inequality, a high value is placed on the privacy of family life, and violence is permitted or occurs in other institutional spheres, such as entertainment or popular culture (Straus & Gelles, 1990; Straus, Gelles, & Steinmetz, 1988).

Violence in the Home

Domestic Violence

GLOBALIZATION AND FAMILIES

The impact of globalization on families depends to a substantial degree on the family's social class and country or region of residence. In this section, we look at the experience of globalization among families, its costs and benefits, and the uneven way in which those costs and benefits are distributed.

Consider the economic and labor market impact of globalization on U.S. families. Among upper- and upper-middle-class families, globalization has increased the demand for men and women with a high degree of skill and formal training as professionals, managers, administrators, and engineers. While low-skilled U.S. workers have been priced out of many sectors of the global job market by their replaceability (lower-wage labor is readily available elsewhere), high-skill labor in fields that are not easily "offshored" or replaced by technology may still benefit, because globalization can produce national economic gains even as it diminishes the prospects of some categories of workers.

About 70% of the U.S. labor force does not hold a four-year college degree. As we see elsewhere in this text, those are the workers who have been hit hardest by global economic change. Writing about domestic manufacturing industries, journalist Louis Uchitelle (2007) observes, "As customers defected, sales plummeted and failed to bounce back. Nowhere was that more apparent than in the auto industry's struggle with [lower-cost] Japanese imports. But nearly every manufacturer was hit, and the steep recession in 1981 and 1982 compounded the damage. The old world has never returned" (p. 8).

Many working-class families have found themselves confronting flat or declining incomes as a result of competition with a global workforce. Household incomes at the bottom of the economic spectrum have declined most dramatically since the 1970s,

DOMESTIC VIOLENCE AND HOMELESSNESS

How are women's experiences of poverty and homelessness linked to the societal phenomenon of domestic violence? In addition to consequences such as physical and psychological injury, violence is both a cause and a consequence of homelessness among women.

According to the National Law Center on Homelessness and Poverty (n.d.), "domestic and sexual violence are leading causes of homelessness nationally, especially for women" (p. 1). The center reports that about a quarter of women in a 2005 study indicated that violence was the immediate precipitating cause of their homelessness. A 2011 study conducted by a Los Angeles women's center reported that nearly half of the women surveyed had experienced domestic violence in their lifetime and a third of homeless women had experienced domestic violence in the past year. Nearly a third of the women surveyed had gone to the women's shelter directly after experiencing domestic violence and/ or assault (Downtown Women's Action Coalition, 2011).

Other violence-linked causes of homelessness are a failure to secure alternative housing, which may be the result of unemployment or denial of resources by a controlling abuser. A 2003 study showed 44% of homeless women in Fargo, North Dakota,

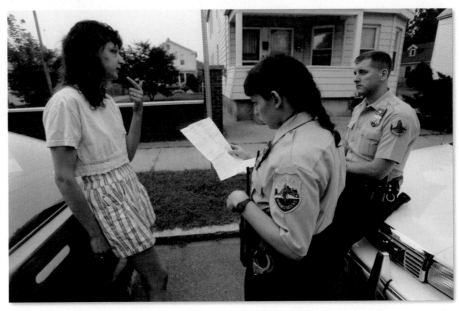

Domestic violence is an underreported crime, and many official reports fail to capture the extent of the problem. Why do you think many people are reluctant to report incidents of domestic violence to the police? ■

reported they had previously stayed in abusive relationships for lack of an alternative place to live; in Minnesota, the figure was 46% (National Coalition for the Homeless, 2007). While women may face violence upon returning home to an abuser, they are also at risk on the streets, since homelessness makes them vulnerable to assault, robbery, rape, and other threats.

Domestic violence is a key precipitator of homelessness, particularly among poor and minority women, who may already face considerable obstacles to finding safe and adequate housing and solid employment opportunities. One societal response is to support safe housing for survivors of domestic violence. A more important one for the long term is to address the causes of abuse, ending or at least reducing domestic violence as a societal phenomenon.

THINK IT THROUGH

■ *How might communities effectively address the problem of domestic violence, as well as associated troubles such as homelessness? Consider issues of both attitudes and policies in answering this question.*

Arlie Hochschild defines the nanny chain thus: "An older daughter from a poor family in a third world country cares for her siblings, while her mother works as a nanny caring for the children of a nanny migrating to a first world country, who, in turn, cares for the child of a family in a rich country" (Hochschild, 2001a). ■

when globalization began to transform the domestic economy. This decline has had a multitude of effects on U.S. families. Recall our earlier discussion of the diminished pool of "marriageable males." Here we see some of the effects of declining job opportunities and wages in manufacturing, which used to offer gainful employment to less educated men.

The need for two incomes to make ends meet is one of the reasons for the dramatic increase in the number of women working outside the home. The movement of women into the paid workforce has, in turn, provided some women with a degree of economic independence and an opportunity to rethink the meaning of marriage. As women join the paid workforce, some postpone marriage until they are older. Couples choose cohabiting as an alternative to marriage, and when they do decide to have children, their families are likely to be smaller. Some may never marry; as we learned earlier, marriage has declined most among those with less education.

Globalization means greater mobility for families and more fluid ways of organizing work and life. The benefits accrued by some U.S. families are accompanied by the losses suffered by others. Globalization may be having the effect of further stratifying U.S. families economically.

The Adoption Option

INTERNATIONAL FAMILIES AND THE GLOBAL WOMAN

We've seen that macro processes of globalization have affected U.S. families at different socioeconomic status levels. In this section, we examine the dual phenomena of *international families* and the *global woman* to emphasize some of the micro-level effects of globalization, and to consider the ways that women, particularly women from the developing world, are experiencing globalization in their own lives.

Anthropologist Christine Ho (1993) has examined what she terms **international families**—that is, *families that result from globalization*. Focusing on mothers who emigrate from the Caribbean to the United States, Ho documents how they often rely on child minding, an arrangement in which extended-family members and even friends cooperate in raising their children while they pursue work elsewhere, often thousands of miles away. This practice adds a global dimension to cooperative child-rearing practices that are a long-standing feature of Caribbean culture.

Ho suggests in her profiles of these female global citizens, most of whom work in lower-wage sectors of the economy including clerical work and child care, that such global family arrangements will enable Caribbean immigrants to avoid becoming fully Americanized: International families and child minding are seen

International families: Families that result from globalization.

as providing a strong sense of continuity with their original Caribbean culture. She predicts that Caribbean immigrants will retain their native cultures by regularly receiving what she characterizes as "bicultural booster shots" through the shuttling of family members between the United States and the Caribbean. At the same time, Ho notes, this process also contributes to the Americanization of the Caribbean region, which may eventually give rise to an ever more global culture.

More recently, sociologist Arlie Russell Hochschild and writer Barbara Ehrenreich (2002) have turned their attention to what they call the global woman. Like Ho, they examine the female migrant leaving home and family to seek work in the wealthy First World. Unlike Ho, however, they take a pointedly critical view of this phenomenon, suggesting that these female workers, most of them engaged in "care work" as nannies or housekeepers (or even prostitutes), are filling a "care deficit" in the wealthier countries, where many female professionals have pursued opportunities outside the home. In doing so the migrants create a new deficit at home, leaving their own children and communities behind: "Third World migrant women achieve their success only by assuming the cast-off domestic roles of middle- and high-income women in the First World—roles that have been previously rejected, of course, by men. And their 'commute' entails a cost we have yet to fully comprehend" (Hochschild & Ehrenreich, 2002, p. 3).

Hochschild and Ehrenreich (2002) argue that Western global power, previously manifested in the extraction of natural resources and agricultural goods, has evolved to embrace an "extraction" of women's labor and love, which is transferred to the well-off at a cost to poorer countries, communities, and—most acutely perhaps—families:

> The lifestyles of the First World are made possible by a global transfer of the services associated with a wife's traditional role—child care, homemaking, and sex—from poor countries to rich ones. To generalize and perhaps oversimplify: in an earlier phrase of imperialism, northern countries extracted natural resources and agricultural products . . . from lands they conquered and colonized. Today, while still relying on Third World countries for agricultural and industrial labor, the wealthy countries also seek to extract something harder to measure and quantify, something that can look very much like love. (p. 4)

While the women from the developing world are, for the most part, agents in their own choice to migrate to the First World in search of work (unless they are trafficked or tricked into migration), Hochschild and Ehrenreich point to powerful social forces that figure into this "choice." On the one hand, many women encounter the "push" factor of poverty, the choice of facing destitution at home or leaving families behind to earn what is a substantial wage abroad. On the other hand, there is the "pull" factor of opportunities abroad: Their services are welcomed and needed. While these women make choices, their decisions are often driven by desperation and carry substantial noneconomic costs.

WHY STUDY FAMILY THROUGH A SOCIOLOGICAL LENS?

In the United States today, there are many possible ways of understanding what constitutes a family. They range from the narrower definitions embraced by both the U.S. government and the socially conservative, to the broader options a growing number of people are recognizing. A sociological perspective helps us to understand the roots of both stasis and change in family life and family formation. The decline of marriage, the rise (and, more recently, the marginal decline) of divorce, and the dramatic increase in nonmarital births are, as Émile Durkheim might have suggested, "social facts," and *social facts can be explained only by other social facts.* These are not changes that appear randomly, but rather complex sociological phenomena with identifiable and interesting social, cultural, and economic antecedents.

Theoretical perspectives on the family and associated sex roles add another layer of analysis to the picture. The functionalist theory of the family looks at its functions for societal stability, emphasizing reproduction, the nurturance and socialization of children, and the allocation of family members into complementary roles that ensure harmony and order. The more conflict-oriented feminist theory looks at the way the family reproduces gender inequality, ignoring the differential experiences and resources of men and women in relationships. The psychodynamic feminist perspective blends psychology and sociology to draw together the experiences of early childhood with relationship choices of adulthood and structural obstacles and opportunities. While all these perspectives have strengths and weaknesses, they offer us a range of possible lenses for considering why families and roles are constituted as they are. The field remains open for new theoretical perspectives, and the family remains a fruitful area of research for sociologists.

Sociologists are concerned with commonalities and differences across families and explanations for these. Class, race, immigration status, health status—all may play a role in the ways that family formation, roles, cultures, and practices are manifested. Macro-level societal changes also have a powerful impact on families; globalization, deindustrialization, and the massive growth of student debt in an era of rapidly rising college costs are all seemingly "nonfamily" phenomena that may, in fact, have a powerful impact on families across the globe. Sociology helps us to make these connections.

The Importance of Family

WHAT CAN I DO WITH A SOCIOLOGY DEGREE?

SKILLS AND CAREERS: QUALITATIVE RESEARCH SKILLS

Sociologists use *qualitative research skills* to gather rigorous, in-depth information on social behaviors, phenomena, and institutions. Qualitative research highlights data that cannot be quantified (that is, cannot be converted into numbers). It relies on the gathering of data through methods such as focus groups, participant and nonparticipant observation, interviews, and archival research. Generally, population samples in qualitative research are small because they focus on deep understanding.

In this chapter, qualitative data was used to research issues as broad as the decline of marriage in the U.S. working class and the struggle for a work-life balance among middle class families. Annette Lareau (2003) used nonparticipant observation and interviews to look at child-rearing practices in middle- and working-class White and Black families. Her work was qualitative because it used a small sample (88 families were interviewed, and 12 were closely observed at home) but sought to develop a detailed and in-depth understanding of how class-associated styles of parenting contribute to the reproduction of class status. Throughout this book you will encounter numerous qualitative research studies, and you will see how they contribute to our knowledge of the social world. As you advance in your sociological studies, you will have the opportunity to learn how to do qualitative sociology. For example, you may learn to prepare interview questions to accurately assess respondents' attitudes toward a particular social trend or to take detailed field notes on observations you make of a practice or population you seek to study.

Knowledge of qualitative research methods is a beneficial skill in today's job market. Learning to collect data through observation, interviews, and focus groups, for instance, prepares you to do a wide variety of *job tasks*, including survey development, questionnaire design, data collection and reporting, and market research. No less importantly, qualitative research experience fosters communication

competencies through the processes of small group management and rapport building, as well as negotiation with study participants. These kinds of tasks are associated with *job titles* such as market research analyst or manager, social science research assistant, program analyst, community engagement analyst, and survey designer, and with *occupational fields* as broad as sociology, psychology, marketing, politics, public relations, community relations, and business and management, among others.

THINK ABOUT CAREERS:

■ *Think about a topic you have read about in your sociology class that was of particular interest to you. What kind of qualitative research method might offer an effective and rigorous way of studying that issue?*

■ *How might you imagine using your knowledge of qualitative research methods in a career field like public relations, community relations, politics, management, or marketing?*

▶ *Access additional web links on the student study site to learn more.*

SUMMARY

To test your knowledge further, find additional study material on the Student Study Site at **www.sagepub.com/chamblissintro**

- The meaning of **family** is socially constructed within a particular culture, and in the United States, as in other modern societies, the meaning and practices of family life have been changing.

- **Marriage**, found in some form in all societies, varies from the most common form—**monogamy**—to many variations like **polygamy**, in which a person has multiple spouses simultaneously.

- The functionalist perspective on the family highlights its functionality in terms of social stability and order, emphasizing such activities as sex role allocation and child socialization.

- The feminist perspectives are more conflict-oriented, highlighting **the sexual division of labor** in society and its stratifying effects. Feminist perspectives also examine the different experiences of men and women in marriage and the way social expectations and roles affect those experiences. The psychodynamic feminist perspective takes a sociopsychological perspective, emphasizing the impact of early mothering on the later assumption of gender roles.

- In modern society, the composition of the family and the roles within it are shifting. The age at first marriage has risen across the board, and marriage has declined, particularly among the less educated, and nonmarital births account for over 40% of all births. Divorce has leveled off but remains at a high level. Same-sex marriage has growing public support, though legislation at the state and federal level legalizing it—and divorce—lags behind changes in public attitudes.

- Socioeconomic class status affects child-rearing practices and family formation patterns. Lower rates of marriage and high rates of nonmarital births occur among the poor and working class.

- The family may be a site of both nurturing and caring, and a site of violence such as spousal and child abuse, which we observe at high rates, and elder abuse.

- In the United States, the effects of globalization include changes in household income and employment opportunities. Women from developing countries often leave home and children to work for families in the developing world.

KEY TERMS

Study terms on the go with the smartphone-friendly key term flashcards, available at **www.sagepub.com/chamblissintro**

family, 239

marriage, 239

monogamy, 239

polygamy, 239

polygyny, 239

polyandry, 239

serial monogamy, 240

endogamous, 240

antimiscegenation laws, 240

extended families, 241

nuclear family, 241

sexual division of labor in modern societies, 242

cohabitation, 246

common law marriage, 246

civil unions, 248

domestic partnerships, 248

domestic or family violence, 257

international families, 260

DISCUSSION QUESTIONS

1. Why do people get married? Why do people not marry? Think about reasons that are individual and sociological. Link your answers to the discussion of marriage trends discussed in the chapter.

2. Lareau's research suggests that middle- and working-class families have different child-rearing styles. How

   does she describe these styles? What are the benefits and consequences of each?

3. Who is the "global woman"? What are the costs and benefits to women and families of a global labor market for care work?

DISCOVER ⊕⊕ STATE STATS

Log-in to the eBook and click on the title to the left for access to State Stats in order to complete the exercise.

In the Population database, find the marriage and divorce rates for 1993 to 2010. Choose five states, including your home state, and for each one compare marriage and divorce rates at three points on this timeline. What trends do you find? What sociological factors can help explain changes in both rates that you see over this time period?

STUDENT STUDY SITE

Visit the Student Study Site at **www.sagepub.com/chamblissintro** to access additional study tools, including eFlashcards, web quizzes, video resources, web resources, audio resources, links to SAGE journal, handbook, and research articles, and much more!

11 EDUCATION AND SOCIETY

WHAT DO YOU THINK?

1. What are the primary reasons that students drop out of college before completing their degree?
2. Why are many U.S. schools still deeply segregated by race and income?
3. Why has the earnings gap between those with a high school diploma and those with a college diploma grown in recent decades?

SOC *VIEW*

Get a closer look with the authors!

A COLLEGE DROPOUT BOOM?

More U.S. students than ever are enrolling in college. According to data from the National Center for Education Statistics (NCES, 2011b), in 2009, fully 70% of high school completers enrolled in college. This figure has risen substantially over time: Consider that in 1960, it was just 45%. As we discuss in several other chapters in this book, in the increasingly globalized workplace and the postindustrial U.S. labor market, education is more critical than ever in ensuring competitiveness in the job market and greater earning potential. Perhaps it is not surprising that more students are seeking to continue their education beyond high school.

Some critical observers, however, point out that all is not well in the hallowed halls of U.S. higher education. In fact, they say, the laudable rate of enrollment obscures a darker and more problematic reality: Many of those students leave college with debt . . . and no degree. Journalist David Leonhardt (2009) writes that "in terms of its core mission—turning teenagers into educated college graduates—much of the system is simply failing."

Leonhardt observes that while the United States does an excellent job getting high school graduates to enroll in higher education, colleges on the whole have been far less successful in retaining students and fostering their timely graduation. For example, according to the group Complete College America (2011), of 100 students who enroll in any public college or university in the state of Texas, only 13 will have graduated with a bachelor's degree within four years. About 79 of 100 students will attend a two-year institution rather than a four-year university, and of those 79 who enroll, only 7 will graduate with a two-year degree within four years (Complete College America, 2011). A study done by the Harvard Graduate School of Education in 2011 notes that in the United States as a whole, just over half of college students (56%) complete four-year degrees in a period of six years—and only 29% of those who enroll in two-year college programs complete them in three years. The low graduation figures put the United States at the bottom of an 18-country Organisation for Economic Co-operation and Development (OECD) list for completion rates, with 46% of students completing college once they begin higher education, far behind countries such as Japan (89%) and Poland (61%).

What happens to these students? Why do they leave? Where do they go? These questions are of critical importance. On the one hand, at the macro level, the U.S. economy needs an educated workforce. Dropouts diminish the potential for productivity and are costly in other ways as well: States paid out about $6.2 billion for four-year colleges and universities between 2003 and 2008 to support the education of students who never returned for a second year of studies (American Institutes of Research, 2010). On the other hand, at the micro level, most workers are better off for having completed college: Median weekly earnings for those who have a bachelor's degree are nearly 50% higher than the earnings for those who have some college, but no degree (U.S. Bureau of Labor Statistics, 2013). The differences are even greater when comparing those without a college degree to those who have graduate, professional, and doctoral degrees. ■

In this chapter, we examine the issue of college dropouts in more detail, looking into the sociological antecedents of this important phenomenon and look at the figures used in public discussions of the issue. We begin with a discussion of the roots of mass public education in the United States and the development of the "credential society" that is driving rising enrollments in higher education today. We continue with a critical look at education, using the functionalist, conflict, and symbolic interactionist perspectives to think about its functions and outcomes in modern society. The chapter then turns to the fundamentally important issue of education and inequality, examining education as a key to understanding how inequality is both reproduced and reduced. We next return to the theme introduced in the opener—that is, higher education in the United States. We consider the relationship between higher education and income, the growing internship phenomenon, and the problem of college dropouts. Finally, we look at education in a global perspective, comparing the United States to other countries in terms of education and employment and discussing the growing interest of U.S. students in studying abroad.

· ·

Education: The transmission of society's norms, values, and knowledge base by means of direct instruction.

Formal education: Education that occurs within academic institutions such as schools.

Mass education: The extension of formal schooling to wide segments of the population.

Literacy: The ability to read and write at a basic level.

EDUCATION, INDUSTRIALIZATION, AND THE "CREDENTIAL SOCIETY"

As societies change, so, too, does the role of **education,** *the transmission of society's norms, values, and knowledge base by means of direct instruction.* For much of human history, education occurred informally, within the family or the immediate community. Children often learned by doing—by working alongside their parents, siblings, and other relatives in the home, in the field, or on the hunt.

With the emergence of industrial society, **formal education,** *education that occurs within academic institutions such as schools,* became increasingly common. As schooling became increasingly important in industrial societies, it came to be seen as the birthright of all society members. **Mass education,** or *the extension of formal schooling to wide segments of the population,* is the norm today. Not only is mass education consistent with the democratic ideals held in most modern and economically advanced or advancing societies, but it is also the principal means by which people acquire the skills they need to participate effectively as workers and citizens in the midst of technological, cultural, and economic change of dramatic proportions.

Modern society requires its members to master a large number of complex skills. People must know how to read and write for productive efficiency. Some will endeavor to organize production, invent new products, or manage accounts—others are engaged in creating art or literature, curing diseases, resolving human conflicts, and addressing scientific challenges like climate change. To create such an educated population requires more than on-the-job training as an apprentice or helper. It requires more than most families are willing or able to pass on from one generation to another.

The first educational institutions in the United States were created in the 17th century by the religious leaders of the New England Puritan communities. Their original intent was to provide religious education; children were taught to read in order to study biblical scripture (Monroe, 1940; Vinovskis, 1995). In 1647, the Massachusetts Bay Colony passed a law requiring every community of 50 or more people to establish a town school. The law was called "The Old Deluder Satan Act," a measure intended to protect New England's youth from acquiescing to the temptations of the devil.

By the 18th century, the goal of education shifted from religious training to cultivating practical and productive skills (Vinovskis, 1995). The emergence of industrial societies not only increased the need for people to be literate—**literacy** is defined as *the ability to read and write at a basic level*—but it also required that they learn skills, work habits, and discipline that would

College and
Social Mobility

In the United States, girls and boys used to be educated separately and unequally in many public schools. Boys were trained in literacy and arithmetic, while girls were educated in cooking and homemaking. ■

prepare them for occupations ranging from industrial laborers, accountants, inventors, and designers to merchandisers, lawyers, and operators of complex machinery (Bergen, 1996).

From the outset, schools in the United States were divided along social class lines. The sons of the middle and upper classes went to private schools that trained them for business and the professions. There were initially few public schools, and they provided working- and lower-class children with the minimal education necessary to acquire the skills and obedience for factory work or farming (Bowles & Gintis, 1976; Wyman, 1997).

When workers began forming labor unions in the 19th century, one of their demands was for free **public education** for their children, a universal education system provided by the government and funded by tax revenues rather than student fees (fees served to exclude economically disadvantaged students from the classroom; Horan & Hargis, 1991). Political activists, philanthropic organizations, and newspapers joined the unions in their demand. By the late 19th century, public elementary schools had been established in most of the industrial centers of the United States, and mass public schooling soon spread throughout the country, though segregated by gender and race. In some places, no schooling was provided for girls or African Americans. In other places, girls and boys were educated separately and unequally, with girls receiving training in cooking and homemaking and

Purpose of Education

boys being educated to be literate (Riordan, 1990; Tyack & Hansot, 1982). Schools for African Americans were segregated by law in the Southern states until the U.S. Supreme Court ruled the practice unconstitutional in 1954; elsewhere in the country, Blacks and Whites attended different schools that offered unequal opportunities in education because they lived in different neighborhoods and schools were locally funded (Aviel, 1997; Bergen, 1996).

In some states, school attendance was compulsory for at least the first six years. The concept of public education was soon expanded to include high schools, and by the turn of the 19th century, the average U.S. student achieved eight years of schooling, while 10% completed high school and 2% completed college or university (Bettelheim, 1982; Vinovskis, 1992; Walters & James, 1992).

With the creation of mass public education, the United States increasingly became a **credential society**, *one in which access to desirable jobs and social status depends on the possession of a certificate or diploma certifying the completion of formal education* (R. Collins, 1979; Vinovskis, 1995). A socially validated credential such as a bachelor's degree or professional degree thus serves as a filter, determining the kinds of jobs and promotions for which a person is eligible. People with a high school diploma have a difficult time competing with those who have a college degree even if they possess a keen intellect and good skills: If a position announcement indicates that a college degree is required, the candidate with only a high school degree is unlikely to be considered at all. Since a person's job is a major determinant of income and social class, educational credentials play a major role in shaping opportunities for social and economic mobility.

Next we look at some different theoretical perspectives on education and its functions in modern society.

THEORETICAL PERSPECTIVES ON EDUCATION

What is the role of the educational system in society? While functionalist theorists highlight the ways in which the educational system is positively functional for society, conflict theorists

Public education: A universal education system provided by the government and funded by tax revenues rather than student fees.

Credential society: One in which access to desirable work and social status depends on the possession of a certificate or diploma certifying the completion of formal education.

School is an important agent of socialization. Among the lessons young children learn in school are obedience to authority and conformity to schedules, imperatives that some sociologists say are rooted in early capitalism's need for compliant workers. ■

point to its role in reinforcing and reproducing social stratification. Symbolic interactionist theories help to illuminate how relational processes in the classroom may contribute to educational success—or failure.

THE FUNCTIONALIST PERSPECTIVE

Émile Durkheim (1956, 1973b), whose work forms a foundation for functionalist theorizing in sociology, wrote about the importance of education in modern societies. According to Durkheim, modern societies are complex, with specialized yet interdependent institutions. This complexity creates a special problem for *social solidarity*—that is, the bonds that unite the members of a social group. Modern society is no longer characterized by communities with high degrees of cultural, religious, or social homogeneity, so social ties have weakened. One function of mass education is to address this problem by socializing members of a society into the norms and values necessary to produce and maintain social solidarity. Durkheim talked about this function in terms of *moral education*, meaning that educational institutions not only provide the knowledge and training necessary for members to fulfill their economic roles in modern society but also function to socialize individuals, building solidarity in the group.

Contemporary functionalist theories echo Durkheim's concerns about social solidarity, emphasizing the function of formal education in socializing people into the norms, values, and skills necessary for society to survive and thrive (Parsons & Mayhew, 1982). Functionalist theory also proposes that education has

both manifest and latent functions (Bourdieu & Coleman, 1991; Merton, 1938/1968). What are these functions?

The manifest, or intended, functions include the transmission of general knowledge and specific skills needed in society and the economy, such as literacy. The latent, or unintended, functions include the propagation of societal norms and values that Durkheim argued should be explicit concerns of *moral education*. For example, beginning with kindergarten, children learn to organize their lives according to schedules, sit at desks, follow rules, and show respect for authority. Sociologist Harry Gracey (1991) has argued that "the unique job of the kindergarten seems . . . to be teaching children the student role. The student role is the repertoire of behavior and attitudes regarded by educators as appropriate to children in school" (p. 448). Having "mastered" the student role, children internalize the external social norms and rules that govern the school day and their academic lives.

Consider other latent functions of the system of mass public education in the United States. For example, in keeping children occupied from about 8 a.m. until 3 p.m., schools serve as supervisors for a large population of children whose parents work in order to contribute to both their own micro economies in the home and the productivity of the macro-level economy. Schools are also sources of peer socialization, offering an environment in which conventional gender roles are enacted and enforced; while some young people challenge expected roles through dress, for example, many opt to conform in order to avoid conflict or ostracism. Can you think of other latent functions that are social, cultural, economic, or political?

■ FIGURE 11.1 Relationship Between U.S. Family Income and Years of Schooling for White Males Aged 35–44, 1962

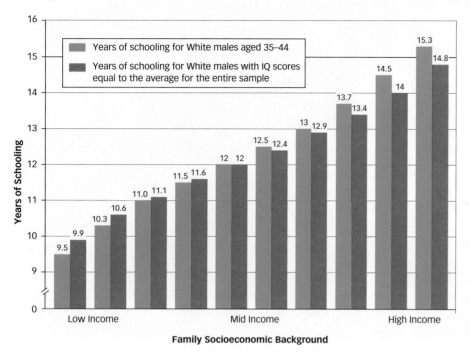

Family Socioeconomic Background

SOURCE: Bowles, Samuel, and Herbert Gintis. *Schooling in Capitalist America: Educational Reform and the Contradictions of Economic Life.* Copyright © 1977 Bowles, Samuel; Gintis, Herbert M. Reprinted by permission of Basic Books, a member of the Perseus Books Group.

What are the weaknesses of the functionalist perspective in fostering our understanding of the system of education? Critics suggest that it ignores schools' contribution to reproducing social inequality. Functionalist theory assumes, for instance, that the educational system educates people in accordance with their abilities and potential, giving credentials to those who deserve them and who can contribute most to society while withholding them from those incapable of doing the most demanding work. Critics, however, say schools function to reproduce the existing class system, favoring those who are already the most advantaged and putting obstacles in the path of those who are disadvantaged. They point to substantial differences in the educational attainment of the different socioeconomic groups (a topic we take up later in this chapter) as evidence that socioeconomic class status is just as important as intellectual capability in influencing educational attainment within the institution of education (Bowles & Gintis, 1976).

Notably as well, although education may socialize students into society's norms and values, it also undermines societal authority by promoting a critical approach to dominant ideas. Education contributes substantially to the development of a capacity for "self-direction" (K. Miller, Kohn, & Schooler, 1986), and students often develop an inquiring, critical spirit because they are exposed to views and ways of thinking that challenge their previously held ideas. For example, Phelan and McLaughlin (1995) found that people with higher levels of education are more sympathetic to and less likely to blame homeless people for their condition than respondents with lower levels of education.

THE CONFLICT PERSPECTIVE

Conflict theorists agree that education trains people in the dominant norms and values of society and the work skills and habits demanded by the economic system. However, they reject the functionalist notion that the system of education channels individuals into the positions for which they are best suited in terms of ambition, skills, and talents. Instead, they believe, it reproduces rather than reduces social stratification and, rather than ensuring that the best people train for and conscientiously perform the most socially important jobs (K. Davis & Moore, 1945), ensures that the discovery of talent will be limited (Tumin, 1953).

According to conflict theory, poor and working-class children have fewer opportunities to demonstrate their talents and abilities because they lack equal access to educational opportunities. Moreover, part of the "hidden curriculum" of the classroom is to socialize members of the working class to accept their class position (Bowles & Gintis, 1976). Children are taught at an early age to define their academic ambitions and abilities in keeping with the social class of their parents. These lowered educational ambitions are reinforced through inferior educational opportunities and labeling and discrimination in the classroom (Bowles & Gintis, 1976; Glazer, 1992; Kozol, 1991; Oakes, 1985; Willis, 1981).

Consider the experience of Malcolm X, a prominent champion of the rights of African Americans who was assassinated in 1965. In his autobiography, Malcolm X recounts how, despite being a top student, he was discouraged by his high school English teacher from becoming a lawyer:

> Mr. Ostrowski looked surprised, I remember . . . He kind of half-smiled and said, "Malcolm, one of life's first needs is for us to be realistic. Don't misunderstand me, now. We all like you, you know that . . . A lawyer—that's no realistic goal for a [black man]. You need to think about something you can be. You're good with your hands—making things . . . Why don't you plan on carpentry? People like you as a person—you'd get all kinds of work." (Haley & Malcolm X, 1964, p. 41)

Poor and minority children still experience lowered expectations and educational opportunities. Author Jonathan Kozol (2000) writes the following:

Many people in Mott Haven [an impoverished neighborhood in the South Bronx] do a lot of work to make sure they are well-informed about the conditions in their children's public schools. Some also know a great deal more about the schools that serve the children of the privileged than many of the privileged themselves may recognize. They know that "business math" is not the same as calculus and that "job-readiness instruction" is not European history or English literature. They know that children of rich people do not often spend semesters of their teenage years in classes where they learn to type an application for an entry-level clerical position; they know that these wealthy children are too busy learning composition skills and polishing their French pronunciation and receiving preparation for the SATs. They come to understand the process by which a texture of enlightenment is stitched together for some children while it is denied to others. They also understand that, as the years go by, some of these children will appear to have deserved one kind of role in life, and some another. (pp. 100–101)

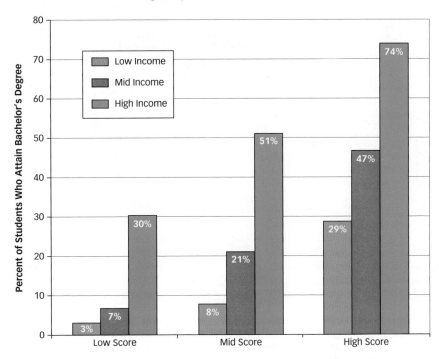

■ **FIGURE 11.2** Correlation Between Performance on Eighth-Grade Math Exam and Attainment of Bachelor's Degree by Income, 2005

SOURCE: Fox, M. A., Connolly, B. A., & Snyder, T. D. (2005). *Youth indicators 2005: Trends in the well-being of American youth* (NCES 2005-050). U.S. Department of Education, National Center for Education Statistics. Washington, DC: U.S. Government Printing Office.

Among the most prominent conflict theorists in the sociology of education are Samuel Bowles and Herbert Gintis, whose 1976 book, *Schooling in Capitalist America,* posited three key arguments. First, these authors argued that schools not only impart cognitive skills but, notably, "prepare people to function well and without complaint in the hierarchical structure of the modern corporation" (Bowles & Gintis, 2002, p. ix). Second, Bowles and Gintis used statistical data to support the argument that parental economic status is passed on to children, at least in part, through unequal educational opportunity, though the advantages conferred on children of higher-social-status families are not limited to their educational preparation. Finally, the authors suggested that the modern school system was not the product of the evolutionary perfection of democratic pedagogy, but rather primarily a reflection of the interests of expanding capitalist enterprises such as factories.

Frequently cited results of Bowles and Gintis's early work include a graph showing the powerful correlation between socioeconomic status (as measured by income) and educational attainment. Using a group of men with similar childhood IQ scores, the data demonstrate an unmistakable relationship between the socioeconomic background of subjects and the average number of years of education they completed (Figure 11.1 on page 270). While a precise update of Bowles and Gintis's data is not available, other data on the correlation between family income category, demonstrated academic potential, and educational attainment show that the same relationship identified by the theorists is still relevant decades later (Figure 11.2).

Critics of conflict theories of education point out that education, even in highly stratified societies, is an important way that the poor and working class can improve their circumstances, and it remains the primary means of upward mobility. It was a crucial path by which generations of U.S. immigrants escaped poverty. Thus, although it may contribute to the reproduction of an unequal socioeconomic structure, the educational system also provides meaningful opportunities for mobility and change.

THE SYMBOLIC INTERACTIONIST PERSPECTIVE

The functionalist and conflict perspectives highlight the role of education in society. Symbolic interactionists, on the other hand, study what occurs in the classroom, alerting us to subtle and not-so-subtle ways in which schools affect the self-image of students. By looking at how students are labeled, for instance, symbolic interactionists shed light on the way schools help to reinforce and perpetuate differences among students.

In a classic study, Rosenthal and Jacobson (1968) conducted an intriguing experiment in which elementary school teachers were intentionally misinformed about the intelligence test scores of

Rosenthal and Jacobson's experiment raises interesting questions: Is intentionally deceptive labeling ethical as it both misinforms the teacher and may confer advantage on some students to the detriment of others? Can it be justified as a social scientific endeavor? ■

selected students. The teachers were told, in confidence, that certain students had scored unusually high on standardized tests the previous year. In fact, these students had been randomly selected and were no different in known intelligence from their peers. Rosenthal and Jacobson then observed the interactions between these students and their teachers and monitored the students' academic performance. The students labeled "exceptional" soon outperformed their peers, a difference that persisted for several years.

The teachers described the labeled students as "more curious" or "more interested" and communicated their heightened expectations of these learners through their voice, facial expression, and use of praise. Enacting a *self-fulfilling prophecy,* the students came to see themselves through their teachers' eyes and began performing as if they were, in fact, more intelligent than their peers, earning still more positive attention from teachers. Younger students, whose self-image was more flexible, exhibited the greatest improvements in performance. Rosenthal and Jacobson concluded that the teachers behaved differently toward some students because they had been labeled "exceptional."

Other studies suggest similar conclusions. A study of student-teacher interaction in a largely African American kindergarten found that such labels as *fast* or *slow*, which the teacher assigned by the eighth day of class, tended to stay with the student throughout the year (Rist, 1970). Another study found that female and Asian American students frequently received classroom grades higher than their actual test scores, while Latino, Black, and White males received lower grades (Farkas et al., 1990a, 1990b). The differences had to do with the teachers' perceptions of their students' "attitude." Those who appeared to be attentive and cooperative were judged to be hard workers and

good students, and were graded up; those who appeared to be indifferent or hostile were graded down.

Classroom labeling has been studied in other countries as well. In one influential study, Paul Willis (1981, 1990) found that British boys from working-class families were systematically labeled as low academic achievers and socialized to think of themselves as capable of doing only working-class jobs. The boys understood quite well that this labeling process worked against them, and they resisted it by the use of humor and other challenges to authority. These behaviors reinforced their teachers' perception that the boys would never make it and would eventually drop out of school and assume their "rightful position" in the working class. The boys thus accepted their teachers' labeling, creating a self-fulfilling prophecy in which they wound up in working-class jobs.

Symbolic interactionism is well suited to studying the ways in which teachers consciously or unintentionally affect their students, but a critic might note that because it focuses on social interaction, it cannot give us a picture of the role of the educational system in society as a whole or help us analyze structural problems such as unequal funding of schools in poor, middle-class, and wealthy areas.

EDUCATION, OPPORTUNITY, AND INEQUALITY

Functionalists argue that education provides a means for mobility and for filling the positions necessary for society to survive and thrive. Conflict theorists posit that the educational system reinforces existing inequalities by unequally according opportunities based on class, race, or gender. In fact, the U.S. educational system may operate to open avenues to mobility *and* create obstacles to achievement among the less privileged—that is, it may both reduce and reproduce inequality. In the following sections we look at issues of education and inequality, focusing in particular on questions about early childhood literacy and later educational achievement, income and poverty, school segregation by race and income, and public school funding.

ILLITERACY AND WORD POVERTY: THE CHILDHOOD CHALLENGE

Researcher Louisa Cook Moats uses the term *word poverty* to characterize the impoverished language environments in which some children grow up. Word poverty is a particular problem in economically disadvantaged homes: Research on a community in California found that by age 5, children in impoverished-language environments had heard 32 million fewer words spoken to them than the average middle-class child. Perhaps not surprisingly, the fewer words that were spoken to children, the fewer they could actively use themselves: In a study of how many words children could produce at age 3, "children from impoverished environments used less than half the number of words already spoken by their more advantaged peers" (Wolf, 2008, pp. 102–103).

Word poverty is also linked to a deficit of books in the homes of many children. Research conducted in three Los Angeles communities found that in the most economically impoverished community in the study, it was common to find no children's books in the home. In low- to middle-income homes, an average of 3 books could be found. By contrast, in the most affluent families, there was an average of 200 books in each home (Wolf, 2008). According to a recent global study (M. Evans, Kelley, Sikora, & Treiman, 2010), the deficit or wealth of books in a home is of significance in children's later schooling: Being raised in a home without books was as likely to affect children's educational attainment as having parents with very low educational attainment. The researchers concluded that "having a 500-book library or having university-educated parents, propel a child 3.2 years further in education, on average" (M. Evans et al., 2010). In the United States, the advantage to having an expansive library was an average of more than two years of education. Commenting on the study, *Science Daily* (2010) noted, "The researchers were struck by the strong effect having books in the home had on children's educational attainment even above and beyond such factors as education level of the parents, the

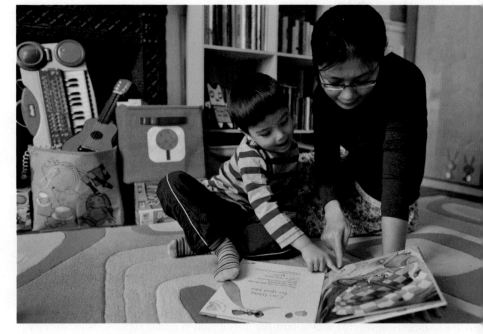

Early literacy has been linked by researchers to later academic achievement. Children who do not learn to read by early elementary school often struggle to catch up later and are at higher risk than their peers of dropping out of high school. ■

country's GDP [gross domestic product], the father's occupation or the political system of the country" (para. 9).

Why is word poverty significant? The answer is that it is linked to low literacy. A fundamental necessity for any country in the modern world is a population that is functionally literate. No less important, literacy is necessary for individual success in education and the job market. Basic **literacy** is defined in one key study as *"using printed and written information to function in society, to achieve one's goals, and to develop one's knowledge and potential"* (The National Assessment of Adult Literacy [NAAL], 2011, para 2). NAAL identifies four categories of literacy: below basic, basic, intermediate, and proficient (Figure 11.3). A large-scale NAAL study using a population of 19,000 representative respondents found the following:

- About 14% of U.S. adults (or 30 million people) fell *below basic* on the literacy test. That is, they could successfully complete "no more than the most *simple* and *concrete* literacy skills," such as locating the intersection of two streets on a clearly labeled map and circling the date of a medical appointment on a hospital appointment slip.
- About 29% of the population (63 million) scored in the *basic* category, meaning they could "perform simple and everyday literacy activities," including finding a table on a specified topic in an almanac and summarizing what articles in a given section of a magazine were about by using information from the table of contents.

■ **FIGURE 11.3** Literacy Rates of U.S. Adults, 2003

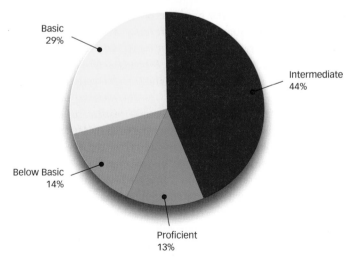

Basic
29%

Intermediate
44%

Below Basic
14%

Proficient
13%

SOURCE: National Center for Education Statistics. (2011). Literacy skills of adults, by type of literacy, proficiency levels, and selected characteristics: 1992 and 2003. *Digest of Education Statistics, 2010.*

· ·

Literacy: The ability to read and write at a basic level.

Global Illiteracy

Gender-segregated classrooms are uncommon in public schools today. Racially segregated classrooms, however, continue to be common. ■

- Another 44% (95 million) fell in to the *intermediate* category. They could "perform moderately challenging literacy activities" such as following directions on a clearly labeled map and finding the age range during which children should receive a given vaccine using a chart on recommended childhood immunizations.
- Finally, about 13% of the population (28 million) were categorized as *proficient*, which indicated they could "perform complex and challenging literacy activities." They could interpret survey data presented in a nested table and contrast financial information presented in a table about the differences between different types of credit cards.

Wolf (2008) suggests that a strong foundation in literacy is a key to later educational success. That is, students who come in with shaky foundations in literacy as a result of early childhood experiences such as word poverty or a deficit of books in the home have a higher probability of high school failure than their peers who grew up in homes with books and parents who read to them at an early age. At the same time, failure to complete high school is likely to affect someone's ability to complete literacy activities successfully (45% of adults in the lowest literacy category had completed high school). If you were to research the correlation between prose literacy and high school completion, how might you proceed? What variables would you choose to study and why? What kind of relationship would you hypothesize?

Higher Education and Race

SCHOOL SEGREGATION

School segregation, *the education of racial minorities in schools that are geographically, economically, and/or socially separated from those attended by the racial majority (Whites),* is a long-standing pattern that is worsening today, despite more than four decades of civil rights legislation intended to alleviate it and reduce its devastating effects. School segregation has long been linked to educational inequality in the United States.

Before slavery was abolished in the United States, it was a crime to teach slaves to read and write; formal education was reserved solely for Whites. Immediately following the abolition of slavery and the end of the Civil War, schools were integrated, but "Jim Crow" laws soon initiated a century of discrimination against Black Americans in the South. "Jim Crow" laws determined, among other things, where Black Americans could live, where they could eat and shop, and where they would be educated. In the North, there were no laws segregating schools by race, but segregated schooling occurred nonetheless as a consequence of racial residential segregation.

Both law and custom created schools segregated by race in the United States until the 1950s (Jordan, 1992). Black activists challenged the constitutionality of segregation, but U.S. courts repeatedly found it did not violate the U.S. Constitution. For example, in its 1896 *Plessy v. Ferguson* decision, the U.S. Supreme Court upheld the states' right to segregate public accommodations as long as they followed the principle of "separate but equal." In 1954, however, the Supreme Court reversed itself. Relying in part on social science research showing that segregated schools were not in fact equal, the Court ruled in *Brown v. Board of Education of Topeka* that laws segregating public schools were unconstitutional (L. Miller, 1995).

This decision met with considerable resistance, especially in the South, where schools were segregated by law. Governor George Wallace of Alabama personally blocked the entrance to the University of Alabama in an effort to stop Black students from enrolling, while a Black college student named James Meredith went to prison for trying to enroll and attend classes at the University of Mississippi. Black and White students who tried to integrate schools were beaten by police and fellow citizens (Branch, 1988; Chong, 1991; McCartney, 1992).

. . . .
School segregation: The education of racial minorities in schools that are separated from those attended by Whites.

Which classroom would you rather be in? One classroom is overcrowded to the point where multiple students are sharing a desk, and the other classroom appears spacious and well supplied. Unequal funding of public schools is a problem that perpetuates disparities in education and upward mobility. ■

Court challenges, civil protests, and mass civil disobedience ultimately broke down barriers, and some racial integration of schools took place across the country. Although the Supreme Court decision in *Brown v. Board of Education* had prohibited purposeful discrimination on the basis of race, it did not provide for specific methods to achieve school integration. The fact that racial and ethnic groups were residentially segregated meant that, in fact, most Blacks would continue to attend schools that were predominantly Black, while Whites would continue to attend mostly White schools.

Subsequent court decisions provided one method of achieving integration: *school busing,* a court-ordered program of transporting public school students to other than their neighborhood schools. Mandated busing proved highly controversial, provoking criticism among some academics and hostility among many parents and policy makers. Controversy erupted in 1974 when Black students were bused into poor Irish neighborhoods in South Boston, whose schools were among the worst in the state. Instead of providing equal educational opportunity, busing worsened racial conflict in some of Boston's most economically disadvantaged neighborhoods. Violence resulted, and over the next 10 years public school enrollment in the city plummeted (Frum, 2000).

Today, despite decades of civil rights activism and laws aimed at promoting integrated schools, racial segregation in U.S. education persists, and in some places it has even worsened. How is this possible?

First, the movement of middle- and upper-class Whites into all-White school districts in suburban or outlying areas has left mostly poor minorities in the inner cities, where some schools have become almost fully racially segregated as a result (Coleman, 1982; Kozol, 2005; Orfield & Eaton, 1996). Because they are located in low-income neighborhoods, highly segregated schools also tend to be the most poorly funded. While there are variations in state formulas for funding schools, the source on which most U.S. school districts still depend most fully is local property taxes. While this system ensures that those who live in areas with high property values will generally accrue adequate—or even excellent—funds for the physical plant and academic programs of their schools, it also puts those who live in poor rural or urban areas at a distinct disadvantage, since even high property tax rates cannot bring in the level of resources that middle- to upper-class area schools enjoy. White families that remain in urban areas often choose to send their children to private schools, too. As a consequence, most students still attend schools with a high degree of racial segregation (Ball, Bowe, & Gewirtz, 1995; Kozol, 2005).

Second, U.S. Supreme Court decisions such as *Board of Education of Oklahoma City v. Dowell, Freeman v. Pitts,* and *Missouri v. Jenkins* have limited the scope of previous laws aimed at promoting racial integration of schools. The Court has ruled that segregated schools resulting from "residential preferences" are a result of people making choices about where to reside and are therefore beyond the scope of the law. The court declared in these cases that school districts that previously had made an effort to integrate schools could send students back to neighborhood schools even if they were segregated and inferior (Orfield & Eaton, 1996).

Latino and Black students are more likely to be in segregated schools today than in earlier decades (Figure 11.4 on page 276). In Chicago in 2005, for instance, more than 87% of students enrolled in public school were either Black or Hispanic; fewer than 10% were White. In Washington, DC, public school enrollment is more than

School Segregation

Educational Resegregation

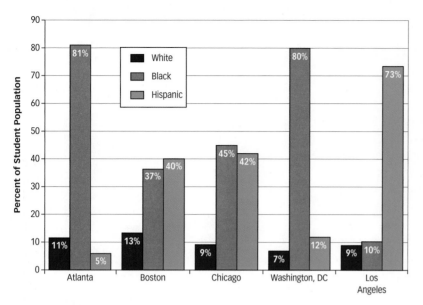

93% African American or Latino—in Detroit is it over 97% (Federal Education Budget Project, 2012). Schools that operate under **de facto segregation** face many daunting problems, including

> low levels of competition and expectation, less qualified teachers who leave as soon as they get seniority, more limited curricula, peer pressure against academic achievement and supportive of crime and substance abuse, high levels of teen pregnancy, few connections with colleges and employers who can assist students, less serious academic counseling and preparation for college, and powerless parents who themselves failed in school and do not know how to evaluate or change schools. (Orfield & Eaton, 1996, p. 54)

By contrast, middle-class Asian American students are almost entirely integrated into schools with Whites. Asian American communities such as "Chinatown" and "Little Saigon" are exceptions to this rule, however, especially among recent immigrants from China, Vietnam, Korea, and other Asian countries (Chen, 1992; Loo, 1991).

American Indians on reservations are the most segregated of all minorities. The various tribes are recognized by treaty as separate nations whose rights are governed by agreements between them and the U.S. government. Their schools are run by the Bureau of Indian Affairs, which employs teachers and sets the curriculum. Treaties between the U.S. government and Indian nations have sought to ensure education that recognizes the value of American Indian culture and tradition. Yet the teachers employed by the Bureau are ordinarily expected to cover the standard subjects of U.S. school curricula, and in English. Problems within the tribal communities have resulted, since Indians often see such instruction as failing to respect their linguistic and cultural differences.

LIVING IN THE PAST? THE U.S. SCHOOL CALENDAR IN MODERN SOCIETY

Some people believe U.S. students are falling behind their international peers because they spend less time in the classroom (Table 11.1). Two popular proposals to expand classroom time are lengthening the school day and lengthening the school year. Below we explore these two ideas, look at the roots of the current calendar, and consider some of its consequences.

"School hours in the United States were developed during the 19th century, in part to allow students to help their families with farm work in the afternoon" (Orzag, 2012, para. 1). Thus, around the time mass schooling began, the school day was designed to accommodate the needs of families sustained by agriculture, needs that are no longer so widespread. Should the school day now be lengthened?

On the one hand, consider that many students participate in after-school sports, clubs, and other activities. No small number of full-time high school students also work; about 16% worked in 2010, although that is about a 50% decline from the 34% employed in 2000 (U.S. Bureau of Labor Statistics, 2011b). Homework loads, particularly at the high school level, may be substantial; a longer school day, unless it included more study time, might impede students' completion of homework. A longer school day would cost taxpayers more: "In 2008, the Center for American

■ **TABLE 11.1** Mandated School Days in Selected Countries, 2009

Country	Average Number of School Days Per Year
United States	180
England	190
France	180
Germany	198
Italy	200
Korea	220
Netherlands	200
Spain	200

SOURCE: International Review of Curriculum and Assessment Frameworks Internet Archive. (2009). Table 15.1: Organisation of school year.

· ·

De facto segregation: School segregation based on residential patterns or student choice, which persists even though legal segregation is now outlawed in the United States.

BEHIND THE NUMBERS

HOW MANY PEOPLE DROP OUT OF HIGH SCHOOL?

According to the National Center for Education Statistics (NCES), in 2009, 8% of U.S. students dropped out of high school. This statistic includes White students with a dropout rate of 5%, Black students with a dropout rate of 9%, Hispanic students with a dropout rate of over 17%, and Asian or Pacific Islander students with a dropout rate of more than 3%. These figures represent the *status dropout rate*, a figure measuring the percentage of 16- through 24-year-olds who are not enrolled in school and have not earned a high school credential, whether a high school diploma or a general equivalency degree (GED) of the civilian, noninstitutionalized population.

Here is another view of the picture. Data from the U.S. Census Bureau show that 3.1% of U.S. students dropped out of high school. Within this category, 3% of Whites dropped out, as well as more than 4% of Black and 5% of Hispanic students (U.S. Census Bureau, 2012). These data represent *event dropout rates*, or the percentage of 10th to 12th graders who dropped out in a single year without completing high school.

High school dropout rates can also be measured with the cohort dropout rate, which measures the outcomes for a single group (cohort) of students over a period of time. For example, a cohort dropout rate might measure the percentage of ninth graders in New York City who are reported as dropouts four years later (having left high school without completing a degree). This measure yields, predictably, the largest dropout rate of the three, because it is stretched across a longer time span. The cohort dropout rate, unlike the status

dropout rate, generally does not count GED credentials as high school completion.

When we read press articles or hear public discussions of the dropout phenomenon in the United States, we are rarely given the source or measurement instrument of the statistics. For example, a *New York Times* article on the cost of dropouts to the U.S. economy notes that "only 7 of 10 ninth graders today will get high school diplomas . . . about 80 percent of white and Asian students graduate from high school, compared with only 55 percent of blacks and Hispanics" (Levin & Rouse, 2012). It is unclear from these figures which of the dropout measures are used or how "dropouts" were defined.

Further, as with poverty and unemployment figures, the institutionalized (imprisoned) population is excluded from most calculations of dropouts. In 1980, the status dropout rate for African Americans in the NCES measure was 19.1%. In 2009, it was 9.3%, a significant decline. On the one hand, this represents more robust efforts on the part of schools to reduce rates of early school leaving and greater educational gains for African Americans overall. On the other hand, it also represents a measurement issue. Because the proportion of African American men who are in prison and are high school dropouts

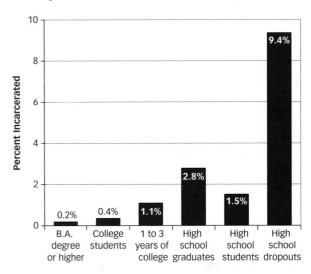

■ FIGURE 11.5 Percent of Incarcerated U.S. Males Aged 16–24 by Educational Attainment, 2006–2007

SOURCE: Sum, A., Khatiwada, I., & McLaughlin, J. (2009). The consequences of dropping out of high school: Joblessness and jailing for high school dropouts and the high cost for taxpayers. *Center for Labor Market Studies Publications,* Paper 23. Retrieved from http://hdl.handle.net/2047/d20000596

is high (see Figure 11.5), the failure to include them gives us a potentially incomplete picture.

It is important for us to be critical consumers of information and to pay attention not only to what is being measured, but also to *how* it is measured, what a statistic illuminates and obscures, and how figures are used in the press and public discourse.

THINK IT THROUGH

■ *Use the search engine of a major national newspaper or other news source to search for the term* high school dropout rates. *You may want to include the name of a state or city in your search as well. Examine what you find. Do the data you find indicate how they were collected? Why is it important to know this?*

Progress estimated that expanding learning time by 30 percent—or adding between 90 minutes and two hours to the school day—would add 6 to 20 percent to school budgets" (Orzag, 2012).

On the other hand, a longer school day has been shown to correlate with academic gains (Dobbie & Fryer, 2011), suggesting one avenue for raising achievement levels as the United States works to build a competitive workforce for the future. As well, about 15 million children, including some as young as 5 years of age, are currently unsupervised by an adult after school (Orzag, 2012). The opportunity to stay longer in a safe learning environment may benefit children who might otherwise have little to do. It might even reduce crime. According to the Office of Juvenile Justice and Delinquency Prevention (2010), most violent juvenile crimes occur in the hours after school. As sociologists we are always aware that correlation is not causation, but this relationship bears close examination. While some of the young people getting into trouble in these hours are dropouts who would not be affected by a longer school day, some offenders and victims are also full-time students.

What about lengthening the school year? In the early part of the 19th century, schoolchildren attended school mostly in the winter and summer, so they could participate in spring and fall planting and harvest seasons (Gold, 2002). By the middle to late 19th century, the average school calendar stretched across those seasons, but summer classes had largely been eliminated—not to accommodate agriculture as is commonly believed, but rather to respond to the desires of a socioeconomic elite for holidays and a break from mental work. In the early 20th century, a time of high immigration from Europe, some "vacation schools" arose in cities to "decongest and decriminalize crowded neighborhoods, assimilate immigrant children, and provide practical skills" (Gold, 2002, p. 5). Later these were replaced by summer schools, the purpose of which was largely to serve those who had fallen behind in school.

Is it time to return to summertime education? Some contend that it would be costly in a time of shrinking budgets. And, as in the middle and late 19th century, the now much larger middle and upper classes might object to a school year that impinges on their holiday calendar.

On the other hand, some research suggests that children may lose up to two months of acquired grade-level skills in math computation skills over the course of the summer. The same study (Cooper, Nye, Charlton, Lindsay, & Greathouse, 1996) found that low-income children, who are about two and a half years behind their better-off peers by Grade 5, also lose the equivalent of two months of reading achievement. A study conducted in Baltimore suggests that about two thirds of the reading achievement gap between ninth graders in lower- and higher-income groups is traceable to differences in summer experiences. Compounding this effect, differences in summer learning activities during elementary school may have an impact on whether a child graduates from high school and matriculates in college (K. Alexander, Entwistle, & Olson, 2007). While many middle- and upper-income students have the opportunity for enriching camp, holiday, and educational experiences in the summer—and middle-class children make small gains in reading achievement during these months—low-income children whose parents may not have the time or resources to offer these advantages are particularly susceptible to what educators term "summer slide," the loss of knowledge and skills gained during the school year.

Should the school day or year be lengthened to serve the new economy, young people, poor families, or other groups? Or should the United States continue to use the model that has been in place for over a century?

EDUCATION, INCOME, AND POVERTY

What is the relationship between education and income? There is a powerful correlation, with greater education generally leading to a higher level of income. For example, in 2011, the mean earnings of a high school graduate were just over $33,000, while for a bachelor's degree holder, they were over $54,000. For those who did not complete high school, mean earnings were just $23,452 (U.S. Bureau of Labor Statistics, 2012).

The relationship between education and income opportunities and prospects has grown in significance as the labor market in the United States has shifted from an industrial to a postindustrial labor market. In the former, positions with solid incomes and security were available in manufacturing for those with a high school education (or less). In particular, men with less education had an opportunity to earn a living wage and advance their economic position over time. In contrast, the postindustrial economy has increased the number of jobs for those with high levels of skill and training, and jobs in the service sector for those with less education. However, service jobs including retail sales, child and elder care, and restaurant jobs fail to provide the standard of living that many manufacturing jobs, particularly those in unionized sectors, once offered. As a result, the income advantage of those with higher education and the relative and absolute disadvantages of those with less education have grown markedly.

The correlation between education and income, and between education and wealth, can be further linked to labor force participation. That is, those with higher incomes are more likely to participate in the paid labor force. U.S. Census data show that in 2010, the labor force participation rate for those without a high school diploma was 46%, while for high school graduates it was over 61% and for college graduates over 76%. The lowest rate of labor force participation was found among African Americans who had not completed high school—just under 39%—while the highest rates were for Hispanic college graduates at almost 82% (U.S. Census Bureau, 2012).

Clearly, low income and poverty are powerfully linked to the lack of human capital among those who have not completed a high school or college education. Are they thus the product of an individual's failure to invest in himself or herself by ambitiously pursuing an education? The sociological imagination suggests a more complex relationship: To paraphrase C. Wright Mills, if in a country of 300 million, only a handful of men or women are poor or undereducated, "we properly look to the character of the man [*sic*], his skills, and his immediate opportunities." But when in a nation of 300 million inhabitants, more than 15%—over 46 million people—are poor and millions have not achieved a high school education (see the box *Behind the Numbers on page 277* in this chapter), we may not hope to find the explanation or solution in the choices, character, or behavior of any given individual. "Both the correct statement of the problem and the range of possible solutions require us to consider the economic and political institutions of the society, and not merely the personal situation and character of a scatter of individuals" (Mills, 1959/2000b, p. 9).

To appreciate the sociological linkages between education and low income or poverty, we need to look not only at the well-established relationship between education and income, but also at factors that affect educational attainment.

We should understand educational attainment as the product of both *agency* and *structure*. Individuals have agency. That is, they make choices about pursuing schooling, sacrificing immediate income for deferred income, or investing time and money in an education. On the other hand, the choices they make are based on the opportunities available to them, and those from more privileged backgrounds typically have more opportunities for good-quality schooling from preschool through college. A higher family income raises the likelihood of finishing high school and, as we will see later in the chapter, college.

The sociological imagination would lead us to conclude that in order to understand the linkage between income and education, we need to look beyond the simple relationship between educational attainment and income level and examine the way socioeconomic status itself influences the level of education an individual achieves, which then further influences income in a cycle that can be challenging to break.

ISSUES IN U.S. HIGHER EDUCATION

In the United States today, nearly three quarters (about 70%) of high school graduates continue on to higher education. The value and even the necessity of higher education in the modern world and economy are common themes in both educational and political discourse. The good jobs of the future, we have been told, will require higher education. Below we look at the general issue of college and income, examining the relationship of education to income today. We continue with an examination of the college internship, a growing phenomenon that has invited both praise and critique. We end with a closer discussion of the topic raised in the opening vignette—that is, the college dropout phenomenon, its dimensions, and its probable causes and possible cures.

■ **FIGURE 11.6** Earnings and Employment by Educational Attainment in the U.S., 2011

SOURCE: U.S. Bureau of Labor Statistics. (2013). *Employment projections: Education pays.* U.S. Department of Labor. Retrieved from http://www.bls.gov/emp/ep_chart_001.htm

COLLEGE AND INCOME

Figure 11.6, published on the U.S. Bureau of Labor Statistics website in 2013, originally appeared under the title "Education Pays." In examining the chart, we see a clear and unequivocal correlation between educational attainment and income, and between educational attainment and vulnerability to unemployment. We've seen in other chapters that educational attainment has grown in importance in the postindustrial era, as the living-wage jobs of the industrial era in sectors such as automobile manufacturing, steel, and textiles have fallen victim to outsourcing and automation. What remains as the foundation of the U.S. economy are advanced professional occupations, which require higher education and often even a graduate degree, and service jobs, which are often part-time, low-pay, and low-benefit positions in sectors such as child and elder care, retail, and hospitality. While some manufacturing has continued to be sited in the United States, new manufacturing jobs are far less likely to be unionized, more likely to be on a shorter-term contract, and characterized by a lower pay scale than similar jobs in the past (see Chapter 14). And a substantial number demand proficiency with high-technology equipment, which may require either college education or other advanced training beyond high school. In this economic environment, education does, indeed, appear to pay—handsomely so.

Yet while college graduates today are still, as a group, outearning their peers with less education, their own income prospects have diminished somewhat in comparison to those of earlier graduates. As Figure 11.7 on page 280 shows, entry-level wages of graduates have dropped from the peak reached at the turn of the millennium, reflecting a larger trend in slowing or stagnating wage growth. In spite of their higher graduation rates, women continue to lag behind their male counterparts. As we will see in the next section of this chapter, some entry-level jobs

College Online   For-Profit Schools

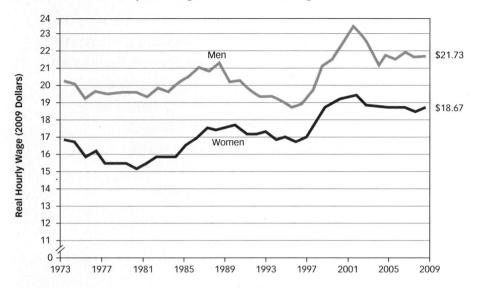

SOURCE: Economic Policy Institute. (2011). New college grads losing ground on wages. *Economic Snapshot—Education.*

have evolved into unpaid internships, rendering the first step on the career ladder more tenuous for new graduates.

At the same time that wages have turned downward, the student debt burden has continued to grow. It is particularly likely to be carried by minority students, more of whom come from homes with lower incomes. For instance, data from the 2007–2008 academic year (prior to the economic recession, when debts continued to balloon) show that a substantial percentage of minority students carry heavy educational debt, defined here as $30,500 or more at graduation. Among bachelor's graduates, 27% of Black students, 16% of White students, 14% of Hispanic students, and 9% of Asian students had heavy educational debt (A. Austin, 2010). Debt presents a substantial challenge to students as they begin their careers.

At the same time, the assertion that "education pays," which headlined the Bureau of Labor Statistics figure, remains essentially correct, particularly in light of the U.S. Department of Labor's projections about the direction of the U.S. economy. A report published in 2005 on growth sectors in the labor market notes that

> professional and related occupations and service occupations . . . which are on opposite ends of the educational attainment and earnings spectrum, are expected to provide about 60 percent of the total job growth from 2004 to 2014. (Hecker, 2005, p. 71)

While both income and debt are critical concerns for students, their families, and the economy as a whole, educational

Affordable Online Education

attainment will continue to grow in importance as a pathway to a professional career and higher earning potential.

INTERNSHIPS AND HIGHER EDUCATION

Thousands of U.S. college students build their résumés and job experience with unpaid internships, which have become a staple of summer or a part of a regular academic year for students living in cities such as Washington, DC, or New York, where opportunities are abundant to work in politics, the fashion industry, public relations, and the like. Many universities require students to complete an internship to earn credit toward a major or graduation. More students than ever are also working in unpaid internships *after* graduation, having been unable to secure a paid entry-level position even with a degree. Critics, however, are raising questions about the legality and morality of employing young people, sometimes full time, without paying them a wage or salary. While some internships offer stipends or pay, most do not.

What are some of the benefits to students of unpaid internships? Both students and their universities often believe internships are a vital component of building human capital in preparation for the world of paid and professional work. Universities have an interest in helping students work outside of campus on activities that can build their knowledge base, and students have an interest in developing skills and social networks that will help them find good jobs after graduation. Many look forward with excitement to the possibility of working with their U.S. representative in Congress, a lawyer, a public relations specialist, a fashion designer, or a favorite nonprofit. For many students, the internship experience is a positive one.

The U.S. Department of Labor Wage and Hour Division (2010) recognizes legal internships as a means for preparing interns for work and has a set of six criteria that most public and private institutions must meet:

- The internship, even though it includes actual operation of the facilities of the employer, is similar to training that would be given in an educational environment.
- The internship experience is for the benefit of the intern.
- The intern does not displace regular employees, but works under close supervision of existing staff.
- The employer that provides the training derives no immediate advantage from the activities of the intern, and on occasion its operations may actually be impeded.
- The intern is not necessarily entitled to a job at the conclusion of the internship.
- The employer and the intern understand that the intern is not entitled to wages for the time spent in the internship.

There is room for interpretation on multiple points. For instance, can we clearly determine whether an employer "derives no immediate advantage from the activities of the intern"? Or that no "regular employees" have been "displaced"?

Another way of looking at internships is to ask how an arrangement intended by law to benefit students and other prospective workers may benefit other entities—perhaps even to the detriment of the intern (Perlin, 2011). Among the points Perlin raises are the following: Universities benefit from mandating student internships for credit, because students are thereby required to pay tuition dollars for an experience that—unlike the classroom experience—costs the university comparably little. And the employer is effectively provided with the services of an often educated and enthusiastic worker—for no pay. Perlin argues that a range of institutions and employers thus exploit the services of young workers for their own economic advantage, in the fashion and finance industries, in politics, and in the nonprofit world.

Who loses in this equation? Perlin (2012) and Eisenbrey (2012) suggest that lower-income students are losers in the internship game. That is, while students from better-off families can afford (at least for a while) to work for nothing in order to secure human and social capital, poor and working-class students need, instead, to work for pay, even if it's in a field unrelated to their area of career interest. Perlin argues that, "Lucrative and influential professions—politics, media and entertainment, to name a few—now virtually require a period of unpaid work, effectively barring young people from less privileged backgrounds" (Perlin, 2012). All students, however, are potentially disadvantaged where jobs that once were or might otherwise have been entry-level jobs are reinvented as unpaid internships, undermining an economically and professionally important stepping-stone for students leaving school with a degree.

There are even broader effects of the internship boom: constricted social and professional mobility, growing inequality, and an economy whose top tier is becoming less and less diverse. Even more seriously, a fundamental ethic in American life is under threat: the idea that a hard day's work demands a fair wage (Perlin, 2011, 2012).

What, then, are we to conclude about internships today, a growing and pervasive phenomenon that will be part of the experience of thousands of students this year and in years to come? It is clear that students benefit from spending time in a professional market that values both formal educational credentials and hands-on work experience. Universities benefit from giving their students opportunities to link classroom learning to experiential learning. And employers benefit from the creativity, skills, and enthusiasm

As an undergraduate student, you may have the opportunity to do an unpaid internship. Interns provide public and private organizations with important yet unpaid labor, while students benefit from getting work experience. ■

of young workers. On the other hand, it remains important that benefits should not accrue disproportionately to the parties with the most power—universities and employers—to the detriment of students. How can students, their schools, and the law ensure opportunity and contribute to making internships meaningful work experiences that provide a foundation for a career? What do you think?

DROPPING IN, DROPPING OUT: WHY ARE COLLEGE DROPOUT RATES SO HIGH?

We began this chapter by looking at the phenomenon of college dropouts, noting that the United States has been tremendously successful in ensuring that a high proportion of high school completers—fully 70%—enroll in higher education. Statistics suggest, however, that many who enroll in college never finish with a degree, though many end their college careers with substantial debt.

College attainment levels have remained flat for generations (Lewin, 2011). A little more than half of those enrolled in four-year institutions go on to graduate, while fewer than half of those enrolled in a two-year institution graduate (Figure 11.8 on page 282). Recent data show that the average graduation rate for 1,575 four-year colleges nationwide was just over 57% (for completion in 6 years), with public colleges at 56% and private colleges at 65%. Figures for two-year institutions are even lower (Collegemeasures.org, 2013). Dropouts can be costly, both to the nation as a whole, which loses potentially educated and productive workers, and to individuals,

The costs of college are a substantial obstacle for many prospective and current students. What can be done to ease this burden on students? ■

accelerated programs that speed the time to degree with rigorous work offered in concentrated time periods (Lewin, 2011).

Many students find it challenging to balance the rigors of school and work. According to Complete College America, the majority of community college students work over 20 hours per week, and a substantial proportion also take care of families. While attending college part-time seems like a viable solution, in fact it substantially lowers the chance that students will ever earn a degree. Only about a quarter of students today fit the stereotypical model of full-time, on-campus students supported largely by their parents.

According to the Organisation for Economic Co-operation and Development (2011), the United States ranks 16th in the percentage of young adults with a college degree (Table 11.2 on page 284). At one time, it topped the list. While everyone may not desire or even need a college degree, the competitive global economic environment has put a premium value on higher education, which offers greater security from unemployment and greater earning potential than a high school credential alone. Understanding why students drop out is the first step to addressing this problem effectively.

Are there other factors you see as important in explaining the high number of U.S. students who leave college without a degree? What should students do to address the problem? What should schools do?

whose earning potential is diminished by the failure to finish a degree.

So what is behind the college dropout phenomenon? Several factors contribute. First, high college costs drive many students out of higher education. A four-year private college education tripled in cost from 1980 to 2010—student loan debt for new bachelor's degree graduates now averages about $23,000 (Carlozo, 2012). Costs are a particularly acute issue for low-income students, who are more likely to drop out than their better-off peers. The financial burden of a college education falls more heavily on those with fewer resources, often even when some grant money is available. As well, low-income students are more likely to attend colleges that "excel in producing dropouts" (Leonhardt, 2009).

Second, the rigors of college work lead some students to drop out. This factor is complex. Some students who enroll in college may indeed be unready for the workload or the level of work. Half of students in associate's degree programs and about a fifth of those in bachelor's programs are required by their institutions to enroll in remedial classes to address academic shortcomings. Some of these courses do not confer college credit, lengthening the time needed to earn a degree and increasing the likelihood that a student will leave without completing college. Advocates for students suggest that colleges can do more to help students stay and succeed with coaching, scheduling that meets the needs of working students, and

■ FIGURE 11.8 U.S. Graduation Rates by Race and Ethnicity, 2009

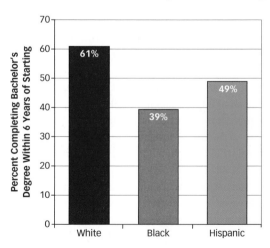

SOURCE: National Center for Education Statistics. (2011). Table 345: Graduation rates of first-time postsecondary students who started as full-time degree/certificate-seeking students, by sex, race/ethnicity, time to completion, and level and control of institution where student started: Selected cohort entry years, 1996 through 2007. *Digest of Education Statistics*.

Cost of a Degree

Future of Public Universities

MCDONALDIZATION AND EDUCATION

Sociologist George Ritzer (2010b) writes that the life experiences of U.S. adults (and a growing number of others across the globe) are influenced from cradle to grave by *McDonaldized institutions*. These institutions have absorbed and put in to practice the key characteristics of the fast-food restaurant: efficiency, calculability (a focus on the quantifiable aspects of what they sell), predictability, and the control of humans by nonhuman technologies. Ritzer follows classical sociologist Max Weber's argument on formal rationality in suggesting that society, including education, is becoming more "formally rationalized," but that while this rationalization serves the profit motive of capitalism well, it does not necessarily serve the individuals who are dehumanized by processes that quantify, control, and "cage" them in a web of rationalized structures.

From preschool to the university level, say Ritzer and others (Hayes & Wynyard, 2002), the experience of education is permeated by the principles of the fast-food restaurant. At the preschool level, Ritzer argues, early education is dominated by child care chains such as KinderCare, which tends to hire short-term employees whose work in the classroom is governed by an "instruction book" that lays out detailed activities for each day, creating an environment that, for better or worse, is predictable from center to center. Individual interpretation and innovation are not encouraged.

Can we also say that higher education is McDonaldized? Ritzer (2010b) writes that "most courses run for a standard number of weeks and hours per week . . . little attention is devoted to determining whether a given subject is best taught in a given number of weeks or hours per week. The focus seems to be on how many students ('products') can be herded through the system and what grades they earn rather than the quality of what they have learned and of the educational experience" (p. 84). Both before and after college, students take standardized examinations with quantifiable results, such as the PSAT, SAT, and GRE. An entire high school or college experience can be summed up in a single number, the grade point average (GPA). Think about your experience at college or university. What aspects of it would you say are McDonaldized?

The growth of online education is another avenue of interest for those who are concerned about the McDonaldization of higher education. According to the National Center for Education Statistics (2011a), in 2007–2008, about a fifth of U.S. students took some kind of distance learning course. The number taking a full program online was smaller—just 3.7%—but rising. As of 2011, the rate of enrollment growth of online programs (10%) was far exceeding the growth rate of enrollment in all higher education (2%; Babson Survey Research Group and College Board, 2011).

A key benefit of online programs is that students who work or are not able to attend classroom lectures can now be part of an active learning community and earn credits toward the completion of a degree. On the other hand, online learning may reduce the "inefficient" human contact that many students and instructors value in education, including debates and discussions, in-class activities such as role-playing, and personal mentoring and encouragement. The collective aspects and pleasures of learning in a course are replaced in some cases by dozens or hundreds of students alone with their computers.

THINK IT THROUGH

■ *Ritzer argues that we are seeing a "dehumanization of education" today. Do you agree with this assertion? How is technology changing education in both positive and negative ways?*

EDUCATION IN A GLOBAL PERSPECTIVE

Education brings gains to individuals, communities, and countries. Today, more people than ever are literate, attending and completing institutions of higher education, and sharing knowledge globally across new communication platforms. It is not unusual for a U.S. classroom to have a partner across the globe so students can "meet" other students through the Internet, sharing interests and ideas. Nor is it unusual to meet U.S. students abroad who are studying for credit and seeing places they might only have read about in books. Education

"Smart classrooms" offer media capabilities, conferencing options, recording, and other technologies that supplement and may even replace traditional lecture-style learning. Some instructors use new technology to link their students with other students across the globe. ■

has the potential to bring people and cultures together to foster greater understanding, innovation, and prosperity. In this section, we take a look at how the United States lines up with its global peers in areas including education, and at what some of its own students are doing in their studies across the planet.

HIGHER EDUCATION AND JOB OPPORTUNITIES

The Organisation for Economic Co-operation and Development (OECD) was formed in 1960 with 18 European member states, the United States, and Canada. Today, it has 34 members across the globe and includes countries as geographically, culturally, and economically diverse as Mexico and Turkey. Its goal is to both foster and track economic and policy development and changes in member states. Among the important data the OECD collects on a regular basis is information about higher education and employment. From this, we can get a basic picture of where the United States falls in relation to other member states in the achievement of educational credentials and the fortunes of its graduates.

In the 34 OECD states, though they include both highly developed states such as the United States and Germany and developing countries such as Mexico and Chile, the correlations we've observed among educational attainment, income, and labor market prospects hold true. The global economic crisis that began in 2008 hit many member countries hard, and unemployment grew in every one. The most heavily affected workers were adults without

post–high school education, whose unemployment rates rose overall from nearly 9% to over 11%. For those with higher education, however, unemployment rates grew only one percentage point between 2008 and 2009 and stayed below 5% in most countries through 2009 (Spain and Turkey were the most notable exceptions). No less important, those with higher education continued to enjoy substantially higher wages than their peers with less education. Clearly, then, education matters across the globe (OECD, 2011).

U.S. STUDENTS MEET THE WORLD

For many U.S. students, the world beckons. Seized by curiosity to see and experience the world outside home, campus, and work, they are taking advantage of a small but growing number of college study-abroad programs (Table 11.3 on page 286). In the academic year 2009–2010, more than 260,000 U.S. students studied abroad for credit, a small increase from the previous year and part of a rising trend. The top destinations have remained largely steady over time and include the United Kingdom, France, Spain, and Italy. In the 2009–2010 academic year, however, almost 14,000 students went to China, compared to just 3,000 a decade earlier. Other destinations that are growing in popularity are India, Israel, Brazil, and New Zealand (Institute of International Education, 2010).

■ **TABLE 11.2** Percentage of Young Adults 25–34 With a College Degree for Selected Countries, 2009

Rank	Country	Percentages
1	Korea	63%
2	Canada	56%
3	Japan	56%
4	Russia	55%
5	Ireland	48%
6	Norway	47%
7	New Zealand	47%
8	Luxembourg	44%
9	United Kingdom	45%
10	Australia	45%
16	United States	41%

SOURCE: Organisation for Economic Co-operation and Development. (2011). Percentage of population that has attained tertiary education, by age group (2009).

Underground College in Iran

Changing Educational Paradigms

Higher Education and Global Issues

MAKING A LINK BETWEEN EDUCATION AND HIV/AIDS IN SUB-SAHARAN AFRICA

What is the connection between HIV/AIDS and education in sub-Saharan Africa? The state of education in countries including Zimbabwe, Zambia, Kenya, Malawi, and Uganda has been significantly affected by the dramatic pandemic of HIV/AIDS in the region: According to United Nations data, the proportion of teachers infected with HIV/AIDS surpasses 20% in parts of Malawi and South Africa and 13% in Zambia (UNAIDS, 2010b). In 2006, there was a shortage of over 45,000 teachers in Tanzania because so many had either died or left the profession because of HIV/AIDS. A recent study in South Africa found that 21% of teachers aged 24–34 were living with HIV/AIDS (UNAIDS, 2006).

In the country of Botswana, over one quarter of the population is infected. According to Avert.org (2010), one of the world's leading HIV/AIDS prevention organizations, an estimated 22.5 million people there have HIV/AIDS. In South Africa alone, more than 5.6 million people are living with the disease (Avert.org, 2010). A substantial share of those infected are adults in their working and child-rearing years, and, significantly for communities, families, and schools, the majority are women. Their incapacitating illnesses and deaths leave behind motherless children and, because most teachers are female, schoolchildren without instruction.

Imagine that 1 out of every 5 teachers in your country was HIV positive. This loss of educators results in overcrowded classrooms and a lack of personnel and talent that could be used to educate the next generation of workers and leaders. ■

Clearly, the loss of educators has a powerful impact on developing economies with a need for more educated workforces, and the loss of teachers is only part of the larger tragedy of HIV/AIDS in sub-Saharan Africa. But not only is the blow to schooling part of the general devastation wrought by the widespread deaths of individuals in their productive years; each death also diminishes the opportunities for members of the next generation to achieve the education they will need to replace the depleted workforce and push forward toward greater prosperity. While the link between the HIV/AIDS pandemic and educational opportunities and institutions in developing countries may not be immediately visible, the discipline of sociology trains us to look beneath the surface to see the myriad ways in which changes or problems in one part of the social system lead to sometimes unexpected changes and problems in other parts.

THINK IT THROUGH

■ *What kinds of creative solutions might both the international and local communities design to address this shortage of educators? Can technology be part of a solution that both addresses HIV/AIDS prevention needs and the need to educate a new generation?*

Any study-abroad experience holds the potential for culture shock, especially venturing to new destinations with cultures quite divergent from those of the mainstream United States. Clearly, though, many students are excited to embrace this possibility. More U.S. students are spending their junior year abroad in places about which they knew little before coming to college, for example, the American University in Cairo or Ibadan University in Nigeria: "These students visit places

Rank	Country
1	United Kingdom
2	Italy
3	Spain
4	France
5	China
6	Australia
7	Germany
8	Mexico
9	Ireland
10	Costa Rica
11	Japan
12	Argentina
13	South Africa
14	India
15	Greece

SOURCE: Data from Institute of International Education (2012). "Study Abroad by U.S. Students Slowed in 2008/09 with More Students Going to Less Traditional Destinations." *Press Release.*

most Americans know only through news reports—the West Bank, Ethiopia and even northern Iraq" (Conlin, 2010).

Part of this growth of academic interest in the Middle East in particular is driven by the availability of new Critical Language Scholarships, created in 2006 by the U.S. Department of State to facilitate the study of languages including Arabic, Pashto, Dari, Azerbaijani, and Punjabi—not the languages available in most U.S. high schools or colleges. Some students desire to be part of the political discourse, study public diplomacy, and witness the potential for change in a tumultuous region of the world. Others want to work in nongovernmental organizations or with the American Foreign Service (Conlin, 2010).

Whether the study-abroad experience takes them to London, Beijing, Beirut, Rio de Janeiro, or Cairo, many students say

Global Achievement Gap

World Poverty and Education

their worldview is forever transformed by the opportunity to live in places they might otherwise know only from books or television. As one student said, "I will never again look at a story about the Middle East with such a one-sided perspective." Another added, "I genuinely enjoyed watching the bottom fall out of every one of my preconceived ideas about the Muslim world" (Conlin, 2010).

WHY STUDY EDUCATION FROM A SOCIOLOGICAL PERSPECTIVE?

Education opens up the world to us. Through education, we have the opportunity to gain new perspectives, to develop a critical approach to problems and the skills to imagine solutions, and to understand other people, cultures, and communities more fully. In an increasingly interdependent and interconnected world, this is a powerful advantage. Opportunities for education are not equally distributed, however, and, as we have seen in this chapter, factors such as socioeconomic status and race are among those that can fundamentally affect access to a good education. This matters because talent that remains unnurtured cannot better individual lives or the life of the community and country.

Sociology helps us look critically at issues such as educational inequality and understand the roots of this problem. It is common in the United States to say that "education is the great equalizer," and, while that goal is certainly possible, it cannot be realized when zip codes determine the quality of schooling, or when low expectations and inadequate resources in poor communities lead to poor educational outcomes. Education may then reproduce rather than reduce inequalities.

Sociology also entreats us to use our sociological imaginations to ask questions about the intersection between personal troubles and public issues. If, for instance, a student is experiencing difficulties balancing work and school, or having trouble financing his or her education, we can easily see this as a *personal trouble*. Recognizing it as part of the larger problem of a substantial proportion of U.S. college enrollees not graduating, however, we begin to see the outlines of a *public issue,* one that cannot be explained by the circumstances of a single case or a dozen cases. In both its causes and consequences, failure to graduate is an authentic public issue, and addressing it requires a critical ability to root out its sociological antecedents. A sociological education in particular helps us gain perspective on the factors that make education increasingly vital today, and those that create obstacles to or opportunities for its attainment.

WHAT CAN I DO WITH A SOCIOLOGY DEGREE?

CAREER DEVELOPMENT: CONSIDERING GRADUATE AND PROFESSIONAL EDUCATION, PART I

According to data published by the American Sociological Association (ASA), 18 months after graduation, about 35% of students who participated in a postgraduation survey were enrolled in graduate or professional schools. The decision to pursue a graduate or professional degree is a significant commitment of time, resources, and energy, and will impact your career options and opportunities. In this chapter, we looked broadly at education through a sociological lens. One of the terms with which you became familiar is *credential society*. We do, in fact, live in a credential society, and in the contemporary world of work, your credentials—specifically, the higher education degree or degrees you earn—will have a big impact on your path to a career. For some students, that path may lead through graduate or professional school.

To consider graduate or professional school, *examine your motivations, assess your career choices, research graduate schools and degree options, and reflect on practical challenges and how you will meet them.* In this chapter feature, we focus on the examination of motivations and assessment of career choices. In the next chapter feature, we turn our attention to researching graduate and professional schools and reflecting on opportunities and challenges.

EXAMINE YOUR MOTIVATIONS

Some students know from an early age that academic study at the advanced level is their goal—aspiring physicians, lawyers, or college professors, for instance, need to plan to continue their studies after earning a bachelor's degree. Other students develop a new interest in an academic or professional area as undergraduates and then decide to stay in school for a second or third degree. Still others know that graduate or professional school may be in their future, but prefer to explore occupational opportunities rather than attending immediately. All options have advantages and disadvantages, but *the best is the one that is best for you.* Take time to reflect on your motivations for graduate or professional study.

Students have various reasons for continuing their education immediately following completion of a bachelor's degree:

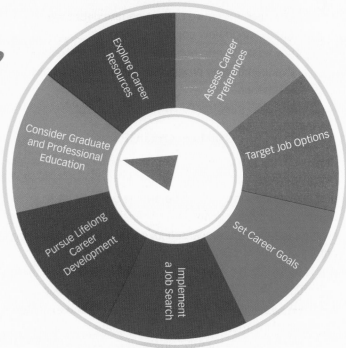

- The effective study skills they have mastered as undergraduates will apply to rigors of graduate or professional school.
- They are motivated now and think they may not return to school later.
- They have few or no family and financial commitments that might prevent them from attending.
- The economy and labor market are challenging, but may improve in a few years.
- They enjoy and succeed in academic settings.
- They lack clarity about pursuing professional opportunities immediately or are anxious about career interests and goals.
- Their desired occupational field or job requires a graduate degree or professional degree for entry-level positions.

Students also consider reasons to postpone graduate school upon completing their bachelor's degree:

- They want to gain work experience to better determine career options.
- Their desired study program requires some employment experience in a professional setting.
- They plan to explore nonacademic options and gain work experience.
- They hope to target employers who will support graduate or professional school expenses.

- They need to reduce undergraduate debt before embarking on new commitments.
- They would like to enhance their application for an advanced degree program with additional accomplishments.

ASSESS YOUR CAREER CHOICES

In considering graduate or professional school, examine your skills, interests, and values to identify likely career options and explore opportunities to determine a career path. *Develop your career goals prior to considering or committing to graduate or professional school so that further education enhances your future and career plans.* One way to do this is to research careers and occupations to determine educational requirements, labor market trends, possible employers, regional employment information, and expected compensation. Another step is to participate in internships as an undergraduate, or following graduation, to gather firsthand knowledge about an organization or profession. You might also test career information by visiting potential employers, speaking to professionals, and networking with alumni to determine which career best fits your aspirations and life goals.

The core knowledge and diverse skills that you acquire as a sociology major prepare you for the rigors of graduate or professional school by helping you develop competencies in research, writing, communication, and critical thinking, among others. If you think that graduate or professional school might be in your future, look at the next chapter's feature to learn about types of degree programs that may fit your aspirations and to explore opportunities and challenges in advanced study.

THINK ABOUT CAREERS:

■ *Have you considered graduate or professional studies?*

■ *Are you interested in testing out professional opportunities before going on to graduate or professional school, or does your desired career choice require further credentials for an entry-level position?*

■ *What would be the advantages and disadvantages for you of choosing to further your studies after earning a bachelor's degree?*

▶ *Access additional web links on the student study site to learn more.*

SUMMARY

To test your knowledge further, find additional study material on the Student Study Site at **www.sagepub.com/chamblissintro**

- **Education** refers to the transmission of society's norms, values, and knowledge base by means of direct instruction.

- **Mass education** spread with industrialization and the need for widespread **literacy**. Today the need is not just for literacy but for specialized training as well. All industrial societies today, including the United States, have a system of **public education** that continues through the high school and frequently university levels. Such societies are sometimes termed **credential societies**, in that access to desirable jobs and social status depends on the possession of a certificate or diploma.

- Functionalist theories of education emphasize the role of the school in serving the needs of society by socializing students and filling positions in the social order, while conflict theories emphasize its role in reproducing rather than reducing social inequality.

- Symbolic interactionist theory, by focusing on the classroom itself, reveals how teachers' perceptions of students—as well as students' self-perceptions—are important in shaping the students' performance.

- Early literacy and later educational attainment are powerfully correlated. Access to books and early reading experiences are among the strongest predictors of basic literacy at an early age. Researchers measure multiple levels of literacy.

- U.S. public schools are highly segregated by race and ethnicity. Before the 1954 U.S. Supreme Court decision in *Brown v. Board of Education,* segregation was legal.

Since that time, schools have continued to show **de facto segregation**, because segregated residential patterns still exist, because many White parents decide to send their children to private schools, and because the courts have recently limited the scope of previous laws aimed at promoting full integration.

- The issues of extending the school day and school year have long been on the educational agenda. The roots of today's calendar help us to understand its evolution and to consider its differential effects on children from different socioeconomic classes.

- Differences in school funding by race, ethnicity, and class reinforce existing patterns of social inequality. In general, the higher someone's social class, the more likely he or she is to complete high school and college. On the other hand, low-income people are often trapped in a cycle of low educational attainment and poverty.

- There is a strong demonstrable relationship between educational attainment, employment prospects, and income. There is also a correlation between the socioeconomic status of a family and the probability of its members' further educational attainment.

- Both the utility and the legality of college internships have become hotly debated. Internships may offer students substantial value in terms of experience, but critics say they also exploit students' labor and skills.

- U.S. college dropout rates are high, exceeding those of many other industrialized countries. Key reasons for dropping out include financial strain, lack of academic preparation, and difficulty balancing competing demands of school, work, and family.

- The correlation between educational attainment and income and employment opportunities holds around the globe.

- U.S. students are studying abroad more often and in more places than in the past. Interest in new destinations, including the Middle East, is opening the world to more young people.

KEY TERMS

Study terms on the go with the smartphone-friendly key term flashcards, available at **www.sagepub.com/chamblissintro**

education, 267

formal education, 267

mass education, 267

literacy, 267

public education, 268

credential society, 268

school segregation, 274

de facto segregation, 276

DISCUSSION QUESTIONS

1. In this chapter, we discussed the phenomenon of college dropouts. What are the primary reasons students drop out? How can identifying specific roots of the problem help us to develop effective policies to address the problem?

2. What historical factors help explain the organization of the modern school day? Should the school day be reorganized to meet new societal needs? What might such a new school day look like?

3. What is the role of internships in higher education today? Who benefits from the growth in students' working in internships? How can internships be structured to maximize student knowledge and employability?

DISCOVER ⌖ STATE STATS

Log-in to the eBook and click on the title to the left for access to State Stats in order to complete the exercise.

Use the Education database to find the averaged freshman graduation rate by state. Look at the most recent data available for three or four states, including your home state. Write a few hypotheses about the sociological roots of differences in graduation rates by state and by region, based on what you learned in the chapter.

STUDENT STUDY SITE

Visit the Student Study Site at **www.sagepub.com/chamblissintro** to access additional study tools, including eFlashcards, web quizzes, video resources, web resources, audio resources, links to SAGE journal, handbook, and research articles, and much more!

12

RELIGION AND SOCIETY

WHAT DO YOU THINK?

1. What is the societal function of religion in a multicultural country such as the United States?
2. Do most people in the United States choose a religion, or are they given a religion?
3. Is religion a source of stability or conflict on a global scale?

SOC**VIEW**

Get a closer look
with the authors!

I PLEDGE ALLEGIANCE...

I pledge allegiance to the flag of the United States of America
And to the Republic for which it stands,
One nation, under God, indivisible, with liberty and justice for all.

In 2004, the U.S. Supreme Court reversed an appeals court ruling that classroom recitation of the Pledge of Allegiance, with the words "under God," was unconstitutional. The basis of the high court's ruling, however, was specifically related to this case: The court argued that the petitioner, a California atheist, did not have standing to sue on behalf of his school-age daughter. The implication was that his daughter could have sued, but he could not sue for her. Thus, a legal question remains about the constitutionality of the pledge in a country with a constitutionally mandated separation of church and state (Pew Forum on Religion and Public Life, 2004).

Jay Sekulow, who filed an *amicus* ("friend of the court") brief on behalf of members of Congress and the Committee to Protect the Pledge, responded to the ruling saying, "By dismissing this case and removing the appeals court decision, the Supreme Court has removed a dark cloud that has been hanging over one of the nation's most important and cherished traditions—the ability of students across the nation to acknowledge the fact that our freedoms in this country come from God, not government" (Pew Forum on Religion and Public Life, 2004, para. 6).

Reverend Barry W. Lynn, executive director of Americans United for Separation of Church and State, suggested, "Students should not feel compelled by school officials to subscribe to a particular religious belief in order to show love of country. America is increasingly diverse in matters of religion, and our public schools should reflect that diversity" (Pew Forum on Religion and Public Life, 2004, para. 4).

The Pledge of Allegiance has been used in public life for over a century, but the phrase "under God" was added by Congress only in 1954. At that time the Solicitor General of the United States argued before the Supreme Court that "under God" is "descriptive" and "ceremonial," rather than a prayer or "religious invocation" (Pew Forum on Religion and Public Life, 2004, p. 1), suggesting that it embodies a civic rather than an overtly religious value.

The First Amendment in the Bill of Rights of the U.S. Constitution contains what is known as the **Disestablishment Clause**: That is, "Congress shall make no law respecting an establishment of religion, or prohibiting the free exercise thereof." How, then, should we interpret the inclusion of "one nation, under God"? What is the function of this brief but provocative phrase? Should we interpret it as *civic or religious*? Is it inclusive or exclusive? And more generally, what is the role of religion in a multicultural United States? ■

In this chapter, we examine the relationship between religion and society, beginning with a consideration of what religion is and what it does in human societies. We explore classical and contemporary theoretical perspectives on religion and society and examine the place of religion in people's private and public lives. We look at different types of religious organizations, as well as the great world religions. The chapter then explores issues of religion in the United States, including the rise of evangelicalism and the decline of religious affiliation among the young. We conclude by looking at global concerns of the sociology of religion.

HOW DO SOCIOLOGISTS STUDY RELIGION?

From a sociological perspective, we define a **religion** as a system of common beliefs and rituals centered on "sacred things" that unites believers and provides a sense of meaning and purpose (Durkheim, 2008). We often think of **theism**, *a belief in one or more supernatural deities*, as basic to religion (the term originates from the Greek word for god, *theos*), but there is no clear conceptual distinction between worship of a spiritual being and worship of an entity such as a nation. Indeed, we could see nationalism as a form of civic religion.

Sociologists look at religion in the context of society, asking about its role and function and identifying its basic social elements. First, religion is a form of culture. Recall from Chapter 3 that culture consists of *the shared beliefs, values, norms, ideas, institutions, and organizations that create a common identity among a group of people*. Religion embodies these characteristics, as it

. . . .

Disestablishment Clause: Part of the First Amendment in the Bill of Rights of the U.S. Constitution, which contains the passage "Congress shall make no law respecting an establishment of religion, or prohibiting the free exercise thereof."

Religion: A system of common beliefs and rituals centered on "sacred things" that unites believers and provides a sense of meaning and purpose.

Theism: A belief in one or more supernatural deities.

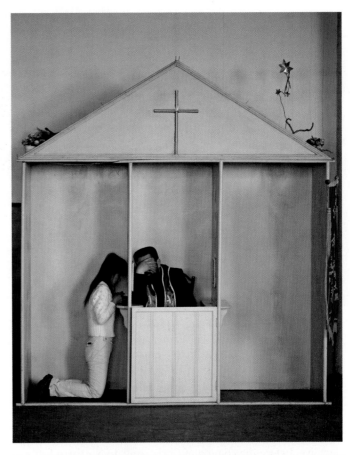

The practice of sacred rites is a characteristic of religions. Among the sacred rites of Catholicism (also called sacraments) is confession. The Church entreats members to cleanse themselves of sin by being contrite, confessing their sins to a member of the clergy, and not repeating their transgression. ■

is constituted by a common worldview that draws together those who identify with it.

Second, religion includes the ritualization and routinization of beliefs. All religions have a behavioral aspect: Adherents engage in practices that identify them as members of the group and create or affirm group bonds. Sociologist Émile Durkheim (2008) argued that religious rituals create and reinforce social cohesion. Robert Merton (1957) added to this idea, suggesting that while rituals have a manifest, or obvious, function, they also have the latent— secondary or unintentional—function of reinforcing group solidarity. The manifest function of the Hopi rain dance was to bring rain; its latent function was to strengthen community ties.

Third, religion provides a sense of purpose and meaning. Religions commonly tell a coherent and compelling story about the forces that transcend everyday life, in ways that other aspects of culture such as a belief in democracy typically cannot (Geertz, 1973; Wuthnow, 1988). Where we may not find empirical answers to fundamental questions about life, death, and fate, faith may stand in.

When sociologists study religion, they do so as sociologists, not as believers or atheists. From the sociological perspective, religion is an important social institution. How, then, do sociologists approach the study of religion in society?

A cow occupies a corner of a fabric shop in India. A statue of the god Krishna riding a cow can be seen in the background. In Hinduism, cows symbolize wealth, strength, abundance, and a full earthly life. They roam freely in many Indian villages and cities. ■

First, they do not study whether religious beliefs are true or false. They regard religious beliefs not as truths decreed by deities, but as the social constructions of human beings. Throughout history humans have told stories about the world in which they live. Before the coming of Christianity to Northern Europe, for instance, people told stories about gods of nature or divinities who brought good fortune or ill fate to explain the tension between good and evil in human existence. Communities have always sought to construct logical frameworks to explain the world around them, and organized religion is only one way they engage in the quest for understanding and control.

Second, sociologists are interested in the social organization of religion. Within Christianity and Judaism, for example, religious practice often occurs in formal organizations, such as churches or synagogues. Yet this is not necessarily true of Hinduism and Buddhism, whose rituals may be practiced in the home or a natural setting. In Islamic societies such as Saudi Arabia and Iran, religious beliefs and practices are incorporated into daily life (P. Hammond, 1992).

Third, sociologists examine the function of religions as sources of solidarity within a group or society. Émile Durkheim (2008, p. 47) writes that religion is a "unified system of beliefs and practices related to sacred things" that are held in awe and elevated above the "profane" elements of daily existence, and that unite believers in a moral community. According to Durkheim (2008), the "god of the clan," the object of worship, is "nothing else than the clan itself, personified and represented to the imagination" (p. 206). This view highlights the importance of the group in constructing and

World's Religions

worshipping, through the objects of devotion, an image of itself.

If a single religion dominates a society, it may function as a key source of social stability. If not, differences between religions or sects may lead to sectarian conflicts. Recent examples of destabilizing religious conflicts include struggles between Sikhs, Hindus, and Muslims in India; between Muslims and Christians in Bosnia and other parts of former Yugoslavia; and between Sunni and Shiite Muslims in Iraq and Pakistan.

Today we experience constant contact between countries that embrace different religious practices, making it relevant to ask whether religion is a stabilizing or destabilizing force on a global level. For instance, some writers see an evolving "clash of civilizations" between the Muslim and Christian worlds (Huntington, 1993, 1997; Lewis, 2010) that will shape the future of international relations.

Finally, sociologists study the ways in which social forces, rather than individual spiritual experiences, affect people's commitment to religion. Religious beliefs are a deeply personal experience for many, creating a profound sense of connection with forces that transcend everyday reality. Sociologists do not question the depth of such feelings, but they do not limit themselves to a spiritual explanation of religious devotion. They examine ways that "getting religion" coincides with community or individual experiences of loss, grief, poverty, or disaster. This perspective has deep historical roots: As far back as the first century B.C., the Latin poet Lucretius saw religion as originating in human fears and needs. He believed "men had dreamed of gods, to whom they attributed omnipotence and immortality. Unable to account for natural phenomena, especially in its more terrifying aspects, men had gone on to ascribe all such things to the gods, whom they consequently feared and sought to propitiate" (Brandon, 1973, p. 93).

THEORETICAL PERSPECTIVES ON RELIGION AND SOCIETY

In this section, we examine classical sociological perspectives on the role of religion in society, but we begin by considering the birth of religion and early human society through the lens of a sister discipline, anthropology. **Anthropology** highlights *the study of human cultures and societies and their development.* Like sociology, it offers different perspectives on questions including the relationship between religion, human civilization, and agriculture, or different theoretical "glasses" we can use to see the development of our common human past.

. . . .

Anthropology: The study of human cultures and societies and their development.

Our story begins in southern Turkey, near the border with Syria. As long as 11,600 years ago, pillars measuring 18 feet and weighing up to 16 tons were raised at Göbekli Tepe, the home of what archeologists believe to be the world's oldest temple (Mann, 2011). Carved into the temple are animal totems, figures that may represent guardian spirits. Still under excavation by archeologists, Göbekli Tepe has challenged a long-held anthropological belief that organized religion arose as a way to establish a social bond when hunter-gatherers evolved from nomadic bands into village communities. Instead, says archeologist Klaus Schmidt, the massive temple shows that organized religion may predate the rise of agriculture and other key aspects of civilization. Lacking evidence of human settlement, Göbekli Tepe may have been a gathering place for foragers living within a hundred-mile radius. Settled agricultural activity may have arisen from a need to ensure adequate food for those drawn to the temple. We may then understand religion—in this instance, "the human impulse to gather for sacred rituals [that] arose as humans shifted from seeing themselves as part of the natural world to seeking mastery over it" (Mann, 2011, para. 29)—as a critical precursor to agriculture and village settlements.

Göbekli Tepe is an ancient sanctuary erected at the top of a mountain ridge in the Southeastern Anatolia Region of Turkey. It is the oldest known human-made religious structure. Archeologists estimate that the temple was erected by hunter-gatherers in the 10th millennium B.C.E. ■

Did organized religion arise in response to a need for cohesion in early human societies, or did religion come first, fostering a shift from nomadic hunting and gathering to settled agricultural communities? These questions shed light on the concerns of both anthropologists and sociologists of religion.

THE CLASSICAL VIEW: RELIGION, SOCIETY, AND SECULARIZATION

Classical sociological theorizing on religion focuses on the relationship between religion and society and includes the work of Karl Marx, Max Weber, and Émile Durkheim. Next we discuss each of these key perspectives.

DURKHEIM: THE FUNCTIONS OF RELIGION Émile Durkheim's *The Elementary Forms of the Religious Life* (2008) set forth one of the most influential and enduring theories in the sociology of religion. Durkheim based his theories on studies of Australian Aborigines, small hunting and gathering tribes who had lived in much the same way for thousands of years. Aborigines divided their world into two parts: the **profane,** *a sphere of routine, everyday*

. . . .

Profane: A sphere of routine, everyday life.

Sacred: That which is set apart from the ordinary, the sphere endowed with spiritual meaning.

Totems: Part of the sacred sphere in which ordinary objects are believed to have acquired transcendent or magical qualities connecting humans with the divine.

life, and the **sacred,** *that which is set apart from the ordinary, the sphere endowed with spiritual meaning.* The sacred sphere included many ordinary objects, which Durkheim called **totems,** *items believed to have acquired transcendent or magical qualities connecting humans with the divine.* Durkheim posited that "totemism" was the most primitive form of religion. Like the ancient worshippers at Göbekli Tepe, early Native Americans elevated elements of the natural world to sacred status and gave particular pride of place to the bison. Another familiar contemporary example of a totem is the wafer and wine used in a Catholic mass, which the devout believe is ritually transformed into the body and blood of Christ.

Sacred activities for the Australian Aborigines included rituals and ceremonies that provided a heightened emotional awareness and a spiritual connection with divine forces and other members of the community. During such rituals, Durkheim suggested, people lost their sense of individuality and merged with the larger group. His key theoretical conclusion was that the realm of the sacred serves an important social function—it brings the community together, reaffirms its norms and values, and strengthens its social bonds. According to Durkheim, the realm of the sacred is society's projection of itself onto divine objects or beings, a view with roots in early history. Xenophanes, a philosopher who lived around 570 B.C., wrote that men have created gods in their own image. The sacred *is* the group, endowed with divine powers and purpose. By worshipping the sacred, society worships itself, becoming stronger and more cohesive as a result.

Durkheim believed the sacred was disappearing from modern industrial society, with the realm of the profane extending over wider areas of life. However, while societies were likely to eventually reject the religiosity of earlier communities, Durkheim believed they could create *secular* forms of religion with the same function but a different form. In the United States, for instance, we

The U.S. Flag Code, adopted by Congress in 1942, says the flag "represents a living country and is itself considered a living thing." National flags, in this respect, can be understood as totems of civil religion by which a country elevates a symbol of worship that embodies its own self. ■

can identify rituals, both religious and civic, that function to create or reinforce a "collective conscience" or group solidarity, such as the Olympic Games, the Pledge of Allegiance, and the national anthem. The U.S. flag carries a symbolic meaning because it stands for the collective nation; in "worshipping" the flag by, for instance, affording it pride of place from classrooms to ballparks, the community venerates itself and its values, beliefs, and practices.

Durkheim's work suggests that one of religion's key functions in society is to create and reinforce the collective bond. Sociologist Herbert Blumer (1969) writes that the meaning of a thing for a person grows out of the ways in which others respond to the object and the person's actions toward it. A flag, as a physical object, is just a swath of colored fabric, but citizens of a country endow it with a meaning that elevates it to a sacred symbol. A wafer is just a wafer unless it is blessed in a Christian religious ceremony, when it becomes a representation of the body of Christ and its consumption an act of worship.

MARX: RELIGION AND INEQUALITY Karl Marx's writings about religion examine its role in society and the capitalist class hierarchy. In his view, religion serves the interests of the ruling class by providing an outlet for human misery that obscures the true source of suffering among the subordinate classes—their exploitation by the ruling class.

Marx wrote that "religion is the sigh of the oppressed creature, the sentiment of a heartless world, and the soul of soulless conditions. It is the opium of the people" (quoted in McLellan, 2010, p. 4). In other words, by promising spiritual solutions such as a better afterlife as the answer to human suffering, religion discourages oppressed people from understanding the nature of their oppression

in the present life and serves the interests of the wealthy and powerful, who then have an easier time maintaining passivity among the economically deprived masses. After all, if there are rewards in the afterlife, then striving for betterment in the present life is not only unnecessary but possibly counterproductive.

Marx also believed that once capitalism was overthrown, religion would no longer be necessary, since the stratification and dire economic disadvantage he saw as inevitable in the capitalist system would no longer exist. Like Durkheim, Marx believed secularization was inevitable. **Secularization** is the *rise in worldly thinking, particularly as seen in the rise of science, technology, and rational thought, and a simultaneous decline in the influence of religion.* While Durkheim was concerned about the fraying of social bonds that he believed would accompany secularization, Marx viewed secularization as a progressive trend, since the social solidarity and harmony promoted by religion was contrary to the interests of the working class and prevented its members' recognition of their oppressive circumstances.

WEBER: RELIGIOUS VALUES AS SOURCES OF SOCIAL CHANGE Religion was a key subject for sociologist Max Weber, who wanted to explain, in particular, why the culture of modern capitalism had emerged first in England, France, and Germany, rather than in India or China—which had once been more advanced than Northern and Western Europe in science, culture, and commerce. Weber concluded that capitalism first appeared where the Protestant Reformation had taken hold, and that the driving force behind its development was Protestantism's religious tenets and the economic behaviors they fostered.

Weber (1958) found that the beliefs of early Protestantism provided fertile ground for capitalism's development. First was the idea that God places each person on earth to fulfill a particular "calling." Whether someone would be saved was predestined by God, but people could find evidence of God's plan in a life dedicated to hard work because economic success was an indicator of salvation. Second, since Protestantism held that consumption-centered lifestyles were sinful, believers were expected to live simple lives, work hard, and save and reinvest their earnings rather than enjoy the immediate gratifications of idleness or acquisition. A hardworking, frugal, sober population reinvesting its earnings in new economic activities was, suggested Weber, a fundamental foundation for economic growth and, significantly, for early capitalism.

Secularization: The rise in worldly thinking, particularly as seen in the rise of science, technology, and rational thought, and a simultaneous decline in the influence of religion.

PRIVATE LIVES, PUBLIC ISSUES

ÉMILE DURKHEIM AND THE FUNCTION OF RELIGION IN SUICIDE

As a sociologist interested in what makes society cohesive and leads to social order, Émile Durkheim wanted to understand why suicide rates varied among different groups in society. He argued that because there are many different personal causes of suicide—mental illness, depression, pride, and even imitation—a general theory of why individuals commit suicide is impossible. A more scientific approach, he argued, is to search for social structural characteristics of different groups and societies that could explain suicide rates, rather than the motivation of individuals to commit suicide.

Durkheim's theory suggests that it is the degree of social solidarity in a society or group that explains the suicide rate: The greater the solidarity, the lower the suicide rate. Durkheim identified a number of different groups within European society to test his theory: He posited that single men compared to married men, widowed men, and women, as well as Catholics compared to Protestants, experienced higher levels of social cohesion and therefore should have lower suicide rates. The data he relied on, although primitive by contemporary standards of statistical sophistication, confirmed his theory.

Durkheim's empirical work led him to label four different types of suicide: egoistic, altruistic, anomic, and fatalistic. Here we focus on the first—*egoistic suicide*, which he understood as stemming from "excessive individuation," or a lack of integration into a community and weakness of community ties. Lack of integration, Durkheim argued, contributes to a sense of purposelessness, whereas integration offers the protection of a "collective conscience" that endows life with a purpose greater than the individual. Of the role of religion in

Sociologist Émile Durkheim identified Catholicism as a religion with strong social bonds. Durkheim's research on suicide suggests that strong bonds make suicide less likely. ■

promoting such a collective conscience, Durkheim (1897/1951) suggested,

> Religion protects man against the desire for self-destruction . . . What constitutes religion is the existence of a certain number of beliefs and practices common to all the faithful, traditional and thus obligatory. The more numerous and strong these collective states of mind are, the stronger the integration of the religious community, also the greater its preservative value. (p. 170)

From Durkheim's perspective, the collective conscience that emerged from being integrated into a religious community was protective. It shielded the individual from the egoism of living only for the fulfillment of his or her own needs, which could not all be met. His sociological perspective places suicide at the intersection of the personal and the social, helping us to examine and empirically test the societal context in which suicide becomes more or less likely. Were we to test Durkheim's theory today we would first identify different groups where the degree of social solidarity varied; then we would compare suicide rates of the different groups. If, for example, Durkheim was correct in saying that Catholics experience a higher level of social solidarity than Protestants (we would have to develop some measure for social solidarity in the two groups), then by comparing their suicide rates we would be able to test Durkheim's theory.

THINK IT THROUGH

■ *Does membership in a religious organization provide a protective social barrier to suicide? What about membership in a civic organization? How would you design a research study to test and compare the protective effects of religious and civic group membership?*

ИМПЕРИАЛИЗМ и РЕЛИГИЯ

The Soviet Union was an atheistic communist state in which religious life was discouraged and sometimes actively persecuted. This Soviet poster from the 1930s makes a link between imperialism, capitalism, and the "poison drug of religion." ∎

Yet Weber also wrote that once capitalism took hold, it became institutionalized and shed the religious ethic that fueled its development. Capitalism, scientific ways of thinking, and bureaucratic forms of organization, he said, would marginalize religion in the drive for productivity and profit. Weber was concerned about the disenchantment he believed would result from secularization and bureaucratization. Modern society, in his well-known metaphor, would become an "iron cage," imprisoning people in "rationalized" but irrational bureaucratic structures, rote work, and lives bereft of spirituality or creativity.

SYNTHESIZING THE CLASSICAL THEORIES Durkheim's observations that sacred rituals and objects function to strengthen community solidarity and embody the community itself were among his most important contributions to the sociology of religion. However, his perspective seems most applicable to highly homogenous and cohesive societies such as the small Australian tribes that provided inspiration for his ideas. In modern, complex societies, which are racially, socially, and ethnically diverse, religion no longer serves such a clear purpose. Durkheim recognized a relationship between modernization and secularization and wrote of the potential for alienation in secular societies, but he also saw that "religion," perhaps in another form, might foster social solidarity.

Marx's insight that religion may divert people from the immediate problems of daily life is illuminating, particularly where the

Religious Economic Perspective

same elite circles hold both religious and political power. Yet his central idea that religion is purely a mystification enabling the ruling class to deceive the masses is problematic for at least two reasons. First, while religions have supported ruling groups in many historical instances, they have also challenged them. Catholicism, along with the labor movement, was a powerful driving force in the social movements that overthrew the Polish communist state through nonviolent mass mobilization, replacing it with a democratic government in 1989.

Second, for many people religious beliefs fill a need that has little to do with political or economic power—a function Marx ignored. When socialist countries such as Cuba or the former Soviet Union sought to follow Marx's ideas and marginalize religion, they were remarkably unsuccessful. Religious beliefs flourished underground, and in countries such as Poland, Ukraine, and Uzbekistan they experienced a resurgence after the fall of communism.

Finally, while Weber's idea that a *religious* ethic of hard work and thrift contributes to economic growth has been used to explain examples of economic success around the world (Berger, 1986; Berger & Hsiao, 1988; Morishima, 1982), it has also been criticized on a number of grounds. First, his conclusions were based on the writings of Protestant theologians, rather than the actual practices of Protestants. During the colonial period he cited as the birthplace of the U.S. capitalist ethic, "Boston's taverns were probably fuller on Saturday night than were its churches on Sunday morning" (Finke & Stark, 1992, p. 23). Second, some scholars argue that capitalism developed among Jews and Catholics—and, for that matter, among Hindus, Muslims, and Confucians—as well as Protestants (Collins, 1980; Hunter, 1987).

No single theoretical perspective can capture the full sociological picture of religion. Together, however, they may explain why religion exists and how it functions in human societies. Below we look at contemporary theorizing on religion, which draws from modern perspectives on economic exchange.

CONTEMPORARY SOCIOLOGICAL THEORY AND THE "RELIGIOUS ECONOMY" PERSPECTIVE

One recent and influential approach to the sociology of religion is tailored to modern societies including the United States, which are home to a wide variety of religious faiths. Taking their cue from economic theory, sociologists developed the **religious economy** approach, which suggests that *religions can be*

Religious economy: Suggests that religions can be fruitfully understood as organizations in competition with one another for followers.

fruitfully understood as organizations in competition with one another for followers (Finke & Stark 1988, 1992, 2005; P. Hammond, 1992; L. Moore, 1994; Stark & Bainbridge, 1987/1996; Warner, 1993). In this view competition is preferable to monopoly for ensuring religious vitality. Compare this view to that of the classical theorists Durkheim, Marx, and Weber, who assumed religion weakens when challenged by competing religious or secular viewpoints.

The religious economy perspective suggests that competition leads to increased engagement in religious organizations for two reasons. First, competition compels each religious group to exert more effort to win followers, reaching out to the masses in a variety of ways in order to capture their attention. Second, the presence of a multitude of religions means there is likely to be something for just about everyone. In a culturally diverse society such as the United States, a single religion will probably appeal to only a limited range of followers, but the presence of Indian gurus, fundamentalist preachers, and mainline churches may encourage broad religious participation.

The religious economy analysis is adapted from the business world, in which competition (in theory) encourages the emergence of specialized products that appeal to specific markets. Sociologists who embrace this perspective even borrow the language of business. According to Finke and Stark (1992), a successful religious group must be well organized for competition, have eloquent preachers who are engaging "sales reps" in spreading the word, offer beliefs and rituals packaged as an appealing product, and develop effective marketing techniques. Religion, in this view, is a business much like any other. Television evangelists, for example, have been effective purveyors of religious "products."

While people's motivations are not easy to pinpoint, a study conducted by the Pew Forum on Religion and Public Life (2010) found about 28% of U.S. adults change their religious affiliation over the course of their lives. If we count those who change their affiliation *within* a religious tradition (for instance, from Baptist to Lutheran, both Protestant religions), the figure rises to 44% (Figure 12.1; Pew Forum on Religion and Public Life, 2010).

The religious economy approach is, of course, also subject to critique. It likely overestimates the extent to which people rationally pick and choose among different religions, as if they were shopping for a new car or a pair of shoes. Among deeply committed believers, particularly in societies or communities that lack religious pluralism, it is not obvious that religion is a matter of rational choice. Even when people are allowed to choose among different religions, most are likely to practice their childhood religion without ever considering alternatives (Roof, 1993). Further, if we consider that the most common shift is from a religious group to the "nonaffiliated" group—7.3% of adults were "unaffiliated" as children, but today over 16% indicate they are not affiliated with a religious group—then it is not clear that U.S. believers are trading one set of beliefs for another better marketed or more enticing set. They would, in fact, seem to be leaving organized religion behind. Can the religious economy perspective account for this large and growing shift? What about the classical perspectives? What do you think?

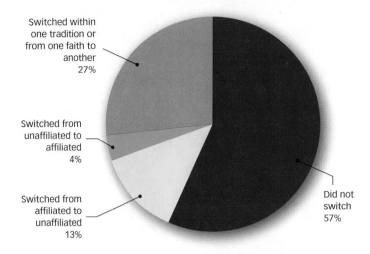

■ **FIGURE 12.1** Changing Religious Affiliations of U.S. Adults, 2007

Switched within one tradition or from one faith to another 27%

Switched from unaffiliated to affiliated 4%

Switched from affiliated to unaffiliated 13%

Did not switch 57%

SOURCE: 2007 U.S. Religious Landscape Survey, reprinted in Pew Forum on Religion and Public Life (2010).

TYPES OF RELIGIOUS ORGANIZATIONS

Sociologist Thomas O'Dea captures an important distinction when he writes that in traditional societies "the same social groups provide satisfaction for both expressive and adaptive needs; in modern societies, organizations which meet adaptive needs tend to be separated out from those which provide an outlet for expressive needs" (1966, p. 36). That is, in modern societies, religion may soothe the fear of death or the future, inject meaning into the routine of daily life, and comfort the sick or grieving, but rarely is it an exclusive channel for education and medical services (though certainly students can attend religious schools from prekindergarten to college, and many private hospitals are affiliated with religious groups).

In modern societies, religion is typically "institutionalized." Max Weber (1921/1963) wrote that after the loss of the charismatic figure from whose life the religion was born, there is a crisis among followers, but there can also be a subsequent "routinization of charisma," which institutionalizes the religion and beliefs into an organizational structure. Early theorists such as Weber, Ernst Troeltsch (1931), and Richard Niebuhr (1929) described religious organizations as falling along a continuum, based on the degree to which they are well established and conventional: Churches, for instance, lie at one end (they are conventional and well established), *cults* lie at the other (they are neither), and *sects* fall somewhere between. These distinctions were based on the study of European and U.S. religions, and there is some debate over how well they apply to the non-Christian world. Also, because the terms *sect* and *cult* have negative connotations today, sociologists sometimes use the phrase *new religious movements* to characterize novel

Religious Cults

Reverend Sun Myung Moon, head of the Unification Church (popularly known as "Moonies"), performs a mass marriage of 30,000 couples in Seoul, Korea. The Unification Church is an example of a religious cult, its unconventional ways lying outside the religious mainstream of the United States and many other countries of the world. ■

religious organizations that lack mainstream credibility (Hadden, 1993; Hexham & Poewe, 1997). Below we look at these different forms religious organizations take.

CHURCH

A **church** is *a well-established religious organization that exists in a fairly harmonious relationship with the larger society* (Finke & Stark, 1992). In everyday terms, churches are respectable, mainstream organizations that reflect a religious community's prevailing values and beliefs. They are likely to be formal, bureaucratically organized, with fairly conventional practices. In the United States, examples include the Presbyterian, United Methodist, Greek Orthodox, and Roman Catholic churches.

A church can take one of two forms. An **ecclesia** is *formally allied with the state and is the official religion of the society.* As such, it is likely to enjoy special rights and privileges that other churches lack. In Greece, for instance, while the practice of other religions is not prohibited or punished, the constitution holds that the Greek Orthodox Church is the "prevailing" religion of the country. A **denomination**, in contrast, is *a church that is not formally allied with the state.* Since there is no established church (or ecclesia) in the United States, all U.S. churches are by definition denominations. The existence of denominations allows for freedom of religious choice, so different denominations may compete with one another for membership, and none enjoys the special favor of the state.

SECT

Unlike a church, which exists in relative harmony with the larger society, a **sect** is a religious organization that has splintered off

What Are Cults?

from an established church, in an effort to restore perceived "true" beliefs and practices believed to have been lost by the established religious organization. Protestant fundamentalist and evangelical religious groups are typically sects.

Sects often tend to hold religious beliefs consistent with the dominant ones in society. Yet because they are splinter groups, they also may exist in tension with more established religious organizations. While churches tend to intellectualize religious practice, sects may emotionalize it, emphasizing heightened personal experience and religious conversion (Finke & Stark, 1992; Stark & Bainbridge, 1987/1996). Sects often appeal more to marginalized than mainstream individuals, drawing followers from among lower-income households, racial and ethnic minorities, and the rural poor.

Yet sects provide a new source of religious ideas and vitality outside mainstream faiths. When they are successful they may grow in size, evolving into churches, becoming bureaucratized, and losing their emotional appeal (Niebuhr, 1929). A new sect may then break off, seeking to return to its religious roots. This occurred within both U.S. Protestantism and Japanese Buddhism in the late 20th century. Disturbed by the increasingly intellectualized and liberal direction taken by mainstream Protestant churches, numerous sects broke off, seeking to return to what they viewed as the biblical roots of the Protestant faith (Finke & Stark, 1992). Similarly, Buddhist sects in Japan sought a return to original Buddhist beliefs in response to what they regarded as the social isolation and irrelevance of mainstream Buddhist groups (W. Davis, 1991).

CULT

A **cult** is *a religious organization that is thoroughly unconventional with regard to the larger society* (Finke & Stark, 1992; J. Richardson, 2009). While sects often originate as offshoots of well-established religious organizations, cults tend to be new, with unique beliefs and practices that typically originate outside the religious mainstream. They may be led by charismatic figures who draw on a wide range of teachings to develop the

- -

Church: A well-established religious organization that exists in a fairly harmonious relationship with the larger society.

Ecclesia: A form of a church that is formally allied with the state and is the "official" religion of the society.

Denomination: A form of a church that is not formally allied with the state.

Sect: A religious organization that has splintered off from an established church in an effort to restore perceived "true" beliefs and practices believed to have been lost by the established religious organization.

Cult: A religious organization that is thoroughly unconventional with regard to the larger society.

ESCHATOLOGY ON THE INTERNET

Eschatology is the study of practices and beliefs related to "end times"—that is, the end of the world as we know it. Religious scholars from many traditions have been drawn to this subject throughout history, and interest appears to have blossomed among evangelical Christians, who make up a growing proportion of the churchgoing population in the United States.

The best-selling "Left Behind" book series chronicles the fictional adventures of a group of evangelical Christians living through the trials of end times, including the rise of an Antichrist, plagues and locusts, the battle of Armageddon, and Jesus's second coming. The Internet plays a dual role in relation to the "Left Behind" series: First, it is an important part of the story line, as the unfolding tale includes a prophet addressing millions of new converts on his website about the biblical meaning of contemporary events. Second, the "Left Behind" site itself (leftbehind.com) purports to serve a similar role, offering to explain "how current events may actually relate to End Times prophecy" and providing a forum for both author and reader testimonials, as well as audio and video resources.

In light of this burgeoning interest in eschatology, dialogue and debate

People have long been fascinated by stories about the end of the world. What makes these stories so powerful and compelling? ■

about the end of the world have become a widespread Internet phenomenon. Websites such as raptureready.com cover a wide range of related topics, including the top 10 signs of the imminence of the end of the world as we know it, message boards, and a long list of frequently asked questions such as "What is hell like?" "How will the Antichrist take over the world?" and "When is the world going to end?"

While religious communities have long been home to self-styled

prophets who claim to know when the world will end, the Internet has proven a powerful tool for the marketing of the ideas and products of evangelical Christianity and the dissemination of beliefs about how the end will occur (Clarke, 2011).

THINK IT THROUGH

■ *Does social media function to capture and reflect public interest in end-times stories—or does it actively create and expand that interest?*

---

group's novel ideas (Stark & Bainbridge, 1987). The presence of a powerful personality can thus define a cult, and the loss of the leader can spell its end.

Cults may have a relationship with larger society characterized by strife and distrust. In recent years, "doomsday cults" that prophecy the end of the world have proliferated. The Church Universal and Triumphant (CUT), for instance, was led by the charismatic leader Elizabeth Clare Prophet. The cult's doctrine amalgamated bits of major religions such as Christianity

and Buddhism, mysticism, astrology, and Western philosophy (Melton, 1996), and a belief in reincarnation (rebirth). Prophet herself, who led the church after the death of her husband Mark Prophet, claimed to have lived past lives as Marie Antoinette, Queen Guinevere of King Arthur's court, and the biblical figure Martha.

In 1990, Prophet predicted that the world would end, and hundreds of her followers fled to bomb shelters near Yellowstone National Park where the CUT had created a self-reliant community.

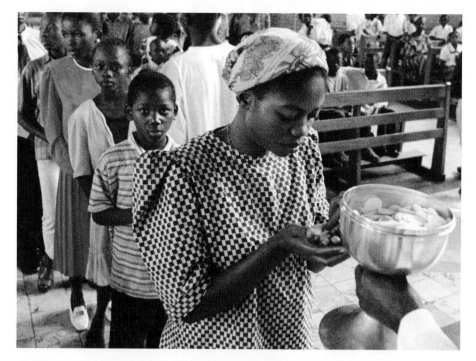

The Catholic Church is finding more new followers in Africa than anywhere else in the world. Catholics on the continent number between 117 and 137 million. The Democratic Republic of Congo is home to more Catholics than any other country in Africa, and about half its population practices the religion (Donadio, 2009). ■

involvement of some well-known celebrities including Tom Cruise and John Travolta with Scientology has further raised its profile, though arguably not its mainstream acceptance.

The youth culture of the 1960s and 1970s was fertile ground for the flowering of religious cults, leading sociologists of religion to adopt a more neutral term to describe them: **new religious movements** (NRMs), or *movements that are new and in key respects different from existing religious movements*. They may be small and based on the charisma of a single leader, evolving out of existence with the leader's death or departure. NRMs were ideal for sociological research into the development of new religions, shedding light on how the world's great religions came into being. There are many—by one estimate, between 1,500 and 2,000 in North America and in Africa perhaps 10,000—but few are enduring (Hadden, 2006). NRMs may, however, evolve into sustained religious movements, such as the Unification Church.

Apparently, the group was also stockpiling weapons in its underground bunkers, and several members were later prosecuted on weapons charges. While the CUT lost members after the failed doomsday prediction, it continued to operate and grew in later years, though Elizabeth Clare Prophet passed away in 2009.

Like sects, cults flourish when there is a breakdown in well-established societal belief systems or when segments of the population feel alienated from the mainstream and seek meaning elsewhere. Cults may originate within or outside the society. In the United States, the Church Universal and Triumphant is "homegrown," while the Reverend Sun Myung Moon's Unification Church ("Moonies"), which originated in Korea, is imported. A cult in one country may be established religious practice in another. Christianity began as an indigenous cult in ancient Jerusalem, and in many Asian countries today, evangelical Protestantism is regarded as a cult imported from the United States.

Mormons, Jehovah's Witnesses, and Seventh-Day Adventists are accepted by most people as members of legitimate religious organizations, though they may be considered a little outside the mainstream. The Unification Church and Scientology, on the other hand, continue to maintain their status as cults, even though both are about 50 years old and have a relatively broad following; the

■ **FIGURE 12.2** The World's Dominant Religions by Percentage of Believers

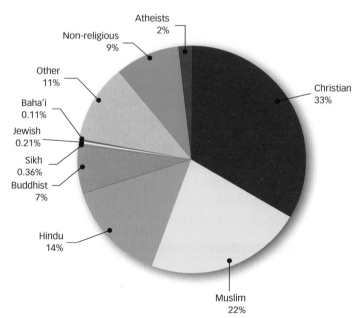

SOURCE: CIA World Factbook. (2013). *World.* Retrieved from https://www.cia.gov/library/publications/the-world-factbook/geos/xx.html

· ·

New religious movements (NRMs): Movements that are new and in key respects different from existing religious movements.

Modern Religious War

Fundamentalism

Nuns vs. Catholic Church

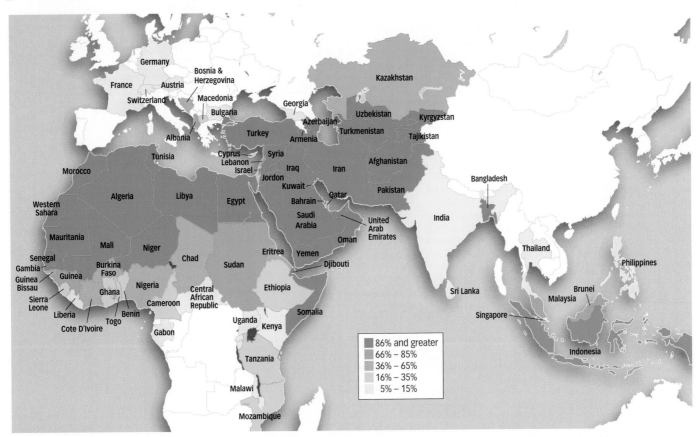

Legend:
- 86% and greater
- 66% – 85%
- 36% – 65%
- 16% – 35%
- 5% – 15%

THE GREAT WORLD RELIGIONS

From its early beginnings, humans' spiritual search for meaning and need for religion as an organizing principle in communities has brought us to a point where thousands of different religions are followed throughout the world. However, just three—Christianity, Islam, and Hinduism—are practiced by nearly three quarters of the people on earth. We look at these below, as well as at Judaism, Buddhism, and Confucianism, all of which have had a powerful influence on global religious and social practices.

CHRISTIANITY

With over 2.1 billion followers—nearly a third of the world's population—Christianity encompasses a broad spectrum of denominations, sects, and even new religious movements (Barrett, 2001). Common to all these is the belief that Jesus of Nazareth was the Messiah or savior foretold in the Hebrew Bible. While doctrinal differences separate the Christian faiths, almost all teach that, at the beginning of time, humans fell from God's grace through their sinful acts, and that acceptance of Christ and his teachings provides the key to salvation. Most Christians also believe in the

....

Monotheism: Belief in a single all-knowing, all-powerful God.

New Testament account of the Resurrection, according to which Jesus rose from the dead on the third day after his crucifixion and then ascended to heaven. Christianity is a form of **monotheism**—*belief in a single all-knowing, all-powerful God*—although in most Christian faiths God is also regarded as a trinity made up of a heavenly Father, His Son the Savior, and His sustaining Holy Spirit.

When Christianity emerged in Palestine some 2,000 years ago, it was a persecuted sect outside the mainstream of Jewish and Roman religious practices. Within four centuries it had become an ecclesia, or official religion, of the Roman Empire. In the 11th century, it divided into the Eastern Orthodox Church (based in Turkey) and the Catholic Church (based in Rome). A second great split occurred within the Catholic branch, when the 16th-century Protestant Reformation gave rise to numerous Protestant denominations, sects, and cults. Protestants tend to emphasize a direct relationship between the individual and God. Catholics, by contrast, emphasize the importance of the church hierarchy as intermediary between the individual and God, with the pope in Rome being the final earthly authority.

ISLAM

With 1.6 billion believers, Islam is the second largest and the fastest-growing religion in the world today. *Muslim* is the term for those who practice *al-Islam,* an Arabic word meaning submission without reservation to God's will. About 60% of Muslims live

In the last month of the Muslim year, thousands of Muslims make an annual pilgrimage (a *hajj*) to a holy shrine called the Ka'aba in Mecca. This site is believed to be the original location of a place of worship that God commanded Abraham and Ishmael to build over 4,000 years ago. ■

in the Asia-Pacific region and about 20% in the Middle East and North Africa. Sub-Saharan Africa, Europe, and the Americas have growing Muslim populations as well (Pew Forum on Religion and Public Life, 2011a).

Although modern Islam dates to the 7th-century Arab prophet Muhammad, Muslims trace their religion to the ancient Hebrew prophet Abraham, also the founder of Judaism. The precepts of Islam as revealed to Muhammad are contained in a sacred book dictated to his followers and called the Koran (or *Qur'an*), which means "recitation." Muhammad's ideas were not initially accepted in his birthplace of Mecca, so in 622 he and his followers moved to Medina (both cities are in today's Saudi Arabia). This migration, called the *hijra,* marks the beginning of Islam, which later spread throughout Arabia. Muhammad is not worshipped by Muslims, who believe in positive devotion to *Allah* (God). Nor is Mohammad a messiah; he is rather a teacher and prophet, the last in a line that includes Abraham, Noah, Moses, and Jesus.

Islam's sacred *sharia* (or way) includes prescriptions for worship, daily life, ethics, and even government. Muslim life is

Women and Conservative Religion

governed by the Five Pillars of Islam, which are (1) accepting Allah as God and Muhammad as Allah's messenger; (2) worshipping according to rituals, including facing toward Mecca and bowing in prayer at five set times each day; (3) observing Ramadan, a month of prayer and fasting during the daylight hours; (4) giving *alms* or donations to those who are poor or in need; and (5) making a holy pilgrimage to Mecca at least once in a lifetime (Weeks, 1988). While all Muslims share these basic tenets, they are broadly divided into Sunnis and Shiites, between whom there may be tension, as in Iraq, which is Shiite dominated but has a strong Sunni minority. Globally, there are more Sunnis than Shiites.

The Koran also invokes *jihad* as a spiritual, personal struggle for enlightenment. Most Islamic terrorist groups including al-Qaeda, however, translate *jihad* as armed struggle against the West and Western values. While some scholars argue that the shift from the struggle for personal enlightenment to armed struggle against Western values reflects "the growing confidence of the community as it developed from being a persecuted sect in Mecca to the triumphant 'super-tribe' of Muhammad's final years" (Ruthven, 2011, p. 83), others argue that it represents diverging attitudes of believers who are divided on the notion of struggle and the legitimate use of violence (Donner, 2012).

JUDAISM

With about 13 million followers worldwide, Judaism is the smallest of the world's major religions. Most Jews live in just two countries: Israel (home to about 42% of the global Jewish population) and the United States (39%), with small populations in many countries (DellaPergola, 2010). Judaism has exerted a strong influence on the world, first as a key foundation of Islam and Christianity. Second, in European and U.S. culture, Jews have played a role disproportionate to their numbers in such diverse fields as music, literature, science, education, and business. Third, the existence of Israel as a Jewish state since 1948 has given the Jewish people and faith international prominence.

Judaism was one of the first religions to teach monotheism. Like many other religions, it teaches that its followers are God's chosen people, but not that they have a duty to convert others to their faith. The primary religious writing for the Jews is the Torah (or "law"), a scroll on which are inscribed the first five books of the Bible. Biblical tradition holds that Jewish law was given by God to Moses when he led the Jews out of slavery in Egypt about 3,500 years ago, and since then it has been elaborated upon by rabbis, or teachers. Today it is codified in books called the Mishnah and the Talmud.

Three principal divisions in Judaism reflect differing perspectives on the nature of biblical law. Orthodox Judaism believes the Bible derives from God, and that its teachings are absolutely binding, while Reform Judaism views the Bible as a historical document containing important ethical precepts, but not literally the word of God. Conservative Judaism occupies a middle ground, maintaining many traditional practices while adapting others to modern society.

Jews have often suffered persecution, and anti-Semitism has a long global history. From the 12th century on, European and Russian Jews were often forced to live in special districts termed *ghettos,* where they lacked full rights as citizens and were sometimes targets of harassment and violence. Partly in reaction to these conditions, and partly because the Torah identifies Jerusalem as the center of the Jewish homeland, some Jews embraced **Zionism**, *a movement calling for the return of Jews to Palestine and the creation of a Jewish state.* (Zion is a biblical name for the ancient city of Jerusalem.)

Zionists established settlements in Palestine early in the 20th century, living for the most part peacefully with their Arab and Palestinian neighbors. Following World War II and the Nazi extermination of 6 million Jews, the State of Israel was created as a homeland for the survivors, an action that both gave refuge to

. . . .

Zionism: A movement calling for the return of Jews to Palestine and the creation of a Jewish state.

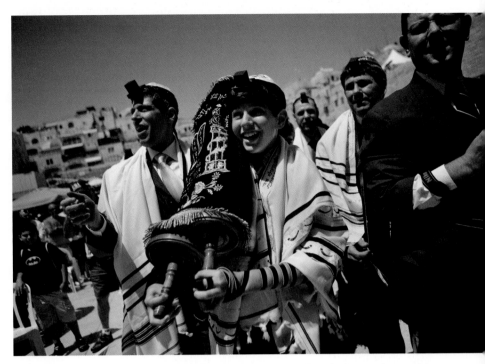

The Bar Mitzvah and Bat Mitzvah rituals are an important rite of passage for Jewish youth. ■

Jews and ignited territorial tensions in the region that continue to this day.

HINDUISM

Hinduism, about 2,000 years older than Christ, is one of the oldest religions in the world and the source of Buddhism and Sikhism. It is not based on the teachings of any single individual, and its followers do not trace their origins to a single deity. It is an broadly defined religion that calls for an ideal way of life. According to the U.S. State Department's 2010 report on international religious freedom, there are between 950 million and 1 billion Hindus throughout the world, primarily in India where they make up the large majority of the population.

Indian social structure is characterized by a caste system, officially abolished in 1949 but still powerful, in which people are believed to be born to a certain status that they must occupy for life. It has its origins in Hindu beliefs that an ideal life is partly achieved by performing the duties appropriate to your caste. Hindus, like Buddhists, believe in *samsara,* the reincarnation of the soul according to a person's *karma,* or actions on earth. Whether someone is reborn into a higher or lower caste depends on the degree to which the person is committed to *dharma,* or the ideal way of life. Although orthodox Hinduism requires observance of caste duties, for the past 500 years religious societies have organized around gurus who break with caste conventions, emphasizing devotional love as the central spiritual act. This tradition influenced Mahatma Gandhi, the leader of India's independence movement, and others who have viewed Hinduism as a vehicle for social reform (Juergensmeyer, 1995).

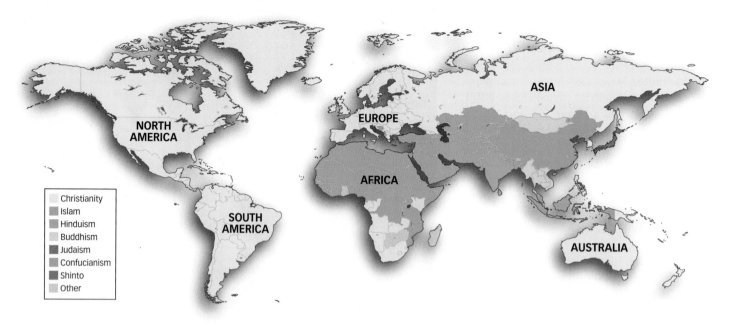

Legend:
- Christianity
- Islam
- Hinduism
- Buddhism
- Judaism
- Confucianism
- Shinto
- Other

Perhaps because Hinduism does not have a central organization or leader, its philosophy and practice are particularly diverse. Religious teachings touch all aspects of life, from the enjoyment of sensual pleasures to stark renunciation of earthly pursuits. Hindus believe in the God-like unity of all things, yet their religion also has aspects of **polytheism**, the belief that *different gods represent various categories of natural forces*. For example, Hindus worship different gods representing aspects of the whole, such as the divine dimension of a spiritual teacher (Basham, 1989).

BUDDHISM

Buddhism was founded in India by Siddhartha Gautama five centuries before Christ. According to legend, the young Siddhartha renounced an upper-caste life of material splendor in search of a more meaningful existence. A lifetime of wandering, occasional poverty, and different spiritual practices eventually taught him the way to achieve enlightenment, and he became the *Buddha*, the awakened or enlightened one. Buddhism is an example of a **nontheistic religion**, in that it believes in *the existence of divine spiritual forces rather than a God or gods*. It is more a set of rules for righteous living than a doctrine of belief in a particular God.

Gautama Buddha's philosophy is contained in the Four Noble Truths. First, all beings—gods, humans, and animals—are caught up in an endless round of suffering and rebirth, the result of their karma or actions. Second, suffering results from desire or attachment. To the extent that we depend on wealth or friends or family or even religious beliefs for satisfaction, we are condemned to suffer unending frustration and loss. Third, suffering can be overcome if we break the endless cycle of karma and rebirth and achieve nirvana—a blissful state of emptiness. Fourth, the means of achieving nirvana are contained in the Eightfold Path, which

advocates ethical behavior, a simple lifestyle, renunciation of material pleasures, meditation, and eventually enlightenment.

Many people practice certain precepts of Buddhism without calling themselves Buddhists, so it is difficult to accurately estimate the number of Buddhists in the world today. Estimates put the figure at about 350 million (CIA World Factbook, 2013). Theravada Buddhism, the "Way of the Elders" or the "Lesser Vehicle," predominates in Myanmar, Thailand, Laos, Cambodia, and Sri Lanka. It is strongly identified with local cultures, and traditional rulers in Thailand and Sri Lanka are religious figures as well. Mahayana Buddhism, the "Greater Vehicle," is practiced in China, Korea, and Japan, where it is not the official religion but mixes with other cultural strands. In China, Buddhism is intertwined with Taoist folk religion and Confucian codes of ethical practice. In Japan, Shinto Buddhism combines emperor worship with elements of **animism**, the belief, common to many religions, *that naturally occurring phenomena, such as mountains and animals, are possessed of indwelling spirits with supernatural powers*.

Buddhism's meditative lifestyle would strike some people as incompatible with life in a modern industrial society, which emphasizes work, consumption, achievement, and all forms of karma that Buddhists regard as a barrier to enlightenment and happiness. On the other hand, it is primarily Buddhist monks rather than ordinary practicing Buddhists who devote extended periods of time to meditation. Perhaps because of its emphasis

• •

Polytheism: The belief that there are different gods representing various categories of natural forces.

Nontheistic religion: Belief in the existence of divine spiritual forces rather than a God or gods.

Animism: The belief, that naturally occurring phenomena, such as mountains and animals, are possessed of indwelling spirits with supernatural powers.

on contemplation and meditation, Buddhism continues to attract followers in Western countries, including celebrities such as actor Orlando Bloom, singer Tina Turner, and the late Steve Jobs of Apple (Lampman, 2006; MacLeod, 2011).

CONFUCIANISM

Confucianism, whose name comes from the English pronunciation of the name of its founder K'ung-Fu-tzu (551–479 B.C.), is more of a philosophical system for ethical living on earth than a religion honoring a transcendental god (Fingarette, 1972). K'ung-Fu-tzu never wrote down his teachings, but his followers compiled many in a book called *The Analects* that became the foundation of official ethics and politics for some 2,000 years in China, until Confucianism was banned after the Communist revolution in 1949. Though there are only about 6 million practitioners of Confucianism—almost all in Asia—this religion has had enormous influence in China, neighboring countries such as Korea and Vietnam, and Japan (Barrett, 2001).

Confucianism emphasizes harmony in social relations, respect for authority and hierarchy, tradition, and the honoring of elders. Rulers are expected to be morally virtuous, setting an example for others to imitate. The group is more important than the individual. The key element in Confucian ethics is *jen,* meaning "love" or "goodness" and calling for faithfulness and altruism; we should never do anything to another person we would not want done to ourselves. Contemporary Confucianism, sometimes called "neo-Confucianism," has mystical elements as well as moral ones, including belief in the Tao (pronounced *dow)*, or "way of being," determined by the natural harmony of the universe.

Confucianism teaches that opposites are not necessarily antagonistic; together they make up a harmonious whole that is constantly in a creative state of tension or change. The two major principles in the universe, *yin* (the female principle) and *yang* (the male principle), are found in all things, and their dynamic interaction accounts for both harmony and change. The *I Ching* (Book of Changes) contains philosophical teachings based on this view, and a technique for determining a wise course of action.

Today many scholars argue that Confucian values such as respect for authority and a highly disciplined work ethic partly explain the rapid economic growth in Singapore, Taiwan, China, and other Asian countries (Berger, 1986; Berger & Hsiao, 1988; MacFarquhar, 1980). On the one hand, this perspective supports Weber's argument that actions rooted in religious beliefs are linked to economic development. On the other hand, it challenges Weber's exclusive emphasis on Western religion, and Protestantism in particular, as the source of this development.

WOMEN AND RELIGION

Although both men and women embrace the major religions of the world, the principal deities, prophets, and leaders are often male. God is depicted as male, beliefs typically emphasize male religious and political superiority, and women are often excluded from positions of theological power. The sociological explanation is straightforward:

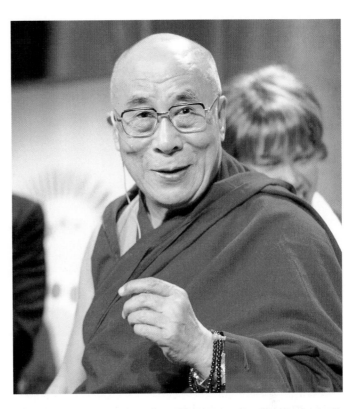

Tibet's Vajrayana tradition of Buddhism intertwines politics and religion and elevates the country's political leader, the Dalai Lama, as the incarnation of Buddha. Communist states have historically been atheist, and in China and Chinese-occupied Tibet, Buddhist practices have been repressed and practitioners persecuted. The Dalai Lama lives in exile in India. ■

These religions were initially developed by men within patriarchal societies and therefore reflect patriarchal norms and values. As we noted above, sociologists see religions as social creations, reflecting the norms, roles, and values embraced by the community and society.

According to the Jewish and Christian Bible, Eve, the first woman, violated God's command and tempted Adam to eat fruit from the Tree of Knowledge, leading to the pair's loss of innocence and expulsion from the Garden of Eden, or paradise. Consequently, all human suffering can be traced to Eve's deception (Genesis 3). The Book of Proverbs instructs the good wife to oversee the servants, to care for her family, and to be kind, fertile, obedient, and submissive to her husband. Even today, Orthodox Jewish males recite a daily prayer thanking God "that thou hast not created me a Gentile [non-Jew], a Slave, or a Woman." For Christians, Saint Paul's teachings instructed wives "to submit yourselves to your husbands as to the Lord. For the husband is the head of the wife, even as Christ is the head of the church. . . . So also wives should submit to their husbands in everything" (Ephesians 5:23–24).

Women have long played an important but unheralded role in religion. For example, Ann Lee (1736–1784), the leader of the

Women and Religious
Self-Identity

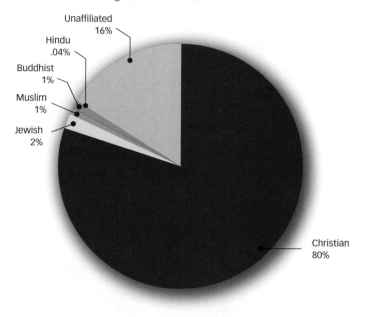

SOURCE: Pew Forum on Religion and Public Life. (2012, December 10). *U.S. religious landscape survey.*

"Shaking Quakers" in England, led a group to the United States and founded the first Shaker settlement in 1776. Alma White (1862–1946) was not only the first female evangelist ordained a bishop in the United States, but also a pioneer in the use of an electronic medium, the radio, to spread beliefs (Stanley, 1993). Aimee Semple McPherson (1890–1944) founded the International Church of the Foursquare Gospel, which today claims some 26,000 churches in 74 countries (D. Epstein, 1993). Mary Baker Eddy (1821–1910) founded Christian Science, along with the newspaper *The Christian Science Monitor*. Her influence was felt not only in religion but also in the early women's movement. Eddy was a strong feminist who argued passionately for women's equality: "In natural law and in religion, the right of women to fill the highest measure of enlightened understanding and the highest places in government is inalienable. . . . This is women's hour, with all its sweet amenities and its moral and religious reforms" (Eddy, 1887/1999, p. 45).

In recent years there has been an upsurge of feminist spirituality, especially within the United States. Some women have turned to religious traditions that predate Judaism and Christianity, including the celebration of goddess-based religions. The goddess acts not only as a literal divine entity but also as a symbol of the historical significance and celebration of the feminine ideal.

Some feminist activists have sought reform within mainstream religions, fighting for the reimagination of God as ungendered, calling for nonsexist language in Scripture and services, and redesigning traditions and rituals along nonsexist lines (Eller, 2000;

Religious Intolerance

Megachurches

New Age Religion

Wallace, 1992; Weidman, 1984). Almost all Protestant denominations now have female clergy, and even some Catholic churches offer women the opportunity to act as lay clergy though the mainstream Catholic Church continues to oppose the practice (Wallace, 1992).

RELIGION IN THE UNITED STATES

Compared to citizens of other modern industrial nations, the population of the United States is unusually religious. While secularization has weakened the power of religious institutions, religious adherence and beliefs remain strong. Most U.S. adults profess an affiliation with a religious group (Figure 12.5); about 80% self-identify as Christian, with smaller numbers identifying as Jewish (2%), Muslim (1%), and Buddhist (1%). About 16% are unaffiliated with a religion: 6% of these say they are religious but unaffiliated, while the rest are secular unaffiliated, agnostic, or atheist. About 39% attend religious services at least weekly, 35% read Scripture weekly, and 58% pray on a daily basis (Pew Forum on Religion and Public Life, 2010).

TRENDS IN RELIGIOUS AFFILIATION

The United States is a more religious country than other economically developed countries. One reason for the continuing high levels of religious group membership is that churches, synagogues, and mosques are an important source of social ties and friendship networks with people who share the same beliefs and values. Another reason is simply that there are an enormous number of such organizations to belong to—supporting the religious economy perspective we examined earlier. The United States is the most religiously diverse country in the world, with more than 1,500 distinct religions (Melton, 1996; T. Smith, 2002). In the remainder of this section we look at two seemingly contrasting trends in U.S. religious life: the rise of conservative Protestantism, specifically evangelicalism, and the declining religious affiliation of young U.S. adults.

The conservative strand of U.S. Protestantism has been growing in both membership and influence in recent years. Conservative Protestants emphasize a literal interpretation of the Bible, Christian morality in daily life as well as public politics, and conversion through evangelizing. Liberal Protestants generally adopt a more flexible, humanistic approach to their religious practices, and moderate Protestants are somewhere in between. While all groups grew from the 1920s through the 1960s, both liberal and moderate churches have since experienced a decline in membership, while the number of conservative Protestants has expanded considerably (Pew Forum on Religion and Public Life, 2008).

A key aspect of this growth is the rise of evangelicalism. **Evangelicalism** is *a belief in spiritual rebirth (being "born again")*. It often includes the admission of personal sin and

Evangelicalism: A belief in spiritual rebirth (conventionally denoted as being "born again").

INEQUALITY MATTERS

WOMEN, HUNGER, AND RELIGIOUS EMPOWERMENT

Women have historically lacked a prominent role in the theologies and hierarchies of mainstream religions. We find an interesting historical counterexample, however, in the fasting women of medieval Europe. In *Fasting Girls* (2000), Joan Jacobs Brumberg writes that among 13th- to 16th-century Catholics, particularly women, food was a symbolic language. "Control of appetite was linked to piety and belief; through fasting, the medieval ascetic strove for perfection in the eyes of her God" (p. 48). According to Brumberg, fasting women of the medieval period spoke of their "hunger" for God and their "inebriation" with the holy wine. Their fasts, lasting from weeks to years, elevated them within their communities as objects of spiritual awe; through this act they claimed religious power, or at least widespread reverence from the religious community. Though their behavior had a label, "anorexia mirabilis," it was not seen as a psychological, biological, or cultural affliction (as anorexia nervosa is today). Rather, it was a demonstration of piety and celebrated as such.

Though the link between fasting behavior and spiritual elevation was somewhat weaker by the end of the 16th century, Brumberg suggests there were still ample instances of female holiness being associated with

the ascetic denial of food and drink, continuing into the Victorian era in both Western Europe and the United States. In this period, there was both skepticism and celebration of "fasting girls," women who seemed to have transcended the worldly body and its physical needs. According to Brumberg, "Many who were pietists or pious Catholics embraced the cause of a particular fasting girl, either because her story reinvigorated the tradition of anorexia mirabilis and Christian miracles or because her existence demonstrated the independence of the spirit from the flesh, a central tenet of Victorian Spiritualism" (p. 64). Spiritualists were those who embraced the idea of transcendence over the material body, and fasting girls offered a focal point for challenging the belief that the body needed food to live.

By the 19th century, food refusal was labeled a disease. No longer did women whose fasts lasted for weeks or months attract celebration and elevation. Rather, they became objects of medical attention, parental concern, and societal curiosity. Anorexia mirabilis, however, whether piety or affliction, remains an interesting premodern manifestation of women's use of food as a symbolic language, and of food refusal as a means to garner attention and, arguably, empowerment. In their emaciation and

Fasting is a cultural staple of some religions. Catherine of Siena, a Roman Catholic, practiced extended fasts, even putting her life in jeopardy for her faith. ■

asceticism, some women found an avenue to affirmation and adoration in early religious communities, though achieved in part through their physical enervation and even death from starvation.

THINK IT THROUGH

■ *From a contemporary perspective, was the historical phenomenon of anorexia mirabilis a manifestation of women's religious marginalization or empowerment?*

---

salvation through acceptance of Christ, a literal interpretation of the Bible, an emphasis on highly emotional and personal spiritual piety, and a commitment to spreading "the Word" to others (Balmer, 1989). (The word *evangel* comes from the Greek for "bringing good news.") We can interpret the rise of evangelicalism

as a response to growing secularism, religious diversity, and, in general, the decline of once-core Protestant values in U.S. life (Wuthnow, 1988).

Conservative Protestants have been an active force in U.S. politics, and their growing numbers may be linked to a

Some evangelical Christian groups have access to extensive resources for recruitment and worship. The facility here used to be home to the Houston Rockets, and was converted to an evangelical church that took about $75 million to renovate. ■

recent rise in their political influence, particularly within the Republican Party. They have, in fact, become a key constituency for Republicans. Data from the past decade (Dionne & Green, 2008) confirm the emergence of a "worship attendance gap" in presidential politics; specifically, "the more observant members of religious communities tend to vote Republican while their less observant co-religionists tend to vote Democratic. This attendance gap has been largest among the white Christian traditions, but has appeared in a more modest form within nearly all religious affiliations." Not only are strongly religious voters more likely to vote Republican, but they seem increasingly more likely to vote at all. That is, they are active in politics to a degree that many other groups are not.

Consider, for instance, the political influence of the Tea Party, a group that affiliates with the Republican Party and draws a substantial degree of support from White evangelical Protestants. Tea Party members are far more likely than registered voters as a whole to say that "religion is the most important factor in determining their opinion on . . . social issues [in politics, such as abortion and same-sex marriage]" (Pew Forum on Religion and Public Life, 2011c). Surveys conducted by the Pew Forum also show that White evangelical Protestants are about 5 times as likely to agree with the ideas of the Tea Party as to disagree (44% vs. 8%), though substantial

numbers also have no opinion or have not heard of the movement (48%). When we consider that the Tea Party, still a nascent political movement in 2010, made up fully 41% of the electorate in November elections that year, the potential for religious communities and beliefs to shape political life in the United States is apparent (Pew Forum on Religion and Public Life, 2011c). (We discuss the Tea Party in greater detail in Chapter 13.)

Many U.S. voters' political beliefs and actions are shaped by religious faith. Not surprisingly, then, many also expect their political leaders to share their faith: A 2011 Pew survey showed that fully 61% of respondents would be less likely to support a presidential candidate who "does not believe in God" (Pew Center on Religion and Public Life, 2011b), a figure that has held steady across recent years.

Paradoxically, recent decades have also seen the decline of religious affiliation in the United States. That is, while U.S. adults are still highly religious compared to their counterparts in other modern states (European states in particular), recent research suggests that a generational shift is taking place with the potential to transform the U.S. religious landscape. While just 16% of U.S. adults report being "unaffiliated" with a religion, fully a quarter of those between 18 and 29 are not affiliated. This is in stark contrast to older generations: Just 14% of those 50–59, 10% of those 60–69, and 8% of those 70 or older do not profess an affiliation. (It may also help explain why more women than men claim religious affiliation—just 13% of women are unaffiliated compared to nearly 20% of men: Due to differences in life expectancy, there are more women in the oldest age groups than men.) Further, today's

Religious Involvement

young adults are less likely than young adults of earlier generations to indicate no religious affiliation; in studies done in the 1970s and 1980s, about half as many young adults identified themselves as unaffiliated with a religion. The study suggests that this change is "a result, in part, of the decision by many young people to leave the religion of their upbringing without becoming involved in a new faith" (Pew Forum on Religion and Public Life, 2010).

Recall the religious economy perspective discussed earlier. Can it help us understand the growing number of young people who do not affiliate with a religion? Does it suggest that religious organizations are failing to "market" themselves effectively? Or does it mean other sources of spiritual or personal fulfillment are available to young adults and act as what Robert Merton called "functional equivalents," fulfilling the functions of religion but assuming a different form?

RELIGION AND DISESTABLISHMENT

Some sociologists call consumption the new U.S. religion. Do U.S. adults seek "salvation" in the abundant goods and services accessible in "Cathedrals of Consumption" such as the Mall of America, Minnesota, shown here? Product ads, like religious appeals, implore us to "better ourselves" and "find ourselves" through consumption, often promising bliss upon purchase. ■

According to Phillip Hammond (1992), religion in the United States has three times undergone **disestablishment**, *a period during which the political influence of established religions is successfully challenged.* One occurred with the 1791 ratification of the first 10 amendments to the U.S. Constitution (the Bill of Rights), the first of which calls for a firm separation of church and state. Some sociologists see this separation as part of a larger trend in industrial societies, in which different institutions specialize in different functions—from economics to medicine, from education to politics. Religion is no exception (J. Alexander & Thompson, 2008; Chaves, 1993, 1994; Parsons, 1951, 1960, 1966). Recall Thomas O'Dea's (1966) suggestion, above, that in traditional societies "the same social groups provide satisfaction for both expressive and adaptive traditional societies' needs," whereas modern societies separate these two functions (p. 36).

The second period of disestablishment occurred between the 1890s and the 1920s, fed by an influx of about 17 million immigrants, mainly European and many Catholic. For the first time, the notion of a predominantly Protestant United States was challenged, and the mainstream Protestant churches never regained their influence in politics or in defining national values. The third period occurred during the 1960s and the 1970s, when core religious beliefs and values were further eroded by the anti–Vietnam

War movement, the fight for racial equality, and experimentation with alternative lifestyles. Fundamental challenges came in the form of more open sexual and lifestyle preferences, the women's movement, and attitudes and laws about birth control (Glock & Bellah, 1976; P. Hammond, 1992; Roof & McKinney, 1990; Wuthnow, 1976, 1978).

Disestablishment of religion reduces its political influence but does not make it less important to individuals. In fact, if religious groups compete with one another for followers, religious practices are more likely to be tailored to public tastes (L. Moore, 1994); this result fits the perspective of religious economy we discussed earlier. We've also seen, however, that conservative Protestant religious organizations have increasingly made their voices heard in U.S. politics. President George W. Bush's period in office was marked by close ties to conservative religious organizations, and some political analysts suggest that his aspirations to democratize the Middle East, for instance, reflected not only pragmatic political considerations but also a spiritual sense that the United States is "called" to be a "beacon of freedom and democracy." More recently, as we noted above, the Tea Party has raised the profile and power of U.S. conservative religious groups.

· ·

Disestablishment: A period during which the political influence of established religions is successfully challenged.

Civil Religion

"CIVIL RELIGION" IN THE UNITED STATES

Some sociologists have argued that the United States has a **civil religion**, *a set of religious beliefs through which a society interprets its own history in light of some conception of ultimate reality* (J. Alexander & Thompson, 2008; Bellah, 1968, 1975; Mathisen, 1989). Civil religion usually consists of "god-language used in reference to the nation," including historical myths about the society's divine origins, beliefs about its sacred historical purpose, and occasionally religious restrictions on societal membership (Wuthnow, 1988).

The infusion of divine meaning into historical events is visible in President Abraham Lincoln's (1809–1865) oratory on the Civil War. In the Gettysburg Address, Lincoln, who was not highly religious himself, drew on religious imagery to attach meaning to the brutal destruction and enormous human cost of the war. He labeled his fellow citizens the "almost chosen people" and called the United States "the last, best hope on earth."

As we noted in the opening vignette, the phrase "under God" was added to the Pledge of Allegiance by Congress in 1954, amid fears of the Cold War and "godless communism." The words are consistent with the construction of a civil religion and a nation worshiping itself, fulfilling a divine destiny. Even though the Bill of Rights of the U.S. Constitution clearly calls for a separation of church and state, this profession of allegiance to "one nation, under God" came to be seen as central to U.S. citizenship. What do you think about the content of the Pledge of Allegiance? Does it endorse religion, or is it a civil rather than a religious declaration? Why do you think different people read this legal question differently?

RELIGION AND GLOBAL SOCIETIES

Thanks in part to the Internet, globalization has transformed religion to a more fluid form that easily crosses boundaries and mixes traditions from different areas. While religions have always evolved, today's sustained and regular contact between them is unprecedented. The embrace of new ideas may create harmony, tension, or even violence.

The global emergence of a scientific-technological culture that colors people's views and behaviors presents a powerful challenge to the world's traditional religions. It means that fewer people may employ religious explanations for natural or social phenomena, probing beyond explanations that refer to a divine plan. Religion may still enrich personal lives, but its role in public life, at least in the most economically advanced countries, has declined.

A second challenge of globalization is the growing contact between large religions with mass followings that claim to possess exclusive accounts of history and the nature of reality. This contact is both a potential and an actual source of tension and conflict, which can fuel "culture wars," as well as real wars that leaders cast as battles between religions and values or even between "good and evil." In fact, rather than leading to a merging of religions (in the manner of a global "culture" of consumption or popular music), globalization may be fostering a backlash against blending that reveals itself as fundamentalism. Fundamentalism is also associated with the rise of religious nationalism.

Religious nationalism is *the linkage of religious convictions with beliefs about a nation or ethnic group's social and political destiny.* It is on the rise in countries around the world, where religious nationalist movements have revived traditional religious beliefs and rejected the separation between religion and the state (Beyer, 1994; Kinnvall, 2004). While the trend is more pronounced among Islamic fundamentalists in some Middle Eastern countries, the United States has also experienced rising political influence of evangelical Protestantism.

The conservative U.S. Christian lobby has been particularly vocal—and often influential—on domestic issues such as abortion and gay marriage, both of which it opposes. It has also had some impact on global policy making. For example, Christian evangelicals have lobbied for U.S. intervention in Sudan, the site of a bloody civil war between Christians and Muslims in the North and a genocide perpetrated by Arab militias (supported by the Sudanese government) against Black Africans in Darfur.

Christian and Islamic religious nationalist movements accept modern technology, politics, and economics; many use Internet technology to disseminate information and ideas. At the same time, they strictly interpret religious values and reject secularization, drawing selectively on traditions and past events to serve their current beliefs and interests. Benedict Anderson (1991) writes about "imagined communities," suggesting that nations are real but not "natural"—that is, they are unified by both real and invented traditions and heroes that legitimate their claims about territories, the past, and the present. Part of the Israeli and Palestinian conflict over land is rooted in different narratives of history that tell diverging stories about who has "true" dominion over the territory.

Religious nationalism can bring communities together or tear them apart. India is the world's largest democracy, one of the world's largest countries with over 1 billion people, and home to Hindus, Muslims, Christians, and believers in dozens of other religions. Diversity and democracy sometimes appear to be on shaky ground, however, particularly when the extreme nationalist ideology of *Hindutva* (or "Hinduness") comes into contact with Muslim extremism. In the northern Indian town of Ayodhya,

The "Sacred" in Modern Society

Catholic Church Renewal

Civil religion: A set of religious beliefs through which a society interprets its own history in light of some conception of ultimate reality.

Religious nationalism: The linkage of religious convictions with beliefs about a nation or ethnic group's social and political destiny.

The Israeli-Palestinian conflict is a deeply entrenched battle between two political-religious groups and their supporters. This conflict has demanded the attention and resources of the United States and other countries as they try to find a diplomatic solution to the conflict. ■

WHY STUDY THE SOCIOLOGY OF RELIGION?

Studying religion from a sociological perspective does not mean embracing or rejecting religious values; it means examining and analyzing an institution that is central to humans on an individual, societal, and global level. In the United States today, the sociology of religion may be especially relevant. First, the question of whether disestablishment is proceeding or receding is an important one. Though the country's political foundations call for the separation of church and state, religious organizations seek to influence politics and public policy. Can religious devotion mix comfortably with domestic and foreign policy, or are the two a volatile brew to be avoided? These are questions of both intellectual and political significance.

bloody clashes between Hindus and Muslims have centered at least symbolically on the destruction by Hindu nationalists of a historic mosque believed to have been built where a Ram temple once stood (Ram is believed to be the incarnation of the Hindu god Vishnu). The disputes date back to the late 19th century, but the violence has escalated since 1990, when Hindu nationalists attacked the mosque, and 1992, when it was destroyed.

Most of the world's religions actively embrace the values of peace, humanity, and charity. Many believe religion is the basis of morality. On the other hand, religion in various forms, including religious nationalism, has been and remains associated with intolerance, discrimination, and violence. How are we to reconcile these two sides of religion as a local, national, and global institution? Is religion as an institution a force for positive change, or a rationale for conflict? Might it be both? What do you think?

Second, on a global level, the "war on terrorism" initiated by President George W. Bush in 2001 in the wake of the terrorist attacks of 9/11 brought questions about religion and politics to the forefront across the globe. For instance, the United States was faulted for failing to recognize why calling the "war on terror" a "crusade" would offend Muslim sensibilities. Tensions between the West and the Muslim world provoked questions about whether there is a "clash of civilizations" that makes conflict difficult to avoid. Some in the United States worry about the "Islamization" of the Middle East and other regions, while others question the power and political influence of religion in their own U.S. government. Debates about religion and its place in communities, societies, and the world will continue to challenge sociologists in the decades to come.

CQR

Religion in Politics

WHAT CAN I DO WITH A SOCIOLOGY DEGREE?

CAREER DEVELOPMENT: CONSIDERING GRADUATE AND PROFESSIONAL EDUCATION, PART II

In the previous chapter's feature essay, we looked at how you might go about assessing your motivations for graduate or professional school and ways you can begin to explore potential career fields associated with graduate or professional study. Below you will learn about degree options available to those who have completed a bachelor's degree and challenges and opportunities associated with advanced study.

Research Degree Options and Graduate Schools

There are several types of graduate degrees. The most traditional are the master's and doctoral degrees. Master's degrees are academic or professional. The *academic* master's degrees, master of arts (MA) and master of science (MS), focus on intellectual development and the mastery of a core of knowledge in a particular discipline. One may, for instance, earn a master's degree in sociology, anthropology, biology, or English. Professional degrees include the master of business administration (MBA) and the master of social work (MSW), which are designed to advance a career or profession in their respective fields.

The doctor of medicine (MD) and juris doctor (JD) degrees focus on the acquisition of advanced skills and knowledge in the areas of medical practice and law, respectively. The typical time required to earn these professional degrees is generally lengthier than the time to a master's-level professional degree such as the MBA or MSW.

The doctor of philosophy degree (PhD), or doctorate, focuses on advancing intellectual knowledge through original research. The focus of doctoral studies is on the broad mastery of disciplinary knowledge, the development of areas of specialization in the discipline, and rigorous, original research that contributes to the discipline and, perhaps, to policy and general societal knowledge of important topics. Consider this chapter's key focus, religion. As we saw, the sociological study of religion highlights the understanding of societal functions of religion. Students interested in the sociology of religion who are studying to earn a PhD might build a doctoral dissertation project around questions like "How do religious beliefs affect political behavior?" or "Why are young Americans less likely to profess a religious affiliation than previous generations?" Doctoral study opens many avenues for students to pursue original research on topics about which they are intellectually curious, though doctoral study is a lengthy commitment, often requiring a minimum of four years.

Once you have considered different degree options, learn about graduate schools through research and speaking to professors in your field of interest. If you are interested in academic master's or doctoral programs, you may also wish to

- get a fuller sense of your interest in and aptitude for research through a research position while an undergraduate student;
- meet with professors to seek recommendations of advanced study programs in particular fields;
- build relationships with professors and seek information about their research;
- volunteer to assist with research projects in the community, local hospitals, or think tanks; and
- identify requirements of graduate programs: for example, credit hours, comprehensive exams, and research and thesis requirements.

Reflect on the Practical Challenges Related to Graduate and Professional School

Advanced study presents both opportunities and challenges. It expands your knowledge horizon, builds your skills, and broadens your career options. Getting there and succeeding, however, also means recognizing in advance some of the challenges inherent in the process of applying and attending. Consider the following questions as you think about graduate or professional study:

- Do you meet the admission requirements? Do you have the undergraduate GPA you need to be competitive? It is not too soon to do the work needed to achieve a competitive GPA.
- Are there entrance exams to complete? Can you take a preparatory course? How soon should you take it?
- How will you finance your education? Are there options for attending graduate school full-time, or will you want or need to attend part-time?
- How will graduate school affect you and your family?
- How have you managed your workload as an undergraduate? Will you be able to meet the challenges of a graduate or professional school workload?
- What is the right time for graduate or professional school in your personal and career path?

Graduate or professional training beyond the bachelor's degree is an option that many students will eventually choose. According to the American Sociological Association, a little over a third of sociology majors were studying in graduate or professional school 18 months after graduation. Of these, just under a quarter were pursuing sociology at the graduate level, but others were studying social work (17%), law (11%), education (11%), psychology/counseling (9%), business/management (5%), or other fields. Choosing whether to pursue advanced study, as well as when to do so, are very individual decisions. Assess your situation—academic, personal, professional, and financial—as you decide. And seek the guidance of professors, career counselors at your school, and your family as you prepare your study and career plan.

THINK ABOUT CAREERS:

■ *If you are interested in graduate or professional studies, with whom might you speak to get advice on selecting schools to apply to or programs that could be suitable for you? Make a list of people you know through your family, school, or work who could be of help in choosing a program or school.*

▶ *Access additional web links on the student study site to learn more.*

- **Religion** is a system of common beliefs and rituals centered on "sacred things" that unites believers and provides a sense of meaning and purpose. Religion may serve many functions in society, lending groups a common worldview, helping to ritualize or routinize behaviors or beliefs, and providing people with a sense of purpose.

- Sociologists who study religion are interested in how religion helps to organize and structure societies and group behavior, along with the functions religion serves for producing and maintaining group solidarity (or, conversely, creates instability in certain circumstances), and how religion becomes a force in society and within the lives of individuals.

- Classical theorists have differing interpretations of religion's sociological function. Marx has emphasized the role of religion in pacifying the oppressed masses; Weber highlighted the role of Protestantism in the development of capitalism; Durkheim looked at the role of religion in reinforcing social solidarity.

- The modern religious economy perspective emphasizes the role of competition between groups as religions seek followers and potential adherents seek affiliations.

- Religions manifest themselves in more than just shared beliefs. They take the form of institutions. Types of religious organizations can be conceptually placed on a spectrum of conventionality in larger society. A **church** would be on the far end of conventionality, and a **cult** would fit on the opposite end of the spectrum.

- **New religious movements (NRMs)** represent a break from existing religious organizations and a push toward new religious practices.

- Christianity, Islam, and Hinduism are the three largest and most practiced religions on earth, but Judaism, Buddhism, and Confucianism are also influential.

- Women have been historically marginalized in major world religions. Today some activists seek to introduce nonsexist language into scripture and services and to expand women's roles and representation in religious beliefs and practices.

- Youth and young adults in the United States today are less likely to claim a religious affiliation than older adults. At the same time, religious faith continues to exercise influence in U.S. life, including in politics.

- **Disestablishment** refers to periods in which the political influence of religion is significantly challenged.

- **Civil religion** refers to the elevation of a nation as an object of worship.

- Globalization has provided challenges and opportunities to religions of the world. Religions may function to bring both peace and conflict at the global level.

KEY TERMS Study terms on the go with the smartphone-friendly key term flashcards, available at **www.sagepub.com/chamblissintro**

DISCUSSION QUESTIONS

1. How might sociologists explain the "generational shift" in religious affiliation in the United States? Do you believe this shift will continue? Why or why not?

2. If religion serves as a source of stability, as functionalists claim, does that mean that a nation of atheists would be less stable than a nation of religious believers? Make a sociological case to support your position.

3. Consider the issue of women and religious roles and beliefs, which was discussed in this chapter. Where societal norms are increasingly progressive, but dominant religious doctrines are traditional, which one might be reasonably expected to change? Explain your reasoning.

DISCOVER ᑫᑭ STATE STATS

Log-in to the eBook and click on the title to the left for access to State Stats in order to complete the exercise.

Classical sociologist Émile Durkheim was one of the first to treat the phenomenon of suicide as a sociological issue—that is, a problem that had not only individual explanations, but social ones. He argued that sociologists should go beyond the study of individual motivations to seek social structural characteristics of groups and societies that could help explain variations in suicide rates. Based on his findings, one would expect to find higher rates of suicide where social cohesion is lower: For example, he believed that more cohesive religious groups would have lower rates of suicide than less cohesive ones. For this activity, you will go to the State Stats database and find the Health statistics. In the Health database, you should find the "Death Rate by Suicide" data. Examine these data and make observations about recorded suicide rates in five states in different parts of the country in the earliest and latest data (by year). Do you find differences over time or space? Write a brief hypothesis that you might test to explain your findings.

STUDENT STUDY SITE

Visit the Student Study Site at **www.sagepub.com/chamblissintro** to access additional study tools, including eFlashcards, web quizzes, video resources, web resources, audio resources, links to SAGE journal, handbook, and research articles, and much more!

13

THE STATE, POLITICS, AND POWER

WHAT DO YOU THINK?

1. Is the rapid spread of social media likely to make young people more politically passive or more politically active?

2. What sociological factors might explain the relatively low rate of voter participation in the United States? Why is the participation rate of young people lower than the average U.S. voter participation rate?

3. How much power does an average person have in a democracy such as the United States? What are specific ways in which average citizens can make their voices heard in the political process?

SOC *VIEW*

Get a closer look with the authors!

ELECTIONS AND THE YOUTH VOTE

I n the 2012 presidential race, the youth vote mattered. While President Barack Obama won under half of the votes of those 30 and older (about 48%), he earned at least 60% of the votes cast by those under 30. By contrast, Republican presidential candidate Mitt Romney won just 36% of votes cast by this group. In the crucial battleground states of Florida, Pennsylvania, Ohio, and Virginia, this significant margin of victory among younger voters was a key factor for the president's reelection (Pew Research Center for the People and the Press, 2012).

Young adults composed about 19% of the total electorate in 2012 (compared to 18% in 2008). The total number of young voters appears to have declined marginally, but, according to the Pew Research Center for the People and the Press (2012), early predictions of dampened youth enthusiasm were exaggerated. According to the center's research, interest in the election grew in the final weeks of the campaigns, and a rising proportion of young people indicated that they were following political developments closely.

Some political commentators have noted that President Obama's success among younger voters reflected not only shared political interests and concerns, but also the Obama campaign's innovative use of social media to ferret out "hidden young voters," few of whom could be found through conventional means because most lacked listed phone numbers. The campaign contacted young supporters and invited them to download a Facebook app that enabled the campaign to see their "friend" lists; over a million of them did this. As well, according to one account, "in those final weeks of the campaign, the team blitzed the supporters who had signed up for the app with requests to share specific online content with specific friends simply by clicking a button. More than 600,000 supporters followed through with over 5 million contacts, asking their friends to register to vote, give money, vote or look at a video designed to change their mind." The logic of this appeal followed what political scientists had already established in 2010: Online social networks can affect voting behavior (Scherer, 2012). In this instance as well, they did.

As we will see later in the chapter, young people have historically been less likely to vote than older generations and have expressed less interest in the process. Will social media transform youth engagement and participation in campaigns? Did social media affect your knowledge and decisions in the last election? ■

We begin this chapter with a discussion of power and the modern nation-state, examining citizenship rights and their provision and then looking at different forms taken by state power and authority. We then examine functionalist and conflict perspectives on state power in order to understand how power and its exercise are understood by sociologists. A discussion of forms of governance in the modern world provides the background for an examination of the U.S. political system, where we consider two-party politics, voter apathy and activism in particular among young people, and how money influences politics.

Obtaining citizenship is a dream for many immigrants to the United States. Every year, thousands take the Naturalization Oath of Allegiance to the United States. ■

THE MODERN STATE

For most of human history, people lived in hundreds of thousands of small and homogenous communities, within which they shared the same language, culture, and customs. Today, however, the world's 7 billion people are distributed across 192 countries. On the world stage, countries are key actors: They are responsible for war and peace, the economic welfare of their citizens, and the quality of our shared environment.

Social scientists (Gellner, 1983) commonly characterize modern countries as **nation-states**—that is, *a single people (a nation) governed by a political authority (a state).* Very few countries neatly fit this model, however. Most are made up of many different peoples brought together through warfare, conquest, immigration, or boundaries drawn by colonial authorities without respect to ethnic or religious differences of the time. For instance, many Native Americans think of themselves as belonging to the Navajo, Lakota, Pawnee, or Iroquois nation rather than only to the

United States. In Great Britain, many residents of Wales, Scotland, and Northern Ireland regard English as a second language and view themselves as Welsh, Irish, or Scottish rather than British. In Nigeria, most people identify primarily with others who are Yoruba, Ibo, or Hausa rather than with a country called Nigeria. Because most political entities are not characterized by the homogeneity implied by the definition of nation-state, we will use the more familiar terms *country* and *state* rather than nation-state.

While not all countries possess them in equal measure, the characteristics we list below represent what Max Weber would term an *ideal-typical model,* a picture that approximates but does not perfectly represent reality. Modern countries emerged along with contemporary capitalism, which benefited from strong central governments and legal systems that regulated commerce and trade both within and across borders (M. Mann, 1986; Wallerstein, 1974; Weber, 1921/1979). This history accounts for several unique features of modern countries, which distinguish them from earlier forms of political organization:

- Underlying the social organization of the modern country is a system of **law**, *the codified rules of behavior established by a government and backed by the threat of force* (Chambliss & Seidman, 1982). The rule of law is a critical aspect of democratic governance.
- The governments of modern countries claim complete and final authority over the people who reside within their borders (Hinsley, 1986).
- People living within a country's borders are divided between **citizens**, *individuals who are part of a political*

. . . .

Nation-state: A single people (a "nation") governed by a political authority (a "state"). Similar to the modern notion of "country."

Law: A system of binding and recognized rules that regulate the actions of people pertaining to a given jurisdiction.

Citizen: A legally recognized inhabitant of a country who bears the rights and responsibilities of citizenship as defined by the state.

The idea of Social Security was first championed by President Truman, but it took a few presidential administrations before President Roosevelt signed it into law in 1935. ■

community in which they are granted certain rights and privileges and, at the same time, have specified obligations and duties, and **noncitizens**, *people who are temporary or permanent residents and who do not have the same rights and privileges as citizens* (Held, 1989).

Citizenship rights may take several forms. *Civil rights,* which protect citizens from injury by individuals and institutions, include the right to equal treatment in places such as the school or workplace regardless of race, gender, sexual orientation, or disabilities. *Political rights* ensure that citizens can participate in governance, whether by voting, running for office, or openly expressing political opinions. *Social rights,* which call for the governmental provision of various forms of economic and social security, include such things as retirement pensions and guaranteed income after losing a job or becoming disabled. Citizens are afforded legal protections from arbitrary rule and in turn are expected to pay taxes, to engage in their own governance through voting or other activities, and to perform military service (specific expectations, of course, vary by country). In reality, the extent to which all people enjoy the full rights of citizenship in any given country varies. Below we discuss two specific aspects of citizenship rights—the first relates to the evolution of state provisions for ensuring social rights; the second relates to the degree to which citizens enjoy freedom in the form of political rights and civil liberties.

THE WELFARE STATE

In most modern countries, political and civil rights evolved and were institutionalized before social rights were realized. The category of social rights is broad and encompasses entitlements that include health care insurance, old age pensions, unemployment benefits, a minimum wage floor for workers, and a spectrum of other benefits intended to ensure social and economic security for the citizenry. Social rights have largely been won by groups of citizens mobilizing (on the basis of the civil and political rights they enjoy) to realize their interests.

Social rights are often embodied in what is termed the **welfare state**, *a political order characterized by the broad provision of social and economic welfare benefits for its citizenry.* It has characterized Western systems of governance in the post–World War II period. In the United States, Social Security, a key social welfare program that ensures an income for retired workers, and Medicare, which provides for at least basic health care for the elderly, are examples of the U.S. welfare state. Social Security was created through the Social Security Act of 1935, signed by President Franklin D. Roosevelt, establishing a social insurance program that provided continuing income for retired workers at age 65 or older (Social Security Administration, 2013). Although it was the vision of President Harry S. Truman, Medicare and Medicaid did not get signed into law until a few decades later, when they were endorsed by President Lyndon B. Johnson. The welfare state has long been a hallmark of advanced and wealthy countries; most developing states have much thinner safety nets, and few have had the resources to provide for retirees or even, oftentimes, for the unemployed or ill.

While it has come to represent a culmination of the three key rights of citizenship in modern countries, the welfare state is shrinking rather than expanding today. Factors such as global wage competition and growing debt loads borne by countries from the United States to Europe and beyond have put pressure on the expansion of social rights. While it is difficult to reduce benefits to already existing constituencies—for example, in the United States, discussion of reducing Social Security payments or even raising the age of eligibility evokes vehement protest from retirees—the economic crises of recent years have led to attempts by lawmakers to curb benefits to less powerful constituencies, including the poor and immigrants.

. . . .

Noncitizens: Individuals who reside in a given jurisdiction but do not possess the same rights and privileges as the citizens who are recognized inhabitants. Sometimes referred to as residents, temporary workers, or aliens.

Welfare state: A government or country's system of providing for the financial and social well-being of its citizens, typically through government programs that provide funding or other resources to individuals who meet certain criteria.

Crimes of the State

Welfare State Debate

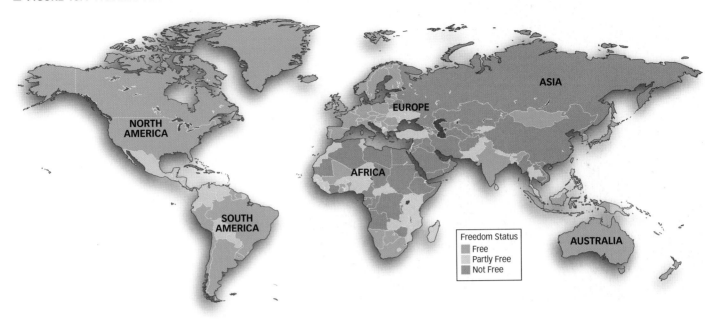

SOURCE: Freedom House. (2012). Freedom in the World. *Issues.*

POLITICAL RIGHTS AND CIVIL LIBERTIES

Every year, Freedom House, an organization dedicated to monitoring and promoting democratic change and human rights, publishes an evaluation of "freedom" in 195 countries, as well as 14 related and disputed territories (Figure 13.1). The report includes ratings that measure *political rights* (based on the electoral process, political pluralism, and participation) and *civil liberties* (based on freedom of expression and belief, rights of association and organization, rule of law, and individual rights).

Even in the United States, which earns top scores in Freedom House's survey, problems with voting procedures have raised the question of whether some voters, especially minorities, have been denied a political voice in elections. Nationwide, over 5 million U.S. citizens, including over 4 million of whom are not in prison, are barred from voting due to felony convictions. In Alabama and Florida, for instance, nearly a third of African American men are permanently disenfranchised (Froomkin, 2010).

Recently, some state legislatures have sought to implement voter identification laws, which require voters to show a photo ID when they vote in person; in 2011, fully 14 states had such laws (Figure 13.2 on page 324). Critics point out that minorities, in particular those who are elderly or poor, are among those least likely to have a photo ID in the form of a driver's license or passport. The practical effect of voter ID laws, they say, is not to combat voter fraud (which has been infrequently documented in the United States), but rather to disenfranchise minorities and the poor (A. Cohen, 2012). What do you think about voter ID laws? Do they bring greater benefits or costs?

Later in this chapter, we discuss more fully the issue of political voice, or the representation of a group's interests in bodies such as state and national legislatures, and ways in which political voice may vary based on variables such as income. Below we turn to broader sociological perspectives on state power, which can give us a fuller context for analyzing contemporary debates on power and politics.

THEORIES OF STATE POWER

Sociologists have developed different approaches to explaining how authority is exercised in modern societies. Below we highlight two theoretical approaches, which disagree about how widely power is shared. These theories are based largely on governance in the United States today, although we can also apply them to other modern societies.

THE FUNCTIONALIST PERSPECTIVE AND PLURALIST THEORY

Functionalist theories of state power assume that most people in a society agree on a set of norms and values. Classical sociologist Émile Durkheim (1922/1956, 1922/1973b) saw government as an institution that translates broadly shared values and interests into fair-minded laws and effective policies. Contemporary functionalist theorists recognize that modern societies do not always enjoy consensus on values and norms. The government,

Affirmative Action

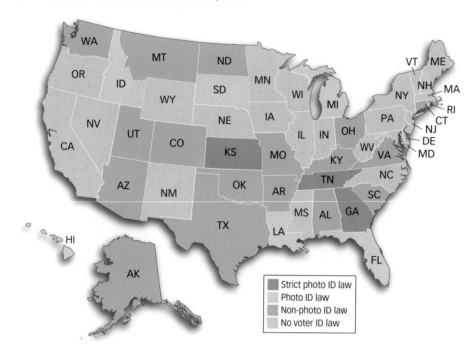

Strict photo ID law
Photo ID law
Non-photo ID law
No voter ID law

SOURCE: National Conference of State Legislatures. (2012). Voter identification requirements. *Legislature & Elections.*

they suggest, is a neutral umpire, balancing the conflicting values, norms, and interests of a variety of competing groups in its laws and actions.

In the United States, most people agree on such general values as liberty, democratic governance, and equality of opportunity, but debate occurs on many other issues such as abortion, the death penalty, the waging of war, funding for medical care when people are old or ill, and the size of government. Recognizing the pluralistic—that is, diverse—nature of contemporary societies, sociologists and political scientists developed theories of government that highlight this aspect of state power.

Pluralist theory tries to answer the question "Given that modern societies are pluralistic, how do they resolve the inevitable conflicts?" To answer this question Robert Dahl (1961, 1982, 1989) studied decision making in New Haven, Connecticut. Dahl (1961) concluded that power was exercised through the political process, which was dominated by different groups of leaders, each having access to a different amalgamation of political resources. Dahl argued that, in their efforts to exert political influence, individuals come together in **interest groups**—*groups comprising people who share the same concerns on a particular issue.* Interest groups may be short-lived, such as a local citizens' group that bands together to have a road repaved or a school built, or they may be long-lasting, such as a labor union or a manufacturers' association.

Dahl's theory argues that interest groups serve the function of seeing that everyone's perspective (values, norms, interests) is

represented in the government. The influence of one group is offset by the power of another. For instance, if several investors band together to seek government approval to clear-cut a forest to build homes, a group of citizens concerned about the environment may coalesce into an interest group to oppose it. The ideal result, according to Dahl, would be a compromise: perhaps limited cutting or the preservation of some particularly sensitive areas. Similarly, big businesses and organized labor routinely face off, so neither exercises disproportionate influence on the political process.

When two powerful interests oppose one another, pluralists see compromise as the likely outcome, and the role of the government is therefore to broker solutions that benefit as many interests as possible. In this view, power is dynamic and fluid, passing from one stakeholder to another over time rather than being concentrated in the hands of a powerful few. This competition and fluidity of power contribute to democratic governance and society.

A critical view of the pluralist characterization of political power points out that modern societies generally lack the assumed consensus and that government is unlikely to represent all interests equally (Chambliss & Seidman, 1982; Domhoff, 2006). Critics also dispute the assumption that government is a neutral mediator between competing interests. They argue that laws may favor some groups over others, so the legal deck is stacked from the beginning. For example, when the U.S. Constitution was framed by White male property owners, only White male property owners could vote: People without property, women, Blacks, and American Indians were excluded from the political process.

As well, some interest groups are far more powerful than others. Governments do not apply the rules neutrally, as the theory claims; rather, they interpret (or even bend) the rules to favor the most powerful groups in society, including big business and other monied interests that finance increasingly costly political campaigns for those who favor them (Domhoff, 2006, 2009; L. Friedman, 1975, 1990).

As a consequence of all these factors, critics contend, even if laws are passed to protect the values and interests of people who are not economically powerful, the laws will not be actively and forcefully implemented. For example, *de facto* racial segregation and discrimination continue to exist, even though school segregation has been outlawed in the United States since 1954

. . . .

Interest groups: Advocacy or lobby groups that utilize their organizational and social resources to influence legislation and the functioning of social institutions.

and most other forms of racial discrimination became illegal in the decade that followed.

THE CONFLICT PERSPECTIVE AND CLASS DOMINANCE THEORY

Social conflict theory highlights power differences between social groups. This perspective recognizes that modern societies are pluralistic, but it argues that the interests of social groups are often incompatible with one another. Furthermore, conflict theory suggests some groups are simply more powerful than others and are therefore more likely to see their interests, values, and norms reflected in government policies and laws. More powerful groups use their power to create

Voter ID laws created controversy in the 2012 federal election campaign. While about three quarters of the population expressed support for the laws, critics pointed out that their implementation risked disenfranchising the populations least likely to have government-issued ID, including the elderly, minorities, and the poor. ■

systems of law, economy, politics, and education that favor them, their children, and other members of their social group.

Unlike pluralistic theory, which views competing interests as having relatively equal and shifting opportunities and access to power, conflict theory sees the concentration of power in the hands of a privileged few groups and individuals. The gains of the elite, conflict theorists suggest, come at the expense of those who have fewer resources, including economic, cultural, and social capital.

The roots of conflict theory are found in the ideas of Karl Marx. You may recall from previous chapters that Marx believed the most important sources of social conflict were economic, and that, as a consequence, class conflict was fundamental to all other forms of conflict. Within a capitalist society, in Marx's view, government represents and serves the interests of the capitalist class or bourgeoisie, the ruling class that exerts disproportionate influence on the government. Still, a well-organized working class can effectively press government for such economic reforms as a shorter working day or the end of child labor.

Contemporary conflict theory extends Marx's concept of the ruling class to include powerful groups besides the capitalist class. **Class dominance theory**, for instance, argues that *power is concentrated in the hands of a relatively small number of individuals who compose a power elite* (Domhoff, 1983, 1990, 2002; Mills, 1956). These individuals have often attended the same elite schools, belong to the same social organizations, and cycle in and out of top positions in government, business, and the military (the so-called revolving door). Class dominance theory complements Marx's

original ideas with a focus on the elite social networks themselves, rather than only on capitalism as a political-economic system.

Domhoff (2002, 2006, 2009) posits that we can show the existence of a dominant class by examining the answers to several basic questions, which he terms "power indicators": *Who benefits? Who governs? Who wins?*

- In terms of "Who benefits?" Domhoff asks us to consider who gets the most of what is valued in society. Who gets money and material goods? What about leisure and travel or status and prestige? "Those who have the most of what people want are, by inference, the powerful," writes Domhoff (2006, p. 13).
- In terms of "Who governs?" he asks who is positioned to make the important political and economic and legal decisions in the country or community. Are all demographic groups relatively well represented? Are some disproportionately powerful? Domhoff suggests, "If a group or class is highly overrepresented or underrepresented in relation to its proportion of the population, it can be inferred that the group or class is relatively powerful or powerless, as the case may be" (2006, p. 14).
- Asking "Who wins?" entails inquiring about which group or groups have their interests realized most often. Domhoff concedes that movements with fewer resources, including, for instance, environmental groups, may "win" desired legislation sometimes. However, we need to look at who has their desires realized most consistently and often. Is it small interest groups representing civil rights, environmental activists, or same-sex marriage advocates? Is it large corporate interests with friends in high places and the ability to write big campaign donation checks?

. . . .

Class dominance theory: The argument that a small and concentrated group of elite or upper-class people dominate and influence societal institutions; compatible with conflict theory.

After examining the power indicators in his book *Who Rules America?* Domhoff concludes that it is the upper class, particularly the owners and managers of large for-profit enterprises, that benefits, governs, and wins. This, he suggests, challenges the premise of pluralist theories that power is not concentrated but dynamic, moving among a variety of interests and groups. Domhoff uses research on corporate America to demonstrate close linkages between corporations, suggesting that a small but powerful inner circle, a **power elite**, is made up of *individuals who are linked to the social upper class, the corporate community, and the policy-formation organizations that influence government policy.* Though member corporations or organizations or individuals may be divided on some issues, Domhoff contends that cooperation is stronger than competition: The power elite is united by a common set of interests, including a probusiness and antiregulation environment, and common enemies, including environmentalists and labor and consumer activists.

From a critical perspective, class dominance theory tends to overemphasize the unified nature of the "ruling class." For instance, Domhoff highlights the fact that many members of the power elite share similar social backgrounds. Often, they attended the same private high schools and colleges, spend their vacations in the same exclusive resorts, and marry into one another's families. They share a strong belief in the importance and value of capitalism and, as Domhoff argues, are steeped in a similar set of worldviews. However, it is difficult to show that they necessarily share the same political beliefs or even economic orientation (Chambliss & Seidman, 1982; Chambliss & Zatz, 1994).

Further, government decisions sometimes appear to be in direct opposition to the expressed interests of powerful capitalist groups. For example, when faced with major conflicts between labor and management during the Depression years of the 1930s, the U.S. government passed laws legalizing trade unions and giving workers the right to bargain collectively with their corporate employers, even though both laws were strongly opposed by corporation executives and owners (Chambliss & Zatz, 1994; Skocpol, 1979; Tilly, 1975). Mark Smith (2000) found that when businesses act to influence public policy to support or oppose some issue, it can often work against them as labor and public interest groups organize in opposition to the perceived power seizure.

Does a power elite exercise disproportionate influence in the political sphere of the United States? Domhoff and other conflict theorists would answer in the affirmative. A pluralist perspective might see corporations, the upper class, and policy organizations as some among many players who compete in the political power game, balanced by other groups such as unions or environmentalists, and answer in the negative. What do you think?

Gun Ownership

POWER AND AUTHORITY

In the section above, we looked at different perspectives on how state power functions and who it serves. Below we turn the question of how states exercise their power in practice by asking the question "How do governments maintain control over their populations?"

One obvious way that states exercise power is through outright **coercion**—*the threat or use of physical violence to force compliance.* Relying solely on coercion, however, is costly and difficult because it requires surveillance and sometimes suppression of the population, particularly those segments that might be inclined to dissent. Governments that ground their authority in coercion are vulnerable to instability, as they generally fail to earn the allegiance of their people. It is more efficient, and in the long run more enduring, if a government can establish **legitimate authority**, *power that is recognized as rightful by those over whom it is exercised.*

One of sociology's founders, Max Weber (1864–1920), was also one of the first social scientists to analyze the nature of legitimate authority, and his ideas have influenced our understanding of power and authority in the modern world. Weber sought to answer the question "Why do people consent to give up power, allowing others to dominate them?" His examination of this question, which was based on detailed studies of societies throughout history, identified three ways authority has historically been legitimized: traditional, rational-legal, and charismatic.

TRADITIONAL AUTHORITY

For most of human history, state power relied on **traditional authority**, *power based on a belief in the sanctity of long-standing traditions and the legitimate right of rulers to exercise authority in accordance with these traditions* (Weber, 1921/1979). Traditional rulers claim power on the basis of age-old norms, beliefs, and practices. When the people being governed accept the legitimacy of traditional authority, it tends to be relatively stable over time. The monarchies of Europe, for example, ruled for hundreds of years based on traditional authority. Their people were considered the king's or queen's "subjects," whose loyalty derived from their recognition of the fundamental legitimacy of monarchical rule, with its long-standing hierarchy and distribution of power on the basis of blood and birth. In modern Europe, however, monarchies such as those in Denmark and Sweden have little more than symbolic power—they have been largely stripped of political power.

. . . .

Power elite: A group of people with a disproportionately high level of influence and resources who utilize their status to influence the functioning of societal institutions.

Coercion: The threat or use of physical force in order to ensure compliance.

Legitimate authority: Power that is recognized as rightful by those over whom it is exercised.

Traditional authority: Power based on a belief in the sanctity of long-standing traditions and the legitimate right of rulers to exercise authority in accordance with those traditions.

Traditional authority, in this instance, coexists with the rational-legal authority exercised by modern elected bodies, which we discuss below.

Traditional authority supports the exercise of power at both the macro and micro levels: While reverence for traditional norms and practices may give legitimacy to a state, a religion, or other government, so too may it drive the decisions and actions of families. If families mark a particular holiday or date with an obligatory ritual, then even if an individual questions the need for that ritual, the reasoning "We've *always* done that" is a micro-level exercise of traditional authority that ensures compliance and discourages challenges by any member of the group.

RATIONAL-LEGAL AUTHORITY

Traditional authority, in Weber's view, was incompatible with the rise of modern capitalist states. Capitalism is based on forms of social organization that favor rational, rule-governed calculation rather than practices grounded in tradition. As capitalism evolved, traditional authority gave way to **rational-legal authority,** *power based on a belief in the lawfulness of enacted rules (laws) and the legitimate right of leaders to exercise authority under such rules* (Weber, 1921/1979). The legitimacy of rational-legal authority derives from a belief in the rule of law. We do something not simply because it has always been done that way, but because it conforms to established rules and procedures.

In a system based on rational-legal authority, leaders are regarded as legitimate as long as they act according to law. Laws, in turn, are enacted and enforced through formal, bureaucratic procedures, rather than reflecting custom and tradition or the whims of a ruler. Weber argued that rational-legal authority is compatible with modern economies, which are based on rational calculation of costs and benefits, profits, and other economic decisions. Rational-legal authority is commonly exercised in the ideal-typical modern state described at the start of this chapter. In practice, we could take the United States, Canada, Japan, or the countries of the European Union as specific examples of states governed by rational-legal authority.

CHARISMATIC AUTHORITY

Weber's third form of authority can threaten both traditional and rational-legal authority. **Charismatic authority** is *power based on devotion inspired in followers by the personal qualities of a leader*

In Great Britain, traditional authority peacefully and functionally coexists with rational-legal authority. In this photo, British Prime Minister David Cameron, who is the head of government, shakes hands with Queen Elizabeth II, who is the constitutional monarch. ■

(Weber, 1921/1979). It derives from widespread belief in a given community that an individual has a "gift" of great—even divine—powers, so it rests most significantly on an individual personality, rather than on that individual's claim to authority on the basis of tradition or legal election or appointment. Charismatic authority may also be the product of a "cult of personality," an image of a leader that is carefully manipulated by the leader and other elites. In North Korea's long-standing dictatorship, power has passed through several generations of the same family, as has the government's careful construction of a "cult of personality" around each leader, which elevates him as supremely intelligent, patriotic, and worthy.

Prominent charismatic leaders in religious history include Moses, Jesus Christ, the Prophet Muhammad, and Buddha. Some military and political rulers whose power was based in large part on charisma are Julius Caesar, Napoleon Bonaparte, Vladimir Lenin, and Adolf Hitler (clearly, not all charismatic leaders are charitable, ethical, or good).

More recently, charismatic leaders have emerged to lead communities and countries toward democratic development. Václav Havel, a dissident playwright in what was then communist Czechoslovakia, challenged the authority of a government that was not elected and that citizens despised; he spent years in prison and doing menial jobs because he was not permitted to work in his artistic field. Later, he helped lead the 1989 opposition movement against the government and, with its fall, was elected president of a new democratic state. (Czechoslovakia no longer exists; its Czech and Slovak populations wanted to establish their own nation-states, and in 1993 they peacefully formed two separate

....

Rational-legal authority: Power based on a belief in the lawfulness of enacted rules (laws) and the legitimate right of leaders to exercise authority under such rules.

Charismatic authority: Power based on devotion inspired in followers by the personal qualities of a leader.

According to a BBC report, "Every night, North Korea's news bulletin begins with a song about the mythical qualities of the country's leader Kim Jong-il" (Williamson, 2011). Political and military leaders in this isolated totalitarian state nurture the image of the late "Dear Leader" and the son who succeeded him. ■

republics.) Similarly, Nelson Mandela, despite spending 27 years in prison, remained a key figure in the opposition movement against the racist policies of apartheid in South Africa. Mandela became South Africa's first democratically elected president in 1994, four years after his release from prison.

Notably, Weber also pointed to a phenomenon he termed the *routinization of charisma*. That is, with the decline, departure, or death of a charismatic leader, his or her authority may be transformed into legal-rational or even traditional authority. While those who follow may govern in the charismatic leader's name, the leader's authority rests either on emulation (traditionalized authority) or on power that has been routinized and institutionalized (rationalized authority).

Authority exists in a larger context, and political authority is often sited in a government. Governance takes place in a variety of forms, which we discuss below.

FORMS OF GOVERNANCE IN THE MODERN WORLD

In the modern world, the three principal forms of governance are authoritarianism, totalitarianism, and democracy. Below we

Authoritarianism

discuss each type, offering ideal-typical definitions, as well as illustrative examples. Two modern global trends in governance are the growth of rational-legal authority and the spread of representative democracy.

AUTHORITARIANISM

In **authoritarian** forms of governance, *ordinary members of society are denied the right to participate in government, while political power is exercised by and for the benefit of a small political elite.* At the same time, authoritarianism is distinguished from totalitarianism (which we will discuss shortly) by the fact that there are at least some social, cultural, and economic institutions that are not under the control of the state. Two prominent types of authoritarianism are monarchies and dictatorships.

Monarchy is *a form of governance in which power resides in an individual or a family and is passed from one generation to the next through hereditary lines.* Monarchies, which derive their legitimacy from traditional authority, were the primary form of governance in many parts of the world, and in Europe until the 18th century. Today, the formerly powerful royal families of Europe have been either dethroned or relegated to peripheral and ceremonial roles. For example, the queens of England, Denmark, and the Netherlands and the kings of Sweden and Spain do not have any significant political power or formal authority to govern. A few countries in the modern world are still ruled by monarchies, including Saudi Arabia, Jordan, Qatar, and Kuwait. Even these monarchs, however, govern with the consent of other powerful religious and social or economic groups.

In the territory of Saudi Arabia, for instance, the royal family, also known as the House of Saud, has ruled for centuries, though the country of Saudi Arabia itself was established only in 1932. The Basic Law of 1992 declared Saudi Arabia to be a monarchy ruled by the sons and grandsons of King Abdul Aziz al-Saud, making the country the only one in the world named after a family. The constitution of the country is the Koran, and, consequently, *sharia* law, which is based on Islamic traditions and beliefs, is in effect. The country does not hold national elections, nor is the formation of independent political parties permitted. However,

Authoritarianism: A form of governance in which ordinary members of society are denied the right to participate in government, while political power is exercised by and for the benefit of a small political elite.

Monarchy: A form of governance in which power resides in an individual or a family and is passed from one generation to the next through hereditary lines.

TWEETING REVOLUTION AND RESISTANCE

Shortly after the new year began in 2011, thousands in Egypt took to the streets to call for regime change and an end to the decades-long authoritarian rule of Hosni Mubarak. They were armed not with weapons, but with mobile phones and laptops. The revolution of the future had arrived. An article on the role of the Internet in Egyptian protest actions (A. Alexander, 2011) noted that "every mass movement needs spaces where political alternatives can be debated and organization can take place . . . In the 1940s, the last time that Egypt saw mass protests on a similar scale, radical bookshops, underground newspapers and illegal trade union meetings played this role . . . For the current generation some of these spaces have been online."

Anonymity gives contemporary organizers power, since digital dissidents can plan, protest, and disseminate their message of resistance in a forum that carries less risk than meetings, which may draw the attention of security forces. Of course authoritarian governments can track dissidents online, as well as on the street, but the digital revolution has brought a new tool to the arsenal of social change, one to which populations even in developing countries have increasing access. It is estimated that in Egypt, about 80 percent of the population has mobile phone access, and even poor and rural areas are accessing the Internet (A. Alexander, 2011).

The Egyptian uprising was sparked at least in part by the

The road to democratic governance in Egypt has not been smooth. After Egypt's democratically elected president, Mohamed Morsi, asserted expanded political powers in November 2012, hundreds of thousands of Egyptians again took to the streets to demonstrate against the perceived threat to democracy. ■

Facebook activism of Wael Ghonim, a young Google executive who became a symbol of Egypt's pro-democracy uprising. A Facebook group created to protest the death of Khaled Said, an activist, at the hands of the Egyptian security apparatus became an organizational core of the protests and eventually was "liked" by nearly 600,000 people (A. Alexander, 2011). In the wake of the protests, Ghonim was quoted as saying, "If you want to liberate a country, give them the internet" (Gustin, 2011).

Some media analysts have suggested that digital media did not cause the revolutionary uprising in Egypt, but it did speed the dissemination of the activist message and drew the attention of the global

media. One social media expert has argued that Facebook and Twitter played different roles in the uprising, suggesting that "Facebook helped to organize the activists inside the country . . . while Twitter functioned to help get the message out to the broader world," adding, "One of the things that social media does is transmission of hope across these countries" (Gustin, 2011).

THINK IT THROUGH

■ *Wael Ghonim called the Egyptian uprising "Revolution 2.0." Is digital media the future of social change? What are the potential rewards and dangers of this new form of resistance to the state and authority?*

Nazi Germany, the Soviet Union under the leadership of Lenin and later Stalin, Chile under August Pinochet, and the Spain of Francisco Franco were examples of totalitarian regimes. This image of "Big Brother," a symbol of totalitarianism's penetration of private as well as public life, comes from the film version of George Orwell's classic book, *1984*. ▓

the royal rulers govern within the bounds of the constitution, tradition, and the consent of religious leaders, the *ulema*.

A more modern form of authoritarianism is **dictatorship**, *a form of governance in which power rests in a single individual.* An example of an authoritarian dictatorship includes the rule of Iraqi president Saddam Hussein, who ruled his country from 1979 to his deposition in 2003. As this case shows, the individual in power is actually closely intertwined with an inner circle of governing elites. In Iraq, for instance, Saddam was linked to the inner circle of the Baath Party. Further, because of the complexity of modern society, even the most heavy-handed authoritarian dictator requires some degree of support from military leaders and an intelligence apparatus. No less important to the dictator's power is the compliance of the masses, whether it is gained through coercion or consent.

We might argue that today it is difficult for a single individual or even a handful of individuals to effectively run a modern country for any length of time. In recent years, many dictators have been deposed by foes or ousted in popular revolutions. Some have even allowed themselves to be turned out of office by relatively peaceful democratic movements, as happened in the former Soviet Union and the formerly communist states of Eastern Europe, such as Czechoslovakia and Hungary. China, which has become

progressively more capitalistic while retaining an authoritarian communist government, remains an exception to this pattern.

TOTALITARIANISM

When authoritarian dictatorships persist and become entrenched, the end result may be a totalitarian form of government. **Totalitarianism** *denies popular political participation in government, but goes one step further by seeking to regulate and control all aspects of the public and private lives of citizens.* In totalitarianism, there are no limits to the exercise of state power. All opposition is outlawed, access to information not provided by the state is stringently controlled, and citizens are required to demonstrate a high level of commitment and loyalty to the system. Totalitarian governments depend more on coercion than legitimacy in exercising power. They thus require a large intelligence apparatus to monitor the citizenry for antigovernment activities, and to punish those who fail to conform. Members of the society are urged to inform on one another if the rules are broken or the leadership is criticized.

One characteristic shared by totalitarian regimes of the 20th century was a ruthless commitment to power and coercion over the rule of law. Soviet leader Vladimir Lenin is quoted as stating that "the dictatorship—and take this into account once and for all—means unrestricted power based on force, not on law" (Amis, 2002 p. 33).

Another characteristic of totalitarian regimes was a willingness to destroy the opposition by any means necessary. Joseph Stalin's regime in the USSR, which lasted from 1922 to 1953, purged millions of perceived, potential, or imagined enemies; Stalin's Great Terror tore apart the ranks of even the Soviet military apparatus. Martin Amis (2002) cites the following statistics in characterizing Stalin's "war" on his own military. From the late 1930s to about 1941, Stalin purged 3 of the 5 marshals, 13 of 15 army commanders, 154 of 186 divisional commanders, and at least 43,000 officers lower down the chain of command (Amis, 2002, p. 175). An often-told story about Stalin cites him telling his political inner circle that each should find two replacements for himself.

Perhaps more than any other political system, totalitarianism is built on terror and the threat of terror—including genocide, imposed famine, purges, deportation, imprisonment, torture, and murder. Fear keeps the masses docile and the dictator in power. Torture has a long, brutal history in the dictatorships of the world, and, in trying to uncover its function, Amis (2002) makes the compelling observation that "torture, among its other applications, was part of Stalin's war against truth. He tortured, not to force you to reveal a fact, but to force you to collude in a fiction" (p. 61).

Today, few totalitiarian states exist. Certainly, in the age of the Internet, control of information is an enormous challenge to states that seek full control of their populations. North Korea remains one of the last remaining totalitarian states, where the citizenry is nearly

. . . .

Dictatorship: A form of governance in which power rests in a single individual.

Totalitarianism: A form of governance that denies popular political participation in government as well as seeks to regulate and control all aspects of the public and private lives of citizens.

fully isolated from the rest of the world and few North Koreans outside the elite have electricity or enough nutritious food, not to speak of Internet connections or computers.

DEMOCRACY

Democracy, *a form of governance in which citizens are able to participate directly or indirectly in their own governance,* literally means "the rule of the people." (The word comes from the Greek *demos,* "the people," and *kratos,* "rule.") The concept of democracy originated in the Greek city-state of Athens during the 5th century B.C., where it took the form of **direct democracy**, in which *all citizens fully participate in their own governance.* This full participation was possible because Athens was a small community by today's standards, and because the vast majority of its people (including women and slaves, on whose labor the economy relied) were excluded from citizenship (E. Sagan, 1992).

Direct democracy is rarely possible today because of the sheer size of most countries and the complexity of their political affairs. One exception is the referendum process that exists in states including California and Oregon. In Oregon, for instance, the signatures of a specified percentage of registered voters can bring a referendum to the ballot. In 2012, Oregonians voted on Ballot Measure 80, which sought to decriminalize personal marijuana usage. Although the signature requirement to have the initative voted on was reached, the ballot measure was ultimately defeated by state voters (CNN, 2012).

Democracy in the modern world more typically takes the form of **representative democracy**, *a political system in which citizens elect representatives to govern them.* In a representative democracy, elected officials are expected to make decisions that reflect the interests of their constituents. Representative democracy first took hold in the industrial capitalist countries of Europe. It is now the principal form of governance throughout the world, although some parts of the population in democratic states may be disenfranchised. For instance, only in recent years have women been legally granted the right to vote in many countries (Figure 13.3). Some countries, such as China, the largest remaining authoritarian society, claim to have free elections for many government positions, though eligibility is limited to members of the Communist Party. Thus even though voting is the hallmark of representative democracy, the mere fact of voting does not ensure the existence of a true democracy.

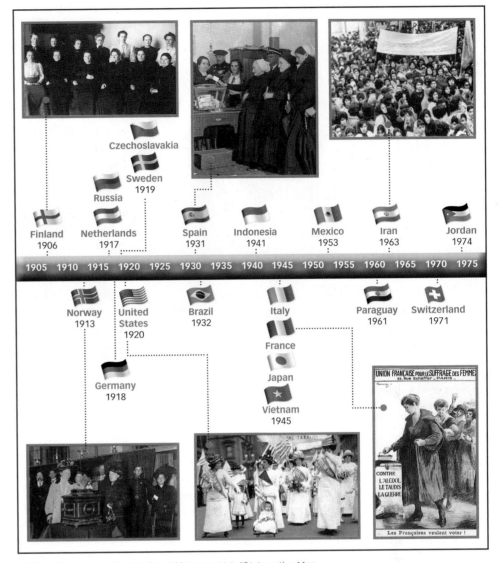

FIGURE 13.3 When Women Won the Right to Vote in Selected Countries, 20th Century

SOURCE: "Women's Suffrage: When Did Women Vote?" Interactive Map.

Democracy: A form of governance in which citizens are able to participate directly or indirectly in their own governance.

Direct democracy: A political system in which all citizens fully participate in their own governance.

Representative democracy: A political system in which citizens elect representatives to govern them.

Politics: The art or science of influencing public policy.

THE U.S. POLITICAL SYSTEM

Politics in democratic societies is structured around competing political parties whose purpose is to gain control of the

Democracy

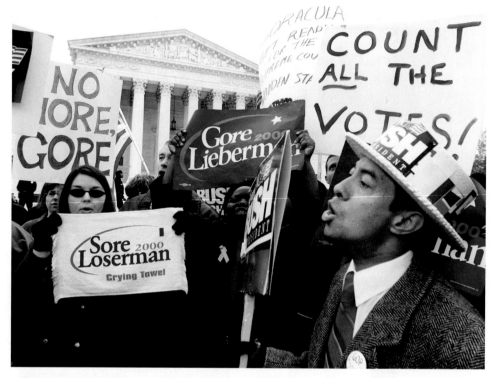

Balloting in the 2000 presidential election produced a disputed result. The Gore campaign sought recounts of ballots in several Florida counties, which the campaign believed could tilt the state's majority toward Gore. In *Bush v. Gore,* the U.S. Supreme Court ruled the planned recount unconstitutional, confirming President Bush's electoral victory. ■

head of the party that has the largest number of seats in the national legislature (typically called a *parliament*). Britain, for example, has a parliamentary system. This arrangement can give a greater degree of influence to minority parties (those that have relatively few representatives in Parliament), since the majority party often requires minority party support to pass legislation, or even to elect a prime minister.

In the United States, the president is chosen by popular vote, though, as happened in the 2000 presidential election, a candidate who wins the popular vote (in this case, Al Gore), will not become president if he fails to win the requisite number of Electoral College votes. Voters in the United States have often chosen a president from one party and a Congress dominated by the other.

The separate election of the president and Congress is intended to help ensure a separation of powers between the executive and legislative branches of the government. At the same time, it weakens the power of minority or third parties, since—unlike the case in parliamentary systems—they are unlikely to have much impact on who will be selected chief of state. In Britain or Germany, by contrast, if a minority party stops voting with the majority party in parliament, its members can force a national election, which might result in a new prime minister. This gives minority parties potential power in parliament to broker deals that serve their interests. No such system exists in the United States, and, as a consequence, third parties play only a minor role in national politics. No third-party candidate has won a presidential election since Abraham Lincoln was elected in 1860.

government by winning elections. Political parties serve this purpose by defining alternative policies and programs, building their membership, raising funds for their candidates, and helping to organize political campaigns. Not only must candidates win elections and retain their offices, but once in office they must make decisions with far-reaching financial and social effects. These decisions ideally reflect the needs and desires of their constituencies, as well as their parties and the entities that contribute to their campaigns. Some politicians argue that their constituents' issues take priority; other observers suggest that politicians are beholden to party or donor interests.

In the section below we discuss electoral politics in the United States. Sociologists take an interest in electoral politics because it is an important site at which power in modern countries is exercised. Thus, key questions that sociologists ask—*How is this functional for society? Who benefits from the existing social order? How do perceptions structure behaviors in the electoral process?*—can be applied to electoral politics.

ELECTORAL POLITICS AND THE TWO-PARTY SYSTEM

Most modern democracies are based on a parliamentary system, in which the chief of state (called a *prime minister*) is the

Electoral College

The domination of the Republican and Democratic Parties of national elections and elected positions is virtually ensured by the current political order. Parties representing well-defined interests are ordinarily eliminated from the national political process, since there are few avenues by which they can exert significant political power. Unlike in many other democracies, there are no political parties in the United States that effectively represent the exclusive interests of labor, environmentalists, or other constituencies at the national level. On the contrary, there is a strong incentive for political groups to support one of the two major political parties, rather than to "waste" their vote on third parties that have no chance at all of winning the presidency; at most, such votes are generally offered as "protest" votes.

ELECTING A U.S. PRESIDENT

"One person, one vote." Is that really how it works when you vote for president?

The sociological imagination suggests that you look beyond your private act of voting and see how your vote fits in to the larger picture of democracy, electoral politics, and power. One place to look is the Electoral College system, written into the U.S. Constitution more than 200 years ago by our country's founders, who feared that direct popular vote for the presidency might lead to (unruly) rule by the masses, even though at the time only about 6% of the population could legally vote.

Under the current electoral system, when you vote for president, you are really voting for your state's "electors." Each state has the same number of electors as its congressional delegation. California, the most populous state, has the most electors (54). Small states including Delaware, Montana, and Vermont have only 3. In nearly all U.S. states, the election is "winner-take-all," so a presidential candidate who gets only one vote more than his leading opponent in a state gets all of that state's electoral votes.

Some critics suggest that you are essentially wasting your vote if you cast it for a third-party candidate, since

On Election Night in the United States, people gather around the TV and at watch parties across the country to see the selection of the president play out in real time. ■

he or she has very little probability of getting elected. Consider that in 1992, a competitive third-party candidate, H. Ross Perot, got about 20% of all votes cast, but *no* electoral votes, since he didn't win the most votes in any individual state. Perot never had a real shot at the presidency, despite his supporters' enthusiasm.

Voting is an important civic activity and a key to political voice in a democracy. Winning the U.S. presidency, however, is about more than just winning the popular vote (Al Gore won the popular vote in 2000

but lost the presidency to George W. Bush). It is the outcome of a complex, historically rooted, and—some would say—problematic political formula that may or may not reflect the wishes of the majority of the electorate.

THINK IT THROUGH

■ *Should the election of the U.S. president be the outcome of a national popular vote rather than the Electoral College system? What might be advantages or disadvantages of making this change?*

Third parties can occasionally play an important, even a decisive, role in national politics, particularly when voters are unhappy with the two dominating parties. The presidential campaign of H. Ross Perot, of the Reform Party, in 1992 was probably significant in taking votes away from Republican George Bush and helping Democrat Bill Clinton to win the presidential election. Perot,

running at the head of his own party organization, won nearly 19% of the popular vote. In 2000, the situation favored Republicans, as Democrat Al Gore probably lost votes to Green Party candidate Ralph Nader; in some states, George W. Bush had fewer votes than Gore and Nader combined, but more than Gore alone. Bush won the electoral votes of those states.

VOTER ACTIVISM AND APATHY IN U.S. POLITICS

One consequence of the lack of political choices in the United States' entrenched two-party system may be a degree of political apathy, reflected in voter turnouts that are among the lowest in the industrialized world. Among democracies, the United States scores in the bottom fifth when it comes to voter participation.

Whereas many European countries typically have voter turnouts between 70% and 90% of the eligible voters, in 2000, about 54% of the "voting eligible" U.S. population participated in the presidential election. The percentage has risen in subsequent presidential election years: Estimates put turnouts for 2004 at about 60% and 2008 at over 61%. Early estimates for the 2012 presidential race suggest that about the same proportion of voting-eligible citizens participated, though differences exist by state: About 70% of New Hampshire voters turned out, while only about half of Arkansans opted to vote (U.S. Elections Project, 2013).

Historically, the proportion of eligible voters turning out for elections has varied by education (Figure 13.4), race and ethnicity (Figure 13.5 on page 335), and age (Figure 13.6 on page 335). Voters who are White, older, and more highly educated have historically had greater influence than other demographic groups on the election of officials and, consequently, on government policies. Interestingly, however, data suggest that President Obama's reelection was driven in part by the votes of young people (60% of voters 18–29 cast a vote for Obama) and minorities (for example, about 70% of ethnic Latino voters cast a ballot for Obama; Pew Research Center for the People and the Press, 2012).

Though the votes of young people and minorities had a notable effect on the outcome of the 2012 presidential election, their lower proportions still beg the question of why people who are poor or working class, minority, and/or young are less likely to be active voters. One thesis (Delli Carpini & Keeter, 1996) is that voters do not turn out if they do not perceive that parties represent their interests. Some of Europe's political parties represent relatively narrow and specific interests. If lower- to middle-class workers can choose a workers' party (for instance, the Labour Party in Britain or the Social Democratic Party in Germany), or environmentalists a Green Party (several European states, including Germany, have active Green Parties), or minority ethnic groups a party of their ethnic kin (in the non-Russian former Soviet states that are now democracies, Russians often

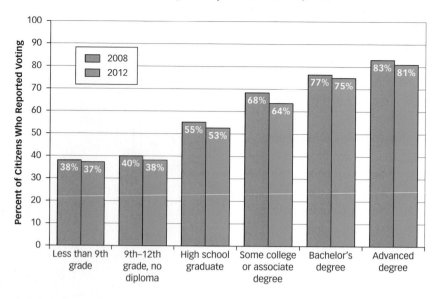

■ **FIGURE 13.4** U.S. Voter Participation by Education Level, 2008–2012

SOURCE: U.S. Census Bureau. (2010). Voting and registration in the election of November 2008: Detailed tables. *Voting and Registration;* U.S. Census Bureau. (2011). Voting and registration in the election of November 2010: Detailed tables. *Voting and Registration.*

have their own political parties), they may be more likely to participate in the process of voting. This is particularly likely if membership in the legislative body—say, a parliament—is proportionally allocated rather than being a "winner-take-all" contest, as it is in the United States.

In the United States, the legislative candidate with the greater number of votes wins the seat; the loser gets nothing. In several European countries, including Germany, parties offer lists of candidates, and the total proportion of votes received by each party determines how many members of the list are awarded seats in parliament. In *proportional voting,* small parties that can break a minimum barrier (in Germany, it is 5% of the total vote) are able to garner at least a small number of seats and enjoy a political voice through coalition building, or by positioning themselves in the opposition.

Consider the winner-take-all system and the proportional division of electoral votes. Is one more representative of the "will of the people" than the other? What do you think?

Some other reasons for low turnout among some demographic groups might be practical; low-wage workers may work two or more jobs and may not be able to visit polling places on the designated day of voting (the first Tuesday following the first Monday of November, usually between about 6 or 8 a.m. and 6 or 8 p.m.). In many European states, Election Day is a national holiday, and workers are given the day off to participate in the voting process. Recently, a growing number of states have offered early voting, extending the opportunity to vote by several days or even weeks at designated polling places. Oregon has allowed voting by mail since 1998. Data suggest these initiatives increase voter participation. However, in advance of the 2012 election, five states either passed

Tea Party Politics

Voter Turnout in Democracies

or attempted to pass legislation that would shorten the time for early voting. Most of the laws involve curbing the number of days in which early voting can take place; for example, Florida reduced the early voting period from 14 days to 8 days.

What about young people? In 1971, the Twenty-Sixth Amendment to the U.S. Constitution gave 18- to 20-year-olds the right to vote. This age group has, however, taken advantage of suffrage in relatively small numbers: 18- to 24-year-olds are less than half as likely to cast a ballot as older citizens, though the 2008 presidential election, in which about 52 percent of those under 20 voted, was a historical exception driven largely by the enthusiasm of the young for Barack Obama's candidacy.

A recent study supported by the Pew Charitable Trust found that young people are generally not apathetic about civic involvement; in fact, many responded that they volunteer and are eager to "give back" to their communities (cited in Center for Information & Research on Civic Learning and Engagement [CIRCLE], 2010). Voting, however, does not appear to inspire the same commitment. The young are less likely to be courted by the parties and candidates, who tailor messages to attract the interests of groups such as the elderly, who vote in larger numbers, or other groups who are historically more likely to turn out at the polls or make campaign donations. Perhaps because of a perception that the candidates and parties do not seem to speak to or for them, younger voters reciprocate with limited participation in the voting process.

■ **FIGURE 13.5** U.S. Voter Participation by Race and Ethnicity, 2008–2012

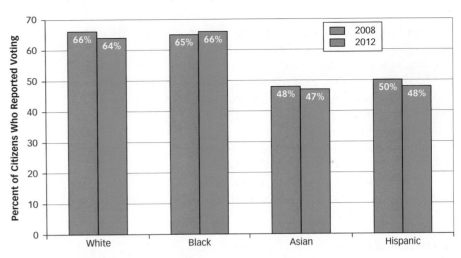

SOURCE: U.S. Census Bureau. (2010). Voting and registration in the election of November 2008: Detailed tables. *Voting and Registration;* U.S. Census Bureau. (2011). Voting and registration in the election of November 2010: Detailed Tables. *Voting and registration.*

Other facts have also been identified as relevant in influencing the youth vote, however, including the accessibility of information about where and when to vote and the level of civic education on issues and candidates. Notably, data show that states offering same-day registration on election day also have higher youth voting rates: In 2008, youth turnout in same-day registration states was about 59%, whereas it was about 50% in states not permitting same-day registration (CIRCLE, 2010).

Before we move on to the next section, which discusses the issue of political influence, we might pause to consider the following questions: How might our elected government and its policies be altered if people turned out to vote in greater numbers? Would higher turnouts among the poor, minorities, and young people make issues particularly pertinent to them higher priorities for decision makers?

POWER AND POLITICS

While part of the general public may show apathy about elections and politics, wealthy and powerful individuals, corporations, labor unions, and interest groups have a great deal at stake. Legislators have the power to make decisions about government contracts and regulations, taxes, federal

■ **FIGURE 13.6** U.S. Voter Participation by Age, 2008–2012

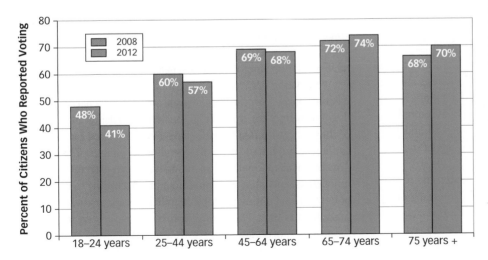

SOURCE: U.S. Census Bureau. (2010). Voting and registration in the election of November 2008: Detailed tables. *Voting and Registration;* U.S. Census Bureau. (2011). Voting and registration in the election of November 2010: Detailed tables. *Voting and Registration.*

Voter Apathy

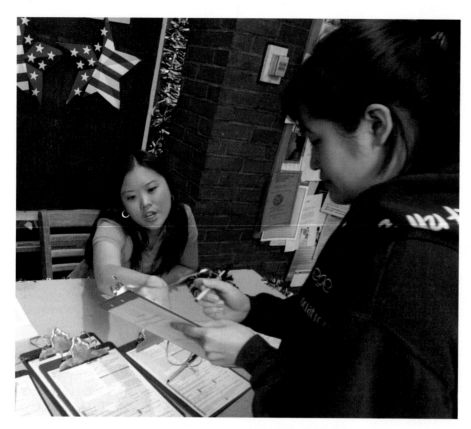

The participation of young adults (18–29) has been higher in the last two presidential elections than in most that preceded them. The volunteer in this picture is helping a college student register to vote so the student can vote via absentee ballot. Do you think increases in youth voting are a trend that will continue to grow? ■

labor and environmental and health standards, and a spectrum of other important policies that affect profits, influence, and the division of power among those competing to have a voice in legislation.

The shortest route to political influence is through campaign contributions. The cost of campaigning has gone up dramatically in recent years, and candidates for public office must spend vast sums of money on getting elected. The 2012 presidential campaign was by far the most expensive in history, with more than $2 billion spent altogether. President Barack Obama's campaign, along with the Democratic National Committee and the super PAC "Priorities USA Action" spent over $1.1 billion, while Mitt Romney's campaign, the Republican National Committee, and super PAC "Restore Our Future" spent between $1 and $1.1 billion. Spending reflected money raised from a range of sources, from very small donors to very large donors (Blake, 2012).

A substantial proportion of the money candidates and parties raise comes from corporate donors and well-funded interest groups. In many instances, companies or well-resourced interest groups donate money to candidates of both parties, in order to ensure a

Stephen Colbert SuperPAC

voice and hand in decision making regardless of the electoral outcome. Clearly, while most politicians would deny that there is an explicit *quid pro quo* (a term that means "something for something") with big donors, most would also admit that money can buy the time and interest of a successful candidate and determine which issues are most likely to be heard. Small interest groups and grassroots organizations lacking financial means may not be able to purchase a pass into the halls of power.

The 2008 presidential election offers a rather different story, however. Democratic nominee Barack Obama raised an unprecedented amount of campaign money, both from big donors and from a massive number of small donations successfully solicited via social media, demonstrating the power of the Internet in political fund-raising. Fund-raising and advertising online first became popular during the 2004 election, particularly after their successful use by Democratic contender Howard Dean and later by the Democratic National Committee. They returned as key strategies in 2012 as well.

The 2012 election also ushered a new player, *super PACs* (political action committees), into electoral politics (as noted above in our description of spending in the 2012 election). **PACs** are *organizations created by groups such as corporations, unions, environmentalists, and other interest groups for the purpose of gathering money and contributing to political candidates that favor the groups' interests.* In 2010, the Supreme Court ruled in *Citizens United v. Federal Election Commission* that the government could not restrict the monetary expenditures of such organizations in political campaigns, citing the First Amendment. This effectively meant that these entities could contribute unlimited amounts of money to PACs. The term *super PAC* is used to describe the numerous, well-funded PACs that have sprung up since the 2010 decision.

While super PACs cannot contribute directly to a specific campaign or party, they can demonstrate support for a particular candidate through, for instance, television advertising. Many critics of the *Citizens United* decision have been disturbed by the implications of unlimited corporate spending in politics. The primary drivers of this new political spending have been extremely wealthy individuals, and often anonymous donors. According to the Center of Responsive Politics, the top 100 individual donors to super PACs make up less than 4% of contributors, but have been responsible for over 80% of donations made (Riley, 2012).

· ·

PACs (political action committees): Organizations created by groups such as corporations, unions, environmentalists, and other interest groups for the purpose of gathering money and contributing to political candidates who favor the groups' interests.

Efforts to influence legislation are not limited to direct or indirect campaign contributions. Special interest groups often hire **lobbyists,** *paid professionals whose job it is to influence legislation.* Lobbyists commonly maintain offices in Washington, DC, or a state capital, and the most powerful lobbies are staffed by full-time employees. Many of the best-funded lobbies represent foreign governments. Lobbying is especially intense when an industry or other interest group stands to gain or lose a great deal through proposed legislation. Oil companies, for instance, take special interest in legislation that opens or limits drilling on U.S. territories, as do environmental groups. In an instance like this, lobbyists from green groups and the oil and gas industry generally stand opposed to one another and seek to influence political decision makers to join their cause.

Lobbyists are often former politicians or high-level government officials. Since lobbyists are often experts on matters that affect their organization's interests, they may help in writing the laws that elected officials will introduce as legislation. Consider the example described below.

In an article titled "A Stealth Way a Bill Becomes a Law," the magazine *Bloomberg Businessweek* (Fitzgerald, 2011) pointed out that that several state-level bills rejecting cap-and-trade legislation (which is intended to reduce carbon dioxide emissions, believed by most scientists to contribute to climate change) used identical wording: "There has been no credible economic analysis of the costs associated with carbon mandates." What was the source of this wording? Those words were penned by the American Legislative Exchange Council (ALEC), an organization supported by companies such as Walmart, Visa, Bayer, ExxonMobil, and Pfizer. In exchange for a large "membership" fee, corporations can buy themselves a seat on the bill-writing "task force," which prepares model legislation, primarily for Republican political decision makers. The group boasts that it gets about 200 state laws passed each year. Is the interaction of private sector corporations and public sector legislators an example of fruitful and appropriate cooperations on matters of mutual interest? When, if ever, is the writing of laws by corporate sponsors appropriate? When is it inappropriate?

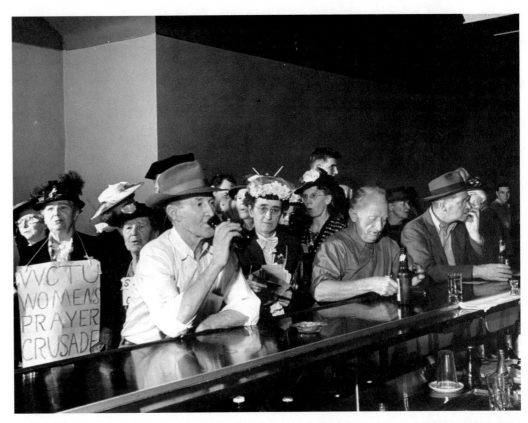

Social movements have the power to create sweeping social change. The temperance movement sought to outlaw the use and sale of alcoholic beverages, and they succeeded, though only temporarily, with the passage of the Eighteenth Amendment. ∎

SOCIAL MOVEMENTS AND POLITICS

Well-organized, popularly based social movements can also be important in shaping public policy. Among the most important social movements of the 19th and 20th centuries was the drive for women's suffrage, which invested half a century of activism to win U.S. women the right to vote. Its leaders fought to overcome the ideas that women ought not vote because their votes were represented by their husbands, because the muddy world of politics would besmirch feminine purity, and because women, like adolescents and lunatics, were not fit to vote.

The suffrage movement was born small in 1869 when Susan B. Anthony and Elizabeth Cady Stanton founded the American Woman Suffrage Association. It took decades to realize its goal: In 1920, the Nineteenth Amendment to the Constitution was ratified and women were granted the right to vote on a national level (some states had granted this right earlier).

The second wave of the women's movements, which began in the 1960s, boasted other important achievements, including the passage of laws prohibiting gender-based job discrimination and rules easing women's ability to independently obtain credit.

Citizens United Ruling

Voter Polarization

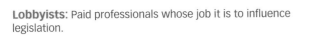

Lobbyists: Paid professionals whose job it is to influence legislation.

MONEY MATTERS: INTEREST GROUPS VERSUS CORPORATIONS

Sociologists understand *interest groups* as groups organized with the goal of pursuing a particular interest and agenda. Environmental interest groups have historically pushed for more aggressive measures to ensure clean air and water, reduce emissions of pollutants, protect fragile ecosystems and endangered species, and the like. Since their efforts sometimes have the effect of regulating industrial activities or imposing antipollution measures that bring new business costs, the interests of environmental groups and those of corporations, whose key interest is the pursuit of profit, are often in conflict. Corporations usually win.

Domhoff (2002) says one way to measure power is to ask the question "Who wins?" We might add, "And how much does victory cost?"

The Center for Responsive Politics reports that in 2009, pro-environmental groups spent about $22.4 million on federal lobbying efforts, an

unprecedented sum for these groups. At the same time, the oil and gas industry initiated an even more costly effort to block new environmental regulations: In 2009, it spent about $175 million on lobbying—fully 8 times what the pro-environmental lobby had invested in its efforts. By July of that year, according to the report, "congressional debate on global warming stopped cold" (Mackinder, 2010).

"Who wins" is not always fully clear. Many pro-environmental groups lauded the passage of the American Clean Energy and Security Act in 2009, which pushed forward with caps on carbon emissions that could help limit climate change. On the other hand, they lamented the loopholes that exempted large parts of the energy and coal industries from the cap, even as those industries argued vehemently that further regulations would cut industry jobs and raise costs.

After the 2010 congressional elections, in which Republicans regained a majority in the House of Representatives and gained seats in the Democratic-majority Senate, the debate over climate change moved lower on the national agenda. In the wake of the 2012 election, President Obama expressed a willingness to push for greater efforts to reduce greenhouse emissions linked to climate change. For the moment, at least, the "winner" is unclear, though the lobbying expenditures on both sides of the issue have been substantial.

THINK IT THROUGH

■ *Well-funded interest groups expend vast sums of money lobbying for their causes. What are available avenues for expressing political opinions and influence for individuals and less well-funded interest groups?*

The temperance movement, symbolized by Carry Nation's pickax attacks on saloons in the early 1900s, sought to outlaw the use and sales of alcoholic beverages. This movement eventually resulted in the 1919 ratification of the Eighteenth Amendment to the Constitution, which made it a crime to sell or distribute alcoholic beverages. The Twenty-First Amendment eventually repealed Prohibition in 1933.

The labor movement grew throughout the first half of the 20th century, providing a powerful counterweight to the influence of business in U.S. politics. Labor unions were critical in getting federal and state laws passed to protect the rights of workers, including minimum wage guarantees, unemployment compensation, the right to strike, and collective bargaining. By

midcentury, at the height of the unions' power, roughly 25% of all U.S. workers belonged to labor unions. Today globalization and the flight of U.S. factories to low-wage areas have contributed to a decline in union membership, and just under 12% belong to a union (U.S. Bureau of Labor Statistics, 2013d). At the same time, large unions including the AFL-CIO have retained a good deal of political power, and candidates, particularly Democrats, vie for the union's endorsement, which brings with it the virtual guarantee of a large block of votes.

On the one hand, social movements provide a counterbalance to the power and influence of large corporate donors, which we discussed above. The movements offer a political voice to grassroots groups representing interests contrary to those of big business, such as labor rights and environmental protection. On the other hand, if we return to Domhoff's (2002) question, "Who wins?" these groups rarely have more influence than large corporations and donors.

2012 Youth Voter Turnout

CONSTITUENTS Wealthy individuals, interest groups, PACs, and lobbyists exert considerable political influence through their campaign contributions. Still, these factors alone are not sufficient to explain political decisions. If they hope to be reelected, elected representatives must also serve their constituents. That is why politicians and their aides poll constituents, read their mail and e-mail, and look closely at the last election results.

One way politicians seek to win their constituents' support is by securing government spending on projects that provide jobs or otherwise help their communities and constituents. If a new prison is to be built, for instance, legislators vie to have it placed in their district. Prisons, while they may seen undesirable, are an economic windfall for a state or region. Among other things, they provide jobs to individuals who may not have the education or training to work in professional sectors of the economy and would otherwise be unemployed or working in the poorly paid service sector.

Projects that legislators push for their home districts are sometimes labeled "pork." Pork may be superfluous or unnecessary for the macro-level economy, but good for the legislator's home district. On the other hand, when a government commission proposes closing military bases, cost-conscious members of Congress will support the recommendation—*unless* the base is in their district.

Politicians spend substantial amounts of time in their home districts. Over the course of the calendar year, Congress is in session for an average of 103 days (Library of Congress, 2012). Congressional representatives are interested in hearing the views of constituents—as well as raising money and getting reelected.

CONTRADICTIONS IN MODERN POLITICS: DEMOCRACY AND CAPITALISM

Leaders in modern democratic capitalist societies like the United States are caught between potentially contradictory demands. They seek widespread popular support, yet they must satisfy the demands of the elites whose financial backing is essential for electoral success. On the one hand, voters are likely to look to their political leaders to back benefits such as retirement income (in the form of Social Security, for instance), housing supports (affordable housing for low-income families or mortgage tax breaks for wealthier ones), and environmental protection. On the other hand, such programs are costly to implement and entail economic costs to corporations, developers, and other members of the elite. Modern governments thus are caught in a conflict between their need to realize the interests of the capitalist class, and their desire to win the support and loyalty of other classes (Held, 1989; Offe, 1984; Wolfe, 1977).

Jurgen Habermas (1976), a contemporary theorist with a conflict orientation, argues that modern countries have integrated their economic and political systems, reducing the likelihood of economic crisis while increasing the chances of a political crisis. He terms this the *legitimation crisis*. Governments have intervened in the market and, to some degree, solved the most acute contradictions of capitalism—including extreme income inequalities and tumultuous economic cycles—that Marx argued could be addressed only in a proletarian revolution. Governments often act to keep inflation and deflation in check, to regulate interest rates, and to provide social assistance to those who have lost a job. Thus economics is politicized, and the citizenry may come to expect that economic troubles will be solved through state structures and social welfare.

To understand Habermas more fully, imagine a postindustrial U.S. city. The loss of jobs and industries manifests itself as a crisis—thousands of jobs in auto or other manufacturing industries move abroad, local businesses suffer as the amount of disposable income held by local people plummets, and economic pain is acute. How, in modern society, does our hypothetical city (which has hundreds of authentic counterparts in the United States) respond? Does it erupt in revolutionary fervor, with displaced laborers calling for class struggle? Or do people look to their local, state, and federal governments to provide relief in the form of tax cuts or credits, unemployment benefits, or plans for attracting new industries?

The citizenry of modern capitalism, says Habermas, do not widely question the legitimacy of capitalism. If there is a "crisis," it is political, and it is "solved" with policies that may smooth capitalism's bumpy ride. In a sense, the state becomes the focus of discontent—in a democracy, political decision makers can be changed and a crisis averted. The economic system that brings many of these crises into being, however, remains in shadow, its legitimacy rarely questioned.

WHY STUDY POLITICS THROUGH A SOCIOLOGICAL LENS?

In the modern world politics and the state directly affect the lives of everyone. Understanding how politics and the state work is therefore essential to having control over your life—and having a voice in politics. In this chapter we have inquired into the processes that directly affect the functioning of the state and politics. In the face of the apparently overwhelming power of the state and the seeming distance of political decision making from the lives of the average person, it is perhaps easy to shrug our shoulders and feel powerless. Yet one of the lessons we learn from the sociological analysis of politics and the state is that both are subject to influence by ordinary citizens, especially when people are mobilized into social movements and interest groups, politically aware, and able to critically evaluate politics and policies. Public ignorance and apathy benefit those who use politics to ensure their own or their social group's well-being; active citizenship is an authentic instrument of power, even where it faces significant obstacles.

The most economically powerful interests in modern states are the best organized to influence political decisions and state policies. In response, ordinary citizens frequently form their own interest groups to counteract the influence of what C. Wright Mills called "the power elite." The civil rights movement, the women's movement, the gay and lesbian equality movement, and antiwar movements all illustrate how ordinary citizens can come together to form organizations that assert an authentic voice in social change. Understanding how these processes work not only empowers you to change what you think needs changing; it also helps make you aware of your responsibility to work for those ideals that are important to you.

WHAT CAN I DO WITH A SOCIOLOGY DEGREE?

SKILLS AND CAREERS: WRITTEN COMMUNICATION SKILLS

Written communication is an essential skill for a broad spectrum of 21st-century careers. Sociology students have many opportunities to practice and sharpen written communication skills. Among others, sociologists learn to write *theoretically*, applying classical and contemporary theories to the understanding of social issues or phenomena, and to write *empirically*, preparing and communicating evidence-based arguments about the social world. Sociology majors write papers in a variety of forms and for a variety of audiences; these may include reaction papers, book reviews, theoretical analyses, research papers, quantitative analysis reports, field note write-ups, letters to decision makers or newspaper editors, and reflections on sociological activities or experiences. Strong written communication skills are absolutely essential in a variety of fields.

In every chapter of the book, we explore the research findings of social scientists. Chapter 13, for instance, discussed the work of classical theorist Max Weber and contemporary sociologist G. William Domhoff. Sociologists need to be able to communicate effectively in writing in order to organize their research projects and to convey their findings to a wider audience (like you!). The success of other professionals is also dependent on writing skills. Consider the broad field of politics, which comprises politicians and their staffs, journalists, lobbyists, public interest advocacy groups, business coalitions, and many more actors. In politics, getting and keeping the attention of valuable constituencies or allies is often done through informed public policy ideas and the astute presentation of arguments. In politics, writing skills are a key foundation of your ability to draft public policy, to persuade voters or donors, to explain political issues, or to report on current events.

Excellent written communication is fundamental in many *occupational fields,* including politics, business and entrepreneurship, communications and marketing, law

and criminal justice, community organizing and advocacy, journalism, higher education, law, and public relations. Effective writing is critical for employees holding *job titles* such as social media writer or webmaster, grant writer, researcher, professor or instructor, public relations writer, journalist or reporter, English as a second language teacher, lawyer or judge, speech writer, editor, or copywriter. You may notice that quite a few of these fields and jobs require graduate or professional education; sharp and organized writing is also a key to success in post-bachelor's educational pursuits.

THINK ABOUT CAREERS:

■ *What are your strengths as a writer? What are your weaknesses? What are your goals for improvement?*

■ *Consider possible career paths that might be of interest to you. What kinds of writing do you think people in those fields do? How can you gain experience in those types of writing?*

▶ *Access additional web links on the student study site to learn more.*

SUMMARY

To test your knowledge further, find additional study material on the Student Study Site at **www.sagepub.com/chamblissintro**

- The world today is politically divided into 192 **nation-states**. Most countries are made up of many different peoples, brought together through warfare, conquest, or boundaries drawn by colonial authorities without respect to preexisting ethnic or religious differences.

- Modern countries are characterized by governments that claim complete and final authority over their **citizens**; a system of **law**; and notions of citizenship that contain obligations as well as civil, social, and political rights.

- State power is typical based on one of three kinds of legitimate authority: **traditional authority**, based on custom and habit; **rational-legal authority**, based on a belief in the law; and **charismatic authority**, based on the perceived inspirational qualities of a leader.

- Functionalist theories of power argue that the role of the government is to neutrally mediate between competing interests; it argues that the influence of one group is usually offset by that of another group with an opposing view.

- Conflict theories of state power draw the opposite conclusion: that the state serves the interests of the most powerful economic and political groups in society. Different versions of social conflict theories emphasize the importance of a **power elite**, structural contradictions, and the relative autonomy of state power from the economic elites.

- Governance in the modern world has taken a number of forms, including **authoritarianism** (including monarchies and dictatorships), **totalitarianism**, and **democracy**.

- Democracy is one of the primary forms of governance in the world today, and most countries claim to be democratic in theory if not in practice. Most democratic countries practice **representative democracy** rather than **direct democracy**.

- The U.S. political system is currently characterized by widespread citizen indifference and apathy toward government, reflected in low voter turnouts. Turnout, however, varies on the basis of demographic variables like age.

- In the United States, elected officials depend heavily on financial support to get elected and to remain in office. Fund-raising is a major part of **politics**, and individuals and organizations that contribute heavily do so in hopes of influencing politicians. Partly as a result, special interests use **lobbyists** to exercise influence in U.S. politics.

- Politicians still depend on their constituents' vote to get elected, and so they must satisfy their voters as well as special interests. Moreover, well-organized social movements can also influence legislation.

KEY TERMS

Study terms on the go with the smartphone-friendly key term flashcards, available at **www.sagepub.com/chamblissintro**

DISCUSSION QUESTIONS

1. In this chapter, you learned about theories of state power. Would you say that U.S. governance today is characterized more by pluralism or by the concentration of power in the hands of an elite? Cite evidence supporting your belief.

2. What is authoritarianism? What potential roles do modern technology and social media play in either supporting or challenging authoritarian governments around the world?

3. The chapter raised the issue of low voting rates for young people. Recall the reasons given in the chapter and then think about whether you can add others. Do most of the young people you know participate in elections? What kinds of factors might explain their participation or nonparticipation?

DISCOVER ๑|๐ STATE STATS

Log-in to the eBook and click on the title to the left for access to State Stats in order to complete the exercise.

In the Population database you will find data on "percent of registered population reported voting" and "percent of eligible population reported voting." Study the maps across multiple years and make some sociological hypotheses about the voting behavior of the U.S. population. What ideas from the chapter might explain this behavior?

STUDENT STUDY SITE

Visit the Student Study Site at **www.sagepub.com/chamblissintro** to access additional study tools, including eFlashcards, web quizzes, video resources, web resources, audio resources, links to SAGE journal, handbook, and research articles, and much more!

14

WORK, CONSUMPTION, AND THE ECONOMY

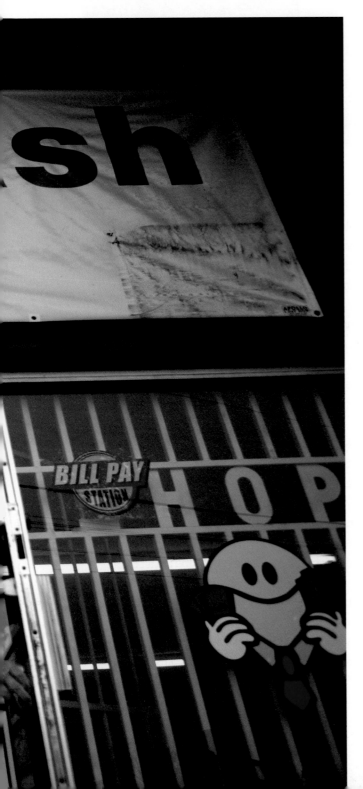

WHAT DO YOU THINK?

1. Do you agree with the societal attitude that parents who are not in the paid labor force, but stay home to care for children or aging parents, "don't work"? How should "work" be defined?

2. Why has average consumer debt grown in recent decades?

3. Should we care about the labor conditions experienced by those who build popular consumer goods such as smartphones, inexpensive clothing, and children's toys?

SOC *VIEW*

Get a closer look
with the authors!

THE LOW-WAGE U.S. LABOR FORCE

I n October 2010, the *Washington Post* reported that a BMW automotive plant, owned by a German parent company, had created 1,000 new jobs for workers in South Carolina. We hear much today about deindustrialization—that is, the decline of U.S. manufacturing, much of which has moved to lower-wage locations overseas. In 1960, for instance, about 35% of nonagricultural workers in the United States produced goods. By the mid-2000s, only about 16% did, though a rise in the number of service jobs is partly responsible, not just a fall in manufacturing jobs (Blinder, 2006). There has, however, been a small but notable movement of manufacturing operations *into* the United States in recent decades, including, very recently, from China. In March 2012, Xinxiang, which produces copper tubing used for air conditioning, refrigeration, and cars, began construction on a new Chinese-owned and -operated plant in Thomasville, Alabama. The plant is expected to create 300 jobs on site (Kavilanz, 2012).

Why are some manufacturers moving their operations to the United States? On the one hand, BMW wanted to have a manufacturing presence in the United States, its largest foreign market. On the other hand, as a representative of the Labor and Industry Group at the Center for Automotive Research pointed out, "We are a low-wage country compared to Germany." Skilled, productive U.S. workers cost BMW about half the hourly wages of their German counterparts, who earn the equivalent of about $33 per hour (Whoriskey, 2010). Another important characteristic of the new BMW jobs is the fact that many workers at the plant do not work for BMW. They are employed through a contractor, which means the positions are less secure and less well paid than those offered directly by BMW.

The phenomenon of contracted work—that is, temporary work that minimizes the commitment of both employer or employee to a long-term economic relationship—has become a key characteristic of the modern U.S. economy, as businesses seek to maximize efficiency, flexibility, and profitability by reducing (or "downsizing") the number of workers with regular "permanent" positions (Figure 14.1). Computer giant Microsoft's use of "permatemps," initiated in the 1990s, was a striking example. During this time, 1,500 "permatemps" worked with the 17,000 regular domestic employees of the company. While they performed comparable tasks, "permatemps," some of whom had been in their jobs for five years or more, not only were denied the same vacation, health, and retirement benefits as other workers; they were also denied discounts at the Microsoft store, opportunities for further job training, and even use of the company basketball court. A class-action suit was filed against Microsoft, and the company agreed to an out-of-court settlement for $97 million (FACE Intel .com, 2000).

In the last 30 to 40 years many businesses have used mass layoffs to "downsize" every aspect of their operations, from factories and production workers to managerial and professional staffs (Uchitelle, 2007). A growing proportion of workers, even in the professional sector, find themselves engaged in short-lived jobs with little security (Greenhouse, 2008). Many more in the service sector are laboring part-time, sometimes in several jobs that lack benefits, mobility, and living wages. Wages at the bottom and in the middle tier have stagnated for a generation, despite a growing U.S. economy.

The clear majority of economic gains in recent decades has streamed upward to the earners already at the top of the ladder. According to the U.S. Census Bureau, today fully half of U.S. aggregate income goes to the top 20% of earners, continuing a long-term trend toward a concentration of gains at the top (U.S. Census Bureau, 2010b). This is the culmination of a longer-term trend. According to economist Emmanuel Saez (2013), from 1993 to 2011, real annual income growth for the bottom 99% of earners was just over 6%, while it was nearly 58% for those in the top 1%. ∎

....

Economy: The social institution that organizes the ways in which a society produces, distributes, and consumes goods and services.

Goods: Objects that have an economic value to others, whether they are the basic necessities we need to survive, or things we simply want.

Services: Economically productive activities that do not result directly in a physical product; they can be relatively simple, or quite complex.

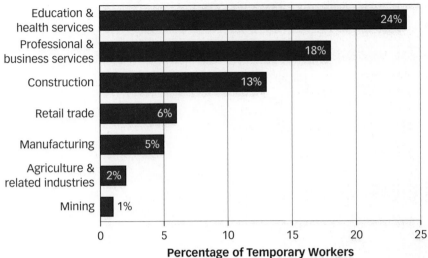

■ **FIGURE 14.1** Temporary Workers in Selected U.S. Industries, 2005

SOURCE: Table 4: Employed contingent and noncontingent workers by occupation and industry, February 2005. U.S. Bureau of Labor Statistics; Contingent and alternative employment arrangements, February 2005. U.S. Department of Labor (USDL 05-1433).

In this chapter, we discuss issues of economic sociology and examine the implications of a new globalized economy—postindustrial, technologically sophisticated, and consumption oriented—for the world and for U.S. society in particular. We begin with a brief historical overview of the three great economic revolutions that have transformed human society. We then look at the two principal types of economic systems that dominated the 20th century and continue to influence the 21st century. We next turn to a discussion of work, and its performance and the generation of income in the formal and informal economies. In this context, we also discuss social and economic issues of consumption, hyperconsumption, and debt. We conclude with a discussion of the changes and challenges globalization has brought to our economic system and prospects.

THE ECONOMY IN HISTORICAL PERSPECTIVE

The **economy** is the social institution that organizes the ways in which a society produces, distributes, and consumes goods and services. By **goods** we mean *objects that have an economic value to others*, whether they are the basic necessities we need to survive (a place to live, food to eat, weather-appropriate clothing) or things we simply want (designer clothing, an iPad or iPhone, popcorn at the movies). **Services** refer to *economically productive activities that do not result directly in a physical product;* they can be relatively simple (shining shoes, working a cash register, or serving cocktails) or quite complex (repairing an airplane engine or computer, or conducting a medical procedure).

The efficiency of both modern machinery and workers ushered in an age of mass-produced and affordable consumer goods. ■

In human history three technological revolutions have brought radically new forms of economic organization. The first led to the growth of agriculture several millennia ago; the second to modern industry some 250 years ago. We are now in the throes of a new revolution that has carried us into a digital and postindustrial age.

THE AGRICULTURAL REVOLUTION AND AGRICULTURAL SOCIETY

The agricultural revolution vastly increased human productivity over that of earlier hunting, gathering, and pastoral societies. This achievement was spurred by the development of innovations such as irrigation and crop rotation methods, as well as expanding knowledge about animal husbandry and the use of animals in agriculture. A simple development such as the plow, which came into use about 5,000 years ago, had a transformational effect on agriculture when it was harnessed to a working animal. Greater productivity led to economic surplus. While the majority of people in agricultural societies still engaged in subsistence farming, an increasing number could produce a surplus, which could be bartered or sold.

Eventually specialized economic roles evolved. Some people were farmers; others were landowners who profited from farmers' labor. A number of families specialized in the making of handicrafts, working independently on items of their own design. This work gave rise to cottage industries—so-called because the work was usually done at home.

The production of an agricultural surplus, as well as handicrafts, created an opportunity for yet another economic role to emerge—that of merchants, who specialized in trading surplus crops and crafted goods. Trading routes developed and permanent cities grew up along them, and the number and complexity of economic activities increased. By about the 15th century, early markets arose to serve as sites for the exchange of goods and services. Prices in markets were set (as they are in free markets today) at the point where *supply* (available goods and services) was balanced by *demand* (the degree to which those goods and services are wanted).

THE INDUSTRIAL REVOLUTION AND INDUSTRIAL SOCIETY

The Industrial Revolution, which began in England with the harnessing of water and steam power to run machines such as looms, increased productivity still further. Cottage industries were replaced by factories, the hallmark of industrial society, and urban areas became centers of economic activity, attracting rural laborers seeking work and creating growing momentum for urbanization. Industrialization spread through Europe and the United States, and then to the rest of the world. The change was massive. In 1810, about 84% of the U.S. workforce worked in agriculture and only 3% in manufacturing; by 1960, just 8% of all U.S. workers labored in agriculture, and fully a quarter of the total workforce was engaged in manufacturing (Blinder, 2006).

Industrial society is characterized by the increased use of machinery and mass production, the centrality of the modern industrial laborer, and the development of a class society rooted in the modern division of labor.

INCREASED USE OF MACHINERY AND MASS PRODUCTION
Machines increase the productive capacity of individual laborers by enabling them to efficiently produce more goods at lower cost. New machines have historically required new sources of energy as well: Waterwheels gave way to steam engines, then the internal combustion engine, and eventually electricity and other modern forms of power.

In 1913, automobile mogul Henry Ford introduced a new system of manufacturing in his factories. **Mass production** is *the large-scale, highly standardized manufacturing of identical commodities on a mechanical assembly line.* Under Ford's new system, a continuous conveyor belt moved the unfinished

. . . .

Mass production: The large-scale, highly standardized manufacturing of identical commodities on a mechanical assembly line.

automobile past individual workers, each of whom performed a specific operation on it: One worker would attach the door, another the windshield, another the wheels. (The term *Fordism* is sometimes used to describe this system.) Mass production resulted in a large number of identical components and products that could be produced efficiently at lower cost. This linked system of production became a foundation for the evolution and expansion of productive industries that went far beyond auto manufacturing.

THE BIRTH OF THE INDUSTRIAL LABORER

With the birth of industry came the rise of the industrial labor force, comprising mostly migrants from poorer rural areas or abroad seeking their fortunes in growing cities. Often, the number of would-be workers competing for available jobs created a surplus of labor. Karl Marx described this as a **reserve army of labor**, *a pool of job seekers whose numbers outpace the available positions and who contribute to keeping wages low and conditions of work tenuous* (those who do not like the conditions of work are easy to replace with those seeking work).

Karl Marx saw industrial workers as "instruments of labor" tethered to an exploitive system. One nineteenth-century British mother described her 7-year-old to a government commission: "He used to work 16 hours a day . . . I have often knelt down to feed him, as he stood by the machine, for he could not leave it or stop" (quoted in Hochschild, 2003, p. 3). ■

If it is possible to create an assembly line where each worker performs a single, repetitive task, why not design those tasks to be as efficient as possible? This was the goal of **scientific management**, *a practice which sought to use principles of engineering to reduce the physical movements of the workers.* Frederick Winslow Taylor's *Principles of Scientific Management,* published in 1911, enabled factory managers to greatly increase their control over the labor process by giving explicit instructions to workers regarding how they would perform their well-defined tasks. While Taylor was focused on the goal of efficiency, "Taylorism" also had the consequence of further deskilling work. Deskilling rendered workers more vulnerable to layoffs, since they—like the components they were making—were standardized and therefore easily replaced (Braverman, 1974/1988).

CLASSES IN INDUSTRIAL CAPITALISM New economic classes developed along with the rise of industrial capitalist society. One important new class was composed of industrialists who owned what Marx called the *means of production*—for example, factories. Another was made up of wage laborers—workers who did not own land, property, or tools. They had only their labor power

to sell at the factory gate. Work in early industrial capitalism was demanding, highly regimented, and even hazardous. Workers labored at tedious tasks for 14 to 16 hours a day, six or seven days a week, and were at risk of losing their jobs if economic conditions turned unfavorable or if they raised too many objections (recall the concept of the "reserve army of labor"). The pool of exploitable labor was expanded by migrant workers from rural areas and abroad, and even children of poor families were sometimes forced to labor for a wage.

Influenced by the poor conditions they saw in 19th-century English factories, Karl Marx and Friedrich Engels posited that these two classes, which they termed the *bourgeoisie* or capitalists and the *proletariat* or working class, would come into conflict. They argued in the *Manifesto of the Communist Party* (1848) that the bourgeoisie exploited the proletariat by appropriating the surplus value of their labor. That is, capitalists paid workers the minimum they could get away with and kept the remainder of the value generated by the finished product for themselves as profit, or as a means to gather more productive capital in their own hands. The exploitation of wage labor by capitalists would, they believed, end in revolution and the end of private ownership of the means of production (such as factories).

While some observers of early capitalism, including Marx and Engels, offered scathing critiques of the social and economic condition of factory laborers, the early and middle decades of the 20th century (with the exception of the period of the Great Depression) witnessed improved conditions and opportunities for the blue-collar workforce in the United States.

Reserve army of labor: A pool of job seekers whose numbers outpace the available positions and who contribute to keeping wages low and conditions of work tenuous.

Scientific management: A practice that sought to use principles of engineering to reduce the physical movements of the workers.

Characteristic	Industrial Society	Postindustrial Society
Principal Technology	Industrial machinery	Advanced technologies, including computers, automation of tasks
Key Types of Labor Categories	Industrial workers and professionals	"Knowledge workers" and service workers
Type of Production	Mass production	Flexible production
Labor Control	"Scientific management"	Outsourcing, threatened and real; technological control of work
Selected Social Stratification Characteristics	Development of modern class society with a dominant economic class, an expanding middle class that may integrate workers, and an economic underclass	Segmentation of the middle class by educational attainment, concentration of wealth and income at the top, and an expanding working poor strata

In the early 20th century, Henry Ford, the patriarch of Fordist production, took the audacious step of paying workers on his Model T assembly line in Michigan fully $5 for an eight-hour day, nearly 3 times the wage of a factory employee in 1914. Ford reasoned that workers who earned a solid wage would become consumers of products such as his Model T. Indeed, his workers bought, his profits grew, and industrial laborers (and, eventually, the workers of the unionized U.S. car industry) set off on a slow but steady path to the middle class (Reich, 2010).

The class structure that emerged from advanced industrial capitalism in the United States, Europe, Japan, Canada, and other modern states boasted substantial middle classes composed of workers who ranged from well-educated teachers and managers to industrial workers and mechanics with a high school or technical education. The fortunes of blue-collar and semiprofessional workers were boosted by a number of factors. Among these were extended periods of low unemployment in which workers had greater leverage in negotiating job conditions (Uchitelle, 2007). Unions supported auto, rail, and many other workers in the negotiation of contracts that ensured living wages, as well as job security and benefits. Unionization surged following the Great Depression and the 1935 passage of the Wagner Act, which "guaranteed the rights of workers to join unions and bargain collectively" (VanGiezen & Schwenk, 2001), growing to more than 27% of the labor force by 1940. At their peak in 1979, U.S. unions claimed 21 million members (Mayer, 2004).

Changes in the U.S. economy, including those we saw illustrated in our opening story, have shaken the relatively stable middle class that emerged around the middle of the 20th century. Since the 1970s, mass layoffs have grown across industries, though manufacturing has been hit hardest (Uchitelle, 2007). As a result, today the industrial laborer—and his or her counterpart in the lower and middle levels of the white-collar workforce—is less likely to belong to a union, less likely to have appreciable job security, and more likely to have experienced a steep decline in wages. Income gains have slipped, and, for many, membership in the U.S. middle class has become tenuous (Table 14.1).

THE INFORMATION REVOLUTION AND POSTINDUSTRIAL SOCIETY

During the past quarter-century the "information revolution," which began with Intel's invention of the microchip in 1971, has altered economic life, accelerating changes in the organization of work that were already under way. Pressured by global competition that intensified by the end of the 1970s, U.S. firms began to move away from the inflexible Fordist system of mass production, seeking ways to accommodate rapid changes in products and production processes and to reduce high labor costs that were making U.S. products less competitive. Postindustrial economic organization is complex, so the sections below focus on only a few of the most important aspects, including the growth of automation and flexible production, reliance on "outsourcing," and the growth of the service economy.

AUTOMATION AND FLEXIBLE PRODUCTION Postindustrial production relies on continual **automation**, *the replacement of human labor by machines in the process of manufacturing.* Today, robots can perform tedious and dangerous work that once required the labor of hundreds of workers. While automation increases efficiency, it has also eliminated jobs, particularly in manufacturing.

Computer-driven assembly lines can be quickly reprogrammed, allowing manufacturers to rapidly shift to new products and designs and to shorten the time from factory to buyer. "Just-in-time" delivery systems also minimize the need for businesses to maintain warehouses full of parts and supplies; instead, parts suppliers ship components to factories on an as-needed basis so they

Low Wage Labor

· ·

Automation: The replacement of human labor by machines in the process of manufacturing.

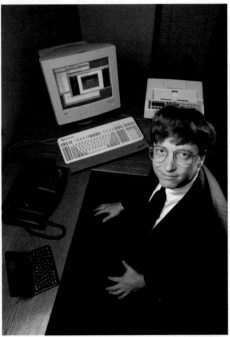

Many of today's highly compensated workers have specialized skills in inventing, designing, or producing innovative technological products. The late Steve Jobs of Apple (left) and Microsoft's Bill Gates have been pioneers of modern technology. ■

move right to the production floor and into the products. Such reliance on more flexible, less standardized forms of production is sometimes termed *post-Fordism*.

RELIANCE ON OUTSOURCING Businesses can perform activities associated with producing and marketing a product "in house," or they can contract some of the work to outside firms, which in turn can do their own subcontracting to other firms. The term *outsourcing* often describes the use of low-cost foreign labor, but it can also mean contracting U.S. workers to do needed tasks, typically for less pay than a company employee would earn. Outsourcing has long been part of industrial production; striking today is the emergence of outsourcing across a wide spectrum of industries. For example, United Airlines used to rely on its own mechanics to service planes. The mechanics were well paid and enjoyed benefits negotiated by their union. By the late 1990s, however, United increasingly turned to nonunionized mechanics operating from lower-cost, lower-wage hangars in the South. The terrorist attacks of September 11, 2001, which temporarily halted air travel, exacerbated financial difficulties of airlines. In spite of billions in government aid and loans, airlines continued to struggle. Major carriers became even more reliant on outsourcing to cut costs (Uchitelle, 2007).

TRANSFORMATION OF THE OCCUPATIONAL AND CLASS STRUCTURE Among the most highly compensated workers in the modern economy are those who invent or design new products, engineer new technologies, and solve problems. They are creative people who "make things happen," organizers who bring people together, administrators who make firms run efficiently, and legal and financial experts who help firms to be profitable (Bell, 1973; Reich, 2010). Workers in this category are sometimes called "symbolic analysts"

(Reich, 1991) or "knowledge workers." Most symbolic analysts are highly educated professionals who engage in mental labor and, in some way, the manipulation of symbols (numbers, computer codes, words). They include engineers, university professors, scientists, lawyers, and financiers and bankers, among others.

While the ranks of symbolic analysts have grown overall in recent decades and the ranks of "routine production workers" in manufacturing have been falling, the most job growth has been concentrated in the service sector. Services are a diverse sector of the labor market. As of 2010, services employed nearly 113 million U.S. workers and accounted for almost 70% of the U.S. workforce (Henderson, 2012). Service jobs include some that require higher education, but they also include retail sales, home health and nurses' aides, food service, and security services. Overall, the service jobs available to workers with a high school education pay less than manufacturing positions, making membership in the middle class less likely and less secure for those without higher education.

Many service positions do not require extensive education or training, and a growing fraction are part-time rather than full-time, are nonunionized, and have few or no benefits. Quite a few of these jobs require people skills stereotypically associated with females and are more often "women's" jobs (but by no means invariably, since private security guards, a growing occupation, tend to be men). By contrast, many routine production jobs were manufacturing jobs that commonly employed men. The decline in manufacturing employment opportunities, with declines in educational attainment among men (a topic we will tackle in Chapter 11), has made unemployment and underemployment particularly acute for some demographic groups, including minority males (Autor, 2010).

Together, these diverse labor market trends point to significant shifts in the U.S. class structure. Economist David Autor

BEHIND THE NUMBERS

COUNTING THE EMPLOYED AND THE UNEMPLOYED IN THE UNITED STATES

According to the U.S. Bureau of Labor Statistics (2013a), in the spring of 2012 the U.S. labor force participation rate (that is, the labor force as a percent of the civilian noninstitutional population) was over 63%, and about 8% of U.S. workers were unemployed (Figure 14.2). Compare to 2005, when the labor force participation rate was 66% and about 5% of U.S. workers were unemployed (U.S. Bureau of Labor Statistics, 2005).

What do these numbers tell us? What do they illuminate, and what do they obscure? The BLS figures are based on the monthly Current Population Survey, which uses a representative sample of 60,000 households and has been conducted every month since 1940. While BLS cannot count every U.S. household, the size of the sample and its configuration are believed to ensure a statistically accurate representation of U.S. employment.

For purposes of the count, the **unemployed** are *people who are jobless, have actively looked for work in the prior four weeks, and are available for work.* Official

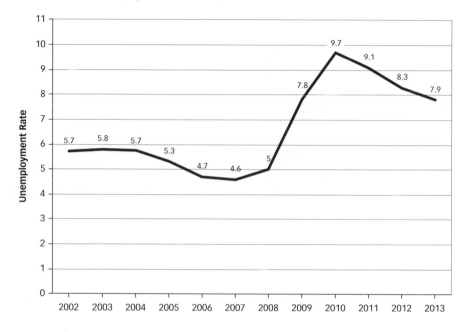

■ **FIGURE 14.2** Unemployment in the U.S., 2002–2013

SOURCE: U.S. Bureau of Labor Statistics. (2013). Labor force statistics from the *Current Population Survey.*

unemployment figures do not include those who, after a brief or extended period of joblessness, have given up looking for work, or whose job seeking is "passive"—for instance, limited to scanning newspaper or online classified ads. Those persons are categorized as **not in the labor force**, because they are *neither officially employed nor officially unemployed.* Persons who would like to work and have searched actively for a job in the past 12 months are categorized as **marginally attached to the labor force.** Widely cited official unemployment statistics omit these categories and may underestimate the number who need and want to work.

(2010) argues that a polarization of job opportunities has taken place, particularly in the past two decades. Autor sees a modern economy characterized by "expanding opportunities in both high-skill, high-wage occupations and low-skill, low-wage occupations, coupled with contracting opportunities in middle-wage, middle-skill, white-collar and blue-collar jobs." He views this as the basis of a split in the middle class, with those whose membership in that group was bolstered by, for instance, good manufacturing jobs now losing ground, and those who occupy the upper, professional rungs of the middle class maintaining their status amid growing opportunities (Figure 14.4 on page 354).

However, not all economists agree with this assessment. Economist Alan Blinder (2006) argues that "many people blithely assume that the critical labor-market distinction is, and will remain, between highly educated (or highly skilled) people and less-educated

Unemployed: People who are jobless, actively looked for work in the prior four weeks, and are available for work.

Not in the labor force: When people are neither officially employed, nor officially unemployed.

Marginally attached to the labor force: Persons who would like to work and have searched actively for a job in the past 12 months.

Some researchers (Western & Petit, 2010) point out that indicators intended to measure the social and economic well-being of the population are distorted because they omit the large U.S. prison population. Prisoners are disproportionately from low socioeconomic backgrounds, yet they do not figure into the Census Bureau's calculation of official poverty, based, like unemployment figures, on a survey of households. Jails and prisons are not households and therefore are not counted, though they house over 2 million people (U.S. Bureau of Justice Statistics, 2010).

Consider the effect of this exclusion on employment figures. In 2008, the incarceration rate of African American men who dropped out of high school was about 37% (Western & Petit, 2010). The distorting effect is considerable if we seek, for instance, to determine how African American men without a high school education are faring in the labor market (Figure 14.3). Western and Petit (2010) write that "[conventional] estimates of the employment rate show that by 2008, around 40 percent of African American male dropouts

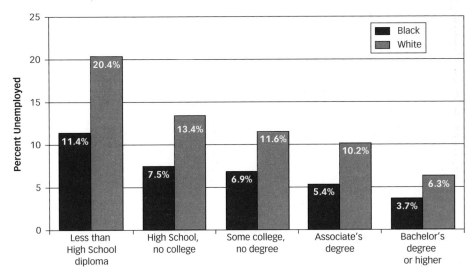

■ **FIGURE 14.3** Unemployment Rate by Educational Attainment for Blacks and Whites 25 and Older in the U.S., 2012

SOURCE: U.S. Bureau of Labor Statistics. (2011). The African-American labor force in the recovery: Chart 3.

were employed" (p. 12). However, when "prison and jail inmates are included in the population count (and among the jobless), we see that employment among young African American men with little schooling fell to around 25 percent by 2008" (Western & Petit, 2010, p. 12).

Clearly, the exclusion of the U.S. incarcerated population from social indicators such as poverty, employment, and unemployment may render an incomplete picture of the economic fortunes (and misfortunes) of some demographic groups, as we learn when we look behind the numbers.

THINK IT THROUGH

■ *Should the institutionalized population of the United States be included in socioeconomic indicators like poverty, employment, and unemployment figures? Can you make a persuasive case to support your position on the question?*

(or less-skilled) people—doctors versus call-center operators, for example. The supposed remedy for the rich countries, accordingly, is more education and a general 'upskilling' of the work force. But this view may be mistaken" (p. 118). Blinder suggests that the more critical social division in the future may not be between jobs that require high levels of education and those that do not, but rather may be between work that can be wirelessly outsourced and work that cannot. Consider the growth of online university education. Whereas a college professor may be able to accommodate 100 or even 500 students in a massive lecture hall, an online instructor can have thousands of students and teach them at a considerable cost savings to the institution—and, in some instances, to the student. Some universities, such as the Massachusetts Institute of Technology (MIT), are offering free college course lectures online (though these are not yet available for credit). While this is not "outsourcing" as we typically imagine it, trends suggest that even many highly educated workers will be vulnerable to technological changes in the decades ahead.

Outsourcing, automation, and the shift to more flexible workplaces characterized by temporary workers are among the factors that have reduced opportunities in the middle-level jobs that built and sustained the once-stable U.S. middle class. Its revival may require new and creative economic and political thinking.

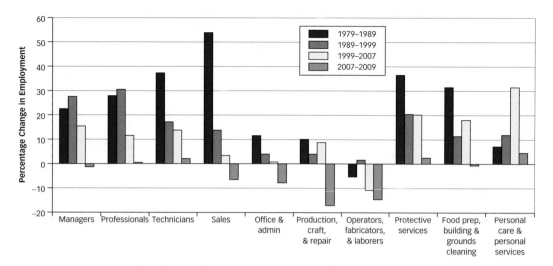

SOURCE: Autor, D. (2010). The polarization of job opportunities in the U.S. labor market: Implications for employment and earnings. Center for American Progress and the Hamilton Project.

TYPES OF ECONOMIC SYSTEMS

Two principal types of economic systems have dominated the 20th century: capitalism and socialism. Industrialization occurred in capitalist economic systems in North America and most of Western Europe, and under socialism in the Soviet Union, Eastern Europe, China, Vietnam, Cuba, and parts of Africa. After 1989, the collapse of socialism in Eastern Europe and the (former) Soviet Union fostered the expansion of capitalist market systems. Orthodox socialism appears to be in decline elsewhere as well, notably in economically growing China. Even Cuba, which remains steadfast in its socialist rhetoric, recently introduced some capitalist-style reforms.

Even though capitalism and socialism share a common focus on economic growth and increased living standards, they differ profoundly in their ideas about how the economy should be organized to achieve these goals. The following descriptions are of "ideal-typical" (that is, model) capitalist and socialist systems. Real economies often include some elements of both.

CAPITALISM

Capitalism is *an economic order characterized by the market allocation of goods and services, production for private profit, and private ownership of the means of producing wealth.* Workers sell their labor to the owners of capital in exchange for a wage, and capitalists are then free to make a profit on the goods their workers produce. Capitalism emphasizes free, unregulated markets and private, rather than government, economic decision making. At the same time, governments in capitalist economies often play a key role in shaping economic life, even in countries such as the United States that have historically tended to keep the government's role to a minimum (which is sometimes referred to as *laissez-faire*

THE GROWING SERVICE ECONOMY AND EMOTIONAL LABOR Many service sector jobs today require a substantial amount of "emotional labor." According to sociologist Arlie Hochschild (2003), **emotional labor** is the *commodification of emotions, including "the management of feeling to create a publicly observable facial and bodily display"* (p. 7). Like physical labor, the symbol of the industrial economy, emotional labor is also "sold for a wage and . . . has exchange value" (Hochschild, 2003, p. 7).

Hochschild (2003) uses the example of flight attendants, who do emotional labor in the management of customers' comfort, good feelings, and sense of safety, but we could also use as examples customer service workers, retail sales associates, or restaurant servers. While these workers may enjoy their jobs, they are also forced to feign positive feelings even when such feelings are absent, and to labor to evoke positive feelings in their customers. The emotional laborer is, in a sense, compelled to "sell" his or her smile in exchange for a wage, just as the industrial laborer sells his or her physical labor. The emotional laborer's actions are programmed for profit and efficiency, as he or she is asked to perform emotions that maximize both. The strain between real and performed feelings, notes Hochschild, leads to an emotive dissonance—that is, a "disconnect" between what the worker really feels and the emotions to be shown or suppressed. Hochschild posits that just as Marx's proletarian laboring in a mill was alienated from the work and from himself or herself, so too is the "emotional laborer" alienated from work and his or her emotional life.

Emotional labor: The management of feelings or emotions to create a publicly observable facial and bodily display in return for a wage.

Capitalism: An economic order characterized by the market allocation of goods and services, production for private profit, and private ownership of the means of producing wealth.

U.S. Jobs for Soviet Women

Capitalism

capitalism—literally, hands-off capitalism). In capitalist countries, the labor market is composed of both public sector jobs and private sector jobs. The **public sector** is *linked to the government (whether national, state, or local) and encompasses production or allocation of goods and services for the benefit of a government and its citizens.* The **private sector** also *provides goods and services to the economy and consumers, but its primary motive is profit.*

Because capitalists compete with one another, they experience persistent pressure from consumers to keep costs and therefore prices down. They can gain a competitive edge by adopting innovative processes such as mass production (think of early Fordism), reducing expensive inventories, and developing new products that either meet existing demands or create a new demand (which sociologists call *manufactured needs*). One important process innovation is minimizing the cost of labor, often by adopting technologies that increase productivity and keep wages low.

Capitalism can create uneven development, inequality, and conflict between workers and employers, whose interests may be at odds. On the other hand, it has been successful in producing diverse and desirable products and services, encouraging invention and creativity by entrepreneurs who are willing to take risks in return for potential profit, and raising living standards in many countries across the globe.

Capitalist systems are based on an individualistic work ethic, which posits that, ideally, if people work hard and diligently pursue their personal goals, both society and the individuals will prosper. The role of the government varies widely among different capitalist economies. In the United States and England, for example, there is greater skepticism about government's role in the private sector and greater emphasis on the private sector as the means for allocating goods and services (though Britain, unlike the United States, has nationalized health care). In contrast, in many European economies, government takes a strong role in individual lives. Sweden and France offer "cradle to grave" social supports with paid parental leave, child allowances, national health insurance, and generous unemployment benefits. Japan, on the other hand, does not expect government to take such a major role but does expect businesses to assume almost family-like responsibility for the welfare of their employees.

A CASE OF CAPITALISM IN PRACTICE: A CRITICAL PERSPECTIVE

Profit is the driving motive of capitalist systems. While the desire for profit spawns creativity and productivity, it may also give rise to greed, corruption, and exploitation. Industries cut costs

. . . .

Public sector: Jobs are linked to the government (whether national, state, or local) and encompass production or allocation of goods and services for the benefit of a state and its citizens.

Private sector: Provides goods and services to the economy and consumers; its primary motive is profit.

in order to increase profits; there is economic logic in such a decision. Cutting costs, however, can also compromise the health and safety of workers and consumers.

What do such compromises look like? We can look at a case study of profit over people in the meat industry in the United States. In the 1930s, Upton Sinclair's classic novel, *The Jungle*, offered a powerful and frightening fictionalized account of the real-life problems of the meat industry. The novel chronicles the struggles of a Lithuanian immigrant family working and struggling in "Packingtown," Chicago's meat district. An excerpt follows:

> It was only when the whole ham was spoiled that it came into the department of Elzbieta. Cut up by the two-thousand-revolutions-a-minute flyers, and mixed with half a ton of other meat, no odor that ever was in a ham could make any difference. There was never the least attention paid to what was cut up for sausage . . . There would be meat stored in great piles in rooms, and the water from leaky roofs would drip over it, and thousands of rats would race about on it . . . Such were the new surroundings in which Elzbieta was placed, and such was the work she was compelled to do. It was stupefying, brutalizing work; it left her no time to think, no strength for anything. She was part of the machine she tended, and every faculty that was not needed for the machine was doomed to be crushed out of existence. (Sinclair, 1906/1995, pp. 143–145)

Sinclair was critical of capitalism and the profit motive, which he felt explained the suffering of the workers and the stomach-turning products churned out in the filthy packinghouses. His work was a stirring piece of social criticism dressed as fiction, and it spurred change. President Theodore Roosevelt's inquiry into the conditions described by Sinclair brought about legislation requiring federal inspection of meat sold through interstate commerce, and the accurate labeling of meat products and ingredients (Schlosser, 2002). The novel had little effect, however, on the conditions experienced by industrial laborers, to which Sinclair had endeavored to draw attention. As he wryly remarked, "I aimed for the public's heart . . . and by accident I hit it in the stomach."

In the years since Sinclair's novel was published, capitalism has evolved (as has regulation), though profit and the need to cut costs have remained basic characteristics. What does cost-cutting look like in today's better-regulated meat industry? In *Fast Food Nation* (2002), writer Eric Schlosser describes his experience in a modern meat plant:

> A man turns and smiles at me. He wears safety goggles and a hardhat. His face is splattered with gray matter and blood. He is the "knocker," the man who welcomes

Upton Sinclair's *The Jungle*, chronicling immigrants' suffering in the unregulated meatpacking industry of the early 20th century, emerged from his investigations of Chicago's Packingtown. In 1904, Sinclair worked in the plants to gather material for a book that eventually spurred disgust and outrage, as well as the 1906 Pure Food and Drug Act. ■

cattle to the building. Cattle walk down a narrow chute and pause in front of him, blocked by a gate, and then he shoots them in the head with a captive bolt stunner . . . For eight and a half hours, he just shoots . . .

When a sanitation crew arrives at a meatpacking plant, usually around midnight, it faces a mess of monumental proportions . . . Workers climb ladders with hoses and spray the catwalks. They get under tables and conveyor belts, climbing right into the bloody muck, cleaning out grease, fat, manure, leftover scraps of meat. (pp. 170–171, 177)

The work is not only brutal; it is also dangerous. Profit still drives the meat industry to endanger its workers' safety, and Schlosser notes the words of a local nurse, who says she always "[knew] the line speed . . . by the number of people with lacerations coming into my office" (2002, pp. 173–174).

Critics of capitalism would suggest that conditions in the meat industry past and present illuminate a fundamental problem of capitalism: Capital accumulation and profit are based on driving down the costs of production. The case of the meat

U.S. Economic Problems

industry shows that the costs are sometimes driven down by compromising worker and consumer safety. The potentially high human cost is a central point of the critique.

SOCIALISM AND COMMUNISM

Modern ideas about communism and socialism originated in the theories of 19th-century philosophers and social scientists, especially those of Karl Marx. **Communism**, in its ideal-typical form, is *a type of economic system without private ownership of the means of production and, theoretically, without economic classes or economic inequality.* In an ideal-typical communist society, the capitalist class has been eliminated, leaving only workers, who manage their economic affairs cooperatively and distribute the fruits of their labor "to each according to his needs, from each according to his abilities." Since Marx believed that governments exist primarily to protect the interests of capitalists, he concluded that once the capitalist class was eliminated, there would be no need for the state, which would, in his words, "wither away."

Marx recognized that there would most likely have to be a transitional form of economic organization between capitalism and communism, which he termed **socialism**. In a socialist system, *the government theoretically manages the economy in the interests of the workers; it owns the businesses, factories, farms, hospitals, housing, and other means of producing wealth and redistributes that wealth to the population through wages and services.* The laborer works for a state-run industrial enterprise, the farmer works for a state-run farm, and the bureaucrat works in a state agency. Profit is not a driving economic imperative.

Before the collapse of the Soviet Union and its socialist allies in Eastern Europe, nearly a third of the world's population lived in socialist countries. Far from withering away as Marx predicted, these socialist governments remained firmly in place until 1989 (1991 in the Soviet Union), when popular revolutions ushered in transformations—not to the classless communist economies Marx envisioned, but to new capitalist states. The largest remaining socialist country in the world—China—has transitioned over the last 20 years into a market economy of a size and scale to nearly rival those of the United States, though the state still exercises control over large industries.

These transformations occurred in part because socialism proved too inflexible to manage a modern economy. Having the central government operate tens of thousands of factories, farms, and other enterprises was a deterrent to economic growth. Further, though the capitalist class was eliminated, a new class emerged—the government bureaucrats and communist officials who managed the economy and who were often inefficient, corrupt, and more

. . . .

Communism: A type of economic system without private ownership of the means of production and, theoretically, without economic classes or economic inequality.

Socialism: Theoretically, when a government manages the economy in the interests of the workers; it owns the businesses, factories, farms, hospitals, housing, and other means of producing wealth and redistributes that wealth to the population through wages and services.

КАЖДЫЙ ДЕНЬ ТРУДА-
ШАГ К КОММУНИЗМУ!

In the socialist period in the Soviet Union and allied countries of Eastern Europe, the state controlled all production, essentially eliminating competition in the marketplace for goods and services. Instead of advertisements in public spaces, political posters and propaganda elevated the achievements and builders of socialism and denigrated the capitalist way of life. ■

interested in self-enrichment than in public service (Djilas, 1957). Moreover, most socialist governments were intolerant of dissent, often persecuting, imprisoning, and exiling those who disagreed with their policies. At the same time, socialist regimes were often successful in eliminating extreme poverty and providing their populations with housing, universal education, health care, and basic social services. Inequality was typically much lower than in capitalist economies—although the overall standard of living was lower as well.

The dramatic rise in economic inequality and poverty in the newly capitalist states of the former Soviet Union and Eastern Europe has created some nostalgia for the socialist past, particularly among the elderly who have a threadbare social safety net in many states. While few miss the authoritarian political regimes, there is some longing for the basic economic and social security socialism offered.

A CASE OF SOCIALISM IN PRACTICE: A CRITICAL PERSPECTIVE

In theory, a driving motive of socialist systems is achievement of a high degree of economic equality. This is achieved in party by creating full-employment economies. In the Soviet Union, full employment gave all citizens the opportunity to earn a basic living, but it also brought about some socially undesirable results. For instance, inefficiency and waste flourished in enterprises that were rewarded for how much raw material they consumed rather than how much output they produced (Hanson, 2003). Human productivity was only partially utilized when work sites had to fill a required number of positions but did not have

meaningful work for all who occupied them. Disaffection and anger grew in workplaces where promotions were as likely to be based on political reliability, connections, and Communist Party membership as on merit. A system that theoretically ensured the use of resources for the good and equality of all workers was undermined by the realities of Soviet-style communism.

In practice, socialist systems such as that of postwar Hungary were characterized by both low wages and low productivity: A popular saying among workers was that "we pretend to work and the state pretends to pay us." Lacking a competitive labor market, workers may not have felt compelled to work particularly hard; unemployment was rare. At the same time, public sector (government) jobs, which made up the bulk of the labor market, were poorly paid; many workers sought supplementary pay in the informal economy (Ledeneva, 1998).

Socialism in practice, according to sociologists Michael Burawoy and Janos Lukács (1992), was in part a performance:

Painting over the sordid realities of socialism is simultaneously the painting of an appearance of brightness, efficiency, and justice. Socialism becomes an elaborate game of pretense which everyone sees through but which everyone is compelled to play . . . The pretense becomes a basis against which to assess reality. If we have to paint

Socialism

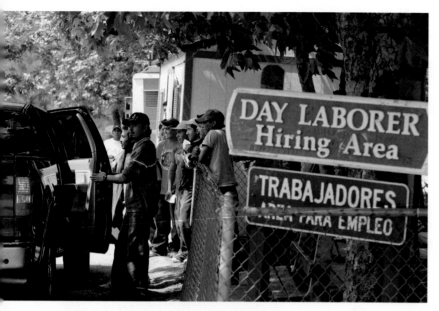

Day laborers often work for low pay in unregulated conditions. Some of them are illegal migrants. Their status and language barriers make it challenging for them to report dangerous or abusive conditions of work. ■

this definition, work includes paid labor in the factory or office, unpaid labor at home, and volunteer work in the community. Workers include rock stars and street musicians, corporate executives and prostitutes, nurses and babysitters. Almost the only activities excluded from this definition of work are those conducted purely for our own pleasure or benefit, such as pursing a hobby or playing a musical instrument for fun.

The concept of work as consisting exclusively of labor that is sold for a wage is a relatively recent development of modern industrial society. Throughout most of human history, work was not ordinarily paid, at least in monetary terms. In agricultural societies, subsistence farming was common: Families often worked their own plots of land and participated with others in the community in a **barter economy**, *based on the exchange of goods and services rather than money*. With the advent of industrial society, however, work shifted largely to the economic setting of a formal, paid, and regulated job. Today, work for pay occurs in two markets: the formal economy and the informal (or underground) economy. We'll look at each of these next.

a world of efficiency and equality—as we do in our [factory] production meetings, our brigade competitions, our elections—we become more sensitive to and outraged by inefficiency and inequality. (p. 129)

In the book, Burawoy, a U.S. sociologist who spent time working in socialist enterprises in Poland and Hungary as part of his study of socialist economies, recounts an instance of such a "painting ritual," when the Hungarian prime minister makes a visit to the Lenin Steel Works. Areas of the factory to be visited are literally painted over in bright hues, debris is swept up, and workers halt their productive tasks to create an "appearance" of productivity, for the prime minister "had to be convinced that the Lenin Steel Works was at the forefront of building socialism" (Burawoy & Lukács, 1992, p. 127). To critics of socialism the case of Hungarian steel in the socialist period highlights a fundamental problem of the system as it was practiced: Its weaknesses were made more rather than less apparent by the "painting" rituals that asked workers to pretend socialism was fundamentally efficient and equal when their own experience showed it was not. This was among the flaws that led to the collapse of socialism in Eastern Europe and the Soviet Union.

THE FORMAL ECONOMY

The **formal economy** describes *all work-related activities that provide income and are regulated by government agencies*. It includes work for wages and salaries, as well as self-employment; it is what people ordinarily have in mind when they refer to work. It has grown in importance since the Industrial Revolution. Indeed, one of the chief functions of government in industrial society is regulation of the formal economy, which contributes to the shape and character of the labor market (Sassen, 1991; Tilly & Tilly, 1994).

In the United States, as in most countries of the world, private businesses are supposed to register with governmental entities ranging from tax bureaus (the Internal Revenue Service) to state and local licensing agencies. Whether they work in the private or the public sector, U.S. workers must pay income, Medicare, and Social Security taxes on their earnings, and employers are expected to withhold such taxes on their behalf and report employee earnings to the government. Numerous agencies regulate wages and working conditions, occupational health and safety, the environmental effects of business activities, product quality, and relationships among firms.

As of 2012, there were over 155 million persons in the U.S. paid workforce, or about two thirds (63%) of all people over 16 years

WORKING ON AND OFF THE BOOKS

Work consists of *any human effort that adds something of value to the goods and services that are available to others.* By

Informal Economy

....

Work: Any human effort that adds something of value to the goods and services that are available to others.

Barter economy: Based on the exchange of goods and services rather than money with others in the community.

Formal economy: All work-related activities that provide income and are regulated by government agencies.

of age who were not in the armed forces (which is also, of course, an employment sector), prisons, or mental hospitals (U.S. Bureau of Labor Statistics, 2013a). When statistical indicators such as employment and unemployment are tabulated by government entities such as the Bureau of Labor Statistics, they rely on data from the formal economy. Work also is done in the informal economy, which is not counted in BLS numbers.

THE INFORMAL OR UNDERGROUND ECONOMY IN THE UNITED STATES

A notable amount of income-generating work avoids formal regulation and is not organized around officially recognized jobs. This part of the economy is termed the **informal** or **underground economy**; it includes *all income-generating activities that are not reported to the government as required by law*. Some of these sources of income are illegal, such as selling guns or pirated DVDs, drug dealing, and sex trafficking. Yet other work activities are not illegal but still operate under the government radar. These include garage sales and most transactions on Internet auction sites such as eBay; housecleaners, gardeners, and babysitters whose employers pay them without reporting the transaction to the government; and food preparers who informally cater neighborhood events. In one way or another, most of us participate in the informal economy at some point in our lives.

Workers' reasons for participating in the informal economy are varied. A worker with a regular job may take up a second job "off the books" to make up a deficit in his or her budget, or someone may be compelled to work outside the legal economy because of his or her undocumented immigration status. Others may find the shadow economy more profitable (Schneider & Enste, 2002). Many of the underground economy's workers occupy the lowest economic rungs of society and are likely to be pursuing basic survival rather than untold riches. They are disproportionately low-income, female, and immigrant, and they lack the protections enjoyed by many jobs in the formal economy, such as health care benefits, unemployment insurance, and job security.

Among the employers in the illegal U.S. underground economy are unlicensed "sweatshop" factories that make clothing, furniture, and other consumer goods (Castells & Portes, 1989; Sassen, 1991). U.S. factories are competing with factories around the world where workers are paid a fraction of U.S. wages. To remain competitive (or to raise profits), U.S. firms sometimes subcontract their labor to low-cost sweatshop firms in the informal sector. Environmental laws, health and safety requirements, mandated contributions to Social Security and other social benefit programs, and taxes lead some businesses to seek to establish themselves off the books. Small businesses may operate without a license, while large firms may illegally subcontract out some of their labor to smaller, unlicensed ones.

While the United States has a broad informal sector, researchers estimate that the underground economy is substantially larger in developing counties than in advanced economies such as those of Western Europe and the United States. For example, a report commissioned by the International Monetary Fund has estimated that the informal economy in developing nations (including Nigeria, Singapore, Bolivia, and others) accounts for 35% to 44% of the national gross domestic product (Schneider & Enste, 2002).

CONSUMERS, CONSUMPTION, AND THE U.S. ECONOMY

In studying the economy from a conflict perspective, we usually focus on issues relating to the means of production. According to Karl Marx, social classes are defined by their relationship to the means of production. Control of the means of production is a key to power, and private ownership of the means of production makes possible class stratification and exploitation. Clearly, production is an important part of the economy and a key part of a sociological analysis of the economy, from a conflict and a functionalist perspective.

THE MEANS OF CONSUMPTION

In modern industrial countries including the United States, production has receded in importance. The economies of advanced capitalist states now rely heavily upon consumption to fuel their continued growth. Today, fully 70% of the U.S. economy is linked to consumption. Thus we need to understand the means of consumption, as well as the means of production, to gain a comprehensive sociological grasp of modern economic organization.

Marx understood the term **means of consumption** as *"commodities that possess a form in which they enter individual consumption of the capitalist and working class"* (quoted in Ritzer, 1999, p. 56). Marx distinguished between the consumption of different classes, suggesting that subsistence consumption ("necessary means of consumption") characterized the working class, whereas luxury consumption was the privilege of the exploiting capitalist class. In sum, Marx's definition of the means of consumption focused on the end products of the exploitive production process.

Sociologist George Ritzer has expanded Marx's concept. He distinguishes between the end product—that is, a consumer good such as a pair of stylish dress shoes, a new car, or a

---

Informal (or underground) economy: Those income-generating economic activities that escape regulation by the governmental institutions that ordinarily regulate similar activities.

Means of consumption: Things that make it possible for consumers to acquire goods and services and, at the same time, foster their control and exploitation as consumers.

Oil Industry Jobs

Underground Pro-Soccer Economy

Worldwide Informal Economy

MUST WORK BE PAID TO BE ECONOMICALLY IMPORTANT?

Being a parent means taking on a spectrum of tasks that are time-consuming and important for the economic, educational, and social care of the family: Housekeeping, child care, cooking, budget management, driving, and teaching are among the key jobs of modern parents. Much of this work is done by women. Today, there are fewer than 160,000 stay-at-home U.S. fathers, while over 5 million mothers with children under 15 are outside the paid labor force as the primary caregivers of their children (U.S. Census Bureau, 2010a). Their work is often treated as marginal. Historian of the family Stephanie Coontz (2012) points out that while men are increasingly sharing the burdens of housework, "[the] real gender inequality in marriage stems from the tendency to regard women as the default parent, the one who, in the absence of family-friendly work policies, is expected to adjust her paid work to shoulder the brunt of domestic responsibilities. Women who quit their jobs or cut their hours suffer a wage penalty that widens over the years, even if they return to the job market

and work continuously for two more decades."

The sociological imagination enables us to understand how ignoring unpaid labor systematically discounts many of women's contributions to society and fails to recognize the consequences and real economic value of work that is not done for pay. The website Salary.com offers an annual calculation of the value of the "mom job," basing its figures on the 10 "typical" job functions of mothers. Using a survey of 28,000 mothers, the site's researchers determined that in 2012 the time spent in these tasks, if compensated, was worth $112,962 for a stay-at-home mother and $66,979 for a mother who worked outside the home (Salary.com, 2013). Unpaid work in the home or community (such as volunteering at schools) can be critical to the well-being of families and

Might the societal devaluation of the unpaid work women do in the home contribute to lower pay scales for "women's work" in the paid labor market? ■

society. It also contributes, if indirectly, to the macro-level economy: Consider that a stay-at-home parent frees up the other parent to work in the formal economy.

THINK IT THROUGH

■ *Why is it conventional in our society to say that stay-at-home parents "don't work"? What explains this devaluation of domestic tasks that have economic value? Is there another label that could be used?*

gambling opportunity—and the means of consumption that allow us to obtain the good—for instance, the shopping mall, the cruise ship, or the Las Vegas casino. For Ritzer (1999), the means of consumption are *"those things that make it possible for people to acquire goods and services and for the same people to be controlled and exploited as consumers"* (p. 57). For example, a venue such as a mall offers the consumer buying options and opportunities, but it is also part of a system of consumer control, through which consumers are seduced into buying what they do not need, thinking they need what they merely want, and spending beyond their means.

Ritzer's concept of the means of consumption also integrates German sociologist Max Weber's ideas about rationalization,

enchantment, and disenchantment. The Weberian perspective holds that premodern societies were more "enchanted." That is, societies or communities, which were often small and homogeneous, were grounded in ideas that were magical and abstract. Individuals and societies defined and pursued goals based on abstract teachings such as the ideals and ideas of a religion rather than on detailed and specific rules and regulations. Even early capitalism was linked to an enchanted world. Weber argued that the early Calvinists saw economic success as an indicator of salvation, and, as part of their faith, they embraced values of thrift, efficiency, and hard work in the so-called Protestant ethic that spurred the rise of capitalism (Weber, 1904–1905/1997).

Modern capitalism, however, lacks enchantment. It is a highly rationalized system characterized by efficiency, predictability, calculability, and control, devoid of spontaneity, spirituality, or surprise. Enchantment, argues Ritzer, is important for controlling consumers, because consumption is, at least in part, a response to a fantasy about the item being consumed. We believe our purchases will make us attractive, popular, envied, and so on. Consequently, disenchanted structures must be "reenchanted" through spectacle and simulation (Baudrillard, 1981). For instance, Disney simulates a kind of childhood dreamworld (think of the Magic Kingdom), Niketown is a sports fantasy, and Las Vegas aims to bring to a single city the dazzle of Egyptian pyramids, New York's towering urban structures, and Paris's Eiffel Tower. One of Disney World's attractions is the Great Outdoors, home of the Country Bears. The Great Outdoors is, of course, outdoors, but it is otherwise fake, a simulation of tree houses and woods. Ironically it not only imitates the real outdoors, but it may replace what really was once "the great outdoors."

In sum, from Ritzer's perspective, the means of consumption are a modern instrument of control not of the *worker,* but of the *consumer,* who is enchanted, led to believe that he or she "needs" certain goods, and given optimal—but inescapable—avenues for acquisition, such as malls with long hallways and few exits to maximize the number of shops a consumer must pass before exiting.

A HISTORICAL PERSPECTIVE ON CONSUMPTION

Consumer society is a political, social, and economic creation. Consider, for instance, that during World War II, the U.S. government asked its citizen-consumers to serve the greater good by reducing consumption. In contrast, in the wake of the terror attacks on the United States in 2001 and the wars that followed, citizen-consumers were encouraged to spend more money to stimulate the economy. Former Secretary of Labor Robert Reich termed this activity "market patriotism."

Taking a broader perspective, economist Juliet Schor (1998) argues that U.S. consumption patterns and the dramatic growth of consumption are heavily driven by our reliance on reference groups. That is, consumers compare themselves and their consumption to the reference groups in their social environment. Significantly, says Schor, those reference groups have changed. In the 1950s, suburban middle-class consumers knew and emulated their neighbors. The substantial number of women outside the paid workforce meant that neighbors were more aware of what others were doing, wearing, and driving. By the 1970s, more women were moving into the workforce; consequently, fewer people knew their neighbors, and the workplace became an important source of reference groups. In contrast to the economically homogeneous neighborhood, however, the workplace is heterogeneous. Low five-figure salaries coexist in the same space as high six-figures, and coworkers may aspire upward and far beyond their means.

The 1980s, 1990s, and 2000s brought further upscaling of ambitions and spending, as television sold a powerful picture of consumer decadence masked as "normal life." In the 1990s, young consumers embraced media referents such as *Friends,* about a group of young professionals living in lavish New York City apartments, wearing ever-changing stylish wardrobes and casually consuming the pleasures around them. Lavish consumption came to seem normal, rather than unreachable for people of average incomes (Schor, 1998). A new generation is now exposed to "reality" TV shows including *The Real Housewives of New Jersey* (and other locales), *Keeping Up With the Kardashians,* and *Say Yes to the Dress,* which emphasize the benefits of conspicuous consumption among celebrities and "ordinary" people alike.

A somewhat different perspective on how the U.S. consumer economy has been built and sustained is offered by Robert Reich (2010). Reich believes the consumption-driven economy originated in a "basic bargain" between workers and employers that offered good pay in sectors such as manufacturing, creating a consumer class that could afford to spend (recall Henry Ford's decision to pay above-average wages so his autoworkers could buy cars). Reich writes that, until about 1970, pay rose more quickly in the middle- and lower-income segments of the U.S. labor pool than it did at the top. Consumption grew with the standard of living.

The real value of workers' pay stagnated in the 1970s, however, profoundly affected by forces including globalization and automation. While income rose at the very top of the economic ladder, in the middle and lower strata it stalled. Consumption continued to rise, however, driven not by gains in income but by the growing credit markets, which offered new ways to spend with or without cash on hand. Next we review the consequences of that shift to credit-driven spending.

CREDIT: DEBT AND MORE DEBT

Do you have a credit card? Do you carry debt? If you answered yes to either or both these questions, you are not alone. In 2011, U.S. consumers held almost 610 million credit cards, and their combined credit card debt was about $886 billion (Woolsey & Schultz, 2012). Each credit card holder had an average of 3.5 cards and owed about $15,700, a huge increase from the 1990 average of roughly $2,966 (Hoffman, Brinker, & Roberts, 2010; Woolsey & Schultz, 2012). By one estimate, the debt payments of nearly 15% of U.S. households exceed 40% of their income (Bricker, Kennickell, Moore, & Sabelbaus, 2012).

Bankruptcies have also become more common. In the early years of the 21st century, "Americans were more likely to go bankrupt than to get divorced" (Quiggin, 2010, p. 26).

Cultural Imperialism and Consumers

Global Consumer Culture

Today, customer service call centers are far more likely than in the past to be located abroad. Whether you are seeking to make an airline reservation or install a computer program, your call from Boston or Des Moines may be picked up in Bangalore or Delhi. ■

As more people joined the ranks of the long-term unemployed and financial insecurities grew, many households cut back on spending. Overall, the average U.S. consumer spent nearly 3% less in 2009 than in 2008; spending was down on consumer items such as meals away from home, apparel, housing, and transportation (U.S. Bureau of Labor Statistics, 2011). These numbers may seem insignificant, but they represent millions of dollars that would normally have flowed into small and large businesses alike.

Consumption (or overconsumption) was not the direct cause of bankruptcies, most of which were precipitated by the loss of a job or unexpected health care costs, but the "culture of indebtedness," the widespread tendency to owe a great deal of money, left people less able to bear any added financial stress. While financial reforms passed into law in 2005 made the declaration of bankruptcy more onerous and less common, the financial crisis that began in 2007 saw another rise in bankruptcies: Over 1.5 million bankruptcy filings were made in 2010 (U.S. Courts, 2011).

Will Rogers commented during the Great Depression that the United States was the first country to drive to the poorhouse in an automobile (quoted in Sullivan, Warren, & Westbrook, 2000, p. 3). Car debt was a particularly notable burden during the late 1990s and early 2000s, when many U.S. drivers opted to purchase "high end" cars, especially aggressively advertised sport utility vehicles. The massive Hummer SUV, manufactured in three different styles by General Motors, became, for many, a symbol of the trend toward bigger and more ostentatious vehicles. Rising gasoline prices through the 2000s, coupled with the economic recession that struck in 2007, reversed the trend, and consumers began opting for fuel-efficient sedans and hybrid vehicles. The Hummer brand failed in 2010.

GLOBALIZATION AND THE NEW ECONOMIC ORDER

The U.S. economic order today has been powerfully affected by the emergence of a unified global economic system. In fact, some writers have argued that it no longer makes sense to think of the United States— or any other country—as an isolated economic society at all: In many respects, we can regard the world as a single economic unit (Friedman, 2005). We conclude this chapter by examining how global economic interdependence and the global labor market have affected work and economic life in the United States and considering the possible shape of a future green global economy.

GLOBAL ECONOMIC INTERDEPENDENCE

The U.S. economy is interwoven with the economies of other countries. Many goods made in the United States are sold in foreign markets, while many goods bought by U.S. consumers are made by foreign workers. Economic integration is multidimensional and can be "shallow" or "deep" (Dicken, 1998). Shallow integration is more characteristic of the globalization of several decades past when a single product (say, a German automobile) was made in a single country, and that country's government would regulate its export, as well as the import of other goods into the country. Countries did business with one another, but their ties were looser and less interdependent.

Deep integration is characteristic of the modern global economy, in which corporations are often multinational rather than just national, products are made of raw materials or parts from a spectrum of countries, and management or engineering may be headquartered in one country, while the sales force or customer service contingent may reside anywhere from Denver to Delhi (Figure 14.5 on page 363). Familiar companies including Nike, Apple, and Ford are among the many with globalized labor forces.

Credit Card Culture

Shift in Economy Production

Labor Force in Africa

A GLOBAL MARKET FOR LABOR

As a result of economic globalization, a growing number of U.S. workers are competing with workers all over the world. This trend may affect the job prospects of all workers, whether they hold high school or advanced degrees. There are substantial wage differences between countries. While the United States is intermediate among industrial countries, its wages are considerably higher than those in developing countries (Figure 14.6).

Jobs will increasingly go wherever on the planet suitable workers can be found. Low labor costs, the decline or absence of labor unions, and governments that enforce worker compliance through repressive measures are all factors influencing the globalization of labor. Some sociologists call this trend a "race to the bottom" (Bonacich & Appelbaum, 2000), in which companies seeking to maximize profits chase opportunities to locate wherever conditions are most likely to result in the lowest costs. This has been the case in, for example, apparel manufacturing; much of the clothing we buy and wear today, including brands sold at popular shops such as H&M and Zara, is made by young workers abroad who labor for very low wages under poor working conditions. A recent *New York Times* article points out that Bangladesh is challenging China as a low-wage destination for manufacturers and is now the world's third biggest garment manufacturer. Bangladesh has the lowest garment manufacturing wages in the world; a relatively well-paid worker profiled by the newspaper earned $64 a month (Bajaj, 2010).

■ **FIGURE 14.5** Global Origins of Boeing 787 Parts

SOURCE: Boeing. (2013). International team facts. *787 Dream Liner.* Retrieved from http://www.boeing.com/commercial/787family/dev_team.html

We've seen above that the emergence of an increasingly global labor market has resulted in job losses and declining wages in many U.S. industries including auto and apparel manufacturing. We may be witnessing the emergence of a *global wage,* equivalent to the lowest worldwide cost of obtaining comparable labor for a particular task, once the costs of operating at a distance are taken into account. For virtually any job, this wage is far lower than U.S. workers are accustomed to receiving.

The global labor market is not limited to manufacturing. A global market is emerging for a wide range of professional and technical occupations as well. In fact, some of the "knowledge worker" jobs touted as the jobs of the future may be among the most vulnerable to globalization. Unlike cars or clothing, engineering designs and computer programs can move around the globe electronically at no cost, and transportation time is, for all practical purposes, nonexistent. Electronic engineering, computer programming, data entry, accounting, insurance claims processing, and other specialized services such as reading medical images can now be inexpensively purchased in such low-wage countries as India, Malaysia, South Korea, the People's Republic of China, and the Philippines, and the work is transmitted digitally back to the United States.

■ **FIGURE 14.6** Hourly Compensation Among Production Workers in Select Countries, 2010

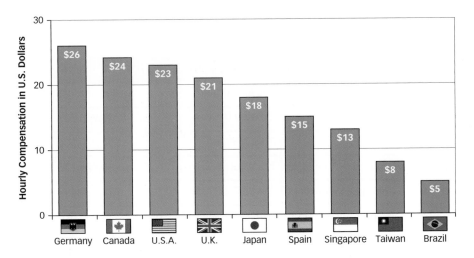

SOURCE: International Labour Organization. (2012, December 7). *A snapshot of comparative pay levels around the world.*

Nature vs. Economics

The green revolution is here, and you are living in the middle of it. Today's economy will demand that companies and countries alike invest in renewable, cleaner energy that will help reduce their carbon footprint and slow the process of climate change and depletion of the earth's natural resources. ■

Also among those selling their labor on the new global market are highly educated professionals from postsocialist countries such as Estonia and Hungary, both of which have full literacy, educated populations, and many individuals fluent in English and other world languages. While we often associate cheap labor with the low-wage factories of developing countries, these post-Soviet European states also advertise their educated workers (on their investment-promoting websites, for instance) as "cheap labor." Indeed, much global labor is low in cost. In 2010, the normal hourly wage in well-educated Estonia was $6.10; in 2008 in rapidly developing China it was $1.36; in India, also a rapidly developing country, the wage per hour was as of 2007 a paltry $1.17 (U.S. Bureau of Labor Statistics, n.d.).

While globalization has had some negative effects on earnings for workers in the lower- to middle-income ranges, corporate executive salaries have skyrocketed. Even in the midst of a plummeting economy (2007–2009), as the federal government was distributing billions of bailout dollars to corporations, banks, and investment firms to prevent them from failing, U.S. chief executive officers were bringing home multiple millions of dollars in compensation (Table 14.2 on page 366). While median CEO pay has declined somewhat during the recession period, it remains, on the whole, far

above the compensation of most employees; after hitting a pinnacle of $15.8 million annually in 2006, it fell to about $8 million in 2009 (Saez, 2013). Figure 14.7 on page 366 compares average CEO compensation to the compensation of the average production worker from 1965 to 2009; as you can see, in 1965 CEOs made about 24.2 times what the average production worker did; by 2009 this number, while down from a turn-of-the-century high of nearly 300 times the average worker's pay, was more than 185 times most workers' salaries.

IS THE FUTURE OF THE GLOBAL ECONOMY GREEN?

Businesses, consumers, and federal officials alike, eager to promote job growth and greater energy independence, are increasingly interested in developing a new "green" economic sector in the United States. In his first State of the Union address, President Barack Obama suggested that "the country that harnesses the power of clean, renewable energy will lead the 21st century." In his second address to the nation, the President urged the creation of clean-energy facilities, rebates for those who make their homes more energy efficient, and tax breaks to encourage businesses to keep the majority of their labor force within the United States (Peters, 2013).

The drive to develop, manufacture, and implement new energy efficient and eco-friendly products and services has been swift and encompasses everything from hybrid, electric, and fuel cell automobiles, solar panels, wind turbines, and alternative fuels (such as ethanol, biodiesel, methanol, hydrogen, and liquefied natural gas), to environmentally friendly versions of consumer products such as dishwashers, stoves, washers, dryers, cleaning products, toothpaste, paper products, clothing, and food.

■ **TABLE 14.2** Annual Compensation of Selected CEOs, 2011

Corporation	CEO	Compensation
Google Inc.	Eric E. Schmidt	$1,137,166,545
Apple Inc.	Timothy D. Cook	$377,996,537
ExxonMobil Corp.	R. W. Tillerson	$34,920,506
Chevron Corp.	J. S. Watson	$24,726,716
Verizon Communications Inc.	Lowell C. McAdam	$23,120,499
JPMorgan Chase & Co.	James Dimon	$23,105,415

Annual compensation includes the value of executives' base salary, bonuses, value of stock and option awards, and other financial compensation vehicles.

SOURCE: American Federation of Labor–Congress of International Organizations. (2012). *CEO pay and the 99%*. Retrieved from http://www.aflcio.org/corporatewatch/paywatch/retirementsecurity/index.cfm

Workers' Rights

DIGITAL SOCIETY

THE DIGITAL SWEATSHOP

The exploitation of labor is a fundamental characteristic of industrial capitalism, according to Karl Marx. While in Western countries today few industrial sites like those he and Upton Sinclair described exist, factories with strikingly poor conditions and large pools of low-wage labor flourish in countries including China and Thailand. Workers in developing countries bear many of the costs of the high technology we enjoy in the form of advanced computers, phones, and other necessities and amenities.

In January 2012, the *New York Times* published an investigative article about Foxconn, one of Apple's key suppliers in China. The article points out that while "Apple and its high-technology peers—as well as dozens of other American industries— have achieved a pace of innovation nearly unmatched in modern history . . . the workers assembling iPhones, iPads and other devices often labor in harsh conditions, according to employees inside those plants, worker advocates and documents published by companies themselves" (Duhigg & Barboza, 2012). Among documented issues noted by workers and their advocates are excessive employee overtime, difficult work conditions that include long hours standing, and work injuries resulting from poisonous chemicals used in the manufacture and cleaning of products such as iPads. The article adds that "under-age workers have helped build Apple's products, and the company's suppliers have improperly disposed of hazardous waste and falsified records" (Duhigg & Barboza, 2012).

Apple representatives argue that the company has conducted investigations into these conditions and has standards to which its

Apple and other global companies have been under scrutiny for the poor conditions under which laborers who produce many of their products work. Some workers in China and Taiwan have responded by conducting strikes—some others by committing suicide. ■

manufacturers must conform (Duhigg & Greenhouse, 2012). Like any modern capitalist enterprise, however, Apple exists in a deeply competitive economic environment, and holding costs down is a path to greater profit. Tightly controlled and rapid manufacturing is also key to maintaining the innovations that drive the technology marketplace.

The *New York Times* article points out that Apple is one of the most admired U.S. brands. A survey the newspaper conducted in 2011 found that fully 56% of respondents could not think of anything negative about the company. Negative opinions were far more likely to be linked to the cost of products (14%) than to overseas labor practices (2%). Without pressure for change from consumers or companies themselves, the voices of laborers are least likely to be heard and their interests least likely to be realized. As an Apple executive interviewed

for the story noted, "You can either manufacture in comfortable, worker-friendly factories, or you can reinvent the product every year, and make it better and faster and cheaper, which requires factories that seem harsh by American standards . . . And right now, customers care more about a new iPhone than working conditions in China" (Duhigg & Barboza, 2012).

THINK IT THROUGH

■ *Consider the interests that come into play in this environment: Apple and its manufacturers are interested in low labor costs, efficient and effective production, and high profits. Consumers are interested in new gadgets and technologies to increase their productivity and pleasure. Workers are interested in safe working conditions and good pay. Can all these interests be realized? What do you think?*

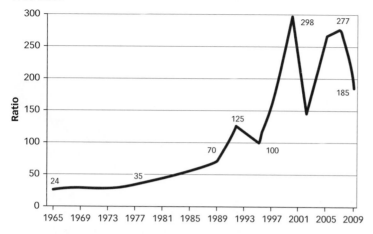

SOURCE: Matthews, D. (2011). Research desk: How has the CEO/employee pay gap changed? Posted at Ezra Klein's Wonkblog, *The Washington Post*, July 25.

In 2005, U.S. consumers of "green" products had spending power of $229 billion (Ryan, 2006). A 2008 United Nations report found that 2.3 million new jobs in renewable energy were created in a span of several years; 406,000 of those were in the United States (United Nations Environment Program, 2008). GroSolar, a solar power system developer and installer, has seen its labor force increase from 2 when it was founded in 1998 to 155 in 2010; likewise, in just three years (2006–2009) its revenues increased 389%, from $11.5 million in 2006 to just over $56 million in 2009 (groSolar, 2010; Inc., 2010).

Relative to other nations, especially China, Brazil, the United Kingdom, Germany, and Spain, the United States has awakened more slowly to the potential of the green economy. China currently leads the world in green (or "clean") industry investments, with an annual commitment of over $100 billion. China is the world leader in the production of solar cells (the main component of solar panels), harnesses more hydropower than any other nation, and in the very near future is poised to surpass other countries in wind power production (Boudreau, 2010). Paradoxically perhaps, it is also a flagrant polluter—the dramatic levels of air pollution in Beijing led some athletes competing in the 2010 Olympics to consider dropping out of the games.

In fact, China has assumed such a dominant position in the new green industrial revolution, thanks to strong policies and production benchmarks set by the powerful centralized government in Beijing, that some U.S. energy experts have expressed fears that if the United States does not soon assume a more dominant position in green technologies, industries, jobs, and research and development, it will lose the opportunity to do so and become dependent on green energy imported from foreign countries, much as it now relies on the importation of oil and fossil fuels. Already 25 of the top 30 green industries are located

Green Jobs in the United States

outside the United States, in countries where "green" has become a requirement, not an option (Boudreau, 2010).

WHY STUDY ECONOMIC SYSTEMS AND TRENDS?

Whether you were born in the 1960s, the 1970s, the 1980s, the 1990s, or earlier, the U.S. economy has experienced some dramatic changes in your lifetime. In 1953, for instance, manufacturing accounted for 30% of the U.S. gross domestic product (Blinder, 2006), and about a third of the workforce was unionized (Reich, 2010). By the mid-2000s, that share of jobs in manufacturing had declined to about 13%, and the proportion of unionized workers had fallen to 12.3%, or 15.3 million people, down from 20% or 17 million people in 1980, the first year for which comparable data are available (U.S. Bureau of Labor Statistics, 2013c).

In the 1960s, over a third of the U.S. nonagricultural workforce was engaged in manufacturing, and about two thirds were in services. Since that time, the service sector's share of jobs has grown by nearly 20%, a massive change that has brought both new opportunities and new challenges, particularly to those workers without higher education.

In the latter years of the 1970s, the United States experienced a steep rise in imports—U.S.-made goods and U.S. workers were increasingly forced to compete with lower-priced goods and lower-priced labor. From this period forward, the share of goods made in the United States and the number of workers making them fell (Uchitelle, 2007).

Starting in the early 1980s, U.S. wages, which had increased for decades, stagnated. Former Secretary of Labor Robert Reich (2010) writes that "contrary to popular mythology, trade and technology have not really reduced the number of jobs available to Americans . . . The real problem [is] that the new [jobs] they got often didn't pay as well as the ones they lost" (pp. 53–54). Today, wages in the middle and lower segments of the economic hierarchy remain flat.

By the 1990s, advances in computer technologies brought a new wave of outsourcing, not of manufacturing jobs, many of which had already moved offshore, but of information technology and, increasingly, customer service jobs (Erber & Sayed-Ahmed, 2005). Countries such as India, with large populations of educated and English-speaking workers, benefited from American firms' pursuit of lower-cost labor not only in manufacturing, but in service as well. This movement of technology jobs and other jobs that, as economist David Autor (2010) pointed out earlier in the chapter, can be done "over the wires" continues unabated today.

The shape of our economy and our economic fortunes have changed in myriad ways and continue to do so. Is the growth of "green" industries the next important shift in the world economy? How will globalization affect today's high-skill, high-wage jobs in the United States and elsewhere? Can the fortunes of the declining middle class be reversed? Understanding economic patterns and trends of the past and present is critical to gaining a perspective on how we as individuals and as a country can both prepare for and shape our economic future.

WHAT CAN I DO WITH A SOCIOLOGY DEGREE?

SKILLS AND CAREERS: DATA AND INFORMATION LITERACY

Paradoxically, in the modern world, we are surrounded by information, but we are not always truly well informed. The ability to distinguish between credible and questionable data, to seek out solid and reliable sources of information, and to use those sources wisely are critical skills in our "information society"—and in today's job market. *Data and information literacy* encompasses the skills to identify information needed to understand an issue or problem, to seek out credible and accurate sources of information, to recognize what a body of data illuminates and what it obscures, and to apply the information to a description and analysis of the issue at hand.

Consider a key topic covered in Chapter 14—unemployment. If you were charged with gathering data on unemployment in the United States or unemployment among particular demographic groups in the United States, where would you begin? Many of us turn to Google or other popular search engines to guide our research. While there is value in these large search engines, experienced researchers are more likely to turn to a credible and frequently updated source of information such as the U.S. Bureau of Labor Statistics, or BLS (www.bls.gov). BLS provides solid data, which can be broken out by demographic categories, states, and other variables. It also provides researchers with information on *how data are gathered*, giving the reader critical information on what the data illuminate and what they obscure. For example, in this chapter's *Behind the Numbers* box on page 352 we learned that the BLS unemployment figures do not take into account the institutionalized population in the United States. With over 2 million people—many of them men of color—incarcerated, this exclusion actually paints an incomplete picture of the dire economic position of this demographic group. This does not mean that the data generated by BLS are not useful. What it means is that we have collected good data—and recognized its limitations. This recognition can help us to use the data more effectively and perhaps to fill in the gaps with information gathered from other sources, such as the U.S. Bureau of Justice Statistics (www.bjs.gov), which provides information on issues related to criminal justice. As a sociology major you will be asked to do research on social issues and problems, and you will learn to use information sources to gather good data. You will have the opportunity to develop key skills that enable you to be a solid researcher and a critical consumer of information.

As a student, data and information literacy is important for tasks including research papers and class presentations. As a consumer, it may guide your decisions about the purchase of a home or a vehicle. As a citizen, it gives you the tools to make informed political choices about which candidates or causes to support. It is no less significant in the world of work. Data and information literacy is a critical part of jobs that involve *tasks* such as research, the assessment of problems and identification of solutions, and the rigorous gathering and organization of bodies of data that inform policy, marketing, or training, among others. This is a skill of significant value in *occupational fields* such as business and management, marketing and advertising, health care administration, information technology, government, education, research, politics and campaign management, polling, insurance, and management consulting. Among the *job titles* one finds in these fields are management/data/information analyst, market researcher, consumer survey adviser, demographic analyst, mass communications analyst, job analyst/labor force and manpower analyst, life quality researcher, policy analyst, program director, research librarian, survey research technician/specialist, and social survey director.

THINK ABOUT CAREERS:

■ *How would you characterize your information literacy skills at this point? What would you like to learn in order to sharpen your skills?*

■ *How would you explain this skill to a potential employer in a field of interest to you?*

▶ *Access additional web links on the student study site to learn more.*

SUMMARY

To test your knowledge further, find additional study material on the Student Study Site at **www.sagepub.com/chamblissintro**

- The **economy**—the social institution that organizes the ways in which a society produces, distributes, and consumes **goods** and **services**—is one of the most important institutions in society.

- Three major technological revolutions in human history have brought radically new forms of economic organization. The first led to agriculture, the second to modern industry, and the third to the postindustrial society that characterizes the modern United States.

- Industrial society is characterized by **automation**, the modern factory, **mass production**, scientific management, and **modern social classes**. Postindustrial society is characterized by the use of computers, the increased importance of higher education for well-paying jobs, flexible forms of production, increased reliance on outsourcing, and the growth of the service economy.

- Although postindustrial society holds the promise of prosperity for people who work with ideas and information, automation and globalization have also allowed for new forms of exploitation of the global workforce and job loss and declining wages for some workers in manufacturing and other sectors.

- **Capitalism** and **socialism** are the two principal types of political-economic systems that emerged with industrial society. While both are committed to higher standards of living through economic growth, they differ on the desirability of private property ownership and the appropriate role of government. Both systems have theoretical and practical strengths and weaknesses.

- **Work** consists of any human effort that adds something of value to goods and services that are available to others. Economists consider three broad categories of work: the **formal economy**, the **informal or underground economy**, and unpaid labor.

- The informal economy is an important part of the U.S. economy even though it does not appear in official labor statistics. Although in industrial societies the informal economy tends to diminish in importance, in recent years this process has reversed itself.

- In the modern economy, consumption replaces production as the most important economic process. The means of consumption, as defined by sociologist George Ritzer (1999), are "those things that make it possible for people to acquire goods and services and for the same people to be controlled and exploited as consumers" (p. 57). A mall offers consumers buying options, but it also is part of a system of consumer control, as consumers are seduced into buying what they do not need.

- We acquire goods in part based on our consideration of reference groups. As consumption reference groups have changed in the past decades, U.S. consumers have increased spending and taken on a much larger debt load.

- Economic globalization is the result of many factors: technological advances that greatly increased the speed of communication and transportation while lowering their costs; increased educational attainment in low- and middle-income countries; and the opening of many national economies to the world capitalist market. Globalization has had profound effects on the U.S. economy.

KEY TERMS

Study terms on the go with the smartphone-friendly key term flashcards, available at **www.sagepub.com/chamblissintro**

economy, 347

goods, 347

services, 347

mass production, 348

reserve army of labor, 349

scientific management, 349

automation, 350

unemployed, 352

not in the labor force, 352

marginally attached to the labor force, 352

emotional labor, 354

capitalism, 354

public sector, 355

private sector, 355

communism, 356

socialism, 356

work, 358

barter economy, 358

formal economy, 358

informal (or underground) economy, 359

means of consumption is on page 359

DISCUSSION QUESTIONS

1. What are the main differences between the formal economy and the informal economy? What are the similarities? What sociological factors explain the existence of the informal economy in the United States?

2. What are the main characteristics of a socialist economic system? Where have such systems been found in recent history?

3. What sociological factors explain the dramatic rise of consumer debt in the United States over the past three to four decades? Why should this be of concern to the population and to policy makers?

DISCOVER ⊓⊓ STATE STATS

Log-in to the eBook and click on the title to the left for access to State Stats in order to complete the exercise.

The Employment and Labor database shows "average annual pay" data by state from 1993 to 2010. There are some substantial differences by state. Choose two states with notably different averages, and construct a sociological hypothesis about the difference. Find and cite another state-level data series of your choice in this database (such as employment-to-population ratio or business failure rate). Do these data lend support to your hypothesis?

STUDENT STUDY SITE

Visit the Student Study Site at **www.sagepub.com/chamblissintro** to access additional study tools, including eFlashcards, web quizzes, video resources, web resources, audio resources, links to SAGE journal, handbook, and research articles, and much more!

15

HEALTH AND MEDICINE

WHAT DO YOU THINK?

1. Should universities and colleges regulate and punish the use of "study drugs"?
2. Do you think that the Internet, like drugs or tobacco or alcohol, can become an addiction?
3. Why are the poor more likely to be obese than their middle-class counterparts? What sociological factors might sociologists look at to understand this correlation?

SOC**VIEW**

Get a closer look
with the authors!

THE RISE OF "STUDY DRUG" USE AMONG U.S. STUDENTS

In the fall of 2011, Duke University in North Carolina added a new bullet point to its list of behaviors that constitute academic dishonesty: "the unauthorized use of prescription medication to enhance academic performance." Duke's policy, which so far has not been adopted at most other universities, represents an attempt to address student use and abuse of so-called study drugs, prescription medications intended to alleviate conditions such as attention deficit/hyperactivity disorder (ADHD). Sales of prescription stimulants such as Ritalin and Adderall have surged in recent years; between 2006 and 2010, they increased from $4 billion to over $7 billion. According to the Higher Education Research Institute, about 5% of incoming freshmen in 2011 had diagnosed ADHD (Johnson, 2011). But the number of students using the drugs prescribed to treat ADHD is higher. By one estimate, as many as a quarter of students on some college campuses have used the drugs in the past year (Trudeau, 2009).

A recent report suggested that those using "study drugs" are more likely to perform below average academically and exhibit poor study habits. At the same time, the use of substances sometimes called "Ivy League Crack" is found among students at all levels of achievement. The drugs are employed to enhance concentration and increase the time a student can spend on a task, though they also carry the risk of irregular heartbeat, panic attacks, addiction, and even death (Johnson, 2011). With more students using them, concerns about their legality and safety have been accompanied, as at Duke, by questions about how institutions of higher education should respond.

Duke administrators, supported by the school newspaper, believe that use of the drugs by students to whom they have not been prescribed constitutes cheating. A recent study suggests that many college students do not agree. In a survey of 1,200 male college freshmen, more respondents labeled the use of performance-enhancing drugs for sports (such as anabolic steroids) as "unethical" than condemned the use of stimulants for the purpose of improving grades.

Why would the use of drugs to enhance performance in one context be judged more harshly than in another? In an interview, Tonya Dodge, one of the authors of the study, suggested that "in sports there can be only one winner so misuse of a substance is less acceptable for achieving success than in academics. In academics, one's success does not necessarily come at the expense of someone else, but in sports it does" (George Washington University, 2012).

Do you agree with Duke University that the use of "study drugs" is a form of academic dishonesty? Or do you believe, as many students in the study suggested, that it is OK because one student's improvements do not come at the expense of his or her peers? Should the drugs be more fully regulated because of their medical dangers—or because they constitute cheating? Or should their use be permitted for those willing to take the health risks? What kinds of policies, if any, should your university or college enact in response to this phenomenon?

At one time, sociology and medicine went their separate ways. In the last half-century, however, this situation has changed significantly (Cockerham & Glasser, 2000; Weitz, 2012). Today it is widely accepted that sociology can contribute to the understanding of mental and physical health and illness, social group disparities in health, and public health issues such as smoking and obesity—and the growing use and abuse of "study drugs" by young people. ∎

In this chapter, we look at health and medicine from a sociological perspective. We focus on the important role that social forces play in health and health care in the United States, as well as issues at the crossroads of medicine, health, public policy, and sociology. We begin by distinguishing health from medicine. We then turn to an examination of the ways in which ideas about

· ·

Health: The extent to which a person experiences a state of mental, physical, and social well-being.

Medicine: An institutionalized system for the scientific diagnosis, treatment, and prevention of illness.

Preventive medicine: Medicine that emphasizes a healthy lifestyle that will prevent poor health before it occurs.

Sick role: The cultural definition of the appropriate behavior of and response to people labeled as sick.

health and illness are socially constructed in culture. We look at health and safety, as well as the relationship between class status and health care and outcomes in the United States. This section also delves into the important issue of health care access and reform in the United States. Further, this chapter highlights sociological issues related to public health, including tobacco use, obesity, and teen pregnancy. We offer ideas about the development of a sociology of HIV/AIDS, a problem that continues to threaten lives, livelihoods, and entire communities and countries. We finish with a consideration of global issues of health and their sociological roots.

CULTURAL DEFINITIONS OF HEALTH AND ILLNESS

Although health and medicine are closely related, sociologists find it useful to distinguish between them. **Health** is the extent to which a person experiences *a state of mental, physical, and social well-being*. It encompasses not merely the absence of illness but a positive sense of soundness as well. This definition, put forth by the World Health Organization (WHO, 2005), draws attention to the interplay of psychological, physiological, and sociological factors in a person's sense of well-being. It makes clear that excellent health cannot be achieved in purely physical terms. Health cannot be realized if the body is disease-free but the mind is troubled or the social environment is harmful.

Medicine is *an institutionalized system for the scientific diagnosis, treatment, and prevention of illness*. It focuses on identifying and treating physiological and psychological conditions that prevent a person from achieving a state of normal health. In this effort medicine typically applies scientific knowledge derived from physical sciences such as chemistry, biology, and physics, as well as psychology. In the United States, we usually view medicine in terms of the failure of health: When people become ill, they seek medical advice to address the problem. Yet, as the above definition suggests, medicine and health can go hand in hand. The field of **preventive medicine**—*medicine emphasizing a healthy lifestyle that will prevent poor health before it occurs*—is of key interest to doctors, patients, and policy makers.

THE SICK ROLE

Cultural definitions of sickness and health and their causes vary widely (Sagan, 1987). There are **sick roles** in every society. Sick roles are rooted in *the cultural definition of the appropriate behavior of and response to people labeled as sick* and are thus sociologically determined (Cockerham & Glasser, 2000; Parsons, 1951,

College Student Drug Use

Mental Health

1975). The sick role of being mentally ill, for instance, varies enormously across time and space (Foucault, 1988). In some societies, mentally ill people have been seen as having unique spiritual qualities, while in others they have been labeled as victims of demonic possession. In modern societies, mental illness is characterized sometimes as a disease with physiological antecedents and at other times as a sign of character weakness.

One of the pioneers in the sociology of medicine, Talcott Parsons (1975), observed that, in the United States, the role of "sick person" includes the right to be excused from social responsibilities and other "normal" social roles. Parsons, whose theories reflect a functionalist perspective on social life, suggested that illness is both biologically and socially defined, because a "normal" state of functioning includes both physiological equilibrium and the ability to enact expected social roles and behaviors.

Even if illness results from a lifestyle that puts a person at risk, society does not usually hold him or her accountable. On the other hand, the sick person has a societal obligation to try to get well and to seek competent medical help in order to do so. Failure to seek help can lead others to refuse to confer on the suffering individual the "benefits" of the sick role.

The notion that a sick person is enacting a social role may remind us of Erving Goffman's (1959) ideas about humans as actors on a social stage. Goffman suggested that life is like a dramatic play, with front and back stages, scripts for certain settings, costumes, and props. In order to define a situation in a way that is favorable to ourselves, he argued, each of us plays a role on the "front stage" that conforms to what is expected and what will show us in the best light.

Imagine a doctor's office as a stage: The doctor arrives wearing a "costume" (often a white lab coat and stethoscope). The patient also wears a "costume" (a cloth or paper gown rather than street clothing). The doctor is expected to greet the patient, ask questions about the illness, examine the patient, and offer advice. The patient is expected to assume a more passive role, submitting to an examination, accepting the diagnosis, and taking advice rather than dispensing it. Now imagine a scenario in which the doctor arrives dressed in evening attire, and the patient gives the doctor medical counsel or refuses to lie on the examining table, choosing instead to sit in the rotating "doctor's chair." The result would be failed expectations about the encounter, as well as an unsuccessful social and medical interaction. As Parsons points out, the sick person has an expected "role," but so too do doctors, nurses, and others who are part of the "sick play."

THE SOCIAL CONSTRUCTION OF ILLNESS

Parsons's model underscores the fact that the sick role is culturally determined. Illnesses that are culturally defined as legitimate,

Internet Addiction

Social Construction
of Illness

such as cancer and heart disease, entitle those who contract them to adopt the role of sick person. The afflicted are forgiven for time missed at work, spending days in bed, and asking others for consideration and assistance. A seriously ill person who persists in leading a "normal" life is given credit for an extraordinary exertion of effort.

Changes in U.S. society's response to alcoholism highlight the importance of cultural definitions of illness. In the middle of the 20th century, people addicted to alcohol were widely seen as weak and of questionable character. In 1956, however, the American Medical Association (2013) declared alcoholism an illness. With the acceptance of this medical model of alcoholism, alcoholics often expect and receive sympathy from family members for their illness, employers may have special programs to help them fight the disease, and the government funds research in an effort to find a cure.

While there also exists a disease model of drug addiction (Le Moal & Koob, 2007), someone addicted to illegal drugs is more likely to be denied the sick role. Cocaine, heroin, or methamphetamine addicts, for example, face the possibility of being sent to prison if they are found in possession of the drugs, and they may or may not be referred for treatment of their addiction. In some states, drug-addicted women are subject to criminal charges if they give birth to babies who test positive for drugs. In Alabama, a statute was enacted in 2006 that made it a crime to place a child in an "environment" in which he or she could be "exposed to, to ingest or inhale, or to have contact with a controlled substance, chemical substance, or drug paraphernalia." While the law when written focused on protecting children from the dangers of methamphetamine labs, some prosecutors interpreted "environment" as encompassing a woman's womb. Consequently, Alabama has brought approximately 60 cases against new mothers (Calhoun, 2012). While there are clear reasons to be concerned about the welfare of infants born to addicted mothers, it is less clear that there are greater benefits to criminally charging new mothers than to supporting their recovery in treatment programs.

Some drug addiction is widely understood as "illness," while some is labeled as "deviance," transforming the status of the individual who carries the label (Goffman, 1963). What explains the difference? Do you think these differing definitions are justified?

HEALTH CARE IN THE UNITED STATES

Health care can be defined as *all those activities intended to sustain, promote, and enhance health.* An adequate health care system includes more than the provision of medical services for those who need them, however. It also includes policies that minimize violence and the chance of accidents, whether on the

Health care: All those activities intended to sustain, promote, and enhance health.

INEQUALITY MATTERS

FEMINIST STANDPOINT THEORY AND THE CONSTRUCTION OF "FEMALE" ILLS

Joan Jacobs Brumberg writes in *The Body Project: An Intimate History of American Girls* (1997),

> According to Victorian medicine, the ovaries—not the brain— were the most important organ in a woman's body.
>
> The most persuasive spokesperson for this point of view was Dr. Edward Clarke, a highly regarded professor at Harvard Medical School, whose popular book *Sex in Education; Or, A Fair Chance for the Girls* (1873) was a powerful statement of the ideology of "ovarian determinism." In a series of case studies drawn from his clinical practice, Clarke described adolescent women whose menstrual cycles, reproductive capacity, and general health were all ruined, in his opinion, by inattention to their special monthly demands . . . Clarke argued against higher education because he believed women's bodies were more complicated than men's; this difference meant that young girls needed time and ease to develop,

free from the drain of intellectual activity. (pp. 7–8)

Medical facts and information are powerful and, because they are cloaked in the credibility of hard science, come to be seen in society as neutral, universal, and true. Feminist standpoint theorists such as Dorothy Smith (1987, 2005) suggest, however, that because "facts," including medical knowledge, have, until quite recently, been produced almost exclusively by men, they reflect a "male standpoint" on the world. Standpoint theorists argue that women's standpoints may well be different from men's, and that "facts" produced from just one standpoint cannot be seen as neutral or universal.

A key part of standpoint theory is the analysis of the power that lies in the production of knowledge, and it asks who has the power to produce "facts."

THINK IT THROUGH

■ *Does the creation of the medical "knowledge" described above about female education and ovulation suggest that men's and women's research and conclusions may be conditioned by their position in*

In the 19th century, female hysteria was a commonly diagnosed "ailment" among women. Today is it not recognized as a medical category at all. In the 19th century, women's ills were almost exclusively labeled by male physicians. Can you see a connection between these facts? ■

society? How likely is it that a female physician or researcher would have come to the scientific conclusion that education interferes with women's menses or reproductive capacity?

---

highways, at work, or at home; a clean, nontoxic environment; ecological protection; and the availability of clean water, fresh air, and sanitary living conditions.

HEALTH AND PUBLIC SAFETY ISSUES

By the standards noted above, few societies come close to providing excellent health care for their citizens. Some, however, do much better than others. The record of the United States in this regard is mixed.

On the one hand, the U.S. government spends vast sums of money in an effort to construct safe highways, provide clean drinking water, and regulate air and ground pollution. Laws regulate working conditions to promote healthy and safe environments: The federal Occupational Safety and Health Administration (OSHA) has stringent laws intended to guard the lives and health of U.S. workers. Local health inspectors visit the premises of restaurants and grocery stores to check that food is handled in a sanitary manner, and agricultural inspectors check the quality of U.S. and imported

DIGITAL SOCIETY

ADDICTION AND THE INTERNET

A recent advertisement for a leading telecommunications company opens with an earnest spokesman meandering through a family's home and declaring, "Today we live online." He adds that in a just a few years, the number of gadgets in our homes will double. Around him, four family members are each engaged in their own electronic worlds, interacting with someone or something other than those in their immediate environment. The scenario is presented as pleasant, progressive, and unproblematic. Might something be missing from this picture?

Scientific studies point to a growing epidemic of technological dependency, even addiction. A recent *Newsweek* article on the issue notes, "In less than the span of a single childhood, Americans have merged with their machines, staring at a screen for at least eight hours a day, more time than we spend on any other activity, including sleeping" (Dokoupil, 2012). Some Internet users neglect sleep, family, and health in favor of the virtual world: In one extreme case, a South Korean couple allowed their infant daughter to starve while nurturing an online baby for hours at a time (BBC News, 2010). At least 10 cases have

been documented of Internet surfers getting fatal blood clots from prolonged sitting at the computer. While most cases are not so acute in their consequences, as of 2013, the *Diagnostic and Statistical Manual of Mental Disorders* (*DSM*), the foundation of modern mental health practice, will include "Internet Addiction Disorder" as a diagnosis "for further study" (Dokoupil, 2012).

A recent publication by psychiatric researchers in Asia, which has very high rates of heavy Internet use, particularly by gamers, points out, "A functional magnetic resonance imaging (MRI) study found that a cue-induced online gaming urge among individuals with Internet gaming abuse activated brain areas similar to those involved in craving in people with drug addiction" (Yen, Yen, & Ko, 2010). Observers suggest that while questions remain about whether brain changes led to

How many hours do members of your family spend online in an average day? What about your friends and you? What are the costs and benefits of our increasing dependence on electronic gadgets and social media? ■

addictive behavior or heavy Internet use fostered brain changes, it is becoming increasingly clear that technology is linked in some way to problems that include addictive behavior, declining attention spans, greater impulsiveness, anxiety, and depression.

THINK IT THROUGH

■ *Is "living online" stigmatized in our society—or celebrated? If Internet or other technology use is addictive and vast swaths of people, particularly the young, are becoming addicted, how should society respond?*

---

food products. States require drivers to use seat belts, motorcyclists to wear helmets, and children to be strapped into car seats, all of which have been shown to reduce injury and fatalities in road accidents. While these efforts do not guarantee the safety of life, work, food, or transport, they contribute to public safety in important ways.

On the other hand, compared to most other modern countries, the United States is more violent, a factor that compromises

safety, in particular for some high-risk groups. Gun violence and firearm accidents leading to death are serious problems in the United States (Table 15.1 on page 377). U.S. children ages 5 to 14 are killed by guns at a rate 11 times higher than the rates of 22 comparable large, high-income countries. A recent analysis of WHO statistics on gun deaths found that fully 80% of the gun deaths in 23 industrialized countries (including the United States) happened in the United States (Richardson &

Hemenway, 2011). Homicide is a leading cause of death among young African American males, and the majority of this violence is perpetrated using guns (Kaiser Family Foundation, 2006; Violence Policy Center, 2010a). Studies have also noted that the rate of homicide victimization is higher in states with high rates of gun ownership. (Miller, Azrael, & Hemenway, 2007).

Domestic violence puts thousands of women at risk: At least 85% of victims of domestic violence are women, and an average of three U.S. women are murdered by a husband or boyfriend every day. In 2008, almost 1,000 women were murdered by an intimate partner (Violence Policy Center, 2010b). The abuse may start young: One in three adolescent females reported being physically and/or sexually abused by a dating partner (Davis, 2008). This occurs in spite of the fact that there are myriad laws against abuse, mechanisms for securing restraining orders against would-be attackers, and shelters for battered women. Efforts to protect victims and potential victims may fall short, because batterers are often given a pass by those hesitant to interfere, and because victims lack resources to leave or fear reprisals.

Different social groups experience different degrees of violence or safety. Black Americans are far more likely to be victims of homicide than Whites, and women are more likely to be killed by intimate partners than are men. Why are some groups in society more vulnerable to violence? Is there a link between physical safety

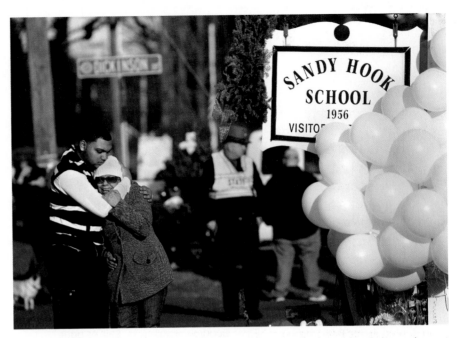

On December 14, 2012, a heavily armed young man killed 20 children and six teachers at Sandy Hook Elementary School in Newtown, Connecticut. The mass shooting has reignited the debate in the United States about gun violence and gun control. Some observers argue that schools should have armed guards. Do you agree or disagree with this proposal? ■

and the power a group has (or does not have) in society? What do you think?

SOCIAL INEQUALITIES IN HEALTH AND MEDICINE

By nearly every measure, health follows the social class curve: Poor people are likely to suffer more chronic illnesses and die earlier. Among children, poverty affects health, food security, housing stability, and maltreatment, with the former two factors playing a significant role in the likelihood of developing chronic illnesses and other negative outcomes such as malnutrition, stunted growth, and suppressed immunity (Henry, 2010). Recessions and economic slumps also hurt families as their ability to afford quality food and health care becomes strained.

Lower-income people are more likely to live in areas that have the highest levels of air pollution, which raise the risk of asthma, heart disease, and cancer (Calderón-Garcidueñas & Torres-Jardón, 2012). Many have a greater probability of exposure to violence and the mental and physical health problems that entails. Their work is also more likely to involve physical and health risks than the work of middle- and upper-class people (Commission on Health, 2009). Figure 15.1 on page 378 highlights class differences in self-perceptions of health and well-being.

The poor often have less healthy diets: Inexpensive foods may be highly processed, fatty, and high in sugar. Fresh fruits and vegetables and lean meats may be out of financial reach for

■ **TABLE 15.1** Gun Homicides for Selected Countries, 2011

	Gun Homicides per 100,000 Population	**Unintentional Gun Deaths per 100,000 Population**
United States	0.2	0.3
France	0.2	0.05
Germany	0.2	0.02
Spain	0.15	0.05
Canada	0.5	−0.08
United Kingdom	0.04	0.01
Japan	0.00	0.01

SOURCE: GunPolicy.org, Sydney School of Public Health, the University of Sydney.

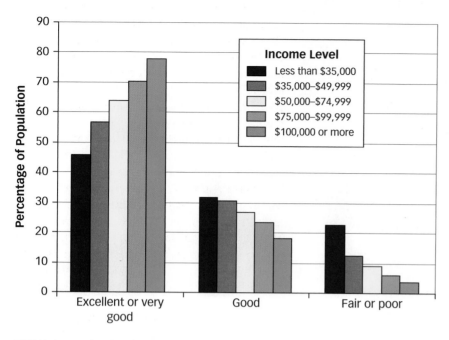

SOURCE: Centers for Disease Control and Prevention. (2012). Table XIII. Crude percent distributions of health status among persons aged 18 years and over, by selected characteristics: United States, 2010. *Summary health statistics for U.S. Adults: National Health Interview Survey, 2010.*

those who struggle to make ends meet, and time pressures can limit a working man's or woman's opportunities to shop for and prepare healthy foods. Children in poor communities may also lack access to safe places for active outdoor play and exercise. Another factor that affects the health of the poorer classes is the fact that they are less likely to perceive the symptoms of illness as requiring a physician (Keeley, Wright, & Condit, 2009).

Because race and class closely intersect in the United States, racial minorities, on average, suffer from poorer health than Whites, which is reflected in the discrepancies in life expectancy (see Figure 15.2 on page 379). The overall life expectancy at birth in 2010 in the United States was 78.7 years. White women's life expectancy was higher at 81.3, while Black women's was lower at 78.2. White men had a life expectancy of 76.6 years, but their Black counterparts had a life expectancy of just 72.1 years (Centers for Disease Control and Prevention [CDC], 2011a).

Inequalities start even before birth, since poor mothers are less likely to have access to prenatal care. A report prepared for the Annie E. Casey Foundation (Shore & Shore, 2009) suggests that "at any age, and at any income, education, or socioeconomic level, an African American mother is twice as likely to lose her infant than a white woman." These

Health and Social Inequality

findings are supported by 2010 data (Table 15.2) showing a mortality rate of 5.52 per 1,000 for White babies and a far higher rate of 12.67 deaths per 1,000 live births for babies of Black mothers (Hoyert & Xu, 2012).

The U.S. medical establishment has also used poor minorities to advance the frontiers of science. In the infamous Tuskegee study, which ran from the 1930s to the 1970s, Black males who had contracted syphilis were intentionally left untreated so researchers could study the progress of the disease (Brandt, 1983; Washington, 2007). During the Cold War, U.S. government agencies funded and conducted hundreds of research tests on unwitting citizens to assess the effects of radiation and other by-products of war (Budiansky, Goode, & Gest, 1994). These tests were usually conducted on the poor and disproportionately on minorities (Washington, 2007). This chapter's *Global Issues* essay on page 380 further explores the issue of medical testing on human beings and the questions that inevitably arise about who benefits from such activities and who loses.

ACCESS TO HEALTH CARE

One important reason why the poor—as well as some families in the working and middle classes—are less likely to experience good health is that a notable proportion are unable to access regular care for prevention and treatment of disease. In the fall of 2010, three years after the start of the Great Recession, the U.S. Census Bureau reported that over 16% of people in the United States were without health care insurance, the highest figure in 23 years (Kaiser Family Foundation, 2010). A key source of this decline was the economic crisis and associated rise in unemployment; most U.S. adults get health insurance coverage from their employers. Workplace coverage is variable, however, and ranges from full benefits requiring little or no financial contribution from the employee to partial benefits paid by shared employer and employee contributions. Cost-saving

■ **TABLE 15.2** Infant Mortality and Birth Weight per 1,000 Live Births Among Black and White Infants in the U.S., 2008

	Infant Mortality	Low Birth Weight	Very Low Birth Weight
Black	12.6	69.6	262.7
White	5.5	47.7	216.7

SOURCE: Centers for Disease Control and Prevention. (2012). Infant mortality statistics from the 2008 period linked birth/infant death data set. *National Vital Statistics Reports, 60*(5).

The Tuskegee experiment, which began in the early 1930s, lasted for four decades. Subjects, all of whom were poor and Black, were never told they had syphilis and were not treated, even after penicillin became available as a remedy in the 1940s. The ethical transgressions of researchers in this study helped to spur tighter human subjects controls in medical experimentation. ■

measures in U.S. workplaces in recent decades have shifted a greater share of the cost of these benefits to the employees themselves.

As the economic picture has improved, more people have gone back to work, but millions of employees are still uninsured or underinsured. According to recent data from the U.S Census Bureau, there were over 49 million uninsured people under the age of 65; including those 65 and older, the figure is nearly 50 million (Gould, 2011). This problem has been worsened by a changing labor market and economic structure that favors part-time or contractual employment, with fewer benefits such as the employer-based coverage that has traditionally applied to full-time employees.

A substantial number of people have access to health care through government-funded programs such as Medicare—an elder insurance program that covers most of those ages 65 and over (about 40 million in 2011) and some younger residents with disabilities (about 8 million in that year)—and Medicaid, a shared federal and state insurance program that provides coverage for many poor adults and children and today reaches about 1 in 6 people in the United States (Kaiser Family Foundation, 2012c; Smith, Gifford, Ellis, Rudowitz, & Snyder, 2011). Medicare was created in 1965 to serve as a federal health insurance program for people age 65 and older, regardless of income or medical history. It covers very diverse populations, since most people over the age of 65 and those with permanent disabilities are entitled to coverage (Kaiser Family Foundation, 2011b).

Medicaid, on the other hand, is the country's major health insurance program designed to assist low-income people of all ages with their health care needs, but it is not available to everyone who needs long-term services; stringent financial qualifications must be met (Kaiser Family Foundation, 2012a).

A contemporary issue related to Medicare is the fact that the post–World War II baby-boom generation (those born between about 1946 and 1964) is now entering the 65+-year-old cohort. As the "boomers" reach eligibility age, their massive numbers will have an effect on the need for health care dollars and resources. The U.S. Census Bureau (Werner, 2011) reports that between 2000 and 2010, the 65+ age cohort grew at a faster rate than the total population; the total population of the United States increased by under 10%, while the population of those 65 years and older grew by over 15%. The increase in eligible Medicare recipients, medical advancements that extend the life of the elderly, and a relatively smaller tax base are the ingredients of a debate over care and government spending that will grow more acute in the years to come (Antos, 2011). The effect of the Obama administration's health care legislation on Medicare is not yet fully clear.

At the opposite end of the age spectrum, the State Children's Health Insurance Program (SCHIP) was created in the late 1990s in an aggressive effort to cover more uninsured children. Because SCHIP is a partnership between states and the federal government, state governments largely dictate its implementation, so the comprehensiveness of coverage and eligibility standards vary by state.

■ **FIGURE 15.2** Life Expectancy in the U.S., 2011

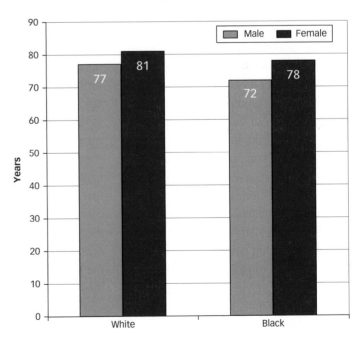

SOURCE: Hoyert, D. L., & Xu, J. (2012). Deaths: Preliminary data for 2011. *National Vital Statistics Reports, 61*(6). Washington, DC: Centers for Disease Control and Prevention.

GLOBAL ISSUES

HOW THE WEST BENEFITS FROM DISEASE IN THE DEVELOPING WORLD

Who benefits from disease and poverty? Your initial response is likely to be a decisive "nobody!" But considered from a conflict-oriented perspective, the question may elicit a different response. As noted in this chapter, U.S. medical science "benefited" from the diseased bodies of the Black men in the Tuskegee study, as well as from their relative powerlessness and lack of knowledge about what was happening to them in the study (Washington, 2007). And Herbert Gans (1972) argued that the nonpoor benefit from having a class of poor people (see Chapter 7). He meant that poverty is *positively functional for the nonpoor* because eliminating it, among other effects, would reduce the numbers of those willing to do health- and life-threatening jobs for low pay and shrink the market for goods or services whose quality the nonpoor would reject.

We can construct a similar conflict-oriented argument around global poverty and disease. Who benefits from global inequality and poverty, or from the poor health that often accompanies economic marginality? Poor, undereducated populations in developing states serve the West by offering pharmaceutical companies relatively unrestricted access to the human subjects they need for testing new medicines they will later sell to patients in wealthier nations. One of the authors of this book, Daina Eglitis (2010), argues that to the degree this is true, it limits incentives for industrialized nations to offer full support to developing nations. Hence, aid to poor states is

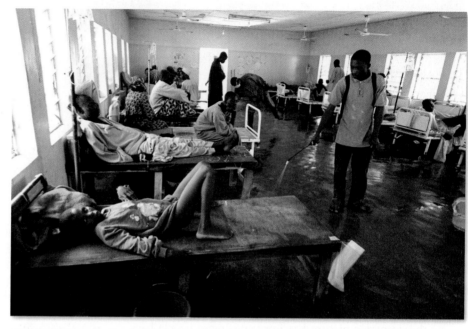

Controls on drug testing in many countries of the developing world are less stringent than in countries such as the United States and Canada. Clinical drug trials run in countries such as Nigeria (shown here) have led to criticism of pharmaceutical company practices. ■

enough to help their populations to survive, but not to thrive.

In terms of health and medicine, the existence of poor, undereducated populations in developing states benefits the West by offering pharmaceutical companies "guinea pigs" on whom to test new medicines where fewer restrictions are in force. Examples were cited by a *Washington Post* investigation in 2000: "[A]n unapproved antibiotic was tested by a major pharmaceutical company on sick children during a meningitis epidemic in Nigeria. The country's lax regulatory oversight, the sense among some doctors that they could not object to experiment conditions for political or economic reasons, the dearth of alternative health care options, combined with the desire of the company to rapidly prepare for market a potential 'blockbuster'

drug underpinned a situation in which disease victims were treated as test subjects rather than patients" (Eglitis, 2010, p. 203).

Looking at global poverty with a critical eye thus demands that we recognize how inhabitants of rich countries *benefit* from the existence of poor states and populations.

THINK IT THROUGH

■ *Would eliminating global poverty be costly for some powerful interests in the West? Might this reduce incentives for rich countries to support fuller development and prosperity in poor states? Are there what sociologist Robert Merton termed functional alternatives for global poverty—that is, can the needs of wealthy countries and populations be met by other means?*

While the care the poorest U.S. adults can access through Medicaid is limited, it is often working poor and other low-income employees who are shut out of insurance coverage altogether. They are most likely to be working in economic sectors such as the service industry (fast-food restaurants, retail establishments, and the like) that provide little or no insurance benefits to employees, while earning too little to afford self-coverage but too much to qualify for government health coverage. The fact, as noted above, that low-income people are more likely to have health problems also affects their ability to get insurance coverage, which has often excluded those with "preexisting conditions" such as diabetes, high blood pressure, or a long bout of illness or disability.

The Patient Protection and Affordable Care Act (PPACA) passed by President Barack Obama in 2010 endeavors to expand insurance coverage to most people in the United States at a time when the numbers of the uninsured have been rising. The goal of the health care overhaul is to bring more people into the insurance fold by making coverage more broadly accessible and affordable, in part by requiring that everyone buy insurance and that private insurance companies offer coverage under new terms that extend benefits to those who may have had difficulty purchasing insurance in the past, such as those with preexisting conditions. While the purchasing mandate begins in 2014, other parts of the PPACA were already in place when the Supreme Court ruled on its constitutionality in June 2012. For example, insurance companies must permit young people to remain on their parents' insurance policy up to age 26 if they do not have other coverage.

Since its passage, the PPACA has been the source of heated political debate. President Obama and other supporters of the act argue that the new law will expand insurance coverage to a broader swath of people, many of whom have been locked out of the insurance market due to preexisting conditions or unaffordability of individual insurance policies. They suggest that the law will support expansion through new state-level insurance markets (or exchanges) that keep prices down by enabling purchasers to buy insurance as part of a group. Those with low incomes may also be eligible for federal subsidies to support insurance purchase. Supporters also note that as the population of uninsured people declines, so will taxpayer-borne costs, including those incurred when the uninsured seek medical care at emergency rooms, which are obligated by law to treat everyone regardless of their ability to pay.

Opponents argue that the U.S. government is overstepping the limits of its powers in requiring that people purchase health insurance or pay a penalty tax for failing to do so. Many see the mandate as an infringement on the freedom to choose whether or

After the passage of President Obama's Patient Protection and Affordable Care Act, several states sued the federal government, calling the act unconstitutional. In June 2012, the Supreme Court ruled that the act's requirement that nearly all citizens secure health insurance is permissible under the taxing authority of the U.S. Congress. ■

not to purchase insurance. There have also been attempts to portray the PPACA as a path to "socialized medicine," though most people will still receive their insurance through private insurance companies rather than the government.

Both supporters and opponents of the PPACA have expressed concerns about the costs of the U.S. health care system. Indeed, the United States spends more per capita on health care than most economically developed states (Figure 15.3 on page 382), though many of its health indicators compare poorly to those of its peers. Opponents of health care reform argue that the PPACA will drive up costs by, for instance, requiring insurers to cover those who have costly health conditions. Supporters point out that having a large pool of uninsured contributes to higher costs when they fail to get preventive care and must resort to far more costly emergency room care. The cost trajectory of health care is not yet clear. Certainly, an aging U.S. population will likely need more, not fewer, health care services in the future. The effect of the PPACA on both U.S. health indicators and access to care will become more clear with the passage of time.

SOCIOLOGY AND ISSUES OF PUBLIC HEALTH IN THE UNITED STATES

Public health is *the science and practice of health protection and maintenance at a community level.* Public health officials

. . . .

Public health: The science and practice of health protection and maintenance at a community level.

Universal Health Care

Teenage Steroid Use

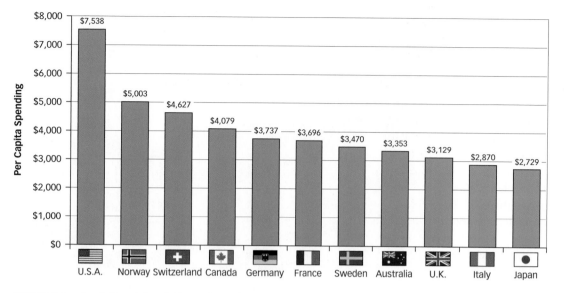

SOURCE: Kaiser Family Foundation. (2011, April). *Health care spending in the United States and selected OECD countries.*

try to control hazards and habits that may harm the health and well-being of the population. They have long sought to educate the public about the hazards of tobacco use, for example, and to prevent young people from taking up smoking. More recently, they have warned that obesity is becoming an ever more serious problem for young and old alike. Teen pregnancies and births have also garnered attention, though rates have fluctuated.

SMOKING

One of the largest and most profitable industries in the United States is the manufacture and sale of tobacco products, estimated to be a $47.1 billion industry. At the same time, tobacco is the number-one cause of premature death in the United States, claiming more than 443,000 lives each year and surpassing the toll from alcohol, homicide, suicide, drugs, auto accidents, and AIDS combined (CDC, 2011d). Even nonsmokers are at risk. The CDC (2011d) estimates that secondhand smoke exposes 88 million nonsmokers to measurable levels of toxic chemicals associated with cigarette smoke. About 90% of men and 80% of women who die of lung cancer are smokers (U.S. Department of Health and Human Services, 2004). While the smoking rate in the United States fell between 2000 and 2005, it has since stalled at about 21%, a figure that translates to over 45 million smokers (CDC, 2011d).

While statistics on **morbidity,** meaning *the rate of illness,* and **mortality,** *the rate of death,* highlight important *medical* aspects of cigarette smoking, we can also use sociological analysis

to illuminate this public health issue. Why do so many people continue to smoke and so many young people take up smoking despite the evidence of its ill effects? Why do more men than women smoke? Why are young women the fastest-growing population of new smokers? (See Figure 15.4.) Why does the government not more stringently regulate the production and sale of an addictive and dangerous product?

Sociology offers us some insight into these questions. Among other things, advertising of cigarettes both constructs and reinforces gender stereotypes (Kilbourne, 1999). Male smoking has been associated with independence, ruggedness, and machismo (think of the Marlboro Man, an iconic figure in U.S. advertising). On the other hand, female smoking has been associated with images that are elegant, chic, and playful or carefree. A symbolic interactionist might highlight the way in which a cigarette is more than just tobacco rolled in paper. To a young teen, it might be a symbol of maturity; to an older teen, it might represent being cool or rebellious. In what other ways do cigarettes function as symbols of self in our society?

■ FIGURE 15.4 Cigarette Smoking in the U.S., 2010

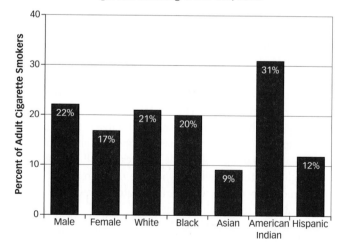

SOURCE: Centers for Disease Control and Prevention. (2012). Adult cigarette smoking in the United States: Current estimate. *Smoking & Tobacco Use.*

Tobacco Use Worldwide

· ·

Morbidity: The rate of illness in a particular population.

Mortality: The rate of death in a particular population.

TWO THEORETICAL PERSPECTIVES ON PUBLIC HEALTH: THE CASE OF CIGARETTES The conflict perspective offers some insight into why cigarettes are not regulated more stringently despite their addictive properties: Who benefits from having a large population of smokers? Who loses?

Smoking may give pleasure to smokers, but its benefits are largely outweighed by its consequences, which include poorer health and a thinner wallet. Smoking does, however, bring profit to the tobacco companies, which have tenaciously defended their product for decades. Tobacco companies are generous contributors to candidates for political office. They are advantaged by wealth and access to the halls of government, where their voices are heard. While the smoker gets a mixed bag of benefits (pleasure) and consequences (addiction, disease, financial cost) from smoking, cigarette companies clearly benefit from those who buy their goods and the recruitment of new smokers—men and boys, women and girls—to replace those who die or quit.

Is the easy availability of cigarettes also functional? A functionalist might suggest that, in fact, it is positively functional in its creation of jobs, which range from tobacco farmers to marketers and lobbyists for the tobacco cause, and in its contribution to rural economies that depend on income from farming tobacco. The highly coveted plant has been subject to human cultivation and use for hundreds of years. Consider its historical functions: Tobacco became a major influence in the development of the economy of early America. During the Revolutionary War, profits from the tobacco trade were used to finance the Revolution by serving as collateral for loans provided to Americans from France (Randall, 1999). In contemporary times, according to the Center for Responsive Politics's *OpenSecrets* blog, the tobacco lobby employed about 133 lobbyists and spent over $17 million on behalf of 25 clients in 2011 alone (Center for Responsive Politics, 2013). The modern tobacco industry is a multimillion-dollar enterprise with a strong political influence despite increased awareness of the deleterious effects that tobacco products have on the human body.

Viewing cigarette smoking through a theoretical lens lets us see it as more than just an individual choice or action. Rather, cigarettes and smoking are social symbols and phenomena with a profound effect on public heath, as well as a source of profit for some and pain for others.

OBESITY

The CDC identifies obesity in the United States as a national health problem: It is a major cause of mortality, second only to smoking. According to the CDC (2012e) and Kaiser Family Health Institute (2011c), over 34% of adults between the ages of 20 and 74 are obese, and over 63% are overweight (this statistic includes those who are classified as obese). The rates of being overweight/obese vary by gender and ethnicity, as we see in Figure 15.5 on page 384.

Children's rate of obesity has risen even faster and is twice what it was in the late 1970s. Children who are much bigger than their peers sometimes experience social ostracism. Further, they

Communications researcher Jean Kilbourne (1999) says female-targeted cigarette ads often contain subtexts about female thinness, using "thin," "slim," or "light" in the product name. Ads also imply that smoking can help women lose weight; in the past Lucky cigarettes urged, "Reach for a Lucky instead of a sweet." ■

may suffer serious health effects. Very obese children have been observed to suffer health problems once believed to affect only older adults, including heart attacks and adult-onset diabetes (CDC, 2012c). With the popularity of sedentary activities, including video games, the Internet, and television viewing, society will likely see this problem increase.

Among the factors to which the rise in size has been attributed is that U.S. families eat more meals outside the home than in the past, and many of these meals are taken in fast-food establishments. As well, the portions diners are offered in restaurants are growing because many ingredients have become very inexpensive. In *Fast Food Nation,* Eric Schlosser (2001) notes that "commodity prices have fallen so low that the fast food industry has greatly increased its portion sizes, without reducing profits, in order to attract customers" (p. 243), a point supported by mathematician and physicist Carson C. Chow, who argues that

The Obesity Problem

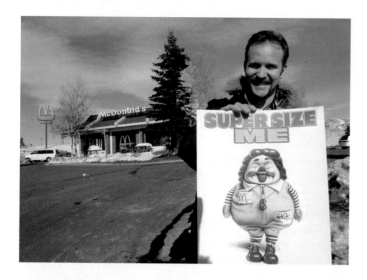

According to the Pew Research Center, 47% of men and 35% of women report eating at a fast-food establishment at least once a week. Among those aged 18–29, the figure was 59%. For his film *Supersize Me* (2004), Morgan Spurlock (pictured) ate only fast food for 30 days. He suffered a variety of health consequences, including a weight gain of 24 pounds. ■

the obesity epidemic in the United States is an outcome of the overproduction of food since the 1970s (Dreifus, 2012). Federal subsidies for food production favor meat and dairy, which soak up almost three quarters of these funds. Just over 10% support the production of sugar, oils, starches, and alcohol. Less than a third of 1% support the growing of vegetables and fruits. These data show that the U.S. Congress has opted to subsidize the production of foods that contribute to obesity rather than those, including fruits and vegetables, recommended in the government's own nutrition pyramid (Rampell, 2010).

Damage to health is not the only harmful effect of obesity. Recent research has found that, on average, the annual individual cost of being obese is $4,879 for women and $2,646 for men. Obese women are also more financially disadvantaged than obese men and suffer 38% more job-related costs, such as absenteeism (Dor, Ferguson, Langwith, & Tan, 2010).

Clearly, being overweight or obese are complex phenomena. They are driven by a variety of factors—biological, genetic, environmental, social, and economic. As you will see below, poverty is also an important factor in understanding the prevalence of obesity. From a sociological perspective, however, consider the connection between the *personal trouble* and the *public issue* of obesity and overweight. That is, if one individual or a handful in a community are obese, that may be a personal trouble, attributable to genetics, illness, eating habits, or any other set of factors. However, when over one third of the U.S. population is obese (CDC,

Obesity and
Healthcare Costs

2012e), including majorities in some communities, this is a public issue and one that, to paraphrase C. Wright Mills, we may not hope to explain by focusing just on individual cases. Rather, we need to seek out its sociological roots.

Consider how this issue might look through the conflict lens. Who benefits, and who loses? While "losers" in this instance are surely those whose health is compromised by excessive weight, there are also macro-level effects, such as lost productivity when employees miss work due to obesity-linked illnesses such as diabetes. In fact, the CDC website published an estimate suggesting that the medical care costs of obesity in the United States total about $147 billion annually (Finkelstein, Trogdon, Cohen, & Dietz, 2009).

Who benefits? The food industry, particularly fast-food companies, arguably benefit when consumers prioritize quantity over quality. By offering bigger portions (which cost only a bit more to provide), restaurants draw bigger crowds and bigger profits. The $60 billion weight-loss industry (Clark, 2011; Market Data Enterprises, 2011) also benefits, since the rise in obesity exists in the presence of widespread societal obsession with thinness. Often, the same companies that market very high-fat, unhealthy foods also peddle "lite" versions (Lemonnier, 2008).

TEEN PREGNANCY

About 750,000 teenage girls become pregnant in the United States each year, and an estimated 444,690 give birth (Kost & Henshaw, 2012). Most of the young mothers (about 81%) are unmarried when they give birth (Henshaw, 2002; Turner, 2003). Figure 15.6 shows changes in the teen birthrate across recent decades.

■ **FIGURE 15.5** Obesity and Overweight Rate in the U.S. by Race and Ethnicity, 2011

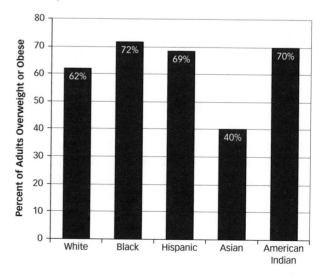

SOURCE: Kaiser Family Foundation. (2011). Overweight and obesity rates for adults by race/ethnicity, 2011. *Statehealthfacts.org.*

PRIVATE LIVES, PUBLIC ISSUES

POVERTY, MALNUTRITION, AND OBESITY

Obesity and being overweight are, in important ways, what many of us would see as "private troubles," reflecting choices individuals make about nutrition, exercise, and health. Clearly, however, these public health problems affect millions in the United States. No less importantly to sociologists, the risk of falling into those categories is not evenly distributed across social groups in this country.

Think for a moment about the problems of hunger and malnutrition. What kinds of images enter your mind? Are you picturing the heartrending scenes of starvation in the world's least-developed countries that are brought to us by the media? Yet hunger and malnutrition are also present in our own country, though their manifestation is often quite different. Poor access to nutritious food in the United States is more likely to be manifested in obesity, not emaciation. Consider, for example, that some of the country's poorest states have the highest obesity rates. In Kentucky 30.4% of adults are obese, in Louisiana 33.4%, and in Mississippi 34.9% (Centers for Disease Control and Prevention [CDC], 2012b).

Among the demographic groups most likely to be poor are also those most at risk of obesity; fully half of African American women are obese, as are 45% of Hispanic women (CDC, 2012b). Those without a high school education are more likely to be obese (32.9%) than those who complete high school (over 29%) or college (nearly 21%; Ogden, Lamb, Carroll, & Flegal, 2010). According to the *Handbook on Obesity,* "In heterogenous and affluent

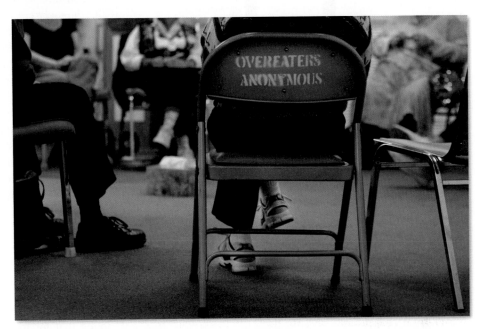

Obesity is not exclusively about overconsumption of food. Factors including the higher cost of healthy meals and the lack of access to recreational spaces also play a key role in understanding why many Americans, particularly the poor, struggle with obesity. ■

societies like the United States, there is a strong inverse correlation of social class and obesity" (quoted in Critser, 2003, p. 117).

Can we use the sociological imagination to examine the relationship between poverty and obesity? What sociological factors are pertinent in understanding this phenomenon? Though individual factors such as bone structure, genes, appetite, and personal choices have an important influence, obesity is also a product of social environment and socioeconomic conditions. Those who are poor are more likely to consume less nutritious food for a host of reasons. Nutritionally poor food is generally less expensive than high-quality goods, and large grocery stores with wide selections and competitive pricing are disproportionately located in suburbs, while convenience stores plying

overpriced, processed foods serve inner-city communities (Critser, 2003), though cities including Washington, DC, have increased incentives for big grocery stores to locate in poor neighborhoods.

The poor are also likely to have more limited access to recreational facilities such as safe playgrounds and sports fields that offer opportunities for exercise. Facing budgetary pressures, some poor schools have cut important physical education programs. Good nutrition and healthy lifestyles and weight are privileges of class in ways we may not have imagined.

THINK IT THROUGH

■ *What kinds of social programs or policies might a sociologist design to address the prevalence of obesity in poor communities?*

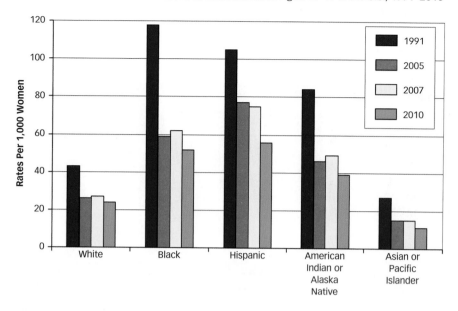

SOURCE: Data from Centers for Disease Control and Prevention. (2012). Birth rates for U.S. teenagers reach historic lows for all age and ethnic groups. *NCHS Data Brief, 89.*

Teenage pregnancy and birth are public health issues because young women who conceive or give birth before their bodies are fully developed put themselves and their babies at risk. Compared to older mothers, teen mothers have worse health, more pregnancy complications, and more stillborn, low-weight, or medically fragile infants. But teen pregnancy and birth are of more than medical concern.

They are also associated with another public health problem: poverty.

Giving birth early and outside marriage compounds the risk that young women and their children will become or remain poor; about 34% of all female-headed households in the United States live below the poverty line, compared with about 7% of married-couple families (DeNavas-Walt, Proctor, & Smith, 2012). Parenthood is a leading cause of dropping out of school among teenage women; teen mothers are at greater risk than their peers of not completing high school—only about 40% of women who become mothers before the age of 18 earn a high school diploma, and fewer than 2% earn a college degree by age 30 (National Campaign to Prevent Teen Pregnancy, 2010).

The relationship between teen pregnancy and birth and poverty is complicated. On the one hand, as noted, early and unwed motherhood compounds the risk of poverty. On the other hand, poverty is itself a risk factor for teenage motherhood: An estimated 80% of teen mothers grew up in low-income households (Shore & Shore, 2009), and poor teens have a higher incidence of early sexual activity, pregnancy, and birth than their better-off peers (National Campaign to Prevent Teen Pregnancy, 2010).

In *Dubious Conceptions* (1996), sociologist Kristin Luker suggests that poverty is a *cause* as well as a *consequence* of teen pregnancy and birth. She argues that poor young women's probability of early motherhood is powerfully affected by "disadvantage and discouragement" (Luker, 1996, p. 111). By *disadvantage* she means the social effects of poverty, which reduce opportunities for a solid education and the realization of professional aspirations. Consider, for instance, a high school senior from an affluent household: She may spend her 18th year contemplating whether to begin college immediately or take a year off for travel abroad. A young woman who hails from poor, rural Louisiana or the Bronx's depressed Mott Haven neighborhood may have received an inferior education in her underfunded school, and having little money, she has no hope for college. Travel beyond her own state or even city is unthinkable. Local jobs in the service industry are an option, as is motherhood. *Discouragement*, according to Luker, is the effect of poverty that may prevent poor young women from exercising agency in confronting obstacles. In an impoverished situation, the opportunity costs—that is, the educational or other opportunities lost due to early motherhood—may seem relatively low.

Notably, a study by Kathryn Edin and Maria Kefalas (2005) found that for many poor young women, early motherhood is

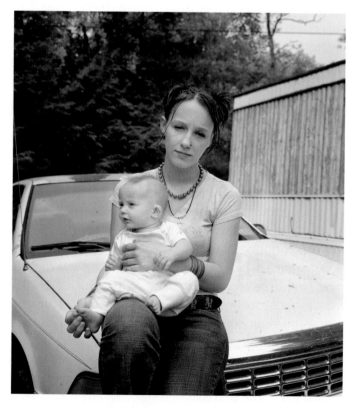

Parenthood is a leading reason that teen women drop out of school. About a third cite this reason for early school leaving. Staying in school, however, is key to job prospects that enable families to stay out of poverty. What might schools do to encourage young mothers to graduate? ■

embraced as an honorable and even desirable choice. It was also seen by some of the women interviewed as something that "saved" them from trouble with drugs or the law and "matured" them. Most of the women they interviewed expressed a desire to marry and embark on a career in the future. At the same time, discouraged by what they perceived as a limited pool of stable partners, whose marriageability is compromised by poor employment prospects and problems such as alcohol and drug use, the women did not put marriage ahead of motherhood, though many retained hopes for marriage at a point when they felt financially independent. In neighborhoods where early motherhood is the norm, many expressed a preference to have their children while young, a norm shared by the young men with whom they had relationships. While few of the pregnancies were planned, many couples also took no steps to avoid pregnancy.

Though they remain higher than in many other economically advanced countries, rates of teen motherhood in the United States have declined in some groups. Among other factors, the use of condoms has increased markedly (U.S. Department of Health and Human Services, 2013), perhaps due to a desire to protect against both pregnancy and sexually transmitted infections. There have also been small drops in the number of teenagers approving of and engaging in premarital sexual activity, and the current rate of birth among teenage women has dropped compared to the rate in earlier decades (Ventura & Hamilton, 2011).

Teen pregnancy and teen birthrates are *social facts*, or phenomena that, according to Émile Durkheim, we can explain only by using other social facts. That is, to understand sociologically both the rise and the fall of teen pregnancies and births, we must recognize that they are not just "personal troubles" or individual issues, but that they are fundamentally tied to other economic, social, and cultural issues in society.

■ **FIGURE 15.8** Estimated New HIV Diagnoses in the United States by Subpopulation, 2009

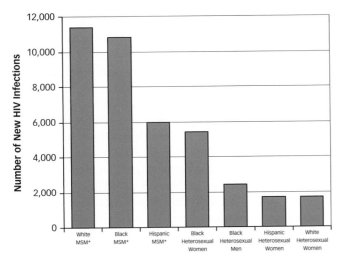

*Men who have sex with men.

SOURCE: Centers for Disease Control and Prevention. (2011). Estimates of new HIV infections in the United States, 2006–2009. *CDC Fact Sheet.*

■ **FIGURE 15.7** HIV/AIDS Prevalence by Race and Ethnicity in the U.S., 2009

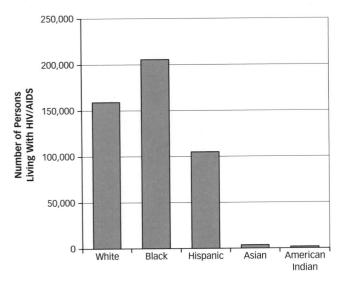

SOURCE: Kaiser Family Foundation. (2009). Estimated numbers of persons living with an AIDS diagnoses, all ages, by race/ethnicity, 2009. *Statehealthfacts.org*

DEVELOPING A SOCIOLOGY OF HIV/AIDS

The case of acquired immunodeficiency syndrome (AIDS) is another example of the importance of understanding the social construction of illness. Perceptions of HIV/AIDS and its sufferers have varied across time, depending upon who its most visible victims have been. As well, the infection—which is a global pandemic—demands a sociological approach because it is closely intertwined with a host of sociological issues, including gender inequality, poverty, violence and conflict, and the pursuit of both medical breakthroughs and profits in a globalizing world.

It is estimated that more than 1 million persons in the United States have HIV/AIDS—of these, about 236,000 or 1 in 5 (about 20%) have not been diagnosed and likely do not know they are infected (CDC, 2011b).

GENDER AND HIV/AIDS

The spread of sexually transmitted diseases, including HIV/AIDS, can be better understood if we examine how these diseases are related to gender and inequality. Globally, the number of women with HIV/AIDS has risen: Fully half of new infections are now diagnosed among women. In some regions, women's infection rates outpace men's: In Sub-Saharan Africa, of the 22.5 million people living with AIDS, 60% are women (UNAIDS, 2010b).

Stigma of HIV

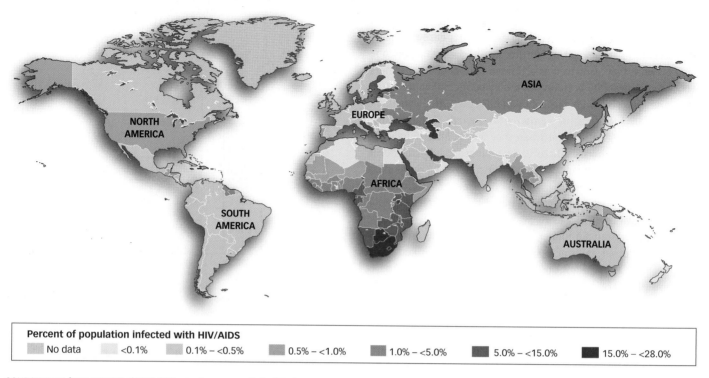

Percent of population infected with HIV/AIDS

No data   <0.1%   0.1% – <0.5%   0.5% – <1.0%   1.0% – <5.0%   5.0% – <15.0%   15.0% – <28.0%

SOURCE: Data from UNAIDS. (2010). HIV prevalence map. *United Nations Programme on HIV/AIDS Global Report 2010.*

Norms and traditions in many regions reinforce women's lower status in society. In some traditional communities in Africa, for example, it is socially acceptable—or even desirable—for men to have multiple partners both before and after marriage. In this case, marriage itself becomes a risk factor for women. Many women also still lack accurate knowledge of sexually transmitted diseases, a problem made more acute by widespread female illiteracy in poor regions. Women who are uninfected may not know how to protect themselves, and women who are infected may not know how to protect their partners.

Gender stereotypes and vulnerability to HIV/AIDS are also pertinent. In a *New York Times Magazine* article on the "down low," a term used to denote the culture of Black men who present themselves to the outside world as heterosexual but engage in homosexual activity, Benoit Denizet-Lewis (2003) writes about a culture of Black masculinity in which Black male bisexuality and homosexuality are little discussed and little accepted. Hence, Black males who want to have sexual relationships with males are often compelled to put on a façade for their families and society. In the words of one man on the down low, "If you're white, you can come out as an openly gay skier or actor or whatever. It might hurt you some, but it's not like if you're black and gay, because it's like you've let down the whole black community, black women, black history, black pride" (Denizet-Lewis, 2003). An important consequence is the fact that some men who are having sex with other men are also having sex with women—wives and girlfriends. Notably, CDC (2010) data show that Blacks made up about half of those found to have HIV in 2008, but only about 3 in 5 have ever been tested. This suggests that many are likely unaware of their status, which puts them, as well as their partners, whether male or female, at risk.

POVERTY AND HIV/AIDS

There is a powerful relationship between the risk of HIV/AIDS and poverty. This relationship holds true across the globe. China, for instance, has experienced a rise in new cases in the past decade. A serious epidemic was detected in central China's Henan Province, where tens of thousands of rural villagers have been infected in the past decade through selling their blood for money under unsafe and unsterile conditions. In China as a whole, it is estimated that at the end of 2005 there were 55,000 commercial blood and plasma donors infected with HIV ("AIDS in China," 2007). In developing countries, economic insecurity and the lack of gainful employment sometimes drive workers (particularly men) to seek work far from home. For example, migrant workers from surrounding countries toil in the mines of South Africa. Away from their families and communities, some men seek out the services of prostitutes, who may be infected (UNAIDS, 2010a).

The sex workers themselves are often victims of dire and desperate economic circumstances. Women in the sex trade, some of whom have been trafficked and enslaved, are highly vulnerable to HIV/AIDS. They have little protection from robbery or rape and limited power to negotiate safe sex with a paying customer, though some countries, such as Thailand, have sought to empower sex workers to demand condom use (UNAIDS, UNFPA, & UNIFEM, 2004).

HIV/AIDS in Poor Countries

Poor states, as well as poor individuals, are vulnerable to the ravages of disease. Consider the cases of many southern African states: HIV prevalence among adults aged 15–49 is about 25% in Botswana, 23% in Lesotho, and 13% in Zimbabwe (Lesotho, 2012; Republic of Botswana, 2012; Zimbabwe, 2012). The high rate of infection and death among young and middle-aged adults also means that countries are left with a diminished workforce. Without productive citizens, the state of a country's economy declines, further reducing the resources that might be put into HIV/AIDS prevention or treatment. Even those who are training the next generation of workers have been hard-hit by the disease: In Zambia, the number of teachers dying of AIDS outpaces those graduating as teachers (Oyoo, 2003). While HIV/AIDS is far from limited to poor victims or poor countries, poverty clearly increases the risk of disease both at the individual and at the national level.

VIOLENCE AND HIV/AIDS

The risk to women of contracting HIV/AIDS is increased by situations of domestic violence. United Nations statistics suggest that up to half the women in the world may experience violence from a domestic partner at some point: This includes forced sex, which is not likely to take place with a condom (UNAIDS, UNFPA, & UNIFEM, 2004).

The rape of men by other males, not uncommon in prison settings, can also be implicated in the spread of the infection. The incidence of HIV/AIDS in prisons is in many countries significantly higher than the incidence of the disease in the noninstitutionalized population. Part of this phenomenon is linked to the sharing of needles among drug-injecting prisoners or to consensual male sexual activity, but part is also linked to the underreported sexual violence behind bars.

HIV/AIDS is a medical issue. It is also a sociological issue. Vulnerability to infection is compounded by factors such as gender stereotypes and poverty. At a time when hope of new treatments and prevention strategies has materialized, but the pandemic continues to ravage communities and countries, a sociological perspective can help us to identify its social roots and to seek the most fruitful paths for combating its spread.

GLOBAL ISSUES IN HEALTH AND MEDICINE

Ever since human beings first began to migrate from their African origins, taking their illnesses with them, the spread of disease has known no global boundaries. Plagues and epidemics have traveled from populations that have developed some degree of biological immunity to others that have not. During the 14th century, the bubonic plague or "Black Death" came to Europe by

The "100% condom" program adopted in Thailand's sex establishments has helped keep the rate of HIV/AIDS infection relatively low. Such programs are rare on a global scale, however, and even with Thailand's 1.5% prevalence rate, AIDS is a leading cause of death there. ■

way of Asia, eliminating a third of the European population in only 20 years. The European conquerors of the Americas brought syphilis and other diseases with them, virtually eliminating the indigenous population in many areas (Thornton, 1987).

U.S. soldiers returning from Europe at the end of World War I carried previously unknown influenza strains, which killed an estimated 20 million people worldwide. Today, tuberculosis, once all but eliminated from the industrial nations, is making a comeback, with new treatment-resistant strains brought by immigrants from poor nations.

Recently, the United States publicly apologized to the nation of Guatemala when it was discovered that in the 1940s, U.S. government researchers deliberately infected hundreds of Guatemalan mental patients with gonorrhea and syphilis for observational purposes and encouraged them to transfer their infections to others (Bazell, 2010). Such unethical experiments endanger larger populations by introducing diseases that can erupt in outbreaks.

Overall, however, the 20th century has witnessed a striking global triumph over many diseases, as sanitation, clean water, sewage systems, knowledge about the importance of diet, and other public health and medical practices and treatments have spread throughout the world. For example, in only a few years, the WHO's plan for "Health for All by the Year 2000" succeeded in immunizing half the world's children against measles, polio, and four other diseases (Steinbrook,

Social Rights in Global Health

Preventing HIV/AIDS

SARS, bird flu, and swine flu, among others, have sickened millions around the globe in recent years. Airports and airplanes, hospitals, classrooms, and other public venues are potential sites of disease dissemination. In this photo, young people in Nashville, Tennessee, wear masks to prevent the spread of swine flu. ■

1988). In 2004, the Gates Foundation, working with the Global Alliance for Vaccines and Immunization, was able to vaccinate an estimated 78% of children in the world against diphtheria, tetanus, and whooping cough (Bill and Melinda Gates Foundation, 2006). Today, the Gates Foundation reports that it is 99% of the way toward eradicating polio, and that a new vaccine will save the lives of an additional 400,000 children per year on a global scale (Bill and Melinda Gates Foundation, 2013). Successes such as these have produced a sharp decline in death rates in most of the world's countries (WHO, 2008).

The AIDS epidemic is the most recent example of the global spread of a fatal disease. What makes it unique is the rapidity with which it spread around the world, to industrialized and less developed nations alike. HIV/AIDS is also a global issue in terms of treatment and prevention. Globalization is both functional and dysfunctional for real and potential victims of the infection. On the one hand, HIV/AIDS was global in its path of spread, and it appears likely that its defeat will also be global, as it was for other once-deadly and widespread diseases such as smallpox, polio, and malaria (Steinbrook, 1988). There is a concerted global effort to combat the disease. Doctors across the globe work together to share information and knowledge on HIV/AIDS and their efforts

Heart Disease in
Developing Countries

to stop it. International organizations including the United Nations are also instrumental in leading information and empowerment campaigns.

On the other hand, globalization has thrown obstacles in the path of expanding the reach of therapeutic drugs that lengthen health and life for those with the infection. The global market in HIV/AIDS treatment has been dominated by Western pharmaceutical companies. Most companies have jealously guarded their patent rights on the drug therapies shown to be most effective for treatment. Their fierce desire to protect patents and profits has made it more difficult for drug makers in developing states to manufacture less expensive generic versions that could save more lives in poor countries.

Together with HIV/AIDS, one of the most threatening diseases in developing countries is malaria: By some accounts, malaria is a threat to no less than half the global population. It kills over 800,000 people every year. The most vulnerable populations are children and pregnant women in Africa, which has the most malaria deaths (CDC, 2012d).

The toll taken by malaria is felt at the individual, community, and national levels. For individual families, malaria is costly in terms of drugs, travel to clinics, lost time at work or school, and burial, among others. For governments, malaria means the potential loss of tourism and productive members of society and the cost of public health interventions including treatments and mosquito nets, which many individuals are unable to afford for themselves (CDC, 2012d). Malaria, together with HIV/AIDS and tuberculosis (TB), has attracted a substantial proportion of available funding from international and national donors and governments seeking to improve the health of populations in the developing world.

Critics of international health spending priorities point to a growing threat in the developing world that has not received substantial funding or attention: chronic disease. Heart disease, stroke, and cancer have long been chronic maladies associated with habits of developed countries such as overeating, lack of exercise, and smoking. One scientist notes that while 80% of global deaths from chronic diseases take place in low- and middle-income countries, those illnesses receive the smallest fraction of donor assistance for health. Of the nearly $26 billion allocated for health in 2009, just 1% targeted chronic disease (Lomborg, 2012).

Chronic disease, however, is a growing threat in the developing world, driven by a dramatic rise in both obesity and smoking. According to the World Health Organization, between 1980 and 2008, global obesity rates doubled. By the WHO estimate, about half the adult populations of Brazil, Russia, and South Africa are overweight. In Africa, around 8% of adults are obese. While these figures are low compared to those in the United States, where two thirds of adults are estimated to be overweight and one third obese, the numbers are rising. A variety of factors contribute to this phenomenon, including growing incomes in many parts of the developing world, which enable more consumption, economic changes that shift work from physical labor to indoor and sedentary labor, and the movement of fast food into new regions that can now afford to splurge for a burger and soda (Kenny, 2012).

While smoking has decreased in many developed countries in recent decades, it has grown dramatically in some parts of the developing world. Today, about 80% of smokers live in the developing world (Qian et al., 2010). By some estimates, China has 350 million smokers (which is more people than live in the United States), and about 60% of men smoke. Tobacco use has grown fourfold in China since the 1970s and has become a key component of China's growing prosperity. Cigarettes, and particularly expensive brands of cigarettes, are given as gifts to friends and family; red cigarettes are special presents for weddings, bringing "double happiness." China also has its own tobacco manufacturing industry, which is run by the government. This creates a conflict of interest, since the same entity that regulates tobacco and might be interested in promoting better public health is also profiting from the large number of tobacco users (PBS News-Hour, 2010). Since 2001, when China joined the World Trade Organization and its markets opened to new goods, Western cigarette makers have also been aggressively marketing their products and targeting relatively untapped consumer categories such as women, who are otherwise less likely than men to smoke (Qian et al., 2010).

Growing income and improvements in the standards of living in developing countries represent important changes. For the most part, these changes are positive and include growing opportunities for education, health care, and access to technology, among others. At the same time, the chronic diseases long associated with the developed world threaten populations in new ways. Whether and how the international community, national governments, and local institutions react to these problems today will have an enormous impact on the health of populations in the decades to come.

WHY SHOULD SOCIOLOGISTS STUDY HEALTH?

Even as our medical and technological knowledge grows, threats to the goal of a healthy society and world continue to

Much progress has been made in developing medicine that helps keep HIV/AIDS under control and maintains one's quality of life, and even better advancements have been made in prevention, awareness, and education on how to avoid contracting HIV. Nevertheless, it is still a global epidemic that continues to claim the lives of millions. In this photo, a mother carries her adult son, who suffers from AIDS. ■

expand. In a globalizing world, no one is isolated from diseases spawned in distant places; we are all part of the same community, linked by communications, travel, and commerce. Neither are we isolated from the far-reaching consequences of health threats that threaten to destabilize regions far from our own. In a world where the very poor exist together with the very wealthy and billions are seeking to scramble further up the ladder of prosperity, the acute illnesses of poverty can be found alongside chronic maladies of affluence. Sociology offers us the tools to examine the sociological antecedents of a spectrum of public health problems.

By using a sociological perspective, we can recognize the ways that medical issues such as HIV/AIDS intersect with social phenomena, such as gender inequality, gender stereotypes, violence, and poverty. We can examine the global obesity epidemic through new eyes when we see that individual choices made by individuals about food and fitness are made in social and economic environments that profoundly affect those choices. While medicine and technology clearly have an enormous amount to contribute to reducing the consequences of serious health issues including HIV/AIDS, obesity, and tobacco-related illnesses, sociology too has a role to take in discovering the social roots of and imagining creative, constructive responses to health problems that threaten so many lives and livelihoods.

WHAT CAN I DO WITH A SOCIOLOGY DEGREE?

SKILLS AND CAREERS: COMMUNITY RESOURCE AND SERVICE SKILLS

Community resource competencies link knowledge of nonprofit, government, and private community resources with the skills to access appropriate services and funding to best serve clients, organizations, and communities. Resources in communities take multiple forms, including individual donors, volunteers, politicians, business owners, religious leaders, schools, libraries and community centers, and public and private service agencies. *Service skills* may be developed through the study of and active participation in community organizations that engage with local populations and issues.

In this chapter, we discussed problems of public health, including the local and global challenge of HIV/AIDS. While public health and medical workers worldwide are doing a commendable job getting effective treatments to more people than ever, much remains to be done. In many communities, HIV/AIDS is stigmatized, and its carriers are regarded with suspicion. Reaching out to individuals and groups who may fear seeking help, or even being tested for HIV/AIDS, requires the services not only of medical personnel, but also of those who have a deep cultural understanding of an affected community and the knowledge to link populations in need with resources that can help prevent and treat HIV/AIDS. Sociology majors develop important intercultural competencies and understandings of diversity. The sociology major also contributes to the development of important occupational skills such as the ability to gather and summarize data in order to effectively characterize community needs and the habits of mind to be resourceful in addressing a problem in a way that takes account of different perspectives. Many educational institutions offer students opportunities for service learning or volunteering in the community, which enable students to become familiar with the particular needs and resources of their own community.

Knowledge of community resources and practice in community service are skills that can be used in a variety of *occupational fields,* ranging from social work and counseling to organizational development, nonprofit management, and criminal justice. *Job titles* in these and related fields include family, school, and health care social worker; volunteer coordinator; psychologist; counselor; social or human service assistant; community resources specialist; city or regional planning aide; and vocational counselors in mental health or rehabilitation.

THINK ABOUT CAREERS

■ *What kinds of opportunities for community service are offered at your college or university? Take some time to research available options for volunteering or service learning, and consider how sharpening your skills and knowledge in this area might be of value to your career plan.*

▶ *Access additional web links on the student study site to learn more.*

SUMMARY

To test your knowledge further, find additional study material on the Student Study Site at www.sagepub.com/chamblissintro

- **Health** refers to the degree to which a person experiences a generalized state of wellness, while **medicine** is an institutionalized approach to the prevention of illness. Although the two are clearly related, they are not the same thing.

- Notions of illness are socially constructed, as are the social roles that correspond to them. The sociological concept of the **sick role** is important to an understanding of societal expectations and perceptions of the ill individual.

- Not all behaviors, such as addictions, are treated the same in society. Some, including alcoholism, are medicalized, while others, including drug use, are criminalized.

- The U.S. health care system does not serve all segments of the population equally. Good health and good **health care** are still often privileges of class and race.

- **Public health** issues such as smoking, obesity, and teen parenthood can be examined through a sociological lens.

- The sociological imagination gives us the opportunity to see the relationship between a private trouble (such as being addicted to tobacco, being obese, or becoming a teen mother) and public issues ranging from the relentless drive for profits in a capitalist country to the persistent poverty of generations.

- The global pandemic of HIV/AIDS demands a sociological approach, as well as a medical approach. The mass spread of the infection is closely intertwined with sociological issues. Gender inequality makes women vulnerable to infection. Poverty renders both individuals and countries more vulnerable to the disease. Violence and war are pathways for the spread of HIV/AIDS.

- Growing standards of living in many parts of the developing world have had many positive effects. But the accompanying sedentary lifestyles and access to fast food and tobacco have also contributed to the increase in chronic diseases associated with obesity and smoking.

KEY TERMS

Study terms on the go with the smartphone-friendly key term flashcards, available at www.sagepub.com/chamblissintro

DISCUSSION QUESTIONS

1. African Americans and Latinos in the United States experience worse health and higher mortality rates than their White and Asian American counterparts. What sociological factors help us to explain this health gap?

2. This chapter looks at cigarettes and smoking through a sociological lens. Recall how we applied the functionalist and conflict perspectives to this topic, and try applying those theories to junk food, such as soda, candy, or fast food.

3. How is HIV/AIDS a sociological as well as medical issue? What are key sociological roots of the spread of this disease in communities and countries?

DISCOVER ⓆⓅ STATE STATS

Log-in to the eBook and click on the title to the left for access to State Stats in order to complete the exercise.

In the Health database under "Personal Health," find the percentage of adults rating their health as fair or poor. Study the map and choose four states in different regions of the country, noting their percentages of self-reporting of fair or poor health. Find another data point of your own choosing in the Health database (such as the incidence of overweight/obesity or asthma). What sociological factors might explain differences in health perception and status in different states or regions?

STUDENT STUDY SITE

Visit the Student Study Site at www.sagepub.com/chamblissintro to access additional study tools, including eFlashcards, web quizzes, video resources, web resources, audio resources, links to SAGE journal, handbook, and research articles, and much more!

16

WAR, TERROR, AND GENOCIDE

WHAT DO YOU THINK?

1. Is war inevitable?
2. Do you agree with the often stated assertion that "one man's terrorist is another man's freedom fighter"?
3. What are the obstacles to preventing or stopping genocide in the modern world?

SOC*VIEW*

Get a closer look
with the authors!

MODERN WAR: A SYRIAN STORY

New York Times writer Janine di Giovanni (2012), observing the evolution of an uprising against the government of President Bashar al-Assad into civil war in Syria in the period from early 2011 to middle 2012, writes of the transformation of place and perception in wartime:

What does it feel like when a war begins? When does life as you know it implode? . . .

For ordinary people, war starts with a jolt: one day you are busy with dentist appointments or arranging ballet lessons for your daughter, and then the curtain drops. One moment the daily routine grinds on; A.T.M.'s work and cellphones function. Then, suddenly, everything stops.

Barricades go up. Soldiers are recruited and neighbors work to form their own defense . . . Fathers disappear. The banks close and money and culture and life as people knew it vanishes. In Damascus, this moment has come. (p. 2)

Technology and Warfare

We are all familiar with war. You are fortunate if you have never experienced it firsthand, or even secondhand through the death, injury, or displacement of a friend or family member. But then you know it from history books, television broadcasts, films, and personal discussions, as well as from debates about wars both historical and contemporary. While frightening and devastating, war is also the object of intense interest and attention. Books about the U.S. Civil War and World War II remain among the most popular nonfiction choices for U.S. readers, and films about these and other wars continue to draw viewers to theaters and televisions. ■

We can also examine wars, their roots, and their consequences from a sociological perspective. The sociological imagination asks us to seek the connections between private troubles and public issues: As we see in the chapter's opening story, the two are intimately intertwined. Daily lives, families, routines, and problems are transformed in the presence of conflict. This chapter begins with a discussion of war and society and an analysis of war from the functionalist and conflict perspectives. We also talk about the important but little discussed phenomenon of rape in war and how it is linked to larger issues of patriarchy and power. The chapter then turns to the issue of terrorism and the U.S. war on terror, initiated in 2001, as well as the question of defining who is a terrorist. We then address genocide, which, while a brutal phenomenon with a long and bloody history, was named as recently as the 20th century and prosecuted only at the end of it. We will ask how regimes, leaders, and individuals come to a decision to target an ethnic, religious, or racial group—and how genocides come to an end.

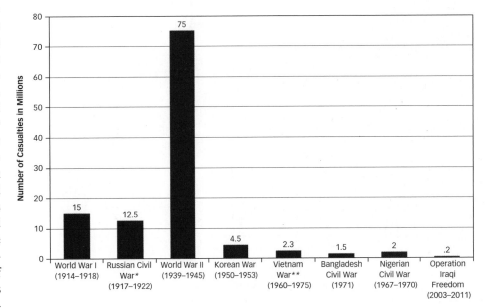

■ **FIGURE 16.1** Combined Military and Civilian Casualties of Some 20th and 21st Century Wars

*Including Soviet-Polish conflict

**Including North Vietnam vs. South Vietnam

SOURCES: Leitenberg, Milton. 2006. "Deaths in Wars and Conflicts in the 20th Century." Cornell University Peace Studies Program, Occasional Paper #29, 3rd edition. Retrieved from http://cissm.umd.edu/papers/files/deathswarsconflictsjune52006.pdf; Fischer, Hannah. 2010. "Iraq Casualties: U.S. Military Forces and Iraqi Civilians, Police, and Security Forces." *Congressional Research Service.* Retrieved from http://fpc.state.gov/documents/organization/145113.pdf.

WAR AND SOCIETY

Conflict between ethnic or religious groups, states, and other social entities has a long history. War has been part of human societies, culture, and practices in some form for millennia. In the 5th century B.C., the ancient Greeks created a game called *petteia,* the first board game known to have been modeled on war. In the 6th century A.D., chess, another game of strategic battle, was born in Northern India, developing into its modern form by the 15th century. Military training in ancient Greece also gave birth to the first Olympics. In the 20th century, war games took on far more advanced forms, ranging from battlefield exercises used to prepare for defensive or offensive war to sophisticated computer simulations used for both popular entertainment and military readiness training (Homans, 2011).

Today, the world spends trillions of dollars preparing for war or fighting in wars. At the same time, armed conflict and associated casualties have declined. Goldstein (2011) suggests that the nature of armed conflict has changed, shifting from larger wars in which powerful global actors confronted one another directly (such as World War II or the Korean War of the 1950s) to asymmetrical guerrilla wars, such as those the United States fought in Iraq and Afghanistan in the past decade. He notes, "Worldwide,

deaths caused directly by war-related violence in the new century have averaged about 55,000 per year, just over half of what they were in the 1990s (100,000 a year), a third of what they were during the Cold War (180,000 a year from 1950 to 1989), and a hundredth of what they were in World War II" (Goldstein, 2011, p. 53; Figure 16.1).

But while war has taken many forms, it has been a key part of the human experience throughout history. What explains its existence and persistence? Recall from earlier chapters that *manifest functions* are intended and obvious, while *latent functions* are hidden, unexpected, or "nonpurposive" (in Robert Merton's words). Functionalists look at phenomena and institutions that exist in society, assert that their existence presupposes a function, and ask what that function is. If something did not serve a function, it would cease to exist. Does war have a function? We begin with a functionalist perspective on war, considering its role and consequences at the macro and micro societal levels.

Drones in Modern Warfare

While armed conflict has declined somewhat, ironically the world may seem like a more violent place. In a technologically advanced age, we are deluged by information about conflict, which comes to us over television, the Internet, smartphones, and tweets. ■

A FUNCTIONALIST PERSPECTIVE ON WAR

What are the manifest functions of war? Historically, one function has been to gain territory. The Roman Empire (27 B.C.–476 A.D.) waged war on surrounding territories, acquiring a substantial swath of the Middle East, including Cleopatra's Egypt, and then holding it with its massive armies. Another manifest function of war is to gain control of the natural resources of another state, while a third is to prevent the disintegration of a territorial unit. The American Civil War (1861–1865) sought to avert the secession of the Southern territories, which still favored slavery, from the North, which sought to abolish slavery.

What about the latent functions of war? First, war has historically operated as a stimulus to the economy: The term **war economy** highlights *the phenomenon of war boosting economic productivity and employment, particularly in capital- and labor-intensive sectors such as industrial production.* Notably, though, the wars in which the United States took part in the 20th century were fought outside its borders, and the benefits to its economy, especially in the World War II era, were not necessarily repeated elsewhere. The Soviet Union, France, Belgium, Poland, and many other European countries on whose territory World War II was waged emerged with shattered economies.

Culture in
Modern Warfare

Privatization of
Military

As well, the United States's first wars of the 21st century—the conflict in Afghanistan that began in October 2001 and the military occupation of Iraq, which began in March 2003—have arguably had a negative effect on U.S. deficits and economic growth and have failed to benefit all but a few large corporations in the defense and energy sectors (Table 16.1 on page 399).

A second latent function is that war can foster patriotism and national pride. In times of war, governments implore their citizens to rally around the national cause, and citizens may display their patriotism with flags or demonstrations. Even those who oppose military action may shy from open opposition in a climate of war-inspired patriotism: During the early years of the conflict in Iraq, officials of President George W. Bush's administration several times chastised those who expressed criticism of the president and his actions "in a time of war," raising the question of whether dissent was unpatriotic.

A third latent function of war is its effect on family life and demographics. In the post–World War II years, the United States (and a number of other countries that had participated in the conflict) experienced a "baby boom," partially the product of the return of men who had been away at war and of childbearing postponed in the war years (note the uptick visible in Figure 16.2).

■ **FIGURE 16.2** U.S. Birth Rates Per 1,000 Women Aged 15–44, 1920–2010

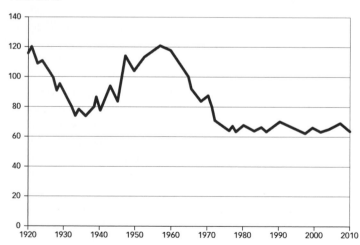

SOURCE: Pew Research Center. (2012, November 29). *U.S. Birth Rate Falls to a Record Low; Decline Is Greatest Among Immigrants.*

War economy: The phenomenon of war boosting economic productivity and employment, particularly in capital- and labor-intensive sectors such as industrial production.

Of course, family life and individual lives are also prone to the deep dysfunctional consequences of war. With the long absence or loss of a father, husband, or son (or mother, wife, or daughter), families may be drawn closer together, or they may break apart. They may experience economic deprivation with the loss of an income. A spouse who has not worked may be compelled by circumstances to join the labor force. War may also have disproportionate effects on different socioeconomic classes, as we discuss in the box *Inequality Matters* on page 400. Clearly, war has a spectrum of manifest and latent functions as well as dysfunctions.

A CONFLICT PERSPECTIVE ON WAR

The conflict perspective suggests that some groups benefit from war at the expense of others. We can turn a conflict-oriented lens on war to ask, "Who benefits from war? Who loses?"

While we might be inclined to answer that the war's victor wins and the defeated state or social group loses, the conflict perspective offers the opportunity to construct a more complex, nuanced picture. Consider the U.S. conflict in Iraq, which spanned from the U.S. occupation of that country in March 2003 to the final withdrawal of troops at the end of 2011. Who benefited from the war in Iraq?

Beneficiaries of any conflict include those who are freed from oppressive state policies or structures or from ongoing persecution by the defeat of a regime. Among the beneficiaries in Iraq we might count the minority Kurdish population, who were victims of Saddam's genocidal attacks in 1987 and 1988 and were threatened by the Iraqi dictator's presence. Were the rest of the people of Iraq beneficiaries? To the degree that Saddam was an oppressive political tyrant, the answer is yes; Saddam's ruling Baath Party also persecuted the majority Shiite Muslim population of the country, particularly after some Shiites sought to foment an uprising at the end of the first Gulf War (1990–1991). Ordinary Sunni Muslims as well had no voice in the single-party state ruled by Hussein with a strong hand. At the same time, the long war led to thousands of civilian and military casualties, fundamentally destabilized the country, and left a badly damaged economy and infrastructure. Today, Iraq continues to be plagued by *sectarian violence*—that is, violence between religious groups.

Other beneficiaries of the Iraq War are corporations (mostly U.S.-based) that have profited from lucrative government contracts to supply weapons and other military supplies. War generates casualties and destruction—it also generates profits. In assessing who benefits from war, we cannot overlook capitalist enterprises for which war is a business and investment opportunity.

■ **TABLE 16.1** Armed Civil and Interstate Conflicts of Recent Decades

Year(s)	Countries Involved	Type
1964–Present	Colombia	Civil
1967–Present	Israel, Palestinian Nation	Interstate
1991–Present	Somalia	Civil
1998–Present	Democratic Republic of Congo; Former Zaire	Interstate
2001–Present	USA (with allies); Afghanistan	Interstate
2002	Algeria, Chad, Mali, Mauritania, Morocco, Niger, Tunisia	Interstate
2002	Ivory Coast	Civil
2004	Yemen, Saudi Arabia	Civil
2008	Cambodia, Thailand	Interstate
2009	Yemen	Civil
2009–Present	Sudan and South Sudan	Interstate
2011–Present	Syria	Civil
2011	Libya	Civil
2011–Present	Yemen	Civil

SOURCE: Pike, J. (2013). The world at war: Current conflicts. *GlobalSecurity.org.*

Among those who benefit directly from war and conflict are private military corporations (PMCs), which provide private military services such as training, transportation, and the protection of human resources and infrastructure. The use of private contractors in war has a long history. The new U.S. government, fighting against the British in the American Revolution, paid private merchant ships to sink enemy ships and steal their cargo. The modern military term, *company*, which is an organized formation of 200 soldiers, comes from the private "companies" of mercenaries who were hired to fight in conflicts of the Middle Ages in Europe.

At the same time, until recently, war in the modern world was largely characterized by wars fought by the citizens of a nation-state. Sociologist Katherine McCoy (2009) writes, "Scholars have long thought of fighting wars as something nation-states did through their citizens. Max Weber famously defined the modern state as holding a monopoly over the legitimate use of violence, meaning that only state agents—usually soldiers or police—were allowed to wield force" (p. 15).

In modern conflicts, governments, including the U.S. government, increasingly rely on PMCs to provide a vast array of services that used to be functions of the government or military, raising critical questions about accountability and control of

DOES THE AMERICAN SOLDIER LOOK LIKE AMERICA?

Is the professional U.S. military, composed of volunteers, a good reflection of the demographics of U.S. society? According to sociologist Christian Appy (1993), 2.5 million young enlisted U.S. men served in Vietnam, 80% from working-class and poor backgrounds. He concludes that "class, not geography, was the crucial factor in determining which Americans fought in Vietnam," adding that "Vietnam, more than any other American war in the twentieth century, perhaps in our history, was a working-class war" (p. xi). Some of the negative sentiment generated by that war reflected the resentment of working-class young men fighting the battles of well-off decision makers comfortably situated in safer places.

Only about a fifth of those who fought in the Vietnam War were drafted; most were enlistees, and they were primarily working class. Well-off students were more likely to be eligible for a draft deferment based on college enrollment (Halbfinger & Holmes, 2003). When they did serve, they were also more likely to sign on for U.S.-based military units such as the National Guard rather than join the regular armed forces bound for Southeast Asia.

What of today's all-volunteer force? About a decade ago, the *New York Times* wrote, "A survey of the American military's . . . demographics paints a picture of a fighting force that is anything but a cross section of America. With minorities overrepresented and the wealthy and the underclass essentially absent, with

The racial and ethnic demographics of the U.S. military today differ from those of the U.S. population, though not dramatically. In 2010, of new recruits, almost 19% were Black, just over 75% were White, and about 5% were Asian American. Hispanics made up about 13% of new recruits, though they are counted in the racial categories as either Black or White. Men still significantly outnumber women: They constituted 85% of the entering group. ■

political conservatism ascendant in the officer corps and Northeasterners fading from the ranks, America's 1.4 million-strong military seems to resemble the makeup of a two-year commuter trade school outside Birmingham or Biloxi far more than that of a ghetto or barrio or four-year university in Boston" (Halbfinger & Holmes, 2003).

More recent analysis of new recruits shows that, while Whites are overrepresented in the more prestigious officer corps, African Americans make up about 13% of the U.S. civilian population but closer to 19% of active-duty enlisted personnel. Few enlistees hail from either the

bottom or the top of the income ladder, but they are not exclusively concentrated in lower-income deciles either (National Priorities Project, 2011b). While the military continues to take a larger share of its recruits from the lower middle classes, the South, and minorities, today it is beginning to resemble the face of the United States.

THINK IT THROUGH

■ *What is the significance of military demographics? Why might it be desirable for a military to reflect the economic, ethnic, and racial composition of the society it serves?*

these private armies, which are motivated by profit rather than patriotism (K. McCoy, 2009). The rise of PMCs has been driven by reductions in the size of armies at the end of the Cold War, the availability of smaller advanced weaponry, and a political-ideological trend toward the privatization and outsourcing of activities previously conducted by the government (Singer, 2003).

The conflict perspective on war also asks, "Who loses?" Losers, of course, include those on both sides of a conflict who lose their lives, limbs, or livelihoods in war. Increasingly, according to some reports, they have been civilians, not soldiers. By one estimate, in World War I, about 5% of casualties were civilians (Swiss & Giller, 1993). In World War II, the figure has been estimated at 50% (Gutman & Rieff, 1999). While some researchers argue that the figure is much higher (Swiss & Giller, 1993), Goldstein (2011) suggests that the ratio of civilian to military casualties has remained at about 50-50 into the 21st century. Specific casualty figures also vary widely, often depending on the methodologies and motivations of the organization or government doing the counting (Table 16.2). This topic is examined in more detail in the *Behind the Numbers* box on page 402.

What about the less apparent "losers"? Who else pays the costs of war? Modern military action has substantial financial costs, which are largely borne by taxpayers. In the decade

A website dedicated to providing information about private military contractors listed more than 60 distinct entities in operation as of March 2013 (PrivateMilitary.org, 2013). PMCs are in the business of war, a trade that continues to be brisk. ■

between 2001, when the United States was the victim of terrorist attacks, and 2011, when the Iraq War ended and the war in Afghanistan began to wind down, the country has spent an estimated $7.6 trillion on defense and homeland security. At the same time, many U.S. domestic programs in education, job training, environmental conservation, and other areas have lost funding as budgets shrink. Growth in the defense and security allocations of the federal budget has not been without costs.

■ **TABLE 16.2** Casualty Estimates for Darfur and Congo Conflicts

Conflict	Estimated Number of Casualties
Congo Conflict, 1998–2008	
International Rescue Committee	5.4 million
Human Security Report Project, Simon Fraser University	900,000
Darfur Conflict, 2003–2005	
Coalition for International Justice	400,000
U.S. Deputy Secretary of State Robert Zoellick	60,000–160,000
United Nations	300,000
Sudanese President Omar Al-Bashir	9,000

SOURCE: Rieff, D. (2011). Millions may die . . . or not. *Foreign Policy* (September/October), pp. 22–25.

RAPE AS A WEAPON OF WAR

The existence of rape in war has a long and grim history. Women, who are often perceived in society as property rather than autonomous individuals, have been taken by soldiers and officers as "spoils of war" for many centuries. In World War I, when Germany invaded Belgium and France, German soldiers terrorized villages by burning houses, raping women, and killing villagers. In World War II, rape was practiced by all sides, with Nazi German forces assaulting girls and women as they beat a path into the Soviet Union. When the war shifted in favor of the Allies, Soviet armies took revenge, in part through brutal assaults on German women. In the Asian theater of conflict in World War II, it is estimated that between 100,000 and 200,000 Korean women were kidnapped by Japanese soldiers and transported to the front lines, where they were pressed into sexual slavery as "comfort women."

In the late 20th and early 21st centuries, wars in Rwanda, the Democratic Republic of Congo (DRC), and the former Yugoslavia

COUNTING THE CIVILIAN CASUALTIES OF WAR

In the U.S.-led occupation of Iraq, begun in 2003, civilian casualties resulted from the actions of multiple actors, including U.S., coalition, and Iraqi forces and armed insurgents, and many followed the sectarian violence between Iraq's Sunni and Shiite Muslim populations. An accurate count of civilians remains difficult to pinpoint. For example, between 2005 and 2008, the Associated Press placed the civilian casualties at 34,832 killed and 40,174 wounded. By contrast, an article published in the medical journal *The Lancet* estimated the total number of deaths to be between 426,000 and 793,600 (H. Fischer, 2008). Clearly the difference between 35,000 and 790,000 deaths is vast, but what accounts for this disparity?

One factor is the way civilian deaths are initially reported. Some may go unreported, some may be reported multiple times, and still others may only be estimated when identifying victims is difficult. Local hospital records are often not accurately maintained in conflict-ridden areas. Finally, some bodies never make it to the hospital if they are taken away by family or are rendered unidentifiable, a tragic but common problem.

The Associated Press tallied the number of individuals listed as killed in news reports and identified as "civilians" (H. Fischer, 2008). Relying only on deaths reported in news accounts likely underestimates the total number. *The Lancet* estimate

Although the deaths of U.S. and allied military personnel are carefully counted, there are no official estimates of the number of Iraqi civilians killed since conflict started in that country in March 2003. Estimates range widely. ■

relied on two cluster sample surveys of Iraqi households but was criticized for, among other problems, a failure to gather demographic information, which might have shed light on the reliability of counts.

A third casualty count, also based on cluster sample surveys, sampled 20 times as many households as the *Lancet* study. Sponsored by the World Health Organization and Iraq Family Health Survey (IFHS), it was nationally representative and had an 89% response rate, and it estimated the number of civilian casualties at just over 115,000 (H. Fischer, 2008).

These counts highlight the fact that casualty statistics can vary depending on how the data are

collected and analyzed. Because casualty figures have been used by states, relief agencies, and international organizations to make the case for intervention, cessation of operations, and budgetary increases, it is important to recognize that different methodologies may render dramatically different figures.

THINK IT THROUGH

■ *Why would it be more difficult to count civilian casualties than military casualties? What kind of counting methodology do you think might be most effective and why? As we saw earlier in the chapter, civilian casualties appear to have risen relative to military casualties in the 20th century. How might this be explained?*

have been scenes of mass sexual violence against women. In the DRC, for example, tens of thousands of women have been raped by armed combatants in the country's civil war. In recent years, scholars have begun to draw attention to the proposition that rape is not just a *product* of war, but also a *policy* of war. That is, rape is a conscious instrument of war for combatant states (Niarchos, 1995).

As in any rape, the victim in war is likely to see the assault and its consequences as a serious personal trouble, which it clearly is. However, the scale of the phenomenon of rape in war suggests that it is not just a private trouble, but a public issue. We examine the sociological roots of rape in war below.

We might begin with the question "What is the role of rape in war?" To ask the question is not to justify rape in war (such a thing is morally impossible), but to analyze how it functions as a practice and policy in conflict. We propose several responses to this question. First, rape has historically been a "normal" component of war and a "right" of the victors. Those who have conquered their enemies may make a claim on the spoils of war, which include female bodies perceived as another form of property to be appropriated or conferred as "rewards." Amnesty International, a nonprofit organization that lobbies for awareness and change in the area of human rights, reported that in Northern Uganda, the Lord's Resistance Army (LRA) was abducting young girls and women and handing them over as "wives" to LRA fighters as prizes for "good behavior," which included following orders to kill villagers and prisoners of war (Amnesty International, 2004; Lough & Denholm, 2005).

Second, rape targets women for political and strategic reasons, including territorial gain. In the former Yugoslavia, for instance, rape and its threat were used to drive women from their homes, contributing to the "ethnic cleansing" that transformed the ethnic composition of towns and villages in, among others, Bosnia-Herzegovina (Thomas & Ralph, 1999). **Ethnic cleansing** is the *physical expulsion of a group from a territory claimed by another group*. It may also be a way of physically destroying a community or group, as the brutality of war rapes can leave women unable to bear children (Frederick & AWARE

In Darfur, Sudan, Arab militias armed by the Sudanese government have used violent measures, including murder and rape, to drive out Black Africans in order to confiscate their lands and resources (http://www.savedarfur.org). The people in this photo are internally displaced, having been driven from their homes. ■

Committee on Rape, 2001). In some areas, raped women are also considered dishonorable and may be shunned by the family and community, as has sometimes been the case in the DRC (J. Moore, 2010).

Third, it has been suggested that rape is a means of communication between male combatants on opposing sides. Where women are considered the "property" of their fathers, husbands, brothers, or the patriarchal social order itself, rape is a symbolic assault on the men who have failed to protect them. This "function" has powerful historical roots: "Even as a system of law [on war] developed, rape was defined as a property crime against the man who owned the raped woman" (Frederick & AWARE Committee on Rape, 2001, p. 12).

Rape in war is thus not just an incidental phenomenon, but a strategic one. Women are targeted as representatives of a community and a gender. They are victimized by their rapists and often again by families and communities that feel shamed by the rape (see as well the box *Private Lives, Public Issues* on page 404 on war rape and HIV/AIDS). This private trouble has, as we see, many links to public issues.

Ethnic cleansing: The physical expulsion of a group from a territory claimed by another group.

Rape in the Vietnam War

POW Abuse

War Crimes

WAR, WOMEN, AND HIV/AIDS

Though it is a painfully private trouble, women's sexual victimization in wartime is an intensely public issue with roots in history, politics, and society—and in the patriarchal cultures and structures that make women particularly vulnerable to sexual violence, degradation, and death. In the modern world, rape in war has also become a pathway for the transmission of HIV/AIDS.

Rape and sexual assault have been widely practiced in the Democratic Republic of Congo (DRC), which suffered serious conflicts from 1996 through the present. An Amnesty International (AI) report on atrocities in that conflict noted that "in conversations with AI delegates, experienced UN and international humanitarian NGO staff were unanimous that they had never come across as many victims of rape in a conflict situation as they had in DRC. They were unanimous, too, in believing that many more victims are still to be identified" (Amnesty International, 2004).

Aside from being a way of terrorizing, moving, destroying, and intimidating populations, rape has also been used by superstitious troops who erroneously believe that it is a way to inoculate themselves against disease. According to Amnesty International (2004), "Some combatants believe that having sex with a pre-pubescent child or post-menopausal women will deliver immunity from diseases, including HIV/AIDS." Thus many rape victims have been very young or old. An estimated 60% of regular troops and militiamen in Congo are infected with HIV/AIDS (Human Rights Watch, 2002). Combatants in Rwanda, Burundi, and Uganda, who have also engaged in mass sexual violence, have shown high rates of infection as well. Predictably, then, the rate of infection of victims is high. The DRC national AIDS program estimates it to be about 20% in the eastern provinces, though it could be much higher.

For rape and HIV/AIDS victims in medically underserved and impoverished Congo, infection is a short-term death sentence. Medical therapies are rarely available, and most Congolese live on less than 20 cents per day; they could not pay for treatment even if it could be obtained (Amnesty International, 2004). Women who have been raped may be stigmatized and rejected in their home communities due to widespread fear of HIV/AIDS, Women are often held responsible for their victimization and are seen as shameful and unclean. Without family support or the possibility of securing a livelihood, they and their children are condemned to desperate and troubled lives.

In many traditional societies, women's "honor" is linked to their perceived sexual purity. While they are in no way complicit in their own violation, raped women may be ostracized from their families and communities, compounding the tragedy of their victimization. The woman in this photo lives in a refugee camp and is infected with HIV. ■

Oxfam International and the Harvard Humanitarian Initiative reported in 2010 that gang rapes by armed combatants are still widespread and rampant; tens of thousands of women were systematically raped by combatant forces between 2004 and 2008. The report also found that rapes committed by civilians dramatically increased during that time frame, suggesting a "civilian adoption of rape" (Rousselot, 2010) and, sadly, its normalization in a society torn by sexual violence.

THINK IT THROUGH

■ *How can rape in war as a policy and practice be publicized and prevented? What means might be available to the international community or to local communities to intervene in cases where mass rape is taking place?*

TERRORISTS AND TERRORISM

The Global War on Terror (GWOT) was initiated in 2001, after the September 11 attacks on the World Trade Center and the Pentagon. GWOT is generally used to refer to the international (though U.S.-led) overt and covert military campaign against the Islamic group al-Qaeda and similar groups believed to be threatening to the United States and its allies. The term was first used by President George W. Bush and other administration officials. President Barack Obama has not adopted the term, and in March 2009, the U.S. Department of Defense dropped the term officially. Though it continues to be used in some political commentary, the designation Overseas Contingency Operation (OCO) has largely replaced GWOT. The focus of U.S. military, diplomatic, and economic efforts on combating terrorism has, however, continued unabated.

The unprecedented events of September 2001 brought terror and terrorists more fully than ever into the U.S. experience and consciousness. The political response was to refocus domestic priorities on the GWOT and homeland security, drawing resources and attention from other areas such as education, immigration reform, and health care. Terrorism became a key theme of U.S. politics, policies, and spending priorities and a subject of intense concern and discussion. The concepts of *terrorist* and *terrorism*, however, are broad and many not be defined or understood in the same way across groups or countries. Acts of violence labeled by one group as terrorism may be embraced as heroic by another. The label of terrorist may be inconsistently applied depending on the ethnicity, religion, actions, and motivations of an individual or a group. Below we examine these concepts and consider their usage with a critical eye.

WHO IS A TERRORIST?

Close your eyes and picture a terrorist. What does your imagined terrorist look like? Why do you think that particular image appeared to you? The images we generate are culturally conditioned by the political environment, the mass media, and the experiences we have, and they therefore differ across communities, countries, and cultures. Every community's idea of a terrorist is not the same because, as we will see further along, violent acts condemned by one community may be embraced as necessary sacrifices in the pursuit of political ends by another.

It has been said that one person's terrorist is another person's freedom fighter. Michael Collins was born in West Cork, Ireland, in 1890. Before he turned 20, he had sworn allegiance to the Irish Republican Brotherhood, a group of revolutionaries struggling for Irish independence from three centuries of British rule, and

A 2010 study by the Harvard Humanitarian Initiative found that between 2004 and 2008, the incidence of rape perpetrated by civilians in the Congo grew 17-fold. The researchers speculate that years of brutal sexual violence during the Congolese conflict, most of which was perpetrated by soldiers, have "normalized" rape (J. Moore, 2010). While some women report sexual crimes and seek medical help, others are reluctant to identify themselves as victims for fear that they will be stigmatized. ■

he worked and fought with them throughout the first decades of the 20th century. In Ireland and Northern Ireland today, Collins is widely regarded as a hero (Coogan, 2002). A 1996 film, *Michael Collins,* starring Liam Neeson and Julia Roberts, cast him in a generally positive light: The film's tagline declared, "Ireland, 1916. His dreams inspired hope. His words inspired passion. His courage forged a nation's destiny."

In Britain, however, Collins is considered by many to be a terrorist. In 1920, while he was the director of intelligence of the Irish Republican Army (IRA), his secret service squad assassinated 14 British officers (Coogan, 2002). The British responded to the IRA with violence as well. Notably, the Continuity Irish Republican Army (CIRA) continues to be on the U.S. Department of State's (2012b) global list of terrorist groups.

Was Michael Collins a terrorist or a hero? How do we judge Britain's violent military response? The label of terrorist is a subjective one, conditioned by whether one rejects or sympathizes with the motives and actions under discussion. As one expert on terrorism notes, "if one party can successfully attach the label *terrorist* to its opponent, then it has indirectly persuaded others to adopt its moral viewpoint" (Hoffman, 2006, p. 23).

Acts of Terror

Terrorism

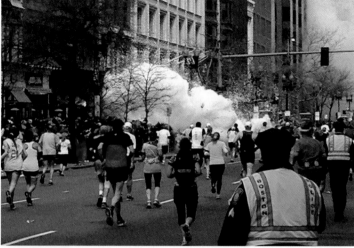

Modern terrorist acts are often intentionally dramatic and calculated to inflict harm, instill fear, and attract media attention. The attacks on the World Trade Center and Pentagon on September 11, 2001 (left), and the Boston Marathon bombing on April 15, 2013 (right), fit this model of terrorism. ■

WHAT IS TERRORISM?

There is no single definition of **terrorism**. The U.S. Department of Defense (2011) defines it as "the unlawful use of violence or threat of violence to instill fear and coerce governments or societies. Terrorism is often motivated by religious, political, or other ideological beliefs and committed in the pursuit of goals that are usually political." This definition highlights the idea that terrorism is intended to provoke both fear and change. Does it then also include the bombings of war, such as the brutal Nazi air attacks on London or the U.S. nuclear bombing of Nagasaki and Hiroshima during World War II? What about genocidal acts against populations? What factors make terrorism difficult to define clearly?

The U.S. Department of State (2011) offers another definition in which terrorism is "premeditated, politically motivated violence perpetrated against noncombatant targets by subnational groups or clandestine agents." This definition highlights that terrorism is committed not by states but by groups, and that its targets are noncombatants. Is it limiting for this definition to suggest that states cannot be agents of terrorism?

We can also understand terrorism as *performative*—that is, it is violence that is intentionally dramatic, enacted for the purpose of attracting attention and publicity and spreading fear. This definition points more deliberately to terrorism as an instrument of horrific political theater whose direct victims are props on the stage of a larger political or ideological play. While such "media-oriented terrorism" does not, by one analysis, make up the majority of the terror acts of the past half-century, it is widespread and has historical roots in the acts of 19th-century anarchists, who pioneered a concept of "propaganda of the deed" (Surette, Hansen, & Noble, 2009).

In some sense the media do offer a "stage" for acts of atrocity, not only functioning as reporters of terror events but also conditioning terrorist groups' selection of targets and actions. Media-oriented terrorism is thus particularly likely in democratic rather than authoritarian states, because democracies allow the wide dissemination of information about events such as terror attacks. Media attention, which has expanded from the print media and television to include the Internet, the "Twitterverse," and other new media, has a powerful multiplier effect on modern terrorism, offering a broad platform of publicity even for small and relatively weak groups whose combat and political capabilities are otherwise very limited (Surette et al., 2009).

Notably, the success of some nations in building strong, centralized militaries may also have contributed to terrorism's spread. As an effective form of asymmetric conflict, terrorism is one of the few avenues open to those who want power attention or change yet lack the military means to directly challenge dominant global powers. Robert Pape (2005) has pointed to terrorism as a weapon of the weak. Based on his analysis of 315 incidences of suicide terrorism between 1980 and 2003, he concluded that a consistent causal logic of these events was the attempt to exercise coercive power against a stronger democratic state perceived as a homeland occupier.

As of 2012, the United Nations Comprehensive Convention on International Terrorism remains in draft form, subject to debate and negotiation, particularly over language that highlights terrorism's roots in the motive to "intimidate a population, or to compel a Government or an international organization to do or abstain from doing any act." At issue here, among other things, is what constitutes the line between an act of terrorism and an act of war. Is an act of war by a state an act of "politically motivated violence" subject to the convention's regulation? Leaders also debate whether to include in the definition of terrorist groups national "liberation movements," examples of which could be the Irish Republican Army, Palestinian movements such as Hamas, or Kurdish militants

. . . .

Terrorism: "The calculated use of violence of the threat of violence to inculcate fear; intended to coerce or to intimidate governments or societies in the pursuit of goals that are generally political, religious, or ideological" (U.S. Department of Defense, 2011).

in Turkey. Those who support the aims of such groups say no. In light of the fact that perceptions of a given act may differ widely between groups and countries, is a global definition of terrorism even possible? Is it necessary, in order to reduce the threat of violence to states and civilian populations? What do you think?

GENOCIDE: THE MASS DESTRUCTION OF SOCIETIES

Genocide can be defined as *a mass, systematic destruction of a people or a nation.* According to the Convention on the Prevention and Punishment of the Crime of Genocide, adopted by the United Nations General Assembly in 1948 when genocide was declared a crime under international law, it means "any of the following acts committed with intent to destroy, in whole or in part, a national, ethnical, racial or religious group, as such:

a. Killing members of the group;

b. Causing serious bodily or mental harm to members of the group;

c. Deliberately inflicting on the group conditions of life calculated to bring about its physical destruction in whole or in part;

d. Imposing measures intended to prevent births within the group;

e. Forcibly transferring children of the group to another group."

The mass killing of people because of their membership in a particular group is ages old. Hans Van Wees (2010) notes that ancient Christian and Hebrew religious texts contain evidence of early religiously motivated mass killings. Roger W. Smith (2002) points out that the Assyrians, Greeks, Romans, and Mongols, among others, engaged in genocide, but their perspective on mass killing was shaped by their time. He notes that rulers boasted about the thousands they killed and the peoples they eliminated. Genocide as both a term and a defined crime is much more recent.

The word *genocide* was coined in the 1940s by Polish émigré Raphael Lemkin, who left his native country in the late 1930s, several years before Adolf Hitler's Nazi army overran it. A lawyer and academic, Lemkin was also a crusader for human rights, and, aware of Nazi atrocities in Europe, he sought to inspire U.S. decision makers to act. In a 1941 radio broadcast, British Prime Minister Winston Churchill decried the "barbaric fury" of the Nazis and declared, "We are in the presence of a crime without a

Once coined, the term *genocide* became a part of a global story about the brutal practices of the Nazi regime. In 1944, the *Washington Post* carried an editorial using the term to label the killing of 1.7 million Jews at Auschwitz-Birkenau between April 1942 and April 1944. ■

name." Lemkin, who heard the broadcast, undertook to name the crime and, through this, to bring an end to it (Power, 2002).

Sociologist Pierre Bourdieu (1991) points to the significance of language in structuring the perception that social agents (such as governments or populations) have of the world around them. The very act of naming a phenomenon confers upon it a social reality. Lemkin sought to use the act of naming as a vehicle for action against Nazi atrocities—and future threats against the physical, political, cultural, and economic existence of collectivities (Shaw, 2010). Lemkin settled on *genocide*, a hybrid of the Greek *geno,* meaning "tribe" or "race," and the Latin *cide* (from *caedere*), or "killing."

The 1948 United Nations Convention on the Prevention and Punishment of the Crime of Genocide created a potentially powerful new political reality, though it narrowed the definition from the broad articulation championed by Lemkin (Shaw, 2010). Theoretically, state sovereignty could no longer shield a country from the consequences of committing genocide, because the nations that signed the UN convention were bound by it to prevent, suppress, and punish such crimes. At the same time, the notion of an obligation to intervene is loose and open to interpretation, as history has shown. As well, other terms can be employed in place of genocide—civil war, ethnic conflict, ethnic cleansing. Many states try to avoid labeling the acts of other governments as

. . . .

Genocide: The mass, systematic destruction of a people or a nation.

Genocide

Armenian Genocide

BOSNIA-HERZEGOVINA (1992-1995)
100,000 to 200,000 Bosnian Muslims killed by Serbs and Croats.

EUROPE (1939-1945)
6 million Jews and 6 million others, including Roma, Slavs, and the handicapped, murdered by the Nazi German state.

OTTOMAN EMPIRE/TURKEY (1914-1923)
1.5 million Armenians, 270,000 to 750,000 Assyrians, and 300,000 to 700,000 Greeks killed by Ottoman Turks.

USSR (1932-1939)
23 million Soviet citizens killed by Soviet government.

TIBET/CHINA (1950-1959)
Unknown number of Tibetan Buddhists killed by Chinese government.

UKRAINE (1932-1933)
1.8 to 7.5 million killed by famine imposed by Soviet government.

GUATAMALA (1981-1983)
Over 200,000 Mayan Indians killed by Guatemalan government.

EAST TIMOR (1995-2000)
100,000 East Timorese killed by Indonesian military.

DARFUR, SUDAN (2003-present)
100,000 to 300,000 ethnic Fur, Zaghawa, and Masalit killed by Sudanese government

IRAQ (1988)
50,000 to 100,000 Kurds killed by Iraqi government.

RWANDA (1994)
500,000 to 1 million ethnic Tutsis killed by Hutus.

BURUNDI (1965-1972)
100,000 to 300,000 ethnic Hutus killed by Tutsis.

CAMBODIA (1975-1979)
1.7 to 1.9 million killed by Khmer Rouge government.

genocide. Humanitarian organizations including Genocide Watch and institutions including the U.S. Holocaust Memorial Museum have sounded the alarm on recent atrocities, often labeling them genocide even while many governments have resisted using the term.

Genocides in the second half of the 20th century include slaughters carried out by the Khmer Rouge in Cambodia in the 1970s, Saddam Hussein's 1987–1988 campaign against ethnic Kurds in Iraq, and Serb atrocities in the former Yugoslav states of Bosnia-Herzegovina and Kosovo in the late 1990s (Figure 16.3). The 21st century has already seen the genocidal destruction of Black Africans, including the Darfuris, Abyei, and Nuba, by Arab militias linked to the government in Sudan.

WHAT EXPLAINS GENOCIDE?

Taking a sociological perspective we might ask, "Who benefits from genocide?" Why do countries or leaders make a choice to pursue or allow it? Genocide is the product of conscious decisions made by those who stand to benefit from it and who anticipate minimal costs for their actions.

Chalk and Jonassohn (1990) suggest that genocide is taken as an option to eliminate a real or perceived threat or to spread fear among enemies, to eliminate a real or potential

Genocide in Darfur and Rwanda

threat to another group, to gain wealth for a dominant group, and/or to realize an ideological goal. Shaw (2010) has noted that "genocide is a crime of social classification, in which power-holders target particular populations for social and often physical destruction" (p. 142).

Anton Weiss-Wendt (2010) points out that, to the degree that genocide "requires premeditation" (p. 81), governments are generally implicated in the crime. Among the necessary parts is also the creation of a "genocidal mentality," not only among the leadership but also among a sufficient number of individuals to ensure participation, or at least support or indifference, from a large proportion of the population (Goldhagen, 1997; Markusen, 2002). Part of creating a "genocide mentality" is dehumanizing the victims. By emphasizing their "otherness" or the idea that the group to be victimized is less than fully human, agents of genocide stamp out sympathy for their targets, replacing it with a sense of threat or disgust. For instance, Rwanda's Hutu labeled their ethnic Tutsi targets "cockroaches." Media have made the process of disseminating the propaganda of dehumanization even easier. Radio broadcasts in Rwanda in the time leading up to the genocide implored Hutus to "kill cockroaches," fostering mass killing (Gourevitch, 1999).

Another mechanism is the "establishment of genocidal institutions and organizations," which construct propaganda to justify and institutions or other means to carry out the genocide. Finally, the recruitment and training of perpetrators is important, as is the establishment of methods of group destruction (Markusen, 2002).

Choosing genocide as a policy incurs costs as well as benefits. Clearly, outside forces can impose costs on a genocidal regime; we've seen that signatories to the 1948 convention are theoretically obligated to intervene. But historically, intervention has often been too little and too late.

Why, in the face of overwhelming evidence of genocide (as in Rwanda or Bosnia-Herzegovina or Sudan), does the international community not step in? One answer is that these states also make choices based on perceived costs and benefits. Intervention in the affairs of another state can be costly, and many leaders avoid it. In a historical overview of U.S. responses to genocide, for instance, Samantha Power (2002) argues,

> American leaders did not act because they did not want to. They believed that genocide was wrong, but they were not prepared to invest the military, financial, diplomatic, or domestic political capital needed to stop it. The U.S. policies crafted in response to each case of genocide [Cambodia, Iraq, Bosnia-Herzegovina, Rwanda] . . . were not the accidental products of neglect. They were concrete choices made by this country's most influential decision makers after unspoken and explicit weighing of costs and benefits. (p. 508)

Is intervention too costly? What benefits to intervention are political leaders likely to see? Does genocide continue to be a viable option for states or regimes wishing to destroy enemy groups? How should outside states—and concerned individuals—respond?

MODERNIZATION AND MASS MURDER

In earlier chapters, we discussed Max Weber's theoretical perspective on the growth of *formal rationality* in modern societies. Formal rationality characterizes societies where pursuit of goals is guided by rule and regulations; Weber's paradigm case of formal rationality was the bureaucracy, with its focus on efficiency, control, predictability, and calculability. These "rationalized" systems, argued Weber, could also be "irrational," trapping people in structures that destroyed creative thinking and reasoning.

Writing after World War II, sociologist Zygmunt Bauman (2001) posited that an extreme of formal rationality had been brutally realized in the Holocaust, writing, "It was the rational world of modern civilization that made the Holocaust thinkable. 'The Nazi mass murder of the European Jewry was not only the technological achievement of an industrial society, but also the organizational achievement of a bureaucratic society'" (p. 13). What did Bauman mean by this? What kind of link did he see between modern society's bureaucratization and technological "progress" and the Nazi genocide? Bauman suggests that the Holocaust was characterized by the formal rationality Max Weber theorized as a key component of modern societies. The focus on efficiency and control, brought to life in the well-organized horrors of mass deportations, concentration camps, and extermination, highlights this point. It was modern "efficiency" and routinization of killing realized by a vast and well-organized bureaucratic structure that supported the systematic slaughter of millions in relatively short order.

Hitler's regime actively embraced eugenics, based on the belief that the Aryan race (which included Germans) could be "improved" by discouraging reproduction of those who did not possess the desired racial characteristics. Eugenics formed an ostensibly scientific foundation for the mass killing of minorities in Germany. Other means for transforming society were also used. The Polish girl pictured in this photo was one of thousands of blonde and blue-eyed children taken by the Nazis and forcibly "Germanized." ■

No less importantly, argues Bauman, modernity also set the stage for the Holocaust with its reverence for science. Nazi science and scientists were committed to eugenics and the pursuit of "perfecting" family, state, and society with the elimination of elements deemed a threat to the healthy body of Aryan society. They not only condoned but also legitimized the extermination of Jews, as well as Gypsies, the mentally handicapped, homosexuals, very ill children, and others in the name of creating a dominant nation.

Modern society, Bauman tells us, has given society norms such as the reverence for science and the pursuit of societal "perfection," as well as tools including a task-driven bureaucracy that prizes efficiency, all of which enabled the enactment of a mass atrocity with shocking proficiency and organization. Ultimately, of course, this "rationality" was highly irrational

Ethnic Wars

because it was used in the service of dehumanization and death. Nonetheless, contends Bauman, the machinery that produced mass murder was rooted in the mechanisms, even the values, of modern society.

This perspective challenges other explanations of genocide, the Holocaust in particular, which suggest that such atrocities are dire deviations from the practices and norms of modern civilization and that perpetrators are unlike the rest of us. Historian William Shirer posited the idea of German exceptionalism in his 1959 book, *The Rise and Fall of the Third Reich* (1959/2011). He argued that Germans were different from other nations and more obedient, and he suggested that this characteristic shed light on their mass complicity in Holocaust atrocities. Psychologist Stanley Milgram, whose famous experiments at Yale University in the 1960s seemed to show that obedience to authority, even when it entailed inflicting pain on others, was by no means a trait exclusive to Germans, challenged this idea.

Milgram's experiments used human subjects, Yale undergraduates who were led to believe they were participating in a memory study. Subjects were directed by a scientist in a white lab coat (the authority in this scenario) to "shock" an unseen learner, who was ostensibly trying to memorize word pairs (Figure 16.4). While no real shocks were ever administered, subjects did not know that and believed they were shocking the learner when he incorrectly recalled a word pair. "Shocks" could reach 450 volts, which subjects were told could be extremely dangerous. In the experiment's first round, fully 65% of subjects followed the scientist's orders to continue giving "shocks,"

War and Disease

even when the learner (who was part of the experiment) pretended to cry out for help.

Milgram (1974/2009) concluded, "Ordinary people, simply doing their jobs, and without any particular hostility on their part, can become agents in a terrible destructive process" (p. 6). His experiments showed that obedience to orders was not a function of ethnic or even personality traits so much as it was a function of the relationship between an authority and a subordinate.

Genocide, then, can be understood through a variety of lenses, some of which place the onus of responsibility on modernity and bureaucracy, some of which highlight the psychology of perpetrators, and some of which point to the perils of blind obedience. No single perspective can capture the full possibility of explanations for either atrocities or the decision of outsiders to act (or not) to stop them. But seeking to more fully grasp the roots of this phenomenon, which stretches back in history and continues today, is a first step toward imagining its elimination from our future.

WHY SHOULD SOCIOLOGISTS STUDY WAR?

Wars are the product of choices made by leaders—usually, the civilian or military leaders of countries or empires. They do not just happen. In understanding war, we benefit from recognizing the ways it confers benefits and incurs costs. Those with power make calculations and choices. Those without power—women and children and sometimes citizens and soldiers—do not make such choices, though they may pay the cost. While war is a reality in our world, we need to move beyond simple understandings of war as an inevitable part of the human experience to recognizing its more complex and less obvious sociological elements. Perhaps a better understanding of war and its motivations and consequences can help to clear a path to greater civility and peace in the world.

Robert Merton (1957) posited the idea of functional alternatives. If we recognize that war has functions (as we saw in this chapter), we might also begin to imagine *functional alternatives*— that is, other means of realizing those functions. For instance, if war has a manifest function of acquiring access to needed or desired natural resources such as oil or water, perhaps greater conservation of the resource would diminish the need for aggressive action to secure access. If war acts as a way of resolving territorial disputes, perhaps creative diplomatic thinking can begin to carry us toward more nonmilitary alternatives. If war is also functional in fostering patriotism, perhaps a country could construct national pride and patriotism on a foundation other than the battlefield of glory and sacrifice, as so many countries do.

Social change demands imagination—a changed world must be imagined before it can be realized. While a future without war seems unimaginable, our expanded understanding of this phenomenon may give us some of the tools needed to make it less probable and less costly to civilians and soldiers alike.

WHAT CAN I DO WITH A SOCIOLOGY DEGREE?

SKILLS AND CAREERS: CONFLICT DYNAMICS AND RESOLUTION SKILLS

Conflict resolution skills are of value when two or more entities—individuals, employees and employers, social groups, businesses, or countries, among others—engage in a process to resolve a disagreement that may be related to values or perceptions, or to social, economic, environmental, or political interests. Sociological study offers students the opportunity to develop competencies in the *analysis of conflict dynamics.* Understanding the dynamics of conflict involves the ability to research and recognize the fundamental issues at the root of conflicts, to take the perspectives of different parties in the conflict, and to communicate effectively with groups in conflict. Understanding conflict dynamics and using this knowledge to resolve conflicts are related to sociology's general orientation toward problem analysis and problem solving.

In Chapter 16, we looked at the most acute manifestation of conflict, war, and we examined some of the functions of war for the participating parties. For example, we considered the fact that war has historically served as a vehicle for countries to pursue dominion over desired natural resources. As the population grows, particularly in poor and developing states, conflicts over natural resources will likely increase at both international and community levels. But violent conflict need not be inevitable. It is in our interest as sociologists and citizens of the world to think in informed and creative ways about averting and addressing conflicts over resources, as well as other sources of tension between states, societies, and groups. As a sociology student, you will have the opportunity to study different theoretical perspectives on conflict and its sources and to become familiar with research studies that delve into the roots of conflicts from the community to the global level.

Understanding conflict dynamics and utilizing that knowledge to address and prevent or resolve conflicts are skills of great value in a heterogeneous and complex social and global environment. These kinds of tasks are

often part of the *job description* of, among others, civil and family mediators, foreign service officers, lawyers, parenting trainers, negotiators, ombudsmen, prison project officers, human rights advocates, and religious leaders such as ministers or rabbis. These jobs may be found in *occupational sectors* such as community organizing, politics, nonprofit management, criminal justice, and international development, among others.

THINK ABOUT CAREERS:

■ *Using what you have learned in sociology to this point, identify some particular conflicts that exist and persist between groups in society. Are people in any of the occupational fields or jobs listed above involved in managing, mediating, or resolving these conflicts?*

■ *Thinking about possible career paths of interest to you, how might the knowledge of conflict dynamics and conflict resolution skills be of value in a future job?*

▶ *Access additional web links on the student study site to learn more.*

SUMMARY

To test your knowledge further, find additional study material on the Student Study Site at **www.sagepub.com/chamblissintro**

- We can examine war from various sociological perspectives. The functionalist perspective asks about the manifest (obvious) and latent (hidden) functions of war and conflict in society. The conflict perspective asks who benefits from war and conflict, and who loses.

- War rape has a long history. Women have often been seen as property rather than people and have been taken as the "spoils of war." Rape in war was recognized as a crime against humanity in the 1990s, after the conflicts in the former Yugoslavia drew attention to the issue.

- The Global War on Terror was initiated in 2001, after the terrorist attacks on U.S. soil. The GWOT encompassed the diplomatic, military, and economic actions taken by the United States and its allies to fight terrorism. The term was replaced in 2009.

- No single image of a terrorist threat is shared across communities and countries and cultures. Irishman Michael Collins is an example of someone regarded as a hero by some and a terrorist by others.

- **Terrorism** is a calculated use of violence to coerce or to inspire fear. It is also "theater"—intended to send a powerful message to a distinct or a global audience.

- **Genocide** is the mass and systematic destruction of a people or a nation. The 1948 United Nations Convention on the Prevention and Punishment of the Crime of Genocide obligates signatories to act against genocide.

- Once it has begun, genocide is difficult to stop without outside intervention. Outside powers may opt to intervene (as in Bosnia-Herzegovina) or not (as in Darfur, Sudan).

- Sociologist Zygmunt Bauman has suggested that the Holocaust may serve as a paradigm of modern bureaucratic rationality. He argues that modern "efficiency" of the bureaucracy and associated institutions facilitated the slaughter of millions in relatively short order.

- Stanley Milgram's 1960s experiments showed the power of authority over ordinary people. He showed that obedience was less a product of particular personalities or cultures, and more a function of the relationship between an authority and a subordinate.

KEY TERMS

Study terms on the go with the smartphone-friendly key term flashcards, available at **www.sagepub.com/chamblissintro**

war economy, 398   ethnic cleansing, 403   terrorism, 406   genocide, 407

DISCUSSION QUESTIONS

1. What are the manifest and latent functions and dysfunctions of war? Review the points made in the chapter. Can you add some of your own?

2. Why has rape been used as a weapon of war? How can understanding the roots of war rape as a phenomenon help communities and countries to prevent or address the problem?

3. What factors make communities vulnerable to genocide? How should other countries respond when genocide seems imminent or is already under way?

DISCOVER STATE STATS

Log-in to the eBook and click on the title to the left for access to State Stats in order to complete the exercise.

Go to the Defense database and search out the percentage of the population who are veterans. Examine the data and note two or three specific data points, such as percentages for some states or percentages at different points in time. Prepare two hypotheses about the sociological significance of this population for U.S. politics, culture, economics, or social life. How are veterans part of the national discourse about war, peace, or politics?

STUDENT STUDY SITE

Visit the Student Study Site at **www.sagepub.com/chamblissintro** to access additional study tools, including eFlashcards, web quizzes, video resources, web resources, audio resources, links to SAGE journal, handbook, and research articles, and much more!

17 POPULATION, URBANIZATION, AND THE ENVIRONMENT

WHAT DO YOU THINK?

1. Should we be concerned about global population growth? What are the costs and benefits of growing populations?
2. Who should bear the costs of the safe and environmentally sound disposal of the electronic gadgets that pervade our lives today?
3. Are the goals of a sustainable environment and a growing economy irreconcilable? Can we have both?

SOC**VIEW**

Get a closer look with the authors!

415

DEMOGRAPHIC DILEMMA: WHERE ARE THE GIRLS?

Millions of women are missing from our planet. According to the United Nations Population Fund (UNFPA, 2007), "one of the most alarming changes in Asia's population dynamics in recent decades has been a dramatic increase in the proportion of males within its local populations . . . if the continent's overall sex ratio was the same as elsewhere in the world, in 2005 Asia's population would have included almost 163 million more women and girls." Where did they go? How could so many girls and women go missing? What are the sociological roots of this dramatic loss?

The missing girls are the result of systematic gender discrimination manifested as a preference for sons. Globally, the natural ratio of male to female births is between 104:100 and 106:100. In some Asian countries, however, male births outpace female births by far more dramatic degrees. In China, the ratio in 2011 was 118 male births for every 100 female births; in Anhui province, the ratio was a dramatic 129:100 in 2010. In Vietnam, the ratio is about 111:100 and in India, the national ratio is 110:100, though individual states, such as Punjab state, record higher figures—in 2008–2010, the male-to-female birth ratio in Punjab was 120:100 (UNFPA, 2012, pp. 19–20).

In all three countries—China, India, and Vietnam—there has been widespread use of prenatal sex selection: That is, parents learn the sex of their fetus prior to birth and are more likely to opt for an abortion if it is female, particularly if the family already has a girl child (UNFPA, 2012). While sex-selective abortion is illegal in all three countries, enforcement of the prohibition has been difficult and often lax. Since this skewed sex ratio was documented beginning around the early 1980s, it has balanced out in several of India's states, thanks in part to central and state government intervention, including implementation of policies to enforce this ban on sex-selective abortions and initiatives that raise awareness and educate Indian families about problems related to the sex-ratio imbalance (UNFPA, 2007).

Reasons for son preference are complex. In India, for instance, it is driven by a widespread belief that boys have greater economic, social, and religious utility for the family. Where a bride's parents are required to pay dowry to the groom's family, the costs to a poor (or even middle-class) family can be great; consequently, girls are often seen as economic liabilities (Mutharayappa, Choe, Arnold, & Roy,

1997; Seager, 2003). Even among families who can afford dowries for their daughters (and, paradoxically, dowry sizes have dropped as brides have become more scarce), boys are more highly valued because they pass on the family line, provide old-age security to parents, and are responsible for fulfilling religious traditions such as lighting the pyre at parents' funerals (International Development Research Centre, n.d.; Mutharayappa et al., 1997).

Interestingly, sex selection is more prevalent among affluent urban dwellers in India than their rural counterparts, though traditional norms are more likely to be associated with the latter. It is significant that the urban population is likely to have greater access to medical technologies such as prenatal sex screening. As well, they are likely to want and have fewer children than rural dwellers, so the perceived urgency of having a son in the first two or three births is more acute (Hvistendahl, 2011).

Son preference has important sociological causes and effects on both the micro and macro levels. Personal decisions based on economic factors, as well as societal and cultural norms, are made in individual families—but they have macro-level consequences. Guilmoto (2011) hypothesizes a coming "marriage squeeze" in China and India. He estimates that between 2020 and 2055, unmarried men may outnumber unmarried women in China by about 60%. In India, he estimates a similar proportion of unmarried men between 2040 and 2060. The men most likely to be pushed out of the marriage market are the poorest and least educated men. An analysis of the Chinese case by Edlund, Hongbin, Junjian, and Junsen (2007) identifies a correlation between rising sex ratios and the incidence of crimes, including, but not limited to, rape, bride abduction, sex trafficking, and prostitution; they concluded that about a seventh of the rise in crime over 20 years of skewed sex ratios could be explained by the phenomenon.

To understand phenomena such as rapid or slow population growth, sex ratios that favor males over females, and rising or falling fertility among women, we must take a sociological perspective that melds private lives and public issues. ■

. . . .

Demography: The science of population size, distribution, and composition.

Dhaka, the capital of Bangladesh, is one of Asia's rapidly growing cities. While urbanization is a key characteristic of modernity, it also brings new health, cultural, political, and economic challenges. ■

In this chapter, we will explore a subfield of sociology called demography. **Demography** is the *science of population size, distribution, and composition* (Keyfitz, 1993). We will discuss issues of global population growth and look at sociological perspectives on rising population. We will also examine issues of urbanization and the growth of megacities around the world. Finally, we will talk about the global environment and some of the ways in which these dual pressures of population growth and urbanization are affecting our planet.

While these three key topics are diverse, they share an important common thread, which we noted in the introductory discussion of son preference—that is, individual choices add up to phenomena that can have a powerful impact. Any individual family may exercise a preference for a son or for seven children rather than one, just as any individual family may opt to move to a city to seek better economic fortunes or may decide to buy a large sport utility vehicle rather than a fuel-efficient automobile. What appears at the micro level as an individual decision with direct effects only on a particular family can add up to macro-level phenomena with national or global effects and consequences.

GLOBAL POPULATION GROWTH

The world's population is growing at a rapid rate, expanding as much since 1950 as it did in the preceding 4 million years.

Hans Rosling on Population

■ FIGURE 17.1 World Population Growth, 1950–2100

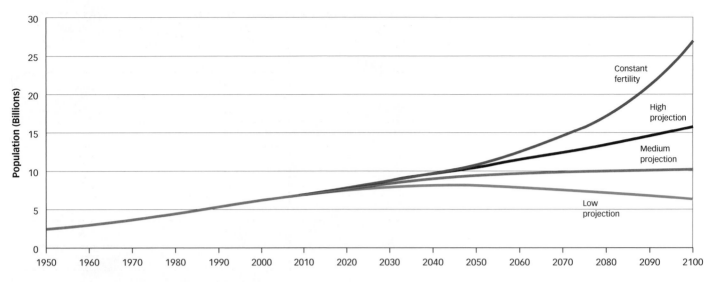

SOURCE: United Nations, Department of Economic and Social Affairs, Population Division. (2011). *World population prospects: The 2010 revision, highlights and advance tables.* Working Paper No. ESA/P/WP.220.

By 1850, global population reached 1 billion people; by 1950, it was 2.3 billion. As of 2012, it had reached over 7 billion people (Figure 17.1).

Population growth on our planet is highly uneven, with the greatest expansion taking place in developing countries. Consider that about half of the increase in global population between 2010 and 2050 is projected to take place in just nine countries, all but one of which are in the developing world: India, Pakistan, Nigeria, Ethiopia, the United States, the Democratic Republic of Congo, Tanzania, China, and Bangladesh. In the United States, most population growth will take place as a result of migration; elsewhere, it is the product of *natural population increase*—that is, it results from births outpacing deaths.

While the global **total fertility rate**—the **TFR** or *average number of births per woman*—was 2.4 in 2012, it differed substantially across countries and regions. The Population Reference Bureau distinguishes between "more developed countries," "less developed countries," and "least developed countries." In the more developed countries in 2012, the TFR was 1.6, in less developed countries it was 2.6, and in the least developed countries it was 3.0 (Haub & Kaneda, 2012; Table 17.1). *Replacement rate fertility* is represented by a TFR of 2.1, which means each parent is just replacing himself or herself (with an allowance of risk for mortality in the fraction above 2.0). Below this rate, populations decline, and above it, they grow.

Central Africa, composed mainly of less and least developed countries, is the fastest-growing region in the world. Its population is expected to grow 129% between 2010 and 2050, and South America's

population is estimated to rise 23% in the same period, while Western Europe will only grow by 0.5%. Other regions will lose populations, including Eastern Europe, where the population is expected to decrease 14% by 2050, due in large part to below-replacement-level fertility rates (Haub, 2010; Table 17.2 on page 419).

■ TABLE 17.1 Total Fertility Rates for Selected Countries, 2012

Country	Total Fertility Rate
Germany	1.4
Japan	1.4
China	1.5
Russia	1.6
United States	1.9
Iran	1.9
Brazil	1.9
Mexico	2.3
South Africa	2.4
India	2.5
Pakistan	3.6
Niger	7.1

SOURCE: Haub, C., & Kaneda, T. (2012). *2012 world population data sheet.* Washington, DC: Population Reference Bureau.

The World Is Getting Bigger

Total fertility rate (TFR): The average number of births per woman.

TABLE 17.2 Projected Population Growth for Global Regions, 2025 and 2050

Region	Current Population (millions)	2025 Projections (millions)	2050 Projections (millions)	Rate of Natural Increase %
World	**7,058**	**8,082**	**9,624**	**1.2**
Sub-Saharan Africa	902	1,245	2,092	2.6
Northern Africa	213	263	346	2.0
Western Africa	324	450	774	2.7
Eastern Africa	342	477	799	2.7
Middle Africa	134	193	352	2.6
Southern Africa	59	63	68	1.0
Northern America	349	391	471	0.5
Central America	160	185	212	1.6
Caribbean	42	46	49	1.1
South America	397	441	479	1.2
Western Asia	244	303	403	1.9
South Central Asia	1,823	2,145	2,565	1.6
Southeast Asia	608	696	801	1.2
East Asia	1,585	1,635	1,516	0.4
Northern Europe	101	111	122	0.3
Western Europe	190	194	194	0.1
Eastern Europe	295	287	259	−0.2
Southern Europe	154	158	157	0.0
Oceania	37	44	57	1.1

SOURCE: Haub, C., & Kaneda, T. (2012). *2012 world population data sheet.* Washington, DC: Population Reference Bureau.

China and India, the world's most populous countries, present interesting cases for looking at population growth. China and India both have over 1 billion inhabitants and high **population momentum**, which is *the tendency of population growth to continue beyond the point when replacement-rate fertility has been achieved because of the high concentration of people of childbearing age.* China has sought to check its population growth with a one-child policy that has slowed its rate of growth and put its total fertility rate below replacement rate (1.5). India's population growth has also declined markedly over time (today the TFR is 2.5), but population momentum remains high (CIA World Factbook, 2012).

· ·

Population momentum: The tendency of population growth to continue beyond the point when replacement-rate fertility has been achieved because of the high concentration of people of childbearing age.

To the east of China is Japan, which, like its close neighbor Russia and distant neighbors in Eastern and Western Europe, is also experiencing population decline: It has a TFR of 1.6 and is expected to see a 25% population drop (unless, of course, the difference is made up by increased immigration). Russia, currently one of the world's most populous countries, has a TFR of 1.6 and is also expected to lose population by midcentury (CIA World Factbook, 2012).

While some developing countries struggle with rapid population growth because it puts strain on basic services like sanitation and education, as well as on the conservation of natural resources, many modern industrialized countries are lamenting a "birth

One Child Per Family

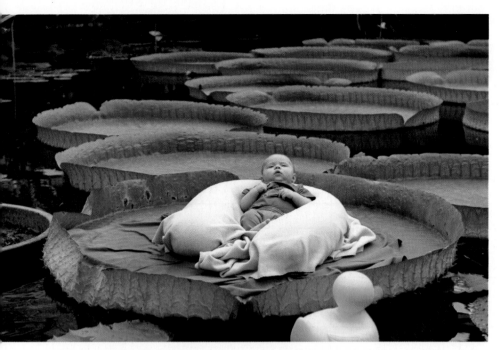

Imagine a pond with a single waterlily that doubles in size each day and covers the entire pond in 30 days. When does it cover just half the pond? The answer (on the 29th day) shows intuitively how population momentum drives rising population sizes, even given a constant growth rate. (Edward O. Wilson, "Is Humanity Suicidal?," New York Times Magazine, May 30, 1993.) ■

dearth" that leaves aging populations dependent for their social welfare (in the form of public retirement benefits, for instance) on the financial contributions of fewer young workers.

DEMOGRAPHY AND DEMOGRAPHIC ANALYSIS

Demographers have developed statistical techniques for predicting future population levels on the basis of current characteristics. Annual population growth or decline in a country is the result of four factors: (1) the number of people born in the country during the year; (2) the number who die; (3) the number who immigrate into the country; and (4) the number who emigrate out. In the language of demographers, population changes are based on **fertility** or *live births,* mortality or *deaths,* and **net migration**, which is *in-migration minus out-migration.*

Let's look at fertility first. Demographers estimate future fertility on the basis of past fertility patterns of women of childbearing age. Although it is possible to make a rough estimate of population growth on the basis of **crude birthrates**—*the number of births each year per 1,000 people*—a far more accurate measure is **age-specific fertility rates**, or *the number of births typical for women of a specific age in a particular population.* Demographers divide women into five-year cohorts—for example, women 15 to 19, 20 to 24, 25 to 29, and so on. If the current average number of live births per 1,000 women is known for each of these age groups, it is relatively easy to project future fertility. Five years from now, for example, today's 15- to 19-year-old women will be 20 to 24, which means that the fertility rates of today's 20- to 24-year-old women can be applied to them. In this way, each successive cohort

of women can be "aged" at five-year intervals, and the result is an estimate of total live births. Since fertility rates in most cultures peak during the late teens and 20s, the largest number of babies will be born to women in these age groups; thereafter, as the cohort ages into the 30s and 40s, the total number of babies born to the group will decline, dropping to zero as the cohort ages out of childbearing altogether.

The second source of population change is mortality. Again, although **crude death rates**—the *number of deaths each year per 1,000 people*—yield a rough measure, demographers prefer to rely on **age-specific mortality rates**, or *estimates of the number of deaths typical in men and women of specific ages in a particular population.* Like age-specific fertility rates, these rates are then applied to successive cohorts of men and women as they age. As you might guess, female mortality rates also affect the number of babies born, since as a cohort of females ages, some of its members will die, leaving fewer women of childbearing age. While in industrialized regions such as Western Europe most women live well beyond their childbearing years, female mortality rates in younger cohorts may have notable effects on birthrates in regions such as Sub-Saharan Africa, where AIDS kills many such women.

One measure of the overall mortality of a society is its **life expectancy**, the *average number of years a newborn is expected to live based on existing health conditions in the country.* In almost all societies, the life expectancy at birth is higher for females than for males. In the United States, for example, in 2010 the average life expectancy at birth for females was 80, while for males it was 75. In some countries of Eastern Europe, the gap between male and female life expectancy is as much as 12 years (Haub, 2010). Some of this gap is attributable to the fact that males are more likely than females to die in early childhood, more likely to die from accidents or violence in young adulthood, and more likely to experience early death from poor health in middle to later life.

. . . .

Fertility: The number of live births in a given population.

Net migration: In-migration minus out-migration.

Crude birthrate: The number of births each year per 1,000 people.

Age-specific fertility rate: The number of births typical in women of a specific age in a particular population.

Crude death rate: The number of deaths each year per 1,000 people.

Age-specific mortality rate: The number of deaths typical in men and women of specific ages in a particular population.

Life expectancy at birth: The average number of years a newborn is expected to live based on existing health conditions in the country.

Life expectancy in general varies enormously among countries of the world (Table 17.3). Japan ranks highest among all countries in terms of life expectancy (83 years), while the African country of Swaziland ranks very low, with a life expectancy at birth of just 48 years (Swaziland has an HIV/AIDS prevalence rate [among adults aged 15–49] of 26%; Haub & Kaneda, 2011, 2012).

It is difficult to make predictions about population growth with precision because they depend on assumptions about human behavior. If a government is effective in implementing family-planning programs, for example, the fertility of the population may differ substantially after a decade or two. An unforeseen epidemic (on a scale such as that of AIDS) may greatly increase mortality; conversely, the development of new drugs (such as new antibiotics or a cure for AIDS) could greatly reduce it. For this reason, demographers typically offer a range of estimates of future populations: a low estimate that assumes high mortality and low fertility; a high estimate that assumes low mortality and high fertility; and an intermediate estimate that represents an informed figure somewhere in between.

Population forecasting also depends on fertility, but again, momentum is critical as well. In 1979 China decided to limit fertility by rewarding one-child families with additional income and

High life expectancy is most common in wealthy and technologically advanced states. The 10 countries with the highest life expectancy at birth are Japan (83), Israel (82), Singapore (82), Iceland (82), Sweden (82), France (82), Switzerland (82), Italy (82), Spain (82), and Australia (82; Haub & Kaneda, 2012). ■

preferential treatment in terms of jobs, housing, health care, and education, while threatening punishment for those who refused to keep their families small. This policy reduced China's TFR to 1.5. Yet this reduction does not mean China's population will decline markedly from the 1.35 billion people it reached in 2012. With about 18% of its population under the age of 15—nearing childbearing years—China has a substantial amount of population momentum. According to the Population Reference Bureau (Haub & Kaneda, 2012), its population will grow to about 1.4 billion in 2025 before likely falling to 1.31 billion by 2050.

THEORY OF THE DEMOGRAPHIC TRANSITION

Extrapolating from the Western model of population change, demographers have argued that many societies go through roughly the same stages of population transition. They suggest that societies begin with an extended stage of low or no growth resulting from high fertility and equally high mortality, pass through a transitional stage of explosive growth resulting from high fertility and low mortality, and end up in a final stage of slow or no growth resulting from low fertility and low mortality (Figure 17.2). This perspective on population change is called the *theory of the first demographic transition*. We outline this transition in more detail below.

Early agricultural societies had high fertility and mortality rates that generally counterbalanced one another. Consequently, the population was either stable or grew very slowly. Crude death

■ **TABLE 17.3** Life Expectancies at Birth for Selected Countries, 2012

Country	Life Expectancy at Birth
South Africa	54
Niger	58
India	65
Pakistan	65
Russia	69
Iran	70
Brazil	74
China	75
Mexico	77
United States	79
Germany	80
Japan	83

SOURCE: Haub, C., & Kaneda, T. (2012). *2012 world population data sheet.* Washington, DC: Population Reference Bureau.

Demographic Transition Theory

About a third of India's 1.2 billion people are under 15, representing momentum for future population growth, even if family planning leads to smaller cohorts in the future. But son preference skews sex ratios at birth in some regions, which may affect the number of future mothers. ■

rates as high as 50 per 1,000 were caused by harsh living conditions, unstable food supplies, poor medical care, and lack of disease control. Epidemics, famines, and wars produced high rates of death, periodically reducing the population even more dramatically. Such societies had to develop strong norms and institutions in support of high fertility to prevent a decline in population. Children were valued for a variety of cultural and economic reasons, particularly where they made a contribution to hunting, farming, herding, weaving, and the other work necessary in a household-based economy (Simon, 1981).

As societies modernized (that is, became more urban and industrial), their birthrates initially remained high. At the same time, mortality rates plummeted due to an improved food supply brought about by growing trade links, sanitation control that accompanied greater public health knowledge and prosperity, and, eventually, modern medicine. Consider, for instance, the discovery that hand washing is important for doctors attending child birthing. While this does not sound revolutionary today, it had a critical impact on maternal and child survival. In the 19th century, women in Europe and the United States had stunning rates of maternal mortality: Up to 25% of women delivering babies at the hospital died from puerperal sepsis, also known as childbed fever. Dr. Ignaz Semmelweis, a Viennese physician practicing in the 1840s, observed this phenomenon and recommended that attending physicians wash their hands with a chlorinated solution before seeing birthing women. Semmelweis and his findings were harshly criticized and

he was ostracized for speaking out; his medical colleagues, nearly all of whom hailed from the upper classes, did not believe that gentlemen (even those attending a birth after dissecting a cadaver) could have dirty hands. As support for germ theory spread, however, Semmelweis's discovery proved to be critically important for the reduction of maternal mortality (Nuland, 2003).

Because people did not initially change their fertility behavior—specifically, they did not stop having many children—as death rates dropped, the result was rapid population growth. Eventually, however, expanding industrialization and urbanization brought about a fall in fertility. Although during the early stages of industrialization children often worked in factories and contributed to family income, the hardships of child labor eventually led to its legal prohibition. Rather than being an economic necessity, then, children became an expense. Urban living was also less amenable to large families than rural life had been. Population growth stabilized as low mortality came to be matched by falling fertility. At this point, the first demographic transition in the industrialized societies of the West was complete.

The theory of the first demographic transition offers a useful perspective based on a pattern observed in Western countries. We can also critique it, however, for the same reason; that is, it describes the historical experience of today's modern, Western societies. It does not describe nearly as well the experience of the developing world, which accounts for most global population growth today. In newly industrializing low-income countries,

■ **FIGURE 17.2** The First Demographic Transition Model in Four Stages

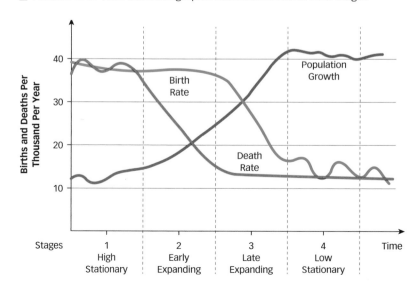

families do not always drastically reduce their fertility. And many low-income nations have not industrialized, yet their mortality rates have declined because populations have access to food, medicine (particularly antibiotics), agricultural and sanitation technologies, and pesticides, which contribute to better health and longer lives. Drops in mortality, however, have not been accompanied by drops in fertility that, in modern industrialized states, stemmed from economic growth, urbanization, industrialization, and expanded educational opportunities.

High fertility combined with low (or relatively low) mortality underlies much of the population explosion in the developing world. Fertility remains high in poor countries for a number of reasons, including health and culture. For instance, families in regions that still experience high child mortality are more likely to have "extra" children to ensure that some survive, and the "ideal" size of families is culturally variable.

Economic factors also shape fertility decisions. Consider the relationship between economic rationality and childbearing. The saying "children are a poor man's riches" highlights the fact that in agricultural societies in particular, children (particularly boy children) are a value more than a cost. In rich and industrialized countries, children, while emotionally valued, are economically costly and contribute little or nothing to the household in terms of economic value. Economic rationality, then, is present in both the decision of a poor household in the

Dr. Ignaz Semmelweis observed higher maternal mortality in Clinic 1 of his hospital, staffed by male obstetricians who performed autopsies, than in Clinic 2, staffed by female midwives who did not. Chlorine washing of male birth attendants' hands reduced maternal mortality until 1850, when Semmelweis left the hospital and old practices resumed. ■

developing world to have many children, and in the decision of a rich household in the developed world to have few.

One of the most important factors contributing to both lowered fertility and improved child survival is the education of women (Figure 17.3). According to a recent study, for every one-year increase in the average education of women in their childbearing years, a country experienced a 9.5% fall in child mortality (Gakidou, Cowling, Lozano, & Murray, 2010). Women who are more educated are more likely to be familiar with family planning methods and more likely to use them. Better-educated women are also more likely to have jobs in the formal labor force and, consequently, to limit their fertility in order to bring in economic resources. Finally, women with some economic resources also tend to have more decision-making power in the family, allowing them to participate in making choices about birth control and family size (United Nations, 1995).

Better health services for children and declining infant and child mortality also have an important effect on fertility decisions. When women have reason to believe that all or most of their offspring will survive into adulthood, they are less likely to have "extra" children, which ensures a few survive (Kibirige, 1997).

Developed countries and the governments of some high-fertility countries have helped finance family-planning programs in order to educate people about birth control. In addition, they have provided condoms, birth control pills, and other means of

■ **FIGURE 17.3** Relationship Between Fertility and Female Education (Scattergram of Countries)

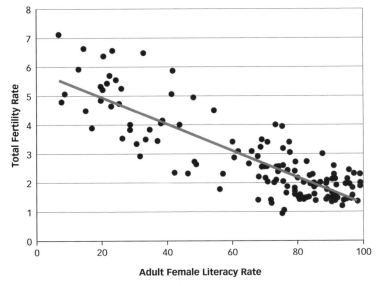

SOURCE: European Environment Agency. (2012). *Correlation between fertility and female education.* Retrieved from http://www.eea.europa.eu/data-and-maps/figures/correlation-between-fertility-and-female-education

Declining Fertility Rates

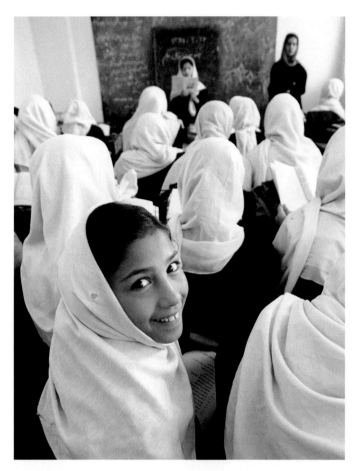

With the assistance of international organizations, Afghanistan has sought to increase the number of girls with access to schooling, but poverty and the cultural priority given to boys' education have kept female literacy low, and few women work in the paid labor force. At 5.5 children per woman, Afghanistan's total fertility rate remains among the world's highest. ■

reducing fertility. While such programs have met with some success, they often run up against deep-seated religious and other cultural values, some of which are found in the developed states as well. For instance, during the Reagan and both Bush presidencies, there were significant cuts in U.S. governmental funding of family planning programs abroad since birth control (and especially abortion) violated the beliefs of conservative supporters of those administrations. It is clear that global efforts in family planning are fraught with problems. It remains to be seen whether they will ultimately succeed in reducing fertility (and hence global population growth).

IS A SECOND DEMOGRAPHIC TRANSITION OCCURRING IN THE WEST?

In the theory of the first demographic transition, population reaches a point of stabilization in Stage 4. What happens after that? Some demographers argue that at least in the most developed countries, stabilization has been followed by a *second demographic transition* (Lesthaeghe, 1995; McNicoll, 2001), characterized by broad changes in family patterns. Countries experiencing a second

demographic transition are said to be characterized by increased rates of divorce and cohabitation, for instance, as well as decreased rates of marriage and fertility and a rise of nonmarital births as a proportion of all births. Germany, France, and Sweden are among these countries, some demographers say. Because changes in family patterns are associated with smaller families, the second demographic transition is often characterized by declines in the **rate of natural increase (RNI)** of populations; the RNI is *the crude birthrate minus the crude death rate.*

If a country has a negative RNI, it can lead to population declines. Russia, for example, is experiencing relatively rapid loss of population: People are dying at a faster rate than they are being born, and Russia can expect to see a population loss of about 10% through the middle of the century (Haub, 2010). The result is an inverted age pyramid, wider at the top and narrower at the bottom (Figure 17.4 on page 425). Some countries with a negative RNI, however, still experience growing populations as a result of immigration. By contrast, countries with above-replacement-rate fertility and growing populations have "normal" pyramids. Figure 17.4 shows Mexico's age pyramid.

What accounts for the second demographic transition? Demographer Ron Lesthaeghe (1995) argues that "the motivations underlying the 'second transition' are clearly different from those supporting the 'first transition,' with individual autonomy and female emancipation more central to the second than to the first" (p. 18). According to this perspective, more people associate personal satisfaction with consumption and personal fulfillment and are not as likely to seek fulfillment through family relationships. Female emancipation has also been broadened by the medical evolution of the "perfectly contracepting society" (Westoff & Ryder, 1977), such that women have unprecedented control over their fertility, and many have chosen smaller families or have opted to remain child free.

Critics suggest that the second transition describes only a fraction of the world's population. However, the number of countries experiencing below-replacement birthrates is rising, and a sociological and demographic perspective such as the theory of the second transition offers sociologists analytical tools to understand these key trends in advanced industrial states.

MALTHUS AND MARX: HOW MANY PEOPLE ARE TOO MANY?

High rates of population growth in some parts of the world may seem daunting, even alarming to some, but numbers alone do not tell the entire story. There is still a great deal of sparsely settled land in the world, and if the planet's nearly 7 billion people were all somehow to be transplanted to the territory of the United States, the resulting crowding would be no greater

. . . .

Rate of natural increase: The crude birth rate minus the crude death rate.

than currently exists in the country of Taiwan.

Is the world overpopulated? Not surprisingly, there are opposing viewpoints on this issue. On one side are those who predict catastrophe if population growth is not slowed or stopped altogether. Activists who fear that a population doomsday is just around the corner often conclude that drastic measures are required, including stringent public policies that promote small families. On the other side are those who argue that while population growth should be slowed, extreme measures are unwarranted. They tend to favor expanded female education, voluntary family-planning programs, and economic policies that raise living standards, making smaller families a more rational economic choice.

MALTHUS: OVERPOPULATION AND NATURAL LIMITS

The argument that the world is overpopulated was first made two centuries ago by British social philosopher Thomas Malthus (1766–1834). Malthus (1798/1926) developed the theory of **exponential population growth**, *the belief that, like compound interest, a constant rate of population growth produces a population that grows by an increasing amount with each passing year.* Malthus also posited that, while population grows exponentially, the food supply does not; the earth's resources are finite. Consequently, though the population may continue to double, the amount of food is more likely to grow at a constant rate. The result, according to Malthus's dire warning, is a growing mismatch between population and food resources. Unless we take steps to control our population growth, Malthus predicted, nature will do it for us: Wars fought over scarce resources, epidemics, and famine will keep population in check. Back when only a billion people occupied the entire planet, Malthus believed doomsday was already on the horizon.

. . . .

Exponential population growth: The belief that a constant rate of population growth produces a population that grows by an increasing amount with each passing year.

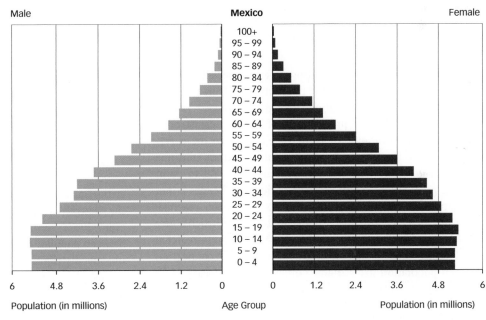

SOURCE: U.S. Census Bureau International Database.

How good was Malthus's prediction? Although war, epidemic, and famine have in fact been sadly evident throughout human history and population has continued to grow exponentially, the food supply has grown along with it. Malthus failed to recognize that modern technology can also be applied to agriculture, yielding an exponential growth in food supplies—at least for a time. A report by the Food and Agriculture Organization of the United Nations concluded that although the world's population may reach 9.1 billion by 2050, "the required increase in food production can be achieved if the necessary investment is undertaken and policies conducive to agricultural production are put in place," along with

Only India and China have reached the 1 billion population mark. While its large population strains the country's resources, India has also experienced steady economic growth and gains in education and innovation. One of the results is a growing middle class with rising incomes (Ablett et al., 2007). ∎

(2000), published posthumously, Simon suggested that *Sudden Modern Progress* (SMP)—the rapid rise in living standards and technology—was the result of population growth and density. Put another way, the great population growth of the modern period was a causal factor of "the great breakthrough" (which is also the title of his book)—that is, population growth brings about technological progress. More people mean more minds and more innovation, so human-generated resources, Simon argues, can overcome limitations on natural resources. Unlike Malthus, Simon was encouraged rather than daunted by the prospect of rising populations.

Indeed, the question of whether more minds can balance the pressure caused by more bodies is an engaging and imperative one. Can population growth be both problematic and powerful? What do you think?

MARX: OVERPOPULATION OR MALDISTRIBUTION OF WEALTH?

Malthus forecast misery and inevitable overpopulation under conditions of growth. Simon saw population growth and density as necessary conditions for economic progress. Karl Marx focused on the unequal distribution of resources across populations.

Marx was concerned about the dominance of an economic system that enabled the wealthy few to consume the world's resources at the expense of the impoverished masses. He was critical of Malthus for having claimed that overpopulation was the central cause of human starvation and misery. In Marx's (1867/1967) view, the central problem was not a mismatch between population size and resource availability, but rather the unequal distribution of resources; in most societies, as well as in the world as a whole, he argued, a small elite enjoyed the lion's share of the wealth and resources, while the majority was left to take up the crumbs that fell from the richly endowed tables of the few.

Parente (2008) notes that even after adjusting for differences in relative prices and gross domestic product per capita, the living standards in the wealthiest industrial countries are about 50 to 60 times greater than in the world's poorest countries. Most of the world's resources and goods are consumed by the West: Western Europe and North America, with 12% of the world's population, accounted for 60% of private consumption expenditures. In contrast, Sub-Saharan Africa and South Asia, which together are home to over one third of humanity, accounted for just over 3% of private consumer expenditures. At the beginning of the new millennium, about two fifths of the earth's inhabitants lived on less than $2 per day (Worldwatch Institute, 2011). Marx argued that such maldistribution was the result of

"policies to enhance access by fighting poverty, especially in rural areas, as well as effective safety net programmes" (United Nations Food and Agriculture Organization, 2009, p. 2).

Although Malthus's predictions of global catastrophe have not been borne out, there may be a limit to the carrying capacity of the planet. World population cannot continue rapid growth indefinitely without consequences. Yet to point out that population growth presents serious challenges is not the same as concluding that the limits have been reached. From Malthus's pessimistic prophecies to Paul Ehrlich's dire warnings in *The Population Bomb* (1968), the long-predicted population doomsday has yet to arrive. In fact, the connection between population growth and human misery appears to be more complicated than many analyses suggest. It is not simply a question of how much additional food will be required to feed more mouths, but whether the food that is produced reaches those who need it. Mass hunger in many countries is as much a product of politics as of true lack of food; in civil conflicts, for instance, hunger may be a weapon, as opposing forces block food shipments to enemy areas.

SIMON: A MODERN CRITIC TAKES ON MALTHUS

Economist Julian Simon (1977, 2000) became well known for his pointedly anti-Malthusian perspective on population. Not only did Simon reject the notion that unchecked population growth would lead humanity down a path to hunger, deprivation, and poverty, but he posited precisely the opposite. He argued that population growth had positive economic effects. In his most recent work a capitalist economic system that divided people into unequal social classes.

Both Malthus and Marx were writing when the world's population was only around 1 billion people. Marx's criticism of Malthus has stood the test of time, since world population has doubled and more than doubled again since Malthus's predictions were made, but global resources have not run dry. Looking critically at Marx's ideas, we might note that although the maldistribution of wealth is an important factor in understanding poverty and human misery, Marx underestimated the importance of population growth itself as a variable.

MALTHUS, MARX, AND MODERNITY

Consider this question: What is the greater threat to the health and survival of our global environment? Is it the rapid growth of the populations of the developing world, or the overconsumption of resources by the small stratum of the wealthy? While some policy makers in the West express concern about the threats posed by unchecked population growth or the use of "dirty" technologies in developing states or the cutting of rainforests in the Amazon and elsewhere, there is little vigorous mainstream debate over the global threat presented by the recklessly wasteful consumption of resources by Western consumers. To cite just one example of the way Western consumption is masked by a focus on the global poor, broad media attention has been given to the millions of acres of rainforest lost to clear-cutting in poor states, not least because of the immense biodiversity that is sacrificed. Many in the United States have donated money to campaigns aimed at saving this precious resource. At the same time, heedless U.S. consumers of steaks, burgers, and barbeques may not recognize that some of the clear-cutting is done by ranchers seeking land on which to farm cattle, the meat from which will be sent to our supermarkets, restaurants, and dinner tables.

The question of whether overpopulation or overconsumption is the greater threat is a provocative one. Neither is without consequences. Malthus feared that population would outpace food production; Marx posited that elites would consume far more than their share. A modern take on this debate points us to the conflict between underdevelopment in some states and "overdevelopment" in others.

As we shall see later in this chapter, environmental stresses have grown substantially since Malthus's and Marx's time, and some scientists believe we are approaching a point of no return in inflicting environmental damage. While overconsumption presents threats to our future, the consequences of the population explosion must also be faced. Since much of the world's population increase is currently concentrated in urban areas, we will next examine the impact of urbanization on modern life, before turning to the environmental effects of urbanization and population growth combined.

. . . .

City: A relatively large, dense, and permanent settlement of socially heterogenous individuals.

URBANIZATION

What is a city? Is it easy or difficult to come up with a definition? Early urban sociologist Louis Wirth (1938) wrote that "a sociologically significant definition of the city seeks to select those elements of urbanism which mark it as a distinctive mode of human group life" (p. 4). For sociological purposes, and thus for ours too, Wirth's definition is useful: A **city** is *"a relatively large, dense, and permanent settlement of socially heterogeneous individuals"* (p. 8).

In the eyes of some literary writers, cities are grim places of human degradation and misery. In the 19th-century poem "The City of Dreadful Night," James Thomson (1874) describes such a place.

> That city's atmosphere is dark and dense,
>
> Although not many exiles wander there,
>
> With many a potent evil influence,
>
> Each adding poison to the poisoned air;
>
> Infections of unalterable sadness,
>
> Infections of incalculable madness,
>
> Infections of incurable despair.

Other writers have praised the modernity, power, and culture of the city, while still others have recognized the contradictions of cities, their beautiful madness, their inhabitants' paradoxical excitement and indifference, and their ability to both attract and repel. Honoré de Balzac wrote of Paris in 1833:

> By dint of taking in everything, the Parisian ends by being interested in nothing. No emotion dominating his face, which friction has rubbed away, it turns gray like the faces of those houses upon which all kinds of dust and smoke have blown . . . [The Parisian] grumbles at everything, consoles himself for everything, jests at everything, forgets, desires, and tastes everything, seizes all with passion, quits all with indifference—his kings, his conquests, his glory, his idols of bronze or glass—as he throws away his stockings, his hats, and his fortune. In Paris, no sentiment can withstand the drift of things.

The city is a place of kings and presidents, as it is a place of thugs and beggars. It is lovely and disgusting, wealthy and poor, rewarding and despairing. Cities have become part of our lives and lore, but they were not always so. Cities have a long history, but until the Industrial Revolution, most people were rural dwellers. Today, most of the world's people live in cities and embody the beauties, miseries, and contradictions of those places. Below we turn a sociological lens on the cities of the United States and the world.

Urbanization and Environment

Urbanization

Like all global cities, Paris has long been a city of contrasts. In a single city, one finds extremes of wealth and poverty, as well as leisure and struggle. ■

THE RISE OF INDUSTRY AND EARLY CITIES

Preindustrial cities, based on both agriculture and trade, first appeared 10,000 to 12,000 years ago. The development of settled agricultural areas enabled farmers to produce an **agricultural surplus**, *food beyond the amount required for immediate survival.* This surplus in turn made it possible to sustain urban populations who were not engaged primarily in farming. The first known cities were small, their populations seldom exceeding a few thousand, since the surplus production of 10 or more farmers was required to support one nonfarming city dweller. The need for access to transportation routes and rich soil for farming figured prominently in the siting of the earliest cities along major river systems (Hosken, 1993). Early city residents included government officials, priests, handicraft workers, and others specializing in nonagricultural occupations, although many city dwellers engaged in some farming as well. Until modern times, very few cities in the world surpassed 100,000 people. Over 2,000 years ago, Rome was considered an enormous metropolis with 800,000 people, though today it would be comparable in population to a U.S. city such as San Francisco, California (Mumford, 1961).

The industrial revolution of the 18th century radically changed the nature of cities. While cities of the past had served primarily as centers of trade, industrial cities now emerged as centers of manufacturing. Although some of the earliest English factories were in smaller cities, by the 19th century industrialization was moving hand in hand with **urbanization**, *the concentration of people in urban areas.* At the beginning of the 19th century, there were barely 100 places in England with more than 5,000 inhabitants; by the end of the century, there were more than 600, together containing more than 20 million people. The city of London grew from 1.1 million to 7.3 million people between 1800 and 1910 (Hosken, 1993), becoming a center of industry, as well as an ever more important hub of commerce and culture. In the United States as well, the explosion of cities coincided with the onset of industrialization at the end of the 19th century. By the early 20th century, most U.S. citizens could be classified as urban, and today, as in Britain and other Western European industrial states, the vast majority live in metropolitan areas.

SOCIOLOGISTS AND THE CITY

The early industrial cities were grimy places, in which people lived in shanties and shacks, often in the shadow of the factories where they spent over a dozen working hours each day. In the absence of proper sanitation and sewage systems, illness and epidemics were common, and many people died of typhoid, cholera, dysentery, and tuberculosis. Writers including Charles Dickens captured the miseries of early urban industrial life, where men, women, and children toiled in dank, squalid conditions and lived lives of deprivation and degradation. Early sociologists too turned their lenses on the city, some viewing urban life as bordering on the pathological. At the same time, most recognized that cities provided opportunities for individuality and creativity.

During the rapid urbanization of the 19th century, some of the earliest sociologists worried about the differences between a presumably serene country life and the "death and decay" of city life

· ·

Agricultural surplus: Food beyond the amount required for immediate survival.

Urbanization: The growing concentration of people in urban areas.

INEQUALITY MATTERS

THE GEOMETRY OF THE CITY

Among the important early urban sociologists at the University of Chicago was Ernest Burgess (1886–1966). Burgess developed the *concentric zone hypothesis* in part to explain how different social groups come to be distributed across urban spaces. It suggests that sociological factors, including socioeconomic class, are relevant to understanding the competition for favorable locations in an urban area.

Burgess believed a key city pattern could be represented by five concentric circles (Figure 17.5). The small inner circle represents the *central business district,* a relatively affluent zone characterized by government buildings, financial institutions, and major retailers. The next ring is a *zone in transition,* with low-rent areas occupied by poor and minority residents and some manufacturing. The third ring from the center is the *workingman's zone* with housing typified by small individual units and apartments. The fourth ring is the *middle-class residential district,* with more upscale housing options. The outer ring is called the *commuters' zone or suburban zone,* with larger housing units and upper-income residences. Burgess noted that as we move from the inner zone to the outer circle, we find decreased population density and increased class status, higher rates of homeownership, lower rates of crime, and smaller families. The patterns could be explained, he argued, by the amount people and businesses were willing to pay for land, with valued commercial space in the center (which has the greatest access to customers) and valued residential space in outer areas.

Burgess's model has been criticized for, among other flaws, hypothesizing a cityscape that has characterized many U.S. cities but cannot capture the patterns of global cities, many of which exhibit the opposite pattern of city class composition, with the wealthiest in the center and suburban districts of poverty at the city's edges. Contemporary gentrification in some U.S. cities has also brought high-rent residences and pricey condominiums to previously poor and neglected urban neighborhoods.

At the same time, Burgess's work is important because it seeks to turn a sociological eye to the U.S. city and to recognize sociological factors that help explain social group distribution across the urban landscape.

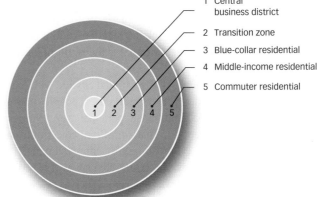

■ **FIGURE 17.5** Burgess's Concentric Zone Hypothesis

1 Central business district
2 Transition zone
3 Blue-collar residential
4 Middle-income residential
5 Commuter residential

THINK IT THROUGH

■ *Can you create a sociological map of your own city or town? What kinds of patterns of commercial activity or residence can you detect, and how would you explain them sociologically?*

(Toennies, 1887/1963). The rural community (*Gemeinschaft* in the original German) was contrasted with urban society (*Gesellschaft*), much to the disadvantage of the latter. Rural community life was said to be characterized by intimate relationships, a strong sense of family, powerful folkways and mores, and stabilizing religious foundations. Urban life, by contrast, was believed to be characterized by impersonal and materially based relationships, family breakdown, and the erosion of traditional beliefs and religious values. Behavior was viewed as governed no longer by long-standing folkways and mores, but by cold cost-benefit calculations, individual preferences rather than group norms, and ever-changing public opinion.

While alienation was assumed to be a product of this chilly urban world, Émile Durkheim put forth the notion that the *mechanical solidarity* of traditional community life (based on homogeneity) could be replaced by the *organic solidarity* of modern societies, with complex divisions of labor in which people were heterogenous but interdependent for survival and prosperity.

During the 1920s and 1930s, researchers at the University of Chicago turned their city into a vast laboratory for urban studies, pioneering urban sociology as a field. Early 20th-century U.S. sociology centered on the study of "social problems," such as hoboes, the mentally ill, juvenile delinquents, criminals, prostitutes, and others who were seen as casualties of urban living. Urbanism was believed to be a specific way of life that resulted from the geographical concentration of large numbers of socially diverse people (see the *Inequality Matters* box on page 429). Sociologists believed one feature of this life was a good deal of mutual mistrust, leading city residents to segregate themselves on the basis of race, ethnicity, class, and even lifestyle into neighborhoods of like-minded people (Wirth, 1938). Of course, as we saw in Chapter 8 on race, self-segregation should be distinguished from imposed segregation that is the result of individual or institutional racism.

Although early sociologists often linked city life with pathology, even in supposedly impersonal cities people maintain intense social networks and close personal ties. Numerous sociological studies have found that significant community relationships persist within even the largest cities (Duneier, 1992; C. Fischer, 1982, 1984; Gans, 1962a, 1962b; Liebow, 1967; Whyte, 1943; Wirth, 1928). Physical characteristics such as size and density do not by themselves account for urban problems. What is important is the way a particular society organizes itself in cities. Below we look at the case of cities in the United States.

CITIES IN THE UNITED STATES

Transportation and communication technologies have played an important role in helping to shape U.S. cities. The automobile and urban rail and subway systems enabled cities to expand outward by allowing people to travel greater distances between home and work. Similarly, modern construction technologies permitted cities to expand skyward, with massive skyscrapers that would take up little land space but create living or work space for thousands.

THE SOCIAL DYNAMICS OF U.S. CITIES AND SUBURBS

Political and economic forces are also key to shaping modern cities. Sociologists John Logan and Harvey Molotch (Logan & Molotch, 1987; Molotch, 1976; K. Warner, Molotch, & Lategola, 1992) have argued that cities are shaped by what they call the **urban growth machine**, consisting of *those persons and institutions that have a stake in an increase in the value of urban land and that constitute a power elite in most cities.* These people and institutions are said to include downtown businesses, real estate owners (particularly those who own commercial and rental property), land developers and builders, newspapers (whose advertising revenues are often tied to the size of the local population), and the lawyers, accountants, architects, real estate agents, construction workers, and others whose income is tied to serving those who own land. The urban growth machine is viewed as dominating local politics in most U.S. cities, with the result that cities often compete with one another to house factories, office buildings, shopping malls, and other economic activities that will increase the value of the land owned by the members of the growth machine.

G. William Domhoff (2002) expands the notion to talk about *growth coalitions,* "whose members share a common interest in intensifying land use in their geographic locale" (p. 39). Growth coalitions are a powerful force in local politics, though they encounter conflicts in their pursuit of growth and profit. Domhoff notes that "neighborhoods are something to be used and enjoyed in the eyes of those who live in them, but they are often seen as sites for further development by growth coalitions, who justify new developments with a doctrine claiming the highest and best use for land" (p. 40).

Consider Domhoff's conflict-oriented analysis of U.S. politics and decision making, which we examined in our chapter on politics and the state (Chapter 13). Recall that he asks us to ponder the questions: *Who benefits? Who governs? Who wins?* Looking at growth politics—the increasing development of already-crowded suburbs or the gentrification of urban neighborhoods at the expense of older neighborhoods—we may ask who has the power and the resources to realize their interests. Are those who favor *use value* (the enjoyment of the neighborhood) or those who favor *exchange value* (the economic development of an area) more powerful? Is the shape of modern cities and suburbs a product primarily of those who inhabit them or those who profit from them?

The post–World War II development of U.S. cities and suburbs illustrates how the growth machine operates at the national level. The rapid growth of suburbs during the 1950s and the 1960s is often attributed to people's preference for suburban living, but it was also a product of economic forces and government policies designed to stimulate the postwar economy (Jackson, 1985; Mollenkopf, 1977). Government influence is illustrated by the 1956 National Interstate and Defense Highways Act, which established a highway trust fund paid for by a federal tax on gasoline. This legislation ensured a self-renewing source of funding to construct high-speed freeways between cities and suburbs across the country. The legislation eventually financed nearly 100,000 miles of highways, characterized by then-president Dwight Eisenhower as "the greatest public works program in history" and enough to build a "Great Wall" around the world 50 feet wide and 9 feet high. The law originated in the planning efforts of a powerful consortium of bankers, corporations, and unions connected with the automobile, petroleum, and construction industries (Mollenkopf, 1977).

The Highways Act, in combination with other government programs, spurred the growth of the U.S. economy, both by improving transportation and by promoting the automobile and construction industries. The existence of freeways encouraged people to buy more cars and to drive additional miles, and, through this, still more gasoline tax revenues were generated for additional highway construction. Large numbers of

. . . .

Urban growth machine: Those persons and institutions that have a stake in an increase in the value of urban land and that constitute a power elite in cities.

people bought houses in the suburbs with federally insured and subsidized loans, commuted on federally financed highways to work in federally subsidized downtown office buildings, and even shopped in malls built in part with federal dollars. All this development ushered in a quarter-century of growth and relative prosperity for working- and middle-class residents of the suburbs.

In fact, one of the most dramatic population shifts in U.S. history has been the rapid growth of suburbs. In 1950, cities contained 33% of the U.S. population, considerably more than their surrounding suburbs (23%). During the 1960s, the suburbs overtook the cities, and by 1990, the suburban population had reached 46% of the U.S. total, while the city population had declined slightly to 31% (Frey & Speare, 1991). In 2000, 46% lived in the suburbs, while the percentage in central cities dropped slightly to 30% (U.S. Census Bureau, 2002). In 2010, over 80% of the U.S. population inhabited metropolitan areas, but the 2010 census also showed a shift back toward urban growth (Mackun & Wilson, 2011).

The emergence of postindustrial society has encouraged further development beyond the economic activity of the urban core. Modern information technology has made it easier to locate high-tech factories and office parks in once-remote suburban or even rural locations, where they take advantage of relatively inexpensive land, wooded landscapes, and other amenities. Since 1980, over two thirds of employment growth has taken place outside central cities, and even manufacturing, while in decline nationally, has found a home in the suburbs; today, about 70% of manufacturing is suburban (Wilson, 2010).

While those who benefit from such relocations tend to be well-educated managerial, technical, and professional specialists, the suburbs are also home to a substantial proportion of entry-level positions. This is significant because it contributes to the loss of employment opportunities in central cities. Sociologist William Julius Wilson (2010) writes of the *spatial mismatch* between urban job seekers and suburban jobs, noting that "opportunities for employment are geographically disconnected from the people who need the jobs" (p. 41). He offers the example of Cleveland where, "although entry-level workers are concentrated in inner-city neighborhoods, 80 percent of the entry-level jobs are located in the suburbs" (Wilson, 2010, p. 41).

. . . .

Urban renewal: The transformation of old neighborhoods with new buildings, businesses, and residences.

Gentrification: The attempt to change the socioeconomic composition of old and poor neighborhoods with the remodeling of old structures and building of new residences and shops to attract new middle- and high-income residents.

The great highway building projects of the postwar period literally paved the roads to America's suburbanized future. Robert Fishman suggests that "every true suburb is the outcome of two opposing forces, an attraction toward the opportunities of the great city and a simultaneous repulsion against urban life" (quoted in Gainsborough, 2001, p. 33). Is this an accurate characterization? Why or why not? ■

The migration of middle- and upper-income families from the cities begun in the postwar era evolved into a critical socioeconomic disparity between the suburbs and central cities. Analyzing the concentrated poverty of urban core areas such as South Chicago, sociologist William Julius Wilson (2010) points out that political forces have led to a "new urban poverty" that plagues inner-city neighborhoods deeply segregated by both race and class. These forces include government support for highway building and a postwar mortgage lending boom to veterans and other predominantly White families, and the decline of the industrial base that long provided economic sustenance to U.S. cities and less educated workers.

The decline of U.S. cities, most visible in the economically distressed urban core of cities including Chicago, Washington, DC, and Baltimore, has fostered efforts toward **urban renewal**, or *the transformation of old neighborhoods with new buildings, businesses, and residences.* Urban renewal is linked to **gentrification**, a process characterized by *the attempt to change the socioeconomic composition of old and poor neighborhoods with the remodeling of old structures and building of new residences and shops to attract new middle- and high-income residents.* On the one hand, gentrification may be successful in transforming dilapidated neighborhoods into flourishing (and more economically valuable) urban spaces that offer cultural and business opportunities to residents and visitors. Cities may benefit from gentrification as the process rebuilds a middle-class base of residents and pushes up the value of taxable property and, consequently, revenues for city governments. On the other hand, rising property values also tend to herald a rise in rents and other costs of living, which may push out low-income residents who cannot afford to be part of the boom in condominiums or the luxury amenities intended to make gentrified spaces inviting to upwardly mobile new residents.

In the fall of 2010, the city of Washington, DC, announced the closing one of the city's few bilingual shelters. The shelter was located in Columbia Heights, a "rapidly developing" neighborhood described as "a focus of city redevelopment efforts" (Rott, 2010). City officials tried to move shelter residents to apartments before the shelter was to be destroyed to make way for condominiums and a new shopping complex. An advocate for the homeless noted, however, that "the remaining shelters are in the poorest parts of the city" (Rott, 2010). What, then, are we to conclude about gentrification? How can urban renewal and efforts to bring upwardly mobile residents back to U.S. city centers be balanced with the needs and aspirations of low-income residents, whether in apartments, houses, or shelters, who may be displaced?

Global cities are an amalgamation of the old and the new: Architectural contrasts are only one among many areas where tradition and modernity meet and sometimes conflict. ■

THE EMERGENCE OF GLOBAL CITIES

We live in the first age of decisive urban dominance. Today, more than half the world's population resides in cities, many of which are massive global centers such as London (population 8.6 million), New York (19.4 million), and Tokyo (36.7 million; Khanna, 2010). **Global cities** are *metropolitan areas that are highly interconnected with one another in their role as centers of global political and economic decision making, finance, and culture* (Sassen, 1991). Their economic role is defined as much by the large role they play in the global economy as by their influence in their immediate geographic region.

Saskia Sassen (1991) identifies four principal functions of global cities: First, they are "command posts" in the organization of the world economy. Second, they serve as key locations for businesses related to finance, accounting, marketing, design, and other highly specialized (and profitable) services that are replacing manufacturing as the leading economic sectors. Third, they are the most important sites of innovation and new product development. Finally, they serve as the principal markets for global businesses. Sassen (2000) adds that "whether at the global or regional level, these cities must inevitably engage each other in fulfilling their functions . . . There is no such entity as a single global city" (p. 4).

In global cities, multinational corporations and international bankers maintain their headquarters and oversee the operation of diverse production and management operations that are spread across the globe. Global cities are sites for the

creation and concentration of enormous economic wealth: By one recent estimate, just 100 cities account for 30% of the world's economy. It is notable that "New York City's economy alone is larger than 46 of sub-Saharan Africa's economies combined" (Khanna, 2010).

At the same time, cities have long been magnets for those who cannot make an adequate living elsewhere, whether in their home countries or in impoverished rural areas or small towns. Low-wage services, low-skill factory production, and sweatshops coexist with the most profitable activities of international businesses in global cities; we find dire poverty and spectacular wealth side by side. In Los Angeles, for example, hundreds of thousands of immigrants from Mexico and Central America work in the shadows of the downtown skyscrapers that house the world's largest banks and corporations. These immigrants labor as janitors, domestics, or workers in small clothing factories that sew apparel for global garment manufacturers (Milkman, 2006; A. Singer, 2012). Cities are places of intense contrasts and contradictions: The inequalities that permeate relationships and institutions and countries are on vivid display in the global cities of the world. The box *Global Issues* on page 433 highlights the particular problem of urbanization and HIV/AIDS.

WORLD URBANIZATION TODAY

Some of the most highly urbanized countries in the world today are those that only a century ago were almost entirely rural. As recently as 1950, only 18% of the inhabitants of developing

Global Governance

. . . .

Global cities: Metropolitan areas that are highly interconnected with one another in their role as centers of global, political, and economic decision making.

URBANIZATION AND THE SPREAD OF HIV/AIDS: THE CASE OF SOUTH AFRICA

One of the critical problems faced by many large cities in developed and developing countries is the spread of HIV/AIDS, primarily through sexual contact and intravenous drug use. Consider urban South Africa, which has experienced rapid urbanization since the end of the racist apartheid regime in 1994. With the lifting of apartheid-era regulations that kept many Black South Africans out of White-dominated cities, urban populations have expanded dramatically. High levels of migration to cities are among a host of sociological factors intertwined with the spread of HIV/AIDS, the prevalence of which has been estimated to be as high as 26% in the city of Johannesburg (Van Donk, 2002).

Urban areas are vulnerable to HIV/AIDS epidemics for a number of reasons. First, the promise of jobs draws migrant laborers from impoverished small towns and rural areas, many of them young males who are unmarried or have left families behind. Some are drawn to the urban sex markets that arise to cater to unattached men, where sexually transmitted infections are rampant and easily passed from person to person. No less significantly, men returning to their villages from cities may carry with them infections they pass to their wives, who do not have the power to ask their men to use prophylactics. Other newcomers to the city, unable to secure legal work, may be drawn into criminal activities such as drugs or prostitution, which also foster an environment conducive to the spread of disease (Van Donk, 2002).

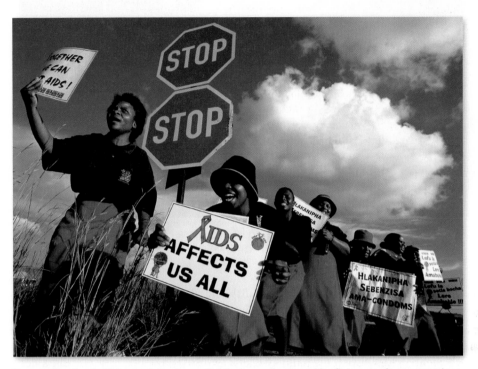

Women in a South African mining town distribute condoms and leaflets on safe sex practices. Some of the women are sex workers, but concern about safe sex is widespread, as HIV/AIDS is a serious threat in mining communities where many male workers are migrants who leave their families for long periods of time and may seek out the services of sex workers. ∎

The Joint United Nations Programme on HIV/AIDS estimates that 5.6 million people in South Africa are infected with HIV/AIDS (UNAIDS, 2011). Many reside in South Africa's cities. Among South Africans between 15 and 49 years of age—who are in both their productive and their reproductive years—there was a prevalence rate of HIV/AIDS of 17.8% in 2009 (Haub & Kaneda, 2011). Increasing levels of ill health and death in this demographic group have the potential to seriously compromise the economic activity and prosperity of the country and its communities and families.

In 2009, South Africa's government announced a new, more vigorous campaign to combat HIV/AIDS and increase access to treatment (Sidibe, 2009). According to South Africa's most recent progress report to the United Nations (Republic of South Africa, 2012), its national HIV counseling and testing program has reached 13 million people, the prevalence of HIV has stabilized, and mortality rates are declining, particularly among women.

THINK IT THROUGH

∎ *How might sociologists go about studying the relationship between rapid urbanization and the spread of disease? How would you measure these variables? How would you design research questions to test whether correlation equals causation?*

Satellite photos from the National Aeronautics and Space Administration show that arctic sea ice cover dropped to a record low on September 16, 2012. NASA scientists say the melt has taken place more rapidly than they predicted. ■

Cities are dynamic places and the centerpiece of modern life in many countries, sites of innovation, creativity, education, and positive social change. They are also often wasteful producers of garbage, pollution, and greenhouse gases. In the next section, we explore the environmental challenges that cities and modern society present for our planet.

THE LOCAL AND GLOBAL ENVIRONMENT

The year 2012 went down as the hottest on record. Across the globe, a spectrum of devastating weather events took place. The U.S. government's National Oceanic and Atmospheric Administration (NOAA) National Climatic Data Center recorded the following:

countries lived in urban areas. In 2012, 51% did. For the first time in history, there are more people living in urban areas than in rural areas throughout the world (Haub & Kaneda, 2012). Today, over 30% of the world's poor inhabit cities—some in the developed countries, most in developing countries. A 2012 UNICEF report identifies urban poverty as a critical and growing problem, particularly for children, noting that, "in fact, hundreds of millions of children today live in urban slums, many without access to basic services. They are vulnerable to dangers ranging from violence and exploitation to the injuries, illnesses and death that result from living in crowded settlements atop hazardous rubbish dumps or alongside railroad tracks" (p. v).

According to the United Nations, as of 2011 there were 456 cities worldwide with 1 million inhabitants or more. Globally, there were 23 **megacities**, usually defined as *cities with a total population of 10 million or more*. This number is projected to increase to 37 megacities by 2025. About 1 in 20 people worldwide currently reside in a megacity, and projections indicate that about 1 in 13 people will reside in a city of more than 10 million people by 2025 (United Nations, 2011). Khanna (2010) suggests that "we need to get used to the idea of nearly 100 million people clustered around Mumbai [India] or Shanghai [China]. Across India, more than 275 million people are projected to move into the country's teeming cities over the next two decades, a population nearly equivalent to that of the United States" (p. 123). By 2025, it is estimated that China will be home to fully 15 cities with an average of 25 million inhabitants.

- In late October 2012, Hurricane Sandy became the largest Atlantic hurricane ever recorded, causing $20 billion worth of damage. The hurricane traveled through the Caribbean, leaving wreckage in Jamaica, Haiti, the Dominican Republic, Puerto Rico, and Cuba before carving a destructive path up the East Coast of the United States. Twenty-four states were affected with the worst damage occurring in New York and New Jersey, where heavy winds and flooding left millions without power. At least 185 people were killed by the storm.
- The period of January–August 2012 was the warmest eight months on record. Thirty-three states were record warm in addition to 12 states that were top-10 warm. The contiguous U.S. temperature average for January–August was 58.7°F, a startling 4.0°F above average.
- A powerful and destructive derecho windstorm, with winds as high as 60–80 miles per hour, blew through the Midwest toward the Atlantic Ocean, hitting the Washington, DC, area in late June 2012. Hundreds of trees were downed, and millions were left without power across the District of Columbia, Maryland, and Virginia.
- The Midwestern farmland states that produce much of our nation's food crops have been experiencing the worst drought in the past 56 years. These dry, arid conditions led to the destruction of 3.6 million acres by wildfires in August 2012 alone.
- Thaws have brought ice levels in the Arctic to record lows. As average global temperatures rise, arctic ice has melted with increasing rapidity. Warming has reduced the thickness of the ice, which also fosters faster melting.

Poor Nations'
Rising Population

Megacities

Megacity: A metropolitan area or city with a total population of 10 million people or more.

The events of 2012 follow on the heels of other recent occurrences of extreme weather, including the U.S. tornado outbreak of 2011; the 2009 heat waves in Argentina; numerous tropical storms and cyclones throughout South Asia in 2008; the 2005 Hurricanes Katrina and Rita, which devastated the Gulf Coast; and the 2004 Indian Ocean tsunami that laid waste to parts of Thailand, Burma, Bangladesh, and Southern India.

What is behind the increase in extreme weather events across the globe? Many scientists suspect it is global warming, also referred to as climate change since not all its effects are manifested in the form of rising temperatures. Global warming is widely understood to occur because so-called greenhouse gases, by-products of industrialization such as carbon dioxide (CO_2) and methane gas, become trapped in the earth's atmosphere and hold heat at the surface. While part of this process is naturally occurring and is related to a climate cycle that keeps the earth at a habitable temperature, the industrial era has

Scientists predict that extreme weather will increasingly become the norm. Drought, wildfires, hurricanes, floods, and tornadoes are among the threats to populations, homes, and businesses. A chain of tornadoes hit Kentucky in March 2012, damaging many homes. ■

seen a growing concentration of greenhouse gases in the atmosphere. The resulting "greenhouse effect" is believed to be causing an unprecedented rise in air temperatures, melting the world's ice caps and glaciers and raising ocean temperatures and sea levels. Warm air also retains more water vapor than cold air, a condition that scientists warn will be linked to greater downpours and a higher probability of floods (McKibben, 2011).

The escalation of climate change and the growing reach of its effects are on the research agenda of climate scientists, biologists, and other physical scientists. Sociologists have also taken an interest. Among their concerns is the way in which this phenomenon, which most climate scientists accept as a credible threat to our planet and its inhabitants, has been framed in the mainstream social and political discourse as a societal problem. Some sociologists have argued that public attention to problems such as climate change depends in part on the presence of a "social scare" (Ungar, 1992)—that is, an event (such as extreme weather) that draws attention to a phenomenon by allowing it to "piggyback on dramatic real-world events" (Ungar, 1992, p. 483).

Recent extreme weather events, however, do not seem to have had an appreciable effect on public concern. Interestingly, while there has been an increase in the availability of information on the science and manifestations of climate change, particularly in the age of the Internet, the proportion of the U.S. population

expressing concern about the issue has remained fairly steady over the last two decades, and even dropped in recent years. In 2012, a Gallup survey found that 42% of respondents indicated they felt "the seriousness of global warming" was "generally exaggerated," about one third believed it to be "generally correct," and about a quarter suggested that it was "generally underestimated" (Saad, 2012).

Why is there little apparent sense of urgency or mobilization of action in the face of an environmental threat such as climate change? There is a spectrum of possible explanations. For example, research suggests that the "creeping nature" of climate change—that is, the fact that effects are not constantly apparent and are perceived to be far in the future—leads some people to discount it as a potential problem (Moser & Dilling, 2004). Some sociologists also point to the **treadmill of production,** *the constant and aggressive growth needed to sustain the modern economy* (Schnaiberg & Gould, 1994). On the political and economic agenda this growth takes precedence over environmental concerns. Governments—as well as companies that drill for oil, mine coal, manufacture products, or engage in other energy-intensive endeavors—are concerned about maintaining profitability in the private sector, which may lead them to ignore, minimize, or even deny the problem.

Are these two imperatives—the need for a vigorous economy and the need for a clean and sustainable environment—irreconcilable? How can we build an economy that can both grow and be green?

Treadmill of production: The constant and aggressive growth needed to sustain the modern economy.

POPULATION GROWTH, MODERNIZATION, AND THE ENVIRONMENT

Industrialization and urbanization, combined with rapid population growth, have taken a toll on the global environment and its resources. Threats to the environment exist in both underdevelopment and over-development. On the one hand, the world's population, surpassing 7 billion people, needs basic resources: water, food, shelter, and energy. These needs tax the earth by impinging upon the natural habitats of unique animal and plant species to make room for human habitation. More importantly, perhaps, the rise of the **global consumer class**—*those who actively use technology, purchase consumer goods, and embrace the culture of consumption*—has meant that more individuals are using more resources per person than ever before.

In Wuhan City in China, young people walk with masks to protect their lungs from a thick haze that settled on the city in June of 2012. Authorities attributed the hazardous air to straw burning, a practice undertaken by some farmers to dispose of surplus crops in the fields. Industrial and automobile pollution are also frequent threats to air quality in Chinese towns and cities—and significant contributors to greenhouse gases. ■

By some estimates, a quarter of the global population are members of the global consumer class. A large percentage of this class lives in developed countries; according to the Worldwatch Institute, the United States and Canada, home to just over 5% of the world's population, account for about 31% of private consumption expenditures, and Western Europe, with around 6% of the globe's people, accounts for over 28% of expenditures. However, the consumer class is expanding. More than half its members now live in areas of advancing prosperity in the developing world (Worldwatch Institute, 2004). The future consumer markets of the world are in developing countries including India and China rather than developed countries, which are characterized by sagging population growth and already high consumption rates.

In many respects, urbanization and industrialization are important achievements in the developing world. More people have the opportunity to meet their needs and realize their dreams, leaving behind the travails of deprivation; though the gulf between rich and poor remains wide, prosperity has advanced around the globe. Development's darker underbelly, however, becomes visible when we look at the problems presented by the consumer class and its growing ranks. Arguably, among the most critical problems of development is overconsumption.

Overconsumption may be understood as a recklessly wasteful use of resources, from fuel to food and consumer goods.

Overconsumption is a symptom of development. Among its health consequences are obesity, or having a body mass index (BMI) of 30 or higher, and being overweight, having a BMI between 25 and 29.9 (a healthy BMI is between 18.5 and 24.9, according to the Centers for Disease Control and Prevention). Over two thirds of U.S. adults (78 million) are overweight or obese, conditions that can lead to heart disease and other dangerous maladies (Ogden, Carroll, Kit, & Flegal, 2012). Globally more than 1 billion people are overweight, and at least 300 million of these are obese. While these problems used to be problems of Western prosperity, more people in developing countries are joining the ranks of the overweight and obese as they move from more traditional diets to "modern" foods (Popkin, Adair, & Ng, 2012). High-fat and high-sugar foods are widely consumed: These foods are aggressively advertised, cheap, and popular, especially among young people.

Rising consumption also threatens the environment, as more people buy, use, and toss away ever more "stuff." The global fleet of passenger cars is over 531 million and growing; in the United States, there are more cars than licensed drivers. Many modern consumers also value size as a sign of material success: The size of SUVs has expanded more rapidly than their fuel efficiency, and new U.S. houses were nearly 38% bigger in 2002 than in 1975, though households on average were smaller (Worldwatch Institute, 2004, 2010). As a comparison, at 2,265 square feet, the average U.S. home today is twice as big as the average European

Cities Are Growing

Global consumer class: Those who actively use technology, purchase consumer goods, and embrace the culture of consumption.

DIGITAL SOCIETY

YOUR COMPUTER AND THE ENVIRONMENT

One of the fastest-growing industries on the planet is the manufacture of electronics, including personal computers and mobile phones. On the one hand, the development is positive. More people than ever before can connect with each other and gain access to the educational, professional, and recreational power of a personal computer. On the other hand, used computers, mobile phones, and other electronics are a growing toxic-waste problem in all countries. A United Nations report suggests that the volume of "e-waste" generated by computers alone could rise by 200% to 400% of 2007 levels in China and South Africa over the coming decade. In India, the report predicts an increase of up to 500% in computer waste (United Nations Environment Programme, 2009).

Computers and mobile devices have demonstrable detrimental environmental and health effects, particularly at the start and end of their useful lives. A recent Bloomberg *Businessweek* article (Simpson, 2012) documented the disturbing origin of tin, which is used in every modern smartphone and tablet. About one third of all tin used in these consumer devices originates in Bangka, an island that is part of Indonesia. About half the mined tin is turned into solder for the electronics industry. The miners—who number between 15,000 and 50,000— work in difficult and dangerous conditions, and "if they're lucky, the members of a crew find enough 'tin sand' to each earn about $5 a day" (Simpson, 2012, p. 52). Tin mines, particularly those dug deep to retrieve the valuable mineral, are vulnerable to collapse and mudslides, among

Nearly all work in Indonesia's tin mines is done by hand with pickaxes and hoes. Global demand by electronics manufacturers has pushed tin mining into the seabed, disrupting the fishing industry which has been a traditional economic staple. One journalist found tin pits dug around Bangka airport's only runway (Simpson, 2012). ■

other hazards. Desperate for money, residents of the island endanger their safety and degrade the environment with deep pits dug legally and illegally to get to tin that can be sold.

At the other end of their productive lives, electronics once again present a serious hazard to human health and the environment. According to some estimates, for every new computer that enters the marketplace each year, another one is discarded into the solid-waste stream, carrying toxic ingredients such as lead, phosphor, barium, and cadmium with it (Worldwatch Institute, 2004). Although making up only 1% to 2% of total waste in the United States, e-waste accounts for 70% of toxic waste (Environmental Protection Agency, 2011). Advanced economies such as the United States use many of the electronics produced around the world and may feel some effects of their disposal. Many

toxic effects, however, are exported abroad. Despite a global ban on trade in hazardous waste, between 50% and 80% of "recycled" computers are believed to end their lives in developing countries such as India, Pakistan, and China, where workers disassembling the machines are exposed to chemicals that can cause organ, nervous system, and brain damage (United Nations Environment Programme, 2009; Worldwatch Institute, 2004).

THINK IT THROUGH

■ *How should we as consumers of computers and other electronic technology respond to the environmental and health problems associated with the production and disposal of that technology? Whose problem is it, and who should pay for the safe disposal of e-waste?*

Massive ships used by developed countries for the transportation of goods and oil end their useful lives on the shores of developing states such as India and Pakistan. Workers at shipbreaking yards deconstruct the giant and complex vessels, a process that releases dangerous toxins into the environment and into their bodies. ■

or Japanese dwelling and 26 times bigger than the typical living space in Africa (Worldwatch Institute, 2010).

As more people across the globe strive, understandably, for prosperity and modernity, it may be wise for us to ask: Can such consumption be sustained? Those who live in the prosperous countries might also ask: Is it hypocritical to raise concerns about the global destruction wrought by overconsumption when the West has been the primary consumer of the world's resources for the past century? (See the *Digital Society* box on page 437 for more on this.) To give you the opportunity to consider these important questions, we discuss below the environmental impacts of population growth in developing states and of consumption growth in developed states and newly prosperous areas.

UNDERDEVELOPMENT AND OVERDEVELOPMENT IN THE MODERN WORLD

Environmental problems that appear in one part of the globe often result from actions taken elsewhere and may have far-reaching effects for all of the planet's inhabitants. They are indeed global. However, many immediate environmental effects are local.

The most degraded local environments tend to be those inhabited by the poorest people. Air pollution is far worse in Bangkok, Mexico City, and Beijing than in the most polluted U.S. cities

Impact on Resources

Regional Planning

such as Los Angeles. China's rapid development has brought new prosperity to many Chinese, but the rising number of factories, power stations, and cars has also brought serious pollution. A 2007 World Health Organization (WHO) study suggests that over 650,000 people in China die each year from causes associated with air pollution; another 95,000 are killed by polluted drinking water (Platt, 2007).

Disease also runs rampant in the large cities of India, where the infrastructure, including sewage systems that carry away waste and ensure the flow of potable water, cannot meet the needs of growing populations. In some coastal areas of India, toxic pollution streams flow from shipbreaking yards, where laborers take apart ships no longer fit to sail the seas. Local environmental problems have also arisen from deforestation in the tropical rainforests of Central America and the destruction of mangrove ponds and wetlands in Asia, as these areas are transformed into agricultural production sites for growing numbers of farmers.

Population pressures in developing countries are important contributors to these problems. However, the world's developed states are also implicated. Consider, for instance, deforestation and wetlands destruction. Some of the rainforest land in the Amazon has been cleared for beef cattle, to be consumed not locally, but in the West. Similarly, the wetlands of some coastal areas of Asia are being transformed into shrimp farms to grow the delicacy enjoyed in wealthy countries. The ships in India's coastal shipbreaking yards are largely the corpses of Western fleets. The consequences of the developed world's consumption

WHAT'S ON THE MENU?

Among the favorite dinner treats of U.S. diners are dishes made with shrimp. Italian restaurants serve shrimp scampi; Chinese and Thai restaurants offer a wide variety of spicy, saucy shrimp dishes; and shrimp cocktail is a popular appetizer. Over 1 billion pounds of shrimp are consumed in the United States each year, 90% of which are imported from overseas (Natural Resources Defense Council, 2011). Where exactly does all that shrimp come from?

A great deal comes from shrimp farms in developing countries. Some governments and wealthy donor nations have encouraged shrimp farming, arguing that it contributes to economic development in poor states and promoting a so-called blue revolution to increase the production of seafood without depleting natural marine stocks.

Community activists, farmers, and environmentalists, however, have questioned the benefits of shrimp farms (Gatsiounis, 2008; Trent, Williams, Thornton, & Shanahan, 2004; Worldwatch Institute, 2004). From a conflict perspective, we might ask who benefits, and who loses, from the expansion of shrimp farming in developing states,

Major beneficiaries include consumers in the United States, Europe, and Japan, who purchase and eat most of the shrimp produced. Thailand, for instance, exports up to 90% of its farmed shrimp (The Fish Site, 2009). Other beneficiaries are the governments of exporting countries, since shrimp exports can bring in

If people know that a particular food is sourced unsustainably, or even unethically, will that alter their choice to purchase the product? What would you predict, and why? ■

substantial revenue, and the private owners of shrimp farms, who are often foreign nationals.

According to some researchers and activists, losers in the blue revolution of shrimp farming are local communities and the marine environment. Common problems include the loss of agricultural land, which is flooded with saline water to create shrimp ponds, and fewer crabs and fish available for consumption and exchange in the local economy (Gatsiounis, 2008; Trent et al., 2004). The salinization process can also pollute supplies of drinking and washing water. In Thailand, "as local fishermen have pulled back from shrimp farming, large-scale conglomerates have filled the void. Behind the small concrete houses . . . backhoes are digging out shrimp ponds

as far as the eye can see. Villagers say there will be 100 ponds in total, owned by industrial conglomerates based in Bangkok, and operated mainly by imported labor" (Gatsiounis, 2008). Shrimp peelers working in Thai factories also absorb the costs, laboring for exploitative wages and under the threat of violence or job loss for taking time off. Many are underage or migrant workers forced into debt slavery to pay off loans to smugglers (Motlagh, 2012).

THINK IT THROUGH

■ *Where did the shrimp in your supermarket or favorite restaurant originate? Should you care? Should other consumers of shrimp care? How can we balance our culinary desires with social justice?*

are, indeed, felt in the furthest corners of the developing world, highlighting the fact that we cannot understand the threat to the earth exclusively in terms of population explosion. We ought also to recognize it as the product of choices made by a small wealthy elite of countries and consumers (Eglitis, 2010).

Industrialization in both the developed and developing worlds is also a critical aspect of the environmental equation. On the one hand, some developing countries such as China are aggressively pursuing industrialization and multisector economic growth. Because of its enormous size and rapid move toward industrialization, China is fast becoming the world's major contributor to greenhouse gases. Coal, a highly polluting source of energy, provides the country with three quarters of its energy, creating so much pollution in some urban areas that residents must wear surgical masks for protection. In the southern and eastern part of the country, where urbanization and industrialization are proceeding at historically unprecedented rates, the environmental damage has been considerable. On the other hand, just as it did in the West, industrialization is also bringing greater prosperity and prospects to many Chinese. This raises the question of whether we must choose between a "good life" and a "good earth." What would it mean to achieve a balance between the needs and desires of people around the world and the needs of the planet? The *Private Lives, Public Issues* box on page 439 looks at the problem of the desires of humans and needs of the planet through the prism of what we choose to eat.

Global Biodiversity

Rising Population
Bad for Environment

WHY STUDY POPULATION AND ENVIRONMENT FROM A SOCIOLOGICAL PERSPECTIVE?

We opened this chapter by describing the effects of son preference in China, India, and South Korea. The global effect of an individual choice is not apparent to us, but populations are the products of millions or billions of such choices, some made by families, some made by states. Demographics are both statistics and lived realities. Whether we live in fast-growth states whose resources may be increasingly taxed by rapidly rising populations, or in no-growth states that may experience economic troubles as workers age without being replaced, our lives will be affected in some way by demographic forces.

Similarly, we make individual choices about consumption and disposal, a topic we looked at in our *Digital Society* box in this chapter. When we purchase a new car or truck, order a meal in a restaurant, toss out bags of old clothes at spring cleaning, or decide to replace an outdated computer, we are part of a mass of other global consumers making similar choices, and our choices—like theirs—affect the economies and environments of countries around the world. Just as there is no "single global city" (in Saskia Sassen's words), there are no single choices about fertility or consumption or disposal that do not cumulatively have a global effect. By understanding the social forces that affect personal choices, as well as the way personal choices affect phenomena such as population growth or decline, rising urban prosperity and poverty, and environmental health or degradation, we become better equipped to recognize and confront some of the paramount global challenges of this century.

WHAT CAN I DO WITH A SOCIOLOGY DEGREE?

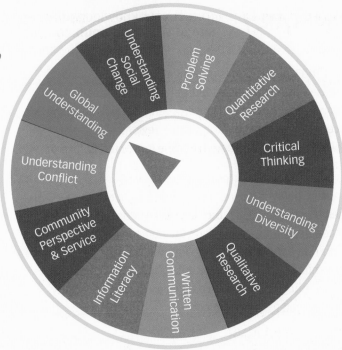

SKILLS AND CAREERS: THE GLOBAL PERSPECTIVE

The study of sociology helps students develop a broad understanding of the social world, which includes relationships between cultures and countries over time and space, and the ability to see the world from a variety of perspectives. A *global perspective* encompasses knowledge and skills. A global perspective evolves through study and experiences that lead to a strong understanding and appreciation of the significance and effects of global cultural, economic, political, and social connections on individuals, communities, and countries. It also encompasses the development of skills to work effectively in intercultural environments.

In Chapter 17, we looked at issues related to population trends, urbanization, and the environment. For example, we examined some urgent problems of the global environment. You know that nearly 200 diverse countries with sometimes competing and even conflicting domestic agendas share a single planet. Borders do not necessarily limit the effects of economic, political, or ecological decisions made by these states. Understanding different cultures, recognizing a diverse spectrum of legitimate political and economic interests, and having the ability to see issues from multiple perspectives are key to global efforts to deal cooperatively with environmental threats to the planet. As a sociology student, you will have the opportunity to develop the kind of thoughtful global perspective that will enable to you make the critical connection between decisions about, for instance, economic consumption or production, which is made at the individual or community or country level, and effects that are experienced globally.

Having a global perspective is of tremendous value in today's globalized labor market and in occupations that demand proficiency in intercultural relationships and communication. *Occupational fields* such as government service, international business, health and medicine, travel and tourism, international development, and diplomacy are just a few of the areas where a global perspective is needed. *Job titles* in these sectors include foreign service officer, intelligence analyst, health worker, global social entrepreneur, cross culture specialist, translator, and human rights organizer. Below you will find a partial list of global industries, companies, and organizations that you can research to learn about opportunities in these exciting areas of employment:

- **Global culture industries:** music, film, and sports, including MTV, Disney, and the NBA
- **Global environment:** World Wildlife Fund, Greenpeace, and Sierra Club
- **Global health:** World Health Organization (WHO) and Centers for Disease Control and Prevention (CDC)

- **Global marketing agencies:** BBDO, J. Walter Thompson, and Leo Burnett
- **Human justice organizations:** Amnesty International and Human Rights Watch
- **International governing agencies:** United Nations, World Bank, and International Monetary Fund
- **International service agencies:** Red Cross, CARE, UNICEF, and Peace Corps
- **International development agencies:** USAID and relief funds
- **International businesses:** Sony, Microsoft, Apple, and GlaxoSmithKline
- **Mass communication:** CNN, ESPN, and foreign correspondence
- **Travel and tourism:** travel agencies, global tours, and cruise lines
- **U.S. government offices and agencies:** Foreign Service and Department of State

THINK ABOUT CAREERS

■ *How is intercultural knowledge developed through sociological study? How can you expand your global perspective outside the classroom? Why is a global perspective of particular importance in the modern world?*

■ *How might a global perspective be of value in some of the career fields of interest to you? Might changes taking place in these fields as a result of globalization or other labor market trends increase the importance of the global perspective?*

▶ *Access additional web links on the student study site to learn more.*

SUMMARY

To test your knowledge further, find additional study material on the Student Study Site at www.sagepub.com/chamblissintro

- The world's population is growing at a rapid rate, having increased as much since 1950 as it did in the preceding 4 million years. Growth is highly uneven, with most taking place in developing countries. Other regions will lose population, including Eastern Europe (projected to face a 14% decline).

- Annual population growth or decline in a country is the result of four factors: (1) the number of people born in the country during the year; (2) the number who die; (3) the number who immigrate into the country; and (4) the number who emigrate out. In the language of demographers, population changes are based on **fertility**, mortality, and net **migration**.

- The theory of the demographic transition proposes that many societies go through roughly the same stages of population growth: low growth resulting from high fertility and equally high mortality, a transitional stage of explosive growth resulting from high fertility and low mortality, and a final stage of slow or no growth resulting from low fertility and low mortality.

- Advanced industrial states may be undergoing a second demographic transition, seen as changes in family patterns that affect population. For instance, in the world's industrialized states divorce has increased, cohabitation has increased, marriage has declined, fertility has fallen, and nonmarital births as a proportion of all births have increased.

- Thomas Malthus developed the theory of **exponential population growth**: the belief that, like compound interest, a constant rate of population growth produces a population that grows by an increasing amount with each passing year. Malthus claimed that while population grows exponentially, the food supply does not; the earth's resources are finite. Others, such as economist Julian Simon, suggest that population growth increases humanity's potential for uncovering talent and innovation.

- Karl Marx was critical of Malthus and felt the central problem was not a mismatch between population size and resource availability, but rather inequitable distribution of resources between the wealthy and the disadvantaged.

- Sociologist Louis Wirth (1938) saw the city as a large, densely populated, and permanent settlement that brought together heterogeneous populations. While cities of the past served primarily as centers of trade, in the 18th century industrial cities emerged as centers of manufacturing. By the 19th century industrialization was advancing hand in hand with **urbanization**.

- Some of the most highly urbanized countries in the world today are those that only a century ago were almost entirely rural. As recently as 1950, only 18% of the inhabitants of developing countries lived in urban areas. In 2010, fully 44% did. By 2015, the proportion of the world's people living in **cities** across the world will approach 50%.

- With the emergence of postindustrial society, **global cities** have appeared. These metropolitan areas are highly interconnected with one another and serve as centers of global political and economic decision making, finance, and culture. Examples include New York, London, Tokyo, Hong Kong, Los Angeles, Mexico City, and Singapore.

- The combination of rapid population growth and modernization, in the form of industrialization and urbanization, takes a toll on the global environment and its resources. Both under- and overdevelopment threaten the environment.

- The study of **demography** and population growth helps us gain a fuller understanding of the ways that micro-level events, such as childbearing decisions in a family, are linked to macro-level issues such as population growth or decline, threats of mortality, and challenges to the sustainability of resources and development.

KEY TERMS

Study terms on the go with the smartphone-friendly key term flashcards, available at www.sagepub.com/chamblissintro

DISCUSSION QUESTIONS

1. What key factors have contributed to the decline of population growth in many modern countries? What are the benefits and consequences of fertility declines?

2. As you saw in the chapter, urbanization continues to increase across the globe. What draws populations to cities? What sociological indicators point to this trend continuing?

3. Are economic growth and environmental protection irreconcilable values? Consider what you have read both in earlier chapters about economic growth and employment and in this chapter about environmental challenges such as climate change, and respond thoughtfully to the question.

DISCOVER STATE STATS

Log-in to the eBook and click on the title to the left for access to State Stats in order to complete the exercise.

Go to the Energy and Environment database and find "gasoline used." Study the available years to determine the national gas consumption per year in this period, then go to the Population database and locate the population of the United States over this period. Does gasoline consumption nationally rise with population? Or does it fall as population rises? Find the answer, and offer a hypothesis to explain your finding.

STUDENT STUDY SITE

Visit the Student Study Site at **www.sagepub.com/chamblissintro** to access additional study tools, including eFlashcards, web quizzes, video resources, web resources, audio resources, links to SAGE journal, handbook, and research articles, and much more!

18

SOCIAL CHANGE AND SOCIAL MOVEMENTS

COUNT ME IN!

WHAT DO YOU THINK?

1. What sociological factors may bring about revolutionary changes in societies?
2. What are the sociological functions of a flash mob?
3. Do people behave differently in crowds than they would individually or in a small group? What explains crowd behavior?

SOC **VIEW**

Get a closer look
with the authors!

OPENING THE FLOODGATES

The events leading to the region-wide revolutionary movement known as the "Arab Spring" began in the most innocuous manner. A young street vendor named Mohamed Bouazizi sat near his stall, which was piled high with a variety of fruits and vegetables, in the local market of the Tunisian city of Sidi Bouzid. Mohamed earned little and used most of it to support his family, including his widowed mother and sister.

Mohamed's work in the marketplace was routine except for regular interruptions by members of the local police force, who continually discovered new reasons to fine him and confiscate his produce and his valuable weighing scales. Coupled with the exorbitant fines he was made to pay, the extortion of his goods left him with a deep sense of grievance. On December 17, 2010, the police came yet another time to take away Mohamed's weighing scales in order to force a bribe out of him. Mohamed could do little—and he might have given in, as he had in the past. But on this occasion he did not passively acquiesce. Instead, outraged and deeply humiliated, he went to the local municipal building in Sidi Bouzid to speak with an official about the harassment he was experiencing. Rather than address Mohamed's complaints, however, the officials simply turned him away.

Determined not to retreat, Mohamed chose to make a dramatic stand. Outside the municipal building, he seized upon a container of flammable liquid and began dousing himself with it. Then, in a final act of defiance, he lit a match and set himself ablaze. Mohamed's act of desperate protest did not fade quietly into the annals of history. With the help of contemporary social media, his immolation was a watershed moment that mobilized people to take action against political oppression in their countries. It became the spark that ignited a conflagration of protest movements and civil uprisings across North Africa and the Middle East. These changes, while uneven and with a still uncertain future, were revolutionary in the changes they wrought.

Mohamed's individual act was just one of many contributing factors that developed into the Arab Spring. It is useful to view Mohamed's experience and act of protest through a sociological lens, and connect the structural conditions of Tunisia to his personal act of setting himself ablaze. It was

Media and Social Movements

not only this one person's initiative that gave birth to the Arab Spring, but rather the widespread political, economic, and cultural grievances that had reached a tipping point in several Arab countries. Collectively referred to as the "Arab Spring," the protest movements occurring across the Middle East and North Africa have resulted in a monumental reorganization of the power structures across both regions. Political leaders in Egypt, Libya, Yemen, and Tunisia have abdicated power or been killed by revolutionary forces. Thousands of people continue to engage in protest actions. Even where new regimes have come to power, aftershocks of change continue to shake the region, as actors in the drama of transformation—government leaders, militaries, modernizers, and Islamic fundamentalists, among others— vie for places of power and prominence in shaping future regimes and societies.

How do sociologists understand events such as those of the Arab Spring? To answer this question, we must understand the ways in which sociological theories approach social change, and we must examine concepts sociologists use to study social movements in history and the contemporary world. ∎

We begin this chapter with an overview of the foundations of sociological theorizing on social change. We continue with an examination of key sources of social change, focusing in particular on collective behavior and resources from which protesters such as those described above draw. Next we provide an overview of forms that social movements take, and we conclude with some reflections on the nature of social change going forward in a rapidly changing and globalized world.

SOCIOLOGICAL PERSPECTIVES ON SOCIAL CHANGE

The concept of social change is all-encompassing. It refers to small group changes, such as when a socially conservative family agrees to permit a 20-year-old daughter to bring her boyfriend home from college to spend the night with her. Social change also incorporates key processes of globalization such as the outsourcing of jobs to low-wage countries and social movements that seek to address climate change.

Notably, when sociologists speak of *social change*, they are generally referring to changes that occur throughout the

. . . .

Differentiation: The development of increasing societal complexity through the creation of specialized social roles and institutions.

social structure of an entire society. *Societies* are understood sociologically as entities comprising those people who share a common culture and common institutions. Social change may refer to changes within small, relatively isolated communities such as those of the Amish or the small, culturally homogenous tribes that dot the Amazon basin; changes across large-scale modern societies such as the United States, Japan, or Germany; or changes common to a number of similar societies, such as economically advanced states of the West or the Arab countries of North Africa and the Middle East.

Three key types of social change theories in sociology are functionalist theories, conflict theories, and cyclical theories. Sociological perspectives on social change begin with particular assumptions about both the social world and basic processes of change. Below we briefly consider each theoretical perspective and discuss its utility in understanding the nature of social change in the world today.

THE FUNCTIONALIST PERSPECTIVE ON SOCIAL CHANGE

Functionalist theories of social change assume that, as societies develop, they become ever more complex and interdependent. Herbert Spencer (1892) argued that what distinguishes modern societies is differentiation—that is, *the development of increasing societal complexity through the creation of specialized social roles and institutions.* Spencer was referring to what Émile Durkheim conceptualized as the division of labor, which occurs when people in a society are divided into interdependent occupational and task categories (and, by extension, class categories). Think of medieval England when craftsmen working at home made tools and shoes that they exchanged for food or clothing, using a broad range of skills to act relatively independently of one another. Compare this to modern society, where factory workers each produce parts of an automobile, managers sell completed cars to dealerships, and salespeople sell them to customers. Now people master a narrow range of tasks within a large number of highly specialized (differentiated) institutional roles and thus are highly interdependent. (Note the similarity here to Durkheim's notion that societies evolve over time from *mechanical* to *organic solidarity*—the former being characteristic of traditional, homogenous societies, while the latter is characteristic of diverse, modern societies.)

The earliest functionalist theories of social change were *evolutionary theories,* which assumed that all societies began as "simple" or "primitive" and eventually developed into more "complicated" and "civilized" forms along a single, unidirectional evolutionary path (L. Morgan, 1877/1964). During the 20th century, however, this notion of unilinear development became increasingly shaky,

Voice of Tunisian Revolution

Arab Spring

Social Change

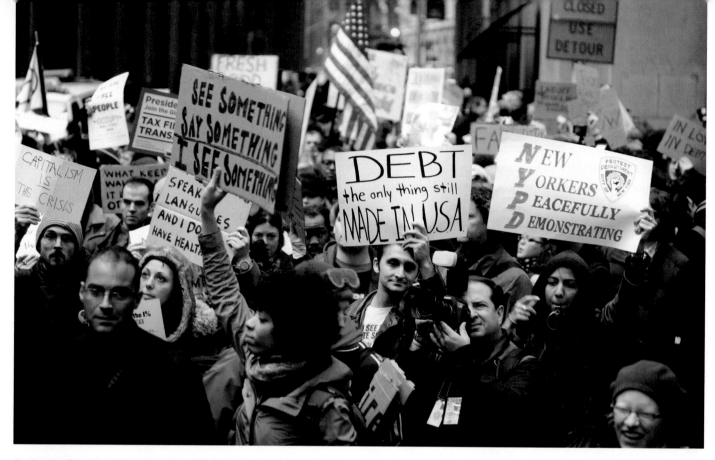

On September 17, 2011, protesters filled the streets around Wall Street in New York City. Many carried signs protesting growing economic inequality in the United States. Occupy Wall Street demonstrators also spoke out for greater environmental protection, union power, campaign finance reform, an end to the war in Iraq, and myriad other social issues. ∎

as anthropologists came to believe that societies evolve in many different ways. More recent evolutionary theories (sometimes termed *multilinear*) argue that multiple paths to social change exist, depending on the particular circumstances of the society (J. Moore, 2004; Sahlins & Service, 1960). In their interplay, technology, environment, population size, and social organization all play a role in determining the path.

Some evolutionary theorists viewed societies as eventually reaching an equilibrium state in which no further change would occur unless an external force set it in motion. For example, Durkheim believed that "primitive," or less developed societies, were basically unchanging unless population growth resulted in such an increase in social relationships that organic solidarity replaced mechanical solidarity. Talcott Parsons (1964) claimed societies were equilibrium systems that constantly sought to maintain balance, or the status quo, unless something external interfered, such as changes in technology or economic relationships with other societies. Parsons later came to argue, however, that societies do change by becoming more complicated systems that are better adapted to their external environments (Parsons, Shils, & Smelser, 2001).

Forward From
Occupy Wall Street

Although no one can deny that modern societies contain many more specialized roles and institutions than earlier ones, evolutionary theories also assume that social changes are progressive, that "modern" (European) societies are "more evolved" than earlier "primitive" ones. Such beliefs appealed to countries whose soldiers, missionaries, and merchants were conquering or colonizing much of the rest of the world, since they helped justify those imperialist actions as part of the "civilizing" mission of a more advanced people. Anthropologists and sociologists eventually rejected these ideas (Nolan & Lenski, 2009). Contemporary functionalists have emphasized Spencer's original notion of differentiation, but with a twist: Instead of viewing differentiation as always contributing to greater functional *interdependence* with society, theorists such as Jeffrey Alexander and Paul Colomy have argued that differentiation can also lead to greater *independence* of some parts of society. This is what Alexander and Colomy call "de-differentiation" (1990). Examples of de-differentiation are legion in the modern world. Consider the French Revolution (1789–1799), the goals of which included "liberty, equality, and brotherhood": At its ideological core was the pursuit of transforming society from one defined by stratified social class positions to one in which groups were "de-differentiated"—or put on equal footing in society. Similarly, the women's rights movements of the 1960s sought to tear down the stringent boundaries between tasks and rights defined legally and normatively as "masculine" or "feminine."

On a more micro level, consider the de-differentiation in the mainstream marital relationship. Traditionally, the man was the "head of the household" and often ruled his wife and children with an iron fist. Both the norm and the reality of marriage today are characterized by a de-differentiation of roles in which men take on domestic responsibilities, and, increasingly, the wife is a major income producer for the family.

Since different parts of society undergo the processes of differentiation and de-differentiation to varying degrees and at different times, considerable conflict between them may arise (J. Alexander, 1998; J. Alexander & Colomy, 1985, 1990; Colomy, 1986, 1990). It is, however, the conflict perspectives that assume conflict as the foundation for social change. We look at those ideas below.

THE CONFLICT PERSPECTIVE ON SOCIAL CHANGE

Conflict theories see conflict as an inherent result of divergent and perhaps irreconcilable social group interests and contradictory goals of social relationships. Even if a population or technology is in a state of stasis rather than change, conflict theorists see social change as inevitable, as people create ways of dealing with the conflicts and contradictions inherent in social life. Responding to the conflicts and contradictions can potentially bring a society to the brink of sharp and sometimes violent breaks with the past.

Unlike their functionalist peers in sociology, conflict theorists do not see social stability as the ultimate goal of social organization. They not only see social change as inevitable, but they also recognize it as a vital, transformative part of social life.

The founder of conflict sociology, Karl Marx, focused his research on the contradictions and conflicts built into capitalist societies, where the world is divided between owners of the means of production and workers, who own only their own labor power and must sell it under conditions not of their own making. In Marx's view, the revolutionary transformation of a society into a new type—from feudalism to capitalism, or from capitalism to socialism, for example—would occur when the consciousness of the people or the concentration of power in one social class was sufficient to create a social movement able to transform the political and economic institutions into new sets of social relationships. As we have seen throughout this text, Marx's conflict theory adhered to its own evolutionary view of social change, in which all societies would advance to the same final destination: a classless, stateless society. We have earlier noted a number of weaknesses in this theory. Of particular importance was Marx's tendency to

By today's standards, Quakers were a highly homogenous society, where consensus of opinion allowed for a type of social organization and structure that would likely not be possible in modern societies. ■

overemphasize economic conflict while underestimating cultural conflict and other noneconomic factors, such as gender, ethnicity, race, and nationalism, which have become increasingly important in the world today.

Later conflict theorists have also addressed key questions about processes of social change, such as how groups come to want and pursue social change. Italian Marxist Antonio Gramsci, for instance, highlighted the importance of ideas in maintaining order and oppression in society (Gramsci, 1971). He observed that the ruling class was often able to create *ideological hegemony,* a generally accepted view of what is of value and how people should relate to their economic status in society. Ideological hegemony may lead people to consent to their own domination by, for instance, socializing them to believe that the existing hierarchy of power is the best or only way to organize society. Consider as well that in the past, women were socialized by agents such as schools, families, and religious institutions to believe they should not have jobs outside the home or vote. The idea that women should not hold positions outside the home could be considered a *hegemonic idea* of this period.

Gramsci also spoke of *organic intellectuals*—those who emerge from oppressed groups to create counterhegemonies that challenge dominant (and dominating) ideas. In the mid-19th century,

Social Movements Theory

Global military and political dominance, sophisticated technology, specialization and division of labor, political institutions, and the social class structure are all strikingly similar between the United States and the fallen Roman Empire. Is there a cautionary tale here about the possible future of the United States? ■

women's suffrage activists including Lucretia Mott and Elizabeth Cady Stanton were organic intellectuals, challenging powerful beliefs that women should be excluded from politics. Over time and through the efforts of activists, the counterhegemonic idea that women should have a voice in politics became, in fact, the hegemonic, or dominant, belief in Western society.

In the 1950s, in response to the dominant functionalist paradigm, sociologist Ralf Dahrendorf published an influential article titled "Out of Utopia" (1958). Dahrendorf argued that functionalist theory, with its emphasis on how social institutions exist to maintain the status quo, overlooked critically important characteristics of society that lead to social conflict, such as the role of power, social change, and the unequal distribution of resources. The distribution of authority in society, said Dahrendorf, is a means of determining the probability of conflict. Where hierarchical structures such as states, private economic entities such as manufacturing firms, and even religious organizations are all dominated by the same elite, the potential for conflict is higher than in societies where authority is more dispersed. Put another way, if Group A dominates all or most key hierarchical authority structures and Group B is nearly always subordinate, conflict will be likely because Group B has little stake in the existing social order. However, if Group B has authority in some hierarchical structures and Group A has authority in others, neither group has great incentives to challenge the status quo.

Conflict Within
Social Movements

Marx emphasized control of the means of production as a source of power and conflict; Gramsci highlighted control of dominant ideas in society as an important source of power and change; and Dahrendorf put authority and its concentration or distribution at the center of his work. Conflict theorists differ in their beliefs about what sources are most likely to underlie social conflict and social change, but all agree that social conflict and social change are both inevitable and desirable components of society and progress.

RISE-AND-FALL THEORIES OF SOCIAL CHANGE

Rise-and-fall theories of social change deny that there is any particular forward direction to social change; rather, they *argue that change reflects a cycle of growth and decline*. Rise-and-fall or cyclical theories are common in the religious myths of many cultures, which view social life as a reflection of the life cycle of living creatures, or the seasons of the year, with the end representing some form of return to the beginning. Sociology, emerging in an era that equated scientific and technological advancement with progress, at first tended to reject such cyclical metaphors in favor of more evolutionary or revolutionary ones that emphasized the forward motion of progress.

There have been a number of significant exceptions, however, among historically oriented social theorists. Pitirim Sorokin (1957/1970, 1962), a historical sociologist of the mid-20th century, argued that societies alternate between three different kinds of mentalities: those that give primacy to the senses, those that emphasize religiosity, and those that celebrate logic and reason. Societies that value hedonism and the satisfaction of immediate pleasures more highly than the achievement of long-term goals give primacy to the senses; religiosity occurs in societies that follow the tenets of a religion over enjoying the senses or solving problems through logic and reason. We tend to think of modern societies as defined largely by the emphasis on logic and reason.

Societies everywhere have contained a mixture of religiosity, an emphasis on the senses, and the celebration of logic and reason. Sorokin's "ideal types" may nonetheless be useful for describing the *relative* emphasis of each of these modes of adaptation in different societies. For example, we might say that the modern Western world puts greater emphasis on logic and reason than on religion or giving primacy to the senses; it would be a mistake, however, to say that there is no emphasis on the senses or religion,

Rise-and-fall theories of social change: Argue that change reflects a cycle of growth and decline.

because these traits too play an important part in shaping the modern Western world.

In *The Rise and Fall of the Great Powers* (1987), historian Paul Kennedy traces the conditions associated with national power and decline during the past five centuries. As nations grow in economic power, he argues, they often seek to become world military powers as well, a goal that in the long run proves to be their undoing. Global military power eventually weakens the domestic economy, undermining the prosperity that once fueled it. Kennedy forecasts that this might well be the fate of the United States. More recently, writer Cullen Murphy (2007) has pointed to parallels between the Roman Empire and the United States, writing that Rome too was characterized by an overburdened and costly military, a deep sense of exceptionalism, and a tendency to denigrate and misunderstand other cultures. He notes as well the Roman pattern of shifting the onus for providing services to citizens away from the public sector to the private sector, seeing this as a form of enrichment for the few but a disadvantage for the many. A key point in rise-and-fall narratives is that social change can be both progressive and regressive—power does not invariably beget more power; it may also beget decline.

The most renowned sociologist considered by some to be a cyclical theorist is Max Weber. Although he took an evolutionary view of society as increasingly moving toward a politically and economically legal-rational society governed by rules and regulations, Weber also emphasized the role of irrational elements in shaping human behavior (Gerth & Mills, 1946). For example, while he wrote about the growing formal rationality of the modern world, he also recognized the possibility that a society's path could be altered by the appearance of a charismatic figure whose singular personal authority transcended institutionalized authority structures. Leaders who drastically changed a nation's trajectory include Haile Selassie, who governed Ethiopia for half a century, Adolf Hitler in Germany, Mao Zedong in China, and Fidel Castro in Cuba. In the United States, Martin Luther King Jr. led the civil rights movement in the 1960s and fundamentally changed race relations.

Cyclical theories have not enjoyed great popularity among sociologists. Even Weber's theory is not truly cyclical; his idea of *charismatic authority* is a sort of wild card, providing an unpredictable twist in an otherwise predictable march of social change between different forms of authority. The more far-reaching versions of cyclical theory, such as Sorokin's theory that society swings between three different worldviews, are framed in such broad terms that it is challenging to prove them right or wrong.

Dr. Martin Luther King Jr. had a transformational dream. His words and deeds inspired and continue to inspire social change. The actions of a single person can be truly significant. ■

SOURCES OF SOCIAL CHANGE

Social change ultimately results from human action. Sociologists studying how change occurs often analyze the mass action of large numbers of people and the institutionalized behaviors of organizations. In this section we examine social change within the context of mass action by groups of people, examining theories of collective behavior and the role played by social movements.

COLLECTIVE BEHAVIOR

Collective behavior is *voluntary, goal-oriented action that occurs in relatively disorganized situations, where society's predominant social norms and values cease to govern individual behavior* (Oberschall, 1973; R. Turner & Killian, 1987). Although collective behavior usually implies a disorganized aggregate of people, it may also occur in a highly regimented social context when order and discipline break down. The Arab Spring movement provides a good example of collective behavior in action. The civil uprisings that occurred in Tunisia, Egypt, and Libya would not have been possible if individuals had not chosen to act in ways contrary to the established social and structural norms of those countries and their governments.

Collective behavior: Voluntary, goal-oriented action that occurs in relatively disorganized situations, in which society's predominant social norms and values cease to govern individual behavior.

DIGITAL SOCIETY

FLASH MOB!

Imagine walking through a heavily populated mall or subway station, and out of the chaos of the crowds there is suddenly order . . . random, well-choreographed order. A flash mob is a form of organized collective behavior in which people gather in large numbers to engage in a coordinated activity to make an artistic or political statement, to provide surprise and "shock value," or to simply have a good laugh—and maybe to get some "hits" on the Internet if a video is posted.

Unlike street protests or politically charged demonstrations, flash mobs usually have a lighter focus. As a form of group recreation, they are typically grounded in having a good time rather than taking a firm political stance. These "mobs" will "flash" or break out suddenly out of chaos, usually with some form of choreography and movements that have been practiced prior to the performance. The core of a flash mob's effectiveness lies in its temporary departure from conventional societal norms and expectations.

Search "flash mob" online, and you will find videos of people engaged in everything from dancing wildly to standing still. Flash mobs are often done just for fun or for positive shock value—but they can also make a political statement or provide artistic expression. ■

You would not expect to see a spontaneous and organized group of people dancing in the middle of Grand Central Station, Times Square, a shopping mall, or the steps of a museum—but flash mobs have occurred in all of those places. Our expectations of "normal" behavior are suspended as the flash mob executes its activity.

THINK IT THROUGH

■ *If you organized a flash mob, what would it look like? What would be its purpose? Which existing concepts or perspectives related to collective behavior can help us understand the flash mob phenomenon? Might we need new approaches to explain it?*

The Arab Spring movement revealed another important feature of collective behavior: It often consists of a group reaction to a provocative—or sometimes seemingly innocuous—situation. From a sociologist's viewpoint, it does not matter what that situation is; it could be street parties that erupt into a group rampage after the local team wins a pennant. Even seemingly spontaneous events may in fact be a group response to larger social conditions such as poverty, long-term and widespread unemployment, or rising food costs, heralding a larger movement for social change. In January 2011, enormous crowds gathered in Tahrir Square in Egypt—and remained there for weeks—to protest the government's

violent response to the demands of demonstrators during the Arab Spring movement. It can be argued that the Tahrir Square protests in Egypt were successful in gaining significant popular support from the people due to the self-immolation by Mohamed Bouazizi in Tunisia. Mohamed's initial act of protest gained widespread attention and broke the gates of a large dam of public discontent. Despite the apparently spontaneous arrival of protesters at Egypt's Tahrir Square—and the important precipitating factor of social media, which we will discuss below—they were in fact responding to long-standing social grievances and frustrations within Egyptian society.

Beginning with the writings of the 19th-century French sociologist Gustave Le Bon (1896/1960), the sociological study of collective behavior has been particularly concerned with the behavior of people in **crowds**—that is, *temporary gatherings of closely interacting people with a common focus*. People in crowds were traditionally seen as prone to being swept up in group emotions, and as losing their ability to make rational decisions as individuals. The "group mind" of the crowd has long been viewed as an irrational and dangerous aspect of modern societies, with crowds believed to consist of rootless, isolated individuals prone to herd-like behavior (Arendt, 1951; Fromm, 1941; Gaskell & Smith, 1981; Kornhauser, 1959).

More recently, however, it seems clear that there can be a fair degree of social organization in crowds. For example, the Occupy Wall Street movement and the Arab Spring revolutions, although representing spontaneous beginnings, quickly developed a degree of predictability and organization, and in turn became social movements. It is important to note that crowds alone do not constitute social movements, but they are a critical ingredient in most cases. We must rethink the very notion of "spontaneity" in a global context, where social media has been a precipitating factor in collective behaviors ranging from flash mobs to street protests to revolutions (see the *Digital Society* box on page 452 on flash mobs).

Sociologists seek to explain the conditions that may lead a group of people to engage in collective behavior, whether violent or peaceful. Below we examine three principal sociological approaches: contagion theories, which emphasize nonsocial factors such as instincts; emergent norm theories, which seek out some kind of underlying social organization that leads the group to generate norms governing collective action; and value-added theories, which combine elements of personal, organizational, and social conditions in order to explain collective behavior.

CONTAGION THEORIES Contagion theories assume that human beings can revert to herd-like behavior when they come together in large crowds. Herbert Blumer (1951), drawing on symbolic interactionism, emphasized the role of raw imitation, which leads people in crowds to "mill about" much like a group of animals, stimulating and goading one another into movement actions, whether peaceful or violent. Individual acts, therefore, become contagious; they are unconsciously copied until they eventually explode into collective action. A skilled leader can effectively manipulate such behavior, "working the crowd" until it reaches a fever pitch.

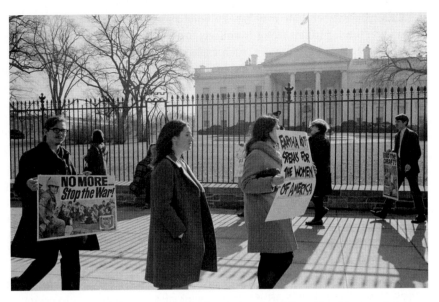

Political activism swept the country in the 1960s and 1970s with widespread demonstrations focused on civil rights, women's rights, and the Vietnam War. The dramatic protests and social transformations of this period helped fuel the reformulation of theories on social change. ■

Sociologists have used the contagion theory perspective to study the panic flights of crowds, "epidemics" of bizarre collective behaviors such as uncontrollable dancing or fainting, and reports of satanic child abuse. After James Holmes opened fire in a Colorado movie theater in July 2012 during the premiere of a popular action film, *The Dark Knight Rises,* some law enforcement officials were concerned that this act of violence would be imitated in other areas of the country. Some sociologists believe that a few well-publicized cases of deviant behavior can trigger imitative behavior until a virtual "epidemic" emerges that then feeds upon itself (Goode, 2009).

How does the contagion actually spread? What are the mechanisms that affect whether people imitate one another's behavior in the interest of grabbing attention or promoting social change? In the case of the Arab Spring, some scholars assert that common variables including language, geographical proximity, and living under the rule of a dictatorship create conditions favorable to the imitation and replication of behavior. Once it was understood that group resistance was plausible and possible to protest the political conditions of their countries, people were more likely to mobilize. An interesting parallel would be the contagion of the Occupy Wall Street movement: As more people realized that there was an avenue to protest the political and economic conditions of the United States, Occupy camps started spreading all over the country. Their decline over time was more gradual.

Flash Mobs

Social Change and Non-Violence

. . . .

Crowd: A temporary gathering of closely interacting people with a common focus.

While copycat behavior may rapidly build momentum, an explanation limited to this factor is unlikely to account fully for collective behavior. Furthermore, such explanations are sometimes used to discredit a particular instance of collective behavior as the result of an irrational (and therefore dangerous) tendency of people to jump on the bandwagon. Critics of the Occupy Wall Street movement often depicted the movement as little more than a copycat action occupying city space, rather than a movement with serious concerns about the state of contemporary society. In the 1960s, some people dismissed the antiwar and civil rights protesters as misled "flower children," rather than people concerned about injustice and war. Sociologists, however, seek ways to determine *why* collective behavior occurs, and to understand the rational and organizational basis for its emergence (Chafetz & Dworkin, 1983; L. Wright, 1993). Let's next look at what some other theories suggest.

EMERGENT NORM THEORIES Most sociologists prefer to look for norms and values that shape conscious human behavior rather than rely on the idea that instincts govern unconscious processes. Some have suggested that emergent norms offer an explanation for collective behavior; we can define **emergent norms** as *norms that are situationally created to support a collective action.* For example, Ralph H. Turner and Lewis M. Killian (1987) argue that even when crowd behavior appears chaotic and disorganized, norms emerge that explain the crowd's actions. Crowd members take stock of what is going on around them, are mindful of their personal motivations, and, in general, collectively define the situation in which they find themselves. In this respect, crowd behavior is not very different from ordinary behavior; there is no need to fall back on "instincts" or "contagion" to explain it.

The "Tea Party" political movement in the United States (which is also discussed in Chapter 13) began as a collective protest against "big government." It soon developed a package of "emergent norms" that morphed into a political movement emphasizing the importance of getting like-minded politicians elected to office, as well as norms that emphasized the importance of adherence to the central ideas of the U.S. Constitution, lower taxes, more limited government, and reduced spending.

The emergent norm approach offers only a partial explanation of collective behavior. First, all crowds do not develop norms that govern their actions; crowds often emerge out of a shared set of norms among the participants. Second, purely spontaneous emotional outbursts may also occur as people act on their immediate impulses. Furthermore, when norms governing crowd behavior do emerge, they are unlikely by themselves to account fully for collective behavior. When a video appeared on the Internet depicting the prophet Muhammad in an unfavorable and even absurd light, some crowds in the Middle East spontaneously gathered to protest against the United States, where the video was made. These crowds were responding to religious leaders who informed their members of the existence of the video and encouraged protests. Emergent norms played little part in these actions; the norms (and grievances) being expressed had long historical standing in the communities where the protests took place.

VALUE-ADDED THEORY Both contagion and emergent norm theories focus primarily on the micro level of individual action and thought, largely ignoring macro-level factors—poverty, unemployment, governmental abuses of authority, and so on—that may explain the emergence of collective behavior. Over 50 years ago, Neil Smelser (1962) sought to develop what he termed a "value-added" approach to understanding collective behavior. He identified a number of both micro- and macro-level factors that each contribute something of value to the outcome, and that must converge in order for collective behavior to occur.

1. *Structural conduciveness* exists when the existing social structure favors the emergence of collective behavior. For example, inequities inherent in the political and economic structures of many Arab and North African countries laid the foundation for the eventual emergence of large-scale protests.

2. *Structural strain* occurs when the social system breaks down. The global economic recession that began in 2007 left many well-educated young people in the Arab Spring countries unemployed and lowered their overall standard of living. These factors produced significant strains within societies already characterized by vast wealth, power, and prestige imbalances, contributing to frustration and anger in key segments of the population.

3. *Generalized beliefs* are shared explanations of the conditions that are troubling people. People must define the problem, identify its causes, and—to use C. Wright Mills's phrase—come to see their personal problems as public issues. Those in the Arab Spring protests attributed their growing hardships not to personal failings, but to the failed policies of their respective governments.

4. *Precipitating factors* are dramatic events that confirm the generalized beliefs of the group, thereby triggering action. Mohamed Bouazizi's suicide and other deaths resulting from official crackdowns on Arab Spring protesters are tangible examples of the failings of many governments.

5. *Mobilization for action* occurs when leaders arise who encourage action. In Egypt, Wael Ghonim, a young technology executive who had been detained by the authoritarian government of Hosni Mubarak, emerged as a leading light of the revolution.

CQR

Occupy Wall Street

Emergent norms: Norms that are situationally created to support a collective action.

INEQUALITY MATTERS

OCCUPYWALLSTREET.ORG—ORGANIZING ONLINE

The Internet has opened new windows of opportunity for civic activism around the globe. *Cyberactivism* is "the act of using the [I]nternet to advance a political cause that is difficult to advance offline" (Howard, 2011, p. 145).

The Occupy Wall Street movement's genesis lies with the Canadian anticonsumerism organization called Adbusters, whose members define themselves as "a global network of culture jammers and creatives working to change the way information flows, the way corporations wield power, and the way meaning is produced in our society" (Adbusters, 2013). On July 13, 2011, Adbusters published an online blog inviting protesters to flood Manhattan's Wall Street sector and peacefully demand democracy while rejecting the influence of corporations.

By mid-October, the Occupy movement had spread like wildfire, with many well-established organizations including labor unions joining the cause. Digital and social media channels such as YouTube, Facebook, Twitter, Instagram, and Tumblr were central to the movement's early success and nationwide proliferation. The movement's website, OccupyWallStreet.org, still contains

information about community organizing, local and nationwide protests, and other resources for those interested in learning about or joining the movement.

In countries such as Egypt, online social media have exposed state violence, police brutality, and blatant injustice that may have otherwise escaped the public eye. Cyberactivism and the increasingly organized utilization of social media contributed to political outcomes such as the removal of President Hosni Mubarak in Egypt, and to the widespread sociopolitical movements and upheavals collectively referred to as the Arab Spring.

It is important, however, to differentiate causal factors from contributing factors. Globalization and developments in telecommunication technologies alone do not give birth to movements for social change; the uprisings of the Arab Spring were born from the poverty and social exclusion that have afflicted much of the population in this region (Rovira,

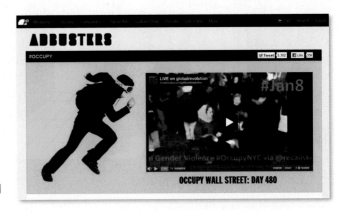

OCCUPY WALL STREET: DAY 480

2011). What social media did in places such as Tunisia, Egypt, Libya, Yemen, and Bahrain was to capture, ignite, and maintain the public's attention and provide a powerful and effective tool for organizing protests and demonstrations. As in the Occupy movement, social media and cyberactivism have been *tools* that operate to further the political movement, not causal factors that initiated the movements themselves.

THINK IT THROUGH

■ *Is cyberactivism effective as a vehicle of social change, or does it also need real collective action in the streets or halls of government to render it effective? Under what conditions could cyberactivism stand alone as a means of protest and change?*

---

6. *The failure of social control* leaves those charged with maintaining law and order unable to do so in the face of mounting pressures for collective action. Many of the governments in power when the Arab Spring movements began attempted to utilize force to exert social control over the protesters and silence their collective voice. However, social media were actively engaged in spreading news about the uprisings. The

widely circulated images and reports of state violence encouraged others to join the protesters.

Smelser's approach has been used to analyze collective behavior in a variety of settings, including self-help groups (D. Smith & Pillemer, 1983), social welfare organizations (M. Smith & Moses, 1980), and nuclear-weapons-freeze activism (Tygart, 1987). The

Sources of Social Change **455**

Psy's video of the song "Gangnam Style" is the most watched YouTube video of all time (at least to this point). It has inspired all manner of imitations and parodies. Interestingly, the song itself is a parody of the lifestyles of residents of an upscale Seoul neighborhood. ■

theory's strength is that it combines societal-, organizational-, and individual-level factors into one comprehensive theory. Yet, it has also been criticized for emphasizing the part that people's reactions play in collective behavior more than the fact that they themselves are conscious agents creating the conditions required for social change.

HOW DO CROWDS ACT?

We have all participated in some form of collective behavior in our social lives. Collective behavior comes in a spectrum of different forms, including riots, fads, fashions, panics, crazes, and rumors. In this section we discuss each of these forms of collective behavior.

RIOTS A **riot** is *an illegal, prolonged outbreak of violent behavior by a large group of people against individuals or property.* Riots represent a form of crowd behavior; often they are spontaneous, although sometimes they are motivated by a conscious set of concerns. Prison and urban riots are common examples. During a riot, conventional norms, including respect for the private property of others, are suspended and replaced with other norms developed within the group. For example, inmates may destroy property to force prison officials to adopt more humane practices, while the theft of property during an urban riot may reflect the desire for a more equitable distribution of resources.

The very use of the term *riot* to characterize a particular action is often highly political. In 1773, a crowd of Bostonians protesting British taxation of the American colonies seized a shipment of tea from a British vessel and dumped it into Boston Harbor. While the British Crown roundly condemned this action as the illegal act of a rioting mob, U.S. history books celebrate the "Boston Tea Party" as the noble act of inspired patriots and an opening salvo in the Revolutionary War.

FADS AND FASHIONS The desire to join others in being different (itself perhaps something of an irony) continually feeds the rise of new looks and sounds. **Fads,** or *temporary, highly imitated outbreaks of mildly unconventional behavior,* are particularly common responses to popular entertainment such as music, movies, and books and require social networks (electronic or otherwise) in order to spread (Iribarren & Moro, 2007). The fads of piercing body parts to wear ornaments and extensive body tattooing have captured several generations and seem to be continuing today. Earlier fads included jeans with holes in the knees, panty raids on sorority houses, and the "hipster" style popularized by young people united by a common interest in alternative music and Pabst Blue Ribbon beer.

As fads become popular, they sometimes cease being fads and instead become **fashions,** that is, *somewhat long-lasting styles of imitative behavior or appearance.* Georg Simmel (1904/1971) first examined the sociological implications of fashions over a century ago. He pointed out that fashions reflect a tension between people's desire to be different and their desire to conform. By adopting a fashion, a person initially appears to stand out from the group, yet the fashion itself reflects group norms. As the fashion catches on, more and more people adopt it, and it eventually ceases to express any degree of individuality. Its very success undermines its attractiveness, so the eventual fate of all fashions is to become unfashionable.

Simmel's observations offer another insight into fashions: Unlike fads, they often grow out of the continuous and well-organized efforts of those who work in design, manufacturing technology, marketing, and media to define what is in style. As "grunge" music became popular, it spawned a profitable clothing industry, and highly paid fashion designers created clothing that was grungy in everything but price. Today there are several fashion trends that resonate with different audiences and subcultures. Whether it is the "hipster" look of skinny jeans, oversized glasses, and an ironic sweatshirt or the EDM (electronic dance music) scene of neon colors, high-waist bottoms, and playful accessories, manufacturers will spend millions of dollars attempting to convince youthful

. . . .

Riot: A prolonged outbreak of violent behavior by a sizable group of people that is directed against people or property and is often illegal.

Fad: A temporary, highly imitated outbreak of mildly unconventional behavior.

Fashion: A style of imitative behavior or appearance that is of a longer duration than a fad.

consumers that they must buy a particular product in order to be fashionable and popular.

PANICS AND CRAZES A **panic** is *a massive flight from something feared*. The most celebrated example was created by an infamous Halloween radio broadcast in 1938: Orson Welles's Mercury Theater rendition of H. G. Wells's science fiction novel *War of the Worlds*. The broadcast managed to convince thousands that Martians had landed in Grover's Mill, New Jersey, and were wreaking havoc with deadly laser beams. People panicked, flooded the telephone lines with calls, and fled to "safer" ground.

Panics often ignite the belief that something is awry in the corporate world or in consumer technology. As the year 2000 approached, the Y2K "computer bug" panic gripped many people, who believed reports that computer systems worldwide would crash when the year 2000 began. A recent example of a panic involved the Mayan calendar, which was projected to "end" during our calendar equivalent of December 2012. The fact that the structure of the Mayan calendar and the Mayan system of counting and noting dates did not pass December 2012 led many to believe that the Mayans predicted the end of the world.

Some panics, like that around Y2K, reflect the fear that, in modern industrial society, we are highly dependent on products and technological processes about which we have little knowledge and over which we have no control.

A **craze** is *an intense attraction to an object, a person, or an activity*. Crazes are like fads but more intense. Body disfigurement has been a periodic craze, ranging from nose piercing to putting rings through nipples, belly buttons, lips, and tongues. The fact that these practices instill horror in some people probably accounts in part for the attraction they hold for others. In many cultures, body disfigurement is considered a necessary condition of beauty or attractiveness. While such practices would be regarded as crazes in the West, they are normal enhancements of beauty in other cultures (D. Brown, Edwards, & Moore, 1988).

Rumors are *unverified forms of information that are transmitted informally, usually originating in an unknown source*. The classic study on rumors was conducted about 60 years ago (Allport & Postman, 1947). In one version of this research, a

A historically notable panic actually happened unintentionally. A 1938 Halloween radio broadcast narrated H. G. Wells's science fiction novel. Many listeners did not realize that the radio was broadcasting a work of fiction, causing them to panic. ■

White student was asked to study a photograph depicting an urban scene: two men on a subway car, one menacing the other. The student was then asked to describe the picture to a second White student, who in turn was asked to pass the information along to a third, and so on. After a certain point, the information became completely changed to reflect the students' previously held beliefs. For example, as the "rumor" in the study took shape, the person engaging in the menacing act was described as Black and the victim as White—even though in the actual photograph the reverse was true.

Allport and Postman's research revealed a number of features unique to rumors. The information they contain is continually reorganized according to the belief systems of those who are passing them along. Some information is forgotten, and some is altered to fit into more familiar frameworks, such as racist preconceptions in the example above. Furthermore, the degree of alteration varies according to the nature of the rumor; it is greatest for rumors that trigger strong emotions or that pass through a large number of people.

For rumors to have an effect, they must tap into collectively held beliefs, fears, or hopes. For some the rumor that the world will imminently end is a hopeful message; for others it is a source of great fear. Rumors often reinforce subcultural beliefs. The rumor that the Central Intelligence Agency and the National Security Agency are planting bugs in everyone's home feeds into the belief that the government is out to control us. Political

. . . .

Panic: A massive flight from something that is feared.

Craze: An intense attraction to an object, a person, or an activity.

Rumor: An unverified form of information that is transmitted informally, usually originating in an unknown source.

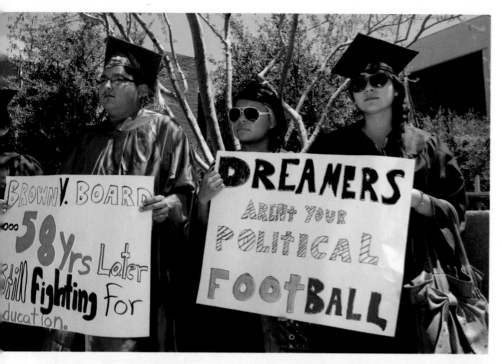

The Dreamer movement consists of people who support immigration reform, including access to opportunities and a legitimate route to residency or citizenship for young people brought to the United States by undocumented parents. Many have been barred from educational institutions or job opportunities due to their immigration status. ■

such routine efforts as lobbying or campaigning; they include noninstitutionalized political actions such as marches, boycotts, demonstrations, and civil disobedience.

On the one hand, social movements often include some degree of formal organization oriented toward achieving longer-term goals, along with a supporting set of beliefs and opinions. On the other hand, their strength often derives from their ability to disrupt the status quo by means of spontaneous, relatively unorganized political actions. The National Association for the Advancement of Colored People's (NAACP) support for the civil rights movement for a long time included advocating the disruption of normal business activities, such as boycotting buses and restaurants in order to force integration. Social movements typically consist of people who are outside the existing set of power relationships in society; they are one of the few forms of political voice available to the relatively powerless (McAdam, McCarthy, & Zald, 1988; Tarrow, 1994). A recent example is the Dreamers, or Dream Act activists, who support immigration reform so that undocumented young people who migrated to the United States with their families can have access to higher education and, over time, permanent residency or citizenship. An executive order signed by President Obama in 2012 would allow the Dreamers to apply for a deferred action permit and avoid deportation under certain conditions. The Dreamer movement is active at the time of this writing.

campaigns are infamous for starting and perpetuating rumors: For example, the rumors that President Barack Obama is not a U.S. citizen, is a Muslim, and is trying to create European-style socialism in the United States have been spread by political opponents. Despite the fact that an abundance of evidence contradicts these rumors, they have been embraced by some groups.

SOCIAL MOVEMENTS

Theories of collective behavior generally emphasize the passive, reactive side of human behavior. Social movement theory, on the other hand, regards human beings as the active makers of their own history—agents who have visions and goals, analyze existing conditions, weigh alternative courses of action, and organize themselves as best they can to achieve success.

A **social movement** is *a large number of people who come together in a continuing and organized effort to bring about (or resist) social change, and who rely at least partially on noninstitutionalized forms of political action.* Social movements thus have one foot outside the political establishment, and this is what distinguishes them from other efforts aimed at bringing about social change. Their political activities are not limited to

The body of research on social movements in the United States is partially the result of movements that began in the late 1950s and gained attention and support in the 1960s and early 1970s. Theories of collective behavior, with their emphasis on the seemingly irrational actions of unorganized crowds, were ill equipped to explain the rise of well-organized efforts of hundreds of thousands of people to change government policies toward the Vietnam War and civil rights for African Americans. As these two social movements spawned others, including the second wave feminist movement, which saw women demand greater rights and opportunities in the workplace, sociologists had to rethink their basic assumptions and develop new theoretical perspectives. In this section, we examine different types of social movements, looking especially at sociological theories about why they arise.

TYPES OF SOCIAL MOVEMENTS

Social movements are typically classified according to the direction and degree of change they seek. For purposes of discussion,

History in Social
Movements

Social Movement
Successes and Failures

. . . .

Social movement: A large number of people who come together in a continuing and organized effort to bring about (or resist) social change, and who rely at least partially on noninstitutionalized forms of political action.

Type	Principal Aims	Examples
Reformist	To bring about change within the existing economic and political system	–U.S. civil rights –Same-sex marriage rights –Climate change activism –Labor movements –International human rights
Revolutionary	To fundamentally change the existing social, political, and/or economic system in light of a detailed alternative vision	–1776 U.S. Revolutionary War –1905 and 1917 Russian Revolution –1991 South African anti-apartheid movement –2010 Arab Spring
Rebellion	To fundamentally alter the existing political, and/or economic system without a detailed alternative vision	–Nat Turner slave rebellion –Urban riots following the assassination of Martin Luther King Jr. –European rebellions in Greece, Spain, and Portugal against austerity measures
Reactionary	To restore an earlier, often mythical social system	–White supremacist organizations in the United States and Europe –German skinheads –Serbian nationalists
Utopian	To withdraw from society and create a utopian community	–Religious communities such as the Quakers, Mennonites, and Mormons –1960s communes in the United States
New social movements	To make fundamental changes in values, culture, and private life	–Gay, lesbian, bisexual, and transgender rights movements –Environmental movements

we will distinguish five different kinds: those that seek reform, revolution, rebellion, reaction, or the formation of community (Table 18.1). In fact, these distinctions are not clear-cut, and categories are not mutually exclusive. Rather, they represent ideal types. In the final section of the chapter, we will also consider some examples of a new sixth category of social movement that aims to change values and beliefs.

REFORMIST SOCIAL MOVEMENTS Reformist social movements seek to *bring about social change within the existing economic and political system* and usually address institutions such as the courts and lawmaking bodies and/or public officials. They are most often found in societies where democratic institutions make it possible to achieve social change within the established political

. . . .

Reformist social movement: A movement seeking to bring about social change within the existing economic and political system.

processes. Yet even reformist social movements can include factions that advocate more sweeping, revolutionary social changes. Sometimes the government fails to respond, or it responds too slowly, raising frustrations. At other times, the government may actively repress the movement, arresting its leaders, breaking up its demonstrations, and even outlawing its activities.

The American Woman Suffrage Association, formed in 1869 by Susan B. Anthony and Elizabeth Cady Stanton, was a reformist organization that resulted in significant social changes. During the latter part of the 19th century, it became one of the most powerful political forces in the United States, seeking to liberate women from oppression and give them the right to vote (Vellacott, 1993) and precipitating the first wave of the women's movement. In 1872, Victoria Woodhull helped to organize the Equal Rights Party, which nominated her for the U.S. presidency (even though, by law, no woman could vote for her); she campaigned on the issues of voting rights for women, the right of women to earn and control their own money, and free love (Underhill, 1995). After a

Revolutionary social movements are not always violent. In Czechoslovakia, the Communist regime led by General Secretary Miloš Jakeš ceded power in 1989 and allowed for a peaceful democratic transition to take place. ■

half-century of struggle by numerous social movement activists, women finally won the right to vote with the ratification of the Nineteenth Amendment to the U.S. Constitution in 1920.

The civil rights movement of the late 1950s and the 1960s called for social changes that would enforce the constitutionally mandated civil rights of African Americans, and nonviolent civil disobedience was often directed at breaking unjust laws. The ultimate aim of the civil rights movement was to change those laws, rather than to change society as a whole. Thus, for example, when Rosa Parks violated the laws of Montgomery, Alabama, by refusing to give up her seat on a city bus to a White person, she was challenging the city ordinance, but not the government itself.

Much early civil rights movement activity was oriented toward registering Southern Blacks to vote, so that by exercising their legal franchise, they could achieve a measure of political power. Yet, within the civil rights movement, there were activists who concluded that the rights of Black Americans would never be achieved through reformist activities alone. Like many social movements, the civil rights movement was marked by internal struggles and debates regarding the degree to which purely reformist activities were adequate to the movement's objectives (Branch, 1988). The Black Panther Party, for example, argued for far more radical changes in U.S. society, advocating "Black power" instead of merely fighting for an end to racial segregation. The Black Panthers often engaged in reformist activities, such as establishing community centers and calling for the establishment and support of more Black-owned businesses. At the same time, they also engaged in revolutionary activities, such as arming themselves against what they viewed to be a hostile police presence within Black neighborhoods.

The experience of U.S. labor unions, another example of reformist social movements, shows the limits of the reformist approach to social change. Organized labor's principal demands have been for fewer hours, higher wages and benefits, job security, and safer working conditions. (In Europe, similar demands have been made, although workers there have sought political power as well.) Labor unions within the United States seldom appeal to a broad constituency beyond the workers themselves, and as a result, their success has depended largely on workers' economic power. U.S. workers have lost much of that power since the early 1970s, as economic globalization has meant the loss of many jobs to low-wage areas. The threat of a strike is no longer quite as menacing, as factories can be closed down and reopened elsewhere in the world.

REVOLUTIONARY MOVEMENTS **Revolutionary social movements** seek to *fundamentally alter the existing social, political, and economic system in keeping with a vision of a new social order.* They frequently result from the belief that reformist approaches are unlikely to succeed because the political or economic system is too resistant. In fact, whether a social movement becomes predominantly reformist or revolutionary may well hinge on the degree to which its objectives can be achieved within the system.

Revolutionary movements call for basic changes in economics, politics, norms, and values, offering a blueprint for a new social order that can be achieved only through mass action, usually by fostering conflict between those who favor change and those who favor the status quo. They are directed at clearly identifiable targets, such as a system of government believed to be unjust or an economy believed to be based on exploitation. Yet even the most revolutionary of social movements are likely to have reformist elements, members or factions who believe some change is possible within the established institutions. In most social movements, members debate the relative importance of reformist and revolutionary activities. While the rhetoric may favor revolution, most day-to-day activities are likely to support reform. Only when a social movement is suppressed and avenues to reform are closed off will its methods call for outright revolution.

Revolutionary social movements sometimes, although by no means always, include violence. In South Africa, for example, the movements that were most successful in bringing about an end to apartheid were largely nonviolent. Those that defeated socialism in the former Soviet Union and Eastern Europe did so with a minimal amount of bloodshed. However, revolutionary movements associated

· ·

Revolutionary social movement: A movement seeking to alter fundamentally the existing social, political, and economic system in keeping with a vision of a new social order.

with the Arab Spring have resulted in considerable violence, most often perpetrated against the protesters by those already in power or their allies. It has yet to be determined whether the Arab Spring movements have been truly revolutionary; some new governments are not radically more democratic than their predecessors. It takes time for political and economic conditions to change within any given country, and while some dictators have been removed from office, it remains to be seen whether these changes in political office will result in the changes desired by constituents.

REBELLIONS Rebellions seek to *overthrow the existing social, political, and economic systems but lack a detailed plan for a new social order.* They are particularly common in societies where effective mobilization against existing structures is difficult or impossible because of their repressive nature. The histories of European feudalism and U.S. slavery are punctuated by examples of rebellions. Nat Turner, an Black American slave,

After the Civil War, the Ku Klux Klan instituted vigilante justice and lynched over 4,000 African Americans for alleged crimes, including looking "the wrong way" at a White woman. White supremacist groups exemplify a resistance or countermovement that rejects racial integration and expansion of civil rights. ■

led other slaves in an 1831 uprising against their White owners in the state of Virginia. Fifty-five Whites were killed before the uprising was suppressed, and Turner and 16 of his followers were hanged (Greenberg, 2003).

REACTIONARY MOVEMENTS Reactionary social movements *seek to restore an earlier social system—often based on a mythical past—along with the traditional norms and values that once presumably accompanied it.* These movements are termed reactionary because they arise in reaction to recent social changes that threaten or have replaced the old order. They are also sometimes referred to as countermovements or resistance movements for the same reason.

For these groups, a mythical past is often the starting point for pursuing goals aimed at transforming the present. The Ku Klux Klan, the White Aryan Resistance, and other White supremacist organizations have long sought to return to a United States where Whites held exclusive political and economic power. Their methods have ranged from spreading discredited social and biological theories that expound the superiority of the "White race," to acts of violence against Black Americans, Asians, Latinos, Jews, gays and lesbians, and others deemed to be inferior or otherwise a threat to the "American way of life" (Gerhardt, 1989; J. Moore, 1991).

· ·

Rebellion: A movement seeking to overthrow the existing social, political, and economic system, but lacking a detailed plan for a new social order.

Reactionary social movement: A movement seeking to restore an earlier social system—often based on a mythical past—along with the traditional norms and values that once presumably accompanied it.

Whether a social movement is reactionary or revolutionary depends to some extent on one's perspective. In Iran, for example, a social movement led by the Ayatollah Khomeini overthrew the pro-U.S. leader in 1979 and created an Islamic republic that quickly reestablished traditional Muslim laws. In the pronouncements of U.S. policy makers and the mass media, the new Iranian regime was reactionary: It required women to be veiled, turned its back on democratic institutions, and levied death sentences on those who violated key Islamic values or otherwise threatened the Islamic state. Yet from the point of view of the clerics who led the upheaval, the movement overthrew a corrupt and brutal dictator who had enriched his family at the expense of the Iranian people, and who had fostered an alien way of life offensive to traditional Iranian values. From this standpoint, the movement claimed to be revolutionary, promising to provide a better life for Iranians.

As globalization threatens traditional ways of life around the world, we might expect to see an increase in reactionary social movements. This is especially likely to be the case if the threat to long-standing traditional values is accompanied by a decline in the standard of living. In Germany, for example, a decline in living standards for many working-class people has spawned a small but significant resurgence of Nazi ideology, and racial supremacist groups blame foreign immigrants for their economic woes. The result has been a vocal campaign by skinhead groups against immigrants, particularly in the former East Germany, which has seen greater economic upheavals.

Guatamalan Social Media

MILLIONS OF DEMONSTRATORS . . . OR NOT

How many demonstrators attended a protest action on a given day in a particular place? This can be a surprisingly contentious issue. For example, how many people attended the Million Man March, a huge 1995 grassroots gathering highlighting issues of concern to urban and minority men and their families? According to National Public Radio (2010), "It depends on whom you ask. According to the U.S. Park Police, about 400,000. But the organizers of the march took issue with that number and asked for a recount. And using different images . . . a crowd counting expert at Boston University estimated the crowd to be closer to 800,000—almost twice the number that the Park Service had."

Once you become familiar with the importance of research methods, you find that the *method* of obtaining information can be at least as important as the information itself. When a statistic, fact, or figure is produced, it is always important to consider the process behind its production. We often hear media accounts that report the number of demonstrators in a given unit of space or time (for instance, there are 200 protesters in New York City, or there are 200,000 demonstrators on the National Mall). During the peak months of the Occupy movement, it was common to read figures ostensibly representing the number of participants attending an action. Where do these numbers come from? Who is keeping count?

In taking a critical look behind the numbers in the U.S. case, we find that

What kind of collective action or issue would bring you out into the street? ■

the National Park Service does not conduct official head counts of the number of demonstrators in a given public space. McPherson Square, a park in Washington, DC, was one of two nuclei for the Occupy movement in that city. The National Park Service conducted periodic estimates of the crowds there to ensure they did not surpass the regulated limit of 500 protesters (Farhi, 2011). Nevertheless, these estimates were not methodologically rigorous. Journalists often rely on best-guess estimates for crowds. Satellite pictures have become a source of information on crowds, though they capture just a few moments in time (NPR, 2010).

So how does one get a good count of the number of participants?

Stephen K. Doig, a professor at the Cronkite School of Journalism at Arizona State University, has a formula (National Public Radio, 2010). He writes that if we know these three variables—the human density of the demonstration, the carrying capacity of the space, and how much of the available space is occupied—we can get closer to the "objective and scientifically accurate" end of the estimating spectrum. A perfect count, however, will likely remain elusive.

THINK IT THROUGH

■ *Why are counts potentially controversial and contested? What makes them significant?*

Sometimes the size of protesting groups—which may be small, but very vocal, or may be awe-inspiring in size—is unclear, as we see in the *Behind the Numbers* box on page 462.

UTOPIAN MOVEMENTS **Utopian social movements** seek to *withdraw from the dominant society by creating their own ideal communities.* The youth movements of the 1960s had a strong utopian impulse; many young (and a few older) people "dropped out" and formed their own communities, starting alternative newspapers, health clinics, and schools and in general seeking to live according to their own value systems outside the established social institutions. Some sought to live communally as well, pooling their resources and sharing tasks and responsibilities. They saw these efforts to create "intentional" communities, based on cooperation rather than competition, as the seeds of a revolutionary new society.

Although religious utopian movements have proved to be somewhat enduring, those based on social philosophy have not. Some "utopian socialist" communities were founded in the United States during the 19th century; some provided models for the socialist collectives of the 1960s. Few lasted for any length of time. The old ways of thinking and acting proved remarkably tenacious, and the presence of the larger society—which remained basically unchanged by the experimentation—was a constant temptation. "Alternative" institutions such as communally run newspapers and health clinics found they had to contend with well-funded mainstream competitors. Most folded or reverted to mainstream forms (Fairfield, 1972; Nordhoff, 1875/1975; Rothschild & Whitt, 1987).

WHY DO SOCIAL MOVEMENTS ARISE?

Although social movements have existed throughout history, modern society has created conditions in which they thrive and multiply. The rise of the modern, democratic nation-state, along with the development of capitalism, has fueled their growth. Democratic forms of governance, which emphasize social equality and the right of political participation, legitimize the belief that people should organize themselves politically to achieve their goals. Democratic nation-states give rise to social movements—and often protect them as well. Capitalism, which raises universal economic expectations while producing some inequality, further spurs their formation.

Given these general historical circumstances, sociologists have advanced a number of theories to explain why people sometimes come together to create or resist social change. Some focus on the micro level, looking at the characteristics and motivations of the people who join social movements. Some focus on the organizational level, looking at the characteristics that result in successful social movement organizations. Some focus on the macro level, examining the societal conditions that give rise to social movements. More recently, theories have emphasized cultural dimensions of social movements, stressing the extent to which social movements reflect—as well as shape—larger cultural understandings. An ideal theory would bridge all these levels, and some efforts have been made to develop one.

MICRO-LEVEL APPROACHES Much research has focused on what motivates individuals to become active members of social movements. Psychological factors turn out to be poor predictors. Neither personality nor personal alienation adequately accounts for activist leanings. Rather, participation seems motivated more by psychological identification with others who are similarly afflicted (Marwell & Oliver, 1993; McAdam, 1982).

Sociology generally explains activism in such terms as having had prior contact with movement members, belonging to social networks that support movement activity, and having a history of activism (McAdam, 1986; Snow, Zurcher, & Ekland-Olson, 1980). Coming from a family background of social activism may also be important. One study, for example, found that many White male activists during the early 1960s social movements had parents who themselves had been activists 30 years earlier (Flacks, 1971). A lack of personal constraints may also be a partial explanation; it is obviously easier to engage in political activity if work or family circumstances afford the necessary time and resources (McCarthy & Zald, 1973). Finally, a sense of moral rightness may provide a powerful motivation to become active, even when the work is difficult and the monetary rewards are small or nonexistent (C. D. Jenkins, 1983).

Social movements always suffer from the **free rider problem**, however, which *arises when people avoid the costs of social movement activism* (such as time, energy, and other personal resources) *and still benefit from its success* (Marwell & Oliver, 1993). Why not let others join the social movement and do the hard work, since if it succeeds everyone will benefit regardless of his or her degree of participation? Clearly it takes a great deal of motivation and commitment, as well as a conviction that their efforts may make a difference, for people devote their time to mailing leaflets or organizing marches; building such motivation is a major challenge faced by all social movements.

ORGANIZATIONAL-LEVEL APPROACHES Some recent research has been devoted to understanding how social movements are consciously and deliberately organized to create social change. This research focuses on **social movement organizations (SMOs)**, *formal organizations that seek to achieve social change through noninstitutionalized forms of political action.* The study of social movement organizations represents a major sociological step away from regarding social change as resulting

....

Utopian social movement: A movement seeking to withdraw from the dominant society by creating its own ideal community.

Free rider problem: A problem that arises because people avoid the costs of social movement activism (such as time, energy, and other personal resources) and still benefit from its success without becoming active participants.

Social movement organizations (SMOs): Formal organizations that seek to achieve social change through noninstitutionalized forms of political action.

from unorganized individuals and crowds. Instead, it places the study of social change within the framework of the sociology of organizations.

Because social movement organizations are a type of formal organization, sociologists use the same concepts and tools to study civil rights organizations and revolutionary groups as to study business firms and government bureaucracies. Researchers conceptualize their actions as rational, their goals as more or less clearly defined, and their organizational structure as bureaucratically oriented toward specific measurable goals (C. D. Jenkins, 1983; McCarthy & Zald, 1977).

Social movement organizations range from informal volunteer groups to professional organizations with a full-time leadership and staff. A single social movement may sustain numerous such organizations: A partial list associated with the 1960s civil rights movement includes the NAACP, the Student Nonviolent Coordinating Committee (SNCC), the Congress of Racial Equality (CORE), the Southern Christian Leadership Conference (SCLC), Students for a Democratic Society (SDS), and the Black Panther Party. As social movements grow, so too do the number of social movement organizations associated with them, each vying for members, financial support, and media attention.

One influential approach to the study of social movement organizations is **resource mobilization theory,** *a theory that focuses on the ability of social movement organizations to generate money, membership, and political support to achieve their objectives.* This approach argues that since discontent and social strain are always present among some members of any society, these factors cannot explain the rise or the relative success of social movements. Rather, what matters are differences in the resources available to different groups and how effectively they use them. The task for sociologists, then, is to explain why some social movement organizations are better able to deploy scarce resources than others (C. D. Jenkins, 1983; McAdam, 1988). Among the most important resources are tangible assets such as money, facilities, and means of communication, as well as such intangibles such as a central core of dedicated, skilled, hardworking members (C. D. Jenkins, 1983).

Much like businesses, then, social movement organizations rise or fall on their ability to be competitive in a resource-scarce environment. Some scholars have even written of "social movement industries," with competing organizations engaging in "social marketing" to promote their particular "brand" of social change (C. D. Jenkins, 1983; Zald & McCarthy, 1980).

Governmental policies are important determinants of the success or failure of social movement organizations. The government may repress the organization, driving it underground so that it has difficulty in operating. Or the government may favor more moderate organizations (for example, Martin Luther King Jr.'s Southern Christian Leadership Conference) over other, more radical ones (such as the Black Panther Party). Other ways in which the government affects social movement organizations are through regulating them, providing favorable tax treatment for those that qualify, and refraining from excessive surveillance or harassment (McAdam et al., 1988).

The success or failure of social movement organizations also depends on their ability to influence the mass media. During the 1960s, the anti–Vietnam War organizations became very effective in commanding the television spotlight, although this effectiveness proved a mixed blessing: Media coverage frequently sensationalized demonstrations rather than presenting the underlying issues, thus contributing to rivalries and tensions within the antiwar movement (Gitlin, 1980). Today, arguably, social media exercise even greater influence on movement success.

Although some scholars have argued that larger, more bureaucratic social movement organizations are likely to be successful in the long run (W. Gamson, 1975), others have claimed that mass defiance, rather than formal organization, is the key to success (Piven & Cloward, 1977). Paradoxically, too much success may undermine social movements, since their strength derives partly from being outside society's power structures, making highly visible demands for social change. Once its demands are met, the group is often drawn inside the very power structures it once sought to change. Its leaders become bureaucrats, their fights are conducted by lawyers and government officials, and rank-and-file members disappear; the militant thrust of the organization is then blunted (Piven & Cloward, 1977).

A related problem is goal displacement, which occurs when the social movement organization's original goals become redirected toward enhancing the organization and its leadership (McCarthy & Zald, 1973). The U.S. labor movement is an example; once labor unions became successful, many of them became large and prosperous bureaucracies that were perceived as distanced from the needs of their rank-and-file members.

In the end, social movement organizations have to motivate people to support their cause, often with dollars as well as votes. Many groups engage in **grassroots organizing,** *attempts to mobilize support among the ordinary members of a community.* This organizing may range from door-to-door canvassing to leafleting to get people to attend massive demonstrations. Most social movements emerge from a group that has some grievance, and their active members consist largely of people who will directly benefit from any social change that occurs.

Some social movement organizations also depend on **conscience constituents,** *people who provide resources for a social movement organization but who are not themselves members of the aggrieved group that the organization champions* (McCarthy & Zald, 1973). Such supporters are motivated by strong ethical convictions rather than by direct self-interest in achieving the social

. . . .

Resource mobilization theory: A theory about social movement organizations that focuses on their ability to generate money, membership, and political support in order to achieve their objectives.

Grassroots organizing: Attempts to mobilize support among the ordinary members of a community.

Conscience constituents: People who provide resources for a social movement organization but who are not themselves members of the aggrieved group that the organization champions.

movement's goals. The National Coalition for the Homeless, for example, consists primarily of public interest lawyers, shelter operators, and others who advocate on behalf of homeless people; only a relatively small number of the homeless are themselves directly involved in the organization. Homeless advocacy groups raise money from numerous sources, including media celebrities and direct mailings to ordinary citizens (J. Blau, 1992).

MACRO-LEVEL APPROACHES Regardless of the efforts particular social movement organizations make, large-scale economic, political, and cultural conditions ultimately determine their movement's success or failure. For a social movement to arise and succeed, conditions must be such that people feel it is necessary and are willing to support it. Therefore social movements emerge and flourish in times of other social change, particularly if people experience that change as disruptive of their daily lives (McAdam et al., 1988; Tilly, 1978). For example, the labor movement arose with the emergence of industrial capitalism, which brought harsh conditions to the lives of many people, while the women's movement reemerged in the 1960s, when expanded educational opportunities for women left many female college graduates feeling marginalized and alienated as full-time homemakers and workplace discrimination threw obstacles in the way of their workplace aspirations.

Some political systems encourage social movements, while others repress them (Gale, 1986). When a government is in crisis, it may respond by becoming more repressive, or it may create a space for social movements to flourish. The former action occurred in China in 1989, when thousands of students and workers, frustrated by deteriorating economic conditions and rigid government controls, took to the streets to demand greater economic and political freedom. The brutal crackdown at Beijing's Tiananmen Square, televised live to a global audience, ended the nascent social movement for democracy. Likewise, government crackdowns on demonstrators and social movement participants have been widespread throughout the Middle East and North Africa as the Arab Spring movements have progressed—Syria's protest movement has, as of this writing, deteriorated into a civil war between the authoritarian government and those who seek its replacement.

Just as economic and political collapse may facilitate the rise of social movements, so too may prosperity. Resources are more abundant, mass media and other means of communication are more likely to be readily available, and activists are more likely to have an independent means of supporting themselves. Prosperous societies are also more likely to have a larger class of well-educated people, a group that has historically provided the leadership in many social movements (McAdam et al., 1988; McCarthy & Zald, 1973; Zald & McCarthy, 1987).

This iconic image shows one man standing in opposition to four tanks in Tiananmen Square, China, on June 5, 1989. Thousands of pro-democracy demonstrators sought political and economic changes in a weeks long occupation of the square. Many were injured or killed in a government crackdown. ■

Finally, even the spatial organization of society has been seen as having an impact on social movements. Dense, concentrated neighborhoods or workplaces facilitate social interaction and spur the growth of social movements. A century and a half ago, Karl Marx recognized that cities and factories were powerful breeding grounds for revolutionary insurgency against capitalism, since they brought previously isolated workers together in single locations. Subsequent research has sustained his conclusion (Marx, 1848/1977; Tilly, 1975). The concentration of students on campuses contributed to the rise of student activism in the 1960s (Lofland, 1985).

CULTURAL-LEVEL STUDIES AND "FRAME ALIGNMENT" Much of the research we have discussed emphasizes the political, economic, and organizational conditions that either help or hinder the rise of social movements. Sociologists have often regarded social movements as by-products of favorable social circumstances, rather than as the active accomplishments of their members. Today, however, rather than stressing how important it is for conditions to be ripe for social movements to thrive, many sociologists are thinking about how social movement organizations themselves are continually interpreting events so as to align themselves better with the cultural understanding of the wider society. The Tea Party movement is a good example. While it has a long list of political goals it wants to achieve, it succeeded in rallying people around the idea that "big government" and taxation are a threat to freedom and liberty. These are ideas that resonate with those who have some suspicion of intrusive government. The movement seeks to create a "good fit" between the social movement and the people who are its likely constituents.

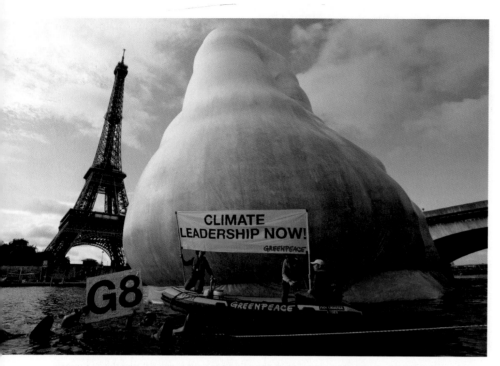

While environmental activism has a long history in the United States, in the past 10 to 15 years it has been reignited and challenged in a debate over climate change. Scientists, academics, and activists are concerned by scientific evidence that global warming is being accelerated by human activity. Today there is a global environmental movement fighting for greater attention and resources. ■

Sociologists think of that fit in terms of **frame alignment**, *the process by which the interests, understandings, and values of the social movement organization are shaped to match those in the wider society.* If their members' understandings align with the understandings of others in a community or society, social movements are likely to be successful; otherwise they are likely to fail. Social movement organizations achieve frame alignment in a variety of ways, ranging from modifying the beliefs of members to attempting to change the beliefs of the entire society (Snow, Rochford, Worden, & Benford, 1986).

In one common situation, people already share the social movement's concerns and understandings but lack the means to bring about the desired changes. In this case, there is no need for the social movement organization to get people to change their thinking about the problem; rather, the task is to get people to support the movement's efforts to do something about it. The social movement organization must "get the word out," whether through informal networks, social media, or direct-mail campaigns.

Sometimes the social movement's concerns are only weakly shared by others. In this case, the challenge for the social movement organization is to get people engaged and concerned enough to take action, perhaps by amplifying their concern that something they strongly believe in requires political action. The environmental movement is a case in point. Many scientists and a large number of other people are convinced that the earth is warming at a rapid rate due to the emission of industrial gases into the atmosphere. The movement has grown rapidly, but it has also produced a large number of skeptics, including politicians, who deny that

climate change is taking place. Groups such as the Sierra Club and Greenpeace and the owners of retail chains such as Patagonia and REI actively provide information to inform the public and spur individuals to action.

Finally, the social movement organization may seek to build support by attempting to entirely change the way people think. Revolutionary social movement organizations, for example, urge people to stop thinking of themselves as victims of bad luck, focusing attention instead on the faults of the political or economic system, which presumably requires a drastic overhaul.

To sum up, social movement organizations are competing for the hearts and minds of their constituents, with whom they must somehow bring their own beliefs and analyses into alignment if they are to succeed.

MICROMOBILIZATION CONTEXTS FOR BUILDING SOCIAL MOVEMENTS

Some conditions are ideal for social movement organizations to spring up. Sociologists call these *micromobilization contexts,* small group settings in which people are able to generate a shared set of beliefs to explain some social problem, along with the necessary social organization to do something about it (McAdam et al., 1988). Both formal and informal social networks usually exist, making it easier for members to understand why a micro-level problem, such as a personal experience of racism, is in fact the result of macro-level social forces, such as institutional racism. The civil rights movement, for example, emerged at a time when the Black community was developing strong local organizations, including schools, churches, and political groups. These highly interconnected institutions provided a fertile ground for the seeds of social activism (McAdam, 1982). Other examples are unions, student support groups, and even friendship networks, which are more elaborate in the age of Facebook, Twitter, and other social media (Beckers, Edwards, & Moody, 2010).

Micromobilization contexts also create the basic organizational framework required to address a problem—including leadership, mass media, and other communications technologies—as well as specific roles for movement activists and motivation to get involved. These incentives range from the emotional rewards that come from belonging to a group dedicated to a common cause to paid salaries. Micromobilization contexts thus serve as the bridge that connects the personal concerns of individuals to collectives hoping to create large-scale social change (Abrahams, 1992; A. Scott, 1990).

· ·

Frame alignment: The process by which the interests, understandings, and values of a social movement organization are rendered congruent with those of the wider society.

Finally, micromobilization contexts provide the starting point for cycles of protest that begin in one place and then spread, to new locations as well as to new social movements (Tarrow, 1983). Members of social movement organizations learn from one another; they copy each other's techniques, acquiring a large repertoire of protest activities in the process (Beckers et al., 2010; Tilly, 1978).

NEW SOCIAL MOVEMENTS

Social movements have often served as a means to an end: People come together to achieve specific objectives, such as improving the conditions of workers, gaining equality for the disadvantaged, or protesting a war. Participation in such social movement organizations was often separate from members' personal lives. Since the 1960s, however, many social movements have sought to break the boundary between politics and personal life. In addition to being a means for changing the world, the social movement organization has come to be seen as a vehicle for personal change and growth (Giugni & Passy, 2012).

In a sense, this progression reflects the *sociological imagination,* which calls for us to understand the relationship between our personal experiences and larger social forces. Social movements that have embraced this perspective have been labeled **new social movements**. While they often address political and economic issues, they *are fundamentally concerned with the quality of private life, often advocating large-scale changes in the way people think and act.*

New social movements may be formally organized with clearly defined roles (leadership, recruiting, etc.), or they may be informal and loosely organized, preferring spontaneous and confrontational methods to more bureaucratic approaches. Part of the purpose of new social movements in protesting, in fact, is not to force a distinction between "them" and "us," but to draw attention to their own right to exist as equals with other groups in society (J. Gamson, 1991; Omvedt, 1992; Tucker, 1991).

The new social movements aim to improve life in a wide range of areas subject to governmental, business, or other large-scale institutional control, from the workplace to sexuality, health, education, and interpersonal relationships. Four characteristics set these movements apart from earlier ones (Melucci, 1989):

1. The new social movements focus not just on the distribution of material goods but also on the control of symbols and information—an appropriate goal for an "information society" in which the production and ownership of knowledge are increasingly valuable.

2. People join new social movement organizations not purely to achieve specific goals but also because they value participation for its own sake (Melucci, 1989). For instance, LGBT (lesbian, gay, bisexual, and transgender)

• •

New social movements: Movements that have arisen since the 1960s and are fundamentally concerned with the quality of private life, often advocating large-scale cultural changes in how people think and act.

movements have provided safe havens for members, in addition to pursuing social change.

3. Rather than large, bureaucratically run, top-down organizations, the new social movements are often networks of people engaged in routine daily activities. For example, a small online movement was begun by a woman who objected to an unannounced $5 charge on her credit card; her protest was joined by thousands of others, and the bank rescinded the charge. Groups trying to raise awareness of climate change and threats to the environment often are loosely organized and register their concerns online and through other media such as newspapers and television talk shows.

4. The new social movements strongly emphasize the interconnectedness of planetary life and may see their actions as tied to a vision of the planet as a whole, rather than centering on narrow self-interest. "Think globally, act locally" is the watchword and includes an acute awareness of environmental issues.

WHY STUDY SOCIAL CHANGE?

Human beings make their own history, but they do not make it out of thin air. Every generation inherits certain *constraints,* characteristics of the society that limit their vision and their choices, and *resources,* characteristics of their society that they can mobilize in new and creative ways. People are constrained by existing institutions and social relationships. Social structures provide the resources for human action, even as the actions themselves are oriented toward changing those structures (Giddens, 1985).

The sociologically significant processes of globalization and technological change provide both resources and constraints for people everywhere. Social movements themselves may become increasingly internationalized (Marx & McAdam, 1994). Economic globalization, like most social processes, has both positive and negative effects. On the one hand, it opens up the possibility of a vast increase in global productive capacity, technological advances, global cooperation, and an increase in the standard of living for people around the world. On the other hand, globalization may also lead to lowered wages and to job losses in high-wage industrial countries, as well as to exploitive labor conditions in the low-wage countries of the world. Concerns about such problems have given rise to labor and environmental groups that operate across national borders (T. Barry & Sims, 1994).

We live at a moment in history that contains enormous possibilities as well as daunting problems. Without an understanding of these social forces, we will be unable to act intelligently to bring about the kind of world we most desire. Your understanding of the forces shaping social change today will enable you and tomorrow's citizens to act more effectively to shape your social world.

Iranian Social Movement

New Social Movements

WHAT CAN I DO WITH A SOCIOLOGY DEGREE?

CAREER DEVELOPMENT: SELECTED SOCIOLOGY CAREER RESOURCES

"Sociology is the study of social life, social change, and the social causes and consequences of human behavior. Sociologists investigate the structure of groups, organizations, and societies, and how people interact within these contexts. The subject matter of sociology ranges from the intimate family to the hostile mob; from organized crime to religious cults; from the divisions of race, gender and social class to the shared beliefs of a common culture; and from the sociology of work to the sociology of sports. In fact, few fields have such broad scope and relevance for research, theory, and application of knowledge."

—*American Sociological Association, 2005*

Sociology offers majors a broad spectrum of knowledge and skills. Majors can also benefit from knowledge of academic, professional, and career resources. *This feature offers an overview of resources that you can use for further research.* Additional resources are available at the book's website.

PROFESSIONAL ASSOCIATIONS FOR SOCIOLOGISTS

- American Anthropological Association: www.aaanet.org
- American Society of Criminology: www.asc41.com
- American Sociological Association: www.asanet.org
- Archaeological Institute of America: www.archaeological .org
- Association for Applied and Clinical Sociology: www .aacsnet.net
- Association for Humanist Sociology: www.ccsu.edu/ page.cfm?p=6817
- Eastern Sociological Society: www.essnet.org
- Good Works Foundation: www.goodworks.org

- International Sociological Association: www.isa-sociology .org
- Midwest Sociological Society: www.themss.org
- National Association for the Practice of Anthropology: www.practicinganthropology.org
- National Organization for Human Service Education: www.nationalhumanservices.org
- North Central Sociological Association: www.ncsanet .org
- Pacific Sociological Association: www.pacificsoc.org
- Social Science Research Council: www.ssrc.org
- Society for American Archaeology: www.saa.org
- Society for Applied Anthropology: www.sfaa.net
- Society for the Study of Social Problems: www.sssp1 .org
- Sociologists for Women in Society: www.socwomen .org
- Southern Sociological Society: www.southern sociologicalsociety.org
- Southwestern Social Science Association: www .sssaonline.org
- Urban Affairs Association: www.urbanaffairsassociation .org

SELECTED OCCUPATIONAL FIELDS FOR SOCIOLOGY MAJORS

- Business and Management
- Community Organizing/Advocacy/Affairs
- Criminal Justice
- Education
- Human Services
- Journalism/Writing
- Law
- Management Consulting
- Marketing and Advertising
- Nonprofit Management/Administration
- Policy Research, Planning, and Development
- Politics
- Program Analysis/Management
- Public Relations
- Social Work
- Sociology
- Youth Services

SAMPLE WORK SETTINGS

- Business/Management
- City Management
- Community Outreach Organizations
- Courts/Law Enforcement Agencies
- Departments of Human Services/Children's Services/Education/Justice/Veterans Affairs
- Elementary, Secondary, and Higher Education
- Federal, State, and Local Government
- Law Firms
- Marketing/Market Research/Sales
- Nonprofits/Nongovernmental Organizations
- Political Campaigns and Offices
- Public Relations/Advertising
- Research Institutes
- Social Service Agencies
- Think Tanks
- Universities and Colleges

INFORMATION ON EMPLOYMENT TRENDS AND EMPLOYMENT SECTORS

- American Enterprise Institute
- American Institutes for Research
- American Sociological Association
- Brookings Institution
- Economic Policy Institute
- Gallup
- National Association of Colleges and Employers
- National Opinion Research Center (NORC)
- O*NET (U.S. Government Occupational Network)
- Partnership for Public Service
- RAND Corporation
- Westat
- Urban Institute
- U.S. Bureau of Labor Statistics
- U.S. Census Bureau
- Your University or College Career Center

ONLINE JOB SEARCH TOOLS

- www.bridgespan.org (nonprofit jobs)
- www.careerbuilder.com (social work jobs)
- www.change.org
- www.geron.org
- www.idealist.org
- www.linkedin.com
- www.nonprofitjobseeker.com
- www.opportunityknocksnow.org
- www.ourpublicservice.org
- www.USAjobs.gov

OTHER RESOURCES

American Sociological Association: www.asanet.org

National Association of Colleges and Employers: www.naceweb.org

Occupational Outlook Handbook, www.bls.gov/ooh/

O*NET: www.onetonline.org

Weigers Vitullo, M. (2009). *Searching for a job with an undergraduate degree in sociology.* American Sociological Association, Academic and Professional Affairs. Retrieved from www.asanet.org

▶ *Access additional web links on the student study site to learn more.*

SUMMARY

To test your knowledge further, find additional study material on the Student Study Site at **www.sagepub.com/chamblissintro**

- Sociologists disagree about whether social change is gradual or abrupt, and about whether all societies are changing in roughly the same direction. The evolutionary, revolutionary, and **rise-and-fall theories of social change** are three approaches to these questions.

- Some early sociologists viewed **collective behavior** as a form of group contagion in which the veneer of civilization gave way to more instinctive, animal-like forms of behavior.

- A more sociological approach, **emergent norm** theory, examines the ways in which crowds and other forms of collective behavior develop their own rules and shared understandings.

- The most comprehensive theory of collective behavior, value-added theory, attempts to take into account the necessary conditions for collective behavior at the individual, organizational, and even societal levels.

- Social movements have been important historical vehicles for bringing about social change. They are usually achieved through **social movement organizations** (SMOs), which we study using the tools and understandings of organizational sociology.

- We can classify social movements as **reformist, revolutionary, rebellious, reactionary, utopian, or "new,"** depending on their vision of social change.

- **Resource mobilization theory** argues that we can explain the success or failure of SMOs not by the degree of social strain that may explain their origins, but by their organizational ability to marshal the financial and personal resources they need.

- In recent years sociologists have sought to explain how **social movements** align their own beliefs and values with those of their potential constituents in the wider society. Frame alignment activities range from modifying the beliefs of the SMO to attempting to change the beliefs of the entire society.

- Many social movements depend heavily on **conscience constituents** for their support. Micromobilization contexts are also important incubators of social movements.

- Globalization has created an opportunity for the formation of global social movements, since many of the problems in the world today are global and require global solutions.

- **New social movements**, organized around issues of personal identity and values, differ from earlier social movements because they focus on symbols and information as well as material issues; participation is frequently seen as an end in itself; they are organized as networks rather than bureaucratically; and they emphasize the interconnectedness of social groups and larger social entities.

KEY TERMS

Study terms on the go with the smartphone-friendly key term flashcards, available at **www.sagepub.com/chamblissintro**

differentiation, 447

rise-and-fall theories of social change, 450

collective behavior, 451

crowd, 453

emergent norms, 454

riot, 456

fad, 456

fashion, 456

panic, 457

craze, 457

rumor, 457

social movement, 458

reformist social movement, 459

revolutionary social movement, 460

rebellion, 461

reactionary social movement, 461

communitarian social movement, 463

free rider problem, 463

social movement organizations (SMOs), 463

resource mobilization theory, 464

grassroots organizing, 464

conscience constituents, 464

frame alignment, 466

new social movements, 467

DISCUSSION QUESTIONS

1. How do fads differ from fashions? Offer some examples of each, and consider whether and how setting phenomena in these different categories can shed light on their roots and functions.

2. Consider what you have learned about social movements and social change in this chapter. How is the global expansion of social media likely to change how people pursue social change? How has it done so already?

3. Design a social movement. What problem or issue would you want to address? How would you overcome the problems of social movements that were identified in this chapter?

DISCOVER STATE STATS

Log-in to the eBook and click on the title to the left for access to State Stats in order to complete the exercise.

Some important social movements addressing problems from pollution to crime to discrimination have been rooted in a particular group's desire to bring about social change. Now that you've gained experience in using the database, you will navigate your own path for this activity. Your goal is to identify a social, political, or economic issue of concern to you as part of an effort to mobilize others to act in the interest of social change. Gather statistical data on your issue of interest and present it in one to two persuasive, data-driven paragraphs intended to convince others to join you in acting on the problem you have identified.

STUDENT STUDY SITE

Visit the Student Study Site at **www.sagepub.com/chamblissintro** to access additional study tools, including eFlashcards, web quizzes, video resources, web resources, audio resources, links to SAGE journal, handbook, and research articles, and much more!

Achieved status: An individual's social position is linked to his or her acquisition of socially valued credentials or skills.

Agency: The ability of individuals and groups to exercise free will and to make changes on a small or large scale.

Age-specific fertility rate: The number of births typical in women of a specific age in a particular population.

Age-specific mortality rate: The number of deaths typical in men and women of specific ages in a particular population.

Agricultural surplus: Food beyond the amount required for immediate survival.

Alliances (or coalitions): Groups that may form between members, enabling them to "gang up" on another member, thereby destabilizing the group.

Animism: The belief, common to many religions, that naturally occurring phenomena, such as mountains and animals, are possessed of indwelling spirits with supernatural powers.

Anomie: A social condition of normlessness; a state of normative uncertainty that occurs when people lose touch with the shared rules and values that give order and meaning to their lives.

Anthropology: Highlights the study of human cultures and societies and their development.

Anticipatory socialization: Adopting the behavior or standards of a group one emulates or hopes to join.

Antimiscegenation laws: Laws passed by states to prohibit interracial sexual relations and marriage.

Ascribed status: An individual's social position is linked to characteristics that are socially significant but cannot generally be altered (such as race or gender).

Assimilation: The absorption of a minority group into the dominant culture.

Atavisms: A word utilized by earlier proponents of biological explanations of deviance that means deviant people are more like primitive humans.

Authoritarianism: A form of governance in which ordinary members of society are denied the right to participate in government, while political power is exercised by and for the benefit of a small political elite.

Automation: The replacement of human labor by machines in the process of manufacturing.

Barter economy: Based on the exchange of goods and services rather than money with others in the community.

Behaviorism: A psychological perspective that emphasizes the effect of rewards and punishments on human behavior.

Beliefs: Particular ideas that people accept as true.

Bias: A characteristic of results that systematically misrepresent the true nature of what is being studied.

Bourgeoisie: The capitalist (or property-owning) class.

Bureaucracies: Formal organizations characterized by written rules, hierarchical authority, and a paid staff, intended to promote organizational efficiency.

Bureaucracy: A type of formal organization based on written procedural rules, arranged into a clear hierarchy of authority, and staffed by full-time paid officials.

Capital offenses: Capital punishment; crimes that are punishable by death.

Capitalism: An economic order characterized by the market allocation of goods and services, production for private profit, and private ownership of the means of producing wealth.

Caste society: A social system in which social status is given for life. Caste societies are closed to social mobility.

Charismatic authority: Power based on devotion inspired in followers by the personal qualities of a leader.

Church: A well-established religious organization that exists in a fairly harmonious relationship with the larger society.

Citizen: A legally recognized inhabitant of a country who bears the rights and responsibilities of citizenship as defined by the state.

City: A relatively large, dense, and permanent settlement of socially heterogenous individuals.

Civil religion: A set of religious beliefs through which a society interprets its own history in light of some conception of ultimate reality.

Civil unions: Legal unions that fall short of marriage but provide some state-level legal rights and benefits.

Class conflict: The product of competition between social classes over the distribution of wealth and power in society.

Class dominance theory: The notion that a small and concentrated group of elite or upper-class people dominate and influence societal institutions; compatible with conflict theory.

Class society: A social system in which social level is open to movement so that changing class status is possible.

Class: A person's economic status in society, usually associated with income, wealth, and occupation, and sometimes associated with political voice.

Class-dominant theories: Propose that what is labeled deviant or criminal—and therefore who gets punished—is determined by the interests of the dominant class in a particular culture or society.

Coercion: The threat or use of physical force in order to ensure compliance.

Coercive organization: An organization in which people are forced to give unquestioned obedience to authority.

Cognitive development: As theorized by Jean Piaget, the increasing ability to make logical decisions as a person grows older.

Cohabitation: Living together as a couple without being legally married.

Collective behavior: Voluntary, goal-oriented action that occurs in relatively disorganized situations, in which society's predominant social norms and values cease to govern individual behavior.

Collective conscience: Encompasses the common beliefs and values that bind a society together.

Common law marriage: A type of relationship in which partners live as if married but without marriage's formal legal framework.

Communism: A type of economic system without private ownership of the means of production and, theoretically, without economic classes or economic inequality.

Communitarian social movement: A movement seeking to withdraw from the dominant society by creating its own ideal community.

Concept: An idea that describes a number of things that have something in common.

Conscience constituents: People who provide resources for a social movement organization but who are not themselves members of the aggrieved group that the organization champions.

Control theory: Explains that the cause of deviance lies in the arena of social control and, specifically, the life experiences and relationships people form.

Conversation analysis: The study of how participants in social interaction recognize and produce coherent conversation.

Correlation: The degree to which two or more variables are associated with one another.

Craze: An intense attraction to an object, a person, or an activity.

Credential society: One in which access to desirable work and social status depends on the possession of a certificate or diploma certifying the completion of formal education.

Crime: An act defined in the law as punishable by fines, imprisonment, or both.

Crimes: An act defined in the law as punishable by fines, imprisonment, or both.

Criminal deviance: deviance that violates established laws.

Critical thinking: The ability to evaluate claims about truth by using reason and evidence.

Crowd: A temporary gathering of closely interacting people with a common focus.

Crude birthrate: The number of births each year per 1,000 people.

Crude death rate: The number of deaths each year per 1,000 people.

Cult: A religious organization that is thoroughly unconventional with regard to the larger society.

Cultural capital: Wealth in the form of knowledge, ideas, verbal skills, and ways of thinking and acting.

Cultural inconsistency: The contradiction between the goals of ideal culture and the practices of real culture.

Cultural pluralism: The coexistence of different racial and ethnic groups characterized by acceptance and respect for one another's differences.

Cultural relativism: A worldview whereby the practices of another society should

be understood sociologically in terms of that society's own norms and values, and not one's own.

Culture: The beliefs, norms, behaviors, and products common to the members of a particular group.

De facto segregation: School segregation based on residential patterns or student choice, which persists even though legal segregation is now outlawed in the United States.

Deductive reasoning: The process of taking an existing theory and logically deducing that if the theory is accurate, we should discover other patterns of behavior consistent with it.

Democracy: A form of governance in which citizens are able to participate directly or indirectly in their own governance.

Demography: The science of population size, distribution, and composition.

Denomination: A form of a church that is not formally allied with the state.

Dependency theory: Argues that the poverty of some countries is a consequence of their exploitation by wealthy states, which control the global capitalist system.

Dependent variable: A variable that changes as a result of changes in another variable.

Deviance: Any behavior, action, practice, or condition, including those that violate cultural norms or societal laws, that results in disapproval, hostility, or sanction if it becomes known.

Dictatorship: A form of governance in which power rests in a single individual.

Differential association theory: Holds that deviant and criminal behavior results from exposure attitudes favorable to acting in ways that are deviant or criminal.

Differentiation: The development of increasing societal complexity through the creation of specialized social roles and institutions.

Direct democracy: A political system in which all citizens fully participate in their own governance.

Discrimination: The unequal treatment of individuals on the basis of their membership in a group.

Disestablishment Clause: Part of the First Amendment in the Bill of Rights of the U.S. Constitution, which contains the passage "Congress shall make no law respecting an establishment of religion, or prohibiting the free exercise thereof."

Disestablishment: A period during which the political influence of established religions is successfully challenged.

Document analysis: Examines written materials or cultural products: previous studies, newspaper reports, court records, campaign posters, digital reports, films, pamphlets, and other forms of text or images produced by individuals, government agencies, or private organizations.

Domestic (family) violence: Physical or sexual abuse committed by one family member against another.

Domestic partnerships: Legal unions that provide a circumscribed spectrum of rights and benefits to same-sex couples.

Double consciousness: An awareness of oneself both as American and as Black, never free of racial stigma.

Doxic: That which is taken for granted as "natural" or "normal" in society, though it may be socially constructed.

Dramaturgical approach: Erving Goffman's theory of social interaction that studies it as if it were governed by the norms of theatrical performance.

Dyad: A group consisting of two persons.

Ecclesia: A form of a church that is formally allied with the state and is the "official" religion of the society.

Economic capital: Money and material that can be used to produce goods and services.

Economy: The social institution that organizes the ways in which a society produces, distributes, and consumes goods and services.

Education: The transmission of society's norms, values, and knowledge base by means of direct instruction.

Ego: According to Sigmund Freud, the part of the mind that is the "self," the core of what is regarded as a person's unique personality.

Egocentric: Experiencing the world as if it were centered entirely on oneself.

Emergent norms: Norms that are situationally created to support a collective action.

Emic perspective: The perspective of the insider, the one belonging to the cultural group in question.

Emotional labor: The management of feelings or emotions to create a publicly observable facial and bodily display in return for a wage.

Endogamous: A characteristic of marriages in which partners are limited to members of the same social group or caste.

Ethnic cleansing: The physical expulsion of a group from a territory claimed by another group.

Ethnicity: The attribution of characteristics to groups of people who share a common cultural (including religious) heritage.

Ethnocentric: Judging other cultures by the standards of one's own culture, and regarding one's own way of life as "normal"—and better.

Ethnocentrism: A worldview whereby one judges other cultures by the standards of one's own culture.

Ethnomethodology: A sociological method that studies the body of commonsense knowledge and procedures by which ordinary members of a society make sense of their social circumstances and interaction.

Etic perspective: The perspective of the outside observer.

Evangelicalism: A belief in spiritual rebirth (conventionally denoted as being "born again").

Experiments: Research techniques for investigating cause and effect under controlled conditions.

Exponential population growth: The belief that a constant rate of population growth produces a population that grows by an increasing amount with each passing year.

Expulsion: The forcible removal of a population.

Extended family: A social group consisting of one or more parents, children, and other kin, often spanning several generations, living in the same household.

Fad: A temporary, highly imitated outbreak of mildly unconventional behavior.

Falsifiability: The ability for a theory to be disproven; the logical possibility for a theory to be tested and proven false.

Family: A group of people who identify themselves as being related to one another, usually by blood, marriage, or adoption, and who share intimate relationships and dependency.

Fashion: A style of imitative behavior or appearance that is of a longer duration than a fad.

Feminist perspective on deviance: Suggests that studies of deviance are biased and that both gender-specific cultural norms and the particular ways in which women are victimized by virtue of their gender account for deviance among women.

Fertility: The number of live births in a given population.

Fieldwork: A research method relying on an in-depth and often extended study of a group or community.

Folkways: Fairly weak norms that are passed down from the past, whose violation is generally not considered serious within a particular culture.

Food deserts: Sites bereft of places selling competitively priced, healthy, and fresh food.

Formal economy: All work-related activities that provide income and are regulated by government agencies.

Formal education: Education that occurs within academic institutions such as schools.

Formal organization: An organization that is rationally designed to achieve its objectives, often by means of explicit rules, regulations, and procedures.

Formal rationality: A characteristic of modern societies, which means that people's pursuit of goals is shaped by rules, regulations, and larger social structures.

Formal social control: Is most often exercised by the state, including the police and courts, and is society's *attempt to officially sanction certain behaviors and visibly punish others.*

Frame alignment: The process by which the interests, understandings, and values of a social movement organization are rendered congruent with those of the wider society.

Free rider problem: A problem that arises because people avoid the costs of social movement activism (such as time, energy, and other personal resources) and still benefit from its success without becoming active participants.

Gender roles: The attitudes and behaviors that are considered appropriately "masculine" or "feminine" in a particular culture.

Gender wage gap: The difference between the earnings of women who work full-time year-round as a group and those of men who work full-time year-round as a group.

Gender: Behavioral differences between males and females that are culturally based and socially learned.

Generalized other: The abstract sense of society's norms and values by which people evaluate themselves.

Genocide: The mass, systematic destruction of a people or a nation.

Gentrification: The attempt to change the socioeconomic composition of old and poor neighborhoods with the remodeling of old structures and building of new residences and shops to attract new middle- and high-income residents.

Glass ceiling: An artificial boundary that allows women to see the next occupational or salary level even as structural obstacles keep them from reaching it.

Glass escalator: The nearly invisible promotional boost men gain in female-dominated occupations.

Global cities: Metropolitan areas that are highly interconnected with one another in their role as centers of global, political, and economic decision making.

Global consumer class: Those who actively use technology, purchase consumer goods, and embrace the culture of consumption.

Global culture: A type of culture—some would say U.S. culture—that has spread across the world in the form of Hollywood films, fast-food restaurants, and popular music heard in virtually every country.

Globalization: The process by which people all around the planet become increasingly interconnected economically, politically, culturally, and environmentally.

GNI-PPP: A comparative economic measure that uses international dollars to indicate the amount of goods and services someone could buy in the United States with a given amount of money.

Goods: Objects that have an economic value to others, whether they are the basic necessities we need to survive, or things we simply want.

Grassroots organizing: Attempts to mobilize support among the ordinary members of a community.

Groupthink: A process by which the members of a group ignore ways of thinking and plans of action that go against the group consensus.

Habitus: The internalization of objective probabilities and subsequent expression of those probabilities as choice.

Health care: All those activities intended to sustain, promote, and enhance health.

Health: The extent to which a person experiences a state of mental, physical, and social well-being.

Hidden curriculum: An unspoken classroom socialization to the norms, values, and roles of a culture that a school provides along with the "official" curriculum.

High culture: The music, theater, literature, and other cultural products that are held in particularly high esteem in society.

Hostile environment harassment: Conditions in the workplace that someone perceives as intimidating, uncomfortable, or otherwise distressing.

Human capital: The skills and knowledge a person possesses that makes them valuable in a particular workplace.

Hypothesis: An idea about the world, derived from a theory that can be disproved when tested against observations.

I: According to George Herbert Mead, the part of the self that refers to the impulse to act; it is creative, innovative, unthinking, and largely unpredictable.

Id: According to Sigmund Freud, the part of the mind that is the repository of basic biological drives and needs.

Ideal culture: The values, norms, and behaviors that people in a given society profess to embrace.

Income: The amount of money a person or household earns in a given period of time, usually a year.

Independent or experimental variable: A variable that causes changes in another variable.

Indirect labor costs: The time, training, or money spent when an employee takes time off to care for sick family members, opts for parental leave, arrives at work late, or leaves a position after receiving employer-provided training.

Individual discrimination: Overt and intentional unequal treatment, often based on prejudicial beliefs.

Inductive reasoning: The process of generalizing to an entire category of phenomena from a particular set of observations.

Inequality: Differences in wealth, power, and other valued resources.

Infant mortality rate: Measures the number of deaths of infants under age 1 per 1,000 live births per year.

Informal (or underground) economy: Those income-generating economic activities that escape regulation by the governmental institutions that ordinarily regulate similar activities.

Informal social control: Most often occurs among ordinary people during the course of their interactions and is the unofficial mechanism through which deviance and deviant behaviors are sanctioned in society.

Institutionalized discrimination: Unequal treatment that has become a part of the routine operation of such major social institutions as businesses, schools, hospitals, and the government.

Interest groups: Advocacy or lobby groups that utilize their organizational and social resources to influence legislation and the functioning of social institutions.

International families: Families that result from globalization.

International governmental organization (IGO): An international organization established by treaties between governments for purposes of commerce, security, promotion of social welfare and human rights, and environmental protection.

International nongovernmental organization (INGO): An international organization established by agreements between the individuals or private organizations making up its membership and existing to fulfill an explicit mission.

Interview: A detailed conversation designed to obtain in-depth information about a person and his or her activities.

Iron law of oligarchy: Robert Michels's theory that there is an inevitable tendency for large-scale bureaucratic organizations to become ruled undemocratically by a handful of people.

Labeling theory: A symbolic interactionist approach holding that deviance is a product of the labels people attach to certain types of behavior.

Labor demand factors: Factors that highlight the needs and preferences of the employer.

Labor supply factors: Factors that highlight reasons that women or men may "prefer" particular occupations.

Language: A system of symbolic verbal, nonverbal, and written representations rooted within a particular culture.

Latent functions: Functions of an object, an institution, or a phenomenon that are not recognized or expected.

Law: A system of binding and recognized rules that regulate the actions of people pertaining to a given jurisdiction.

Laws: Codified norms or rules of behavior.

Leading question: A question that solicits a particular response.

Legitimate authority: A type of power that is recognized as rightful by those over whom it is exercised.

Legitimate authority: Power that is recognized as rightful by those over whom it is exercised.

Liberal feminism: The belief that women's inequality is primarily the result of imperfect institutions, which can be corrected by reforms that do not fundamentally alter society itself.

Life chances: The opportunities and obstacles one will encounter in education, social life, work, and other areas critical to social mobility.

Life expectancy: The average number of years a person of a given age can expect to live based on existing health conditions in the country.

Literacy: The ability to read and write at a basic level.

Literacy: The ability to read and write at a basic level.

Lobbyists: Paid professionals whose job it is to influence legislation.

Looking-glass self: The concept developed by Charles Horton Cooley that our self-image results from how we interpret other people's views of us.

Macro-level paradigm: Theories of the social world that are concerned with large-scale patterns and institutions.

Mandatory minimum sentences: Federal and state legislators in the 1980s passed legislation stipulating that a person found guilty of a particular crime had to be sentenced to a minimum number of years in prison. This reduced judges' ability to use their discretion in sentencing and led to a substantial increase in the average prison term.

Manifest functions: Functions of an object, an institution, or a phenomenon that are obvious and intended.

Marriage: A culturally approved relationship, usually between two individuals, which provides a degree of economic cooperation, intimacy, and sexual activity.

Mass education: The extension of formal schooling to wide segments of the population.

Mass media: Forms of communication that permit a flow of information from a single source to a wide audience.

Mass production: The large-scale, highly standardized manufacturing of identical commodities on a mechanical assembly line.

Material culture: The physical objects that are created, embraced, or consumed by society that help shape people's lives.

Matrix of domination: A system of social positions in which any individual may concurrently occupy a status (for example, gender, race, class, or sexual orientation) as a member of a dominated group and a status as a member of a dominating group.

Me: According to George Herbert Mead, the part of the self through which we see ourselves as others see us.

Means of consumption: Things that make it possible for consumers to acquire goods and services and, at the same time, foster their control and exploitation as consumers, as they spend beyond their needs and means.

Means of production: The sites and technology that produce the goods we need and use.

Medicine: An institutionalized system for the scientific diagnosis, treatment, and prevention of illness.

Megacity: A metropolitan area or city with a total population of 10 million people or more.

Meritocracy: A society in which personal success is based on talent and individual effort.

Micro-level paradigm: Models or images of the world that are concerned with social relations and interactions in specific, individual situations.

Minorities: Groups of people who are discriminated against on the basis of socially constructed characteristics.

Mixed contacts: Interactions between those who are stigmatized and those who are "normal."

Modernization theory: A market-oriented development theory that envisions development as evolutionary and guided by modern institutions and cultures.

Monarchy: A form of governance in which power resides in an individual or a family and is passed from one generation to the next through hereditary lines.

Monogamy: A form of marriage in which a person may have only one spouse at a time.

Monotheism: Belief in a single all-knowing, all-powerful God.

Morbidity: The rate of illness in a particular population.

Mores: Strongly held norms, violation of which would seriously offend the standards of acceptable conduct of most people within a particular culture.

Mortality: The rate of death in a particular population.

Multicultural feminism: The belief that inequality must be understood—and ended—for all women, regardless of race, class, nationality, age, sexual orientation, physical ability, or other characteristics.

Multiculturalism: A commitment to respect cultural differences rather than to try to submerge them into a larger, dominant culture.

Nation-state: A single people (a "nation") governed by a political authority (a "state"). Similar to the modern notion of "country."

Negative correlation: One variable increases as the other decreases.

Net financial assets: A measure of wealth that excludes such personal assets as home and car.

Net migration: In-migration minus out-migration.

New religious movements (NRMs): Movements that are new and in key respects different from existing religious movements.

"New" social movements: Movements that have arisen since the 1960s and are fundamentally concerned with the quality of private life, often advocating large-scale cultural changes in how people think and act.

Noncitizens: Individuals who reside in a given jurisdiction but do not possess the same rights and privileges as the citizens who are recognized inhabitants. Sometimes referred to as residents, temporary workers, or aliens.

Nonmaterial culture: The abstract creations of human cultures, including language and social practices.

Nontheistic religion: Belief in the existence of divine spiritual forces rather than a God or gods.

Normative organization: An organization that people join of their own will to pursue a morally worthwhile goal, without expectation of material reward; sometimes called a voluntary association.

Norms: Accepted social behaviors and beliefs.

Norms: The common rules of a culture that govern the behavior of people belonging to that culture.

Nuclear family: A social group consisting of one or two parents and their biological, dependent children with no other kin.

Objectivity: The ability to represent the object of study accurately.

Occupation: A person's main vocation or paid employment.

Occupational segregation by gender: The concentration of men and women in different occupations.

Official poverty line: The dollar amount set by the government as the minimum amount of money needed to meet the basic needs for a family.

Operational definition: Definition of a concept that allows it to be observed and measured.

Operational definition: Definition of a concept that allows it to be observed and measured.

Opportunity theory: Argues that people differ not only in their motivation to engage in deviant acts, but also in their *opportunity* to do so.

Organization: A group with an identifiable membership that engages in concerted collective actions to achieve a common purpose.

Organized crime: Crimes committed by groups that provide illegal goods and services.

PACs (political action committees): Organizations created by groups such as corporations, unions, environmentalists, and other interest groups for the purpose of gathering money and contributing to political candidates who favor the groups' interests.

Panic: A massive flight from something that is feared.

Patriarchy: Any set of social relationships in which men dominate women.

Personal power: Power that derives from a leader's personality.

Phrenology: A theory that the skull shapes of deviant individuals differ from those of nondeviants.

Pluralistic societies: Societies made up of many diverse groups with different norms and values.

Political power: The ability to exercise influence on political institutions and/or actors in order to realize personal or group interests.

Politics: The art or science of influencing public policy.

Polyandry: A form of marriage in which a woman may have multiple husbands.

Polygamy: A form of marriage in which a person may have more than one spouse at a time.

Polygamy: The act of having multiple wives.

Polygyny: A form of marriage in which a man may have multiple wives.

Polytheism: The belief that there are different gods representing various categories of natural forces.

Popular culture: The entertainment, culinary, and athletic tastes shared by the masses.

Population momentum: The tendency of population growth to continue beyond the point when replacement-rate fertility has been achieved because of the high concentration of people of childbearing age.

Population: The whole group of people studied in sociological research.

Positional power: Power that stems officially from the leadership position itself.

Positivist: Science that is based on facts alone.

Power elite: A group of people with a disproportionately high level of influence and resources who utilize their status to influence the functioning of societal institutions.

Power: The ability to mobilize resources and achieve goals despite the resistance of others.

Prejudice: A belief about an individual or a group that is not subject to change on the basis of evidence.

Presentation of self: The creation of impressions in the minds of others in order to define and control a social situation.

Preventive medicine: Medicine that emphasizes a healthy lifestyle that will prevent poor health before it occurs.

Primary deviance: A term developed by Edwin Lemert; the first step in the labeling of deviance, it occurs at the moment an activity is labeled deviant (see also *secondary deviance*).

Primary group: A small group characterized by intense emotional ties, face-to-face interaction, intimacy, and a strong, enduring sense of commitment.

Primary groups: Groups characterized by intense emotional ties, intimacy, and identification with membership in the group.

Principle of falsification: The principle, advanced by philosopher Karl Popper, that a scientific theory must lead to testable hypotheses that can be disproved if they are wrong.

Private sector: Provides goods and services to the economy and consumers; its primary motive is profit.

Profane: A sphere of routine, everyday life.

Proletariat: The working class; wage workers.

Property crime: Involves violating the ownership rights of someone else and includes crimes like burglary, larceny/theft, arson, and motor vehicle theft.

Psychoanalysis: A psychological perspective that emphasizes the complex reasoning processes of the conscious and unconscious mind.

Public education: A universal education system provided by the government and funded by tax revenues rather than student fees.

Public health: The science and practice of health protection and maintenance at a community level.

Public sector: Jobs are linked to the government (whether national, state, or local) and encompass production or allocation of goods and services for the benefit of a government and its citizens.

Qualitative research: Typically highlights data that cannot be quantified (or converted into numbers), focusing instead on generating in-depth knowledge of social life, institutions, and processes.

Qualitative variables: Variables that express a quality and do not have a numerical value.

Qualitative variables: Variables that express a quality and do not have a numerical value.

Quantitative research: Gathers data that can be quantified and offers insight into patterns of social behavior and social attitudes.

Quantitative variables: Factors we can count.

Quantitative variables: Factors we can count.

Quid pro quo sexual harassment: The demand or implication that a sexual favor will buy a promotion or an opportunity to keep one's job.

Race: A group sharing apparent physical traits deemed by society to be socially significant.

Racism: Institutionalized relationships between dominant and minority groups that create a structure of economic, social, and political inequality based on socially constructed racial or ethnic categories.

Radical feminism: The belief that women's inequality underlies all other forms of inequality, including economic inequality.

Random sample: A sample in which everyone in the population of interest has an equal chance of being chosen for the study.

Rape culture: A social culture that provides an environment conducive to rape.

Rate of natural increase: The crude birth rate minus the crude death rate.

Rational-legal authority: Power based on a belief in the lawfulness of enacted rules (laws) and the legitimate right of leaders to exercise authority under such rules.

Reactionary social movement: A movement seeking to restore an earlier social system—often based on a mythical past—along with the traditional norms and values that once presumably accompanied it.

Real culture: The values, norms, and behaviors that people in a given society actually embrace and exhibit.

Rebellion: A movement seeking to overthrow the existing social, political, and economic system, but lacking a detailed plan for a new social order.

Reference group: A group that provides standards for judging one's attitudes or behaviors.

Reformist social movement: A movement seeking to bring about social change within the existing economic and political system.

Reliability: The extent to which researchers' findings are consistent with different studies of the same thing, or with the same study over time.

Religion: A system of common beliefs and rituals centered on "sacred things" that unites believers and provides a sense of meaning and purpose.

Religious economy: Suggests that religions can be fruitfully understood as organizations in competition with one another for followers.

Religious nationalism: The linkage of religious convictions with beliefs about a nation or ethnic group's social and political destiny.

Replication: The repetition of a previous study using a different sample or population to verify or refute the original findings.

Representative democracy: A political system in which citizens elect representatives to govern them.

Research method: A specific technique for systematically gathering data.

Reserve army of labor: A pool of job seekers whose numbers outpace the available positions and who contribute to keeping wages low and conditions of work tenuous.

Resocialization: The process of altering an individual's behavior through control of his or her environment, for example, within a total institution.

Resource mobilization theory: A theory about social movement organizations that focuses on their ability to generate money, membership, and political support in order to achieve their objectives.

Revolutionary social movement: A movement seeking to alter fundamentally the existing social, political, and economic system in keeping with a vision of a new social order.

Riot: A prolonged outbreak of violent behavior by a sizable group of people that is directed against people or property and is often illegal.

Rise-and-fall theories of social change: Argue that change reflects a cycle of growth and decline.

Role-taking: The ability to take the role of others in interaction.

Rumor: An unverified form of information that is transmitted informally, usually originating in an unknown source.

Sacred: That which is set apart from the ordinary, the sphere endowed with spiritual meaning.

Sample: A portion of the larger population selected to represent the whole.

School segregation: The education of racial minorities in schools that are geographically separated from those attended by whites.

Scientific management: A practice that sought to use principles of engineering to reduce the physical movements of the workers.

Scientific method: A way of learning about the world that combines logically constructed theory and systematic observation to provide explanations of how things work.

Scientific theories: An explanation of how and why scientific observations are as they are.

Scientific: A way of learning about the world that combines logically constructed theory and systematic observation.

Second shift: A phrase used by sociologists to characterize the unpaid housework that women typically do after they come home from their paid employment.

Secondary deviance: A term developed by Edwin Lemert; the second step in the labeling of deviance, it occurs when a person labeled deviant accepts the label as part of his or her identity and, as a result, begins to act in conformity with the label (see also *primary deviance*).

Secondary group: A group that is large and impersonal and characterized by fleeting relationships.

Secondary groups: Large, impersonal groups with minimal emotional and intimate ties.

Sect: A religious organization that has splintered off from an established church, in an effort to restore perceived "true" beliefs and practices believed to have been lost by the established religious organization.

Secularization: The rise in worldly thinking, particularly as seen in the rise of science, technology, and rational thought, and a simultaneous decline in the influence of religion.

Segregation: The physical and social separation of different categories of people.

Serial monogamy: The practice of having more than one wife or husband, but only one at a time.

Services: Economically productive activities that do not result directly in a physical product; they can be relatively simple, or quite complex.

Sex category: The socially required identification display that confirms someone's membership in a given category.

Sex: Anatomical or other biological differences between males and females that originate in the genetic differences.

Sexual division of labor in modern societies: The phenomenon of dividing production functions by gender and designating different spheres of activity, the "private" to women and the "public" to men.

Sexual harassment: Unwelcome sexual advances, requests for sexual favors, or physical conduct of a sexual nature when such conduct is used as a condition of employment, instruction, evaluation, benefits, or other opportunities; or when such conduct interferes with an individual's performance or contributes to an intimidating, hostile, or offensive environment.

Sexuality: The ways in which people construct their sexual desires and relationships, including the norms governing sexual behavior.

Sick role: The cultural definition of the appropriate behavior of and response to people labeled as sick.

Significant others: According to George Herbert Mead, the specific people who are important in children's lives and whose views have the greatest impact on their self-evaluations.

Social bonds: Our connections to others (see also *control theory*).

Social capital: The social knowledge and connections that enable people to accomplish their goals and extend their influence.

Social categories: People sharing a common characteristic without necessarily interacting or identifying with one another.

Social class reproduction: The way that class status is reproduced from generation to generation, with parents "passing on" a class position to their offspring.

Social closure: The ability of groups to strategically and consciously exclude outsiders or those deemed "undesirable" from participating in the group or enjoying the group's resources.

Social conflict paradigm (conflict perspective): A theory that seeks to explain social organization and change in terms of the conflict that is built into social relations.

Social control: Refers to the attempts by certain people or groups in society to control the behaviors of other individuals and groups in order to increase the likelihood that will conform to established norms or laws.

Social diversity: The social and cultural mixture of different groups in society and the recognition of difference as significant.

Social dynamics: The laws that govern social change.

Social embeddedness: The idea that economic, political, and other forms of human behavior are fundamentally shaped by social relations.

Social epidemiology: Studies communities and their social status, practices, and problems to understand patterns of health and disease.

Social facts: Qualities of groups that are external to individual members yet constrain their thinking and behavior.

Social inequality: A high degree of disparity in income, wealth, power, prestige, and other resources.

Social learning: The way people adapt their behavior in response to social rewards and punishments.

Social mobility: The upward or downward status movement of individuals or groups over time.

Social movement organizations (SMOs): Formal organizations that seek to achieve social change through noninstitutionalized forms of political action.

Social movement: A large number of people who come together in a continuing and organized effort to bring about (or resist) social change, and who rely at least partially on noninstitutionalized forms of political action.

Social power: The ability to exercise social control.

Social solidarity: The bonds that unite the members of a social group.

Social statics: The way society is held together.

Social stratification: The systematic ranking of different groups of people in a hierarchy of inequality.

Socialism: Theoretically, when a government manages the economy in the interests of the workers; it owns the businesses, factories, farms, hospitals, housing, and other means of producing wealth and redistributes that wealth to the population through wages and services.

Socialist feminism: The belief that women's inequality results from the combination of capitalistic economic relations and male domination, arguing that both must be transformed fundamentally before women can achieve equality.

Socialization: The process by which people learn the culture of their society.

Sociological imagination: The ability to grasp the relationship between our individual lives and the larger social forces that help to shape them.

Sociological theories: Logical, rigorous frameworks for the interpretation of social life that make particular assumptions and ask particular questions about the social world.

Sociology: The scientific study of human social relations, groups, and societies.

Standpoint epistemology: A philosophical perspective that argues that what we can know is affected by the position we occupy in society.

Standpoint theory: A perspective that says the knowledge we create is conditioned by where we stand, or our subjective social position.

State crime: Criminal acts committed by state and government officials in the pursuit of their jobs as representatives of the government.

Statistical data: Quantitative information obtained from government agencies, businesses, research studies, and other entities that collect data for their own or others' use.

Status: The prestige associated with a social position.

Stereotyping: Generalizing a set of characteristics to all members of a group.

Stigma: An attribute that is deeply discrediting to an individual or a group because it overshadows other attributes and merits the individual or group may possess.

Stigmatized: Branded as highly disgraceful (see also *labeling theory*).

Strain theory: Argues that societal pressures inhibit the ability for people to fulfill their needs, causing them to experience stress, or strain, and turn to crime to satisfy those needs.

Structural contradiction theory: Argues that conflicts generated by fundamental contradictions in the structure of society produce deviance laws defining certain deviant acts as criminal.

Structural functionalism (functionalist perspective): A theory that seeks to explain social organization and change in terms of the roles performed by different social structures and institutions.

Structural strain: In Robert K. Merton's reformulation of Durkheim's functionalist theory, a form of anomie that occurs when a gap exists between society's culturally defined goals and the means

society makes available to achieve those goals.

Structuralism: The idea of an overarching structure within which culture and other aspects of society must be understood.

Structure: Patterned social arrangements that have an effect on agency.

Subcultural theories: Explain deviance in terms of the conflicting interests of more and less powerful segments of a population.

Subcultures: Cultures that exist together with a dominant culture, but differ in some important respects from that dominant culture.

Superego: According to Sigmund Freud, the part of the mind that consists of the values and norms of society, insofar as they are internalized, or taken in, by the individual.

Survey: A questionnaire or interviews administered to a group of people in person or by telephone or e-mail to determine their characteristics, opinions, and behaviors.

Symbolic interactionism: A microsociological perspective that posits that both the individual self and society as a whole are the result of social interactions based on language and other symbols.

Symbols: Cultural representations of social realities.

Symbols: Representations of things that are not immediately present to our senses.

Taboos: Powerful mores, the violation of which is considered serious and even unthinkable.

Technology: The practical application of knowledge to transform natural resources for human use.

Terrorism: "The calculated use of violence of the threat of violence to inculcate fear; intended to coerce or to intimidate governments or societies in the pursuit of goals that are generally

political, religious, or ideological" (U.S. Department of Defense, 2011).

The "war on drugs": Actions taken by the U.S. government that are intended to curb the illegal drug trade and reduce drug use.

Theism: A belief in one or more supernatural deities.

"Three strikes" laws: Many states and the federal government can sentence anyone to life in prison who is found guilty of committing three felonies, or serious crimes punishable by a minimum of one year in jail.

Total fertility rate (TFR): The average number of births per woman.

Total institution: An institution that isolates individuals from the rest of society in order to achieve administrative control over most aspects of their lives.

Totalitarianism: A form of governance that denies popular political participation in government as well as seeks to regulate and control all aspects of the public and private lives of citizens.

Totems: Part of the sacred sphere in which numerous ordinary objects are believed to have acquired transcendent or magical qualities connecting humans with the divine.

Traditional authority: Power based on a belief in the sanctity of long-standing traditions and the legitimate right of rulers to exercise authority in accordance with those traditions.

Transactional leader: A leader who is concerned with accomplishing the group's tasks, getting group members to do their jobs, and making certain that the group achieves its goals.

Transformational leader: A leader who is able to instill in the members of a group a sense of mission or higher purpose, thereby changing the nature of the group itself.

Transgender: An umbrella term used to describe all those who identify outside of their assigned sex or outside the gender binary.

Transsexuals: People who use surgery and hormones to change their sex to match their preferred gender.

Treadmill of production: The constant and aggressive growth needed to sustain the modern economy.

Triad: A group consisting of three persons.

Urban growth machine: Those persons and institutions that have a stake in an increase in the value of urban land and that constitute a power elite in cities.

Urban renewal: The transformation of old neighborhoods with new buildings, businesses, and residences.

Urbanization: The growing concentration of people in urban areas.

Utilitarian organization: An organization that people join primarily because of some material benefit they expect to receive in return for membership.

Validity: The degree to which concepts and their measurements accurately represent what they claim to represent.

Value neutrality: Freedom from personal beliefs and opinions that would influence the course of research.

Values: The general standards in society that define ideal principles, like those governing notions of what is right or wrong.

Variable: A concept or its empirical measure that can take on multiple values.

Variable: A concept or its empirical measure that can take on multiple values.

Verstehen: The German word for interpretive understanding.

Violent crime: Involves force or threat of force and includes robbery, murder, assault, and rape.

War economy: the phenomenon of war boosting economic productivity and employment, particularly in capital- and labor-intensive sectors such as industrial production

Wealth (or net worth): The value of everything a person owns, minus the value of everything owed.

Welfare state: A government or country's system of providing for the financial and social well-being of its citizens, typically through government programs that provide funding or other resources to individuals who meet certain criteria.

White-collar crime: Crimes committed by people of high social status in connection with their work.

Work: Any human effort that adds something of value to the goods and services that are available to others.

World systems theory: Argues that the global capitalist economic system has long been shaped by a few powerful economic actors, who have ordered it in a way that favors their economic and political interests.

Zionism: A movement calling for the return of Jews to Palestine and the creation of a Jewish state.

ABC News. (2005, April 18). *Secret FBI report highlights domestic terrorism.* Retrieved from http://abcnews.go.com/WNT/Investigation/story?id=681288&page=1#.T8knBMWdySo

Ablett, J., Baijal, A., Beinhocker, E., Bose, A., Farrell, D., Gersch, U., . . . Gupta, S. (2007). *The "bird of gold": The rise of India's consumer market.* McKinsey Global Institute. Retrieved from http://www.mckinsey.com/Insights/MGI/Research/Asia/The_bird_of_gold

Abrahams, N. (1992). Towards reconceptualizing political action. *Sociological Inquiry, 62*(Summer), 327–347.

Achen, A. C., & Stafford, F. P. (2005). Data quality of housework hours in the panel study of income dynamics: Who really does the dishes? *PSID Technical Series Paper #05–04.* Retrieved from http://psidonline.isr.umich.edu/Publications/Papers/tsp/2005-04_Data_Qual_of_Household_Hours-_Dishes.pdf

Ackbar, S. (2011). *Constructions and socialization of gender and sexuality in lesbian-/gay-headed families.* Doctoral dissertation, University of Windsor. Retrieved from ProQuest (NR77959).

Aclemo, R., Hernandez-Tejada, M., Muzzy, W., & Steve, K. (2009). *The national elder mistreatment study.* Washington, DC: National Institute of Justice. Retrieved from https://www.ncjrs.gov/pdffiles1/nij/grants/226456.pdf

Adachi, P. J. C., & Willoughby, T. (2011). The effect of video game competition and violence on aggressive behavior: Which characteristic has the greatest influence? *Psychology of Violence, 1*(4), 259–274.

Adams, J., Parkinson, L., Sanson-Fisher, R. W., & Walsh, R. A. (2008). Enhancing self-report of adolescent smoking: The effects of bogus pipeline and anonymity. *Addictive Behaviors, 33*(10), 1291–1296.

Adbusters. (2013). *Culture jammer network.* Retrieved from https://www.adbusters.org/

Adler, F. (1975). *Sisters in crime: The rise of the new female criminal.* New York: McGraw-Hill.

Adorno, T. (1975). The culture industry reconsidered. *New German Critique, 6*(Fall), 12–19.

Ahmed, A., & Little, D. (2008). Chicago, America's most segregated big city. *Chicago Tribune,* December 26. Retrieved from http://articles.chicagotribune.com/2008-12-26/news/0812250194_1_racial-steering-douglas-massey-neighborhoods

Ahola, A. S., Christianson, S., & Hellstrom, A. (2009). Justice needs a blindfold: Effects of gender and attractiveness on prison sentences and attributions of personal characteristics in a judicial process. *Psychiatry, Psychology, and Law, 16*(S1), S90–S100.

AIDS in China: Blood debts. (2007). *The Economist,* January 18. Retrieved from http://www.economist.com/node/8554778

Aina, O. E., & Cameron, P. A. (2011). Why does gender matter? Counteracting stereotypes with young children. *Dimensions of Early Childhood, 39*(1), 11–19.

Albanese, J. S. (1989). *Organized crime in America.* New York: Anderson.

Alcindor, Y., Bello, M., & Welch, W. M. (2012). Trayvon Martin's killing is now a murder case. *USA Today,* April 12. Retrieved from http://www.usatoday.com/news/nation/story/2012-04-12/george-zimmerman-charges-trayvon-martin-shooting/54191768/1

Aldrich, H. E., & Marsden, P. V. (1988). Environments and organizations. In N. J. Smelser (Ed.), *Handbook of sociology* (pp. 361–392). Newbury Park, CA: Sage.

Alexander, A. (2011). Internet role in Egypt's protests. *BBC News,* February 9. Retrieved from http://www.bbc.co.uk/news/world-middle-east-12400319

Alexander, J. C. (1998). *Neofunctionalism and after.* Malden, MA: Blackwell.

Alexander, J. C., & Colomy, P. (1990). *Differentiation theory and social change.* New York: Columbia University Press.

Alexander, J. C., & Thompson, K. (2008). *A contemporary introduction to sociology: Culture and society in transition.* Boulder, CO: Paradigm.

Alexander, K., Entwisle, D., & Olson, L. (2007). Lasting consequences of the summer learning gap. *American Sociological Review, 72,* 167–180.

Alexander, M. (2010). *The new Jim Crow: Mass incarceration in the age of colorblindness.* New York: The New Press.

Alfano, S. (2009). Poll: Women's movement worthwhile. *CBS News,* February 11. Retrieved from http://www.cbsnews.com/2100-500160_162-965224.html

Al Jazeera. (2011). *Country profile: Tunisia.* Retrieved from http://www.aljazeera.com/indepth/features/2011/10/20111012115318525711.html

Allport, G., & Postman, L. (1947). *The psychology of rumor.* New York: Holt.

Alpers, P., & Wilson, M. (2013). *Guns in the United States: Facts, figures and firearm law.* Sydney School of Public Health, The University of Sydney. Retrieved from http://www.gunpolicy.org/firearms/compare/194/rate_of_gun_homicide/31,66,69,172,192,91

American Academy of Child and Adolescent Psychiatry. (2011). Children and watching TV. *Facts for Families, 54*(4). Retrieved from http://www.aacap.org/cs/root/facts_for_families/children_and_watching_tv

American Association of University Women. (1993). *Hostile hallways: Bullying, teasing, and sexual harassment in school.* Washington, DC: Author.

American Federation of Labor–Congress of International Organizations. (2012). *CEO pay and the 99%.* Retrieved from http://www.aflcio.org/corporatewatch/paywatch/retirementsecurity/index.cfm

American Institute for Research. (2010). *College dropouts cost cash-strapped states billions.* Retrieved from http://www.air.org/news/index.cfm?fa=viewContent&content_id=988

American Jewish Yearbook. (2006). New York: American Jewish Committee.

American Medical Association. (2013). 1941–1960. *AMA history timeline.* Retrieved from http://www.ama-assn.org/ama/pub/about-ama/our-history/ama-history-timeline.page

American Sociological Association. (2005, January 8). *Society and social life.* Retrieved from http://www2.asanet.org/student/career/careers.html

Amis, M. (2002). *Koba the dread.* New York: Miramax.

Amnesty International. (2004, October 26). *Democratic Republic of Congo: Mass* rape —*Time for remedies.* Retrieved from http://www.amnesty.org/es/library/asset/AFR62/022/2004/es/97ac3942-d571-11dd-bb24-1fb85fe8fa05/afr620222004en.pdf

Amnesty International. (2012). Jalila al-Salman and Mahdi 'Issa Mahdi Abu Dheeb: Prisoners of conscience. *Our work: Cases.* Retrieved from http://www.amnestyusa.org/our-work/cases/bahrain-jalila-al-salman-mahdi-issa-mahdi-abu-dheeb

Andersen, G. S. (2006). *Biological influences on criminal behavior.* Boca Raton, FL: CRC Press.

Andersen, M. L., & Collins, P. H. (1992). *Race, class, and gender: An anthology.* Stamford, CT: Wadsworth.

Anderson. B. (1991). *Imagined communities: Reflections on the origin and spread of nationalism.* London and New York: Verso.

Anderson, C., Berkowitz, L., Donnerstein, E., Huesmann, L. R., Johnson, J., Linz, D., . . . Wartella, E. (2003). The influence of media violence on youth. *The Psychological Science in the Public Interest, 4*(3), 81–110.

Anderson, E. (1999). *Code of the street: Decency, violence and the moral life of the inner city.* New York: Norton.

Anderson, K. J. (2000). Internet use among college students: An exploratory study. *Journal of American College Health, 50*(1), 21–26.

Anderson, N. (1940). *Men on the move.* Chicago: University of Chicago Press.

Anderson, T. D. (2000). Sex-role orientation and care-oriented moral reasoning: An online test of Carol Gilligan's theory. *Dissertation Abstracts International, 61*(4), 1618-A. Retrieved from http://search.proquest.com.proxygw.wrlc.org/socabs/docview/60390650/13C8E238511536831E/1?accountid=11243

Andre, F. E., Boy, R., Bock, H. L., Clemens, J., Datta, S. K., John, T. J., . . . Schmitt, H. J. (2008). Vaccination greatly reduces disease, disability, death and inequity worldwide. *Bulletin of the World Health Organization, 86*(2). Retrieved from http://www.who.int/bulletin/volumes/86/2/07-040089/en/

Angier, N. (2000). Do races differ? Not really, genes show. *The New York Times,* August 22. Retrieved from http://www.nytimes.com/2000/08/22/science/do-races-differ-not-really-genes-show.html?pagewanted=all&src=pm

Antos, J. (2011). Medicare reform and fiscal reality. *Journal of Policy Analysis & Management, 30*(4), 934–942.

Anzaldua, G. (Ed.). (1990). *Making face, making soul: Haciendo caras.* San Francisco: Aunt Lute Foundation.

Appelbaum, R. P. (1986). Testimony on "A report to the secretary on the homeless and emergency shelters." In J. Erickson & C. Wilhelm (Eds.), *Housing the homeless.* New Brunswick, NJ: Rutgers University Center for Urban Policy Research.

Appelbaum, R. P., Dolny, M., Dreier, P., & Gilderbloom, J. (1991). Scapegoating rent control: Masking the cause of homelessness. *Journal of the American Planning Association, 57,* 153–164.

Appy, C. (1993). *Working class war: American combat soldiers and Vietnam.* Chapel Hill: University of North Carolina Press.

Arab American Institute. (2012). Arab Americans. Retrieved from http://www.aaiusa.org/pages/arab-americans/

Arab American Institute Foundation. (2010). Quick facts about Arab Americans. Retrieved from http://aai.3cdn.net/afb-c33810b07728c5a_oim6bx98f.pdf

Archer, D., & Gartner, R. (1984). *Violence and crime in cross-national perspective.* New Haven, CT: Yale University Press.

Arendt, H. (1951). *The origins of totalitarianism.* New York: Harcourt, Brace.

Armstrong, L., Phillips, J. G., & Saling, L. L. (2000). Potential determinants of heavier Internet use. *International Journal of Human-Computer Studies, 53*(4), 537–550.

Asch, S. (1952). *Social psychology.* Englewood Cliffs, NJ: Prentice-Hall.

Asencio, E. K., & Burke, P. J. (2011). Does incarceration change the criminal identity? A synthesis of labeling and identity theory perspectives on identity change. *Sociological Perspectives, 54*(20), 163–182.

Asimov, N. (1995). Stereotypes, affect testing, study finds: Results rebut bell curve argument on race. *San Francisco Chronicle,* August 12, p. A15.

Aubrey, J., & Harrison, K. (2004). The gender-role content of children's favorite television programs and its link to their gender-related perceptions. *Media Psychology, 6,* 111–146.

Austin, A. (2010). Briefing paper #282: Graduate employment gap: Students of color losing ground. *Economic Policy Institute,* October 28. Retrieved from http://www.epi.org/publication/graduate_employment_gap_students_of_color_losing_ground/

Austin, J., Dimas, J., & Steinhart, D. (1992). *Over-representation of minority youth in the California juvenile justice system.* Report prepared for the California State Advisory Group on Juvenile Justice and the California Office of Criminal Justice Planning. Washington, DC: National Council on Crime and Delinquency.

Autor, D. (2010). *The polarization of job opportunities in the U.S. labor market: Implications for employment and earnings.* Center for American Progress and the Hamilton Project, April 30. Retrieved from http://www.americanprogress.org/issues/2010/04/job_polarization.html

Avert.org. (2010). Sub-Saharan Africa HIV and AIDS statistics. Retrieved from http://www.avert.org/africa-hiv-aids-statistics.htm

Aviel, D. (1997). Issues in education: A closer examination of American education. *Childhood Education, 73*(3), 130–132.

Azuz, C. (2012, August 22). Survey: 17% of high schoolers drink, smoke, use drugs during school day. *CNN News Online.* Retrieved from http://schoolsofthought.blogs.cnn.com/2012/08/22/survey-17-of-high-schoolers-drink-smoke-use-drugs-during-school-day/

Babbie, E. R. (1998). *The practice of social research.* Belmont, CA: Wadsworth.

Babcock, P., & Marks, M. (2010). Leisure college, USA: The decline in student study time. *Research Education Outlook No. 7.* American Enterprise Institute for Public Policy. Retrieved from http://www.aei.org/article/education/higher-education/leisure-college-usa/

Babson Survey Research Group and College Board. (2011). *Going the distance: Online education in the United States.* Retrieved from http://sloanconsortium.org/publications/survey/going_distance_2011

Bachar, E., Canetti, L., Bonne, O., DeNour, A., & Shalev, A. (1997). Physical punishment and signs of mental distress in normal adolescents. *Adolescence, 38*(128), 945–952.

Bajaj, V. (2010). Bangladesh, with low wages, moves in on China. *The New York Times,* July 16. Retrieved from http://www.nytimes.com/2010/07/17/business/global/17textile.html?pagewanted=all

Baldwin, J. D., & Baldwin, J. I. (1986). *Behavior principles in everyday life.* Engelwood Cliffs, NJ: Prentice Hall.

Baldwin, J. D., & Baldwin, J. I. (1988). Factors affecting aids-related sexual risk-taking behavior among college students. *Journal of Sex Research, 25*(2), 181–196.

Ball, S. J., Bowe, R., & Gewirtz, S. (1995). Circuits of schooling: A sociological exploration of parental choice of school in social class contexts. *The Sociological Review, 43*(1), 52–77.

Balmer, Z. (1989). *Mine eyes have seen the glory: A journey into the Evangelical subculture in America.* New York: Oxford University Press.

Bandura, A. (1977). *Social learning theory*. Engelwood Cliffs, NJ: Prentice Hall.

Bandura, A., & Walters, R. H. (1963). *Social learning and personality development*. New York: Holt, Rinehart & Winston.

Banks, S., & Renwick, L. (1997). Technology remains promise, not panacea. *Los Angeles Times*, June 8.

Barber, B. K. (1992). Family, personality, and adolescent problem behaviors. *Journal of Marriage and the Family, 54*(2), 69–79.

Barner, M. (1999). Sex-role stereotyping in FCC-mandated children's educational television. *Journal of Broadcasting & Electronic Media, 43*(4), 551–564.

Barnes, R. (2012). Justices decline to consider whether Constitution requires insanity defense. *Washington Post*. Retrieved from http://articles.washingtonpost.com/2012-11-26/politics/35510546_1_insanity-defense-justices-decline-jeffrey-1-fisher

Barrera, M. (1979). *Race and class in the Southwest*. Notre Dame, IN: University of Notre Dame Press.

Barrett, D. B. (2001). *World Christian encyclopedia*. New York: Oxford University Press.

Barringer, F. (1993). Pride in a soundless world: Deaf oppose a hearing aid. *The New York Times*, May 16. Retrieved from http://www.nytimes.com/1993/05/16/us/pride-in-a-soundless-world-deaf-oppose-a-hearing-aid.html?pagewanted=all&src=pm

Barry, K. (1979). *Female sexual slavery*. Engelwood Cliffs, NJ: Prentice Hall.

Barry, T., & Sims, B. (1994). *The challenge of cross-border environmentalism: The U.S.-Mexico case*. Albuquerque, NM: Resource Center Press.

Basham, A. L. (1989). *The origins and development of classical Hinduism*. New York: Oxford University Press.

Basow, S. (2004). The hidden curriculum: Gender in the classroom. In M. Paludi (Ed.), *Praeger guide to the psychology of gender* (pp. 117–132). Westport, CT: Praeger.

Bassuk, E. L. (2005). *Written submission to the U.N. regional consultation on women and the right to adequate housing in North America*. Needham, MA: National Center on Family Homelessness.

Baudrillard, J. (1981). *Simulacra and simulation* (S. F. Glaser, trans.). Ann Arbor: University of Michigan Press.

Baum, S., & O'Malley, M. (2003). College on credit: How borrowers perceive their education debt. *NASFAA Journal of Student Financial Aid, 33*(3), 7–19.

Bauman, Z. (2001). *Modernity and the Holocaust*. Ithaca, NY: Cornell University Press.

Baumgardner, J., & Richards, A. (2010). *Manifesta: Young women, feminism, and the future*. New York: Farrar, Straus, and Giroux.

Bazell, R. (2010). U.S. apologizes for Guatemala STD experiments. *NBC News*, October 1. Retrieved from http://www.msnbc.msn.com/id/39456324/ns/health-sexual_health/t/us-apologizes-guatemala-std-experiments/#.ULbLqe-igkI

BBC News. (2008). Rwanda: How the genocide happened. Retrieved from http://news.bbc.co.uk/2/hi/1288230.stm

BBC News. (2010). S Korea child "starves as parents raise virtual baby." *World News*, March 5. Retrieved from http://news.bbc.co.uk/2/hi/asia-pacific/8551122.stm

Beaver, K. M., Wright, J. P., DeLisi, M., & Vaughn, M. G. (2008). Genetic influences on the stability of low self-control: Results from a longitudinal sample of twins. *Journal of Criminal Justice, 36*, 478–485.

Beckers, V., Edwards, A., & Moody, R. (2010). *Micro-mobilization, social media and coping strategies*. Paper presented at Public Policy Conference, Oxford, England, Oxford University, St. Anne's College, September 16–17, 1–34.

Beiner, T. M. (2007). Sexy dressing revisited: Does target dress play a part in sexual harassment cases? *Duke Journal of Gender Law & Policy, 14*, 125–152.

Beinhocker, E. D., Farrell, D., & Zainulbhai, A. S. (2007). Tracking the growth of India's middle class. *McKinsey Quarterly*, August. Retrieved from http://www.mckinsey-quarterly.com/Tracking_the_growth_of_Indias_middle_class_2032

Belasco, A. (2010). The cost of Iraq, Afghanistan, and other global war on terror operations since 9/11. *Congressional Research Service*, September 2. Retrieved from http://www.fas.org/sgp/crs/natsec/RL33110.pdf

Bell, D. (1973). *The coming of post-industrial society: A venture in social forecasting*. New York: Basic Books.

Bellah, R. N. (1968). Meaning and modernization. *Religious Studies, 4*(1), 37–45.

Bellah, R. N. (1975). *The broken covenant: American civil religion in time of trial*. New York: Seabury Press.

Berger, P. L. (1986). *The capitalist revolutions: Fifty propositions about prosperity, equality, and liberty*. New York: Basic Books.

Berger, P. L., & Hsiao, H.-H. M. (Eds.). (1988). *In search of an East Asian development model*. Piscataway, NJ: Transaction Books.

Berlin, L. J., Ispa, J. M., Fine, M. A., Malone, P. S., Brooks-Gunn, J., Brady-Smith, C., . . . Bai, Y. (2009). Correlates and consequences of spanking and verbal punishment for low-income White, African American, and Mexican American toddlers. *Child Development, 80*(5), 1403–1420.

Berdal, M., & Serrano, M. (2002). *Transnational organized crime and international security: Business as usual?* Boulder, CO: Rienner.

Berenbaum, S. A., Blakemore, J. E. O., & Beltz, A. M. (2011). A role for biology in gender-related behavior. *Sex Roles, 64*, 804–825.

Bergen, T. J., Jr. (1996). The social philosophy of public education. *School Business Affairs, 62*(6), 22–27.

Bernard, J. (1981). *The female world*. New York: Free Press.

Bernard, J. (1982). *The future of marriage*. New Haven, CT: Yale University Press.

Bernhardt, A. (2012). *The low-wage recovery and growing inequality*. New York: National Employment Law Project. Retrieved from http://www.nelp.org/page/-/Job_Creation/LowWageRecovery2012.pdf?nocdn=1

Berns, R. (1989). *Child, family, community: Socialization and support*. New York: Holt, Rinehart & Winston.

Bettelheim, B. (1979). *Surviving and other essays*. New York: Knopf.

Bettelheim. B. (1982). Difficulties between parents and children: Their causes and how to prevent them. In N. Stinner DeFrain, K. H. Lingren, G. Rowe, S. VanZandt, & R. Williams (Ed.), *Family strengths 4: Positive support systems* (pp. 5–14). Lincoln: University of Nebraska Press.

Beyer, P. (1994). *Religion and globalization*. London: Sage.

Bhanot, R. T., & Jovanovic, J. (2005). Do parents' academic gender stereotypes influence whether they intrude on their children's homework? *Sex Roles, 52*(9/10), 597–607.

Bilal, M., Zia-ur-Rehman, M., & Raza, I. (2010). Impact of family friendly policies on employees' job satisfaction and turnover intention (A study on work-life balance at workplace). *Interdisciplinary Journal of Contemporary Research in Business, 2*(7), 378–395.

Bill and Melinda Gates Foundation. (2006). *Ensuring the world's poorest children benefit from lifesaving vaccines*. Retrieved from http://www.gatesfoundation.org/learning/Documents/GAVI.pdf

Bill and Melinda Gates Foundation. (2013). *What we do: Vaccine delivery strategy*.

Retrieved from http://www.gatesfoundation.org/vaccines/Documents/vaccines-fact-sheet.pdf

Bishaw, A., & Macartney, S. (2010). Poverty: 2008 and 2009. *American Community Survey Briefs*. Washington, DC: U.S. Census Bureau. Retrieved from http://www.census.gov/prod/2010pubs/acsbr09-1.pdf

Bishop, M., & Hicks, S. L. (Eds.). (2009). *Hearing, mother father deaf*. Washington, DC: Gallaudet University Press.

Blackburn, B. (2010). University of Maryland student brutally beaten by police after basketball game. *ABC World News*. Retrieved from http://abcnews.go.com/WN/video-shows-university-maryland-student-beaten-county-police/story?id=10362033#.UMX8hJPjmBN

Blake, A. (2012). Both Romney and Obama ran $1 billion campaigns. *The Washington Post*, December 7. Retrieved from http://www.washingtonpost.com/blogs/the-fix/wp/2012/12/07/both-romney-and-obama-ran-1-billion-campaigns/

Blalock, H. (1967). *Toward a theory of minority group relations*. New York: Wiley.

Blau, J. (1992). *The visible poor: Homelessness in the United States*. New York: Oxford University Press.

Blau, P. M. (1964). *Exchange and power in social life*. New York: Wiley.

Blau, P. (1977). *Inequality and heterogeneity*. New York: The Free Press.

Blau, P. M., & Meyer, M. (1987). *Bureaucracy in modern society* (3rd ed.). New York: Random House.

Blinder, A. S. (2006). Offshoring: The next industrial revolution? *Foreign Affairs, 85*(2), 113–128.

Block, A., & Chambliss, W. J. (1981). *Organizing crime*. New York: Elsevier.

Block, A., & Weaver, A. (2004). *All is clouded by desire: Global banking, money laundering, and international organized crime*. Westport, CT: Praeger.

Block, J. J. (2008). Issues for *DSM-V*: Internet addiction. *American Journal of Psychiatry, 165*(3), 306–307.

Blumberg, J. (2007). A brief history of the Salem witch trials. *Smithsonian*. Retrieved from http://www.smithsonianmag.com/history-archaeology/brief-salem.html

Blumberg, R. (1995). *Engendering wealth and well-being: Empowerment for global change*. Boulder, CO: Westview.

Blumer, H. (1951). Collective behavior. In A. M. Lee (Ed.), *Principles of sociology* (pp. 166–222). New York: Barnes & Noble.

Blumer, H. (1969). *Symbolic interactionism: Perspective and method*. Engelwood Cliffs, NJ: Prentice Hall.

Blumer, H. (1970). *Movies and conduct*. New York: Arno Press.

Boeing. (2013). International team facts. *787 Dream Liner*. Retrieved from http://www.boeing.com/commercial/787family/dev_team.html

Bohnert, D., & Ross, W. H. (2010). The influence of social networking web sites on the evaluation of job candidates. *Cyberpsychology, Behavior, and Social Networking, 13*, 341–347.

Bonacich, E., & Applebaum, R. (2000). *Behind the label: Inequality in the Los Angeles garment industry*. Berkeley: University of California Press.

Boncar, T. P., & Beck, A. J. (1997). *Lifetime likelihood of going to state or federal prison*. Bureau of Justice Statistics, Special Report, NCJ-160092. Washington, D.C: Office of Justice Programs, U.S. Department of Justice.

Bonnie, R. J., & Wallace, R. B. (2003). *Elder mistreatment: Abuse, neglect and exploitation in aging America*. Washington, DC: National Academies Press.

Borgeson, C. A. (2001). *Parenting strategies: Does corporal punishment lead to antisocial behavior?* Blacksburg, VA: Southern Sociological Society.

Bos, H., & Sandfort, T. G. M. (2010). Children's gender identity in lesbian and heterosexual two-parent families. *Sex Roles, 62*(1–2), 114–126.

Boswell, A. A., & Spade, J. Z. (1996). Fraternities and collegiate rape culture: Why are some fraternities more dangerous places for women? *Gender and Society, 10*, 133–147.

Boswell, T. (Ed.). (1989). *Revolution in the world system*. New York: Greenwood Press.

Boudreau, J. (2010). Silicon Valley races fierce global competition in Cleantech. *Mercury News*, May 11. Retrieved from http://www.mercurynews.com/green-energy/ci_14233459

Bourdieu, P. (1977). *Outline of a theory of practice*. New York: Cambridge University Press.

Bourdieu, P. (1984). *Distinction: A social critique of the judgment of taste*. Cambridge, MA: Harvard University Press.

Bourdieu, P. (1991). *Language and symbolic power*. New York: Cambridge University Press.

Bourdieu, P. (1999). *Language and symbolic power*. Boston: Harvard University Press.

Bourdieu, P., & Coleman, J. S. (1991). *Social theory for a changing society*. Boulder, CO: Westview Press.

Bowles, S., & Gintis, H. (1976). *Schooling in capitalist America: Educational reform and the contradictions of economic life*. New York: Basic Books.

Bowles, S., & Gintis, H. (2002). Schooling in capitalist America revisited. *Sociology of Education, 75*(1), 1–18.

Boxer, S. (1997). One casualty of the women's movement: Feminism. *The New York Times*, December 14. Retrieved from http://www.nytimes.com/1997/12/14/weekinreview/ideas-trends-one-casualty-of-the-women-s-movement-feminism.html

Branch, T. (1988). *Parting the waters: America in the King years, 1954–1963*. New York: Simon & Schuster.

Brandon, S. G. (1973). *Ancient empires*. New York: Newsweek Books.

Brandt, A. M. (1983). Racism and research: The case of the Tuskegee syphilis study. In J. W. Leavitt & R. L. Numbers (Eds.), *Sickness and health in America* (pp. 392–404). Madison: University of Wisconsin Press.

Branson, C., & Cornell, D. (2009). A comparison of self and peer reports in the assessment of middle school bullying. *Journal of Applied School Psychology 25*, 5–27.

Braverman, H. (1988). *Labor and monopoly capital: The degradation of work in the 20th century*. New York: Monthly Review Press. (Original work published 1974)

Bremer, C. (2012, March). *Economic commentary* (T. Vaughn, managing director). Retrieved from http://www.tom-vaughn.com/Economic-Commentary----March-2012.c3472.htm

Bremer, J., & Rauch, P. K. (1998). Children and computers: Risks and benefits. *Journal of the American Academy of Child and Adolescent Psychiatry, 37*, 559–560.

Brenner, V., & Fox, R. (1998). Parental discipline and behavior problems in young children. *Journal of Genetic Psychology, 159*(2), 251–259.

Bricker, J., Kennickell, A. B., Moore, K. B., & Sabelhaus, J. (2012). Changes in U.S. family finances from 2007 to 2010: Evidence from the survey of consumer finances. *Federal Reserve Bulletin, 98*(2). Retrieved from http://www.federalreserve.gov/pubs/bulletin/2012/PDF/scf12.pdf

Brock, J., & Cocks, T. (2012). Insight: Nigeria oil corruption highlighted by audits. *Reuters*, March 8. Retrieved from http://www.reuters.com/article/2012/03/08/us-nigeria-corruption-oil-idUSBRE8270GF20120308

Brown, D. (1991). *Wondrous times on the frontier*. Little Rock, AK: August House.

Brown, D. (2010). A mother's education has a huge effect on a child's health. *The Washington Post*, September 16. Retrieved from http://www.washingtonpost.com/wp-dyn/content/article/2010/09/16/AR2010091606384.html

Brown, D. E., Edwards, J. W., & Moore, R. B. (1988). *The penis inserts of Southeast Asia*. Berkeley, CA: Center for South and Southeast Asian Studies.

Brown, M., Haughwout, A., Lee, D., Mabutas, M., & van der Klaauw, W. (2012, March 5). *Grading student loans*. Federal Reserve Bank of New York. Retrieved from http://libertystreeteconomics.newyorkfed.org/2012/03/grading-student-loans.html

Brumberg, J. J. (1997). *The body project: An intimate history of American girls*. New York: Vintage Books.

Brumberg, J. (2000). *Fasting girls: The history of anorexia nervosa*. New York: Vintage Books.

Buchwald, E., Fletcher, P., & Roth, M. (2005). *Transforming a rape culture*. Minneapolis, MN: Milkweed Editions. (Original work published in 1993)

Budiansky, S., Goode, E. E., & Gest, T. (1994). The cold war experiments. *U.S. News & World Report*, January 16. Retrieved from http://www.usnews.com/usnews/news/articles/940124/archive_012286.htm

Buechler, S. M. (1990). *Women's movements in the United States: Women's suffrage, equal rights, and beyond*. New Brunswick, NJ: Rutgers University Press.

Burawoy, M., & Lukács, J. (1992). *The radiant past: Ideology and reality in Hungary's road to capitalism*. Chicago: University of Chicago Press.

Bureau of Labor Statistics. (2012). Education pays. *Employment projections*. Washington, DC: U.S. Government Printing Office. Retrieved from http://www.bls.gov/emp/ep_chart_001.htm

Burgess, E. W. (1925). The growth of the city. In R. E. Park, E. Burgess, & R. McKenzie (Eds.), *The city*. Chicago: University of Chicago Press.

Burgess, R. L., & Akers, R. L. (1996). A differential association-reinforcement theory of criminal behavior. *Social Problems, 14*(2), 128–147.

Burns, J. M. (1978). *Leadership*. New York: Harper & Row.

Burt, M. R. (1992). *Over the edge: The growth of homelessness in the 1980s*. New York: Sage.

Byers, B. D., & Crider, B. W. (2002). Hate crimes against the Amish: A qualitative analysis of bias motivation using routine activities theory. *Deviant Behavior, 23,* 115–148.

Cabeza, M. F., Johnson, J. B., & Tyner, L. J. (2011). Glass ceiling and maternity leave as important contributors to the gender wage gap. *Southern Journal of Business and Ethics, 3,* 73–85.

Calderón-Garcidueñas, L., & Torres-Jardón, R. (2012). Air pollution, socioeconomic status and children's cognition in megacities: The Mexico City scenario. *Frontiers in Developmental Psychology.* Retrieved from http://www.frontiersin.org/Developmental_Psychology/10.3389/fpsyg.2012.00217/full

Calhoun, A. (2012). The criminalization of bad mothers. *New York Times Magazine,* April 25. Retrieved from http://www.nytimes.com/2012/04/29/magazine/the-criminalization-of-bad-mothers.html?pagewanted=all&_r=0

Camarota, S. (2005). *Birth rates among immigrants in America: Comparing fertility in the U.S. and home countries*. Washington, DC: Center for Immigration Studies. Retrieved from http://www.cis.org/articles/2005/back1105.pdf

Campbell, A. (1984). *The girls in the gang*. New Brunswick, NJ: Rutgers University Press.

Campbell, A., & Muncer, S. (Eds.). (1998). *The social child*. East Sussex, UK: Psychology Press.

Campbell, K., Klein, D. M., & Olson, K. (1992). Conversation activity and interruptions among men and women. *Journal of Social Psychology, 132,* 419–421.

Carlozo, L. (2012). Why college students stop short of a degree. *Reuters,* March 27. Retrieved from http://www.reuters.com/article/2012/03/27/us-attn-andrea-education-dropouts-idUSBRE82Q0Y120120327

Carson, R. (1962). *Silent spring*. New York: Houghton Mifflin.

Castells, M., & Portes, A. (1989). World underneath: The origins, dynamics, and effects of the informal economy. In A. Portes, M. Castells, & L. A. Benton (Eds.), *The informal economy: Studies in advanced and less developed countries* (pp. 11–37). Baltimore: Johns Hopkins University Press.

Catalyst. (1997). *Women of color in corporate management: A statistical portrait*. New York: Author.

Catalyst. (1999). *Women of color in corporate management: Opportunities and barriers, executive summary*. New York: Author.

Catan, T. (2010). U.S. sues KBR on security costs. *The Wall Street Journal,* April 2. Retrieved from http://online.wsj.com/article/SB10001424052702303960604575158220281487044.html

Cavalli-Sforza, L. L., Menozzi, P., & Piazza, A. (1996). *The history and geography of human genes*. Princeton, NJ: Princeton University Press

Cawley, J. (2001). The impact of obesity on wages. *The Journal of Human Resources, 39,* 451–474.

CBS News. (2011, November 25). 7 arrested on hate crime charges in Amish hair cutting attacks. Retrieved from http://www.cbsnews.com/8301-504083_162-57331265-504083/7-arrested-on-hate-crime-charges-in-amish-hair-cutting-attacks/

Center for American Progress. (2011). *The Black and White labor gap in America*. Washington, DC. Retrieved from http://www.americanprogress.org/issues/labor/report/2011/07/25/9992/the-black-and-white-labor-gap-in-america/

Center for Immigration Studies. (2012). *Immigrants in the United States: A profile of America's foreign-born population*. Retrieved from http://cis.org/2012-profile-of-americas-foreign-born-population

Center for Information & Research on Civic Learning and Engagement. (2010). Why youth voting matters. *CIRCLE: Youth Voting*. Retrieved from http://www.civicyouth.org/quick-facts/youth-voting/

Center for Responsible Lending. (2011). *Disparities in mortgage lending and foreclosures*. Retrieved from http://www.responsiblelending.org/mortgage-lending/researchanalysis/lost-ground-2011.html

Center for Responsive Politics. (2012). 2012 presidential race: Fundraising. *OpenSecrets*. Retrieved from http://www.opensecrets.org/pres12/index.php?q13

Center for Responsive Politics. (2013). Industry profile, 2011: Annual lobbying on tobacco. *OpenSecrets,* March 4. Retrieved from http://www.opensecrets.org/lobby/indusclient.php?id=A02&year=2011

Centers for Disease Control and Prevention. (2010a, December). *CDC vital signs: HIV testing in the U.S.* Retrieved from http://www.cdc.gov/vitalsigns/pdf/2010-12-vital signs.pdf

Centers for Disease Control and Prevention. (2010b). *National intimate partner and sexual violence survey*. Washington, DC: U.S. Government Printing Office. Retrieved from http://www.cdc.gov/ViolencePrevention/pdf/NISVS_FactSheet-a.pdf

Centers for Disease Control and Prevention. (2011a). *Deaths: Final data for 2010.* Retrieved from http://www.cdc.gov/nchs/data/dvs/deaths_2010_release.pdf

Centers for Disease Control and Prevention. (2011b). Estimates of new HIV infections in the United States, 2006–2009. *CDC Fact Sheet.* Retrieved from http://www.cdc.gov/nchhstp/newsroom/docs/HIV-Infections-2006-2009.pdf

Centers for Disease Control and Prevention. (2011c). HIV surveillance—United States, 1981–2008. *Morbidity and Mortality Weekly Report.* Retrieved from http://www.cdc.gov/mmwr/preview/mmwrhtml/mm6021a2.htm

Centers for Disease Control and Prevention. (2011d). Prevalence of self-reported obesity among U.S. adults. *Behavioral Risk Factor Surveillance System.* Washington, DC. Retrieved from http://www.cdc.gov/obesity/data/adult.html

Centers for Disease Control and Prevention. (2011e). Vital signs: Current cigarette smoking among adults Aged ≥ 18 Years—United States, 2005–2010. *Morbidity and Mortality Weekly Report.* Retrieved from http://www.cdc.gov/mmwr/preview/mmwrhtml/mm6035a5.htm

Centers for Disease Control and Prevention. (2012a). Adult cigarette smoking in the United States: Current estimate. *Smoking & Tobacco Use.* Retrieved from http://www.cdc.gov/tobacco/data_statistics/fact_sheets/adult_data/cig_smoking/index.htm

Centers for Disease Control and Prevention. (2012b). Adult obesity facts. *Overweight and Obesity.* Retrieved from http://www.cdc.gov/obesity/data/adult.html

Centers for Disease Control and Prevention. (2012c). Basics about childhood obesity. *Overweight and Obesity.* Retrieved from http://www.cdc.gov/obesity/childhood/basics.html

Centers for Disease Control and Prevention. (2012d). Estimated pregnancy rates and rates of pregnancy outcomes for the United States, 1990–2008. *National Vital Statistics System.* Retrieved from http://www.cdc.gov/nchs/data/nvsr/nvsr60/nvsr60_07.pdf

Centers for Disease Control and Prevention. (2012e). *Impact of malaria.* Retrieved from http://www.cdc.gov/malaria/malaria_worldwide/impact.html

Centers for Disease Control and Prevention. (2012f). *National Vital Statistics System: Birth Data.* Washington, DC: U.S. Government Printing Office. Retrieved from http://www.cdc.gov/nchs/births.htm

Centers for Disease Control and Prevention. (2012g). Prevalence of obesity in the United States, 2009–2010. *NCHS Data Brief 82.* Washington, DC: U.S. Department of Health and Human Services. Retrieved from http://www.cdc.gov/nchs/data/databriefs/db82.pdf

Centers for Disease Control and Prevention. (2012h). Prevalence of self-reported obesity among U.S. adults. BRFSS, 2011. *Adult Obesity Facts.* Retrieved from http://www.cdc.gov/obesity/data/adult.html

Centers for Disease Control and Prevention. (2012i). *Tobacco use: Targeting the nation's leading killer at a glance 2011.* Retrieved from http://www.cdc.gov/chronicdisease/resources/publications/aag/osh.htm

Centers for Disease Control and Prevention. (2013). *Provisional number of marriages and marriage rate: United States, 2000–2011.* Washington, DC: U.S. Government Printing Office. Retrieved from http://www.cdc.gov/nchs/nvss/marriage_divorce_tables.htm

Cevallos, D. (2013). Shrimp industry devastating mangrove forests. *Tierramerica.* Retrieved from http://www.tierramerica.info/nota.php?lang=eng&idnews=822

Chafetz, J. S. (1984). *Sex and advantage: A macrostructural perspective on gender stratification.* Totowa, NJ: Rowan and Allenheld.

Chafetz, J. S. (1997). Feminist theory and sociology: Underutilized contributions for mainstream theory. *Annual Review of Sociology, 23,* 97–120.

Chafetz, J. S., & Dworkin, A. G. (1983). Macro and micro process in the emergence of feminist movements: Toward a unified theory. *Western Sociological Review, 14*(1), 27–45.

Chalk, F., & Jonassohn, K. (1990). *The history and sociology of genocide: Analyses and case studies.* New Haven, CT: Yale University Press.

Chambliss, W. J. (1973). The Saints and the Roughnecks. *Society 11*(1), 24–31.

Chambliss, W. J. (1988a). *Exploring criminology.* New York: Macmillan.

Chambliss, W. J. (1988b). *On the take: From petty crooks to presidents.* Bloomington: Indiana University Press.

Chambliss, W. J. (1999). *Power, politics, and crime.* Boulder, CO: Westview Press.

Chambliss, W. J. (2001). *Power, politics and crime.* Boulder, CO: Westview Press.

Chambliss, W. J., & King, H. (1984). *Boxman: A professional thief's journey.* New York: Macmillan.

Chambliss, W. J., Michalowski, R., & Kramer, R. C. (2011). *State crime in the global age.* London: Willan.

Chambliss, W. J., & Seidman, R. B. (1982). *Law, order, and power.* Reading, MA: Addison-Wesley.

Chambliss, W. J., & Zatz, M. (1994). *Making law: The state, law and structural contradictions.* Bloomington: Indiana University Press.

Chaves, M. (1993). Denominations as dual structures: An organizational analysis. *Sociology of Religion, 54*(2), 147–169.

Chaves, M. (1994). Secularization as declining religious authority. *Social Forces, 72*(3), 749–774.

Chen, H. S. (1992). *Chinatown no more: Taiwan immigrants in contemporary New York.* Ithaca, NY: Cornell University Press.

Chesney-Lind, M. (1989). Girls' crime and woman's place: Toward a feminist model of female delinquency. *Crime & Delinquency, 33*(1), 5–29.

Chesney-Lind, M. (2004). Beyond bad girls: Feminist perspectives on female offending. In C. Sumner (Ed.), *The Blackwell companion in criminology.* Oxford: Blackwell.

Chesney-Lind, M., & Pasko, L. (2004). *The female offender: Girls, women, and crime.* Thousand Oaks, CA: Sage.

Chia, R. C., Allred, L. J., Grossnickle, W. F., & Lee, G. W. (1988). Effects of attractiveness and gender on the perception of achievement-related variables. *The Journal of Social Psychology, 138*(4), 471–477.

Chiang, S. (2009). Personal power and positional power in a power-full "I": A discourse analysis of doctoral dissertation supervision. *Discourse and Communication, 3*(3), 255–271.

Childhelp. (2010). *Child abuse in America.* Scottsdale, AZ: Author. Retrieved from http://www.childhelp.org/pages/statistics#gen-stats

Chodorow, N. (1999). *The reproduction of mothering: Psychoanalysis and the sociology of gender.* Berkeley: University of California Press.

Chong, D. (1991). *Collective action and the civil rights movement.* Chicago: University of Chicago Press.

Christiansen, K. O. (1977). Preliminary study of criminality among twins. In S. A. Mednick & K. O. Christiansen (Eds.), *Biosocial bases of criminal behavior.* New York: Gardner Press.

Christy, B. (2009). *The lizard king: The true crimes and passions of the world's greatest reptile smugglers.* New York: Grand Central.

Church, W. T., II, Jaggers, J. W., & Taylor, J. K. (2012). Neighborhood, poverty, and negative behavior: An examination of differential association and social control theory. *Children and Youth Services Review, 34*(5), 1035–1041.

CIA World Factbook. (2012). *Total fertility rate: Country comparison to the world.* Washington, DC: Central Intelligence Agency. Retrieved from https://www.cia.gov/library/publications/the-world-factbook/fields/2127.html

CIA World Factbook. (2013). *World.* Retrieved from https://www.cia.gov/library/publications/the-world-factbook/geos/xx.html

Cichowski, L., & Nance, W. E. (2004). More marriages among the deaf may have led to doubling of common form of genetic deafness in the U.S. *Virginia Commonwealth University News Center.* Retrieved from http://www.news.vcu.edu/news/More_marriages_among_the_deaf_may_have_led_to_doubling_of_common

City of Sanford, Florida. (n.d.). Transcript of George Zimmerman's call to the police. *Mother Jones.* Retrieved from http://www.motherjones.com/documents/326700-full-transcript-zimmerman

Clark, B. (2011). The weight loss industry (and public health) dilemma. *24K Marketing,* January 18. Retrieved from http://24kmarketing.com/2011/01/weight-loss-industry-and-public-health.html

Clark, H. (2006). Are women happy under the glass ceiling? *Forbes.* Retrieved from http://www.forbes.com/2006/03/07/glass-ceiling-opportunities--cx_hc_0308glass.html

Clarke, S. (2011). 2012 end-of-the-world countdown based on Mayan calendar starts today. *ABCnews.com.* Retrieved from http://abcnews.go.com/blogs/headlines/2011/12/2012-end-of-the-world-countdown-based-on-mayan-calendar-starts-today/

Cloward, R. A., & Ohlin, L. E. (1960). *Delinquency and opportunity: A theory of delinquent gangs.* Glencoe, IL: Free Press.

CNN. (2010). More Americans say they attend church, mosque, synagogue. Retrieved from http://religion.blogs.cnn.com/2010/06/30/more-americans-say-they-attend-church-mosque-synagogue/

CNN. (2012). Oregon Measure 80: Legalize marijuana. *Election Center: Races & Results,* November 14. Retrieved from http://www.cnn.com/election/2012/results/state/OR/ballot/01

Cockerham, W. C., & Glasser, M. (2000). *Readings in medical sociology* (2nd ed.). Englewood Cliffs, NJ: Prentice Hall.

Cohen, A. K. (1955). *Delinquent boys: The culture of the gang.* Glencoe, IL: Free Press.

Cohen, A. (2012). How voter ID laws are being used to disenfranchise minorities and the poor. *The Atlantic,* March 16. Retrieved from http://www.theatlantic.com/politics/archive/2012/03/how-voter-id-laws-are-being-used-to-disenfranchise-minorities-and-the-poor/254572/

Cohen, L. J., & Debenedet, A. T. (2012). Penn State cover-up: Groupthink in action. *Time,* July 17, p. 26.

Coleman, J. (1982). *High school achievement.* New York: Basic Books.

Coleman, J. S. (1990). *The foundations of social theory.* Cambridge, MA: Harvard University Press.

Coleman, J., & Hang, Y. (2008). Beyond nature and nurture: The influence of lay gender theories on self-stereotyping. *Self & Identity, 7*(1), 34–53.

Colen, C. G., Geronimus, A. T., Bound, J., & James, S. A. (2006). Maternal upward socioeconomic mobility and Black-White disparities in infant birthweight. American *Journal of Public Health,* 96(11), 2032–2039.

College Board. (2010). Mean SAT scores of college-bound seniors, 1972–2010. *SAT Trends.* Retrieved from http://professionals.collegeboard.com/profdownload/2010-sat-trends.pdf

Collegemeasures.com. (2010). *Performance of four-year colleges in the United States.* Retrieved from http://collegemeasures.org/4-year_colleges/national/scorecard/strategic-measures/

Collins, P. H. (1990). *Black feminist thought: Knowledge, consciousness and the politics of empowerment.* New York: Routledge.

Collins, R. (1979). *The credential society: An historical sociology of education and stratification.* New York: Academic Press.

Collins, R. (1980). Weber's last theory of capitalism: A systematization. *American Sociological Review, 45*(6), 925–942.

Collins, R. (1990). Conflict theory and the advance of macro-historical sociology. In George Ritzer (Ed.), *Frontiers of social theory: The new synthesis* (pp. 68–87). New York: Columbia University Press.

Colomy, P. (Ed.). (1990). *Functionalist sociology.* Brookfield, VT: Elgar.

Colomy, P. (1986). Recent developments in the functionalist approach to change. *Sociological Focus, 19,* 139–158.

Coltrane, S., & Ishii-Kuntz, M. (1992). Remarriage, stepparenting, and household labor. *Journal of Family Issues, 13*(2), 215–233.

Commission on Health. (2009). Race and socioeconomic factors affect opportunities for better health. *Issue Brief 5: Race and socioeconomic factors.* Retrieved from http://www.commissiononhealth.org/PDF/506edea1-f160-4728-9539-aba2357047e3/Issue%20Brief%205%20April%2009%20-%20Race%20and%20Socioeconomic%20Factors.pdf

Complete College America. (2011). Texas 2011. *2011 College Completion Data.* Retrieved from http://www.completecollege.org/docs/Texas.pdf

Comte, A. (1975). In G. Lenzer (Ed.), *Auguste Comte and positivism: The essential writings.* New York: Harper Torchbooks.

Condry, J. C. (1989). *The psychology of television.* Hillsdale, NJ: Erlbaum.

Conley, D. (1999). *Being Black, living in the red: Race, wealth and social policy in America.* Berkeley: University of California Press.

Conlin, J. (2010). For American students, life lessons in the Mideast. *The New York Times,* August 6. Retrieved from http://www.nytimes.com/2010/08/08/fashion/08Abroad.html?pagewanted=all

Connell, R. W. (2005). Change among the gatekeepers: Men, masculinities, and gender equality in the global arena. *Signs: Journal of Women in Culture and Society, 30*(3), 1801–1826.

Connell, R. W. (2010). Masculinities. Retrieved from http://www.raewynconnell.net/p/masculinities_20.html

Connell, R. W., & Messerschmidt, J. W. (2005). Hegemonic masculinity: Rethinking the concept. *Gender & Society, 19*(6), 829–859.

Cooley, C. H. (1909). *Social organization: A study of the larger mind.* New York: Charles Scribner's Sons.

Cooley, C. H. (1964). *Human nature and the social order.* New York: Schocken Books. (Original work published 1902)

Coontz, S. (2000). Historical perspectives on family studies. *Journal of Marriage and the Family, 62*(2), 283–297.

Coontz, S. (2005). *Marriage, a history: From obedience to intimacy, or how love conquered marriage.* New York: Penguin Group.

Coontz, S. (2012). Five myths about marriage. *The Washington Post,* May 25. Retrieved from http://www.washingtonpost.com/opinions/five-myths-aboutmarriage/2012/05/25/gJQAofiMqU_story.html

Cooper, H., Nye, B., Charlton, K., Lindsay, J., & Greathouse, S. (1996). The effects of summer vacation on achievement test scores: A narrative and meta-analytic review. *Review of Educational Research, 66*, 227–268.

Core Group Las Vegas. (2004, June 6). *Private military contractors preserving peace through protection.* Retrieved from http://www.unitedpmc.com/

Corsaro, W. A. (1997). *The sociology of childhood.* Newbury Park, CA: Pine Forge Press.

Critser, G. (2003). *Fatland: How Americans became the fattest people in the world.* New York: Houghton Mifflin.

Crocker, W. H. (1986). Canela body painting. *Review: Latin American Literature and Arts, 36,* 24–26.

Crocker, W. H. (1990). The Canela (Eastern Timbira), I: An ethnographic introduction. *Smithsonian Contributions to Anthropology, 33.* Washington, DC: Smithsonian Institution Press.

Crocker, W. H. (1994). *The Canela: Bonding through kinship, ritual, and sex (Case studies in cultural anthropology).* Fort Worth, TX: Harcourt Brace College.

Crumley, B. 2010. *The Game of Death—France's shocking TV experiment. Time,* March 17. Retrieved from http://www.time.com/time/arts/article/0,8599,1972981,00.html

Curtiss, S. (1977). Genie: A *psycholinguistic study of a modern-day "wild child."* Boston: Academic Press.

Cutright, P., & Fernquist, R. M. (2000). Effects of societal integration, period, region, and culture of suicide on male age-specific suicide rates: 20 developed countries, 1955–1989. *Social Science Research, 29,* 148–172.

Dahl, R. A. (1961). *Who governs?* New Haven, CT: Yale University Press.

Dahl, R. A. (1982). *Dilemmas of a pluralist democracy: Autonomy vs. control.* New Haven, CT: Yale University Press.

Dahl, R. A. (1989). *Democracy and its critics.* New Haven, CT: Yale University Press.

Dahrendorf, R. (1958). *Out of utopia.* New York: Ardent Media.

Dahrendorf, R. (1959). *Class and class conflict in industrial society.* Stanford, CA: Stanford University Press.

Dahrendorf, R. (1967). *New perspectives on the theory of social and political conflict.* London: Longmans.

Daniels, R. (2004). Incarceration of the Japanese Americans: A sixty year perspective. *The History Teacher, 35*(3), 297–310.

D'Augelli, A. R., Pilkington, N. W., & Hershberger, S. L. (2002). Incidence and mental health impact of sexual orientation victimization of lesbian, gay, and bisexual youths in high school. *School Psychology Quarterly, 17*(2), 148–167.

David, D. S., & Brannon, R. (1976). *The forty-nine percent majority: The male sex role.* New York: Random House.

Davis, A. (2008). Interpersonal and physical dating violence among teens. *The National Council on Crime and Delinquency Focus.* Retrieved from http://www.nccdglobal.org/publications/interpersonal-and-physical-dating-violence-among-teens-focus

Davis, F. J. (1991). *Who is Black? One nation's definition.* University Park: Pennsylvania State University Press.

Davis, K., & Moore, W. (1945). Some principles of stratification. *American Sociological Review, 10,* 242–249.

Davis, S. N., Greenstein, T. N., & Marks, J. P. (2007). Effects of union type on division of household labor: Do cohabiting men really perform more housework? *Journal of Family Issues, 28*(9), 1246–1272.

Davis, W. (1991). *Fundamentalism in Japan: Religious and political.* Chicago: University of Chicago Press.

Death Penalty Information Center. (2010). *Executions.* Retrieved from http://www.deathpenaltyinfo.org/executions-united-states

de Balzac, H. (1833). *The girl with the golden eyes.* Philadelphia, PA: George Barrie & Son.

de Balzac, H. (1985). *Les employés.* French & European Publications.

DeBeaumont, R. (2009). Occupational differences in the wage penalty for obese women. *Journal of Socio-Economics, 38,* 344–349.

DeFrancisco, V. L. (1991). The sounds of silence: How men silence women in marital relations. *Discourse & Society, 2*(4), 412–423.

DellaPergola, S. (2010). World Jewish population, 2010. *Current Jewish Population Reports, 2.* Retrieved from http://www.jewishdatabank.org/Reports/World_Jewish_Population_2010.pdf

Delli Carpini, M. X., & Keeter, S. (1996). *What Americans know about politics and why it matters.* New Haven, CT: Yale University Press.

DeNavas-Walt, C., Proctor, B. D., & Smith, J. C. (2012a). Income, poverty, and health insurance coverage in the United States: 2011. *Current Population Reports.* Washington, DC: U.S. Census Bureau.

DeNavas-Walt, C., Proctor, B. D., & Smith, J. C. (2012b). Table 232: Meaning earnings by highest degree earned: 2009. *Statistical Abstract of the United States: 2012.* U.S. Census Bureau. Retrieved from http://www.census.gov/compendia/statab/2012/tables/12s0231.pdf

Denizet-Lewis, B. (2003). Double lives on the down low. *The New York Times Magazine,* August 3. Retrieved from http://www.nytimes.com/2003/08/03/magazine/double-lives-on-the-down-low.html?pagewanted=all&src=pm

Denno, B. W. (1990). *Biology and violence from birth to adulthood.* Cambridge: Cambridge University Press.

Denyer, S., & Lakshmi, R. (2011). Anna Hazare inspires young, middle-class awakening in India. *The Washington Post,* August 19. Retrieved from http://www.washingtonpost.com/world/asia-pacific/anna-hazare-inspires-young-middle-class-awakening-in-india/2011/08/19/gIQA-1NaCQJ_story.html

de Paul, J., & Domenech, L. (2000). Childhood history of abuse and child abuse potential in adolescent mothers: A longitudinal study. *Child Abuse and Neglect, 24*(5), 701–713.

DeSantis, A., & Kayson, W. A. (1997). Defendants' characteristics of attractiveness, race, sex and sentencing decisions. *Psychological Reports, 81,* 679–683.

De Vise, D. (2012, May 21). Is college too easy? As study time falls, debate rises. *The Washington Post.* Retrieved from http://www.washingtonpost.com/local/education/is-college-too-easy-as-study-time-falls-debate-rises/2012/05/21/gIQAp7uUgU_story.html

Diaz, J. D. (1999). *Suicide in the Las Vegas homeless population: Applying Durkheim's theory of suicide.* PhD dissertation, University of Nevada, Las Vegas.

Dicken, P. (1998). *The global shift: Transforming the world economy* (3rd ed.). New York: Guilford Press.

di Giovanni, J. (2012). Life during wartime. *The New York Times, Sunday Review,* July 22, pp. 2, 6.

Dilmac, B. (2009). Psychological needs as a predictor of cyberbullying: A preliminary report on college students. *Educational Sciences: Theory and Practice, 9*(3), 1308–1325.

DiMaggio, P. J., & Powell, W. (1983). The iron cage revisited: Institutional isomorphism and collective rationality in organizational fields. *American Sociological Review, 48,* 147–160.

Dion, K., Berscheid, E., & Walster, E. (1972). What is beautiful is good. *Journal of Personality and Social Psychology, 24*(3), 285–290.

Dionne, E. J., Jr., & Green, J. C. (2008). *Religion and American politics: More secular, more evangelical . . . or both?* Washington, DC: Brookings Institution. Retrieved from http://www.brookings.edu/papers/2008/02_religion_green_dionne.aspx

Dishion, T. J., McCord, J., & Poulin, F. (1999). When interventions harm: Peer groups and problem behavior. *American Psychologist, 54,* 755–764.

Djilas, M. (1957). *The new class: An analysis of the communist system.* New York: Harvest Books.

Dobbie, W., & Fryer, R. G. (2011). Getting beneath the veil of effective schools: Evidence from New York City. *American Economic Journal: Applied Economics, 3*(3), 158–187.

Dokoupil, T. (2012a). Is the web driving us mad? *Newsweek,* July 9. Retrieved from http://www.thedailybeast.com/newsweek/2012/07/08/is-the-internet-making-us-crazy-what-the-new-research-says.html

Dokoupil, T. (2012b). Tweets, texts, email, posts: Is the onslaught making us crazy? *Newsweek,* July 16, pp. 24–30.

Dollard, J. (1957). *Caste and class in a Southern town* (3rd ed.). New York: Anchor Books.

Dolnick, E. (1993). Deafness as culture. *The Atlantic, 272*(3), 37–53.

Domhoff, G. W. (1983). *Who rules America now?* New York: Simon and Schuster.

Domhoff, G. W. (1990). *The power elite and the state: How policy is made in America.* Hawthorne, NY: Aldine de Gruyter.

Domhoff, G. W. (2002). *Who rules America? Power and politics* (4th ed.). New York: McGraw-Hill.

Domhoff, G. W. (2006). *Who rules America? Power, politics, & social change* (5th ed.). New York: McGraw-Hill.

Domhoff, G. W. (2009). *Who rules America? Challenges to corporate and class dominance* (6th ed.). New York: McGraw-Hill.

Domhoff, G. W. (1990). *The power elite and the state: How policy is made in America.* New York: Aldine De Gruyter.

Donadio, R. (2009). On Africa trip, Pope will find place where church is surging amid travail. *The New York Times,* March 15. Retrieved from http://www.nytimes.com/2009/03/16/world/africa/16pope.html

Donner, F. M. (2012). *Muhammad and the believers: At the origins of Islam.* Boston: Harvard University Press.

Dor, A., Ferguson, C., Langwith, C., & Tan, E. (2010). *A heavy burden: The individual costs of being overweight and obese in the United States.* George Washington University. Retrieved from http://sphhs.gwu.edu/departments/health-policy/dhp_publications/pub_uploads/dhpPublication_35308C47-5056-9D20-3DB157B39AC53093.pdf

Douglas, D. (2013). Attorney general says big banks' size may inhibit prosecution. *The Washington Post,* March 6, p. A12.

Downs, E., & Smith, S. (2010). Keeping abreast of hypersexuality: A video game character content analysis. *Sex Roles, 62*(11), 721–733.

Downtown Women's Action Coalition. (2011). *2010 Downtown Women's needs assessment.* Los Angeles, CA: Author. Retrieved from dwcweb.org/needs/DWAC_NeedsAssessment2010.pdf

Dreifus, C. (2012). A mathematical challenge to obesity. *The New York Times,* May 14. Retrieved from http://www.nytimes.com/2012/05/15/science/a-mathematical-challenge-to-obesity.html

Du Bois, W. E. B. (1968). *The souls of Black folk.* New York: Fawcett World Library. (Original work published 1903)

Du Bois, W. E. B. (2011). *The souls of Black folk.* New York: Tribeca Books. (Original work published 1903)

Dugger, R. (2004). How they could steal the election this time. *The Nation,* August 16. Retrieved from http://www.thenation.com/article/how-they-could-steal-election-time?page=0,3#

Duhigg, C., & Barboza, D. (2012). In China, human costs are built into an iPad. *The New York Times,* January 25. Retrieved from http://www.nytimes.com/2012/01/26/business/ieconomy-apples-ipad-and-the-human-costs-for-workers-in-china.html?_r=2&pagewanted=print

Duhigg, C., & Greenhouse, S. (2012). Electronic giant vowing reforms in China plants. *The New York Times,* March 29. Retrieved from http://www.nytimes.com/2012/03/30/business/apple-supplier-in-china-pledges-changes-in-working-conditions.html?pagewanted=all

Duneier, M. (1992). *Slim's table: Race, respectability, and masculinity.* Chicago: University of Chicago Press.

Dunner, D. L., Gershon, E. S., & Barrett, J. S. (1988). *Relatives at risk for mental disorder.* New York: Ravens Press.

Durkheim, É. (1951). *Suicide.* New York: Free Press. (Original work published 1897)

Durkheim, É. (1956). *Education and sociology* (S. L. Fox, trans.). New York: Free Press. (Original work published 1922)

Durkheim, É. (1964). *The division of labor in society.* New York: Free Press. (Original work published 1893)

Durkheim, É. (1964). *The rules of sociological method.* New York: Free Press. (Original work published 1895)

Durkheim, É. (1973a). *Émile Durkheim on morality and society* (Heritage of Sociology Series). Chicago: University of Chicago Press. (Original work published 1922)

Durkheim, É. (1973b). *Moral education: A study in the theory and application of the sociology of education.* New York: Free Press. (Original work published 1922)

Durkheim, É. (1997a). *The division of labor in society with an introduction by Lewis Coser.* New York: Free Press. (Original work published 1892)

Durkheim, É. (1997b). *Suicide: A study in sociology.* New York: Free Press. (Original work published 1897)

Durkheim, É. (2008). *The elementary forms of the religious life.* New York: Dover.

Duster, T. (1995). Symposium on "The Bell Curve." *Contemporary Sociology, 24*(2), 157–161.

Dworkin, A. (1981). *Pornography: Men possessing women.* New York: Pedigree.

Dworkin, A. (1987). *Intercourse.* New York: Free Press.

Dworkin, A. (1989). *Letters from the war zone: Writings, 1976–1987.* New York: Dutton.

Dwoskin, E. (2012). Will you marry me (after I pay off my student loans)? *Bloomberg Businessweek,* March 28. Retrieved from http://www.businessweek.com/articles/2012–03–28/will-you-marry-me-after-i-pay-off-my-student-loans/

Dwyer, C. (1976). *Research report.* Princeton, NJ: Educational Testing Service.

Eddy, M. B. (1999). *Christian science: No and yes.* Boston: Author. (Original work published 1887)

Edin, K., & Kefalas, M. (2005). *Promises I can keep: Why poor women put motherhood before marriage.* Berkeley: University of California Press.

Edlund, L., Hongbin, L., Junjian, Y., & Junsen, Z. (2007). *Sex ratios and crime: Evidence from China's one child policy.* IZA Discussion Papers 3214, Institute for the Study of Labor (IZA).

Edwards, K. E. (2007). *"Putting my man face on": A grounded theory of college men's gender identity development.* Doctoral dissertation, University of Maryland-College Park. Retrieved from ProQuest Dissertations & Theses (3260431).

Eglitis, D. S. (2010). The uses of global poverty: How economic inequality benefits the West. In J. J. Macionis & N. V. Benokraitis (Eds.), *Seeing ourselves: Classic, contemporary, and cross-cultural readings in sociology* (8th ed., pp. 199–206). New York: Pearson.

Ehrenreich, B. (2001). *Nickel and dimed: On (not) getting by in America.* New York: Metropolitan Books.

Ehrlich, P. (1986). *The population bomb.* Cutchogue, NY: Buccaneer Books.

Eichler, A. (2012). Unpaid overtime: Wage and hour lawsuits have skyrocketed in the last decade. *The Huffington Post,* May 30. Retrieved from http://www.huffingtonpost.com/2012/05/30/wage-hour-lawsuits_n_1556484.html

Eisenbrey, R. (2012). Pushing back against illegal unpaid internships. *EPI Blog,* March 2.

Eliade, M. (1959). *The sacred and the profane: The nature of religion.* Orlando, FL: Harcourt.

Eller, C. (2000). *The myth of matriarchal prehistory: Why an inventive past won't give women a future.* Boston: Beacon Press.

Ellis, B. (2011). Average student loan debt tops $25,000. *CNN Money,* November 3. Retrieved from http://money.cnn.com/2011/11/03/pf/student_loan_debt/index.htm

Eliot, L. (2009). *Pink brain, blue brain: How small differences grow into troublesome gaps—and what we can do about it.* New York: Houghton Mifflin Harcourt.

Emerson, R. M. (1962). Power-dependence relations. *American Sociological Review, 27,* 31–41.

Emmanuel, A. (1972). *Unequal exchange: A study of the imperialism of trade.* New York: Monthly Review.

Engels, F. (1942). *The origins of family, private property, and the state.* New York: International. (Original work published 1884)

Environmental Protection Agency. (2011). *Electronics waste management in the United States through 2009.* Washington, DC: Author.

Epps, G. (2012). The history of Florida's "Stand Your Ground" law. *The American Prospect,* March 21. Retrieved from http://prospect.org/article/history-floridas-stand-your-ground-law

Epstein, C. F. (1988). *Deceptive distinctions: Sex, gender, and the social order.* New Haven, CT: Yale University Press.

Epstein, D. M. (1993). *Sister Aimee: The life of Aimee Semple McPhearson.* New York: Harcourt Brace.

Erber, G., & Sayed-Ahmed, A. (2005). Offshore outsourcing—A global shift in the present IT industry. *Intereconomics, 40*(2), 100–112.

Erlanger, S. (2009, August 31). Burqa furor scrambles French politics. *The New York Times.* Retrieved from http://www.nytimes.com/2009/09/01/world/europe/01france.html

Etter, G. (1998). Common characteristics of gangs: Examining the cultures of the new urban tribes. *Journal of Gang Research, 5*(2), 19–33.

Etzioni, A. (1975). *A comparative analysis of complex organizations: On power, involvement, and their correlates.* New York: Free Press.

Evans, L., & Davies, K. 2000. No sissy boys here: A content analysis of the representation of masculinity in elementary school reading. *Sex Roles, 42*(3–4), 255–270.

Evans, M. D. R., Kelley, J., Sikora, J., & Treiman, D. J. (2010). Family scholarly culture and educational success: Books and schooling in 27 nations. *Research in Social Stratification and Mobility, 28*(2), 171–197.

FACE Intel. (2000). A huge victory for the worker. *Related Class Action Lawsuits.* Retrieved from http://www.faceintel.com/relatedclassactions.htm

Facebook. (2012). Key facts. *Newsroom.* Retrieved from http://newsroom.fb.com/content/default.aspx?NewsAreaId=22

Farhi, P. (2011). Occupy D.C.: They're occupying, but who's counting? *Washington Post,* October 31. Retrieved from http://www.washingtonpost.com/lifestyle/style/occupy-dc-theyre-occupying-but-whos-counting/2011/10/31/gIQAZBecaM_story.html

Fair Elections Legal Network. (2012). *Restrictive voting laws and legislation in 2011–2012.* Retrieved from http://www.fairelectionsnetwork.com/webfm_send/10

Fairfield, R. (1972). *Communes USA.* Baltimore: Penguin.

Faludi, S. (1991). *Backlash: The undeclared war against American women.* New York: Crown.

Farkas, G., Grobe, R. P., Sheehan, D., & Shuan, Y. (1990a). Cultural resources and school success: Gender, ethnicity, and poverty groups within an urban school district. *American Sociological Review, 55,* 127–142.

Farkas, G., Grobe, R. P., & Sheehan, D. (1990b). Coursework mastery and school success: Gender, ethnicity, and poverty groups within an urban school district. *American Educational Research, 27*(4), 807–827.

Farr, K. (2004). *Sex trafficking: The global market in women and children.* New York: Worth.

Fausto-Sterling, A. (2000). *Sexing the body: Gender politics and the construction of sexuality.* New York: Basic Books.

FBI Uniform Crime Report. (2009). *Crime in the United States—2009.* Retrieved from http://www.fbi.gov/about-us/cjis/ucr/crime-in-the-u.s/2009/crime2009

FBI Uniform Crime Report. (2010). *Crime in the United States—2010.* Retrieved from http://www.fbi.gov/about-us/cjis/ucr/crime-in-the-u.s/2010/crime-in-the-u.s.-2010/persons-arrested

Federal Education Budget Project. (2012). Comparative analysis of funding, student demographics and achievement data. *New America Foundation.* Retrieved from http://febp.newamerica.net/k12/GA/1300120

Federal Election Commission. (1997). *Congressional fundraising and spending up again in 1996.* Retrieved from http://www.fec.gov/press/canye96.htm

Fenstermaker Berk, S. (1985). *The gender factory: the apportionment of work in American households.* New York: Plenum Press.

Fenstermaker, S., & West, C. (2002). *Doing gender, doing difference: Inequality, power, and institutional change.* New York: Routledge.

Ferguson, S. J. (Ed.). (1997). *Shifting the center: Understanding contemporary families.* Mountain View, CA: Mayfield.

Ferment, C. A. (1989). Political practice and the rise of an ethnic enclave: The Cuban American case. *Theory and Society, 18*(January), 47–48.

Ferraris, C., & Carveth, R. (2003). *NASA and the* Columbia *disaster: Decision-making by groupthink?* Presented at the Proceedings of the Association for Business and Communication National Convention.

Fingarette, H. (1972). *Confucius: The secular as sacred.* Long Grove, IL: Waveland Press.

Finke, R., & Stark, R. (1988). Religious economies and sacred canopies: Religious mobilization in American cities, 1906. *American Sociological Review, 53,* 41–49.

Finke, R., & Stark, R. (1992). *The churching of America, 1776–1980: Winners and losers in our religious economy.* New Brunswick, NY: Rutgers University Press.

Finke, R., & Stark, R. (2005). *The churching of America, 1776–2005: Winners and losers in our religious economy.* New Brunswick, NY: Rutgers University Press.

Finkelstein, E. A., Trogdon, J. G., Cohen, J. W., & Dietz, W. (2009). Annual medical spending attributable to obesity: Payer- and service-specific estimates. *Health Affairs, 28*(5), 822–831.

Firestone, S. (1971). *The dialectic of sex.* London, England: Paladin.

Fischer, C. (1982). *To dwell among friends: Personal networks in town and city.* Chicago: University of Chicago Press.

Fischer, C. (1984). *The urban experience* (2nd ed.). New York: Harcourt Brace Jovanovich.

Fischer, H. (2008). *Iraqi civilian deaths estimate.* Congressional Research Service, U.S. Library of Congress, August 27. Retrieved from http://www.fas.org/sgp/crs/mideast/RS22537.pdf

Fischer, R., & Lane, H. (Eds.). (1993). *Looking back: A reader on the history of deaf communities and their sign languages.* Hamburg, Germany: Signum Press; Washington, DC: Distributer for the U.S., Gallaudet University Press.

Fishman, P. (1978). Women's work in interaction. *Social Problems, 25*(4), 397–406.

The Fish Site. (2009). Thai shrimp exporters expect a good year. *News*, September 24. Retrieved from http://www.thefishsite.com/fishnews/10852/thai-shrimp-exporters-expect-a-good-year

Fitzgerald, A. (2011). A stealth way a bill becomes a law. *Bloomberg Businessweek Magazine*, July 28. Retrieved from http://www.businessweek.com/magazine/a-stealth-way-a-bill-becomes-a-law-07282011.html

Flacks, R. (1971). *Youth and social change.* Chicago: Markham.

Ford, L. K., Jr. (1988). Republican ideology in a slave state. *Journal of Southern History, 54*, 405–424.

Forsythe-Brown, I. (2007). *An exploratory analysis of gender, kinscripts and the work of transnational kinship among Afro-Caribbean immigrant families.* Doctoral dissertation. University of Maryland. Retrieved from ProQuest (3307758).

Foucault, M. (1988). *Madness and civilization: A history of insanity in the age of reason.* New York: Vintage Press.

Fouts, G., & Burggraf, K. (2000). Television situation comedies: Female weight, male negative comments, and audience reactions. *Sex Roles, 42*(9–10), 925–932.

Fox, M. A., Connolly, B. A., & Snyder, T. D. (2005). *Youth indicators 2005: Trends in the well-being of American youth* (NCES 2005–050). U.S. Department of Education, National Center for Education Statistics.

Washington, DC: U.S. Government Printing Office.

Frank, A. G. (1966). The development of underdevelopment. *Monthly Review, 18*, 9.

Frank, A. G. (1979). *Dependent accumulation and underdevelopment.* London, UK: Macmillan.

Frederick, S., & AWARE (Association of Women for Action and Research) Committee on Rape. (2001). *Rape: Weapon of terror.* River Edge, NJ: Global.

Freedom House. (2013). Freedom in the world. *Issues.* Retrieved from http://www.freedomhouse.org/report-types/freedom-world

Freedom to Marry. (2012). *States.* Retrieved from http://www.freedomtomarry.org/states/

Freire, P. (1972). *Pedagogy of the oppressed.* New York: Herder & Herder.

Freud, S. (1905). Three essays on sexuality. In *Standard Edition* (Vol. 7). London: Hogarth.

Freud, S. (1929). Civilization and its discontents. In *Standard Edition* (Vol. 21). London: Hogarth.

Freud, S. (1933). *New introductory lectures on psychoanalysis.* New York: Norton.

Freund, C. P. (2002). In praise of vulgarity. *Reason, 33*(10), 24–35.

Frey, W. H., & Speare, A. (1991). U.S. metropolitan area church growth, 1960–1990: Census trends and explanations. *Research Reports, 91*(212). Ann Arbor: University of Michigan Population Studies Center.

Friedan, B. (1963). *The feminine mystique.* New York: Norton.

Friedan, B. (1981). *The second stage.* New York: Summit.

Friedl, E. (1975). *Women and men: An anthropologist's view.* New York: Holt, Rinehart, and Winston.

Friedman, L. (1975). *The legal system: A social science perspective.* New York: Sage.

Friedman, L. (1990). *The republic of choice: Law, authority, and culture.* Cambridge, MA: Harvard University Press.

Friedman, S., Squires, G. D., & Chadwick, J. (2006). Cybersegregation: Are Neil Kelly and Greg Baker more desirable tenants than Tyrone Jackson or Jorge Rodriguez? A research proposal. *SAGE Race Relations Abstracts, 31*(2), 26–31.

Friedman, S., Squires, G., & Galvan, C. (2010). *Cybersegregation in Dallas and Boston: Is Neil amore desirable tenant than Tyrone or Jorge?* Unpublished paper presented at Population Association of America, Dallas, TX.

Friedman, T. (2000). *The Lexus and the olive tree: Understanding globalization.* New York: Anchor Books.

Friedman, T. (2005). *The world is flat.* New York: Farrar, Straus & Giroux.

Fromm, E. (1941). *Escape from freedom.* New York: Farrar & Rinehart.

Froomkin, D. (2010). How do you disenfranchise 1 in 8 Black men? *The Huffington Post*, May 17. Retrieved from http://www.huffingtonpost.com/2010/03/17/how-do-you-disenfranchise_n_502178.html

Frum, D. (2000). *How we got here: The '70s.* New York: Basic Books.

Frye, N. K., & Breaugh, J. A. (2004). Family-friendly policies, supervisor support, work-family conflict, family-work conflict, and satisfaction: A test of a conceptual model. *Journal of Business and Psychology, 19*(2), 197–220.

Gahran, A. (2012). Smartphone users report more phone problems, survey says. *CNN Tech*, August 3. Retrieved from http://www.cnn.com/2012/08/03/tech/mobile/pew-smartphone-problems/index.html

Gainsborough, J. F. (2001). *Fenced off: The suburbanization of American politics.* Washington, DC: Georgetown University Press.

Gakidou, E., Cowling, K., Lozano, R., & Murray, C. J. L. (2010). Increased educational attainment and its impact on child mortality in 175 countries between 1970 and 2009: A systematic analysis. *The Lancet, 376*(9745), 959–974.

Gale, R. P. (1986). Social movements and the state: The environmental movement, counter movement, and governmental agencies. *Sociological Perspectives, 29*, 202–240.

Gallaudet Research Institute. (2005). *A brief summary of estimates for the size of the deaf population in the USA based on available federal data and published research.* Retrieved from http://research.gallaudet.edu/Demographics/deaf-US.php

Gamble, J. L., & Hess, J. J. (2012). Temperature and violent crime in Dallas, Texas: Relationships and implications of climate change. *Western Journal of Emergency Medicine, 13*(3), 239–246.

Gamson, J. (1991). Silence, death, and the invisible enemy: AIDS activism and social movement "newness." *Sociology*, Paper 1.

Gamson, W. (1975). *The strategy of social protest.* England: Dorsey Press.

Gamson, W. (1988). Political discourse and collective action. In B. Kandermans et al. (Eds.), *From structure to action: Comparing social movements research across cultures.* Greenwich, CT: JAI Press.

Gans, H. (1962a). *The urban villagers.* New York: Free Press.

Gans, H. (1962b). Urbanism and suburbanism as ways of life. In A. Rose (Ed.), *Human behavior and social processes*. Boston: Houghton Mifflin.

Gans, H. J. (1972). The positive functions of poverty. *The American Journal of Sociology, 78*(2), 275–289.

Gardner, H. (1983). *Frames of mind: The theory of multiple intelligences*. New York: Basic Books.

Garfinkel, H. (1963). A conception of, and experiments with, "trust" as a condition of stable concerted actions. In O. J. Harvey (Ed.), *Motivation and social interaction* (pp. 187–238). New York: Ronald Press.

Garfinkel, H. (1985). *Studies in ethnomethodology*. New York: Blackwell.

Gaskell, G., & Smith, P. (1981). The crowd in history. *New Society, 57*(August 20), 303–304.

Gatsiounis, I. (2008). In Thailand, pollution from shrimp farms threatens a fragile environment. *The New York Times*, March 20. Retrieved from http://www.nytimes.com/2008/03/20/business/worldbusiness/20iht-rbogcoast.1.11278833.html?_r=0

Gauntlett, D. (2008). *Media, gender, and identity: An introduction* (2nd ed.). New York: Taylor & Francis Group.

Geertz, C. (1973). *The interpretation of cultures*. New York: Basic Books.

Gellner, E. (1983). *Nations and nationalism*. Ithaca, NY: Cornell University Press.

George Washington University. (2012). Drug use for better grades deemed more acceptable than for athletics, GW professor finds. *Media Relations News Release*, June 1. Retrieved from http://mediarelations.gwu.edu/drug-use-better-grades-deemed-more-acceptable-athletics-gw-professor-finds

Ger, G. (2005). Religion and consumption: The profane sacred. *Advances in Consumer Research, 32*(1), 79–81.

Gerhardt, K. F. G. (1989). *The silent brotherhood: Inside America's racist underground*. New York: Free Press.

Geronimus, A. (1992). The weathering hypothesis and the health of the African-American women and infants: Evidence and speculations. *Ethnicity and Disease, 2*(3), 207–221.

Gerstel, N., & Gallagher, S. (1994). Caring for kith and kin: Gender, employment and the privatization of care. *Social Problems, 41*(4), 519–539.

Gerth, H., & Mills, C. W. (Eds.). (1946). *From Max Weber: Essays in sociology*. New York: Oxford University Press.

Gerth, H. H., & Mills, C. W. (Eds.). (1958). *From Max Weber: Essays in sociology*. Oxford: Oxford University Press.

Geybullayeva, A. (2012). Azerbaijani blogs talk about Armenians: Introducing Hate 2.0. *Osservatorio balcani e caucaso*, February 3. Retrieved from http://www.balcani-caucaso.org/eng/Regions-and-countries/Azerbaijan/Azerbaijani-blogs-talk-about-Armenians-introducing-Hate-2.0-111320

Ghosh, B. N. (2001). *Dependency theory revisited*. London, UK: Ashgate.

Gibbs, N. (2009). The state of the American woman: What women want now. *Time*, October 14. Retrieved from http://www.time.com/time/specials/packages/article/0,28804,1930277_1930145_1930309,00.html

Giddens, A. (1985). *The constitution of society*. Berkeley: University of California Press.

Giedd, J. N. (2004). Structural magnetic resonance imaging of the adolescent brain. *Annals of the New York Academy of Sciences, 1021*, 77–85.

Gilbertson, G. A., & Gurak, D. T. (1993). Broadening the enclave debate: The labor market experiences of Dominican and Colombian men in New York City. *Sociological Forum, 8*(June), 205–220.

Gilligan, C. (1982). *In a different voice: Psychological theory and women's development*. Cambridge, MA: Harvard University Press.

Gilligan, C., Ward, J. V., & Taylor, J. M. (Eds.). (1989). *Mapping the moral domain: A contribution of women's thinking to psychological theory and education*. Cambridge, MA: Harvard University Press.

Gilman, C. P. (1898). *Women and economics: A study of the economic relation between men and women as a factor in social evolution*. Boston: Small, Maynard & Co.

Gitlin, T. (1980). *The whole world is watching: Mass media in the making and unmaking of the new left*. Berkeley: University of California Press.

Giugni, M., & Passy, F. (2012). *Social movements and policy change: Direct, indirect or join effect*. Paper presented at Public Policy Conference, Oxford, England, Oxford University, St. Anne's College, September 16–17, pp. 1–34.

Glazer, N. (1992). The real world of education. *The Public Interest* (Winter), 57–75.

Glazer, N. (1997). *We are all multiculturalists now*. Cambridge, MA: Harvard University Press.

Glenny, M. (2009). *McMafia: A journal through the global criminal underworld*. New York: Knopf.

Global Commission on Drug Policy. (2011, June). *Report*. Retrieved from http://www.globalcommissionondrugs.org/wp-content/themes/gcdp_v1/pdf/Global_Commission_Report_English.pdf

Glock, C. Y., & Bellah, R. N. (1976). *The new religious consciousness*. Berkeley: University of California Press.

Goffman, E. (1959). *The presentation of self in everyday life*. New York: Doubleday.

Goffman, E. (1961). *Asylums: Essays on the social situation of mental patients and other inmates*. Garden City, NY: Anchor Books.

Goffman, E. (1963a). *Behavior in public place*. New York: Free Press.

Goffman, E. (1963b). *Stigma: Notes on the management of spoiled identity*. Englewood Cliffs, NJ: Prentice Hall.

Goffman, E. (1967). *Interaction ritual: Essays on face to face behavior*. Garden City, NY: Anchor.

Goffman, E. (1972). *Relations in public: Microstudies of the public order*. New York: Harper & Row.

Goffman, E. (1973). *The presentation of self in everyday life*. New York: Doubleday.

Gokcearslan, A. (2010). The effect of cartoon movies on children's gender development. *Procedia: Social and Behavior Sciences, 2*(2), 5202–5207.

Gold, K. M. (2002). *School's in: The history of summer education in American public schools*. New York: Peter Lang.

Goldhagen, D. J. (1997). *Hitler's willing executioners*. New York: Vintage Books.

Goldschieder, F. K., & Waite, L. J. (1991). *New families, no families? The transformation of the American home*. Berkeley: University of California Press.

Goldstein, J. S. (2011). World peace could be closer than you think. *Foreign Policy*, September/October, pp. 53–56.

Goldstone, J. A. (2001). Towards a fourth generation of revolutionary theory. *Annual Review of Political Science, 4*, 139–187.

Goode, E. (2000). How culture molds habits of thought. *The New York Times*, August 8. Retrieved from http://www.nytimes.com/2000/08/08/science/how-culture-molds-habits-of-thought.html?pagewanted=all&src=pm

Goode, E. (2009). *Moral panics: The social construction of deviance*. Chichester, UK: Wiley-Blackwell.

Goodwin, P. Y., Mosher, W. D., & Chandra, A. (2010). Marriage and cohabitation in the United States: A statistical portrait based on Cycle 6 (2002) of the National Survey of

Family Growth. *Vital Health Stat, 23*(28). National Center for Health Statistics. Retrieved from http://www.cdc.gov/nchs/data/series/sr_23/sr23_028.pdf

Goody, J. (1983). *The development of the family and marriage in Europe.* Cambridge: Cambridge University Press.

Gottfredson, M. R., & Hirschi, T. (1990). *A general theory of crime.* Stanford, CA: Stanford University Press.

Gottlieb, L. (2011). How to land your kid in therapy. *The Atlantic*, July. Retrieved from http://www.theatlantic.com/magazine/archive/2011/07/how-to-land-your-kid-in-therapy/8555/

Gould, E. (2011). 2010 marks another year of decline for employer-sponsored health insurance coverage. *Economic Policy Institute*. Retrieved from http://www.epi.org/publication/2010-marks-year-decline-employer-sponsored/

Gould, S. J. (1994). Curveball. In S. Fraser (Ed.), *The Bell Curve wars: Race, intelligence, and the future of America* (pp. 11–22). New York: Basic Books.

Gourevitch, P. (1999). *We wish to inform you that tomorrow we will be killed with our families: Stories from Rwanda.* New York: Farrar, Straus & Giroux.

Graca, M. (1995). *Impact of armed conflict on children.* UNICEF Report. Retrieved from http://www.unicef.org/graca/

Gracey, H. L. (1991). Learning the student role: Kindergarten as academic boot camp. *Down to earth sociology: Introductory readings.* New York: The Free Press.

Gramsci, A. (1971). *Selections from the prison notebooks* (Q. Hoare & G. N. Smith, eds. and trans.). London: Lawrence and Wishart.

Grant, R. (1991). The sources of gender bias in international relations theory. In R. Grant & K. Newland (Eds.), *Gender and international relations* (pp. 8–26). Bloomington: Indiana University Press.

Gray, J. (1998). *Men are from Mars, women are from Venus.* New York: Harper.

Green, P., & Ward, T. (2004). *State crime: Governments, violence and corruption.* London: Pluto Press.

Greenberg, K. S. (1996). *The confessions of Nat Turner and related documents.* Boston: Bedford Books of St. Martin's Press.

Greenberg, K. S. (2003). *Nat Turner: A slave rebellion in history and memory.* New York. Oxford University Press.

Greene, K., & Kramar, M. (2005). Predicting exposure to and liking of media violence: A uses and gratification approach. *Communication Studies, 56*(1), 71–93.

Greenhouse, S. (2008). *The big squeeze: Tough times for the American worker.* New York: Anchor Books.

Grey, S. (2006). *Ghost plane: The true story of the CIA torture program.* New York: MacMillan. (1978). *Woman and nature: The roaring within her.* New York: Harper & Row.

Griffin, S. (1979). *Rape, the power of consciousness.* New York: Harper & Row.

Griffin, S. (1981). *Pornography as silence: Culture's revenge against nature.* New York: Harper & Row.

Grogan, S. (2008). *Body image: Understanding body dissatisfaction in men, women, and children.* New York: Routledge.

groSolar. (2010). *groSolar history.* Retrieved from http://www.grosolar.com/company/our-story

Grossman, D. (1996). *On killing: The psychological cost of learning to kill in war and society.* New York: Back Bay Books.

Gruber, J. E., & Fineran, S. (2008). Comparing the impact of bullying and sexual harassment victimization on the mental and physical health of adolescents. *Sex Roles, 59*(1–2), 1–13.

Grusky, O., Bonacich, P., & Webster, C. (1995). The coalition structure of the four person family. *Current Research in Social Psychology 2,* 16–28.

Guerino, P., Harrison, P. M., & Sabol, W. (2011). *Prisoners in 2010.* Washington, DC: Bureau of Justice Statistics.

Guilmoto, C. Z. (2007). Characteristics of sex-ratio imbalance in India, and future scenarios. Report from the *Fourth Asia Pacific Conference on Reproductive and Sexual Health and Rights.* Hyderabad, India: United Nations Population Fund.

Guilmoto, C. Z. (2011). Skewed sex ratios at birth and future marriage squeeze in China and India, 2005–2100. *Working Papers du CEPED, 15.* Paris: CEPED.

Gump, L. S., Baker, R. C., & Roll, S. (2000). Cultural and gender differences in moral judgment: A study of Mexican Americans and Anglo-Americans. *Hispanic Journal of Behavioral Sciences, 22*(1), 78–93.

Gunnell, J. J., & Ceci, S. J. (2010). When emotionality trumps reason: A study of individual processing style and juror bias. *Behavioral Sciences & the Law, 28*(6), 850–877.

Gunnoe, M. L. (1997). Toward a developmental contextual model of the effects of parental spanking on children's aggression. *Archives of Pediatrics and Adolescence, 151*(8), 768–775.

Gura, D. (2012). From middle class to working poor. *Marketplace: The Real Economy,* March 5. Retrieved from http://www.marketplace.org/topics/life/real-economy/middle-class-working-poor

Gustin, S. (2011). Social media sparked, accelerated Egypt's revolutionary fire. *Wired*, February 11. Retrieved from http://www.wired.com/business/2011/02/egypts-revolutionary-fire/

Gutman, R., & Rieff, D. (1999). *Crimes of war: What the public should know.* New York: Norton.

Habermas, J. (1976). *Legitimation crisis.* London: Heinemann.

Hadden, J. K. (1993). *Religion and the social order: The handbook on cults and sects in America.* Bingley, UK: Emerald Group.

Hadden, J. K. (2006). *New religious movements.* Retrieved from http://hirr.hartsem.edu/denom/new_religious_movements.html

Haggerty, R. A. (Ed.). (1991). *Dominican Republic and Haiti: Country studies* (2nd ed.). Washington, DC: Federal Research Division, Library of Congress.

Haj-yahia, M. M., & Cohen, H. C. (2009). On the lived experience of battered women residing in shelters. *Journal of Family Violence, 24*(2), 95–109.

Halbfinger, D. M., & Holmes, S. A. (2003). A nation at war: The troops; military mirrors a working-class America. *The New York Times,* March 30. Retrieved from http://www.nytimes.com/2003/03/30/us/a-nation-at-war-the-troops-military-mirrors-a-working-class-america.html?pagewanted=all&src=pm

Haley, A., & Malcolm X. (1964). *The autobiography of Malcolm X.* New York: Ballantine Books.

Hall, E. (1973). *The silent language.* New York: Doubleday.

Hall, P. M. (2003). Interactionism, social organization, and social processes: Looking back there, reflecting now here, and moving ahead then. *Symbolic Interaction, 26,* 33–55.

Hamermesh, D. S. (2011). *Beauty pays: Why attractive people are more successful.* Princeton, NJ: Princeton University Press.

Hamermesh, D. S., & Parker, A. (2005). Beauty in the classroom: Professorial pulchritude and putative pedagogical productivity. *Economics of Education Review, 24,* 369–376.

Hamilton, D. (2011, July 15). Milgram's experiment, *Horrible Bosses* and Dwight Shrute co-workers. Retrieved from http://drdiane hamilton.wordpress.com/2011/07/15/

milgram%E2%80%99s-experiment-horrible-bosses-and-dwight-shrute-co-workers/

Hamm, M. S. (2002). Apocalyptic violence: The seduction of terrorist subcultures. *Theoretical Criminology, 8*(3), 323–339.

Hammond, E. M., Berry, M. A., & Rodriguez, D. N. (2011). The influence of rape myth acceptance, sexual attitudes, and belief in a just world on attributions of responsibility in a date rape scenario. *Legal and Criminological Psychology, 16*(2), 242–252.

Hammond, P. E. (1992). *Religion and personal autonomy: The third disestablishment in America*. Columbia: University of South Carolina Press.

Handlin, O. (1991). *Boston's immigrants, 1790–1880: A study in acculturation*. Cambridge, MA: Belknap of Harvard University Press.

Haney, C., Banks, W. C., & Zimbardo, P. G. (1973). Interpersonal dynamics in a simulated prison. *International Journal of Criminology and Penology, 1*, 69–97.

Haninger, K., & Thompson, K. M. (2004). Content and ratings of teen-rated video games. *JAMA, 291*(7), 856–865.

Hansen, C. (1992). *A Daoist theory of Chinese thought*. New York: Oxford University Press.

Hanson, P. (2003). *An economic history of the USSR, 1945–1991*. New York: Longman.

Harjo, S. S. (1993). The American Indian experience. In H. P. McAdoo (Ed.), *Family and ethnicity: Strength in diversity* (pp. 63–71). Newbury Park, CA: Sage.

Harper, B. (2000). Beauty, stature and the labour market: A British cohort study. *Oxford Bulletin of Economics and Statistics, 62*, 771–800.

Harrell, B. (1981). Lactation and menstruation in cultural perspective. *American Anthropologist, 83*, 796–823.

Harring, H. A., Montgomery, K., & Hardin, J. (2011). Perceptions of body weight, weight, weight management strategies, and depressive symptoms among US college students. *Journal of American College Health, 59*(1), 43–50.

Harrington, M. (1963). *The other America: Poverty in the United States*. New York: Simon & Schuster.

Harris, J. R. (2009). *The nurture assumption: Why children turn out the way they do* (2nd ed.). New York: Free Press.

Harris Interactive. (2009). Firefighters, scientists and doctors seen as most prestigious occupations. *The Harris Poll #86*. Retrieved from http://www.harrisinteractive.com/vault/Harris-Interactive-Poll-Research-Pres-Occupations-2009-08.pdf

Harth, E. (2001). *Last witnesses: Reflections on the wartime internment of Japanese Americans*. United Kingdom: Palgrave-MacMillan.

Hartmann, H. (1984). The unhappy union of Marxism and feminism: Toward a more progressive union. In A. M. Jaggar & P. S. Rothenberg (Eds.), *Feminist frameworks*, (pp. 172–188). New York: McGraw-Hill.

Harvard Graduate School of Education. (2011). *Pathways to prosperity project*. Retrieved from http://www.gse.harvard.edu/news_events/features/2011/Pathways_to_Prosperity_Feb2011.pdf.

Harvard Medical School. (2010). Marriage and men's health. *Harvard Men's Health Watch Newsletter*, July. Retrieved from http://www.health.harvard.edu/newsletters/Harvard_Mens_Health_Watch/2010/July/marriage-and-mens-health

Hattery, A. J. (2001). *Families on crisis: Men and women's perceptions of violence in partner relationships*. Blacksburg, VA: Southern Sociological Society.

Haub, C. (2010). *2010 World population data sheet*. Washington, DC: Population Reference Bureau.

Haub, C. (2012). Sex ratio at birth trend in India grows more mixed. *Behind the numbers: The PRB blog on population, health, and the environment*. Washington, DC: Population Reference Bureau. Retrieved from http://prbblog.org/index.php/2012/02/23/india-sex-ratio-at-birth-2/comment-page-1/

Haub, C., & Kaneda, T. (2011). *2011 World population data sheet*. Washington, DC: Population Reference Bureau.

Haub, C., & Kaneda, T. (2012). *2012 World population data sheet*. Washington, DC: Population Reference Bureau.

Hauser, R. M. (1995). Symposium on "The Bell Curve." *Contemporary Sociology, 24*(2), 149–153.

Hausmann, R., Tyson, L. D., & Zahidi, S. (2011). *The global gender gap report*. New York: World Economic Forum. Retrieved from http://reports.weforum.org/global-gender-gap-2011/#=

Hayes, D., & Wynyard, D. (2002). *The McDonaldization of higher education*. Westport, CT: Bergin & Garley.

Hecker, D. E. (2005). Occupational employment projections to 2014. *Monthly Labor Review*. Retrieved from http://www.bls.gov/opub/mlr/2005/11/art5full.pdf

Hedwig, L. (2011). Inequality as an explanation for obesity in the United States. *Sociology Compass, 5*(3), 215–232.

Hegewisch, A., & Liepmann, H. (2012). *The gender wage gap by occupation fact sheet*. Washington, DC: Institute for Women's Policy Research. Retrieved from http://www.iwpr.org/publications/pubs/the-gender-wage-gap-by-occupation

Hegewisch, A., Williams, C., & Harbin, V. (2012). *The gender wage gap by occupation fact sheet*. Washington, DC: Institute for Women's Policy Research. Retrieved from http://www.iwpr.org/publications/pubs/the-gender-wage-gap-by-occupation-1

Held, D. (1989). *Political theory and the modern state*. Stanford, CA: Stanford University Press.

Helmich, N. (2009). "Eat your vegetables": For kids, it means fries. *USA Today*, March 3. Retrieved from http://www.usatoday.com/news/health/2009-03-01-vegetables-fries_N.htm

Henderson, R. (2012). Employment outlook: 2010–2020. *Industry Employment*. Bureau of Labor Statistics. Retrieved from http://www.bls.gov/opub/mlr/2012/01/art4full.pdf

Henley, N. M., Hamilton, M., & Thorne, B. (1984). *Womanspeak and manspeak: Sex differences and sexism in communication, verbal and nonverbal*. St. Paul, MN: West.

Henry, T. (2010). Even short-term poverty can hurt kids' health. *CNN Health: The Chart*. Retrieved from http://thechart.blogs.cnn.com/2010/11/15/even-short-term-poverty-can-hurt-kids-health/

Henshaw, S. K. (2002). *Unplanned pregnancy rates in the United States, 1981–2002*. The National Campaign. Retrieved from http://www.thenationalcampaign.org/national-data/pdf/Unplanned-pregnancy-rates-by-age.pdf

Heppner, C. M. (1992). *Seeds of disquiet: One deaf woman's experience*. Washington, DC: Gallaudet University Press.

Heritage, J., & Greatbatch, D. (1991). On the institutional character of institutional talk: The case of news interviews. In D. H. Zimmerman & D. Boden (Eds.), *Talk and social structure* (pp. 93–137). Cambridge, UK: Polity.

Herrnestein, R. J., & Murray, C. J. (1994). *The Bell Curve: Intelligence and class structure in American life*. New York: Free Press

Hersey, P., Blanchard, K., & Natemeyer, W. (1987). *Situational leadership, perception, and the use of power*. Escondido, CA: Leadership Studies.

Hersi, A. A. (2012). Transnational immigration and education: A case of an Ethiopian immigrant high school student. *Creative Education, 3*(1), 149–154.

Hess, H. (1973). *Mafia and mafiosi: The structure of power*. Farnborough, UK: Saxon House.

Hesse-Biber, S. (1997). *Am I thin enough yet? The cult of thinness and the commercialization of identity*. New York: Oxford University Press.

Hexham, I., & Poewe, K. (1997). *New religions as global cultures: Making the human sacred*. Boulder, CO: Westview Press.

Hill, C., & Kearl, H. (2011). *Crossing the line: Sexual harassment at school*. Washington, DC: American Association of University Women. Retrieved from http://www.aauwmi .org/state/High%20School%20Girls/ CrossingTheLine.pdf

Hill, L. E., & Johnson, H. P. (2002). *How fertility changes across immigrant generations*. San Francisco: Public Policy Institute of California. Retrieved from http://www.ppic .org/content/pubs/rb/RB_402LHRB.pdf

Himes, S. M., & Thompson, J. K. (2007). Fat stigmatization in television shows and movies: A content analysis. *Obesity, 15*, 712–718.

Hine, T. (2000). *The rise and fall of the American teenager*. New York: Bard/Avon.

Hinsley, F. H. (1986). *Sovereignty* (2nd ed.). Cambridge: Cambridge University Press.

Hirschi, T. (1969). *Causes of delinquency*. Berkeley: University of California Press.

Hirschi, T. (2004). Self-control and crime. In R. F. Baumeister & K. D. Vohs (Eds.), *Handbook of self-regulation: Research, theory and applications* (pp. 537–552). New York: Guilford.

Ho, C. (1993). The internationalization of kinship and the feminization of Caribbean migration: The case of Afro-Trinidadian immigrants in Los Angeles. *Human Organization, 52*(1), 32–40.

Hoare, R. (2012). Meet Fortune 500's female powerbrokers. *CNN*, May 9. Retrieved from http:// edition.cnn.com/2012/05/08/business/ f500-leading-women/index.html

Hochschild, A. (2001a). The nanny chain. *The American Prospect*, December 19. Retrieved from http://prospect.org/article/ nanny-chain

Hochschild, A. R. (2001b). *The time bind: When work becomes home and home becomes work*. New York: Holt.

Hochschild, A. (2003). *The managed heart: Commercialization of human feeling*. Berkeley: University of California Press.

Hochschild, A. R., & Ehrenreich, B. (2002). *Global woman: Nannies, maids, and sex workers in the new economy*. New York: Metropolitan Books.

Hochschild, A. R., & Machung, A. (2003). *The second shift*. New York: Penguin Group.

Hoffman, B. (2006). *Inside terrorism*. New York: Columbia University Press.

Hoffman, Brinker & Roberts. (2010). *Credit card debt statistics*. Retrieved from http:// www.hoffmanbrinker.com/credit-card- debt-statistics.html

Holt, J. (1994). *Demographic aspects of deafness: Questions and answers* (3rd ed.). Washington, DC: Gallaudet Research Institute, Center for Assessment and Demographic Studies.

Holt, T. (1977). *Black over White: Negro political leadership in South Carolina during reconstruction*. Urbana: University of Illinois Press.

Homans, C. (2011). Anthropology of an idea: War games. *Foreign Policy*, September/ October, pp. 30–31.

Hooton, E. A. (1939). *The American criminal: An anthropological study*. Cambridge, MA: Harvard University Press.

Hopper, R. (1991). Hold the phone. In D. H. Zimmerman & D. Boden (Eds.), *Talk and social structure* (pp. 217–231). Cambridge, UK: Polity.

Horan, P. M., & Hargis, P. G. (1991). Children's work and schooling in the late nineteenth century family economy. *American Sociological Review, 56*, 583–596.

Horkheimer, M. (1947). *The eclipse of reason*. Oxford, UK: Oxford University Press.

Hosken, F. (1993). City. In *American academic encyclopedia* (Online edition). Danbury, CT: Grolier Electronic.

Hossain, Z., Roopnarine, J. L. (1993). Division of household labor and child care in dual-earner African-American families with infants. *Sex Roles, 29*, 571–583.

Howard, P. N. (2011). *The digital origins of dictatorship and democracy: Information technology and political Islam*. Oxford: Oxford University Press.

Hoyert, D. L., & Xu, J. (2012). Deaths: Preliminary data for 2011. *National Vital Statistics Reports, 61*(6). Washington, DC: Centers for Disease Control and Prevention. Retrieved from http://www.cdc.gov/nchs/ data/nvsr/nvsr61/nvsr61_06.pdf

Huber, J. (1990). Macro-micro links in gender stratification: 1989 presidential address. *American Sociological Review, 55*, 1–10.

Huber, J. (1993). Gender role change in families: A macrosociological view. In T. Brubaker (Ed.), *Family relations: Challenges for the future*. Newbury Park, CA: Sage.

Huber, J. (2006). Comparative gender stratification. In J. Saltzman Chafetz (Ed.), *Handbook of the sociology of gender* (pp. 65–80). New York: Springer.

Hudson, J. I., Hiripi, E., Pope, H. G., & Kessler, R. C. (2007). The prevalence and correlates of eating disorders in the National Comorbidity Survey Replication. *Biological Psychiatry, 61*, 248–258.

Huffman, M. L., & Torres, L. (2002). It's not only "Who you know" that matters: Gender, personal contacts, and job lead quality. *Gender & Society, 16*, 793–813.

Human Rights Campaign. (2013). *Pass ENDA now*. Retrieved from http://www.hrc.org/ campaigns/employment-non-discrimina tion-act

Human Rights Watch. (2002). *The war within the war: Sexual violence against women and girls in Eastern Congo*. New York: Author.

Hunt, K. (2007). Gingrich: Bilingual classes teach "ghetto" language. *The Washington Post*, April 1. Retrieved from http://www .washingtonpost.com/wp-dyn/content/ article/2007/03/31/AR2007033100992.html

Hunter, J. D. (1987). *Evangelicalism: The coming generation*. Hutchinson, KS: de Wit Books.

Huntington, S. (1993). The clash of civilizations? *Foreign Affairs, 72*(3), 22–49.

Huntington, S. (1997). *The clash of civilizations and the remaking of world order*. New York: Simon and Schuster.

Hutcheon, D. (1999). *Building character and structure*. Westport, CT: Praeger.

Hvistendahl, M. (2011). *Unnatural selection: Choosing boys over girls, and the consequences of a world full of men*. New York: Public Affairs.

Hyman, H. H. (1942). The psychology of status. *Archives of Psychology, 38*(15), 147–165.

Immerwahr, D. (2007). Caste or colony? Indianizing race in the United States. *Modern Intellectual History, 4*(2), 275–301.

Inc. (2010). *groSolar 2010 statistics*. Retrieved from http://www.inc.com/inc5000/profile/ grosolar

Ingraham, C. (1999). *White weddings: Romancing heterosexuality in popular culture*. New York: Routledge.

Institute of International Education. (2010). Study abroad by U.S. students slowed in 2008/09 with more students going to less traditional destinations. *Press Release*, November. Retrieved from http://www.iie .org/Who-We-Are/News-and-Events/Press- Center/Press-Releases/2010/2010-11-15- Open-Doors-US-Study-Abroad

Institute for the Study on Homelessness and Poverty at the Weingart Center. (2004).

Homelessness in Los Angeles: A summary of recent research. Los Angeles, CA: Author. Retrieved from http://www.bringlahome.org/docs/Homelessness_rsch.pdf

Institute for Women's Policy Research. (2011). Gender wage gap by occupation. *IWPR #C350a.* Retrieved from http://www.iwpr.org/initiatives/employment-job-quality/#publications

International Campaign to Ban Landmines. (2012). States not party. *Mine ban treaty.* Retrieved from http://www.icbl.org/index.php/icbl/Universal/MBT/States-Not-Party

International Development Research Centre. (n.d.). *The daughter deficit: Exploring declining sex ratios in India.* Ottawa, Canada: Women's Rights and Citizenship. Retrieved from http://web.idrc.ca/uploads/user-S/12040457571daughter_deficit.pdf

International Review of Curriculum and Assessment Frameworks Internet Archive. (2009). *Table 15.1: Organisation of school year.* Retrieved from http://www.inca.org.uk/Table15.pdf

International Telecommunication Union. (2011). The world in 2011: ICT facts and figures. Retrieved from http://www.itu.int/ITU-D/ict/facts/2011/material/ICTFactsFigures2011.pdf

Internet Systems Consortium. (2012). Internet host count history. *ISC Domain Survey.* Retrieved from https://www.isc.org/solutions/survey/history

Internet World Stats. (2012). World Internet usage and population statistics, December 31, 2011. *Usage and population statistics.* Retrieved from http://www.internetworldstats.com/stats.htm

Iribarren, J. L., & Moro, E. (2007). Information diffusion epidemics in social networks. *Physical Review Letters, 103.*

Issel, W. (1985). *Social change in the United States: 1945–1983.* New York: Schocken Books.

Jackson, K. T. (1985). *Crabgrass frontier: The suburbanization of America.* New York: Oxford University Press.

Jaffee, S., & Hyde, J. (2000). Gender differences in moral orientation: A meta analysis. *Psychological Bulletin, 126*(5), 703–726.

Jaggar, A. (1983). *Feminist politics and human nature.* Totowa, NJ: Rowman & Allanheld.

Jamieson, R., South, N., & Taylor, I. (1997). *Economic liberalization and cross-border crime.* Salford, Canada: Institute for Social Research.

Janis, I. L. (1972). *Victims of groupthink.* Boston: Houghton Mifflin.

Janis, I. L. (1989). *Crucial decisions: Leadership in policy making and crisis management.* New York: Free Press.

Janis, I. L., & Mann, L. (1977). *Decision making: A psychological analysis of conflict, choice, and commitment.* New York: Free Press.

Jaschik, S. (2009). Probe of extra help for men. *Inside Higher Ed,* November 2. Retrieved from http://www.insidehighered.com/news/2009/11/02/admit

Jenkins, C. D. (1983). Social environment and cancer mortality in men. *New England Journal of Medicine, 308,* 395–408.

Jenkins, C. J., & Eckert, C. M. (1986). Channeling Black insurgency: Elite patronage and professional social movement organizations in the development of the Black movement. *American Sociological Review, 51*(December), 812–829.

Jhally, S. (Producer & Director). (2007). *Dreamworlds 3: Desire, sex & power in music video* [Motion picture]. United States of America: Media Education Foundation.

Johnson, J. (2011). College administrators worry that use of prescription stimulants is increasing. *The Washington Post,* November 27. Retrieved from http://articles.washingtonpost.com/2011-11-27/local/35281941_1_prescription-drugs-study-drugs-prescription-stimulants

Johnson, J. M., & Ferraro, K. J. (1984). The victimized self: The case of battered women. In J. A. Kotarba & A. Fontana (Eds.), *The existential self in society* (pp. 119–130). Chicago: University of Chicago Press.

Johnston, L. D., Bachman, J. G., & O'Malley, P. M. (2010). *Monitoring the future: Questionnaire responses from the nation's high school seniors, 2009.* Ann Arbor, MI: Institute for Social Research.

Johnston, L. D., O'Malley, P. M., Bachman, J. G., & Schulenberg, J. E. (2011a). Demographic subgroup trends for various licit and illicit drugs, 1975–2010. *Monitoring the Future Occasional Paper No. 74.* Ann Arbor, MI: Institute for Social Research. Retrieved from http://www.monitoringthefuture.org/pubs/occpapers/mtf-occ74.pdf

Johnston, L. D., O'Malley, P. M., Bachman, J. G., & Schulenberg, J. E. (2011b). *National results on adolescent drug use: Overview of key findings, 2010.* Monitoring the Future. Ann Arbor: Institute for Social Research, University of Michigan.

Jordan, M. (1992). Big city schools become more segregated in the 1980s, a study says. *Washington Post,* January 9, p. A3.

Josephson Institute Center for Youth Ethics. (2012). *2012 report card on the ethics of American youth.* Retrieved from http://charactercounts.org/programs/reportcard/2012/index.html

Juergensmeyer, M. (1995). The social significance of Radhasoami. In D. Lorenzen (Ed.), *Bhakti Religion in North India: Community identity and political action* (pp. 67–89). Albany: SUNY Press.

Kagay, M. R. (1994). Poll on doubt of Holocaust is corrected: Roper says 91% are sure it occurred. *New York Times,* July 8.

Kahlenberg, S. G., & Hein, M. M. (2010). Progression on Nickelodeon? Gender-role stereotypes in toy commercials. *Sex Roles, 62*(11–12), 830–847.

Kahlor, L. A., & Morrison, D. (2007). Television viewing and rape myth acceptance among college women. *Sex Roles, 56*(11/12), 729–739.

Kaiser Family Foundation. (1998). *American values: 1998 national survey of Americans on values.* Retrieved from http://www.kff.org/kaiserpolls/1441-index.cfm

Kaiser Family Foundation. (2006). *Race, ethnicity, & healthcare: Fact sheet.* Washington, DC. Retrieved from http://www.kff.org/minorityhealth/upload/7541.pdf

Kaiser Family Foundation. (2008). Eliminating racial/ethnic disparities in health care: What are the options? *Health Care and the 2008 Elections.* Retrieved from http://www.kff.org/minorityhealth/upload/7830.pdf

Kaiser Family Foundation. (2009). Estimated numbers of persons living with an AIDS diagnosis, all ages, by race/ethnicity, 2009. *Statehealthfacts.org* Retrieved from http://www.statehealthfacts.org/comparetable.jsp?ind=848&cat=11

Kaiser Family Foundation. (2010a). Census Bureau: Recession fuels record number of uninsured Americans. *Kaiser Health News,* September 17. Retrieved from http://www.kaiserhealthnews.org/daily-reports/2010/september/16/uninsured-census-statistics.aspx

Kaiser Family Foundation. (2010b). *Role of government survey.* Retrieved from http://www.washingtonpost.com/wp-srv/special/politics/Post-Kaiser-Harvard-Role-of-Government-2010.pdf

Kaiser Family Foundation. (2011a). Health care spending in the United States and selected OECD countries. *Snapshots: Health Care Costs.* Retrieved from http://www.kff.org/insurance/snapshot/oecd042111.cfm

Kaiser Family Foundation. (2011b). Overweight and obesity rates for adults by race/

ethnicity, 2011. *Statehealthfacts.org*. Retrieved from http://www.statehealthfacts.org/comparebar.jsp?ind=91&cat=2

Kaiser Family Foundation. (2011c). Percent of adults who are overweight or obese, 2011. *State Health Facts*. Retrieved from http://www.statehealthfacts.org/comparemaptable.jsp?ind=89&cat=2

Kaiser Family Foundation. (2012a). Medicaid and long-term care services and supports. *Kaiser Commission on Medicaid Facts*. Retrieved from http://www.kff.org/medicaid/upload/2186-09.pdf

Kaiser Family Foundation. (2012b). Medicare at a glance. *The Kaiser Family Foundation Medicare Policy*. Retrieved from http://www.kff.org/medicare/1066.cfm

Kaiser Family Foundation. (2012c). Total number of Medicare beneficiaries, 2012. *Statehealthfacts.org* Retrieved from http://www.statehealthfacts.org/comparemaptable.jsp?ind=290&cat=6#notes-1

Kamin, L. J. (1986). Is crime in the genes? The answer may depend on who chooses what evidence. *Scientific American*, February, pp. 22–27.

Kanazawa, S., & Still, M. C. (2000). Parental investment as a game of chicken. *Politics and the Life Sciences, 19,* 17–26.

Kandal, T. R. (1988). *The woman question in classical sociological theory*. Gainesville: University of Florida Press.

Kane, E., & Sanchez, L. (1994). Family status and criticism of gender inequality at home and work. *Social Forces, 72,* 1079–1102.

Kanter, R. M. (1983). *The change masters: Innovation for productivity in the American corporation*. New York: Simon & Schuster.

Kappeler, V. E., Sluder, R. D., & Alpert, G. P. (1998). *Forces of deviance: Understanding the dark side of policing*. Prospect Heights, IL: Waveland Press.

Kapuscinski, R. (2001). *The shadow of the sun*. New York: Vintage Books.

Kara, S. (2009). *Sex trafficking: Inside the business of modern slavery*. New York: Columbia University Press.

Karpinski, A., & Duberstein, A. (2009). *A description of Facebook use and academic performance among undergraduate and graduate students*. Ohio State University: Retrieved from http://researchnews.osu.edu/archive/facebook2009.jpg

Kasarda, J. (1993). Urban industrial transition and the underclass. In W. J. Wilson (Ed.), *The ghetto underclass* (pp. 43–64). Newbury Park, CA: Sage.

Katz, J., & Chambliss, W. J. (1995). Biology and crime. In J. F. Sheley (Ed.), *Criminology*. Belmont, CA: Wadsworth.

Katz, J., & Jhally, S. (2000a). Manhood on the mat: The problem is not that pro wrestling makes boys violent: The real lesson of the wildly popular pseudo-sport is more insidious. *The Boston Globe*, February 13. Retrieved from http://www.jacksonkatz.com/pub_manhood.html

Katz, J., & Jhally, S. (2000b). Put the blame where it belongs: On men. *Los Angeles Times*, June 25. Retrieved from http://articles.latimes.com/2000/jun/25/opinion/op-44616

Kaufman, J. M. (2009). Gendered responses to serious strain: The argument for a general strain of deviance. *Justice Quarterly, 26*(3), 410–444.

Kavilanz, P. (2012). China offshores manufacturing to U.S. *CNN Money*, April 26. Retrieved from http://money.cnn.com/2012/04/24/smallbusiness/china-us-manufacturing/index.htm?hpt=hp_t2

Kavner, L. (2012). "Compliance," a low budget indie, might be the most disturbing movie ever made. *The Huffington Post,* August 15. Retrieved from http://www.huffingtonpost.com/2012/08/15/compliance-movie-film_n_1779123.html

Keeley, B., Wright, L., & Condit, C. M. (2009). Functions of health fatalism: Fatalistic talk as face saving, uncertainty management, stress relief and sense making. *Sociology of Health and Illness, 31*(5), 734–747. Retrieved from http://onlinelibrary.wiley.com/doi/10.1111/j.1467-9566.2009.01164.x/abstract

Kellner, D. (1990). *Television and the crisis of democracy*. Boulder, CO: Westview Press.

Kennedy, P. (1987). *The rise and fall of the great powers: Economic change and military conflict from 1500 to 2000*. New York: Random House.

Kenning, C., & Halladay, J. (2008). Cities study dearth of healthy food. *USA Today,* January 25. Retrieved from http://usatoday30.usatoday.com/news/health/2008-01-24-fooddesert_N.htm

Kenny, C. (2012). The global obesity bomb. *Bloomberg Businessweek*, June 4. Retrieved from http://www.businessweek.com/articles/2012-06-04/the-global-obesity-bomb

Kenworthy, L., & Malami, M. (1999). Gender inequality in political representation: A worldwide comparative analysis. *Social Forces, 78*(1), 235–268.

Kessler, E.-M., Racoczy, K., & Staudinger, U. (2004). The portrayal of older people in prime time television series: The match

with gerontological evidence. *Ageing and Society, 24*(4), 531–552.

Keyfitz, N. (1993). Thirty years of demography and *Demography*. *Demography, 30*(4), 533–549.

Khanna, P. (2010). Beyond city limits: The age of nations is over. The new urban era has begun. *Foreign Policy*. Retrieved from http://www.foreignpolicy.com/articles/2010/08/16/beyond_city_limits?page=full

Khondker, H. (2011). Role of the new media in the Arab Spring. *Globalizations, 8*(5), 675–679. doi:10.1080/14747731.2011.621287

Kibirige, J. S. (1997). Population growth, poverty, and health. *Social Science & Medicine, 45,* 247–259.

Kilbourne, J. (1999). *Deadly persuasion: Why women and girls must fight the addictive power of advertising*. New York: The Free Press.

Kimmel, M. S. (1995). *The politics of manhood*. Philadelphia: Temple University Press.

Kimmel, M. S. (1996). *Manhood in America: A cultural history*. New York: Free Press.

Kimmel, M. S. (1986). Toward men's studies. *American Behavioral Scientist, 29*(5), 517–529.

Kimmel, M. S. (2000). *The gendered society*. New York: Oxford University Press.

King, H., & Chambliss, W. J. (1984). *Harry King: A professional thief's journey*. New York: Macmillan.

Kinnvall, C. (2004). Globalization and religious nationalism: Self, identity, and the search for ontological security. *Political Psychology, 25*(4), 741–767.

Kluckhohn, F. R., & Strodtbeck, F. L. (1961). *Variations in value orientations*. Evanston, IL: Row, Peterson.

Kochhar, R., Fry, R., & Taylor, P. (2011). Wealth gaps rise to record highs between Whites, Blacks, Hispanics. *Pew Social & Demographic Trends*. Retrieved from http://www.pewsocialtrends.org/2011/07/26/wealth-gaps-rise-to-record-highs-between-whites-blacks-hispanics/

Kohlberg, L. (1969). Stage and sequence: The cognitive-developmental approach to socialization. In A. Goslin (Ed.), *Handbook of socialization theory and research* (pp. 347–480). Chicago, IL: Rand McNally.

Kohlberg, L. (1983). *The philosophy of moral development*. New York: Harper & Row.

Kohlberg, L. (1984). *The psychology of moral development* (Vol. 2). New York: Harper & Row.

Kohn, M. L. (1977). *Class and conformity: A study in values*. Chicago: University of Chicago Press.

Kohn, M. (1989). *Class and conformity: A study in values.* Chicago: University of Chicago Press.

Kolowich, S. (2011). What students don't know. *Inside Higher Ed*, August 22. Retrieved from http://www.insidehighered.com/news/2011/08/22/erial_study_of_student_research_habits_at_illinois_university_libraries_reveals_alarmingly_poor_information_literacy_and_skills

Kornhauser, W. (1959). *The politics of mass society.* Glencoe, IL: Free Press.

Kost, K., & Henshaw, S. (2012). *U.S. teenage pregnancies, births and abortions, 2008: National trends by age, race and ethnicity.* Guttmacher Institute. Retrieved from http://www.guttmacher.org/pubs/USTPtrends08.pdf

Kowinski, W. S. (1985). *The malling of America.* New York: William Morrow.

Kozol, J. (1991). *Savage inequalities: Children in American schools.* New York: HarperCollins.

Kozol, J. (1995). *Amazing grace: Lives of our children and the conscience of a nation.* New York: Crown.

Kozol, J. (2000). *Ordinary resurrections: Children in the years of hope.* New York: Crown Books.

Kozol, J. (2005). *The shame of the nation: The restoration of apartheid schooling in America.* New York: Three Rivers Press.

Kozol, J. (2010). *Shame of the nation: The restoration of apartheid schooling in America.* New York: Three Rivers Press.

Kramer, R. C., & Michalowski, R. J. (2005). War, aggression and state crime: A criminological analysis of the invasion and occupation of Iraq. *British Journal of Criminology, 45,* 446–469.

Kraut, R., Patterson, M., Lundmark, V., Kiesler, S., Mukopadhayay, T., & Scherlis, W. (1998). Internet paradox: A social technology that reduces social involvement and psychological well-being? *The American Psychologist, 53,* 1017–1032.

Kristof, N., & WuDunn, S. (2009). *Half the sky: Turning oppression into opportunity for women worldwide.* New York: Knopf.

Kubota, Y. (2009, June 8). Tokyo firm rents fake family, friends for weddings. *Reuters.* Retrieved from http://www.reuters.com/article/2009/06/08/us-japan-weddings-idUSTRE5571IY20090608

Kubrin, C. E. (2005). Gangstas, thugs, and hustlas: Identity and the code of the street in rap music. *Social Problems, 52*(3), 360–378.

Kurdek, L. A. (2007). The allocation of household labor by partners in gay and lesbian couples. *Journal of Family Issues, 28,* 132–148.

Kutnick, P., & Manson, I. (1998). Social life in the primary school: Towards a relational concept of social skills for use in the classroom. In A. Campbell & S. Muncer (Eds.), *The social child* (pp. 165–185). East Sussex, UK: Psychology Press.

Lamont, M., & Lareau, A. (1988). Cultural capital: Elisions, gaps, and glissandos in recent theoretical developments. *Sociological Theory, 6*(2), 153–168.

Lampman, J. (2006). American Buddhism on the rise. *The Christian Science Monitor,* September 14.

Lane, C. (1994). The tainted sources of the Bell Curve. *New York Review of Books,* December 1, pp. 14–19.

Lane, H. (1984). *The deaf experience: Classics in language and education.* Cambridge, MA: Harvard University Press.

Lane, H. (1992). *The mask of benevolence: Disabling the deaf.* New York: Random House.

Lane, H. (2005). Ethnicity, ethics, and the deaf world. *Journal of Deaf Studies and Deaf Education, 10*(3), 291–310.

Lareau, A. (2002). Invisible inequality: Social class and childrearing in Black families and White families. *American Sociological Review, 67*(5), 747–776.

Lareau, A. (2003). *Unequal childhoods: Class, race, and family life.* Berkeley and Los Angeles: University of California Press.

Lareau, A. (2011). *Unequal childhoods: Class, race, and family life* (2nd ed.). Berkeley and Los Angeles: University of California Press.

LaRosa, J. (2011). U.S. weight loss market worth $60.9 billion. *PRWeb,* May 9. Retrieved from http://www.prweb.com/releases/2011/5/prweb8393658.htm

Laub, J., & Sampson, R. J. (2003). *Shared beginnings, divergent lives.* Cambridge, MA: Harvard University Press.

Lauzen, M., Dozier, D., & Horan, N. (2008). Constructing gender stereotypes through social roles in primetime television. *Journal of Broadcasting & Electronic Media, 52*(2), 200–214.

Leaper, C., Breed, L., Hoffman, L., & Perlman, C. A. (2002). Variations in the gender-stereotyped content of children's television cartoons across genres. *Journal of Applied Social Psychology, 32*(8), 1653–1662.

Leaper, C., & Robnett, R. D. (2011). Women are more likely than men to use tentative language, aren't they? A meta-analysis testing for gender differences and moderators. *Psychology of Women Quarterly, 35*(1), 129–142.

Le Bon, G. (1960). *The crowd: A study of the popular mind.* New York: Viking Press. (Original work published 1896)

Lederman, D. (2011). An investigation abandoned. *Inside Higher Ed*, March 16. Retrieved from http://www.insidehighered.com/news/2011/03/16/civil_rights_commission_ends_inquiry_into_admissions_preferences_for_men_and_title_ix

Ledeneva, A. V. (1998). *Russia's economy of favours: Blat, networking and informal exchange.* Cambridge, MA: Cambridge University Press.

Lee, M. M., Carpenter, B., & Meyers, L. S. (2007). Representations of older adults in television advertisements. *Journal of Aging Studies, 21*(1), 23–30.

Lemann, N. (1991). *The promised land: The great Black migration and how it changed America.* New York: Vintage Books.

Lemert, E. (1951). *Social pathology.* New York: McGraw-Hill.

Le Moal, M., & Koob, G. F. (2007). Drug addiction: Pathways to the disease and pathophysiological perspectives. *European Neuropsychopharmacology, 17*(6), 377–393. Retrieved from http://www.european-neuropsychopharmacology.com/article/S0924-977X(06)00231-8/abstract

Lemonnier, J. (2008). Big players in diet industry shift focus to online presences. *The Consumer Lab,* February 18. Retrieved from http://consumerlab.wordpress.com/2008/02/18/big-players-in-diet-industry-shift-focus-to-online-presences/

Lempert, D. (2007). *Women's increasing wage penalties from being overweight and obese.* U.S. Bureau of Labor Statistics. Retrieved from http://www.bls.gov/osmr/abstract/ec/ec070130.htm

Lenning, E. (2007). Execution for body parts: A case of state crime. *Contemporary Justice Review, 10*(2), 173–191.

Leonhardt, D. (2009). Colleges are failing in graduation rates. *The New York Times,* September 8. Retrieved from http://www.nytimes.com/2009/09/09/business/economy/09leonhardt.html

Lesotho. (2012). *Global AIDS response country progress report.* Retrieved from http://www.unaids.org/en/dataanalysis/knowyourresponse/countryprogressreports/2012countries/ce_LS_Narrative_Report%5B1%5D.pdf

Lester, D. (Ed.). (2000). *Suicide prevention—resources for the millennium.* Philadelphia: Brunner-Routledge.

Lesthaeghe, R. (1995). The second demographic transition in Western countries: An interpretation. In K. O. Mason & A. Jensen (Eds.), *Gender and family change in industrialized countries* (pp. 17–62). Oxford: Clarendon Press.

Levin, H. M., & Rouse, C. (2012). The true cost of high school dropouts. *The New York Times,* Retrieved from http://www.nytimes.com/2012/01/26/opinion/the-true-cost-of-high-school-dropouts.html?_r=0

Levine, M., & Crowther, S. (2008). The responsive bystander: How social group membership and group size can encourage as well as inhibit bystander intervention. *Journal of Interpersonal Psychology, 95*(6), 1429–1439.

Levine, S., & Laurie, N. O. (Eds.). (1974). *The American Indian today.* Baltimore: Penguin Books.

Levitt, P. (2004). Transnational migrants: When "home" means more than one country. *Migration Fundamentals.* Washington, DC: The Migration Policy Institute.

Lewin, T. (2011). College graduation rates are stagnant even as enrollment rises, a study finds. *The New York Times,* September 27. Retrieved from http://www.nytimes.com/2011/09/27/education/27remediation.html

Lewis, B. (2010). *Faith and power: Religion and politics in the Middle East.* New York: Oxford University Press.

Lewontin, R. C., Rose, S., & Kamin, L. J. (1984). *Not in our genes: Biology, ideology, and human behavior.* New York: Pantheon.

Library of Congress. (2012). *Days in session calendars: 112th Congress 2nd session.* Retrieved from http://thomas.loc.gov/home/ds/h1122.html

Liebow, E. (1967). *Talley's corner: A study of Negro streetcorner men.* Boston: Little, Brown.

Light, H. K., & Martin, R. E. (1996). American Indian families. *Journal of American Indian Education, 26*(1). Retrieved from http://jaie.asu.edu/v26/V26S1ame.htm

Light, I. H., & Bonacich, E. (1988). *Immigrant entrepreneurs: Koreans in Los Angeles, 1965–1982.* Berkeley: University of California Press.

Lindsey, E. W., & Mize, J. (2001). Contextual differences in parent-child play: Implications for children's gender role development. *Sex Roles, 44,* 155–176.

LinkedIn. (2012). About us. *Press Center.* Retrieved from http://press.linkedin.com/about

Linz, D. G. 1989. "Exposure to Sexually Explicit Materials and Attitudes Toward Rape: A Comparison of Study Results." *Journal of Sex Research, 26*(February), 50–84.

Lips, H. (2008). *Sex and gender: An introduction* (6th ed.). Boston: McGraw-Hill.

Living Tongues Institute for Endangered Languages. (n.d.). *Who we are.* Retrieved from http://www.livingtongues.org/aboutus.html

Livingstone, S., & Brake, D. R. (2010). On the rapid rise of social networking sites: New findings and policy implications. *Children and Society, 24,* 75–83.

Lofland, J. (1985). *Protest: Studies of collective behavior and social movements.* New Brunswick, NJ: Transaction.

Lofquist, D., Lugaila, T., O'Connell, M., & Feliz, S. (2012). *Households and Families: 2010.* U.S. Census Bureau. Washington, DC: U.S. Government Printing Office. Retrieved from http://www.census.gov/prod/cen2010/briefs/c2010br-14.pdf

Logan, J., & Molotch, H. L. (1987). *Urban fortunes: The political economy of place.* Berkeley: University of California Press.

Lomborg, B. (2012). The high cost of heart disease and cancer. *Slate,* April 30. Retrieved from http://www.slate.com/articles/technology/copenhagen_consensus_2012/2012/04/copenhagen_consensus_ideas_for_reducing_cancer_and_heart_disease.html

Lombroso, C. (1896). *L'homme Criminel.* Felix: Alcan.

Lonsway, K. A., Banyard, V. L., Berkowitz, A. D., Gidycz, C. A., Katz, J. T., Koss, M. P., . . . Ullman, S. E. (2009). Rape prevention and risk reduction: Review of the literature for practitioners. *Applied Research Forum,* National Online Resource Center on Violence Against Women. Retrieved from http://oregonsatf.org/wp-content/uploads/2012/05/AR_RapePrevention.pdf

Loo, C. M. (1991). *Chinatown: Most time, hard time.* New York: Praeger.

Lough, R., & Denholm, E. (2005, July 17). *Violence against women in Northern Uganda.* Retrieved from http://www.amnesty.org/en/library/asset/AFR59/001/2005/en/c0fde617-d4ca-11dd-8a23-d58a49c0d652/afr590012005en.pdf

Lubeck, S. (1985). *Sandbox society: Early education in Black and White America.* London: Falmer.

Lucas, J. W., & Lovaglia, M. J. (1998). Leadership status, group size, and emotion in face to face groups. *Sociological Perspectives, 41*(3), 617–637.

Luker, K. (1996). *Dubious conceptions: The politics of teenage pregnancy.* Cambridge, MA: Harvard University Press.

Lunsford, J. L., & Glader, P. (2007). Boeing's nuts-and-bolts problem. *The Wall Street Journal.* Retrieved from http://online.wsj.com/article/SB118220599199739686.html

Maas, P. (1997). *Serpico.* New York: HarperTorch.

MacFarquhar, R. (1980). The post-Confucian challenge. *The Economist, 9,* 67–72.

Mackinder, E. (2010). Pro-environment groups outmatched, outspent in battle over climate change legislation. *OpenSecrets,* August 23. Center for Responsive Politics. Retrieved from http://www.opensecrets.org/news/2010/08/pro-environment-groups-were-outmatc.html

MacKinnon, C. A. (1982). Feminism, Marxism, method and the state: An agenda for theory. *Signs, 7*(3), 515–544.

MacKinnon, C. (1989). *Toward a feminist theory of the state.* Cambridge, MA: Harvard University Press.

Mackun, P., & Wilson, S. (2011). *Population distribution and change: 2000 to 2010.* U.S. Census Bureau. Retrieved from http://www.census.gov/prod/cen2010/briefs/c2010br-01.pdf

MacLeod, C. (2011). In China, tensions rising over Buddhism's quiet resurgence. *USAtoday.com.* Retrieved from http://www.usatoday.com/news/religion/story/2011-11-01/tibetan-buddhism-china-communist-tension/51034604/1

Madlock, P. E., & Westerman, D. (2011). Hurtful cyber-teasing and violence: Who's laughing out loud? *Journal of Interpersonal Violence, 26*(17), 3542–3560.

Maher, J. K., Herbst, K. C., Childs, N. M., & Finn, S. (2008). Racial stereotypes in children's television commercials. *Journal of Advertising Research, 48*(3), 80–93.

Maher, L. (1997). *Sexed work: Gender, race, and resistance in a Brooklyn drug market.* New York: Oxford University Press.

Majka, L. C., & Majka, T. J. (1982). *Farm workers, agribusiness, and the state.* Philadelphia: Temple University Press.

Malacrida, C. (2005). Discipline and dehumanization in a total institution: Institutional survivors' descriptions of time-out rooms. *Disability & Society, 20*(5), 523–537.

Malinauskas, B. M., Raedeke, T. D., Aeby, V. G., Smith, J. L., & Dallas, M. B. (2006). Dieting practices, weight perceptions, and body composition: A comparison of normal weight, overweight, and obese college females. *Nutrition Journal, 5,* 11.

Malthus, T. (1926). *First essay on population.* London: Macmillan. (Original work published 1798)

Mann, C. C. (2011). The birth of religion. *National Geographic,* June, pp. 34–59.

Mann, C. R., & Zatz, M. S. (Eds.). (1998). *Images of color, images of crime.* Los Angeles: Roxbury.

Mann, M. (1986). *The sources of social power: Vol. 1, A history of power from beginning until 1760.* New York: Cambridge University Press.

Manning, R. D. (2005). *Living with debt: A life stage analysis of changing attitudes and behaviors.* Rochester, NY: Lending Tree.

Manning, S. (2009). Is anything made in the U.S.A. anymore? You'd be surprised. *The New York Times,* February 20. Retrieved from http://www.nytimes.com/2009/02/20/business/worldbusiness/20iht-wbmake.1.20332814.html

Marche, S. 2012. Is Facebook making us lonely? *The Atlantic Magazine,* May. Retrieved from http://www.theatlantic.com/magazine/archive/2012/05/is-facebook-making-us-lonely/308930/

Marcuse, H. (1964). *One-dimensional man.* Boston: Beacon Press.

Margolis, E. (2001). *The hidden curriculum in higher education.* New York: Routledge.

Marini, M. M. (1990). Sex and gender: What do we know? *Sociological Forum, 5*(1), 95–120.

Markert, J. (2010). The changing face of racial discrimination: Hispanics as the dominant minority in the United States—A new application of power-threat theory. *Critical Sociology, 36*(2), 307–327.

Market Data Enterprises. (2011). The U.S. weight loss and diet control market (11th ed.). *Report #FS22.* Retrieved from http://www.marketdataenterprises.com/FullIndustryStudies.htm#WeightLoss Websites

Markusen, E. (2002). Mechanisms of genocide. In C. Rittner, J. Roth, & J. M. Smith (Eds.), *Will genocide ever end?* (pp. 83–90). St. Paul, MN: Paragon House.

Marlowe, C. M., Schneider, S. L., & Nelson, C. E. (1996). Gender and attractiveness biases in hiring decisions: Are more experienced managers less biased? *Journal of Applied Psychology, 81,* 11–21.

Marschak, M., Rhoten, C., & Fabich, M. (2007). Effects of cochlear implants on children's reading and academic achievement. *Journal of Deaf Studies and Deaf Education, 12*(3), 269–282. Retrieved from http://jdsde.oxfordjournals.org/content/12/3/269.full

Martin, D. S. (2012). Vets feel abandoned after secret drug experiments. *CNN,* March 1. Retrieved from http://edition.cnn.com/2012/03/01/health/human-test-subjects/

Martin, C. L., & Fabes, R. A. (2001). The stability and consequences of young children's same-sex peer interactions. *Developmental Psychology, 37,* 431–446.

Martineau, H. (1837). *Society in America.* New York: Saunders & Otley.

Marwell, G., & Oliver, P. (1993). *The critical mass in collective action: A micro-social theory.* New York: Cambridge University Press.

Marx, G. T., & McAdam, D. (1994). *Collective behavior and social movements: Process and structure.* Englewood Cliffs, NJ: Prentice Hall.

Marx, K. (1967). *Capital.* New York: International. (Original work published 1867)

Marx, K. (1977). "The Communist Manifesto." In David McClellan (ed.), *Karl Marx: Selected writings.* London: Oxford University Press. (Original work published 1848)

Marx, K. (1992a). *Capital: A critique of political economy* (Vol. 1). New York: Penguin Classics. (Original work published 1867)

Marx, K. (1992b). *Capital: A critique of political economy* (Vol. 2). New York: Penguin Classics. (Original work published 1885)

Marx, K. (1992c). *Capital: A critique of political economy* (Vol. 3). New York: Penguin Classics. (Original work published 1894)

Marx, K., & Engels, F. (1998). *The communist manifesto.* New York: Verso. (Original work published 1848)

Massey, D. S. (2011). Epilogue: The past and future of Mexico-U.S. migration. In O.-V. Mark (Ed.), *Beyond la Frontera: The history of Mexico-U.S. migration* (pp. 241–265). New York: Oxford University Press.

Massey, D. S., & Denton, N. A. (1993). *American apartheid: Segregation and the making of the underclass.* Boston: Harvard University Press.

Mathews, T. J., & MacDorman, M. F. (2012). Infant mortality statistics from the 2008 period linked birth/infant death data set. *National Vital Statistics Reports, 60*(5). Centers for Disease Control and Prevention. Retrieved from http://www.cdc.gov/nchs/data/nvsr/nvsr60/nvsr60_05.pdf

Mathisen, J. A. (1989). Twenty years after Bellah: Whatever happened to American civil religion? *Sociological Analysis, 50*(2), 129–146.

Mauer, M. (2009). The changing racial dynamics of the war on drugs *The Sentencing Project.* Retrieved from http://www.sentencingproject.org/doc/dp_raceanddrugs.pdf

Mayer, G. (2004). *Union membership trends in the United States.* Congressional Research Service: Cornell University ILR School. Retrieved from http://digitalcommons.ilr.cornell.edu/cgi/viewcontent.cgi?article=1176&context=key_workplace

Mazur, E., & Richards, L. (2011). Adolescents' and emerging adults' social networking online: Homophily or diversity? *Journal of Applied Developmental Psychology, 32*(4), 180–188.

Mazzella, R., & Feingold, A. (1994). The effects of physical attractiveness, race, socioeconomic status, and gender of defendant and victims on judgments of mock jurors: A meta-analysis. *Journal of Applied Social Psychology, 24,* 1315–1344.

McAdam, D. (1982). *Political process and the development of Black insurgency, 1930–1970.* Chicago: University of Chicago Press.

McAdam, D. (1986). Recruitment to high-risk activism: The case of freedom summer. *American Journal of Sociology, 92,* 64–90.

McAdam, D. (1988). *Freedom summer: The idealists revisited.* New York: Oxford University Press.

McAdam, D., McCarthy, J. D., & Zald, M. N. (1988). Social movements. In N. J. Smelser (Ed.), *Handbook of sociology* (pp. 695–737). Newbury Park, CA: Sage.

McCarthy, E. (2012). A court's conundrum: When same-sex partners want to split. *The Washington Post,* April 9. Retrieved from http://www.washingtonpost.com/lifestyle/style/a-courts-conundrum-when-same-sex-partners-want-to-split/2012/04/09/gIQAvhep6S_story.html

McCarthy, J. D., & Zald, M. N. (1973). *The trend of social movements in America: Professionalization and resource mobilization.* Morristown, NJ: General Learning.

McCarthy, J., & Zald, M. N. (1977). Resource mobilization and social movements: A partial theory. *The American Journal of Sociology, 82*(6), 1212–1241.

McCartney, J. T. (1992). *Black power ideologies: An essay in African American political thought.* Philadelphia: Temple University Press.

McCoy, A. W. (1991). *The politics of heroin: CIA complicity in the global drug trade.* New York: Lawrence Hill.

McCoy, K. (2009). Uncle Sam wants them. *Contexts* (Winter), pp. 15–19.

McDonald, S., Lin, N., & Ao, D. (2009). Networks of opportunity: Gender, race, and job leads. *Social Problems, 56*(3), 385–402.

McDonald, S., & Day, J. C. (2010). Race, gender, and the invisible hand of social capital. *Sociology Compass, 4*(7), 532–543.

McDonald, S., & Mair, C. A. (2010). Social capital across the life course: Age and gendered patterns of network resources. *Sociological Forum, 25*, 335–359.

McGirk, T. (2009). Behind the Taliban's resurgence in Afghanistan. *Time*, September 16. Retrieved from http://www.time.com/time/world/article/0,8599,1923303,00.html

McGuire, L. C., Okoro, C. A., Goins, R. T., & Anderson, L. A. (2008). Characteristics of American Indian and Alaska native adult caregivers, Behavioral Risk Factor Surveillance System, 2000. *Ethnicity & Disease, 18*(4), 520.

McIntosh, P. (1990). White privilege: Unpacking the invisible knapsack. *Independent School*, pp. 31–36.

McKee, L., Roland, E., Coffelt, N., Olson, A. L., Forehand, R., Massari, C., . . . Zens, M. S. (2007). Harsh discipline and child problem behaviors: The roles of positive parenting and gender. *Journal of Family Violence, 22*(4), 187–196.

McKenna, K. Y. A., & Bargh, J. A. (1998). Coming out in the age of the Internet: Identity "demarginalization" through virtual group participation. *Journal of Personality and Social Psychology, 75*(3), 681–694.

McKibben, B. (2011). Resisting climate reality. *The New York Review of Books*, April 7. Retrieved from http://www.nybooks.com/articles/archives/2011/apr/07/resisting-climate-reality/?pagination=false

McLean, B., & Nocera, J. (2010). *All the devils are here: The hidden history of the financial crisis*. New York: Penguin/Portfolio.

McLean, B., & Elkind, P. (2003). *The smartest guys in the room: The amazing rise and scandalous fall of Enron*. New York: Penguin/Portfolio.

McLellan, D. (2010). *Karl Marx: Selected writings*. New York: Classic Books International.

McLoyd, V., & Smith, J. (2002). Physical discipline and behavior problems in African American, European American, and Hispanic children: Emotional support as a moderator. *Journal of Marriage and Family, 64*(1), 40–53.

McMurray, S. (2011). 2011 wedding cost update 3.4% decrease from 2010 spending. *The Wedding Report*. Retrieved from http://www.theweddingreport.com/bz/index.php/2011-wedding-cost-update-3-4-decrease-from-2010-spending/

McNeely, C. L. (1995). *Constructing the nation-state: International organization and prescriptive action*. Westport, CT: Greenwood.

McNicoll, G. (2001). Government and fertility in transitional and post-transitional societies. *Population and Development Review, 27*, 129–159.

McPhail, C. (1991). *The myth of the madding crowd*. New York: de Gruyter.

Mead, G. H. (1934). *Mind, self, and society*. Chicago: University of Chicago Press.

Mead, G. H. (1938). *The philosophy of the act*. Chicago: University of Chicago Press.

Mednick, S. A., Gabrielli, W. F., Jr., & Hutchings, B. (1987). Genetic factors in the etiology of criminal behavior. In S. A. Mednick, T. E. Moffitt, & S. A. Stack (Eds.), *The causes of crime: New biological approaches*. Cambridge: Cambridge University Press.

Mednick, S. A., Moffitt, T. E., & Stack, S. A. (1987). *The causes of crime: New biological approaches*. Cambridge: Cambridge University Press.

Mehra, A., Dixon, A. L., Brass, D. J., & Robertson, B. (2006). The social network ties of group leaders: Implications for group performance and leader reputation. *Organization Science, 17*(1), 64–79.

Melton, J. G. (1996). *Encyclopedia of American religions* (5th ed.). New York: Gale Research.

Melucci, A. (1989). *Nomads of the present: Social movements and individual needs in contemporary society*. Philadelphia: Temple University Press.

Merton, R. K. (1938). Social structure and anomie. *American Sociological Review, 3*, 672–682.

Merton, R. (1957). *Social theory and social structure*. New York: Free Press.

Merton, R. K. (1967). *Social theory and social structure*. New York: Free Press.

Merton, R. K. (1968a). Social structure and anomie. *American Sociological Review, 3*, 672–682. (Original work published 1938)

Merton, R. K. (1968b). *Social theory and social structure*. New York: Free Press. (Original work published 1938)

Merton, R. K. (1996). *On social structure and science* (Heritage of Sociology Series). Chicago: University of Chicago Press.

Messerschmidt, J. W. (1986). *Capitalism, patriarchy and crime: Towards a socialist feminist criminology*. Totowa, NJ: Rowman & Littlefield.

Meyerson, H. (2012). Labor's power gap. *The Washington Post*, September 3, p. A17.

Meyrowitz, J. (1985). *No sense of place: The impact of electronic media on social behavior*. New York: Oxford University Press.

Michalowski, R., & Dubisch, J. (2001). *Run for the wall: Remembering Vietnam on a motorcycle pilgrimage*. New Brunswick, NJ: Rutgers University Press.

Migration Policy Institute. (2011). *The relationship between immigration and nativism in Europe and America*. Retrieved from http://www.migrationpolicy.org/pubs/Immigration-Nativism.pdf

Migration Policy Institute. (2012). *Region of birth as a percentage of the total immigrant population, 1960–2011*. Retrieved from http://www.migrationinformation.org/datahub/charts/fb.2.shtml

Milgram, S. (1963). Behavioral studies in obedience. *Journal of Abnormal Psychology, 67*, 371–378.

Milgram, S. (2009). *Obedience to authority*. New York: Harper & Row. (Original work published 1974)

Milkman, R. (2006). *L.A. story: Immigrant workers and the future of the U.S. labor movement*. New York: Russell Sage Foundation.

Miller, K. A., Kohn, M. A., & Schooler, C. (1986). Educational self-direction and personality. *American Sociological Review, 5*, 372–390.

Miller, L. P. (1995). Tracking the progress of *Brown*. *Teachers College Record, 96*(4), 609–613.

Miller, T., Govil, N., McMurria, J., & Maxwell, R. (2002). *Global Hollywood*. London, UK: British Film Institute.

Miller, M., Azrael, D., & Hemenway, D. (2007). State-level homicide victimization rates in the U.S. in relation to survey measures of household firearm ownership, 2001–2003. *Social Science and Medicine, 64*, 656–664.

Millett, K. (1970). *Sexual politics*. Garden City, NY: Doubleday.

Mills, C. W. (1956). *The power elite*. New York: Oxford University Press.

Mills, C. W. (2000a). *The power elite*. New York: Oxford University Press. (Original work published 1956)

Mills, C. M. (2000b). *The sociological imagination* (40th anniversary ed.). New York: Oxford University Press. (Original work published 1959)

Miner, H. (1956). Body ritual among the Nacirema. *American Anthropologist, 58*(3), 503–507.

Mishel, L., Bivens, J., Gould, E., & Shierholz, H. (2012). *The state of working America* (12th ed.). Ithaca, NY: Cornell University Press, Economic Policy Institute.

Mizruchi, M. S., & Potts, B. B. (1998). Centrality and power revisited: Actor success in group decision making. *Social Networks, 20*(4), 353–387.

Mollenkopf, J. (1977). The postwar politics of urban development. In J. Walton & D. E. Carns (Eds.), *Cities in change* (2nd ed., pp. 549–579). Boston: Allyn & Bacon.

Moloney, C. (2012). *The buffalo slaughter and the conquest of the West.* Master's thesis, George Washington University.

Molotch, H. L. (1972). *Managed integration: Dilemmas of doing good in the city.* Berkeley: University of California Press.

Molotch, H. L. (1976). The city as a growth machine. *American Journal of Sociology, 82,* 309–333.

Molotch, H., & Boden, D. (1985). Talking social structure: Discourse, dominance, and the Watergate hearings. *American Sociological Review, 50,* 273–288.

Monroe, P. (1940). *Founding of the American public school system.* New York: Macmillan.

Montague, A. (1995). *Race and IQ* (Expanded ed.). New York: Oxford University Press.

Moore, J. (1991). *Going down to the barrio: Homeboys and homegirls in change.* Philadelphia: Temple University Press.

Moore, J. D. (2004). *Visions of culture: An introduction to anthropological theories and theorists.* Walnut Creek, CA: Altamira Press.

Moore, J. (2010). Congo war leaves legacy of sexual violence against women. *The Christian Science Monitor,* June 30. Retrieved from http://www.csmonitor.com/World/Africa/2010/0630/Congo-war-leaves-legacy-of-sexual-violence-against-women

Moore, J. (2012). Son fulfills dream that racism denied his mother. *National Public Radio,* May 18. Retrieved from http://www.npr.org/2012/05/18/152935623/son-fulfills-dream-racism-denied-to-his-mother

Moore, J., & Pinderhughes, R. (2001). The Latino population: The importance of economic restructuring. In M. L. Anderson & P. Hill-Collins (Eds.), *Race, class, and gender: An anthology* (4th ed., pp. 251–258). New York: Wadsworth.

Moore, L. R. (1994). *Selling God: American religion in the marketplace culture.* New York: Oxford University Press.

Morgan, J. (1999). *When chickenheads come home to roost: A hip hop feminist breaks it down.* New York: Touchstone.

Morgan, L. H. (1964). *Ancient society, or researches in the lines of human progress, from savagery through barbarism to civilization.* Cambridge, MA: Harvard University Press. (Original work published 1877)

Morgenstern, J. (2008). "Slumdog" finds rare riches in poor boy's tale. *Wall Street Journal,* November 14. Retrieved from http://online.wsj.com/article/SB122661670370126131.html

Morishima, M. (1982). *Why has Japan "succeeded"? Western technology and the Japanese ethos.* New York: Cambridge University Press.

Morrison, M. K. C. (1987). *Black political mobilization: Leadership, power, and mass behavior.* Albany: State University of New York Press.

Moser, S., & Dilling, L. (2004). Making climate hot: Communicating the urgency and challenge of global climate change. *Environment, 46*(10), 32–46.

Motlagh, J. (2012). In a world hungry for cheap shrimp, migrants labor overtime in Thai sheds. *The Washington Post,* September 19. Retrieved from http://www.washingtonpost.com/world/asia_pacific/in-a-world-hungry-for-cheap-shrimp-migrants-labor-overtime-in-thai-sheds/2012/09/19/3435a90e-01a4-11e2-b257-e1c2b3548a4a_story.html

Moxley, M. (2011). Deaths rise with smoke. *Inter Press Service News Agency,* February 16. Retrieved from http://ipsnews.net/news.asp?idnews=54496

Mukhopadhyay, C. C., & Higgins, P. (1988). Anthropological studies of women's status revisited: 1977–87. *Annual Review of Anthropology, 17,* 461–495.

Muller, T., & Espenshade, T. J. (1986). *The fourth wave.* Washington, DC: Urban Institute.

Mumford, L. (1961). *The city in history: Its origins, its transformations, and its prospects.* New York: Harcourt.

Muncer, S. J., & Campbell, A. (2000). Comments on "Sex differences in beliefs about aggression: Opponent's sex and the form of aggression" by J. Archer and A. Haigh. *The British Journal of Social Psychology, 39*(2), 309–311.

Murdock, G. P. (1949). *Social structure.* New York: Macmillan.

Murphy, C. (2007). *Are we Rome? The fall of an empire and the fate of America.* New York: Houghton Mifflin Harcourt.

Murphy, R. (1988). *Social closure: The theory of monopolization and exclusion.* Oxford, UK: Clarendon.

Mutchler, J. E., Baker, L. E., & Lee, S. (2007). Grandparents responsible for grandchildren in Native-American families. *Social Science Quarterly, 88*(4), 990–1009.

Mutharayappa, R., Choe, M. K., Arnold, F., & Roy, T. K. (1997). Son preference and its effect on fertility in India. *National Family Survey Subject Reports 3.* Retrieved from http://scholarspace.manoa.hawaii.edu/bitstream/handle/10125/3475/NFHSsubjrpt003.pdf?sequence=1

Narayan, U., & Harding, S. (2000). *Decentering the center: Philosophy for a multicultural, postcolonial, and feminist world.* Bloomington: Indiana University Press.

National Alliance to End Homelessness. (2012). Executive summary. *The state of homelessness in America 2012.* Washington, DC. Retrieved from http://www.endhomelessness.org/content/article/detail/4361/

National Assessment of Adult Literacy. (2011). *Definition of literacy.* Retrieved from http://nces.ed.gov/naal/fr_definition.asp

National Association of the Deaf. (2000). *NAD position statement on cochlear implants.* Silver Spring, MD: Author. Retrieved from http://www.nad.org/issues/technology/assistive-listening/cochlear-implants

National Association of Realtors. (2006). *Annual report.* Retrieved from http://archive.realtor.org/article/national-association-realtors®-2006-annual-report

National Campaign to Prevent Teen Pregnancy. (2010). Teen pregnancy, poverty, and income disparity. *Why It Matters.* Retrieved from http://www.thenationalcampaign.org/why-it-matters/pdf/poverty.pdf

National Center for Charitable Statistics. (2009). Number of nonprofit organizations in the United States, 1999—2009. *Nonprofit data and statistics.* Washington, DC: Urban Institute. Retrieved from http://nccs.urban.org/statistics/profiles.cfm

National Center for Education Statistics. (2009). *NAEP 2009 high school transcript study: Gender, grade point average.* Washington, DC: U.S. Department of Education. Retrieved from http://www.nationsreportcard.gov/hsts_2009/gender_gpa.asp

National Center for Education Statistics. (2011a). *Fast facts: Distance learning.* Retrieved from http://nces.ed.gov/fastfacts/display.asp?id=80

National Center for Education Statistics. (2011b). Table 208: Recent high school completers and their enrollment in college, by sex: 1960 through 2010. *Digest of Education Statistics.* Retrieved from http://nces.ed.gov/programs/digest/d11/tables/dt11_209.asp

National Center for Education Statistics. (2011c). Table 345: Graduation rates of first-time postsecondary students who started as full-time degree/certificate-seeking students, by sex, race/ethnicity, time to completion, and level and control of institution where student started: Selected cohort entry years, 1996 through 2007. *Digest of Education Statistics.* Retrieved from http://nces.ed.gov/programs/digest/d11/tables/dt11_345.asp

National Center for Education Statistics. (2011d). Table 393: Literacy skills of adults, by type of literacy, proficiency levels, and selected characteristics: 1992 and 2003. *Digest of Education Statistics 2010.* Retrieved from http://nces.ed.gov/programs/digest/d10/tables/dt10_393.asp

National Center for Health Statistics. (2010). Births, marriages, divorces, and deaths: Provisional data for 2009. *National Vital Statistics Reports, 58*(25), 1–6.

National Center for Injury Prevention and Control. (2010). *The national intimate partner and sexual violence survey: 2010 summary report.* Washington, DC: U.S. Government Printing Office. Retrieved from http://www.cdc.gov/ViolencePrevention/pdf/NISVS_Report2010-a.pdf

National Coalition for the Homeless. (2007). *Domestic violence and homelessness fact sheet.* Washington, DC: Author. Retrieved from http://www.nationalhomeless.org/publications/facts/domestic.pdf

National Coalition for the Homeless. (2009). *Employment and homelessness fact sheet.* Retrieved from http://www.nationalhomeless.org/factsheets/employment.html

National Conference of State Legislatures. (2013). Voter identification requirements. *Legislature & Elections,* March 4. Retrieved from http://www.ncsl.org/legislatures-elections/elections/voter-id.aspx

National Institute of Mental Health. (2010). The numbers count: Mental disorders in America. *Health Topics: Publications.* Retrieved from http://www.nimh.nih.gov/health/publications/the-numbers-count-mental-disorders-in-america/index.shtml#Hudson

National Law Center on Homelessness and Poverty. (2010). *Homelessness & poverty in America: Real solutions.* Washington, DC. Retrieved from http://www.nlchp.org/hapia.cfm

National Law Center on Homelessness and Poverty. (n.d.). *Some facts on homelessness, housing, and violence against women.* Retrieved from http://www.nlchp.org/content/pubs/Some%20Facts%20on%20Homeless%20and%20DV.pdf

National Low Income Housing Coalition. (2009). Out of reach: Persistent problems, new challenges for renters. *Fact sheet.*

Washington, DC. Retrieved from http://www.nationalhomeless.org/factsheets/employment.html#1

National Opinion Research. (2003). *General Social Surveys 1972–2002.* Retrieved from http://www.cpanda.org/data/a00006/gsscbk.pdf

National Organization for Women. (N.d.). *Education & Title XI.* Washington, DC: Author. Retrieved from http://www.now.org/issues/title_ix/index.html

National Priorities Project. (2011a, August 26). *End of the year military spending wrap-up.* Retrieved from http://nationalpriorities.org/en/analysis/2011/end-year-military-spending-wrap-up/

National Priorities Project. (2011b, June 30). *Military recruitment 2010 analysis.* Retrieved from http://nationalpriorities.org/en/analysis/2011/military-recruitment-2010/

National Public Radio. (2010). Counting crowds: Results may very. *Talk of the Nation,* November 5. Retrieved from http://www.npr.org/templates/story/story.php?storyId=131099075

National Survey of Student Engagement. (2012). *NSSE annual results 2011: Fostering student engagement campus-wide.* Bloomington: Indiana University. Retrieved from http://nsse.iub.edu/html/annual_results.cfm

Natural Resources Defense Council. (2011). Meals of mass destruction: Shrimp. *Smarter living: Shopping wise,* July 8. Retrieved from http://www.nrdc.org/living/shoppingwise/meals-mass-destruction-shrimp.asp

Naylor, N. T. (2002). *Wages of crime: Black markets, illegal finance and the underworld economy.* Ithaca, NY: Cornell University Press.

Netcraft. (2012). March 2012 web server survey. *News.* Retrieved from http://news.netcraft.com/archives/2012/03/05/march-2012-web-server-survey.html

Neuman, W. L. (2000). *Social research methods: Qualitative and quantitative approaches.* Toronto, Canada: Allyn and Bacon.

Newcomb, T. C. (2008). *Parameters of parenting in Native American families.* Doctoral dissertation. Oklahoma State University. Retrieved from ProQuest (3320882).

Newport, F. (2012). Half of Americans support legal gay marriage. *Gallup Politics,* May 8. Retrieved from http://www.gallup.com/poll/154529/half-americans-support-legal-gay-marriage.aspx

Neyazi, T. A. (2010). Cultural imperialism or vernacular modernity? Hindi newspapers

in a globalizing India. *Media, Culture and Society, 32*(6), 907–924.

Niarchos, C. N. (1995). War and rape: Challenges facing the International Tribunal for the Former Yugoslavia. *Human Rights Quarterly, 17*(4).

Nicholas, S. E. (2009). "I live Hopi, I just don't speak it"—The critical intersection of language, culture and identity in the lives of contemporary Hopi youth. *Journal of Language, Identity & Education, 8*(5), 321–334.

Niebuhr, H. R. (1929). *The social sources of denominationalism.* New York: Meridian Books.

Nielsen. (2010). *Social media, games, email dominate web time.* New York: Author.

Nielsen. (2011). *State of the media: TV usage trends: Q3 and Q4 2010.* New York: Author.

Nisbet, R. (1970). *The social bond: An introduction to the study of society.* New York: Knopf.

Nolan, P., & Lenski, G. (2009). *Human societies: An introduction to macrosociology.* Boulder, CO: Paradigm.

Nordhoff, C. (1975). *The communistic societies of the United States.* New York: Harper & Row. (Original work published 1875)

Norris, M. (2011). Why Black women, infants lag in birth outcomes. *National Public Radio,* July 8. Retrieved from http://www.npr.org/2011/07/08/137652226/-the-race-gap

NPD Group. (2006). *Report from the NPD Group shows 45 percent of heavy video gamers are in the six- to 17-year-old age group.* Port Washington, NY: Author. Retrieved from http://www.businesswire.com/news/home/20060919005153/en/Report-NPD-Group-Shows-45-Percent-Heavy

Nuland, S. B. (2003). *The doctors' plague: Germs, childbed fever, and the strange story of Ignac Semmelweis.* New York: Norton.

Oakes, J. (1985). *Keeping track: How schools structure inequality.* New Haven, CT: Yale University Press.

Oberschall, A. (1973). *Social conflict and social movements.* Englewood Cliffs, NJ: Prentice Hall.

O'Dea. T. (1966). *The sociology of religion.* Upper Saddle River, NJ: Prentice Hall.

Offe, C. (1984). *Contradictions of the welfare state.* Cambridge, MA: MIT Press.

Office of Justice Programs, Bureau of Justice Statistics. (2013a). National Crime Victimization Survey property crime trends. *Key Facts at a Glance.* Retrieved http://bjs.ojp

.usdoj.gov/content/glance/tables/proptrd
tab.cfm

Office of Justice Programs, U.S. Bureau of Justice Statistics. (2013b). National Crime Victimization Survey violent crime trends. *Key Facts at a Glance.* Retrieved from http://bjs.ojp.usdoj.gov/content/glance/tables/viortrdtab.cfm

Office of Juvenile Justice and Delinquency Prevention. (2010). Juveniles as offenders. *OJJDP Statistical Briefing Book.* U.S. Department of Justice—Office of Justice Programs. Retrieved from http://www.ojjdp.gov/ojstatbb/offenders/qa03301.asp

Office of Planning and Research. (1965). *The Negro family: The case for national action.* Washington, DC: U.S. Government Printing Office, U.S. Department of Labor.

Office of Research Integrity. (n.d.). Nuremberg Code: Directives for human experimentation. *U.S. Department of Health & Human Services.* Retrieved from http://ori.dhhs.gov/education/products/RCRintro/c03/b1c3.html

Ogden, C., & Carroll, M. (2010). Prevalence of obesity among children and adolescents: United States, trends 1963–1965 through 2007–2008. *NCHS Health E-Stat,* June 4. Centers for Disease Control and Prevention. Retrieved from http://www.cdc.gov/nchs/data/hestat/obesity_child_07_08/obesity_child_07_08.htm

Ogden, C. L., Carroll, M. D., Kit, B. K., & Flegal, K. M. (2012). Prevalence of obesity in the United States, 2009–2010. *NCHS Data Brief 82.* Washington, DC: Centers for Disease Control and Prevention.

Ogden, C. I., Lamb, M. M., Carroll, M. D., Flegal, K. M. (2010). Obesity and socioeconomic status in adults, 2005–2008. *NCHS Data Brief No. 50.* Retrieved from http://www.cdc.gov/nchs/data/databriefs/db50.pdf

Ogunwole, S. U., Drewery, N. P., Jr., & Rios-Vargas, M. (2012). *The population with a bachelor's degree or higher by race and Hispanic origin: 2006–2010.* Washington, DC: U.S. Department of Commerce, Economics and Statistics Administration, U.S. Census Bureau. Retrieved from http://www.census.gov/prod/2012pubs/acsbr10-19.pdf

O'Leary, A. (2012). In virtual play, sex harassment is all too real. *The New York Times,* August 2. Retrieved from http://www.nytimes.com/2012/08/02/us/sexual-harassment-in-online-gaming-stirs-anger.html

Omvedt, G. (1992). "Green earth, woman's power, human liberation": Woman in peasant movements in India. *Development of Dialogue, 1*(2), 116–130.

O'Neill, T. (2007). Curse of the black gold: Hope and betrayal on the Niger Delta. *National Geographic,* February. Retrieved from http://ngm.nationalgeographic.com/2007/02/nigerian-oil/oneill-text

Orfield, G., & Eaton, S. E. (1996). *Dismantling desegregation: The quiet reversal of* Brown v. Board of Education. New York: Norton.

Organisation for Economic Co-operation and Development. (2011). Percentage of population that has attained tertiary education, by age group (2009). *Education at a Glance.* Retrieved from http://www.oecd.org/education/highereducationandadultlearning/48630299.pdf

Orszag, P. (2012). Get rid of the 3 p.m. school day. *The Washington Post,* April 19. Retrieved from http://articles.washingtonpost.com/2012-04-19/opinions/35452521_1_school-day-school-budgets-student-achievement

Oxfam America. (2012). *Community finance.* Boston: Author. Retrieved from http://www.oxfamamerica.org/issues/community-finance

Oyoo, G. O. (2003). Impact of HIV/AIDS on education in the Sub-Saharan Africa. *East African Medical Journal, December,* pp. 609–610. Retrieved from http://ajol.info/index.php/eamj/article/viewFile/8775/1904

Padden, C., & Humphries, T. (1988). *Deaf in America: Voices from a culture.* Cambridge, MA: Harvard University Press.

Paglen, T., & Thompson, A. C. (2006). *Torture taxi: On the trail of the CIA's rendition flights.* United Kingdom: Melville House.

Paludneviciene, R., & Leigh, I. W. (Eds.). (2011). *Cochlear implants: Evolving perspectives.* Washington, DC: Gallaudet University Press.

Paoli, L. (2003). *Mafia brotherhoods: Organized crime Italian style.* Oxford: Oxford University Press.

Pape, R. (2005). *Dying to win: The strategic logic of suicide terrorism.* New York: Random House.

Parente, S. L. (2008). Narrowing the economic gap in the 21st century. *2008 Index of economic freedom.* Washington, DC: The Heritage Foundation.

Park, P. (1993). *Voices of change: Participatory research in the United States and Canada.* Westport, CT: Bergin & Garvey.

Park, R. E. (1972). *The crowd and the public and other essays* (Henry Elsner Jr., ed.). Chicago: University of Chicago Press.

Park, R. E., & Burgess, E. (1921). *An introduction to the science of sociology.* Chicago: University of Chicago Press

Parker-Pope, T. (2010). Is marriage good for your health? *New York Times Magazine,* April 14. Retrieved from http://www.nytimes.com/2010/04/18/magazine/18marriage-t.html?pagewanted=all

Parkin, F. (1979). Social closure and class formation. In A. Giddens & D. Held (Eds.), *Classes, power, and conflict* (pp. 175–184). Los Angeles: University of California Press.

Parrado, E. A., & Morgan, S. P. (2008). Intergeneration fertility among Hispanic women: New evidence of immigrant assimilation. *Demography, 45*(3), 651–671. Retrieved from http://www.ncbi.nlm.nih.gov/pmc/articles/PMC2782440/

Parsons, T. (1951). *The social system.* New York: Free Press.

Parsons, T. (1954a). *Essays in sociological theory.* New York: The Free Press.

Parsons, T. (1954). The kinship system of the contemporary United States. In *Essays in Sociological Theory* (pp. 189–194). New York: Free Press.

Parsons, T. (1960). Some principle characteristics of industrial societies. In T. Parson (Ed.), *Structure and process in modern societies* (pp. 132–168). New York: Free Press.

Parsons, T. (1964). *The social system.* New York: Free Press.

Parsons, T. (1966). *Societies; evolutionary and comparative perspectives.* Upper Saddle River, NJ: Prentice Hall.

Parsons, T. (1967). *The structure of social action.* New York: Free Press.

Parsons, T. (1970). On building social system theory: A personal history. *Daedalus, 99*(4), 826–881.

Parsons, T. (1975). The sick role and the role of the physician reconsidered. *The Milbank Memorial Fund Quarterly, Health and Society, 53*(3), 257–278.

Parsons, T. (2007). *Social structure and personality.* New York: Free Press. (Original work published 1964)

Parsons, T., & Bales, R. F. (1955). *Family, socialization and interaction process.* Glencoe, IL: The Free Press.

Parsons, T., & Mayhew, H. D. (1982). *On institutions and social evolution: Selected writings.* Chicago: University of Chicago Press.

Parsons, T., Shils, E., & Smelser, N. J. (2001). *Toward a general theory of action, theoretical foundations for the social sciences.* Cambridge, MA: Harvard University Press.

Parsons, T., & Smelser, N. J. (1956). *Economy and society.* New York: Free Press.

Pascoe, C. J. (2011). *Dude, you're a fag.* Berkeley: University of California Press.

Patterson, D. (1989). *Power in law enforcement: Subordinate preference and actual use of power base in special weapons teams (SWAT).* Doctoral dissertation, Fielding Institute, Santa Barbara, CA.

PBS. (2011). Caught in the crossfire: Arab Americans. *9/11 stories.* Retrieved from http://www.pbs.org/itvs/caughtinthecrossfire/arab_americans.html

PBS NewsHour. (2010, May 31). China faces growing health threat from prevalent tobacco use. Retrieved from http://www.pbs.org/newshour/bb/health/jan-june10/tobacco_05–31.html

Pearlstein, S. (2010). The costs of rising economic inequality. *The Washington Post,* October 6. Retrieved from http://www.washingtonpost.com/wp-dyn/content/article/2010/10/05/AR2010100505535.html

Peek, K. L. (1999). *The good, the bad, and the "misunderstood": A study of the cognitive moral development theory and ethics in the public sector.* Fort Lauderdale, FL: Nova Southeastern University.

Perlin, R. (2011). *Intern nation: How to earn nothing and learn little in the brave new economy.* New York: Verso. Retrieved from http://www.epi.org/blog/pushing-back-illegal-unpaid-internships/

Perlin, R. (2012). These are not your father's internships. *The New York Times,* February 6. Retrieved from http://www.nytimes.com/roomfordebate/2012/02/04/do-unpaid-internships-exploit-college-students/todays-internships-are-a-racket-not-an-opportunity

Peters, G. (2013). *The American Presidency Project: State of the Union Addresses and Messages.* Retrieved from http://www.presidency.ucsb.edu/sou.php

Pettit, B. (2012). *Invisible men: Mass incarceration and the myth of black progress.* New York: Russell Sage Foundation.

Pettit, K., & Reuben, K. (2010). *Investor-owners in the boom-bust.* Washington, DC: Urban Institute. Retrieved from http://metrotrends.org/mortgagelending.html

Pew Forum on Religion and Public Life. (2004). *Supreme Court upholds "under God" in Pledge of Allegiance.* Pew Research Center, June 14. Retrieved from http://www.pewforum.org/Press-Room/Press-Releases/Supreme-Court-Upholds-Under-God-in-Pledge-of-Allegiance.aspx

Pew Forum on Religion and Public Life. (2008). *Summary of key findings: U.S. Religious Landscape Survey.* Washington, DC: Pew Research Center.

Pew Forum on Religion and Public Life. (2010). *Religion among the Millennials.* Pew Research Center. Retrieved from http://www.pewforum.org/Age/Religion-Among-the-Millennials.aspx#affiliation

Pew Forum on Religion and Public Life. (2011a). *The future of the global Muslim population, projections for 2010–2030.* Pew Research Center. Retrieved from http://pewforum.org/Global-Muslim-Population.aspx

Pew Forum on Religion and Public Life. (2011b). Republican candidates stir little enthusiasm. Retrieved from http://people-press.org/2011/06/02/republican-candidates-stir-little-enthusiasm/

Pew Forum on Religion and Public Life. (2011c). *The Tea Party and religion.* Retrieved from http://pewforum.org/Politics-and-Elections/Tea-Party-and-Religion.aspx

Pew Hispanic Center. (2008). National survey of Latinos/Hispanics. Retrieved from http://www.google.com/search?client=safari&rls=en&q=pew+hispanic+center+2008&ie=UTF-8&oe=UTF-8

Pew Research Center. (2006). *Overview: Pentecostalism in Asia.* Retrieved from http://www.pewtrusts.org/news_room_detail.aspx?id=21872

Pew Research Center. (2012a). Hispanic origins profiles. Pew Hispanic Center. Retrieved from http://www.pewhispanic.org/2012/06/27/country-of-origin-profiles/

Pew Research Center. (2012b, April 25). *More support for gun rights, gay marriage than in 2008 or 2004.* Retrieved from http://pewresearch.org/pubs/2251/social-issues-gun-rights-gay-marriage-abortion-presidential-campaign

Pew Research Center. (2012c). The rise of Asian Americans. *Pew Social & Demographic Trends.* Retrieved from http://www.pewsocialtrends.org/2012/06/19/the-rise-of-asian-americans/

Pew Research Center for the People and the Press. (2012, November 26). *Young voters supported Obama less, but may have mattered more.* Retrieved from http://www.people-press.org/2012/11/26/young-voters-supported-obama-less-but-may-have-mattered-more/

Phelan, A. M., & McLaughlin, H. J. (1995). Educational discoveries: The nature of the child and practices of new teachers. *Journal of Teacher Education, 46*(3), 165–174.

Phelps, R. J., et al. (1982). *Wisconsin female juvenile offender study project summary report.* Wisconsin: Youth Policy and Law Center, Wisconsin Council on Juvenile Justice.

Piaget, J. (1926). *The language and thought of the child.* New York: Harcourt, Brace.

Piaget, J. (1928). *Judgment and reasoning in the child.* New York: Harcourt, Brace.

Piaget, J. (1930). *The child's conception of physical causality.* New York: Harcourt, Brace.

Piaget, J. (1932). *The moral judgment of the child.* New York: Harcourt, Brace.

Pike, J. (2013). The world at war: Current conflicts. *GlobalSecurity.org.* Retrieved from http://www.globalsecurity.org/military/world/war/

Pilkington, E. (2010). Tyler Clementi, student outed as gay on Internet, jumps to his death. *The Guardian,* September 30. Retrieved from http://www.guardian.co.uk/world/2010/sep/30/tyler-clementi-gay-student-suicide

Pinterest. (2012). What is Pinterest? Retrieved from http://pinterest.com/about/

Pipes, D., & Duran, K. (2002). *Muslim immigrants in the United States.* Washington, DC: Center for Immigration Studies. Retrieved from http://www.cis.org/articles/2002/back802.html

Piven, F. F., & Cloward, R. A. (1977). *Poor people's movements: Why they succeed, how they fail.* New York: Random House.

Platt, K. H. (2007). Chinese air pollution deadliest in the world, report says. *National Geographic News.* Retrieved from http://news.nationalgeographic.com/news/2007/07/070709-china-pollution.html

Podsakoff, P., & Schriesheim, C. (1985). Field studies of French and Raven's bases of power: Critique, reanalysis, and suggestions for future research. *Psychological Bulletin, 97*(3), 387–411.

Polaris Project. (2013). *Human trafficking statistics.* Retrieved from http://www.polaris-project.org

Polivy, J., & Herman, P. (2007). Is the body the self? Women and body image. *Collegium Anthropologicum, 31,* 63–67.

Ponton, L. (2000). *The sex lives of teenagers.* New York: Dutton.

Popkin, B. M., Adair, L. S., & Ng, S. W. (2012). Global nutrition transition and the pandemic of obesity in developing countries. *Nutrition Reviews, 70*(1), 3–21.

Popper, K. (1939). *The logic of scientific discovery.* New York: Basic Books.

Popper, K. (1959). *The logic of scientific discovery.* New York: Basic Books.

Population Reference Bureau. (2011). *2011 World Population Data Sheet.* Retrieved from http://www.prb.org/pdf11/2011population-data-sheet_eng.pdf

Population Reference Bureau. (2012). *2012 World Population Data Sheet.* Retrieved from http://www.prb.org/pdf12/2012-population-data-sheet_eng.pdf

Poteet, G. A. (2007). *Perceptions of pretty people: An experimental study of interpersonal attractiveness.* Master's dissertation, Washington State University. Retrieved from http://www.dissertations.wsu.edu/Thesis/Spring2007/a_poteet_050307.pdf

Pough, G. D. (2004). *Check it while I wreck it: Black womanhood, hip hop culture, and the public sphere.* Boston: Northeastern University Press.

Powell, B., Bolzendahl, C., Geist, C., & Steelman, L. C. (2010). *Counted out: Same-sex relations and Americans' definitions of family.* New York: Russell Sage Foundation.

Power, S. (2002). *"A problem from hell": America and the age of genocide.* New York: Basic Books.

Prell, R. (1999). *Fighting to become Americans: Jews, gender, and the anxiety of assimilation.* Boston: Beacon.

Pressley, S. A. (1993). The people ask: What's in a name for the Navajo? *Washington Post,* December 17, p. B-5.

Preston, P. (1994). *Mother father deaf: Living between sound and silence.* Cambridge, MA: Harvard University Press.

Preves, S. (2003). *Intersex and identity: The contested self.* Piscataway, NJ: Rutgers University Press.

PrivateMilitary.org. (2013, March 1). *Private military companies (PMCs).* Retrieved from http://www.privatemilitary.org/private_military_companies.html

Putnam, R. (2000). *Bowling alone: The collapse and revival of American community.* New York: Simon & Schuster.

Qian, J., Cai, M., Gao, J., Tang, S., Xu, L., & Critchley, J. A. (2010). Trends in smoking and quitting in China from 1993 to 2003: National Health Service survey data. *Bulletin of the World Health Organization.* Retrieved from http://www.who.int/bulletin/volumes/88/10/09-064709/en/index.tml

Queen, S. A., Habenstein, R. W., & Adams, J. B. (1961). *The family in various cultures.* Chicago: Lippincott.

Quiggin, J. (2010). *Zombie economics: How dead ideas still walk among us.* Princeton, NJ: Princeton University Press.

Quinney, R. (1970). *Crime and justice in America.* New York: Little, Brown and Co.

Rabiner, S. (2012). Facebook friend suggestion gets man charged with bigamy. *Reuters News Agency,* March 12. Retrieved from http://blogs.findlaw.com/legally_weird/2012/03/facebook-friend-suggestion-gets-man-charged-with-bigamy.html

Rampell, C. (2010). Why a Big Mac costs less than a salad. *The New York Times,* March 9. Retrieved from http://economix.blogs.nytimes.com/2010/03/09/why-a-big-mac-costs-less-than-a-salad/

Randall, V. R. (1999). History of tobacco. *Boston University Medical Center.* Retrieved from http://academic.udayton.edu/health/syllabi/tobacco/history.htm#industry

Rashid, A. (2000). *Taliban: Militant Islam, oil, and fundamentalism in Central Asia.* New York: I. B. Tauris & Co Ltd.

Ratner, M., & Ray, E. (2004). *Guantánamo: What the world should know.* New York: Chelsea Green.

Raven, B., & Kruglianski, W. (1975). Conflict and power. In P. Swingle (Ed.), *Structure of conflict* (pp. 177–219). New York: Academic Press.

Reaney, P., & Goldsmith, B. (2008). Husbands create 7 hours of extra housework a week: Study. *Reuters Life,* April 4. Retrieved from http://www.reuters.com/article/2008/04/04/us-housework-husbands-idUSN0441782220080404

Reich, R. (1991). *The work of nations: Preparing ourselves for 21st century capitalism.* New York: First Vintage Books.

Reich, R. (2001). The case (once again) for universal health insurance. *The American Prospect,* April 9. Retrieved from http://prospect.org/article/case-once-again-universal-health-insurance

Reich, R. (2010). *Aftershock: The next economy and America's future.* New York: Knopf.

Reiman, J. (2003). *The rich get richer and the poor get prison.* Upper Saddle River, NJ: Prentice Hall.

Reiman, J., & Leighton, P. (2012). *The rich get richer and the poor get prison.* New York: Prentice Hall.

Reinders, G. (2006). *Women's reactions to a realistic rape portrayal and the influence of feminist identity and rape myth acceptance.* Doctoral dissertation, University of Missouri. Retrieved from https://mospace.umsystem.edu/xmlui/bitstream/handle/10355/4482/research.pdf?sequence=3

Renjini, D. (2000). *Nayar women today: Disintegration of matrilineal system and the status of Nayar women in Kerala.* India: India Classical Publishing Company.

Renzetti, C. M., & Curran, D. J. (1992). *Women, men, and society* (2nd ed.). Boston: Allyn & Bacon.

Republic of Botswana. (2012). *Progress report of the national response to the 2011 declaration of commitments on HIV and AIDS.* National AIDS Coordinating Agency. Retrieved from http://www.unaids.org/en/dataanalysis/knowyourresponse/countryprogressreports/2012countries/ce_BW_Narrative_Report%5B1%5D.pdf

Republic of South Africa. (2012). *Global AIDS response progress report 2012.* South African National AIDS Council.

Reskin, B., & Padavic, I. (2002). *Women and men at work* (2nd ed.). Thousand Oaks, CA: Sage.

Residents of Hull House. (1895). *Hull House maps and papers.* New York: Thomas Y. Crowell.

Rhodes, C. (2010). *A certain "Je ne sais quoi": The origin of foreign words used in English.* New York: Reader's Digest.

Richards, C. (2012). Playing under surveillance: Gender, performance and the conduct of the self in a primary school playground. *British Journal of Sociology of Education, 33,* 373–390.

Richardson, E. G., & Hemenway, D. (2011). Homicide, suicide, and unintentional firearm fatality: Comparing the United States with other high-income countries, 2003. *Journal of Trauma, Injury, Infection, and Critical Care, 70*(1), 238–43.

Richardson, J. (2009). Satanism in America: An update. *Social Compass, 56*(4), 552–563.

Ridgeway, C. L., & Smith-Lovin, L. (1999). The gender system and interaction. *Annual Review of Sociology, 25,* 191–217.

Ridgeway, C., & Correll, S. (2004). Unpacking the gender system: A theoretical perspective on gender beliefs and social relations. *Gender & Society, 18*(4), 510–531.

Ridley, M. (1998). *The origins of virtue: Human instincts and the evolution of cooperation.* New York: Viking.

Rieff, D. (2011). Millions may die . . . or not. *Foreign Policy* (September/October), pp. 22–25

Riley, C. (2012). Can 46 rich dudes buy an election? *CNN Money,* March 26. Retrieved from http://money.cnn.com/2012/03/26/news/economy/super-pac-donors/index.htm

Riordan, C. (1990). *Girls and boys in school: Together or separate?* New York: Teachers College Press.

Risch, E. (1981). *Supplying Washington's army*. Washington, DC: Center of Military History.

Rist, R. S. (1970). Student, social class, and teacher expectations: The self-fulfilling prophecy in ghetto education. *Harvard Educational Review, 40*, 411–451.

Ritzer, G. (1999). *Enchanting a disenchanted world: Revolutionizing the means of consumption*. Thousand Oaks, CA: Pine Forge Press.

Ritzer, G. (2007). *The globalization of nothing*. Thousand Oaks, CA: Pine Forge Press.

Ritzer, G. (2010a). *Globalization: A basic text*. Walden, MA: Wiley Blackwell.

Ritzer, G. (2010b). *The McDonaldization of society* (5th ed.). Thousand Oaks, CA: Sage.

R.L.G. (2010). Of dialects, armies and navies. *The Economist*. Retrieved from http://www.economist.com/blogs/johnson/2010/08/languages_and_dialects

Roberts, S. (2010). Report finds shift toward extended families. *The New York Times*, March 18. Retrieved from http://www.nytimes.com/2010/03/19/us/19family.html

Roof, W. C. (1993). *A generation of seekers: Spiritual journeys of the baby boom generation*. San Francisco, CA: HarperSanFrancisco.

Roof, W. C., & McKinney, W. (1990). *American mainline religion: Its changing shape and future*. New Brunswick, NJ: Rutgers University Press.

Roschelle, A. R., & Kaufman, P. (2004). Fitting in and fighting back: Stigma management strategies among homeless kids. *Symbolic Interaction, 27*(1), 23–46. Retrieved from http://onlinelibrary.wiley.com/doi/10.1525/si.2004.27.1.23/abstract

Rosellini, L., & Mulrine, A. (1998). When to spank. *U.S. News and World Report*, April 13, pp. 52–53, 55.

Rosenthal, R., & Jacobson, L. (1968). *Pygmalion in the classroom*. New York: Holt, Rinehart & Winston.

Rosoff, S., Pontell, H., & Tillman, R. (2010). *Profit without honor: White collar crime and the looting of America*. Upper Saddle River, NJ: Prentice Hall.

Rosser, P. (1989). *The SAT gender gap: Identifying the causes*. Washington, DC: Center for Women Policy Studies.

Rostow, W. W. (1961). *The stages of economic growth*. Cambridge, England: Cambridge University Press.

Rothe, D. L. (2009). *State criminality: The crime of all crimes*. Lanham, MD: Lexington Books.

Rothschild, J., & Whitt, A. (1987). *The cooperative work place: Potentials and dilemmas of organizational democracy and participation*. New York: Cambridge University Press.

Rothschild-Whitt, J. (1979). The collectivist organization: An alternative to rational-bureaucratic models. *American Sociological Review, 44*, 509–527.

Rothstein, R. (1993). Low wages in developing countries = Poverty in the U.S. *Poverty and Race, 2*(March), 6–7.

Rott, N. (2010). Bilingual D.C. homeless shelter to close. *The Washington Post*, October 2. Retrieved from http://www.washingtonpost.com/wp-dyn/content/article/2010/10/01/AR2010100107181.html

Rousselot, J. (2010). Sexual violence still prevalent in the DCR. *Human Rights Now Blog*, April 15. Amnesty International. Retrieved from http://blog.amnestyusa.org/africa/sexual-violence-still-prevalent-in-the-drc/

Rovira, J. (2011, February). *Interview with Manuel Castells*. Retrieved from http://www.uoc.edu/portal/en/sala-de-premsa/actualitat/entrevistes/2011/manuel_castells.html

Rowbotham, S. (1973). *Woman's consciousness, man's world*. Middlesex, UK: Pelican.

Rubenstein, R. E. (1970). *Rebels in Eden*. Boston: Little, Brown

Rubenstein, R. E., & Crocker, J. (1994). Challenging Huntington. *Foreign Policy, 96*(Autumn), 113–128.

Rubin, B. (1996). *Shifts in the social contract: Understanding change in American society*. Thousand Oaks, CA: Pine Forge.

Rule, J. B. (1999). Silver bullets or land rushes? Sociologies of cyberspace. *Contemporary Sociology, 28*(6), 661–664.

Russell, D. E. H. (2001a). Defining femicide and related concepts. In D. E. H. Russell & R. A. Harmes (Eds.), *Femicide in global perspective* (pp. 12–28). New York: Teachers College Press, Columbia University.

Russell, D. E. H. (2001b). Introduction: The politics of femicide. In D. E. H. Russell & R. A. Harmes (Eds.), *Femicide in global perspective* (pp. 3–11). New York: Teachers College Press, Columbia University.

Ruskin, J. S., & Washington, M. M. (1973). The beginning of the national club movement. In G. Lerner (Ed.), *Black women in White America: A documentary history* (pp. 440-446). New York: Vintage Books. (Original work published 1929)

Ruthven, M. (2011). The birth of Islam: A different view. *The New York Review of Books, LVIII*(6), 80–84.

Ryan, B. (2006). Green consumers: A growing market for many local businesses. *Let's Talk Business, 123*. Retrieved from http://www.uwex.edu/CES/cced/downtowns/ltb/lets/LTB1106.pdf

Ryan, R. A. (1981). Strengths of the American Indian family: State of the art. In F. Hoffman (Ed.), *The American Indian family: Strengths and stresses*. Isleta, NM: American Indian Social Research and Development Associates.

Rymer, R. (1993). *Genie: A scientific tragedy*. New York: HarperCollins.

Rymer, R. (2012). Vanishing voices. *National Geographic*, July, 60–93.

Saad, L. (2012). In U.S., global warming views steady despite warm weather. *Gallup Politics*, March 30. Retrieved from http://www.gallup.com/poll/153608/Global-Warming-Views-Steady-Despite-Warm-Winter.aspx

Sadker, D., & Sadker, M. (1997). *Failing at fairness: How our schools cheat girls*. New York: Scribner.

Sadker, D., & Zittleman, K. (2009). *Still failing at fairness: How gender bias cheats girls and boys in school and what we can do about it*. New York: Scribner.

Sadker, D. M., Zittleman, K., & Sadker, M. P. (2003). *Teachers, schools, and society*. New York: McGraw-Hill.

Saez, E. (2010). *Striking it richer: The evolution of top incomes in the United States* (updated with 2008 estimates). Retrieved from http://elsa.berkeley.edu/~saez/saez-UStopincomes-2008.pdf

Saez, E. (2013). *Striking it richer: The evolution of top incomes in the United States*. Retrieved from http://elsa.berkeley.edu/~saez/saez-UStopincomes-2011.pdf

Sagan, E. (1992). *The honey and the hemlock: Democracy and paranoia in ancient Athens and modern America*. New York: Basic Books.

Sagan, L. L. (1987). *The health of nations: True causes of sickness and well-being*. New York: Basic Book.

Sahlins, M. D., & Service, E. R. (1960). *Evolution and culture*. Ann Arbor, MI: Ann Arbor Paperbacks.

Salaita, S. (2005). Ethnic identity and imperative patriotism: Arab Americans before and after 9/11. *College Literature, 32*(2), 146–168.

Salary.com. (2013). *Salary.com's 12th annual mom salary survey*. Retrieved from http://swz.salary.com/momsalarywizard/htmls/mswl_momcenter.html

Sampson, R. J., & Laub, J. H. (1990). Crime and deviance over the life course: The salience of adult social bonds. *American Sociological Review, 55*(5), 609–627.

Sanchez-Ayendez, M. (1986). Puerto-Rican elderly women: Shared meanings and informal supportive networks. In J. Cole (Ed.), *All-American women: Lines that divide, ties that bind*. New York: Free Press.

Sanday, P. R. (1990). *Fraternity gang rape: Sex, brotherhood, and privilege on campus*. New York: New York University Press.

Sanders, T. (2011). The lighter the skin, the shorter the prison term? *The Root*, July 9. Retrieved from http://newamericamedia.org/2011/07/the-lighter-the-skin-the-shorter-the-prison-term.php

Sandoz, M. (1961). *These were the Sioux*. New York: Dell.

Sassen, S. (1991). *The global city: New York, London, Tokyo*. Princeton, NJ: Princeton University Press.

Sassen, S. (2000). The global city: Strategic site/new frontier. *American Studies, 41*(2–3).

Scahill, J. (2009). U.S. war privatization results in billions lost in fraud, waste and abuse—Report. *Common Dreams*, June 10. Retrieved from http://www.commondreams.org/headline/2009/06/10-5

Schabner, D. (2012). Trump won't bar transsexual beauty queen from shot at Miss Universe Canada title. *ABC News*, April 2. Retrieved from http://abcnews.go.com/blogs/entertainment/2012/04/trump-wont-bar-transsexual-beauty-queen-from-shot-at-miss-universe-canada-title/

Schaefer, D. R. (2011). Resource characteristics in social exchange networks: Implications for positional advantage. *Social Networks, 33*(2), 143–151.

Schaefer, R. T. (2009). *Race and ethnicity in the United States*. New Jersey: Pearson Education.

Scheff, T. (1966). *Being mentally ill*. Chicago: Aldine.

Scheff, T. J. (1988). Shame and conformity: The deference/emotion system. *American Sociological Review, 53*, 395–406.

Schegloff, E. (1990). On the organization of sequences as a source of "coherence" in talk-in-interaction. In B. Dorval (Ed.), *Conversational organization its development* (pp. 55–77). Norwood, NJ: Ablex.

Schegloff, E. (1991). Reflections on talk and social structure. In D. H. Zimmerman & D. Boden (Eds.), *Talk and social structure* (pp. 44–70). Cambridge, UK: Polity.

Scherer, M. (2012). Friended: How the Obama campaign connected with youth voters. *Time*, November 20. Retrieved from http://swampland.time.com/2012/11/20/friended-how-the-obama-campaign-connected-with-young-voters/

Schlosser, E. (2002). *Fast food nation: The dark side of the all-American meal*. New York: Perennial.

Schnaiberg, A., & Gould, K. A. (1994). *Environment and society: The enduring conflict*. New York: St. Martin's Press.

Schneider, D. M., & Gough, K. (1974). *Matrilineal kinship*. Berkeley: University of California Press.

Schneider, F., & Enste, D. (2002). Hiding in the shadows: The growth of the underground economy. *Journal of Economic Issues, 30*. Retrieved from http://www.imf.org/external/pubs/ft/issues/issues30/index.htm

Schor, J. B. (1998). *The overspent American: Why we want what we don't need*. New York: HarperPerennial.

Schulhofer, S. J. (2000). *Unwanted sex: The culture of intimidation and the failure of law*. Cambridge, MA: Harvard University Press.

Science Daily. (2010). Books in home as important as parents' education in determining children's education level. Retrieved from http://www.sciencedaily.com/releases/2010/05/100520213116.htm

Scott, A. (1990). *Ideology and the new social movements*. London and Boston: Unwin Hyman.

Scott, J. (2005). Life at the top in America isn't just better, it's longer. *The New York Times*, May 16. Retrieved from http://www.nytimes.com/2005/05/16/national/class/HEALTH-FINAL.html?pagewanted=all

Scott, J. C., Tehranian, J., & Mathias J. (2002). The production of legal identities proper to states: The case of the permanent family surname. *Comparative Studies in Society and History, 44*(1), 4–44.

Scott, W. R., & Meyer, J. W. (1994). *Institutional environments and organizations: Structural complexity and individualism*. Newbury Park, CA: Sage.

Seager, J. (2003). *The Penguin atlas of women in the world*. New York: Penguin Group.

Sebald, H. (2000). *Adolescence: A social psychological approach* (4th ed.). Englewood Cliffs, NJ: Prentice Hall.

Sellin, T. (1938). *Culture, conflict and crime*. New York: Social Science Research Council.

Sennett, R. (1998). *The corrosion of character: The personal consequences of work in the new capitalism*. New York: Norton.

The Sentencing Project. (2009). *The changing racial dynamics of the war on drugs*. Washington, DC. Retrieved from http://www.sentencingproject.org/doc/dp_race-anddrugs.pdf

The Sentencing Project. (2011). *Felony disenfranchisement*. Retrieved from http://www.sentencingproject.org/template/page.cfm?id=133

The Sentencing Project. (2012). *Trends in U.S. corrections: State and federal prison population, 1925–2010*. Retrieved from http://sentencingproject.org/doc/publications/inc_Trends_in_Corrections_Fact_sheet.pdf

Shahani-Denning, C. (2003). Physical attractiveness bias in hiring: What is beautiful is good. *Hofstra University Office for Research and Sponsored Programs*. Retrieved from http://www.hofstra.edu/pdf/orsp_shahani-denning_spring03.pdf

Shamir, R. (2011). Mind the gap: The commodification of corporate social responsibility. *Symbolic Interaction, 28*(2), 229–253. Retrieved from http://onlinelibrary.wiley.com/doi/10.1525/si.2005.28.2.229/abstract

Shattuck, R. (1980). *The forbidden experiment*. New York: Farrar, Straus, Giroux.

Shaw, M. (2010). Sociology and genocide. In D. Bloxham & A. D. Moses (Eds.), *The Oxford Handbook of Genocide Studies* (pp. 142–161). New York: Oxford University Press.

Sheldon, W. H. (1949). *Varieties of delinquent youth: An introduction to constitutional psychiatry*. New York: Harper.

Shelton, B. A., & John, D. (1996). The division of household labor. *Annual Review of Sociology, 22*, 299–322.

Shierholz, H. (2011). New college grads losing ground on wages. *Economic Snapshot—Education*, August 31. Economic Policy Institute. Retrieved from http://www.epi.org/publication/new_college_grads_losing_ground_on_wages/

Shierholz, H., Sabadish, N., & Wething, H. (2012). *Wages of young college graduates have failed to grow in the last decade*. Washington, DC: Economic Policy Institute.

Shin, H. B., & Kominski, R. A. (2010). Language use in the United States: 2007. *American Community Survey Reports*, U.S. Census Bureau. Retrieved from http://www.census.gov/hhes/socdemo/language/data/acs/ACS-12.pdf

Shirer, W. (2011). *The rise and fall of the third reich: A history of Nazi Germany.* New York: Simon & Schuster. (Original work published 1959)

Shore, R., & Shore B. (2009). Reducing infant mortality. *KIDS COUNT Indicator Brief.* Baltimore, MD: Annie E. Casey Foundation. Retrieved from http://www.aecf.org/~/media/Pubs/Initiatives/KIDS%20COUNT/K/KIDSCOUNTIndicatorBriefReducing InfantMortalit/ReducingInfantMortality.pdf

Shukoor, H. (2010). Taliban tries to stop the music in Afghanistan—again. *McClatchy.* Retrieved from http://www.mcclatchydc.com/2010/09/03/100136/taliban-tries-to-stop-the-music.html

Sidibe, M. (2009). *South Africa's reinvigorated AIDS response* (Speech). Pretoria, South Africa: UNAIDS. Retrieved from http://data.unaids.org/pub/SpeechEXD/2009/20091201_ms_speech_wad09_en.pdf

Silva, E. B. (2001). *White supremacy and racism in the post–civil rights era.* Boulder, CO: Rienner.

Silverman, R. M. (2005). Community socioeconomic status and disparities in mortgage lending: An analysis of Metropolitical Detroit. *The Social Science Journal, 42,* 479–486.

Simmel, G. (1955). *Conflict and the web of group affiliations* (K. Wolf, trans.). Glencoe, IL: Free Press.

Simmel, G. (1971). "Fashion." In Donald Levine (ed.), *Georg Simmel* (pp. 324–339). Chicago: University of Chicago Press. (Original work published 1904)

Simon, J. (1977). *The economics of population growth.* Princeton, NJ: Princeton University Press.

Simon, J. (1981). *The ultimate resource.* Princeton, NJ: Princeton University Press.

Simon, J. (2000). *The great breakthrough and its cause.* Ann Arbor: University of Michigan Press.

Simon Wiesenthal Center. (2011). *Social media must do more to thwart subculture of hate fueling lone wolf terrorism.* Retrieved from http://www.wiesenthal.com/site/apps/nlnet/content2.aspx?c=lsKWLbPJLnF&b=4441467&ct=11675937

Simpson, C. (2012). Tech's tragic secret. *Bloomberg Businessweek,* August 27–September 2, pp. 48–57.

Simpson, M. E., & Conklin, G. H. (1989). Socioeconomic development, suicide, and religion: A test of Durkheim's theory of religion and suicide. *Social Forces, 67,* 945–964.

Sinclair, U. (1995). *The jungle.* New York: Doubleday, Page. (Original work published 1906)

Singer, A. (2012). *Immigrant workers in the U.S. labor force.* Washington, DC: Brookings Institution. Retrieved from http://www.brookings.edu/research/papers/2012/03/15-immigrant-workers-singer#8

Singer, P. W. (2003). *Corporate warriors: The rise of the privatized military industry.* Ithaca, NY: Cornell University Press.

Skinner, B. F. (1938). *The behavior of organisms.* Cambridge, MA: B. F. Skinner Foundation.

Skinner, B. F. (1953). *Science and human behavior.* Cambridge, MA: B. F. Skinner Foundation.

Skocpol, T. (1979). *States and social revolutions.* New York: Cambridge University Press.

Slovak, K., & Singer, J. B. (2011). School social workers' perceptions of cyberbullying. *Children & Schools, 33*(1), 1–16.

Smelser, N. J. (1962). *The theory of collective behavior.* New York: Free Press.

Smith, B. (1990). Racism and women's studies. In G. Anzaldua (Ed.), *Making face, making soul: Haciendo caras.* San Francisco: Aunt Lute Foundation.

Smith, D. (1987). *The everyday world as problematic: A feminist sociology.* Boston: Northeastern University Press.

Smith, D. (1990). *The conceptual practices of power: A feminist sociology of knowledge.* Boston: Northeastern University Press.

Smith, D. (2005). *Institutional ethnography: A sociology for people.* Lanham, MD: AltaMira Press.

Smith, D. H., & Pillemer, K. (1983). Self help groups as social movement organizations: Social structure and social change. *Research in Social Movements, Conflicts and Change, 5,* 203–233.

Smith, K. (2005). Prebirth gender talk: A case study in prenatal socialization. *Women & Language, 28*(1), 49–53.

Smith, M. (2000). *American business and political power: Public opinions, elections, and democracy.* Chicago: University of Chicago.

Smith, M. J., & Moses, B. (1980). Social welfare agencies and social reform movements: The case of the single parent family. *Journal of Sociology and Social Welfare, 7*(January), 125–136.

Smith, P. (2009). *Obesity among poor Americans? Is public assistance the problem?* Nashville, TN: Vanderbilt University Press.

Smith, P. K., Mahdavi, J., Carvalho, M., Fisher, S., Russell, S., & Tippett, N. (2008). Cyberbullying: Its nature and its impact in secondary school pupils. *Journal of Child Psychology and Psychiatry, 49*(4), 376–385.

Smith, R. W. (2004, July 30). American self-interest and the response to genocide. *The Chronicle of Higher Education,* pp. B6–B9.

Smith, R. W. (2002). As old as history. In C. Rittner, J. K. Roth, & J. M. Smith (Eds.), *Will genocide ever end?* (pp. 31–34). St. Paul, MN: Paragon House.

Smith, S. (2001). *Allah's mountains: The battle for Chechnya.* London: I. B. Tauris & Co. Ltd.

Smith, T. W. (2002). Religious diversity in America: The emergence of Muslims, Buddhists, Hindus, and Others. *Journal for the Scientific Study of Religion, 41*(3), 577–585.

Smith, V. K., Gifford, K., Ellis, E., Rudowitz, R., & Snyder, L. (2011). Moving ahead amid fiscal challenges: A look at Medicaid spending, coverage and policy trends. *Kaiser Commission on Medicaid and the Uninsured.* Retrieved from http://www.kff.org/medicaid/upload/8248.pdf

Smits, D. (1994). The frontier army and the destruction of the Buffalo: 1865–1883. *The Western Historical Quarterly, 25*(3), 312–338.

Smock, P. J., Manning, W. D., & Porter, E. (2000). Everything's there except money: How money shapes decisions to marry among cohabitating adults. *Journal of Marriage and the Family, 67,* 680–696.

Snow, D. A., Rochford, E. B., Jr., Worden, S. K., & Benford, R. D. (1986). Frame alignment processes, micromobilization, and movement participation. *American Sociological Review, 51*(August), 464–481.

Snow, D. A., Zurcher, L. A., Jr., & Ekland-Olson, S. (1980). Social networks and social movements: A microstructural approach to differential recruitment. *American Sociological Review, 45*(October), 787–801.

Social Security Administration. (2013). Social Security history. *Social Security Online,* February 4. Retrieved from http://www.ssa.gov/history/

Society for Human Resource Management. (2008). Mensa membership, Kennedy kinship students. *Journal of American College Health,* 59(1), 43–50.

Sokoloff, N. J., & Raffel, B. (1995). *The criminal justice system and women: Offenders, victims, workers* (2nd ed.). New York: McGraw-Hill.

Sorokin, P. (1962). *Society, culture, and personality: Their structure and dynamics.* New York: Cooper Square.

Sorokin, P. (1970). *Social and cultural dynamics: A study of change in major systems of art, truth, ethics, law and social relationships.* Boston: Extending Horizons Books, Porter Sargent Publishers. (Original work published 1957)

Souder, W. (2012). *On a farther shore: The life and legacy of Rachel Carson.* New York: Crown.

Southern Poverty Law Center. (2011). *Hate and extremism.* Retrieved from http://www.splcenter.org/what-we-do/hate-and-extremism

Sparrow, R. (2005). Defending deaf culture: The case of cochlear implants. *The Journal of Political Philosophy, 13*(2), 135–152. Retrieved from http://www.neiu.edu/~gmoreno1/Special_Education__Courses_with_Dr._Moreno/Module_Nine_files/ActivitySix.pdf

Spencer, H. (1892). *Essays, scientific, political and speculative* (2 vols.). New York: Appleton.

Spicher, C. H., & Hudak, M. A. (1997). Gender role portrayal on Saturday morning cartoons: An update. *Proceedings from American Psychological Association's 105th Annual Convention.* Chicago: Allegheny College.

Spitzer, S. (1975). Toward a Marxian theory of deviance. *Social Problems, 22*(5), 641–651.

Squires, G. D., Friedman S., & Saidat, C. E. (2002). Experiencing residential segregation: A contemporary study of Washington, DC. *Urban Affairs Review, 38*(2), 155–183.

Squires, G. D. (2003). Racial profiling, insurance style: Insurance redlining and the uneven development of Metropolitan America. *Journal of Urban Affairs, 24*(4), 391–410.

Stanley, S. C. (1993). *Feminist pillar of fire: The life of Alma White.* Cleveland: The Pilgrim Press.

Stanton, G. H. (2005, June 15). *The 12 ways to deny a genocide.* Retrieved from http://www.genocidewatch.org/genocide/12waystodenygenocide.html

Stark, R., & Bainbridge, W. S. (1996). *A theory of religion.* New York: Peter Lang. (Original work published 1987)

Steele, C. M., Spencer, S. J., & Lunch, M. (1993). Self-image resilience and dissonance: The role of affirmational resources. *Journal of Personality and Social Psychology, 64*(6), 885–896.

Steffensmeier, D., & Allen, E. (1998). The nature of female offending: Patterns and explanations. In Zaplin (Ed.), *Female offenders: Critical perspectives and effective intervention.* Gaithersburg, MD: Aspen.

Steinbrook, R. (1988). AIDS summit delegates adopt a unanimous call for action. *Los Angeles Times*, January 29. Retrieved from http://articles.latimes.com/1988-01-29/news/mn-26467_1_aids-control

Stepick, A., III, & Grenier, G. (1993). Cubans in Miami. In J. Moore & R. Pinderhughes (Eds.), *In the barrios: Latinos and the underclass debate* (pp. 79–100). New York: Sage.

Stiglitz, J. E. (2012). *The price of inequality: How today's divided society endangers our future.* New York: Norton.

Stokes, R., & Chevan, A. (1996). Female-headed families: Social and economic context of racial differences. *Journal of Urban Affairs, 8*(3), 245–268.

Stolle, D. (1998). Why do bowling and singing matter? Group characteristics, membership, and generalized trust. *Political Psychology, 19*(3), 497–525.

Straus, M. A., & Gelles, R. J. (Eds.). (1990). *Physical violence in American families: Risk factors and adaptations to violence in 8,145 families.* New Brunswick, NJ: Transaction.

Straus, M. A., Gelles, R. J., & Steinmetz, S. K. (1988). *Behind closed doors: Violence in the American family.* Newbury Park, CA: Sage.

Straus, M. A., Sugarman, D. B., & Giles-Sims, J. (1997). Spanking by parents and subsequent antisocial behavior of children. *Archives of Pediatrics and Adolescence, 151*, 761–767.

Strickler, A. (2010). KBR chastised in Iraq contract review. CBSnews.com, March 31. Retrieved from http://www.cbsnews.com/stories/2010/03/29/cbsnews_investigates/main6344690.shtml

Subrahmanyam, K., & Lin, G. (2007). Adolescents on the net: Internet use and well-being. *Adolescence, 42*(168), 659–677.

Substance Abuse and Mental Health Services Administration. (2011). *Results from the 2010 National Survey on Drug Use and Health: Volume I.* Rockville, MD: Author. Retrieved from http://www.samhsa.gov/data/NSDUH.aspx

Sullivan, T. A., Warren, E., & Westbrook, J. (2000). *The fragile middle class: Americans in debt.* Binghamton, NY: Vail-Ballou Press.

Sum, A., Khatiwada, I., & McLaughlin, J. (2009). The consequences of dropping out of high school: Joblessness and jailing for high school dropouts and the high cost for taxpayers 22% daily jailing rate for young Black men who drop out of high school. *Northeastern University Labor Market Studies Report.*

Summers, C. H. (2000). The war against boys. *The Atlantic Monthly*, May. Retrieved from http://www.theatlantic.com/magazine/archive/2000/05/the-war-against-boys/304659/

Sumner, W. G. (1959). *Folkways: A study of the sociological importance of usages, manners, customs, mores, and morals.* Boston: Ginn. (Original work published in 1906)

Surette, R., Hansen, K., & Noble, G. (2009). Measuring media oriented terrorism. *Journal of Criminal Justice, 37*, 360–370.

Sutherland, E. H. (1929). The person v. the act in criminology. *Cornell Law Quarterly, 14*, 159–167.

Swiss, S., & Giller, J. E. (1993). Rape as a crime of war. *Journal of the American Medical Association, 270*(5), 619–622.

Tannen, D. (2001). *You just don't understand: Women and men in conversation.* New York: HarperCollins.

Tannenbaum, F. (1938). *Crime and the community.* New York: Columbia University Press.

Tarrow, S. G. (1983). *Struggling to reform: Social movements and policy changes during cycles of protest.* Ithaca, NY: Cornell University Press.

Tarrow, S. G. (1994). *Power in movement: Social movements, collective action, and politics.* New York: Cambridge University Press.

Taslitz, A. (1999). *Rape and the culture of the courtroom.* New York: University Press.

Tavernise, S. (2012). Education gap grows between rich and poor, studies say. *The New York Times*, February 9. Retrieved from http://www.nytimes.com/2012/02/10/education/education-gap-grows-between-rich-and-poor-studies-show.html?pagewanted=all

Taylor, H. (1995). Ringing "The Bell Curve." *Contemporary Sociology, 24*(2), 153–157.

Taylor, P., Parker, K., Cohn, D., Passel, J. S., Wang, W., & Pattern, E. (2011). *Barely half of U.S. adults are married—A record low.* Washington, DC: Pew Research Center. Retrieved from http://www.pewsocialtrends.org/2011/12/14/barely-half-of-u-s-adults-are-married-a-record-low/

Taylor, P., Passel, J. S., Wang, W., Kiley, J., Velasco, G., & Dockterman, D. (2010). *Marrying out: One-in-seven new U.S. marriages is interracial or interethnic.* Washington, DC: Pew Research Center.

Taylor, S., & Butcher, M. (2007). *Extra-legal defendant characteristics and mock juror ethnicity re-examined.* Proceedings from British Psychological Society Annual Conference, York Conference Park.

Taylor, V., & Whittier, N. (1992). Collective identity in social communities: Lesbian feminist mobilization. In A. D. Morris & C. M. Mueller (Eds.), *Frontiers in social movement theory* (pp. 104–130). New Haven, CT: Yale University Press.

Teichner, G., Ames, E. W., & Kerig, P. K. (1997). The relation of infant crying and the sex of the infant to parents' perceptions of their infant and themselves. *Psychology: A Journal of Human Behavior, 34,* 59–60.

Tenenbaum, H., & Leaper, C. (2003). Parent-child conversations about science: The socialization of gender inequities? *Developmental Psychology, 39*(1), 34–47.

Tews, M. J., Stafford, K., & Zhu, J. (2009). Beauty revisited: The impact of attractiveness, ability, and personality in the assessment of employment suitability. *International Journal of Selection and Assessment, 17*(1), 92–100.

Thomas, D. Q., & Ralph, R. E. (1999). Rape in war: The case of Bosnia. In S. P. Ramet (Ed.), *Gender politics in the Western Balkans: Women and society in Yugoslavia and the Yugoslav successor states* (pp. 203–218). University Park: Pennsylvania State University Press.

Thomas, G. M., Meyer, J. W., Ramirez, F. O., & Boli, J. (1987). *Institutional structure: Constituting state, society, and the individual.* Newbury Park, CA: Sage.

Thomas, W. I., & Thomas, D. S. (1928). *The child in America: Behavior problems and programs.* New York: Knopf.

Thompson, T. L., & Scantlin, R. M. (2007). Gender representation in cartoons. In J. J. Arnett (Ed.), *Encyclopedia of children, adolescents, and the media* (pp. 141–144). Thousand Oaks, CA: Sage.

Thomson, J. (1874). The city of dreadful night. *National Reformer.*

Thorne, B. (1993). *Gender play: Girls and boys in school.* New Brunswick, NJ: Rutgers University Press.

Thornton, R. (1987). *American Indian holocaust and survival: A population history since 1492.* Norman: University of Oklahoma Press.

Tilly, C. (1975). *The formation of national states in Europe.* Princeton, NJ: Princeton University Press.

Tilly, C. (1978). *From mobilization to revelation.* Reading, MA: Addison-Wesley.

Tilly, C. (1993). *European revolutions, 1492–1992.* Cambridge, MA: Blackwell.

Tilly, C., & Tilly, L. (1994). Capitalist work and labor markets. In N. J. Smelser & R. Swedberg (Eds.), *The handbook of economic sociology.* Princeton, NJ: Princeton University Press.

Timoney, J. F. (2012). Florida's disastrous self-defense law. *The New York Times,* March 23. Retrieved from http://www.nytimes.com/2012/03/24/opinion/floridas-disastrous-self-defense-law.html

Toennies, F. (1963). *Gemeinschaft and Gesellschaft.* New York: Harper & Row. (Original work published 1887)

Tolan, P., Gorman-Smith, D., & Henry, D. (2005). Family violence. *Annual Review of Psychology 57,* 557–583.

Tourangeau, R., Smith, T. W., & Rasinki, K. A. (1997). Motivation to report sensitive behaviors on surveys: Evidence from a bogus pipeline experiment. *Journal of Applied Social Psychology, 27*(3), 209–222.

Tragle, H. I. (1971). *The Southampton slave revolt of 1931: A compilation of source material.* Amherst: University of Massachusetts Press.

Transparency International. (2011). *Corruption perceptions index 2011.* Retrieved from http://cpi.transparency.org/cpi2011/results/

Trent, S., Williams, J., Thornton, C., & Shanahan, M. (2004). *Farming the sea, costing the earth: Why we must green the blue revolution.* London: Environmental Justice Foundation. Retrieved from http://www.ejfoundation.org/pdf/farming_the_sea_costing_the_earth.pdf

Trimble, L. B., & Kmec, J. A. (2011). The role of social networks in the job attainment process. *Sociology Compass, 5,* 165–178.

Troeltsch, E. (1931). *The social teaching of the Christian churches* (Vol. 1). New York: Macmillan.

Trudeau, M. (2009). More students turning illegally to "smart" drugs. *NPR,* February 5. Retrieved from http://www.npr.org/templates/story/story.php?storyId=100254163

Trust for America's Health. 2010. "F as in Fat: How Obesity Threatens America's Future." Retrieved from http://healthyamericans.org/reports/obesity2010/

Tucker, K. H. (1991). How new are the new social movements? *Theory, Culture and Society, 8*(May), 75–98.

Tumin, M. M. (1953). Some principles of stratification: A critical analysis. *American Sociological Review, 18*(8), 387–393.

Tumin, M. M. (1963). On inequality. *American Sociological Review, 28,* 19–26.

Tumin, M. M. (1985). *Social stratification: The forms and functions of inequality* (2nd ed.). Englewood Cliffs, NJ: Prentice Hall.

Turner, J. S. (2003). *Dating and sexuality in America: A reference handbook.* Santa Barbara, CA: ABC-CLIO.

Turner, M. A, Popkin, S. J., & Rawlings, L. (2009). *Public housing and the legacy of segregation.* Washington, DC: Urban Institute Press.

Turner, M., & McDade, Z. (2012). *Immigration brings diversity to neighborhoods where African Americans live.* Washington, DC: The Urban Institute. Retrieved from http://www.metrotrends.org/commentary/diversity2.cfm

Turner, R. H., & Killian, L. M. (1987). *Collective behavior* (3rd ed.). Englewood Cliffs, NJ: Prentice Hall.

Tyack, D., & Hansot, E. (1982). *Managers of virtue: Public school leadership in America, 1820–1980.* New York: Basic Books.

Tygart, C. E. (1987). Social structure linkages among social movement participants: Toward a synthesis of micro and macro paradigms. *Sociological Viewpoints, 3*(1), 71–84.

Tyman, K., Saylor, C., Taylor, L. A., & Comeaux, C. (2010). Comparing children and adolescents engaged in cyberbullying with matched peers. *Cyberpsychology, Behavior and Social Networking, 13*(2), 195–199.

Uchitelle, L. (2007). *The disposable American: Layoffs and their consequences.* New York: Vintage Books.

Ulaby, N. (2012). TV writers script safe sex "product placement." NPR: *All Things Considered,* September 6. Retrieved from http://www.npr.org/2012/09/06/160634572/tv-writers-script-safe-sex-product-placement

UNAIDS. (2006). *2006 Report on the global AIDS epidemic.* Retrieved from http://www.unaids.org/en/media/unaids/contentassets/dataimport/pub/report/2006/2006_gr_en.pdf

UNAIDS. (2010a). HIV prevalence map. *United Nations Programme on HIV/AIDS Global Report 2010.* Retrieved from http://www.unaids.org/documents/20101123_2010_HIV_Prevalence_Map_em.pdf

UNAIDS. (2010b). *Malawi HIV and AIDS monitoring and evaluation report: 2008–2009*. Retrieved from http://www.unaids.org/en/dataanalysis/knowyourresponse/countryprogressreports/2010countries/malawi_2010_country_progress_report_en.pdf

UNAIDS. (2010c). Sub-Saharan Africa. *Global Report Fact Sheet*. Retrieved from http://www.unaids.org/documents/20101123_FS_SSA_em_en.pdf

UNAIDS. (2011). *World AIDS day report 2011: How to get to zero faster, smarter, better.* Joint United Nations Programme on HIV/AIDS.

UNAIDS, UNFPA, & UNIFEM. (2004). *Women and HIV/AIDS: Confronting the crisis.* Retrieved from http://www.unfpa.org/upload/lib_pub_file/308_filename_women_aids1.pdf

Underhill, B. (1995). *The woman who ran for president: The many lives of Victoria Woodhull.* New York: Bridge Works.

Ungar, S. (1992). The rise and (relative) decline of global warming as a social problem. *The Sociological Quarterly, 33*(4), 483–501.

UNICEF. (2012). *The state of the world's children, 2012: Children in an urban world.* New York: Author.

Union of International Associations. (2011). Historical overview of number of international organizations by type, 1909–2011. *Yearbook of International Organizations, 2011/2012 Edition.* Herndon, VA: Brill.

United to End Genocide. (2012, March 9). Stop Sudan's weapons of mass starvation: March 16th day of action. Retrieved from http://endgenocide.org/stop-sudans-weapons-of-mass-starvation-organize-in-your-community/

United Nations. (1995). *Women's education and fertility behavior: Recent evidence from the demographic and health surveys.* New York: Author.

United Nations. (2011). *World urbanization prospects: The 2011 revision.* New York: United Nations Department of Economic and Social Affairs.

United Nations Environment Programme. (2008). *Green jobs: Towards decent work in a sustainable, low-carbon world.* Retrieved from http://www.ilo.org/empent/units/green-jobs-programme/about-the-programme/WCMS_158727/lang—en/index.htm

United Nations Environment Programme. (2009). *Recycling: From e-waste to resources.* Berlin, Germany: Author. Retrieved from http://www.unep.org/PDF/Press Releases/E-Waste_publication_screen_FINALVERSION-sml.pdf

United Nations Food and Agriculture Organization. (2009). *How to feed the world in 2050.* Retrieved from http://www.fao.org/fileadmin/templates/wsfs/docs/expert_paper/How_to_Feed_the_World_in_2050.pdf

United Nations High Commissioner for Refugees. (2010). *UNHCR statistical yearbook 2010.* Retrieved from http://www.unhcr.org/4ef9c8d10.html

United Nations Population Fund. (2007). *Characteristics of sex-ratio imbalance in India and future scenarios: Executive summary, India.* Fourth Asia Pacific Conference on Reproductive and Sexual Health and Rights, Hyderabad, India, October 29–31. Retrieved from http://www.unfpa.org/gender/docs/studies/summaries/india_summary.pdf

United Nations Population Fund. (2012). *Sex imbalances at birth: Current trends, consequences, and policy implications.* Bangkok, Thailand: Author. Retrieved from http://www.unfpa.org/webdav/site/global/shared/documents/publications/2012/Sex%20Imbalances%20at%20Birth.%20PDF%20UNFPA%20APRO%20publication%202012.pdf

University of Chicago Map Collection. (2001). *Major "racial" groups and Hispanic population by census tract: Chicago and vicinity, 2000.* Retrieved from http://www.lib.uchicago.edu/e/collections/maps/chi2000.html

University of Nevada, Reno. (2010). Books in home as important as parents' education in determining children's education level. *ScienceDaily.* Retrieved from http://www.sciencedaily.com/releases/2010/05/100520213116.htm

U.S. Bureau of Justice Statistics. (2005). *Family violence statistics: Including statistics on strangers and acquaintances.* Retrieved from http://bjs.ojp.usdoj.gov/content/pub/pdf/fvs.pdf

U.S. Bureau of Justice Statistics. (2010). Number of state prisoners declined by almost 3,000 during 2009; federal prison population increased by 6,800. *Press Release,* June 23. Retrieved from http://bjs.ojp.usdoj.gov/content/pub/press/pim09stpy09acpr.cfm

U.S. Bureau of Justice Statistics. (2011a). *National Crime Victimization Survey report.* Washington, DC: U.S. Department of Justice. Retrieved from http://bjs.ojp.usdoj.gov/content/pub/pdf/cv10.pdf

U.S. Bureau of Justice Statistics. (2011b). Prisoners in 2010. *Bureau of Justice Statistics Bulletin.* Retrieved from http://bjs.ojp.usdoj.gov/content/pub/pdf/p10.pdf

U.S. Bureau of Justice Statistics. (2011c). Sexual victimization reported by adult correctional authorities, 2007–2008. *Special Report.* Retrieved from http://bjs.ojp.usdoj.gov/content/pub/pdf/svraca0708.pdf

U.S. Bureau of Justice Statistics. (2011d). *Women in prison.* Retrieved from http://bjs.ojp.usdoj.gov/index.cfm?ty=pbdetail&iid=569

U.S. Bureau of Justice Statistics. (2012). *Intimate partner violence, 1993–2010.* Retrieved from http://bjs.ojp.usdoj.gov/content/pub/pdf/ipv9310.pdf

U.S. Bureau of Labor Statistics. (2005). The employment situation—October 2005. *News Release* (USDL 05–2118). Retrieved from http://www.bls.gov/news.release/archives/empsit_11042005.pdf

U.S. Bureau of Labor Statistics. (2010). Production workers: Hourly compensation costs in U.S. dollars. Retrieved from http://www.bls.gov/news.release/ichcc.t08.htm

U.S. Bureau of Labor Statistics. (2011a). The African-American labor force in the recovery: Chart 3. Retrieved from http://www.dol.gov/_sec/media/reports/blacklaborforce/

U.S. Bureau of Labor Statistics. (2011b). *Consumer expenditures in 2009.* Retrieved from http://www.bls.gov/cex/csxann09.pdf

U.S. Bureau of Labor Statistics. (2011c). *Labor force status of persons 16 to 24 years old by school enrollment, educational attainment, sex, race, and Hispanic or Latino ethnicity.* Retrieved from http://www.bls.gov/news.release/hsgec.t02.htm

U.S. Bureau of Labor Statistics. (2012a). *American time use survey: 2011 results.* Retrieved from http://www.bls.gov/news.release/pdf/atus.pdf

U.S. Bureau of Labor Statistics. (2012b). America's young adults at 24: School enrollment, training, and employment transitions between ages 23 and 24 summary. *Economic News Release.* Washington, DC: U.S. Government Printing Office. Retrieved from http://www.bls.gov/news.release/nlsyth.nr0.htm

U.S. Bureau of Labor Statistics. (2012c). Consumer expenditures—2011. *News Release,* September 25. Retrieved from http://www.bls.gov/news.release/pdf/cesan.pdf

U.S. Bureau of Labor Statistics. (2012d). *Highlights of women's earnings in 2011.* Retrieved from http://www.bls.gov/cps/cps-wom2011.pdf

U.S. Bureau of Labor Statistics. (2012f). Table 7: Median usual weekly earnings of full-time wage and salary workers by selected characteristics, annual averages. *Economic News Release.* Washington, DC: U.S. Government Printing Office. Retrieved from http://www.bls.gov/news.release/wky-eng.t07.htm

U.S. Bureau of Labor Statistics. (2012g). Table 11: Employed persons by detailed occupation, sex, race, and Hispanic or Latino ethnicity. *Household Data Annual Averages.* Washington, DC: U.S. Government Printing Office. Retrieved from http://www.bls.gov/cps/cpsaat11.pdf

U.S. Bureau of Labor Statistics. (2012h). Table 39: Median weekly earnings of full-time wage and salary workers by detailed occupation and sex. *Household Data Annual Averages.* Washington, DC: U.S. Government Printing Office. Retrieved from http://www.bls.gov/cps/cpsaat39.pdf

U.S. Bureau of Labor Statistics. (2013a). Employment projections: Education pays. *United States Department of Labor,* January 28. Retrieved from http://www.bls.gov/emp/ep_chart_001.htm

U.S. Bureau of Labor Statistics. (2013b). The employment situation—February 2013. *News Release,* March 8. Retrieved from http://www.bls.gov/news.release/pdf/empsit.pdf

U.S. Bureau of Labor Statistics. (2013c). Table A-1. Employment status of the civilian population by sex and age. *Economic News Release,* March 8. Retrieved from http://www.bls.gov/news.release/empsit.t01.htm

U.S. Bureau of Labor Statistics. (2013d). *Union members—2012.* U.S. Department of Labor (USDL-13–0105). Retrieved from http://www.bls.gov/news.release/pdf/union2.pdf

U.S. Bureau of Labor Statistics. (2013e). Union members summary. *Economic News Release,* January 23. Retrieved from http://www.bls.gov/news.release/union2.nr0.htm

U.S. Bureau of Labor Statistics. (n.d.). Estonia, China, India. *International Labor Comparisons.* Retrieved from http://www.bls.gov/fls/

U.S. Census Bureau. (1991). *The Asian and Pacific Islander population in the United States: March 1991 and 1990* (P-20 No. 459). Washington, DC: U.S. Government Printing Office.

U.S. Census Bureau. (2002). *Demographic trends in the twentieth century: Census 2000 special reports.* Retrieved from http://www.census.gov/prod/2002pubs/censr-4.pdf

U.S. Census Bureau. (2003). *Statistical Abstract of the United States, No. HS-12. Households by Type and Size: 1900 to 2002.* Washington, DC: U.S. Government Printing Office. Retrieved from http://www.census.gov/statab/hist/HS-12.pdf

U.S. Census Bureau. (2009). *2009 national population projections.* Retrieved from http://www.census.gov/population/projections/data/national/2009.html

U.S. Census Bureau. (2010a). Census Bureau reports families with children increasingly face unemployment. *Newsroom.* Retrieved from http://www.census.gov/newsroom/releases/archives/families_households/cb10-08.html

U.S. Census Bureau. (2010b). *Households, families, subfamilies, and married couples: 1980 to 2010, Table 59.* Washington, DC: U.S. Government Printing Office. Retrieved from http://www.census.gov/compendia/statab/2012/tables/12s0059.pdf

U.S. Census Bureau. (2010c). Nation's foreign-born population nears 37 million. *Newsroom,* October 19. Retrieved from http://www.census.gov/newsroom/releases/archives/foreignborn_population/cb10-159.html

U.S. Census Bureau. (2010d). POV46: Poverty status by state: 2010. *Annual social and economic (ASEC) supplement.* Washington, DC: U.S. Government Printing Office.

U.S. Census Bureau. (2010e). *Selected measures of household income dispersion 1967–2009* (Table A-2). Retrieved from http://www.census.gov/hhes/www/income/data/historical/inequality/taba2.pdf

U.S. Census Bureau. (2010f). U.S. Census reports nearly 6 in 10 advanced degree holders age 25–29 are women. *Newsroom,* April 20. Washington, DC: U.S. Government Printing Office. Retrieved from http://www.census.gov/newsroom/releases/archives/education/cb10-55.html

U.S. Census Bureau. (2010g). Voting and registration in the election of November 2008—Detailed tables. *Voting and Registration,* November 9. Retrieved from http://www.census.gov/hhes/www/socdemo/voting/publications/p20/2008/tables.html

U.S. Census Bureau. (2011a). 2010 Census shows America's diversity: Hispanic and Asian populations grew fastest during the decade. *Newsroom,* March 24. Retrieved from http://2010.census.gov/news/releases/operations/cb11-cn125.html

U.S. Census Bureau. (2011b). *America's families and living arrangements: 2011, Table C2.* Washington, DC: U.S. Government Printing Office. Retrieved from http://www.census.gov/hhes/families/data/cps2011.html

U.S. Census Bureau. (2011c). Census Bureau releases estimates of same-sex married couples. *Newsroom,* September 27. Washington, DC: U.S. Government Printing Office. Retrieved from http://www.census.gov/newsroom/releases/archives/2010_census/cb11-cn181.html

U.S. Census Bureau. (2011d). More working women than men have college degrees, Census Bureau reports. *Newsroom,* April 26. Washington, DC: U.S. Government Printing Office. Retrieved from http://www.census.gov/newsroom/releases/archives/education/cb11-72.html

U.S. Census Bureau. (2011e). *Poverty thresholds by size of family and number of children, 2011.* Retrieved from http://www.census.gov/hhes/www/poverty/data/threshld/

U.S. Census Bureau. (2011f). *Profile America facts and figures: American Indian and Alaska Native heritage month: November 2011.* Washington, DC: U.S. Government Printing Office. Retrieved from http://www.census.gov/newsroom/releases/archives/facts_for_features_special_editions/cb11-ff22.html

U.S. Census Bureau. (2011g). Voting and registration in the election of November 2010—Detailed tables. *Voting and Registration,* November 2. Retrieved from http://www.census.gov/hhes/www/socdemo/voting/publications/p20/2010/tables.html

U.S. Census Bureau. (2012a). *Civilian labor force and participation rates by educational attainment, sex, race, and Hispanic origin.* Retrieved from http://www.census.gov/compendia/statab/2012/tables/12s0593.pdf

U.S. Census Bureau. (2012b). *High school dropouts by race and Hispanic origin.* Retrieved from http://www.census.gov/compendia/statab/cats/education/elementary_and_secondary_education_completions_and_dropouts.html

U.S. Census Bureau. (2012c). *Historical poverty tables: People.* Retrieved from http://www.census.gov/hhes/www/poverty/data/historical/people.html

U.S. Conference of Mayors. (2011). *Hunger and homelessness survey.* Washington, DC: Author.

U.S. Courts. (2011). *2010 report of statistics required by the Bankruptcy Abuse Prevention and Consumer Protection Act of 2005.* Retrieved from http://www.uscourts.gov/uscourts/Statistics/Bank

ruptcyStatistics/BAPCPA/2010/2010
BAPCPA.pdf

U.S. Department of Commerce Economics and Statistics Administration. (2010, January). *Middle class in America*. Prepared for the Office of the Vice President of the United States Middle Class Task Force. Retrieved from http://www.commerce.gov/sites/default/files/documents/migrated/Middle%20Class%20Report.pdf

U.S. Department of Defense. (2011). *Dictionary of military terms*. Retrieved from http://www.dtic.mil/doctrine/dod_dictionary/

U.S. Department of Education. (2012). *Trends in high school dropout and completion rates in the United States: 1972–2009*. Retrieved from http://nces.ed.gov/pubs2012/2012006.pdf

U.S. Department of Health and Human Services. (2004). The health consequences of smoking: A report of the Surgeon General. Retrieved from http://www.surgeongeneral.gov/library/reports/smoking-consequences/index.html

U.S. Department of Health and Human Services. (2010). *Child maltreatment 2010*. Washington, DC: U.S. Government Printing Office. Retrieved from http://www.acf.hhs.gov/programs/cb/stats_research/index.htm#can

U.S. Department of Health and Human Services. (2013). *Healthy people 2020*. Washington, DC: U.S. Government Report. Retrieved from http://healthypeople.gov/2020/

U.S. Department of Health and Human Services, National Center for Health Statistics. (2013). Live births and birth rates, by Year. *Infoplease*. Retrieved from http://www.infoplease.com/ipa/A0005067.html

U.S. Department of Homeland Security. (2011). *2010 yearbook of immigration statistics*. Retrieved from http://www.dhs.gov/xlibrary/assets/statistics/yearbook/2010/ois_yb_2010.pdf

U.S. Department of Justice. (2005). *Family violence statistics: Including statistics on strangers and acquaintances*. Washington, DC: U.S. Government Printing Office. Retrieved from http://bjs.ojp.usdoj.gov/content/pub/pdf/fvs02.pdf

U.S. Department of Labor Wage and Hour Division. (2010). *Internship programs under the Fair Labor Standards Act*. Retrieved from http://www.dol.gov/whd/regs/compliance/whdfs71.pdf

U.S. Department of State. (2008). *Nontraditional students enrich college campuses: Older students value challenging courses with real-world implications*. Washington, DC: U.S. Government Printing Office. Retrieved from http://www.america.gov/st/educ-english/2008/April/200804281212291CJsamohT0.3335382.html

U.S Department of State. (2010). *International religious freedom report for 2010*. Retrieved from http://www.state.gov/j/drl/rls/irf/2010/index.htm

U.S. Department of State. (2011, September 13). *Terrorism*. National Institute of Justice. Retrieved from http://www.nij.gov/topics/crime/terrorism/welcome.htm

U.S. Department of State. (2012a). *Background note: India*. Washington, DC: Bureau of South and Central Asian Affairs. Retrieved from http://www.state.gov/r/pa/ei/bgn/3454.htm

U.S. Department of State. (2012b). Foreign terrorist organizations. *Bureau of Counterterrorism*, September 28. Retrieved from http://www.state.gov/j/ct/rls/other/des/123085.htm

U.S. Department of State. (2012c). *Trafficking in persons report, June 2012*. Washington, DC: U.S. Government Printing Office.

U.S. Elections Project. (2013, February 9). *2012 general election turnout rates*. Retrieved from http://elections.gmu.edu/Turnout_2012G.html

U.S. Energy Information Administration. (2012). *International energy outlook 2011*. Retrieved from http://www.eia.gov/forecasts/ieo/ieo_tables.cfm

U.S. Fish and Wildlife Service, Office of Law Enforcement Intelligence Unit. (2003). *U.S. wildlife trade: An overview for 1997–2003*. Washington, D.C: Department of the Interior.

U.S. Government Accountability Office. (2011). *Child maltreatment: Strengthening national data on child fatalities could aid in prevention* (GAO-11-599). Washington, DC: U.S. Government Printing Office. Retrieved from http://www.gao.gov/new.items/d11599.pdf

U.S. News and World Report. (2012). *Best colleges*. Retrieved from http://colleges.usnews.rankingsandreviews.com/best-colleges

Valentine, G. (2006). Globalizing intimacy: The role of information and communication technologies in maintaining and creating relationships. *Women's Studies Quarterly, 34*(1), 365–393.

Valenzuela Arce, J. M. (1992). Permanencia y cambio en las identidades ethnicas: La poblacion de origen Mexicano en Estados Unidos. *Estudios Sociologicos, 10*(January–April), 103–125.

Valette, A. (1893). *Socialism and sexualism*. Paris: Verneuil.

Van DeBosch, H., & Van Cleemput, K. (2008). Defining cyberbullying: A qualitative research into the perceptions of youngsters. *Cyberpsychology & Behavior, 11*(4), 499–503.

Van den Berghe, P. (1963). Dialectic and functionalism: Toward reconciliation. American *Sociological Review, 28*(October): 695–705.

van Dijke, M., & Poppe, M. (2006). Striving for personal power as a basis for social power dynamics. *European Journal of Social Psychology, 36*(4), 537–566.

Van Donk, M. (2002). HIV/AIDS and urban poverty in South Africa. *The role of cities in poverty alleviation*. South Africa Cities Network.

VanGiezen, R., & Schwenk, A. E. (2001). Compensation before World War I through the Great Depression. *Compensation and Working Conditions* (Fall). Bureau of Labor Statistics. U.S. Department of Labor. Retrieved from http://www.bls.gov/opub/cwc/cm20030124ar03p1.htm

Van Wees, H. (2010). Genocide in the ancient world. In D. Bloxham & A. D. Moses (Eds.), *The Oxford handbook of Genocide studies* (pp. 239–258). New York: Oxford University Press.

Veblen, T. (1899). *The theory of the leisure class*. New York: Macmillan.

Vellacott, J. (1993). *From liberal to labor*. Montreal: McGill-Queens Press.

Venkatesh, S. (2006). *Off the books: The underground economy of the urban poor*. Cambridge, MA: Harvard University Press.

Venkatesh, S. (2008). *Gang leader for a day: A rogue sociologist takes to the streets*. New York: Penguin Press.

Ventura, S. J., & Hamilton, B. E. (2011). U.S. teenage birth rate resumes decline. *National Center for Health Statistics Data Brief, 58*. Centers for Disease Control and Prevention. Retrieved from http://www.cdc.gov/nchs/data/databriefs/db58.pdf

Viglione, J., Hannon, L., & DeFina, R. (2011). The impact of light skin on prison time for Black female offenders. *The Social Science Journal, 48*, 250–258.

Vinovskis, M. A. (1992). Schooling and poor children in 19th-century America. *American Behavioral Scientist, 35*(3), 313–331.

Vinovskis, M. A. (1995). *Education, society, and economic opportunity: A historical perspective on persistent problems*. New Haven, CT: Yale University Press.

Violence Policy Center. (2010a). *Black homicide victimization in the United States: An analysis of 2007 homicide data*. Washington, DC. Retrieved from http://www.vpc.org/studies/blackhomicide10.pdf

Violence Policy Center. (2010b). *When men murder women: An analysis of 2008 homicide data*. Washington, DC. Retrieved from http://www.vpc.org/studies/wmmw2010.pdf

Vlasic, B. (2011). Detroit sets its future on a foundation of two-tier wages. *The New York Times*, September 13. Retrieved from http://www.nytimes.com/2011/09/13/business/in-detroit-two-wage-levels-are-the-new-way-of-work.html?_r=1&pagewanted=all

Wacquant, L. (2002). From slavery to mass incarceration. *New Left Review, 13*(2), 40–61.

Wade, C., & Tavris, C. (1997). *Psychology*. New York: Longman.

Walberg, M. (2009). Officer's bar beating trial opens, and video is played: cop's lawyer says it was self-defense, and female bartender takes the stand. *Chicago Tribune*, June 2. Retrieved from http://articles.chicagotribune.com/2009-06-02/news/0906010513_1_female-bartender-anthony-abbate-beating

Wallace, R. (1992). *They call him Pastor: Married men in charge of Catholic parishes*. Mahwah, NJ: Paulist Press.

Wallerstein, I. M. (1974). *The modern world-system*. New York: Academic Press.

Wallerstein, I. (2011a). *The modern world system, I: Capitalist agriculture and the origins of the European world-economy in the sixteenth century* (revised ed. with new prologue). San Francisco: University of California Press. (Original work published 1974)

Wallerstein, I. (2011b). *The modern world system II: Mercantilism and the consolidation of the European world-economy, 1600–1750* (revised ed. with new prologue). San Francisco: University of California Press. (Original work published 1980)

Wallerstein, I. (2011c). *The modern world system III: The second era of great expansion of the capitalist world-economy, 1730–1840s* (revised ed. with new prologue). San Francisco: University of California Press. (Original work published 1989)

Wallerstein, I. (2011d). *The modern world system IV: Centrist liberalism triumphant, 1789–1914*. San Francisco: University of California Press. New York: The New Press.

Walters, P. B., & James, R. J. (1992). Schooling for some: Child labor and school enrolment of Black and White children in the early 20th century South. *American Sociological Review, 57*(5), 635–650.

Wang, W., & Parker, K. (2011). *Women see value and benefits of college: Men lag on both fronts, survey finds*. Washington, DC: Pew Research Center. Retrieved from http://www.pewsocialtrends.org/2011/08/17/women-see-value-and-benefits-of-college-men-lag-on-both-fronts-survey-finds/4/

Warner, K., Molotch, H. L., & Lategola, A. (1992). *Growth of control: Inner workings and external effects*. Berkeley: University of California Press.

Warner, R. S. (1993). A work in progress toward a new paradigm for the sociological study of religion in the United States. *American Journal of Sociology, 98*(5), 1044–1093.

Washington, H. (2007). *Medical apartheid: The dark history of medical experimentation on Black Americans from colonial times to the present*. New York: Doubleday.

Wasserman, I. M. (1999). *African Americans and the criminal justice system: An explanation for changing patterns of Black male suicide*. Paper presented at the annual conference of the Midwest Sociological Society, Minneapolis, MN.

Watanbe, T. (1992). Rent-A-Family fills emotional need in busy Japan. *Los Angeles Times*, May 13. Retrieved from http://community.seattletimes.nwsource.com/archive/?date=19920513&slug=1491524

Watkins, S., & Sherk, J. (2008). Who serves in the U.S. military? The demographics of enlisted troops and officers. *The Heritage Foundation*, August 21. Retrieved June 7, 2012 http://www.heritage.org/research/reports/2008/08/who-serves-in-the-us-military-the-demographics-of-enlisted-troops-and-officers

Watson, J. B. (1924). *Behaviorism*. New York: People's Institute.

Weber, M. (1946). *From Max Weber: Essays in sociology* (H. Gerth & C. W. Mills, trans. and eds.). New York: Oxford University Press. (Original work published 1919)

Weber, M. (1947). *The theory of social and economic organization*. New York: Free Press.

Weber, M. (1958). *The Protestant ethic and the spirit of capitalism*. New York: Charles Scribner's Sons.

Weber, M. (1963). *The sociology of religion*. Boston: Beacon Press. (Original work published 1921)

Weber, M. (1968). *On charisma and institution building*. Chicago: University of Chicago Press.

Weber, M. (1977). *The Protestant ethic and the spirit of capitalism*. New York: Macmilllan. (Original work published 1904–1905)

Weber, M. (1979). *Economy and society: An outline of interpretive sociology*. Berkeley: University of California Press. (Original work published 1921)

Weber, M. (1979). *Economy and society: An outline of interpretive sociology* (Vols. 1 & 2). Berkeley: University of California Press.

Weber, M. (2002). The Protestant Ethic and the Spirit of Capitalism, *and other writings*. New York: Penguin. (Original work published 1904–1905)

Weber, M. (2012). *The theory of social and economic organization*. Eastford, CT: Martino Fine Books. (Original work published 1921)

The Wedding Report. (2012). United States complete market report: Wedding statistics summary for United States. Retrieved from http://www.theweddingreport.com/wmdb/index.cfm?action=db.viewdetail&t=s&lc=00&setloc=y

Weeks, J. R. (1988). The demography of Islamic nations. *Population Bulletin, 43*(4), 5–54.

Weiss-Wendt, A. (2010). The state and genocide. In Donald Bloxham A. Dirk Moses (eds.), *The Oxford handbook of genocide studies* (pp. 81–101). New York: Oxford University Press.

Weitz, E. D. (2003). *A century of genocide: Utopias of race and nation*. Princeton, NJ: Princeton University Press.

Weitz, R. (2012). *The sociology of health, illness, and health care: A critical approach* (6th ed.). Boston: Wadsworth Cengage Learning.

Weitzer, R., & Kubrin, C. E. (2009). Misogyny in rap music: A content analysis of prevalence and meanings. *Men and Masculinities, 12*(1), 3–29.

Weller, C. E., Ajinka, J., & Farrel, J. (2011). *The state of communities of color in the U.S. economy*. Washington, DC: Center for American Progress. Retrieved from http://www.americanprogress.org/issues/poverty/report/2012/04/12/11423/the-state-of-communities-of-color-in-the-u-s-economy/

Wellman, B., & Hampton, K. (1999). Living networked on and offline. *Contemporary Sociology, 28*(6), 648–654.

Welsh, R. (1998). Severe parental punishment and aggression: The link between corporal punishment and delinquency. In I. A. Hyman & J. H. Wise (Eds.), *Corporal* punishment in American education: Readings in history, practice and alternatives (pp. 126–142). Philadelphia: Temple University Press. Retrieved from http://www.nospank.net/welsh3.htm

Werdigier, J. (2010). J. P. Morgan penalized by regulator in Britain. *The New York Times*, June 4, p. B3.

Werner, C. (2011). The older population: 2010. *2010 Census Briefs*. Washington, DC: U.S. Census Bureau. Retrieved from http://www.census.gov/prod/cen2010/briefs/c2010br-09.pdf

Wertheimer, B. (1977). *We were there: The story of working women in America*. New York: Pantheon.

West, C. (1979). Against our will: Male interruptions of females in cross-sex conversations. *Annals of the New York Academy of Sciences, 327*, 81–97.

West, C., & Zimmerman, D. H. (1977). Woman's place in everyday talk: Reflections on parent-child interactions. *Social Problems, 24*, 521–529.

West, C., & Zimmerman, D. H. (1983). Small insults: A study of interruptions in conversations between unacquainted persons. In B. Thorne & N. Henley (Eds.), *Language, gender, and society* (pp. 102–117). Rowley, MA: Newbury House.

West, C., & Zimmerman, D. H. (1987). Doing gender. *Gender and Society, 1*(2), 125–151.

Western, B., & Petit, B. (2010). Incarceration and social inequality. *Daedalus* (Summer), 8–18.

Westoff, C. F., & Ryder, N. B. (1977). *The contraceptive revolution*. Princeton, NJ: Princeton University Press.

Whalen, J., & Zimmerman, D. H. (1987). Sequential and institutional contexts in calls for help. *Social Psychology Quarterly, 50*, 172–185.

Whalen, J., & Zimmerman, D. H. (1990). Describing trouble: Epistemology in citizen calls to the police. *Language in Society, 19*, 465–492.

Whalen, J., Zimmerman, D. H., & Whalen, M. R. (1990). When words fail: A single case analysis. *Social Problems, 35*, 335–362.

Whitelaw, K. (2001). A verdict against rape: War crimes convictions. *U.S. News & World Report,* March 5, p. 36.

Whoriskey, P. (2010). BMW finding skilled workers for less at S.C. plant. *The Washington Post*, November 13. Retrieved from http://seattletimes.com/html/businesstechnology/2013389893_bmwworkers14.html

Whyte, W. F. (1943). *Street corner society: The social structure of an Italian slum*. Chicago: University of Chicago Press.

Whyte, W. F. (1991). *Participatory action research*. Newbury Park, CA: Sage.

Widen, S. C., & Russell, J. A. (2002). Gender and preschoolers' perception of emotion. *Merrill-Palmer Quarterly, 48*(3), 248–262. Retrieved from http://muse.jhu.edu/login?auth=0&type=summary&url=/journals/merrill-palmer_quarterly/v048/48.3widen.pdf

Wiedman. J. L. (Eds.). (1984). *Christian feminism: Visions of a new humanity*. New York: Harper & Row.

Williams, A. (2010). The new math on campus. *The New York Times*, February 7. Retrieved from http://www.nytimes.com/2010/02/07/fashion/07campus.html?pagewanted=all

Williams, C. (1995). *Still a man's world: Men who do women's work*. Berkeley: University of California Press.

Williams, J. (2002). The role of civil society in disarmament issues: Realism vs. idealism? *International Campaign to Ban Landmines*. Retrieved from http://www.icbl.org/index.php/icbl/About-Us/Inspiration/Realism-vs.-Idealism

Williams, J. P., & Kirschner, D. (2012). Coordinated action in the massively multiplayer online game *World of Warcraft*. *Symbolic Interaction* [Early View]. Retrieved from http://onlinelibrary.wiley.com/doi/10.1002/j.1533-8665.2012.00022.x/abstract

Williams, R. M., Jr. (1970). *American society: A sociological interpretation* (3rd ed.). New York: Knopf.

Williams-Meyers, A. J. (1996). Slavery, rebellion, and revolution in the Americas: A historiographical scenario on the theses of Genovese and others. *Journal of Black Studies, 26*(4), 381–400.

Williamson, L. (2011). Delving into North Korea's mystical cult of personality. *BBC News*, December 27. Retrieved from http://www.bbc.co.uk/news/world-asia-16336991

Willis, P. (1990). *Common culture*. Boulder, CO: Westview Press.

Willoughby, T., Adachi, P. J. C., & Good, M. (2012). A longitudinal study of the association between violent video game play and aggression among adolescents. *Developmental Psychology, 48*(4), 1044–1057.

Wilson, B., Kunkel, D., Linz, D., Potter, J., Donnerstein, E., Smith, S., . . . Berry, M. (1997). Violence in television programming. *National Television Violence Study, 2*, 3–178. Thousand Oaks, CA: Sage.

Wilson, B., Donnerstein, E., Linz, D., Kunkel, D., Potter, J., Smith, S., . . . Grey, T. (1998). Content analysis of entertainment television: The importance of context. In J. Hamilton (Ed.), *Television violence and public policy* (pp. 13–54). Ann Arbor: University of Michigan Press.

Wilson, B., Potter, J., Linz, D., Donnerstein, E., Kunkel, D., Smith, S., . . . Grey, T. (1998). Content analysis of entertainment television: Results for 1994–95. In J. Hamilton (Ed.), *Television violence and public policy* (pp. 55–104). Ann Arbor, MI: University of Michigan Press.

Wilson, E. O. (1993). Is humanity suicidal? *New York Times Magazine*, May 30.

Wilson, T. P. (1991). Social structure and the sequential organization of interaction. In D. H. Zimmerman & D. Boden (Eds.), *Talk and social structure* (pp. 22–43). Cambridge, UK: Polity.

Wilson, W. J. (1987). *The truly disadvantaged: The inner city, the underclass, and public policy*. Chicago: University of Chicago Press.

Wilson, W. J. (1997). *When work disappears: The world of the new urban poor*. New York: Vintage Books.

Wilson, W. J. (2010). *More than just race: Being black and poor in the inner city*. New York: Norton.

Wingfield, A. H. (2008). Racializing the glass escalator: Reconsidering men's experiences with women's work. *Gender & Society, 23*(1), 5–26.

Wirth, L. (1928). *The ghetto*. Chicago: University of Chicago Press.

Wirth, L. (1938). Urbanism as a way of life. *The American Journal of Sociology, 44*(1), 1–24.

Wirth, L. (1945). The problem of minority groups. In R. Linton (Ed.), *The science of man in the world crisis* (pp. 347–372). New York: Columbia University Press.

Wittstock, L. W., & Salinas, E. J. (1998). *A brief history of the American Indian movement*. Retrieved from http://www.aimovement.org/ggc/history.html

Woldoff, R. A. (2011). *White flight/Black flight: The dynamics of racial change in an American neighborhood*. Ithaca, NY: Cornell University Press.

Wolf, M. (2008). *Proust and the squid: The story and science of the reading brain*. New York: Harper Perennial.

Wolfe, A. (1977). *The limits of legitimacy*. New York: Free Press.

Wolfson, A. (2005). A hoax most cruel: Caller coaxed McDonald's managers into strip-searching a worker. The *Courier Journal Online*, October 9. Retrieved from http://www.courier-journal.com/apps/pbcs.dll/article?AID=/20051009/NEWS01/510090392&loc=interstitialskip&nclick_check=1

Wollstonecraft, M. (1792). *A vindication of the rights of women: With strictures on political and moral subjects*. Boston: Peter Edes.

Wonacott, M. (2002). What is a gold-collar worker? *Eric Digest, 234.* Retrieved from http://www.calpro-online.org/ERIC/docs/dig234.pdf

Wood, G. S. (1993). *The radicalism of the American Revolution.* New York: Vintage Books.

Wood, R. G., Goesling, B., & Avellar, S. (2007). *The effects of marriage on health: A synthesis of recent research evidence.* Princeton, NJ: Mathematica Policy Research. Retrieved from http://www.mathematicampr.com/publications/PDFs/marriagehealth.pdf

Woodiwiss, M. (2000). Organized crime: The dumbing of discourse. *British Society of Criminology.* Retrieved from http://www.britsoccrim.org/volume1/017.pdf

Woodiwiss, M. (2005). *Gangster capitalism: The United States and the global rise of organized crime.* New York: Carroll and Graf.

Woolsey, B., & Schulz, M. (2012). *Credit card statistics, industry facts, debt statistics.* Retrieved from http://www.creditcards.com/credit-card-news/credit-card-industry-facts-personal-debt-statistics-1276.php

Workman, J. E., & Freeburg, E. W. (1999). An examination of date rape, victim dress and perceiver variables within the context of attribution theory. *Sex Roles, 41,* 261–277.

World Health Organization. (2005). *Widespread misunderstandings about chronic disease—And the reality.* Retrieved from http://www.who.int/chp/chronic_disease_report/media/Factsheet2.pdf

World Health Organization. (2012). Health workforce—Aggregated data, density per 1,000. *Data Repository: World Health Statistics.* Retrieved from http://apps.who.int/ghodata/?vid=92100_

World Health Organization. (2013). Maternal mortality country profiles. *Global Health Observatory (GHO).* Retrieved from http://www.who.int/gho/maternal_health/countries/en/index.html#U

Worldwatch Institute. (2004). *State of the world: Consumption by the numbers.* Washington, DC: Author.

Worldwatch Institute. (2010). *State of the world: Transforming cultures from consumerism to sustainability.* Washington, DC: Author.

Worldwatch Institute. (2011). *State of the world: Innovations that nourish the planet.* Washington, DC: Author.

Wright, E. O. (1998). *Classes* (2nd ed.). New York: Verso.

Wright, J. P., Tibbetts, S. G., & Daigle, L. E. (2008). *Criminals in the making: Criminality across the life course.* Thousand Oaks, CA: Sage.

Wright, L. (1993). Remember Satan—Part II. *The New Yorker*, May 24, pp. 54–76

Wrong, D. H. (1959). The functional theory of stratification: Some neglected considerations. *American Sociological Review, 24,* 772–782.

Wuthnow, R. (1976). *The consciousness reformation.* Berkeley: University of California Press.

Wuthnow R. (1978). *Experimentation in American religion: The new mysticisms and their implications for churches.* Berkeley: University of California Press.

Wuthnow, R. (1988). *The restructuring of American religion: Society and faith since World War II,* Princeton, NJ: Princeton University Press.

Wyman, A. (1997). *Rural women teachers in the United States: A sourcebook.* Lanham, MD: Scarecrow Press.

Wyss, S. (2007). "This was my hell": The violence experienced by gender non-conforming youth in US high schools. *International Journal of Qualitative Studies in Education, 17*(5), 709–730.

Yen, C., Yen, J., & Ko, C. (2010). Internet addiction: Ongoing research in Asia. *World Psychiatry, 9*(2), 97. Retrieved from http://www.ncbi.nlm.nih.gov/pmc/articles/PMC2911088/

Young, S., & Martin, D. S. (2012). CNN readers share stories about secret army drug testing program. *CNN*, March 9. Retrieved from http://edition.cnn.com/2012/03/09/health/soldier-guinea-pigs/index.html

Young, T. R. (1989). Symbolic interactional theory: Hard times and hard tomatoes. In N. K. Denizen (Ed.), *Studies in symbolic interaction* (pp. 473–481). Greenwich, CT: JAI Press.

Zald, M., & McCarthy, J. D. (1980). Social movement industries: Competition and cooperation among movement organizations. In Louis Kriesberg (Ed.), *Research in social movements, conflicts and change* (Vol. 3). Greenwich, CT: JAI Press.

Zimbabwe. (2012). *Global AIDS response progress report 2012.* Zimbabwe Country Report. Retrieved from http://www.unaids.org/en/dataanalysis/knowyourresponse/countryprogressreports/2012countries/ce_ZW_Narrative_Report.pdf

Zimbardo, P. G. (1974). On "obedience to authority." *American Psychologist, 29*(7), 566–567.

Zimbardo, P. G., Ebbesen, E. B., & Maslach, C. (1977). *Influencing attitudes and changing behavior.* Reading, MA: Addison-Wesley.

Zimmerman, D. H. (1984). Talk and its occasion: The case of calling the police. In D. Schiffrin (Ed.), *Meaning, form, and use in context: Linguistic applications* (pp. 210–228). Washington, DC: Georgetown University Press.

Zimmerman, D. H. (1992). The interactional organization of calls for emergency assistance. In P. Drew & J. Heritage (Eds.), *Talk at work: Interaction in institutional settings* (pp. 418–469) New York: Cambridge University Press.

Zimmerman, D. H., & West, C. (1975). Sex roles, interruptions and silences in conversations. In B. Thorne & N. Henley (Eds.), *Language, gender, and society* (pp. 105–129). Rowley, MA: Newbury House.

Zimmerman, D. H., & West, C. (1980). Language and social interaction. *Sociological Inquiry. 50,* 3–4.

Zinn, M. B., Weber, L., Higginbotham, E., & Dill, B. T. (1986). The costs of exclusionary practices in women's studies. *Signs: Journal of Women in Culture and Society, 11*(2), 290–303.

Zinsser, J. (1993). *History and feminism: A glass half full (The feminist impact on the arts and sciences).* Woodbridge: CT: Twayne.

SOURCES/REFERENCES FOR *WHAT CAN I DO WITH A SOCIOLOGY DEGREE?*

CAREER DEVELOPMENT AND THE JOB SEARCH

Career Center, University of North Carolina. (n.d.). *Sociology careers.* Retrieved from http://uncw.edu/career/sociology.html

Career Services, University of Tennessee. (2013). *Explore majors and careers.* Retrieved from http://career.utk.edu/exploremajors.php

Department of Sociology and Anthropology, Elon University. (2013). *What is sociology and anthropology?* Retrieved from http://www.elon.edu/e-web/academics/elon_college/sociology/default.xhtml

COMMUNITY RESOURCE AND SERVICE SKILLS

The Community Tool Box. (2013). Retrieved from http://ctb.ku.edu/en/default.aspx

National Service Learning Clearinghouse. (2013). *Beyond needs assessments: Identifying a community's resources and hopes.* Retrieved from http://www.servicelearning.org

CONFLICT DYNAMICS AND RESOLUTION

Conflict Resolution Network. (n.d.). *12 conflict resolution skills summary.* Retrieved from http://www.crnhq.org/pages.php?pID=10

CRITICAL THINKING

Sociology Department, Thompson Rivers University. (2013). *Sociology.* Retrieved from http://www.tru.ca/arts/socanth/sociology.html

DIVERSITY

Department of Sociology, University of California at San Diego. (2013). *Why major in sociology?* Retrieved from http://sociology.ucsd.edu/undergraduates/why.shtml

Stanford Center for Opportunity Policy in Education, Stanford University. (2013). Retrieved from http://edpolicy.stanford.edu/

GLOBAL UNDERSTANDING

Department of Sociology, Belmont University. (n.d.). *Marketable skills learned from sociology.* Retrieved from http://www.belmont.edu/sociology/graduates/soc_marketable_skills.html

Sage Publications. *Understanding our social world.* Retrieved from www.sagepub.com/

INFORMATION LITERACY

American Library Association, Association of College and Research Libraries, Anthropology and Sociology Section, Instruction and Information Literacy Committee Task Force on Standards. (2008, January 15). *Information literacy standards for anthropology and sociology students.* Retrieved from www.ala.org/acrl/standards/anthro_soc_standards

Goodfellow, M., & Wade, B. *Confronting statistical literacy in the undergraduate social science curriculum. Appendix I: Worry questions.* Retrieved from www.pasocsociety.org

Lohr, S. (2012). The age of big data. *New York Times,* February 12. Retrieved from www.nytimes.com

OCCUPATION AND JOB TITLE RESOURCES

Bureau of Labor Statistics, U.S. Department of Commerce. (2013). *Occupational outlook handbook, 2012–13 edition.* Retrieved from www.bls.gov

U.S. Department of Labor, Employment and Training Administration. (n.d.). *O*NET. Resource Center.* Retrieved from www.onetcenter.org

U.S. Office of Personnel Management. (n.d.). *USAJOBS: The federal government's official jobs site.* Retrieved from www.usajobs.gov

PROBLEM SOLVING

Barrie, L. (2013). *Best careers for problem solvers.* Retrieved from http://education.yahoo.net/articles/problem-solving_careers.htm

Department of Sociology, Memorial University. (2013). *Careers in sociology.* Retrieved from www.mun.ca/soc/Careers_In_Sociology.php

Employment Spot. (2012). *Careers for people who like to problem solve.* Retrieved from www.employmentspot.com/employment-articles/careers-for-people-who-like-to-problem-solve

Kisielewski, M., Senter, M. S., Spalter-Roth, R., & Van Vooren, N. (2012). Recruiting sociology majors: What are the effects of the Great Recession, concepts, changes, and careers. American Sociological Association. Retrieved from www.asanet/org

Little, D. (2012). Why sociology major? *The Huffington Post.* Retrieved from www.huffingtonpost.com

QUALITATIVE RESEARCH

Neill, J. (2007, February). *Qualitative versus quantitative research: Key points in a classic debate, features of qualitative and quantitative research.* Retrieved from www.wilderdom.com/research/QualitativeVersusQuantitativeResearch.html

Smith College Libraries, Smith College. (2009, June 4). *Sociology majors research skills.* Retrieved from www.smith.edu/libraries/services/faculty/infolit/ilprograms/sociologyskills

QUANTITATIVE RESEARCH

Neill, J. (2007, February 28). *Qualitative versus quantitative research: Key points in a classic debate, features of qualitative and quantitative research.* Retrieved from www.wilderdom.com/research/Qualitative VersusQuantitativeResearch.html

Smith College Libraries, Smith College. (2009, June 4). *Sociology majors research skills.* Retrieved from www.smith.edu/libraries/services/faculty/infolit/ilprograms/sociologyskills

SYNTHESIS AND ANALYSIS

Cooper, H., Hedges, L. V., & Valentine, J. C. (2009). *The handbook of research synthesis and meta-analysis* (Amazon Book Description). Retrieved from http://www.amazon.com/The-Handbook-Research-Synthesis-Meta-Analysis/dp/0871541637/ref=sr_1_1?ie=UTF8&qid=1363290064&sr=8-1&keywords=The+Handbook+of+Research+Synthesis+and+Meta-Analysis

LinkedIn. (2013). *Skills and expertise: Data analysis.* Retrieved from www.linkedin.com/skills/skill/Data_Analysis

Murphy, K. A. (2007). *Vehicle for enrichment: University of Wisconsin–Madison's undergraduate concentration in analysis and research.* American Sociological Association, Academic and Professional Affairs Program. Retrieved from www.asanet.org

SOCIAL CHANGE

American Sociological Association, Sociology and General Education, Task Force on Sociology and General Education. (2007). *Report of the Task Force on Sociology and General Education.* Retrieved from http://www.asanet.org/images/asa/docs/pdf/Task%20Force%20on%20Sociology%20and%20General%20Education.pdf

Fairchild, Denise G., Community Learning Partnership. (n.d.). *Development skills for social and community change.* Retrieved from www.communitylearningpartnership.org/docs/developskils.doc

UNDERSTANDING SOCIAL PROBLEMS

Career Services, University of Tennessee. (2013). *Explore majors and careers.* Retrieved from www.career.utk.edu/exploremajors.php

PHOTO CREDITS

Chapter 1: CO Photo, page xxiv. © Ashley Cooper/Corbis; Photo 1.1, page 2. © Bob Sacha/Corbis; Photo 1.2, page 3. © Scott Houston/Corbis; Photo 1.3, page 4. © iStockphoto.com/raw206; Photo 1.4, page 5. Mario Tama/Getty Images News/Getty Images; Photo 1.5, page 7. Mark Wilson/Getty Images News/Getty Images; Photo 1.6, page 8. © PRISMA ARCHIVO/Alamy; Photo 1.7, page 9. The Granger Collection, NYC — All rights reserved.; Photo 1.8, page 10. The Granger Collection, NYC — All rights reserved.; Photo 1.9, page 10. © Pictorial Press Ltd/Alamy; Photo 1.10, page 11. International Institute of Social History in Amsterdam, Netherlands, Public Domain; Photo 1.11, page 12. © Everett Collection Historical/Alamy; Photo 1.12, page 13. Public domain – Library of Congress; Photo 1.13, page 14. Fritz Goro/Time & Life Pictures/Getty Images; Photo 1.14, page 15. Library of Congress; Photo 1.15, page 17. REUTERS/Alessandro Bianchi; Photo 1.16, page 18. Melanie Stetson Freeman/Christian Science Monitor/Getty Images; Photo 1.17, page 20. AP Photo/Richard Vogel; Photo 1.18, page 21. © iStockphoto.com/LanceB

Chapter 2: CO Photo, page 26. © Marianna Day Massey/ZUMA/Corbis; Photo 2.1, page 28. © Ringo Chiu/ZUMA Press/Corbis; Photo 2.2, page 31. Jewel Samad/AFP/Getty Images; Photo 2.3, page 32. © Martin Ruetschi/Keystone/Corbis; Photo 2.4, page 33. © Ed Kashi/Corbis; Photo 2.5, page 36. Mario Tama/Getty Images News/Getty Images; Photo 2.6, page 39. © Janine Wiedel Photolibrary/Alamy; Photo 2.7, page 41. Nigel Treblin/DDP/Getty Images; Photo 2.8, page 42. Wikimedia Commons/Dmitry Valberg's l; Photo 2.9, page 45. © iStockphoto.com/stevecoleimages; Photo 2.10, page 46. Library of Congress, Prints & Photographs Division, New York World Telegram Collection, LC-DIG-ppmsca-19290;

Chapter 3: CO Photo, page 50. Jeronimo Rivero/LatinContent Editorial/Getty Images; Photo 3.1, page 52. © Catherine Karnow/Corbis; Photo 3.2, page 54. New York Daily News Archive/New York Daily News/Getty Images; Photo 3.3, page 55. © Trinity Mirror/Mirrorpix/Alamy; Photo 3.4, page 56. © Corbis; Photo 3.5, page 57. © AF archive/Alamy; Photo 3.6a, page 58. CBS Photo Archive/CBS/Getty Images; Photo 3.6b, page 58. ABC Photo Archives/Disney ABC Television Group/Getty Images; Photo 3.6c, page 58. The Granger Collection, NYC — All rights reserved; Photo 3.7, page 59. REUTERS/Stefano Rellandini; Photo 3.8a, page 61. © ALEX LEE/epa/Corbis; Photo 3.8b, page 61. © Nengah Januartha/Demotix/Corbis; Photo 3.8c, page 61. © Bob Sacha/Corbis; Photo 3.9, page 92. © ZUMA Press, Inc./Alamy; Photo 3.10, page 63. © Remy de la Mauviniere/AP/Corbis; Photo 3.11, page 66. © iStockphoto.com/kupicoo; Photo 3.12, page 68. © Andria Patino/Corbis; Photo 3.13, page 69. ©Warner Bros./Courtesy Everett Collection; Photo 3.14, page 70. Scott Gries/Getty Images Entertainment/Getty Images; Photo 3.15, page 71. Massoud Hossaini/AFP/Getty Images; Photo 3.16, page 72. © Joachim Ladefoged/VII/Corbis

Chapter 4: CO Photo, page 76. © Jim Mahoney/Dallas Morning News/Corbis; Photo 4.1, page 78. © Najlah Feanny/Corbis; Photo 4.2, page 79. Toshifumi Kitamura/AFP/Getty Images; Photo 4.3, page 80. Nina Leen/Time & Life Pictures/Getty Images; Photo 4.4, page 82. © Bettmann/CORBIS; Photo 4.5, page 83. © Kelly-Mooney Photography/Corbis; Photo 4.6, page 86© iStockphoto.com/MichaelDeLeon; Photo 4.7, page 87. © Pixland/Pixland/Thinkstock; Photo 4.8a, page 90. © Andy Ryan/Corbis Outline; Photo 4.8b, page 90. Getty Images/Getty Images Entertainment/Getty Images; Photo 4.8c, page 90. Silver Screen Collection/Moviepix/Getty Images; Photo 4.9, page 91. © MARTON MAGOCSI/epa/Corbis; Photo 4.10, page 92. ©Touchstone Pictures/Courtesy Everett Collection; Photo 4.11, page 93. © Philip Gould/CORBIS; Photo 4.12, page 94. Mary Evans/TURNER ENTERTAINMENT/Ronald Grant/Everett Collection(10369945); Photo 4.13, page 95. © iStockphoto.com/Leontura

Chapter 5: CO Photo, page 100. REUTERS/Donald Chan; Photo 5.1, page 102. Patrick Smith/Stringer/Getty Images News/Getty Images; Photo 5.2, page 103. © iStockphoto.com/track5; Photo 5.3, page 105. REUTERS/Bobby Yip; Photo 5.4, page 108. © Peter Turnley/CORBIS; Photo 5.5, page 109. Granted by permission of Alexandra Milgram; Photo 5.6, page 110. © Stock Illustrations Ltd/Alamy; Photo 5.7, page 111. © iStockphoto.com/EdStock; Photo 5.7, page 113. © Sygma/Corbis; Photo 5.9, page 114. JOE SONGER/Birmingham News/Landov; Photo 5.10, page 116. REUTERS/Lucy Nicholson; Photo 5.11, page 118. AP Photo/ASSOCIATED PRESS; Photo 5.12, page 120. AP Photo/Andy Manis

Chapter 6: CO Photo, page 126. REUTERS/Shannon Stapleton; Photo 6.1, page 128. Kevork Djansezian/Getty Images News/Getty Images; Photo 6.2, page 129. © Neville Elder/Corbis; Photo 6.3, page 130. Topical Press Agency/Stringer/Hulton Archive/Getty Images; Photo 6.4, page 131. SPL/Science Source; Photo 6.5, page 132. © Simon Jarratt/Corbis; Photo 6.6, page 134. REUTERS/Lucy Nicholson; Photo 6.7, page 136. © Oliver Burston/Ikon Images/Corbis; Photo 6.8, page 137. © Jérome Sessini/Corbis; Photo 6.9, page 139. © PETER DEJONG/AP/Corbis; Photo 6.11, page 142. © iStockphoto.com/DrGrounds; Photo 6.12, page 143. Library of Congress. New York World-Telegram & Sun Collection. Photograph by Al Ravenna, World Telegram staff photographer

Chapter 7: CO Photo, page 152. © Lisa Wiltse/Corbis; Photo 7.1, page 154. Drew Angerer/Stringer/Getty Images News/Getty Images; Photo 7.2, page 155. AP Photo/Ben Margot; Photo 7.3, page 156. © Bettmann/CORBIS; Photo 7.4, page 157. Robert Nickelsberg/3rd Party – Agents/Getty Images; Photo 7.5, page 159. © Bob Rowan/Progressive Image/Corbis; Photo 7.6, page 161. John Moore/Getty Images News/Getty Images; Photo 7.7, page 162. Dimas Ardian/Stringer/Getty Images News/Getty Images; Photo 7.8, page 163. © iStockphoto.com/Kangah; Photo 7.9, page 166. © iStockphoto.com/EdStock; Photo 7.10, page 168. © Jeremy Horner/CORBIS; Photo 7.11, page 170. © Andrew Lichtenstein/Corbis; Photo 7.12a, page 174. © Ed Kashi/Corbis; Photo 7.12b, page 174. © Adrian Arbib/Adrian Arbib/Corbis; Photo 7.13, page 175. © Kevin Frayer//AP/Corbis

Chapter 8: CO Photo, page 180. © Gideon Mendel/Corbis; Photo 8.1, page 182. Missouri State University; Photo 8.2, page 184. © David Turnley/CORBIS; Photo 8.3, page 187. Library of Congress. Russell Lee photographer; Photo 8.4, page 188. © Julie Dermansky/Corbis; Photo 8.5, page 189. National Archives and Records Administration. Original photographers: McPherson and Oliver; Photo 8.6, page 190. © Ken McKimm/Icon SMI/Corbis; Photo 8.7, page 191. © iStockphoto.com/EdStock; Photo 8.8, page 192. REUTERS/Jim Bourg; Photo 8.9, page 193. © Scott Houston/Corbis; Photo 8.10, page 196. Stephan Gladieu/Getty Images News/Getty Images; Photo 8.11, page 199. © ZUMA Press, Inc./Alamy; Photo 8.12, page 200. Library of Congress. Photograph by Ansel Adams; Photo 8.13, page 202. © Detroit Publishing Company

Chapter 9: CO Photo 9, page 206. © Jake Warga/Corbis; Photo 9.1, page 208. John Nordell/Christian Science Monitor/Getty Images; Photo 9.2, page 209. © Jason Edwards/National Geographic Society/Corbis; Photo 9.3, page 210. Esther Lin/Forsa LLC/UFC/Getty Images; Photo 9.4a, page 211. Kristian Dowling/TB/Editorial Specials/Getty Images; Photo 9.4b, page 211. AP Photo/Aaron Vincent Elkaim; Photo 9.5, page 212. © ROBIN UTRECHT FOTOGRAFIE/HillCreek Pictures/Corbis; Photo 9.6, page 213. © Sandy Huffaker/Corbis; Photo 9.7, page 215. AP Photo/Rui Vieira; Photo 9.8, page 216. AP/Rich Pedroncelli; Photo 9.9, page 221. © iStockphoto.com/Photomorphic; Photo 9.10, page 223. © Shine Pictures/Corbis; Photo 9.11a, page 225. © Alex Milan Tracy/Demotix/Demotix/Corbis; Photo 9.11b, page 225. Keystone/Hulton Archive/Getty Images; Photo 9.13a, page 227. Murray Close/©Lionsgate/Courtesy Everett Collection; Photo 9.13b, page 227. © AF archive/Alamy; Photo 9.14, page 229. AP Photo/Andy Wong; Photo 9.15, page 230. REUTERS/POOL New; Photo 9.16, page 231. Tim Graham/Getty Images News/Getty Images; Photo 9.17, page 232. © Karen Kasmauski/Science Faction/Corbis

Chapter 10: CO Photo, page 236. The India Today Group/The India Today Group/Getty Images; Photo 10.1, page 238. © Bryan Denton/Corbis; Photo 10.2, page 240. Stephan Gladieu/Getty Images News/Getty Images; Photo 10.3, page 241. Boston Globe/Boston Globe/Getty Images; Photo 10.4a, page 242. Bruce Bennett/Getty Images Sport/Getty Images; Photo 10.4b, page 242. Fox/Getty Images Entertainment/Getty Images; Photo 10.5, page 244. © Patrick Semansky//AP/Corbis; Photo 10.6a, page 245. Lambert/Archive Photos/Getty Images; Photo 10.6b, page 245. The Granger Collection, NYC — All rights reserved.; Photo 10.7, page 247. © Gideon Mendel/Corbis; Photo 10.8, page 248. © Noah K. Murray/Star Ledger/Corbis; Photo 10.9, page 252. © Ann Johansson/Corbis; Photo 10.10, page 253. Andy Nelson/Christian Science Monitor/Getty Images; Photo 10.11, page 254. © Gene J. Puskar//AP/Corbis; Photo 10.12, page 255. © Mia Song/Star Ledger/Corbis; Photo 10.13, page 257. © Studio DL/Corbis; Photo 10.14, page 258. © Viviane Moos/CORBIS; Photo 10.15, page 259. © Lara Solt/Dallas Morning News/Corbis; Photo 10.16, page 260. © Catherine Karnow/Corbis

Chapter 11: CO Photo, page 264. © Michael Reynolds/epa/Corbis; Photo 11.1, page 266. © Darron Cummings/AP/Corbis; Photo 11.2, page 268. Library of Congress; Photo 11.3, page 269. © iStockphoto.com/sjlocke; Photo 11.4, page 272. © Gideon Mendel/Corbis; Photo 11.5, page 273. © Alex Brandon/AP/Corbis; Photo 11.6, page 274. Library of Congress. Photograph by Frances Benjamin Johnston; Photo 11.7a, page 275. © Najlah Feanny/Corbis; Photo 11.7b, page 275. Spencer Grant/Photo Researchers, Inc.; Photo 11.8, page 281. Boston Globe/Boston Globe/Getty Images; Photo 11.9, page 282. The Washington Post/The Washington Post/Getty Images; Photo 11.10, page 284. © Bryan Denton/Corbis

Chapter 12: CO Photo, page 290. © Gideon Mendel/CORBIS; Photo 12.1, page 292. AP Photo/Paul Sakuma; Photo 12.2, page 293. © Andrew Holbrooke/Corbis; Photo 12.3, page 294. Wikipedia; Photo 12.4, page 295. Donald Miralle/Edit/Getty Images; Photo 12.5, page 296. REUTERS/Alessandro Bianchi; Photo 12.6, page 297. © Tim Farrell/Star Ledger/Corbis; Photo 12.7, page 298. Spencer Platt/Getty Images News/Getty Images; Photo 12.8, page 300. © Bettmann/CORBIS; Photo 12.9, page 301. REUTERS/Peter Andrews; Photo 12.10, page 302. NICHOLAS © Kazuyoshi Nomachi/Corbis; Photo 12.11, page 304. © Kevin Frayer/AP/Corbis; Photo 12.12, page 305. Wikipedia; Photo 12.13, page 307. Wikipedia; Photo 12.14, page 309. AP Photo/Jessica Kourkounis; Photo 12.15, page 310. © Kye R. Lee/Dallas Morning News/Corbis; Photo 12.16, page 311. Abbas Momani/AFP/Getty Images; Photo 12.17, page 313. Wikipedia

Chapter 13: CO Photo, page 318. © Paul A. Souders/CORBIS; Photo 13.1, page 320. Marc Piscotty/Getty Images News/Getty Images; Photo 13.2, page 321. © ARISTIDE ECONOMOPOULOS/Star Ledger/Corbis; Photo 13.3, page 322. Library of Congress; Photo 13.4, page 325. © Felix Adamo/ZUMA Press/Corbis; Photo 13.5, page 327. © Kirsty Wigglesworth//AP/Corbis; Photo 13.6, page 328. © Vincent Yu//AP/Corbis; Photo 13.7, page 329. Mohammed Abed/AFP Getty Images; Photo 13.8, page 330. © AF archive/Alamy; Photo 13.9, page 332. Library of Congress, Prints & Photographs Division, NYWT&S Collection, [reproduction number, e.g., LC-USZ62-111157]; Photo 13.10, page 333. KIM HONG-JI/Reuters/Landov; Photo 13.11, page 336. © Reuters/CORBIS; Photo 13.12, page 337. Boston Globe/Boston Globe/Getty Images

Chapter 14: CO Photo, page 344. © Lara Solt/Dallas Morning News/Corbis; Photo 14.1, page 346. Bloomberg/Bloomberg/Getty Images; Photo 14.3, page 349. Photo by Lewis Wickes Hines; Photo 14.4a, page 351. AP Photo/Kristy Macdonald; Photo 14.4b, page 351. © Matthew Mcvay/CORBIS; Photo 14.5, page 356. © Matthew Mcvay/CORBIS; Photo 14.6, page 357. Library of Congress; Photo 14.7, page 358. © Swim Ink 2, LLC/CORBIS; Photo 14.8, page 360. © iStockphoto.com/BassittART; Photo 14.9, page 362. LUCAS JACKSON/X01783/Reuters/Corbis; Photo 14.10 , page 364. ©iStockphoto.com/emre563; Photo 14.11, page 365. © Fredrik Renander/Alamy

Chapter 15: CO Photo, page 370. © Richard T. Nowitz/CORBIS; Photo 15.1, page 372. © iStockphoto.com/kickstand; Photo 15.2, page 375. © iStockphoto.com/TommL; Photo 15.3, page 376. © PARIS PIERCE/Alamy; Photo 15.4, page 377. © iStockphoto.com/Maica; Photo 15.5, page 379. REUTERS/Shannon Stapleton; Photo 15.6, page 380. The National Archives. Department of Health, Education, and Welfare. Public Health Service. Health Services and Mental Health Administration. Center for Disease Control. Venereal Disease Branch (1970 - 1973); Photo 15.7, page 381. The Washington Post/Washington Post/Getty Images; Photo 15.8, page 383. © Ken Cedeno/Corbis; Photo 15.9, page 384. © Bettmann/CORBIS; Photo 15.10, page 385. Randall Michelson Archive/WireImage/Getty Images; Photo 15.11, page 386. © ZUMA Wire Service/Alamy; Photo 15.12, page 389. © Scott Houston/Corbis; Photo 15.13, page 390. Madaree Tohlala/AFP/Getty Images; Photo 15.14, page 391. © Daniel Lai/Aurora Photos/Corbis

Chapter 16: CO Photo, page 394. John Moore/Edit/Getty Images; Photo 16.1, page 396.

REUTERS/Goran Tomasevic; Photo 16.2, page 398. Benjamin Lowy/Getty Images News/Getty Images; Photo 16.3, page 400. © Leif Skoogfors/CORBIS; Photo 16.4, page 401. © Leif Skoogfors/CORBIS; Photo 16.5, page 402. Matt Moyer/Edit/Getty Images; Photo 16.6, page 403. REUTERS/Handout; Photo 16.7, page 404. © Lynsey Addario/VII/Corbis; Photo 16.8, page 405. © Marco Baroncini/Corbis; Photo 16.9a, page 406. © U.S. Navy - digital version copy/Science Faction/Corbis; Photo 16.9b, page 406. Staff Sergeant Preston Chasteen; Photo 16.10, page 407. National Archives. Photo by Lt. A. E. Samuelson; Photo 16.11, page 409. ullstein bild/The Granger Collection, NYC — All rights reserved

Chapter 17: CO Photo, page 414. REUTERS/Vivek Prakash; Photo 17.1, page 416. AFP/AFP/Getty Images; Photo 17.2, page 417. © Karen Kasmauski/Science Faction/Corbis; Photo 17.3, page 420. © iStockphoto.com/ROMAOSLO; Photo 17.4, page 421. John Moore/Getty Images News/Getty Images; Photo 17.5, page 422. Deshakalyan Chowdhury/AFP/Getty Images; Photo 17.6, page 423. © Heritage Images/Corbis; Photo 17.7, page 424. ullstein bild/The Granger Collection, NYC — All rights reserved.; Photo 17.8, page 426. © ZUMA Wire Service/Alamy; Photo 17.9a, page 428. © Can Stock Photo Inc./sborisov; Photo 17.9b, page 428. Library of Congress, Prints & Photographs Division, HABS [or HAER or HALS], Reproduction number [e.g., "HABS ILL, 16-CHIG, 33-2 "]; Photo 17.10, page 431. The Washington Post/The Washington Post/Getty Images; Photo 17.11, page 432. © iStockphoto.com/King_Louie; Photo 17.12, page 433. Brent Stirton/Getty Images News/Getty Images; Photo 17.13, page 434. REUTERS/ERIC THAYER; Photo 17.14, page 435. REUTERS/Stringer Indonesia; Photo 17.15, page 436. REUTERS/Zahid Hussein; Photo 17.16, page 437. © Imaginechina/Corbis; Photo 17.17, page 438. © iStockphoto.com/NNehring; Photo 17.18, page 439. © iStockphoto.com/NNehring

Chapter 18: CO Photo, page 444. © Carl & Ann Purcell/Corbis; Photo 18.1, page 446. REUTERS/Handout; Photo 18.2, page 448. © Amy Sussman/Corbis; Photo 18.3, page 449. © Egbert van Heemskerk the Elder/The Bridgeman Art Library/Getty Images; Photo 18.4, page 450. © Historical Picture Archive/CORBIS; Photo 18.5, page 451. AFP/AFP/Getty Images; Photo 18.6, page 452. Getty Images/Getty Images Entertainment/Getty Images; Photo 18.7, page 453. Library of Congress. Photograph by Thomas J. O'Halloran; Photo 18.8, page 455. occupywallstreet.org; Photo 18.9, page 456. © Lee Jin-man//AP/Corbis; Photo 18.10, page 457. The Granger Collection, NYC — All rights reserved.; Photo 18.11, page 458. © Parker Haeg/Demotix/CorbisLicense Type:Rights Managed (RM); Photo 18.12, page 460. © David Turnley/CORBIS; Photo 18.13, page 461. © JIM LO SCALZO/epa/Corbis; Photo 18.14, page 462. © iStockphoto.com/Alija; Photo 18.15, page 465. AP Photo/Jeff Widener; Photo 18.16, page 466. REUTERS/Gonzalo Fuentes

INDEX

Page numbers in italics *indicate illustrations, figures and tables.*

Occupational segregation by gender or gender occupational segregation, 218, 220–221, *221, 222*

Occupational segregation by gender or gender occupational segregation defined, 218

Occupational transformation, 351–353

Occupy movements, *448,* 453–454, 455, 462

O'Dea, T., 299

OECD (Organisation for Economic Co-operation and Development), 266–267, 282, 284

"Off the books" jobs, 359

Ohlin, L., 132–133

Operational definition, 32

Operation Enduring Freedom Afghanistan, 141, *397,* 398, 401

Operation Iraqi Freedom (Iraq War), *397,* 399, 401, 402

Opportunity theory, 132–133, 149

Organic intellectuals, 449–450

Organisation for Economic Co-operation and Development (OECD), 266–267, 282, 284

Organizational-level theory, 463–465

Organizations. *See also* Bureaucracies; Groups and organizations
 summary of, 112–114
 anti-slavery organization and, 113
 coercive organization defined and, 114
 coercive organizations and, 114
 formal organization defined and, 112
 nonnormative organization defined and, 114
 normative organizations and, 114
 organization defined and, 112
 utilitarian organization defined and, 112
 utilitarian organizations and, 112, 114

Organized crime, 142

Orshansky, M., 173

OSHA (Occupational Safety and Health Administration), 375–376

Outsourcing, 346, 351

Oxfam America, 230, *232*

Oxfam International, 404

Pacific Islanders, and high school dropouts, 277

PACs (political action committees), 336

Pakistan
 infant mortality rates and, 171
 population growth and, 418

Pakistan, and sex trafficking, 230

Palestinian-Israeli conflict, 312, *313*

Panic defined, 457

Panics, *457,* 457–458

Park, R. E., 13

Parliamentary system, 332

Parsons, T., 16, 57, 88, 224, 241–242, 374, 448

Participatory research, 43

Pascoe, C. J., 212

Patient Protection and Affordable Care Act (PPACA), 167, 381, *381*

Patriarchy defined, 226

Pavlov, I., 80

Peers. *See also* Schools and teachers
 fads and, 88
 fashions and, 88
 gender concepts and, 212
 sexual harassment among, 222
 socialization and, 86, 88

Perot, H. R., 333

Personal power, 108

Peru, 136, *197*

Petraeus, D., *140,* 141

Pew Charitable Trust, 335

Pew Forum on Religion and Public Life, 299

Pew Research Center, 219, 240

Pharmaceutical company drug testing, 380, *381*

Phelan, A. M., 270

Phrenology defined, 130

Piaget, J., 83

Piketty, T., 164

Pledge of Allegiance, 292, 293, 312

Plessy v. Ferguson (1896), 274

Pluralistic societies
 summary of, 129–130, 149
 definition of, 129

Pluralist theory, 324

PMCs (private military corporations), 399, 401, *401, 402*

Poland, 54, 267, 298, 358, 398

Police corruption and brutality, 143–144

Political action committees (PACs), 336

Political action committees (super PACs), 336

Political power defined, 160

Political rights, 322, 323, 341

Political voice, 160

Politics
 definition of, 332
 electoral politics and, *332,* 332–333, *333*
 political activism in U.S. and, *453*
 political power in U.S. and, 335–337, *339*
 political rights and, 322, 323, 341
 political system in U.S. and, *331,* 331–339, *332, 339,* 341
 politics defined and, 332
 religion in U.S. and, 313, 315
 social movements in U.S. and, *339*
 state power and, 331–332, 341

Polyandry defined, 239–240

Polygamy defined, 129, 239, *240*

Polygyny defined, 239

Polytheism defined, 306

Poor populations, and correlation with HIV/AIDS, 388–389, *389. See also* Poverty in U.S.

Popper, K., 37, 91

Popular culture. *See also* Culture
 summary of, 74

definition of, 64
socialization and, 78–79

Population defined, 38

Population growth rate, 424–427

Population momentum defined, 419

Population Reference Bureau, 418

Populations
 summary of, 417, 440
 age-specific fertility rates defined and, 420
 age-specific mortality rates defined and, 420
 agricultural surplus defined and, 427
 cities and, 427–434, 442
 cities in U.S. and, 430–432, *431*
 city defined and, 427
 consumption of goods and, 436–438
 crude birthrates defined and, 420
 crude death rates defined and, 420
 demographic analysis and, 420–421, 442
 demographic transition in the West theory and, 423–424, 442
 demographic transition theory and, 421–423, *422, 422,* 442
 demography defined and, 417
 environmental impact of computers and mobile devices and, 437
 exponential population growth defined and, 425
 exponential population growth theory and, 425–426, 427, 442
 fertility correlation with female education and, 422, *422, 424*
 fertility defined and, 420, 442
 gentrification defined and, 431
 geometric model of cities and, 429, *429*
 global cities and, 432, *432,* 442
 global cities defined and, 432
 global consumer class defined and, 436
 global environment and, 434–440, *435,* 442
 global population growth and, 417–420, *418, 419*
 global urbanization and, 432–434
 global warming and, 434–435
 HIV/AIDS correlation with cities and, 433, *433*
 industrialization correlation with cities and, 427–428
 inequitable distribution of resources theory of Marx and, 426–427, 442
 life expectancy and, *420,* 420–421, *421*
 life expectancy defined and, 420
 local environment and, 438–440
 megacities defined and, 434
 migration and, 442
 net migration defined and, 420
 population defined and, 38
 population growth rate viewpoints and, 424–427
 population momentum defined and, 419
 rate of natural increase and, 424, *425*

racism and, 187–188
racism defined and, 187
scapegoating defined and, 192
segregation and, 185–186, *186, 188,* 204
segregation defined and, 185
social construction of, 183–185
social epidemiology and, 194, *194*
social epidemiology defined and, 194
soldiers in U.S. armed forces and, 400, *400*
stereotyping and, 189–190, *190,* 204
stereotyping defined and, 198
stigma and, 188–189
stigma defined and, 188
symbolic interaction theory and racism
   and, 188–189
technologies of discrimination and, 191
theoretical approaches and, 187–189
U.S. and, *184, 195,* 195–201, *201,* 204
voter activism or apathy and, 334, *335*
White Americans and, 200–201
White Americans and segregation and,
   186, *186*
White separatist and supremacist groups
   and, 192
Racism
   definition of, 187
   race and ethnicity and, 187–188
   theoretical approaches to, 187–189
Radical feminism defined, 226, 237
Random sampling defined, 38
Rape (sexual assault), 67–69, 74, 389, 401,
   403, 403–405, 412
Rape as weapon of war, 401, *403,*
   403–405, 412
Rape culture, 68–69, 74
Rate of natural increase (RNI), 424, *425*
Rational-legal authority
   definition of, 327
   state power and, 327, *327,* 341
Reactionary social movements, *459,* 461,
   461, 461–463, 470
Real culture
   summary of, 57–58, 60, 74
   definition of, 57
Rebellions
   definition of, *459*
   social movements and, 461, 470
Reference group defined, 81
Reformist social movements
   definition of, 459
   social movements and, *459,* 459–460, 470
Reich, R., 168, 361
Reimer, J., 134
Reliability defined, 35, 48. *See also* Validity
   and reliability
Religion
   summary of, 293, 312, 315
   animism defined and, 306
   anthropology and, 294–295
   anthropology defined and, 294
   atheism and, 88, 293, *302*
   atheists and, *302*

Buddhism and, *302,* 306, *307*
Catholicism and, *302,* 309, *309*
charismatic leaders and, 327
Christianity and, 302, *302,* 303, 312
church and, 300, 315
church defined and, 300
civil religion and, 312, 315
Confucianism and, 306–307
conservative Protestantism and, 309–310
consumption of goods and services and,
   296, *311,* 312, 315
cult and, 300–302, 315
cult defined and, 300
denomination defined and, 300
disestablishment and, 293, 311–312, 315
Disestablishment Clause and, 293
disestablishment defined and, 311
ecclesia defined and, 300
economic development correlation
   with, 307
eschatology and, 301, *301*
evangelicalism and, 308–309, *310,* 312
evangelicalism defined and, 308
fasting women and, 309, *309*
feminism and, 308
functionalism and, 295–296
globalization and, 312–313, *313,* 315
Hinduism and, *294,* 302, *302,* 305, 313
Islam and, 302, *302, 303,* 303–304, *304,*
   312, 313
Judaism and, *302,* 304–305, *305,* 312, *313*
mass media and, 307
monotheism defined and, 303
new religious movements and, 302, 315
new religious movements defined
   and, 302
nontheistic religion defined and, 306
Pledge of Allegiance and, 292, 293, 312
politics and, 313, 315
polytheism defined and, 306
profane defined and, 295
Quakers and, 307
religion defined and, 293
religious affiliation in U.S. and, 308–311
religious economy and, 298–299,
   299, 315
religious economy defined and, 298–299
religious nationalism and, 312–313
religious nationalism defined and, 312
religious organizations and, 297, 298,
   299–302, 315
sacred defined and, 295
sect defined and, 300
secularization defined and, 296
socialization and, 88
sociological study of, 293–294, 315
suicide rates and, 297
synthesis of theories and, 298
Tea Party movement and, 310, 312
theism defined and, 293
theories and, 294–299, 315
totems defined and, 295, *296*

U.S. as multicultural and, 292–293,
   308–312
women and, 307–308, 309, 315
world religions and, *302,* 302–307, *306*
young adults in U.S. and, 311, 315
Zionism defined and, 305
Religious affiliation in U.S., 308–311, 315
Religious economy, 298–299, *299,* 315
Religious nationalism, 312–313
Religious organizations, 297, 298, 299–302,
   315. *See also* Religion; *and specific*
   religious organizations
Replication defined, 37, 48
Representative democracy, 331, 341
Republican Party, 309–310, 332, 337
Research methods, 37, 44, 48. *See also*
   Sociological research; Statistical data
Reserve army of labor defined, 349
Resocialization, 90, 92, 98. *See also*
   Socialization
Resource mobilization theory, 464, 470
Revolutionary social movements, 11, 330,
   459, 460, *460,* 460–461, 470
Riot defined, 456
Riots, 456–457
Rise-and-fall social change or cyclical
   theories, *450,* 450–451, 470
Rise-and-fall theories of social change
   defined, 450
Ritzer, G., 71, 283, 359–361, 368
RNI (rate of natural increase), 424, *425*
Role-taking defined, 82
Roosevelt, F. D., *322*
Roosevelt, T., 65, 355
Rosenthal, R., 272, *272*
Rostow, W., 171
Rothschild-Whitt, J., 118
Rousseau, J.-J., 9, 224
Rumors, 457–458
Rumors defined, 457
Rural health care, 229, *230*
Russia. *See also* Soviet Union
   capitalism and, 354
   immigrants from, 195, 201
   obesity and, 390
   organized crime and, 142, *142*
   politics and, 334
   population growth and, 419, 424
   rate of natural increase and, 424, *425*
   revolutionary social movements and, 11
   state power and, 121
   UN and, 119
Rwanda, 184, 202, 403, 404, 408–409

Sacred defined, 295
Saez, E., 164
"Salad bowl," 63
Salinas, Elaine J., 198
al-Salman, J., 120
Same-sex partners in U.S., 247, *247,*
   248, 248–249, *249. See also* Sexual
   orientation

inequality armed forces and, 400, *400*
internment camps in, 199
Jews and, 304
life expectancy and, 421, *421*
low-wage labor force in, 346
marriage in, *242, 244,* 247, 248
Medicaid and, 322, 379, 381
Medicare and, 322, 358, 379
"melting pot" or "salad bowl" in, 63
middle class families in, 256–257
middle class in, 256–257
minimum wage debate in, 166
modernization theory and, 172, 173
modern society families in, 245–246, *246,* 263
modern society in, 245–246, *246,* 263
obesity in, 34, *34, 35, 383,* 383–385, *384*
Pledge of Allegiance and, 292, 293, 312
PMCs and, 399, 401, *402*
political activism in, *453,* 458, 464
political power in, 335–337
political system in, *331,* 331–339, *332, 339,* 341
politics religion in, 313, 315
population growth and, 418, *419*
prejudice in, 199, *200*
presidential elections in, 333, *333*
public health issues in, 381–387, *382,* 393
race and ethnicity and, *184, 195,* 195–201, *201,* 204
race and ethnicity in, 198–199, *199*
race and ethnicity in armed forces and, 400, *400*
race and ethnicity in armed forces in, 400, *400*
rational-legal authority and, 327
reactionary social movements and, 451, *451*
religion and, 300, 311, 315
religion and politics in, 313, 315
religion in, 292–293, 308–312
religious affiliation in, 308–311, 315
same-sex partners in, 247, *247, 248,* 248–249, *249*
social change and, 447, 451
social dynamics of cities and suburbs in, 430–432, *431*
social movements and political power in, *339*
social movements correlation with state power in, 337–338, *339*
social movements in, *339*
socioeconomic class, and families in, 253–257, *255, 256,* 263
socioeconomic class in, 253–257, *255, 256*
sociology history in, 13, 24
soldiers in armed forces in, 400, *400*
state power and, 121
state power in, 335–337
teen pregnancy in, 384, *386,* 386–387

thinness culture in, 59
traditional families in, *242,* 244–245, *245*
traditional marriage in, *242, 244,* 247, 248
UN and, 119
unemployment in, *352,* 352–353, *353*
voter identification in, 323, *324, 325*
war economy and, 398
women's suffrage and, 14, *331,* 337, 459–460
young adults and religion in, 311, 315
Urban growth machine defined, 430
Urbanization. *See also* Cities
definition of, 428, 442
global urbanization and, 432–434
HIV/AIDS and, 433, *433*
populations and, 427–434, 442
population shifts and, 9
urban growth machine defined and, 430
urban renewal defined and, 431
Urban renewal defined, 431
U.S. Bureau of Justice Statistics, 41, 257
U.S. Bureau of Labor Statistics, 159, 221, 257, 279–280, 352, 359
U.S. Census Bureau, 31, 34, 41, 155, 164, 186, 197, 204, 217, 220, 247, 252, 347, 353, 378, 379
U.S. Commission on Civil Rights, 218
U.S. Department of State, 175, 230, 285, 405, 406
U.S. Park Police, 462
Utilitarian organization, 112, 114, 123
Utopian social movements, *449, 459,* 463

Valette, F., 14
Validity and reliability
theories and hypotheses and, 35, 48
validity defined and, 35
Value-added theory, 454–456
Value neutrality defined, 37
Value neutral research, 37, 227
Values, 56–57, 74
Van Wees, H., 407
Variable defined, 32
Variables relationships
summary of, 32–34
dependent variable defined and, 40
independent or experimental variable defined and, 40
qualitative variable defined and, 32, 48
quantitative variable defined and, 32, 48
variable defined and, 32
Venkatesh, A. A., 28–29, 30, 39, 40
Verstehen defined, 12
Vietnam
immigration and, 199, 276
religion and, 307
sex ratios and, 416
socialism and, 354
Vietnam War and, 225, 228, 311, *397,* 400, *450, 453,* 458, 464

Violence and culture. *See also* Violent crimes
summary of, 67–69
rape culture and, 68–69, 74
rape culture defined and, 68
Violent crimes. *See also* Violence and culture
summary of, *141,* 141–142, 149
violent crime defined and, 141
Viswanathan, S., 175
Voltaire, 9
Voter activism or apathy, *334,* 334–335, *335*
Voter identification in U.S., 323, *324, 325*
Voting rights, 14, *331,* 335, 337, 459–460
Voting rights (suffrage), 14, *331,* 335, 337, 459–460

Waite, L. J., 216
Wallerstein, I., 172, 174
Walls, M. J. P., 182–183
War economy, 398
War on drugs, 146, 149
Wars. *See also specific conflicts and wars*
summary of, 396–397, 410, 412
authority and subordinate relationship and, 410, 412
birth rates and, 398, *398*
casualties of, *397,* 401, *401,* 402, *402*
civilian casualties of, 402, *402*
conflict theory and, 399, *399,* 399–400
ethnic cleansing and, 403, 408
ethnic cleansing defined and, 403
eugenics and, 409, *409*
family life and, 398–399
formal rationality and, 409, 412
functional alternatives and, 410
functionalism and, 397–398, 410
genocide and, *407,* 407–410
genocide defined and, 407, 412
GWOT and, 405, 412
HIV/AIDS transmission during, 404
inequality in U.S. armed forces and, 400, *400*
nationalism and, 398
obedience to authority and, 410, *410*
PMCs and, 399, 401, *401, 402*
rape as weapon of war and, 401, *403,* 403–405, 412
society and, *397,* 397–401, *398*
sociological perceptive on genocide and, 408–409
soldiers in U.S. armed forces and, 400, *400*
terrorism defined and, 406, 412
terrorists and terrorism and, 405–406, 412
terrorists described and, 405
war economy defined and, 398
Washington, M. M., 113
Watson, J., 80
"Way of being" (Tao), 307

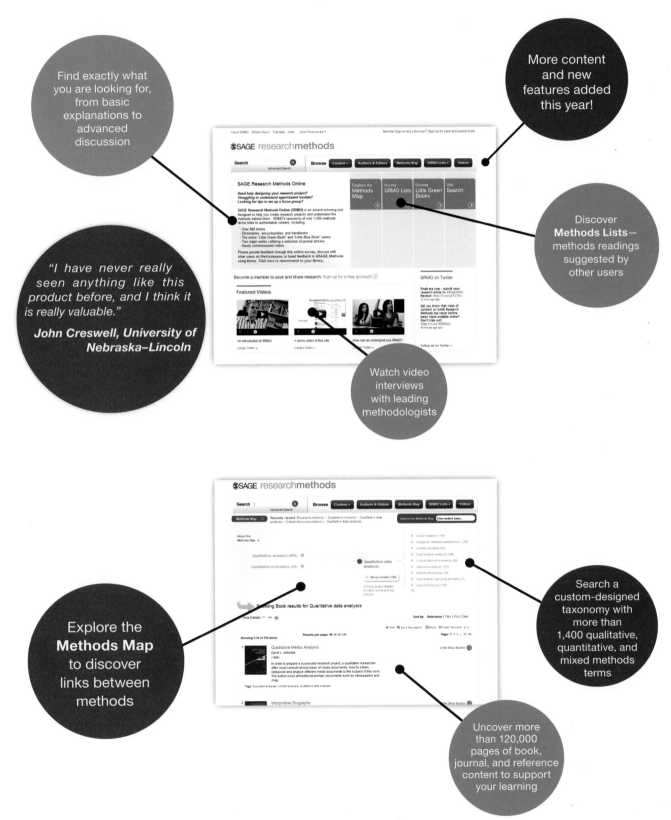

⑤SAGE researchmethods

The essential online tool for researchers from the world's leading methods publisher

Find exactly what you are looking for, from basic explanations to advanced discussion

More content and new features added this year!

"I have never really seen anything like this product before, and I think it is really valuable."

John Creswell, University of Nebraska–Lincoln

Discover **Methods Lists**— methods readings suggested by other users

Watch video interviews with leading methodologists

Explore the **Methods Map** to discover links between methods

Search a custom-designed taxonomy with more than 1,400 qualitative, quantitative, and mixed methods terms

Uncover more than 120,000 pages of book, journal, and reference content to support your learning

Find out more at
www.sageresearchmethods.com